Autodesk Fusion 360

A Power Guide for Beginners and Intermediate Users (8th Edition): 2026

A premium provider of learning products and solutions

www.cadartifex.com

Autodesk Fusion 360: A Power Guide for Beginners and Intermediate Users (8th Edition): 2026

Author: Sandeep Dogra
Email: info@cadartifex.com

Published by
CADArtifex
www.cadartifex.com

ISBN: 978-9394074361

NOTICE TO THE READER

The publisher and the author make no representations or warranties with respect to the accuracy or completeness of the contents of this work/text and specifically disclaim all warranties, including without limitation warranties of fitness for a particular purpose. The publisher does not guarantee any of the products described in the text nor has performed any independent analysis in connection with any of the product information contained in the text. No warranty may be created or extended by sales or promotional materials. This work is sold with the understanding that the publisher is not engaged in rendering legal, accounting, or other professional services. Neither the publisher nor the author shall be liable for damages arising here from. Further, readers should be aware that Internet websites listed or referenced in this work may have changed or may have been removed in the time between the writing and the publishing of this work.

Examination Copies

Textbooks received as examination copies in any form such as paperback or eBook are for review only and may not be made available for the use of the student. These files may not be transferred to any other party. Resale of examination copies is prohibited.

Electronic Files

The electronic file/eBook in any form of this textbook is licensed to the original user only and may not be transferred to any other party.

Disclaimer

The author has made sincere efforts to ensure the accuracy of the material described herein, however the author makes no warranty, expressed or implied, with respect to the quality, accuracy, or freedom from error of this document or the products it describes.

www.cadartifex.com

Dedication

First and foremost, I would like to thank my parents for being a great support throughout my career and while writing this book.

Heartfelt gratitude goes to my wife and my sisters for their patience and endurance in supporting me to take up and successfully accomplish this challenge.

I would also like to acknowledge the efforts of the employees at CADArtifex for their dedication in editing the contents of this book.

Video Courses by CADArtifex

Contents at a Glance

Table of Contents

Part 3. Working with Assemblies

Part 4. Creating Animation

Part 5. Creating Drawings

Preface

Autodesk Fusion is a product of Autodesk Inc., one of the biggest providers of technology for the engineering, architecture, construction, manufacturing, media, and entertainment industries. It offers robust software tools for 3D design, engineering, and entertainment industries that let you design, visualize, simulate, and publish your ideas before they are built or created. Moreover, Autodesk continues to develop a comprehensive portfolio of state-of-the-art CAD/CAM/CAE software for the global market.

Autodesk Fusion delivers a rich set of integrated tools that are powerful and intuitive to use. It is the first cloud-based 3D CAD/CAM/CAE software that combines the entire product development cycle into a single cloud-based platform. It allows you to design feature-based, parametric mechanical designs by using simple but highly effective 3D modeling tools. Autodesk Fusion provides a wide range of tools that allow you to create real-world components and assemblies. These components and assemblies can be converted into 2D engineering drawings for production and used for validating designs by simulating their real-world conditions and assessing the environmental impact of your products. It also enables you to create photorealistic renderings, animations, and toolpaths for CNC machines, in addition to creating rapid prototypes of your design by using the 3D printing workflow.

Autodesk Fusion 360: A Power Guide for Beginners and Intermediate Users (8th Edition): 2026 is designed for both instructor-led training and self-paced learning, this textbook is an essential resource for engineers, designers, and students aiming to master 3D mechanical design.

This comprehensive guide spans 14 chapters and 768 pages, covering key Autodesk Fusion workspaces, including DESIGN, ANIMATION, and DRAWING. It provides a structured approach to creating parametric 3D solid components, assemblies, animations, and detailed 2D drawings. Serving as both a valuable learning tool for beginners and an effective teaching aid for instructors.

This edition has been developed using **Autodesk Fusion version 2701.1.27 (March 2026)** to ensure compatibility with the latest features and enhancements..

This textbook goes beyond simply teaching the tools and commands of Autodesk Fusion by also emphasizing design principles. Each chapter includes **step-by-step tutorials** that guide users through the creation of mechanical designs and drawings with ease. Additionally, every chapter concludes with **hands-on test drives**, enabling users to practice and explore the powerful and intuitive capabilities of Autodesk Fusion.

Who Should Read This Textbook

This textbook is designed to benefit a wide range of Autodesk Fusion users, from beginners to advanced users, as well as Autodesk Fusion instructors. The easy-to-follow chapters ensure that readers can easily grasp various design techniques, Autodesk Fusion tools, and design principles.

What Is Covered in This Textbook

Autodesk Fusion 360: A Power Guide for Beginners and Intermediate Users (8th Edition): 2026 is designed to help you learn everything you need to get started with Autodesk Fusion through straightforward, step-by-step tutorials. This textbook covers the following topics:

*Chapter 1, "**Introducing Autodesk Fusion**,"* introduces the Autodesk Fusion user interface and various workspaces. It also explains how to manage data by using the **Data Panel**, save a design file, convert between design files, export a design to other CAD formats, open an existing design file, open different versions of a design, work in the offline mode, recover unsaved design data, share design, invoke a Marking Menu, and export your design for 3D printing.

*Chapter 2, "**Drawing Sketches with Autodesk Fusion**,"* discusses how to invoke a new design file in Autodesk Fusion and start creating a sketch by selecting a sketching plane. It explains how to specify the unit system as well as the grids and snaps settings. Besides, this chapter introduces methods for drawing lines, midpoint line, rectangles, circles, arcs, polygons, ellipses, slots, conic curves, splines, and so on by using the respective sketching tools. This chapter also discusses methods for editing a spline, creating sketch points, and inserting text in a sketch.

*Chapter 3, "**Editing and Modifying Sketches**,"* introduces various editing and modifying operations such as trimming unwanted sketch entities, extending sketch entities, offsetting, mirroring, patterning, scaling, breaking sketch entities, and creating fillets and chamfers by using various editing/modifying tools.

*Chapter 4, "**Applying Constraints and Dimensions**,"* introduces the concept of fully defined sketches encompassing the application of constraints and dimensions. It discusses various types of constraints and the application of constraints and dimensions to sketch entities. It explains methods for controlling the display of applied constraints and modifying or editing the dimensions of sketch entities. It also describe how to apply constraints and diamensions automatically. This chapter also introduces you to the different states of a sketch and various tools of the **SKETCH PALETTE** dialog box.

*Chapter 5, "**Creating Base Feature of Solid Models**,"* discusses how to create extrude and revolve base features by using the **Extrude** and **Revolve** tools. This chapter also explains how to navigate a model by using mouse buttons, ViewCube, and navigating tools such as **Pan**, **Zoom**, and **Fit**. It also teaches how to control the navigation settings like other CAD software you might be familiar with. Additionally, this chapter discusses changing the visual style of a model.

*Chapter 6, "**Creating Construction Geometries**,"* explains that the three default planes: Front, Top, and Right may not be enough for creating models having multiple features. Therefore, the chapter discusses how to create additional reference planes. Additionally, methods for creating a construction axis and a construction point are discussed.

*Chapter 7, "**Advanced Modeling - I**,"* introduces advanced options for creating extrude and revolve features. Methods for creating cut features and creating features by only keeping the intersecting material between them are discussed. This chapter explains how to create a new body and a component by using the **Extrude** and **Revolve** tools. Besides, it teaches how to work with a sketch having multiple profiles and project edges of existing features onto the currently active sketching plane. This chapter also discusses methods for editing an existing feature, a sketch, and a sketching plane. Additionally, the chapter discusses about creating 3D curves by using the **Project To Surface**, **Intersection Curve**, and

Intersect tools, in addition to methods for assigning material properties, calculating the mass properties of a model, and measuring the distance between objects.

*Chapter 8, "**Advanced Modeling - II**,"* discusses how to create sweep features, loft features, rib features, web features, emboss features, holes, threads, and primitive shapes such as solid rectangular boxes, cylinders, spheres, and torus. It also discusses methods for creating helical and spiral coils, pipes, automated modelling, and 3D sketches. The chapters also discuss creating cosmetic and modeled threads by using the **Thread** tool, in addition to creating simple, counterbore, and countersink holes by using the **Hole** tool.

*Chapter 9, "**Patterning and Mirroring**,"* introduces various patterning and mirroring tools. After completing this chapter, you can create different types of patterns such as rectangular patterns, circular patterns, and patterns along a path in addition to mirroring features, faces, bodies, or components about a mirroring plane.

*Chapter 10, "**Editing and Modifying 3D Models**,"* discusses how to modify or edit a 3D solid model by using the **Press Pull** tool. By using the **Press Pull** tool, you can offset the face of a model, fillet an edge of the model, and extrude a sketch profile dynamically in the graphics area. It also discusses creating constant and variable radius fillets to remove the sharp edges of a model, creating a fillet by specifying its chord length, creating full round fillets and rule fillets, along with various methods for creating a chamfer on the edges of a model. The chapter also discusses methods for creating a shell feature, adding drafts, scaling objects, combining solid bodies by performing different Boolean operations, offsetting faces, and splitting faces/bodies.

*Chapter 11, "**Working with Assemblies - I**,"* discusses how to create assemblies by using the bottom-up assembly approach. The chapter introduces the application of rigid, revolute, slider, cylindrical, pin-slot, planar, and ball joints to assemble components and define relative motion concerning each other. It also explains how to insert components in a design file, ground the first component, apply various types of joints, define joint origin, edit joints, define joint limits, animate a joint, animate a model, lock/unlock the motion between two joints, and group components together. Besides, this chapter discusses applying constraints and enabling contact sets between the components and capturing the position of components.

*Chapter 12, "**Working with Assemblies - II**,"* discusses how to create assemblies by using the top-down assembly approach. This chapter introduces the application of As-Built joints between the components of the assembly by using the **As-Built Joint** tool. Besides, it explains defining a joint origin on a component and editing components of an assembly.

*Chapter 13, "**Creating Animation of a Design**,"* discusses how to create an animation of a design/assembly in the **ANIMATION** Workspace. To animate an assembly, you need to capture various views and actions on the Timeline of a storyboard. The chapter explains how to capture views and actions on the **Timeline**. It also discusses methods for creating exploded views of the assembly (manually or automatically), turning on or off the visibility of the components, and creating callouts. Besides, it teaches customizing and deleting views and actions on the **Timeline**, creating new storyboards, turning on or off the recording of the views, and publishing animation in a *.avi* file format.

*Chapter 14, "**Working with Drawings**,"* discusses how to create 2D drawings of components and assemblies using manual and automatic methods. The chapter introduces the concept and definition of the angle of projections and editing the document and sheet settings, in addition to creating sketches, applying dimensions, adding notes, geometries such as center marks and centerlines, and surface texture symbols in drawing views. Besides, it discusses how to create the Bill of Material (BOM)/Part List, add balloons, renumber balloons, add drawing sheets, create a drawing template, and methods for exporting a drawing.

Icons/Terms used in this Textbook

The following icons and terms are used in this textbook:

Note

Note: Notes highlight information requiring special attention.

Tip

Tip: Tips provide additional advice, which increases the efficiency of the users.

Drop-down Menu

A drop-down menu is a menu in which a set of tools is grouped, see Figure 1.

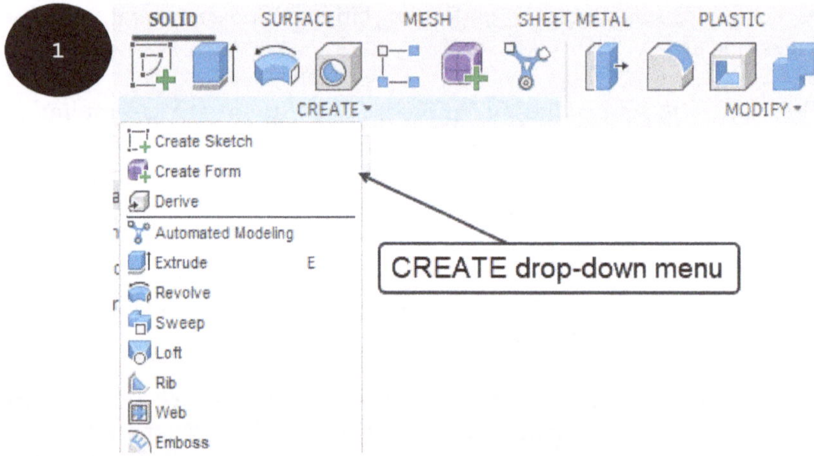

Drop-down List

A drop-down list is a list in which a set of options is grouped, see Figure 2.

Field

A Field allows you to enter a new value, or modify an existing/default value, as per your requirement, see Figure 2.

Button

A Button appears as a 3D icon and is used for confirming or discarding an action, see Figure 2.

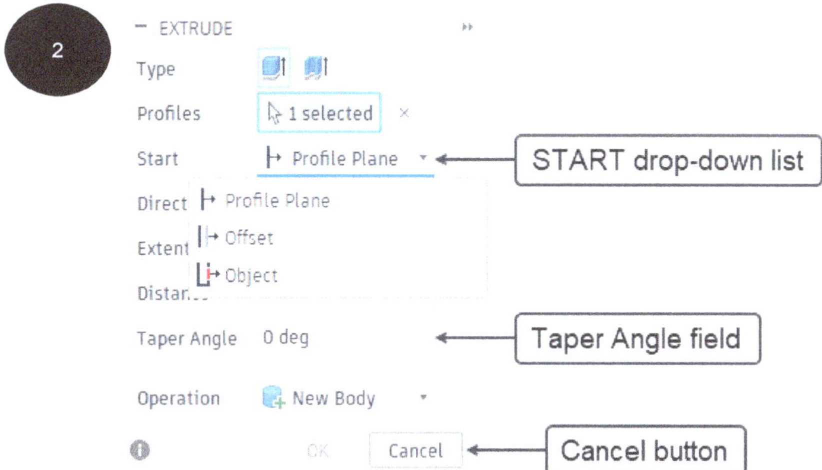

Rollout

A rollout is an area in which drop-down lists, fields, selection options, check boxes, and so on are available to specify various parameters, see Figure 3. A rollout can either be in the expanded or collapsed form. You can expand or collapse a rollout by clicking on the arrow available on the left side of its title bar.

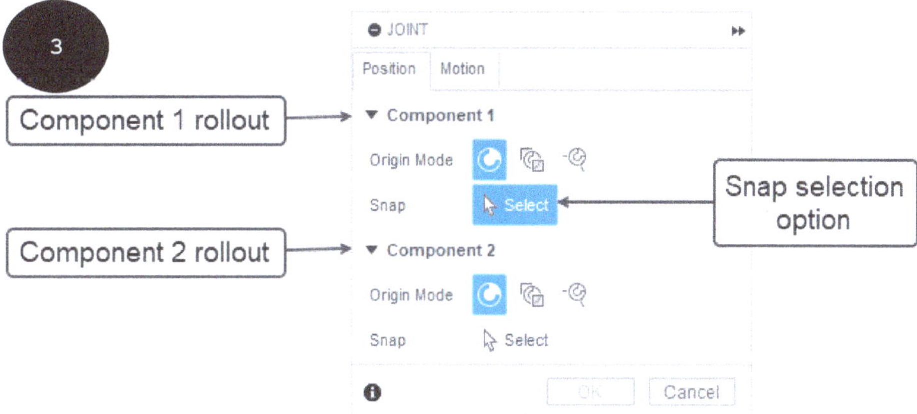

Check box

A check box allows you to turn on or off the uses of a particular option, see Figure 4.

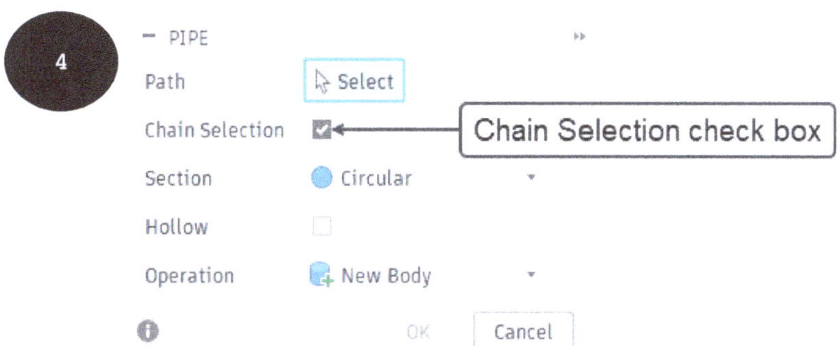

How to Download Online Resources

To download the free online teaching and learning resources of the textbook, log in to our website (*cadartifex.com/login*) and navigate to the respective textbook page to access and download its resources. If you are a new user, you need to first sign up (*cadartifex.com/register*) for downloading the online resources of the textbook.

Students and faculty members can download all parts/models used in the illustrations, Tutorials, and Hand-on Test Drives (exercises) of the textbook. In addition, faculty can also download PowerPoint Presentations (PPTs) of each chapter of the textbook.

Interactive Support for Your Learning

In the book, you'll find QR **codes** next to key tutorial steps for certain tutorials. Scan these codes to access video demonstrations, designed to help you through any challenging parts of the process.

How to Contact the Author

We truly value your feedback and suggestions. Please feel free to reach out to us at *info@cadartifex*.com or visit ***www.cadartifex.com*** to share your feedback and download additional learning resources.

Thank you for choosing **Autodesk Fusion 360: A Power Guide for Beginners and Intermediate Users (8th Edition): 2026**. We hope the knowledge and concepts presented in this textbook support you in achieving your professional objectives.

1

Introducing Autodesk Fusion

In this chapter, the following topics will be discussed:

- Installing Autodesk Fusion
- Getting Started with Autodesk Fusion
- Understanding the Part Design User Interface
- Invoking a New Design File
- Setting the Default Design Type
- Switching Between Design Types
- Working with Workspaces
- Managing Data by Using the Data Panel
- Saving a Design File
- Exporting a Design to Other CAD Formats
- Opening an Existing Design File
- Working in the Offline Mode
- Sharing a Design Using a Link
- Recovering Unsaved Data
- Invoking a Marking Menu
- 3D Printing

Welcome to the world of Computer-Aided Design (CAD) with Autodesk Fusion. Autodesk Fusion is a product of Autodesk Inc., one of the leading technology providers for the engineering, architecture, construction, manufacturing, media, and entertainment industries. It offers robust 3D design tools that allow you to design, visualize, simulate, and publish your ideas before they are built or manufactured. Moreover, Autodesk continues to develop a comprehensive portfolio of state-of-the-art CAD/CAM/CAE software solutions for global markets.

Autodesk Fusion delivers a rich set of integrated tools that are powerful and intuitive to use. It is a cloud-based 3D CAD/CAM/CAE software platform that combines the entire product development cycle into a single environment. It allows you to create feature-based, parametric mechanical designs using effective 3D modeling tools. Autodesk Fusion also enables you to create assemblies, engineering 2D drawings, photorealistic renderings, animations, CNC toolpaths, and rapid prototypes using 3D printing workflows.

Autodesk Fusion enables multiple design teams to work collaboratively on a single project. It allows you to securely save designs in the cloud with access from anywhere and share them with partners and colleagues. Autodesk Fusion also tracks different versions of designs, improving collaboration and shortening the design cycle. It is compatible with Windows and macOS operating systems.

Installing Autodesk Fusion

If you do not have installed Autodesk Fusion in your system, you first need to get it installed. However, before you start installing Autodesk Fusion, you need to evaluate the system requirements and ensure that you have a system capable of running it adequately. Below are the system requirements:

- **Operating Systems:** Microsoft® windows 11, 23H2 (Build 22631 or newer), macOS 14 sonoma (macOS 15.7 Sequoia, macOS 26 Tahoe, or newer recommended)
- **CPU Type:** x86-based 64-bit processor (Example: Intel Core i3, AMD Ryzen 3, or similar)
- **RAM:** 8 GB RAM (32 GB or more recommended)
- **Disk Space:** 8.5 GB of storage (10 GB or more recommended)
- **Graphics Card:** Supported for DirectX 11 (Direct3D 10.1 or greater), Dedicated GPU with 1 GB or more of VRAM, or Integrated graphics with 6 GB or more of RAM

For more information about the system requirements, visit: *knowledge.autodesk.com/support/fusion-360/troubleshooting/caas/sfdcarticles/sfdcarticles/System-requirements-for-Autodesk-Fusion-360.html*

Once the system is ready, install Autodesk Fusion by using the downloaded Autodesk Fusion software setup files. You can download the setup files by logging in to your Autodesk account.

Getting Started with Autodesk Fusion

Once Autodesk Fusion is installed on your system, launch the software by double-clicking the **Autodesk Fusion** icon on your desktop. After the necessary files are loaded, the Autodesk Fusion startup interface appears with the default design type (Part Design), as shown in Figure 1.1.

1.1

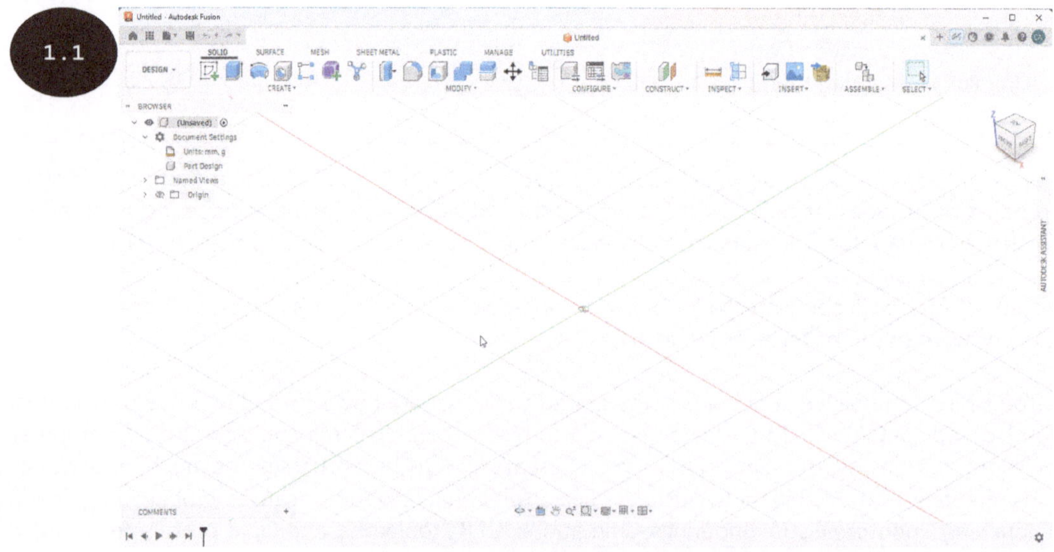

Note: Each time Autodesk Fusion is launched, a new design document with the default name "**Untitled**" is opened automatically. By default, Part Design is set as the default design type that opens automatically when Autodesk Fusion is started. It allows you to create solid, surface, and sheet metal components. However, if required, you can change the default design type at any time using the **Preferences** dialog box. You will learn about setting the default design type later in this chapter.

If you are not already logged into your Autodesk account, the **Welcome to Fusion** window appears when Autodesk Fusion is launched, see Figure 1.2. In this window, click on the **Sign In** button to display the **Sign in** page in the default browser, see Figure 1.3. Enter your **E-mail ID** and click on the **NEXT** button. On the **Welcome** page that appears, enter the password and click on the **SIGN IN** button. After signing in, click on the **Go to product** button displayed in the browser to open Autodesk Fusion.

1.2

1.3

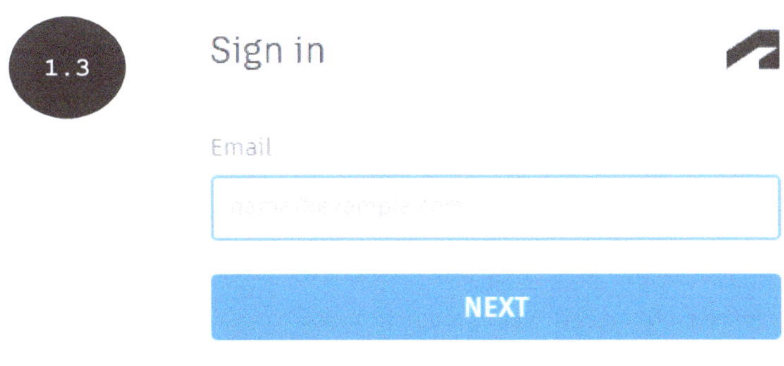

Understanding the Part Design User Interface

It is evident from the startup user interface of the Part Design file that it is intuitive and user-friendly. The various components of the startup user interface are shown in Figure 1.4 and are discussed next.

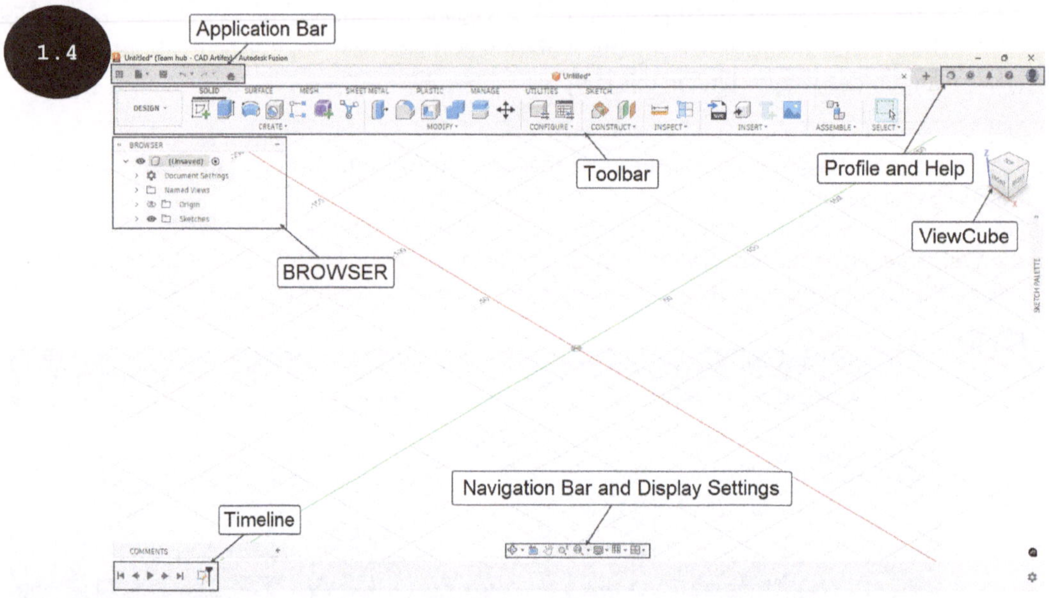

Application Bar

Application Bar consists of frequently used tools to access design files, manage data, create a new design file, export data, save design files, and undo/redo operations, see Figure 1.5. You will learn about these tools later in this chapter.

Toolbar

Toolbar provides access to various tools for accomplishing different tasks depending on the activated workspace, see Figure 1.6.

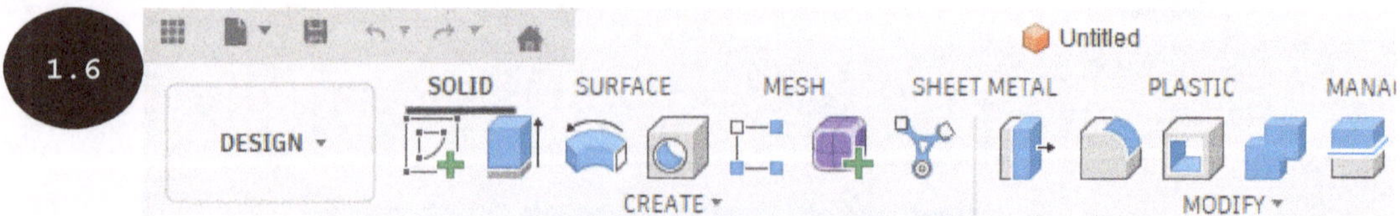

You can activate a workspace by using the **Workspace** drop-down menu of the **Toolbar**, see Figure 1.7. By default, the **DESIGN** workspace is activated in the **Workspace** drop-down menu of the **Toolbar**. As a result, the tools for creating and editing solid 3D parts, surface models, mesh designs, sheet metal components, and plastic parts are available in the **SOLID**, **SURFACE**, **MESH**, **SHEET METAL**, and **PLASTIC** tabs of the **Toolbar**, respectively. You will learn more about the different workspaces available in Autodesk Fusion later in this chapter.

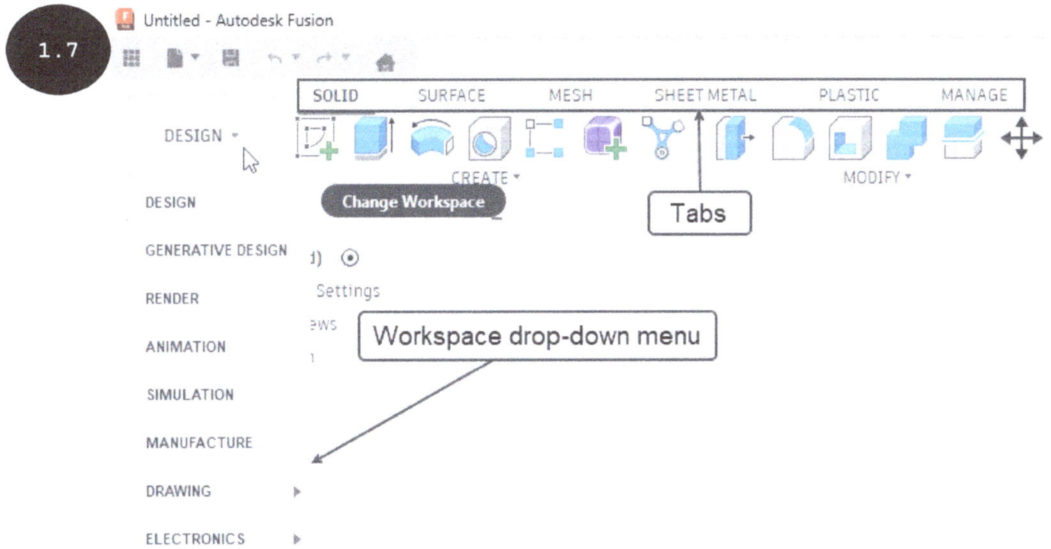

BROWSER

BROWSER appears on the left side of the graphics area and keeps a record of all objects in the design which includes sketches, bodies, components, and construction geometries, see Figure 1.8. You can use **BROWSER** to control the visibility of each object of the design. For example, to toggle the visibility of an object in the graphics area, click on the **Show/Hide** icon of the object, see Figure 1.8. In **BROWSER**, a set of similar objects are grouped under different nodes.

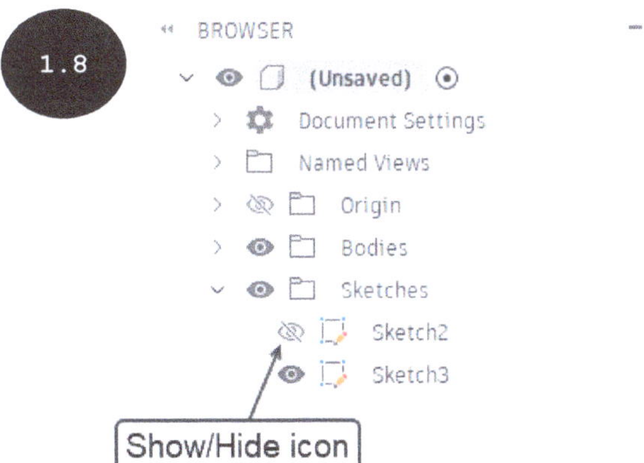

Profile and Help Menus

Profile and **Help** menus appear in the upper right corner of the interface. The **Profile** menu allows you to control your profile, account settings, and design preferences settings, see Figure 1.9.

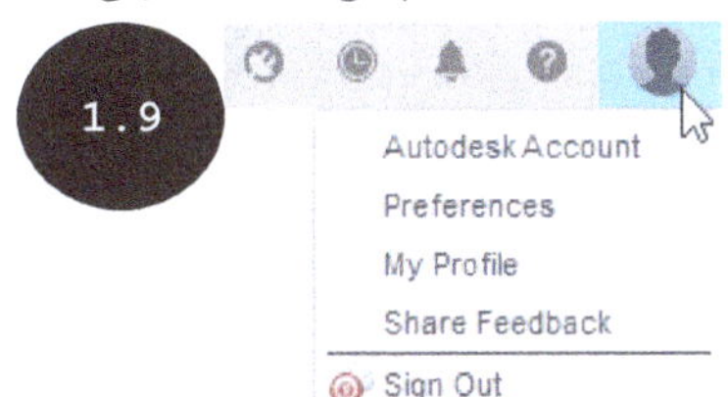

The **Help** menu allows you to access help documents, community forums, what's new in Autodesk Fusion information, and so on, see Figure 1.10.

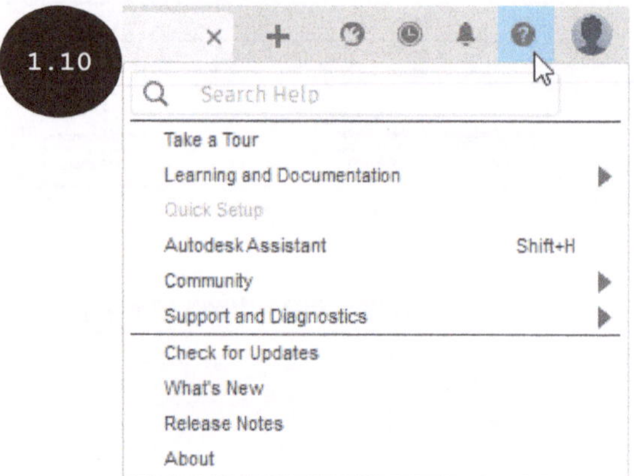

ViewCube

ViewCube is available at the upper right corner of the graphics area and is used for navigating the design, see Figure 1.11. You can orbit or switch between the standard and isometric views of a model by using ViewCube. You will learn to navigate a design by using ViewCube in later chapters.

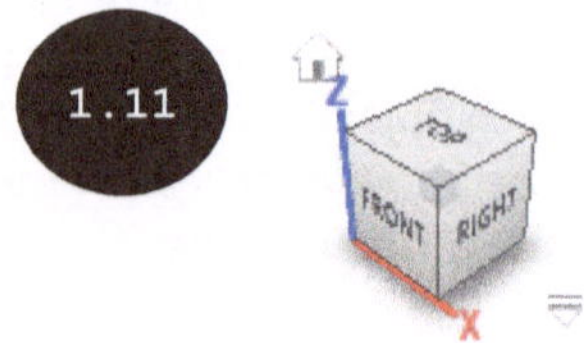

Timeline

Timeline appears in the lower left corner of the interface and keeps a record of all features or operations performed on the design, see Figure 1.12. Note that the features appear in the **Timeline** in the order they are created. The Rollback Bar appears on the right side of the last feature in the **Timeline**. You can drag the Rollback Bar to the left or right in the **Timeline** to step forward or backward through the regeneration order of the features. Note that the features present after the Rollback Bar get suppressed and do not appear in the graphics area.

Navigation Bar

Navigation Bar is available at the lower middle part of the graphics area, see Figure 1.13. **Navigation Bar** contains navigation tools such as **Zoom**, **Pan**, and **Orbit** to navigate the design, as well as tools to control the display settings such as the appearance of the interface and the visual style of the design. You will learn about navigating and display settings in later chapters.

Invoking a New Design File

As discussed earlier, every time Autodesk Fusion is launched, a new design file with the default name "**Untitled**" and the default design type is opened automatically, see Figure 1.14. Various components of the startup user interface, such as the **Application Bar**, **Toolbar**, **Browser**, and **Timeline**, have already been discussed.

1.14

New Design File (Untitled)

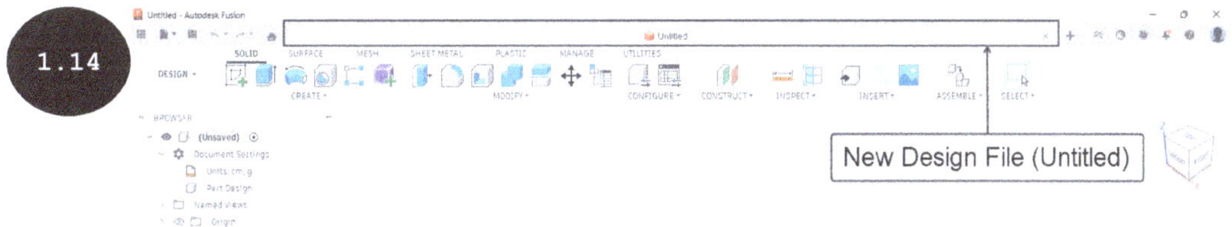

In addition to the default design file, you can open a new design file using the **New** tool. To do so, invoke the **File** drop-down menu in the **Application Bar** and then click on the **New** tool, see Figure 1.15. The **What do you want to design?** dialog box appears, see Figure 1.16. This dialog box allows you to choose the required design environment to be opened.

1.15

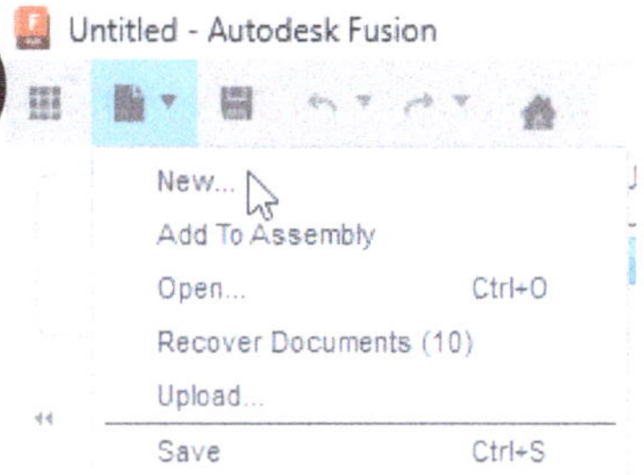

Untitled - Autodesk Fusion
New...
Add To Assembly
Open... Ctrl+O
Recover Documents (10)
Upload...
Save Ctrl+S

1.16

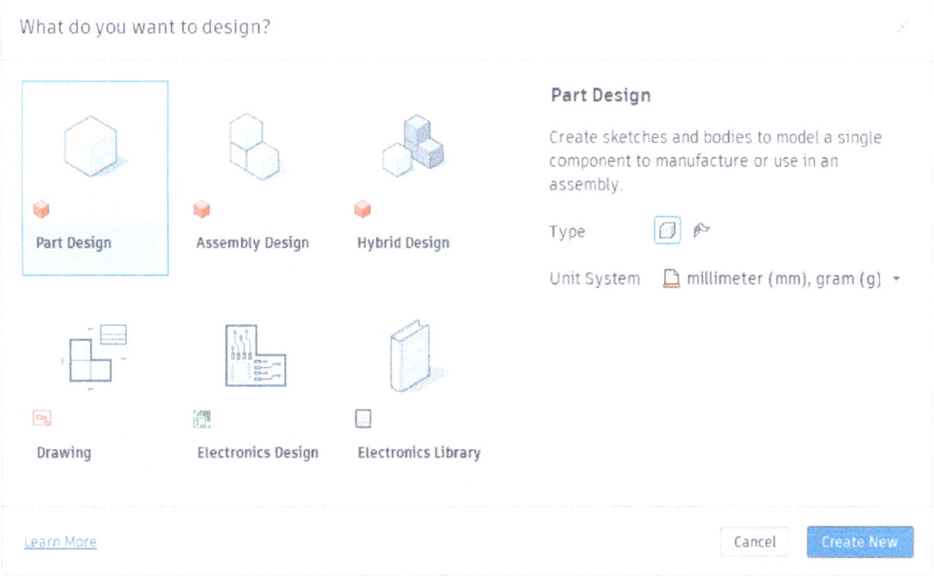

What do you want to design?
Part Design
Assembly Design
Hybrid Design
Drawing
Electronics Design
Electronics Library
Part Design
Create sketches and bodies to model a single component to manufacture or use in an assembly.
Type
Unit System
millimeter (mm), gram (g)
Learn More
Cancel
Create New

In the **What do you want to design?** dialog box, Autodesk Fusion prompts you to specify the type of design you want to open, such as Part Design, Assembly Design, Hybrid Design, or Drawing. Based on the selected option, Autodesk Fusion opens the corresponding design environment for creating a part, assembly, or drawing.

You can also click on the **+** sign next to the name of the existing design file to access the **What do you want to design?** dialog box, see Figure 1.17. The methods for opening different design environments using the **What do you want to design?** dialog box are discussed next.

Invoking a New Part Design File

To invoke a new Part Design file, select the **Part Design** button in the **What do you want to design?** dialog box. You can further specify the type of component to be created by choosing either the **Standard** or **Sheet Metal** option in the **Type** area of the dialog box, see Figure 1.18. By default, the **Standard** option is selected and is used for creating a solid component.

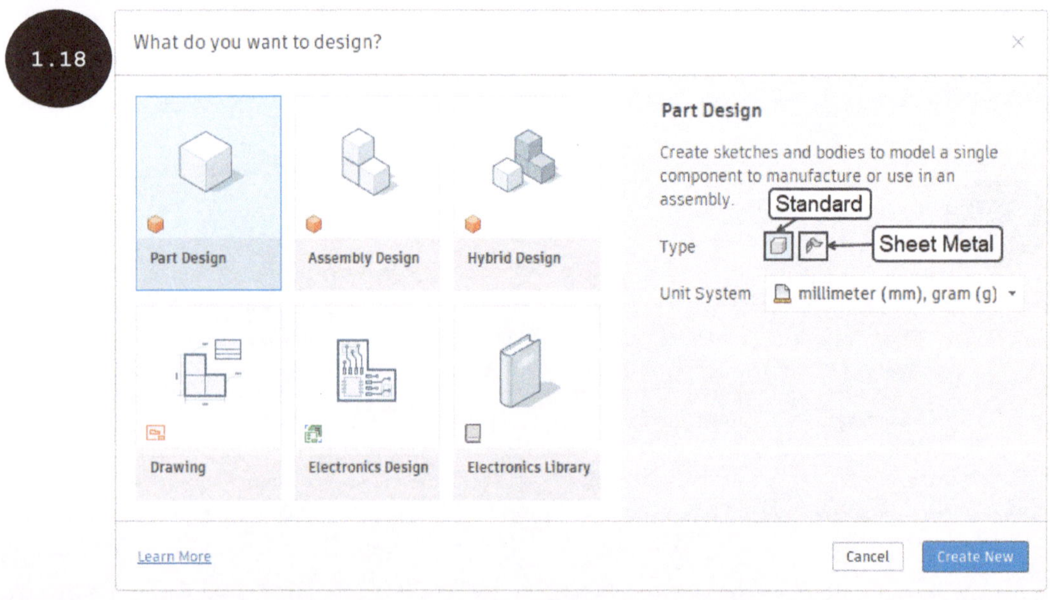

Note: Autodesk Fusion allows you to create solid, sheet metal, and surface designs within the same Part Design file by accessing their respective tools. The methods for accessing these tools are discussed later in this chapter.

Next, specify the desired unit system, such as **millimeter (mm), gram (g)**; **centimeter (cm), gram (g)**; or **meter (m), kilogram (kg)**, using the **Unit System** drop-down list of the dialog box. The unit system of a design file can be modified at any stage during the design process. Units and their management are discussed in more detail in later chapters.

After selecting **Part Design** and the required unit system, click on the **Create New** button. A new Part Design file with the default name "**Untitled (n)**" is opened in a separate tab, see Figure 1.19. The interface appears with various tools displayed in the **Toolbar**.

1.19

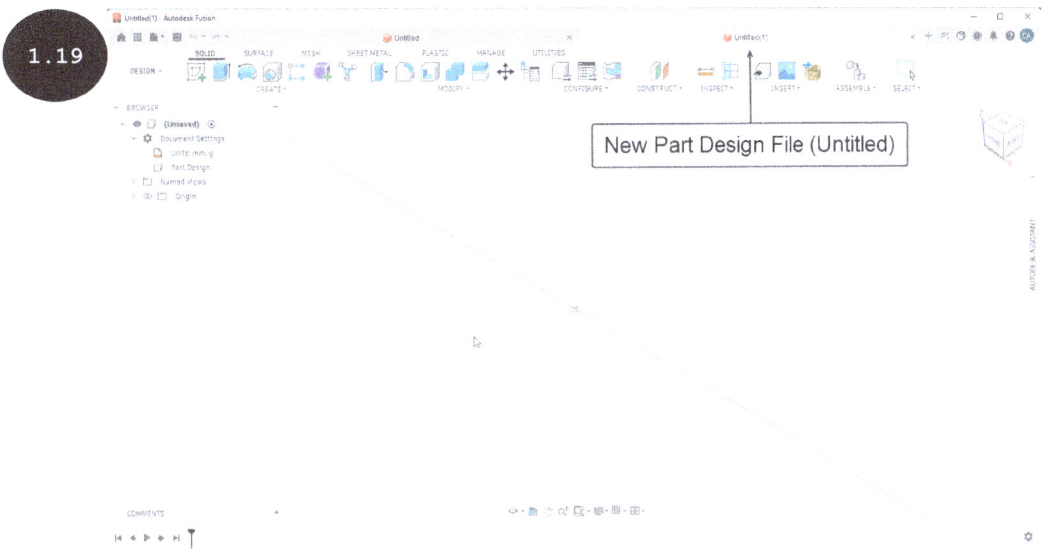

Invoking an Assembly Design File

An Assembly Design file allows you to insert external components to build assemblies by defining relationships between them. It also allows you to create an assembly by creating multiple components within the same Assembly Design file. Figure 1.20 shows an example of an assembly.

1.20

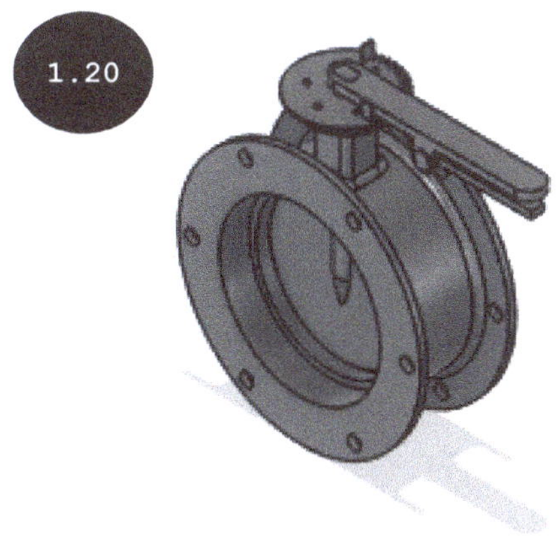

To invoke an Assembly Design file for creating an assembly, select the **Assembly Design** button in the **What do you want to design?** dialog box, see Figure 1.21.

1.21

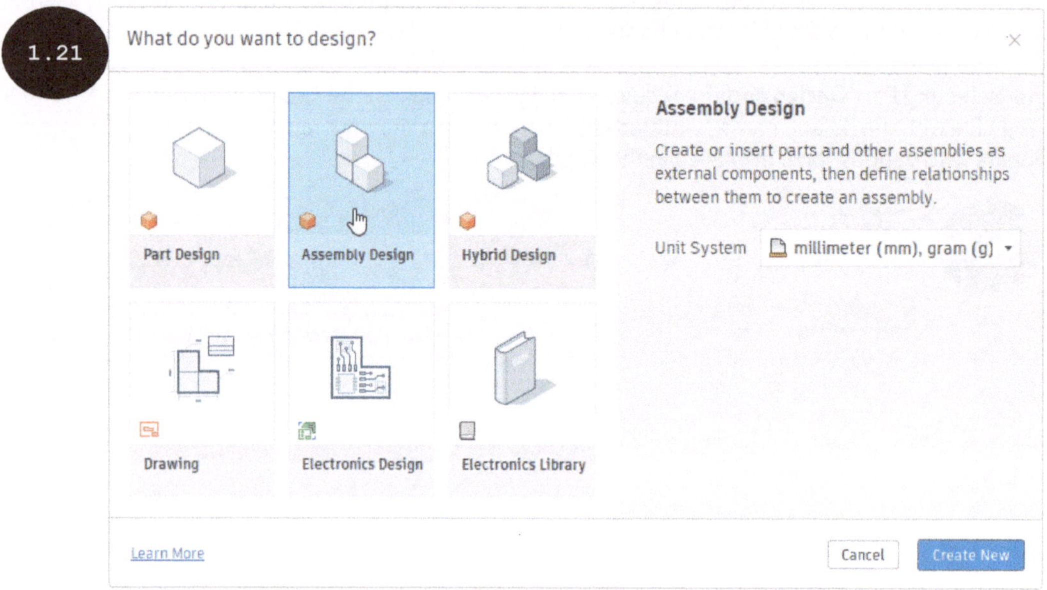

After selecting the **Assembly Design** button, specify the desired unit system, such as **millimeter (mm), gram (g)**; **centimeter (cm), gram (g)**; or **meter (m), kilogram (kg)**, using the **Unit System** drop-down list. Next, click on the **Create New** button. A new Assembly Design file with the default name "**Untitled (n)**" is opened in a separate tab with tools for creating an assembly, see Figure 1.22.

1.22

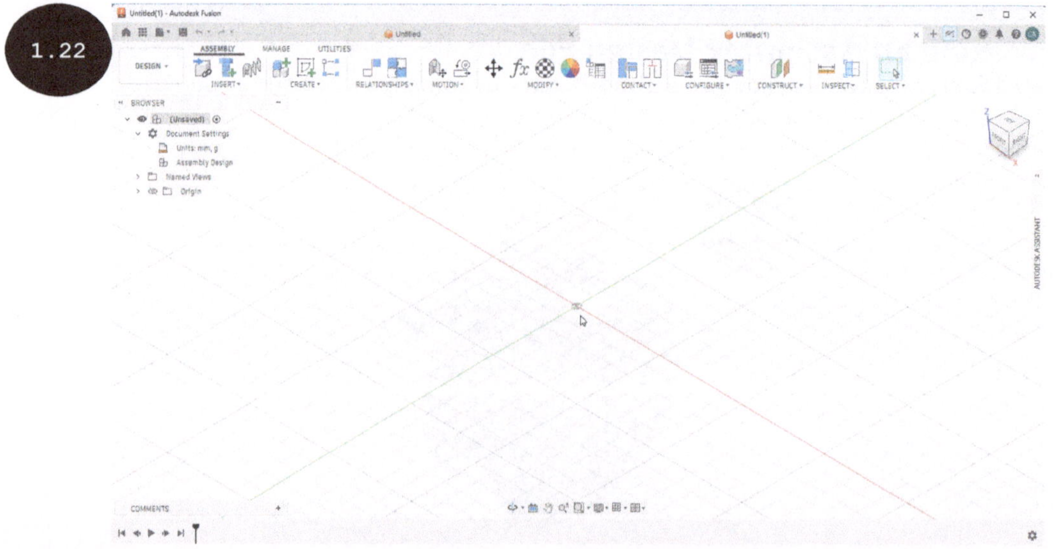

Note that the user interface components of the Assembly Design file such as the **Application Bar**, **BROWSER**, **Profile** and **Help** menus, **ViewCube**, and **Timeline** are similar to those in the Part Design environment. However, the **Assembly** tab in the **Toolbar** provides tools specifically used for creating and managing assemblies. You will learn about creating assemblies in detail in later chapters.

Invoking a Hybrid Design File

A Hybrid Design file allows you to work in an environment where parts and assemblies can be created and managed within a single file. Similar to the Part Design file, it enables you to create solid, surface, and sheet metal components. In addition, like the Assembly Design file, it allows you to create components and insert external components to build assemblies by defining relationships between them.

To invoke the Hybrid Design environment, select the **Hybrid Design** button in the **What do you want to design?** dialog box. Next, specify the desired unit system, such as **millimeter (mm), gram (g); centimeter (cm), gram (g)**; or **meter (m), kilogram (kg)** using the **Unit System** drop-down list.

After selecting **Hybrid Design** and the required unit system, click the **Create New** button. A new Hybrid Design file is created with the default name "**Untitled (n)**," providing access to both part modeling tools and assembly tools, as shown in Figure 1.23.

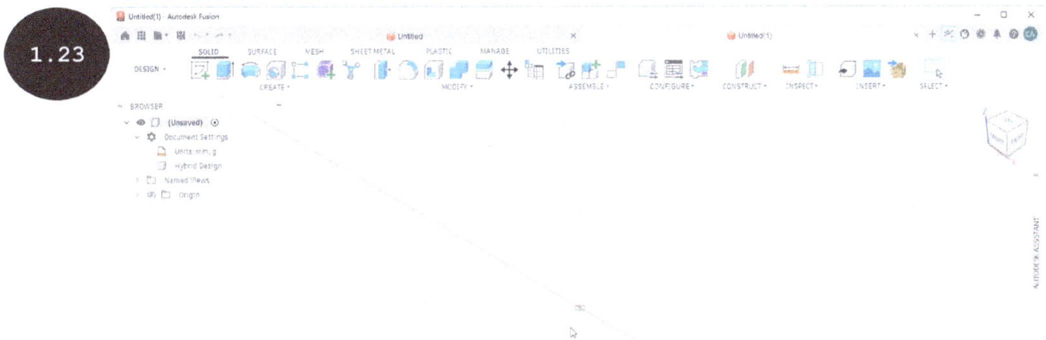

1.23

Invoking a Drawing File

To create a drawing of a component or an assembly, you need to access the Drawing environment. To do this, select the **Drawing** button in the **What do you want to design?** dialog box, see Figure 1.24.

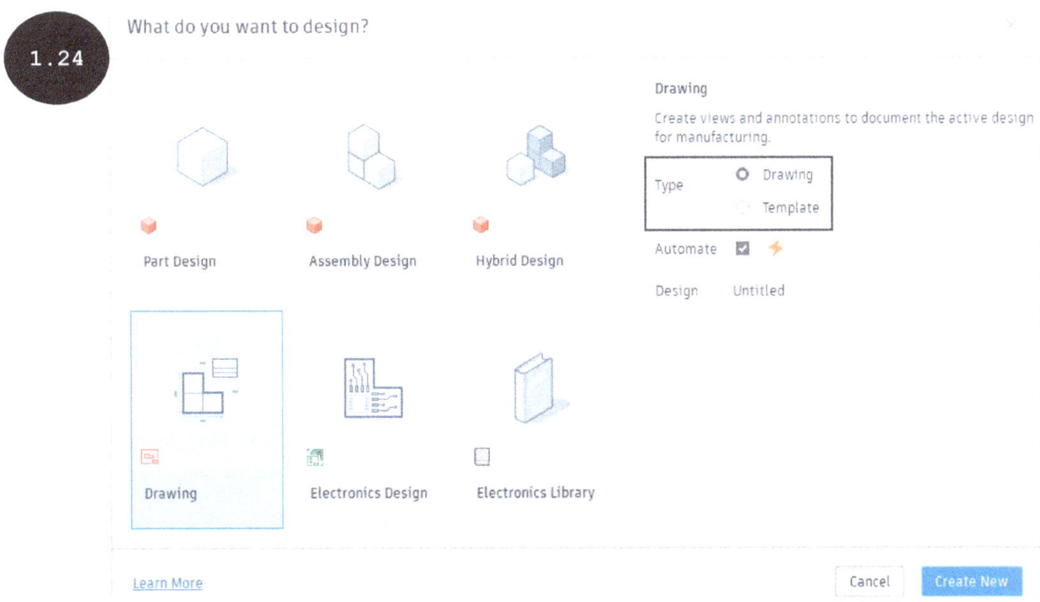

1.24

In the **Type** area, you can specify whether to create a new drawing of a design or a template file by selecting the appropriate radio button, refer to Figure 1.24. By default, the **Drawing** radio button is selected and is used to create 2D drawings of a design. You will learn more about creating drawings and templates in Chapter 14.

Figure 1.25 shows the Drawing environment startup interface, and Figure 1.26 shows a sample drawing of a design for reference.

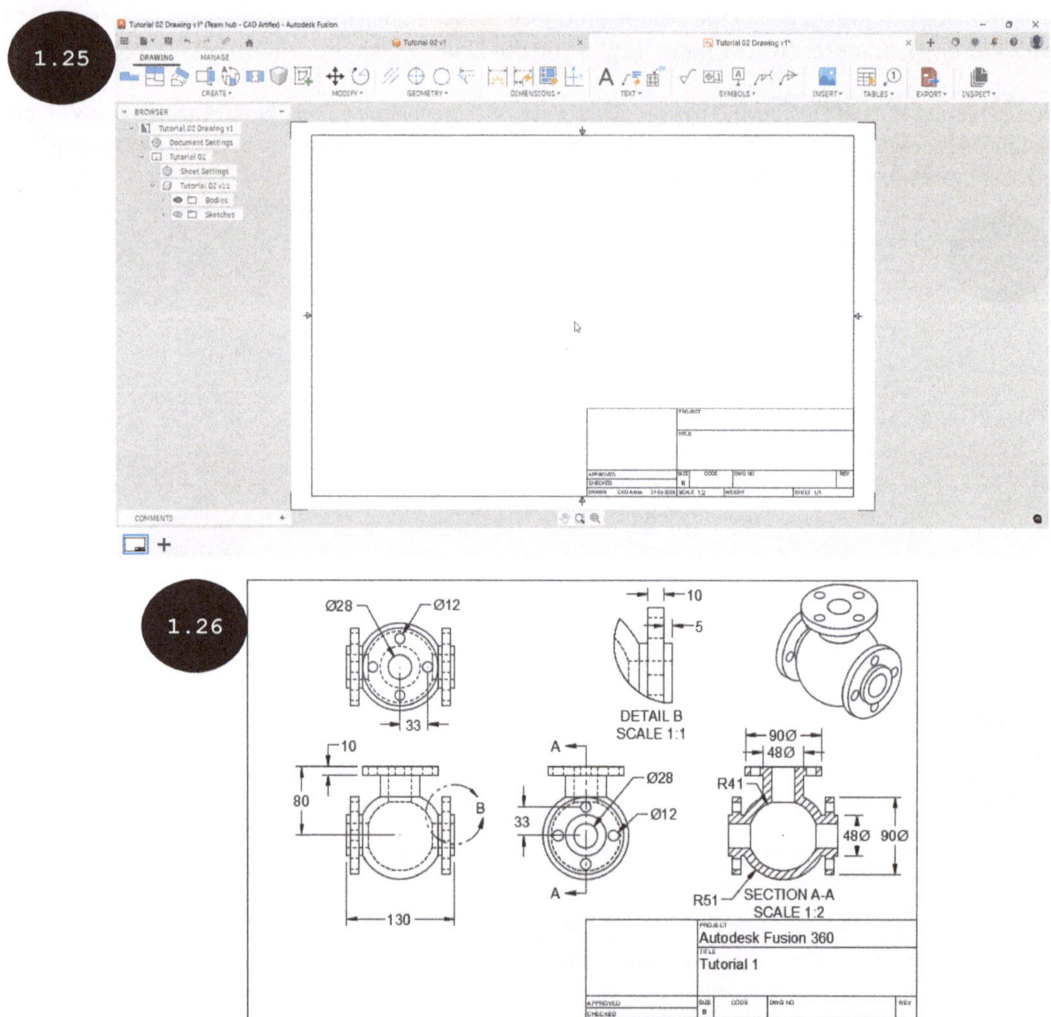

1.25

1.26

Invoking an Electronics Design File

To access the Electronics Design environment for creating and managing schematics, 2D PCB, and 3D PCB designs, select the **Electronics Design** button in the **What do you want to design?** dialog box, and then click the **Create New** button. Figure 1.27 shows the startup user interface of the Electronics Design file used to create schematics, 2D PCB, and 3D PCB designs.

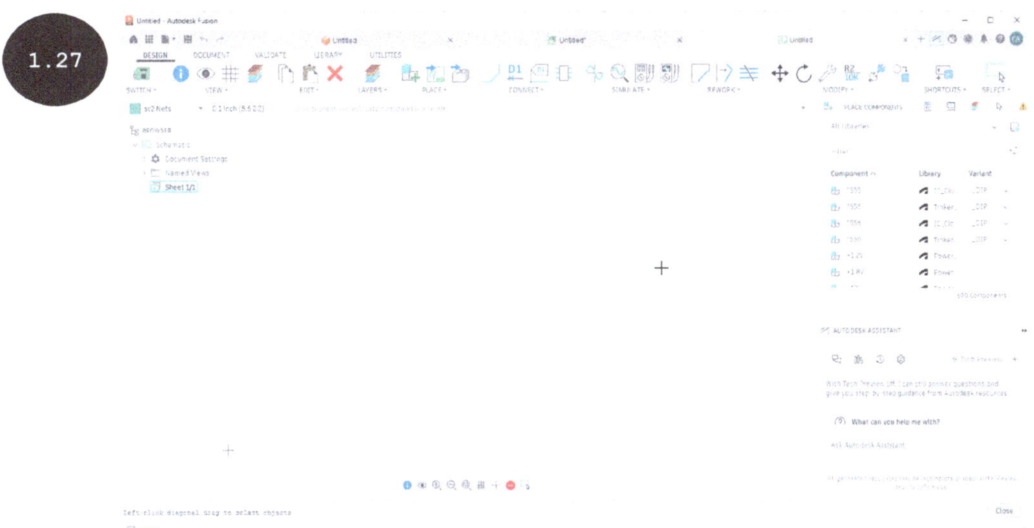

Invoking an Electronics Library File

To access the Electronics Library environment for creating and managing components used in electronics designs, select the **Electronics Library** button in the **What do you want to design?** dialog box and then click the **Create New** button.

Figure 1.28 shows the startup user interface of the Electronics Library file used for creating components for electronics designs.

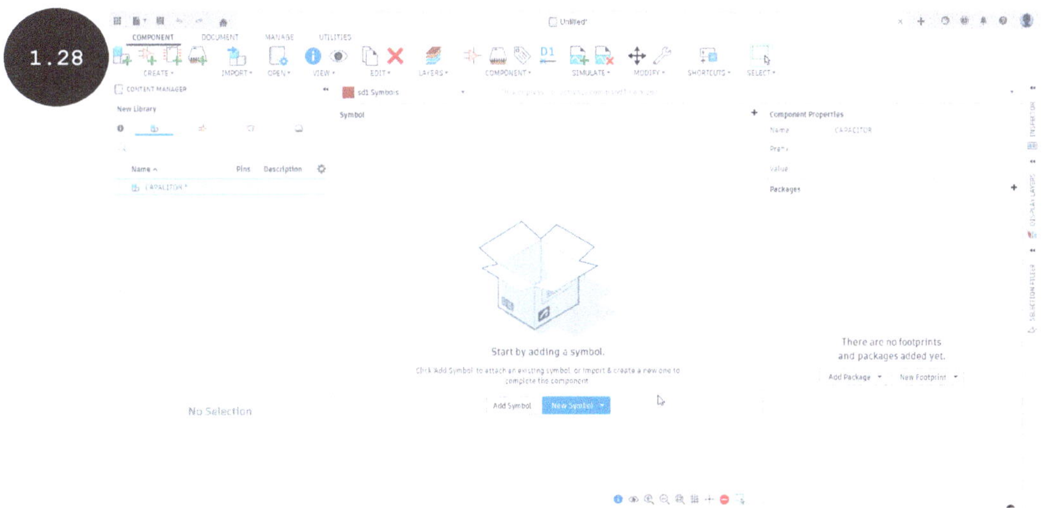

Setting the Default Design Type

By default, Part Design is set as the default design type that opens automatically each time Autodesk Fusion is launched. It provides direct access to the Part Design environment for creating solid, surface, and sheet metal components. However, if required, you can set any desired design type (Part Design, Assembly Design, Hybrid Design, or Drawing) as the default one using the **Preferences** dialog box.

To set a design type as the default one, click on your profile image in the upper-right corner. The **User Account** drop-down menu appears, see Figure 1.29. In this menu, click on the **Preferences** tool to open the **Preferences** dialog box, refer to Figure 1.30.

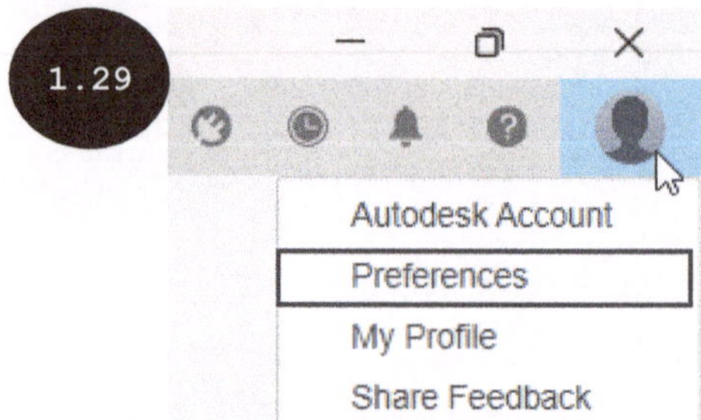

In the **Preferences** dialog box, invoke the **Default design type** drop-down list and select the required design type as the default one, see Figure 1.30. After selecting the required design type, click on the **Apply** button and then click on the **OK** button to apply the changes and close the dialog box. The next time Autodesk Fusion is launched, the newly defined default design type will open automatically.

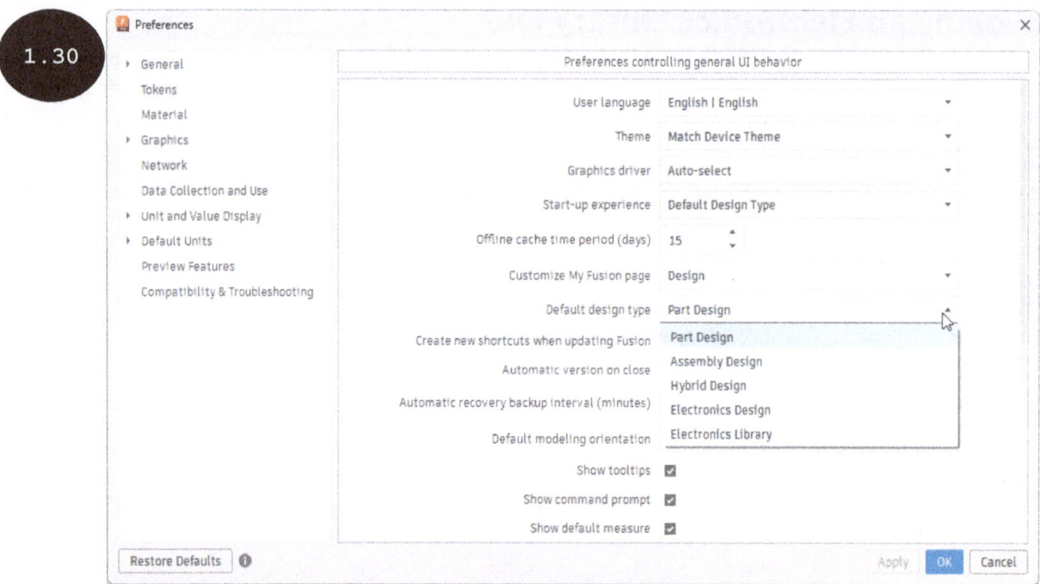

Switching Between Design Types

The expanded **Document Settings** node in the **BROWSER** displays the name of the current design type, see Figure 1.31. This figure indicates that the current file is a Part Design file.

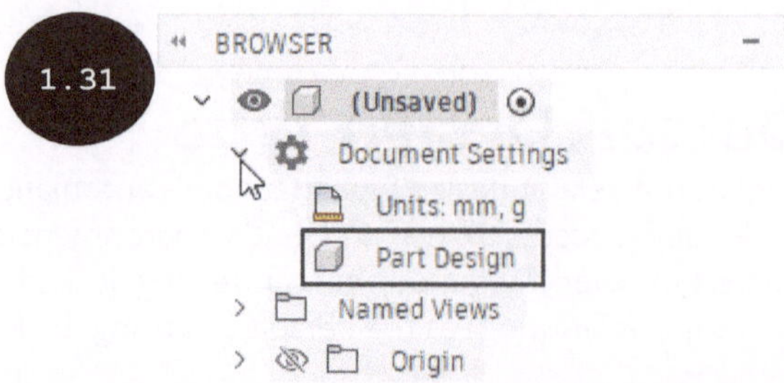

However, you can easily convert a Part Design file to an Assembly Design or Hybrid Design file, and vice versa, as required. To do this, move the cursor over the **Part Design** option under the **Document Settings** node in the **BROWSER**, see Figure 1.32. Then, click the **Convert Design Type** icon that appears. The **CONVERT UNTITLED** dialog box appears, see Figure 1.33.

In the drop-down list of this dialog box, select the desired design type and click the **Convert** button. The current file is then converted to the selected design type.

In Autodesk Fusion, the tools available in the **Toolbar** of a design file depend on the active workspace. By default, the **DESIGN** workspace is active. As a result, in a Part Design file, tools related to creating 3D solid components, surface models, mesh designs, and sheet metal components are available in different tabs of the **Toolbar**. The various workspaces available in Autodesk Fusion are discussed next.

Working with Workspaces

Workspaces are defined as task-oriented environments in which different tools and commands are organized according to design objectives.

In Autodesk Fusion, different workspaces namely, **DESIGN**, **GENERATIVE DESIGN**, **RENDER**, **ANIMATION**, **SIMULATION**, **MANUFACTURE**, **DRAWING**, and **ELECTRONICS** are available. You can switch between these workspaces by using the **Workspace** drop-down menu of the **Toolbar**, see Figure 1.34. Different workspaces are discussed next.

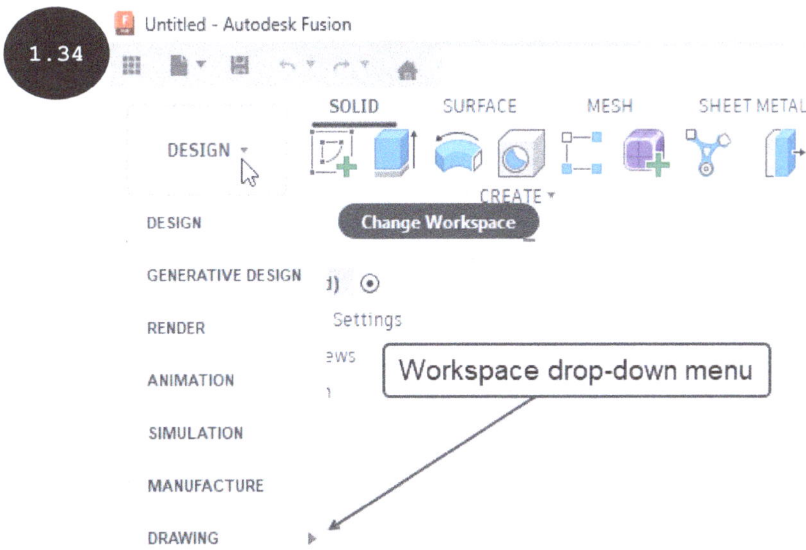

DESIGN Workspace

The **DESIGN** workspace consists of different sets of tools that are used for creating 3D solid models, surface models, mesh models, sheet metal models, as well as free-form 3D solid or surface models in the respective tabs of the **Toolbar**. Different tabs of the **Toolbar** in the **DESIGN** workspace are discussed next.

SOLID

The **SOLID** tab consists of different sets of tools that are used for creating 3D solid models, which includes designing 3D solid components and assemblies, see Figure 1.35.

1.35

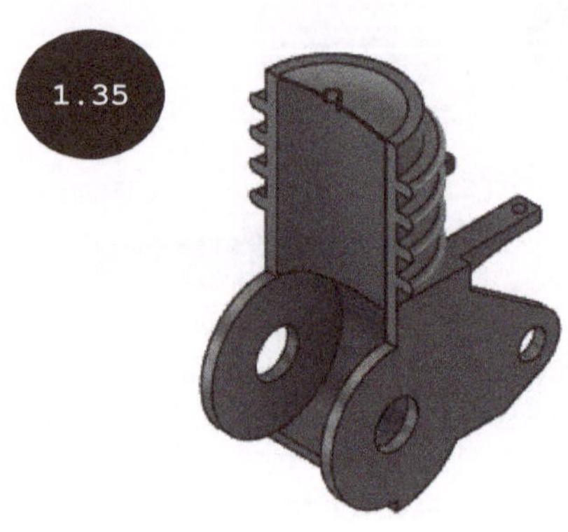

SURFACE

The **SURFACE** tab consists of different sets of tools that are used for creating surface models, see Figure 1.36. Surface models have zero thickness and are generally used for creating models with complex structures, see Figure 1.37.

1.36

1.37

Note: To learn about creating surface designs and sculpting with T-Spline surfaces, refer to the **"Autodesk Fusion 360 Surface Design and Sculpting with T-Spline Surfaces (8th Edition)"** textbook by CADArtifex.

MESH

The **MESH** tab consists of different sets of tools that are used for creating mesh bodies, see Figure 1.38. A mesh body is a collection of polygonal faces composed of vertices and edges, see Figure 1.39. Mesh bodies have no thickness and are generally used in additive manufacturing.

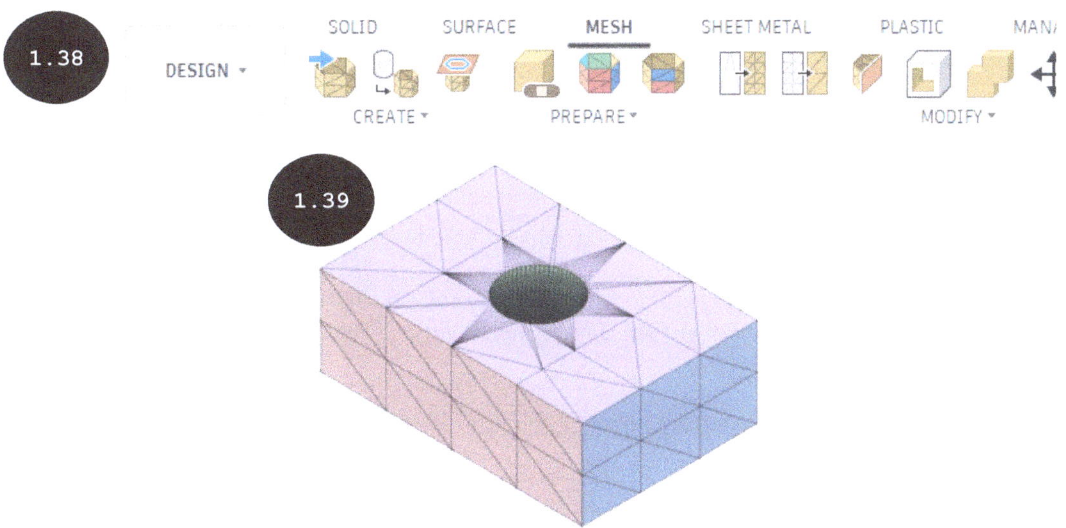

SHEET METAL

The **SHEET METAL** tab consists of different sets of tools that are used for creating sheet metal components, see Figures 1.40 and 1.41.

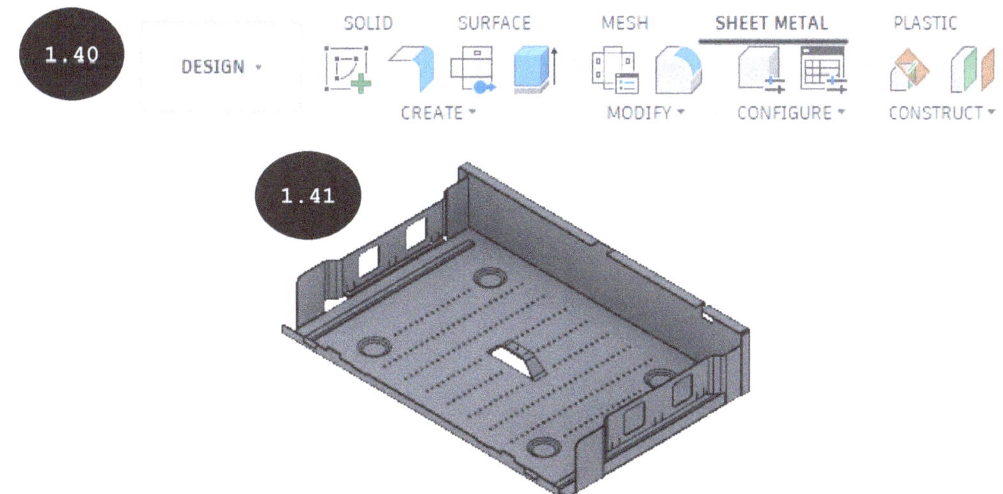

FORM

The **FORM** contextual tab is provided with different sets of tools that are used for creating or editing free-form T-Spline surface models of desired shapes, see Figure 1.42.

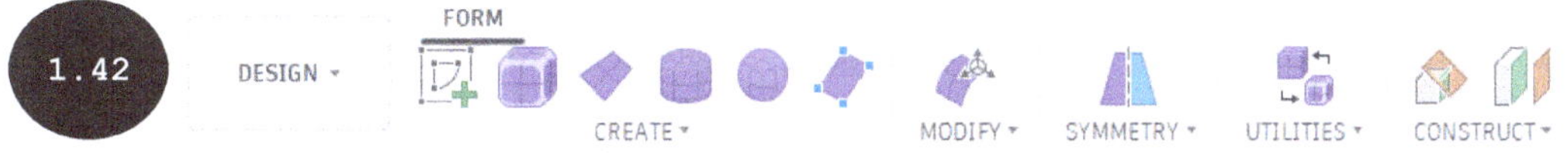

Note that the **FORM** contextual tab is the sub-environment of the **DESIGN** Workspace and can be invoked by clicking on the **Create Form** tool in the **CREATE** panel of the **SOLID** tab in the **DESIGN**

workspace, see Figure 1.43. To return to the **SOLID** tab, you need to click on the **FINISH FORM** tool in the **Toolbar**.

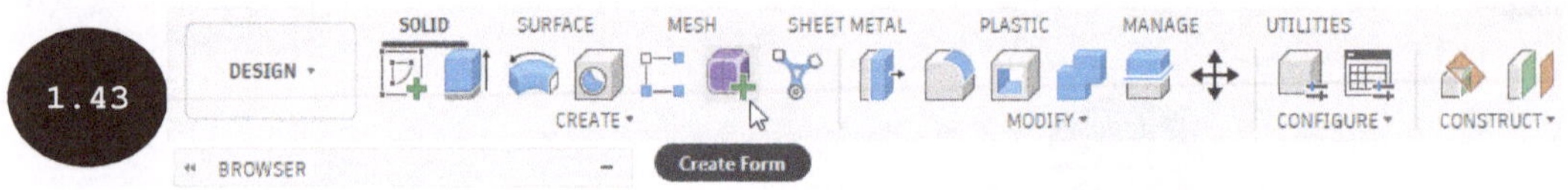

Note: To learn about creating surface designs and sculpting with T-Spline surfaces, refer to the **"Autodesk Fusion 360 Surface Design and Sculpting with T-Spline Surfaces (8th Edition)"** textbook by CADArtifex.

SKETCH

The **SKETCH** contextual tab is provided with different sets of tools that are used for creating sketches for the solid, surface, and sheet metal models, see Figure 1.44. Note that the **SKETCH** contextual tab is invoked by clicking on the **Create Sketch** tool in the **CREATE** panel of the **DESIGN** workspace, see Figure 1.45.

UTILITIES

The **UTILITIES** tab is provided with different sets of tools that are used for creating 3D prints of the design, determining the area and volume of models, detecting interference between components, and so on, see Figure 1.46.

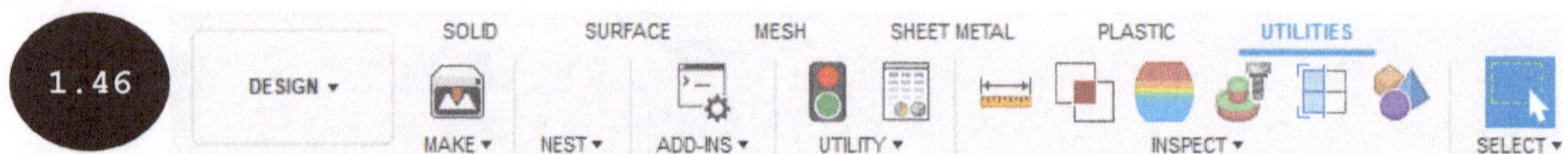

GENERATIVE DESIGN Workspace

The **GENERATIVE DESIGN** workspace consists of different sets of tools that are used for generating different design alternatives to fulfill the design goals and constraints set by the designer or the engineer, see Figure 1.47.

RENDER Workspace

The RENDER workspace consists of different sets of tools that are used for rendering photo-realistic images, see Figure 1.48.

ANIMATION Workspace

The ANIMATION workspace consists of different sets of tools that are used for creating exploded views of an assembly as well as animation of a design to represent how the components of an assembly are assembled, operated, or repaired, see Figure 1.49.

SIMULATION Workspace

The SIMULATION workspace allows you to perform various types of finite element analysis on a design for simulating its performance under applied loads and conditions, see Figure 1.50. It helps engineers to bring product performance knowledge into the early stages of the design cycle.

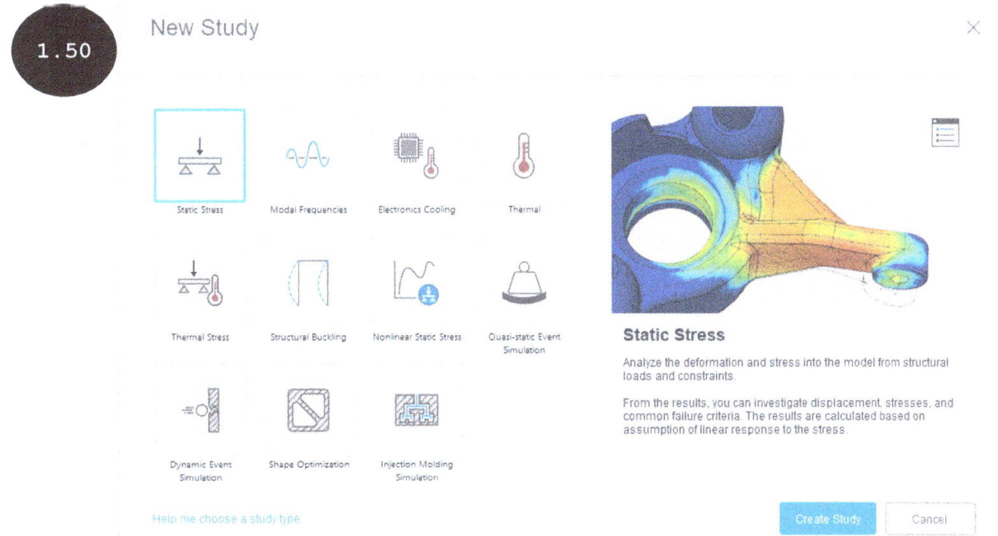

MANUFACTURE Workspace

The MANUFACTURE workspace consists of different sets of tools that are used for creating toolpaths for CNC machines, see Figure 1.51.

DRAWING Workspace

The **DRAWING** workspace consists of different sets of tools that are used for creating 2D drawings of a design (component or assembly), see Figure 1.52.

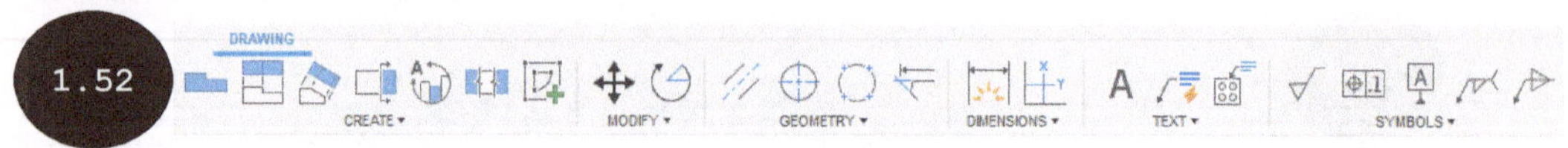

ELECTRONICS Workspace

The **ELECTRONICS** workspace allows you to access the Electronics Design and Electronics Library environments for creating and managing schematics, 2D PCB and 3D PCB designs, and components for electronics designs, respectively, see Figure 1.53.

Managing Data by Using the Data Panel

Autodesk Fusion is a cloud-based 3D CAD/CAM/CAE software that allows you to store all your designs safely and securely in the cloud using the **Data Panel**. It is a smart new approach to managing data in the cloud. To access the **Data Panel**, click on the **Show Data Panel** tool in the **Application Bar**, see Figure 1.54. The **Data Panel** appears on the left, see Figure 1.55.

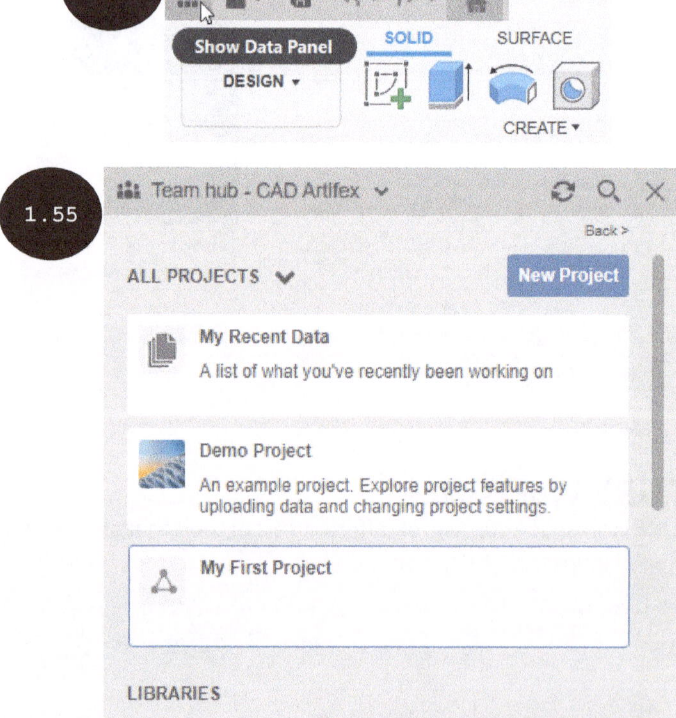

The homepage of the **Data Panel** is divided into three areas: **PROJECTS**, **LIBRARIES**, and **SAMPLES**. The **PROJECTS** area allows you to create a new project folder and sub-folders to save the files, upload files, collaborate with other users, and access recently used data.

The **LIBRARIES** area allows you to store projects that contain assets used by Autodesk Fusion including templates, libraries, and other configuration files.

The **SAMPLES** area provides access to sample projects and training exercises. The methods for creating a new project folder and sub-folders, uploading files, and collaborating with other users are discussed next.

Creating a New Project Folder and Sub-Folders

In Autodesk Fusion, the first and foremost step is to organize the **Data Panel** by creating the project folder and sub-folders to save files. To do this, invoke the **Data Panel** and then click on the **New Project** button, see Figure 1.56. A new project folder is created in the **PROJECTS** area of the **Data Panel** and its default name "**New Project**" appears in an edit field, see Figure 1.56. Write the name of the project in this edit field and then press ENTER. The new project folder is created in the **PROJECTS** area of the **Data Panel** with the specified name.

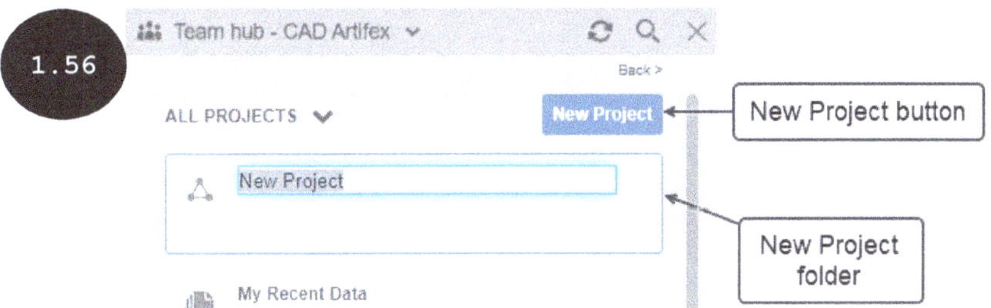

After creating the project folder, you can access it to save files. You can also create sub-folders in the project folder to organize sets of similar project files. To do this, double-click on the name of the project folder in the **PROJECTS** area of the **Data Panel**. The selected project folder is opened in the **Data Panel** and its name appears at the top, see Figure 1.57. Next, click on the **New Folder** button. A new sub-folder is created, and its default name "**New Folder**" appears in an edit field, see Figure 1.57. Write the name of the sub-folder in this edit field and then press ENTER. A sub-folder with the specified name is created inside the selected project folder. Similarly, you can create multiple sub-folders in a project folder.

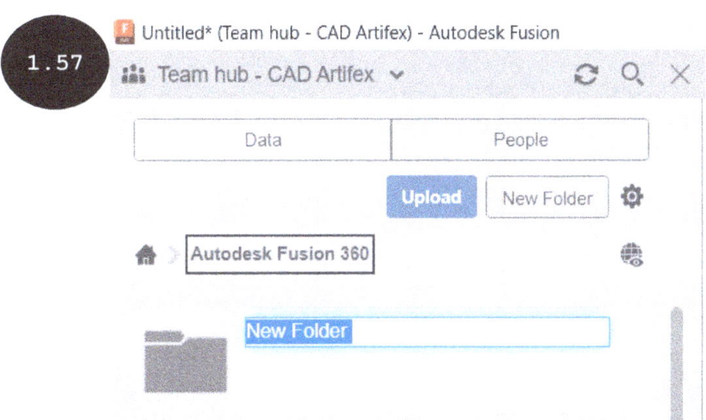

Note: If you are not connected to the Internet or have lost your Internet connection, you cannot create project folders and sub-folders in the **Data Panel**. However, you can continue to work on your designs in the offline mode. You will learn more about offline mode later in this chapter.

Uploading Existing Files in a Project

In Autodesk Fusion, you can also upload one or more existing files to an active project in the **Data Panel**. To do this, click on the **Upload** button available at the top of the activated project or sub-folder in the **Data Panel**. The **Upload** dialog box appears, see Figure 1.58.

1.58

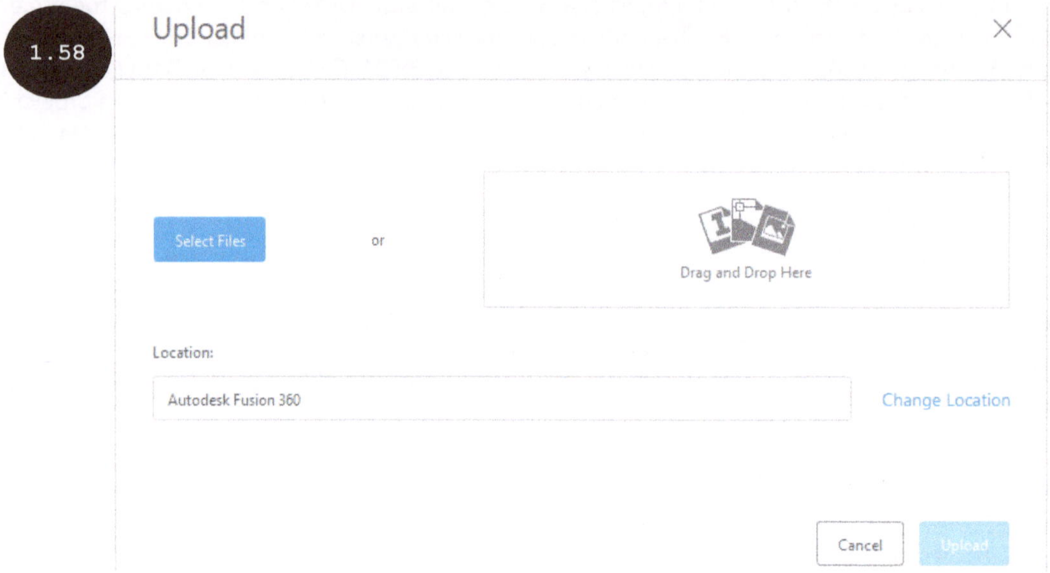

In the **Upload** dialog box, the **Location** field displays the location for uploading files in the **Data Panel**. You can change the location by using the **Change Location** option available to the right of the **Location** field. After specifying the location for uploading the files, click on the **Select Files** button. The **Open** dialog box appears. By using the **Open** dialog box, you can select the following types of files:

- All Files (*.*)
- Alias Files (*.wire)
- AutoCAD DWG Files (*.dwg)
- Autodesk Fusion Files (*.f3d, *.f3z)
- Autodesk Inventor Files (*.iam, *.ipt)
- Catia V5 Files (*.CATProduct, *.CATPart)
- DXF Files (*.dxf)
- FBX Files (*.fbx)
- IGES Files (*.iges, *.ige, *.igs)
- NX Files (*.prt)
- OBJ Files (*.obj)
- Parasolid Binary Files (*.x_b)
- Parasolid Text Files (*.x_t)

- Pro/ENGINEER and Creo Parametric Files (*.asm, *.prt)
- Pro/ENGINEER Neutral Files (*.neu)
- Rhino Files (*.3dm)
- SAT/SMT Files (*.sab, *.sat, *.smb, *.smt)
- SolidWorks Files (*.prt, *.asm, *.sldprt, *.sldasm)
- SolidEdge Files(*.par, *.asm, *.psm)
- STEP Files (*.ste, *.step, *.stp)
- STL Files (*.stl)
- 3MF Files (*3mf)
- SketchUp Files (*.sku)
- 123D Files(*.123dx)

Tip: You can also drag and drop the files to be uploaded in the **Upload** dialog box.

Select one or more files in the **Open** dialog box and then click on the **Open** button. The selected file(s) appear in the **Upload** dialog box. Then, click the **Upload** button to begin uploading the file(s) to the specified location. The upload progress is displayed at the bottom of the **Data Panel**. Once the upload is complete, the thumbnails of the uploaded file(s) appear in the specified location within the **Data Panel**.

To open an uploaded file in Autodesk Fusion, double-click its thumbnail in the **Data Panel**. The file opens in Autodesk Fusion, allowing you to edit it as needed.

Collaborating with Other Users

Autodesk Fusion enables multiple design teams to work together on a single project for collaborative product development. To collaborate with other users or to share the design with your partners, subcontractors, and colleagues, click on the **People** tab in the **Data Panel**, see Figure 1.59. The **People** tab gets activated and displays the list of people working on the project. Also, the **Invite** field appears in the **Data Panel**, see Figure 1.60.

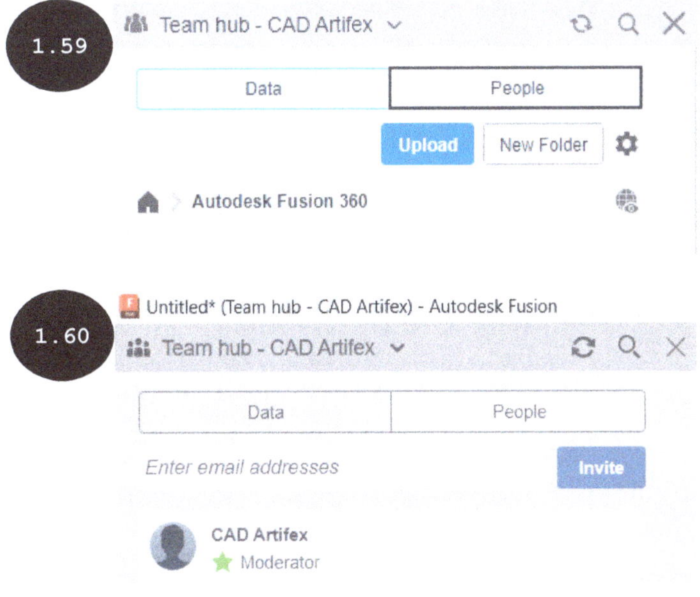

Note: After activating the **People** tab in the **Data Panel**, if the **Manage Members** option appears, click it to open the web browser, where you can view and manage project members.

Now, you can enter an e-mail ID in the **Invite** field of the **Data Panel** and then click on the **Invite** button to allow specified people to access your design.

In Autodesk Fusion, you can join or switch between team hubs using the **Team hub** switcher located in the top-left corner of the **Data Panel**, see Figure 1.61. A team hub serves as a collaborative environment for storing and managing design data, enabling you to work independently or collaborate with others effectively. To switch hubs, click the drop-down arrow next to your name in the **Team hub** switcher. A list of team hubs you are a member of appears in the drop-down menu. Select the desired team hub to access its projects and files.

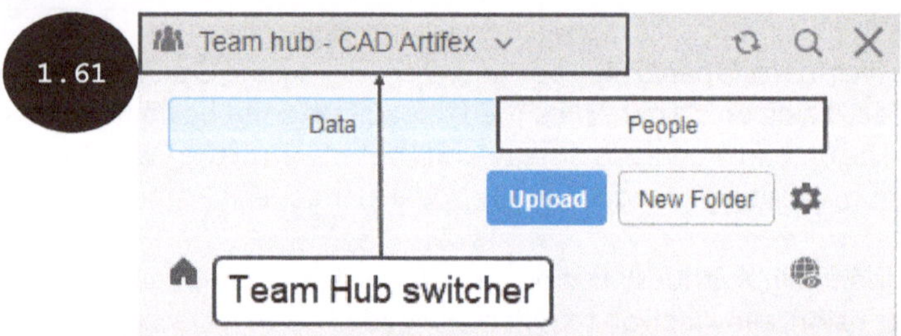

To find and join a new team hub, click on the **Find hubs** button, see Figure 1.62. This opens the **Find Hub** window, where you can follow the instructions to locate and join a new team hub.

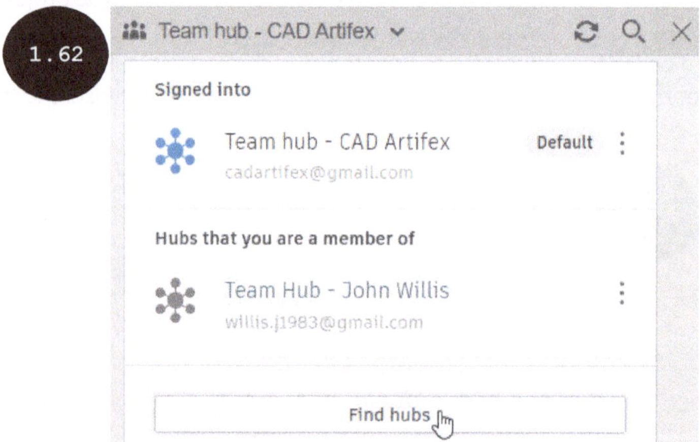

Filtering Project Display in the Data Panel

You can organize the display of projects in the **Data Panel** by using the drop-down list located in the upper left corner of the **Data Panel**, see Figure 1.63. From this list, you can choose the desired option to view all projects, pinned projects, owned projects, or shared projects, enabling efficient project navigation. Additionally, you can use the **Filter** field at the bottom of the **Data Panel** to further refine the project display and quickly locate specific projects.

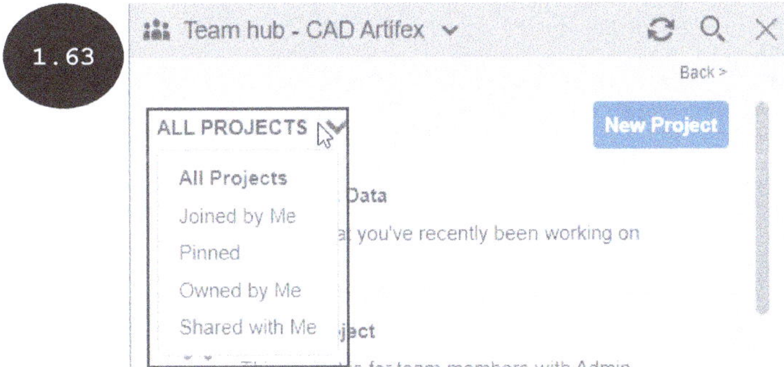

Opening Data Panel in Web Browser

In Autodesk Fusion, you can also view and manage a project on a web browser. To do this, open the project folder by double-clicking on its name in the **Data Panel** and then click on the **Open on the Web** tool available at the top right side of the **Data Panel**, see Figure 1.64. The selected project opens in the default web browser, and you can perform various operations such as uploading a file, deleting a file, creating folders, and so on in the project.

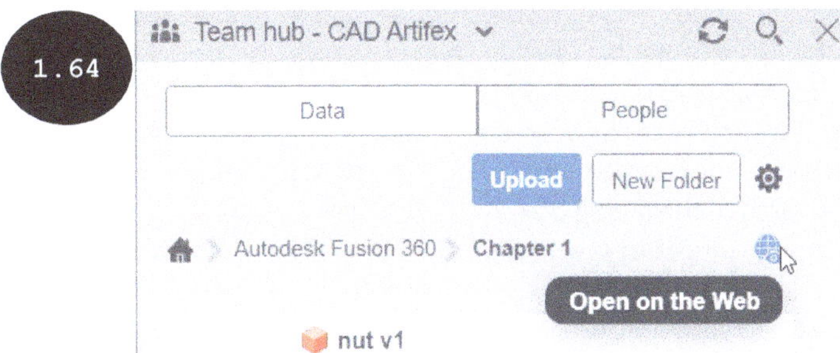

Saving a Design File

To save a design file created in any of the workspaces of Autodesk Fusion, click on the **Save** tool in the **Application Bar**, see Figure 1.65. The **Save** dialog box appears.

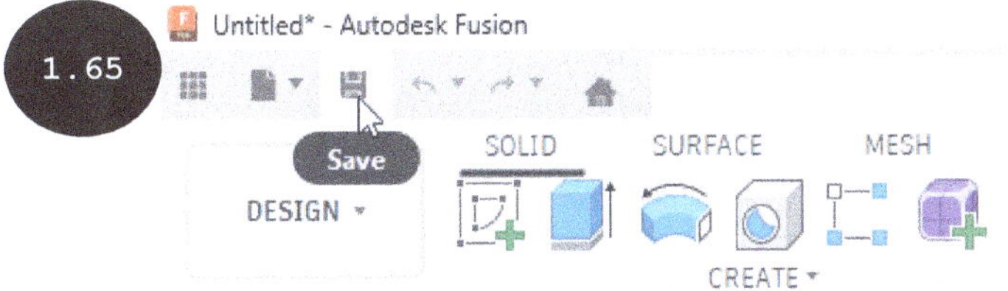

In this dialog box, enter the name of the design file in the **Name** field. The **Location** field of the dialog box displays the current location for saving the file. To specify a new location for saving the file, click on the down arrow next to the **Location** field of the dialog box. The **Save** dialog box gets expanded, see Figure 1.66.

1.66

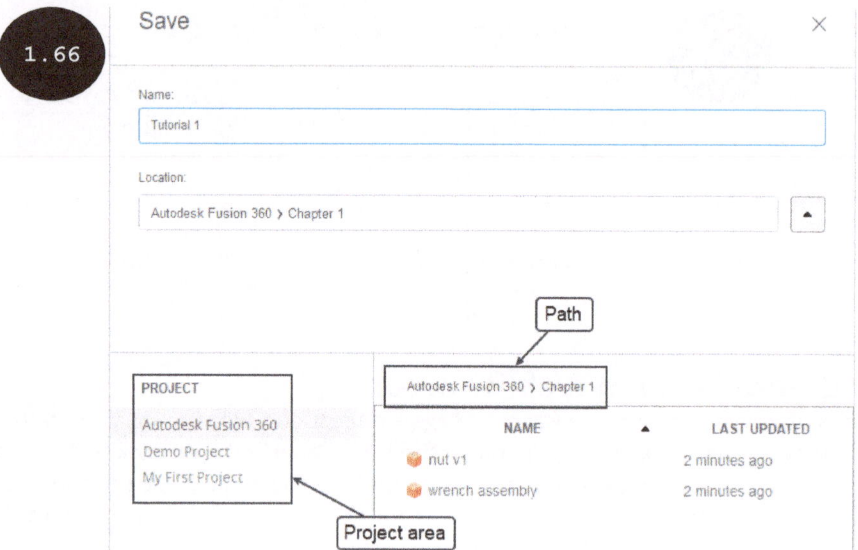

In the expanded **Save** dialog box, you can specify the location to save the file. The **Project** area of the dialog box displays the list of projects. You can select the required project folder to save the file in this area. On selecting the project folder, its sub-folders appear on the right panel of the dialog box. You can double-click on the sub-folder to access it to save the file. Note that the **Path** area of the dialog box displays the current path/location for saving the file. You can also click on the project folder or sub-folder in the **Path** area of the dialog box to change the location. Besides, you can also create a new project and sub-folders by using the **New Project** and **New Folder** buttons of the dialog box, respectively.

After specifying the name and location, click on the **Save** button. The design file is saved at the specified location.

In Autodesk Fusion, every time you save a file by using the **Save** tool, a new version of the file is saved because Autodesk Fusion keeps track of each version of your design. By default, when you open a design file, the latest version of the file will be opened in Autodesk Fusion. However, you can also open an older version of the design file as well. You will learn about opening design files later in this chapter.

You can also save an already saved design file with a different name. To do this, invoke the **File** drop-down menu in the **Application Bar** and then click on the **Save As** tool, see Figure 1.67. The **Save As** dialog box appears. In this dialog box, specify a new name for the design file and the location for saving it. Next, click on the **Save** button. The design file gets saved with the specified name.

1.67

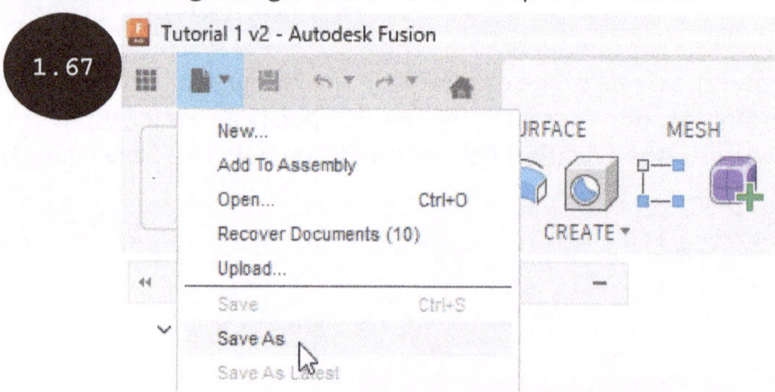

You can also save an older version of a design as the latest version. To do this, open an older version of a design that you want to save as the latest version. Next, invoke the **File** drop-down menu in the **Application Bar** and then click on the **Save As Latest** tool. A **Warning** window appears. In this window, click on the **Continue** button. The **Save As Latest** dialog box appears. Specify a version description in the dialog box, if required. Next, click on the **OK** button. The version gets saved as the latest version of the design file.

Exporting a Design to Other CAD Formats

In Autodesk Fusion, you can also export the Fusion design files to other CAD formats, neutral file formats, or the native Fusion file format. To do this, invoke the **File** drop-down menu in the **Application Bar** and then click on the **Export** tool. The **Export** dialog box appears, see Figure 1.68.

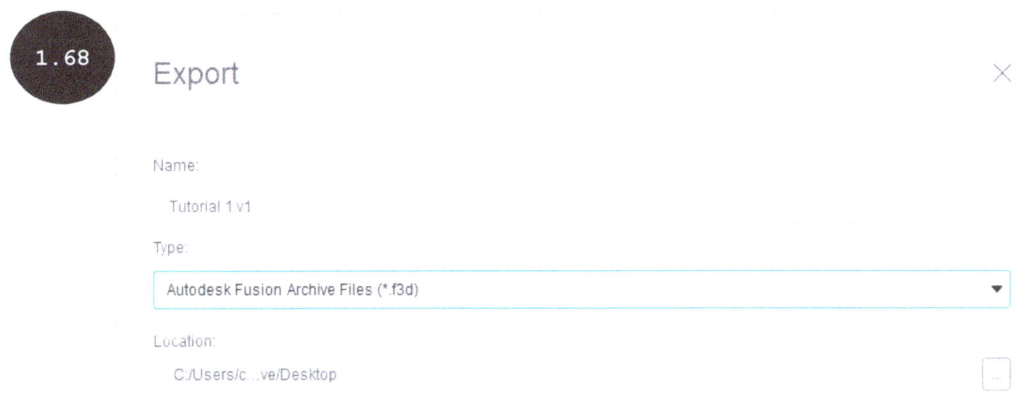

In the **Type** drop-down list of the **Export** dialog box, select the required file format [**Autodesk Fusion Files (*.f3d), 3MF Files (*.3mf) , Autodesk Inventor 2024 Files (*.ipt), DWG Files (*.dwg), DXF Files (*.dxf), FBX Files (*.fbx), IGES Files (*.igs *.iges), OBJ Files (*.obj), SAT Files (*.sat), SketchUp Files (*.skp),**] in which you want to export the file. To specify the location for saving the file in a local drive of your computer, click on the **Browse** button. The **Save As** dialog box appears. In this dialog box, specify a location to save the file and then click on the **Save** button. The file is saved in the specified file format.

Opening an Existing Design File

In Autodesk Fusion, you can open an existing design file of a project from the **Data Panel** or the **Open** dialog box. You can also open an existing **Autodesk Fusion, IGES, SAT/SMT, STEP,** etc. file that is saved on your local computer. The various methods for opening an existing file are discussed next.

Opening an Existing File from the Data Panel

To open an existing design file of a project from the **Data Panel,** click on the **Show Data Panel** tool of the **Application Bar**. The **Data Panel** gets invoked.

Next, browse to the location of the file to be opened and then double-click on it. The selected file gets opened in Autodesk Fusion.

Alternatively, right-click on the file to be opened and then click on the **Open** option in the shortcut menu that appears, see Figure 1.69.

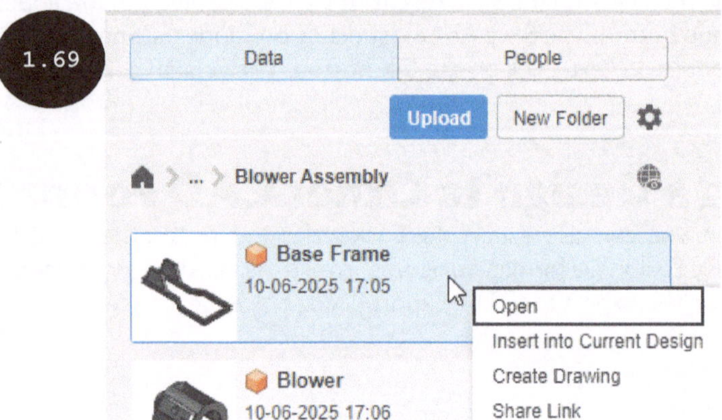

By default, when you open a design file, its latest version will get opened in Autodesk Fusion. However, you can also open an older version of the file. To do this , click on the Version icon V5▾ available in the lower right corner of the design thumbnail in the **Data Panel**, see Figure 1.70. All the versions of the respective design file appear in the **Data Panel**, see Figure 1.71. Note that in this figure, the **V5** icon indicates that a total of 5 versions are available for the selected design file.

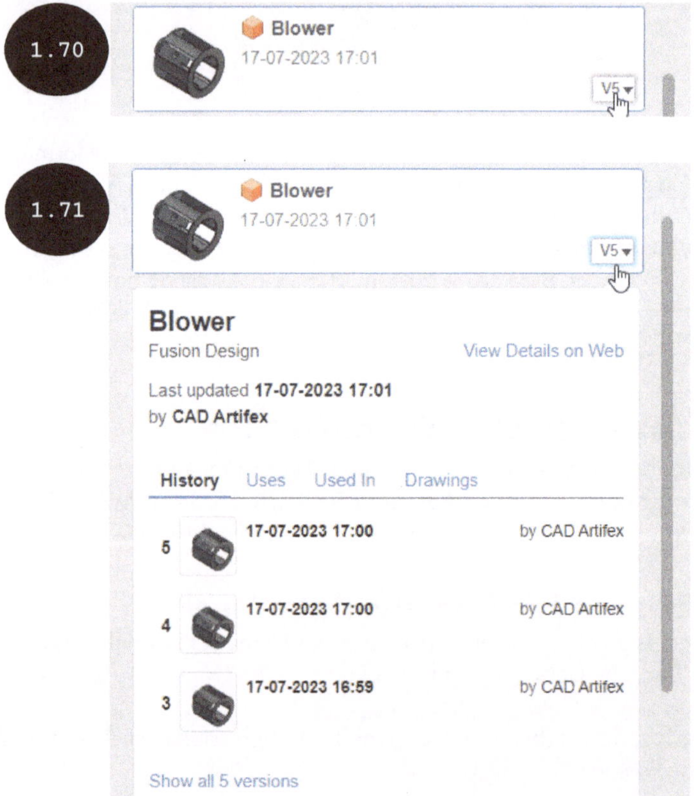

Then, click on the three dots that appears on its right to display a drop-down menu, see Figure 1.72. Click on the Open button in this menu to open the selected version of the file.

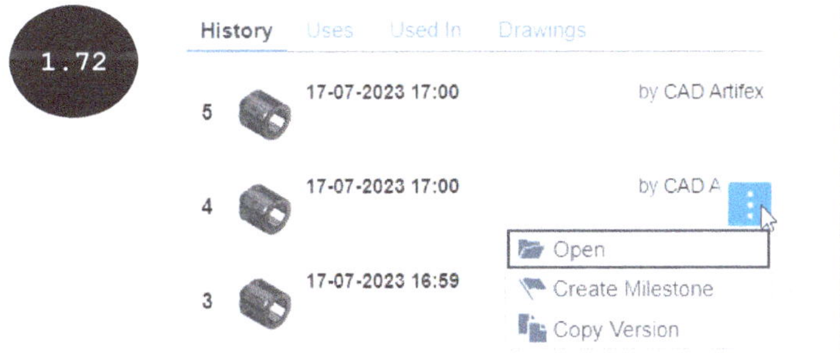

If all versions of the selected files do not appear in the **Data Panel**, then click on the **Show all versions** option in the **Data Panel**.

Note: You can also access the older versions of a file from the **BROWSER**. To do this, open the design file, right-click on the name of the file (top browser node) in the **BROWSER** and then click on the **History** tool in the shortcut menu that appears, see Figure 1.73. The **HISTORY** dialog box appears, see Figure 1.74. In this dialog box, double-click on the version of the design file to be opened. The selected version of the design gets opened.

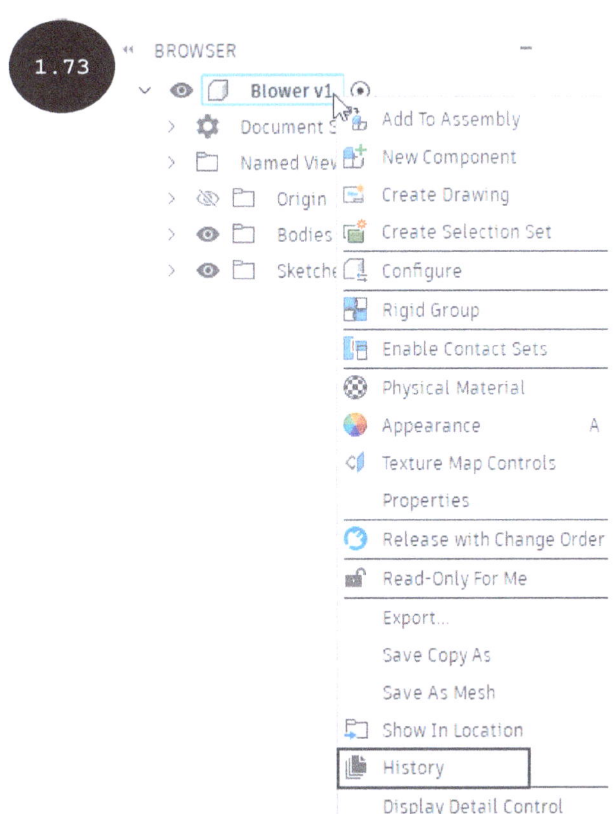

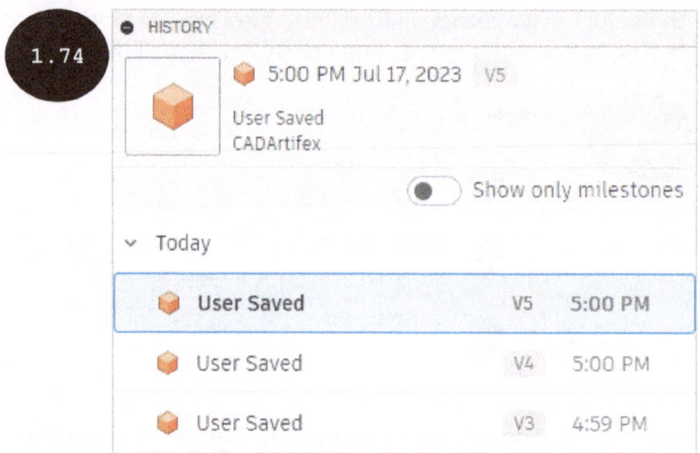

Opening an Existing File by using the Open tool

To open an existing design file of a project by using the **Open** tool, invoke the **File** drop-down menu in the **Application Bar** and then click on the **Open** tool, see Figure 1.75. The **Open** dialog box appears, see Figure 1.76.

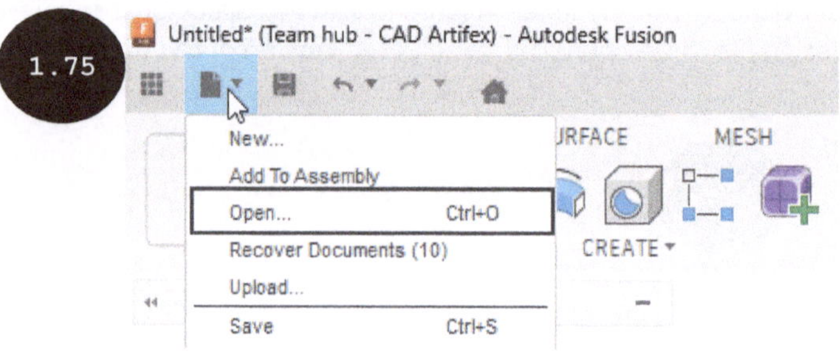

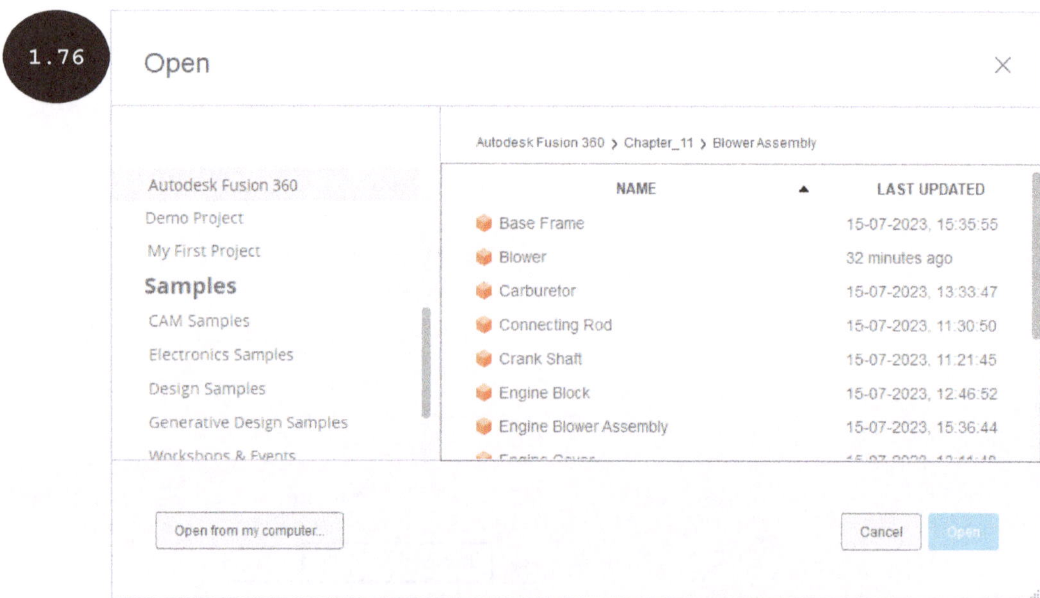

In the **Open** dialog box, click on the name of the project that appears on the left panel of the dialog box. All the sub-folders or files of the selected project appear on the right panel of the dialog box. Select the required design file to be opened from the right panel of the dialog box.

Note that if the design file to be opened is saved in a sub-folder of the selected project, then you need to double-click on the sub-folder to display its files. After selecting the design file, click on the **Open** button in the dialog box. The selected file gets opened.

Opening an Existing File from the Local Computer

As discussed earlier, you can also open an existing **Autodesk Fusion, IGES, SAT/SMT, STEP**, etc. file that is saved on your local computer. To do this, invoke the **Open** dialog box, as discussed earlier and then click on the **Open from my computer** button, refer to Figure 1.76. Another **Open** dialog box appears. In this dialog box, browse to the location where the file to be opened is saved. You can open **Alias** files, **AutoCAD DWG** files, **Autodesk Fusion** files, **Autodesk Inventor** files, **Catia V5** files, **NX** files, **IGES** files, **STEP** files, and so on.

After selecting the desired file, click the **Open** button in the dialog box. The file begins uploading, with its progress displayed at the bottom of the **Data Panel**. Once the upload is complete, a notification appears in the top-right corner of the screen in the **Notification Center**. You can click **Open** in this notification to access the file in Autodesk Fusion. If you open a native Fusion file, it will open directly in Autodesk Fusion.

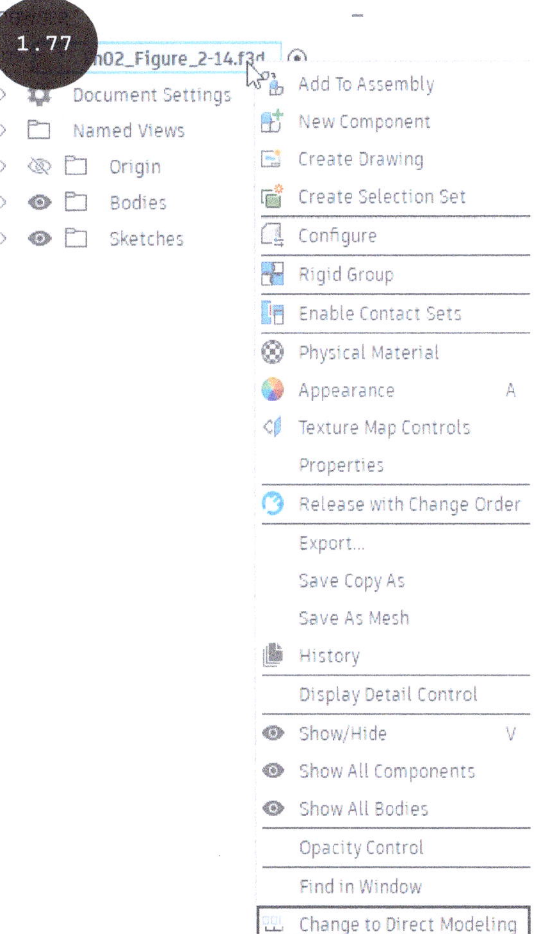

Once the file is opened, you can edit it by adding new features as required. Note that any newly added features will be automatically recorded in the **Timeline**.

If you want to switch to Direct Modeling mode for editing the model, right-click the file name (top browser node) in the **BROWSER** and select the **Change to Direct Modeling** option, see Figure 1.77. This option allows you to edit the existing features of the model without capturing the design history.

To switch back to Parametric Modeling, right-click the file name (top browser node) in the **BROWSER** and select the **Change to Parametric Modeling** option. After making the necessary modifications, you can save the file to the desired location in the **Data Panel** using the **Save** button.

Working in the Offline Mode

Autodesk Fusion automatically goes to offline mode when you are not connected to the Internet, lose the Internet connection, an unexpected outage is detected, or the service is under maintenance. However, Autodesk Fusion allows you to continue working on your designs in the offline mode.

You can also switch between the online and offline modes, manually. To do this, click on the **Job Status** icon in the upper right corner of the screen, see Figure 1.78. The **Job Status** flyout appears, see Figure 1.79. In this flyout, click on the **Working Online** icon. The offline mode gets activated and the **Working Offline** icon appears in the flyout.

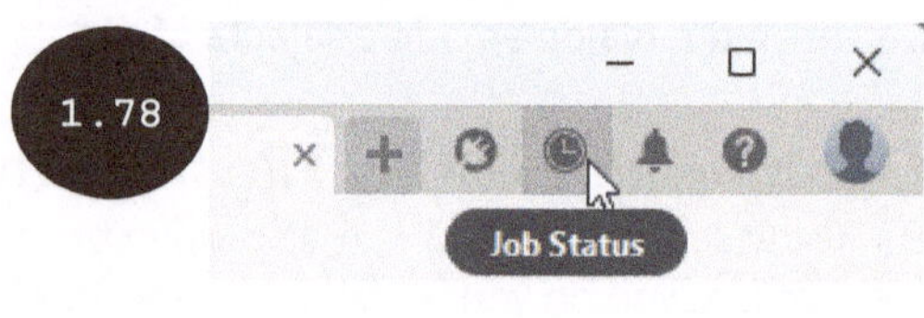

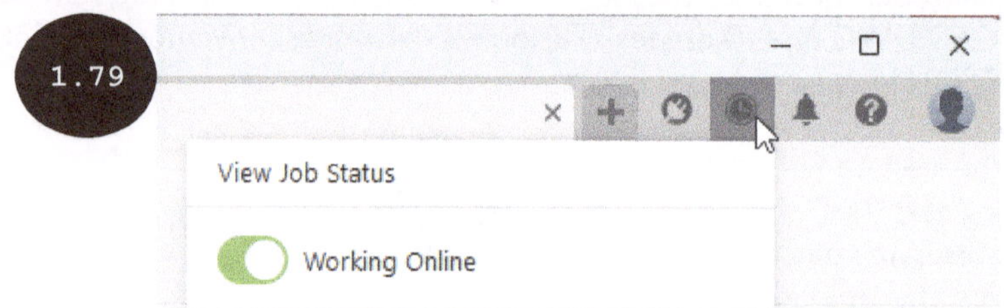

As discussed, Autodesk Fusion allows you to work in the offline mode. However, certain file operations such as uploading files, creating project folders, and sub-folders cannot be performed. Note that the designs saved in the offline mode will be automatically synced and uploaded to the **Data Panel** when you are back to the online mode. However, when you save a design in offline mode, only the last saved version of the design is captured.

Sharing a Design Using a Link

In Autodesk Fusion, you can share your design with others using a link. To do this, open the **File** drop-down menu in the **Application Bar** and select the **Share File Link** tool, see Figure 1.80. This action opens the **Share** window.

In the **Share** window, enable the **Share the latest version with anyone using this link** check box, see Figure 1.81. A unique link is then generated and displayed in the window. Click the **Copy** button to copy the link, which you can share via email or other communication methods to provide access to your design.

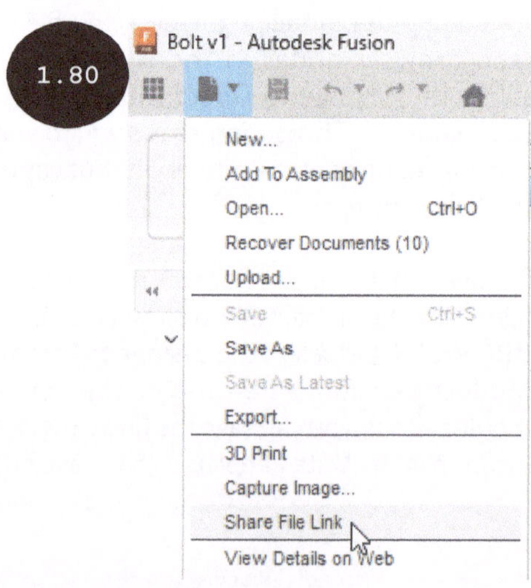

You can also manage privacy settings, such as allowing the item to be downloaded or requiring a password to access the link, by using the respective check boxes in the **Privacy Settings** area of the **Share** window. By default, the **Allow item to be downloaded** check box is selected, enabling anyone with the link to download the file.

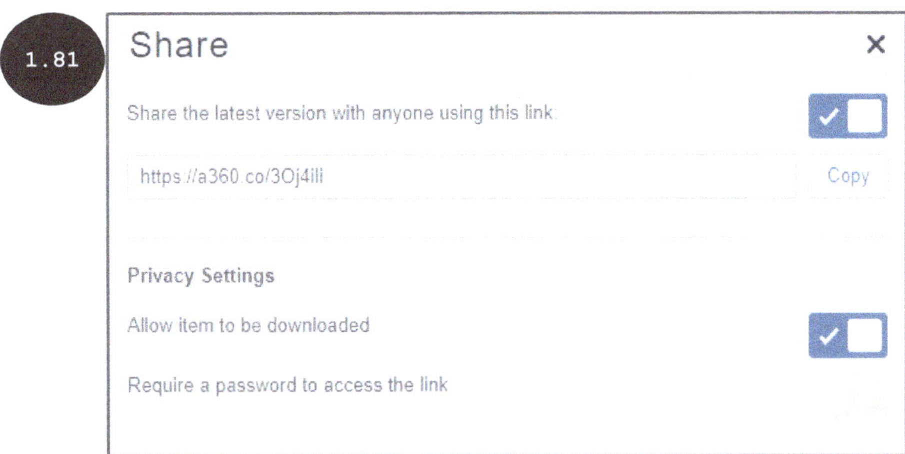

Recovering Unsaved Data

Autodesk Fusion allows you to recover the data in case an unexpected error occurs and Fusion closes automatically. To do this, invoke the **File** drop-down menu in the **Application Bar** and then click on the **Recover Documents** tool. The **File Recovery** window appears. In this window, click on the unsaved file to be recovered and then click on the **Open** tool in the menu that appears. The file is recovered and opened in Autodesk Fusion. Note that the **Recover Documents** tool is only active if unsaved data is available for recovery. To delete a recovered file from the list, select the **Delete** tool in the menu that appears by clicking the name of the recovered file.

Invoking a Marking Menu

The Marking Menu gets invoked when you right-click in the graphics area. It provides quick access to the most frequently used tools in the Wheel. It also includes an Overflow menu that provides quick access to navigation tools and a workspace selection menu, see Figure 1.82. Note that the availability of the tools in the Marking Menu depends on the active workspace.

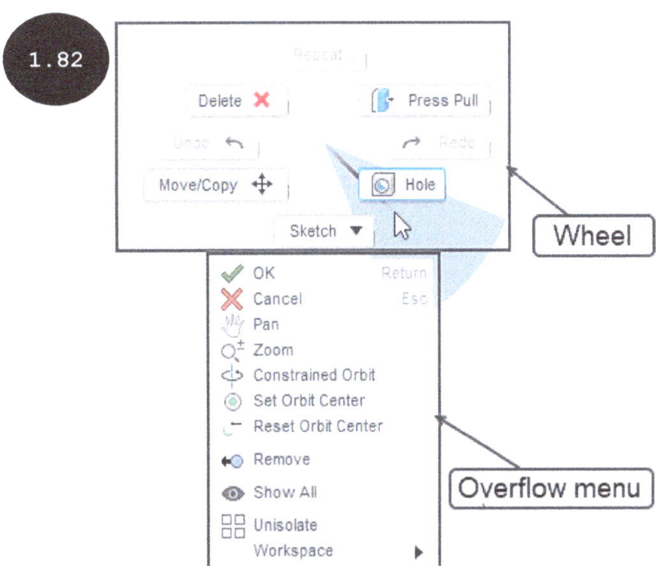

3D Printing

After creating a design in Autodesk Fusion, you can create a prototype of your design by using additive manufacturing or 3D printing. You can also export your design in a .3MF or .OBJ file format. Additive manufacturing is a technique where a 3D printer builds the model in 3 dimensions by joining material layer by layer as per the design. Generally, different grades of plastic material are used for building the 3D prototype of your design. However, you can also use metal material for building the prototype.

Note that for creating a 3D prototype of your design by using 3D printing, you need to export your design in a .STL file as input to a 3D printer, since the .STL file is the most popular file format for 3D printing. The method for exporting your design in .STL file format for 3D printing is discussed next.

Exporting a Design in .STL File Format for 3D Printing

1. Invoke the **MAKE** drop-down menu in the **UTILITIES** tab of the **DESIGN** workspace and then click on the **3D Print** tool, see Figure 1.83. The **3D PRINT** dialog box appears, see Figure 1.84. The availability of options in this dialog box depends upon the option selected in the **Preparation Type** drop-down list. Alternatively, you can also click on **File > 3D Print** in the **Application Bar** to invoke the **3D PRINT** dialog box.

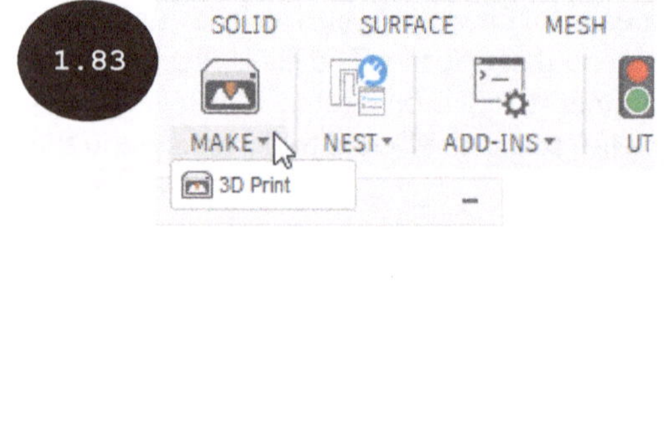

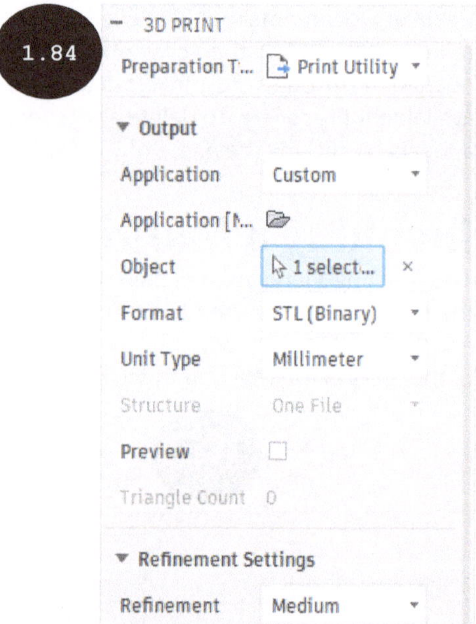

TIP: You can also right-click on the name of the model in the **BROWSER** (*top browser node*) and then click on the **Save As Mesh** tool in the shortcut menu that appears. The **SAVE AS MESH** dialog box appears. In this dialog box, specify the required parameters to export the design for the 3D printing.

2. Select the appropriate option in the **Preparation Type** drop-down list of the dialog box, such as **Manufacturing**, **Export**, or **Print Utility**, depending on your needs. The available options in the dialog box adjust dynamically depending on your selection, refer to Figure 1.80. In this figure, the **Print Utility** option is selected.

Manufacturing: Selecting this option creates a new additive setup in the Manufacture workspace, preparing your model for 3D printing.

Export: This option allows you to export your design in STL, OBJ, or 3MF file formats, which are commonly used for 3D printing.

Print Utility: The Preform option prepares your model for printing specifically using a Formlabs printer.

3. Select a component in the graphics area to be exported as .stl file for a 3D printer.

4. Select the **STL (Binary)** option in the **Format** drop-down list to export the design in .STL file format for 3D printing. You can also export the design in STL(ASCII), .3MF or .OBJ file format by selecting the respective option in the **Format** drop-down list.

5. Select the required unit in the **Unit Type** drop-down list. Next, select the **Preview** check box in the dialog box. The mesh preview of the model appears in the graphics area as per the default refinement settings.

6. Select the required option in the **Refinement** drop-down list to define the refinement quality of the mesh. You can further define the refinement settings by expanding the **Refinement Settings** rollout of the dialog box.

7. Ensure that the **PreForm** option is selected in the **Application** drop-down list of the **Output** rollout to send the .STL file directly to the PreForm utility application for 3D printing. You can also choose the **Custom** option in this drop-down list and select a custom application for 3D printing.

8. Specify the other related settings in the dialog box, then click **OK**. The process of loading the selected utility starts, and once it's complete, the selected utility is invoked, see Figure 1.85. This figure shows the PreForm utility. If the selected utility is not installed on your computer, you will need to download and install it using the link provided in the dialog box.

1.85

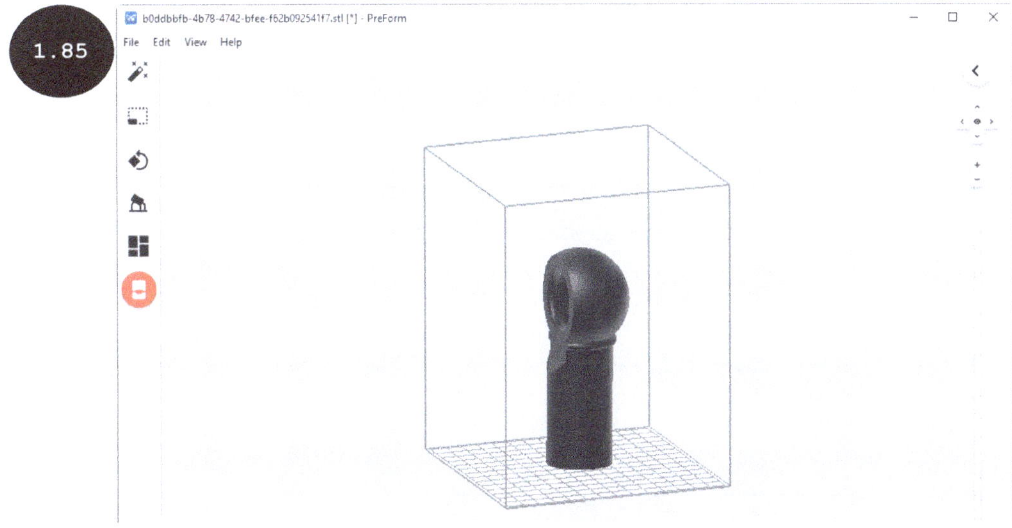

Now, you can define the settings for 3D printing such as orientation, placement of the model on the printing tray, scale, repair model for any geometrical defects, add supports for overhanging parts, and so on. Also, you need to connect your computer to a 3D printer. After defining all the parameters for 3D printing, click on the **Start a print** tool in the toolbar to print the model.

TIP: Instead of sending the design file directly to a 3D print utility, you can export it to your local computer by selecting the **Export** option from the **Preparation Type** drop-down list in the **3D PRINT** dialog box. The design file, saved in the specified format (.3MF, .STL, or .OBJ), can later be imported into a 3D print utility application for 3D printing.

Summary

In this chapter, you learned about the system requirements for installing Autodesk Fusion and the steps to begin a new design file. The chapter introduced the Fusion user interface, its various workspaces, and essential data management techniques using the **Data Panel**. Additionally, you explored how to save and export design files, open existing files and their versions, work offline, recover unsaved data, share your designs, use the Marking Menu, and prepare designs for 3D printing. These topics provide you with the foundational knowledge needed to effectively use Autodesk Fusion for your design projects.

Questions

Complete and verify the following sentences:

- In Autodesk Fusion, the _________ workspace consists of different sets of tools that are used for creating 3D solid models.
- The _________ workspace is used for creating exploded views of an assembly as well as animation of a design.
- The _________ appears in the lower left corner of the interface and keeps a record of all features or operations performed on the design.
- The _________ tool is used for opening an existing **Autodesk Fusion**, **IGES**, **SAT**, or **STEP** file.
- The _________ tool is used for turning ON the process of capturing design history in the **Timeline** for an imported design.
- Autodesk Fusion allows you to store all your designs in the cloud by using the _________.
- The _________ tool in the **Application Bar** is used for exporting designs in other CAD formats.
- In Autodesk Fusion, every time you save a file by using the **Save** tool, a new version of the file gets saved. (True/False)
- Autodesk Fusion does not allow you to work in the offline mode. (True/False)

2

Drawing Sketches with Autodesk Fusion

In this chapter, the following topics will be discussed:

- Invoking a New Design File
- Creating Sketches
- Working with Selection of Planes
- Specifying Units
- Specifying Grids and Snaps Settings
- Drawing a Line Entity
- Drawing a Midpoint Line
- Drawing a Tangent Arc by Using the Line Tool
- Drawing a Rectangle
- Drawing a Circle
- Drawing an Arc
- Drawing a Polygon
- Drawing an Ellipse
- Drawing a Slot
- Drawing Conic Curves
- Drawing a Spline
- Editing a Spline
- Creating Sketch Points
- Inserting Text into a Sketch

Autodesk Fusion is a feature-based, parametric solid modeling software for mechanical design and automation. Before creating 3D models in Autodesk Fusion, it is important to understand that designing a 3D model requires building its features one at a time, see Figures 2.1 and 2.2. Features are divided into two main categories: sketch-based features and placed features. A feature created using a sketch is called a sketch-based feature, while a feature created on an existing feature without a sketch is known as a placed feature. Among these two categories, sketch-based features are typically the first to be created in any real-world component, making it important to focus initially on drawing accurate sketches.

Figure 2.1 illustrates a component that includes an extrude feature and a chamfer. The extrude feature is created using a sketch, making it a sketch-based feature. Conversely, the chamfer is a placed feature, as it does not require a sketch for its creation. Figure 2.2 depicts the process for creating this model.

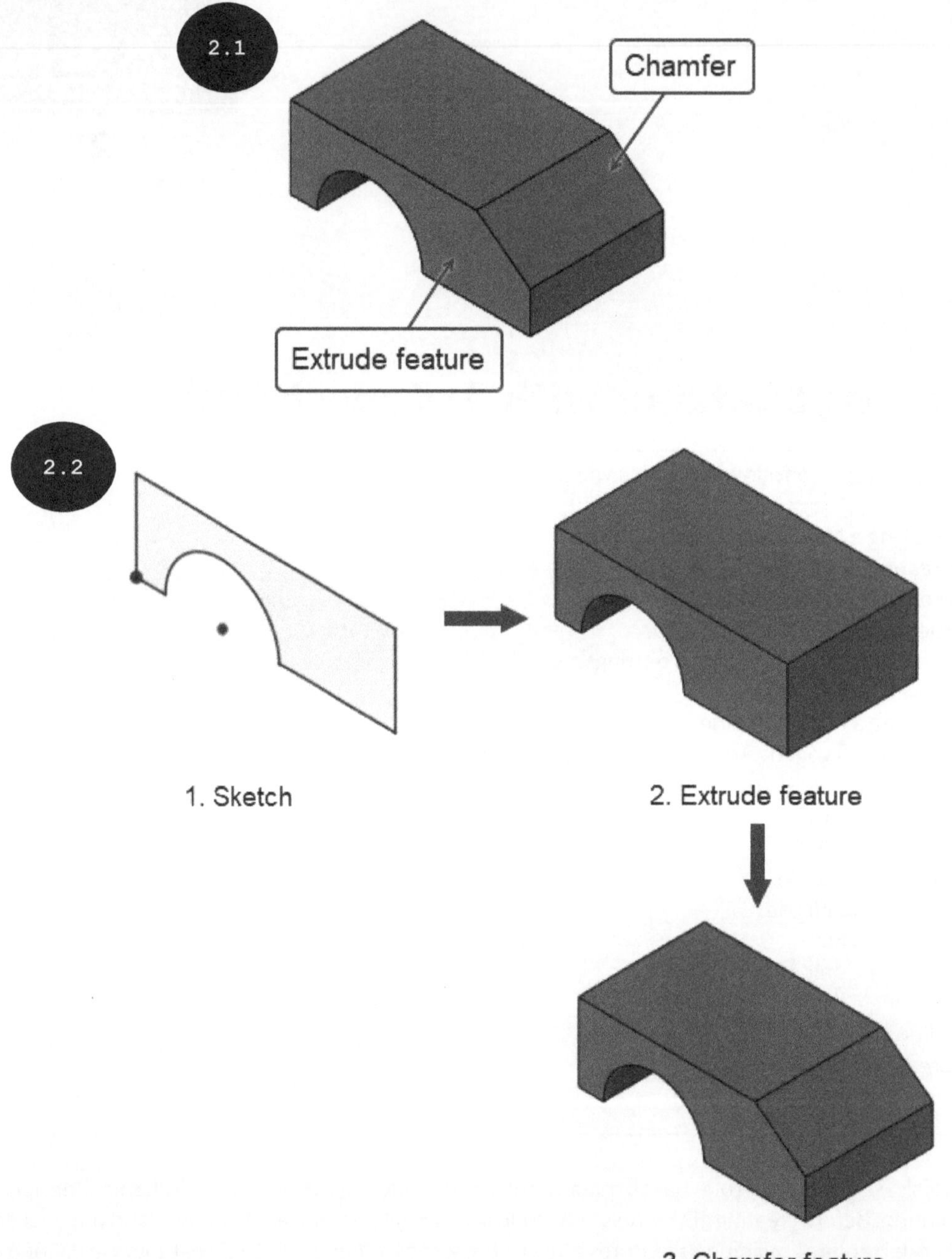

To begin designing a component in Autodesk Fusion, mastering sketch creation is essential, as the base or first feature of any component is typically sketch-based. In Autodesk Fusion, sketches can be created using a variety of sketching tools that are accessible within a Part Design file.

Invoking a New Part Design File

Start Autodesk Fusion by double-clicking on the **Autodesk Fusion** icon on your desktop. After the necessary files are loaded, the Autodesk Fusion startup interface appears with the default Part Design file opened with the default name **"Untitled"** and displays various tools in the **Toolbar**, see Figure 2.3. The main components of the Part Design interface, including the **Application Bar**, **Toolbar**, **BROWSER**, and **Timeline**, are discussed in Chapter 1.

2.3

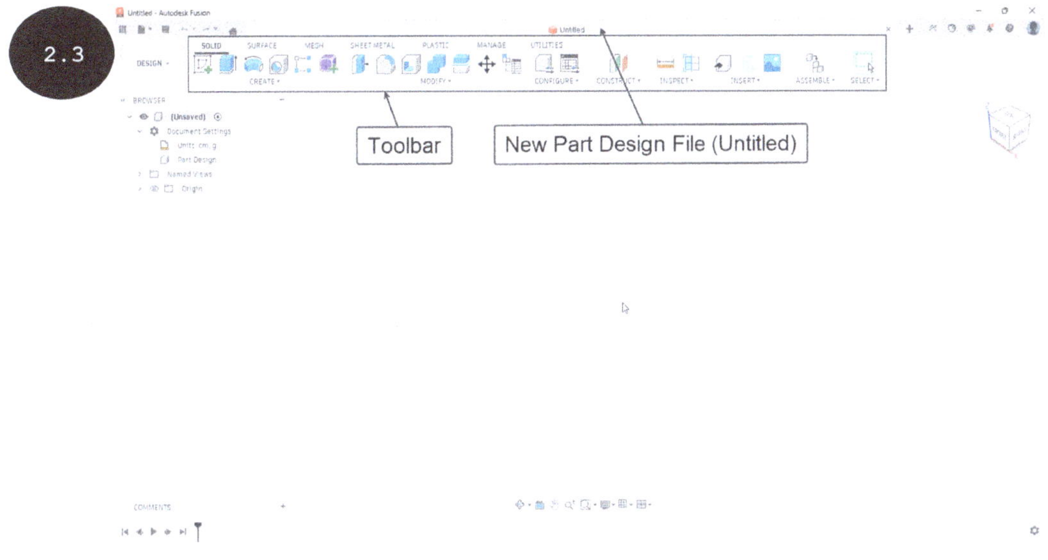

Note: By default, Part Design is set as the design type that opens automatically when Autodesk Fusion is started. It allows you to directly create solid, surface, and sheet metal components. However, if required, you can change the default design type at any time using the **Preferences** dialog box. The procedure for setting the default design type is discussed in Chapter 1.

Note that you can open multiple new design files within a single session of Autodesk Fusion. To open a new design file, click **File** > **New** from the **Application Bar**, see Figure 2.4. This opens the **What do you want to design?** dialog box, see Figure 2.5.

2.4

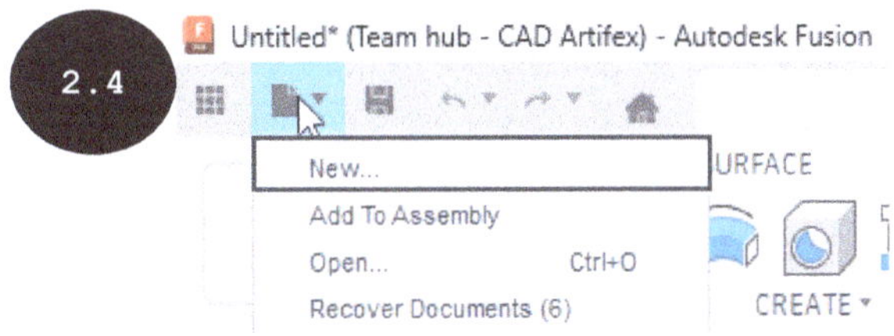

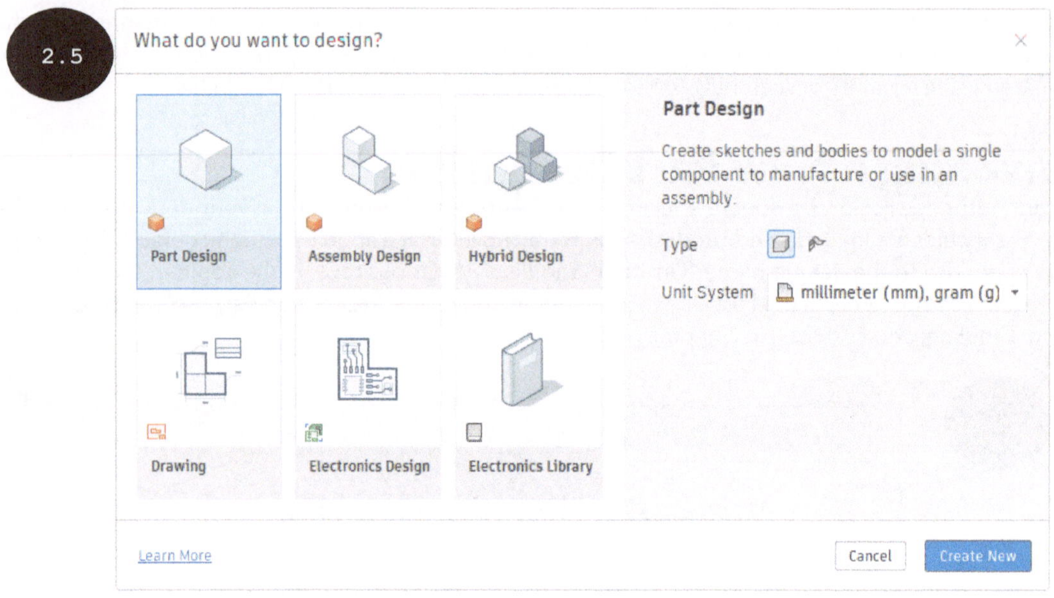

Note: As per the latest updates in Autodesk Fusion, when opening a new design file, you are first required to specify the design type such as Part Design or Assembly Design to ensure that the appropriate design environment is used for the intended modeling task.

In the **What do you want to design?** dialog box, after selecting **Part Design** and the required unit system, click on the **Create New** button. A new Part Design file is opened with the default name "**Untitled(1)**" in a separate tab and is activated automatically.

Alternatively, you can press **Ctrl + N** on the keyboard or click the + icon next to the name of the currently active design file (see Figure 2.6) to open the **What do you want to design?** dialog box and start a new design file. Each newly opened design file appears in a separate tab, allowing you to work on multiple designs within the same Autodesk Fusion session.

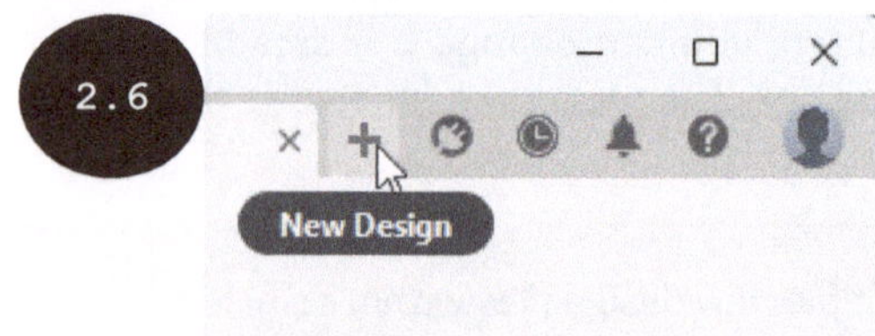

As discussed earlier, the tools available in the **Toolbar** of a design file depend on the currently active workspace. By default, the **DESIGN** workspace is activated. As a result, the tools used for creating 3D mechanical solid, surface, and sheet metal models are available in the corresponding tabs of the **Toolbar**, see Figure 2.7.

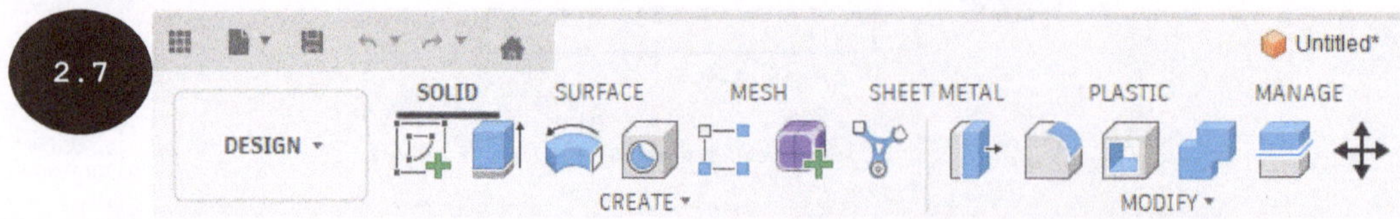

If needed, you can switch among the workspaces using the **Workspace** drop-down menu in the **Toolbar**, see Figure 2.8.

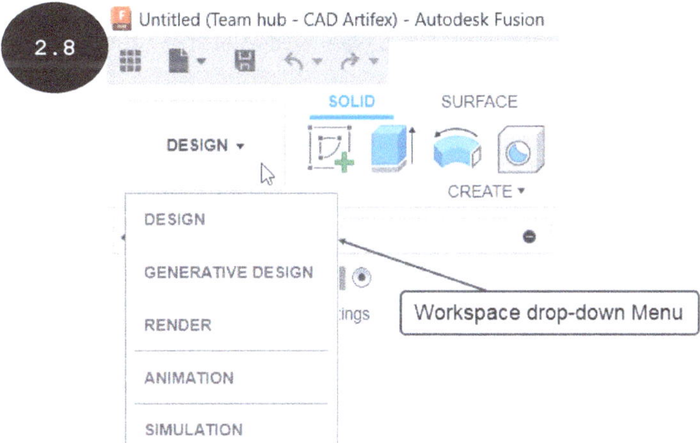

Creating Sketches

After invoking a new Part Design file, you can access the sketching tools and begin creating the sketch for the first feature of a 3D model. To do this, click the **Create Sketch** tool in the **SOLID** tab of the **Toolbar**, see Figure 2.9. The three default reference planes: Front, Top, and Right, which are mutually perpendicular to each other, appear in the graphics area, see Figure 2.10.

2.9

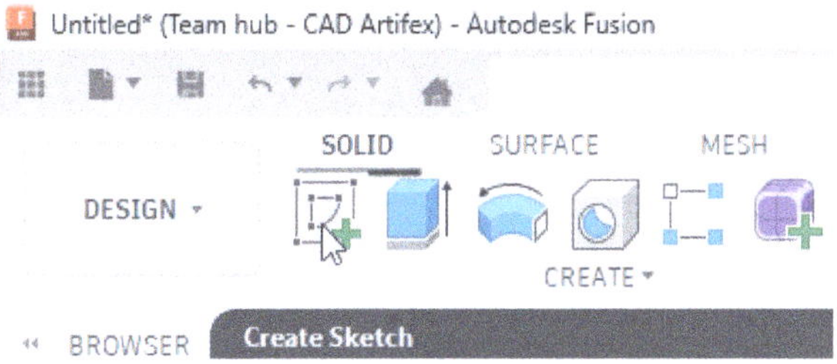

2.10

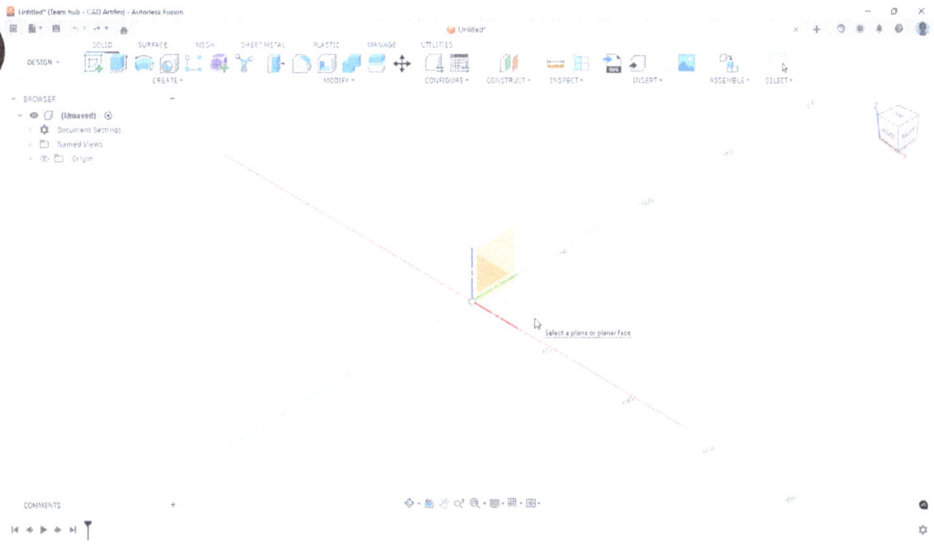

You can select any one of these default planes as the sketching plane for creating the sketch. To select a plane, move the cursor over the desired plane and click the left mouse button when it is highlighted in the graphics area, refer to Figure 2.10. Once the plane is selected, the **SKETCH** contextual tab appears in the **Toolbar** (see Figure 2.11), and the selected plane becomes the active sketching plane.

The selected plane is automatically oriented normal to the viewing direction, allowing you to create the sketch easily using the sketching tools available in the **SKETCH** contextual tab of the **Toolbar**. In addition, the **SKETCH PALETTE** dialog box appears in the drawing area, see Figure 2.11. The options in this dialog box provide quick access to certain display settings. You will learn about the options available in the **SKETCH PALETTE** dialog box in later chapters.

2.11

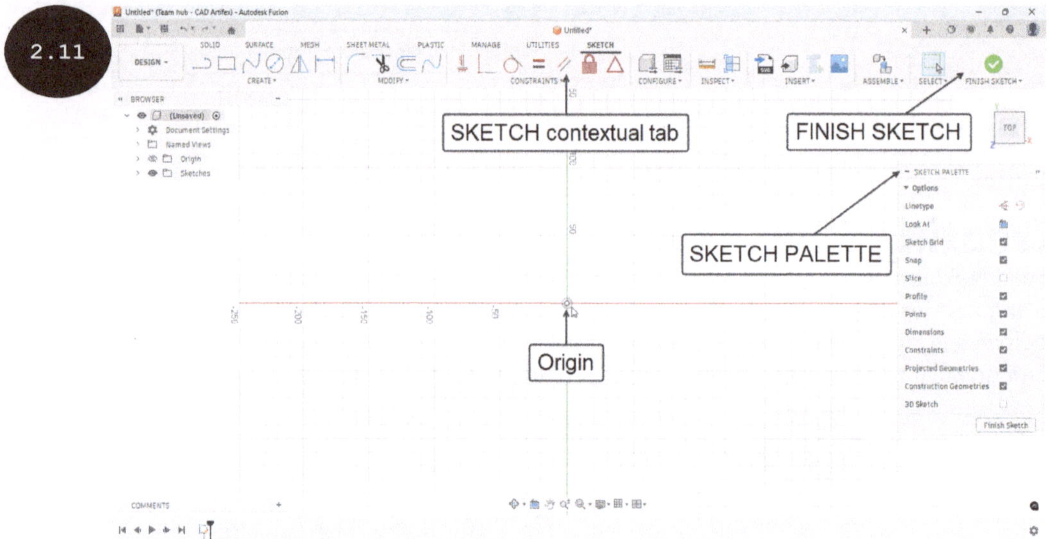

Also, a point with two perpendicular axes appears at the center of the drawing area. This point represents the origin (0,0). You can now start creating the sketch using the sketching tools available in the **SKETCH** contextual tab. However, before you begin drawing the sketch, it is important to understand the selection of sketching planes, the procedure for setting the unit of measurement, and the grid settings.

Working with Selection of Planes

As discussed earlier, you can start creating the sketch by selecting a plane as the sketching plane. Selection of the correct plane is very important in defining the right orientation of the model. Figure 2.12 shows the isometric view of a model having a length of 200 mm, width of 100 mm, and height of 40 mm.

2.12

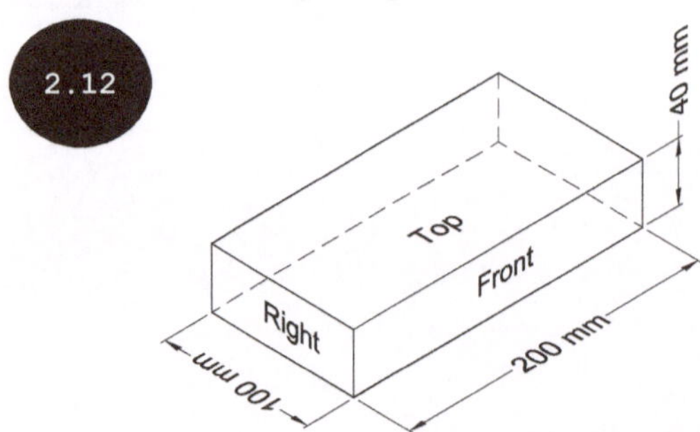

To create this model with the same orientation, select the Top plane as the sketching plane and then draw a rectangular sketch of 200 mm X 100 mm. However, if you select the Front plane as the sketching plane for creating this model then you need to draw a rectangular sketch of 200 mm X 40 mm. Likewise, if you select the Right plane as the sketching plane then you need to draw a rectangular sketch of 100 mm X 40 mm.

Specifying Units

To change the default unit system of the currently active design document, expand the **Document Settings** node in the **BROWSER** by clicking the arrow next to it, see Figure 2.13. The **Units** option appears within the expanded **Document Settings** node. Next, move the cursor over the **Units** option to display the **Change Active Units** tool, see Figure 2.14.

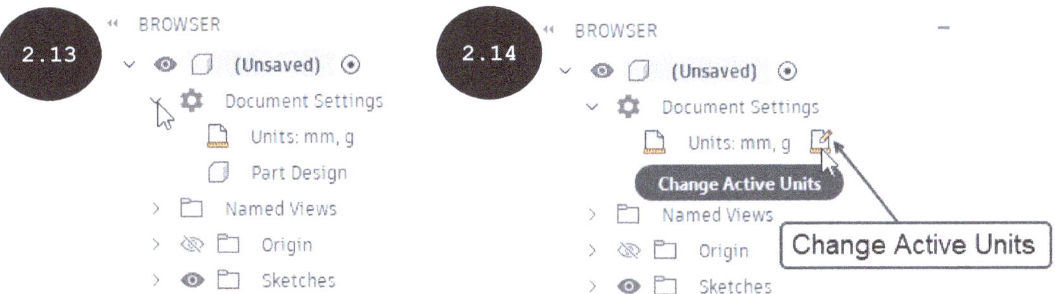

Click the **Change Active Units** tool, the **CHANGE ACTIVE UNITS** dialog box appears to the right of the graphics area, see Figure 2.15. In this dialog box, the currently specified unit is selected in the **Unit System** drop-down list. You can select the required unit system for the active design file from this list.

Note: If you select the **Set as Default** check box in the **CHANGE ACTIVE UNITS** dialog box, the selected unit system becomes the default unit system for all newly created design files.

After specifying the required unit system, click the **OK** button to apply the change.

Alternatively, you can control the default unit settings using the **Preferences** dialog box. To open this dialog box, click your profile image in the upper-right corner. The **User Account** drop-down menu appears, see Figure 2.16. From this menu, click the **Preferences** tool to open the **Preferences** dialog box.

In the **Preferences** dialog box, click the **Design** option under the **Default Units** section in the left panel, see Figure 2.17. Next, select the required unit from the **Default units for new design** drop-down list to set it as the default unit for all new documents. After selecting the required unit, click the **Apply** button and then click the **OK** button to accept the changes and close the dialog box.

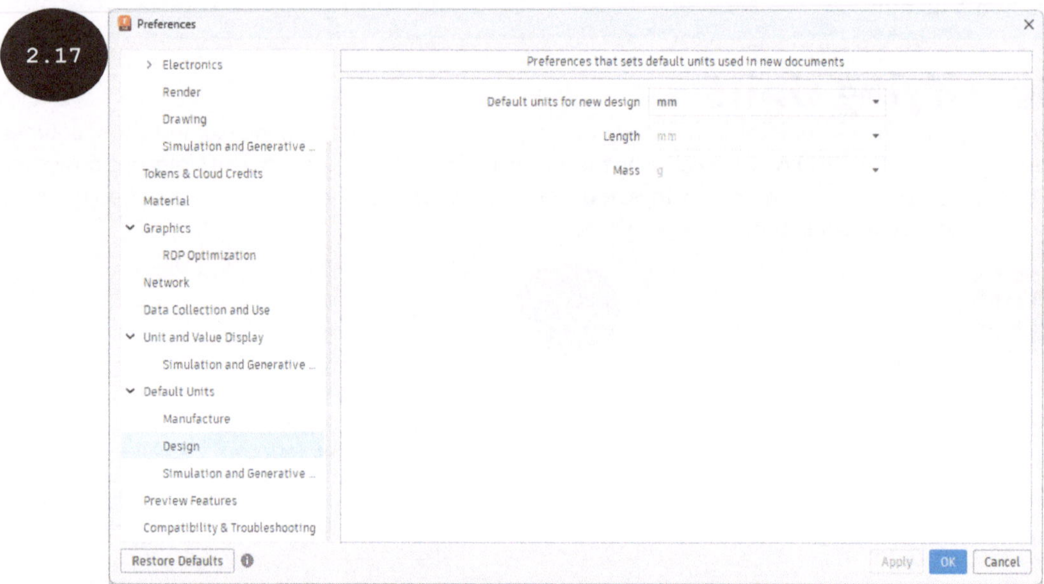

Specifying Grids and Snaps Settings

Grids help you to specify points in the drawing area while creating sketch entities and acting as reference lines. By default, the display of grids is turned on in the drawing area since the **Sketch Grid** check box is selected in the **SKETCH PALETTE** dialog box, by default, see Figure 2.18. You can turn on or off the display of grids in the drawing area by using the **Sketch Grid** check box of the **SKETCH PALETTE** dialog box.

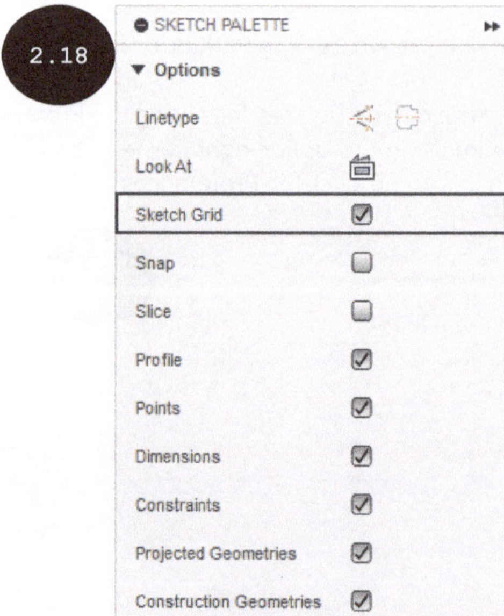

You can also turn on the snap mode to restrict or snap the movement of the cursor at the intersection of grid lines while drawing the sketch entities. To do this, select the **Snap** check box in the **SKETCH PALETTE** dialog box. Alternatively, invoke the **Grid and Snaps** flyout in the **Navigation Bar** available at the bottom of the drawing area, see Figure 2.19. Next, select the **Snap to Grid** check box in this flyout to snap the movement of the cursor to the grid lines.

In addition to controlling the display of grid lines in the drawing area, you can also specify the grid settings as needed. To do this, invoke the **Grid and Snaps** flyout in the **Navigation Bar**, see Figure 2.19. Next, click on the **Grid Settings** tool in this flyout.

The **GRID SETTINGS** dialog box appears, see Figure 2.20. The options in the **GRID SETTINGS** dialog box are discussed next.

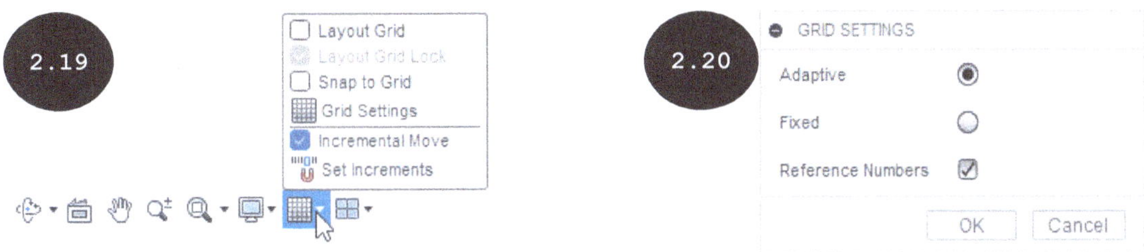

Adaptive

By default, the **Adaptive** radio button is selected in the **GRID SETTINGS** dialog box. As a result, the size of the grid adjusts automatically when you zoom in and out of the drawing display area.

Fixed

The **Fixed** radio button is used for specifying the grid size which remains the same and does not change or adjust when you zoom in or out of the drawing display area.

On selecting the **Fixed** radio button, the **Major Grid Spacing** and **Minor Subdivisions** fields appear in the dialog box, see Figure 2.21. The **Major Grid Spacing** field is used for specifying the distance between two major grid lines and the **Minor Subdivisions** field is used for specifying the number of divisions between two major grid lines. For example, if you enter 5 in the **Minor Subdivisions** field, then two major grid lines will be divided into 5 smaller areas horizontally or vertically.

Reference Numbers

The **Reference Numbers** check box is used for turning on or off the display of the grid's reference numbers in the drawing area, see Figure 2.22. In this figure, the grid's reference numbers are turned on by selecting the **Reference Numbers** check box.

After specifying the grid settings, click on the **OK** button in the **GRID SETTINGS** dialog box to accept the changes made and exit the dialog box.

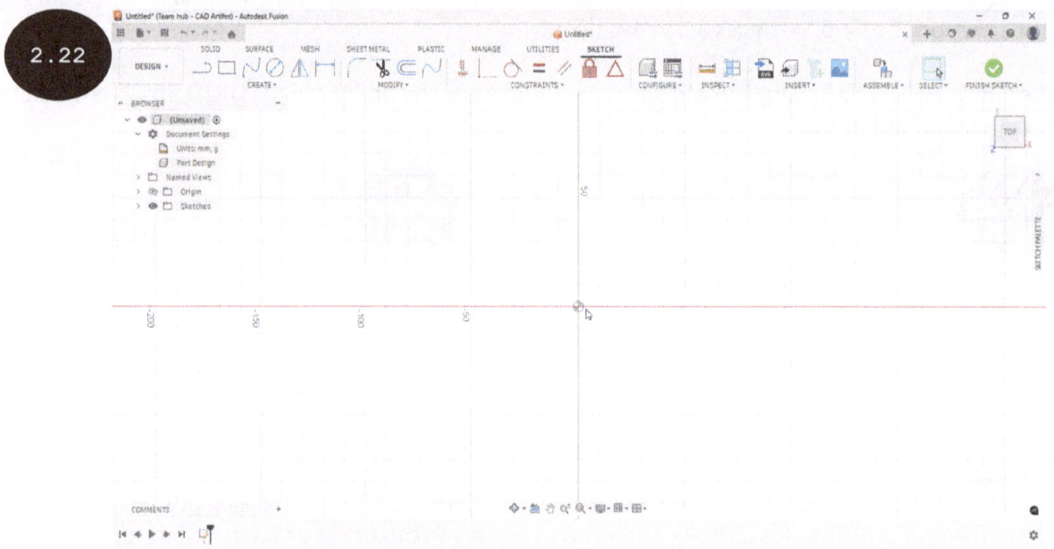

2.22

Drawing a Line Entity

A line is defined as the shortest distance between two points. To draw a line, click the **Line** tool in the **CREATE** panel of the **SKETCH** contextual tab, see Figure 2.23. The **Line** tool is activated.

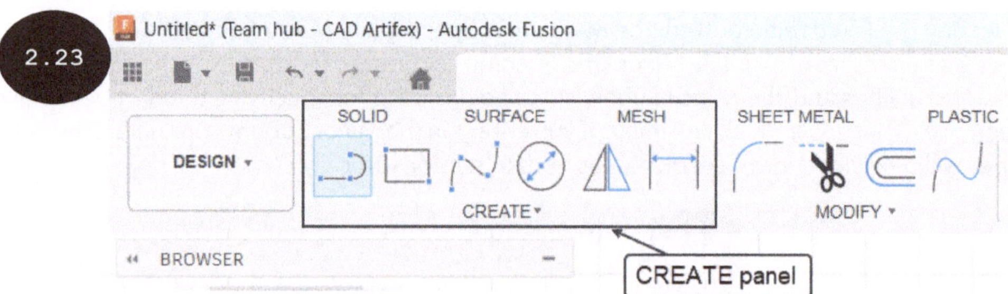

2.23

You can also press the **L** key on the keyboard to invoke the **Line** tool. Alternatively, right-click in the drawing area to display the Marking Menu. From this menu, click the **Sketch** tool or hover the cursor over it, see Figure 2.24. The second level of the Marking Menu appears, displaying frequently used sketching tools, see Figure 2.25. Next, click the **Line** tool from the Marking Menu. The method for drawing a line is discussed below:

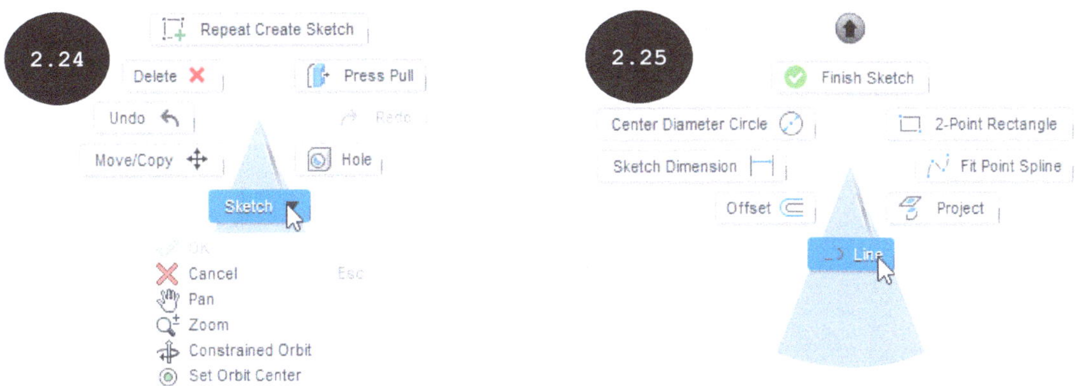

1. Click on the **Line** tool in the **Toolbar** or press the **L** key. The **Line** tool gets activated.

2. Click to specify the start point of the line.

3. Move the line cursor away from the start point. A rubber band line appears with one of its ends fixed at the start point and the other end attached to the cursor. Notice that as you move the cursor, the length of the rubber band line changes and appears in the dimension box, see Figure 2.26.

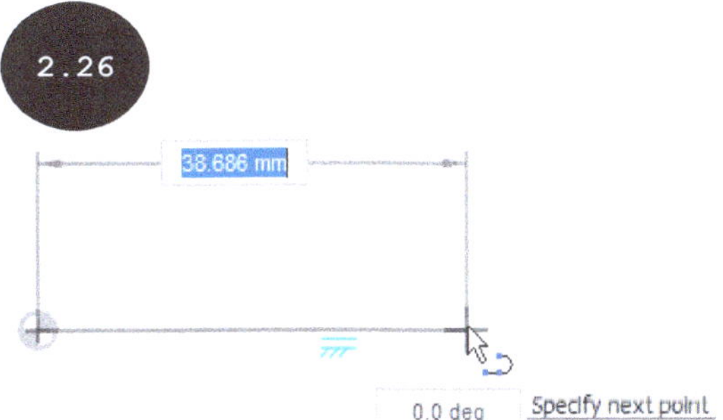

Note: When you move the cursor horizontally or vertically after specifying the start point of the line, the symbol of horizontal or vertical constraint appears near the line. These symbol of constraint indicates that if you click the left mouse button to specify the endpoint of the line, the corresponding constraint will be applied. You will learn more about constraints in later chapters.

4. Click the left mouse button in the drawing area to specify the endpoint of the line. A line between the specified points is drawn. Also, notice that the rubber band line is still displayed with one of its ends fixed to the last specified point and the other end attached to the cursor. This indicates that a chain of continuous lines can be drawn by clicking the left mouse button in the drawing area.

Note: You can also enter the length of the line in the dimension box and then press ENTER. On doing so, a line of the specified length is drawn, and the dimension is applied to the line. Also, the **Line** tool is no longer active.

As Autodesk Fusion is a parametric 3D solid modeling software, you can draw a sketch by specifying points arbitrarily in the drawing area and then apply dimensions. You will learn about dimensioning sketch entities in later chapters.

5. After drawing all the line entities of the sketch, click on the tick-mark that appears near the last line segment in the drawing area to end the creation of continuous lines, see Figure 2.27. Note that

the **Line** tool is still activated. To exit the **Line** tool, press the ESC key or right-click in the drawing area and then click on the **OK** tool in the Marking Menu that appears.

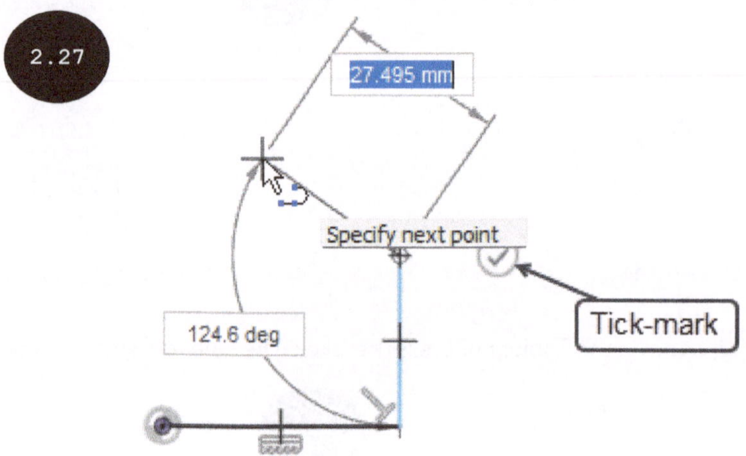

Note: The **CREATE** panel of the **SKETCH** contextual tab displays some of the most commonly used sketching tools, by default. You can customize to add more tools to the **CREATE** panel from the **CREATE** drop-down menu of the **SKETCH** contextual tab. To do this, invoke the **CREATE** drop-down menu in the **SKETCH** contextual tab (see Figure 2.28), and then move the cursor over the tool to be added to the **CREATE** panel. Next, click on the three dots ⋮ that appear near the tool, see Figure 2.28. A cascading menu appears. In this menu, select the **Pin to Toolbar** check box. The selected tool gets added to the **CREATE** panel of the **Toolbar**. Note that on clearing the **Pin to Toolbar** check box, you can remove the selected tool from the **CREATE** panel of the **Toolbar**. The **Pin to Shortcuts** check box is used for adding the tool in the **Shortcuts** dialog box that appears on pressing the S key in the drawing area. You can also remove an existing tool from the **Toolbar** by dragging it out of the **Toolbar**.

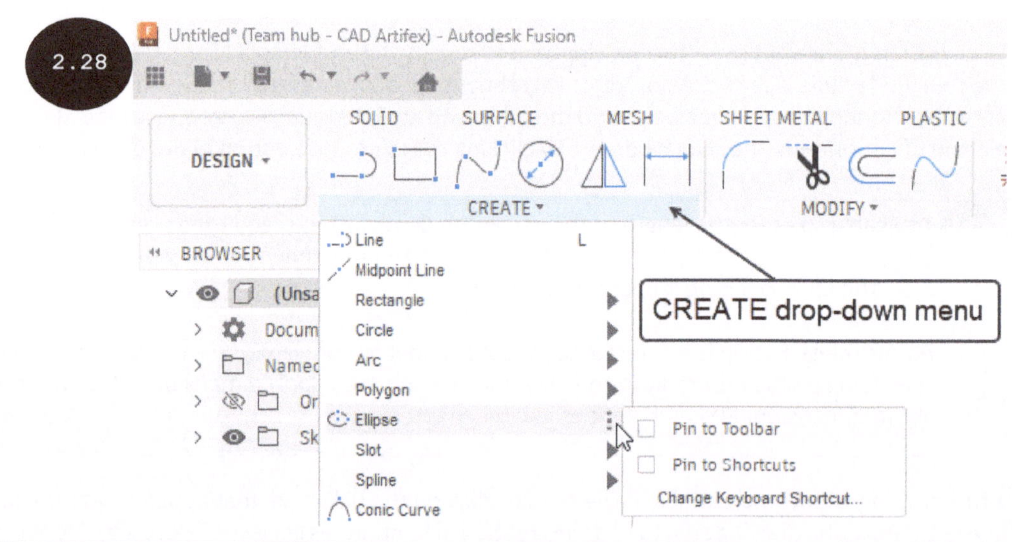

Tutorial 1

Draw a sketch of the model shown in Figure 2.29. The dimensions and the model shown in the figure are for your reference only. All dimensions are in mm.

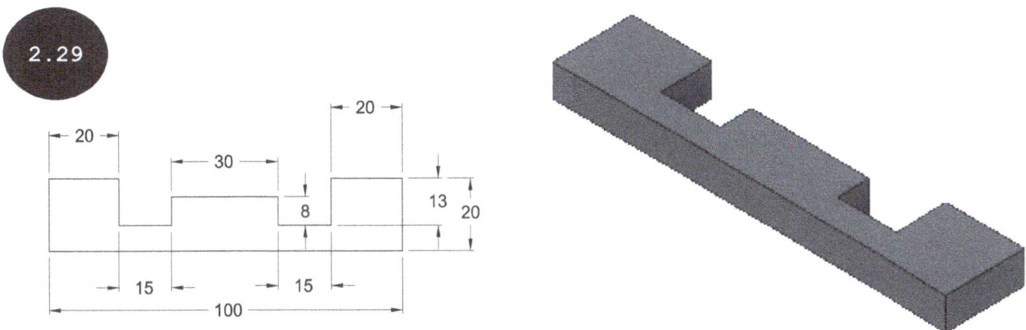

Section 1: Starting Autodesk Fusion

1. Start Autodesk Fusion by double-clicking on the **Autodesk Fusion** icon on your desktop. After the necessary files are loaded, the Autodesk Fusion startup interface appears with the default Part Design file and displays various tools in the **Toolbar**, see Figure 2.30.

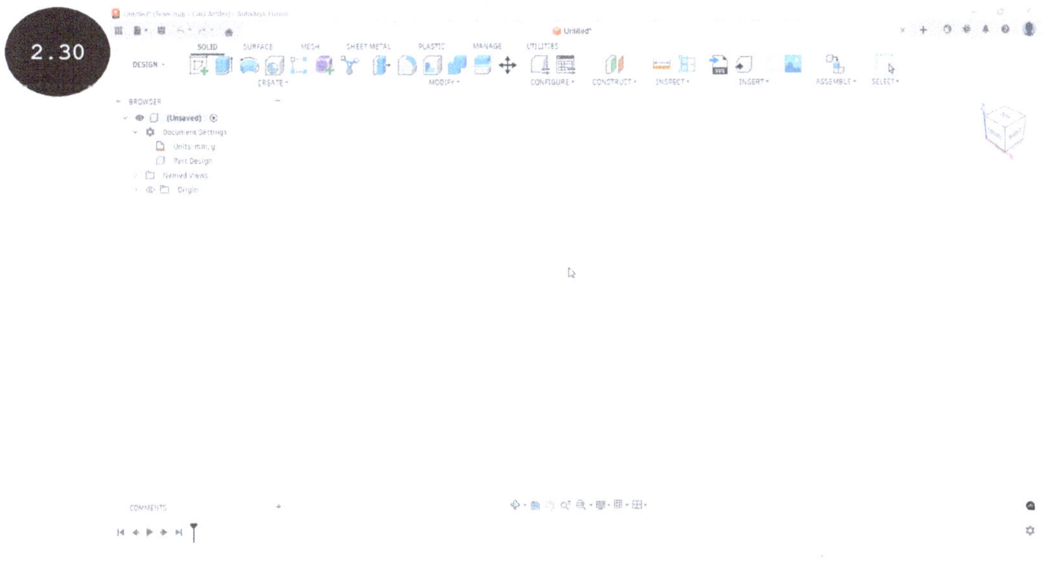

Note: Alternatively, click **File > New** in the **Application Bar** to display the **What do you want to design?** dialog box, see Figure 2.31.

In this dialog box, select the **Part Design** button and choose the **millimeter (mm), gram (g)** unit system from the **Unit System** drop-down list. Next, click on the **Create New** button. A new Part Design file is opened with the default name in a separate tab.

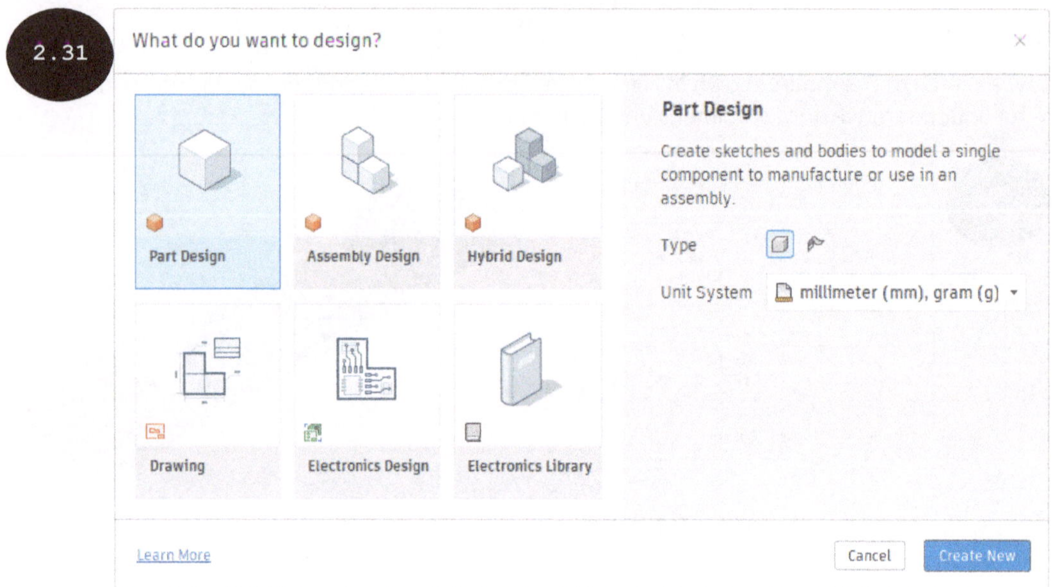

Section 2: Organizing Data Panel

Before you begin creating a design, you can organize the **Data Panel** by creating a project folder and sub-folders to save your design files.

1. Click on the **Show Data Panel** tool in the **Application Bar**, see Figure 2.32. The **Data Panel** appears, see Figure 2.33.

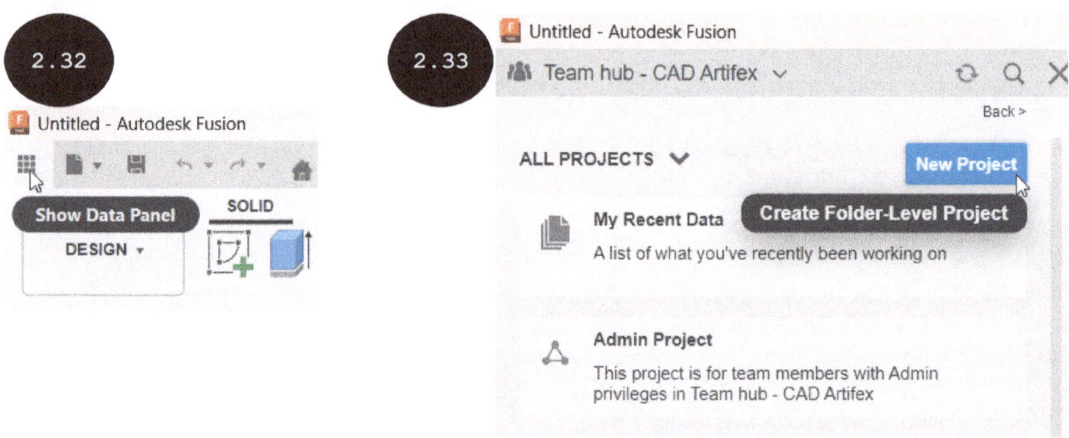

2. Click on the **New Project** button at the top right corner of the **Data Panel**, refer to Figure 2.33. The new project is added to the **Data Panel** and its default name *New Project* appears in an edit field. You can edit or change the default name of the newly added project.

3. Enter **Autodesk Fusion 360** in the edit field as the name of the newly added project and then click anywhere in the drawing area. A new project with the name **Autodesk Fusion 360** is created in the **Data Panel**, see Figure 2.34.

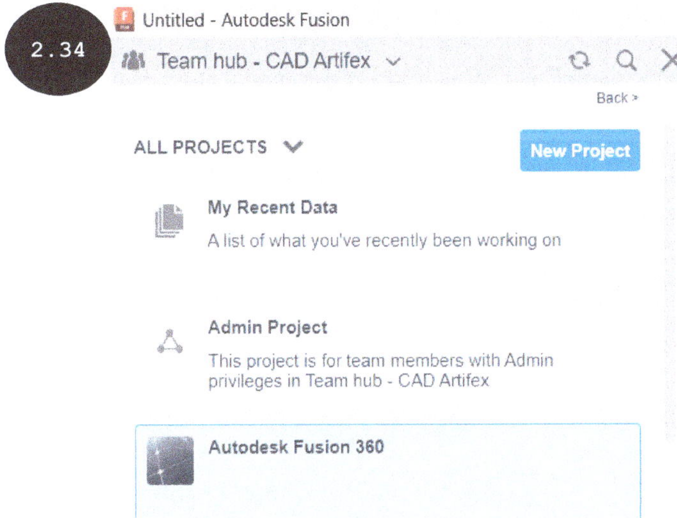

Now, you need to create sub-folders inside the **Autodesk Fusion 360** project.

4. Double-click on the **Autodesk Fusion 360** project in the **Data Panel**. The project is opened and appears in the **Data Panel**, see Figure 2.35.

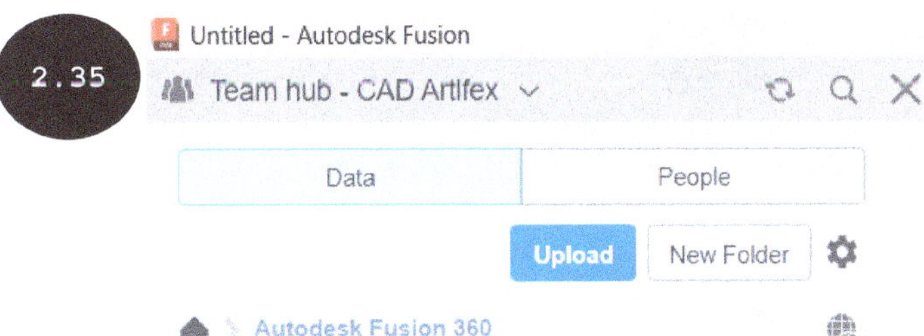

5. Click on the **New Folder** button to create a folder inside the project. The new folder is added inside the project and its default name *New Folder* appears in an edit field.

6. Enter **Chapter 02** in the edit field as the name of the folder (see Figure 2.36) and then click anywhere in the drawing area. The new folder with the name **Chapter 02** is created inside the **Autodesk Fusion 360** project in the **Data Panel**.

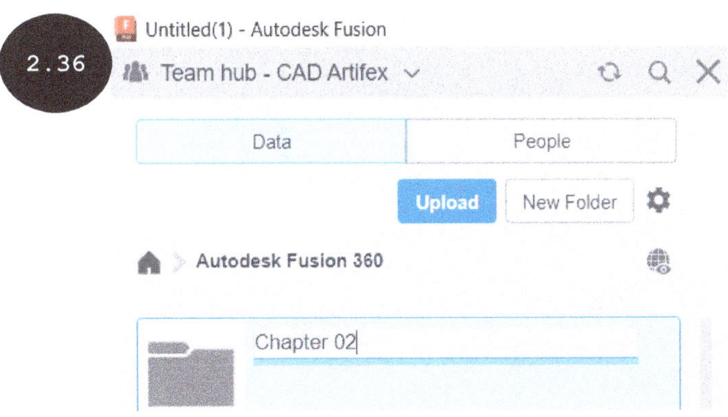

7. Similarly, create a sub-folder inside the **Chapter 02** folder with the name **Tutorial**.

8. After organizing the **Data Panel**, close it by clicking on the cross-mark × at its top right corner.

Section 3: Specifying Units

1. Expand the **Document Settings** node in the **BROWSER** and then move the cursor over the **Units** option. The **Change Active Units** tool appears, see Figure 2.37.

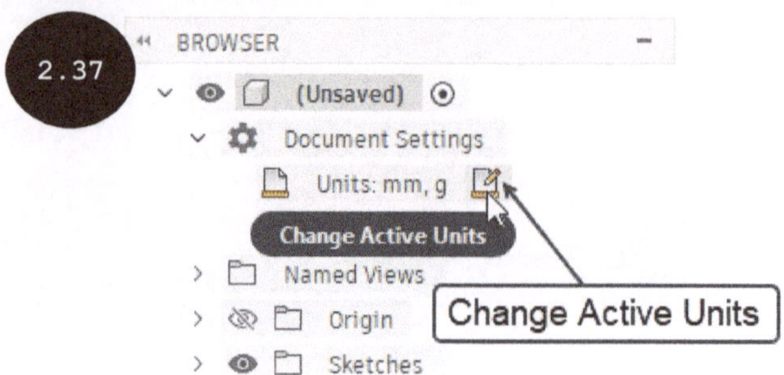

2. Click on the **Change Active Units** tool. The **CHANGE ACTIVE UNITS** dialog box appears on the right side of the graphics area, see Figure 2.38.

3. Ensure that the **Millimeter (mm), gram (g)** unit system is selected in the **Unit System** drop-down list of this dialog box. Next, click on the **OK** button.

Section 4: Specifying Grid Settings

1. Invoke the **Grid and Snaps** flyout in the **Navigation Bar**, see Figure 2.39.

2. Click on the **Grid Settings** tool in the **Grid and Snaps** flyout. The **GRID SETTINGS** dialog box appears, see Figure 2.40.

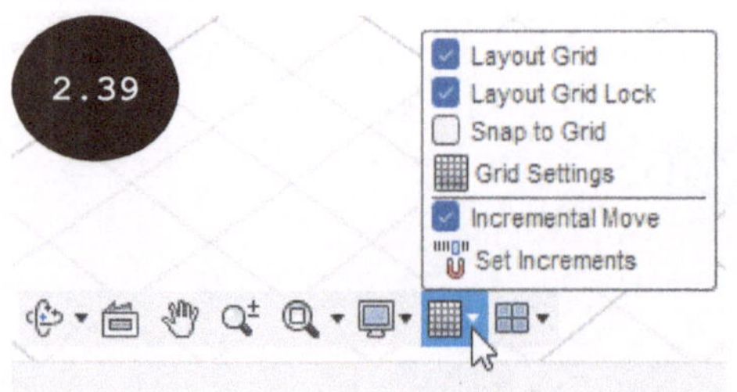

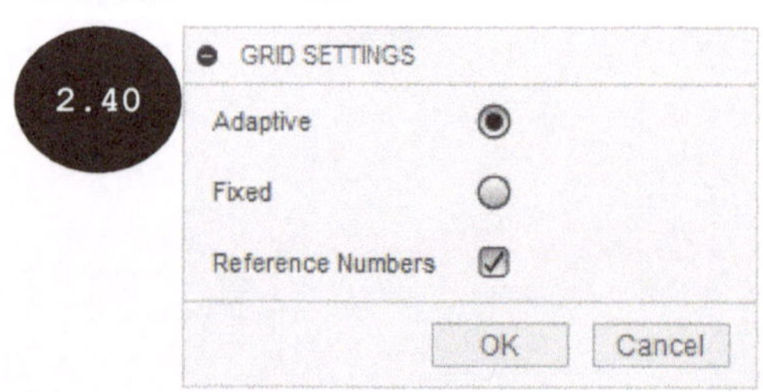

3. Ensure that the **Adaptive** radio button is selected in the **GRID SETTINGS** dialog box to adjust the grid size automatically, as you zoom into or out of the drawing view.

4. Click on the **OK** button in the **GRID SETTINGS** dialog box.

Section 5: Creating Sketch

1. Click on the **Create Sketch** tool in the **Toolbar**, see Figure 2.41. Three default planes: Front, Top, and Right, which are mutually perpendicular to each other appear in the graphics area, see Figure 2.42.

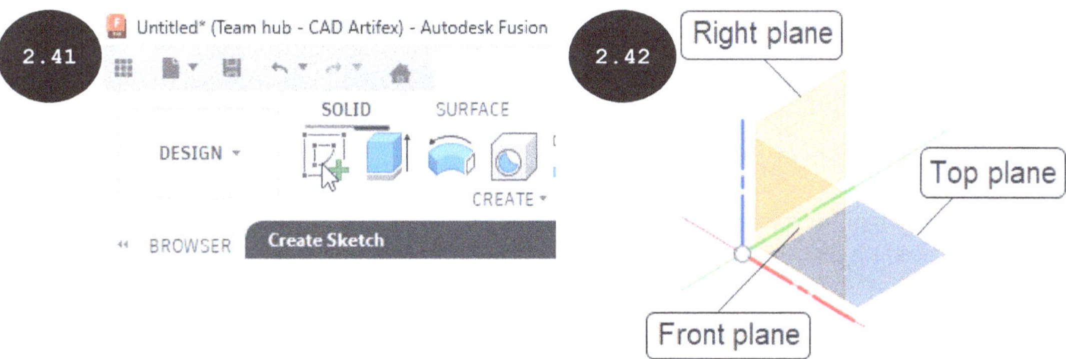

2. Move the cursor over the Top plane and then click the left mouse button when it gets highlighted in the drawing area. The Top plane becomes the sketching plane for creating the sketch and it is oriented normal to the viewing direction. Also, the **SKETCH** contextual tab and the **SKETCH PALETTE** dialog box appear, see Figure 2.43.

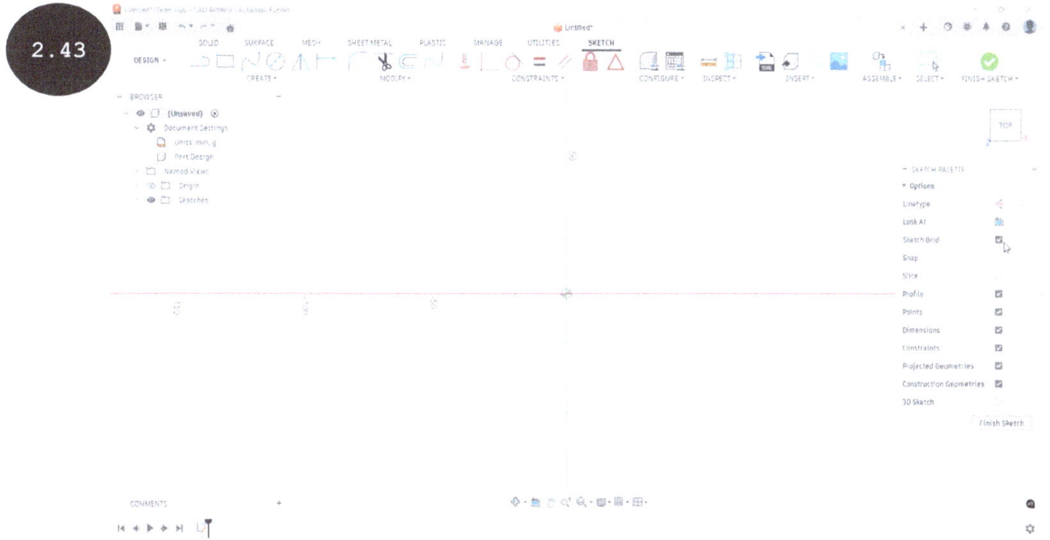

3. Ensure that the **Sketch Grid** and **Snap** check boxes are selected in the **SKETCH PALETTE** dialog box to display the grids and to snap the movement of the cursor on the grid lines.

Now, you can create the sketch.

4. Click on the **Line** tool in the **Toolbar**, see Figure 2.44. The **Line** tool gets activated. Alternatively, press the L key to activate the **Line** tool.

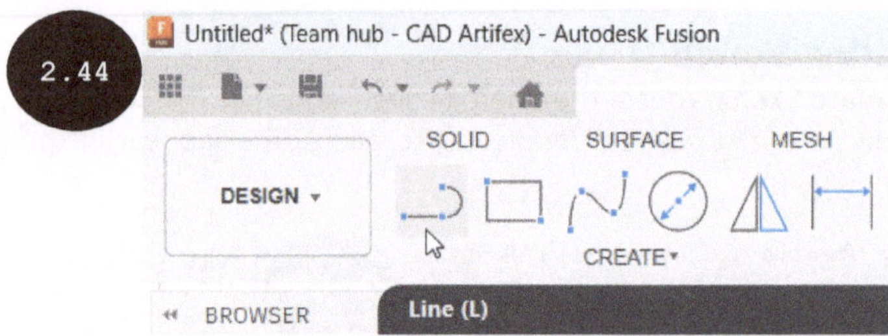

5. Move the cursor to the origin and then click to specify the start point of the line when the cursor snaps to the origin.

6. Move the cursor horizontally toward the right and then click to specify the endpoint of the line when the length of the line appears 100 mm in the dimension box, see Figure 2.45.

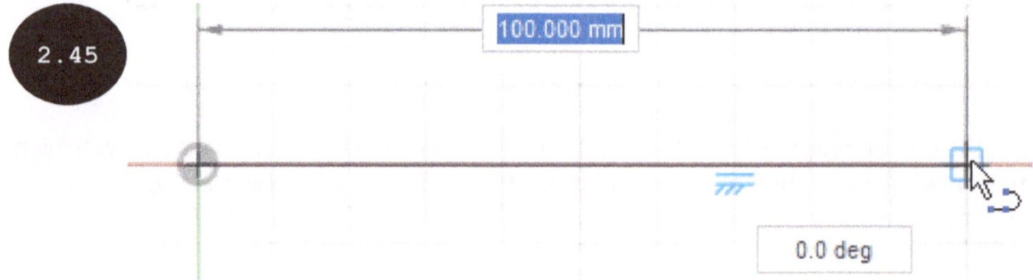

7. Move the cursor vertically upward and then click the left mouse button when the length of the line appears 20 mm, see Figure 2.46.

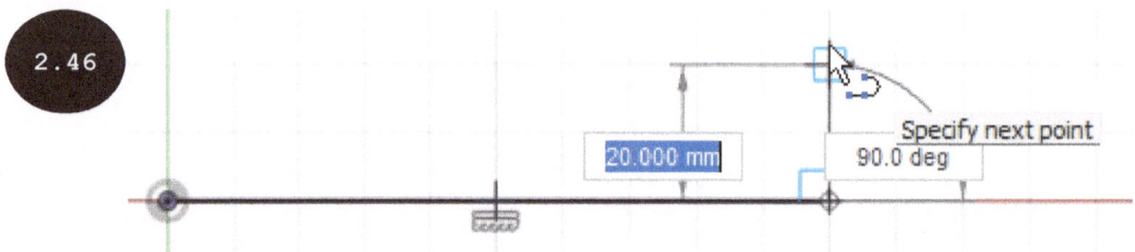

8. Move the cursor horizontally toward the left and then click when the length of the line appears 20 mm.

9. Move the cursor vertically downward and then click when the length of the line appears 13 mm in the dimension box, see Figure 2.47. Note that you need to zoom into the drawing view to adjust the grid size so that the cursor snaps to the grid lines when the length of the line is measured as 13 mm. You can zoom in to or zoom out of the drawing area by scrolling the middle mouse button.

2.47

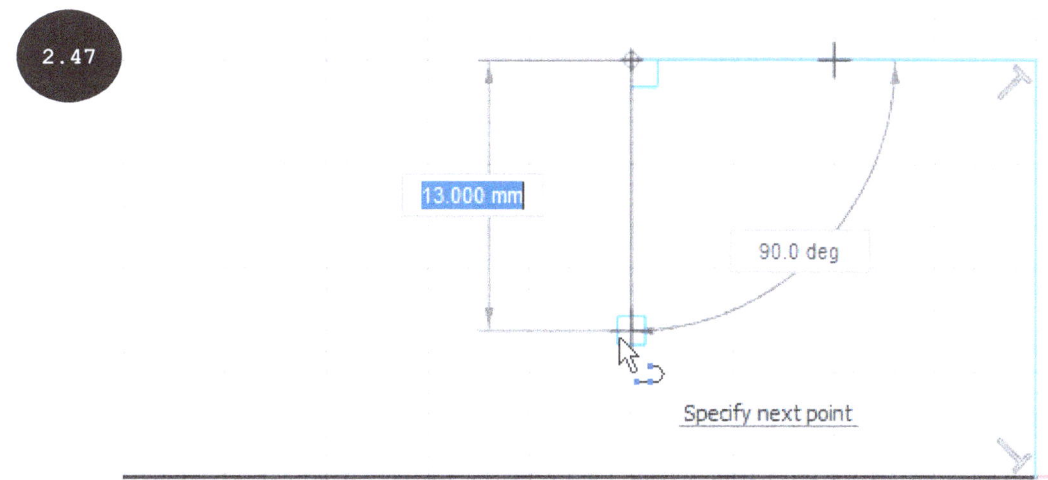

10. Move the cursor horizontally toward the left and then click when the length of the line appears 15 mm.

Note: You need to zoom into the drawing view by using the middle mouse button so that the grid size adjusts automatically and the cursor snaps to the required location.

11. Move the cursor vertically upward and then click when the length of the line appears as 8 mm.

12. Move the cursor horizontally toward the left and then click when the length of the line appears as 30 mm.

13. Move the cursor vertically downward and then click when the length of the line appears as 8 mm.

14. Similarly, draw the remaining sketch entities. Figure 2.48 shows the sketch after all the sketch entities have been drawn.

2.48

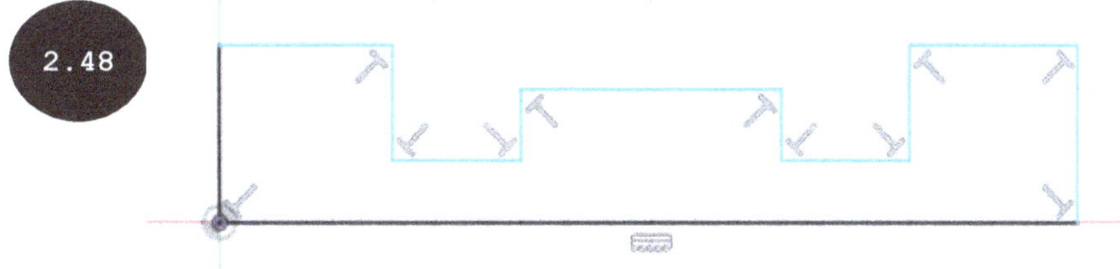

15. Right-click in the drawing area, the Marking Menu appears. In this Marking Menu, click on the **OK** tool to exit the **Line** tool.

Section 6: Saving the Sketch

1. Click on the **Save** tool in the **Application Bar**. The **Save** dialog box appears.

2. Enter **Tutorial 1** in the **Name** field of the dialog box.

3. Click on the down arrow next to the **Location** field in the dialog box. The expanded **Save** dialog box appears with the **PROJECT** area on its left side, refer to Figure 2.49.

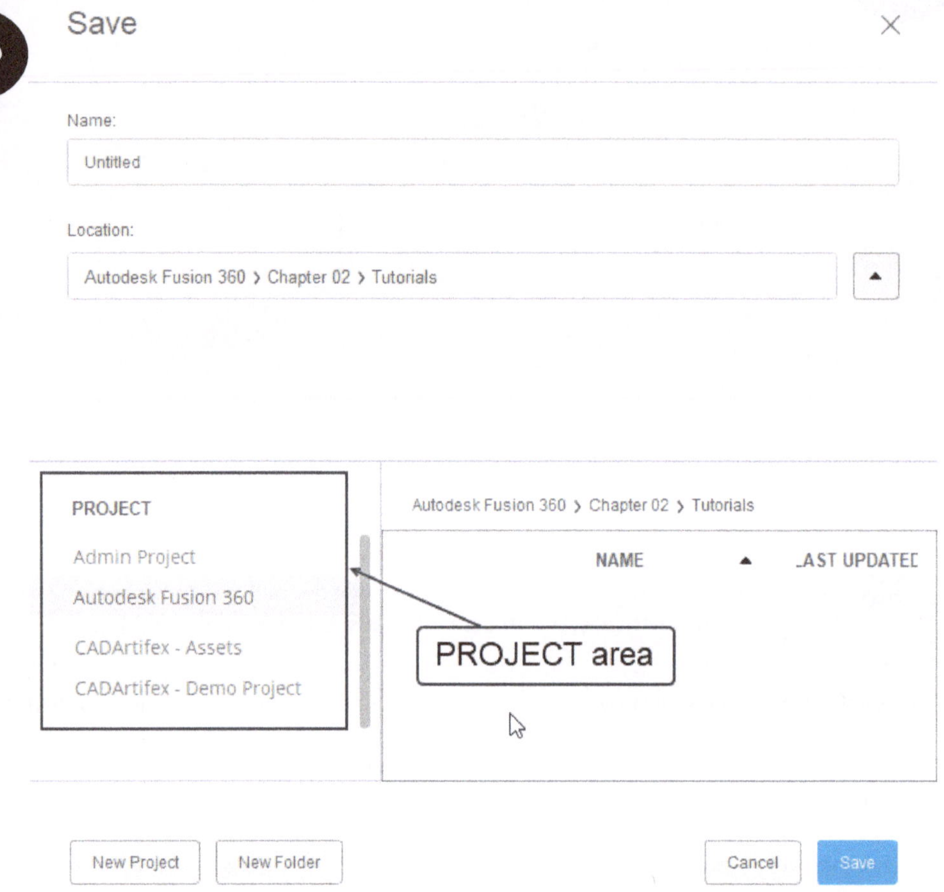

4. Ensure that the **Autodesk Fusion 360** project is selected in the **PROJECT** area. Note that all the folders created in the selected project appear on the right panel of the dialog box.

5. Specify the location ***Autodesk Fusion 360 > Chapter 02 > Tutorial*** to save the sketch. Note that you need to double-click on the folder/sub-folder of the project in the right panel of the dialog box to access the required location for saving the sketch.

6. Click on the **Save** button in the dialog box. The sketch is saved with the name Tutorial 1 in the specified location (***Autodesk Fusion 360 > Chapter 02 > Tutorial***).

Hands-on Test Drive 1

Draw a sketch of the model, as shown in Figure 2.50. The dimensions and the model shown in the figure are for your reference only. You will learn about applying dimensions and creating 3D models in later chapters. All dimensions are in mm.

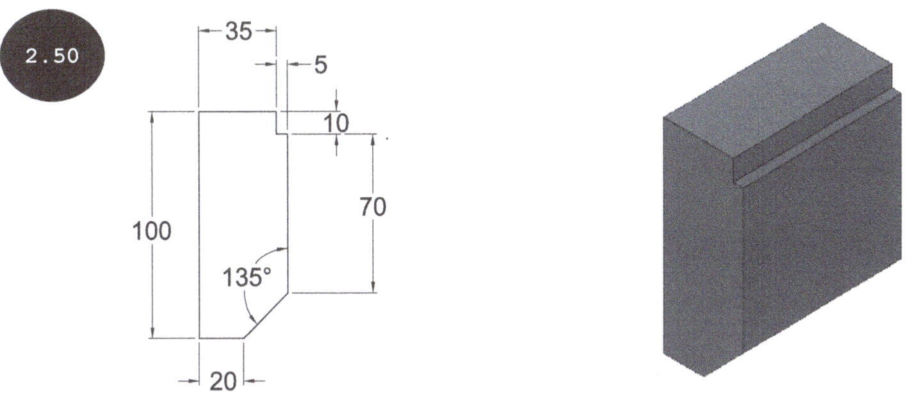

Drawing a Midpoint Line

The **Midpoint Line** tool is created symmetrically about its midpoint. In Autodesk Fusion, you draw midpoint lines using the **Midpoint Line** tool. The method for drawing a midpoint line is discussed below:

1. Invoke the **CREATE** drop-down menu in the **SKETCH** contextual tab of the **Toolbar** and then click on the **Midpoint Line** tool, see Figure 2.51.

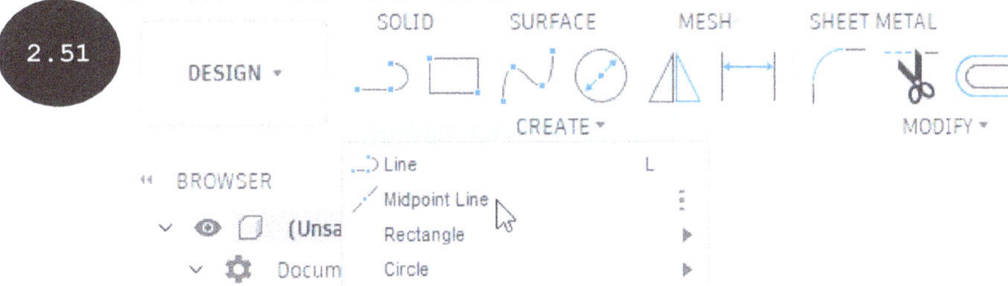

2. After activating the **Midpoint Line** tool, click to specify the midpoint of the line in the drawing area.

3. Move the cursor to the required location to define the endpoint of the line. As you move the cursor, a preview of a line, symmetrical about the specified midpoint appears, see Figure 2.52.

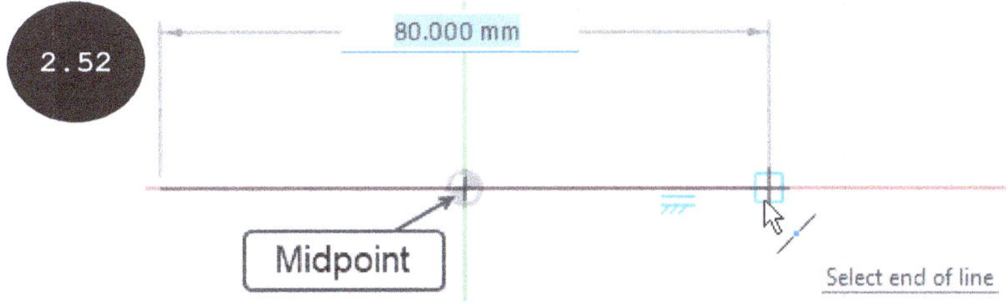

4. Click to specify the endpoint of the line. The midpoint line is created.

Drawing a Tangent Arc by Using the Line Tool

In Autodesk Fusion, you can draw a tangent arc using the **Tangent Arc** tool, which is discussed later in this chapter. Additionally, you can create a tangent arc with the **Line** tool, provided that at least one line or arc entity is already drawn in the drawing area. The method for drawing a tangent arc by using the **Line** tool is discussed below:

1. Invoke the **Line** tool and then draw a line by specifying two points in the drawing area. Once the line is drawn, do not exit the **Line** tool.

2. Move the cursor over the last specified point. Next, drag the cursor by pressing and holding the left mouse button toward the other side of the line. The arc mode is activated, and the preview of a tangent arc appears in the drawing area, see Figure 2.53.

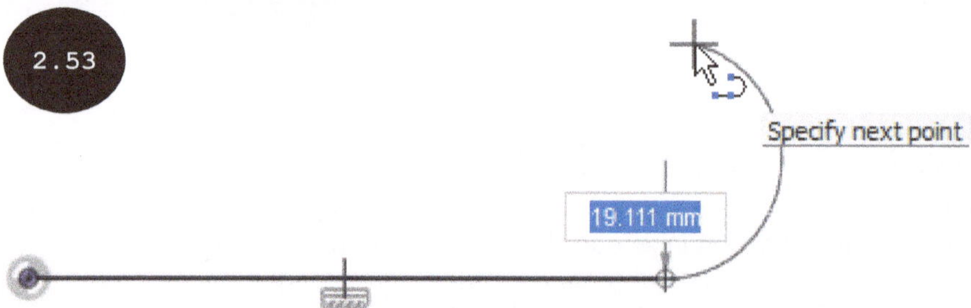

3. Release the left mouse button to specify the endpoint of the arc. The arc is drawn, and the line mode is activated again. You can continue with the creation of line entities or move the cursor back to the last specified point and then drag it to invoke the arc mode again.

Note: The tangency of arc depends upon how you drag the cursor from the last specified point in the drawing area. Figure 2.54 shows the possible movements of the cursor and the creation of arcs in the respective movements.

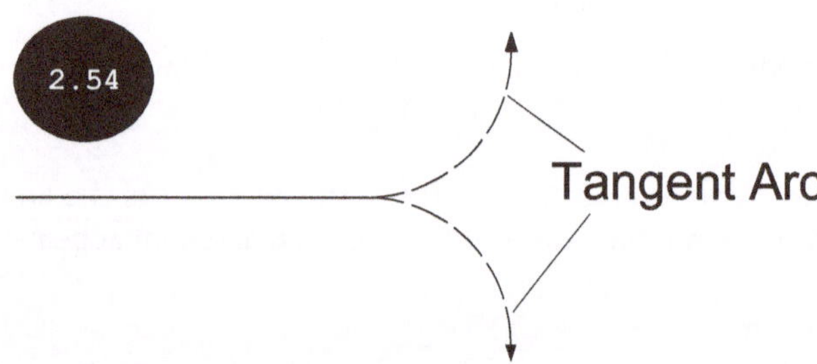

4. Once you have created all the entities of the sketch, right-click in the drawing area and then click on the **OK** tool in the Marking Menu that appears to exit the **Line** tool.

Tutorial 2

Draw a sketch of the model, as shown in Figure 2.55 by using the **Line** tool. The dimensions and the model shown in the figure are for your reference only. You will learn about applying dimensions and creating 3D models in later chapters. All dimensions are in mm.

2.55

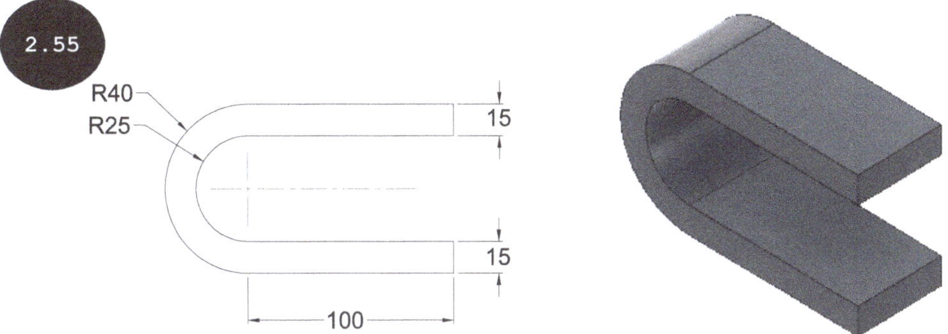

Section 1: Starting a New Part Design File

1. Click **File** > **New** in the **Application Bar** to display the **What do you want to design?** dialog box, see Figure 2.56.

2.56

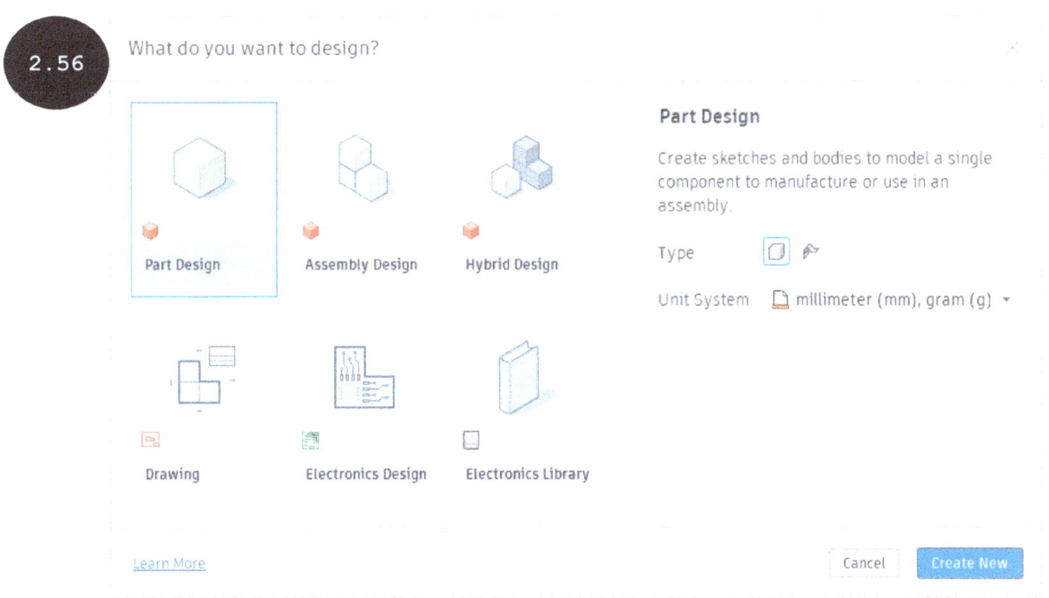

2. In **What do you want to design?** dialog box, select the **Part Design** button. Also, select the **millimeter (mm), gram (g)** unit system from the **Unit System** drop-down list.

3. After specifying the required options, click the **Create New** button. A new Part Design file is opened with the default name, refer to Figure 2.57.

Note: If you are starting a new Autodesk Fusion session, the Part Design file opens automatically because it is set as the default design type. The method for setting the default design type is discussed in Chapter 1.

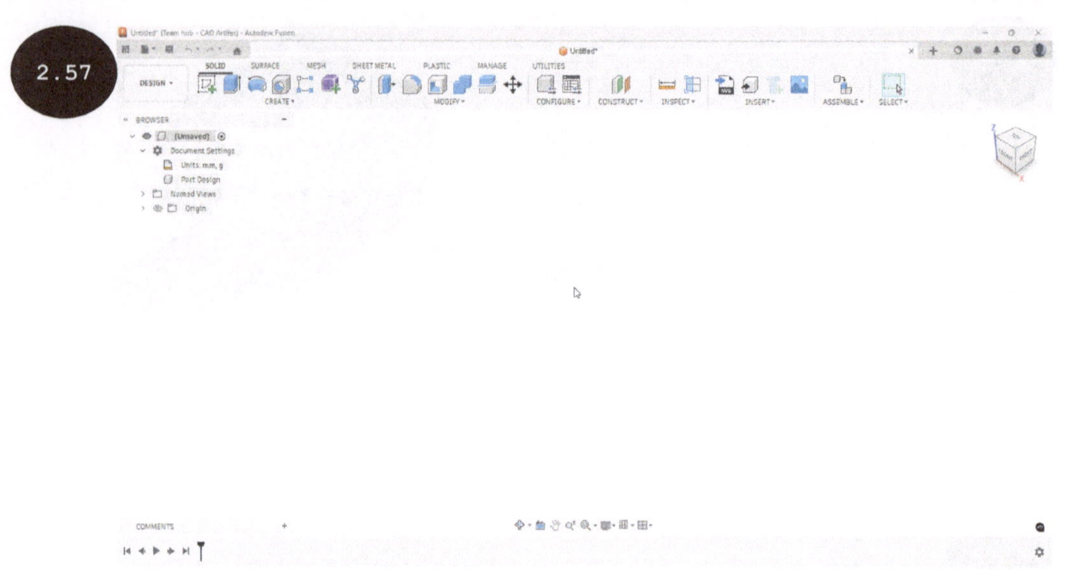

Section 2: Organizing Data Panel

Before you begin creating a design, you can organize the **Data Panel** by creating a project folder and sub-folders to save your design files.

1. Click on the **Show Data Panel** tool in the **Application Bar**, see Figure 2.58. The **Data Panel** appears, see Figure 2.59.

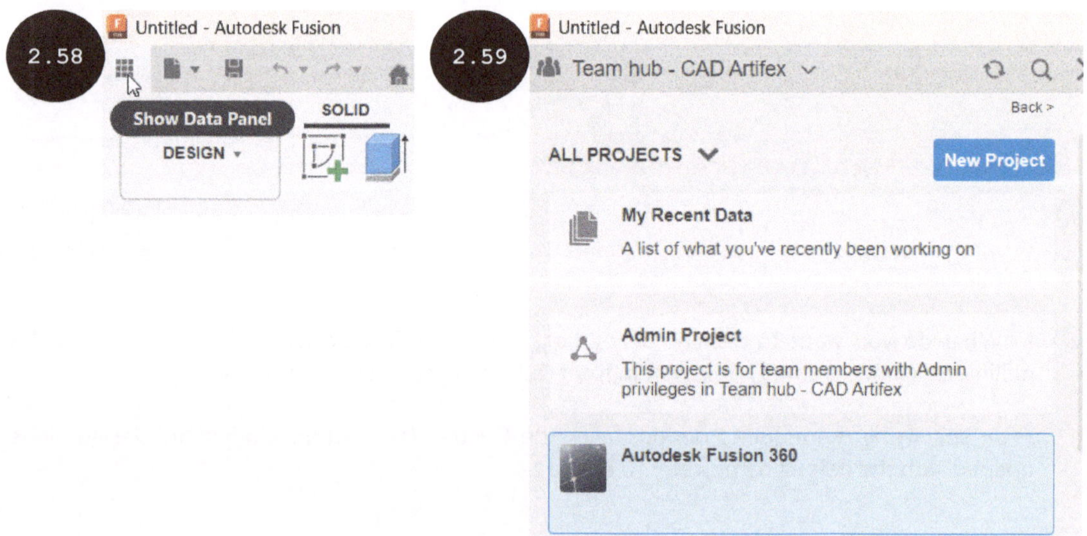

2. Create a new project '**Autodesk Fusion 360**', if not created earlier by using the **New Project** tool.

3. Create the **Chapter 02** folder inside the **Autodesk Fusion 360** project and then the **Tutorial** sub-folder inside the **Chapter 02** folder, if not created earlier.

Note: If you have already created *Autodesk Fusion 360 > Chapter 02 > Tutorial* folders, then you can skip the steps of this section.

4. Click on the cross-mark × at the top right corner of the **Data Panel** to close it.

Section 3: Specifying Grid Settings

It is evident from Figure 2.55 that all the sketch entities are multiples of 5 mm. Therefore, you can set the grid settings such that the cursor snaps to an increment of 5 mm only.

1. Invoke the **Grid and Snaps** flyout in the **Navigation Bar**, see Figure 2.60.

2. Click on the **Grid Settings** tool in the **Grid and Snaps** flyout. The **GRID SETTINGS** dialog box appears, see Figure 2.61.

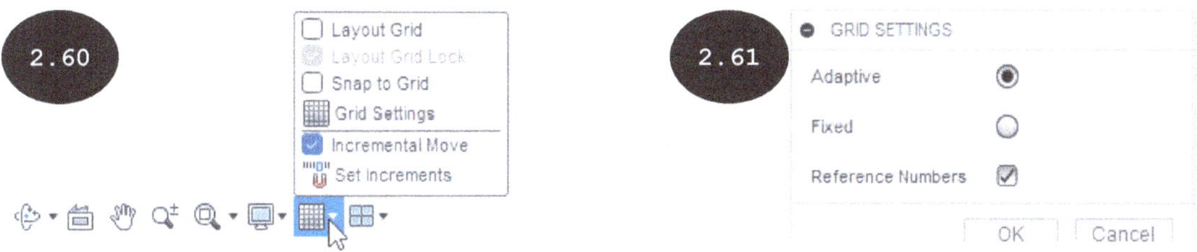

3. Select the **Fixed** radio button in the **GRID SETTINGS** dialog box to specify the fixed grid size. The **Major Grid Spacing** and **Minor Subdivisions** fields appear in the dialog box.

4. Enter **20** mm in the **Major Grid Spacing** field and **4** in the **Minor Subdivisions** field in the dialog box.

5. Click on the **OK** button in the **GRID SETTINGS** dialog box.

Section 4: Creating the Sketch

1. Click on the **Create Sketch** tool in the **Toolbar**, see Figure 2.62. Three default planes: Front, Top, and Right, which are mutually perpendicular to each other appear in the graphics area, see Figure 2.63.

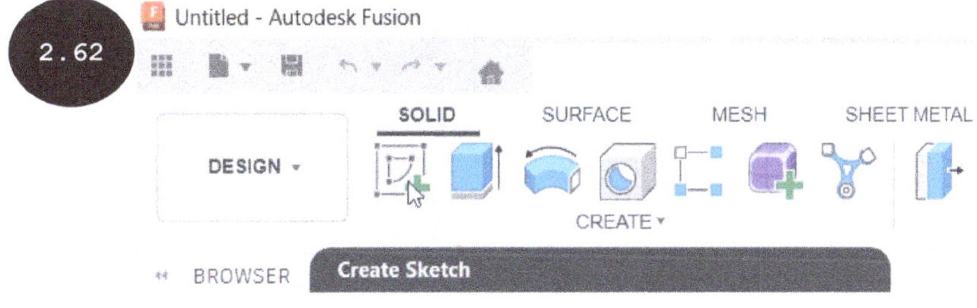

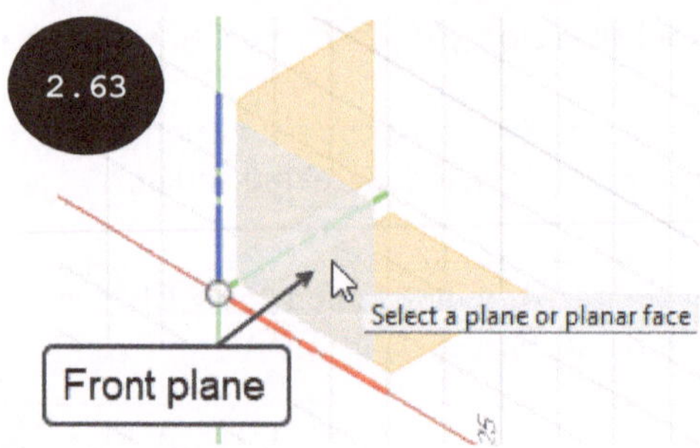

2. Move the cursor over the Front plane and then click the left mouse button when it gets highlighted in the drawing area, refer to Figure 2.63. The Front plane becomes the sketching plane for creating the sketch and it is oriented normal to the viewing direction. Also, the **SKETCH** contextual tab and the **SKETCH PALETTE** dialog box appear, see Figure 2.64.

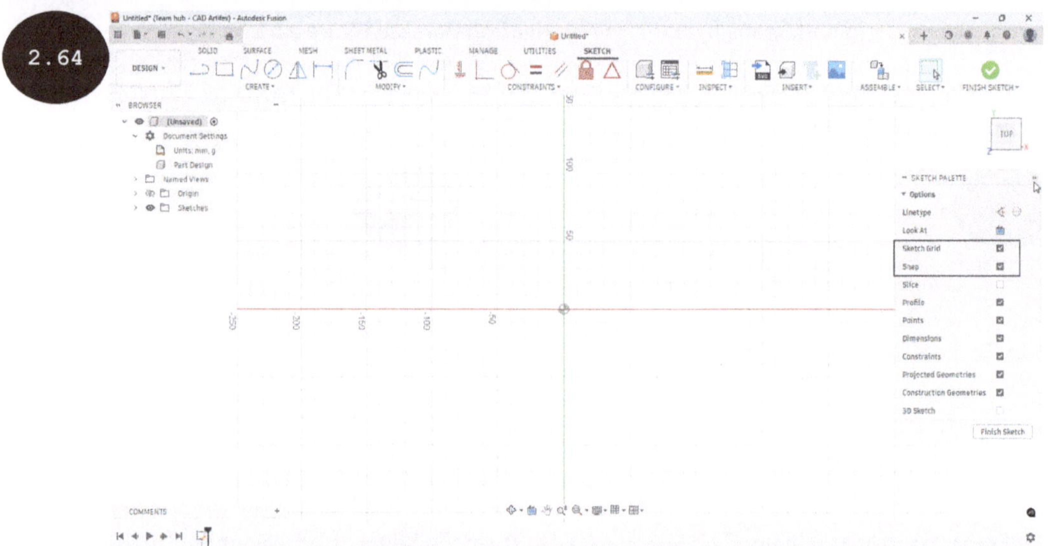

3. Ensure that the **Sketch Grid** and **Snap** check boxes are selected in the **SKETCH PALETTE** dialog box to display the grids and to snap the movement of the cursor on the grid lines.

   Now, you can create the sketch entities of the sketch.

4. Click on the **Line** tool in the **Toolbar**, see Figure 2.65. The **Line** tool is activated. Alternatively, press the L key to activate the **Line** tool.

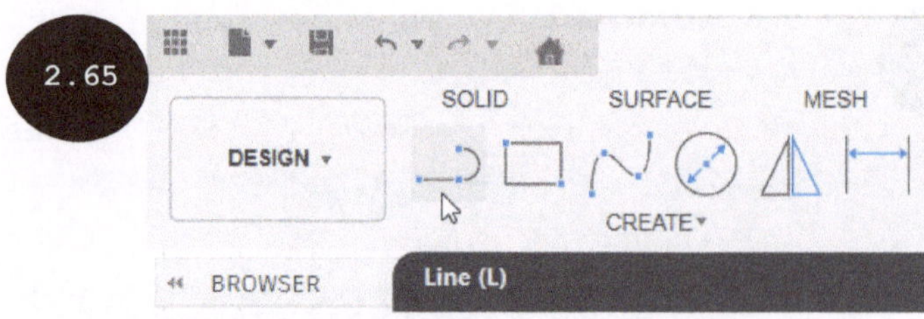

5. Move the cursor to the origin and then click to specify the start point of the line when the cursor snaps to the origin.

6. Move the cursor horizontally toward the left and then click to specify the second point of the line when the length of the line appears as 100 mm in the dimension box, see Figure 2.66. Notice that when you move the cursor in the drawing area, it snaps gradually to a distance of 5 mm.

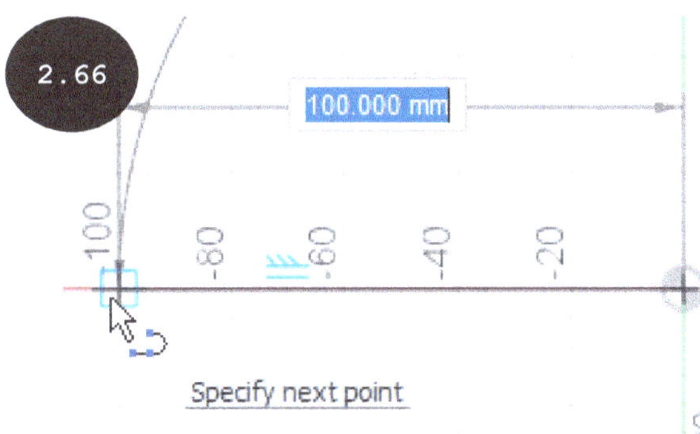

7. Move the cursor to the last specified point. Next, drag the cursor toward the left to a distance and then vertically upward by pressing the left mouse button. The arc mode is activated and the preview of the tangent arc appears in the drawing area, see Figure 2.67.

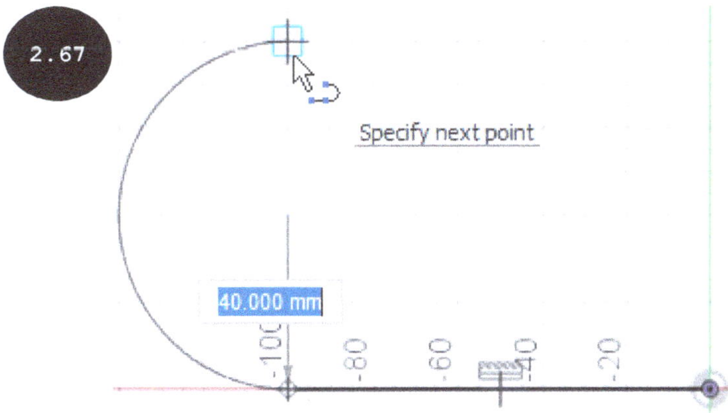

8. Release the left mouse button when the radius of the arc appears as 40 mm in the dimension box, refer to Figure 2.67. An arc of radius 40 mm is created and the line mode gets activated again.

9. Move the cursor horizontally toward the right and click when the length of the line appears as 100 mm.

10. Move the cursor vertically downward and click when the length of the line appears as 15 mm.

11. Move the cursor horizontally toward the left and click when the length of the line appears as 100 mm.

12. Move the cursor to the last specified point. Next, drag the cursor toward the left to a distance and then vertically downward by pressing the left mouse button. The arc mode is activated and the preview of the tangent arc appears in the drawing area, see Figure 2.68.

13. Release the left mouse button when the radius of the arc appears as 25 mm in the dimension box, see Figure 2.68. An arc of radius 25 mm is created and the line mode gets activated again.

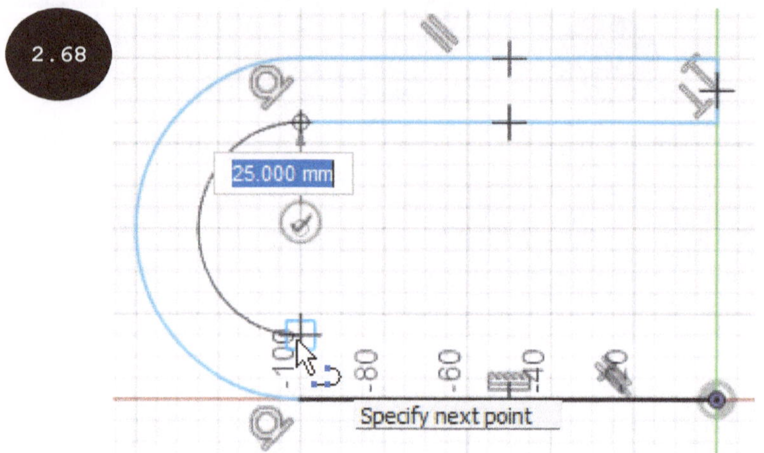

14. Move the cursor horizontally toward the right and then click when the length of the line appears as 100 mm.

15. Move the cursor vertically downward and then click when the cursor snaps to the start point of the first sketch entity. The sketch is drawn, see Figure 2.69.

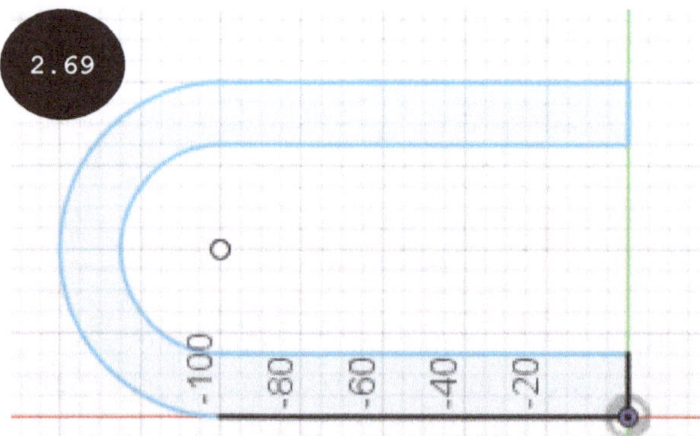

Note: In Figure 2.69, the display of automatically applied constraints such as horizontal and vertical is turned off. To do this, clear the **Constraints** check box in the **SKETCH PALETTE** dialog box.

16. Right-click in the drawing area. The Marking Menu appears. In this Marking Menu, click on the **OK** tool to exit the **Line** tool.

Section 5: Saving the Sketch

1. Click on the **Save** tool in the **Application Bar**. The **Save** dialog box appears.

2. Enter **Tutorial 2** in the **Name** field of the dialog box.

3. Ensure that the location to save the file is specified as ***Autodesk Fusion 360 > Chapter 02 > Tutorial*** in the **Location** field of the dialog box, see Figure 2.70. To specify the location, you need to expand the **Save** dialog box by clicking on the down arrow available next to the **Location** field of the dialog box, as discussed earlier.

4. Click on the **Save** button in the dialog box. The sketch is saved with the name Tutorial 2 in the specified location (***Autodesk Fusion 360 > Chapter 02 > Tutorial***).

Hands-on Test Drive 2

Draw a sketch of the model shown in Figure 2.71. The dimensions and the model shown in the figure are for your reference only. Draw all entities of the sketch by using the **Line** tool. All dimensions are in mm.

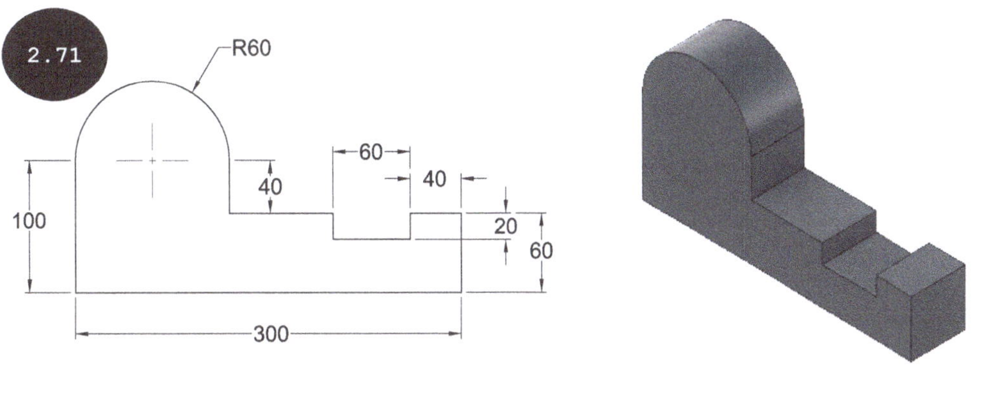

Drawing a Rectangle

In Autodesk Fusion, you can draw a rectangle using the **2-Point Rectangle**, **3-Point Rectangle**, and **Center Rectangle** tools. You can access these tools in the **CREATE** drop-down menu of the **SKETCH** contextual tab in the **Toolbar**, see Figure 2.72. The tools for drawing a rectangle are discussed next.

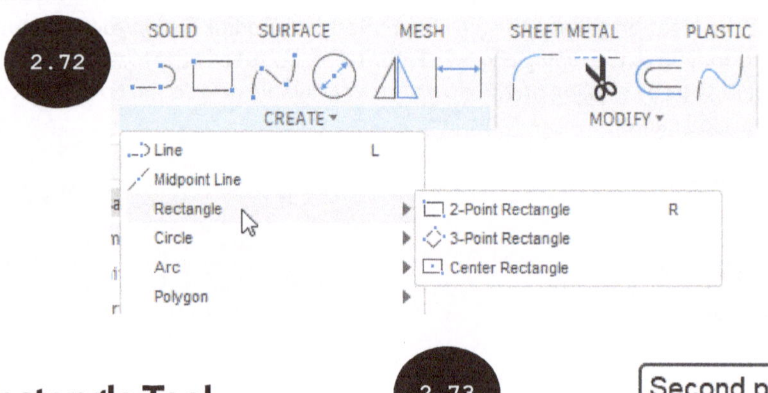

2-Point Rectangle Tool

The **2-Point Rectangle** tool is used to draw a rectangle by specifying two diagonally opposite corners. The first specified point defines the position of the rectangle, while the second point defines the length and width of the rectangle, see Figure 2.73. The method for drawing a rectangle using the **2-Point Rectangle** tool is discussed below:

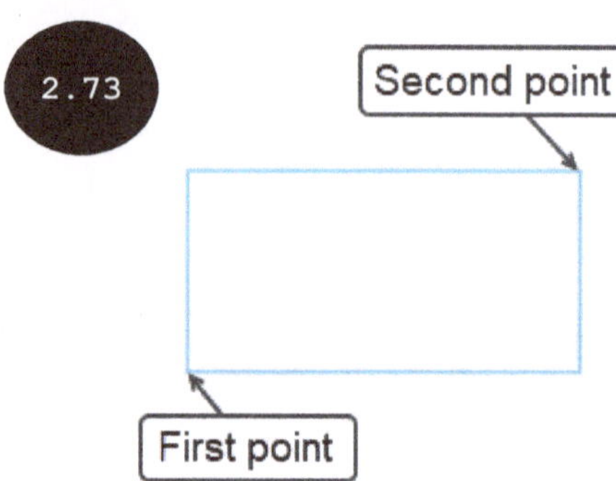

1. Click on the **2-Point Rectangle** tool in the **CREATE** panel of the **SKETCH** contextual tab, see Figure 2.74 or press the **R** key. The **2-Point Rectangle** tool gets activated. Alternatively, invoke the **CREATE** drop-down menu in the **SKETCH** contextual tab of the **Toolbar** and then move the cursor over the **Rectangle** option, refer to Figure 2.72. A cascading menu appears. In this menu, click on the **2-Point Rectangle** tool. The **2-Point Rectangle** tool gets activated.

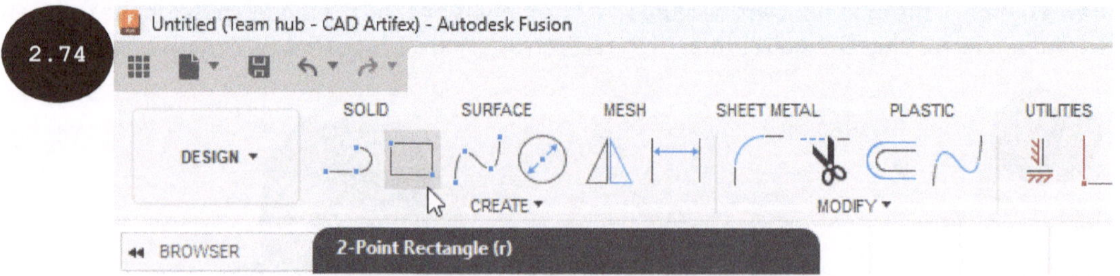

You can also activate this tool by using the Marking Menu. To do this, right-click in the drawing area and then click on the **Sketch** tool in the Marking Menu that appears. The second level of the Marking Menu appears with frequently used sketching tools, see Figure 2.75. In this Marking Menu, click on the **2-Point Rectangle** tool.

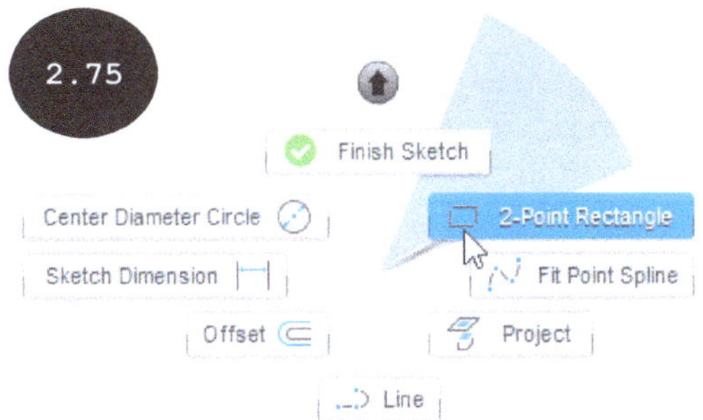

Note: As soon as the **2-Point Rectangle** tool is activated, the **Feature Options** rollout appears in the **SKETCH PALETTE** dialog box with all rectangle tools, see Figure 2.76. You can switch between the rectangle tools by activating them in this **Feature Options** rollout.

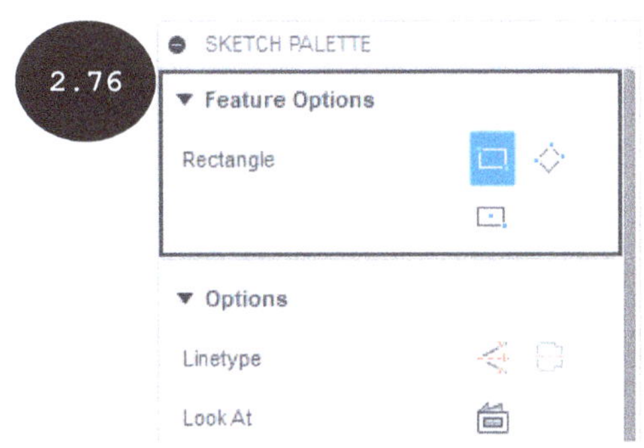

2. Click to specify the first point (corner) of the rectangle in the drawing area.

3. Move the cursor away from the first specified point, see Figure 2.77.

4. Click to specify the second point (corner) of the rectangle in the drawing area. The rectangle is drawn.

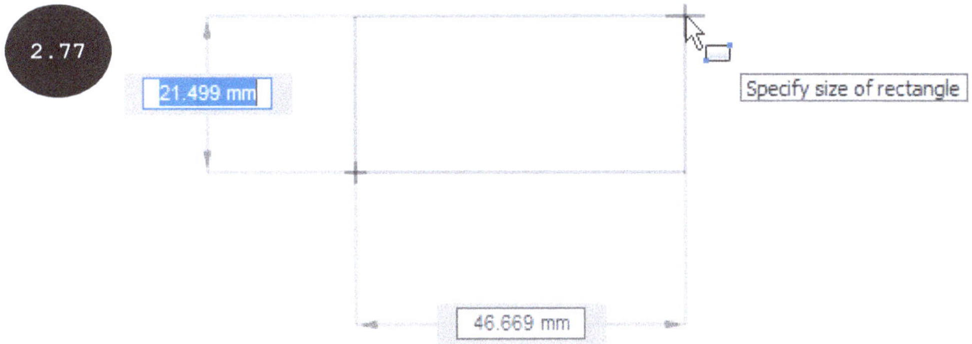

3-Point Rectangle Tool

The **3-Point Rectangle** tool is used to draw a rectangle by specifying 3 points in the drawing area. The first two points define the width and orientation of the rectangle third point defines the length of the rectangle, see Figure 2.78. The method for drawing a rectangle using the **3-Point Rectangle** tool is discussed below:

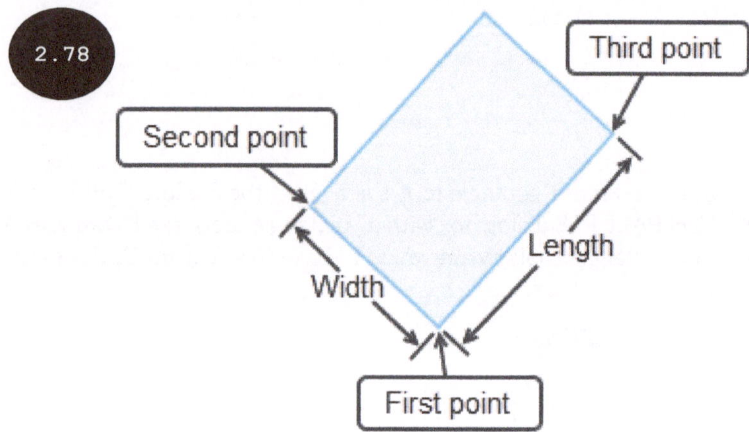

1. Invoke the **CREATE** drop-down menu in the **SKETCH** contextual tab of the **Toolbar** and then move the cursor over the **Rectangle** option, see Figure 2.79. A cascading menu appears. In this menu, click on the **3-Point Rectangle** tool. The **3-Point Rectangle** tool gets activated.

Tip: You can also customize to add this tool in the **CREATE** panel of the **SKETCH** contextual tab. To do this, move the cursor over the **3-Point Rectangle** tool in the **CREATE** drop-down menu and then click on the three dots ⋮ that appear near the tool. A cascading menu appears. Next, select the **Pin to Toolbar** check box in the cascading menu. The selected tool gets added in the **CREATE** panel of the **SKETCH** contextual tab.

2. Click to specify the first point (corner) of the rectangle in the drawing area.

3. Move the cursor away from the first specified point in the drawing area. An inference line appears attached to the cursor, see Figure 2.80.

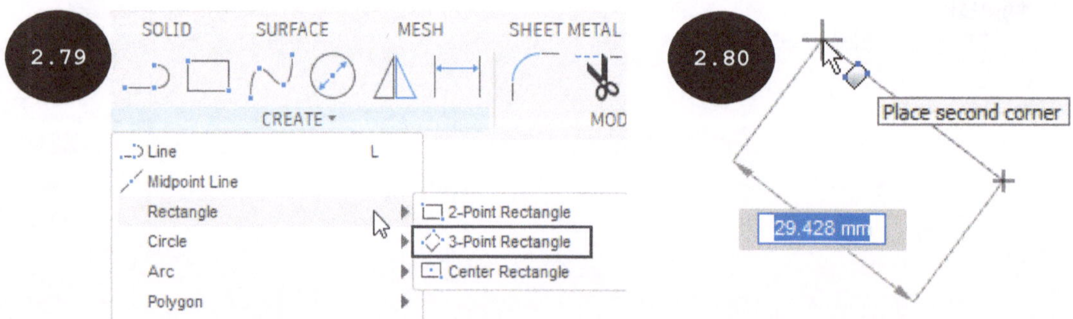

4. Click to specify the second point (corner) of the rectangle in the drawing area.

5. Move the cursor to a distance in the drawing area. A preview of the rectangle appears, see Figure 2.81.

6. Click to specify the third point of the rectangle. The rectangle is drawn.

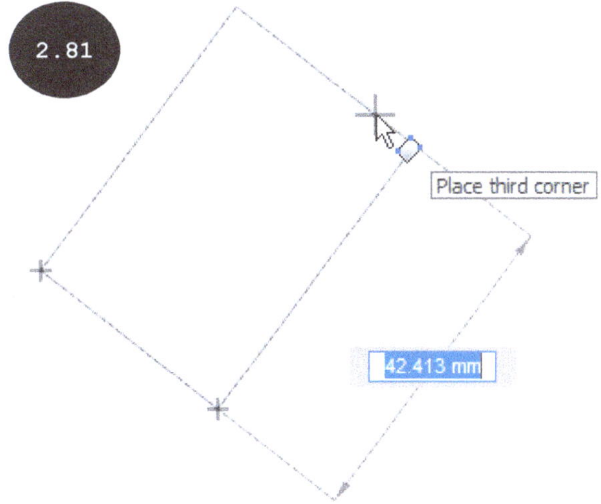

Center Rectangle Tool

The **Center Rectangle** tool is used to draw a rectangle by specifying a center point and a corner point, see Figure 2.82. The method for drawing a rectangle using the **Center Rectangle** tool is discussed below:

1. Invoke the **CREATE** drop-down menu in the **SKETCH** contextual tab of the **Toolbar** and then move the cursor over the **Rectangle** option. A cascading menu appears. In this menu, click on the **Center Rectangle** tool. The **Center Rectangle** tool gets activated.

2. Click to specify the center point of the rectangle in the drawing area.

3. Move the cursor to a distance. A preview of the rectangle appears, see Figure 2.83.

4. Click to specify the corner of the rectangle in the drawing area. The rectangle is drawn.

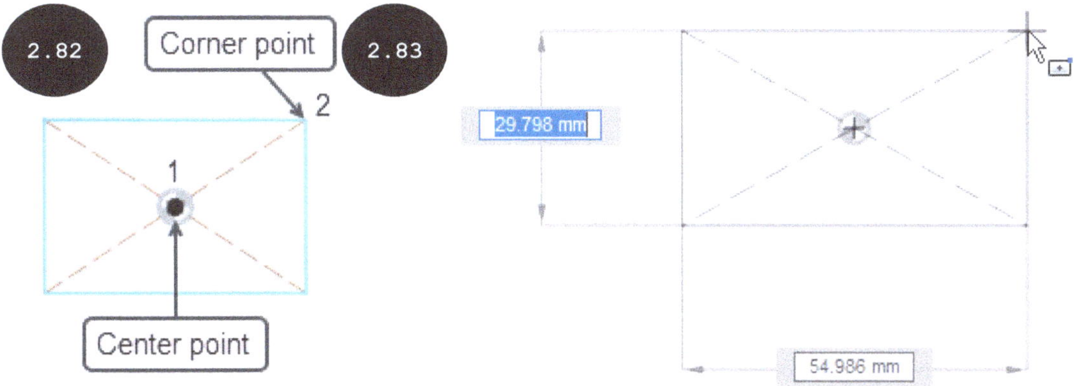

Drawing a Circle

In Autodesk Fusion, you can draw a circle using the various tools: **Center Diameter Circle**, **2-Point Circle**, **3-Point Circle**, **2-Tangent Circle**, and **3-Tangent Circle**. You can access these tools in the **CREATE** drop-down menu of the **Toolbar**, see Figure 2.84. The tools for drawing a circle are discussed next.

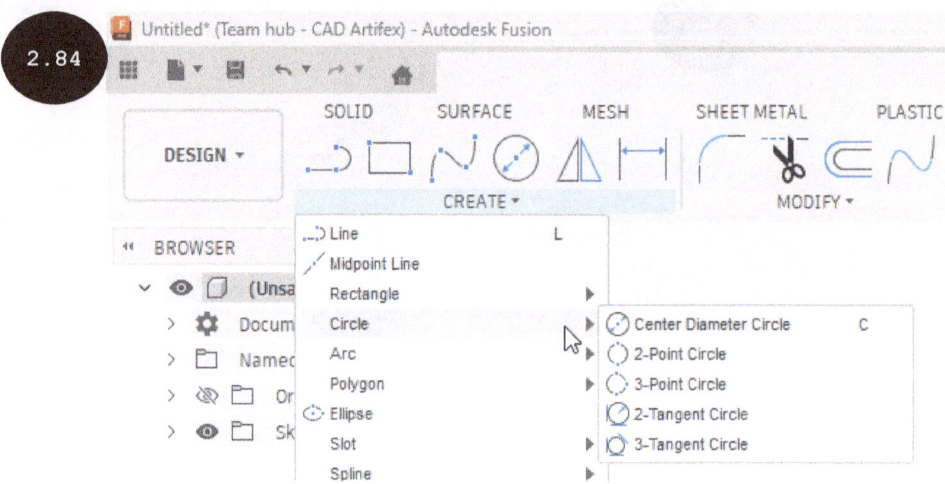

Center Diameter Circle Tool

The **Center Diameter Circle** tool is used to draw a circle by specifying the center point and a point on the circumference of the circle, see Figure 2.85. The method for drawing a circle using the **Center Diameter Circle** tool is discussed below:

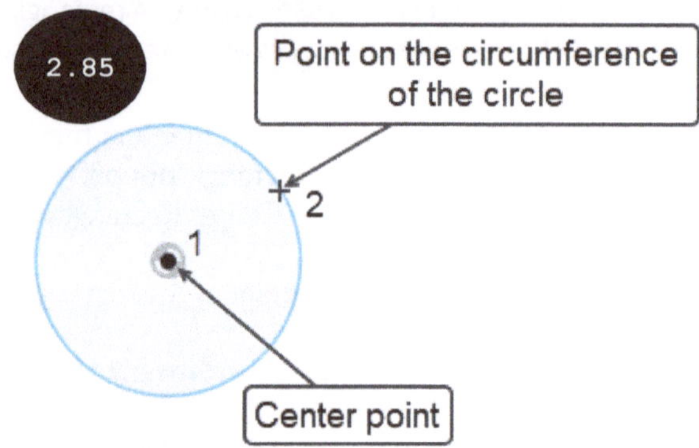

1. Invoke the **CREATE** drop-down menu in the **SKETCH** contextual tab of the **Toolbar** and then move the cursor over the **Circle** option, refer to Figure 2.84. A cascading menu appears. In this menu, click on the **Center Diameter Circle** tool. The **Center Diameter Circle** tool gets activated. Alternatively, press the C key or click on the **Center Diameter Circle** tool in the **CREATE** panel to activate this tool.

   You can also activate this tool using the Marking Menu. To do this, right-click in the drawing area and then click on the **Sketch** tool in the Marking Menu that appears. The second level of the Marking Menu appears, see Figure 2.86. In this Marking Menu, click on the **Center Diameter Circle** tool.

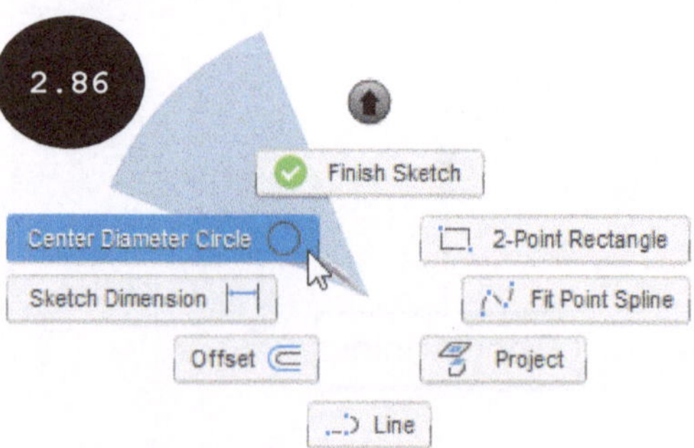

Tip: As soon as the **Center Diameter Circle** tool is activated, the **Feature Options** rollout appears in the **SKETCH PALETTE** dialog box with all circle tools, see Figure 2.87. You can switch between different circle tools by activating them in this **Feature Options** rollout.

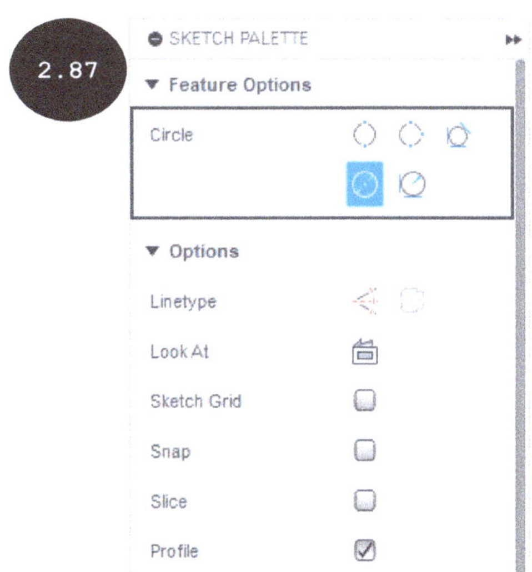

2. Click to specify the center point of the circle in the drawing area.

3. Move the cursor to a distance in the drawing area. A preview of the circle appears with its diameter dimension, see Figure 2.88.

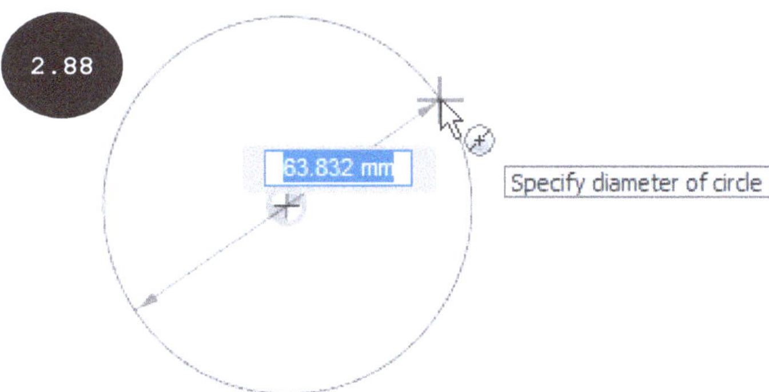

4. Click to specify a point in the drawing area. The circle is drawn.

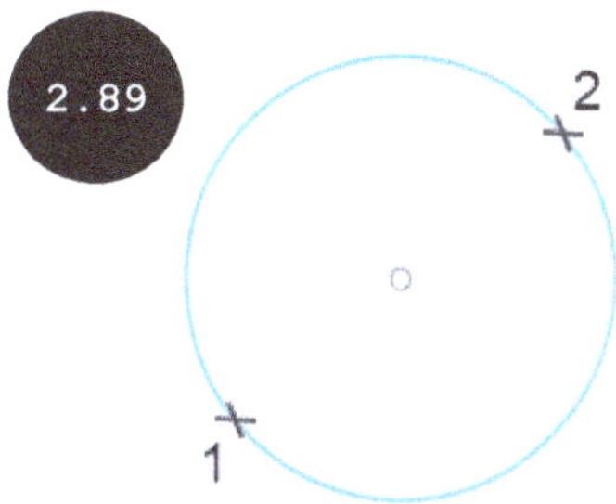

2-Point Circle Tool

The **2-Point Circle** tool is used to draw a circle by specifying two diametrically opposite points on the circumference of the circle, see Figure 2.89. The method for drawing a circle by using the **2-Point Circle** tool is discussed below:

1. Invoke the **CREATE** drop-down menu in the **SKETCH** contextual tab of the **Toolbar** and then move the cursor over the **Circle** option, see Figure 2.90. A cascading menu appears. In this menu, click on the **2-Point Circle** tool. The **2-Point Circle** tool gets activated.

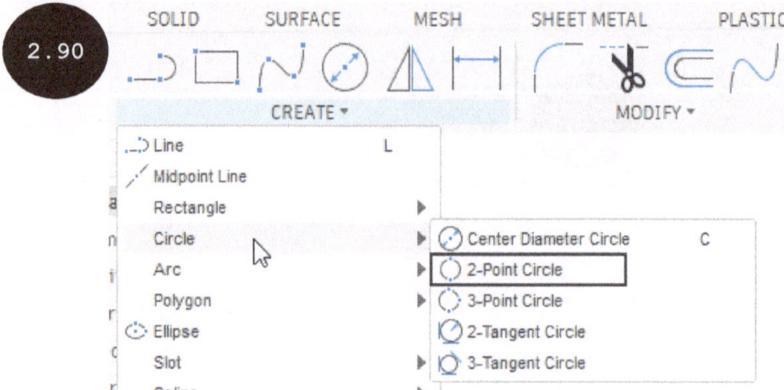

2. Click to specify the first point in the drawing area.

3. Move the cursor away from the first specified point. A preview of the circle appears.

4. Click to specify the second point in the drawing area. The circle is drawn by defining two diametrically opposite points on its circumference.

3-Point Circle Tool

The **3-Point Circle** tool is used for drawing a circle by specifying three points on the circumference of the circle, see Figure 2.91. The method for drawing a circle using the **3-Point Circle** tool is discussed below:

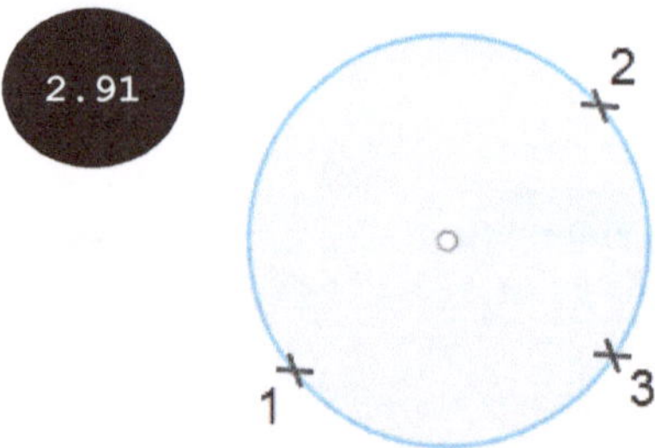

Note: In this chapter, some of the figures are numbered for your reference only, refer to Figure 2.91. These numbers represent the sequence of points specified in the drawing area for creating an object by clicking the left mouse button.

1. Invoke the **CREATE** drop-down menu in the **SKETCH** contextual tab of the **Toolbar** and then move the cursor over the **Circle** option. A cascading menu appears. In this menu, click on the **3-Point Circle** tool. The **3-Point Circle** tool gets activated.

2. Click to specify the first point in the drawing area.

3. Click to specify the second point in the drawing area.

4. Move the cursor away from the second specified point. A preview of the circle appears.

5. Click to specify the third point in the drawing area. The circle is drawn by defining three points on its circumference.

2-Tangent Circle Tool

The **2-Tangent Circle** tool is used to draw a circle that is tangent to two line entities. To do this, you need to define two line entities and the radius of the circle, see Figure 2.92. The method for drawing a circle by using the **2-Tangent Circle** tool is discussed below:

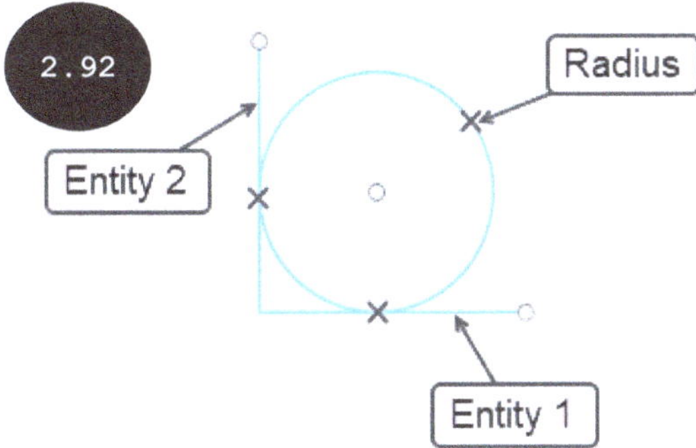

1. Invoke the **CREATE** drop-down menu in the **SKETCH** contextual tab of the **Toolbar** and then move the cursor over the **Circle** option. A cascading menu appears. In this menu, click on the **2-Tangent Circle** tool, see Figure 2.93. The **2-Tangent Circle** tool gets activated.

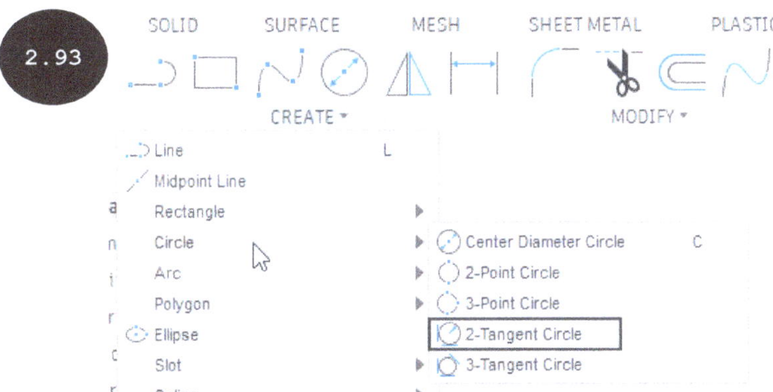

2. Click to select the first line entity in the drawing area.

3. Click to select the second line entity in the drawing area. A preview of the circle appears and you are prompted to specify the radius of the circle.

4. Click in the drawing area to specify the radius of the circle. Alternatively, you can enter the radius in the dimension box and then click in the drawing area to specify the position of the circle. A circle tangent to the selected entities is drawn.

3-Tangent Circle Tool

The **3-Tangent Circle** tool is used for drawing a circle that is tangent to three line entities, see Figure 2.94. The method for drawing a circle by using the **3-Tangent Circle** tool is discussed below:

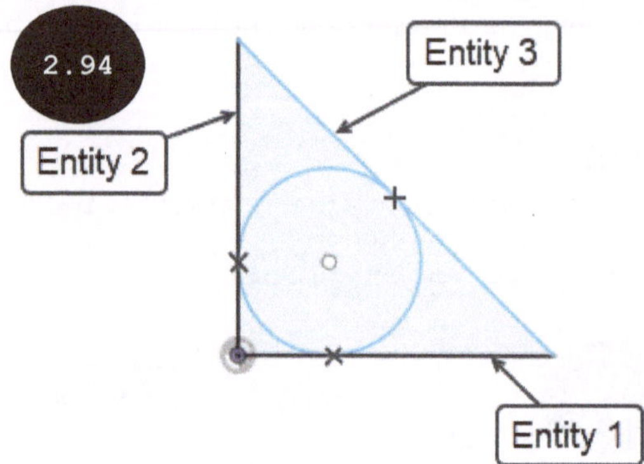

1. Invoke the **CREATE** drop-down menu in the **SKETCH** contextual tab of the **Toolbar** and then move the cursor over the **Circle** option. A cascading menu appears. In this menu, click on the **3-Tangent Circle** tool.

2. Click to select the first line entity in the drawing area.

3. Click to select the second line entity in the drawing area.

4. Click to select the third line entity in the drawing area. A circle tangent to the selected entities is drawn.

Drawing an Arc

In Autodesk Fusion, you can draw an arc using the **3-Point Arc**, **Center Point Arc**, and **Tangent Arc** tools. You can access these tools in the **CREATE** drop-down menu of the **SKETCH** contextual tab, see Figure 2.95. The tools for drawing an arc are discussed next.

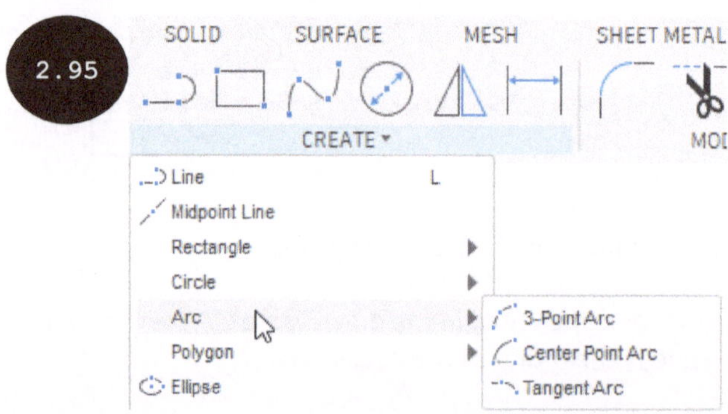

3-Point Arc Tool

The **3-Point Arc** tool is used to draw an arc by defining three points on its arc length, see Figure 2.96. The method for drawing an arc using the **3-Point Arc** tool is discussed below:

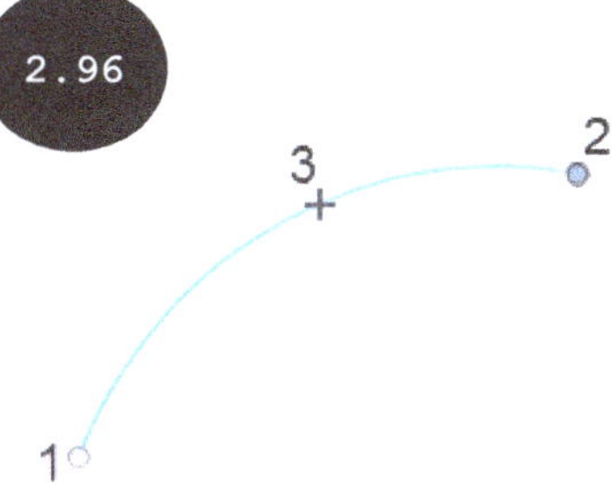

1. Invoke the **CREATE** drop-down menu in the **SKETCH** contextual tab and then click on **Arc > 3-Point Arc**, see Figure 2.97. The **3-Point Arc** tool gets activated. Also, the **Feature Options** rollout appears in the **SKETCH PALETTE** dialog box with all arc tools, see Figure 2.98. You can switch between different arc tools by activating them in this **Feature Options** rollout.

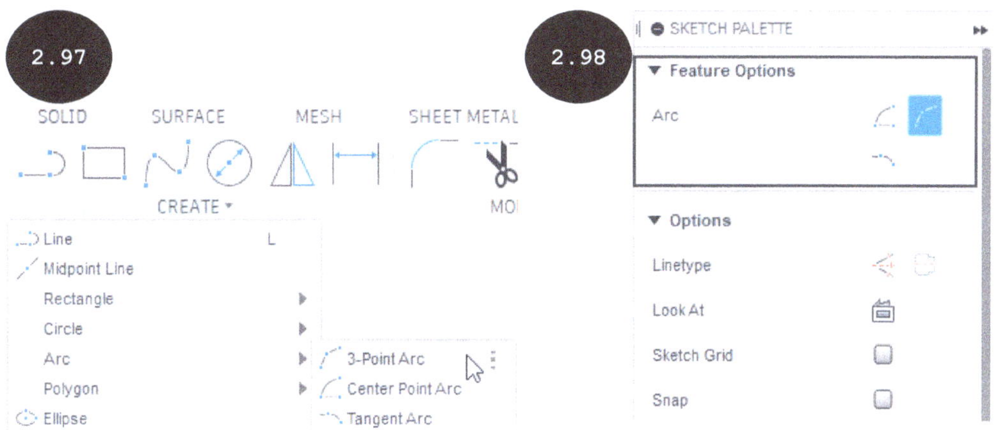

2. Click to specify the first point of the arc in the drawing area, see Figure 2.99.

3. Click to specify the second point of the arc in the drawing area, see Figure 2.99.

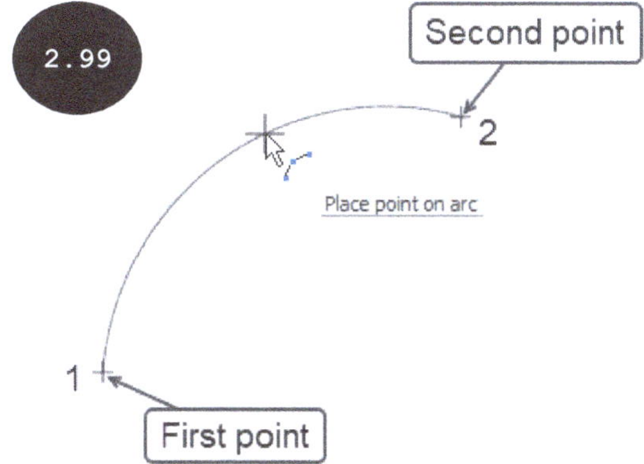

4. Move the cursor to a distance. A preview of the arc appears in the drawing area, refer to Figure 2.99. Next, click to specify a point on the arc length. The arc is drawn.

Center Point Arc Tool

The **Center Point Arc** tool is used to draw an arc by defining its center point, start point, and endpoint, see Figure 2.100. The method for drawing an arc using the **Center Point Arc** tool is discussed below:

1. Invoke the **CREATE** drop-down menu in the **SKETCH** contextual tab of the **Toolbar** and then click on **Arc > Center Point Arc**. The **Center Point Arc** tool gets activated.
2. Click to specify the center point of the arc in the drawing area.
3. Move the cursor to a distance and then click in the drawing area to define the start point of the arc.
4. Move the cursor clockwise or anti-clockwise. A preview of the arc appears in the drawing area.
5. Click to specify the endpoint of the arc in the drawing area. The arc is drawn, see Figure 2.100.

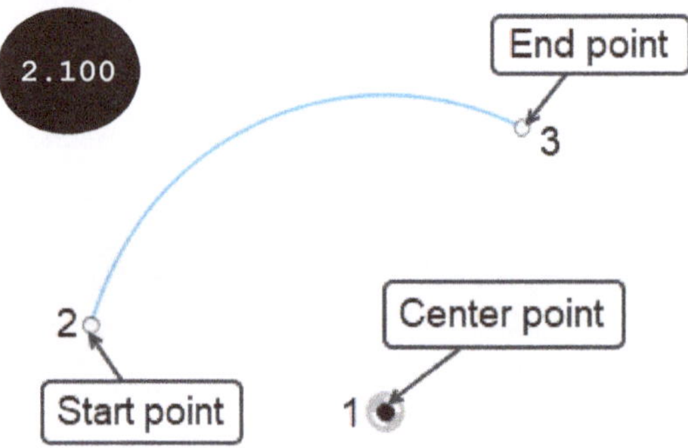

Note: As mentioned earlier, in this chapter, some of the figures are numbered for your reference only, see Figure 2.100. These numbers represent the sequence of points specified in the drawing area for creating an object by clicking the left mouse button.

Tangent Arc Tool

The **Tangent Arc** tool is used to draw an arc tangent to an existing entity, see Figure 2.101. You can draw an arc tangent to a line, an arc, or a spline entity using this tool. The method for drawing an arc using the **Tangent Arc** tool is discussed below:

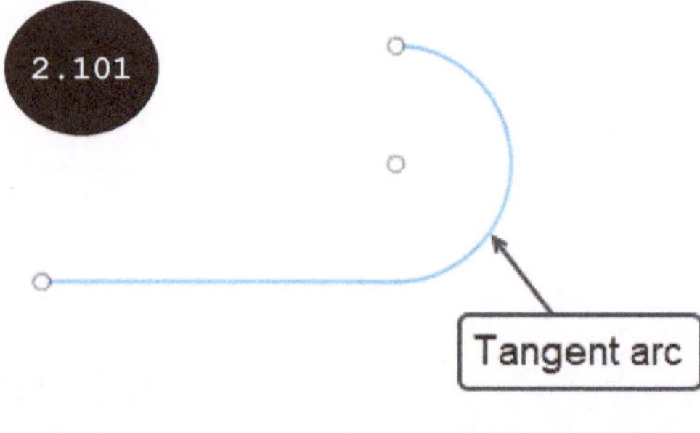

1. Invoke the **CREATE** drop-down menu in the **SKETCH** contextual tab and then click on **Arc > Tangent Arc**. The **Tangent Arc** tool gets activated.
2. Move the cursor to the endpoint of an existing entity (line, arc, or spline) in the drawing area and then click to specify the start point of the tangent arc when the cursor snaps to the endpoint.

3. Move the cursor to a distance. A preview of the tangent arc appears in the drawing area such that its endpoint is attached to the cursor.

Note: The tangency of an arc depends upon how you move the cursor in the drawing area. Figure 2.102 shows the possible movements of the cursor and the creation of arcs in the respective movements.

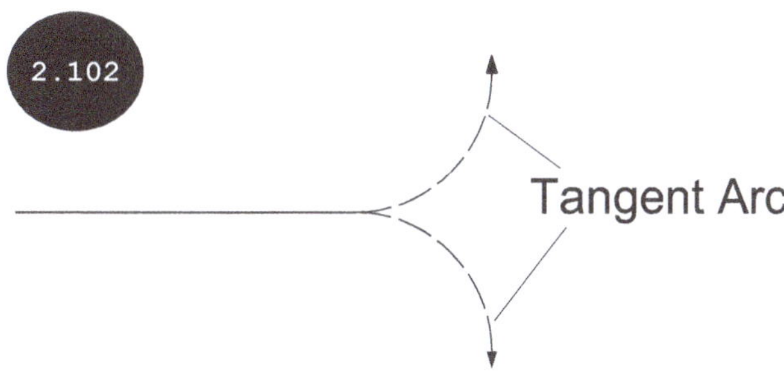

4. Click to specify the endpoint of the tangent arc in the drawing area. The tangent arc is drawn. Also, the **Tangent Arc** tool remains activated. As a result, you can continue drawing tangent arcs by specifying the start and end points in the drawing area.

5. After drawing the tangent arcs, right-click in the drawing area. The Marking Menu appears. In this Marking Menu, click on the **OK** tool to exit the **Tangent Arc** tool.

Drawing a Polygon

A polygon is a closed multi-sided geometry having equal sides as well as equal angles between all sides. Figure 2.103 shows a polygon having six sides. In Autodesk Fusion, you can draw a polygon using the **Circumscribed Polygon**, **Inscribed Polygon**, and **Edge Polygon** tools. You can access these tools in the **CREATE** drop-down menu of the **SKETCH** contextual tab, see Figure 2.104. The tools for drawing a polygon are discussed next.

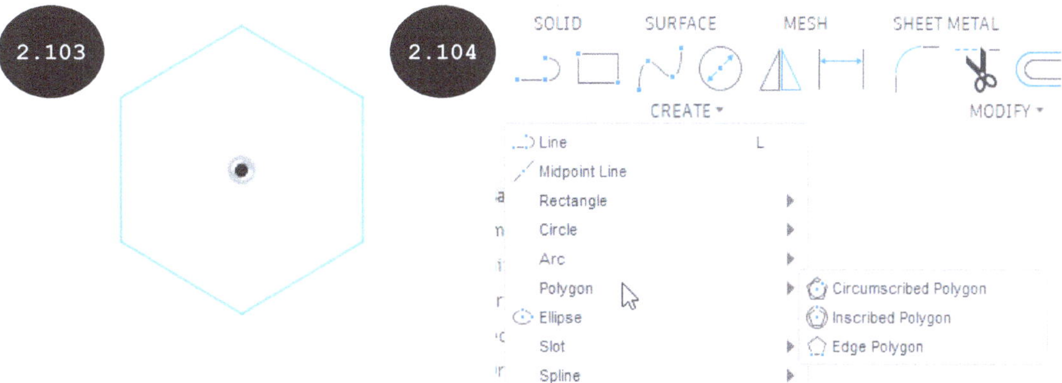

Circumscribed Polygon Tool

The **Circumscribed Polygon** tool is used to draw a circumscribed polygon that is created outside an imaginary circle such that the midpoints of the polygon sides touch the imaginary circle, see Figure 2.105. You can draw a circumscribed polygon by specifying the center point, the number of polygon sides, and the midpoint of any side of the polygon or the radius of the imaginary circle. The method for drawing a polygon using the **Circumscribed Polygon** tool is discussed below:

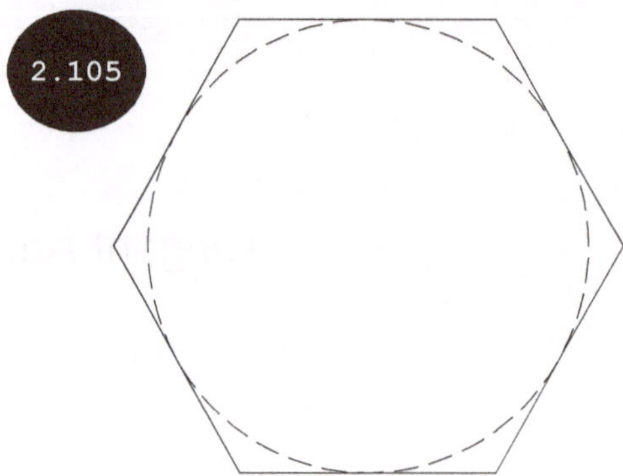

Circumscribed Polygon

1. Invoke the **CREATE** drop-down menu in the **SKETCH** contextual tab and then click on **Polygon > Circumscribed Polygon**. The **Circumscribed Polygon** tool gets activated.

2. Click to specify the center point of the polygon in the drawing area. A preview of the polygon with an imaginary circle appears in the drawing area, see Figure 2.106.

3. Enter the number of polygon sides in the **Edge Number** box that appears in the drawing area.

4. Click to specify the midpoint of any side of the polygon in the drawing area to define the radius of the imaginary circle. Alternatively, enter the radius value in the dimension box that appears in the drawing area and then press ENTER. The polygon is drawn and the **Circumscribed Polygon** tool is still active.

5. Right-click in the drawing area and then click on the **OK** tool in the Marking Menu that appears to exit the tool. Alternatively, press the ESC key to exit the tool.

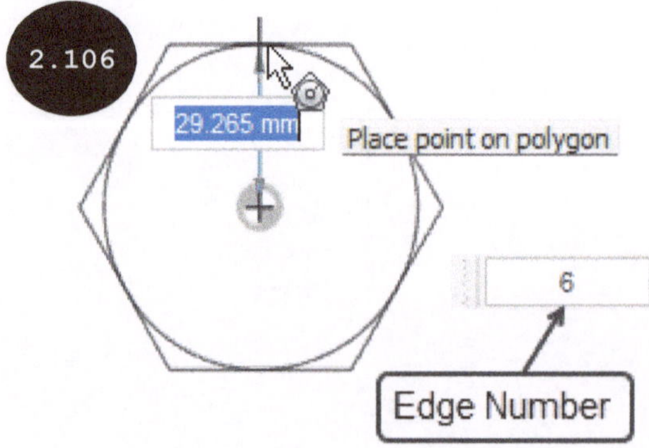

Inscribed Polygon Tool

The **Inscribed Polygon** tool is used to draw an inscribed polygon that is created inside an imaginary circle such that its vertices touch the imaginary circle, see Figure 2.107. You can draw an inscribed polygon by specifying the center point, the number of polygon sides, and a vertex of the polygon or the radius of the imaginary circle. The method for drawing a polygon using the **Inscribed Polygon** tool is discussed below:

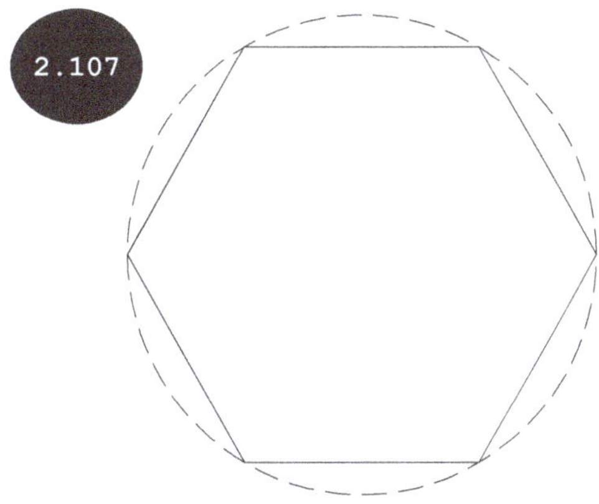

Inscribed Polygon

1. Invoke the **CREATE** drop-down menu in the **SKETCH** contextual tab and then click on **Polygon > Inscribed Polygon**. The **Inscribed Polygon** tool gets activated.

2. Click to specify the center point of the polygon in the drawing area. A preview of the polygon with an imaginary circle appears in the drawing area, see Figure 2.108.

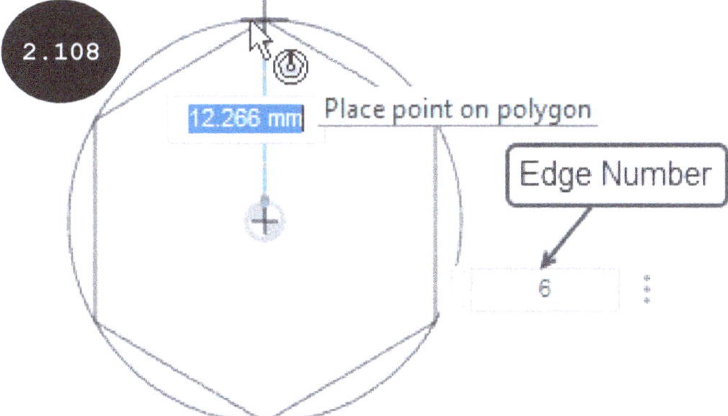

3. Enter the number of polygon sides in the **Edge Number** box that appears in the drawing area.

4. Click to specify a vertex of the polygon to define the radius of the imaginary circle or enter the radius value in the dimension box that appears in the drawing area and then press ENTER. The polygon is drawn.

5. Right-click in the drawing area and then click on the **OK** tool in the Marking Menu that appears to exit the tool. Alternatively, press the ESC key to exit the tool.

Edge Polygon Tool

The **Edge Polygon** tool is used to draw a polygon by specifying the start and end points of an edge of the polygon, and the number of polygon sides. The method for drawing a polygon using the **Edge Polygon** tool is discussed below:

1. Invoke the **CREATE** drop-down menu in the **SKETCH** contextual tab and then click on **Polygon > Edge Polygon**. The **Edge Polygon** tool gets activated.
2. Click to specify the start point of an edge of the polygon in the drawing area, see Figure 2.109.
3. Click to specify the endpoint of the polygon edge in the drawing area. A preview of the polygon appears in the drawing area with the **Edge Number** box, see Figure 2.109.

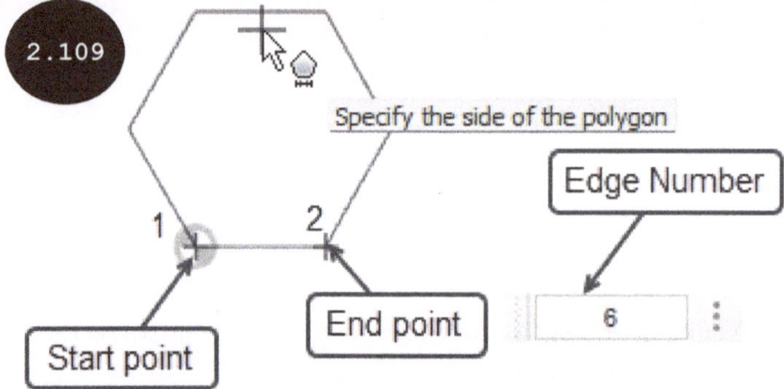

4. Enter the number of polygon sides in the **Edge Number** box that appears in the drawing area.
5. Click in the drawing area to specify the orientation of the polygon. The polygon is drawn and the **Edge Polygon** tool is still active.
6. Right-click in the drawing area and then click on the **OK** tool in the Marking Menu that appears, to exit the tool. Alternatively, press the ESC key to exit the tool.

Drawing an Ellipse

An ellipse is drawn by defining its major axis and minor axis, see Figure 2.110. You can draw an ellipse using the **Ellipse** tool. The method for drawing an ellipse is discussed below:

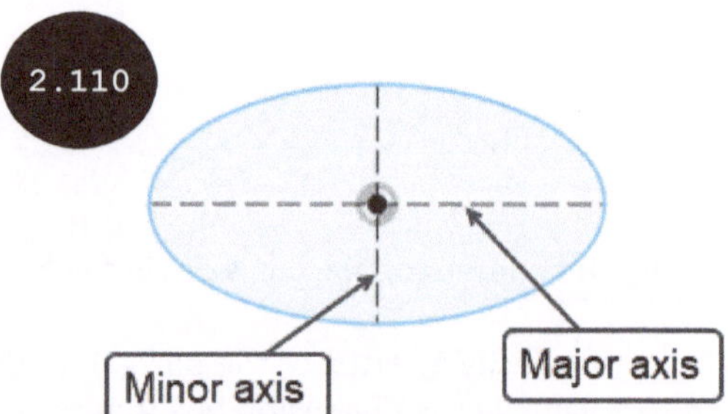

1. Invoke the **CREATE** drop-down menu in the **SKETCH** contextual tab of the **Toolbar** and then click on the **Ellipse** tool.
2. Click to specify the center point of the ellipse.
3. Move the cursor away from the specified center point and then click to define the major axis of the ellipse.

4. Move the cursor to a distance in the drawing area. A preview of the ellipse appears.

5. Click to specify the minor axis of the ellipse. The ellipse is drawn.

6. Right-click in the drawing area and then click on the **OK** tool in the Marking Menu that appears, to exit the **Ellipse** tool or press the ESC key to exit the tool.

Drawing a Slot

In Autodesk Fusion, you can draw straight and arc slots using various slot tools: **Center to Center Slot**, **Overall Slot**, **Center Point Slot**, **Three Point Arc Slot**, and **Center Point Arc Slot**. You can access these tools in the **CREATE** drop-down menu of the **SKETCH** contextual tab, see Figure 2.111. The tools for drawing slots are discussed next.

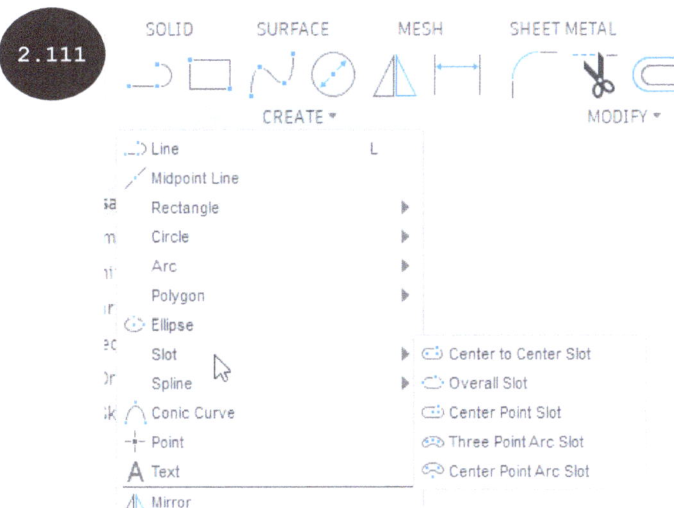

Center to Center Slot Tool

The **Center to Center Slot** tool is used for drawing a straight slot by defining the centers of both slot arcs and a point that determines the width of the slot, see Figure 2.112. The method for drawing a slot by using the **Center to Center Slot** tool is discussed below:

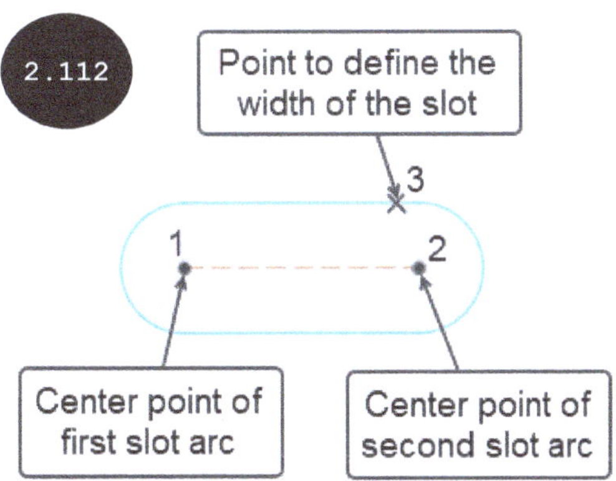

1. Invoke the **CREATE** drop-down menu in the **SKETCH** contextual tab of the **Toolbar** and then click on **Slot** > **Center to Center Slot**.

2. Click to specify the center point of the first slot arc in the drawing area, refer to Figure 2.112.

3. Move the cursor to a distance in the drawing area and then click the left mouse button to define the center point of the second slot arc, refer to Figure 2.112.

4. Move the cursor to a distance in the drawing area. A preview of the slot appears.

5. Click to specify a point in the drawing area to define the width of the slot. You can also enter the width of the slot in the dimension box and then press ENTER. A straight slot is drawn.

6. Press the ESC key to exit the tool.

Overall Slot Tool

The **Overall Slot** tool is used for drawing a straight slot by defining the start and end points of the overall slot length, and a point to define the width of the slot, see Figure 2.113. The method for drawing a slot using the **Overall Slot** tool is discussed below:

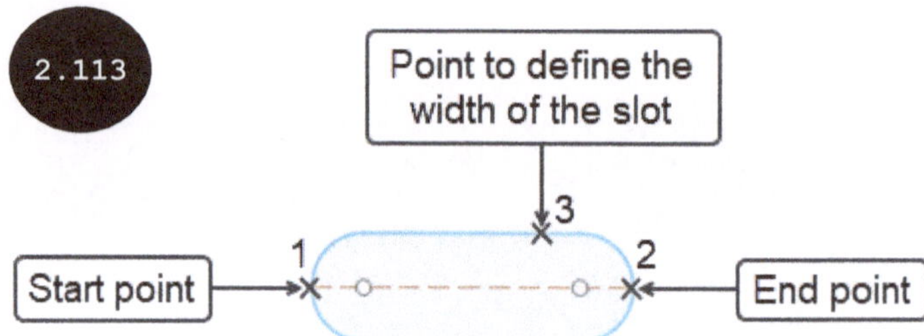

1. Invoke the **CREATE** drop-down menu in the **SKETCH** contextual tab of the **Toolbar** and then click on **Slot** > **Overall Slot**.

2. Click to specify the start point of the overall slot length, refer to Figure 2.113.

3. Move the cursor to a distance in the drawing area. A straight rubber band line with one of its ends attached to the cursor appears.

4. Click the left mouse button in the drawing area to define the endpoint of the overall slot length, refer to Figure 2.113.

5. Move the cursor to a distance in the drawing area. The preview of the slot appears.

6. Click to specify a point in the drawing area to define the width of the slot. You can also enter the width of the slot in the dimension box and then press ENTER. A straight slot is drawn.

7. Press the ESC key to exit the tool.

Center Point Slot Tool

The **Center Point Slot** tool is used for drawing a straight slot by defining the slot center point, the center point of a slot arc, and a point to define the width of the slot, see Figure 2.114. The method for drawing a slot using the **Center Point Slot** tool is discussed below:

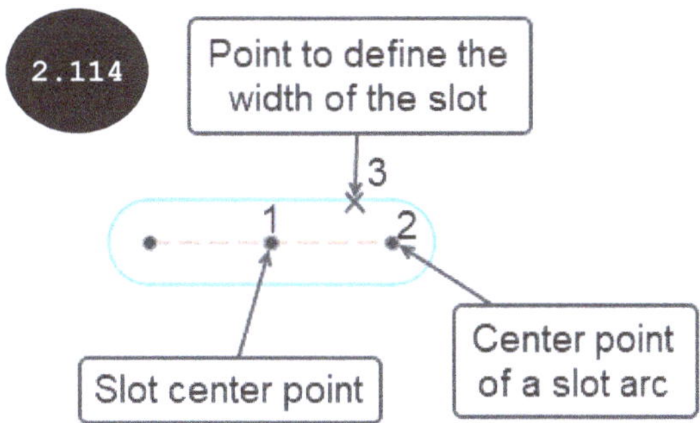

1. Invoke the **CREATE** drop-down menu in the **SKETCH** contextual tab of the **Toolbar** and then click on **Slot > Center Point Slot**.

2. Click to specify the slot center point in the drawing area, refer to Figure 2.114.

3. Move the cursor in the drawing area and then click to specify the center point of a slot arc, refer to Figure 2.114.

4. Move the cursor to a distance in the drawing area. A preview of the slot appears.

5. Click to specify a point in the drawing area to define the width of the slot. You can also enter the width of the slot in the dimension box and then press ENTER. A straight slot is drawn.

6. Press the ESC key to exit the tool.

Three Point Arc Slot Tool

The **Three Point Arc Slot** tool is used for drawing an arc slot by defining three points on the slot center arc and a point to define the width of the slot, see Figure 2.115. The method for drawing a slot using the **Three Point Arc Slot** tool is discussed below:

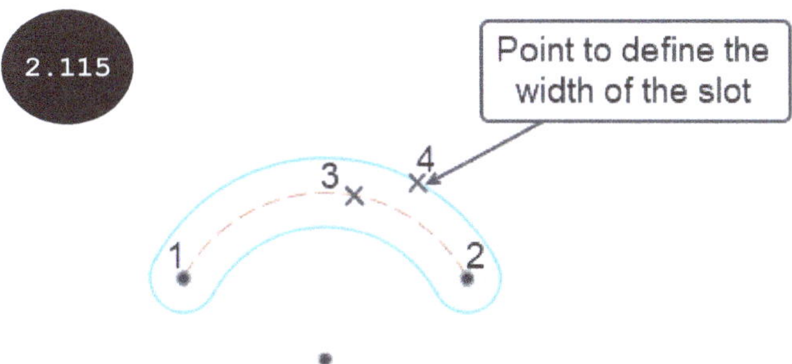

1. Invoke the **CREATE** drop-down menu in the **SKETCH** contextual tab of the **Toolbar** and then click on **Slot > Three Point Arc Slot**.

2. Click to specify the first point (Point 1) of the slot center arc in the drawing area, refer to Figure 2.115.

3. Move the cursor in the drawing area and then click to specify the second point (Point 2) of the slot center arc, refer to Figure 2.115.

4. Move the cursor to a distance in the drawing area. A preview of the slot center arc appears.

5. Click to specify the third point (Point 3) of the slot center arc, refer to Figure 2.115. The preview of the arc slot appears in the drawing area.

6. Click to specify a point in the drawing area to define the width of the slot. You can also enter the width of the slot in the dimension box and then press ENTER. The arc slot is drawn. Next, press the ESC key to exit the tool.

Center Point Arc Slot Tool

The **Center Point Arc Slot** tool is used for drawing an arc slot by defining the center point of the slot, the center points of both the slot arcs, and a point to define the width of the slot, see Figure 2.116.

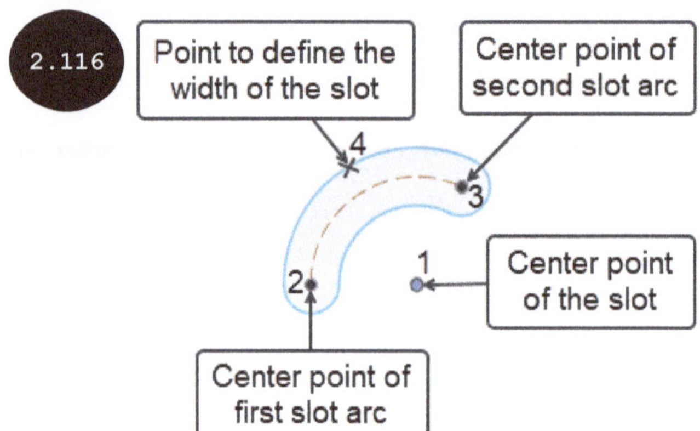

The method for drawing a slot using the **Center Point Arc Slot** tool is discussed below:

1. Invoke the **CREATE** drop-down menu in the **SKETCH** contextual tab and then click on **Slot > Center Point Arc Slot**.

2. Click to specify the center point of the slot in the drawing area, refer to Figure 2.116.

3. Move the cursor in the drawing area and then click to specify the center point of the first slot arc, refer to Figure 2.116.

4. Move the cursor clockwise or anti-clockwise. A preview of the slot center arc appears in the drawing area.

5. Click to specify the center point of the second slot arc in the drawing area, refer to Figure 2.116. A preview of the slot appears in the drawing area.

6. Click to specify a point in the drawing area to define the width of the slot. You can also enter the width of the slot in the dimension box and then press ENTER. An arc slot is drawn.

7. Press the ESC key to exit the tool.

Drawing Conic Curves

Autodesk Fusion allows you to draw conic curves by specifying the start point, endpoint, top vertex, and Rho value, see Figure 2.117. You can draw conic curves using the **Conic Curve** tool in the **CREATE** drop-down menu of the **SKETCH** contextual tab. The method for drawing conic curves is discussed below:

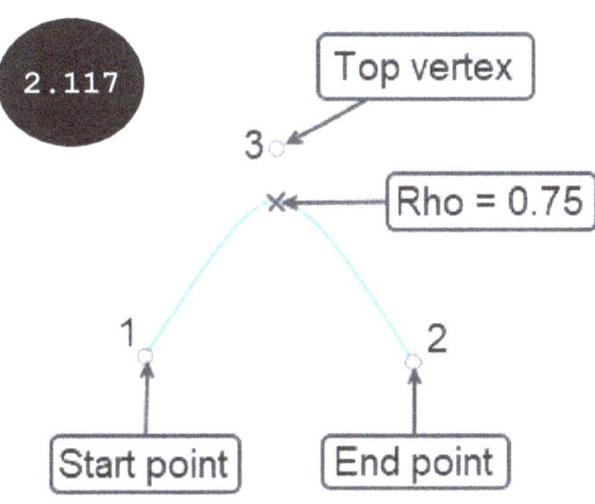

1. Invoke the **CREATE** drop-down menu in the **SKETCH** contextual tab and then click on the **Conic Curve** tool, see Figure 2.118.

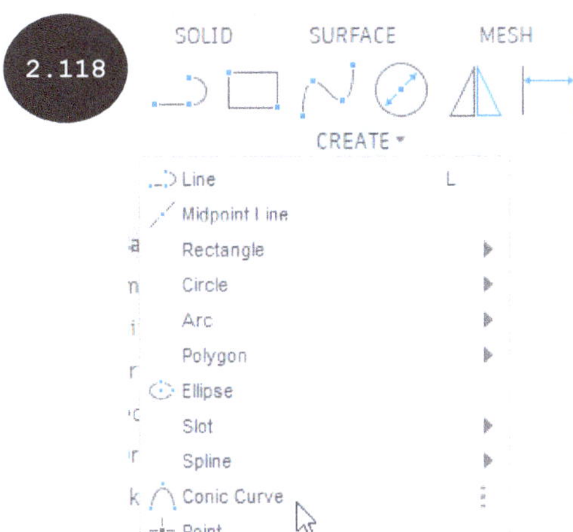

2. Click to specify the start point of the curve in the drawing area, see Figure 2.119.

3. Move the cursor away from the specified start point. A rubber band line appears.

4. Click to specify the endpoint of the curve, see Figure 2.119.

5. Move the cursor to a distance in the drawing area. A preview of the curve appears.

6. Click to specify the top vertex of the conic curve. The **Rho** box and an arrow appear in the drawing area, see Figure 2.119.

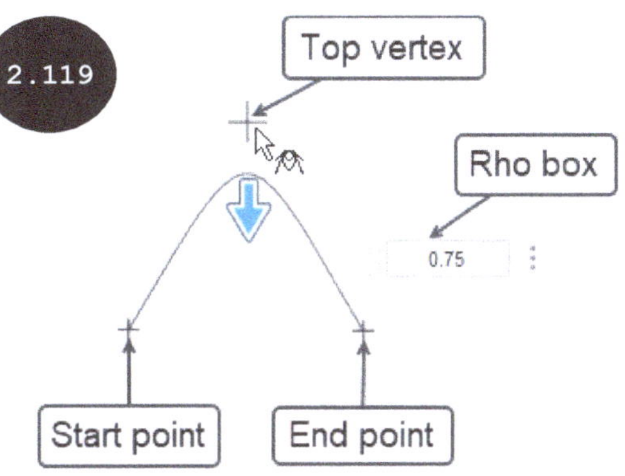

7. Enter the Rho value of the conic curve in the **Rho** box. Alternatively, drag the arrow upward or downward to a distance. The preview of the conic curve gets modified, and its current Rho value appears in the **Rho** box.

Note: The Rho value of the conic curve defines the type of curve. If the Rho value is less than 0.5 then the conic curve will be an ellipse. If the Rho value is equal to 0.5 then the conic curve will be a parabola. If the Rho value is greater than 0.5 then the conic curve will be a hyperbola.

8. After entering the required Rho value in the **Rho** box, press the ENTER key. The respective conic curve is drawn.

Drawing a Spline

A Spline is defined as a curve having a high degree of smoothness and is used for creating free-form features. You can draw a spline by specifying two or more points in the drawing area. In Autodesk Fusion, you can draw a spline using **Fit Point Spline** and **Control Point Spline** tools. You can access these tools in the CREATE drop-down menu of the SKETCH contextual tab, see Figure 2.120. The tools for drawing splines are discussed next.

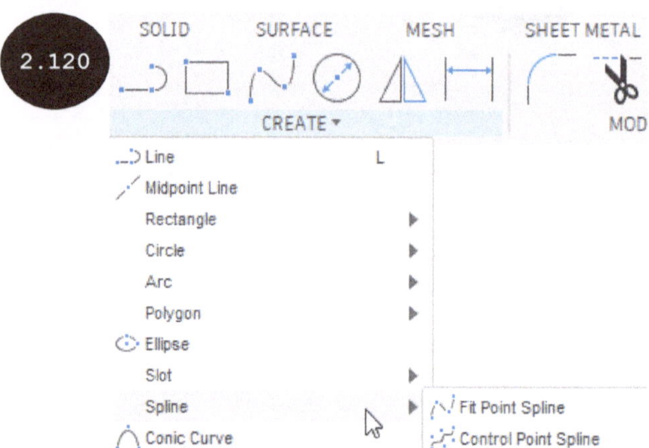

Fit Point Spline Tool

The **Fit Point Spline** tool is used to draw a spline by defining two or more fit points in the drawing area, see Figure 2.121. Note that the spline is created such that it passes through the specified fit points. The method for drawing a spline using the **Fit Point Spline** tool is discussed below:

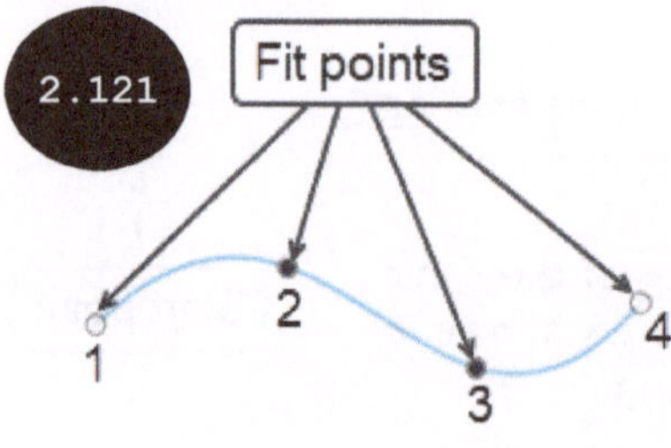

1. Invoke the **CREATE** drop-down menu in the **SKETCH** contextual tab and then click on **Spline > Fit Point Spline** tool, refer to Figure 2.120. You can also click on the **Fit Point Spline** tool in the **CREATE** panel of the **SKETCH** contextual tab. Alternatively, right-click in the drawing area and then click on the **Sketch** tool in the Marking Menu that appears. The second level of the Marking Menu appears, see Figure 2.122. Next, click on the **Fit Point Spline** tool.

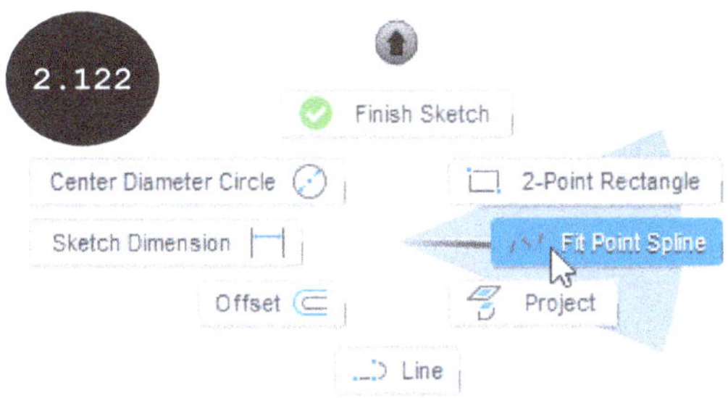

2. Click to specify the first fit point of the spline in the drawing area.

3. Move the cursor to a distance. A reference curve appears in the drawing area whose one end is fixed at the specified point and the other end is attached to the cursor.

4. Click to specify the second fit point of the spline and then move the cursor. A preview of the spline appears such that it passes through the specified fit points, see Figure 2.123.

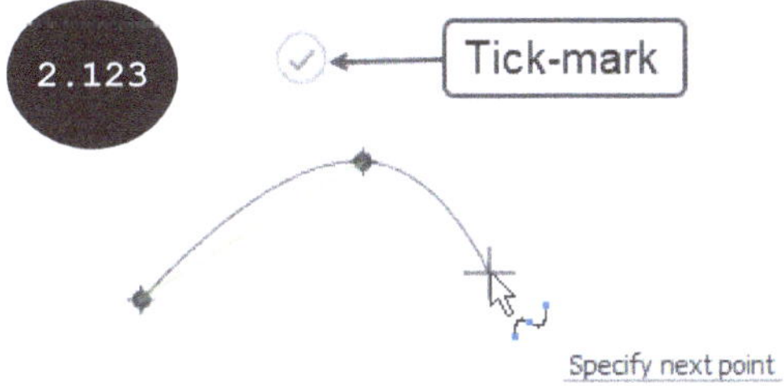

5. Click to specify the third fit point of the spline. Similarly, you can specify multiple fit points.

6. Once all fit points have been specified for drawing the spline, click on the tick-mark, refer to Figure 2.123. The spline is drawn, and the **Fit Point Spline** tool is still active. To exit the **Fit Point Spline** tool, right-click in the drawing area and then click on the **OK** tool in the Marking Menu.

   Figure 2.124 shows a spline with its tangent handles. You can edit the spline by using its tangent handles. Click anywhere in the drawing area to exit the editing mode of the spline.

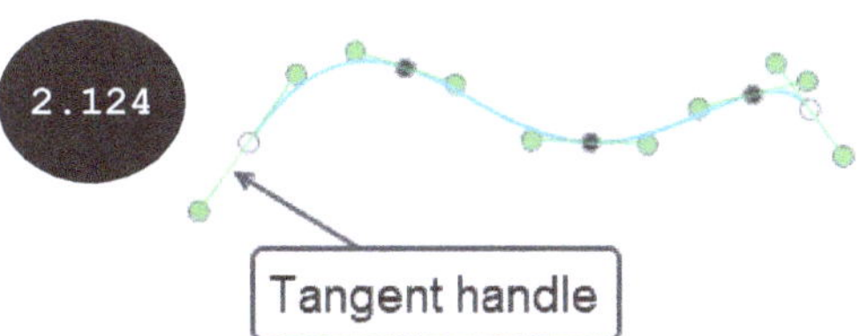

Note: To create a closed spline, right-click in the drawing area after specifying three or more than three fit points of the spline. A Marking Menu appears. Next, click on the **Close Spline Curve** tool in the Marking Menu.

Control Point Spline Tool

The **Control Point Spline** tool is used to create a spline by defining two or more control points in the drawing area. Note that the spline is created such that it passes near the control points specified in the drawing area, see Figure 2.125. In this figure, four control points have been specified in the drawing area to create a spline using the **Control Point Spline** tool. The method for drawing a spline using the **Control Point Spline** tool is discussed below:

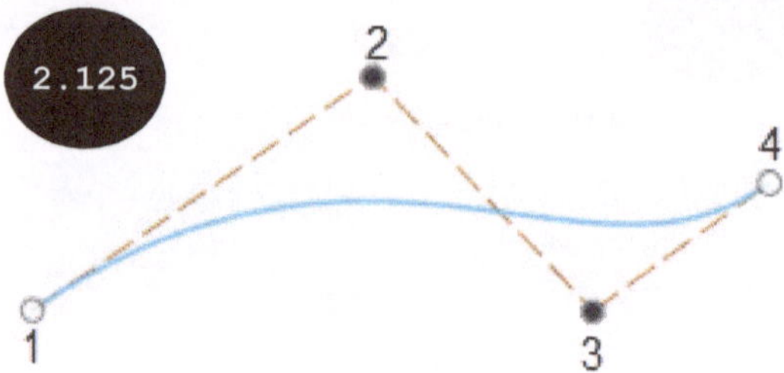

1. Invoke the **CREATE** drop-down menu in the **SKETCH** contextual tab and then click on **Spline > Control Point Spline** tool.

2. Click to specify the first control point of the spline in the drawing area.

3. Move the cursor to a distance. A reference curve appears in the drawing area whose one end is fixed at the specified point and the other end is attached to the cursor.

4. Click to specify the second control point of the spline and then move the cursor. A preview of the spline appears such that it passes near the specified control points, see Figure 2.126.

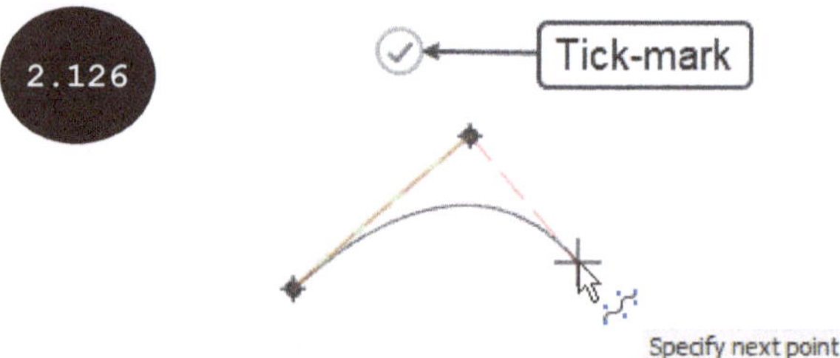

5. Click to specify the third control point of the spline. Similarly, you can specify multiple control points for drawing the spline.

6. Once all control points have been specified for drawing the spline, click on the tick-mark that appears in the drawing area, refer to Figure 2.126. The spline is drawn and the **Control Point Spline** tool is still active. To exit the **Control Point Spline** tool, right-click in the drawing area and then click on the **OK** tool in the Marking Menu that appears.

Editing a Spline

Editing a spline is essential for achieving complex shapes while maintaining a high degree of smoothness and curvature. In Autodesk Fusion, you can edit a spline created with the **Fit Point Spline** tool by adjusting its fit points and tangent handle. To do this, click on the fit point of the spline to be modified.

The selected fit point gets highlighted and appears with its tangent handle in the drawing area, see Figure 2.127. Also, the **Curvature display** and **Tangent display** tools appear in the **Contextual Options** rollout of the **SKETCH PALETTE** dialog box, see Figure 2.128.

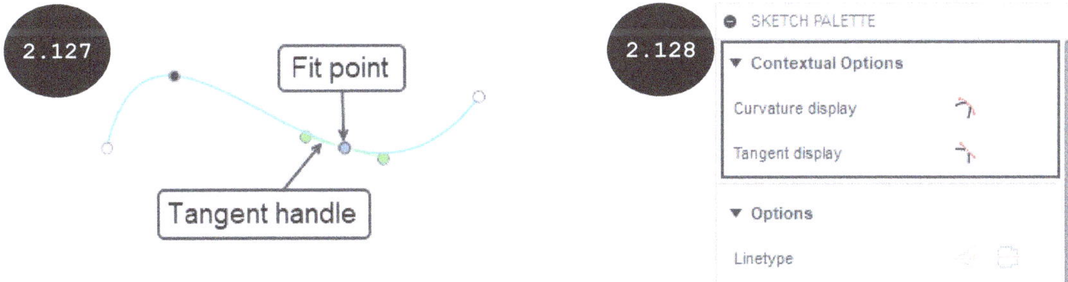

You can drag the selected fit point by pressing and holding the left mouse button to change its location in the drawing area. You can drag the endpoints of the tangent handle to edit the tangency of the spline. To edit the curvature continuity of the spline, click on the **Curvature display** tool in the **Contextual Options** rollout of the **SKETCH PALETTE** dialog box. The curvature handle of the selected fit point appears in the drawing area. Now, you can drag the endpoints of the curvature handle to edit the curvature continuity of the spline.

Similarly, you can edit a spline that is drawn by using the **Control Point Spline** tool using its control points. You can also change the degree of a spline that is drawn by using the **Control Point Spline** tool. To do this, select a spline in the graphics area. The **Change Spline Degree** drop-down list appears in the **Contextual Options** rollout of the **SKETCH PALETTE** dialog box, see Figure 2.129. In this drop-down list, you can select the required degree of spline in the range from 1 to 9.

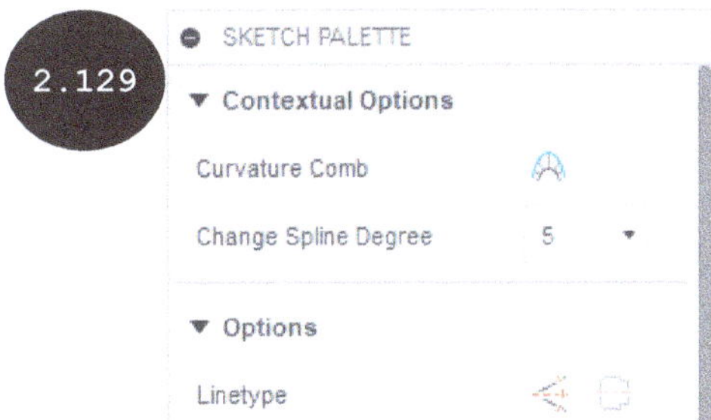

Adding Fit/Control Points in a Spline

To add a fit or a control point in a spline, select the spline and then right-click to display the Marking Menu in the drawing area. Next, click on the **Insert Spline Fit Point** or **Insert Spline Control Point** tool in the Marking Menu, see Figures 2.130 and 2.131.

Note that the **Insert Spline Fit Point** tool appears in the Marking Menu when the selected spline is drawn using the **Fit Point Spline** tool, whereas the **Insert Spline Control Point** tool appears when the selected spline is drawn using the **Control Point Spline** tool.

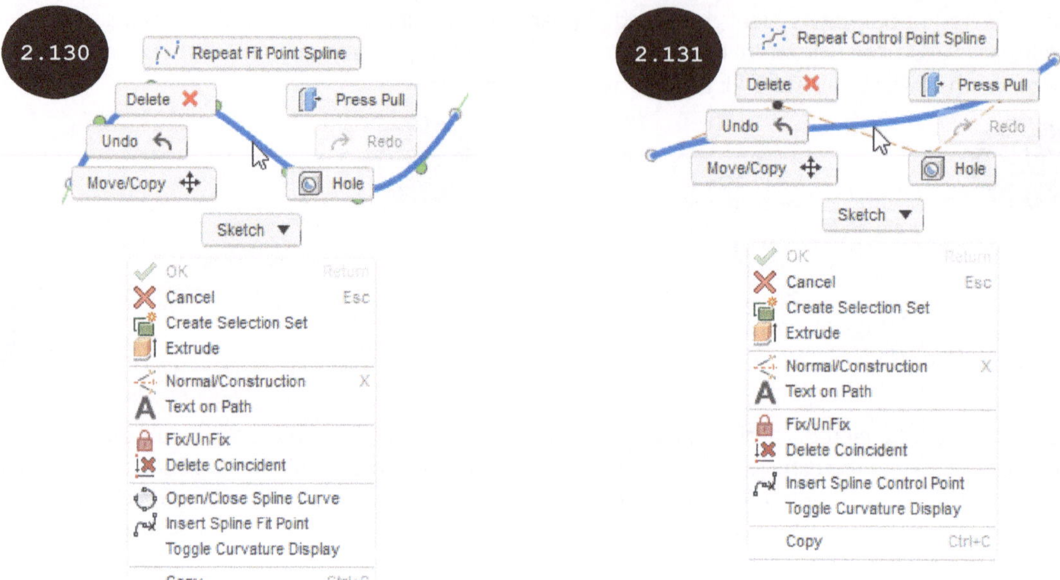

After selecting the required tool in the Marking Menu, you are prompted to specify the location of the fit or control point in the spline. Move the cursor over the spline in the location where you want to add the point and then click on the left mouse button. The point gets added in the specified location of the spline. Similarly, you can add multiple points in the spline by clicking on the left mouse button in the required locations of the spline. After adding the points in the spline, right-click in the drawing area and then click on the **OK** tool in the Marking Menu that appears to exit the tool.

Controlling the Curvature Display of a Spline

You can also turn on or off the curvature display of the spline. To do this, select the spline in the drawing area and then click on the **Toggle Curvature Display** tool in the **Contextual Options** rollout of the **SKETCH PALETTE** dialog box. Alternatively, right-click in the drawing area after selecting the spline and then click on the **Toggle Curvature Display** tool in the Marking Menu that appears, see Figure 2.132. The curvature display of the spline appears in the drawing area, see Figure 2.133. Also, the **SETUP CURVATURE DISPLAY** dialog box appears in the drawing area. By using the **Density** and **Scale** sliders of this dialog box, you can control the density and scale of the curvature display in the spline, respectively. Next, click on the **OK** button in the dialog box. To turn off the curvature display of the spline, select the spline and then click on the **Toggle Curvature Display** tool in the **Contextual Options** rollout of the **SKETCH PALETTE** dialog box.

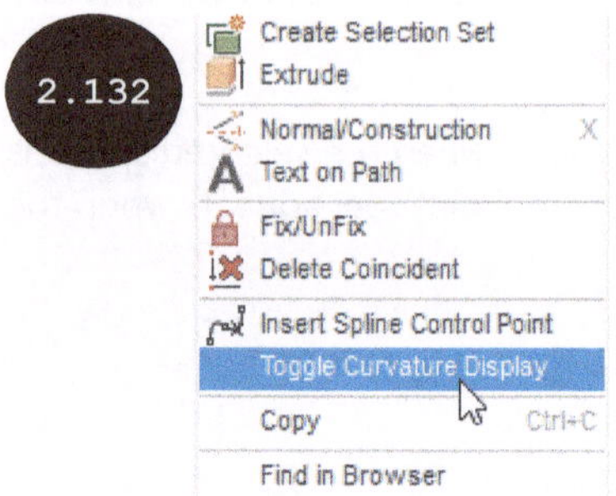

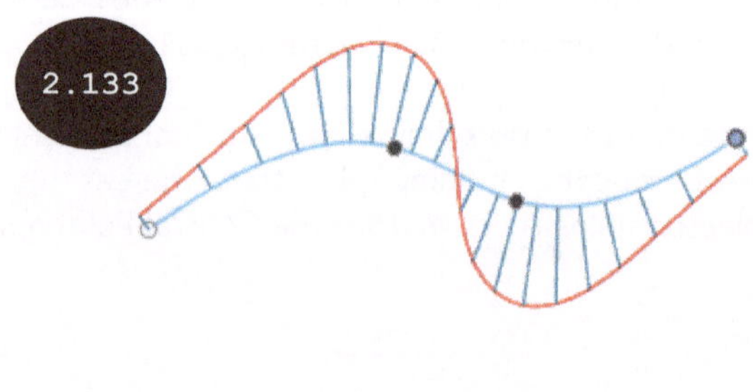

Creating Sketch Points

In Autodesk Fusion, you can create multiple sketch points in the drawing area using the **Point** tool of the **CREATE** drop-down menu in the **SKETCH** contextual tab. The sketch points act as reference entities within the sketching environment and can be used for creating other entities of the sketch. You can also use sketch points to position hole features and create reference planes, axes, etc. You will learn about creating reference planes and axes in later chapters.

To create sketch points, invoke the **CREATE** drop-down menu in the **SKETCH** contextual tab and then click on the **Point** tool. Next, click on the left mouse button in the drawing area where you want to position the sketch point. The sketch point is created. Similarly, you can create multiple sketch points in the drawing area by clicking on the left mouse button. After creating the sketch points, right-click in the drawing area and then click on the **OK** button in the Marking Menu that appears to exit the **Point** tool.

Inserting Text into a Sketch

In Autodesk Fusion, you can insert text into an active sketch by drawing a rectangular frame and then writing text into it or writing text along a path. Both these methods are discussed next.

Inserting Text by Drawing a Rectangular Frame

To insert text by drawing a rectangular frame, invoke the **CREATE** drop-down menu in the **SKETCH** contextual tab and then click on the **Text** tool. The **TEXT** dialog box appears, see Figure 2.134.

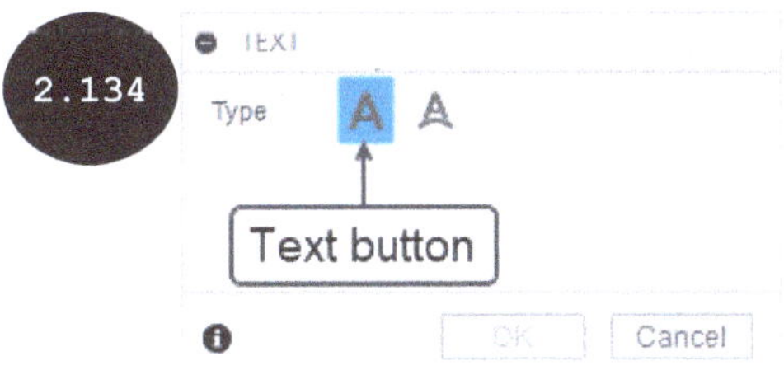

In this dialog box, ensure that the **Text** button is selected. Next, draw a rectangular window by specifying two diagonally opposite corners in the drawing area, see Figure 2.135. After drawing a rectangular window, the **TEXT** dialog box gets updated with additional options, see Figure 2.136. Also, a preview of the sample text inside the rectangular frame, along with the orientation handle appears in the drawing area, see Figure 2.137.

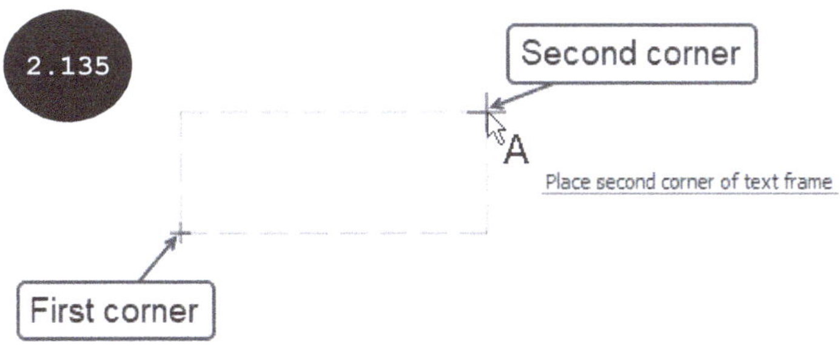

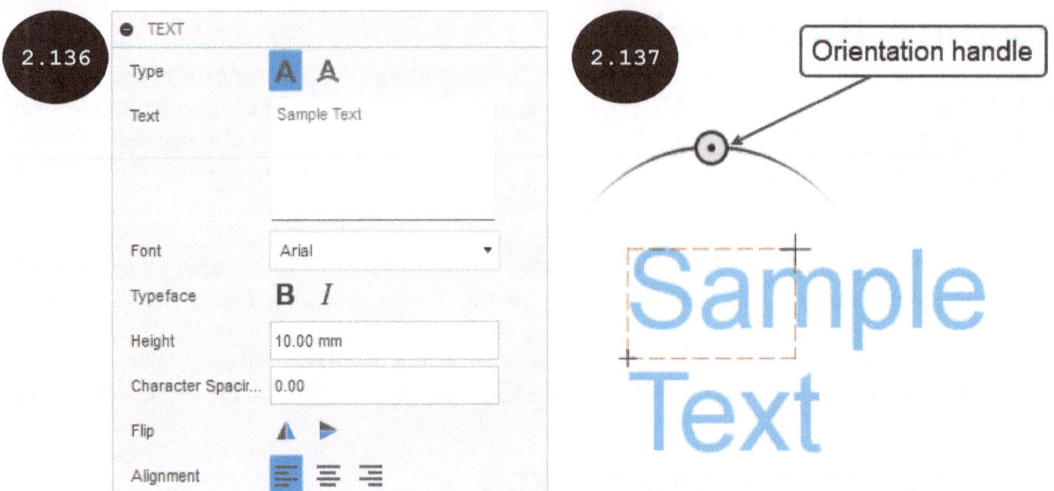

Enter the text in the **Text** field of the dialog box or the rectangular frame in the drawing area. You can specify the height, typeface, alignment, character spacing, and font of the text by using the respective options in the dialog box. You can also flip the text, horizontally and vertically, by using the **Horizontal Flip** and **Vertical Flip** buttons of the dialog box, respectively. You can also drag the Orientation handle that appears in the drawing area to rotate the text in the drawing area. After specifying all the parameters, click on the **OK** button. The text is inserted in the drawing area.

Inserting Text along a Path

To insert text along a path in the active sketch, invoke the **TEXT** dialog box, as discussed earlier. Next, in the **Type** area of the TEXT dialog box, select the **Text on Path** button. The **Path** selection option appears in the dialog box, see Figure 2.138. Select a path in the drawing area along which the text is to be inserted. You can select a line, curve, spline, or edge as the path. Next, enter the text in the **Text** field of the dialog box. A preview of the text appears along the selected path in the drawing area, see Figure 2.139.

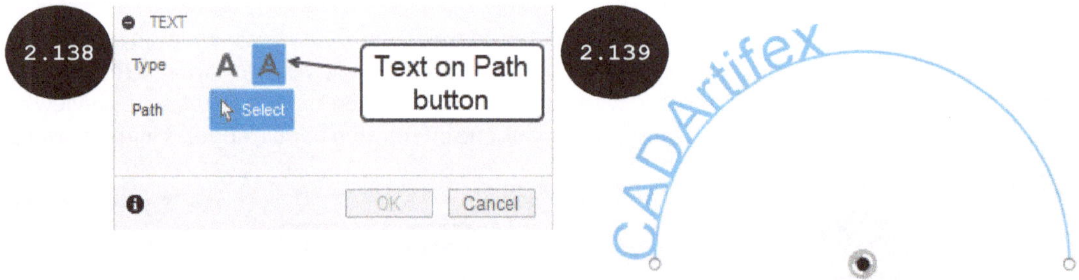

After entering the text in the **Text** field, you can specify the text height, alignment, character spacing, and font using the respective options in the dialog box. You can also flip the text, horizontally and vertically, by using the **Horizontal Flip** and **Vertical Flip** buttons, respectively. You can define the placement of the text above or below the path by selecting the **Place text above path** or **Place text below path** option in the **Placement** area of the dialog box, respectively. You can also choose to fit the complete text along the path by selecting the **Fit to Path** check box in the dialog box. After specifying all the parameters, click on the **OK** button. The text is inserted along the selected path in the drawing area.

Tutorial 3

Draw the sketch of the model shown in Figure 2.140. The dimensions and the model shown in the figure are for your reference only. All dimensions are in mm. You will learn about applying dimensions and creating 3D models in later chapters.

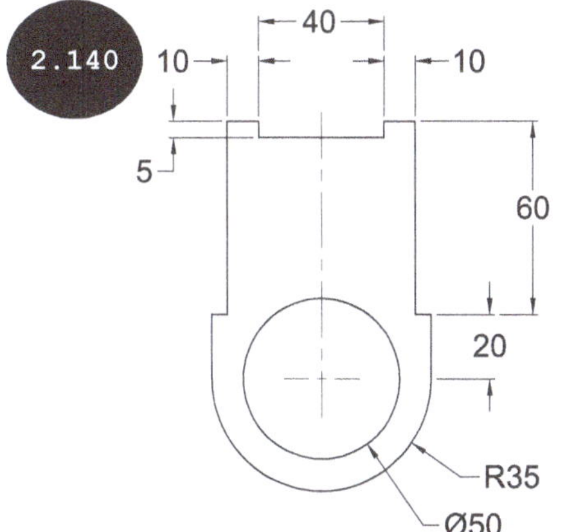

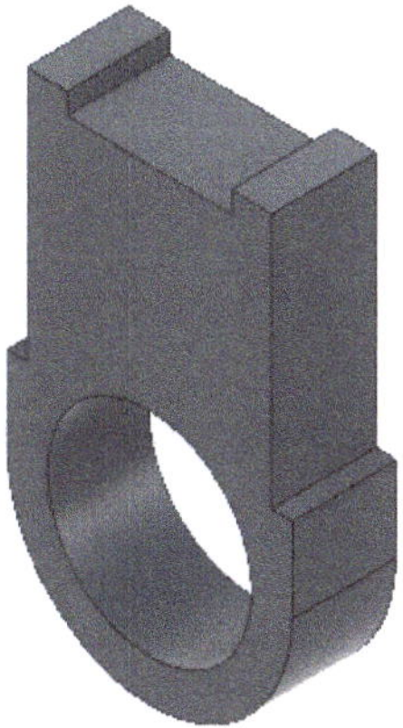

Section 1: Starting a New Part Design File

1. Click **File** > **New** in the **Application Bar** (see Figure 2.141) to display the **What do you want to design?** dialog box, see Figure 2.142.

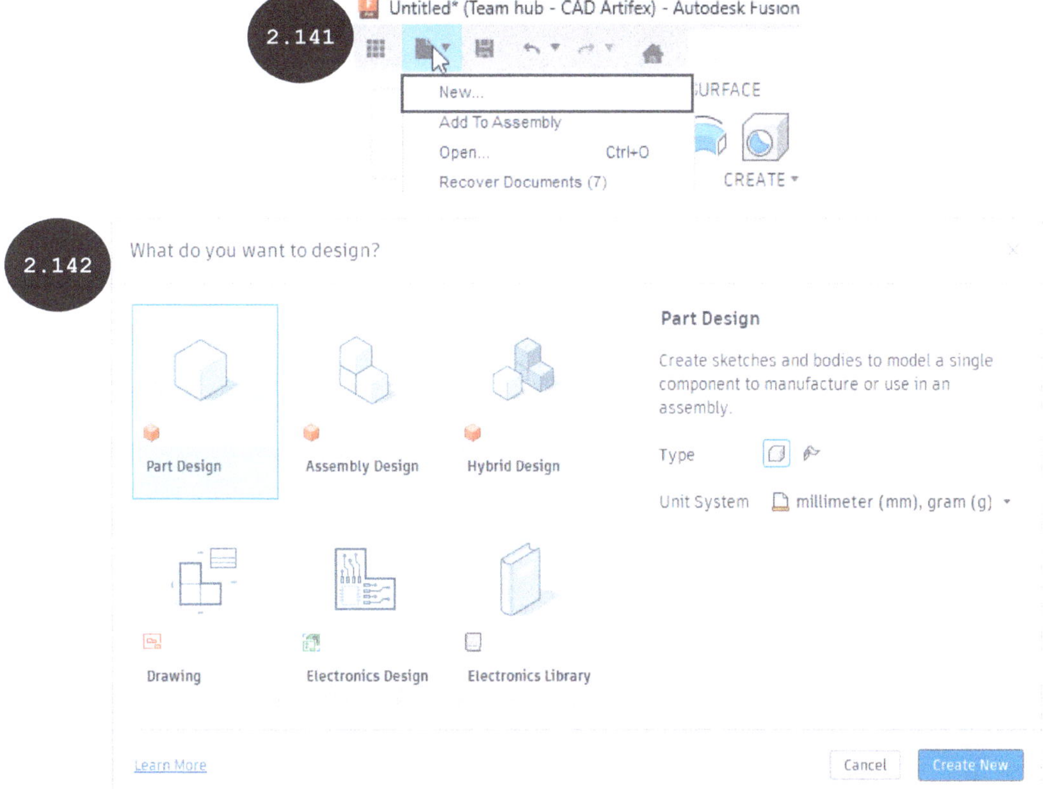

Note: If you are starting a new Autodesk Fusion session, the Part Design file opens automatically because it is set as the default design type. In this case, ensure that the **millimeter (mm), gram (g)** unit system is set for the opened Part Design file.

2. In the **What do you want to design?** dialog box, select the **Part Design** button and choose the **millimeter (mm), gram (g)** unit system from the **Unit System** drop-down list.

3. After specifying the required options, click the **Create New** button. A new Part Design file is opened with the default name in a separate tab.

Section 2: Organizing the Data Panel

Before you begin creating a design, you can organize the **Data Panel** by creating a project folder and sub-folders to save your design files.

1. Click on the **Show Data Panel** tool in the **Application Bar**, see Figure 2.143. The **Data Panel** appears, see Figure 2.144.

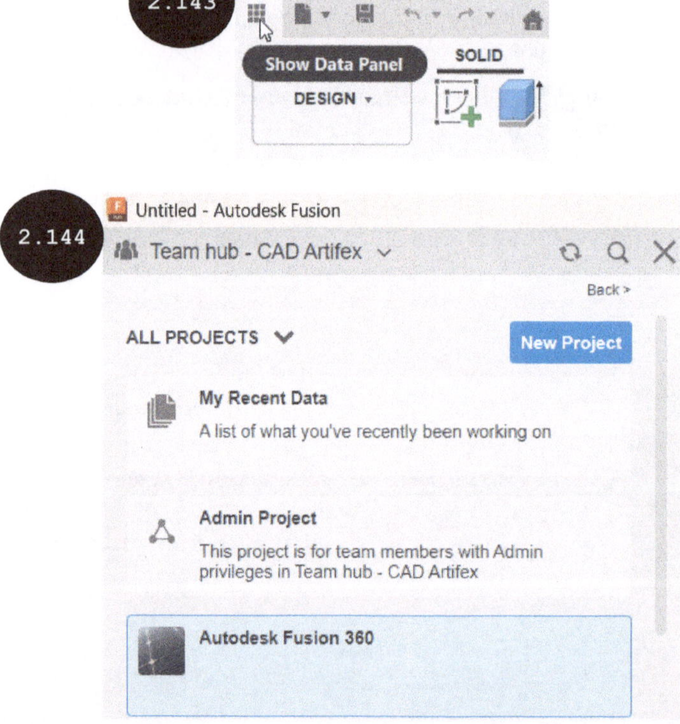

2. Create a new project '**Autodesk Fusion 360**', by using the **New Project** tool, if not created earlier.

Note: If you have already created the project folder and sub-folders "*Autodesk Fusion 360 > Chapter 02 > Tutorial*" in the **Data Panel**, you can skip steps 3 and 4 in this section.

3. Double-click on the **Autodesk Fusion 360** project in the **Data Panel** and then create the "**Chapter 02**" folder by using the **New Folder** tool of the **Data Panel**.

4. Double-click on the **Chapter 02** folder in the **Data Panel** and then create the "**Tutorial**" sub-folder by using the **New Folder** tool of the **Data Panel**, if not created earlier. Next, click on the cross-mark ✕ at the top right corner of the **Data Panel** to close it.

Section 3: Specifying Grid Settings

1. Invoke the **Grid and Snaps** flyout in the **Navigation Bar**, see Figure 2.145.

2. Click on the **Grid Settings** tool in the **Grid and Snaps** flyout. The **GRID SETTINGS** dialog box appears, see Figure 2.146.

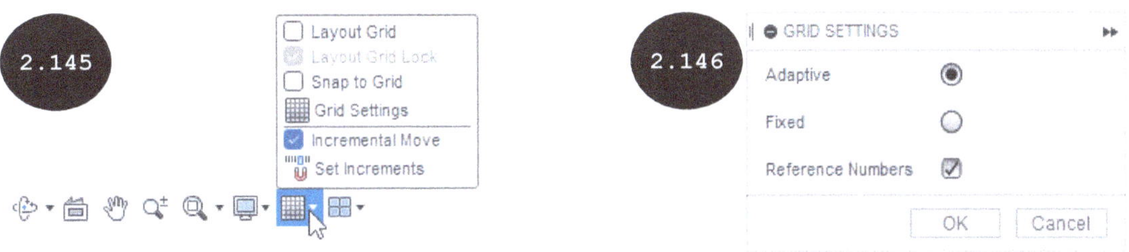

3. Ensure that the **Adaptive** radio button is selected in the **GRID SETTINGS** dialog box to adjust the grid size, automatically, as you zoom into or out of the drawing view.

4. Click on the **OK** button in the **GRID SETTINGS** dialog box.

Section 4: Creating the Sketch

1. Click on the **Create Sketch** tool in the **Toolbar**, see Figure 2.147. Three default planes: Front, Top, and Right, which are mutually perpendicular to each other appear in the graphics area, see Figure 2.148.

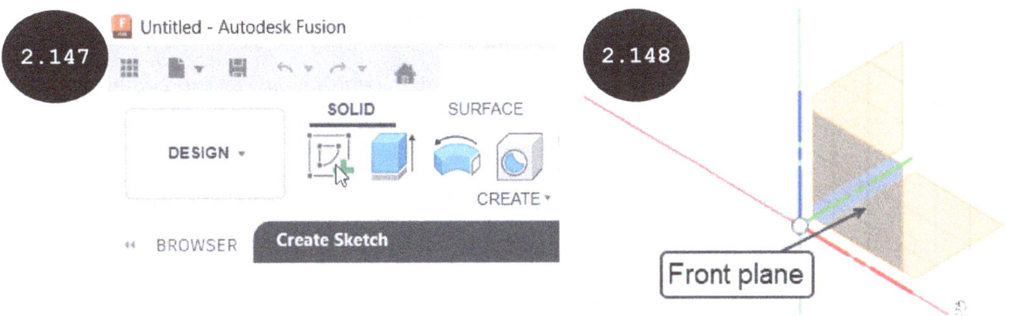

2. Move the cursor over the Front plane and then click the left mouse button when it gets highlighted in the drawing area. The Front plane becomes the sketching plane for creating the sketch and it is oriented normal to the viewing direction. Also, the **SKETCH** contextual tab and the **SKETCH PALETTE** dialog box appear, see Figure 2.149.

2.149

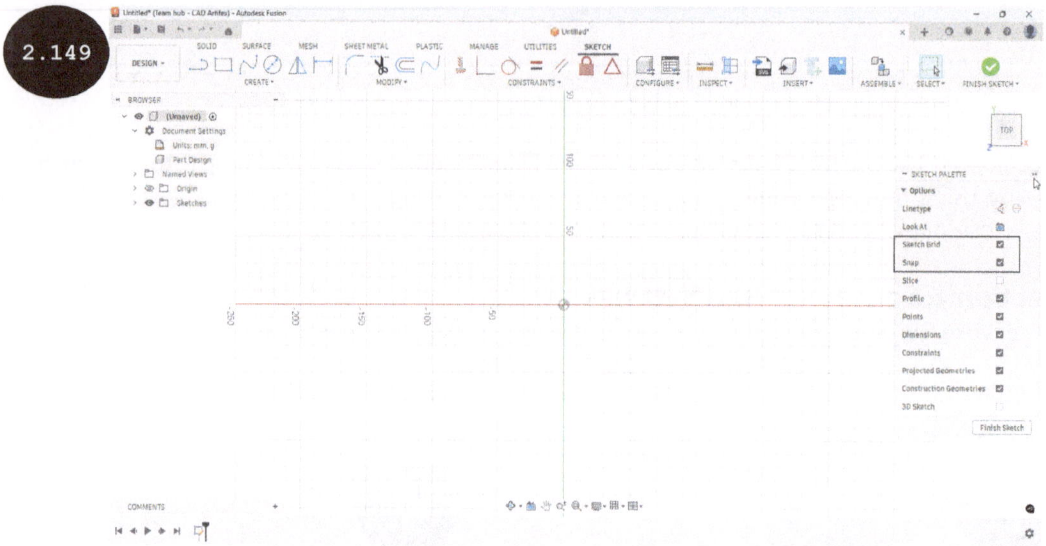

3. Ensure that the **Sketch Grid** and **Snap** check boxes are selected in the **SKETCH PALETTE** dialog box to display the grids and to snap the movement of the cursor on the grid lines.

   Now, you can create the entities of the sketch.

4. Click on the **Center Diameter Circle** tool of the **CREATE** panel in the **SKETCH** contextual tab, see Figure 2.150. The **Center Diameter Circle** tool gets activated. Alternatively, press the C key to activate the **Center Diameter Circle** tool.

2.150

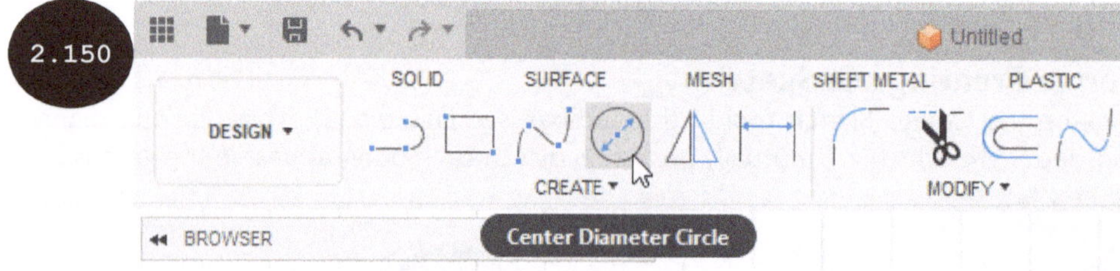

5. Move the cursor to the origin and then click to specify the center point of the circle when the cursor snaps to the origin.

6. Move the cursor horizontally toward the right and then click to specify a point when the diameter of the circle appears 50 mm in the dimension box, see Figure 2.151. A circle of diameter 50 mm is drawn. Note that you may need to zoom into or out of the drawing view to adjust the grid size so that the cursor snaps to the grid lines when the diameter of the circle measures 50 mm.

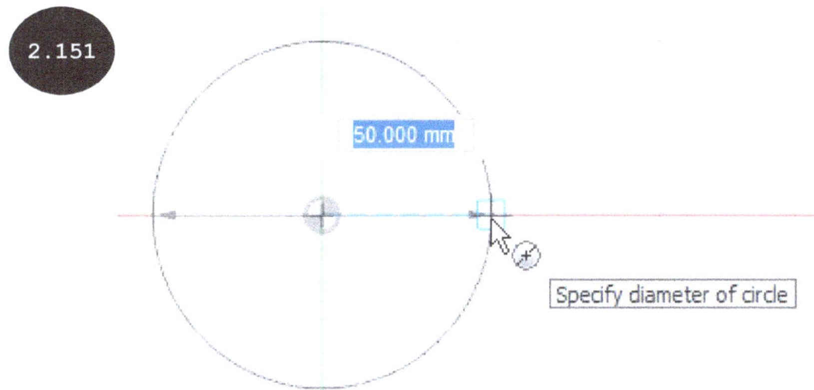

7. Right-click in the drawing area and then click on the **OK** tool in the Marking Menu to exit the **Center Diameter Circle** tool.

8. Invoke the **CREATE** drop-down menu in the **SKETCH** contextual tab of the **Toolbar** and then click on **Arc** > **Center Point Arc**, see Figure 2.152. The **Center Point Arc** tool gets activated.

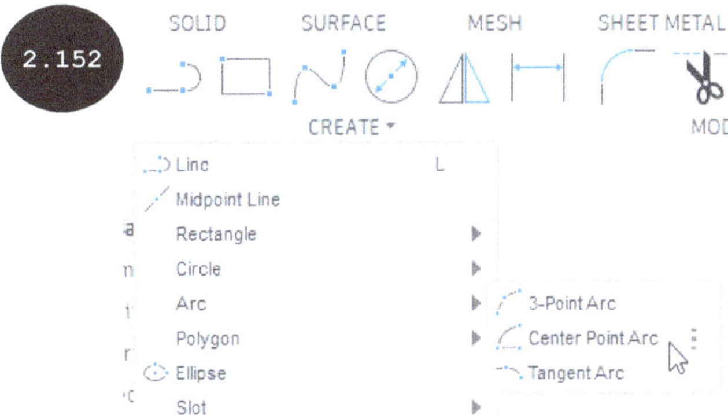

9. Move the cursor to the origin and then click to specify the center point of the arc when the cursor snaps to the origin.

10. Move the cursor horizontally toward the right and then click to specify the start point of the arc when the radius of the arc appears as 35 mm in the dimension box, see Figure 2.153.

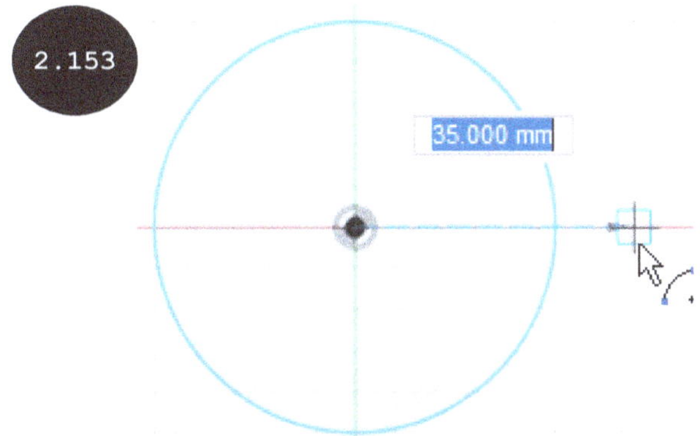

11. Move the cursor clockwise in the drawing area. The preview of an arc appears. Next, click to specify the endpoint of the arc when the angle value appears as 180 degrees, see Figure 2.154. The arc is drawn. Next, press the **ESC** key to exit the tool.

12. Click on the **Line** tool in the **Toolbar**, see Figure 2.155. The **Line** tool gets activated. Alternatively, press the L key to activate the **Line** tool.

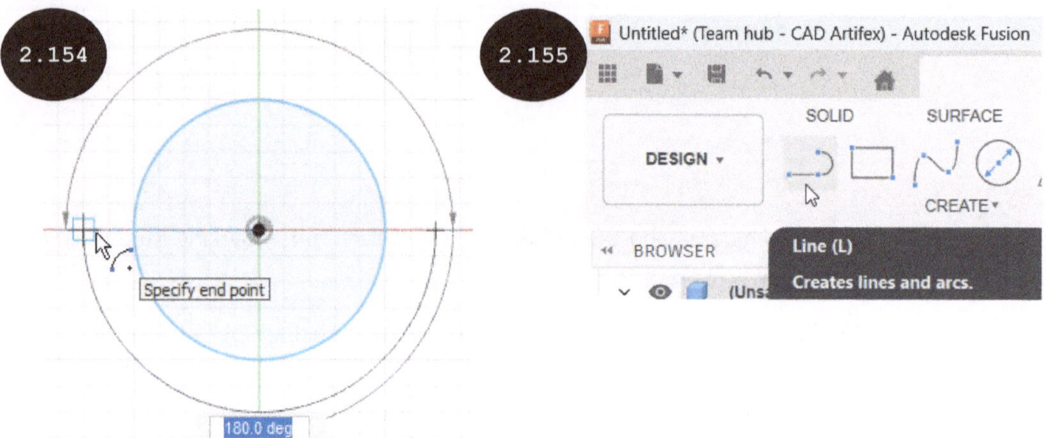

13. Move the cursor to the start point of the previously drawn arc and then click the left mouse button when the cursor snaps to it, see Figure 2.156.

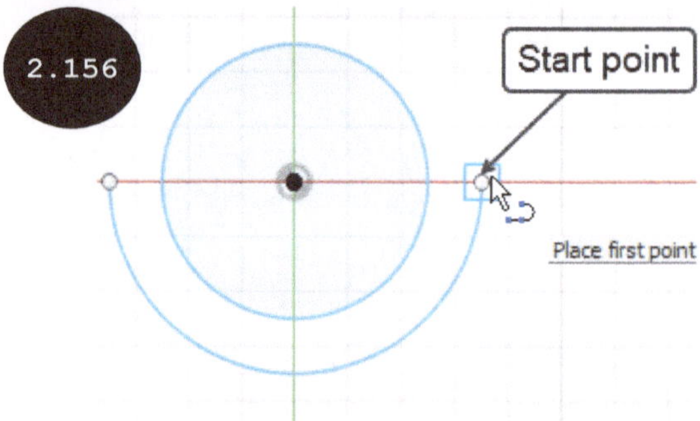

14. Move the cursor vertically upward and click when the length of the line appears as 20 mm in the dimension box. A line of length 20 mm is drawn.

15. Move the cursor horizontally toward the left and click when the length of the line appears as 5 mm.

16. Move the cursor vertically upward and click when the length of the line appears as 60 mm.

17. Move the cursor horizontally toward the left and click when the length of the line appears as 10 mm.

18. Move the cursor vertically downward and click when the length of the line appears as 5 mm.

19. Move the cursor horizontally toward the left and click when the length of the line appears as 40 mm.

20. Move the cursor vertically upward and click when the length of the line appears as 5 mm.

21. Move the cursor horizontally toward the left and click when the length of the line appears as 10 mm.

22. Move the cursor vertically downward and click when the length of the line appears as 60 mm.

23. Move the cursor horizontally toward the left and click when the length of the line appears as 5 mm.

24. Move the cursor vertically downward and click when the cursor snaps to the endpoint of the arc, see Figure 2.157.

25. Right-click in the drawing area and then click on the **OK** tool in the Marking Menu that appears to exit the **Line** tool. Figure 2.158 shows the final sketch.

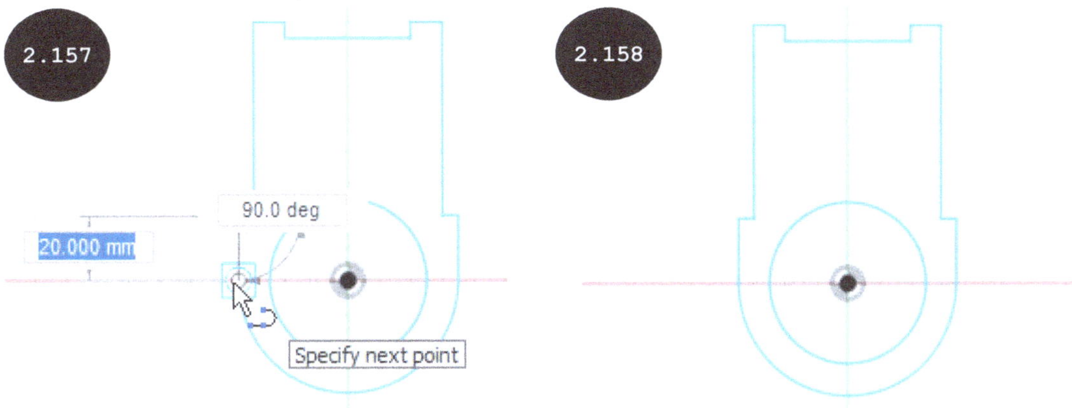

Note: In Figures 2.157 and 2.158, the display of automatically applied constraints (horizontal and vertical) is turned off. To turn off the display of constraints in the drawing area, clear the **Constraints** check box in the **SKETCH PALETTE** dialog box.

Section 5: Saving the Sketch

1. Click on the **Save** tool in the **Application Bar**. The **Save** dialog box appears.

2. Enter **Tutorial 3** in the **Name** field of the dialog box.

3. Click on the down arrow next to the **Location** field in the dialog box. The expanded **Save** dialog box appears with the **PROJECT** area on its left, see Figure 2.159.

4. Ensure that the **Autodesk Fusion 360** project is selected in the **PROJECT** area.

5. Specify the location ***Autodesk Fusion 360 > Chapter 02 > Tutorial*** to save the sketch. Note that you need to double-click on the folder/sub-folder of the project in the right panel of the dialog box to access the required location for saving the sketch.

6. Click on the **Save** button in the dialog box. The sketch is saved with the name Tutorial 3 in the specified location (***Autodesk Fusion 360 > Chapter 02 > Tutorial***).

2.159

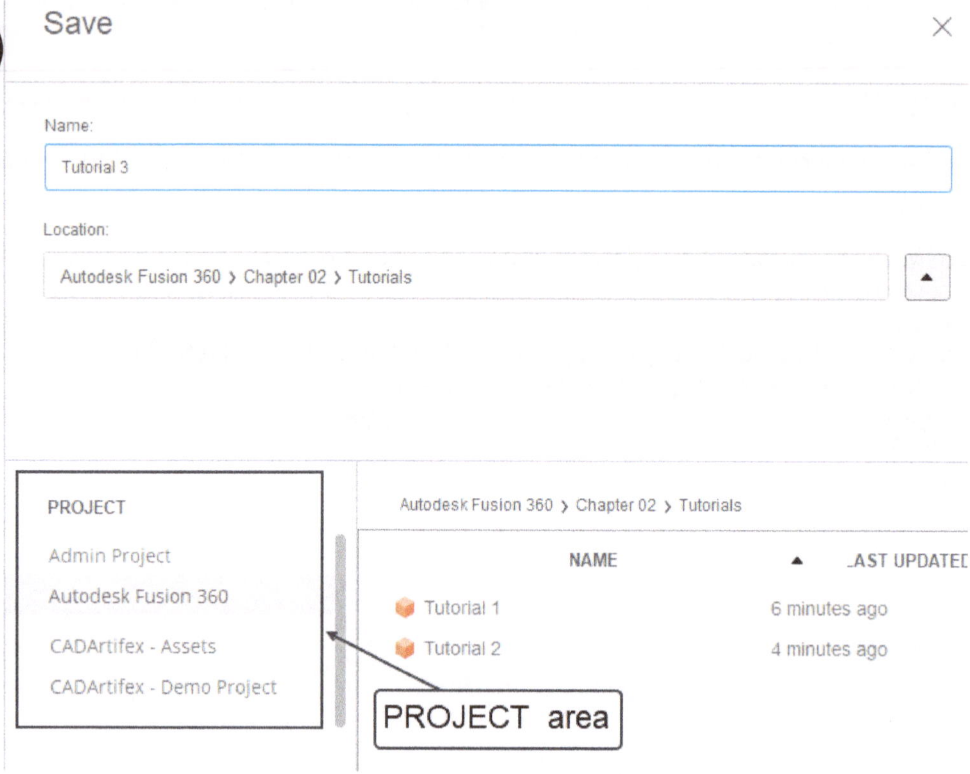

Save
Name:
Tutorial 3
Location:
Autodesk Fusion 360 > Chapter 02 > Tutorials
PROJECT
Admin Project
Autodesk Fusion 360
CADArtifex - Assets
CADArtifex - Demo Project
Autodesk Fusion 360 > Chapter 02 > Tutorials
NAME
LAST UPDATED
Tutorial 1
6 minutes ago
Tutorial 2
4 minutes ago
PROJECT area

Tutorial 4

Draw the sketch of the model shown in Figure 2.160. The dimensions and the model shown in the figure are for your reference only. All dimensions are in mm. You will learn about applying dimensions and creating a model in later chapters.

2.160

R70
Ø40
R10
120
100
R40
R30
10
20
30
40
10

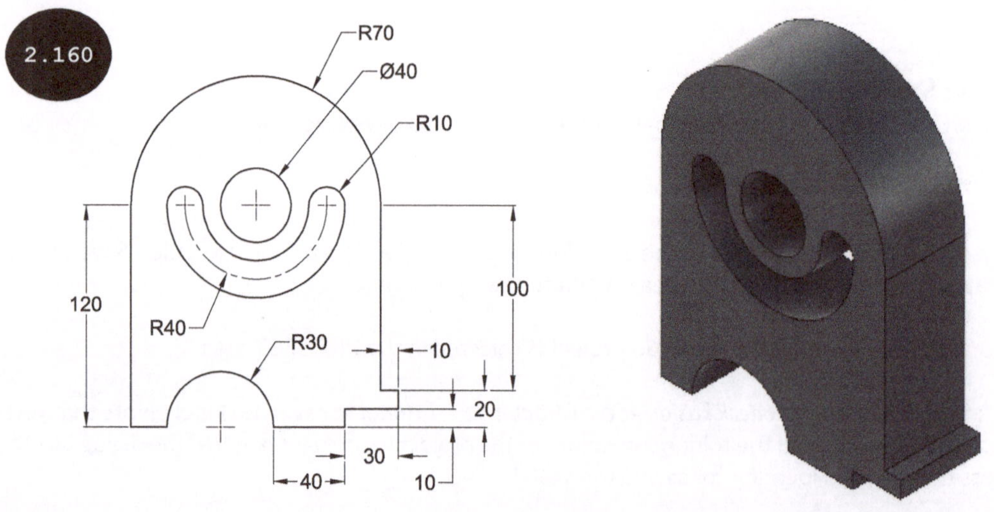

Section 1: Starting a New Design File

1. Click **File** > **New** in the **Application Bar** (see Figure 2.161) to display the **What do you want to design?** dialog box, see Figure 2.162.

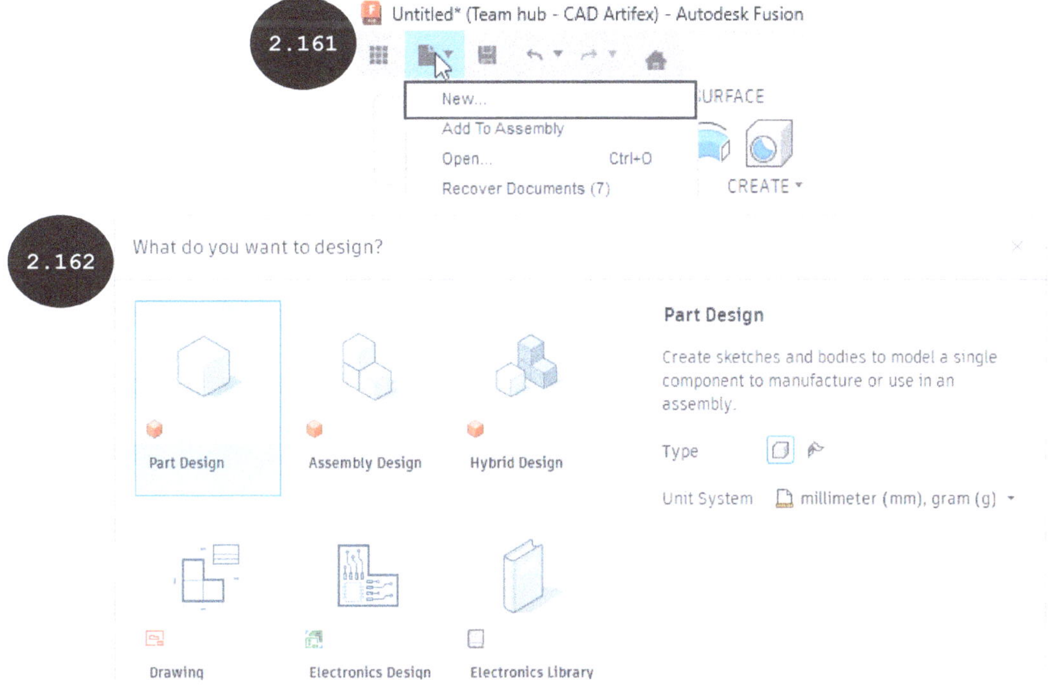

Note: If you are starting a new Autodesk Fusion session, the Part Design file opens automatically because it is set as the default design type. In this case, ensure that the **millimeter (mm), gram (g)** unit system is set for the opened Part Design file.

2. In the **What do you want to design?** dialog box, select the **Part Design** button and choose the **millimeter (mm), gram (g)** unit system from the **Unit System** drop-down list.

3. After specifying the required options, click the **Create New** button. A new Part Design file is opened.

Section 2: Organizing the Data Panel

Now, you can organize the **Data Panel** by creating a project folder and sub-folders to save files.

1. Click on the **Show Data Panel** tool in the **Application Bar**, see Figure 2.163. The **Data Panel** appears.

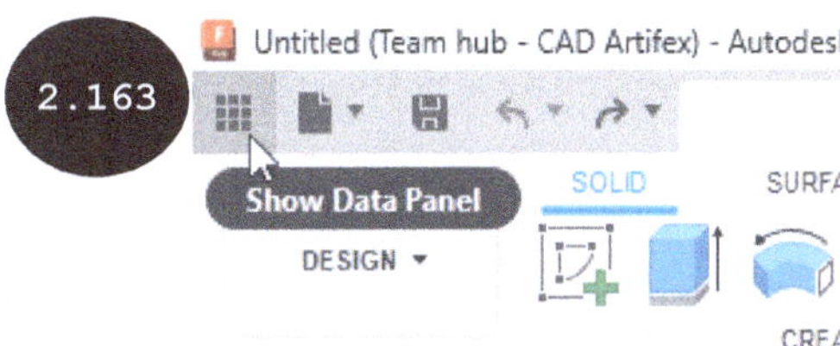

2. Ensure that the **Autodesk Fusion 360** > **Chapter 02** > **Tutorial** folders are created in the **Data Panel**. You need to create these project folders, if not created earlier.

3. Click on the cross-mark ✕ at the top right corner of the **Data Panel** to close it.

Section 3: Specifying Grid Settings

1. Invoke the **Grid and Snaps** flyout in the **Navigation Bar**, see Figure 2.164.

2. Click on the **Grid Settings** tool in the **Grid and Snaps** flyout. The **GRID SETTINGS** dialog box appears, see Figure 2.165.

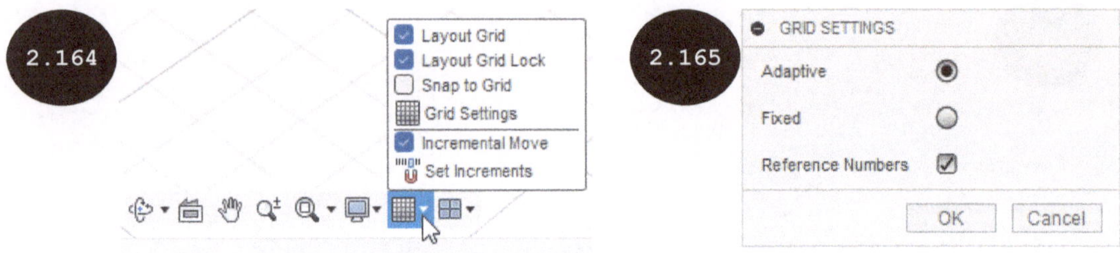

3. Ensure that the **Adaptive** radio button is selected in the **GRID SETTINGS** dialog box to adjust the grid size, automatically, as you zoom into or out of the drawing view.

4. Click on the **OK** button in the **GRID SETTINGS** dialog box.

Section 4: Creating the Sketch

1. Click on the **Create Sketch** tool in the **Toolbar**, see Figure 2.166. Three default planes: Front, Top, and Right, which are mutually perpendicular to each other appear in the graphics area, see Figure 2.167.

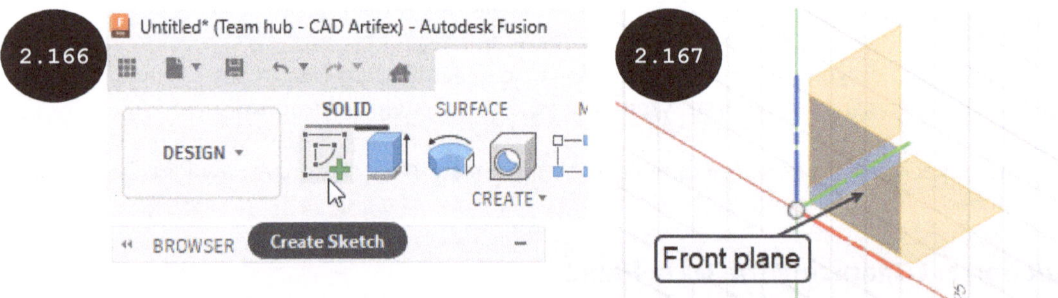

2. Move the cursor over the Front plane and then click the left mouse button when it gets highlighted in the drawing area, refer to Figure 2.167. The Front plane becomes the sketching plane for creating the sketch and it is oriented normal to the viewing direction. Also, the **SKETCH contextual** tab and the **SKETCH PALETTE** dialog box appear, see Figure 2.168.

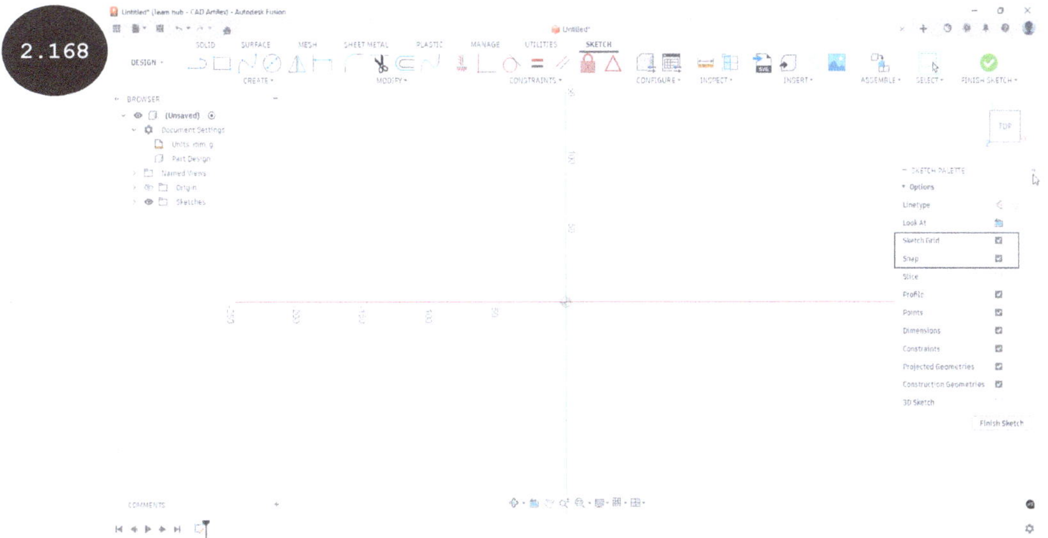

3. Ensure that the **Sketch Grid** and **Snap** check boxes are selected in the **SKETCH PALETTE** dialog box to display the grids and to snap the movement of the cursor on the grid lines.
   Now, you can create the entities of the sketch.

4. Invoke the **CREATE** drop-down menu of the **SKETCH** contextual tab of the **Toolbar** and then click on **Arc > Center Point Arc**, see Figure 2.169. The **Center Point Arc** tool gets activated.

5. Move the cursor to the origin and then click to specify the center point of the arc when the cursor snaps to the origin.

6. Move the cursor horizontally toward the right and then click to specify the start point of the arc when the radius of the arc appears as 30 mm in the dimension box, see Figure 2.170.

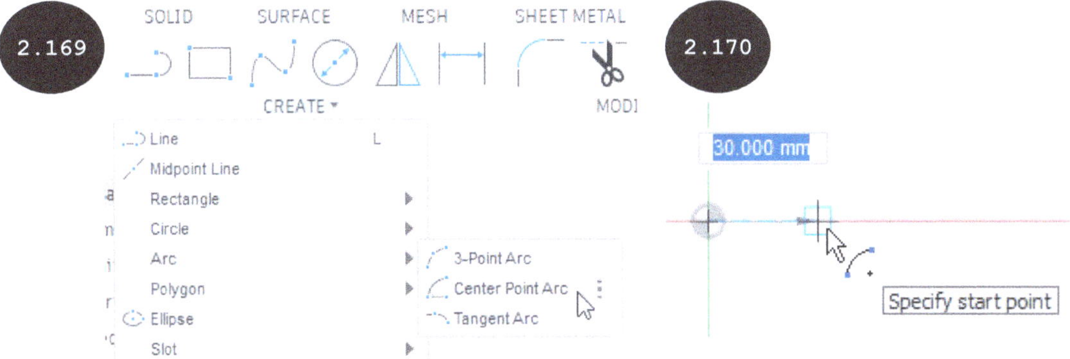

7. Move the cursor anti-clockwise in the drawing area. The preview of the arc appears. Next, click the left mouse button when the angle value appears as 180 degrees, see Figure 2.171. Next, press the ESC key to exit the **Center Point Arc** tool.

8. Click on the **Line** tool in the **Toolbar**, see Figure 2.172. The **Line** tool gets activated. Alternatively, press the L key to activate the **Line** tool.

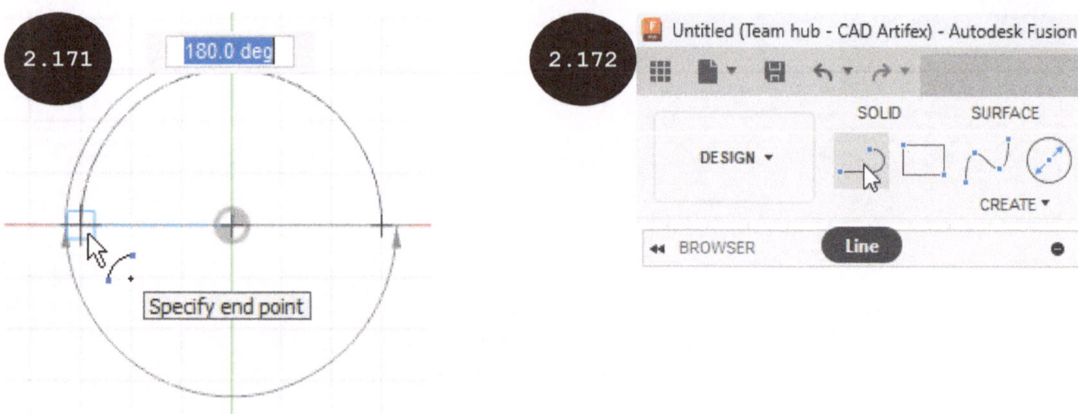

9. Move the cursor to the start point of the previously drawn arc and then click the left mouse button when the cursor snaps to it, see Figure 2.173.

10. Move the cursor horizontally toward the right and click when the length of the line appears as 40 mm, see Figure 2.174.

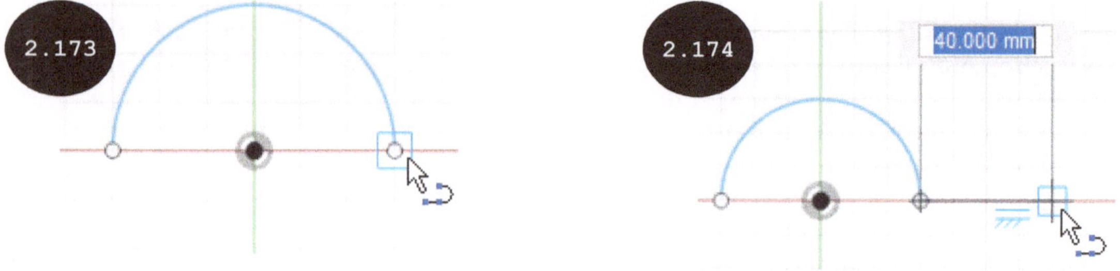

11. Move the cursor vertically upward and click when the length of the line appears as 10 mm.

12. Move the cursor horizontally toward the right and click when the length appears as 30 mm.

13. Move the cursor vertically upward and click when the length of the line appears as 10 mm.

14. Move the cursor horizontally toward the left and click when the length appears as 10 mm.

15. Move the cursor vertically upward and click when the length of the line appears as 100 mm.

16. Move the cursor over the last specified point. Next, drag the cursor upward to a distance and then horizontally toward the left by pressing and holding the left mouse button. The arc mode is activated and the preview of the tangent arc appears in the drawing area, see Figure 2.175.

17. Click to specify the endpoint of the arc when the radius value of the arc appears as 70 mm, see Figure 2.175.

18. Move the cursor vertically downward and click when the length of the line appears as 120 mm.

19. Move the cursor horizontally toward the right and click when the cursor snaps to the endpoint of the arc. The outer closed loop of the sketch is drawn, see Figure 2.176. Next, press the **ESC** key to exit the tool.

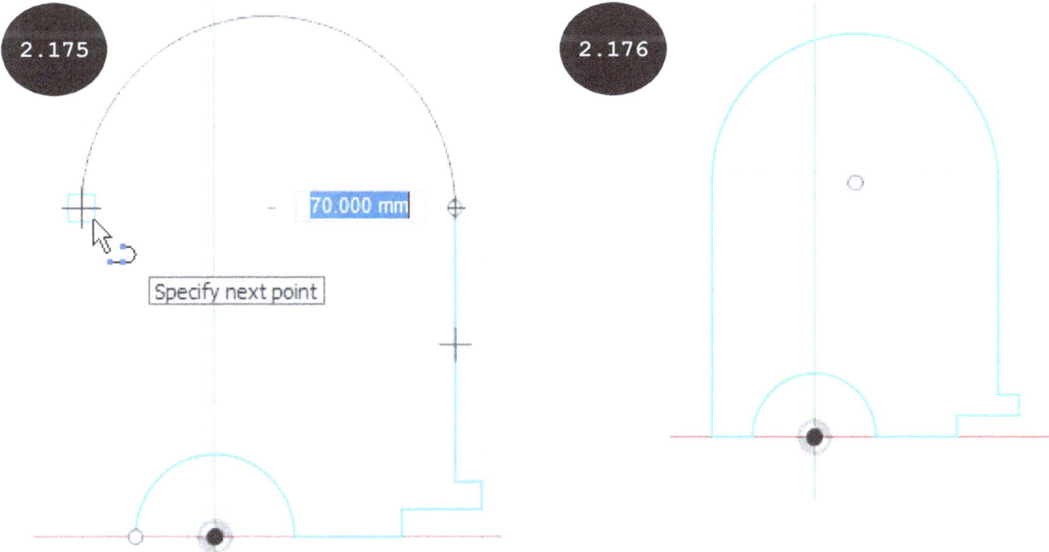

Section 5: Drawing the Slot and the Circle of the Sketch

1. Click on the **Center Diameter Circle** tool of the **CREATE** panel in the **SKETCH** contextual tab. The **Center Diameter Circle** tool is activated. Alternatively, press the C key to activate the **Center Diameter Circle** tool.

2. Move the cursor toward the center point of the upper arc of the sketch, see Figure 2.177 and then click when the cursor snaps to it.

3. Move the cursor horizontally toward the right and click when the diameter of the circle appears as 40 mm. A circle of diameter 40 mm is drawn. Next, press the ESC key to exit the tool.

Now, you need to create the arc slot.

4. Invoke the **CREATE** drop-down menu of the **SKETCH** contextual tab and then click on **Slot > Center Point Arc Slot**, see Figure 2.178. The **Center Point Arc Slot** tool gets activated.

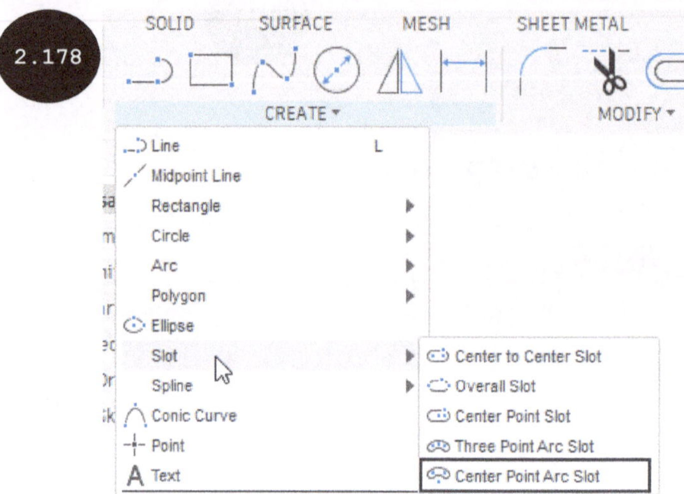

5. Move the cursor to the center point of the previously drawn circle and then click the left mouse button when the cursor snaps to it. The center point of the arc slot is specified.

6. Move the cursor horizontally toward the right and click when the radius appears as 40 mm.

7. Move the cursor clockwise in the drawing area. A preview of the slot center arc appears. Next, click to specify the endpoint of the slot when the angle value appears as 180 degrees.

8. Move the cursor toward the left and click when the width appears as 20 mm, see Figure 2.179. The arc slot is drawn. Next, press ESC to exit the tool. Figure 2.180 shows the final sketch.

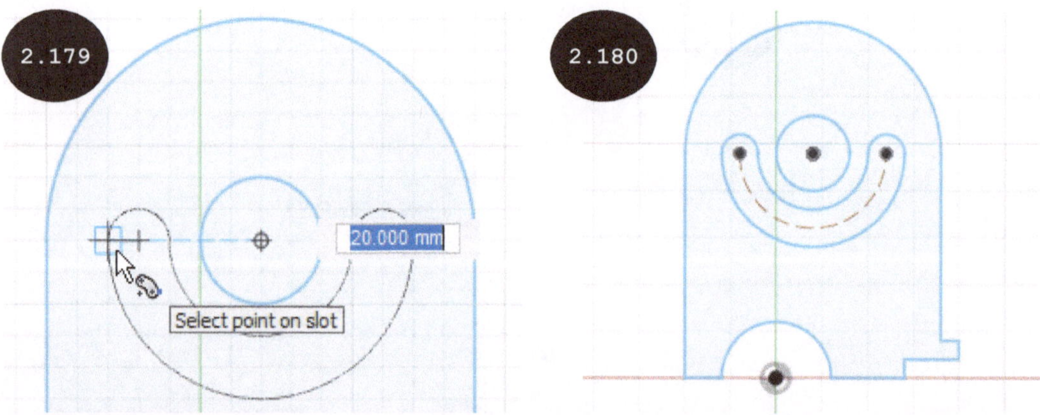

Section 6: Saving the Sketch

1. Click on the **Save** tool in the Application Bar. Next, enter **Tutorial 4** in the **Name** field of the **Save** dialog box that appears.

2. Ensure the location ***Autodesk Fusion 360 > Chapter 02 > Tutorial*** is specified in the **Location** field of the dialog box to save the file of this tutorial. To specify the location, you need to expand the Save dialog box by clicking on the down arrow next to the Location field of the dialog box.

3. Click on the Save button in the dialog box. The sketch is saved with the name Tutorial 4 in the specified location (***Autodesk Fusion 360 > Chapter 02 > Tutorial***).

Hands-on Test Drive 3

Draw a sketch of the model shown in Figure 2.181. The dimensions and the model shown in the figure are for your reference only. All dimensions are in mm.

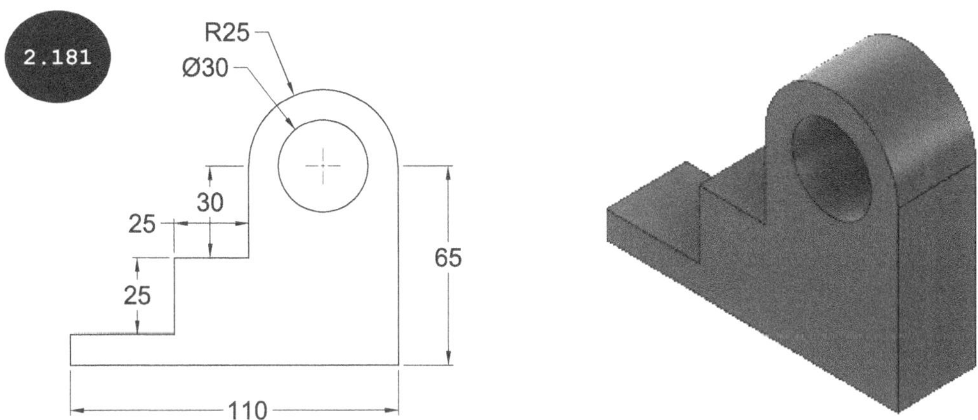

Hands-on Test Drive 4

Draw a sketch of the model shown in Figure 2.182. The dimensions and model shown in the figure are for your reference only. All dimensions are in mm.

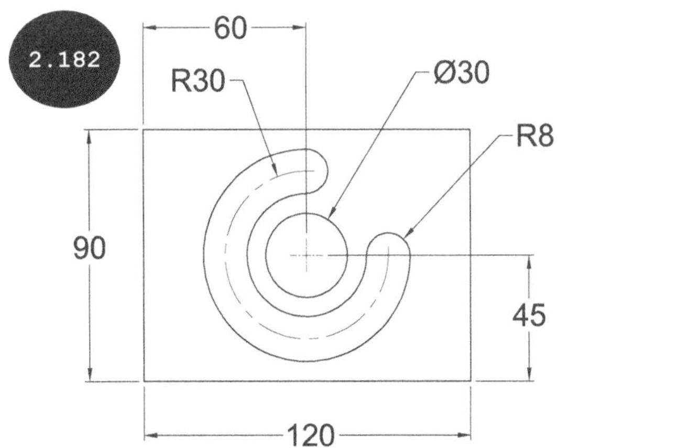

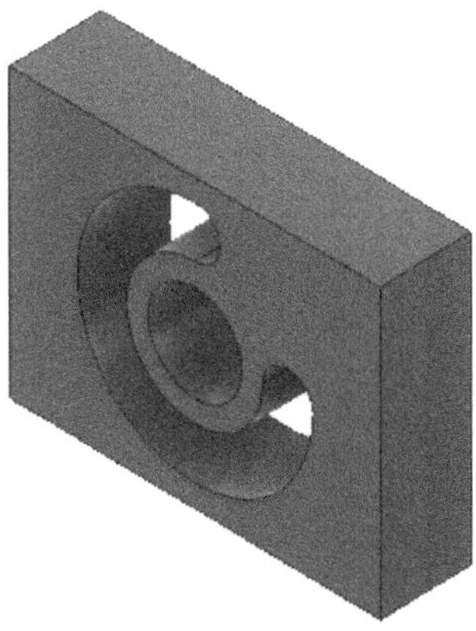

Hands-on Test Drive 5

Draw a sketch of the model shown in Figure 2.183. All dimensions are in mm.

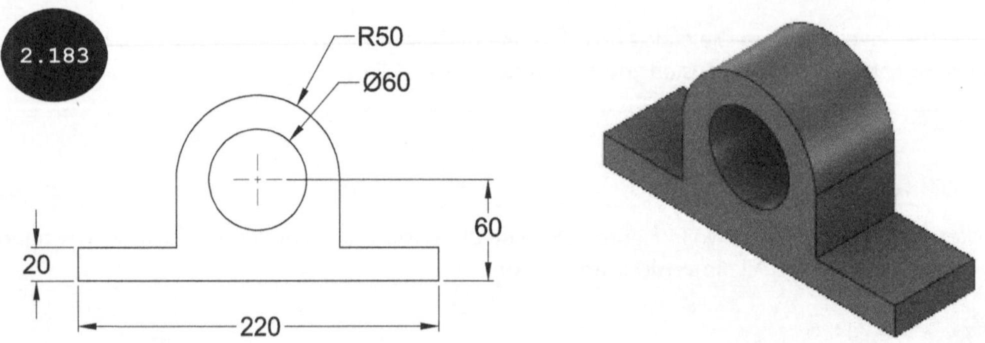

Summary

This chapter discussed how to invoke a new design file in Autodesk Fusion and start creating a sketch by selecting a sketching plane. You explored how to configure the unit system and set up grids and snap settings. The chapter also introduced tools for drawing various shapes, such as lines, rectangles, circles, arcs, polygons, ellipses, slots, conic curves, and splines. Additionally, you learned how to edit splines, create sketch points, and insert text into your sketches. These techniques are essential for building accurate and detailed sketches in your designs.

Questions

Complete and verify the following sentences:

- Features are divided into two main categories: _________ and _________.
- The _________ feature of any real-world component is sketch-based.
- You can turn on or off the display of grids in the drawing area by using the _________ check box of the **SKETCH PALETTE** dialog box.
- To draw an ellipse, you need to define its _________ axis and _________ axis.
- If the Rho value of a conic curve is less than 0.5 then the conic curve is an _______.
- The _______ tool is used for drawing a rectangle by specifying two diagonally opposite corners.
- The _______ tool is used for drawing an arc slot by defining three points on the slot center arc and a point to define the width of the slot.
- You cannot draw a tangent arc by using the **Line** tool. (True/False)
- A fillet feature is known as a placed feature. (True/False)

3

Editing and Modifying Sketches

In this chapter, the following topics will be discussed:

- Trimming Sketch Entities
- Extending Sketch Entities
- Offsetting Sketch Entities
- Creating Construction Entities
- Mirroring Sketch Entities
- Patterning Sketch Entities
- Creating a Sketch Fillet
- Creating a Sketch Chamfer
- Scaling Sketch Entities
- Breaking Sketch Entities

Editing and modifying a sketch is an important step in giving the sketch its desired shape. In Autodesk Fusion, various editing operations such as trimming unwanted sketch entities, extending sketch entities, mirroring, patterning, scaling, moving, and rotating sketch entities, can be performed in a sketch. The various editing operations are discussed next.

Trimming Sketch Entities

You can trim the unwanted sketch entities to their nearest intersection using the **Trim** tool. To do this, click on the **Trim** tool in the **MODIFY** panel of the **SKETCH** contextual tab, see Figure 3.1. Alternatively, to activate the **Trim** tool, invoke the **MODIFY** drop-down menu in the **SKETCH** contextual tab and click on the **Trim** tool, see Figure 3.2. You can also activate the **Trim** tool by pressing the T key.

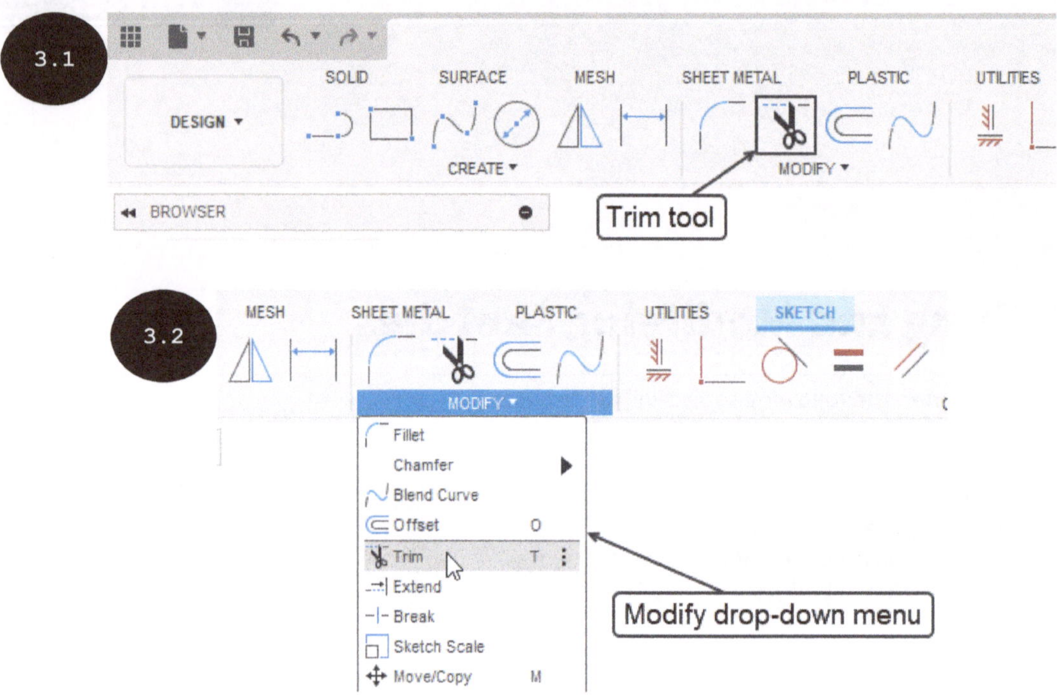

After activating the **Trim** tool, place the cursor over the entity to be trimmed and pause. The portion of the entity highlights up to its nearest intersection in the drawing area, see Figure 3.3. Next, click the left mouse button to trim the highlighted portion of the entity. Figure 3.4 shows the sketch after the entity trimmed.

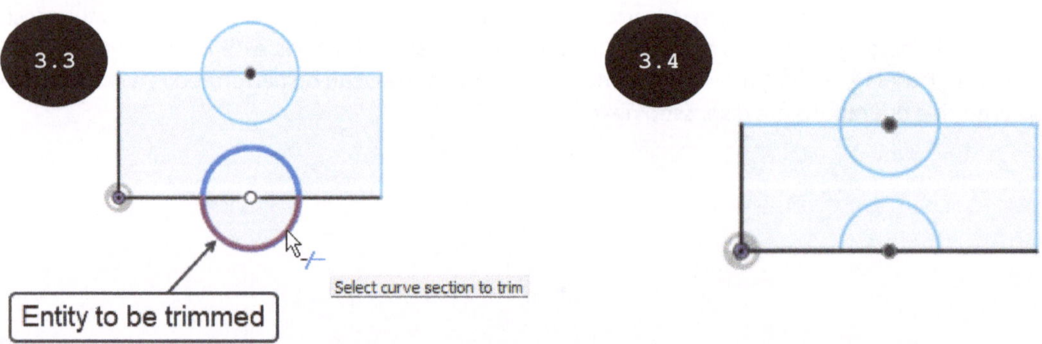

Similarly, you can continue trimming entities up to their next intersection one by one, by clicking the left mouse button multiple times. Figure 3.5 shows the sketch after trimming all the unwanted entities of the sketch shown in Figure 3.3.

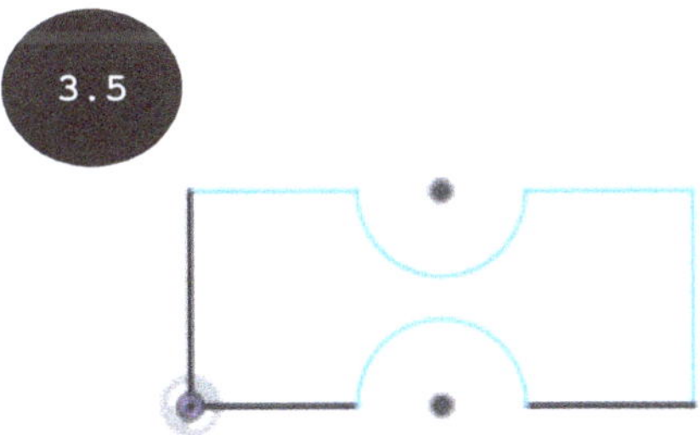

In addition to trimming entities by clicking the left mouse button, you can also drag the cursor over the entities to be trimmed. To do this, after activating the **Trim** tool, press and hold the left mouse button while dragging the cursor over the entities to be trimmed. A square box follows the cursor, and the sketch entities that intersect this box get trimmed to their nearest intersection. Figure 3.6 shows the sketch before trimming the entities, while Figure 3.7 displays the same sketch after trimming the entities that intersect the square box.

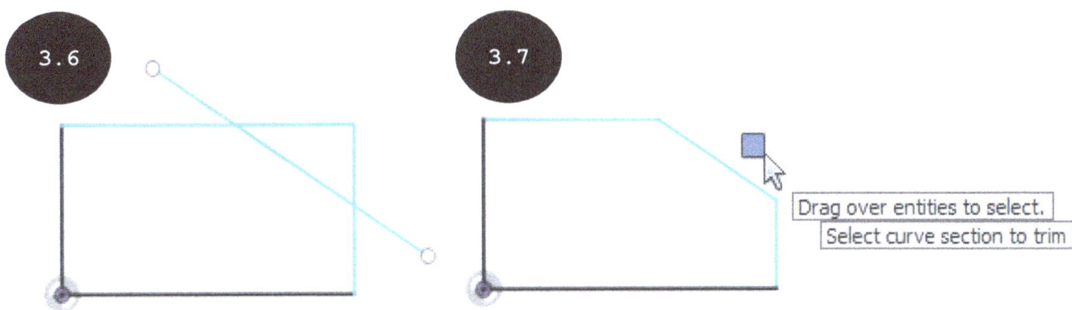

After trimming undesired entities of a sketch, right-click in the drawing area and then click on the **OK** tool in the Marking Menu to exit the **Trim** tool. You can also press the ESC key to exit the tool.

Note: If an intersection is not detected in the entity to be trimmed, then the entity will be deleted from the sketch.

Extending Sketch Entities

You can extend sketch entities up to their nearest intersection using the **Extend** tool. Figure 3.8 shows the entity to be extended, while Figure 3.9 illustrates the resultant sketch after the entity has been extended. The method for extending entities using the **Extend** tool is discussed below:

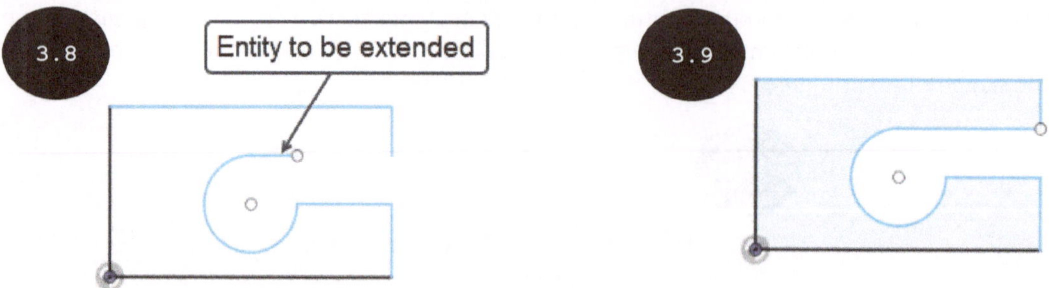

1. Invoke the **MODIFY** drop-down menu in the **SKETCH** contextual tab of the **Toolbar** and then click on the **Extend** tool, see Figure 3.10. The **Extend** tool is activated.

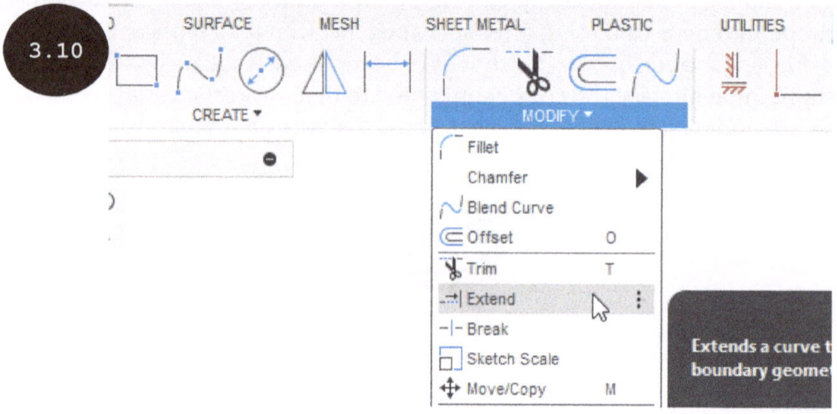

2. Move the cursor over the entity to be extended. The preview of the extended line appears up to its next intersection in the drawing area, see Figure 3.11.

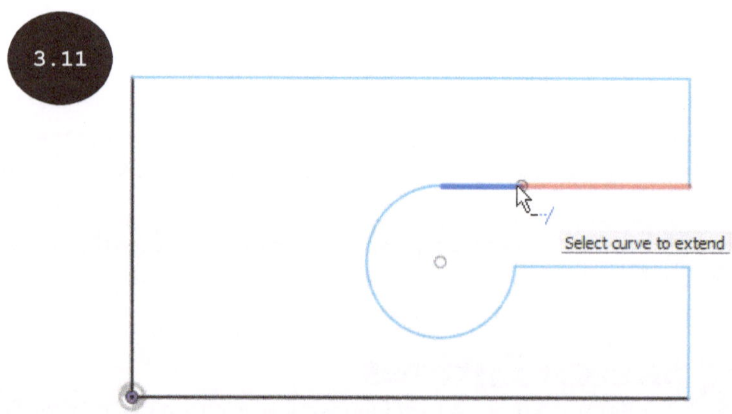

Note: The direction of an extended entity depends upon the position of the cursor over the entity. The endpoint of the entity, which is closer to the position of the cursor will be extended. To change the direction of extension, move the cursor to the other side of the sketch entity.

3. Click on the left mouse button when the preview of the extended line appears. The selected entity is extended up to the next intersection.

4. Similarly, you can extend other sketch entities. Once you have extended all the sketch entities, press the ESC key to exit the **Extend** tool.

Offsetting Sketch Entities

You can offset the entities of a sketch or the edges of a feature at a specified distance using the **Offset** tool. The method for offsetting entities using the **Offset** tool is discussed below:

1. Click on the **Offset** tool in the **MODIFY** panel of the **SKETCH** contextual tab, see Figure 3.12. The **OFFSET** dialog box appears, see Figure 3.13. Alternatively, invoke the **MODIFY** drop-down menu in the **SKETCH** contextual tab and click on the **Offset** tool. You can also press the O key to invoke this tool.

Curves: By default, the **Curves** selection option is activated in the **OFFSET** dialog box. As a result, you can select an entity to offset in the drawing area.

Chain Selection: By default, the **Chain Selection** check box is selected in the **OFFSET** dialog box. As a result, on selecting an entity to offset in the drawing area, all the contiguous entities (closed or open loop) of the selected entity get automatically selected in the drawing area.

2. Select or clear the **Chain Selection** check box in the **OFFSET** dialog box, as required.

3. Click the entity (sketch entity or edge) to offset. Depending on whether the **Chain Selection** check box is selected or cleared, a preview of either a chain of entities or an individual entity appears in the drawing area, refer to Figures 3.14 and 3.15.

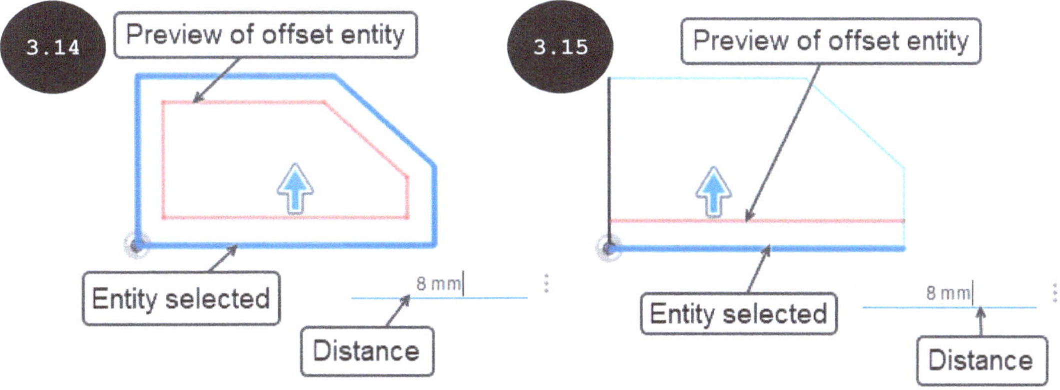

Note: The Figure 3.14 shows the preview of the offset entities when the **Chain Selection** check box is selected, whereas Figure 3.15 shows the preview of the offset entity when the **Chain Selection** check box is cleared.

Distance: On selecting one or more entities to offset, the **Distance** field appears in the **OFFSET** dialog box as well as in the drawing area. In this field, you can enter an offset distance value by which you want to offset the selected entity or entities.

4. Enter the required offset distance value in the **Distance** field that appears. You can also drag the arrow that appear in the drawing area to set the offset distance.

Direction: The options in the **Direction** drop-down list are used to define the direction of the offset entities, see figure 3.16. These options are discussed next.

One Side: The **One Side** option is used to define the direction of the offset on the either side of the selected entity.

Two Sides: The **Two Sides** option is used to offset geometry on both side of the original sketch entity. When this option is selected, the **Distance 1**, and **Distance 2** fields appears in the dialog box. You can enter the required offset values for the entity in the respective distance field with diffrent distance value see figure 3.17.

Symmetric: The **Symmetric** option is used to offset geometry equally on both sides of the original sketch entity.

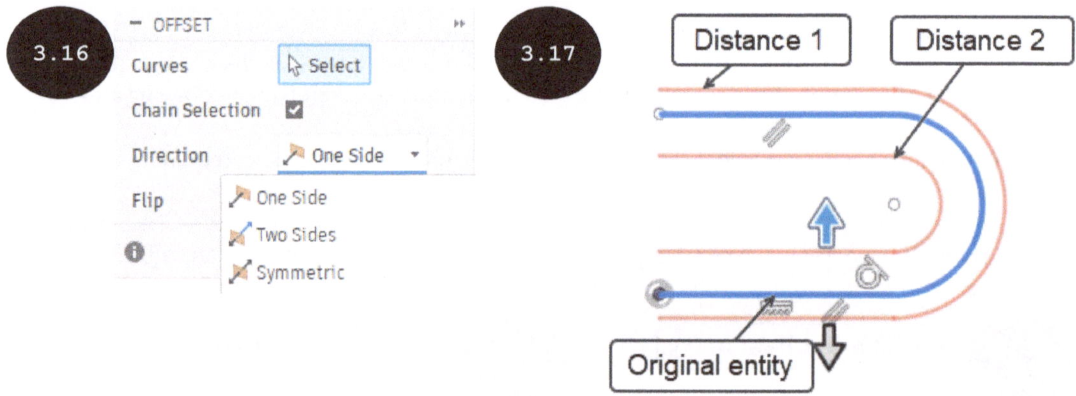

5. Select the required option (**One Side**, **Two Sides**, or **Symmetric**) in the **Direction** drop-down list, as discussed above.

6. Click on the **Flip** button or drag the arrow that appear in the drawing area on the other side of the selected entity to reverse the offset direction, if needed. You can also enter a negative value in the **Distance** field to reverse the offset direction.

7. Click on the **OK** button in the dialog box or press **ENTER**. The offset entities are created.

Note: To edit the parameters of an already created offset, double click on the offset symbol that appears near the offset geometry in the drawing area, see Figure 3.18. The **EDIT OFFSET** dialog box appears. By using this dialog box, you can edit the offset parameters, as required. Note that, if the offset symbol does not appear in the drawing area, then you need to select the **Constraints** check box in the **SKETCH PALETTE** dialog box to turn on the display of constraint symbols.

3.18

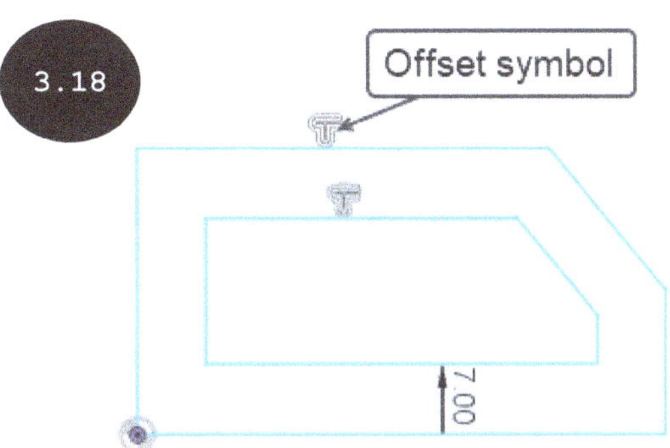

Creating Construction Entities

In Autodesk Fusion, you can activate the construction mode to create construction entities in the drawing area by using the **Construction** tool available in the **Linetype** area of the **SKETCH PALETTE** dialog box, see Figure 3.19. By default, this tool is deactivated in the **SKETCH PALETTE** dialog box. As a result, you can only create solid sketch entities using the sketching tools available in the **CREATE** drop-down menu of the **SKETCH** contextual tab in the **Toolbar**.

3.19

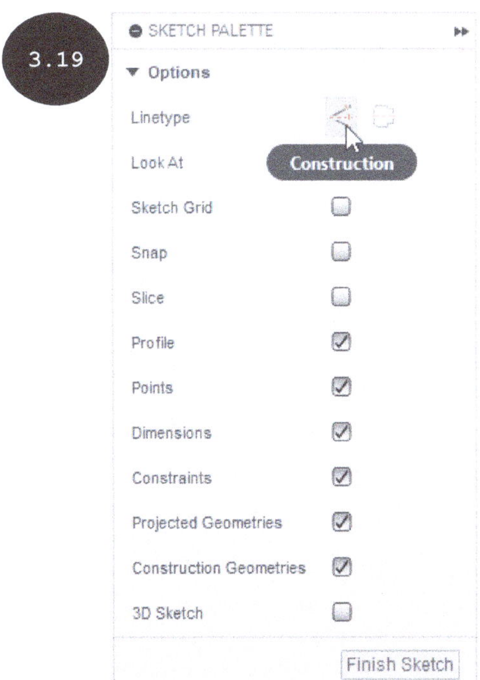

To create construction entities, click on the **Construction** tool in the **Linetype** area of the **SKETCH PALETTE** dialog box. This activates the construction mode. Now, any sketch entities you create in the drawing area by using the sketching tools will act as construction entities and can only be used as references. Figure 3.20 shows a line created with the **Line** tool, while Figure 3.21 displays a circle created with the **Center Diameter Circle** tool after activating the **Construction** tool.

Note: To deactivate the construction mode, click on the **Construction** tool again. It functions as a toggle tool.

You can also convert an existing solid sketch entity into a construction entity or vice versa. To do this, select the entity in the drawing area and then click on the **Construction** tool in the **Linetype** area of the **SKETCH PALETTE** dialog box. The selected solid entity is converted to a construction entity or vice versa.

Mirroring Sketch Entities

You can mirror sketch entities about a mirroring line using the **Mirror** tool CREATE drop-down menu of the SKETCH contextual tab in the **Toolbar**, see Figures 3.22 and 3.23. Figure 3.22 shows the entities to be mirrored along with the mirroring line, while Figure 3.23 shows the resultant sketch after mirroring the entities about the mirroring line. The method for mirroring entities by using the **Mirror** tool is discussed below:

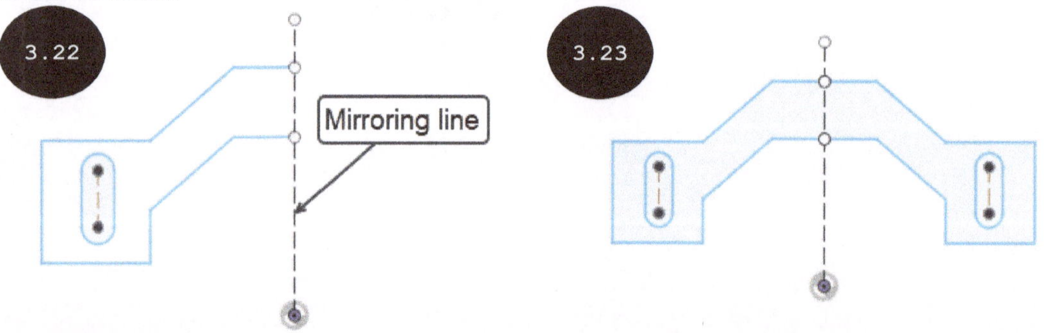

Note: When you mirror entities, a symmetric relation is applied between the original entities and the mirrored entities with respect to the mirroring line. As a result, on modifying the original entities, the mirrored entities get automatically modified and vice-versa. You will learn more about relations in later chapters.

1. Click on the **Mirror** tool in the **CREATE** panel of the **SKETCH** contextual tab of the **Toolbar**. The **MIRROR** dialog box appears, see Figure 3.24. Alternatively, invoke the **CREATE** drop-down menu in the **SKETCH** contextual tab and then click on the **Mirror** tool.

2. Select the entities to be mirrored in the drawing area either by clicking on them one by one with the left mouse button or by drawing a window around the entities you want to mirror.

3. Click on the **Mirror Line** selection option in the **MIRROR** dialog box.

4. Select a mirroring line in the drawing area about which the selected entities are to be mirrored. You can select a centerline, a construction entity, or a regular sketch entity as the mirroring line. The preview of the mirrored entities appears in the drawing area. Note that, if a centerline is present in the drawing area, then it will automatically be selected as a mirroring line on invoking the **MIRROR** dialog box.

5. Click on the **OK** button in the **MIRROR** dialog box. The selectsed entities are mirrored about the mirroring line.

Note: To draw a centerline, activate the **Line** tool in the **CREATE** panel and then activate the **Centerline** tool in the **Linetype** area of the **SKETCH PALETTE** dialog box, see Figure 3.25. Next, draw the centerline by defining two points in the drawing area.

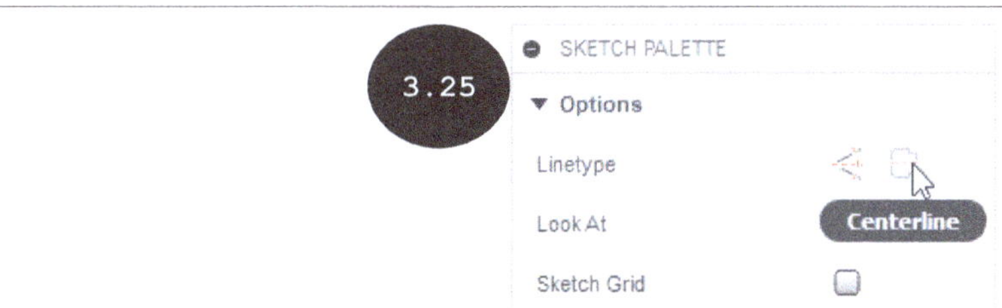

Patterning Sketch Entities

In Autodesk Fusion, you can create rectangular and circular patterns of sketch entities using the **Rectangular Pattern** and **Circular Pattern** tools, respectively. Both tools are discussed next.

Rectangular Pattern Tool

The **Rectangular Pattern** tool is used to create multiple instances of one or more sketch entities in linear directions. To do this, invoke the **CREATE** drop-down menu of the **SKETCH** contextual tab in the **Toolbar** and then click on the **Rectangular Pattern** tool, see Figure 3.26. The **RECTANGULAR PATTERN** dialog box appears, see Figure 3.27. The options in this dialog box are discussed next.

3.26

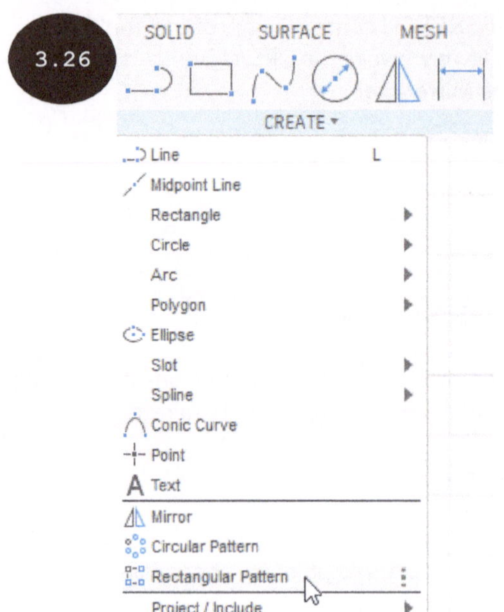

3.27

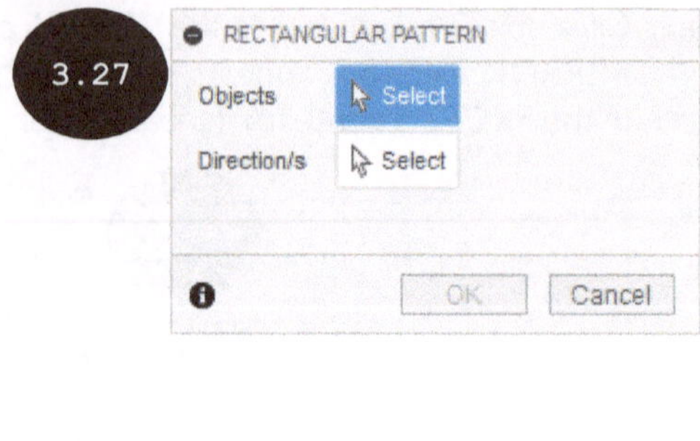

3.28

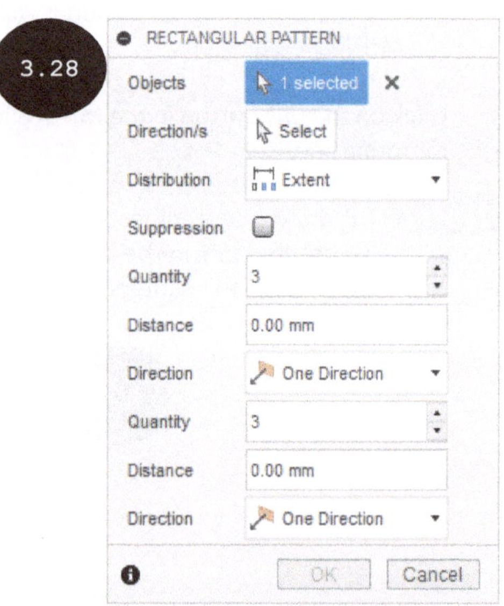

Objects

The **Objects** selection option in the dialog box is used for selecting one or more sketch entities to be patterned. By default, this option is activated, allowing you to select entities one by one by clicking the left mouse button or by drawing a window around them. After selecting an entity to be patterned, the **RECTANGULAR PATTERN** dialog box updates to display additional options for creating a rectangular pattern, see Figure 3.28. These options are discussed next. Note that after selecting an entity to be patterned, the **RECTANGULAR PATTERN** dialog box gets modified and displays additional options for creating a rectangular pattern, see Figure 3.28. These options are discussed next.

Direction/s

The **Direction/s** selection option is used to define the first and second linear directions of the pattern. By default, the selected entities get patterned along the X-axis and Y-axis. However, by activating this selection option, you can select linear edges or sketch entities as the first and second linear directions of the pattern. Figure 3.29 shows the preview of a pattern along the default X-axis direction, while Figure 3.30 shows the preview of a pattern along an inclined sketch entity.

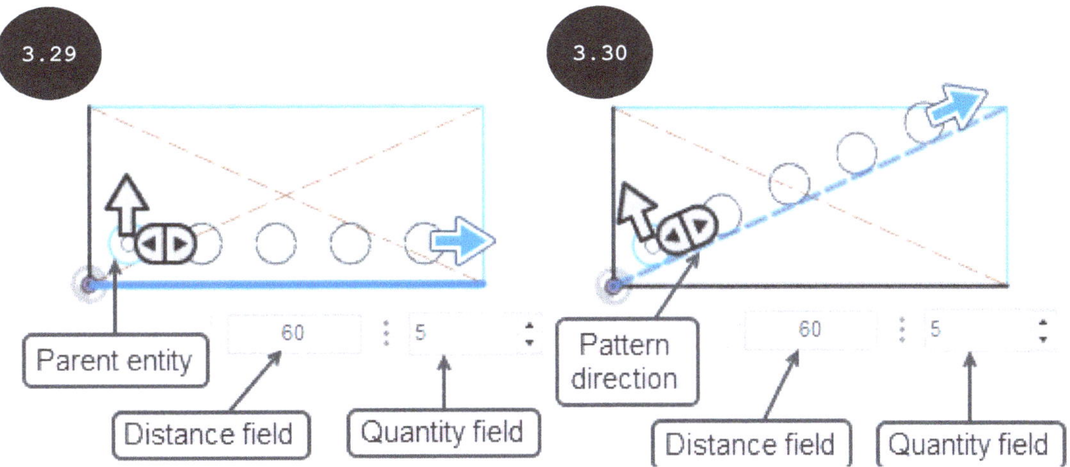

Distribution

The **Distribution** drop-down list is used to specify the type of distance measurement between the pattern instances. By default, the **Extent** option is selected. This means that the distance value specified in the **Distance** field is used as the spacing between the first and last pattern instances (total pattern distance). If you select the **Spacing** option from the **Distribution** drop-down list, the distance value in the **Distance** field will be used as the spacing between two consecutive pattern instances.

Quantity

The **Quantity** fields in **Direction 1** and **Direction 2** areas of the dialog box are used to specify the number of pattern instances to be created in direction 1 and direction 2, respectively, see Figures 3.31 and 3.32. Figure 3.31 shows the **Direction 1** and **Direction 2** areas in the dialog box, while Figure 3.32 shows the preview of a rectangular pattern with 5 instances in direction 1 and 3 instances in direction 2. You can also specify the number of pattern instances in the **Quantity** field that appears in the drawing area, refer to Figure 3.30. Alternatively, you can drag the spinner arrows that appear near the parent entity in the preview of the pattern to increase or decrease the number of pattern instances.

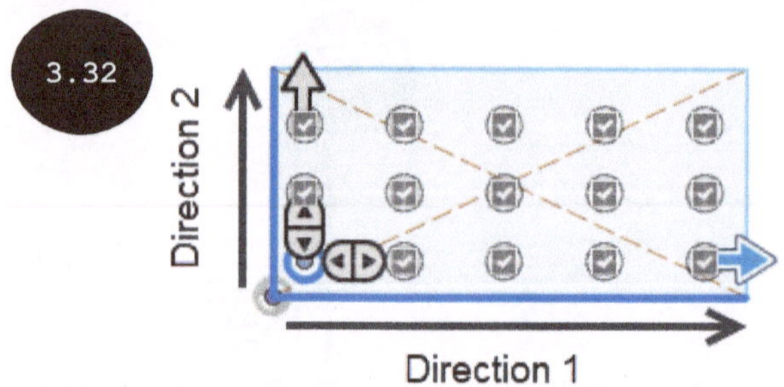

Note: The number of pattern instances specified in the **Quantity** field includes the parent or original instance. For example, if you specify 6 in the **Quantity** field, a total of 6 pattern instances will be created, which includes the parent instance in the respective pattern direction.

Distance

The **Distance** fields in **Direction 1** and **Direction 2** areas of the dialog box are used to specify the spacing between pattern instances in their respective directions. Note that the distance value specified in these fields depends upon the option selected in the **Distribution** drop-down list of the dialog box. You can also specify the spacing between pattern instances in the **Distance** field that appears in the drawing area, refer to Figure 3.30. Alternatively, you can drag the arrow that appears on the last pattern instance in the preview of the pattern to increase or decrease the spacing between the pattern instances. Additionally, to reverse the pattern direction, you can enter a negative distance in the **Distance** field.

Direction

The **Direction** drop-down lists in the **Direction** 1 and **Direction** 2 areas of the dialog box are used to define the pattern direction either on one side or symmetric about the parent entity/entities by selecting the **One Direction** or **Symmetric** option, respectively, see Figures 3.33 and 3.34. Figure 3.33 shows the preview of a rectangular pattern when the **One Direction** option is selected for both direction 1 and direction 2. In contrast, Figure 3.34 shows the preview of a rectangular pattern when the **Symmetric** option is selected for direction 1.

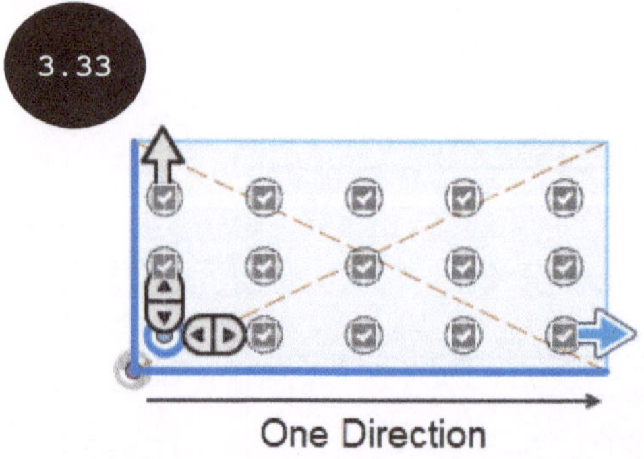

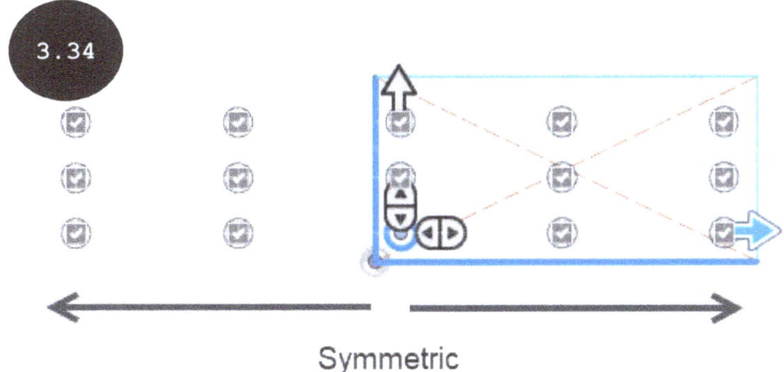

Suppression

On selecting the **Suppression** check box in the **RECTANGULAR PATTERN** dialog box, a check box appears at the center of each pattern instance in the drawing area. You can clear the check boxes of the pattern instances that you want to skip or remove from the resultant pattern. You can do so by clicking the left mouse button on the instance to be removed from the pattern. To recall or include the skipped instances of the pattern, select the respective check boxes that appear in the preview of the pattern.

After defining parameters for patterning the entities in the **RECTANGULAR PATTERN** dialog box, click on the **OK** button. The rectangular pattern is created.

Note: To edit the parameters of an already created rectangular pattern, double-click on the symbol of rectangular pattern that appears near the parent entity in the drawing area, see Figure 3.35. The **EDIT RECTANGULAR PATTERN** dialog box appears. By using this dialog box, you can edit the parameters of the rectangular pattern. Note that, if the symbol of rectangular pattern does not appear in the drawing area, then you need to select the **Constraints** check box in the **SKETCH PALETTE** dialog box to turn on the display of constraints.

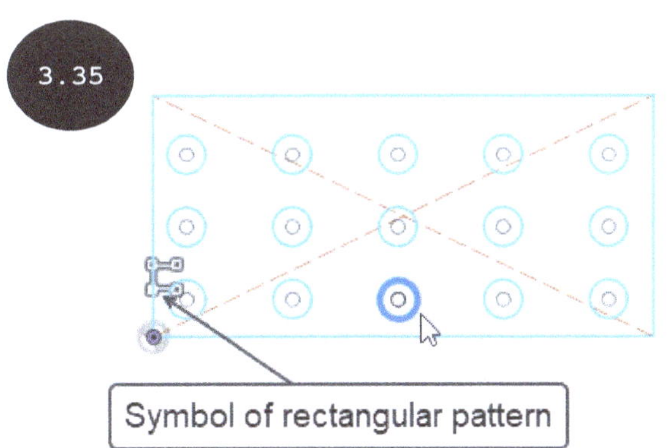

Circular Pattern Tool

The **Circular Pattern** tool is used to create multiple instances of one or more sketch entities in a circular manner about a center point. To do this, invoke the **CREATE** drop-down menu of the **SKETCH** contextual tab in the **Toolbar** and then click on the **Circular Pattern** tool. The **CIRCULAR PATTERN** dialog box appears, see Figure 3.36. The options in this dialog box are discussed next.

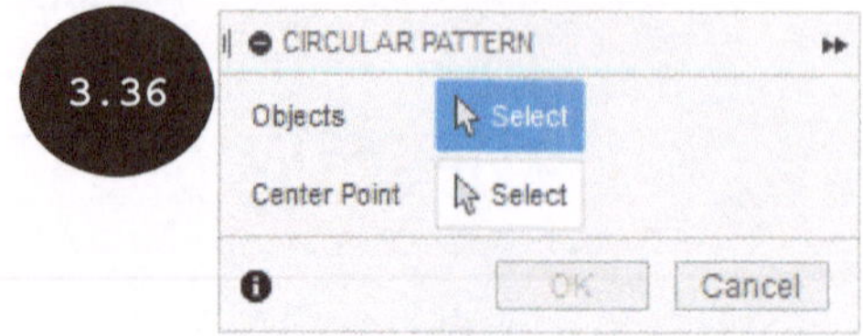

Objects

The **Objects** selection option of the dialog box is used to select the sketch entities to be patterned. By default, this option is activated, allowing you to select entities one by one by clicking the left mouse button or by drawing a window around them. After selecting an entity to be patterned, the **CIRCULAR PATTERN** dialog box updates to display additional options for creating a circular pattern, see Figure 3.37. These options are discussed next.

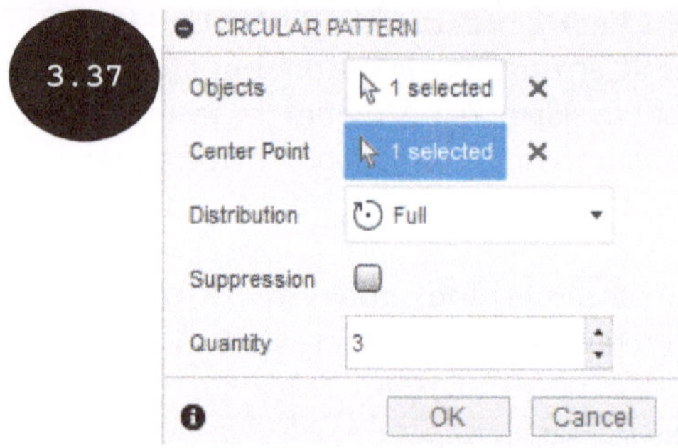

Center Point

The **Center Point** selection option is used for selecting a point as the center point of the circular pattern for circularly patterning the instances about the selected point. To do this, click on the **Center Point** selection option in the dialog box to activate it. Next, click on a point in the drawing area as the center point of the circular pattern. The preview of the circular pattern appears in the drawing area with default parameters, see Figure 3.38.

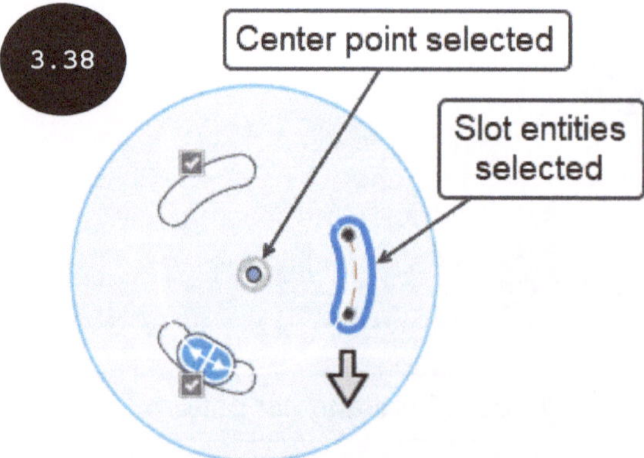

Distribution

By default, the **Full** option is selected in the **Distribution** drop-down list in the dialog box as well as in the drawing area. This setting creates a circular pattern that covers 360 degrees, with the number of pattern instances specified in the **Quantity** field distributed equally across the entire 360 degrees. On selecting the **Angle** option in the **Distribution** drop-down list, the **Total Angle** field appears in the dialog box, see Figure 3.39. In this field, you can specify the total angle value of the pattern, as required. You can also drag the arrow that appears near the last pattern instance to increase or decrease the total angle value. Note that the pattern instances automatically adjust within the specified total angle value.

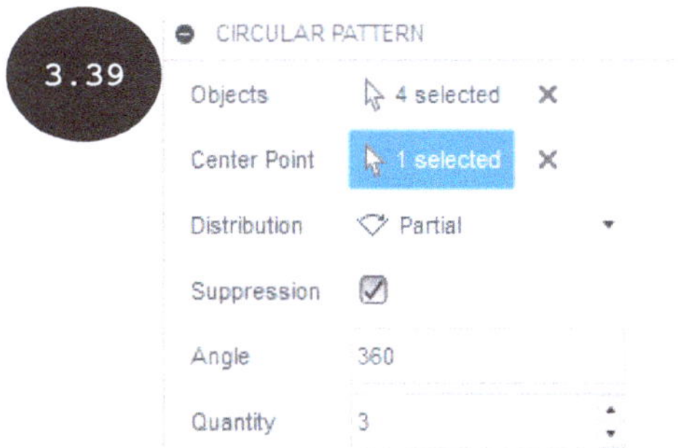

On selecting the **Symmetric** option in the **Distribution** drop-down list, you can create a circular pattern symmetric about the parent entity/entities selected.

Quantity

The **Quantity** field is used to specify the number of pattern instances to be created. You can specify the number of pattern instances in the **Quantity** field in the dialog box or the drawing area. You can also drag the spinner arrows that appear near the parent entity/entities in the preview of the pattern to increase or decrease the number of pattern instances.

Note: The number of pattern instances specified in the **Quantity** field is counted along with the parent or original instance. For example, if 6 is specified in the **Quantity** field, then 6 pattern instances will be created including the parent instance.

Suppression

On selecting the **Suppression** check box in the **CIRCULAR PATTERN** dialog box, a check box appears near each pattern instance in the drawing area. You can clear the check boxes of the pattern instances that you want to skip or remove from the resultant pattern. To recall or include the skipped instances of the pattern, select the check boxes that appear in the preview of the pattern.

After defining parameters for patterning the entities in the **CIRCULAR PATTERN** dialog box, click on the **OK** button. A circular pattern is created.

Note: To edit the parameters of an already created circular pattern, select the symbol of the circular pattern that appears in the drawing area, see Figure 3.40. Next, double-click on the symbol of the circular pattern. The **EDIT CIRCULAR PATTERN** dialog box appears. By using this dialog box, you can edit the parameters of the circular pattern. Note that, if the symbol of circular pattern does not appear in the drawing area, then you need to select the **Constraints** check box in the **SKETCH PALETTE** dialog box to turn on the display of constraints.

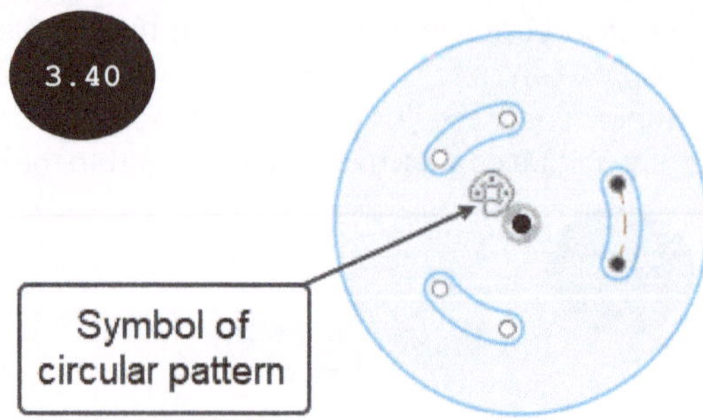

Creating a Sketch Fillet

A sketch fillet is used to remove the corner at the intersection of two sketch entities (lines or arcs) by creating a tangent arc of constant radius, see Figure 3.41. You can create sketch fillets using the **Fillet** tool in the **MODIFY** panel of the **SKETCH** contextual tab. The method for creating a sketch fillet is discussed below:

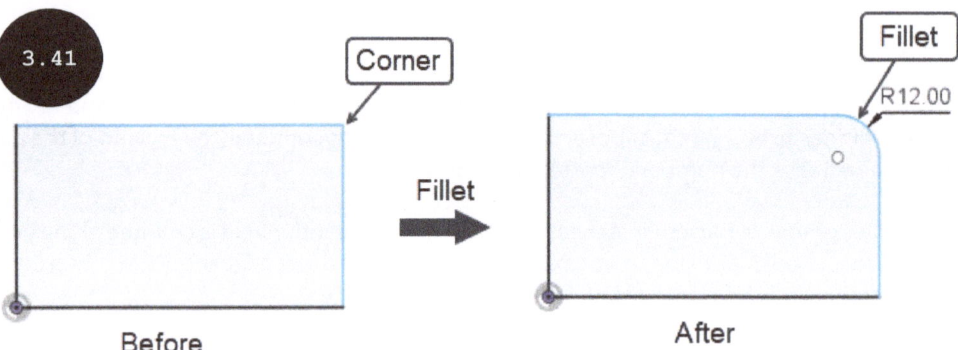

1. Click on the **Fillet** tool in the **MODIFY** panel of the **SKETCH** contextual tab, see Figure 3.42. The **Fillet** tool gets activated. Alternatively, invoke the **MODIFY** drop-down menu in the **SKETCH** contextual tab and then click on the **Fillet** tool.

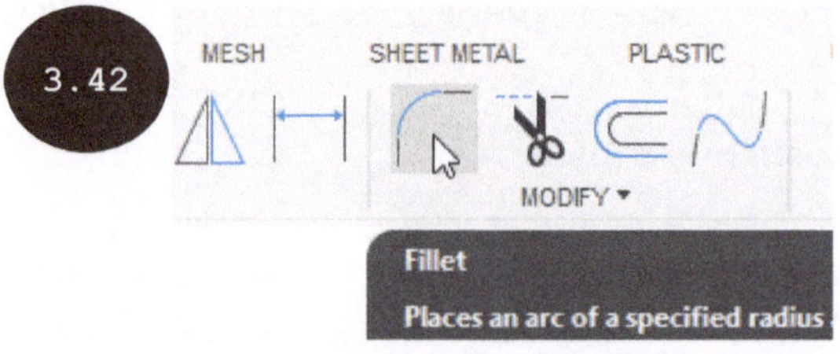

2. Move the cursor over a corner/vertex created by two intersecting lines, arcs, or a line and an arc of the sketch. The preview of the fillet is highlighted in the drawing area. You can also select two intersecting or parallel lines one by one to create a fillet between them.

3. Click on the left mouse button when the preview of the fillet gets highlighted. The **Fillet radius** field appears in the drawing area. Also, a radius manipulator handle appears along with the fillet preview, see Figure 3.43.

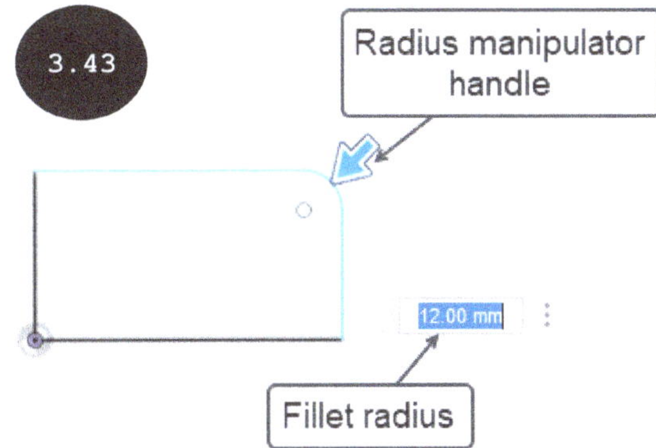

4. Enter the fillet radius in the **Fillet radius** field. You can also drag the radius manipulator handle that appears in the preview to adjust the fillet radius. The preview of the fillet gets modified as per the fillet radius specified.

5. Similarly, click on the other corners of the sketch one by one to create fillets of a specified radius.

6. After creating the fillets, right-click in the drawing area and then click on the OK tool in the Marking Menu that appears.

Creating a Sketch Chamfer

A sketch chamfer is a beveled corner created at the intersection of any two non-parallel line entities, see Figure 3.44. You can create sketch chamfers using the **Equal Distance Chamfer**, **Distance and Angle Chamfer**, and **Two Distance Chamfer** tools in the **MODIFY** panel of the **SKETCH** contextual tab. These tools are discussed next.

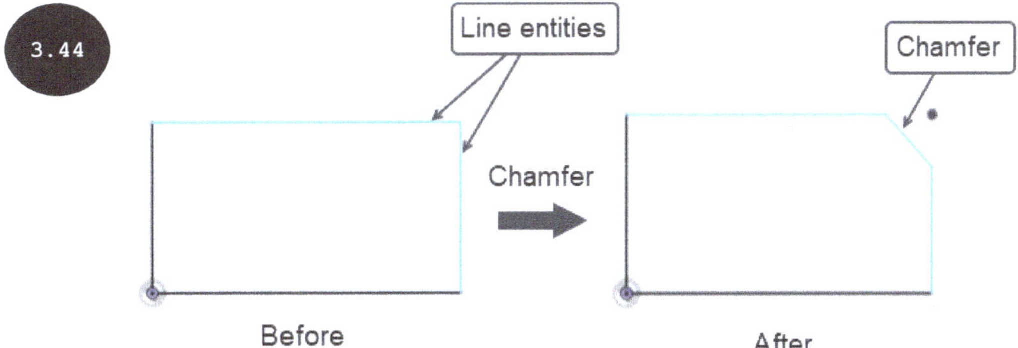

Equal Distance Chamfer

The **Equal Distance Chamfer** tool is used for creating a chamfer at an equal distance from the intersection of both the selected line entities. The method for creating an equal distance sketch chamfer is discussed below:

1. Click on **Chamfer** > **Equal Distance Chamfer** tool in the **MODIFY** drop-down menu of the **SKETCH** contextual tab, see Figure 3.45. The **Equal Distance Chamfer** tool gets activated.

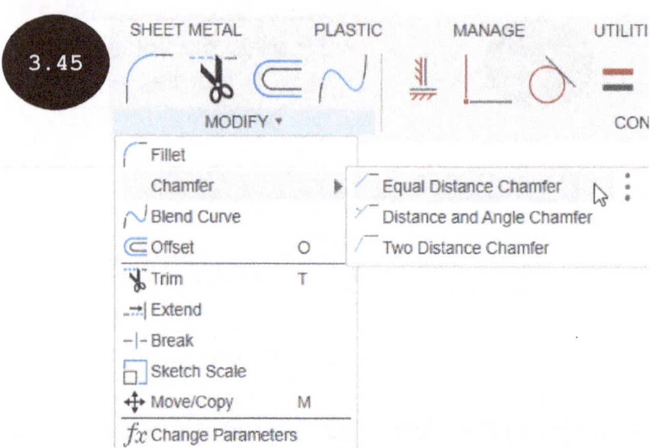

2. Move the cursor over a corner or a vertex created by two intersecting lines of the sketch. The preview of the chamfer is highlighted in the drawing area. You can also select two intersecting or non-parallel lines one by one to create a chamfer between them.

3. Click on the left mouse button when the preview of the chamfer gets highlighted. The **Distance** field appears in the drawing area. Also, a distance manipulator handle appears along with the chamfer preview, see Figure 3.46.

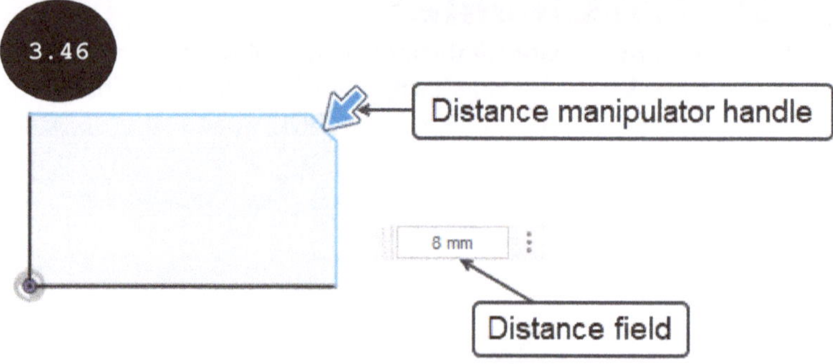

4. Enter the chamfer distance value in the **Distance** field for creating a chamfer at a specified distance from the intersection of both the selected line entities. You can also drag the distance manipulator handle that appears in the preview to adjust the chamfer distance. The preview of the chamfer gets modified as per the distance specified.

5. Similarly, you can click on the other corners of the sketch one by one to create multiple chamfers of specified distance.

6. After creating the chamfer, right-click in the drawing area and then click on the **OK** tool in the Marking Menu that appears. An equal distance chamfer is created, see Figure 3.47.

Distance and Angle Chamfer

The **Distance and Angle Chamfer** tool is used to create a chamfer by specifying an angle from the first selected line entity and a distance from its intersection with the second selected line entity. The method for creating distance and angle sketch chamfer is discussed below:

1. Click on **Chamfer** > **Distance and Angle Chamfer** tool in the **MODIFY** drop-down menu of the **SKETCH** contextual tab. The **Distance and Angle Chamfer** tool gets activated.

2. Select two intersecting or non-parallel lines one by one to create a chamfer between them. You can also select a corner or a vertex of a sketch. The preview of a chamfer along with the **Distance** field appears in the drawing area. Also, a distance manipulator handle and an angle manipulator handle appear along with the chamfer preview, see Figure 3.48.

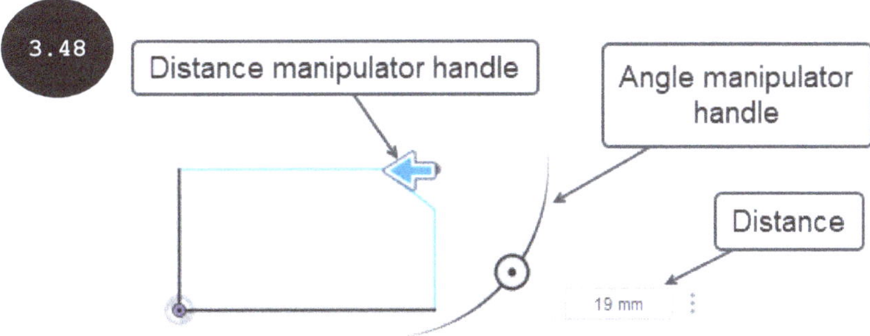

3. Enter the chamfer distance value in the **Distance** field. You can also drag the distance manipulator handle that appears in the preview to adjust the chamfer distance. The preview of the chamfer gets modified as per the distance specified.

4. After defining the chamfer distance, click on the angle manipulator handle to activate it. The **Angle** field appears in the drawing area. Next, enter the angle value in the **Angle** field. You can also drag the angle manipulator handle that appears in the preview to adjust the chamfer angle. The preview of the chamfer gets modified as per the angle value specified.

5. Similarly, you can click on other corners of the sketch one by one to create multiple chamfers of specified angle and distance values.

6. After creating the chamfer, right-click in the drawing area and then click on the **OK** tool in the Marking Menu that appears. A distance and angle chamfer gets created, see Figure 3.49.

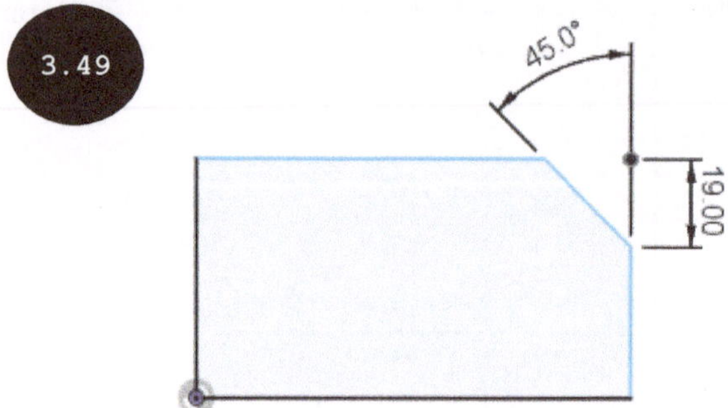

Two Distance Chamfer

The **Two Distance Chamfer** tool is used to create a chamfer by specifying different distance values from the intersection of each selected line entity. The method for creating a two-distance sketch chamfer is discussed below:

1. Click on **Chamfer > Two Distance Chamfer** in the **MODIFY** drop-down menu of the **SKETCH** contextual tab. The **Two Distance Chamfer** tool gets activated.

2. Select two intersecting or non-parallel lines one by one to create a chamfer between them. You can also select a corner or a vertex of a sketch. The preview of a chamfer along with the **Distance 1** field appears in the drawing area. Also, two distance manipulator handles appear along with the chamfer preview, see Figure 3.50.

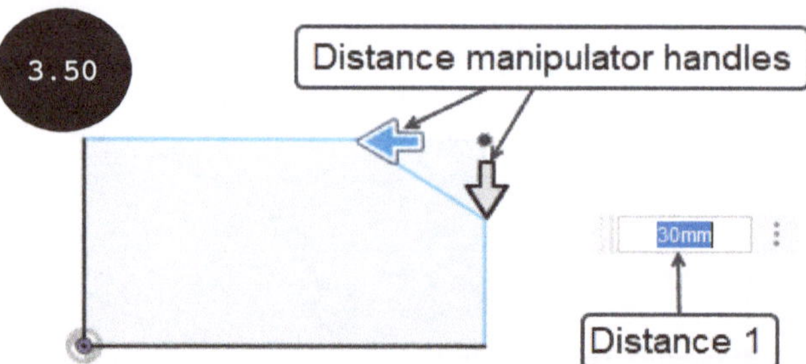

3. Enter the first chamfer distance value in the **Distance 1** field. You can also drag an active distance manipulator handle that appears in the preview to adjust the first chamfer distance. The preview of the chamfer gets modified as per the distance specified.

4. Click on the other distance manipulator handle to activate it. The **Distance 2** field appears in the drawing area. Next, enter the second chamfer distance value in the **Distance 2** field. You can also drag the active distance manipulator handle that appears in the preview to adjust the second chamfer distance. The preview of the chamfer gets modified as per the distance value specified.

5. Similarly, you can click on other corners of the sketch to create multiple chamfers with specified different distance values.

6. After creating the chamfer, right-click in the drawing area and then click on the **OK** tool in the Marking Menu that appears. A chamfer gets created, see Figure 3.51.

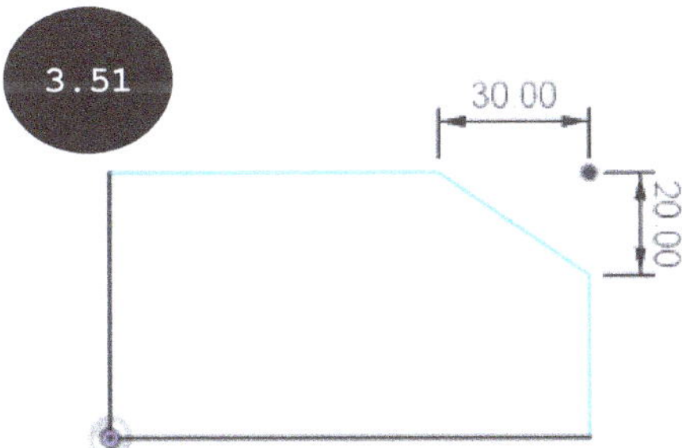

Scaling Sketch Entities

You can increase or decrease the scale of entities using the **Sketch Scale** tool. To do this, invoke the **MODIFY** drop-down menu in the **SKETCH** contextual tab of the **Toolbar** and then click on the **Sketch Scale** tool. The **SKETCH SCALE** dialog box appears, see Figure 3.52. The options in this dialog box are discussed next.

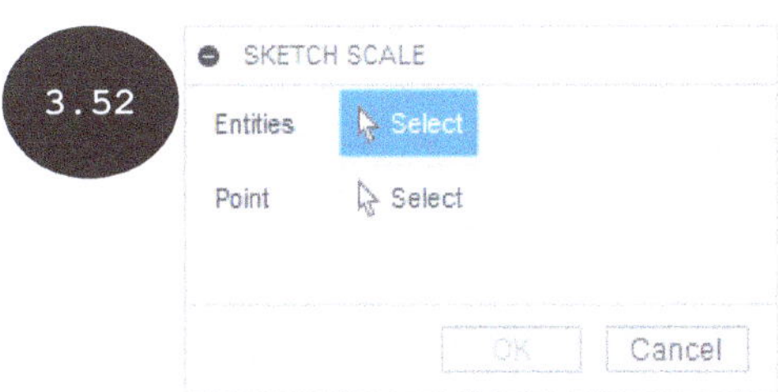

Entities

The **Entities** selection option is used to select the entities to be scaled. By default, this option is activated in the dialog box, allowing you to select entities either one by one by clicking the left mouse button or by drawing a window around the entities. You can choose entities before or after invoking the **SKETCH SCALE** dialog box.

Point

The **Point** selection option is used to select a point as the base point for scaling the selected entities. To do this, click on the **Point** selection option in the dialog box to activate it, and then click on a point in the drawing area. The point is selected and represents the base point for scaling the entities. Note that an arrow appears near the base point in the drawing area, see Figure 3.53. Also, the **Scale Factor** field appears in the drawing area as well as in the dialog box. In Figure 3.53, the origin is selected as the base point for scaling the selected entities.

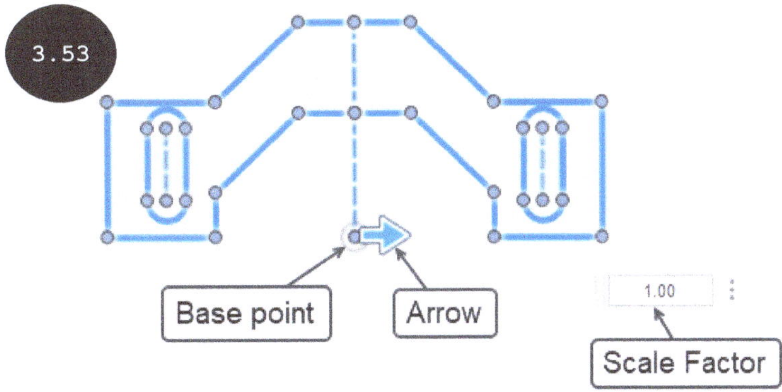

Next, enter the scale factor in the **Scale Factor** field. The preview of the scaled sketch entities as per the specified scale factor appears, see Figure 3.54. Note that to enlarge the sketch entities, you need to specify a scale factor greater than 1, whereas, to shrink the entities, you need to specify a scale factor lesser than 1. You can also drag the arrow that appears in the drawing area to adjust the scale factor. In Figure 3.54, the scale factor is specified as 0.5. As a result, a shrunk image of the selected entities appears in the preview. Next, click on the **OK** button in the dialog box. The selected entities are scaled.

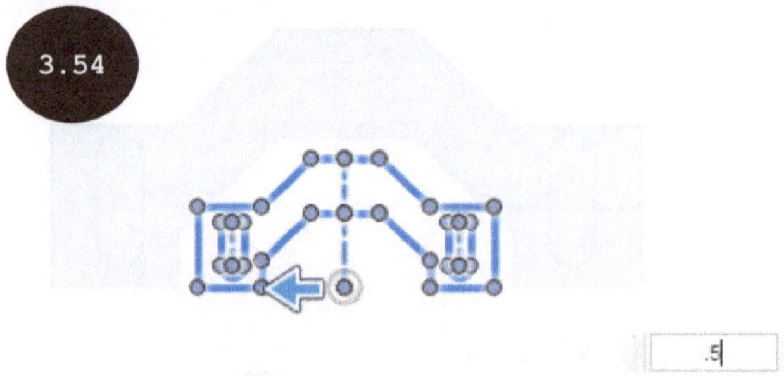

Breaking Sketch Entities

In Autodesk Fusion, you can break a sketch entity into two or more segments at its intersection with other entities by using the **Break** tool of the **MODIFY** drop-down menu. The method for breaking a sketch entity into multiple segments is discussed below:

1. Invoke the **MODIFY** drop-down menu in the **SKETCH** contextual tab of the **Toolbar** and then click on the **Break** tool, see Figure 3.55.

2. Move the cursor over the entity to be broken and then pause the cursor over it. The nearest intersection points of the selected entity are highlighted in the drawing area, see Figure 3.56. Note that if the entity does not have any intersection with other entities, then it cannot be broken.

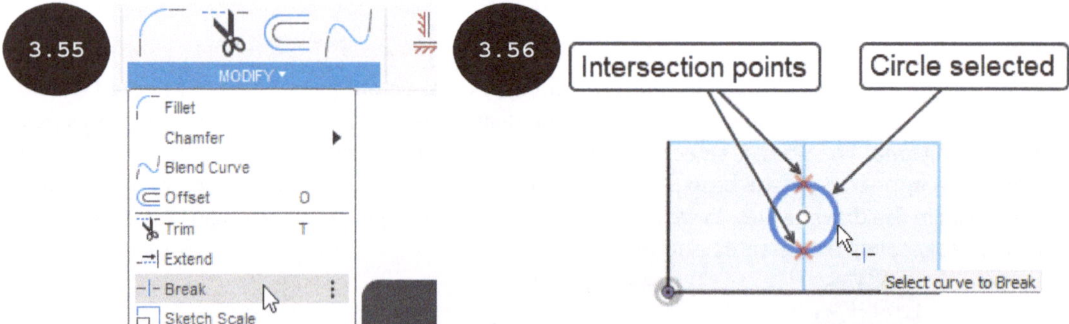

3. Click the left mouse button when the intersection points get highlighted in the drawing area. The selected entity is broken into two segments at its nearest intersection points.

4. Similarly, you can continue breaking the sketch entities at their nearest intersection by clicking the left mouse button.

5. Right-click in the drawing area and then click on the **OK** tool in the Marking Menu that appears to exit the **Break** tool.

Tutorial 1

Draw the sketch of the model, as shown in Figure 3.57. The dimensions and the model shown in this figure are for your reference only. You will learn about applying dimensions and creating 3D models in later chapters.

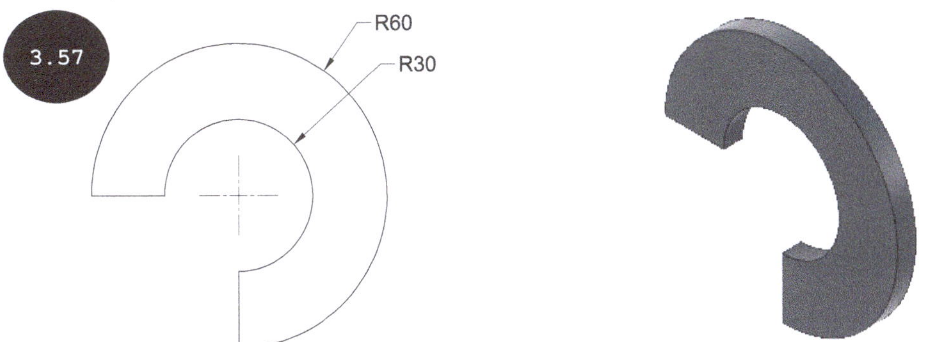

Section 1: Starting a New Part Design File

1. Click **File** > **New** in the **Application Bar** (see Figure 3.58) to display the **What do you want to design?** dialog box, see Figure 3.59.

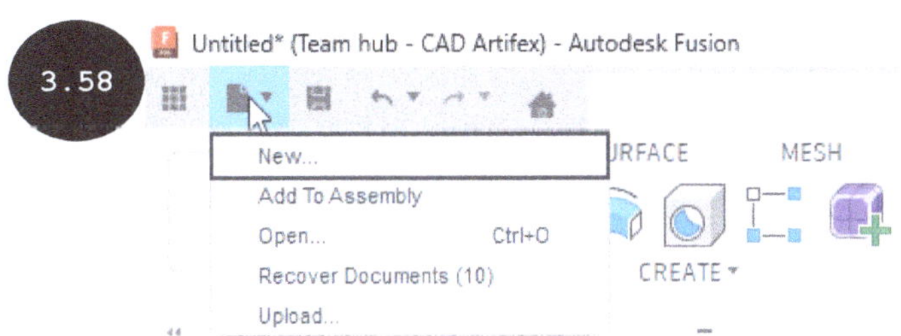

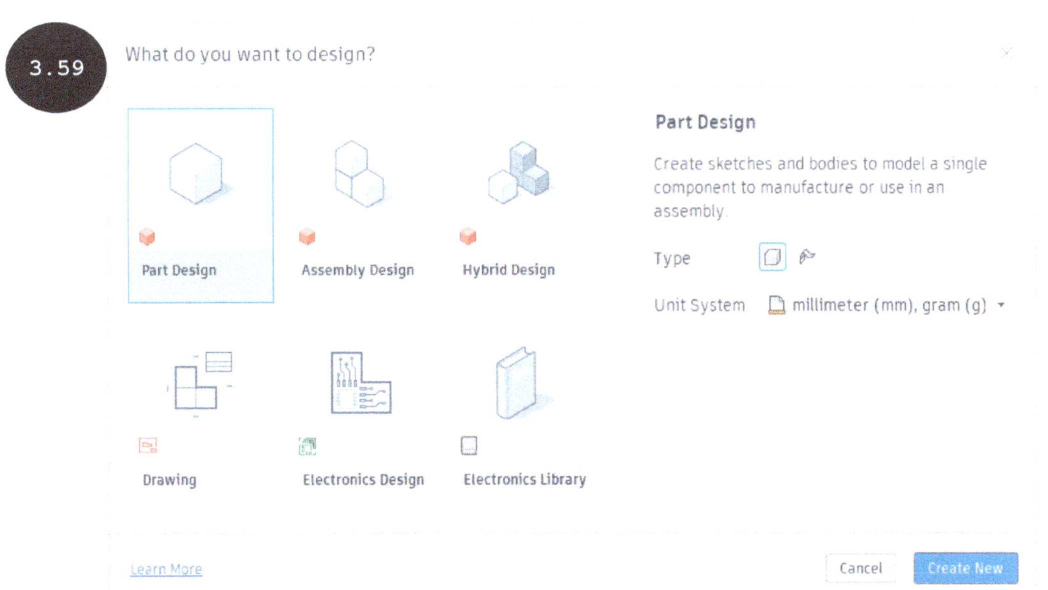

Note: If you are starting a new Autodesk Fusion session, the Part Design file opens automatically because it is set as the default design type. In this case, ensure that the **millimeter (mm), gram (g)** unit system is set for the opened Part Design file.

2. In the **What do you want to design?** dialog box, select the **Part Design** button and choose the **millimeter (mm), gram (g)** unit system from the **Unit System** drop-down list.

3. After specifying the required options, click the **Create New** button. A new Part Design file is created with the default name "**Untitled**", refer to Figure 3.60.

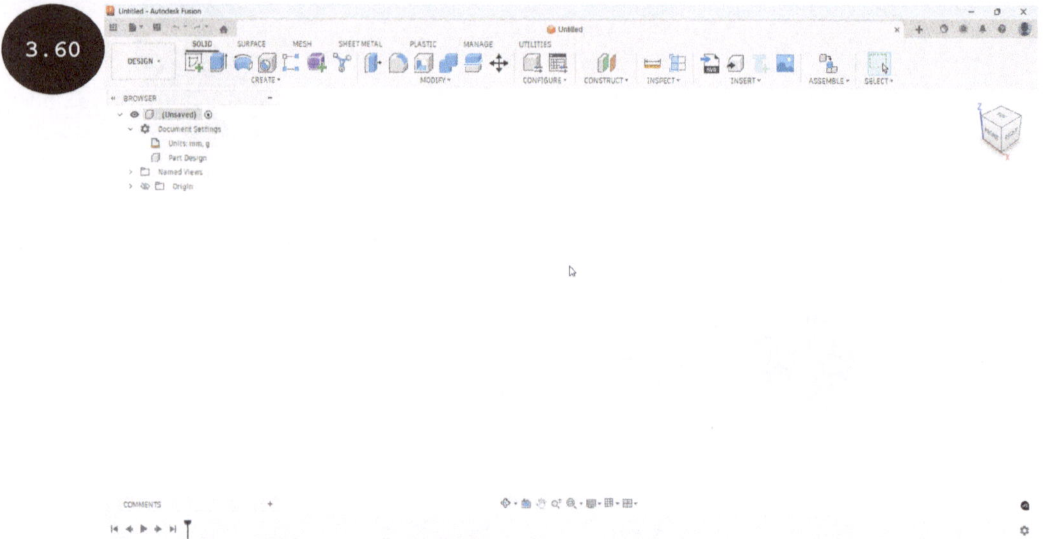

3.60

Section 2: Organizing the Data Panel

Now, you can organize the **Data Panel** by creating a project folder and sub-folders to save your design files.

1. Click on the **Show Data Panel** tool in the **Application Bar**, see Figure 3.61. The **Data Panel** appears, see Figure 3.62.

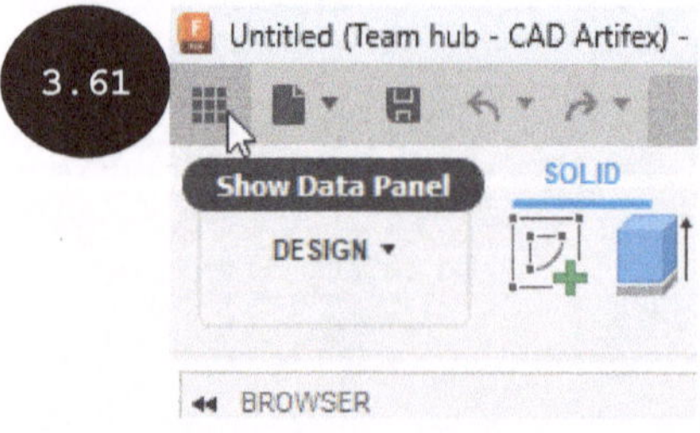

3.61

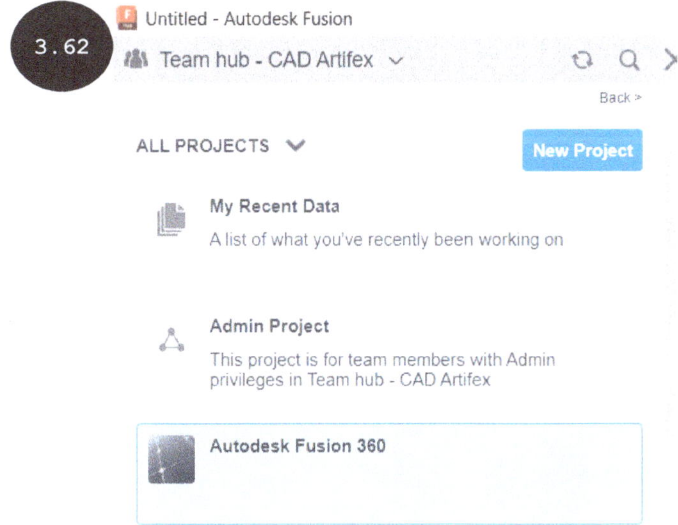

2. Create a new project named "**Autodesk Fusion 360**" using the **New Project** tool if it has not been created earlier.

3. Double-click on the **Autodesk Fusion 360** project in the **Data Panel** then create the "**Chapter 03**" folder using the **New Folder** tool in the **Data Panel**.

4. Double-click on the **Chapter 03** folder in the **Data Panel,** and then create the "**Tutorial**" sub-folder using the **New Folder** tool of the **Data Panel**.

5. Click on the cross-mark ✕ at the top right corner of the **Data Panel** to close it.

Section 3: Specifying Grid Settings

1. Invoke the **Grid and Snaps** flyout in the **Navigation Bar**, see Figure3.63.

2. Click on the **Grid Settings** tool in the **Grid and Snaps** flyout. The **GRID SETTINGS** dialog box appears, see Figure 3.64.

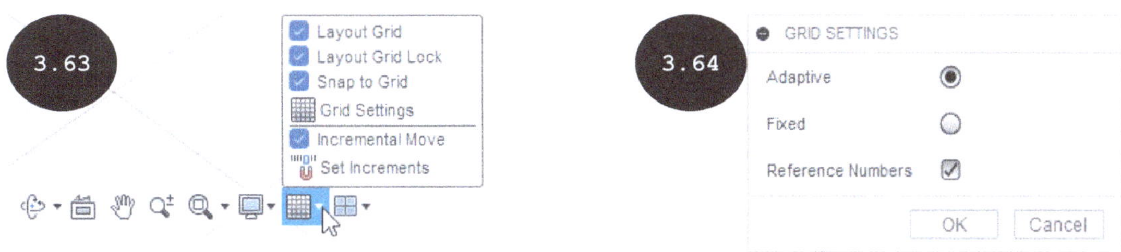

3. Ensure that the **Adaptive** radio button is selected in the **GRID SETTINGS** dialog box to adjust the grid size automatically as you zoom into or out of the drawing view.

4. Click on the **OK** button in the **GRID SETTINGS** dialog box.

Section 4: Creating the Sketch

1. Click on the **Create Sketch** tool in the **Toolbar**, see Figure 3.65. Three default planes: Front, Top, and Right, which are mutually perpendicular to each other appear in the graphics area, see Figure 3.66.

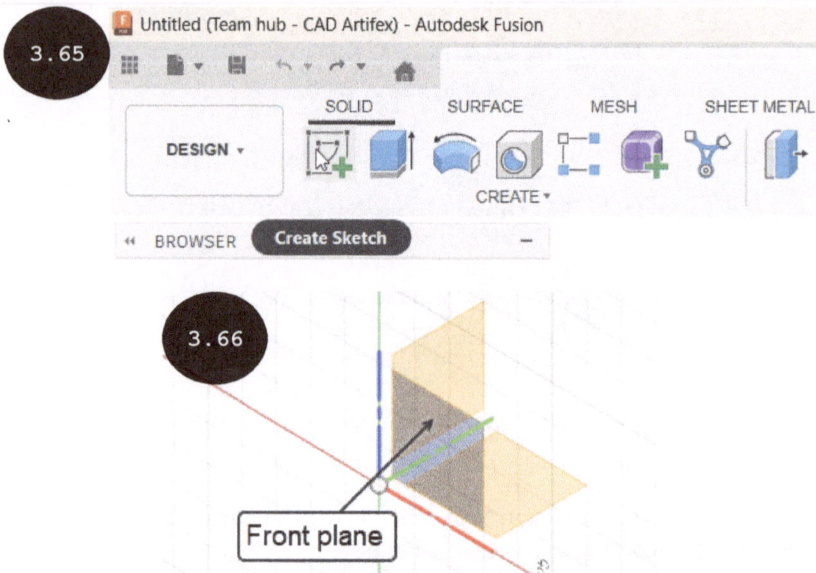

2. Move the cursor over the Front plane and then click on the left mouse button when it gets highlighted in the graphics area. The Front plane becomes the sketching plane for creating the sketch and it is oriented normal to the viewing direction. Also, the **SKETCH** contextual tab and the **SKETCH PALETTE** dialog box appear.

3. Ensure that the **Sketch Grid** and **Snap** check boxes are selected in the **SKETCH PALETTE** dialog box to display the grids and to snap the movement of the cursor on the grid lines.

   Now, you can create the entities of the sketch.

4. Click on the **Center Diameter Circle** tool of the **CREATE** panel in the **SKETCH** contextual tab, see Figure 3.67. The **Center Diameter Circle** tool gets activated. Alternatively, press the **C** key to activate the **Center Diameter Circle** tool.

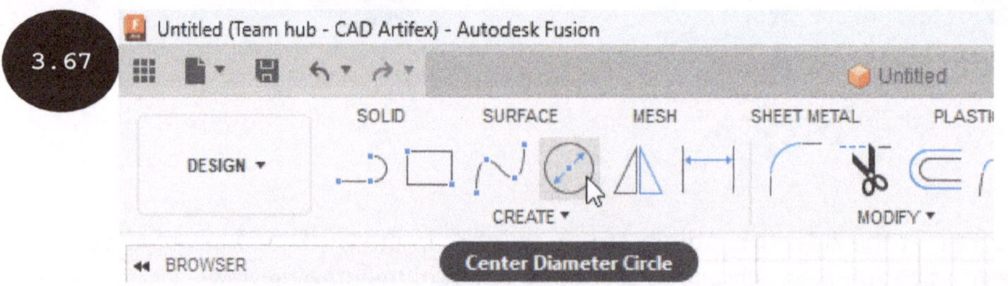

5. Move the cursor to the origin and then click to specify the center point of the circle when the cursor snaps to the origin.

6. Move the cursor horizontally toward the right and then click to specify a point when the diameter of the circle appears 120 mm in the dimension box, see Figure 3.68. A circle of diameter 120 mm is drawn, and the **Center Diameter Circle** tool is still active.

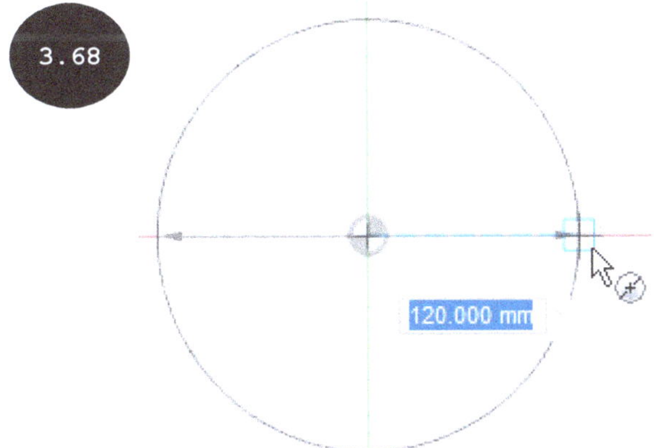

Note: You may need to zoom into or out of the drawing view to adjust the grid size so that the cursor snaps at the required distance measurement.

7. Move the cursor to the origin and then click to specify the center point of another circle when the cursor snaps to the origin.

8. Move the cursor horizontally to the right and click when the diameter of the circle appears as 60 mm, see Figure 3.69. A circle diameter of 60 mm is drawn.

9. Right-click in the drawing area and then click on the **OK** tool in the Marking Menu that appears to exit the **Center Diameter Circle** tool, see Figure 3.70.

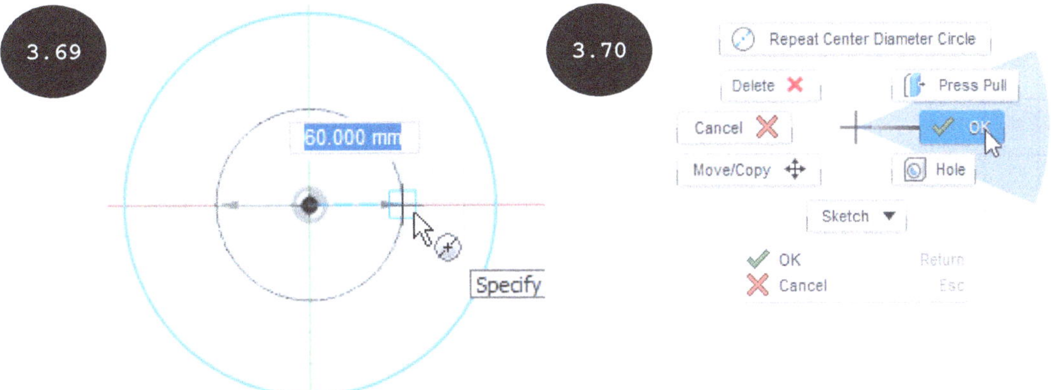

10. Click on the **Line** tool in the **Toolbar** or press the **L** key. The **Line** tool gets activated.

11. Specify the start point of the line at the origin and then move the cursor horizontally toward the left.

12. Click to specify the endpoint of the line when the length of the line appears as 60 mm and the cursor snaps to the outer circle, see Figure 3.71. A line is created, and the **Line** tool is still active.

13. Move the cursor to the origin and click to specify the start point of the other line when the cursor snaps to the origin.

14. Move the cursor vertically downward and click to specify the endpoint of the line when the length of the line appears as 60 mm and the cursor snaps to the outer circle, see Figure 3.72.

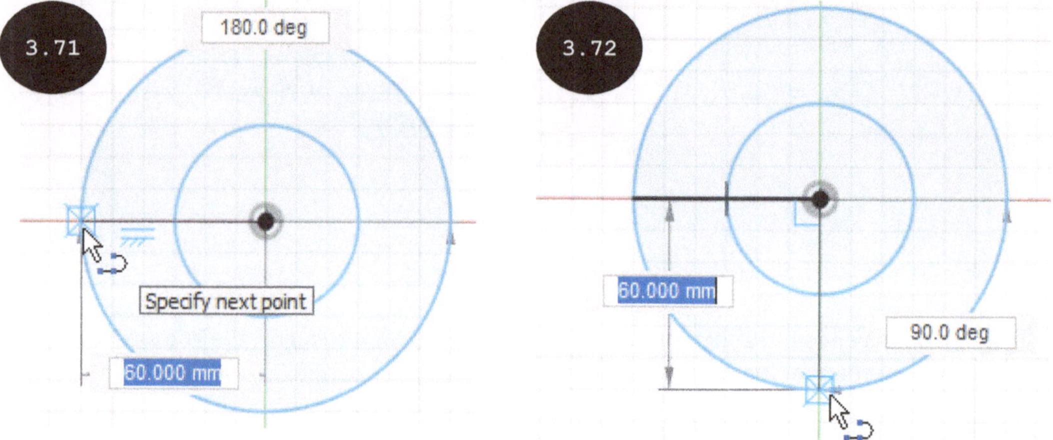

15. Right-click in the drawing area and then click on the **OK** tool in the Marking Menu that appears to exit the **Line** tool.

Section 5: Trimming Sketch Entities

1. Click on the **Trim** tool in the **MODIFY** panel of the **SKETCH** contextual tab. Alternatively, press the **T** key to activate the **Trim** tool.

2. Move the cursor over the lower left portion of the outer circle, see Figure 3.73 and then click the left mouse button when it is highlighted in the drawing area. The selected portion of the outer circle is trimmed, see Figure 3.74.

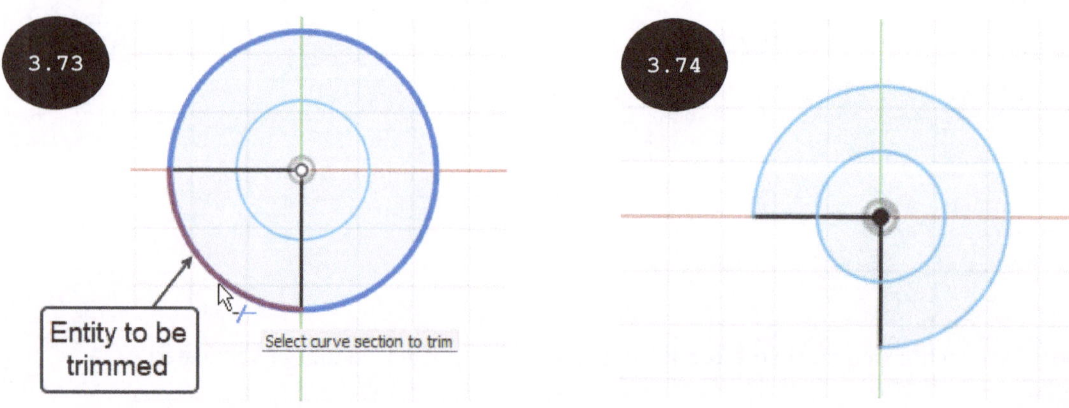

3. Similarly, trim the other unwanted portions of the sketch entities by clicking the left mouse button. Figure 3.75 shows the entities to be trimmed and Figure 3.76 shows the sketch after trimming all the unwanted entities.

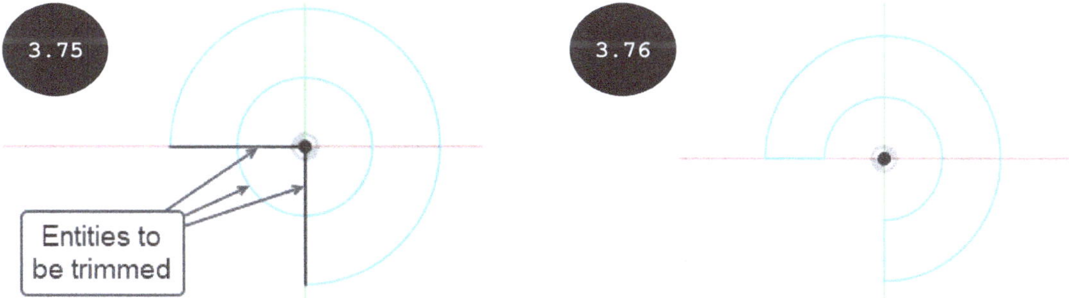

4. Right-click in the drawing area and then click on the **OK** tool in the Marking Menu that appears to exit the **Trim** tool.

Section 6: Saving the Sketch

1. Click on the **Save** tool in the **Application Bar**. The **Save** dialog box appears.

2. Enter **Tutorial 1** in the **Name** field of the dialog box.

3. Ensure that the location ***Autodesk Fusion 360 > Chapter 03 > Tutorial*** is specified in the **Location** field of the dialog box to save the file of this tutorial. To specify the location, you need to expand the **Save** dialog box by clicking on the down arrow next to the **Location** field of the dialog box.

4. Click on the **Save** button in the dialog box. The sketch is saved with the name Tutorial 1 in the specified location (***Autodesk Fusion 360 > Chapter 03 > Tutorial***).

Tutorial 2

Draw the sketch of the model shown in Figure 3.77. The dimensions and the model shown in the figure are for your reference only. You will learn about applying dimensions and creating a model in later chapters.

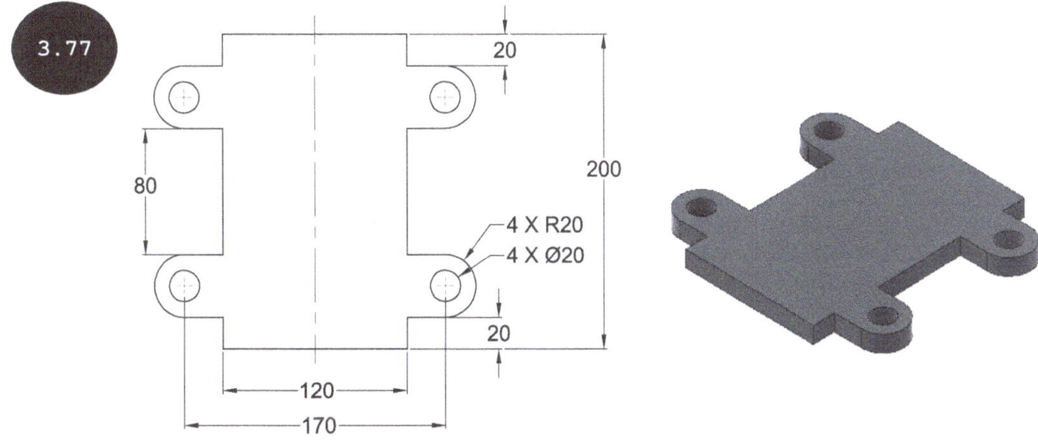

Section 1: Starting a New Part Design File

1. Click **File** > **New** in the **Application Bar** (see Figure 3.78) to display the **What do you want to design?** dialog box, see Figure 3.79.

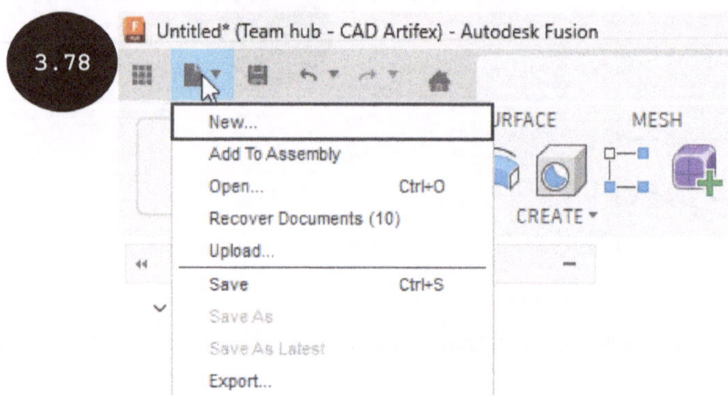

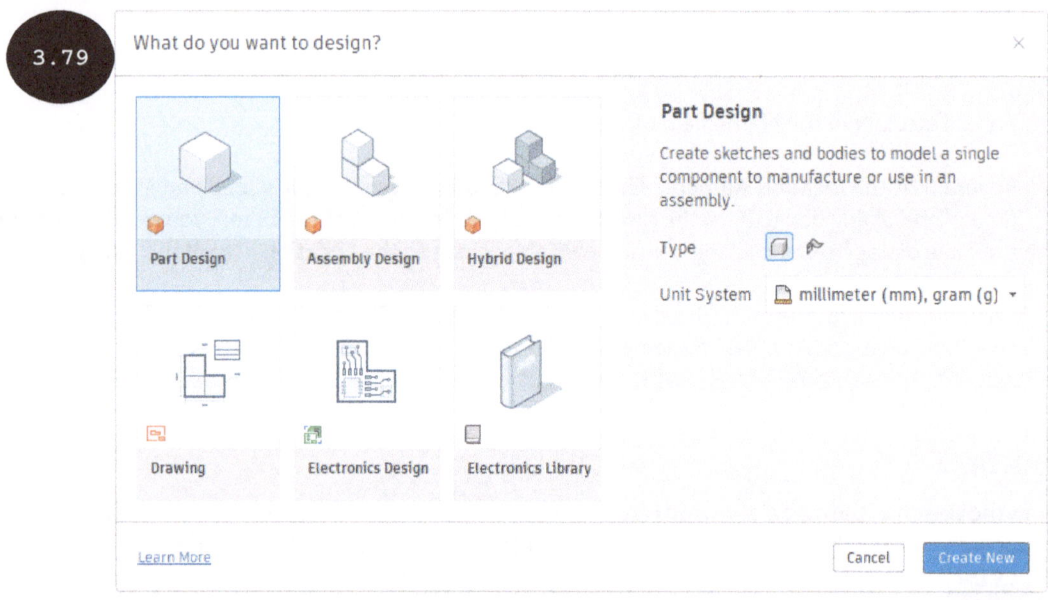

Note: If you are starting a new Autodesk Fusion session, the Part Design file opens automatically because it is set as the default design type. In this case, ensure that the **millimeter (mm), gram (g)** unit system is set for the opened Part Design file.

2. In the **What do you want to design?** dialog box, select the **Part Design** button and choose the **millimeter (mm), gram (g)** unit system from the **Unit System** drop-down list.

3. After specifying the required options, click the **Create New** button. A new Part Design file is created with the default name "**Untitled**", refer to Figure 3.80.

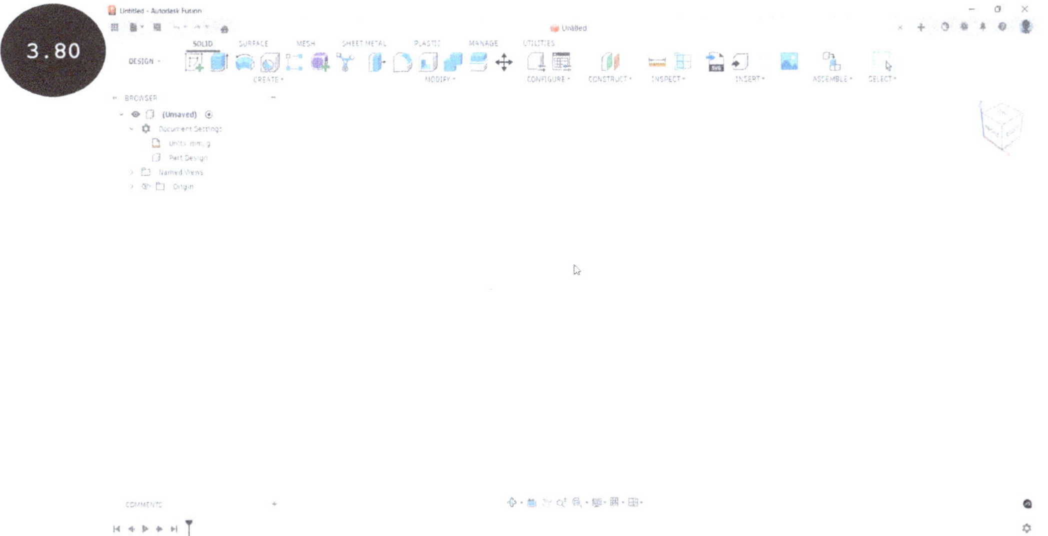

Section 2: Organizing the Data Panel

Now, you can organize the **Data Panel** by creating a project folder and sub-folders to save your design files.

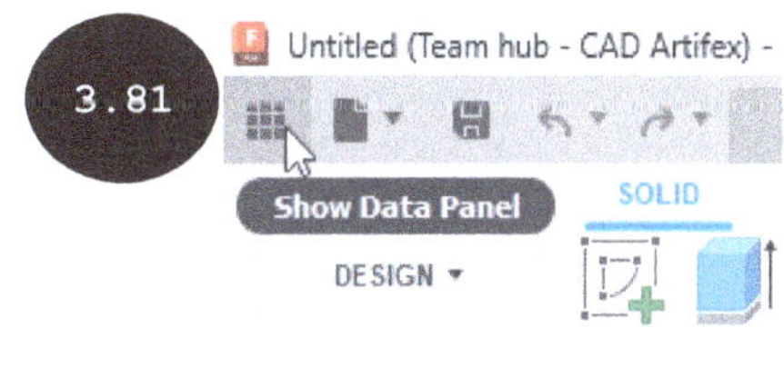

1. Click on the **Show Data Panel** tool in the **Application Bar**, see Figure 3.81. The **Data Panel** appears.

2. Ensure that the **Autodesk Fusion 360 > Chapter 03 > Tutorial** folders are created in the **Data Panel**. You need to create these project folders, if not created earlier.

3. Click on the cross-mark ✕ at the top right corner of the **Data Panel** to close it.

   Now, you need to specify the grid settings.

Section 3: Specifying Grid Settings

1. Invoke the **Grid and Snaps** flyout in the **Navigation Bar**, see Figure 3.82.

2. Click on the **Grid Settings** tool in the **Grid and Snaps** flyout. The **GRID SETTINGS** dialog box appears, see Figure 3.83.

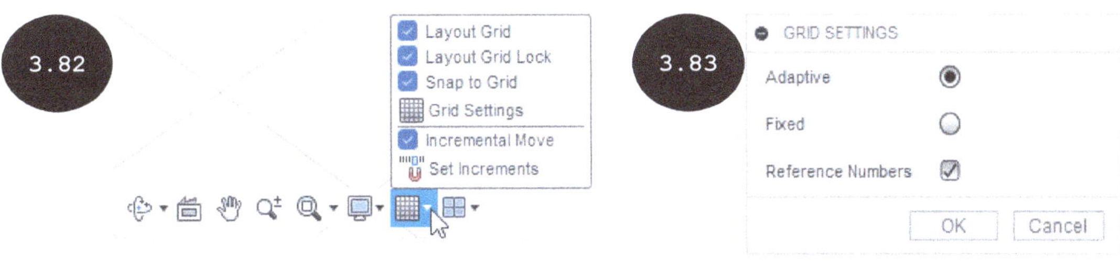

3. Ensure that the **Adaptive** radio button is selected in the **GRID SETTINGS** dialog box.

4. Click on the **OK** button in the **GRID SETTINGS** dialog box.

Section 4: Creating the Sketch

1. Click on the **Create Sketch** tool in the **Toolbar**, see Figure 3.84. Three default planes: Front, Top, and Right, which are mutually perpendicular to each other appear in the graphics area.

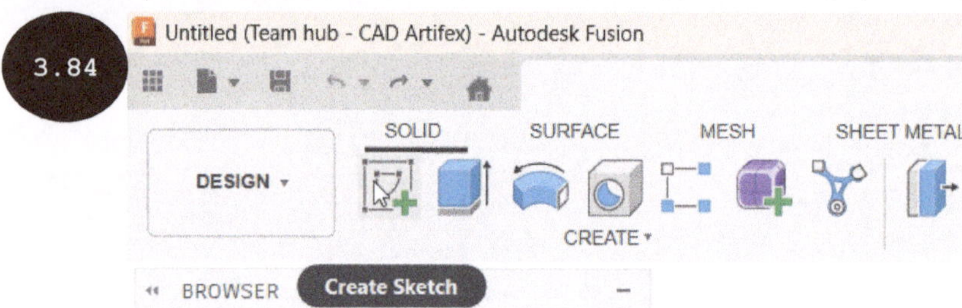

2. Move the cursor over the Top plane and then click the left mouse button when it gets highlighted in the graphics area. The Top plane becomes the sketching plane for creating the sketch and it is oriented normal to the viewing direction. Also, the **SKETCH** contextual tab and the **SKETCH PALETTE** dialog box appear.

3. Ensure that the **Sketch Grid** and **Snap** check boxes are selected in the **SKETCH PALETTE** dialog box to display the grids and to snap the movement of the cursor in the grid lines.

   Now, you can create the sketch. It is evident from Figure 3.77 that the sketch is symmetric about its centerline, therefore, you can create the right half of the sketch and then mirror it to create its left half.

4. Click on the **Line** tool in the **CREATE** panel of the **SKETCH** contextual tab or press the **L** key to activate the **Line** tool.

5. Move the cursor to the origin and then click to specify the start point of the line when the cursor snaps to the origin.

6. Move the cursor horizontally toward the right and then click to specify the endpoint of the first line when the length of the line appears as 60 mm, see Figure 3.85.

7. Move the cursor vertically upward and then click to specify the endpoint of the second line entity when the length of the line appears as 20 mm, see Figure 3.86.

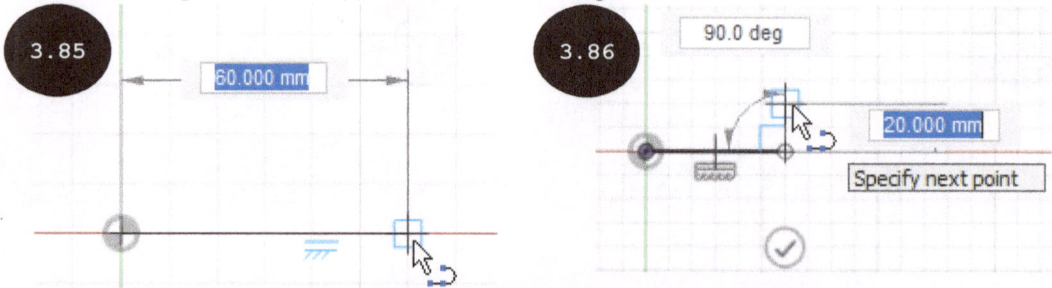

8. Move the cursor horizontally toward the right and click to specify the endpoint of the line when the length of the line appears as 25 mm. Note that you need to zoom into the drawing view to adjust the size of the grids so that the cursor snaps to a distance of 25 mm.

   Now, you need to create an arc of radius 20 mm. To create an arc, you can use the arc tools.

   However, in this tutorial, you will create arcs by using the **Line** tool.

9. Move the cursor over the last specified endpoint in the drawing area and then drag the cursor toward the right and then vertically upward by pressing and holding the left mouse button. A preview of the tangent arc appears in the drawing area, see Figure 3.87.

10. Click to specify the endpoint of the arc when the radius of the arc appears as 20 mm, see Figure 3.87. The arc is created, and the line mode is invoked again.

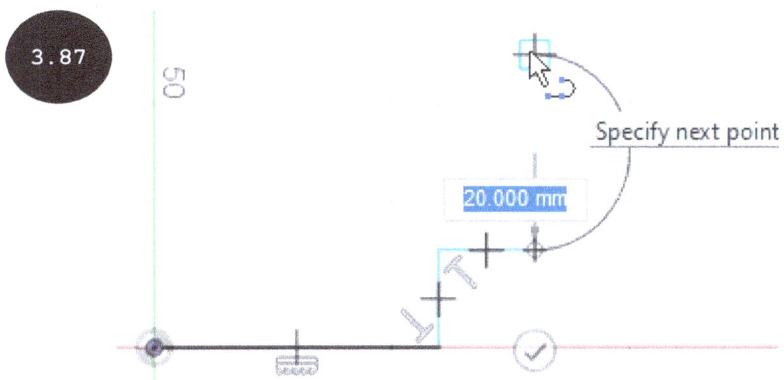

11. Move the cursor horizontally toward the left and click when the length appears as 25 mm.

12. Move the cursor vertically upward and click when the length of the line appears as 80 mm.

13. Move the cursor horizontally toward the right and then click when the length of the line appears as 25 mm.

    Now, you need to create an arc of radius 20 mm.

14. Move the cursor over the last specified endpoint in the drawing area and then drag the cursor toward the right and then vertically upward by pressing and holding the left mouse button. A preview of the tangent arc appears in the drawing area, see Figure 3.88.

15. Click to specify the endpoint of the arc when the radius of the arc appears as 20 mm, see Figure 3.88. The arc is created, and the line mode is invoked again.

16. Move the cursor horizontally toward the left and click when the length of the line appears as 25 mm.

17. Move the cursor vertically upward and click when the length of the line appears as 20 mm.

18. Move the cursor horizontally toward the left and then click when the length of the line appears as 60 mm. The right half of the sketch is created, see Figure 3.89. Next, right-click in the drawing area and then click on the **OK** tool in the Marking Menu that appears to exit the **Line** tool.

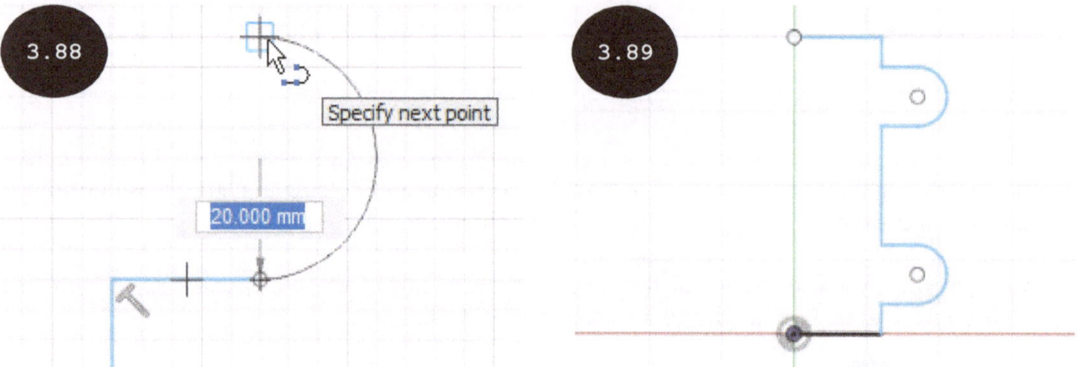

Now, you need to create circles

19. Press the **C** key to activate the **Center Diameter Circle** tool. Alternatively, click on the **Center Diameter Circle** tool in the **CREATE** panel in the **SKETCH** contextual tab.

20. Move the cursor toward the center point of the lower arc of the sketch and then click the left mouse button when the cursor snaps to it, see Figure 3.90.

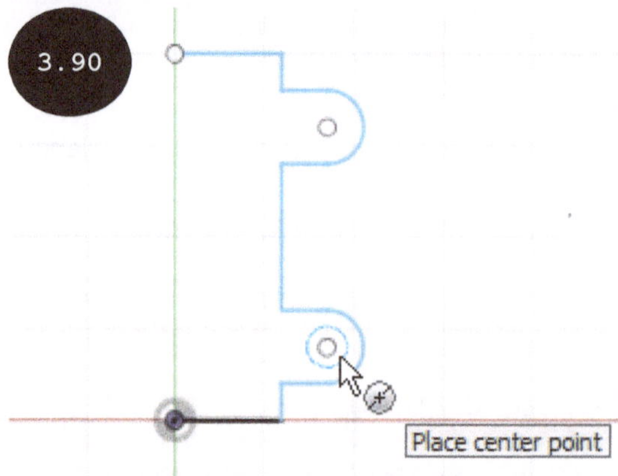

21. Move the cursor horizontally toward the right and click the left mouse button when the diameter of the circle appears as 20 mm. A circle of diameter 20 mm is created.

22. Similarly, create another circle of diameter 20 mm at the center point of the upper arc of the sketch.

23. Press the ESC key to exit the **Center Diameter Circle** tool.

Section 5: Drawing a Construction Line

After creating the right half of the sketch, you can mirror it about a centerline to create the left half of the sketch.

1. Click on the **Line** tool in the **Toolbar** or press the **L** key to activate the **Line** tool.

2. Click to activate the **Centerline** tool in the **Linetype** area of the **SKETCH PALETTE** dialog box, see Figure 3.91. Now, you can create a centerline.

3. Move the cursor to the origin and then click to specify the start point of the centerline when the cursor snaps to the origin.

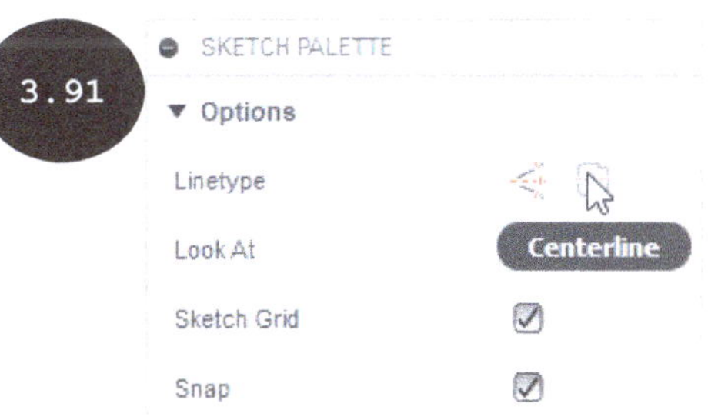

4. Move the cursor vertically upward and then click to specify the endpoint of the vertical centerline, see Figure 3.92. Next, press the ESC key to exit the **Line** tool.

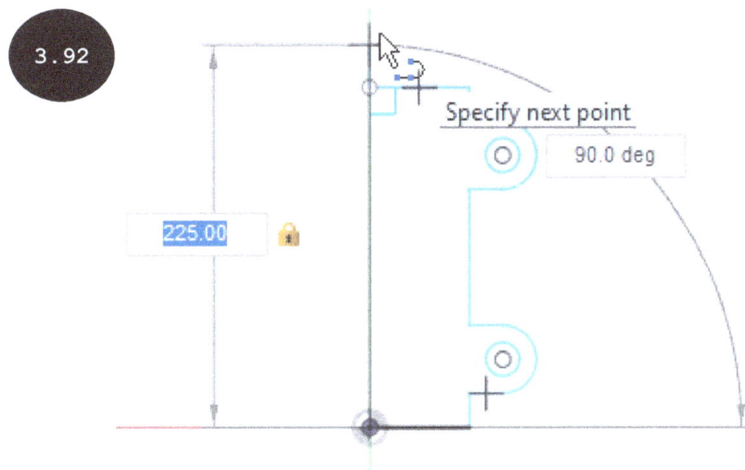

Section 6: Mirroring Sketch Entities

After creating the centerline, you need to mirror the sketch.

1. Click on the **Mirror** tool in the **CREATE** panel of the **SKETCH** contextual tab. The **MIRROR** dialog box appears, see Figure 3.93. Note that the centerline automatically gets selected as the mirror line.

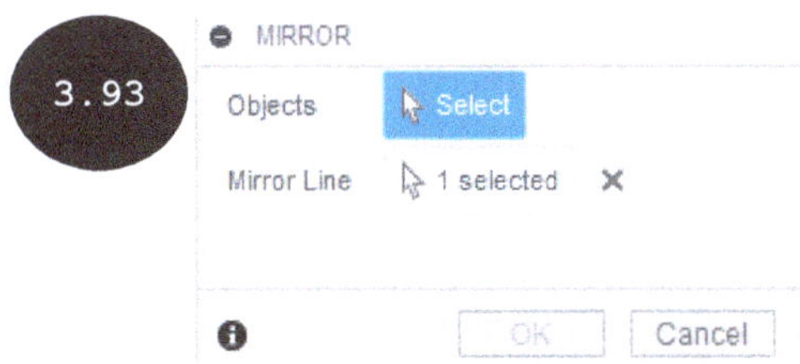

2. Select all the sketch entities one by one, except the centerline, by clicking the left mouse button or by drawing a window around the entities, see Figure 3.94. You can draw a window around the entities to be selected by dragging the cursor after pressing and holding the left mouse button. The preview of the mirror entities appears.

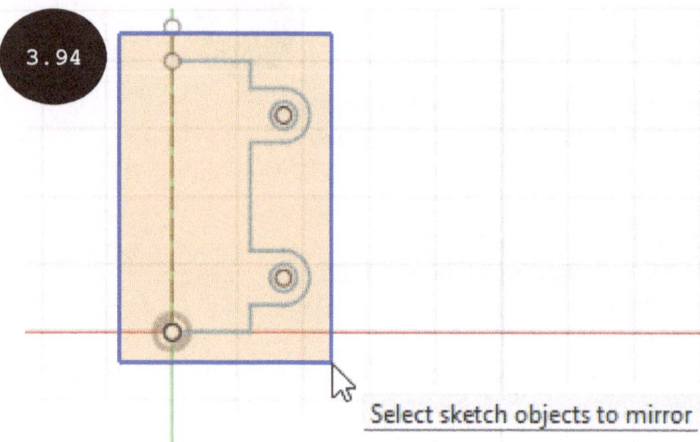

3. Click on the **OK** button in the dialog box. The selected entities get mirrored about the centerline, see Figure 3.95.

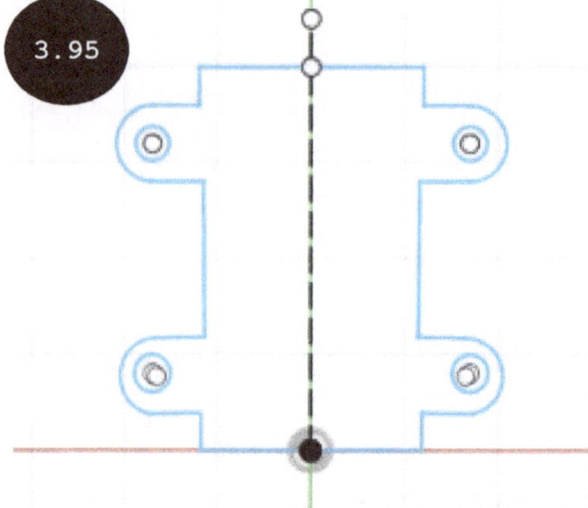

Section 7: Saving the Sketch

1. Click on the **Save** tool in the **Application Bar**. The **Save** dialog box appears.

2. Enter **Tutorial 2** in the **Name** field of the dialog box.

3. Ensure that the location ***Autodesk Fusion 360 > Chapter 03 > Tutorial*** is specified in the **Location** field of the dialog box to save the file of this tutorial. To specify the location, you need to expand the **Save** dialog box by clicking on the down arrow next to the **Location** field of the dialog box.

4. Click on the **Save** button in the dialog box. The sketch is saved with the name Tutorial 2 in the specified location (***Autodesk Fusion 360 > Chapter 03 > Tutorial***).

Tutorial 3

Draw the sketch of the model shown in Figure 3.96. The dimensions and the model shown in the figure are for your reference only. You will learn about applying dimensions and creating 3D models in later chapters. All dimensions are in mm.

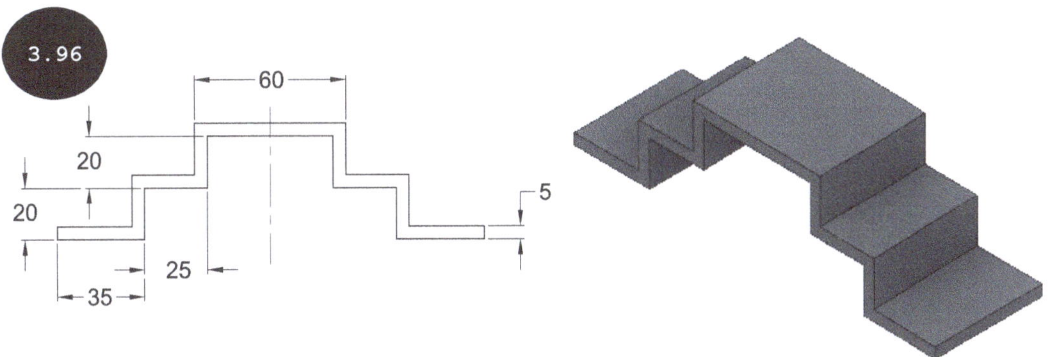

Section 1: Starting a New Part Design File

1. Click **File** > **New** in the **Application Bar** (see Figure 3.97) to display the **What do you want to design?** dialog box, see Figure 3.98.

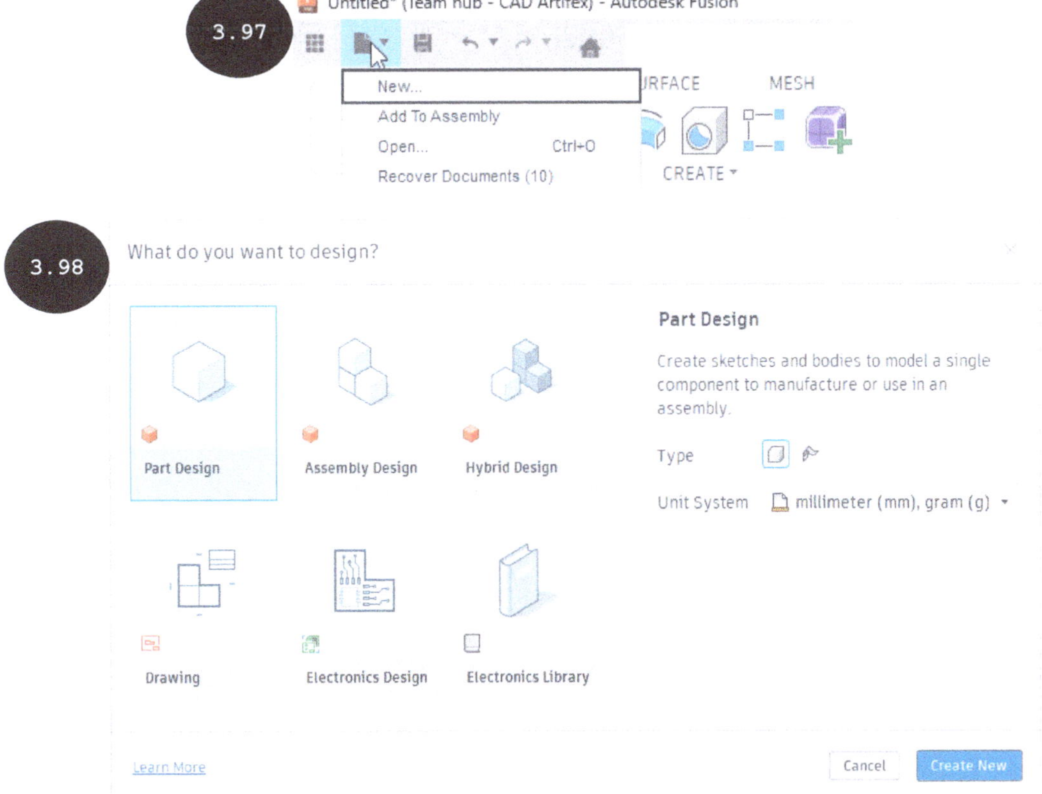

2. In the **What do you want to design?** dialog box, select the **Part Design** button and choose the **millimeter (mm), gram (g)** unit system from the **Unit System** drop-down list.

3. After specifying the required options, click the **Create New** button. A new Part Design file is created with the default name, refer to Figure 3.99.

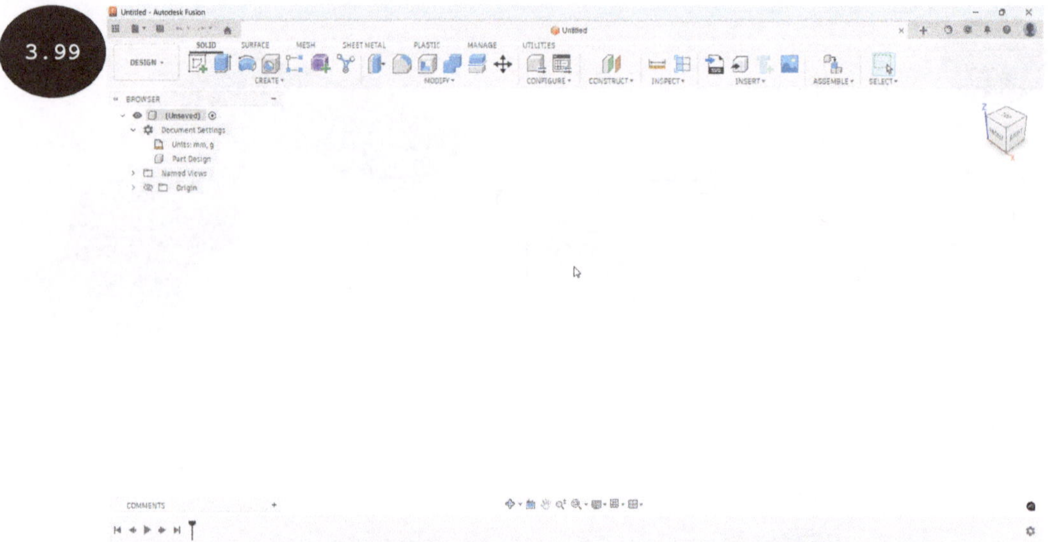

Section 2: Organizing the Data Panel

Now, you need to organize the data panel by creating the project folder and sub-folders to save the files.

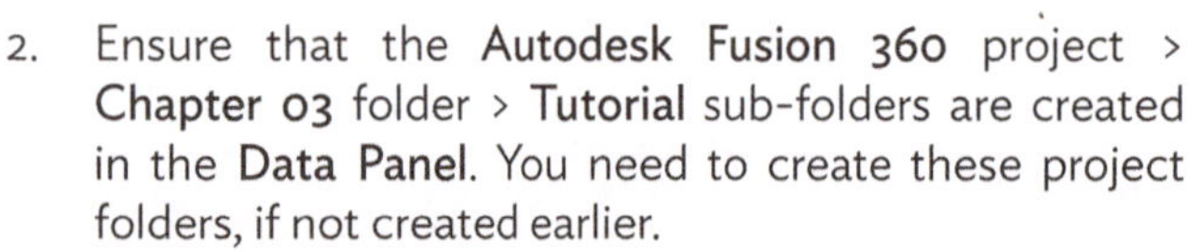

1. Click on the **Show Data Panel** tool in the **Application Bar**, see Figure 3.100. The **Data Panel** appears.

2. Ensure that the **Autodesk Fusion 360** project > **Chapter 03** folder > **Tutorial** sub-folders are created in the **Data Panel**. You need to create these project folders, if not created earlier.

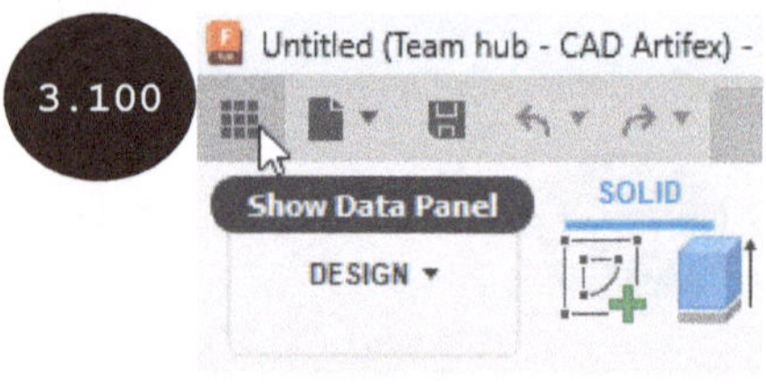

3. Click on the cross-mark at the top right corner of the **Data Panel** to close it.

Section 3: Specifying Grid Settings

1. Invoke the **Grid and Snaps** flyout in the **Navigation Bar**, see Figure 3.101.

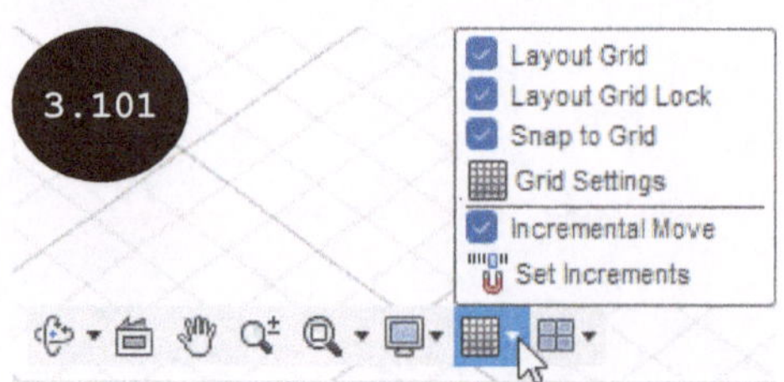

2. Click on the **Grid Settings** tool in the **Grid and Snaps** flyout. The **GRID SETTINGS** dialog box appears, see Figure 3.102.

3. Ensure that the **Adaptive** radio button is selected in the **GRID SETTINGS** dialog box.

4. Click on the **OK** button in the **GRID SETTINGS** dialog box.

Section 4: Creating the Sketch

1. Click on the **Create Sketch** tool in the **Toolbar**, see Figure 3.103. Three default planes: Front, Top, and Right, which are mutually perpendicular to each other appear in the graphics area.

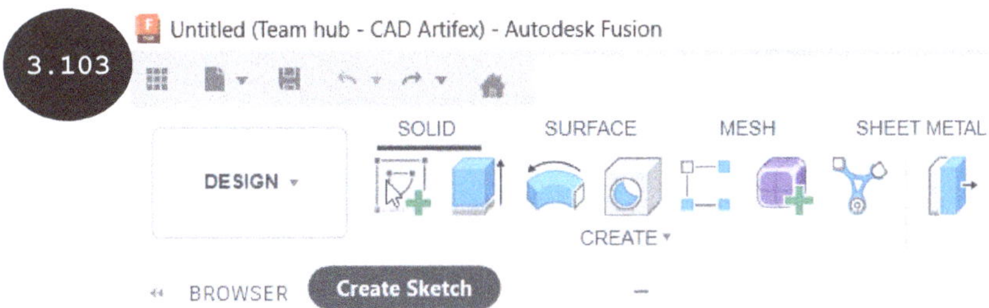

2. Move the cursor over the Front plane and then click the left mouse button when it gets highlighted in the graphics area. The Front plane becomes the sketching plane for creating the sketch and it is oriented normal to the viewing direction. Also, the **SKETCH** contextual tab and the **SKETCH PALETTE** dialog box appear.

3. Ensure that the **Sketch Grid** and **Snap** check boxes are selected in the **SKETCH PALETTE** dialog box to display the grids and to snap the movement of the cursor on the grid lines.

   Now, you can create the sketch.

4. Click on the **Line** tool in the **Toolbar** or press the **L** key. The **Line** tool gets activated.

5. Move the cursor toward the origin and then click the left mouse button when the cursor snaps to the origin.

6. Move the cursor horizontally toward the right and then click to specify the endpoint of the first line when the length of the line appears as 35 mm, see Figure 3.104. A horizontal line of length 35 mm is created.

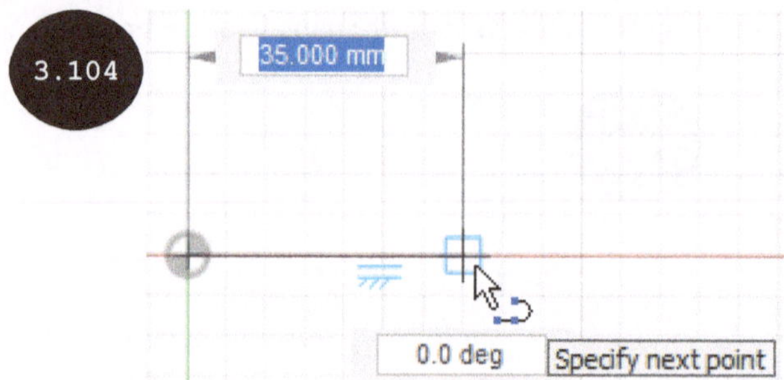

7. Move the cursor vertically upward and then click to create a vertical line of length 20 mm.

8. Move the cursor horizontally toward the right and then click to create a horizontal line of length 25 mm.

9. Move the cursor vertically upward and then click to create a vertical line of length 20 mm.

10. Similarly, create the other line entities of the lower loop of the sketch, see Figure 3.105.

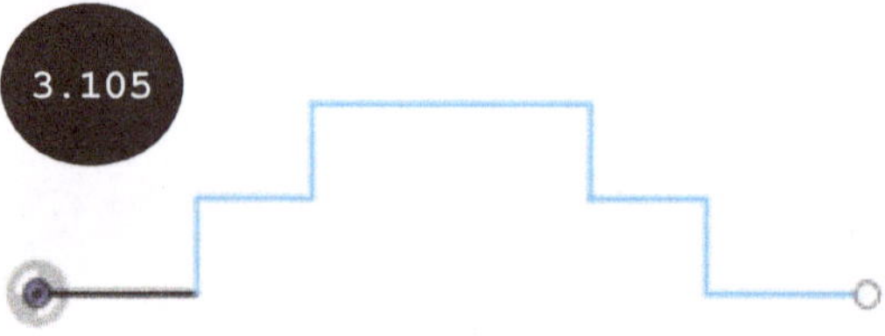

Note: In Figure 3.105, the display of grids is turned off for clarity of the image. You can turn on or off the display of grids by selecting or clearing the **Sketch Grid** check box in the **SKETCH PALETTE** dialog box respectively.

Section 5: Offsetting the Sketch Entities

After creating the lower loop of the sketch, you need to offset its entities to a distance of 5 mm to create the upper loop of the sketch.

1. Click on the **Offset** tool in the **MODIFY** panel of the **SKETCH** contextual tab. The **OFFSET** dialog box appears, see Figure 3.106. Alternatively, press the **O** key to invoke the **OFFSET** dialog box.

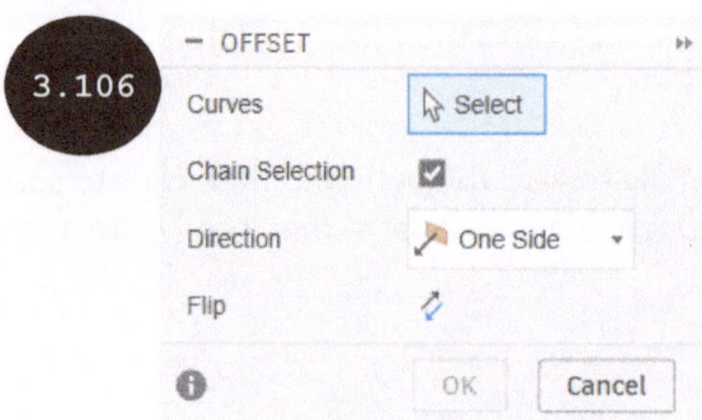

2. Ensure that the **Chain selection** check box is selected in the **OFFSET** dialog box.

3. Select an entity of the lower loop of the sketch in the drawing area. All contiguous entities of the selected entity get selected, and the preview of offset entities appears in the drawing area, see Figure 3.107. Also, the **Distance** field appears in the dialog box as well as in the drawing area.

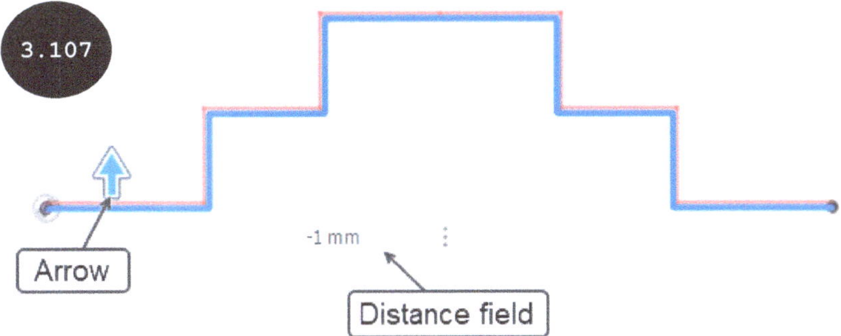

4. Enter **5** in the **Distance** field of the dialog box. The preview of the offset entities gets modified, see Figure 3.108.

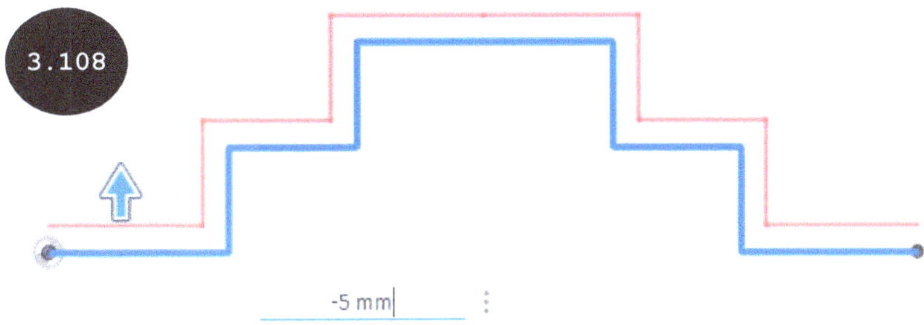

Note: Ensure that the direction of offset entities is on the upper side of the sketch. To reverse the direction of offset entities, you can click on the **Flip** button in the dialog box or enter **-5** in the **Distance** field.

5. Click on the **Flip** button in the dialog box to reverse the direction of offset entities toward the upper side of the sketch, if required.

Note: If the default offset direction is the upper side of the sketch then you can skip step 5.

6. Click on the **OK** button in the dialog box. The offset entities are created.

Now, you need to close the sketch by creating lines on both sides of the sketch.

7. Invoke the **Line** tool and then create lines on both the open ends of the sketch one by one. Figure 3.109 shows the final sketch after creating lines on both the open ends of the sketch.

8. Press the ESC key to exit the **Line** tool.

Section 6: Saving the Sketch

1. Click on the **Save** tool in the **Application Bar**. The **Save** dialog box appears.

2. Enter **Tutorial 3** in the **Name** field of the dialog box.

3. Ensure that the location ***Autodesk Fusion 360 > Chapter 03 > Tutorial*** is specified in the **Location** field of the dialog box to save a file of this tutorial. To specify the location, you need to expand the **Save** dialog box by clicking on the down arrow next to the **Location** field of the dialog box.

4. Click on the **Save** button in the dialog box. The sketch is saved with the name Tutorial 3 in the specified location (***Autodesk Fusion 360 > Chapter 03 > Tutorial***).

Hands-on Test Drive 1

Draw the sketch of the model shown in Figure 3.110. The dimensions and the model are for your reference only. All dimensions are in mm.

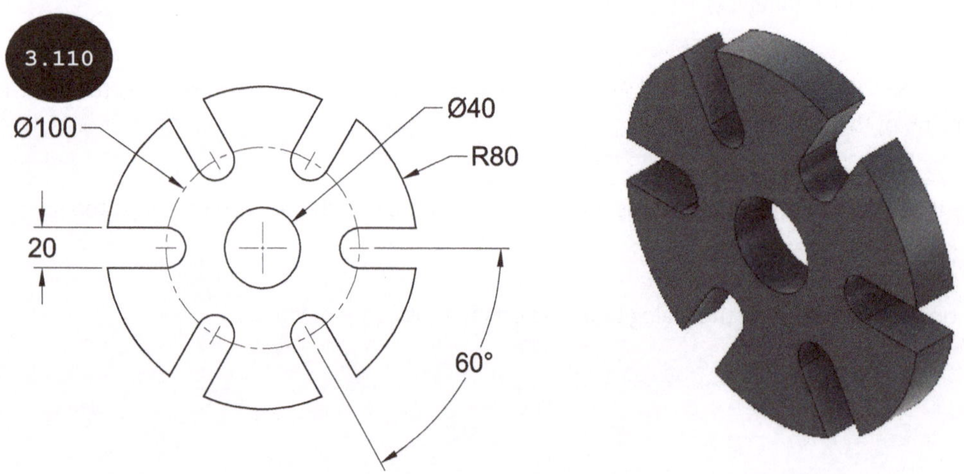

Hands-on Test Drive 2

Draw the sketch of the model shown in Figure 3.111. The dimensions and the model are for your reference only. All dimensions are in mm.

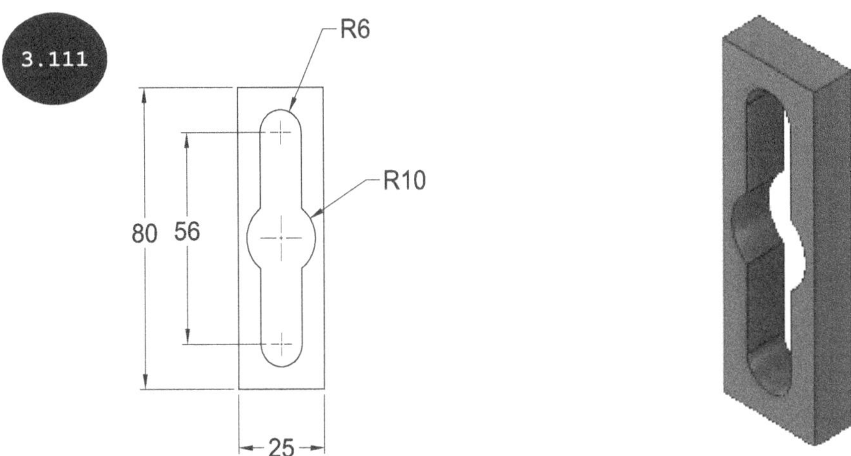

Summary

In this chapter, you learned about various editing and modifying operations in Autodesk Fusion, utilizing tools such as **Trim**, **Extend**, **Offset**, **Mirror**, **Rectangular Pattern**, **Circular Pattern**, **Fillet**, and **Chamfer**. You explored how to create rectangular and circular sketch patterns and discovered methods for creating construction sketch entities using the **Construction** tool. Additionally, you learned how to break sketch entities into segments using the **Break** tool. These skills will help you edit and modify sketches effectively in Autodesk Fusion.

Questions

Complete and verify the following sentences:

- The _________ tool is used for offsetting sketch entities at a specified offset distance.
- You can increase or decrease the scale of sketch entities by using the _________ tool.
- While offsetting sketch entities, if you select the _______ check box in the **OFFSET** dialog box, all the contiguous entities of the selected entity get automatically selected.
- You can trim the unwanted sketch entities to their nearest intersection by using the _________ tool.

- On activating the _________ tool in the **Linetype** area of the **SKETCH PALETTE** dialog box, you can create construction entities in the drawing area.
- The _________ tool is used for breaking a sketch entity into two or more segments at its point of intersection with other entities.
- The _________ tool is used for extending sketch entities up to their nearest intersection.
- The number of pattern instances specified in the **Quantity** field includes the parent or original instance selected to be patterned. (True/False)
- You cannot recall the skipped pattern instances. (True/False)

4

Applying Constraints and Dimensions

In this chapter, **the following topics will be discussed:**

- Working with Constraints
- Applying Constraints
- Controlling the Display of Constraints
- Applying Dimensions
- Applying Constraints/Dimensions Automatically
- Modifying/Editing Dimensions
- Working with Different States of a Sketch
- Working with SKETCH PALETTE

Once you have finished creating a sketch using the sketching tools, the next step is to make your sketch fully defined by applying the necessary constraints and dimensions. A fully defined sketch is one in which all degrees of freedom are constrained, meaning its shape and position cannot be altered by simply dragging its entities. You will learn more about fully defined sketches later in this chapter. Before that, it is essential to understand constraints and dimensions.

Working with Constraints

Constraints are used to restrict the degrees of freedom of a sketch. You can apply constraints to a sketch entity, between sketch entities, and between sketch entities and planes, axes, edges, or vertices. Some constraints, such as horizontal, vertical, and coincident, are applied automatically while drawing sketch entities.

For example, when drawing a line entity, if you move the cursor horizontally toward the left or right, a symbol of horizontal constraint appears near the cursor, see Figure 4.1 (a). This indicates that if you specify the endpoint of the line, the horizontal constraint will be applied to the line entity. Likewise, if you move the cursor vertically upward or downward, a symbol of vertical constraint appears near the cursor, see Figure 4.1 (b). This indicates that if you specify the endpoint of the line, a vertical constraint will be applied to the line. The various geometric constraints are discussed next.

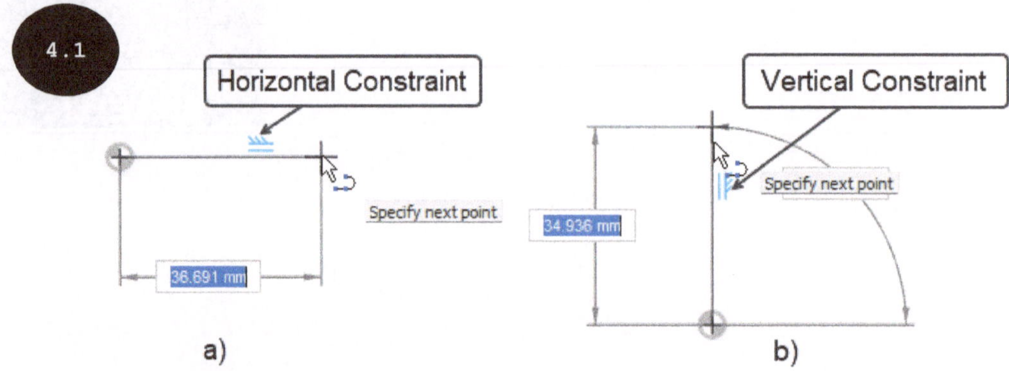

Horizontal Constraint

The horizontal constraint is used to change the orientation of an entity to horizontal and ensure that it remains in that position.

Vertical Constraint

The vertical constraint is used to change the orientation of an entity to vertical and ensure that it remains in that position.

Coincident Constraint

The coincident constraint is used to make two points or vertices coincide and ensures that they remain coincident with each other. This constraint can be applied between two points or between a point and a line, arc, circle, or ellipse. Additionally, you can apply a coincident constraint between a sketch point and the origin.

Collinear Constraint

The collinear constraint is used to make two lines collinear, ensuring that they remain aligned with each other. You can also apply this constraint to make a line collinear with a linear edge.

Perpendicular Constraint

The perpendicular constraint is used to make two line entities perpendicular to each other and ensures that they remain perpendicular. You can also apply this constraint to make a line perpendicular to a linear edge.

Parallel Constraint

The parallel constraint is used to make two line entities parallel to each other and ensures that they remain parallel. You can also apply this constraint to make a line parallel to a linear edge.

Tangent Constraint

The tangent constraint is used to make two sketch entities, such as a circle and a line, tangent to each other. You can also apply this constraint to make two circles, two arcs, two ellipses, or a combination of these entities tangent to each other. Additionally, it can be used to make a sketch entity (line, circle, arc, or ellipse) tangent to a linear or circular edge.

Concentric Constraint

The concentric constraint is used to make two arcs, two circles, two ellipses, or a combination of these entities concentric to each other. When this constraint is applied, the selected entities share the same center point, ensuring they remain concentric.

Equal Constraint

The equal constraint is used to make two entities, such as arcs, circles, or lines, equal in size. When this constraint is applied, the length of the selected line entities becomes equal, and the radii of the selected arcs or circles become the same.

Midpoint Constraint

The midpoint constraint is used to make a point coincident with the midpoint of a line entity. This constraint ensures that the selected point remains at the midpoint of the line. You can apply the midpoint constraint between a sketch point and a line or between a sketch point and a linear edge.

Symmetry Constraint

The symmetry constraint is used to make two points, lines, arcs, circles, or ellipses symmetric about a line entity. This constraint ensures that the selected entities remain mirrored or symmetrically positioned with respect to the designated symmetry line, maintaining equal distances and orientation.

Curvature Constraint

The curvature constraint is used for maintaining smooth curvature continuity at the transition point between two sketch entities, such as two splines or a spline and a line.

Fix Constraint

The Fix constraint is used for locking the current position and size of a sketch entity, preventing it from being moved or resized. However, for a fixed line or arc entity, the endpoints can still move independently without altering the overall position of the entity.

Polygon Constraint

The Polygon constraint is used to define a closed sketch profile with equal side lengths and angles as a regular polygon. When applied, all sides of the sketch remain equal, and the shape maintains its regular form during modification.

Applying Constraints

In Autodesk Fusion, you can apply constraints using the constraints tools available in the **CONSTRAINTS** panel of the **SKETCH** contextual tab in the **Toolbar**, see Figure 4.2.

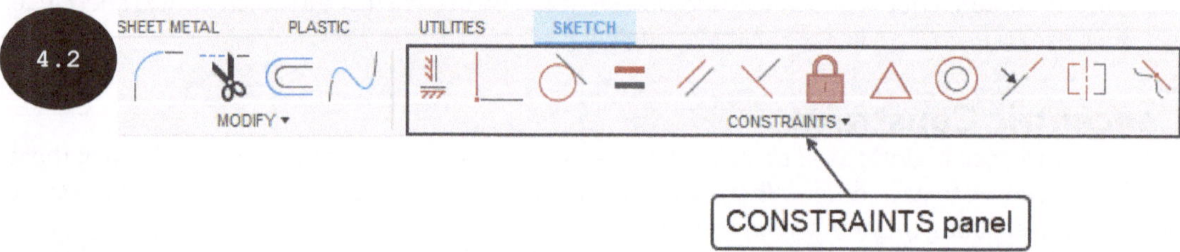

To apply a constraint, click on its tool in the **CONSTRAINTS** panel of the **SKETCH** contextual tab and then select the entities in the drawing area. For example, to apply a concentric constraint between an arc and a circle, click on the **Concentric** tool in the **CONSTRAINTS** panel. Next, click on the arc and then the circle in the drawing area one by one. The concentric constraint is applied, and the selected entities become concentric to each other such that they share the same center point, see Figure 4.3. Also, the symbol of concentric constraint appears near the entities in the drawing area.

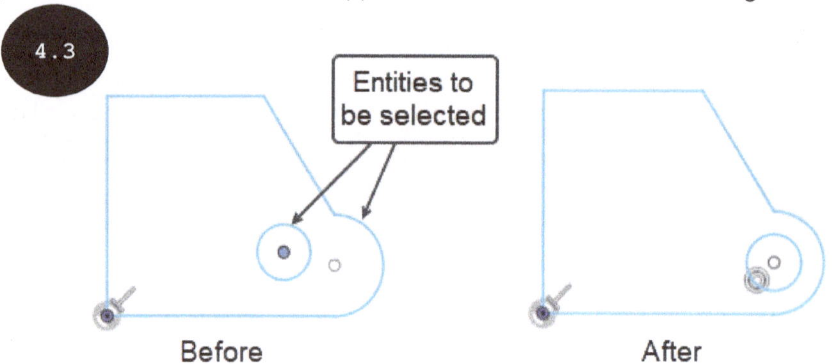

Note: You can select entities for applying a constraint either before or after invoking the required constraint tool in the **CONSTRAINTS** panel.

Tip: Most of the time, the second selected entity moves to fulfil the applied constraint condition. However, sometimes due to the other applied constraints, the first selected entity moves to fulfil the constraint condition.

To apply a horizontal/vertical constraint to an inclined line, click on the **Horizontal/Vertical** tool in the **CONSTRAINTS** panel of the **SKETCH** contextual tab, see Figure 4.4.

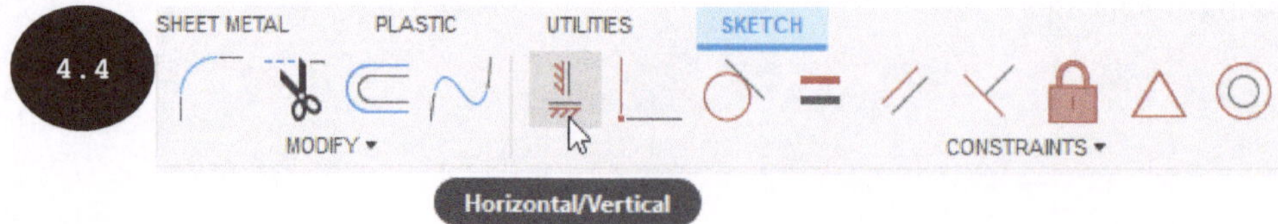

Next, click on the inclined line in the drawing area. A horizontal or vertical constraint is applied to the selected line depending on whether the inclined line is closest to the horizontal or vertical orientation, respectively, see Figure 4.5. In this figure, a horizontal constraint is applied to the inclined line. This is because the selected line is closest to the horizontal orientation.

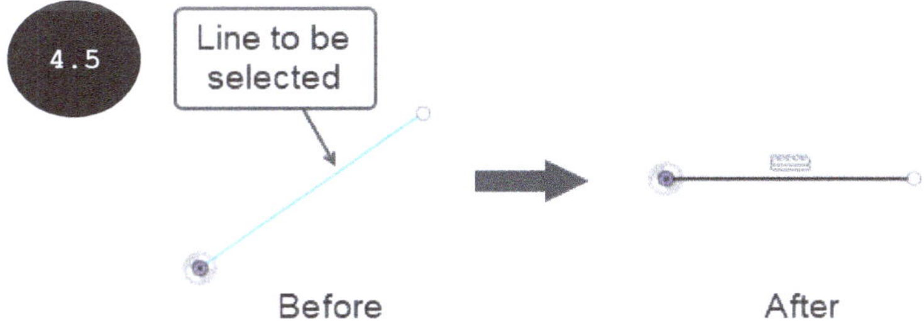

Similarly, you can apply other constraints to the sketch entities using the respective constraint tools available in the **CONSTRAINTS** panel, as needed.

Tip: You can also apply a constraint between the selected entities using the Marking Menu. To do this, select the sketch entities between which a constraint is to be applied and then right-click in the drawing area. The Marking Menu appears with a list of all the possible constraints that can be applied between the selected set of entities, see Figure 4.6. This figure shows the Marking Menu after selecting two circles in the drawing area. Next, click on the required constraint in the Marking Menu. The selected constraint gets applied between the entities.

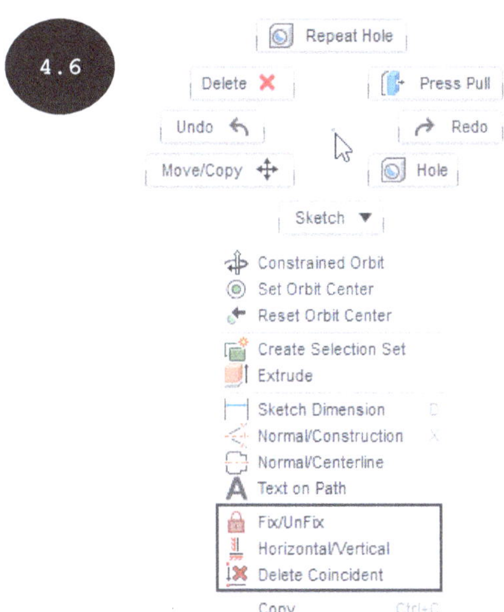

Note: After applying a constraint, the constraint tool remains activated. You need to press the ESC key to deactivate the constraint tool. You can also click on the **SELECT** tool in the **Toolbar**. Alternatively, right-click in the drawing area and then click on the **CANCEL** tool in the Marking Menu that appears to exit the tool.

Controlling the Display of Constraints

You can control the visibility of the applied constraints in the drawing area. To turn on or off the display of the applied constraints, select or clear the **Constraints** check box, in the **Options** rollout of the SKETCH PALETTE dialog box, respectively, see Figure 4.7.

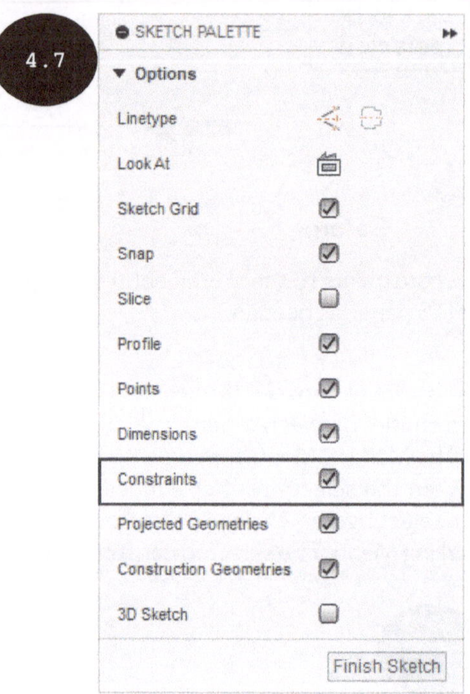

Tip: You can also delete an already applied constraint by selecting it in the drawing area and then pressing the DELETE key.

Applying Dimensions

Once a sketch has been drawn and the necessary constraints have been applied, the next step is to apply dimensions to the sketch. Since Autodesk Fusion is a parametric software, the parameters of sketch entities, such as length and angle, are controlled by dimensions. Modifying a dimension value results in the corresponding sketch entity being adjusted accordingly. You can apply dimensions using the **Sketch Dimension** tool, which can be activated through one of the following methods:

- Click on the **Sketch Dimension** tool in the **CREATE** panel of the **SKETCH** contextual tab, see Figure 4.8.

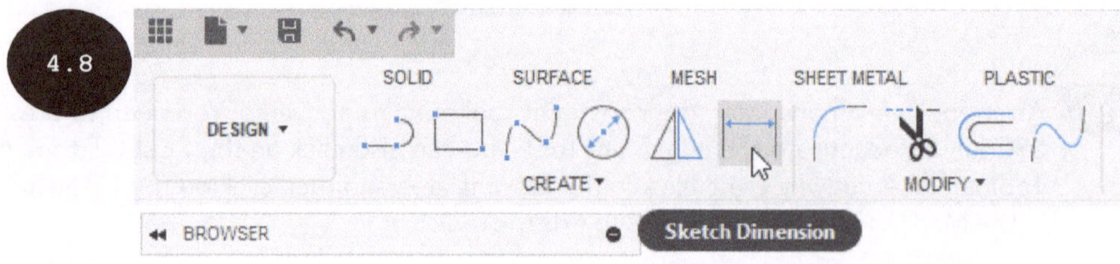

- Press the D key.
- Invoke the **CREATE** drop-down menu of the **SKETCH** contextual tab and then click on the **Sketch Dimension** tool.
- Right-click in the drawing area. The Marking Menu appears. Next, click on the **Sketch** tool or hover the cursor over the **Sketch** tool in the Marking Menu, see Figure 4.9. The second level of the Marking Menu appears with frequently used sketching tools, see Figure 4.10. Next, click on the **Sketch Dimension** tool in the Marking Menu.

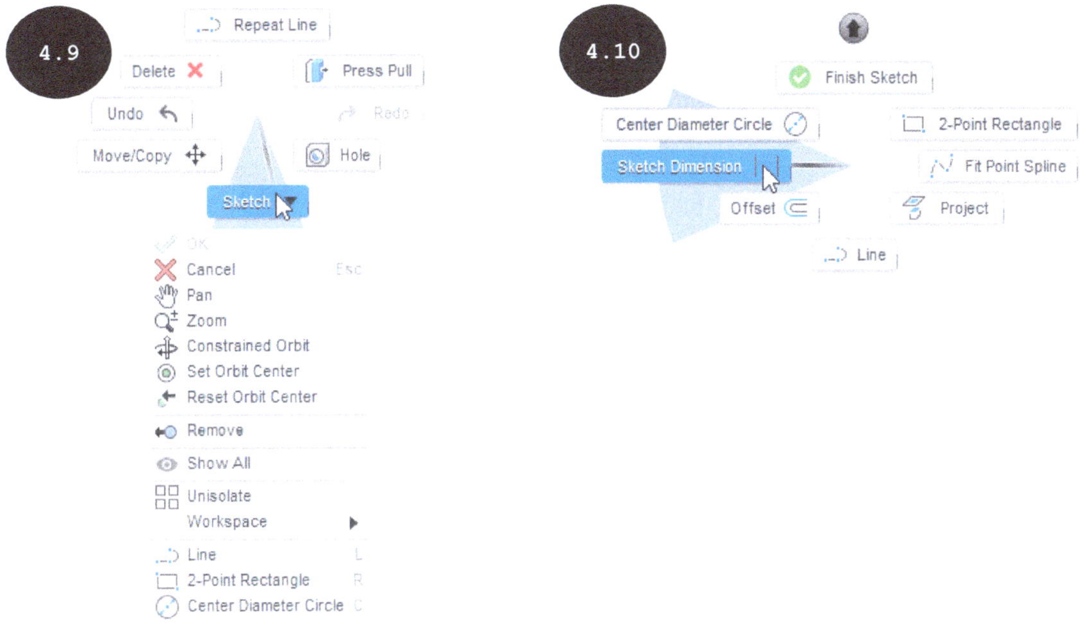

The **Sketch Dimension** tool is used for applying dimensions, depending upon the type of entity selected. For example, if you select a circle, the diameter dimension is applied, and if you select a line, the linear dimension is applied. You can apply horizontal, vertical, aligned, angular, diameter, radius, and linear diameter dimensions by using this tool. The methods for applying dimensions by using the **Sketch Dimension** tool are discussed next.

Applying a Horizontal Dimension

The method for applying a horizontal dimension is discussed below:

1. Press the D key to activate the **Sketch Dimension** tool, or click on the **Sketch Dimension** tool in the **CREATE** panel of the **SKETCH** contextual tab.
2. Select the required sketch entity or entities. You can choose a horizontal sketch entity, an inclined sketch entity, two points, or two vertical entities to apply the horizontal dimension, see Figure 4.11. After selecting the entities, their current dimension value appears attached to the cursor.

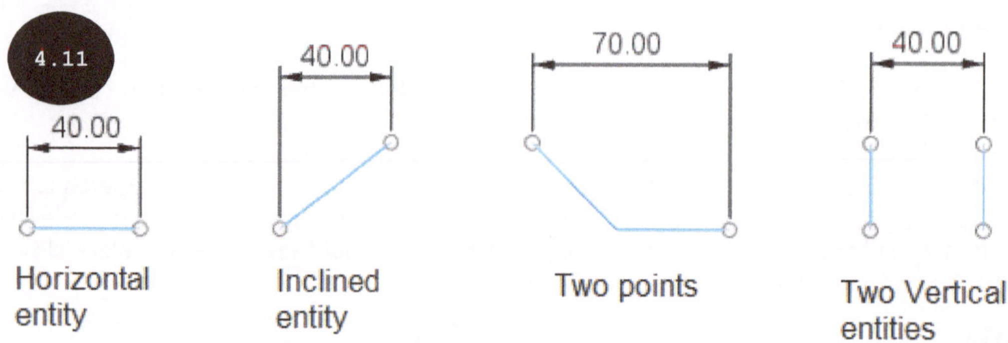

3. Move the cursor vertically up or down, then click the left mouse button in the drawing area to specify the placement point for the horizontal dimension. A dimension box appears in the drawing area with the current dimension value.

4. Enter the required dimension value in this dimension box and press ENTER. The horizontal dimension is applied.

Tip: After selecting an inclined entity or two sketch points, if you move the cursor in a direction other than vertically up or down, then notice that the vertical or aligned dimension gets attached to the cursor.

Applying a Vertical Dimension

Similar to applying a horizontal dimension by using the **Sketch Dimension** tool, you can apply a vertical dimension to a vertical sketch entity, an inclined sketch entity, between two points, or between two horizontal sketch entities, see Figure 4.12. Note that to apply a vertical dimension, you need to move the cursor horizontally toward the right or left after selecting one or more entities.

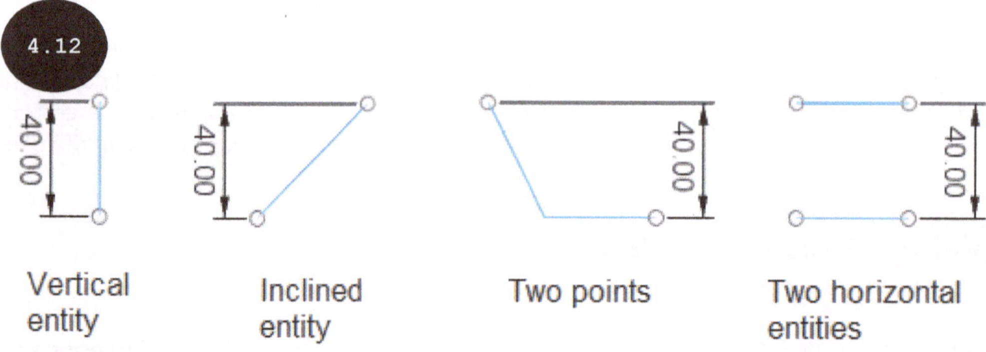

Applying an Aligned Dimension

Similar to applying horizontal and vertical dimensions using the **Sketch Dimension** tool, you can apply an aligned dimension to an aligned sketch entity or between two points, see Figure 4.13.

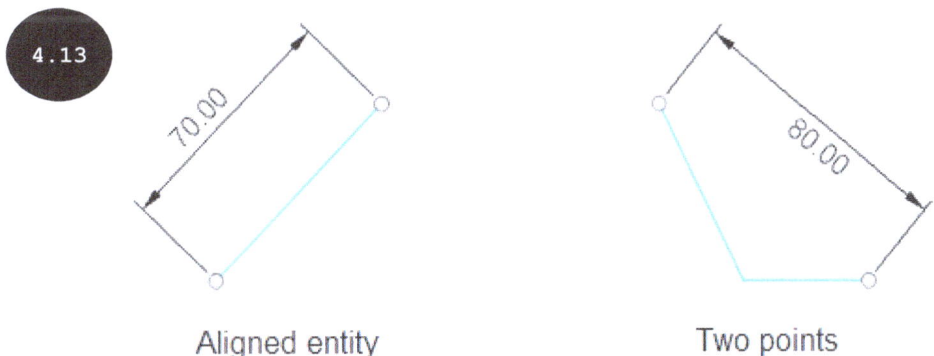

The aligned dimension is generally used for measuring the aligned length of an inclined line. Note that after selecting one or more entities for applying aligned dimension, you need to move the cursor perpendicular to the selected entity to specify the placement point. Alternatively, after selecting one or more entities, right-click in the drawing area and then click on the **Aligned** option in the Marking Menu that appears for applying the aligned dimension, see Figure 4.14.

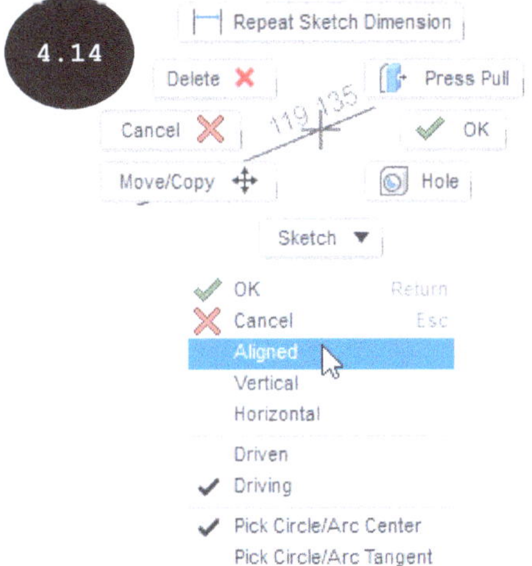

Applying an Angular Dimension

You can apply an angular dimension between two non-parallel line entities or three points using the **Sketch Dimension** tool. To do this, activate the **Sketch Dimension** tool and then select two non-parallel line entities in the drawing area. The angular dimension between the selected entities gets attached to the cursor, see Figure 4.15. Next, move the cursor to a location where you want to place the dimension and then click to specify the placement point. A dimension box appears in the drawing area. Enter the required angular value in this box and then press ENTER. An angular dimension is applied between the selected entities. Note that an angular dimension is applied between the selected entities depending on the location of the placement point in the drawing area, see Figure 4.16.

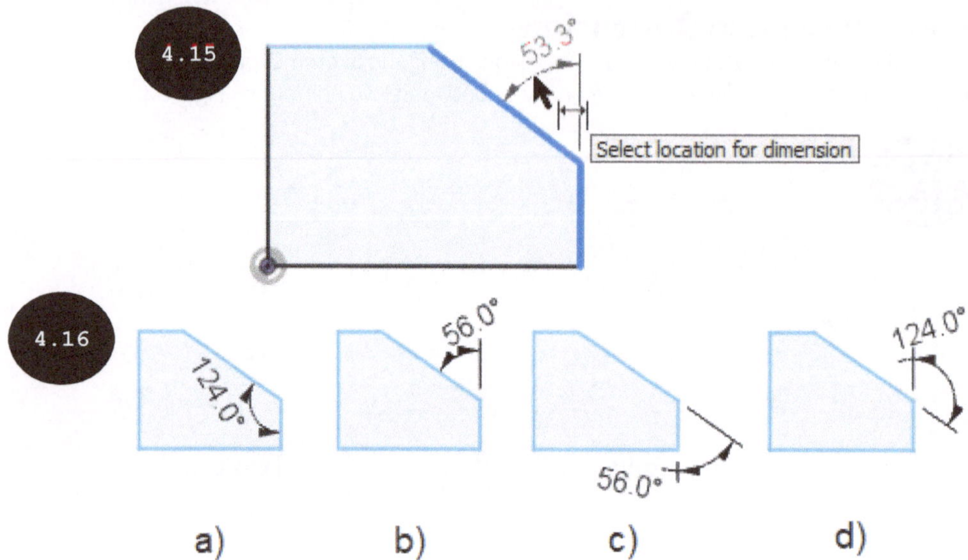

To apply an angular dimension between three points, activate the **Sketch Dimension** tool and then select three points one by one in the drawing area, see Figure 4.17. The angular dimension between the selected points gets attached to the cursor. Next, move the cursor to a location where you want to place the attached angular dimension and then click to specify the placement point. A dimension box appears. Enter the required angular value in this box and then press ENTER. An angular dimension is applied between the three selected points, see Figure 4.17.

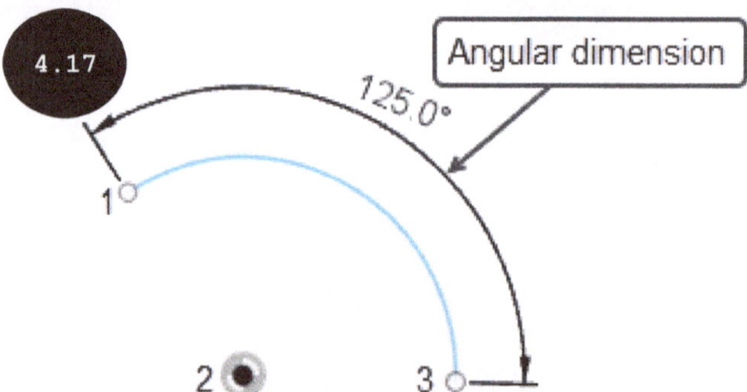

Applying a Diameter Dimension

You can apply a diameter dimension to a circle by using the **Sketch Dimension** tool. To do this, activate the **Sketch Dimension** tool and then select a circle. The diameter dimension gets attached to the cursor. Next, move the cursor to the required location and then click to specify a placement point in the drawing area. A dimension box appears. Enter the diameter value in this box and then press ENTER. The diameter dimension is applied, see Figure 4.18.

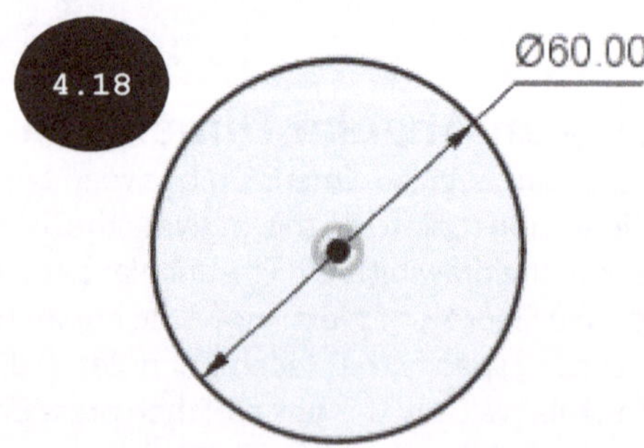

Tip: By default, the diameter dimension is applied to a circle. However, you can also apply a radius dimension to a circle. To do this, after selecting a circle to apply dimension, right-click in the drawing area and then click on the **Radius** option in the Marking Menu that appears. The radius dimension gets attached to the cursor. Next, click to specify the placement point in the drawing area. A dimension box appears. Enter the radius value in this box and then press ENTER.

You can also convert the already applied diameter dimension to the radius dimension. To do this, right-click on the diameter dimension in the drawing area and then click on the **Toggle Radius** option in the Marking Menu that appears.

Applying a Radius Dimension

You can apply a radius dimension to an arc by using the **Sketch Dimension** tool. To do this, activate the **Sketch Dimension** tool and then click on the arc. The radius dimension gets attached to the cursor. Move the cursor to the required location and then click to specify a placement point in the drawing area. A dimension box appears. Enter the radius value in this box and then press ENTER. The radius dimension is applied, see Figure 4.19.

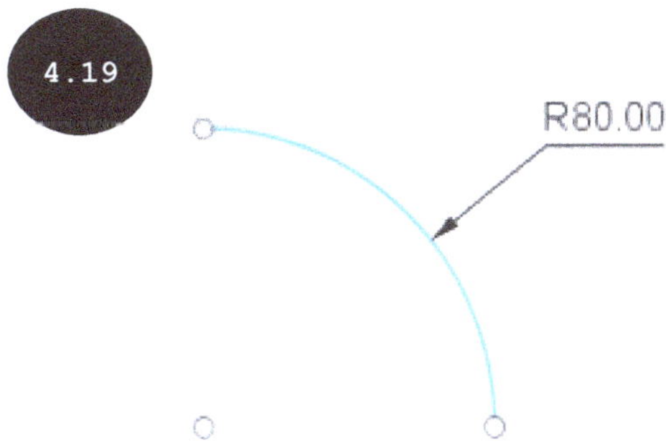

Tip: By default, the radius dimension is applied to an arc. However, you can also apply the diameter dimension to an arc. To do this, after selecting the arc to apply dimension, right-click in the drawing area and then click on the **Diameter** option in the Marking Menu that appears. The diameter dimension gets attached to the cursor. Next, click to specify the placement point in the drawing area. A dimension box appears. Enter the diameter value in this box and then press ENTER.

You can also convert the already applied radius dimension to a diameter dimension. To do this, right-click on the radius dimension in the drawing area and then click on the **Toggle Diameter** option in the Marking Menu that appears.

Applying a Linear Diameter Dimension

You can apply a linear diameter dimension to a sketch of a revolved feature, see Figure 4.20. To do this, activate the **Sketch Dimension** tool and then select a linear entity (line, centerline, or construction line) as the revolving axis of the sketch, see Figure 4.20. In this figure, the construction line is selected as the revolving axis of the sketch. Next, select a linear sketch entity of the sketch.

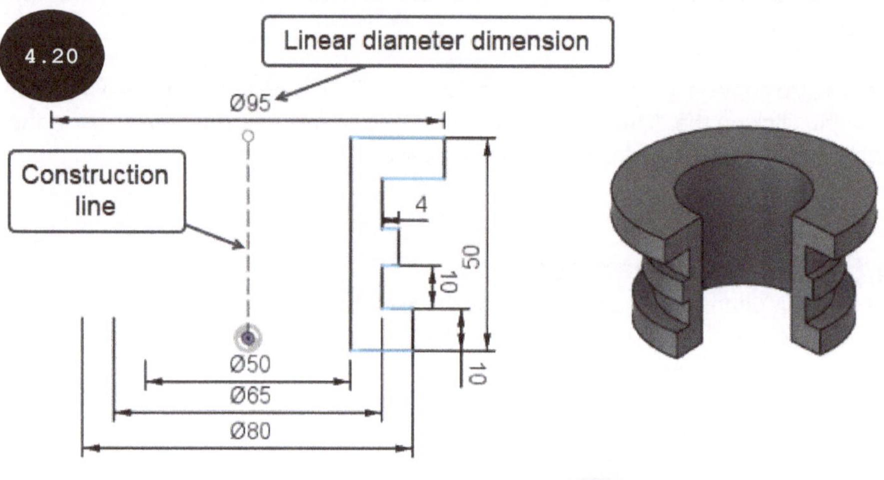

The linear dimension between the selected entities gets attached to the cursor. Next, right-click in the drawing area. The Marking Menu appears, see Figure 4.21. In this Marking Menu, click on the **Diameter Dimension** option. The linear diameter dimension gets attached to the cursor. Move the cursor to the other side of the entity selected as the axis of revolution and then click to specify the placement point. A dimension box appears. Enter the linear diameter value in this box and then press ENTER. The linear diameter dimension is applied.

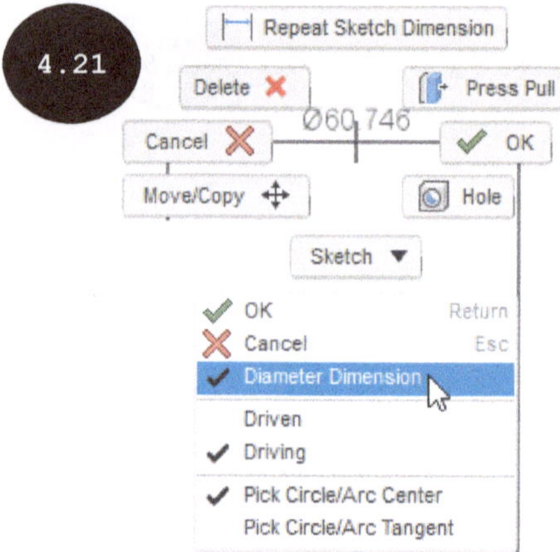

Note: If a centerline is selected as the revolving axis of the sketch, then on selecting the second linear sketch entity, the linear diameter dimension gets automatically attached to the cursor. Click to specify the placement point. A dimension box appears. Enter the linear diameter value in this box and then press ENTER. The linear diameter dimension is applied.

Applying Constraints/Dimensions Automatically

In Autodesk Fusion, you can automatically apply geometric constraints and dimensions to an entire sketch based on the type of sketch entities using the **Auto Constrain** and **Auto Constrain from Datum** tools. Both tools are available in the **CONSTRAINTS** drop-down menu of the **SKETCH** contextual tab, see Figure 4.22. These tools are discussed next.

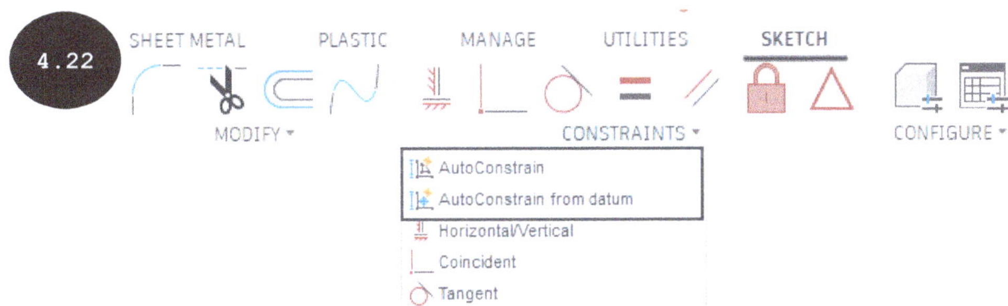

AutoConstrain Tool

The **Auto Constrain** tool is used to automatically apply geometric constraints and dimensions to all sketch entities based on their shape, orientation, and relationships with respect to the origin. The method for applying geometric constraints and dimensions using this tool is discussed below:

1. Invoke the **CONSTRAINTS** drop-down menu and click **AutoConstrain** tool, see Figure 4.23. The **AUTOCONSTRAIN** dialog box appears, and the process of applying geometric constraints and dimensions to the sketch entities begins.

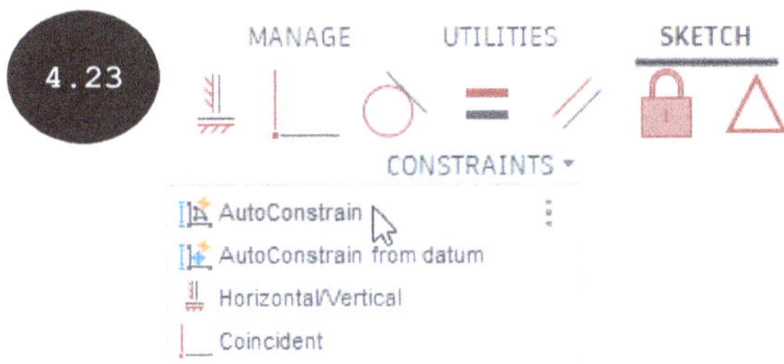

2. After the process is complete, multiple results for a fully defined sketch appears in the dialog box. You can select the result that best fits your design intent. A preview of the selected result is displayed in the drawing area.

3. If needed, you can generate additional options by clicking the **Generate More** button in the dialog box.

4. After selecting the required result, click **OK**. The sketch becomes fully defined with all dimensions and constraints applied relative to the origin, see Figure 4.24.

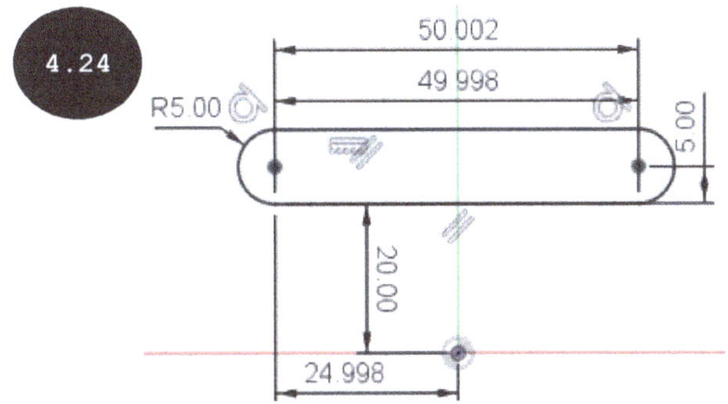

AutoConstrain from datum Tool

The **AutoConstrain from datum** tool is used to automatically apply geometric constraints and dimensions to all sketch entities with respect to the datum point. The method for applying geometric constraints and dimensions using this tool is discussed below:

1. Invoke the **CONSTRAINTS** drop-down menu and click **AutoConstrain from datum** tool, see Figure 4.25. You are prompted to select a point to place the datum.

4.25

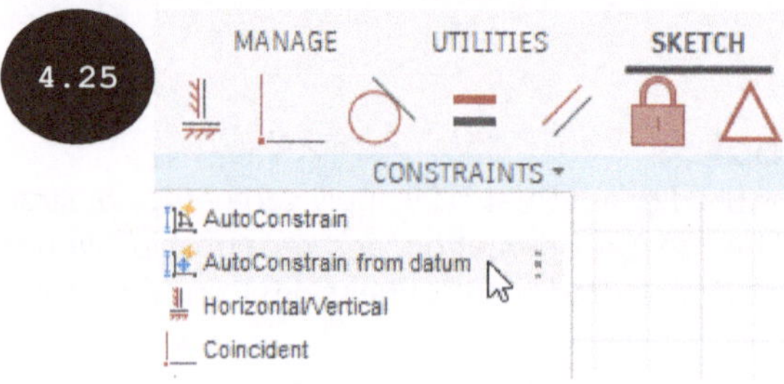

2. Select a point as the datum in the drawing area. The **AUTOCONSTRAIN FROM DATUM** dialog box appears, and the process of applying geometric constraints and dimensions to the sketch entities begins.

3. After the process is complete, multiple results for a fully defined sketch appears in the dialog box. You can select the result that best fits your design intent.

4. If needed, you can generate additional options by clicking the **Generate More** button in the dialog box.

5. After selecting the required result, click **OK**. The sketch becomes fully defined with all dimensions and constraints applied relative to the selected datum point, see Figure 4.26.

4.26

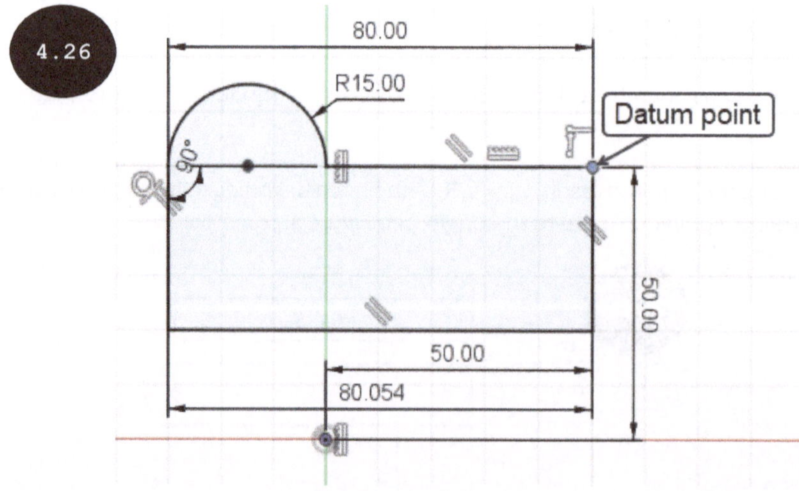

Modifying/Editing Dimensions

After applying dimensions, you may need to modify them due to changes in the design, revisions in the design, and so on. To modify an already applied dimension, double-click on the dimension value to be modified. A dimension box appears with the display of the current dimension value in the drawing area, see Figure 4.27. Enter the new dimension value in this box and then press ENTER. The selected dimension value gets modified. Also, the length of the entity is changed, accordingly.

Working with Different States of a Sketch

In Autodesk Fusion, a sketch can be either under defined or fully defined. Both these states of a sketch are discussed next.

Under Defined Sketch

An under-defined sketch is a sketch, whose all degrees of freedom are not fixed. This means that the entities of the sketch can change their shape, size, and position upon being dragged. Figure 4.28 shows a rectangular sketch in which the length of the rectangle is defined as 50 mm. However, the width and the position of the rectangle concerning the origin are not defined. This means that the width and position of the rectangle can be changed by dragging the respective entities of the rectangle. Note that the entities of an under-defined sketch appear in blue color in the drawing area.

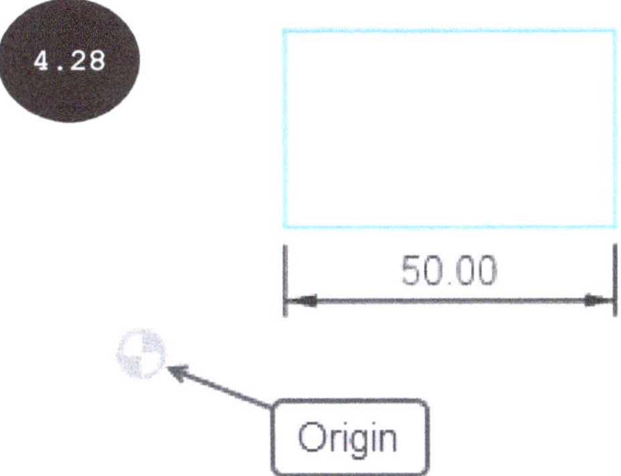

Fully Defined Sketch

A fully defined sketch is a sketch, whose all degrees of freedom are fixed. This means that the entities of the sketch cannot change their shape, size, and position upon being dragged. Figure 4.29 shows a rectangular sketch in which the length, width, and position of the sketch are defined. Note that the entities of a fully defined sketch appear in black. Also, a small lock icon appears on the sketch under the expanded **Sketches** folder in the **BROWSER**, see Figure 4.30.

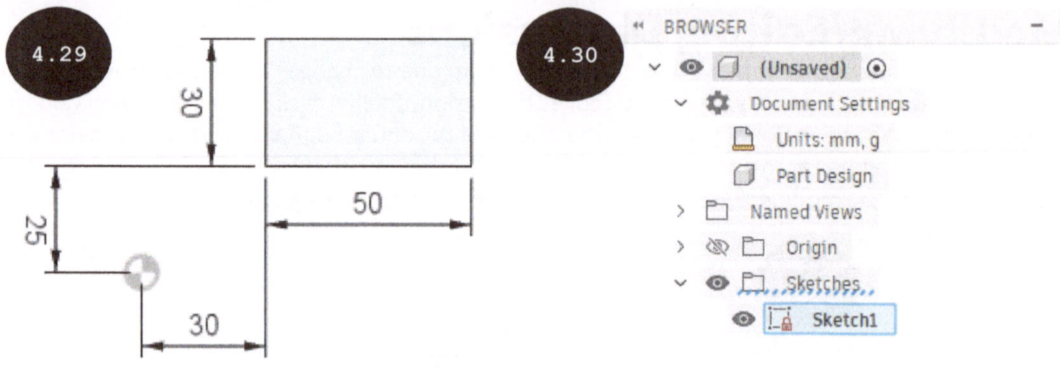

Tip: The sketch shown in Figure 4.29 is a fully defined sketch as all its entities are dimensioned and the required constraints have been applied. The constraints applied in this sketch are horizontal to the horizontal entities and vertical to the vertical entities. Horizontal and vertical constraints are applied automatically to the entities while drawing them.

Note: When you apply a dimension to a fully defined sketch, the **Over-constrained sketch** message window appears (see Figure 4.31), informing you that adding this dimension would over-constrain the sketch and suggests applying it as the driven dimension. Click on the **OK** button to apply the dimension as the driven dimension. The newly applied dimension becomes a driven dimension and acts as a reference dimension only. As a result, the sketch does not become over-constrained. Figure 4.32 shows a sketch with driven dimension applied on a vertical entity.

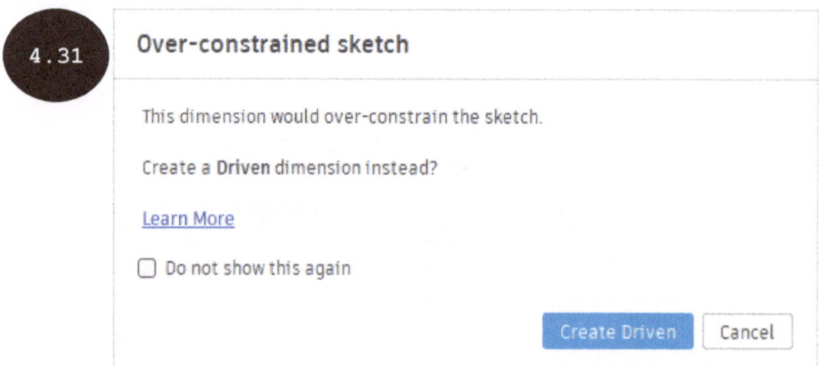

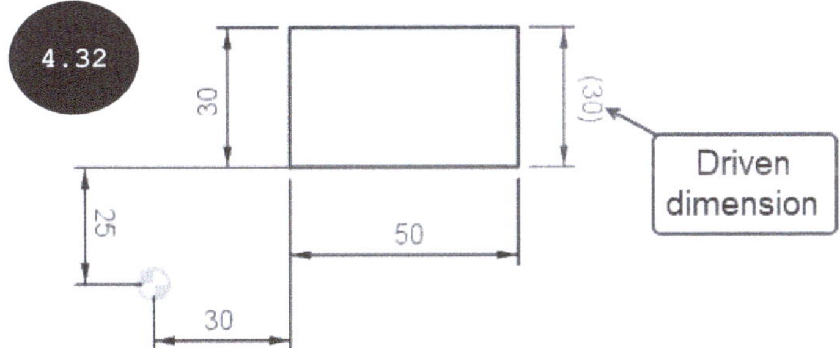

Working with SKETCH PALETTE

The **SKETCH PALETTE** dialog box appears every time a sketch is active. It provides quick access to commonly used sketch options and display settings, see Figure 4.33. Some of the options of the **SKETCH PALETTE** dialog box have been discussed earlier. The remaining options are discussed next.

Look At

The **Look At** tool is used for changing the orientation of the sketching plane, normal to the viewing direction. By default, the orientation of the sketching plane sets normal to the viewing direction, automatically. However, if its orientation has been changed while creating a sketch then you can click on the **Look At** tool in the **Options** rollout of the **SKETCH PALETTE** dialog box to change the orientation of the sketching plane normal to the viewing direction.

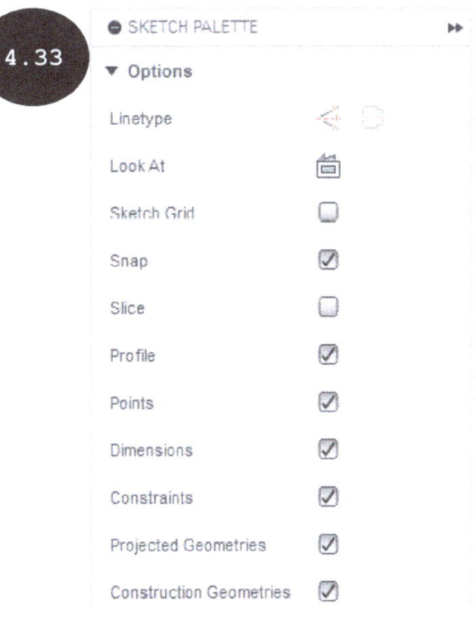

Slice

The **Slice** check box is used for cutting an object by using the sketching plane of the sketch. If you are creating a sketch on a sketching plane that is passing through an object, then you can select the **Slice** check box to cut the object such that the sketch appears in front of it, see Figure 4.34.

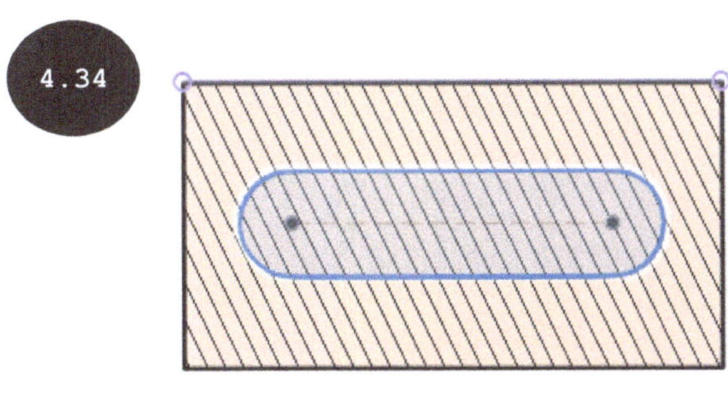

Front view

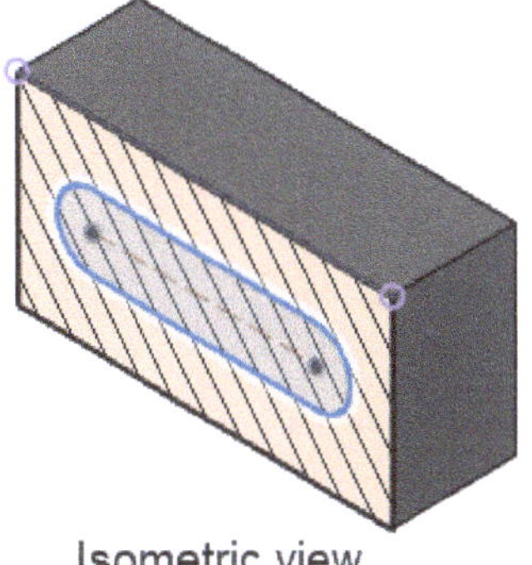

Isometric view

Profile

The **Profile** check box is used for displaying the shaded closed profiles in a sketch. By default, this check box is selected in the **Options** rollout of the **SKETCH PALETTE** dialog box. As a result, all the closed profiles of the sketch appear in a shaded display, see Figure 4.35. This helps to easily identify whether the profiles of the sketch are fully closed or not. Figures 4.35 (a) and (b) show a sketch with the **Profile** check box selected and cleared, respectively.

4.35

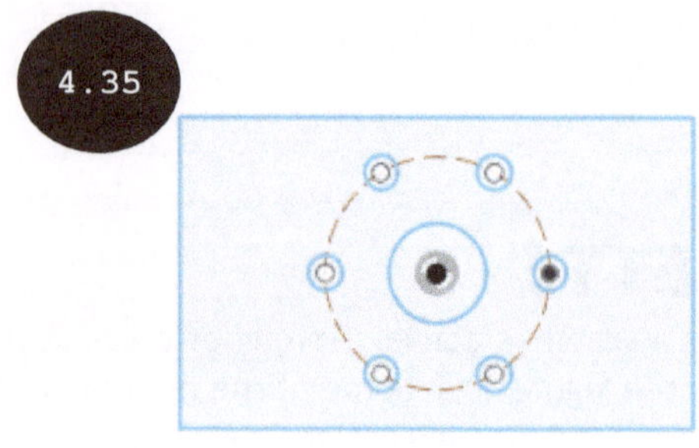

a) Profile check box is selected

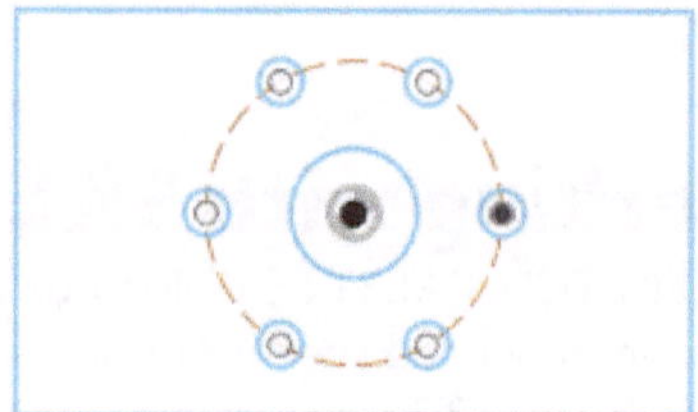

a) Profile check box is cleared

Points

The **Points** check box is used for displaying points on the open ends of the sketch. This helps in easily identifying the open connections of the sketch.

Dimensions

The **Dimensions** check box is used for turning on or off the visibility of the applied dimensions of the sketch in the drawing area. By default, this check box is selected in the **SKETCH PALETTE** dialog box. As a result, all the applied dimensions appear in the drawing area. You can temporarily disable the display of dimensions by clearing this check box.

Constraints

The **Constraints** check box is used for turning on or off the display of constraints symbols in the drawing area.

Projected Geometries

The **Projected Geometries** check box is used for turning on or off the display of projected geometries in the drawing area. You will learn about projecting geometry in later chapters.

3D Sketch

On selecting the **3D Sketch** check box, you can create a 3D sketch by using sketching tools such as **Line** and **Spline**. You will learn about creating 3D sketches in Chapter 8.

Tutorial 1

Draw the sketch of the model shown in Figure 4.36 and make it fully defined by applying all dimensions and constraints. The model shown in this figure is for your reference only. You will learn how to create 3D models in the later chapters. All dimensions are in mm.

4.36

R140
Ø120
2X R100
2X Ø50
2X R50
550
750

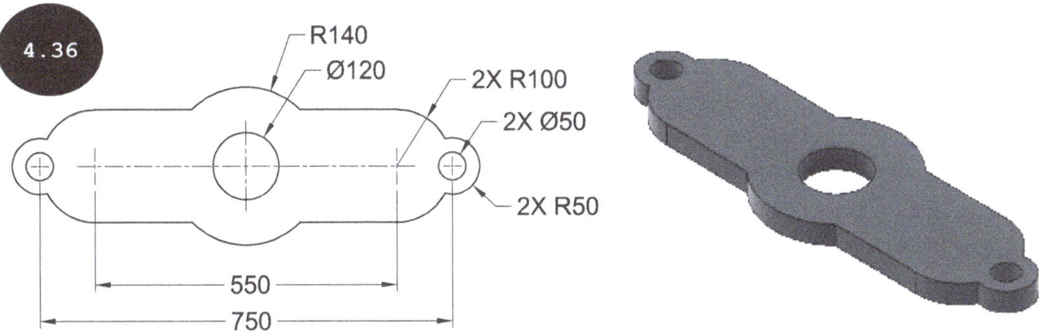

Section 1: Starting a New Part Design File

1. Click **File > New** in the **Application Bar** (see Figure 4.37) to display the **What do you want to design?** dialog box, see Figure 4.38.

4.37

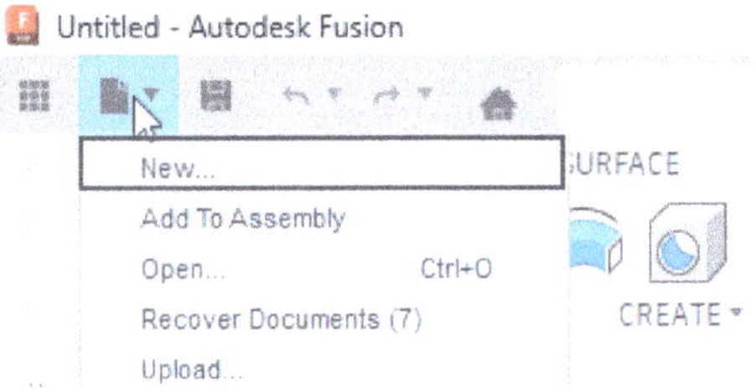

Untitled - Autodesk Fusion
New...
Add To Assembly
Open... Ctrl+O
Recover Documents (7)
Upload...
CREATE

4.38

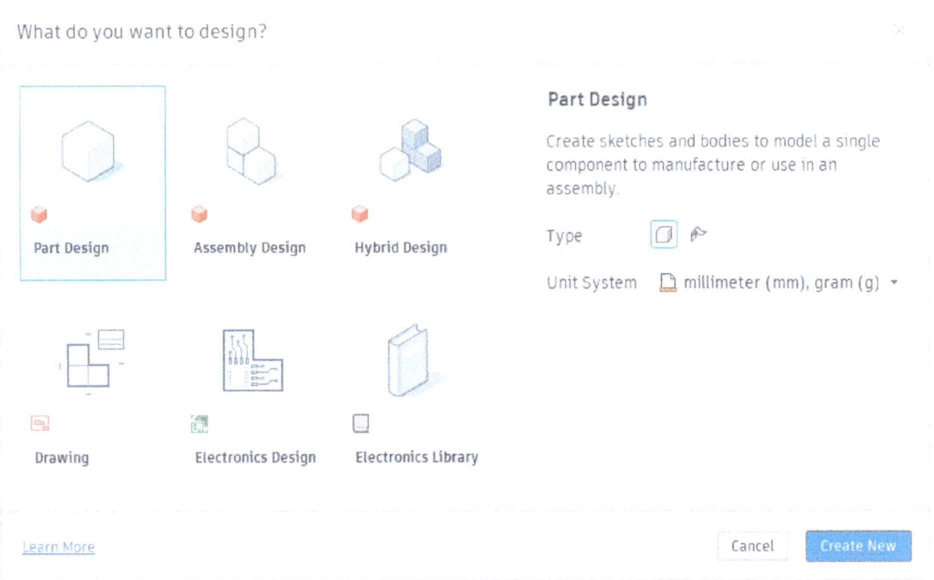

What do you want to design?
Part Design
Assembly Design
Hybrid Design
Drawing
Electronics Design
Electronics Library
Part Design
Create sketches and bodies to model a single component to manufacture or use in an assembly.
Type
Unit System
millimeter (mm), gram (g)
Learn More
Cancel
Create New

Note: If you are starting a new Autodesk Fusion session, the Part Design file opens automatically because it is set as the default design type. In this case, ensure that the **millimeter (mm), gram (g)** unit system is set for the opened Part Design file.

2. In the **What do you want to design?** dialog box, select the **Part Design** button and choose the **millimeter (mm), gram (g)** unit system from the **Unit System** drop-down list.

3. After specifying the required options, click the **Create New** button. A new Part Design file is created with the default name.

Section 2: Organizing the Data Panel

Now, you can organize the **Data Panel** by creating a project folder and sub-folders to save files.

1. Click on the **Show Data Panel** tool in the **Application Bar**, see Figure 4.39. The **Data Panel** appears.

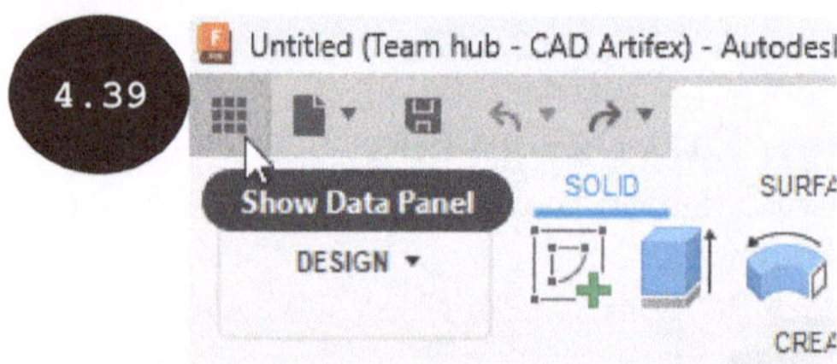

2. Create a new project named "**Autodesk Fusion 360**" using the **New Project** tool if it has not been created earlier.

3. Double-click on the **Autodesk Fusion 360** project in the **Data Panel** and then create the "**Chapter 04**" folder using the **New Folder** tool in the **Data Panel**.

4. Double-click on the **Chapter 04** folder in the **Data Panel** and then create the "**Tutorial**" sub-folder using the **New Folder** tool in the **Data Panel**.

5. Click on the cross-mark ✕ at the top right corner of the **Data Panel** to close it.

Section 3: Specifying Grid Settings

1. Invoke the **Grid and Snaps** flyout in the **Navigation Bar**, see Figure 4.40.

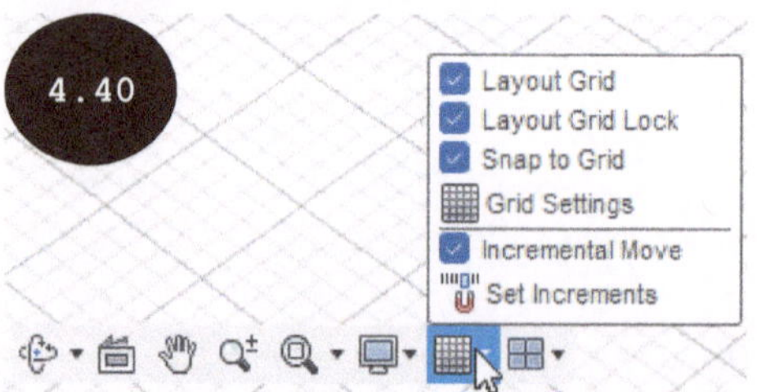

2. Click on the **Grid Settings** tool in the **Grid and Snaps** flyout. The **GRID SETTINGS** dialog box appears, see Figure 4.41.

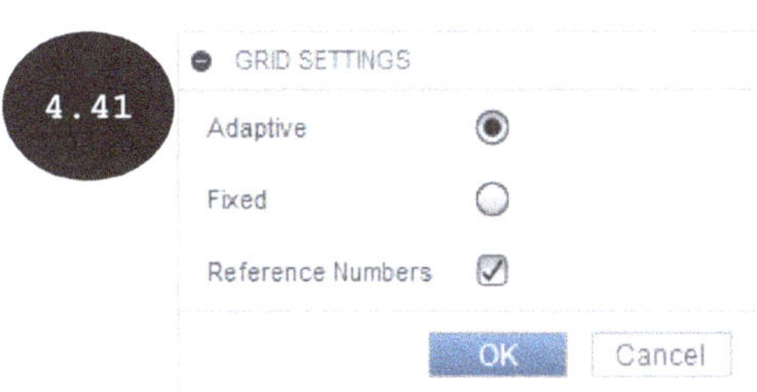

3. Ensure that the **Adaptive** radio button is selected in the **GRID SETTINGS** dialog box.

4. Click on the **OK** button in the **GRID SETTINGS** dialog box.

Section 4: Creating the Sketch

1. Click on the **Create Sketch** tool in the **Toolbar**, see Figure 4.42. Three default planes: Front, Top, and Right, which are mutually perpendicular to each other, appear in the graphics area.

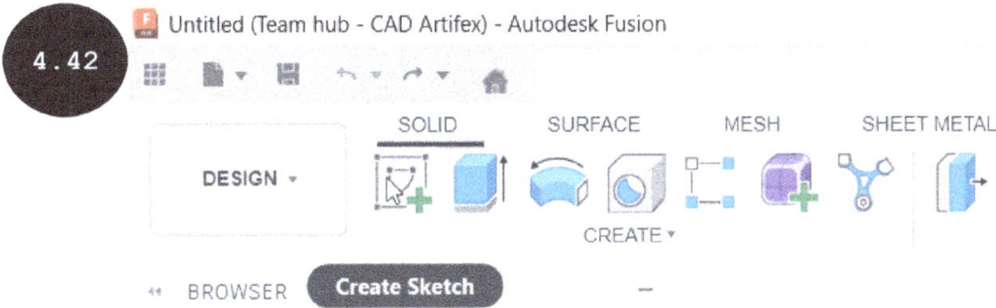

2. Move the cursor over the Top plane and then click the left mouse button when it gets highlighted in the graphics area. The Top plane becomes the sketching plane for creating the sketch and it is oriented normal to the viewing direction. Also, the **SKETCH** contextual tab and the **SKETCH PALETTE** dialog box appear.

3. Ensure that the **Sketch Grid** and **Snap** check boxes are selected in the **SKETCH PALETTE** dialog box to display the grids and to snap the movement of the cursor on the grid lines.

   Now, you can create the entities of the sketch.

4. Click on the **Center Diameter Circle** tool of the **CREATE** panel in the **SKETCH** contextual tab, see Figure 4.43. The **Center Diameter Circle** tool is activated. Alternatively, press the **C** key to activate the **Center Diameter Circle** tool.

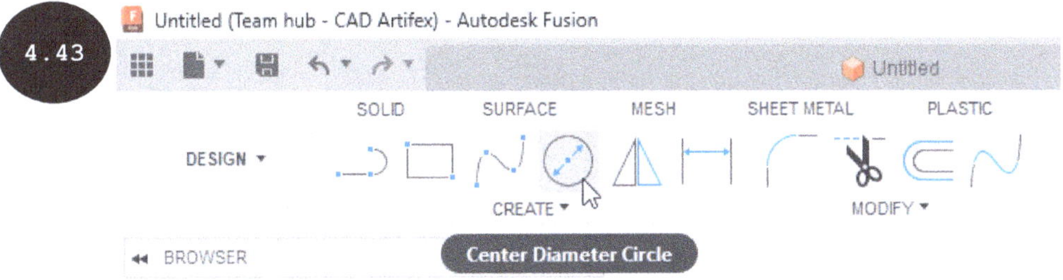

5. Move the cursor to the origin and then click to specify the center point of the circle when the cursor snaps to the origin.

6. Move the cursor horizontally toward the right and then click to specify a point when the diameter of the circle appears as 120 mm in the dimension box, see Figure 4.44. A circle of diameter 120 mm is drawn, and the **Center Diameter Circle** tool is still active.

4.44

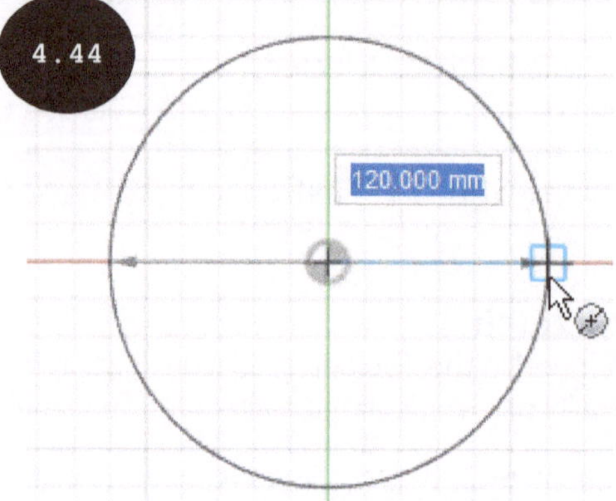

7. Move the cursor to the origin and click to specify the center point of another circle when the cursor snaps to the origin.

8. Move the cursor horizontally toward the right and click when the diameter of the circle appears as 280 mm. The circle is created, and the **Center Diameter Circle** tool remains activated.

Tip: While drawing sketch entities, you may need to zoom into or zoom out of the drawing display area. To do this, scroll the middle mouse button. Alternatively, click on the **Zoom** tool in the **Navigation Bar**, which is available in the lower middle section of the screen. Next, drag the cursor upward or downward.

9. Right-click in the drawing area and then click on the **OK** tool in the Marking Menu that appears to exit the **Center Diameter Circle** tool.

10. Invoke the **CREATE** drop-down menu in the **SKETCH** contextual tab of the **Toolbar** and then click on **Slot > Center Point Slot**, see Figure 4.45. The **Center Point Slot** tool is activated.

4.45

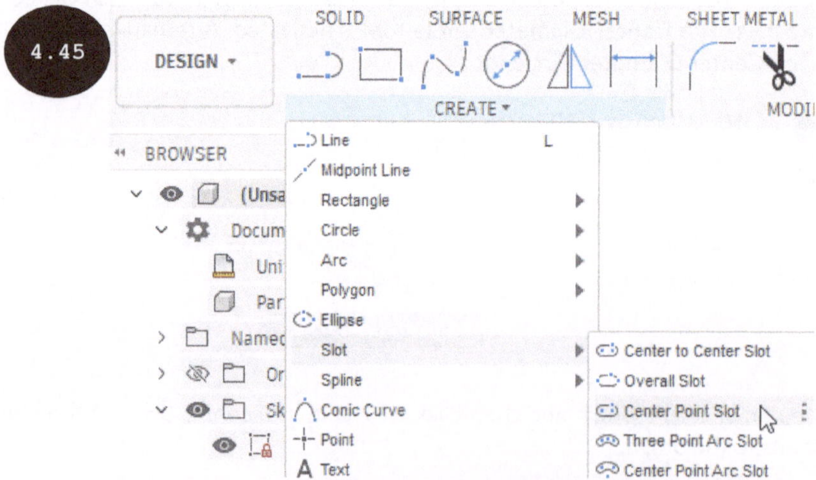

11. Move the cursor to the origin and then click to specify the center point of the slot when the cursor snaps to the origin.

12. Move the cursor horizontally toward the right and click when the half length of the slot appears as 275 mm (550/2 = 275), see Figure 4.46. Next, move the cursor to a distance in the drawing area. A preview of the slot appears.

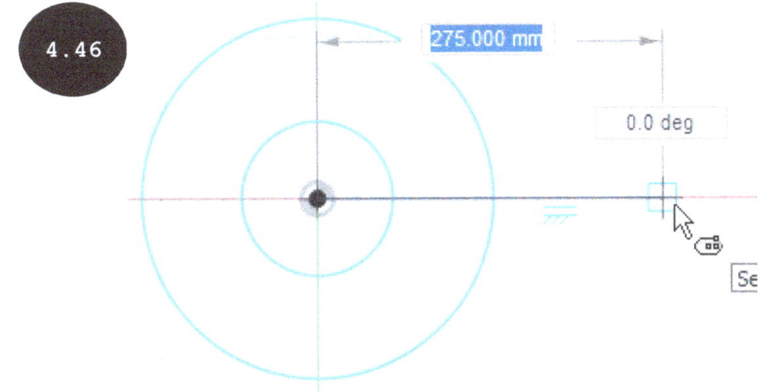

13. Click on the left mouse button when the width of the slot appears as 200 mm, see Figure 4.47. The slot is created. Next, press the ESC key to exit the **Center Point Slot** tool.

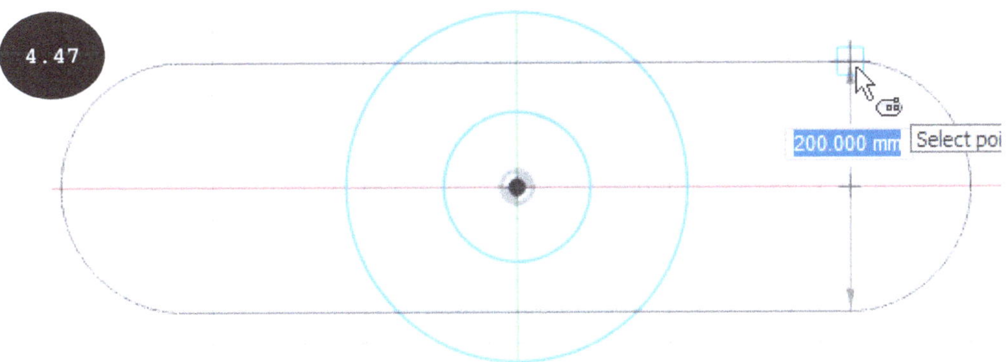

14. Click on the **Center Diameter Circle** tool in the **CREATE** panel of the **SKETCH** contextual tab or press the C key. The **Center Diameter Circle** tool gets activated.

15. Move the cursor toward the midpoint of the right slot arc, see Figure 4.48 and then click to specify the center point of the circle when the cursor snaps to the midpoint of the slot arc.

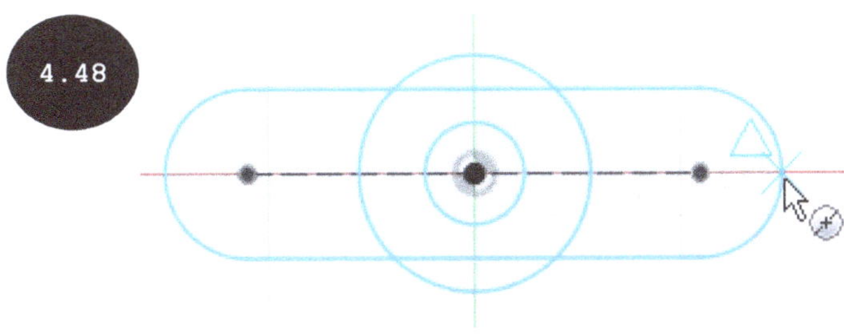

16. Move the cursor horizontally toward the right and click when the diameter of the circle appears as 50 mm. A circle of diameter 50 mm is created, and the **Center Diameter Circle** tool remains activated.

17. Move the cursor to the center point of the previously created circle of diameter 50 mm and then click to specify the center point of another circle when the cursor snaps to it.

18. Move the cursor horizontally toward the right and click when the diameter of the circle appears as 100 mm. The circle is created, see Figure 4.49.

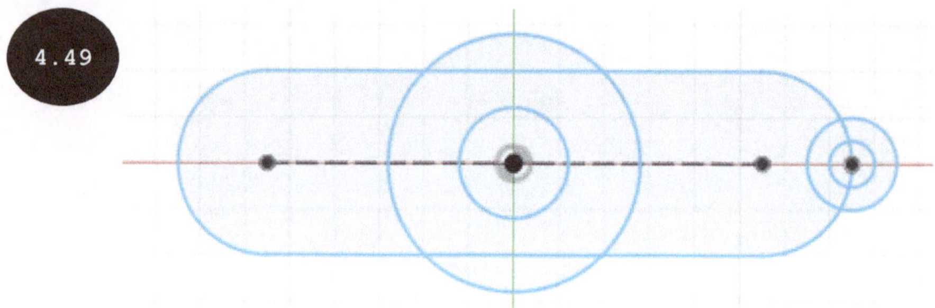
4.49

19. Similarly, create two circles of diameters 50 mm and 100 mm on the left side of the slot, see Figure 4.50. Next, press the ESC key to exit the **Center Diameter Circle** tool.

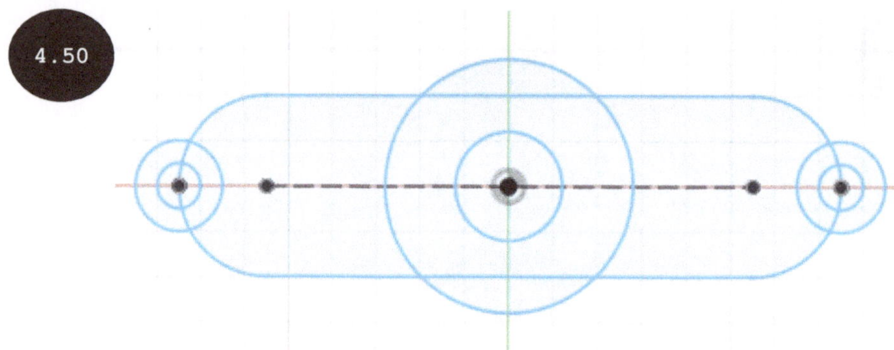
4.50

Now, you need to create a vertical construction line.

20. Click on the **Line** tool in the **Toolbar** or press the **L** key. The **Line** tool gets activated.

21. Click on the **Construction** tool in the **Linetype** area of the **Options** rollout of the **SKETCH PALETTE** dialog box to activate the construction mode, see Figure 4.51.

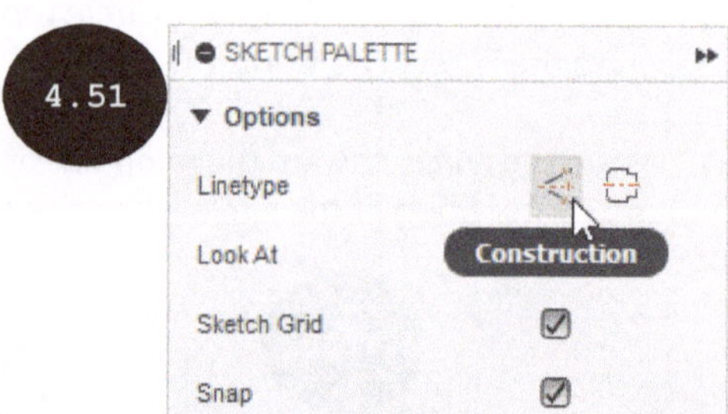

4.51

22. Create a vertical construction line of any length starting from the origin, see Figure 4.52. Next, press the ESC key to exit the **Line** tool. Note that in Figure 4.52, the display of grids is turned off for clarity of the image.

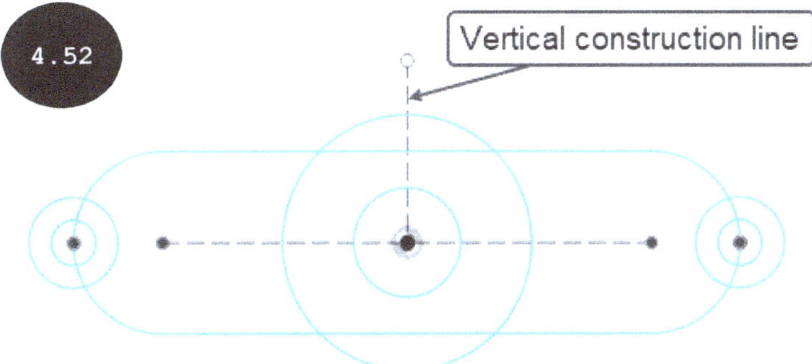

Section 5: Trimming Sketch Entities

Now, you need to trim the unwanted entities of the sketch.

1. Click on the **Trim** tool in the **MODIFY** panel of the **SKETCH** contextual tab or press the T key. The **Trim** tool gets activated. 

2. Move the cursor over the portion of the lower horizontal slot entity which lies inside the outer circle, see Figure 4.53. Next, click the left mouse button when it is highlighted. The selected portion of the entity is trimmed, see Figure 4.54. Also, a warning message appears at the lower right section of the drawing area which informs you that the constraints or dimensions were removed during the trimming operation. Ignore this warning message.

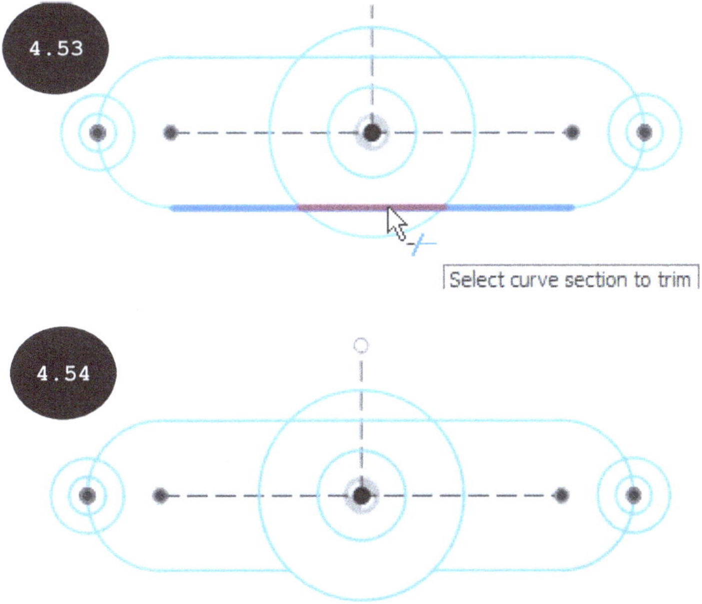

3. Similarly, click on the other unwanted entities of the sketch one by one to trim them. Figure 4.55 shows the sketch after trimming all the unwanted entities.

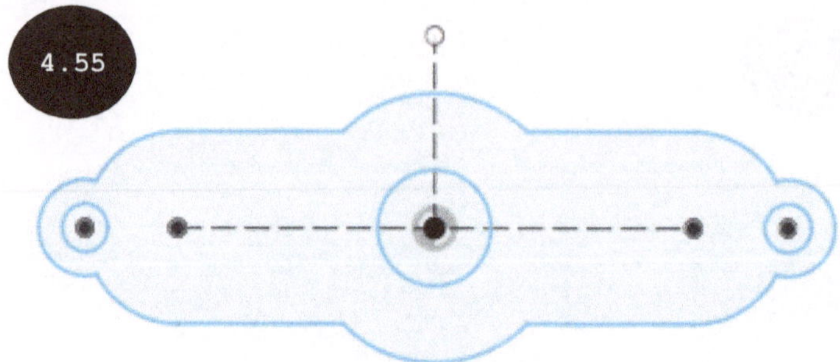

Tip: While trimming sketch entities, you may need to zoom in to or out of the drawing display area. To do this, scroll the middle mouse button. Alternatively, click on the **Zoom** tool in the **Navigation Bar** and then drag the cursor upward or downward. To exit the tool, press ESC.

4. Once you have completed the trimming operation, press the ESC key to exit the **Trim** tool.

Section 6: Applying Dimensions

After creating the sketch, you need to make it fully defined by applying the required dimensions and constraints to the sketch entities.

1. Click on the **Sketch Dimension** tool in the **CREATE** panel of the **SKETCH** contextual tab or press the **D** key to activate the **Sketch Dimension** tool.

2. Select a circle whose center point is at the origin. The diameter dimension of the selected circle gets attached to the cursor, see Figure 4.56.

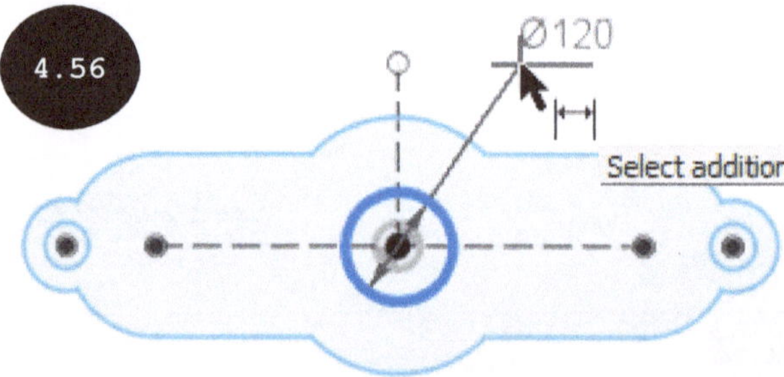

3. Move the cursor to a location where you want to place the dimension in the drawing area and then click to specify the placement point. A dimension box appears, see Figure 4.57.

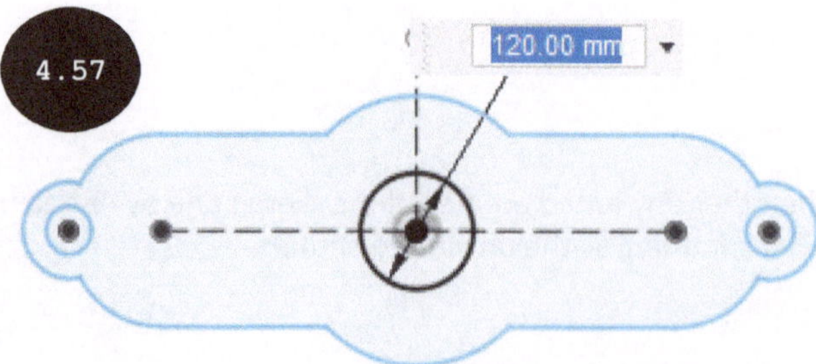

4. Ensure that the value 120 mm is entered in the dimension box as the diameter of the circle.

5. Press ENTER. The diameter dimension is applied to the circle. Also, the **Sketch Dimension** tool remains activated.

6. Click on the right-side circle of the sketch. The diameter dimension of the selected circle gets attached to the cursor, see Figure 4.58.

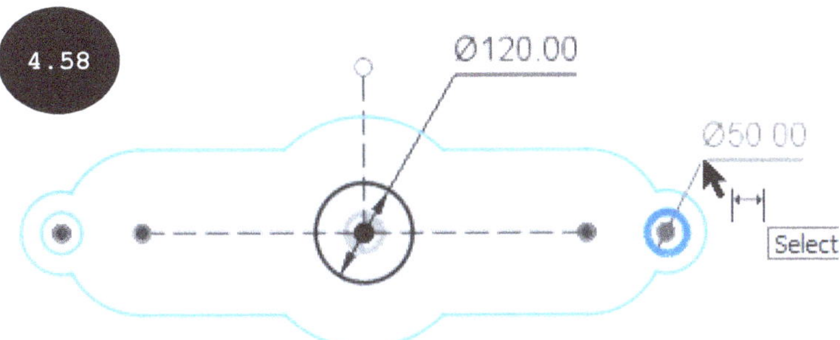

7. Click to specify the placement point in the drawing area. A dimension box appears.

8. Ensure that the value 50 mm is entered in the dimension box as the diameter of the circle. Next, press the ENTER key. The diameter dimension is applied to the circle.

9. Similarly, apply the remaining dimensions of the sketch. Figure 4.59 shows the sketch after applying all the required dimensions.

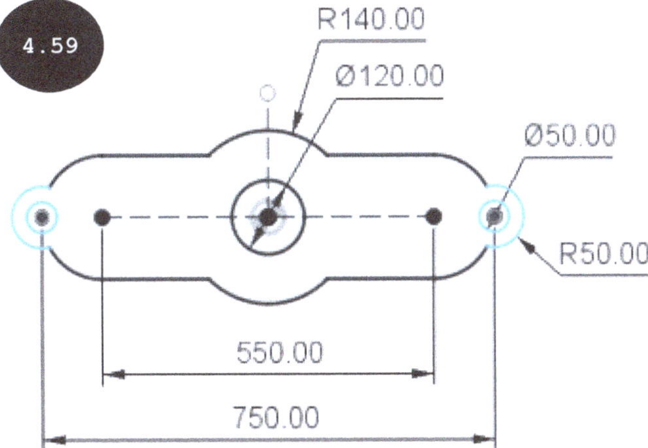

Note that even after applying the dimensions as shown in Figure 4.59, the sketch is not fully defined and some of its entities appear in blue. You need to apply the required constraints to make the sketch fully defined.

Section 7: Applying Constraints

Now, you need to apply the constraints to the sketch.

1. Click on the **Equal** tool in the **CONSTRAINTS** panel in the **SKETCH** contextual tab of the **Toolbar** to apply an equal constraint between the entities having equal dimensions.

2. Click on a circle of diameter 50 mm, see Figure 4.60 and then click on the other circle with the same diameter, see Figure 4.61. An equal constraint is applied between the selected circles. The **Equal** constraint tool remains activated.

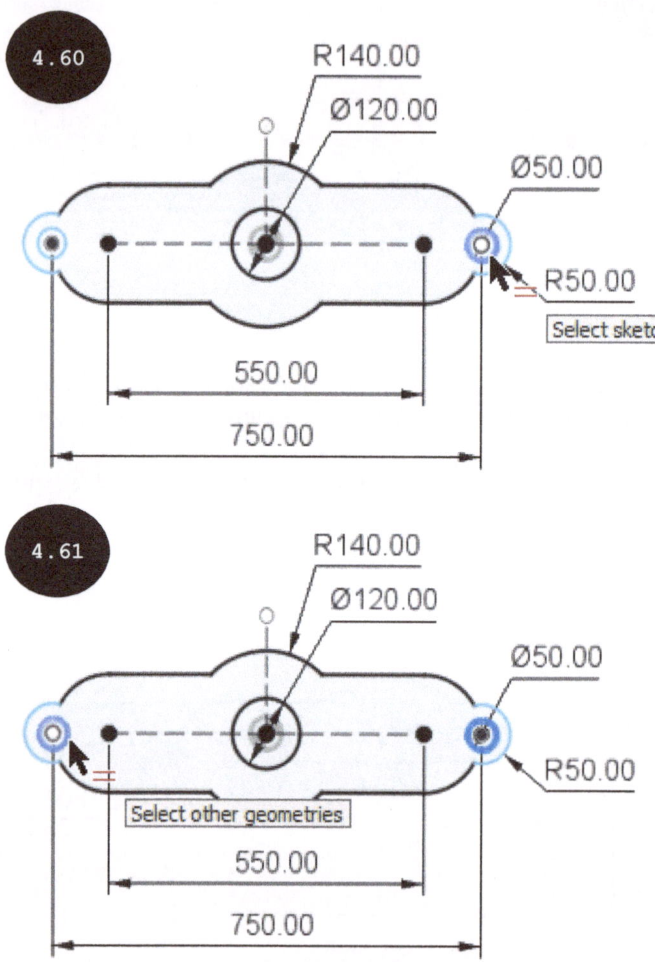

3. Similarly, click on both the arcs of radius 50 mm one by one to apply an equal constraint between them. Next, press the ESC key to exit the **Equal** constraint tool.

   Now, you need to apply symmetric constraints to the sketch entities.

4. Click on the **Symmetry** tool in the **CONSTRAINTS** panel in the **SKETCH** contextual tab of the **Toolbar** to apply symmetric constraints between the entities.

5. Select the center points of the two circles of diameter 50 mm and the vertical construction line one by one, see Figure 4.62. A symmetric constraint is applied between the selected center points and the vertical construction line. Also, the sketch becomes fully defined and all its entities appear in black, see Figure 4.63.

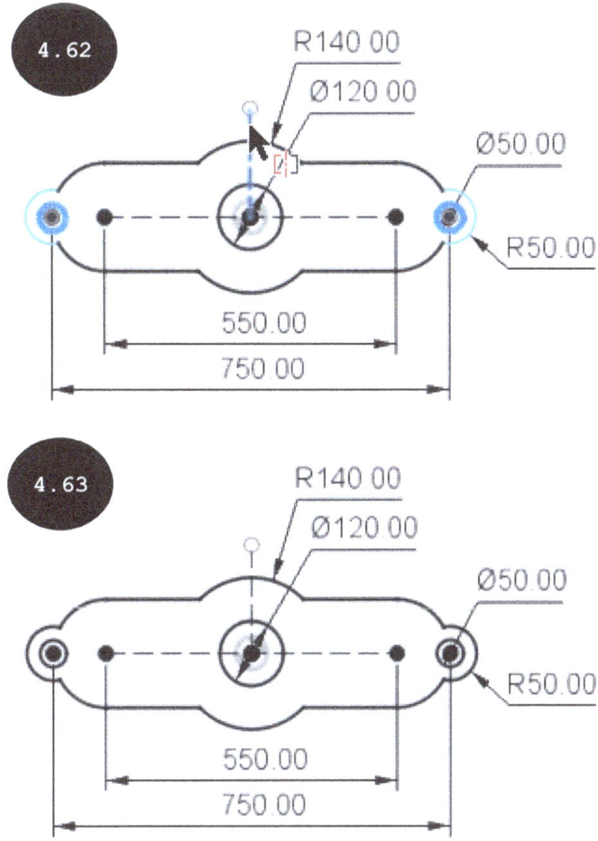

Note: In Figure 4.63, the display of constraints is turned off. You can turn on or off the display of the constraints in the drawing area by selecting or clearing the **Constraints** check box in the **Options** rollout of the **SKETCH PALETTE** dialog box, respectively.

Section 8: Saving the Sketch

1. Click on the **Save** tool in the **Application Bar** and then enter **Tutorial 1** in the **Name** field of the **Save** dialog box that appears.

2. Ensure the location *Autodesk Fusion 360 > Chapter 04 > Tutorial* is specified in the **Location** field of the dialog box to save the file of this tutorial. To specify the location, you need to expand the **Save** dialog box by clicking on the down arrow next to the **Location** field of the dialog box.

3. Click on the **Save** button in the dialog box. The sketch is saved with the name Tutorial 1 in the specified location (*Autodesk Fusion 360 > Chapter 04 > Tutorial*).

Tutorial 2

Draw the sketch shown in Figure 4.64 and make it fully defined by applying the dimensions and constraints. The model shown in this figure is for your reference only. You will learn how to create 3D models in the later chapters. All dimensions are in mm.

4.64

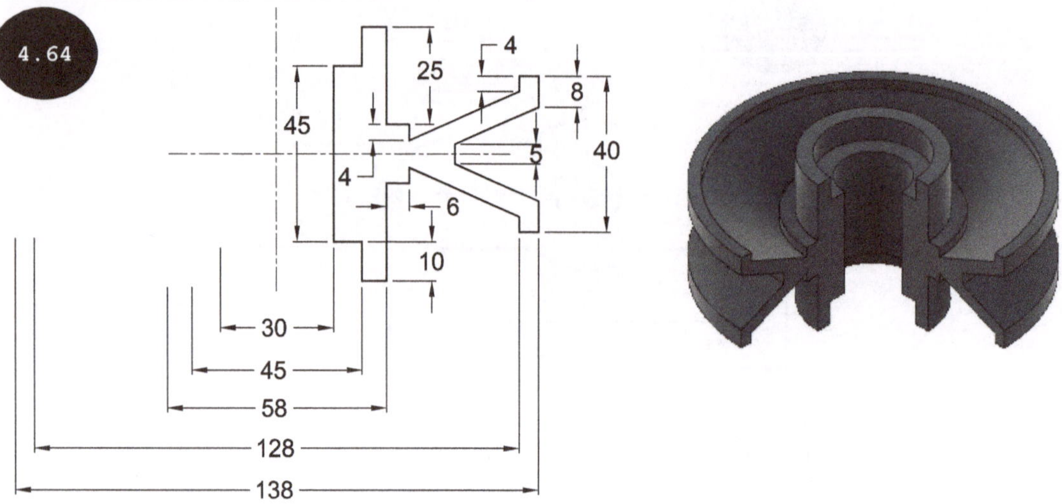

Section 1: Starting a New Design File

1. Click **File** > **New** in the **Application Bar** (see Figure 4.65) to display the **What do you want to design?** dialog box, see Figure 4.66.

4.65

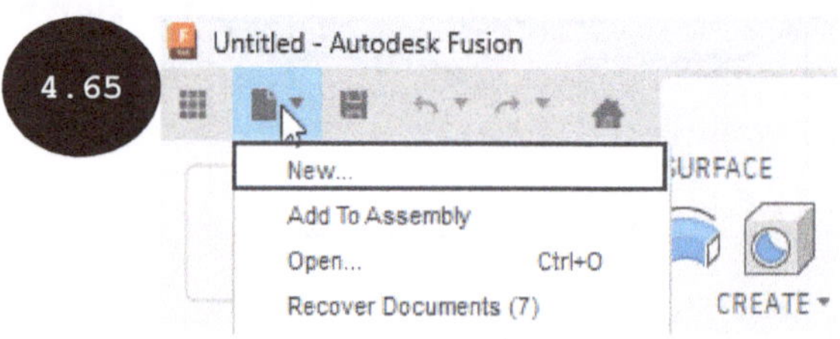

4.66

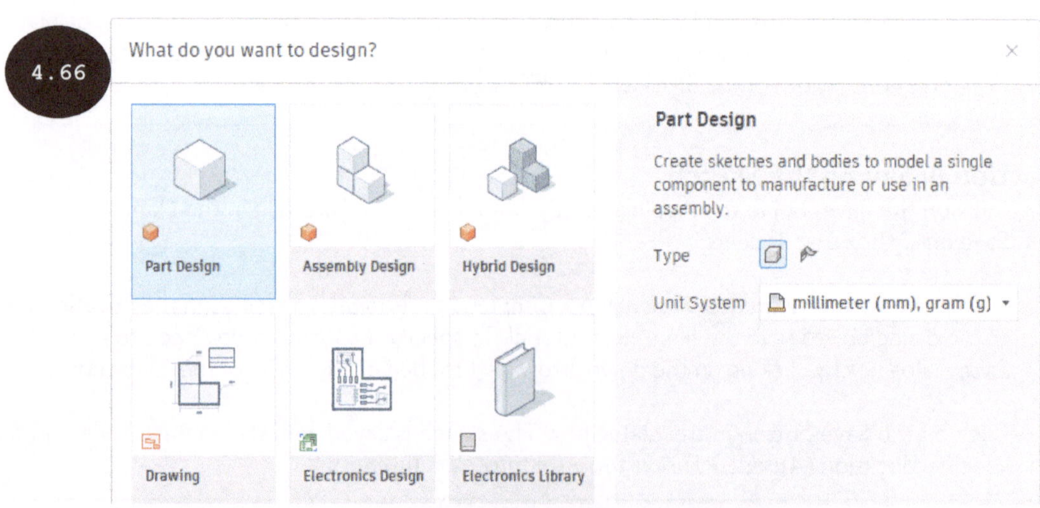

Note: If you are starting a new Autodesk Fusion session, the Part Design file opens automatically because it is set as the default design type. In this case, ensure that the **millimeter (mm), gram (g)** unit system is set for the opened Part Design file.

2. In the **What do you want to design?** dialog box, select the **Part Design** button and choose the **millimeter (mm), gram (g)** unit system from the **Unit System** drop-down list.

3. After specifying the required options, click the **Create New** button. A new Part Design file is created with the default name "**Untitled**".

Section 2: Organizing the Data Panel

1. Click on the **Show Data Panel** tool in the **Application Bar**, see Figure 4.67. The **Data Panel** appears.

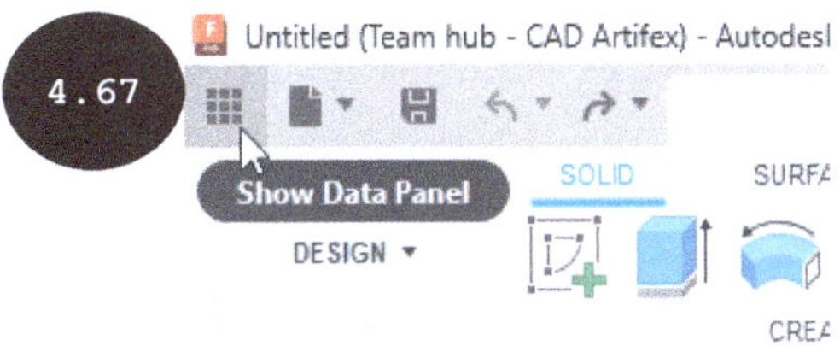

2. Ensure that the **Autodesk Fusion 360** project > **Chapter 04** folder > **Tutorial** sub-folders are created in the **Data Panel**. You need to create these project folders, if not created earlier.

3. Click on the cross-mark ✕ at the top right corner of the **Data Panel** to close it.

Section 3: Creating the Sketch

1. Click on the **Create Sketch** tool in the **Toolbar**, see Figure 4.68. Three default planes: Front, Top, and Right, which are mutually perpendicular to each other, appear in the graphics area.

2. Move the cursor over the Front plane and then click the left mouse button when it gets highlighted. The Front plane becomes the sketching plane for creating the sketch and it is oriented normal to the viewing direction. Also, the **SKETCH** contextual tab and the **SKETCH PALETTE** dialog box appear.

Now, you need to turn off the grids and snap modes. As Autodesk Fusion is parametric software, you can turn off the grids and snap modes and create a sketch by specifying points arbitrarily in the drawing area and then applying the required dimensions.

3. Clear the **Sketch Grid** and **Snap** check boxes in the **SKETCH PALETTE** dialog box to turn off the grids and snap modes.

   Now, you can create the sketch.

4. Click on the **Line** tool in the **Toolbar** or press the **L** key. The **Line** tool gets activated.

5. Click on the **Construction** tool in the **Linetype** area of the **SKETCH PALETTE** dialog box to create construction lines in the drawing area.

6. Create vertical and horizontal construction lines of any length starting from the origin one by one, see Figure 4.69. After creating the construction lines, do not exit the **Line** tool.

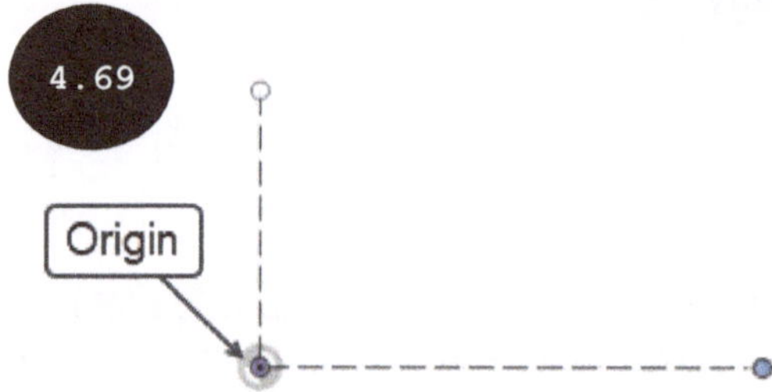

7. Deactivate the construction mode by clicking on the **Construction** tool again in the **SKETCH PALETTE** dialog box.

8. Move the cursor over the horizontal construction line, see Figure 4.70 and then click to specify the start point of the line.

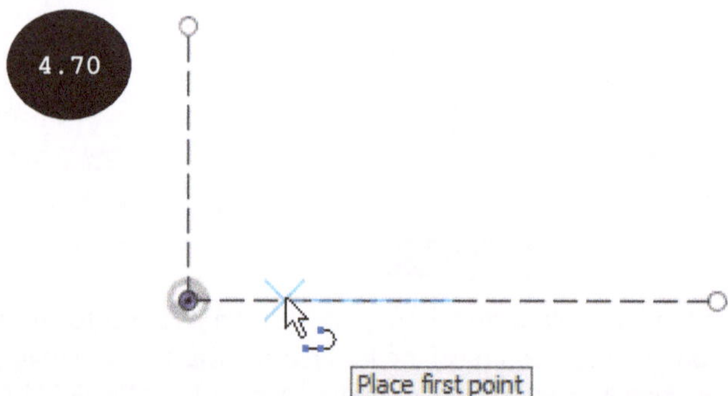

9. Move the cursor vertically upward and then click to specify the endpoint of the line when the length of the line appears close to 22.5 mm near the cursor, see Figure 4.71. A vertical line of length close to 22.5 mm is created.

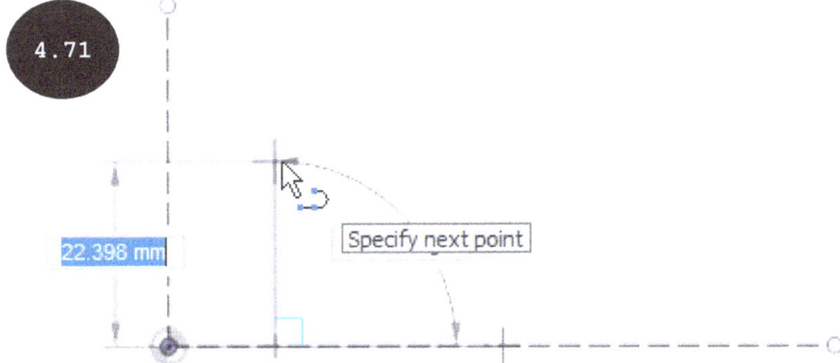

10. Move the cursor horizontally toward the right and click to specify the endpoint of the second line when the length of the line appears close to 7.5 mm. A horizontal line of length close to 7.5 mm is created.

11. Move the cursor vertically upward and click to specify the endpoint of the line when the length of the line appears close to 10 mm. A vertical line of length close to 10 mm is created.

12. Move the cursor horizontally toward the right and click when the length of the line appears close to 6.5 mm. A horizontal line of length close to 6.5 mm is created.

13. Move the cursor vertically downward and click when the length of the line appears close to 25 mm.

14. Move the cursor horizontally toward the right and click when the length of the line appears close to 6 mm.

15. Move the cursor vertically downward and click when the length of the line appears close to 4 mm.

16. Move the cursor toward the right at an angle, see Figure 4.72 and then click to specify the endpoint of the inclined line when the line appears similar to the one shown in Figure 4.72.

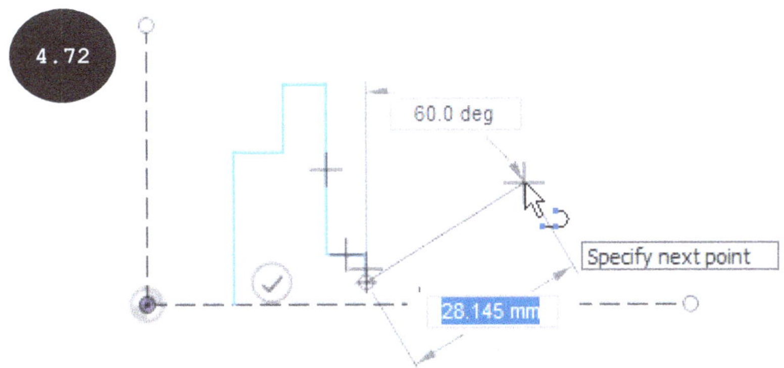

17. Move the cursor vertically upward and click when the length of the line appears close to 4 mm.

18. Move the cursor horizontally toward the right and click when the length of the line appears close to 5 mm.

19. Move the cursor vertically downward and click when the length of the line appears close to 8 mm.

20. Move the cursor parallel to the inclined line toward the left (see Figure 4.73) and then click on the left mouse button just above the horizontal construction line, see Figure 4.73.

    Note that if the symbol of parallel constraint does not appear, then first move the cursor over the existing inclined line and then move it parallel to the existing inclined line.

4.73

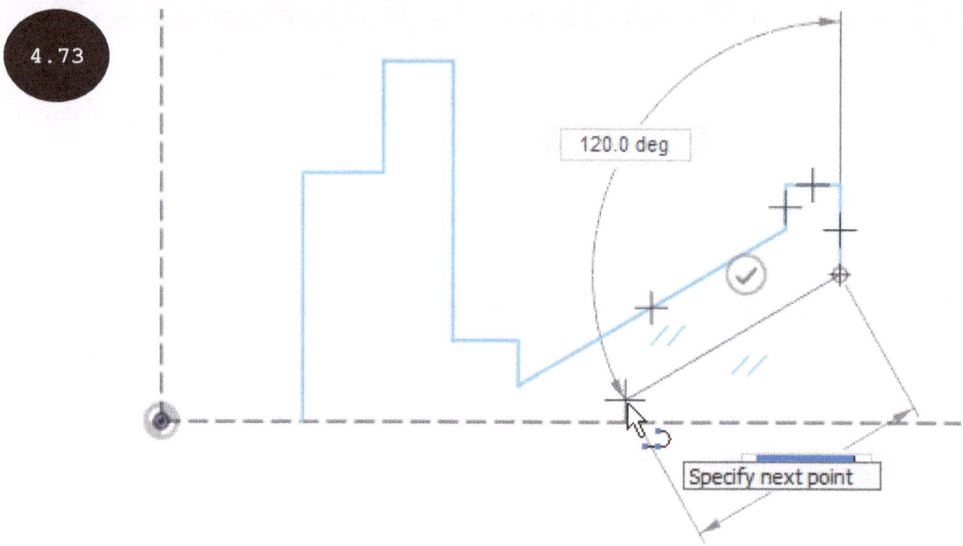

21. Move the cursor vertically downward and then click the left mouse button when the cursor snaps to the horizontal centerline.

22. Press the ESC key to exit the **Line** tool. Figure 4.74 shows the sketch after creating its upper half.

4.74

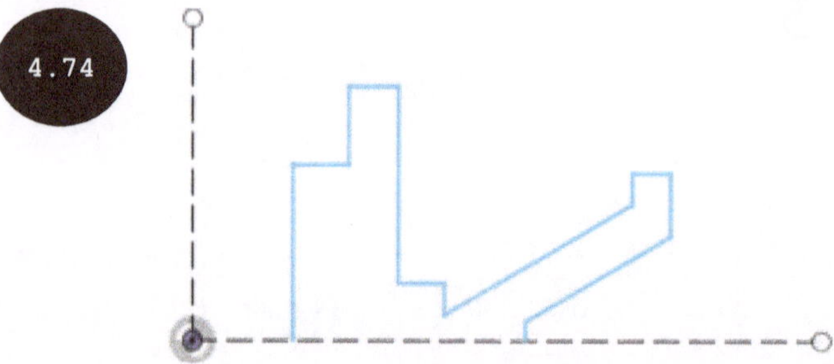

Section 4: Mirroring Sketch Entities

After creating the upper half of the sketch, you need to mirror it to create the lower half of the sketch.

1. Click on the **Mirror** tool in the **CREATE** panel in the **SKETCH** contextual tab of the **Toolbar**. The **MIRROR** dialog box appears, see Figure 4.75.

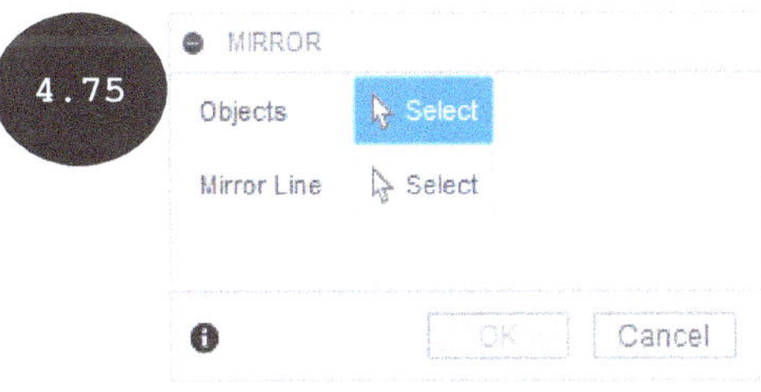

2. Select all the sketch entities except the vertical and horizontal construction lines as the entities to be mirrored. You can select the entities one by one by clicking the left mouse button or by drawing a window around the entities to be selected, see Figure 4.76. You can draw a window by dragging the cursor.

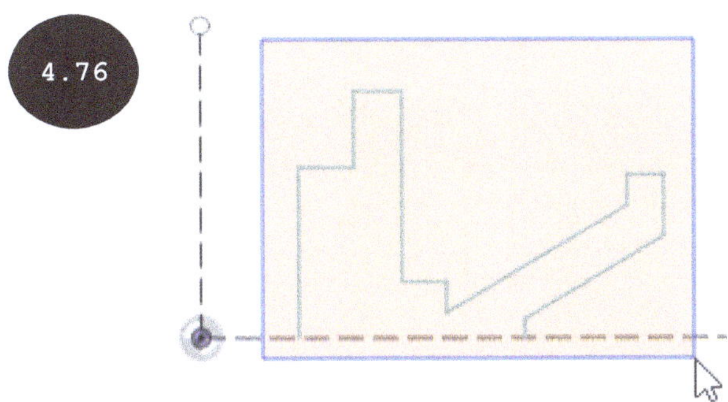

3. Click on the **Mirror Line** selection option in the **MIRROR** dialog box to activate it and then click on the horizontal construction line as the mirroring line in the drawing area. A preview of the lower half of the sketch appears.

4. Click on the **OK** button in the **MIRROR** dialog box. The lower half of the sketch is created, see Figure 4.77.

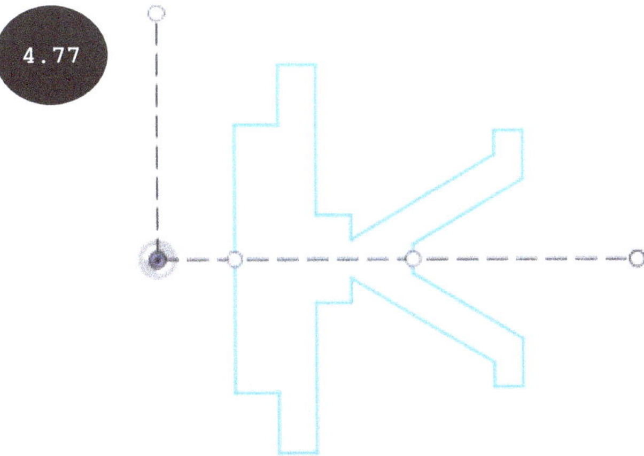

Section 5: Applying Dimensions

Now, you need to apply dimensions to make the sketch fully defined. Constraints such as horizontal, vertical, and parallel are already applied to the sketch entities while drawing them.

1. Press the D key. The **Sketch Dimension** tool gets activated.
2. Click to select both the endpoints of the vertical line to the extreme left of the sketch one by one, see Figure 4.78. The nb appears attached to the cursor.

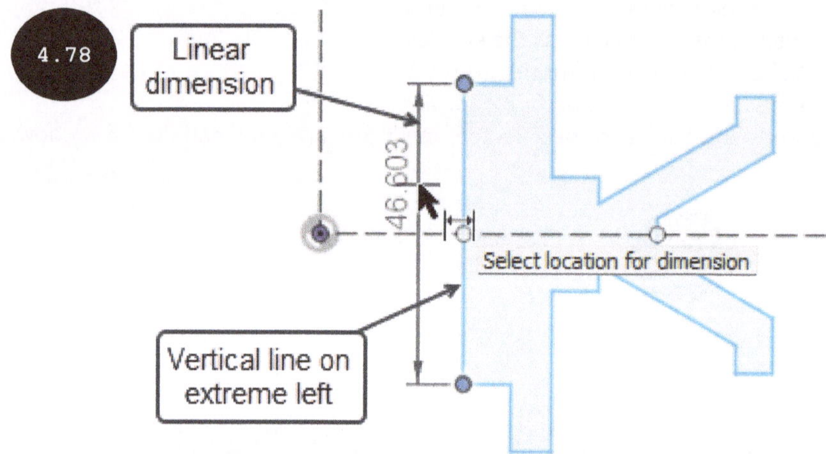

3. Move the cursor toward the left to a distance and then click to specify the placement point. A dimension box appears.
4. Enter **45** in the dimension box and then press ENTER. The length of the line is modified, and the dimension is applied, see Figure 4.79. Also, the **Sketch Dimension** tool remains active.
5. Click on the next vertical line, see Figure 4.80. The linear dimension is attached to the cursor. Next, move the cursor toward the left to a distance and then click to specify the placement point. A dimension box appears.

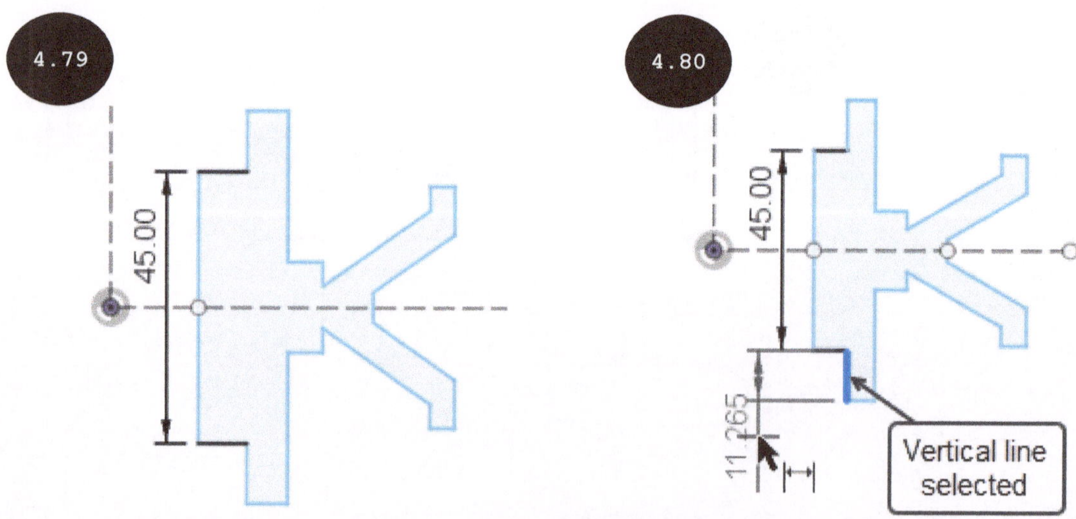

6. Enter **10** in the dimension box and then press ENTER. The length of the line is modified to 10 mm and the linear dimension is applied. Also, the **Sketch Dimension** tool remains active.

7. Similarly, apply the remaining linear dimensions to the sketch entities, see Figure 4.81.

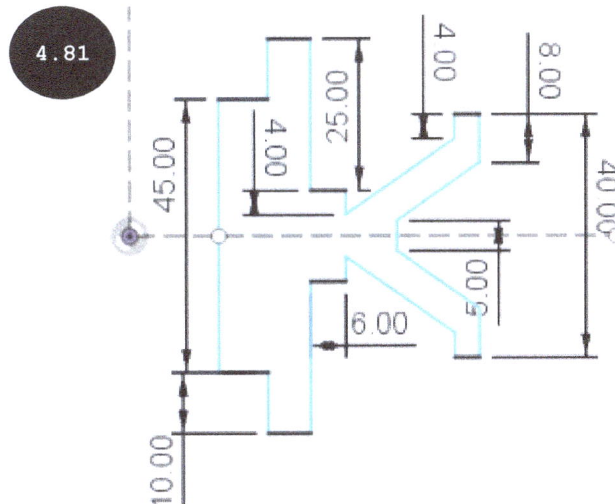

After applying the linear dimensions, you need to apply the linear diameter dimensions.

8. Ensure that the **Sketch Dimension** tool is activated, and then select the vertical construction line. The linear dimension of the vertical construction line is attached to the cursor. Next, select the vertical sketch line to the extreme left. The linear dimension between the selected entities is attached to the cursor, see Figure 4.82.

9. Right-click in the drawing area and then click on the **Diameter Dimension** option in the Marking Menu that appears, see Figure 4.83. The linear diameter dimension appears attached to the cursor. Next, click to specify the placement point. A dimension box appears.

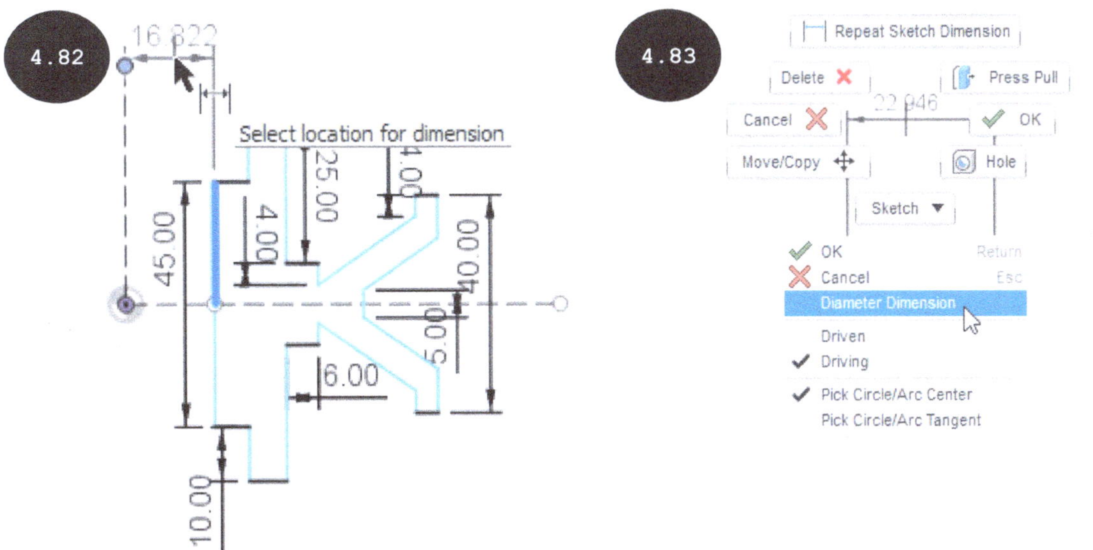

10. Enter **30** in the dimension box and then press ENTER. The linear diameter dimension is applied, see Figure 4.84.

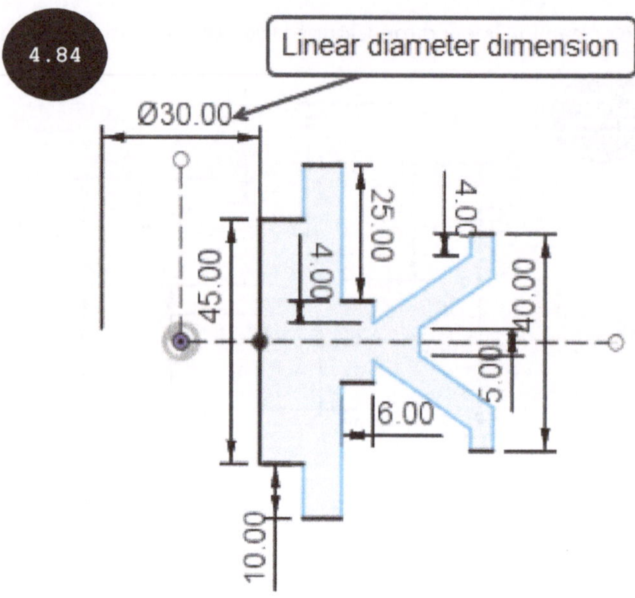

11. Similarly, apply the remaining linear diameter dimensions to the sketch, see Figure 4.85. Note that to apply the linear diameter dimensions, you need to first select the vertical construction line and then the sketch entity. This is because the first selected entity will be used as the revolving axis for applying the diameter dimension.

12. Press the ESC key to exit the **Sketch Dimensions** tool. Figure 4.85 shows the fully defined sketch after applying all the dimensions.

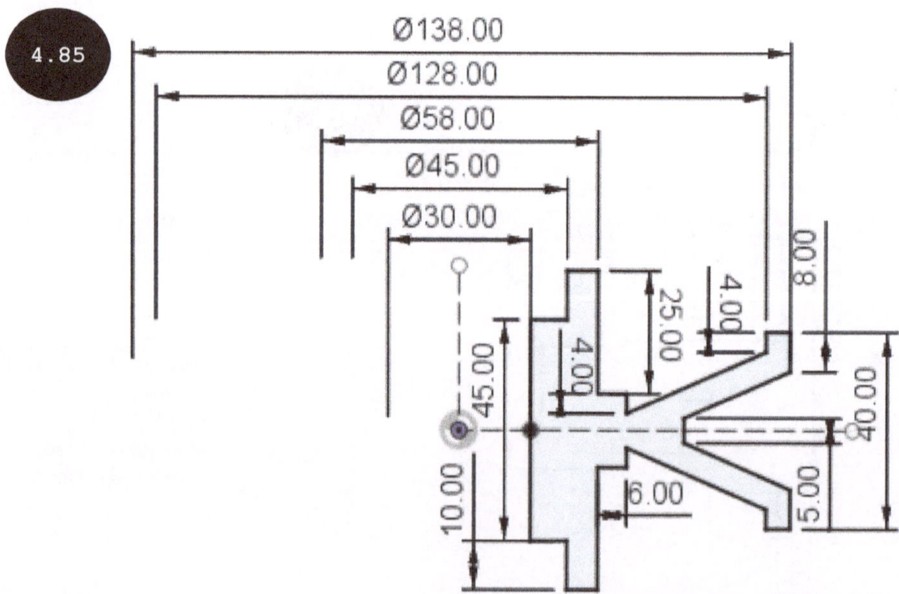

Section 6: Saving the Sketch

After creating the sketch, you need to save it.

1. Click on the **Save** tool in the **Application Bar**. The **Save** dialog box appears.

2. Enter **Tutorial 2** in the **Name** field of the dialog box.

3. Ensure that the location ***Autodesk Fusion 360 > Chapter 04 > Tutorial*** is specified in the **Location** field of the dialog box to save the file of this tutorial. To specify the location, you need to expand the **Save** dialog box by clicking on the down arrow next to the **Location** field of the dialog box.

4. Click on the **Save** button in the dialog box. The sketch is saved with the name Tutorial 2 in the specified location (***Autodesk Fusion 360 > Chapter 04 > Tutorial***).

Tutorial 3

Draw the sketch shown in Figure 4.86 and make it fully defined by applying all dimensions and constraints. The model shown in this figure is for your reference only. You will learn about creating 3D models in later chapters. All dimensions are in mm.

4.86

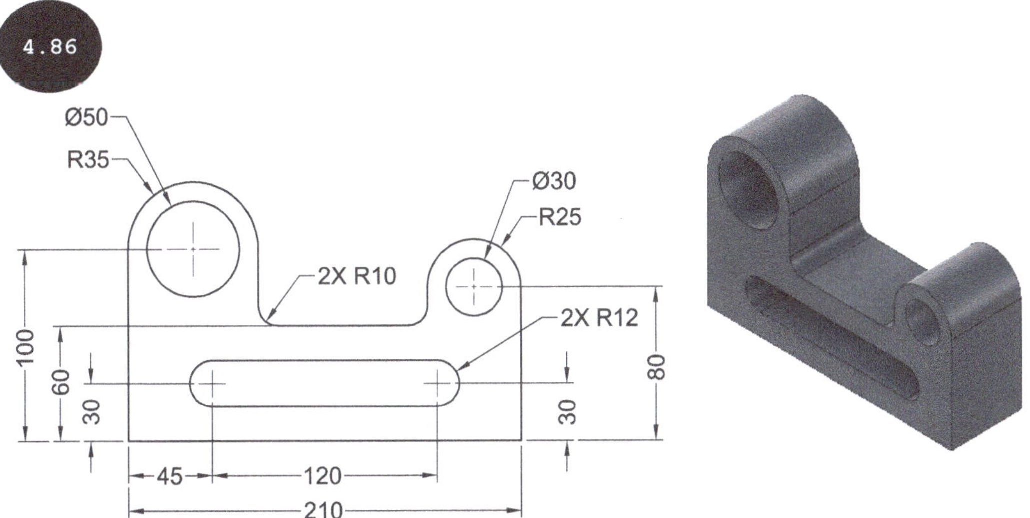

Section 1: Starting a New Part Design File

1. Click **File > New** in the **Application Bar** (see Figure 4.87) to display the **What do you want to design?** dialog box, see Figure 4.88.

4.87

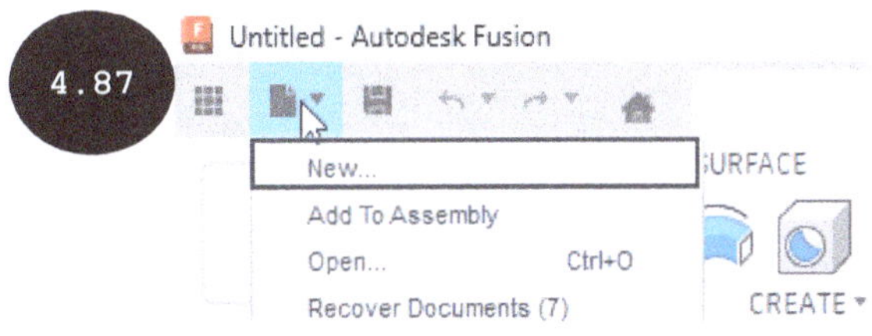

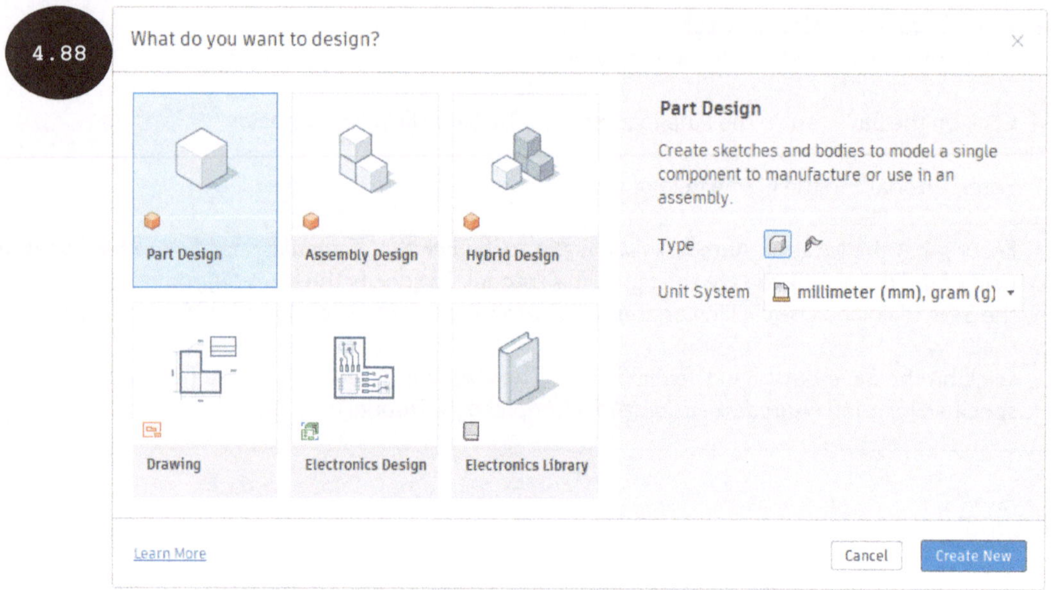

2. In the **What do you want to design?** dialog box, select the **Part Design** button and choose the **millimeter (mm), gram (g)** unit system from the **Unit System** drop-down list.

3. After specifying the required options, click the **Create New** button. A new Part Design file is created with the default name **"Untitled"**.

4. Click on the **Show Data Panel** tool in the **Application Bar**, see Figure 4.89. The **Data Panel** appears.

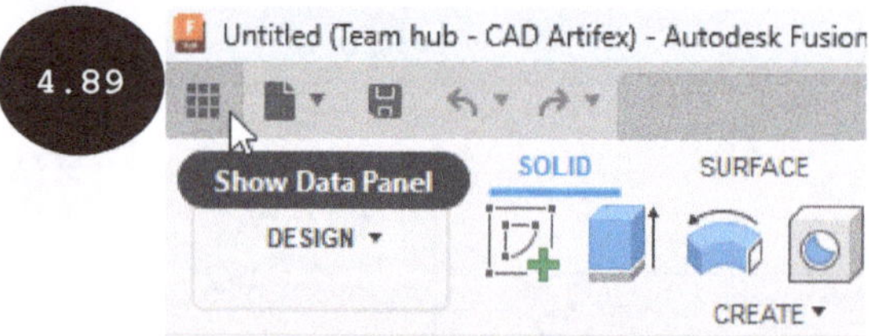

5. Ensure that the **Autodesk Fusion 360** project > **Chapter 04** folder > **Tutorial** sub-folders are created in the **Data Panel**. You need to create these project folders, if not created earlier.

6. Click on the cross-mark at the top right corner of the **Data Panel** to close it.

Section 2: Creating the Sketch

1. Click on the **Create Sketch** tool in the **Toolbar**, see Figure 4.90. Three default planes: Front, Top, and Right, which are mutually perpendicular to each other appear in the graphics area.

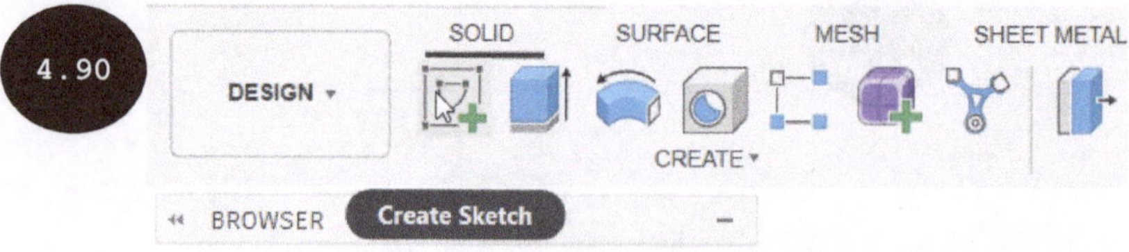

2. Move the cursor over the Front plane and then click the left mouse button when it gets highlighted in the graphics area. The Front plane becomes the sketching plane for creating the sketch and it is oriented normal to the viewing direction. Also, the **SKETCH** contextual tab and the **SKETCH PALETTE** dialog box appear.

   Now, you need to turn off the grids and snap modes. As Autodesk Fusion is parametric software, you can turn off the grids and snap modes, and create the sketch by specifying points arbitrarily in the drawing area and then apply the required dimensions.

3. Clear the **Sketch Grid** and **Snap** check boxes in the **SKETCH PALETTE** dialog box to turn off the grids and snap modes.

   Now, create the sketch.

4. Press the **L** key to invoke the **Line** tool or click on the **Line** tool in the **Toolbar**.

5. Move the cursor to the origin and then click to specify the start point of the line when the cursor snaps to the origin.

6. Move the cursor horizontally toward the right and click to specify the endpoint of the line when the length is close to 210 mm and the symbol of horizontal constraint appear near the cursor, see Figure 4.91. A horizontal line of length close to 210 mm is created. Also, a horizontal constraint is applied to the line.

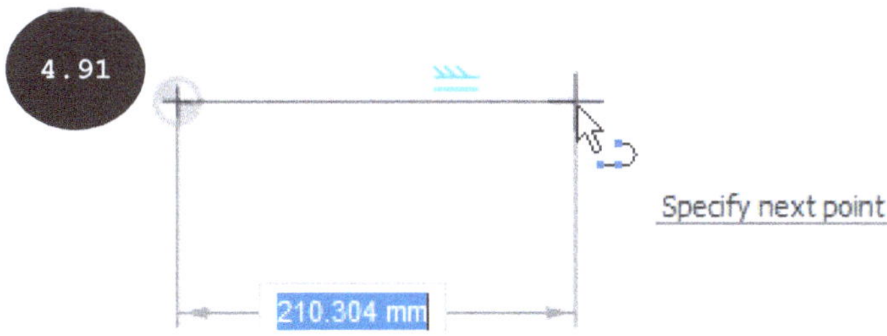

Note: If you specify a point in the drawing area, when a horizontal or vertical constraint appears near the cursor, the respective constraint is applied to the entity.

Tip: While drawing sketch entities, you may need to increase or decrease the drawing display area. You can zoom into or out of the drawing display area by scrolling the middle mouse button. Alternatively, click on the **Zoom** tool in the **Navigation Bar** and then drag the cursor upward or downward. Next, to exit the tool, press the ESC key.

7. Move the cursor vertically upward and create a vertical line of length close to 80 mm.

Now, you need to create a tangent arc.

8. Move the cursor over the last specified point in the drawing area. Next, drag the cursor vertically upward to a distance and then horizontally toward the left by pressing and holding the left mouse button. The arc mode is activated, and the preview of a tangent arc appears, see Figure 4.92.

9. Release the left mouse button to specify the endpoint of the tangent arc when the radius of the arc appears close to 25 mm, see Figure 4.92. The tangent arc is created, and the line mode is activated again.

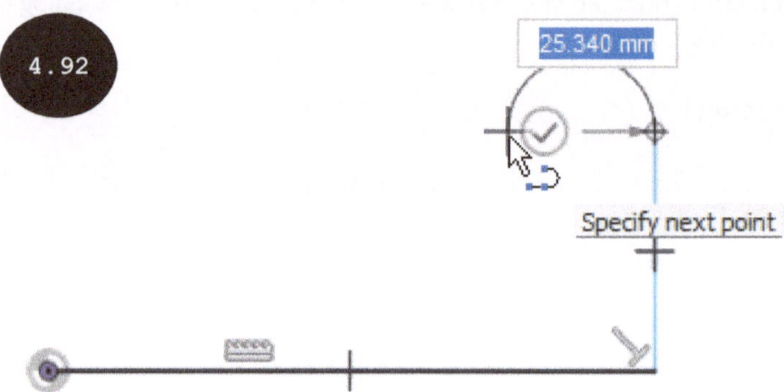

10. Move the cursor vertically downward and create a vertical line of length close to 20 mm.

11. Move the cursor horizontally toward the left and create a horizontal line close to 90 mm.

12. Move the cursor vertically upward and create a vertical line of length close to 40 mm.

Now, you need to create a tangent arc.

13. Move the cursor over the last specified point in the drawing area. Next, drag the cursor vertically upward to a distance and then horizontally toward the left by pressing and holding the left mouse button. The arc mode is activated, and the preview of a tangent arc appears, see Figure 4.93.

14. Release the left mouse button to specify the endpoint of the tangent arc when the radius of the arc appears close to 35 mm and the endpoint of the tangent arc is aligned to the start point of the first line entity, see Figure 4.93. The tangent arc is created, and the line mode is activated again.

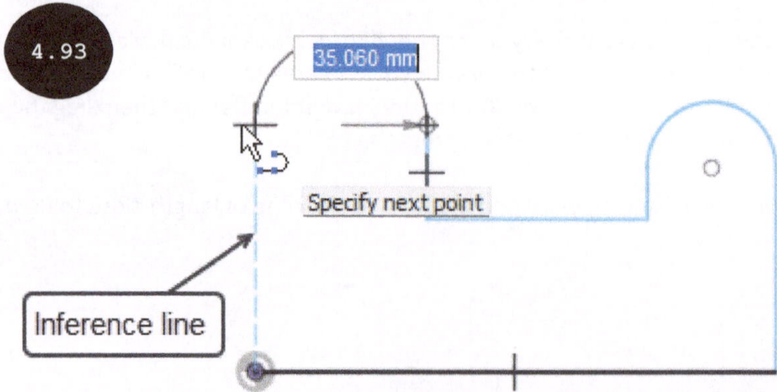

Note: To align the endpoint of the tangent arc to the start point of the first line entity, you need to first drag the cursor to the origin and then vertically upward to display the vertical inference line, refer to Figure 4.93.

15. Move the cursor vertically downward and click to specify the endpoint of the line when the cursor snaps to the start point of the first line entity. The outer closed loop of the sketch is created, see Figure 4.94. Next, press the ESC key to exit the **Line** tool.

    Now, you need to create circles of the sketch.

16. Drag the cursor vertically downward by pressing and holding the right mouse button and then pause. The second level of the Marking Menu appears, see Figure 4.95.

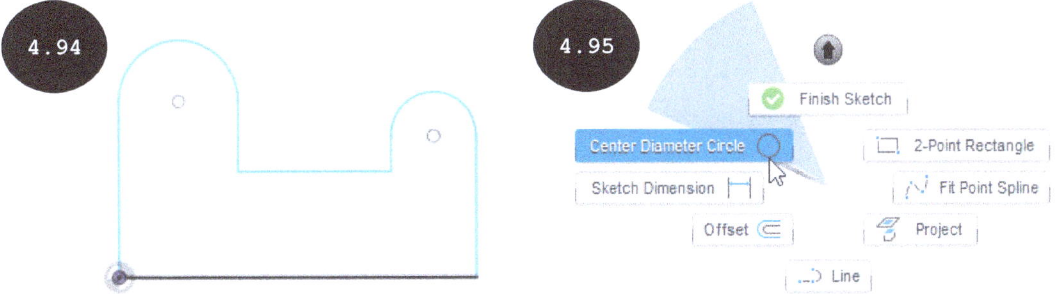

17. Move the cursor over the **Center Diameter Circle** tool in the Marking Menu and then release the right mouse button. The **Center Diameter Circle** tool is activated. You can also activate this tool by pressing C or by clicking **Circle > Center Diameter Circle** in the **CREATE** drop-down menu.

18. Create two circles of diameters close to 50 mm and 30 mm, see Figure 4.96. Next, exit the **Center Diameter Circle** tool.

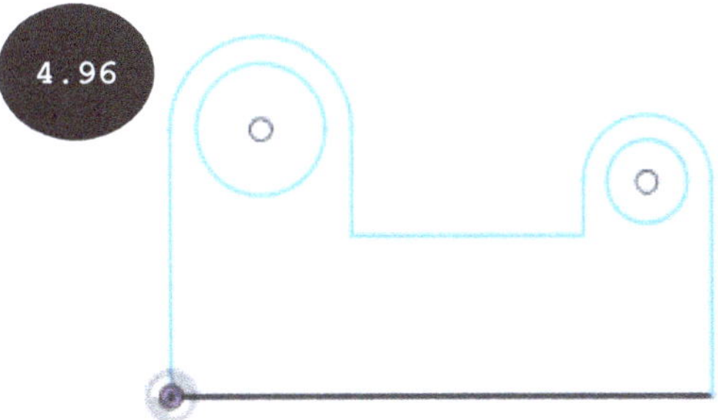

19. Invoke the **CREATE** drop-down menu in the **SKETCH** contextual tab and then click on **Slot > Center to Center Slot**, see Figure 4.97. The **Center to Center Slot** tool gets activated.

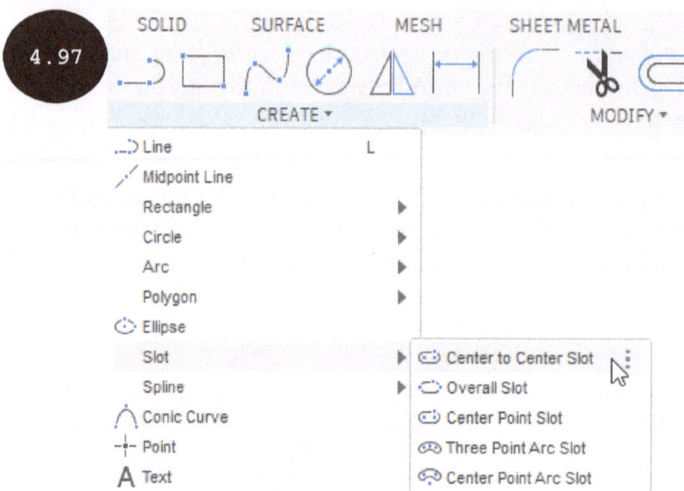

20. Create a straight slot similar to the one shown in Figure 4.98 and then exit the tool. You can create a slot of any parameters as later in this tutorial, you will be required to apply dimensions to make the sketch fully defined.

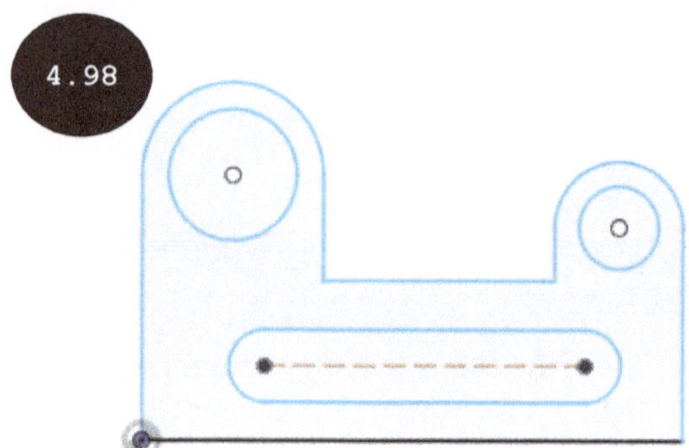

Now, you need to create fillets in the sketch.

21. Click on the **Fillet** tool in the **MODIFY** panel in the **SKETCH** contextual tab of the **Toolbar**.

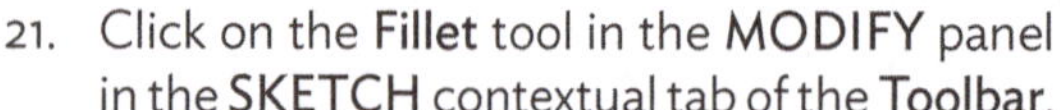

22. Move the cursor over the upper right vertex of the sketch, see Figure 4.99. The preview of the fillet is highlighted. Next, click on the left mouse button to accept the fillet preview. The **Fillet radius** field appears in the drawing area.

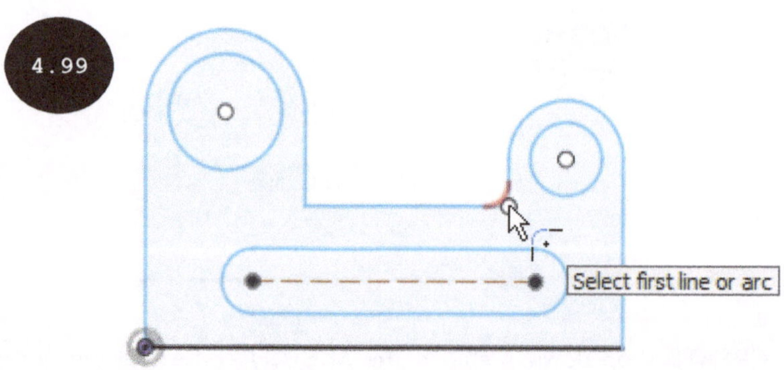

23. Enter **10** in the **Fillet radius** field and then move the cursor over the upper left vertex of the sketch, see Figure 4.100. The preview of the fillet appears. Next, click on the left mouse button to accept the fillet preview.

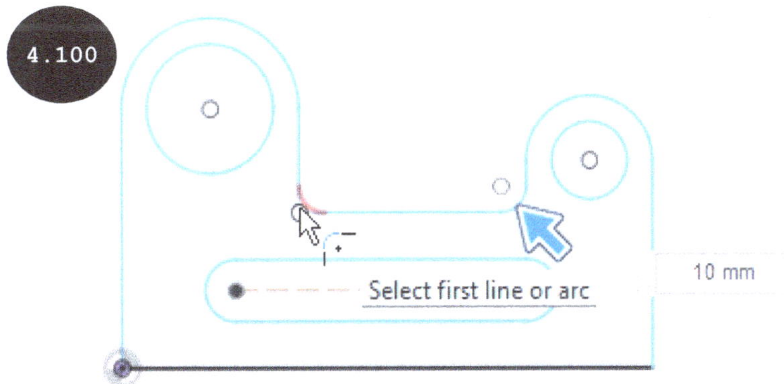

24. Press the ENTER key. Fillets of radius 10 mm are created. Also, a radius dimension is applied to the first fillet and equal constraint between both fillets.

Section 3: Applying Dimensions

After creating the sketch, you need to apply the required constraints and dimensions to make the sketch fully defined. In this sketch, all the required constraints have been applied automatically while creating the entities. Therefore, you need to apply dimensions only.

1. Press the D key. The **Sketch Dimension** tool gets activated.

2. Click on the lower horizontal line of the sketch and then move the cursor downward. The linear dimension is attached to the cursor, see Figure 4.101.

3. Click to specify the placement point for the attached linear dimension in the drawing area. A dimension box appears.

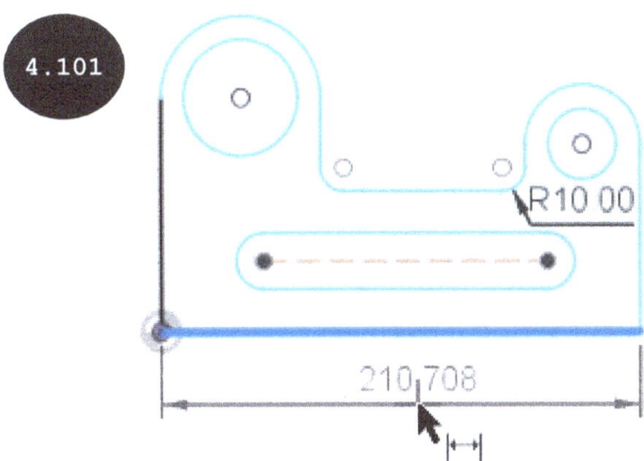

4. Enter **210** in the dimension box and then press ENTER. The length of the line is modified to 210 mm and the linear dimension is applied.

5. Similarly, apply the remaining dimensions to the sketch by using the **Sketch Dimension** tool, see Figure 4.102. Next, press the ESC key to exit the tool. Figure 4.102 shows the final sketch.

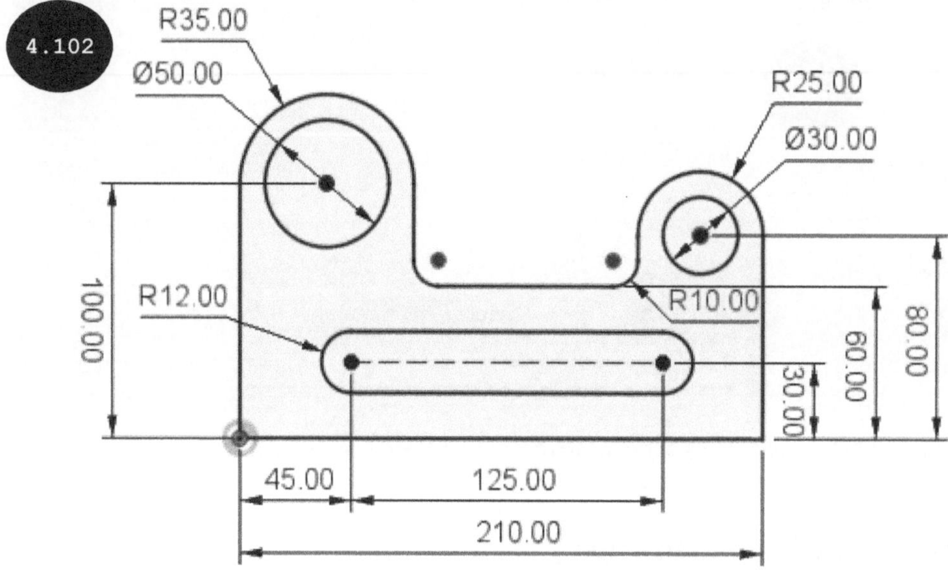

Tip: After placing a dimension in the required location, you may need to further change its location to place other dimensions. To change the location of an existing dimension, press and hold the left mouse button over the dimension and then drag the dimension to the new location. Next, release the left mouse button.

Note: If the sketch is not fully defined even after applying all dimensions, then you need to ensure that the horizontal constraint is applied to all the horizontal lines, vertical constraint is applied to vertical lines, and tangent constraint is applied between the connecting lines and arcs of the sketch.

Section 4: Saving the Sketch

1. Click on the **Save** tool in the **Application Bar** and then enter **Tutorial 3** in the **Name** field of the **Save** dialog box that appears.

2. Ensure the location ***Autodesk Fusion 360 > Chapter 04 > Tutorial*** is specified in the **Location** field of the dialog box to save the file of this tutorial. To specify the location, you need to expand the **Save** dialog box by clicking on the down arrow next to the **Location** field of the dialog box.

3. Click on the **Save** button in the dialog box. The sketch is saved with the name Tutorial 3 in the specified location (***Autodesk Fusion 360 > Chapter 04 > Tutorial***).

Hands-on Test Drive 1

Draw a sketch of the model shown in Figure 4.103. You need to apply constraints and dimensions to make it fully defined. The model shown in the figure is for your reference only. You will learn about creating 3D models in later chapters. All dimensions are in mm.

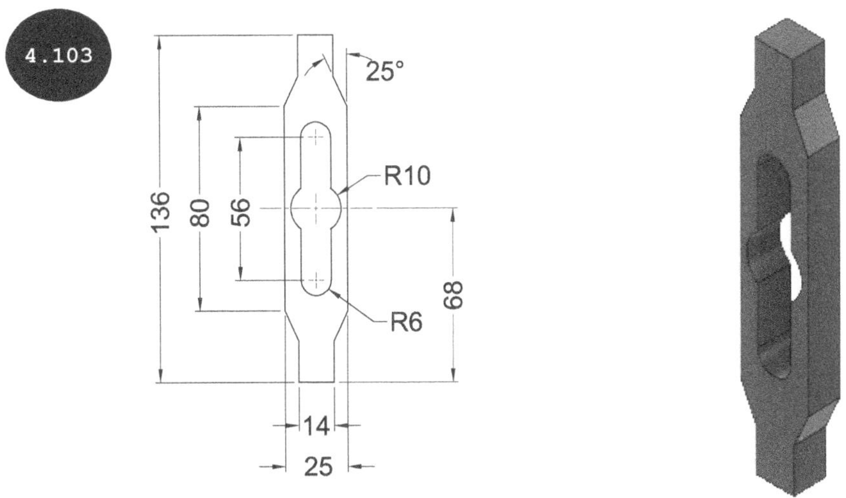

Hands-on Test Drive 2

Draw a sketch of the model shown in Figure 4.104. You need to apply dimensions to make it fully defined. The model shown in the figure is for your reference only. You will learn about creating 3D models in later chapters. All dimensions are in mm.

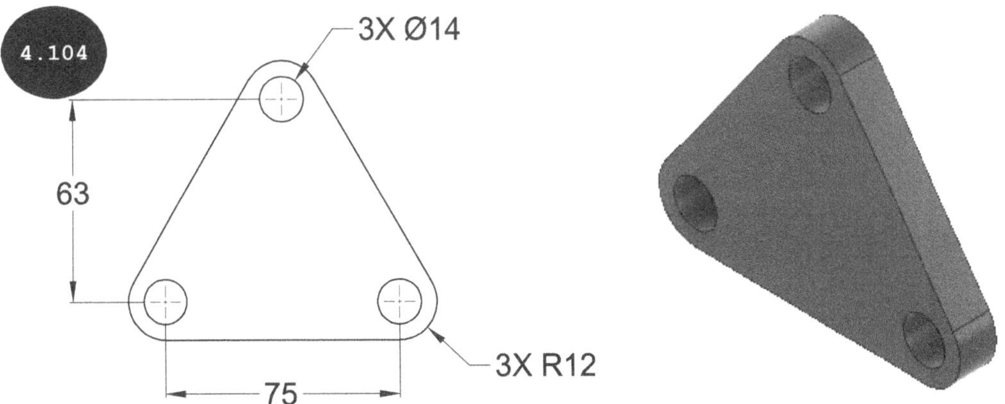

Summary

In this chapter, you learned about the concept of fully defined sketches, highlighting the critical role of constraints and dimensions. You explored various types of constraints and methods for applying them to sketch entities, as well as techniques for controlling the display of these constraints. Additionally, you discovered how to modify and edit the dimensions of sketch entities effectively. The chapter concludes by discussing the different states of a sketch and the tools available in the **SKETCH PALETTE** dialog box, providing you with a comprehensive foundation for understanding sketching techniques in design.

Questions

Complete and verify the following sentences:

- The _________ constraint is used for coinciding a sketch point onto a line, an arc, or an elliptical entity.
- You can control the display or visibility of the applied constraints by using the _________ check box of the **SKETCH PALETTE** dialog box.
- The _________ dimension is applied to a sketch representing revolve features.
- All degrees of freedom of a _______ sketch are fixed.
- You can apply constraints by using the constraints tools available in the _______ panel of the **SKETCH** contextual tab.
- The _______ tool is used for applying dimensions, depending upon the type of entity selected.
- The _______ tool is used for changing the orientation of the sketching plane normal to the viewing direction.
- The _______ check box of the **SKETCH PALETTE** dialog box is used for cutting the object by using the sketching plane of the sketch.
- You cannot modify the dimensions once they have been applied. (True/False)
- You cannot delete the constraints that have already been applied between the selected entities. (True/False)
- Constraints are used for restricting some degrees of freedom of a sketch. (True/False)

Creating Base Features of Solid Models

In this chapter, the following topics will be discussed:

- Creating an Extrude Feature
- Creating a Revolve Feature
- Navigating a 3D Model in Graphics Area
- Changing the Visual Style of a Model

Once a sketch has been created and fully defined, you can convert it into a 3D solid feature using the feature modeling tools, see Figure 5.1.

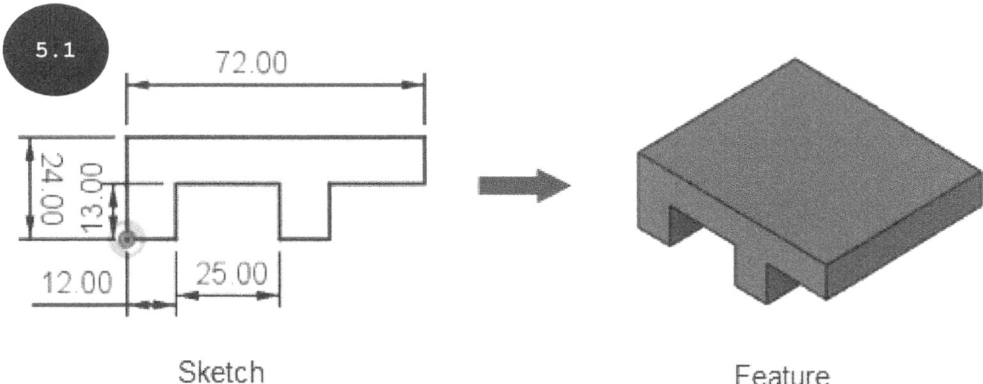

All features modeling tools are available in the **CREATE** drop-down menu of the **SOLID** tab in the **Toolbar**, see Figure 5.2. To create a 3D solid model, you need to create each of its features individually using these feature modeling tools, see Figure 5.3. The first feature you create for a model is known as the base feature or the parent feature of the model.

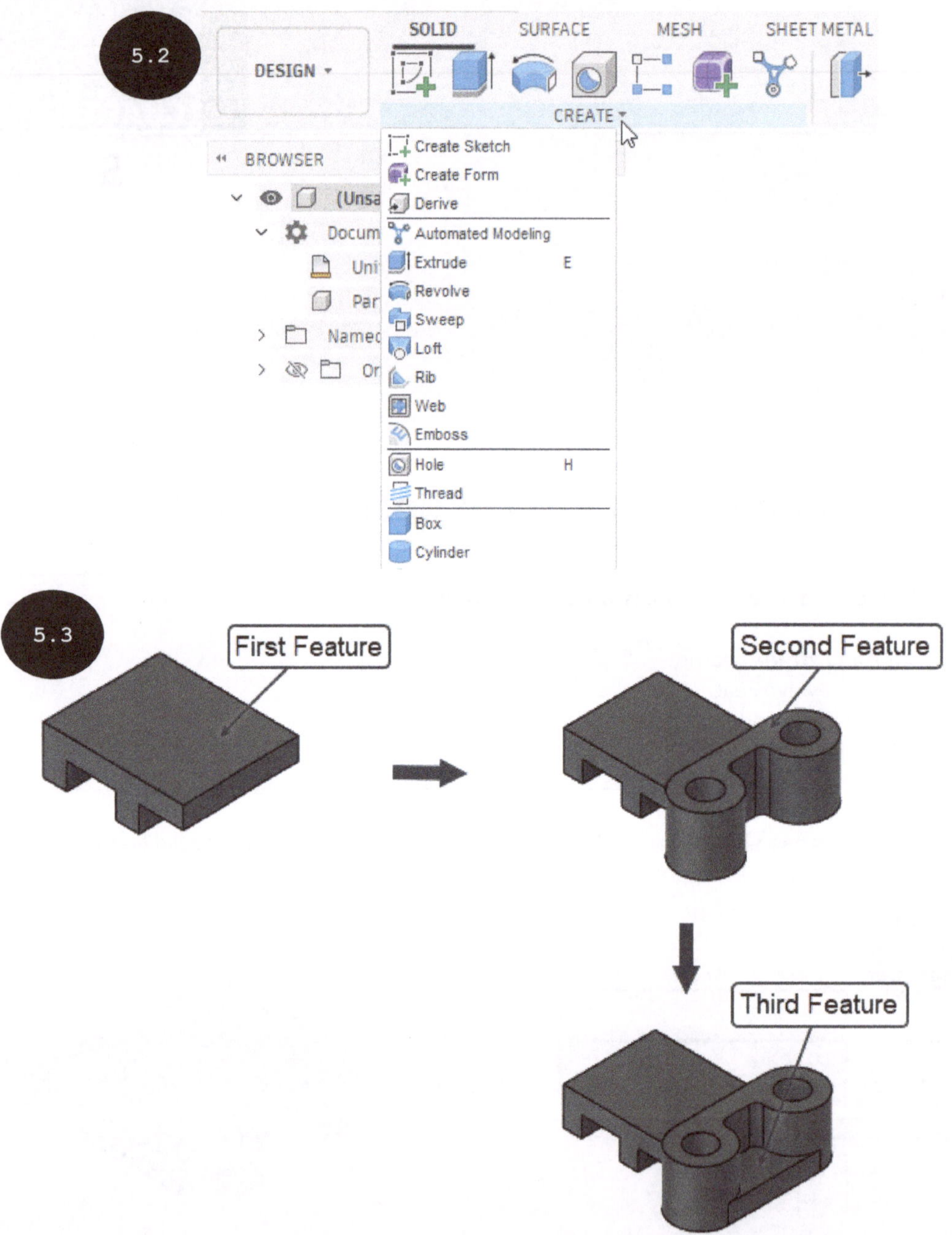

In Autodesk Fusion, you can create a base feature using various feature modeling tools, including **Extrude**, **Revolve**, **Sweep**, and **Loft**. In this chapter, you will focus on creating a base feature using the **Extrude** and **Revolve** tools. The remaining tools will be covered in later chapters.

Creating an Extrude Feature

An extrude feature is created by adding or removing material, normal to the sketching plane. Note that the sketch of the extruded feature defines its geometry. The first or base extrude features are essentially created by adding material. Figure 5.4 shows different base extrude features that are created from the respective sketches. In Autodesk Fusion, you can create an extrude feature using the **Extrude** tool in the CREATE panel of the SOLID tab in the **Toolbar**.

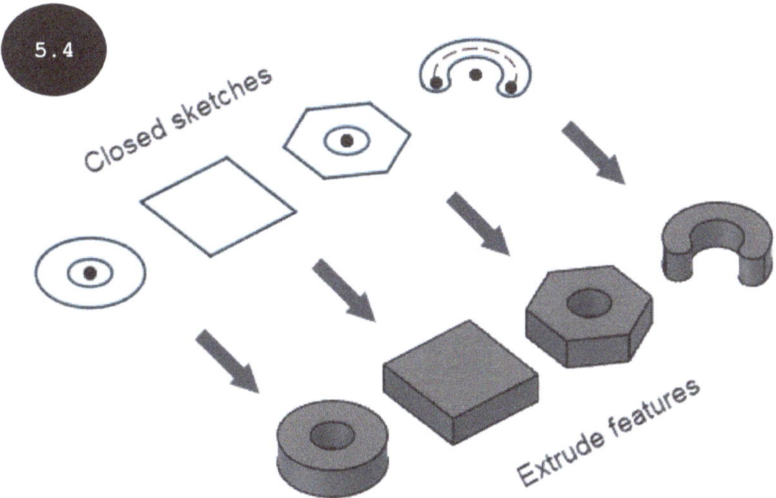

After creating the sketch using the sketching tools, activate the SOLID tab in the **Toolbar**. Then, click on the **Extrude** tool in the CREATE panel, see Figure 5.5 or select it from the CREATE drop-down menu, see Figure 5.6. The EXTRUDE dialog box appears, see Figure 5.7, and the orientation of the sketch changes to an isometric view.

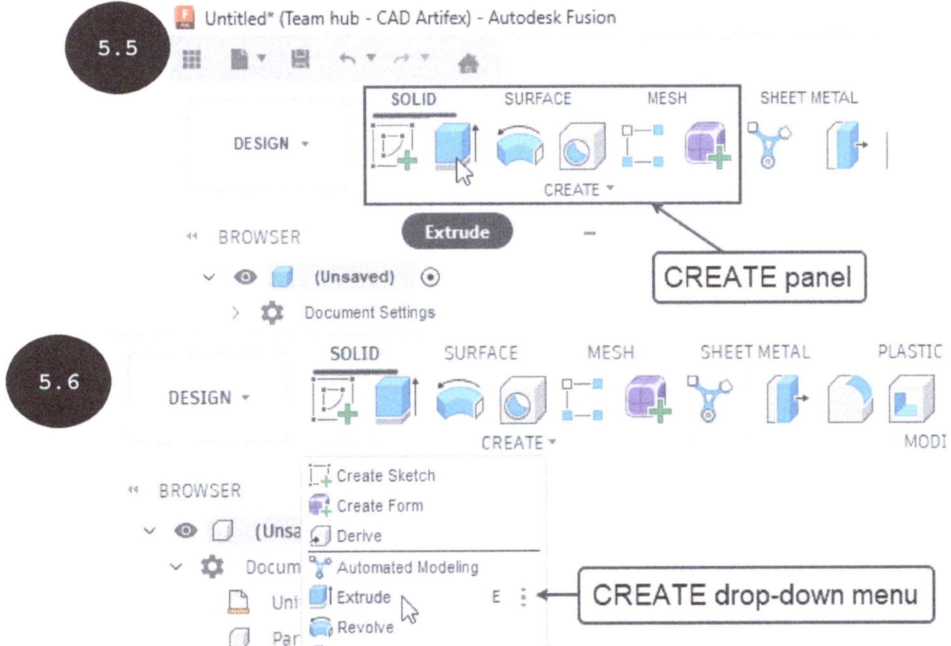

5.7

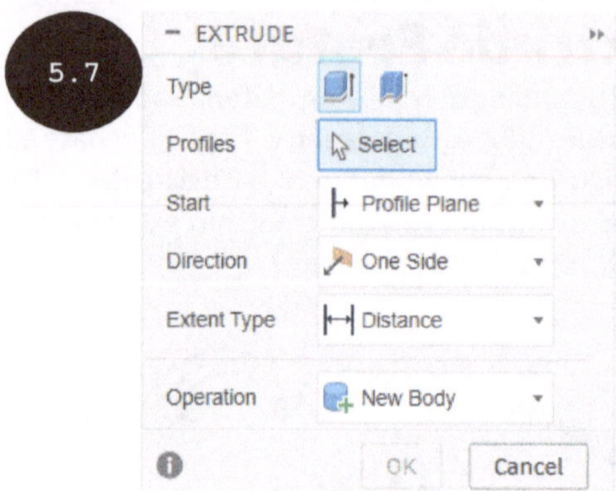

Note: After creating the sketch, you can also finish the creation of the sketch first by clicking on the **FINISH SKETCH** tool in the **SKETCH** contextual tab of the **Toolbar** and then invoke the **Extrude** tool for extruding the sketch.

The options in the **EXTRUDE** dialog box allow you to specify parameters for extruding the sketch. Some of the options in this dialog box are discussed next.

Type

The **Extrude** button in the **Type** area of the dialog box is activated by default. This creates a solid extrude feature by adding material to a closed sketch profile, see Figure 5.8.

5.8

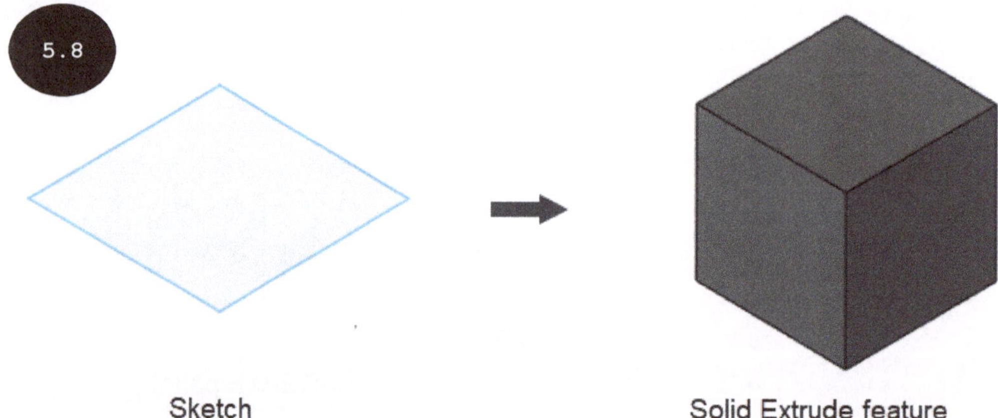

When you select the **Thin Extrude** button, a thin extrude feature is created by adding a specified thickness value to either an open or closed sketch profile, see Figure 5.9. In this figure, a thin extrude feature is created by adding thickness to a closed sketch profile.

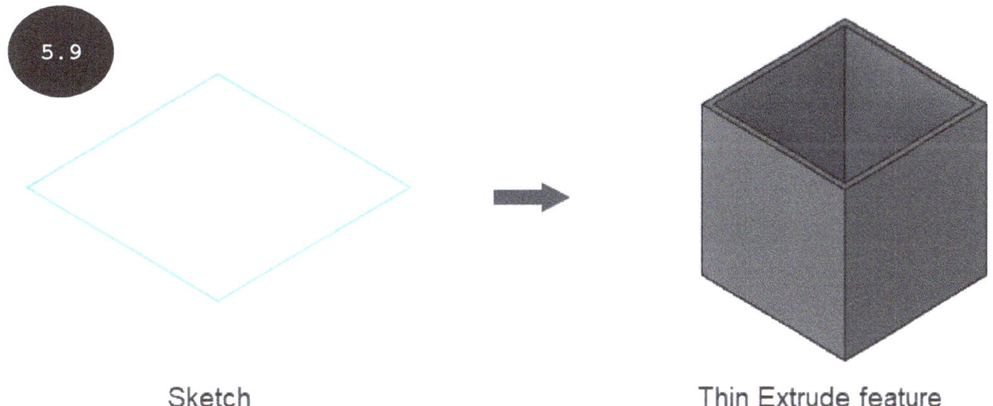

Profiles

The **Profiles** selection option in the **EXTRUDE** dialog box is activated by default, allowing you to select either an open or closed sketch profile to add or remove material. When creating a base feature, you can only extrude the profile by adding material. Additionally, you can select multiple open or closed profiles to create an extrude feature.

Tip: To remove an already selected profile or a profile selected by mistake, click again on the selected profile, or press and hold the CTRL or SHIFT key and then click on the profile to be removed from the selection set.

Chaining

The **Chaining** check box is selected by default in the dialog box. As a result, on selecting an entity of an open sketch profile while creating a thin extrude feature, all its tangentially connected entities also get selected. Note that this check box is available only when the **Thin Extrude** button is activated in the **Type** area of the **EXTRUDE** dialog box.

Start

The options in the **Start** drop-down list of the dialog box are used for specifying the start condition for extruding the sketch profile, see Figure 5.10. These options are discussed next.

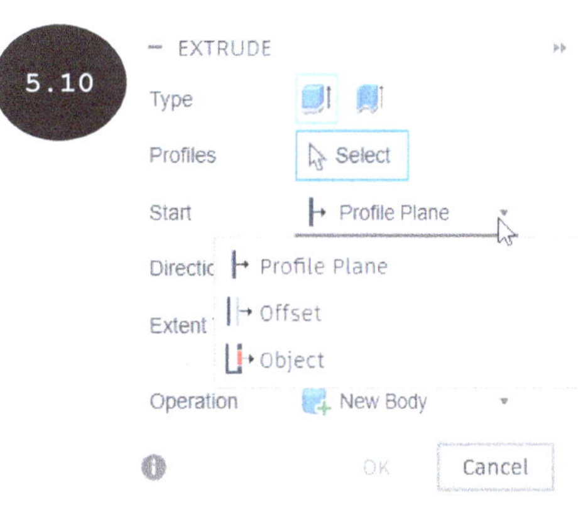

Profile Plane

By default, the **Profile Plane** option is selected in the **Start** drop-down list of the **EXTRUDE** dialog box. As a result, extrusion starts exactly from the sketching plane of the sketch. Figure 5.11 shows the preview of an extruded feature from its front when the **Profile Plane** option is selected.

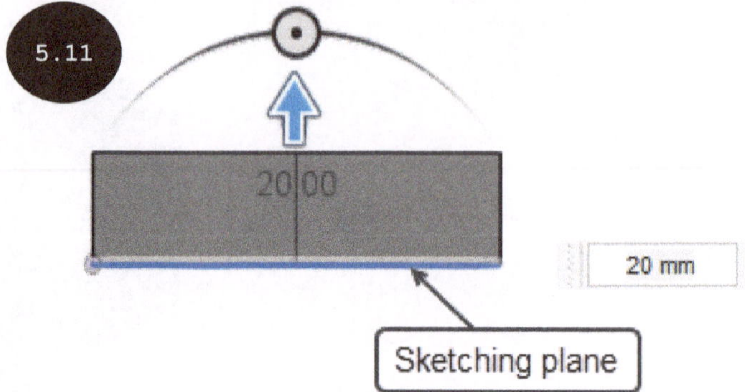

Offset

The **Offset** option is used to create an extrude feature at a specified distance from the sketching plane. On selecting this option, the **Offset** field appears in the **EXTRUDE** dialog box, see Figure 5.12. By default, the value entered in the **Offset** field is 0 (zero). You can enter the required offset value in this field. Figure 5.13 shows the preview of an extruded feature from its front after specifying an offset distance.

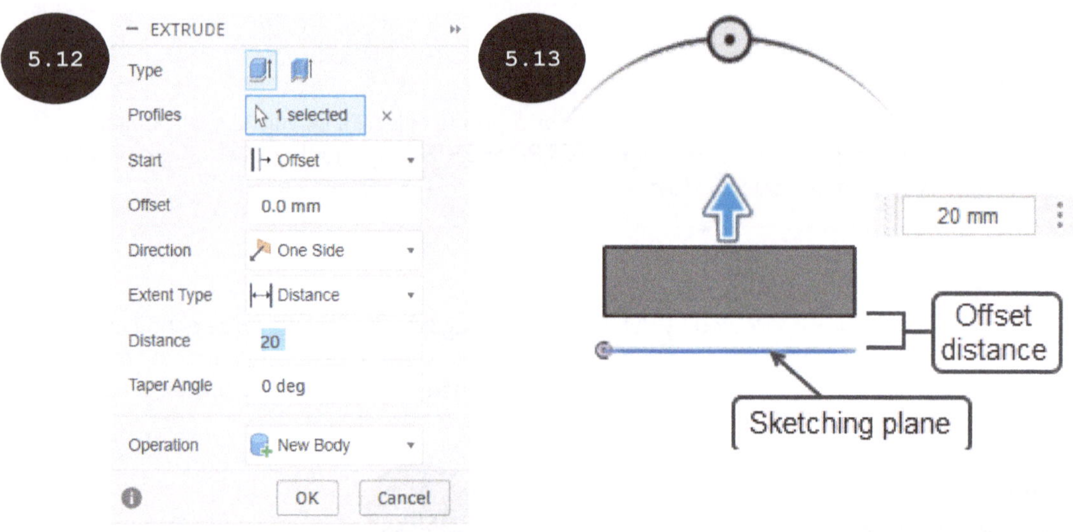

Note: The **Object** option of the **Start** drop-down list is used while creating the second and further features of the model and is discussed in later chapters.

Direction

The options in the **Direction** drop-down list of the **EXTRUDE** dialog box are used to define the direction of the extrusion, see Figure 5.14. These options are discussed next.

One Side

The **One Side** option of the **Direction** drop-down list is used to define the direction of extrusion on either side of the sketching plane. Note that to reverse the direction of extrusion, you need to enter a negative distance value in the **Distance** field of the dialog box.

Two Sides

The **Two Sides** option of the **Direction** drop-down list is used to extrude the sketch profile on both sides of the sketching plane. On selecting this option, the **Side 1** and **Side 2** rollouts appear in the dialog box, see Figure 5.15. The options available in both rollouts are the same, with the only difference being that the **Side 1** rollout defines the extrusion parameters for one side of the sketching plane, while the **Side 2** rollout defines the parameters for the other side.

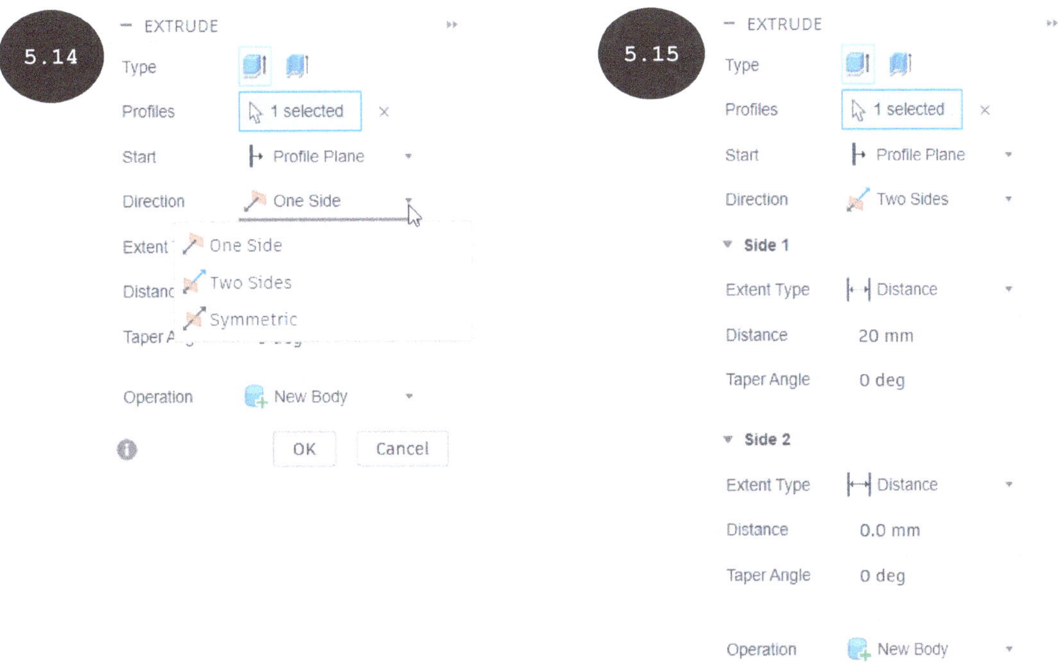

Symmetric

The **Symmetric** option of the **Direction** drop-down list is used to extrude the sketch profile symmetrically on both sides of the sketching plane, see Figure 5.16. On selecting this option, the **Half Length** and **Whole Length** buttons appear below the **Direction** drop-down list in the dialog box, see Figure 5.17.

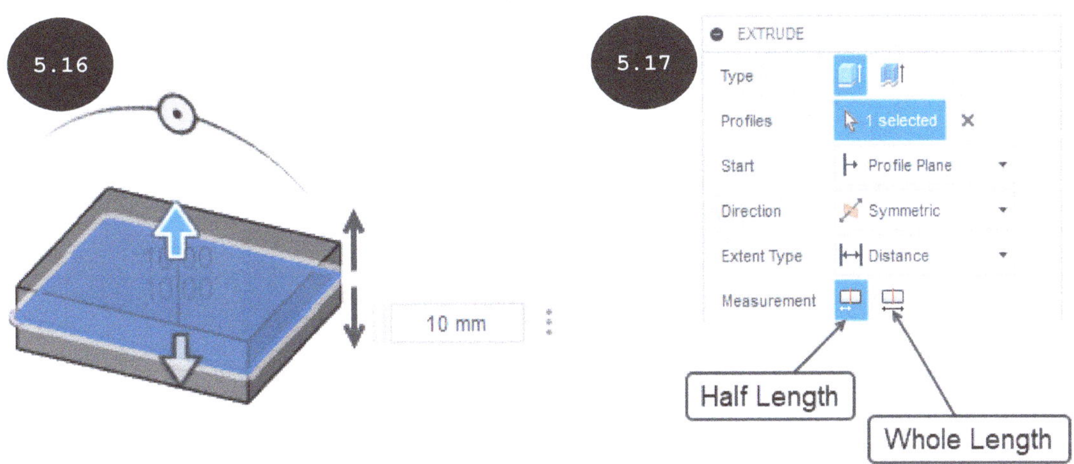

The **Half Length** button is activated by default. As a result, the distance value specified in the **Distance** field of the dialog box is measured as the half length of the extrusion. For example, if the specified distance value is 10 mm, then the resultant feature will be created by adding material 10 mm on each side (side 1 and side 2) of the sketching plane. On activating the **Whole Length** button, the distance value specified in the **Distance** field is measured as the total length of the extrusion. For example, if the specified distance value is 10 mm, then the resultant feature will be created by adding material 5 mm on each side (side 1 and side 2) of the sketching plane.

Extent Type

The options in the **Extent Type** drop-down list of the dialog box are used to specify the extent or end condition for extruding the sketch profile, see Figure 5.18. The options in the **Extent Type** drop-down list are discussed next.

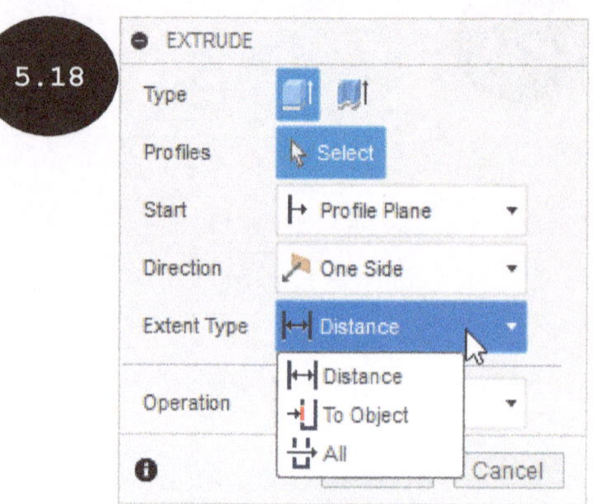

Distance

The **Distance** option is used to specify the extent or end condition of the extrusion by specifying the distance value in the **Distance** field of the dialog box.

Note: The other options such as **To Object** and **All** are used while creating the second and subsequent features of the model and will be discussed in later chapters.

Distance

The **Distance** field of the dialog box is used to specify the distance of extrusion. You can enter the distance of extrusion in this field or in the **Distance** box that appears in the graphics area. You can also drag the arrow that appears along with the preview of the extrude feature in the graphics area to set the distance of extrusion dynamically, see Figure 5.19. To reverse the direction of extrusion from one side to the other side of the sketch profile, you need to enter a negative distance value in the **Distance** field of the dialog box. Note that the **Distance** field is available in the dialog box when the **Distance** option is selected in the **Extent** drop-down list of the dialog box.

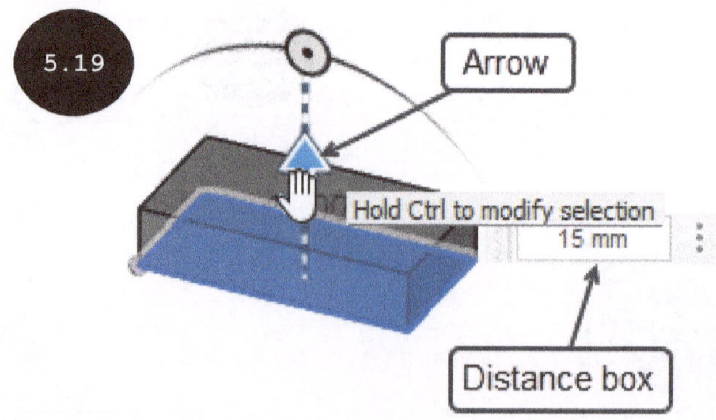

Taper Angle

The **Taper Angle** field of the dialog box is used to add tapering in the extrude feature. By default, this field is set to 0 (zero), resulting in an extrude feature created without any tapering. You can enter the required taper angle in this field. You can also drag the manipulator handle that appears along with the preview of the extrude feature in the graphics area to set the taper angle, dynamically, see Figure 5.20 which shows the preview of an extrude feature having a taper angle value set to 15 degrees. Note that to reverse the taper direction from the outward to the inward side of the sketch or vice-versa, you need to enter a negative value for the taper angle in the **Taper Angle** field of the dialog box.

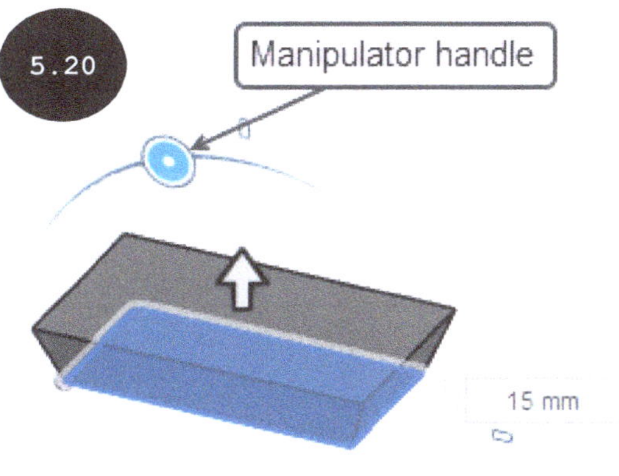

Wall Thickness

The **Wall Thickness** field of the dialog box is used to specify the a thickness value for creating a thin extrude feature. Note that this field is available only when the **Thin Extrude** button is activated in the **Type** area of the **EXTRUDE** dialog box.

Wall Location

On selecting the required option (**Side 1**, **Side 2**, or **Center**) in the **Wall Location** drop-down list (see Figure 5.21), you can add thickness value to either side of the sketch profile or symmetrically on both sides of the sketch profile, respectively. Note that this drop-down list is available only while creating a thin extrude feature.

Operation Drop-down list

The options in the **Operation** drop-down list of the dialog box are used to specify the type of operation for creating the extrude feature, see Figure 5.22. The options are discussed next.

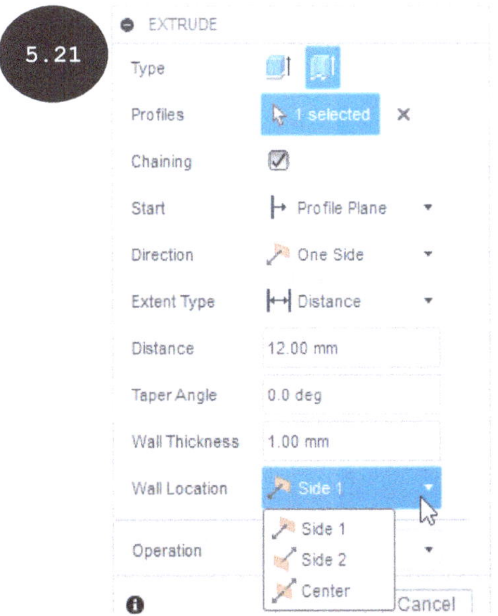

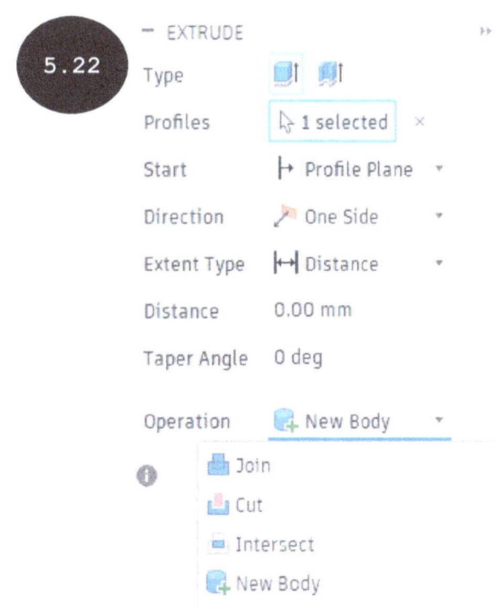

New Body

When creating the first or base feature of a model, the **New Body** option is automatically selected in the **Operation** drop-down list. This option creates a base extrude feature by adding material and forming a new body. After the base feature of a part is created as a body, you can use the **Join**, **Cut**, and Intersect options to build the additional features of the part.

Join

The **Join** option is used to extrude the sketch by adding material and merging it with existing features of the model.

Cut

The **Cut** option is used to extrude the sketch by subtracting material from the model and creating a cut feature.

Intersect

The **Intersect** option is used to create a feature by retaining only the intersecting or common material between the existing feature and the new one.

You will learn about creating features by using the **Join**, **Cut**, and **Intersect** options in later chapters.

If you are creating the first or base feature of a model, then the **New Body** option is selected in the **Operation** drop-down list, by default. The resultant base extrude feature is created by adding material and acts as a new body. After creating the base feature as a body, you can create the second or remaining features of the model (body) by using the **Join**, **Cut**, or **Intersect** options of the **Operation** drop-down list. The **Join** option is used for extruding the sketch by adding material and merging/joining the feature with the existing features of the model. The **Cut** option is used for extruding the sketch by removing the material from the model creating a cut feature. The **Intersect** option is used for creating a feature by only keeping the intersecting or common material between the existing feature and the feature being created.

After specifying all the parameters for extruding a sketch profile, click on the **OK** button in the **EXTRUDE** dialog box. The extrude feature is created.

Creating a Revolve Feature

A revolve feature is created by adding or removing material through the process of revolving a sketch around an axis of revolution. Note that the sketch to be revolved should be on either side of the axis of revolution. You can use a line, a construction line, a centerline, or a linear edge as the axis of revolution. In Autodesk Fusion, you can create a revolve feature by using the **Revolve** tool. Note that the base revolves features are essentially created by adding material. Figure 5.23 shows sketches and the resultant base revolve features created by revolving the sketch around the respective axes of revolution.

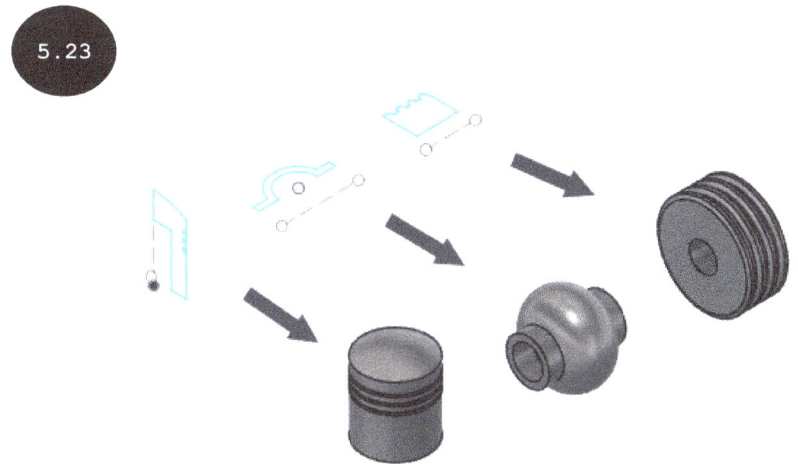

After drawing the sketch of a revolve feature along with the axis of revolution, activate the **SOLID** tab and click on the **Revolve** tool in the **CREATE** panel, see Figure 5.24. Alternatively, invoke the **CREATE** drop-down menu in the **SOLID** tab and then click on the **Revolve** tool. The **REVOLVE** dialog box appears, see Figure 5.25. Also, the orientation of the sketch is changed to isometric.

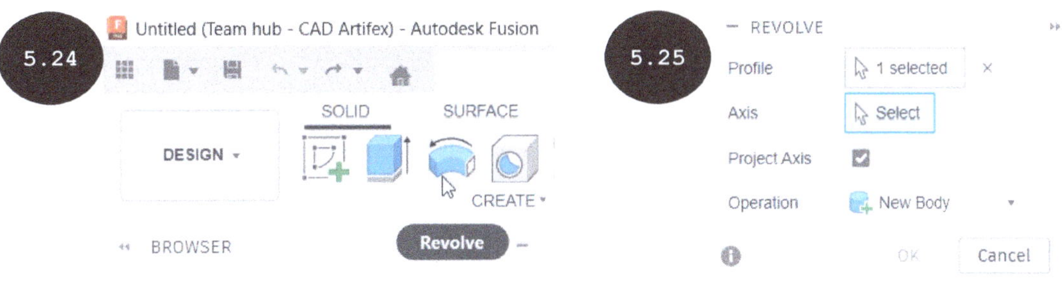

Tip: After creating the sketch, you can also finish the creation of sketch first by clicking on the **FINISH SKETCH** tool in the **SKETCH** contextual tab of the **Toolbar** and then invoke the **Revolve** tool to revolve the sketch.

The options in the **REVOLVE** dialog box are used to specify parameters for revolving the sketch. Some of the options in this dialog box are discussed next.

Profile

The **Profile** selection option in the **REVOLVE** dialog box is activated by default, allowing you to select a closed sketch profile to revolve around the axis of revolution. When creating a base feature, you can only revolve the profile by adding material. You can also select multiple closed profiles to create a revolve feature.

Tip: To remove an already selected profile or a profile selected by mistake, click again on the selected profile, or press and hold the CTRL or SHIFT key and then click on the profile to be removed from the selection set.

Axis

The **Axis** selection option is used to select an axis of revolution. To do this, click on the **Axis** selection option in the dialog box to activate it and then select an axis of revolution. You can select a line, a construction line, a centerline, or an edge as the axis of revolution. After selecting a closed profile and an axis of revolution, the preview of the revolve feature appears in the graphics area, see Figure 5.26.

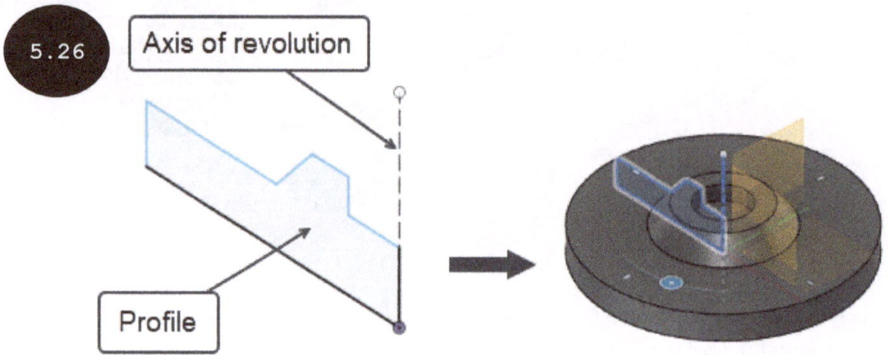

Project Axis

On selecting the **Project Axis** check box, the selected axis of a revolve feature gets projected onto the sketching plane of the profile for creating a revolve feature. If the **Project Axis** check box is cleared, the axis of the revolve feature will remain in its original plane or location for creating a revolve feature. Note that this option works better if the axis of the revolve feature is defined on a plane other than the plane of the profile.

Extent Type

The options in the **Extent Type** drop-down list are used to specify the end condition for revolving the sketch profile around the axis, see Figure 5.27. These options are discussed next.

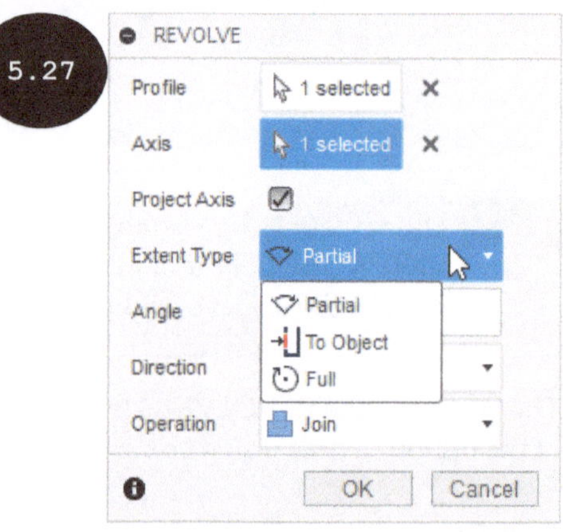

Partial

The **Partial** option in the **Extent Type** drop-down list is used to specify the end condition of the revolution by specifying the angle value in the **Angle** field of the dialog box.

Full

The **Full** option is used to revolve a sketch 360 degrees around the axis of revolution.

Note: The **To Object** option of the **Extent Type** drop-down list is used while creating the second and further features of a model and is discussed in later chapters.

Angle

The **Angle** field of the dialog box is used to specify the angle of revolution. You can enter the angle of revolution in this field of the dialog box or in the **Angle** box that appears in the graphics area. You can also drag the manipulator handle that appears along with the preview of the revolve feature in the graphics area to set the angle of revolution dynamically, see Figure 5.28. To reverse the direction of revolution from one side to the other side of the profile, you need to enter a negative angle value in the **Angle** field of the dialog box. Note that the **Angle** field is not available in the dialog box when the **Full** option is selected in the **Extent Type** drop-down list of the dialog box.

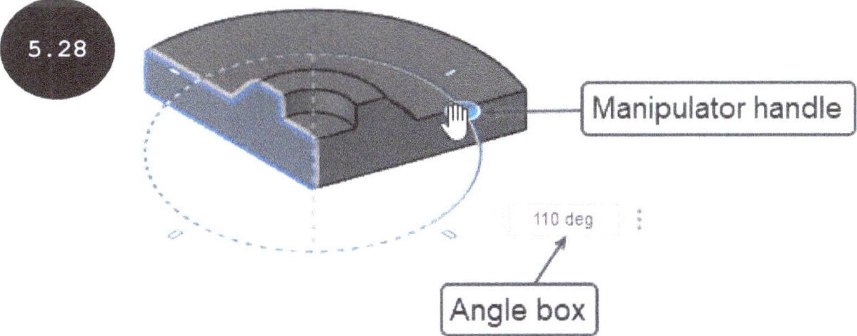

Direction

The options in the **Direction** drop-down list of the **REVOLVE** dialog box are used to define the direction of revolution, see Figure 5.29. These options are discussed next.

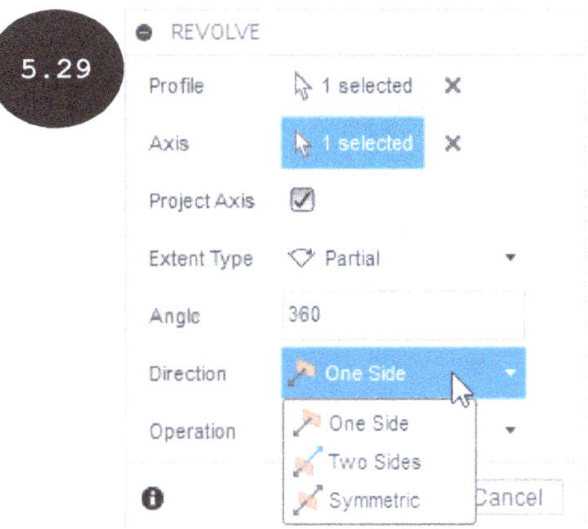

One Side

The **One Side** option is used to define the direction of revolution on either side of the sketching plane. Note that to reverse the direction of revolution, you need to enter a negative angle value in the **Angle** field of the dialog box.

Two Sides

The **Two Sides** option is used to revolve the sketch profile on both sides of the sketching plane. On selecting this option, two **Angle** fields (Angle 1 and Angle 2) appear in the dialog box, see Figure 5.30. In these fields, you can specify different angle values for revolving the sketch on both sides of the sketching plane, see Figure 5.31.

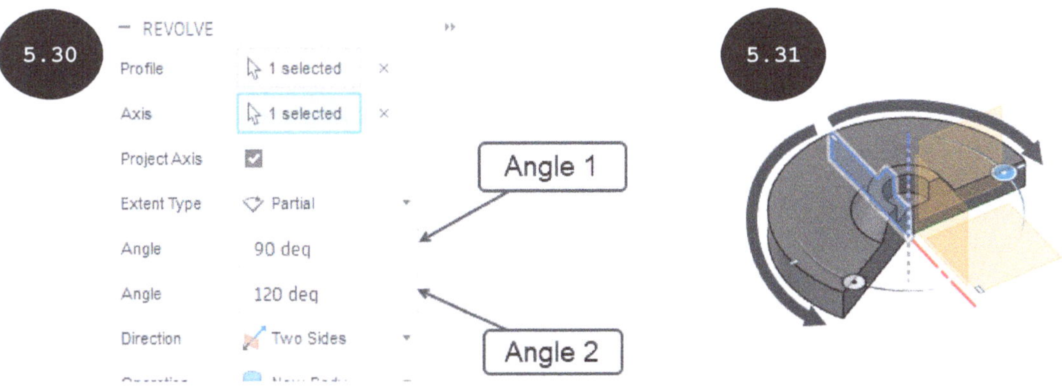

Symmetric

The **Symmetric** option is used to revolve the sketch profile symmetrically on both sides of the sketching plane, see Figure 5.32. For example, if you specify the angle value as 120 degrees in the **Angle** field, then the resultant feature will be created by revolving the profile 120 degrees on each side of the sketching plane.

Operation

The options in the **Operation** drop-down list of the dialog box are used to specify the type of operation for creating a revolve feature, see Figure 5.33.

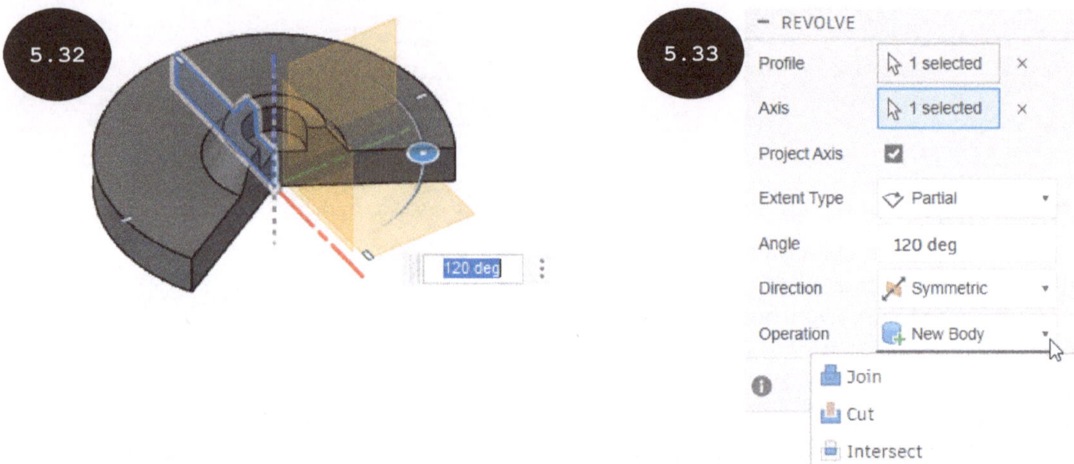

When creating the first or base feature of a model, the **New Body** option is selected by default in the **Operation** drop-down list. This results in a revolve feature that adds material and acts as a new body.

After creating the base feature, you can create additional features for the model (body) using the **Join**, **Cut**, or **Intersect** options in the **Operation** drop-down list. You will learn about these options in later chapters.

After specifying all the parameters for revolving a sketch profile, click on the **OK** button in the **REVOLVE** dialog box. The revolve feature is created.

Navigating a 3D Model in Graphics Area

In Autodesk Fusion, you can navigate a model using the mouse buttons and navigation tools. You can access the navigation tools in the **Navigation Bar** available in the lower middle section of the graphics area, see Figure 5.34. Alternatively, you can navigate a model using ViewCube. Before you begin navigating, it's important to understand the navigation settings. Autodesk Fusion allows you to control the shortcuts for panning, zooming, and orbiting a model, similar to other CAD packages like Alias, Inventor, Tinkercad, PowerMill, or SolidWorks. The method for adjusting these navigation settings is discussed next.

5.34

Controlling the Navigation Settings

In Autodesk Fusion, you can control the navigation settings by using the **Preferences** dialog box. To invoke the **Preferences** dialog box, click on your profile image in the upper right corner of Autodesk Fusion. The **User Account** drop-down menu appears, see Figure 5.35. In this drop-down menu, click on the **Preferences** tool. The **Preferences** dialog box appears, see Figure 5.36.

5.35

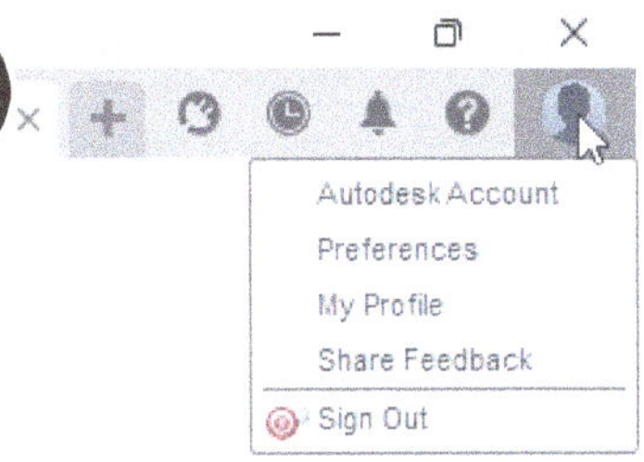

5.36

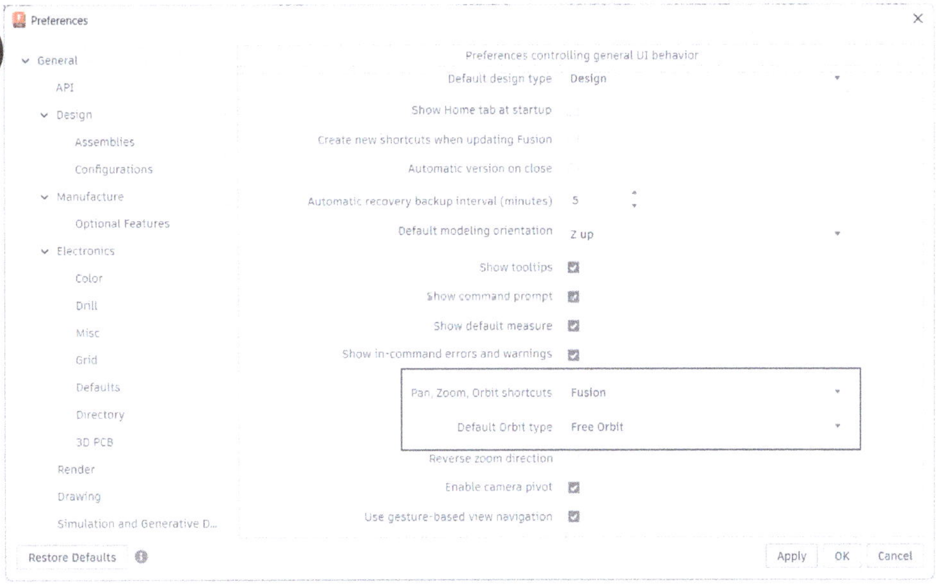

In the **Preferences** dialog box, ensure that the **General** option is selected in the left panel of the dialog box. The options to control the navigation settings appear on the right panel of the dialog box, refer to Figure 5.36. Next, in the **Pan, Zoom, Orbit shortcuts** drop-down list of the dialog box, select the **Fusion**, **Alias**, **Inventor**, **Solidworks**, **Tinkercad**, or **PowerMill** option, see Figure 5.37. Note that depending upon the option selected in the **Pan, Zoom, Orbit shortcuts** drop-down list, you can navigate the model by using the shortcuts used in the respective CAD package, see the Table given below:

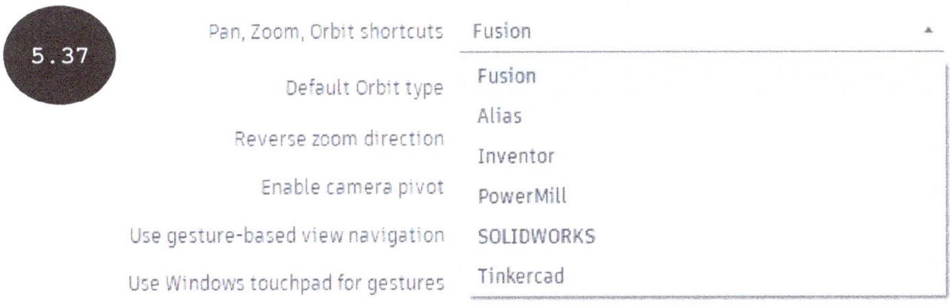

5.37

	Pan	Zoom	Orbit
Fusion	Hold the Middle Mouse Button 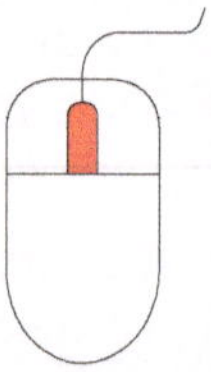	Scroll Middle Mouse Button 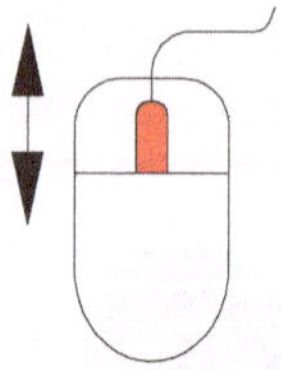	SHIFT + 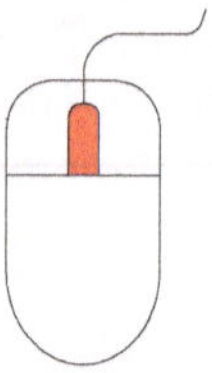
Alias	SHIFT + ALT + 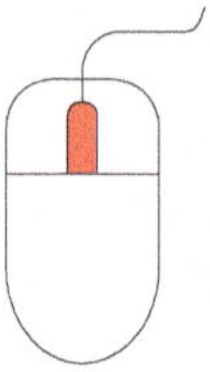	SHIFT + ALT + 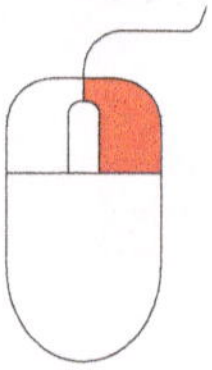	SHIFT + ALT + 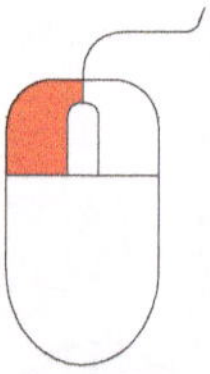
Inventor	F2 + 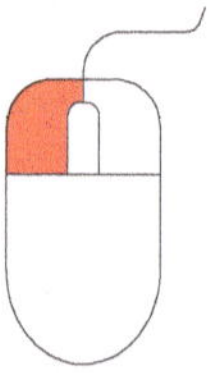	F3 + 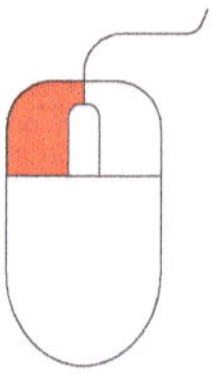	F4 + 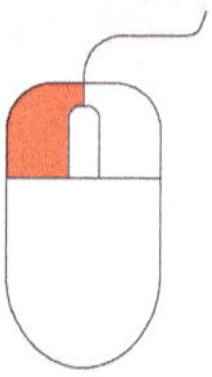
SolidWorks	CTRL + 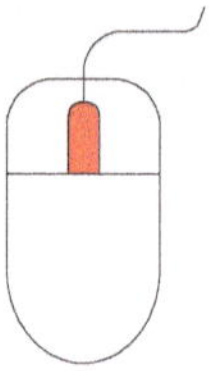	SHIFT + 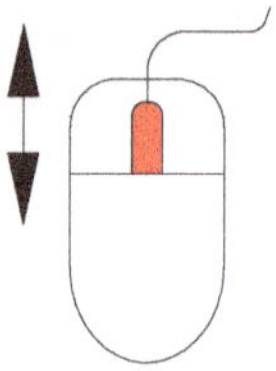	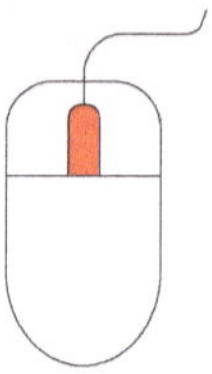
Tinkercad	Hold the Middle Mouse Button 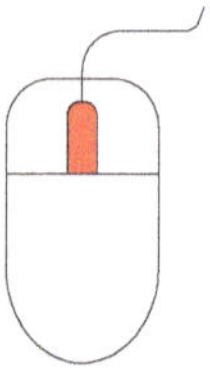	Scroll Middle Mouse Button 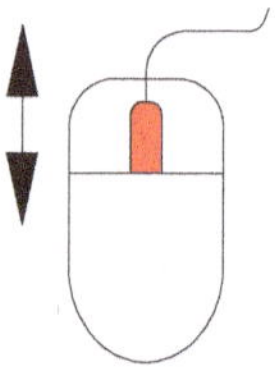	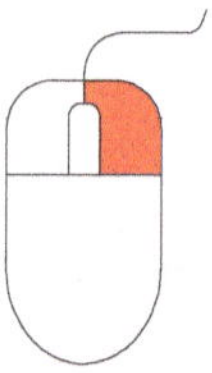
PowerMill	SHIFT + 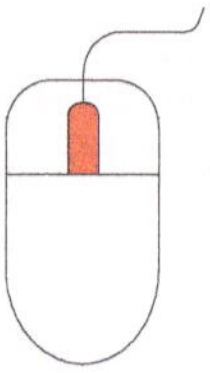	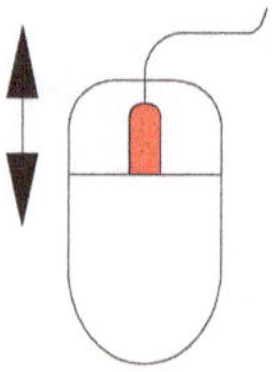	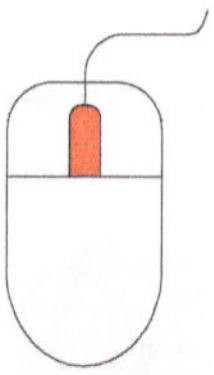

You can also set the default option to orbit the model: **Constrained Orbit** or **Free Orbit** using the **Default Orbit type** drop-down list of the dialog box.

After specifying the navigation settings, as per the requirement, click on the **Apply** button and then on the **OK** button in the **Preferences** dialog box.

Now, you can navigate the model as per the navigation settings specified in the **Preferences** dialog box. The various navigation tools are discussed next.

Note: In this textbook, the default navigation settings are used for panning, zooming, and orbiting the model. The Autodesk Fusion navigation settings are the default settings.

Pan

You can pan or move a model in the graphics area using the **Pan** tool. To do this, click on the **Pan** tool in the **Navigation Bar**, see Figure 5.38. The **Pan** tool gets activated. Next, drag the cursor after pressing and holding the left mouse button.

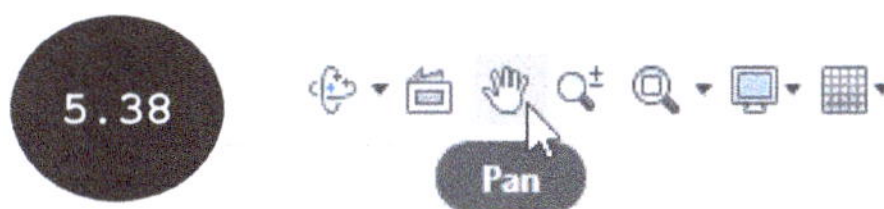

Alternatively, you can also pan the model by dragging the cursor after pressing and holding the middle mouse button.

Zoom

You can zoom into or out of the graphics area dynamically using the **Zoom** tool. In other words, you can enlarge or reduce the view of a model dynamically using the **Zoom** tool. To do this, click on the **Zoom** tool in the **Navigation Bar**. The **Zoom** tool gets activated. Next, drag the cursor upward or downward in the graphics area by pressing and holding the left mouse button. On dragging the cursor upward, the view gets reduced, whereas on dragging the cursor downward, the view gets enlarged. You can also reverse the zoom direction. To do this, invoke the **Preferences** dialog box, as discussed earlier, and then select the **Reverse zoom direction** check box, see Figure 5.39. Note that in the process of zooming in or zooming out, the scale of the model remains the same. However, the viewing distance gets modified to enlarge or reduce the view of the model.

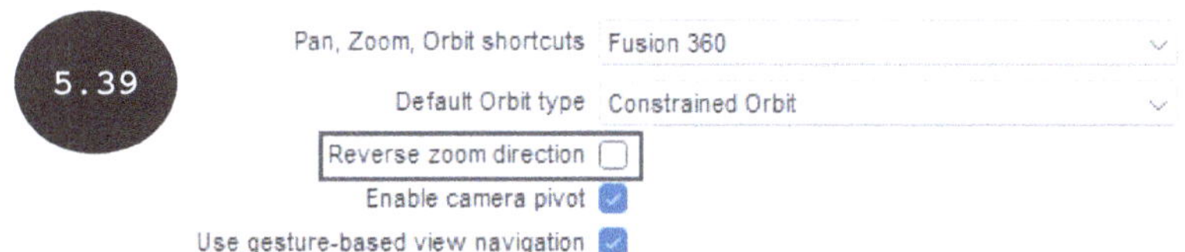

Alternatively, you can also zoom in or zoom out by scrolling the middle mouse button in the graphics area.

Zoom Window

The **Zoom Window** tool is used to zoom in on a particular portion or area of a model by defining a window. To do this, invoke the **Zoom** flyout in the **Navigation Bar** by clicking on the arrow next to the active Zoom tool, see Figure 5.40. Next, click on the **Zoom Window** tool and then draw a window by dragging the cursor around the portion or area of the model to be zoomed. The area inside the window is enlarged.

5.40

Zoom Window
Fit F6

Fit

The **Fit** tool is used to fit a model completely inside the graphics area. To do this, invoke the **Zoom** flyout in the **Navigation Bar** by clicking on the arrow next to the active Zoom tool, refer to Figure 5.40 and then click on the **Fit** tool. The model fits completely inside the graphics area. You can also press the **F6** key to fit the model completely inside the graphics area.

Free Orbit

The **Free Orbit** tool is used to rotate the model freely inside the graphics area. To do this, invoke the **Orbit** flyout by clicking on the arrow next to the active orbit tool in the **Navigation Bar** (see Figure 5.41) and then click on the **Free Orbit** tool. A circular rim with lines at its four quadrants and a cross mark at its center appears in the graphics area, see Figure 5.42.

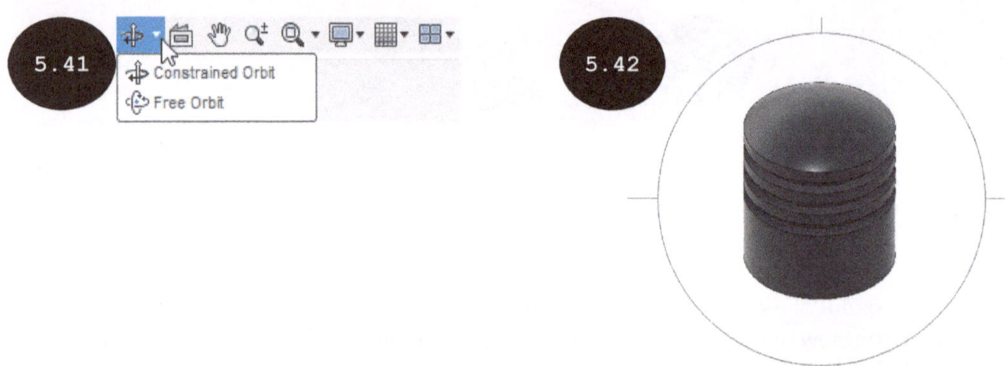

To rotate a model freely, drag the cursor after pressing and holding the left mouse button in the graphics area. Alternatively, drag the cursor after pressing and holding the SHIFT key and middle mouse button.

To rotate a model about the vertical axis, move the cursor over the horizontal line at the right or left quadrant of the circular rim. The cursor icon changes to a horizontal elliptical arrow. Next, drag the cursor by pressing the left mouse button to rotate the model about the vertical axis. Similarly, you can rotate the model about the horizontal axis by dragging the cursor after positioning it over a vertical line at the top or bottom quadrant of the circular rim.

Constrained Orbit

The **Constrained Orbit** tool is used to rotate the model by constraining the view of the model along the XY plane of the Z axis. To do this, invoke the **Orbit** flyout in the **Navigation Bar** (refer to Figure 5.41) and then click on the **Constrained Orbit** tool. Next, drag the cursor after pressing and holding the left mouse button. You can also rotate the model around the vertical or horizontal axis by using the horizontal or vertical lines of the circular rim that appear in the graphics area respectively, as discussed earlier.

Look At

The **Look At** tool is used to display the selected face of a 3D model normal to the viewing direction. To do this, click on the **Look At** tool in the **Navigation Bar** and then click on a face. The selected face becomes normal in the viewing direction. If you are in the Sketching environment, then you can use this tool to make the current sketching plane normal to the viewing direction.

Navigating a 3D Model by Using the ViewCube

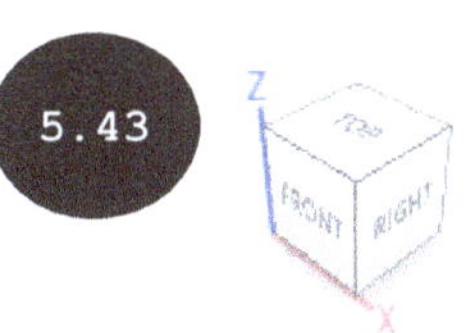

ViewCube is available at the upper right corner of the graphics area, see Figure 5.43. It is used to change the view or orientation of the model easily.

By using ViewCube, you can switch between standard and isometric views.
By default, it is in an inactive state. When you move the cursor over ViewCube, it becomes active and works as a navigation tool. You can navigate a model by using the ViewCube components, see Figure 5.44. The various ViewCube components are discussed next.

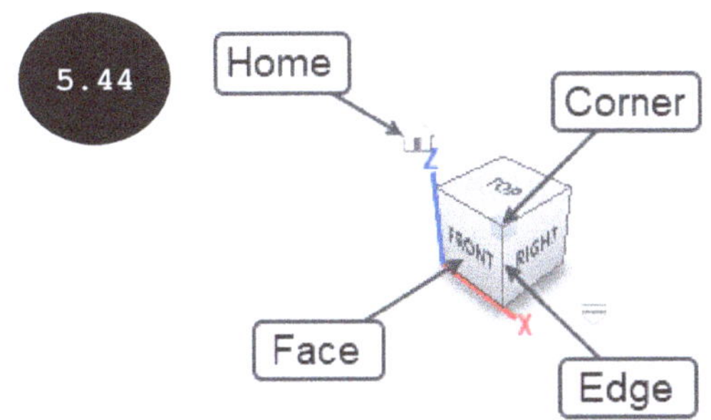

Home

The **Home** icon of ViewCube is used to return the current view of the model to the default home or isometric view.

Corner

A corner of ViewCube is used to obtain an isometric view or to rotate the view freely in all directions. To get an isometric view, click on a corner of the ViewCube. To rotate the view freely in all directions, drag a corner of the ViewCube by pressing and holding the left mouse button.

Edge

An edge of the ViewCube is used to obtain an edge-on view or to rotate the view freely in all directions. To achieve an isometric view, click on an edge of the ViewCube. To rotate the view freely in all directions, drag an edge by pressing and holding the left mouse button.

Face

A face of the **ViewCube** is used to obtain an orthogonal view, such as top, front, or right. For instance, to get the top view of the model, click on the top face of the **ViewCube**.

You can also display additional options to control the view of a model or the ViewCube settings. To do this, click on the arrow available at the bottom of the ViewCube to display options for controlling the ViewCube settings, see Figure 5.45. Alternatively, right-click on the ViewCube to display these options. Some of the options are discussed next.

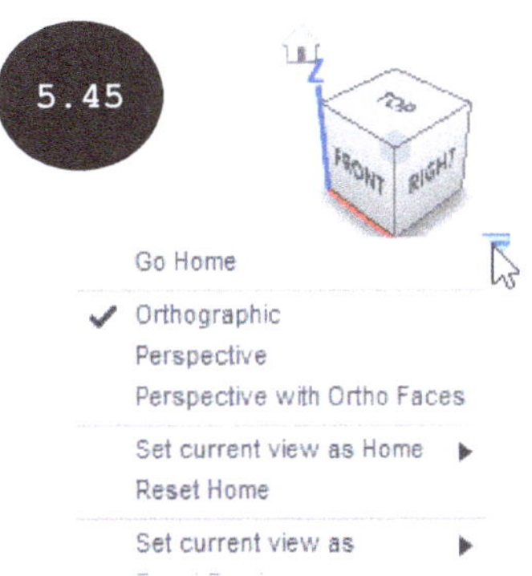

Go Home

The **Go Home** option is used to revert the current view of the model back to the default home view.

Orthographic

By default, the **Orthographic** option is selected. As a result, the model appears in the orthographic view in the graphics area.

Perspective

The **Perspective** option is used to display a model in a perspective view, providing a more realistic representation of depth.

Perspective with Ortho Faces

The **Perspective with Ortho Faces** option is used to display a model in the perspective view with orthographic faces.

Set current view as Home

In Autodesk Fusion, you can set the current view of a model as the home view with a fixed distance or fit to view. To do this, move the cursor over the **Set current view as Home** option. A cascading menu appears with the **Fixed Distance** and **Fit to View** options, see Figure 5.46. The **Fixed Distance** option is used to set the current view of the model as the home view with a fixed view distance as it is currently set for the model. The **Fit to View** option is used to set the current view of the model as the home view with the fit to view distance. This means that the model view adjusts automatically and fits in the graphics area.

5.46

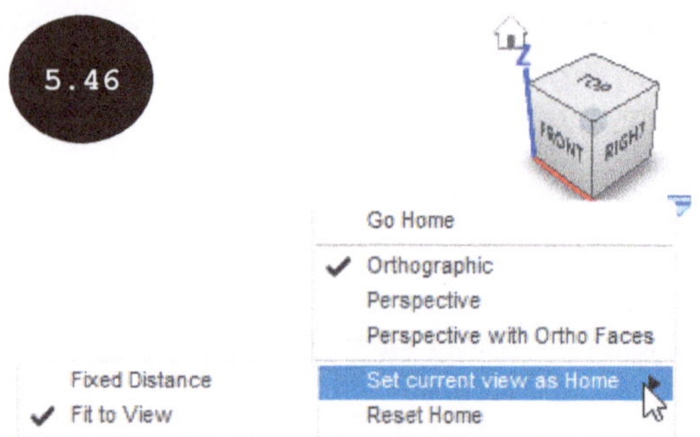

Reset Home

The **Reset Home** option is used to rest the home view of the model to the default settings.

Set current view as

You can set the current view of the model as the Front or Top view. To do this, move the cursor over the **Set current view as** option. A cascading menu appears with the **Front** and **Top** options. Click on the required option in this menu.

Reset Front

The **Reset Front** option is used for resetting the Front view of the model to the default settings.

Changing the Visual Style of a Model

You can change the visual or display style of a model to shaded, shaded with hidden edges, shaded with visible edges, wireframe, wireframe with hidden edges, or wireframe with visible edges. You can access the tools to change the visual style of the model by clicking on **Display Settings > Visual Style** in the **Navigation Bar**, see Figure 5.47. The tools are discussed next.

5.47

Shaded

The **Shaded** tool is used to display a model in a 'shaded' visual style. In this style, the model is displayed in shaded mode with the display of edges turned off, see Figure 5.48.

Shaded with Hidden Edges

The **Shaded with Hidden Edges** tool is used to display a model in a 'shaded with hidden edges' visual style. In this style, the model is displayed in shaded mode with the display of visible and hidden edges turned on, see Figure 5.49.

5.48 5.49

Shaded with Visible Edges Only

The **Shaded with Visible Edges Only** tool is used to display the model in a 'shaded with visible edges' visual style. In this style, the model is displayed in shaded mode with only the display of visible edges turned on, see Figure 5.50. This tool is activated by default. As a result, the model is displayed in a 'shaded with visible edges' visual style in the graphics area, by default.

Wireframe

The **Wireframe** tool is used to display the model in a 'wireframe' visual style. In this style, the edges (visible and hidden) of the model are displayed in solid lines, see Figure 5.51.

Wireframe with Hidden Edges

The **Wireframe with Hidden Edges** tool is used for displaying the model in a 'wireframe with hidden edges' visual style. In this style, the hidden edges of the model are displayed in dotted lines and the visible edges of the model are displayed in solid lines, see Figure 5.52.

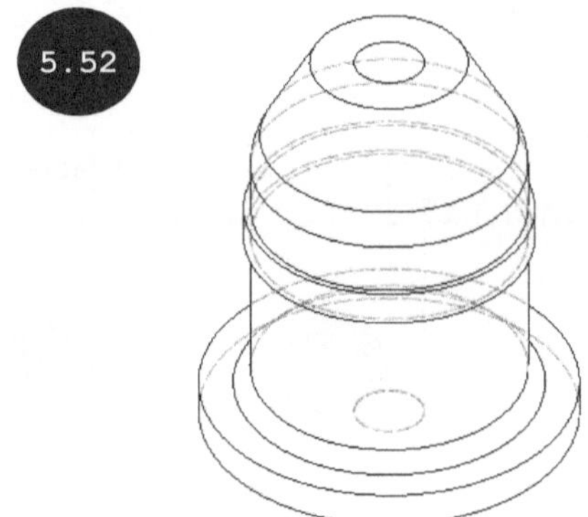

Wireframe with Visible Edges Only

The **Wireframe with Visible Edges Only** tool is used for displaying the model in a 'wireframe with visible edges' visual style. In this style, the display of the hidden edges of the model is turned off and only the visible edges of the model are displayed in solid lines, see Figure 5.53.

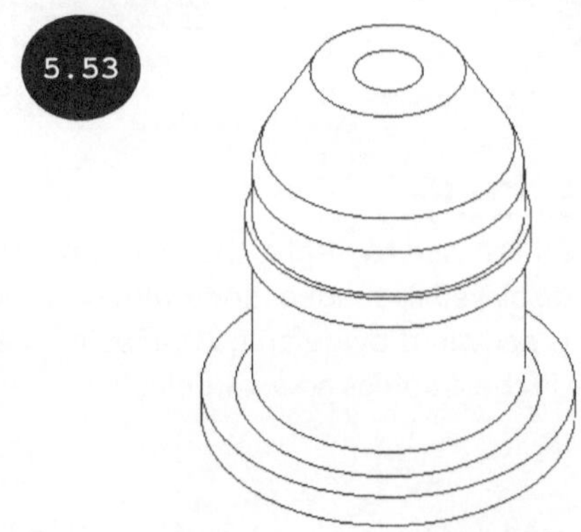

Tutorial 1

Create an extruded model shown in Figure 5.54. The depth of extrusion is 15 mm. All dimensions are in mm.

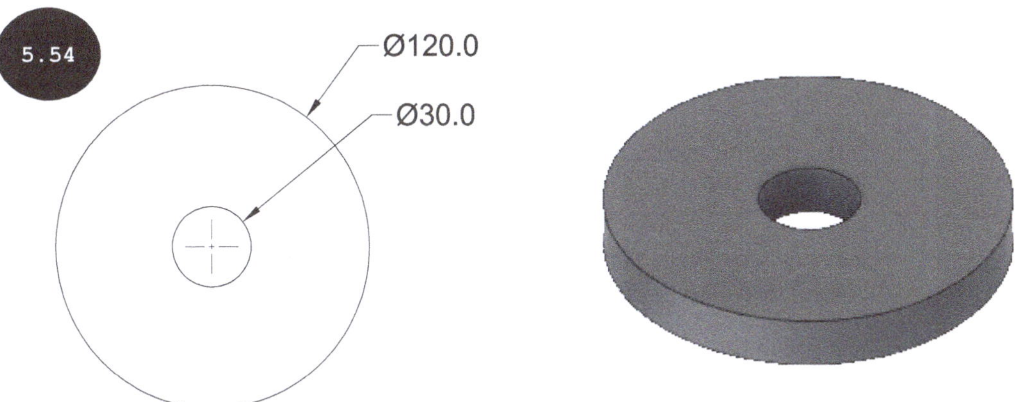

Section 1: Starting a New Part Design File

1. Click **File** > **New** in the **Application Bar** (see Figure 5.55) to display the **What do you want to design?** dialog box, see Figure 5.56.

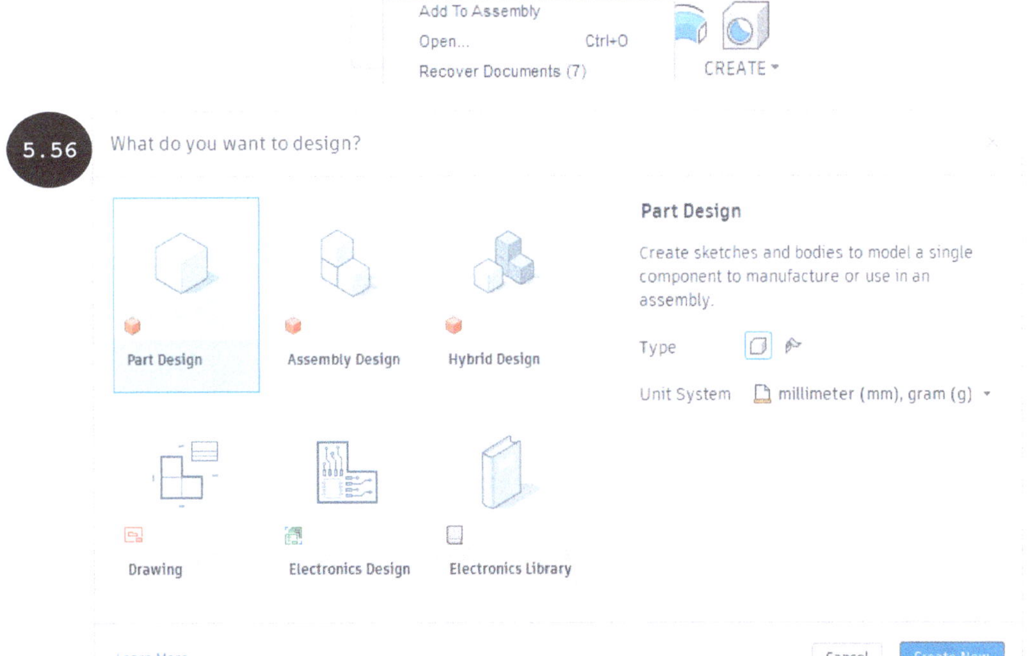

Note: If you are starting a new Autodesk Fusion session, the Part Design file opens automatically because it is set as the default design type. In this case, ensure that the **millimeter (mm), gram (g)** unit system is set for the opened Part Design file.

2. In the **What do you want to design?** dialog box, select the **Part Design** button and choose the **millimeter (mm), gram (g)** unit system from the **Unit System** drop-down list.

3. After specifying the required options, click the **Create New** button. A new Part Design file is created with the default name "**Untitled**".

Section 2: Organizing the Data Panel

1. Invoke the **Data Panel** and then ensure that the '**Autodesk Fusion 360**' project is created in the **Data Panel.**

2. Double-click on the **Autodesk Fusion 360** project in the **Data Panel** and then create the "**Chapter 05**" folder by using the **New Folder** tool in the **Data Panel.**

3. Double-click on the **Chapter 05** folder in the **Data Panel** and then create the "**Tutorial**" sub-folder. Next, close the **Data Panel.**

Section 3: Creating the Sketch

1. Click on the **Create Sketch** tool in the **Toolbar** and then select the Top plane as the sketching plane for creating the sketch of the feature.

2. Create the sketch (two concentric circles), see Figure 5.57. Note that the center points of the circles are at the origin. Also, you need to apply the diameter dimensions to the circles.

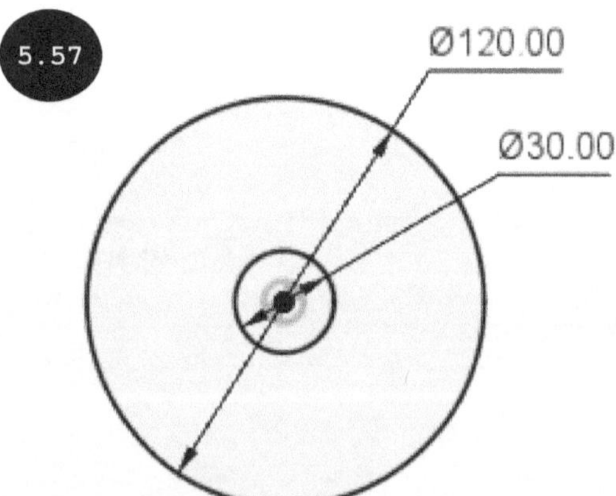

Section 4: Extruding the Sketch

After creating the sketch, you can convert it into a 3D solid feature.

1. Click on the **SOLID** tab in the **Toolbar** to display the solid modeling tools.

2. Click on the **Extrude** tool in the **SOLID** tab, see Figure 5.58 or press the **E** key. The **EXTRUDE** dialog box appears, see Figure 5.59.

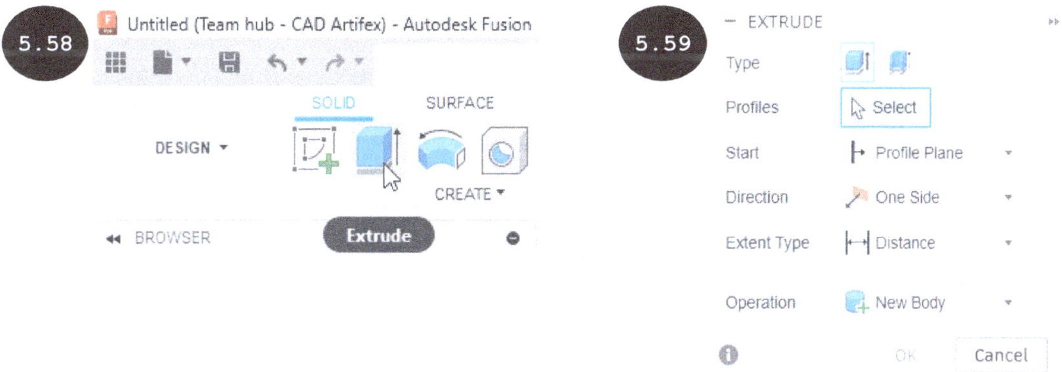

3. Change the orientation of the sketch to isometric by clicking on the **Home** icon of ViewCube, if the orientation is not changed by default.

4. Move the cursor over the outer closed profile of the sketch and then click when it gets highlighted in the graphics area, see Figure 5.60.

5. Enter **15** as the extrusion distance in the **Distance** field of the **EXTRUDE** dialog box. The preview of an extruded feature appears in the graphics area.

6. Click on the **OK** button in the dialog box. The extrude feature is created, see Figure 5.61.

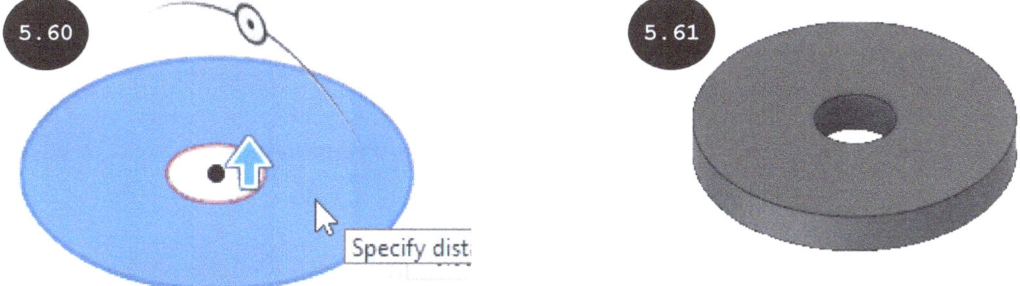

Section 5: Saving the Model

1. Click on the **Save** tool in the Application Bar. The **Save** dialog box appears.

2. Enter **Tutorial 1** in the **Name** field of the dialog box.

3. Ensure that the location *Autodesk Fusion 360 > Chapter 05 > Tutorial* is specified in the **Location** field of the dialog box to save the file of this tutorial. To specify the location, you need to expand the **Save** dialog box by clicking on the down arrow next to the **Location** field of the dialog box.

4. Click on the **Save** button in the dialog box. The model is saved with the name **Tutorial 1** in the specified location (***Autodesk Fusion 360 > Chapter 05 > Tutorial***).

Tutorial 2

Open the sketch created in Tutorial 1 of Chapter 4 see Figure 5.62 and then create a solid model (extrude feature) by extruding it to a depth of 40 mm, see Figure 5.63.

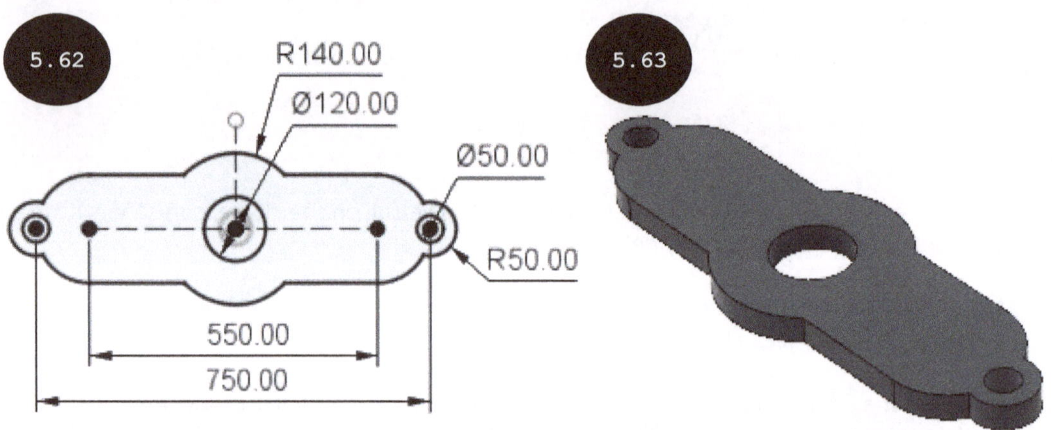

Section 1: Opening the Sketch of Tutorial 1, Chapter 4

1. Launch Autodesk Fusion, if it is not already running.

   Now, you need to open the sketch of Tutorial 1 created in Chapter 4.

2. Click on the **Show Data Panel** tool in the **Application Bar**, see Figure 5.64. The **Data Panel** appears.

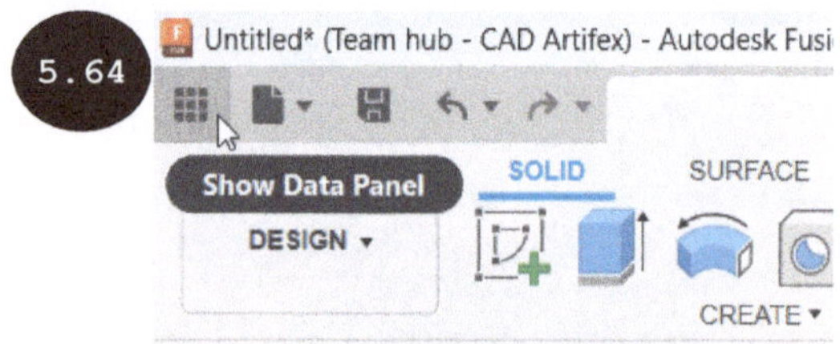

3. Browse to the ***Autodesk Fusion 360 > Chapter 04 > Tutorial*** in the **Data Panel**. All the tutorial files created in Chapter 4 appear in the **Data Panel**.

4. Double-click on the **Tutorial 1** file which is created in Chapter 4. The sketch of Tutorial 1, created in Chapter 4, is opened in the current session of Autodesk Fusion, see Figure 5.65.

Note: If you have not created Tutorial 1 of Chapter 4 then you need to first create it, as discussed in Chapter 4.

5. Close the **Data Panel** by clicking on the cross-mark × at its top right corner.

Section 2: Saving the Sketch

Now, you need to save the sketch with the name "Tutorial 2" in the *Chapter 5* folder.

1. Invoke the **File** drop-down menu in the **Application Bar** and then click on the **Save As** tool, see Figure 5.66. The **Save As** dialog box appears.

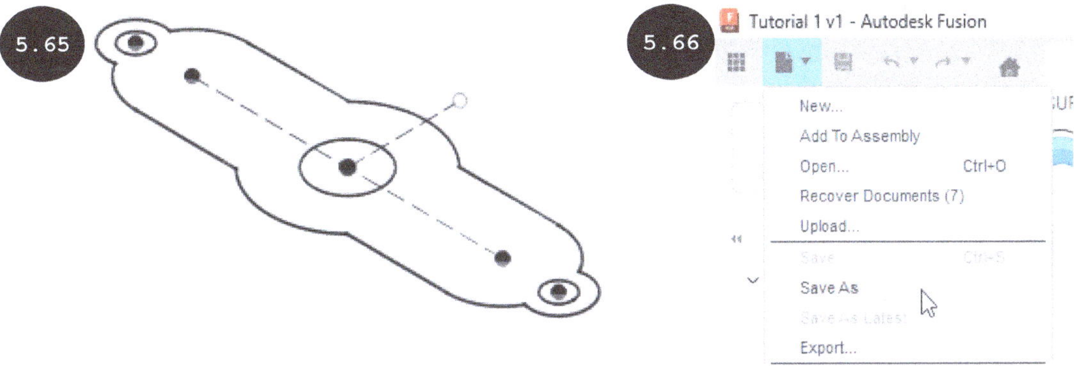

2. Enter **Tutorial 2** in the **Name** field of the dialog box, see Figure 5.67.

3. Ensure the location ***Autodesk Fusion 360 > Chapter 05 > Tutorial*** is specified in the **Location** field of the dialog box to save the file. To specify the location, you need to expand the **Save As** dialog box by clicking on the down arrow next to the **Location** field, refer to Figure 5.66. Note that you need to create these folders inside the **Autodesk Fusion 360** project, if not created earlier.

4. Click on the **Save** button in the dialog box. The sketch is saved as **Tutorial 2** in the *Autodesk Fusion 360 > Chapter 05 > Tutorial* location of the **Data Panel**.

Note: It is important to save the sketch in a different location or with a different name before making any modification, so that the original file does not get modified.

Section 3: Extruding the Sketch

Now, you can extrude the sketch and convert it into a feature.

1. Click on the **Extrude** tool in the **SOLID** tab of the **Toolbar**, see Figure 5.68. The **EXTRUDE** dialog box appears, see Figure 5.69. You can also press the **E** key to activate the **Extrude** tool.

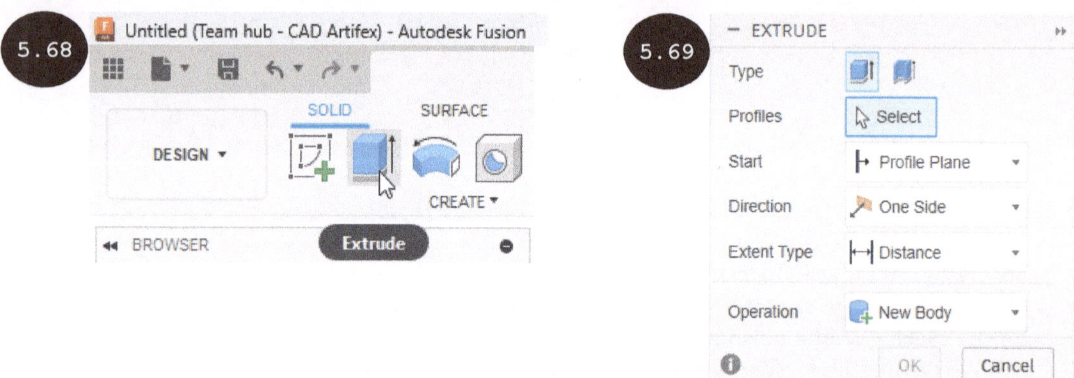

2. Move the cursor over the outer closed profile of the sketch and then click when it gets highlighted in the graphics area, see Figure 5.70. The profile gets selected. Also, an arrow, manipulator handle, and **Distance** box appear in the graphics area, see Figure 5.71.

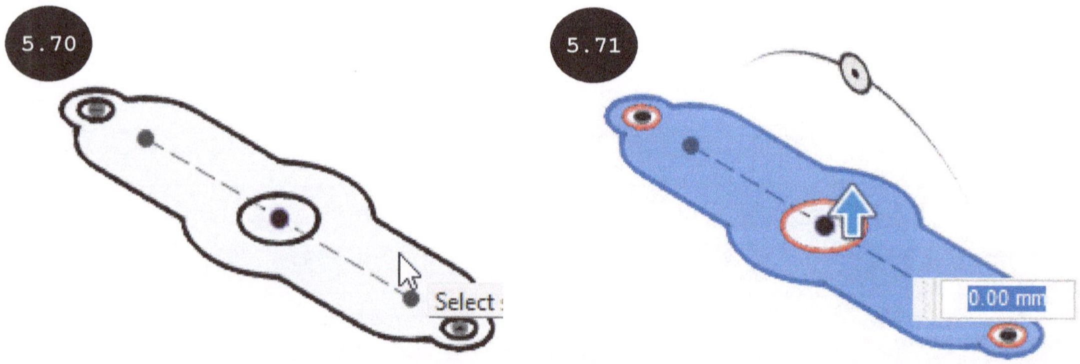

3. Enter **40** in the **Distance** field of the **EXTRUDE** dialog box as the extrusion distance. A preview of the extruded feature appears in the graphics area, see Figure 5.72.

Tip: You can also drag the arrow that appears in the graphics area to set the extrusion distance in the graphics area, dynamically. The manipulator handle appearing along with the preview in the graphics area is used for setting the taper angle of extrusion in the graphics area.

4. Accept the remaining default specified options in the dialog box and then click on the **OK** button. The extrude feature is created, see Figure 5.73.

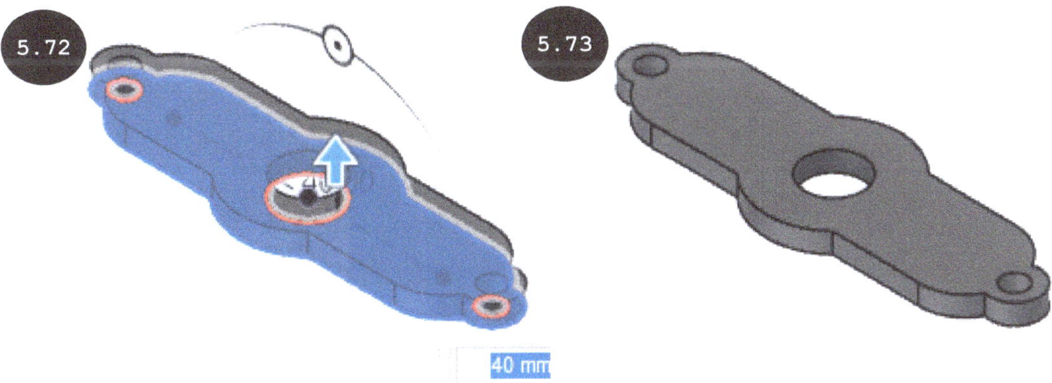

Section 4: Saving the Model

Now, you need to save the model.

1. Click on the **Save** tool in the **Application Bar**. The **Save** window appears, see Figure 5.74. Note that as the design file is already saved, the **Save** window appears. In this window, you can enter the description for the new version of the file.

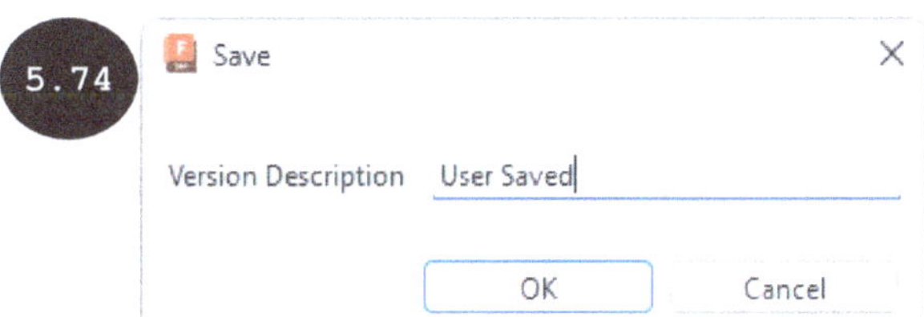

Note: In Autodesk Fusion, every time you save an existing file after making changes, a new version is created without overwriting the previous ones. Fusion keeps all versions, with the latest one being the active version. To access an earlier version, browse to the file's location in the **Data Panel**, and click on the version icon (V1, V2, etc.) in the lower right corner of the file's thumbnail to display a list of all saved versions. Next, hover over the version you want to open, and when the **Open** icon appears, click on it to open that version.

2. Accept the default **Version description** in the **Save** window and then click on the **OK** button. The new version of the file is saved.

3. Close the file by clicking on the cross-mark on its tab, see Figure 5.75.

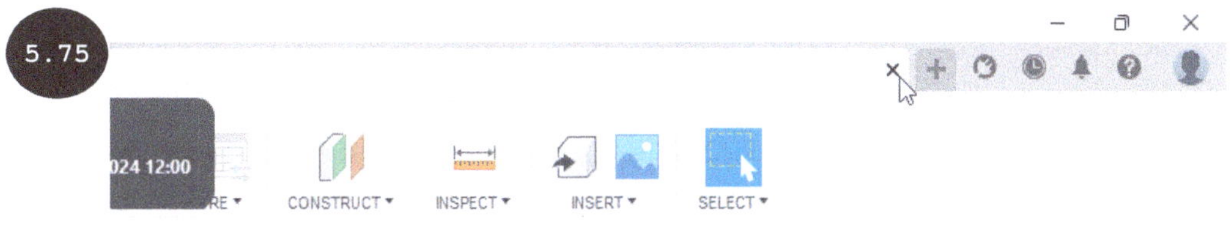

Tutorial 3

Open the sketch created in Tutorial 2 of Chapter 4, see Figure 5.76, and then revolve it around the vertical construction line at an angle of 270 degrees, see Figure 5.77. Also, change the display style of the model to the 'wireframe with visible edges only' visual style.

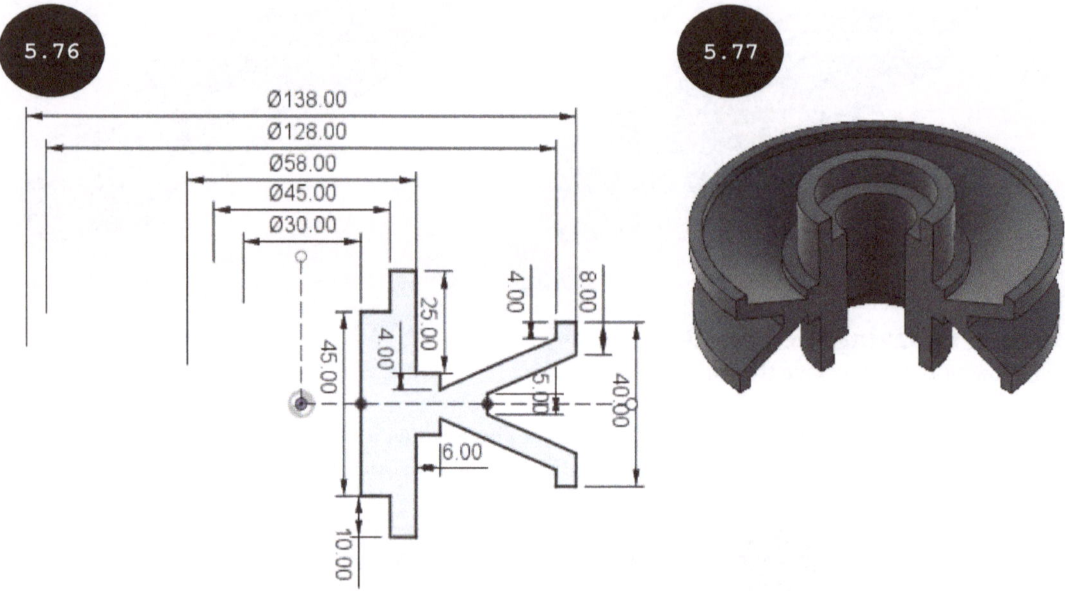

Section 1: Opening the Sketch of Tutorial 2, Chapter 4

1. Launch Autodesk Fusion, if it is not already running.

   Now, you need to open the sketch of Tutorial 2 created in Chapter 4.

2. Click on the **Show Data Panel** tool in the **Application Bar**, see Figure 5.78. The **Data Panel** appears.

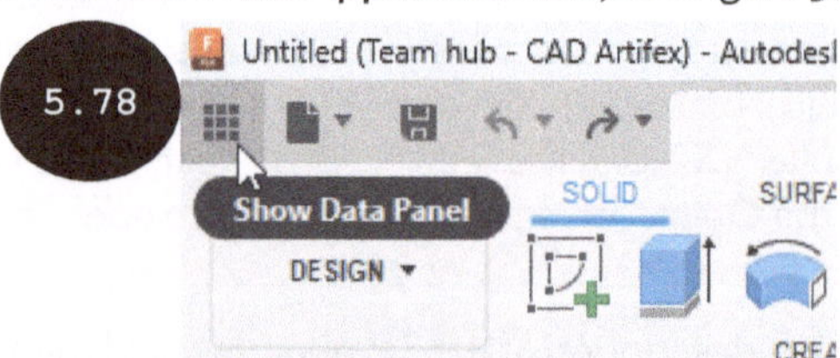

3. Browse to the ***Autodesk Fusion 360 > Chapter 04 > Tutorial*** in the **Data Panel**. All the tutorial files created in Chapter 4 appear in the **Data Panel**.

4. Double-click on the **Tutorial 2** file which is created in Chapter 4. The sketch of Tutorial 2, created in Chapter 4, is opened in the current session of Autodesk Fusion, see Figure 5.79.

Note: If you have not created Tutorial 2 of Chapter 4, then you need to first create it, as discussed in Chapter 4.

5. Close the **Data Panel** by clicking on the cross-mark × at its top right corner.

Section 2: Saving the Sketch

Now, you need to save the sketch with the name "Tutorial 3" in the *Chapter 5* folder.

1. Invoke the **File** drop-down menu in the **Application Bar** and then click on the **Save As** tool, see Figure 5.80. The **Save As** dialog box appears.

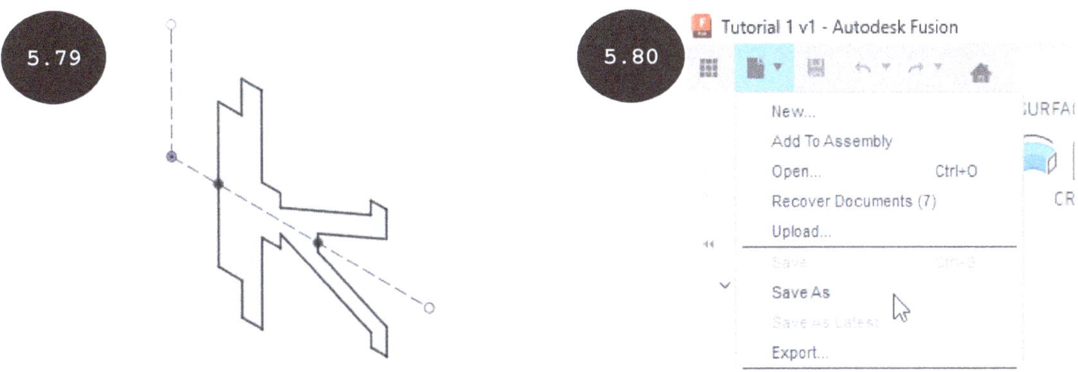

2. Enter **Tutorial 3** in the **Name** field of the dialog box.

3. Ensure the location *Autodesk Fusion 360 > Chapter 05 > Tutorial* is specified in the **Location** field of the dialog box to save the file of this tutorial. To specify the location, you need to expand the **Save As** dialog box by clicking on the down arrow next to the **Location** field. Note that you need to create these folders inside the Autodesk Fusion 360 project, if not created earlier.

4. Click on the **Save** button in the dialog box. The sketch is saved as **Tutorial 3** in the ***Autodesk Fusion 360 > Chapter 05 > Tutorial*** location of the **Data Panel**.

Note: It is important to save the sketch in a different location or with a different name before making any modification, so that the original file does not get modified.

Section 3: Revolving the Sketch

Now, you need to revolve the sketch and convert it into a feature.

1. Click on the **Revolve** tool in the **SOLID** tab of the **Toolbar**, see Figure 5.81. The **REVOLVE** dialog box appears, see Figure 5.82. Also, the closed profile of the sketch gets selected automatically and you are prompted to select an axis of revolution.

Note: In Autodesk Fusion, if a single valid profile is available in the graphics area, then it gets selected automatically on invoking the **EXTRUDE** or **REVOLVE** tool.

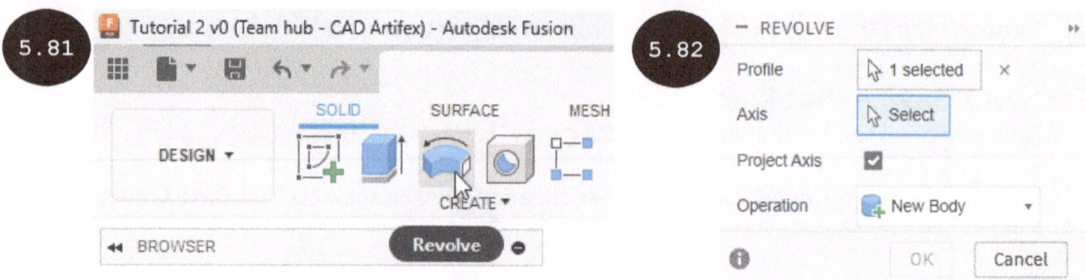

2. Click on the vertical construction line of the sketch as the axis of revolution. The preview of the revolve feature appears in the graphics area with a default angle of revolution.

3. Ensure that the **Partial** option is selected in the **Extent Type** drop-down list of the dialog box.

4. Enter **270** in the **Angle** field of the **REVOLVE** dialog box. The preview of the revolve feature gets modified in the graphics area, see Figure 5.83.

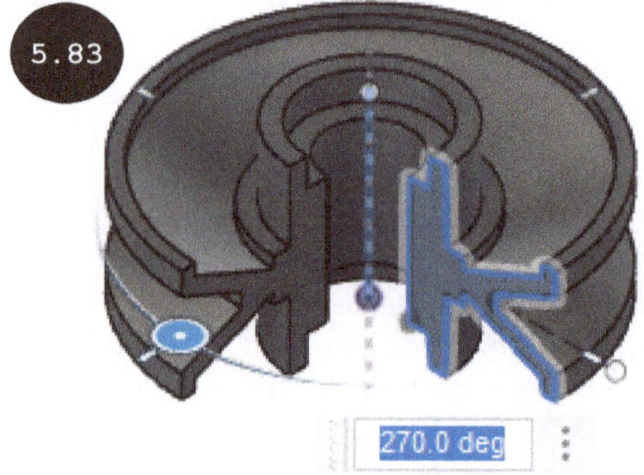

Tip: You can also drag the manipulator handle that appears along with the preview of the feature in the graphics area, to set the angle of revolution of the feature, dynamically.

5. Accept the remaining default specified options in the dialog box and then click on the **OK** button. The revolve feature is created, see Figure 5.84.

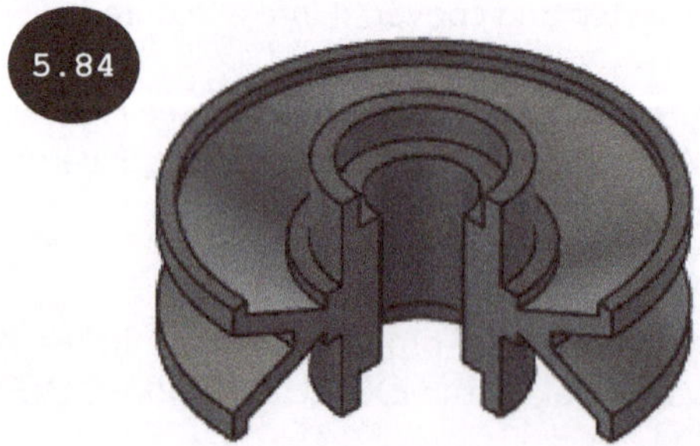

Section 4: Changing the Visual Style

As mentioned in the tutorial description, you need to change the visual style of the model to the 'wireframe with visible edges only' visual style.

1. Click on **Display Settings > Visual Style > Wireframe with Visible Edges Only** in the **Navigation Bar**, see Figure 5.85. The visual style of the model is changed to the 'wireframe with visible edges only' style, see Figure 5.86.

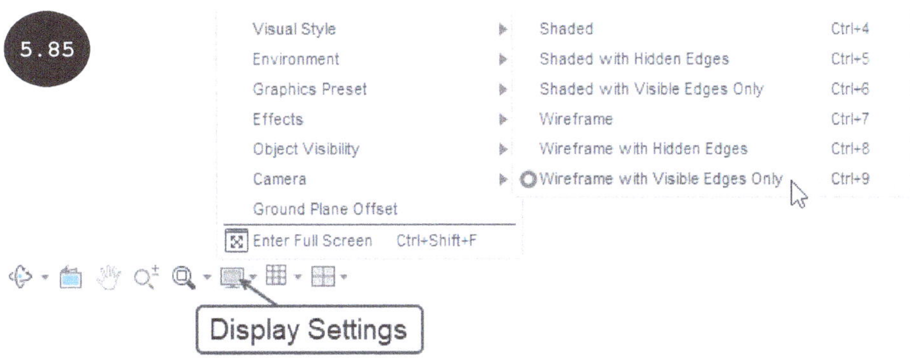

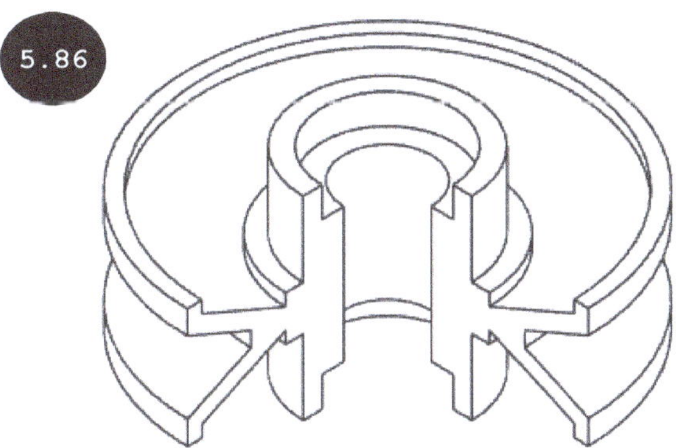

Section 5: Saving the Model

Now, you need to save the model.

1. Click on the **Save** tool in the **Application Bar**. As this Tutorial is already saved, the **Save** window appears. In this window, you can enter the description for the new version of the file.

Note: In Autodesk Fusion, every time you save an existing file after making changes, a new version is created without overwriting the previous ones. Fusion keeps all versions, with the latest one being the active version. To access an earlier version, browse to the file's location in the **Data Panel**, and click on the version icon (**V1**, **V2**, etc.) in the lower right corner of the file's thumbnail to display a list of all saved versions. Next, hover over the version you want to open, and when the **Open** icon appears, click on it to open that version.

2. Accept the default version description in the **Add Version Description** window and then click on the **OK** button. The new version of the file is saved in the same location (***Autodesk Fusion 360 > Chapter 05 > Tutorial***).

3. Close the file by clicking on the cross-mark on its tab.

Hands-on Test Drive 1

Create the revolve model, as shown in Figure 5.87. All dimensions are in mm.

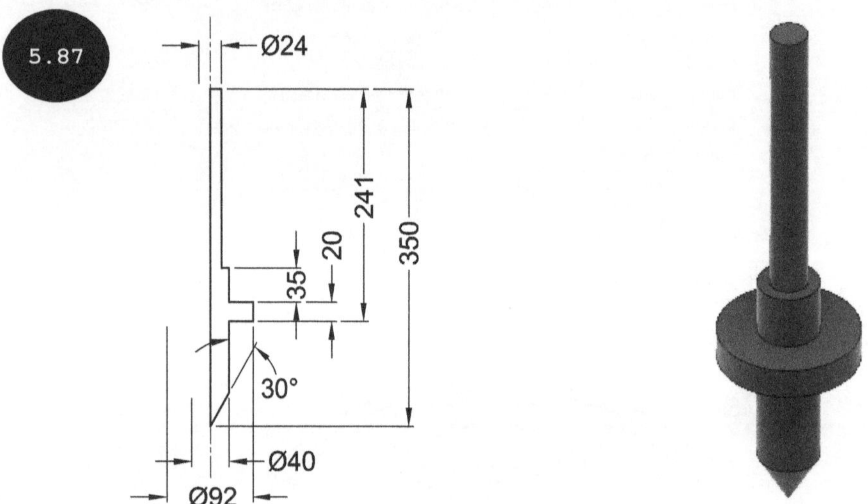

Hands-on Test Drive 2

Create the extruded model, as shown in Figure 5.88. The depth of extrusion is 2 mm. All dimensions are in mm.

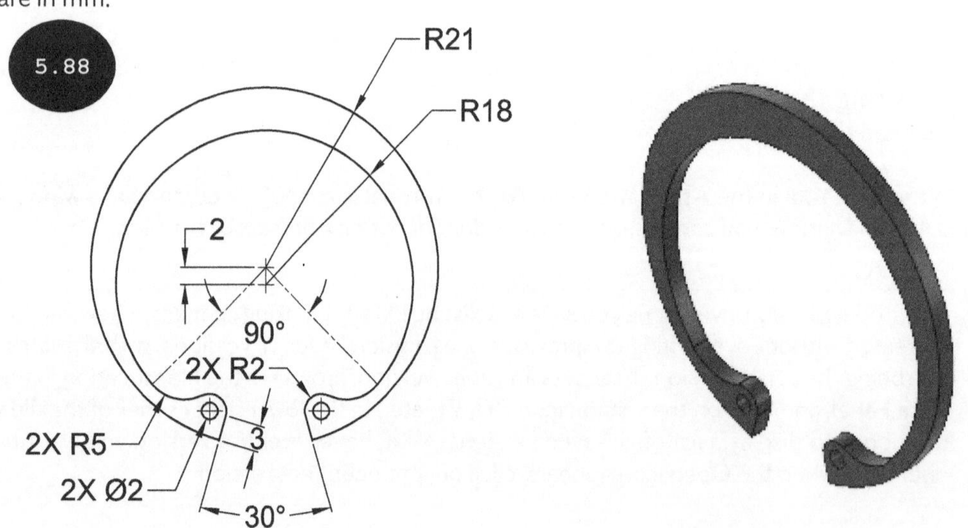

Hands-on Test Drive 3

Open the sketch created in Tutorial 3 of Chapter 4, see Figure 5.89 and then extrude it to an extrusion distance of 60 mm symmetrically about the sketching plane, see Figure 5.90.

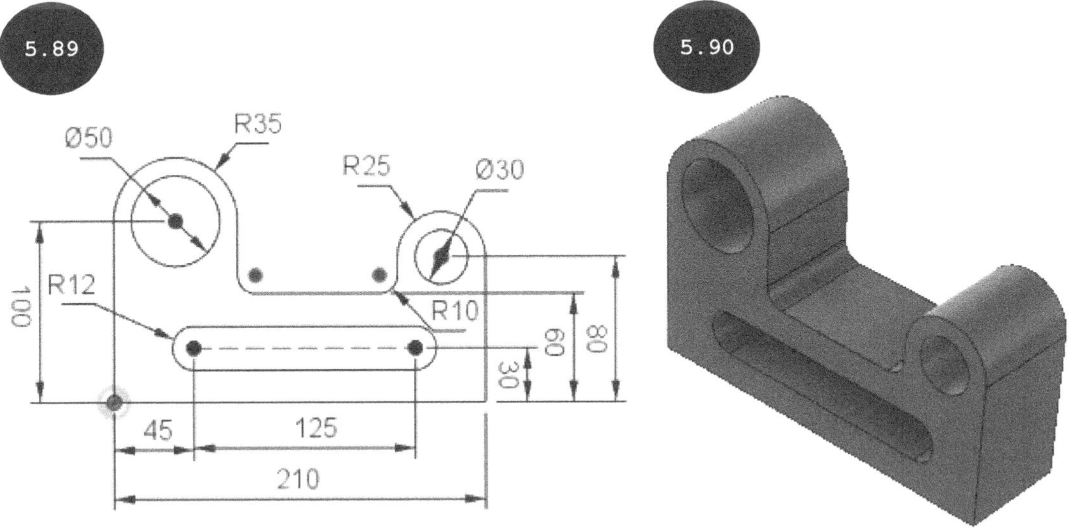

Summary

In this chapter, you learned how to create base features using the **Extrude** and **Revolve** tools, essential for building 3D models. The chapter also covered how to efficiently navigate a model using mouse controls, **ViewCube**, and navigation tools such as **Pan**, **Zoom**, and **Fit**, along with managing navigation settings similar to other CAD software. Additionally, you explored methods for adjusting the visual style of a model, ensuring a solid grasp of both model creation and navigation techniques to enhance your design workflow.

Questions

Complete and verify the following sentences:

- The _________ tool is used for creating a feature by adding or removing material normal to the sketching plane.
- The _________ tool is used for creating a feature by revolving the sketch around a centerline as the axis of revolution.
- The _________ tool is used for fitting a model completely inside the graphics area.
- The _______ field of the **EXTRUDE** dialog box is used to add tapering in the extrude feature.

- The ______ option is used for extruding or revolving a feature symmetrically about the sketching plane.
- The first created feature of a model is known as the ______ feature.
- In the ______ visual style, the model is displayed in shaded mode with the display of visible edges turned on.
- The ______ tool is used for zooming a particular portion of a model by defining a window.
- The ______ option in the **Start** drop-down list of the **EXTRUDE** dialog box is used for creating an extrude feature at an offset distance from the sketching plane.
- In Autodesk Fusion, you cannot navigate a model by using the mouse buttons. (True/False)
- In Autodesk Fusion, to remove an already selected profile, press and hold the SHIFT key and then click on the profile to be removed from the selection set. (True/False)

CHAPTER
6

Creating Construction Geometries

In this chapter, the following topics will be discussed:

- Creating a Construction Plane
- Creating a Construction Axis
- Creating a Construction Point

In Autodesk Fusion, three default construction planes, Front, Top, and Right, are available for creating features of a model, such as extrude and revolve, as discussed in earlier chapters. However, for more complex, real-world models, additional construction planes may be necessary, as the default planes might not be sufficient for all features. To address this, Autodesk Fusion provides the flexibility to create additional construction planes as needed. You can create various types of construction planes using the tools available in the **CONSTRUCT** drop-down menu of the **Toolbar**, see Figure 6.1.

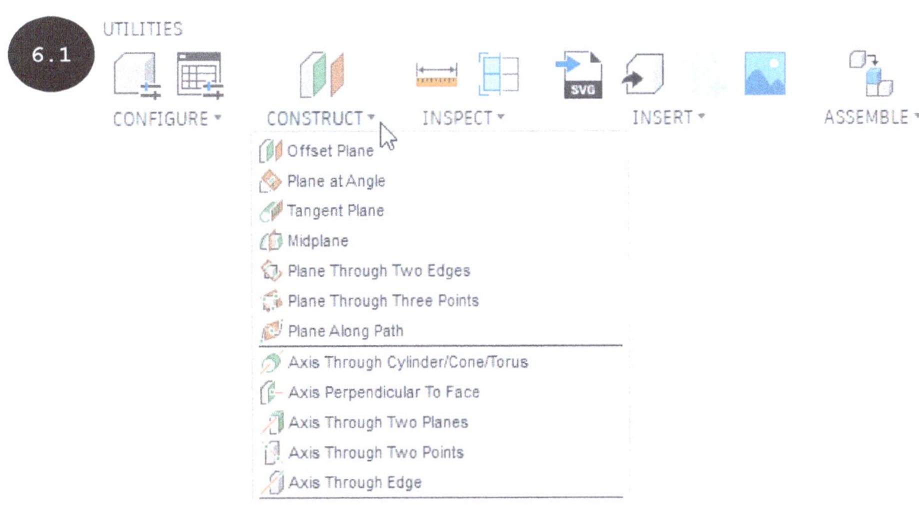

Figure 6.2 shows a model created by sequentially building its features. The first feature is an extruded feature with the sketch drawn on the Right plane. The second feature is a user-defined construction plane, positioned at an angle to the top front edge of the first extruded feature. The third feature is another extruded feature created on the user-defined construction plane. This demonstrates how an additional construction plane is used to create a feature of a model.

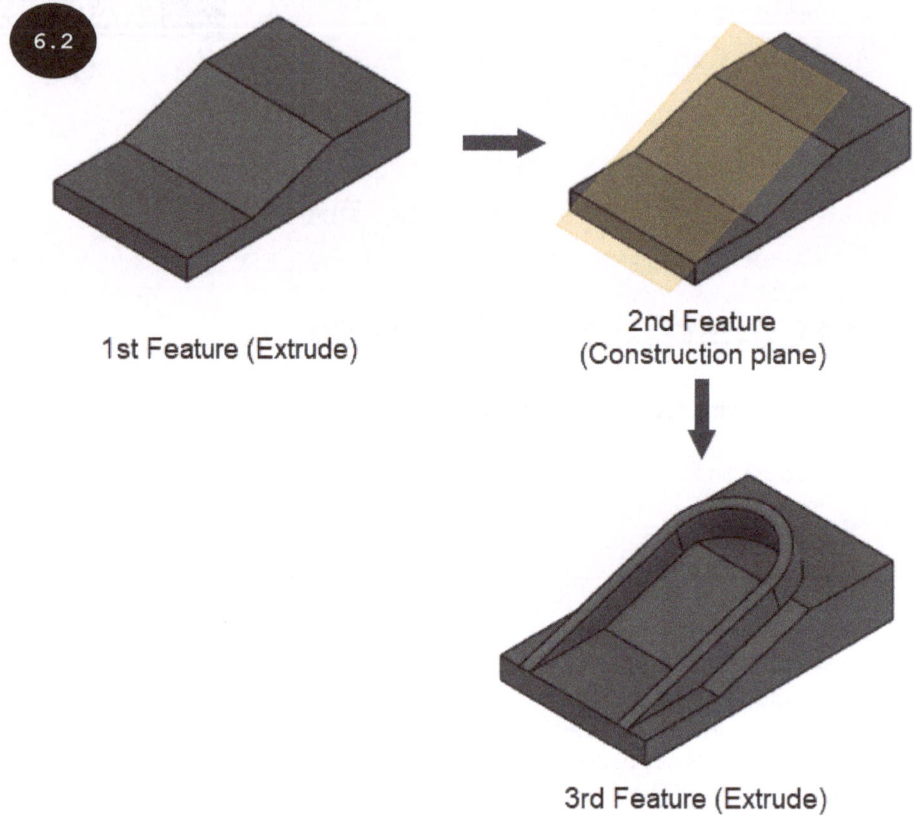

Note: It is clear from the above figure that additional construction planes may be required for creating features of a model.

In addition to creating additional construction planes, you can also create construction axes and construction points. The tools for creating various types of construction planes, axes, and points are available in the CONSTRUCT drop-down menu in the Toolbar and are discussed next.

Creating a Construction Plane

In Autodesk Fusion, you can create a construction plane at an offset distance from an existing plane or planar face, at an angle to an existing plane or planar face, tangent to a cylindrical or conical face, passing through two edges, and so on. The methods for creating different types of construction planes are discussed next.

Creating a Plane at an Offset Distance

1. Invoke the CONSTRUCT drop-down menu in the **Toolbar** and click the **Offset Plane** tool, see Figure 6.3. The **CONSTRUCTION GEOMETRY** dialog box appears with the **Plane** option activated by default in the **Type** area, see Figure 6.4.

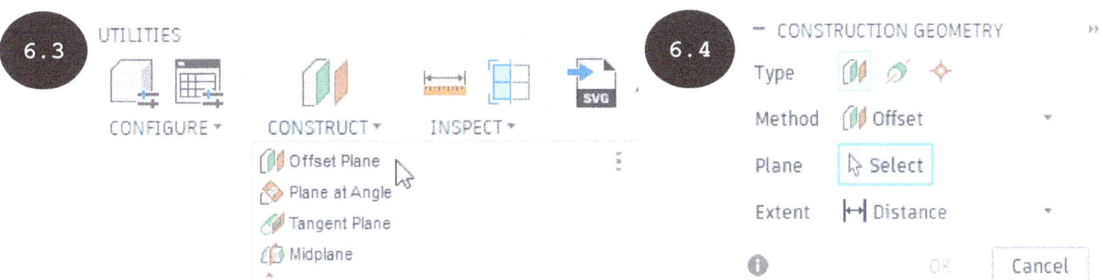

You can switch between different geometry creation tools, such as **Plane**, **Axis**, or **Point** by activating the required option in the **Type** area of the dialog box. You will learn about creating construction axes and points later in this chapter.

2. Ensure that the **Offset** option is selected in the **Method** drop-down list to create a construction plane at a specified offset distance from a selected plane or planar face.

3. Click on a planar face or a plane in the graphics area. A preview of the offset plane appears with 0 (zero) offset distance, see Figure 6.5. Also, the **Distance** field appears in the dialog box as well as in the graphics area. This is because, the **Distance** option is selected in the **Extent** drop-down list of the dialog box, by default.

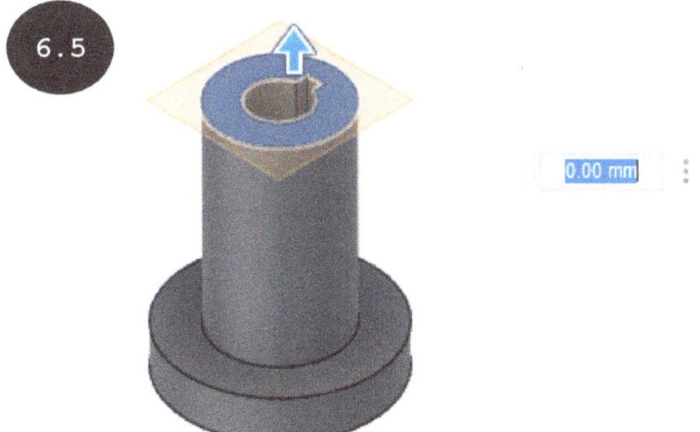

Extent: By default, the **Distance** option is selected in this drop-down list. As a result, you can create a plane at a specified offset distance from the selected planar face. On selecting the **To Object** option, you can create a plane up to a reference point, a sketch point, or a vertex.

4. Enter the required offset distance value in the **Distance** field. The preview of the construction plane gets modified as per the specified offset distance. You can also drag the arrow that appears in the graphics area to adjust the offset distance of the construction plane dynamically.

Note: To reverse the direction of the construction plane, you need to either enter a negative offset distance value or drag the arrow to the other side of the selected planar face.

5. Click on the **OK** button in the dialog box. A construction plane at the specified offset distance is created, see Figure 6.6.

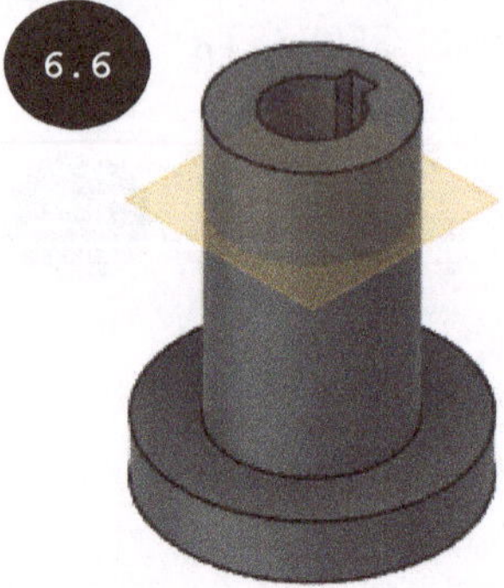

Creating a Plane at an Angle

1. Invoke the **CONSTRUCT** drop-down menu in the **Toolbar** and then click on the **Plane at Angle** tool, see Figure 6.7. The **CONSTRUCTION GEOMETRY** dialog box appears, see Figure 6.8.

2. Ensure that the **At Angle** option is selected in the **Method** drop-down list to create a construction plane at a specified angle to an existing plane or planar face.

3. Click on a linear edge, a sketch line, or an axis as the axis of revolution for the construction plane. A preview of the construction plane appears with the 0-degree angle of revolution, see Figure 6.9. Also, the **Angle** field appears in the dialog box as well as in the graphics area.

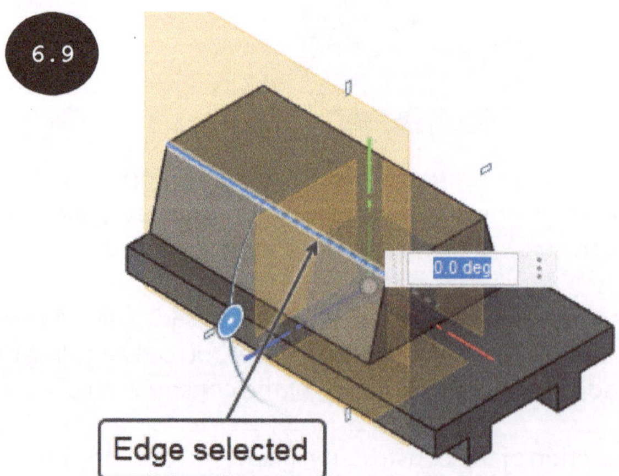

4. Enter the required angle value in the **Angle** field. A preview of the construction plane gets modified as per the specified angle value. You can also drag the manipulator handle, appearing in the graphics area, to dynamically specify the angle of revolution for the construction plane.

Note: To reverse the direction of the construction plane, you need to either enter a negative angle value or drag the manipulator handle to the other direction.

5. Click on the **OK** button in the dialog box. A construction plane at the specified angle is created, see Figure 6.10.

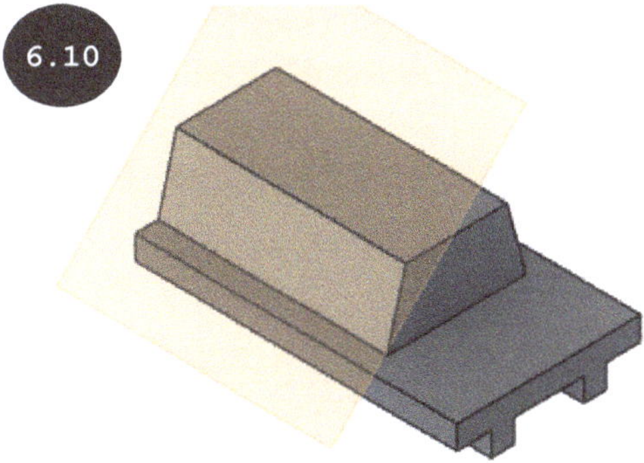
6.10

Creating a Plane Tangent to a Cylindrical or Conical Face

1. Invoke the **CONSTRUCT** drop-down menu in the **Toolbar** and then click on the **Tangent Plane** tool. The **CONSTRUCTION GEOMETRY** dialog box appears, see Figure 6.11.

2. Ensure that the **Tangent** option is selected in the **Method** drop-down list to create a construction plane tangent to an existing cylindrical or conical face.

3. Click on a cylindrical or conical face of the model. A preview of the plane tangent to the selected face appears in the graphics area, see Figure 6.12.

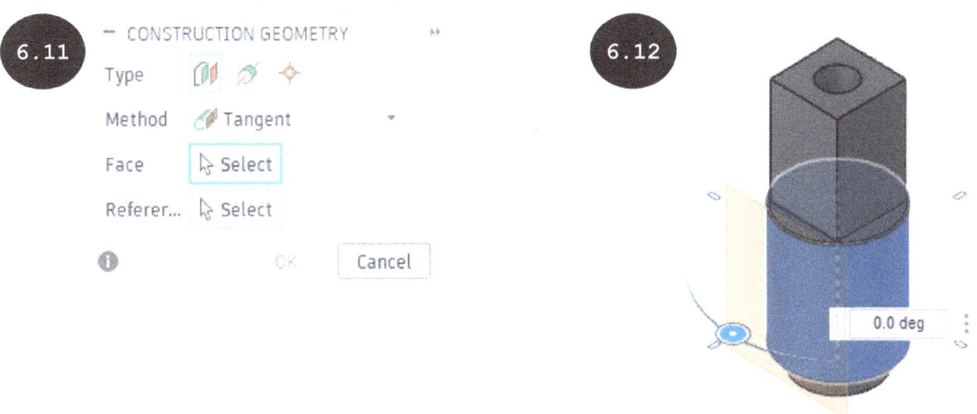

6.11 6.12

4. Enter the required angle value in the Angle field to set the position of the tangent plane. Alternatively, you can drag the manipulator handle displayed in the graphics area to dynamically adjust the position of the tangent plane.

Note: Instead of specifying an angle value, you can also select a point or vertex as a reference object to create a plane tangent to the selected face and aligned with the selected reference object.

5. Click on the **OK** button in the dialog box. A construction plane tangent to the selected cylindrical or conical face is created.

Creating a Plane at the Middle of Two Faces/Planes

1. Invoke the **CONSTRUCT** drop-down menu in the **Toolbar** and then click on the **Midplane** tool. The **CONSTRUCTION GEOMETRY** dialog box appears, see Figure 6.13.

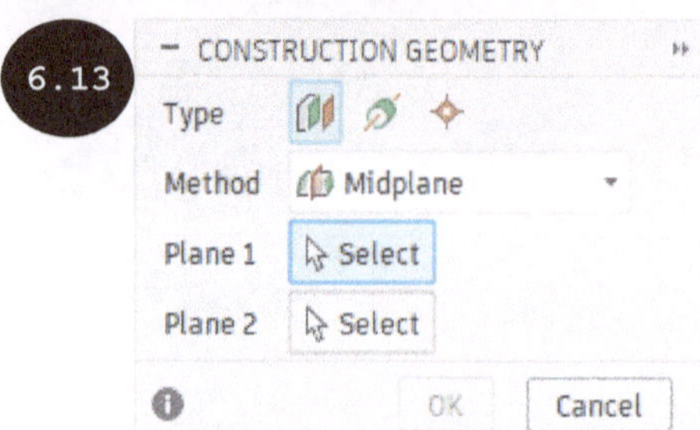

2.. Ensure that the **Midplane** option is selected in the **Method** drop-down list to create a construction plane exactly at the middle of two selected planar faces.

3. Select two planar faces or planes one by one in the graphics area. A preview of the construction plane passing through the middle of two selected faces appears, see Figure 6.14.

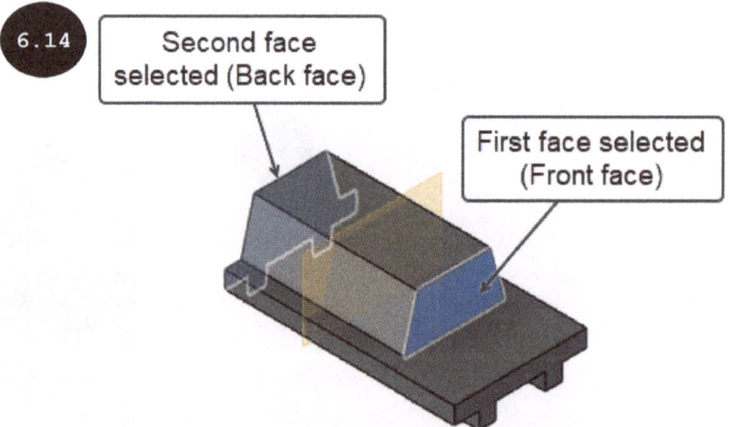

Note: In Figure 6.14, the visual style of the model has been changed to "shaded with hidden edges" visual style for the visualization of the back face of the model selected.

4. Click on the **OK** button in the dialog box. A construction plane in the middle of the two selected faces is created.

Creating a Plane Passing Through Two Edges

1. Invoke the **CONSTRUCT** drop-down menu in the **Toolbar** and then click on the **Plane Through Two Edges** tool. The **CONSTRUCTION GEOMETRY** dialog box appears, see Figure 6.15.

2. Ensure that the **Through Two Edges** option is selected in the **Method** drop-down list to create a construction plane passing through two selected edges or axes.

3. Select two linear edges or axes one by one in the graphics area, see Figure 6.16. A preview of the construction plane passing through two linear edges or axes appears.

Note: The two selected linear edges or axes must either intersect or be parallel to each other.

4. Click on the **OK** button in the dialog box. A construction plane passing through two selected linear edges or axes is created, see Figure 6.16.

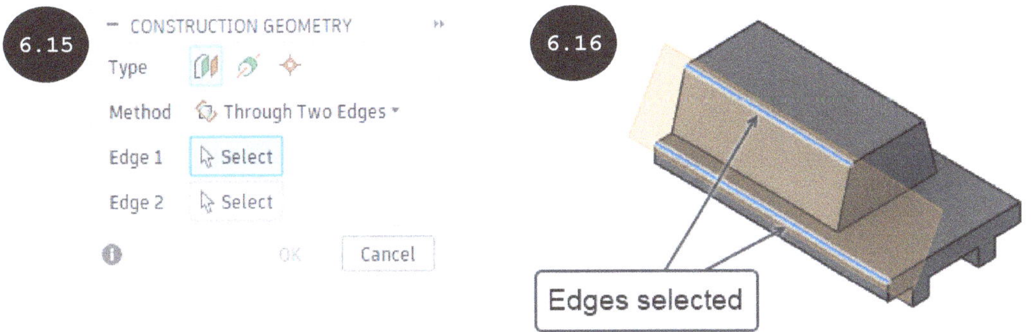

Creating a Plane Passing Through Three Points

1. Invoke the **CONSTRUCT** drop-down menu in the **Toolbar** and then click on the **Plane Through Three Points** tool. The **CONSTRUCTION GEOMETRY** dialog box appears, see Figure 6.17.

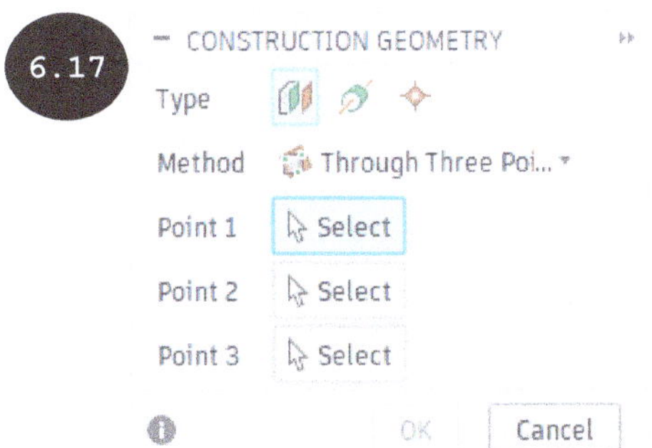

2. Ensure that the Through Three Points option is selected in the Method drop-down list to create a construction plane passing through three selected points or vertices.

3. Select three vertices, points, or sketch points one by one in the graphics area, see Figure 6.18. A preview of the construction plane passing through three points appears, see Figure 6.18.

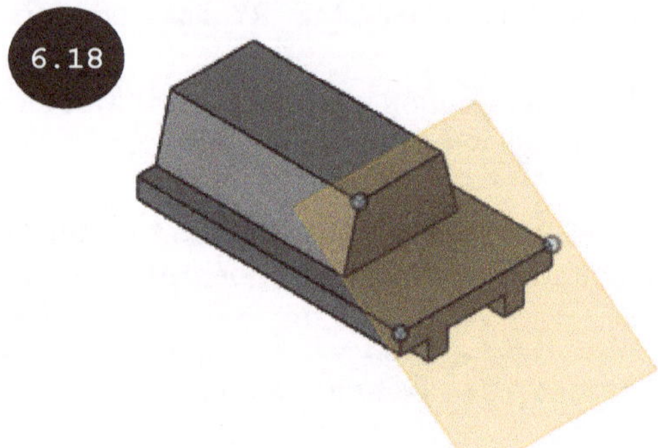

4. Click on the **OK** button in the dialog box. A construction plane passing through three points is created.

Creating a Plane Along a Path

1. Invoke the **CONSTRUCT** drop-down menu in the **Toolbar** and then click on the **Plane Along Path** tool. The **CONSTRUCTION GEOMETRY** dialog box appears.

2. Ensure that the **Along Path** option is selected in the **Method** drop-down list to create a construction plane along a curve.

3. Select an edge or a sketch curve as the path to create the construction plane. A preview of the construction plane normal to the curve at the point of selection appears, see Figure 6.19. Also, the **Extent Type** drop-down list and **Distance** field appear in the dialog box.

4. Enter the distance value in terms of percentage (0 to 1) in the **Distance** field to define the location of the plane along the path. This is done because, the **Proportional** option is selected in the **Extent Type** drop-down list of the dialog box, by default.

   On selecting the **Absolute** option, you can specify the actual distance value in the **Distance** field to define the position of the plane on the selected path. Note that the distance is measured from the endpoint of the curve/edge selected. You can also drag the handle that appears in the graphics area to dynamically specify the location of the plane along the path.

5. Click on the **OK** button in the dialog box. A construction plane along the path is created, see Figure 6.20.

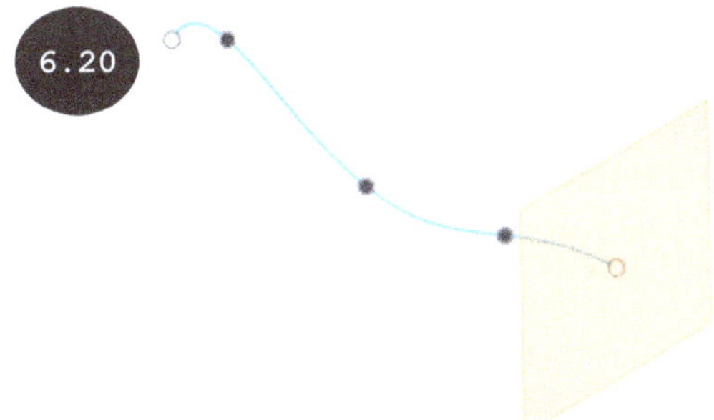

Creating a Construction Axis

In Autodesk Fusion, you can create different types of construction axes in addition to construction planes. A construction axis can be used as the axis of revolution for creating features like revolved and circular patterns. The methods for creating different types of construction axes are discussed next.

Creating an Axis Passing Through a Cylinder/Cone/Torus

1. Invoke the CONSTRUCT drop-down menu in the **Toolbar** and then click on the **Axis Through Cylinder/Cone/Torus** tool, see Figure6.21. The CONSTRUCTION GEOMETRY dialog box appears, with the **Axis** button activated by default in the **Type** area, see Figure 6.22.

As discussed earlier, you can switch between different geometry creation tools, such as **Plane**, **Axis**, or **Point** by activating the required option in the **Type** area of the dialog box.

2. Select a cylindrical face, a conical face, or a toroidal face of the model in the graphics area. A preview of the construction axis coincident with the axis of the selected face appears in the graphics area, see Figures 6.23 and 6.24.

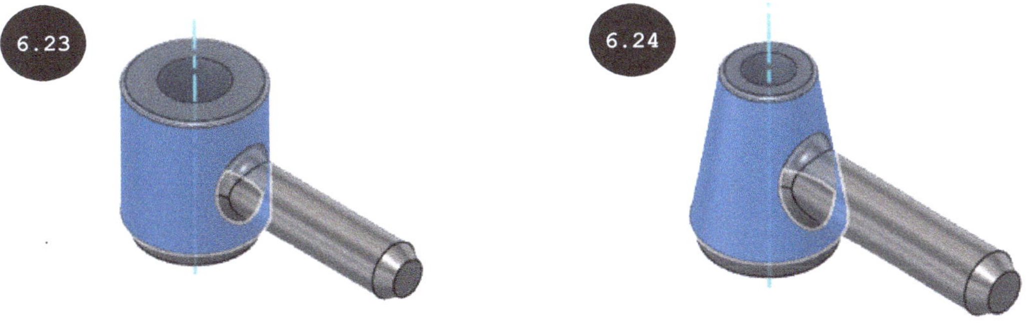

3. Click on the **OK** button in the dialog box. A construction axis passing through the center of the cylinder/cone/torus is created.

Creating an Axis Perpendicular to a Face at a Point

1. Invoke the **CONSTRUCT** drop-down menu in the **Toolbar** and then click on the **Axis Perpendicular to Face** tool. The **CONSTRUCTION GEOMETRY** dialog box appears, see Figure 6.25.

2. Select a face of the model in the graphics area. A preview of the construction axis, perpendicular to the selected face at the point of selection appears, see Figure 6.26.

Now, you can also select a point to create a reference axis that is perpendicular to the selected face and passes through the selected point.

3. Select a point or a vertex in the graphics area. The preview of the construction axis updates such that it is perpendicular to the selected face and passes through the selected point, refer to Figure 6.26.

4. Click on the **OK** button in the dialog box. A construction axis perpendicular to the face at the point of selection is created.

Creating an Axis Passing Through Two Planes

1. Invoke the **CONSTRUCT** drop-down menu in the **Toolbar** and then click on the **Axis Through Two Planes** tool. The **CONSTRUCTION GEOMETRY** dialog box appears, see Figure 6.27.

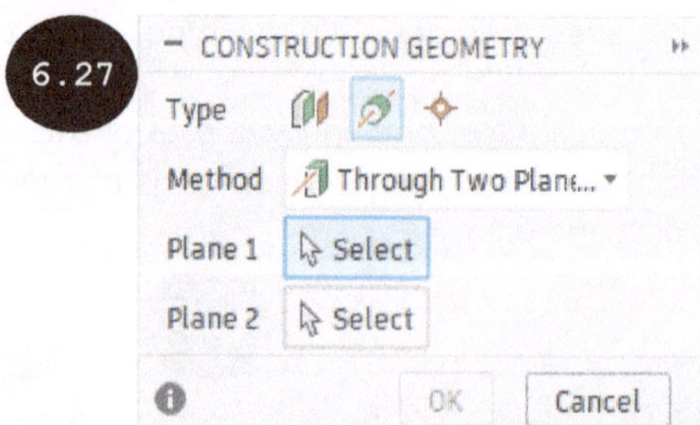

2. Select two planes or planar faces one after another. A preview of the construction axis at the intersection of two selected planes/faces appears, see Figure 6.28.

3. Click on the **OK** button in the dialog box. A construction axis at the intersection of two selected planes/faces is created, see Figure 6.28.

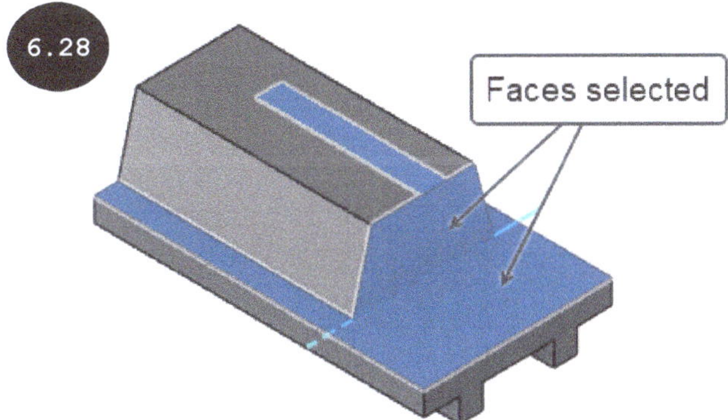

Creating an Axis Passing Through Two Points

1. Invoke the **CONSTRUCT** drop-down menu in the **Toolbar** and then click on the **Axis Through Two Points** tool. The **CONSTRUCTION GEOMETRY** dialog box appears, see Figure 6.29.

2. Select two vertices, points, or sketch points in the graphics area. A preview of the construction axis passing through the selected points appears, see Figure 6.30.

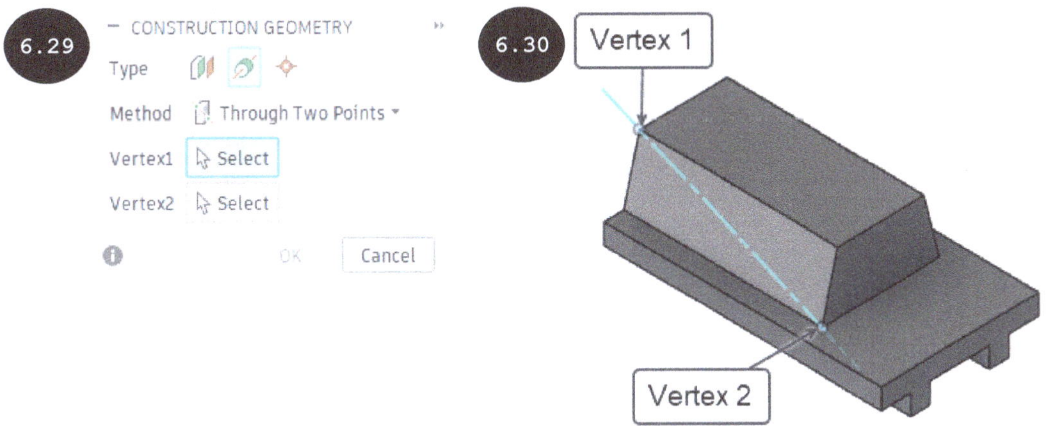

3. Click on the **OK** button in the dialog box. A construction axis passing through two points is created.

Creating an Axis Passing Through an Edge

1. Invoke the **CONSTRUCT** drop-down menu in the **Toolbar** and then click on the **Axis Through Edge** tool. The **CONSTRUCTION GEOMETRY** dialog box appears, see Figure 6.31.

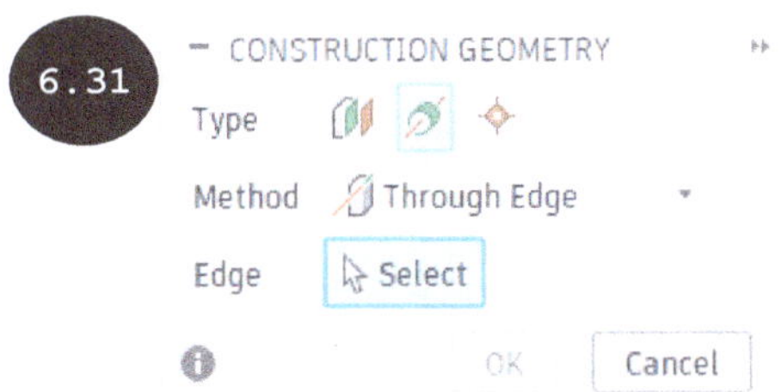

2. Select an edge, axis, or sketch line in the graphics area. A preview of the construction axis along the selected entity appears in the graphics area.

3. Click on the **OK** button in the dialog box. A construction axis passing through the edge is created, see Figure 6.32.

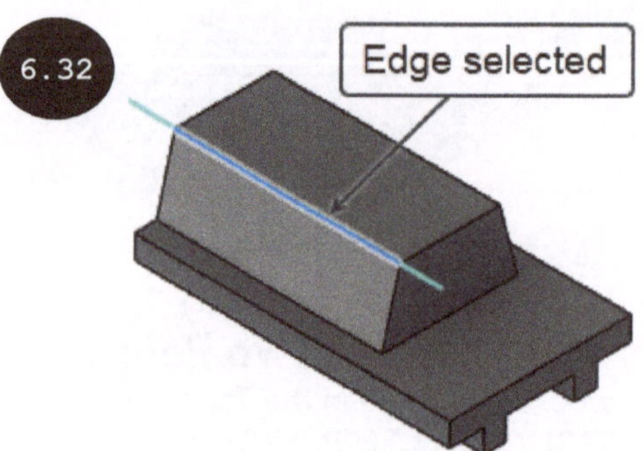

Creating a Construction Point

A construction point is used as a reference point for measuring distance, creating planes, and so on. The different methods for creating construction points are discussed next.

Creating a Point at Vertex

1. Invoke the **CONSTRUCT** drop-down menu in the **Toolbar** and then click on the **Point At Vertex** tool, see Figure 6.33. The **CONSTRUCTION GEOMETRY** dialog box appears with the **Point** button activated by default in the **Type** area, see Figure 6.34.

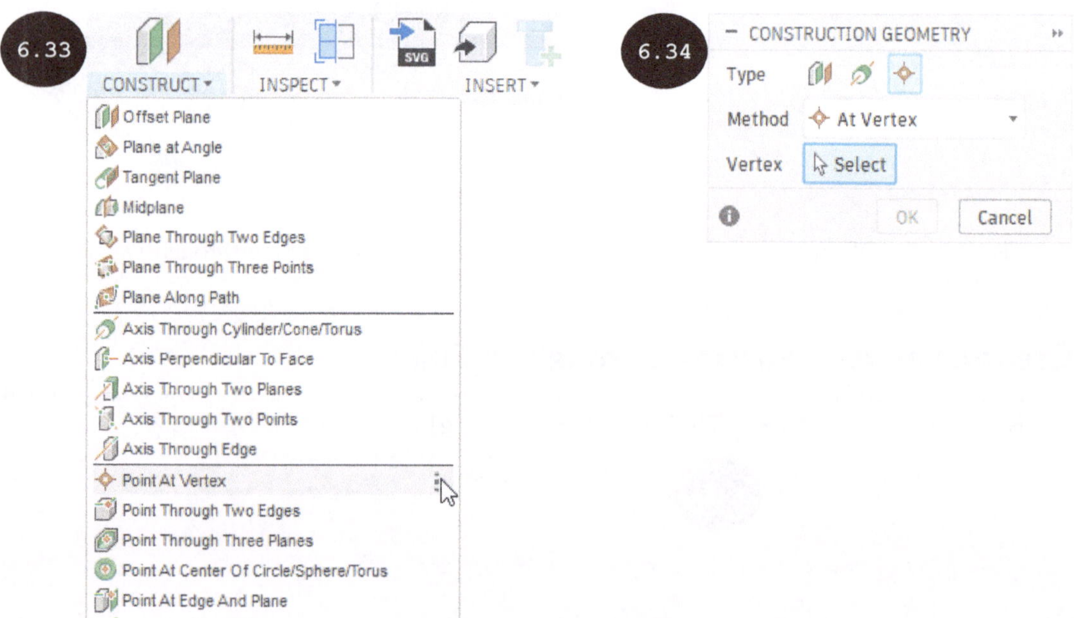

2. Select a vertex, a point, or a sketch point in the graphics area. A preview of the construction point coincident with the selected entity appears in the graphics area.

3. Click on the **OK** button in the dialog box. A construction point at the selected vertex/point is created.

Creating a Point at the Intersection of Two Edges

1. Invoke the **CONSTRUCT** drop-down menu in the **Toolbar** and then click on the **Point Through Two Edges** tool. The **CONSTRUCTION GEOMETRY** dialog box appears, see Figure 6.35.

2. Select two edges, axes, or sketch entities in the graphics area, see Figure 6.36. A preview of the construction point at the intersection of the selected edges appears.

3. Click on the **OK** button in the dialog box. A construction point at the intersection of edges is created, see Figure 6.36.

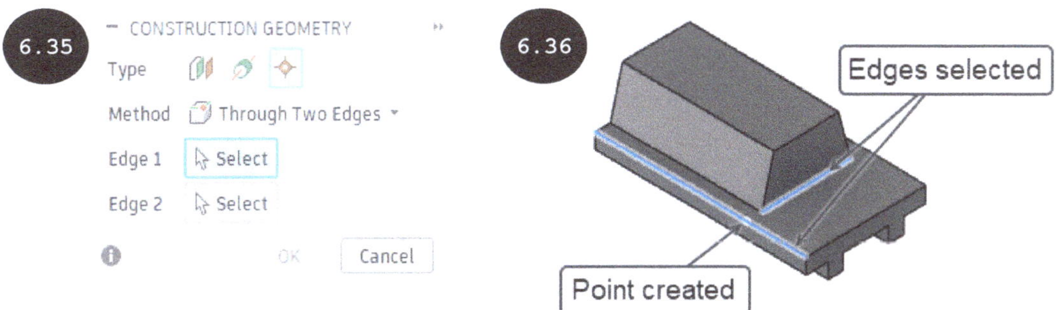

Creating a Point at the Intersection of Three Planes

1. Invoke the **CONSTRUCT** drop-down menu in the **Toolbar** and then click on the **Point Through Three Planes** tool. The **CONSTRUCTION GEOMETRY** dialog box appears, see Figure 6.37.

2. Select three planes, planar faces, or sketch profiles in the graphics area, see Figure 6.38. A preview of the construction point at the intersection of the selected planes/planar faces appears.

3. Click on the **OK** button in the dialog box. A construction point at the intersection of selected planes/ planar faces is created, see Figure 6.38.

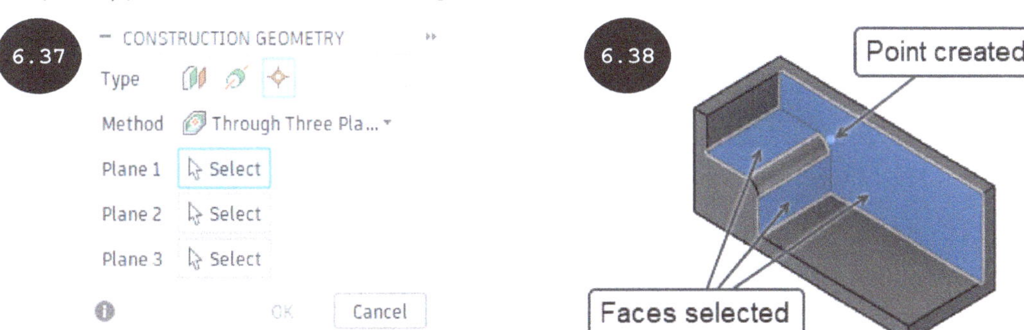

Creating a Point at the Center of Circle/Sphere/Torus

1. Invoke the **CONSTRUCT** drop-down menu in the **Toolbar** and then click on the **Point At Center Of Circle/Sphere/Torus** tool. The **CONSTRUCTION GEOMETRY** dialog box appears.

2. Select a circular edge, a spherical face, or a toroidal face of the model in the graphics area. A preview of the construction point at the center of the selected circular edge, spherical face, or toroidal face appears, see Figures 6.39 through 6.41.

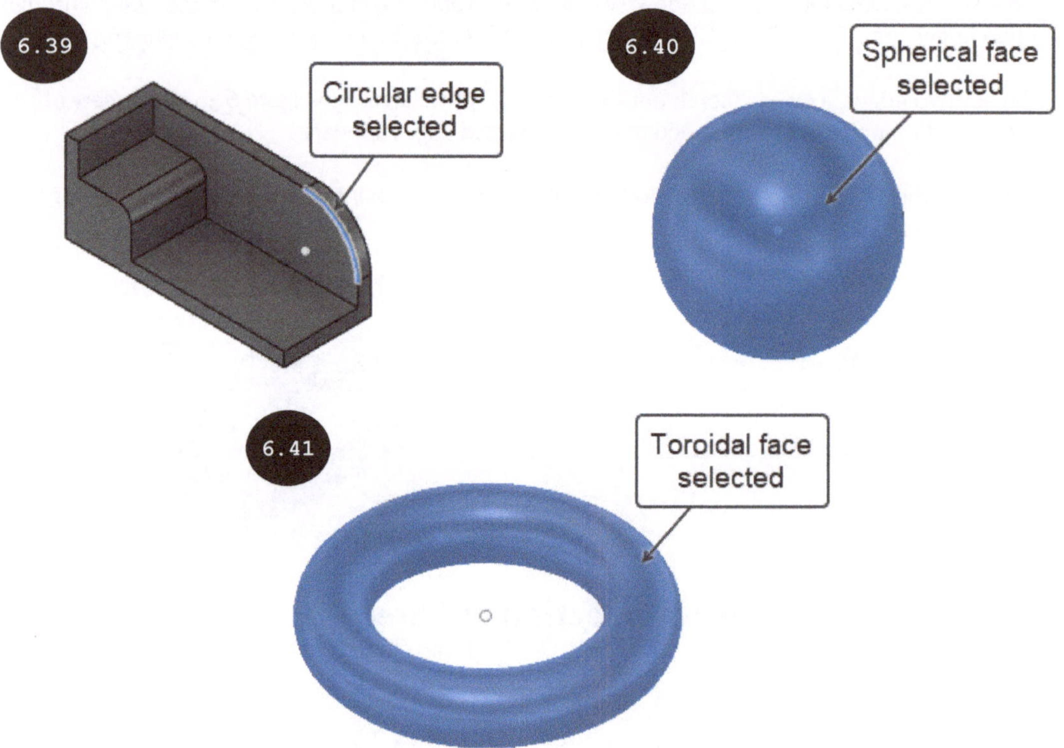

3. Click on the **OK** button in the dialog box. A construction point at the center of the selected circular edge/spherical face/toroidal face is created.

Creating a Point at the Intersection of an Edge and a Plane

1. Invoke the **CONSTRUCT** drop-down menu in the **Toolbar** and then click on the **Point At Edge And Plane** tool. The **CONSTRUCTION GEOMETRY** dialog box appears.

2. Select a linear edge, an axis, or a sketch line and a planar face, a plane, or a sketch profile in the graphics area, see Figure 6.42. A preview of the construction point at the intersection of the selected entities appears.

3. Click on the **OK** button in the dialog box. A construction point at the intersection of the selected entities is created, see Figure 6.42.

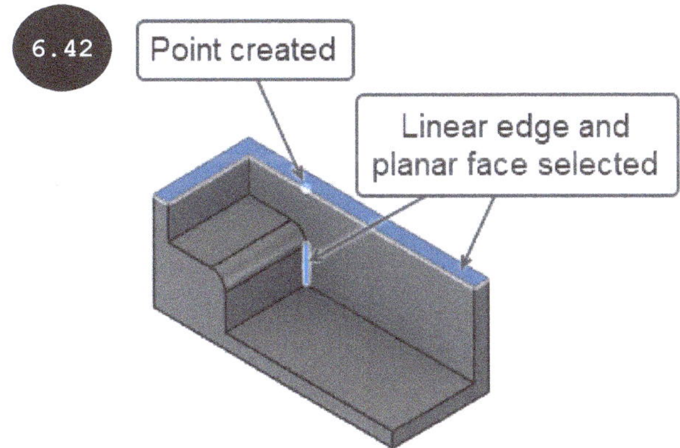

Creating a Point Along a Path

1. Invoke the **CONSTRUCT** drop-down menu in the **Toolbar** and then click on the **Point Along Path** tool. The **CONSTRUCTION GEOMETRY** dialog box appears.

2. Select an edge or a sketch curve as the path to create the construction point. A preview of the construction point at the point of selection appears, see Figure 6.43. Also, the **Extent Type** drop-down list and **Distance** field appear in the dialog box.

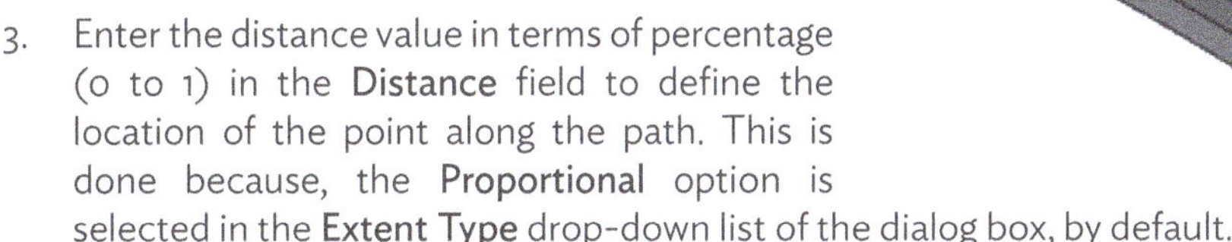

3. Enter the distance value in terms of percentage (0 to 1) in the **Distance** field to define the location of the point along the path. This is done because, the **Proportional** option is selected in the **Extent Type** drop-down list of the dialog box, by default.

   On selecting the **Absolute** option, you can specify the actual distance value in the **Distance** field to define the position of the point on the selected path. Note that the distance is measured from the endpoint of the curve/edge selected. You can also drag the handle that appears in the graphics area to dynamically specify the location of the point along the path.

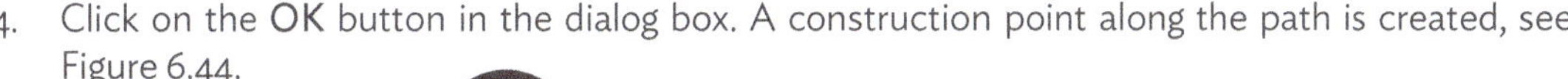

4. Click on the **OK** button in the dialog box. A construction point along the path is created, see Figure 6.44.

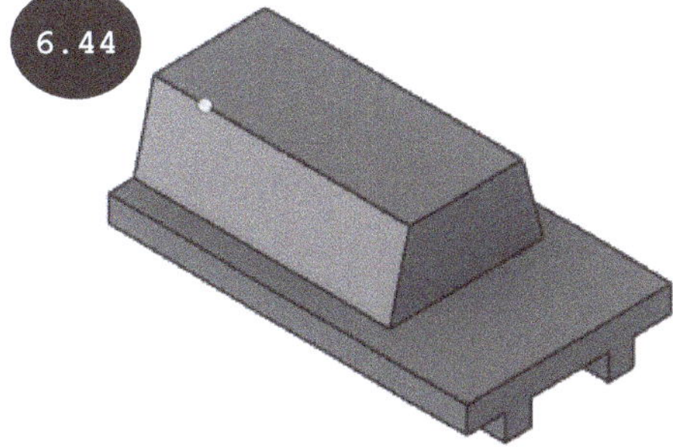

Tutorial 1

Create the multi-feature model shown in Figure 6.45. You need to create the model by creating all its features one by one. All dimensions are in mm.

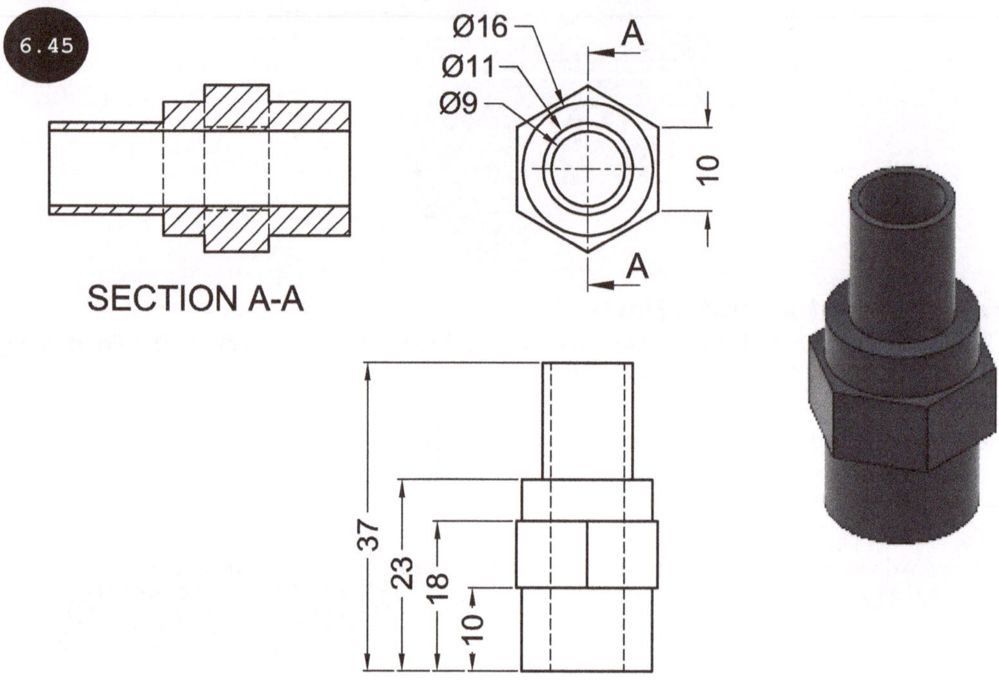

Section 1: Starting a New Part Design File

1. Click **File** > **New** in the **Application Bar** (see Figure 6.46) to display the **What do you want to design?** dialog box, see Figure 6.47.

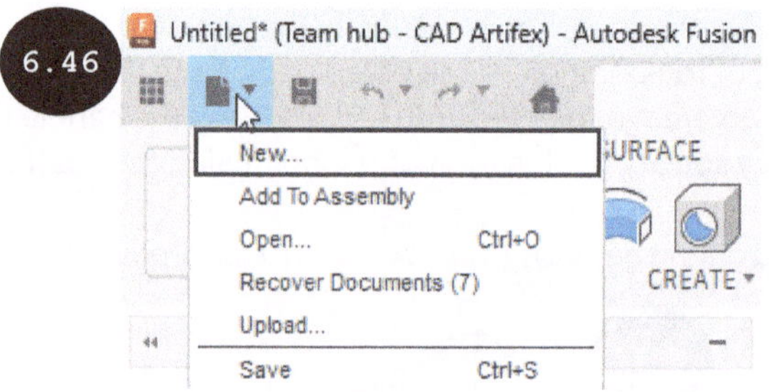

Note: If you are starting a new Autodesk Fusion session, the Part Design file opens automatically because it is set as the default design type. In this case, ensure that the **millimeter (mm), gram (g)** unit system is set for the opened Part Design file.

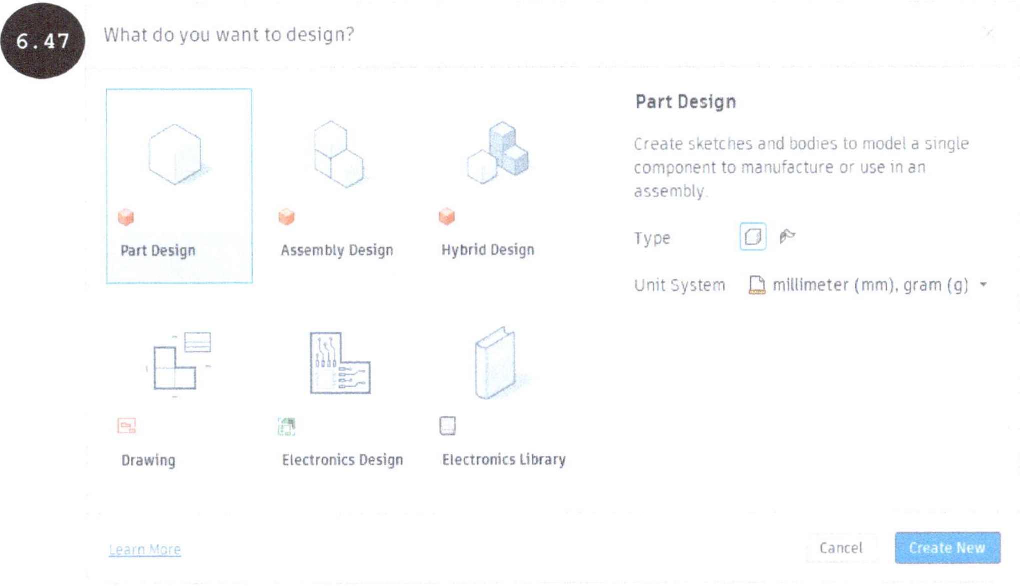

2. In the **What do you want to design?** dialog box, select the **Part Design** button and choose the **millimeter (mm), gram (g)** unit system from the **Unit System** drop-down list.

3. After specifying the required options, click the **Create New** button. A new Part Design file is created with the default name "**Untitled**".

Section 2: Organizing the Data Panel

1. Click on the **Show Data Panel** tool in the **Application Bar**, see Figure 6.48. The **Data Panel** appears.

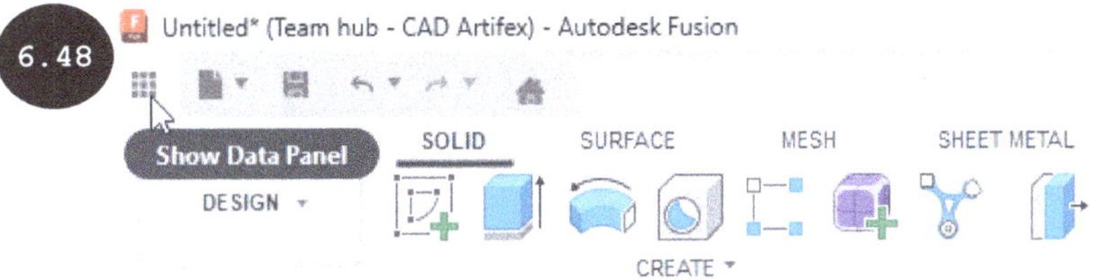

2. Ensure that the '**Autodesk Fusion 360**' project is created in the **Data Panel**.

3. Double-click on the **Autodesk Fusion 360** project in the **Data Panel** and then create the "**Chapter 06**" folder using the **New Folder** tool of the **Data Panel**.

4. Double-click on the "**Chapter 06**" folder in the **Data Panel** and then create the "**Tutorial**" sub-folder using the **New Folder** tool of the **Data Panel**. Next, click on the cross-mark × at the top right corner of the **Data Panel** to close it.

Section 3: Creating the Base Feature

Now, you can create the base/first feature of the model.

1. Click on the **Create Sketch** tool in the **Toolbar**, see Figure 6.49. The three default planes: Front, Top, and Right, which are mutually perpendicular to each other appear in the graphics area.

2. Select the Top plane as the sketching plane. It is oriented normal to the viewing direction. Also, the **SKETCH** contextual tab and the **SKETCH PALETTE** dialog box appear.

3. Create two circles of diameters 9 mm and 16 mm as the sketch of the base feature, see Figure 6.50. Ensure that the center points of the circles are at the origin.

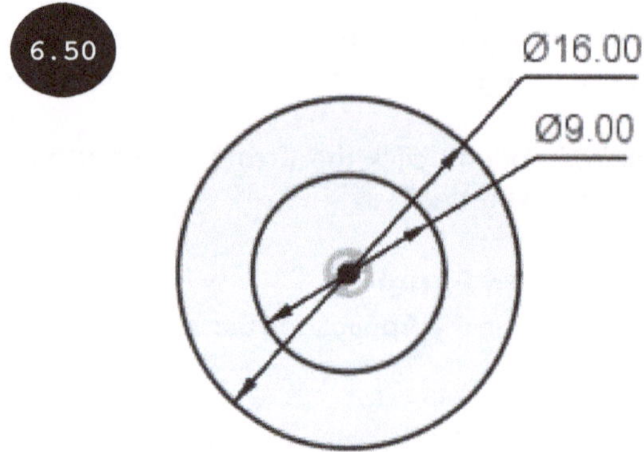

4. Click on the **SOLID** tab in the **Toolbar** to display the solid modeling tools.

5. Click on the **Extrude** tool in the **CREATE** panel of the **SOLID** tab, see Figure 6.51 or press the E key. The **EXTRUDE** dialog box appears.

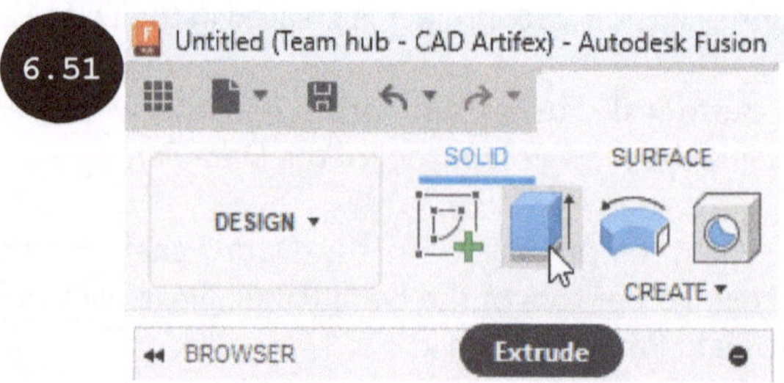

6. Move the cursor over the outer closed profile of the sketch and then click when it gets highlighted in the graphics area, see Figure 6.52.

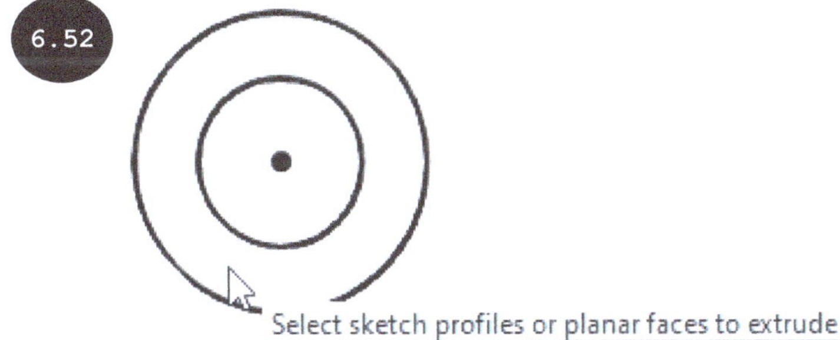

7. Enter **10** in the **Distance** field of the **EXTRUDE** dialog box. A preview of the extruded feature appears in the graphics area.

8. Click on the **OK** button in the dialog box. The base feature is created, see Figure 6.53.

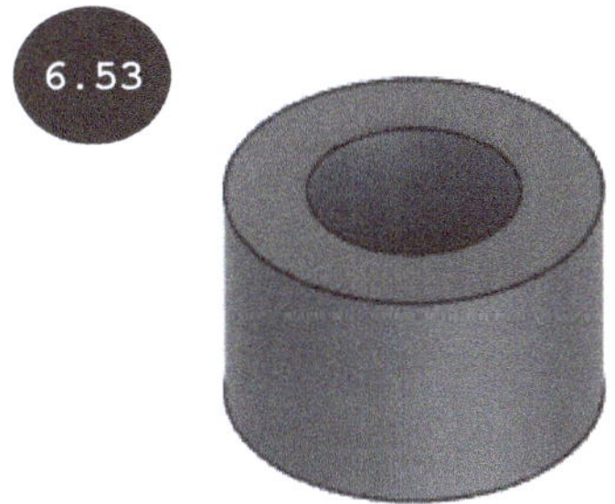

Section 4: Creating the Second Feature

1. Click on the **Create Sketch** tool in the **Toolbar**. Three default planes: Front, Top, and Right which are mutually perpendicular to each other appear in the graphics area and you are prompted to select a sketching plane.

2. Click on the top planar face of the base feature, see Figure 6.54. The top planar face of the base feature becomes the sketching plane for creating the sketch and it is oriented normal to the viewing direction.

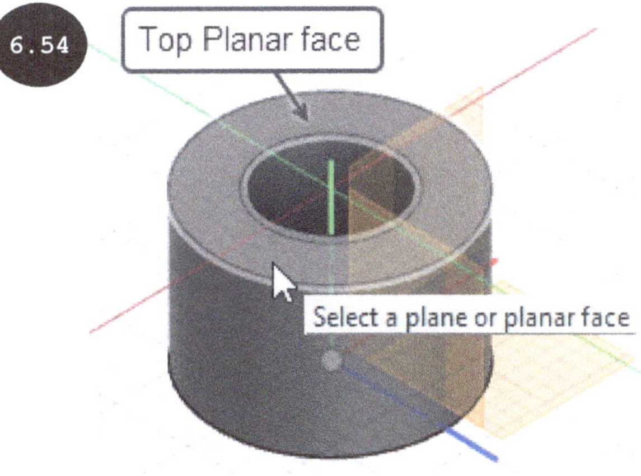

3. Create a polygon of 6 sides using the **Inscribed Polygon** tool as the sketch of the second feature, see Figure 6.55. Note that besides dimension, you need to apply a vertical constraint to a vertical line of the polygon to make it fully defined.

4. Click on the **SOLID** tab in the **Toolbar** and then click on the **Extrude** tool, see Figure 6.56 or press the **E** key. The **EXTRUDE** dialog box appears.

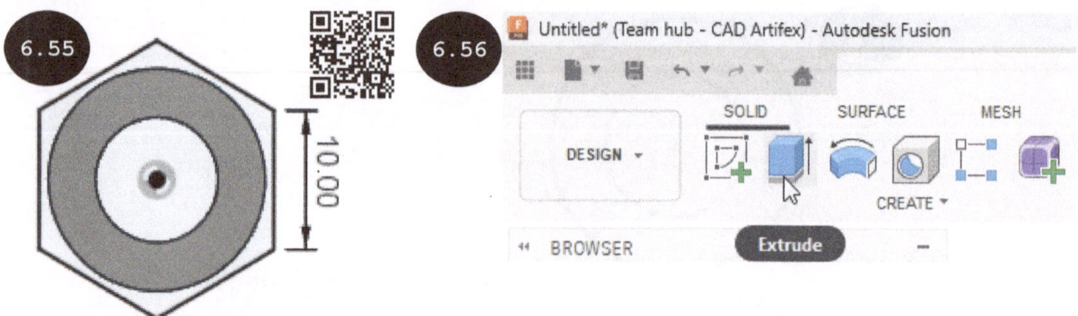

5. Change the orientation of the model to isometric by clicking on the **Home** icon of ViewCube, if the orientation is not changed by default.

6. Select the outer two closed profiles of the sketch one by one in the graphics area, see Figure 6.57.

7. Enter **8** in the **Distance** field of the **EXTRUDE** dialog box. A preview of the extrude feature appears in the graphics area, see Figure 6.58.

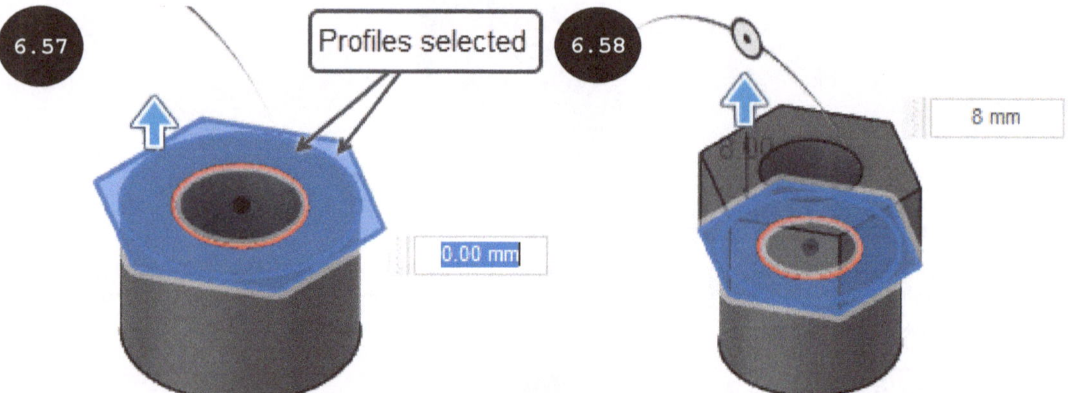

8. Ensure that the **Join** option is selected in the **Operation** drop-down list of the dialog box to join the feature with the base feature of the model. In doing so, both features will act as a single body.

9. Click on the **OK** button in the dialog box. The extrude feature is created, see Figure 6.59.

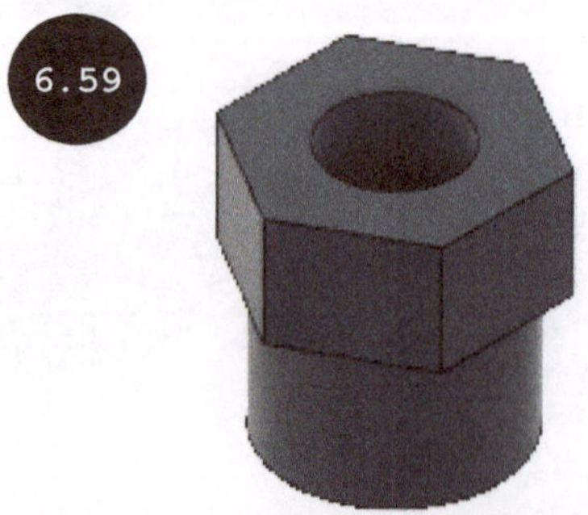

Section 5: Creating the Third Feature

1. Click on the **Create Sketch** tool in the **Toolbar** and then select the top planar face of the second feature as the sketching plane, see Figure 6.60. The top planar face of the second feature becomes the sketching plane, and it is oriented normal to the viewing direction.

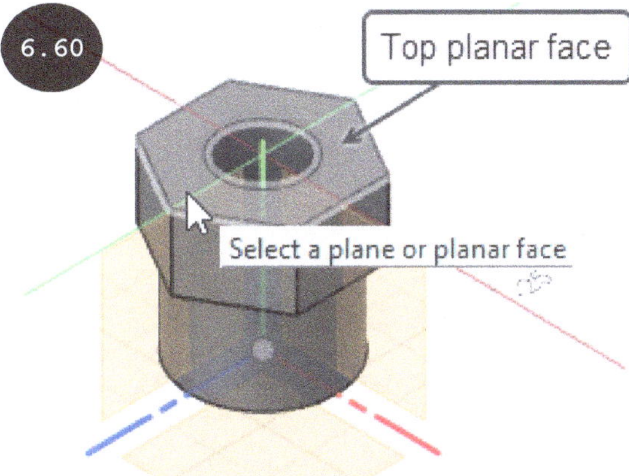

2. Create a circle of diameter 16 mm as the sketch of the third feature and apply the diameter dimension, see Figure 6.61.

3. Press the **E** key to activate the **Extrude** tool. The **EXTRUDE** dialog box appears.

4. Change the orientation of the model to isometric by clicking on the **Home** icon of ViewCube, if the orientation is not changed by default.

5. Select a closed profile of the sketch in the graphics area, see Figure 6.62.

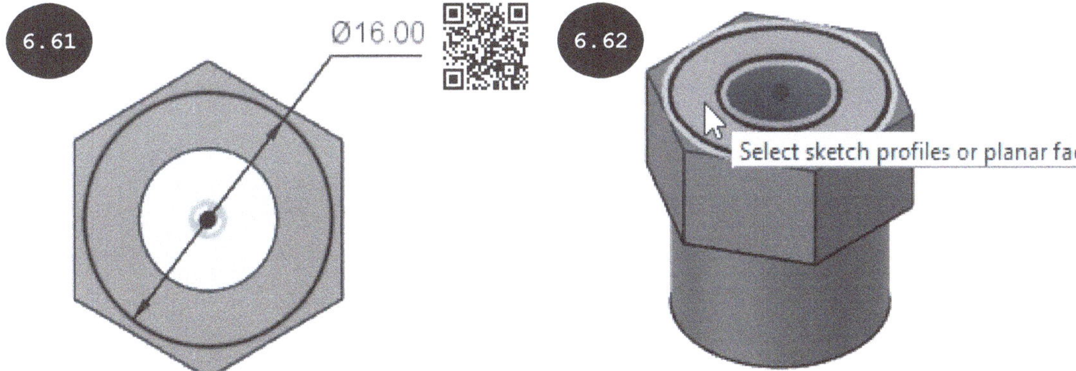

6. Enter **5** in the **Distance** field of the **EXTRUDE** dialog box. A preview of the extruded feature appears in the graphics area, see Figure 6.63.

7. Ensure that the **Join** option is selected in the **Operation** drop-down list of the dialog box to join the feature with the existing features of the model. In doing so, all features of the model will act as a single body.

8. Click on the **OK** button in the dialog box. The extrude feature is created, see Figure 6.64.

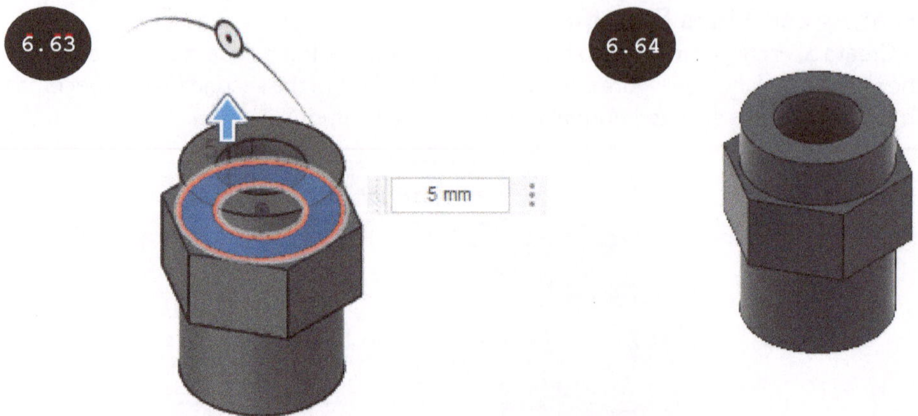

Section 6: Creating the Fourth Feature

1. Click on the **Create Sketch** tool in the **Toolbar** and then select the top planar face of the third feature as the sketching plane.

2. Create a circle of diameter 11 mm as the sketch of the fourth feature and apply the diameter dimension, see Figure 6.65.

3. Press the **E** key to activate the **Extrude** tool. The **EXTRUDE** dialog box appears.

4. Change the orientation of the model to isometric by clicking on the **Home** icon of ViewCube.

5. Select a closed profile of the sketch in the graphics area, see Figure 6.66.

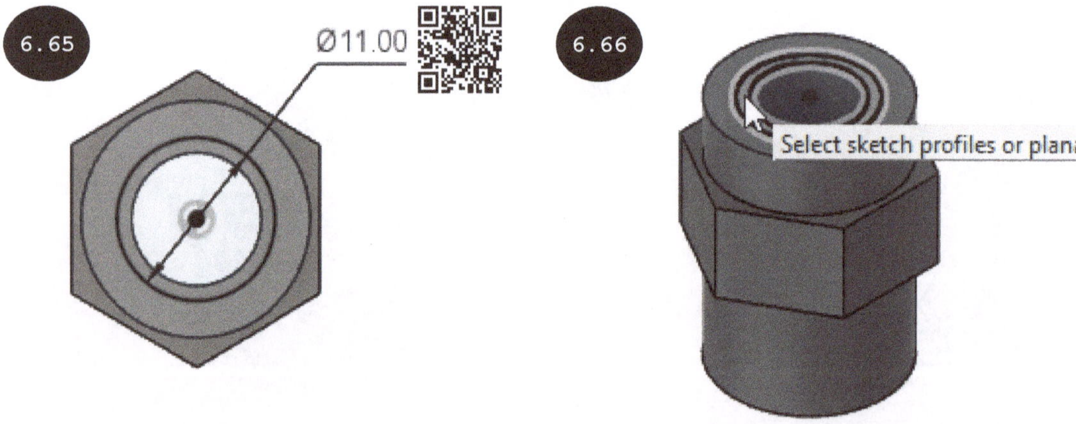

6. Enter **14** in the **Distance** field of the **EXTRUDE** dialog box. A preview of the extruded feature appears in the graphics area.

7. Ensure that the **Join** option is selected in the **Operation** drop-down list of the dialog box to join the feature with the existing features of the model.

8. Click on the **OK** button in the dialog box. The extrude feature is created. Figure 6.67 shows the final model after creating all its features.

6.67

Section 7: Saving the Sketch

1. Click on the **Save** tool in the **Application Bar**. The **Save** dialog box appears.

2. Enter **Tutorial 1** in the **Name** field of the dialog box.

3. Ensure that the location ***Autodesk Fusion 360 > Chapter 06 > Tutorial*** is specified in the **Location** field of the dialog box to save the file of this tutorial. To specify the location, you need to expand the **Save** dialog box by clicking on the down arrow next to the **Location** field of the dialog box.

4. Click on the **Save** button in the dialog box. The model is saved with the name Tutorial 1 in the specified location (***Autodesk Fusion 360 > Chapter 06 > Tutorial***).

Tutorial 2

Create the model, as shown in Figure 6.68. All dimensions are in mm.

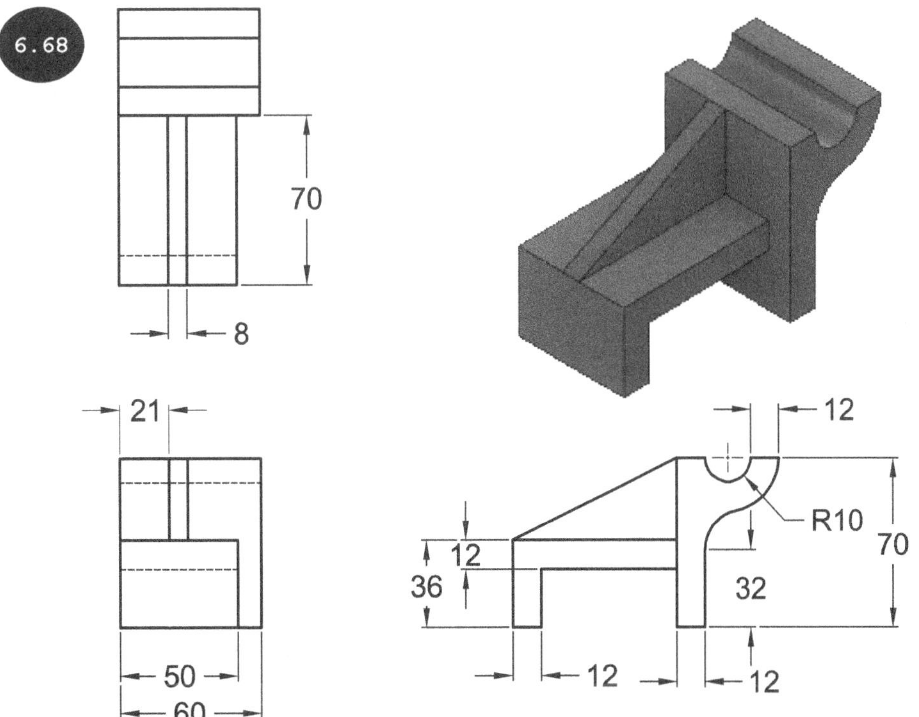

Section 1: Starting a New Design File

1. Click **File** > **New** in the **Application Bar** (see Figure 6.69) to display the **What do you want to design?** dialog box, see Figure 6.70.

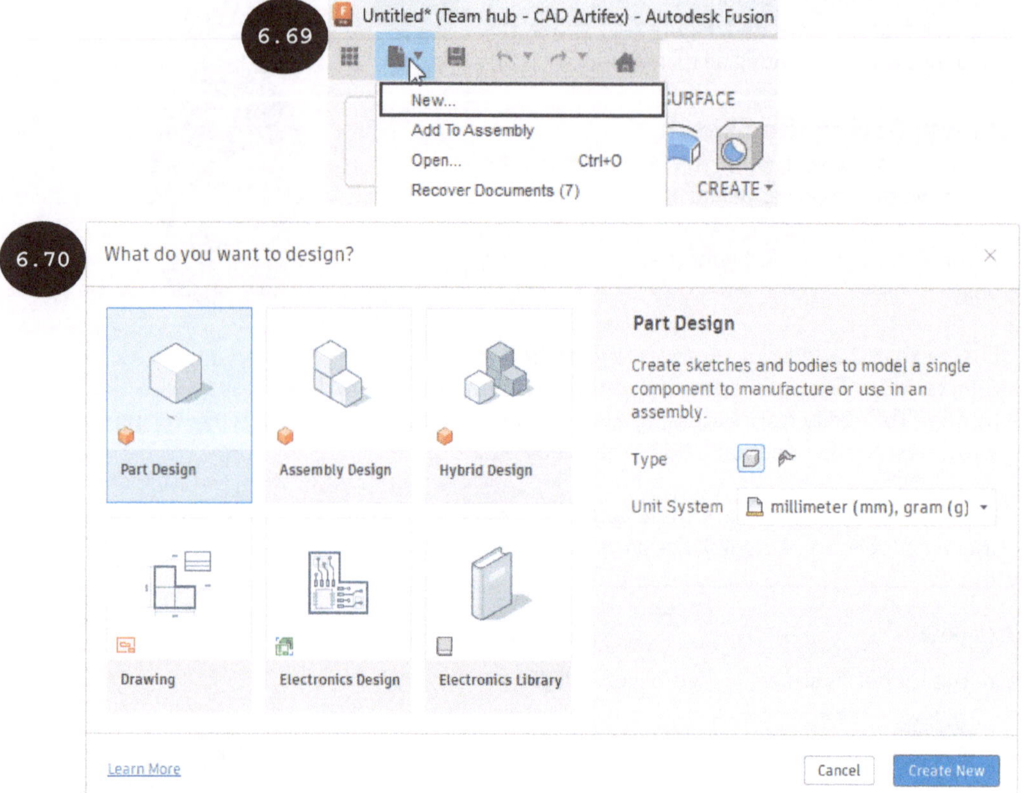

2. In the **What do you want to design?** dialog box, select the **Part Design** button and choose the **millimeter (mm), gram (g)** unit system from the **Unit System** drop-down list.

3. After specifying the required options, click the **Create New** button. A new Part Design file is created with the default name.

Section 2: Organizing the Data Panel

1. Invoke the **Show Data Panel**, see Figure 6.71 and then ensure that the ***Autodesk Fusion 360*** *project* > ***Chapter 06*** *folder* > ***Tutorial*** *sub-folders* are created. You need to create these project folders, if not created earlier.

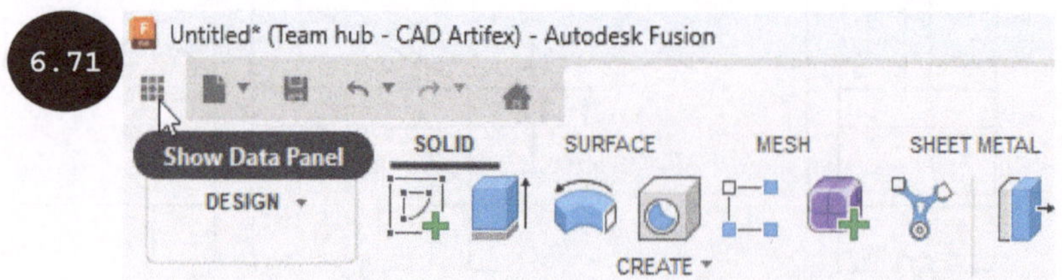

2. Close the **Data Panel** by clicking on the cross-mark ✕ at its top right corner.

Section 3: Creating the Base/First Feature

1. Click on the **Create Sketch** tool in the **Toolbar**, see Figure 6.72. Three default planes that are mutually perpendicular to each other appear in the graphics area.

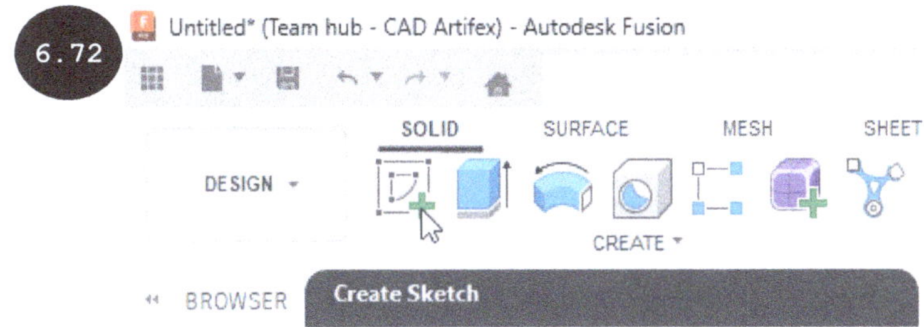

2. Select the Right plane as the sketching plane for creating the sketch of the base feature. The Right plane becomes the sketching plane and is oriented normal to the viewing direction.

3. Create the sketch of the base feature and then apply the required constraints and dimensions to the sketch, see Figure 6.73.

Tip: To fully define the sketch, apply a tangent constraint between line 2 and arc 3, as well as between arc 3 and arc 4, refer to Figure 6.74. Additionally, apply a concentric constraint between arc 4 and arc 6. You may also need to apply a horizontal constraint between the endpoints of line 5 and 7. Note that the sketch in Figure 6.74 has been numbered for reference only. Horizontal and vertical constraints are applied automatically when you draw horizontal and vertical lines in the sketch.

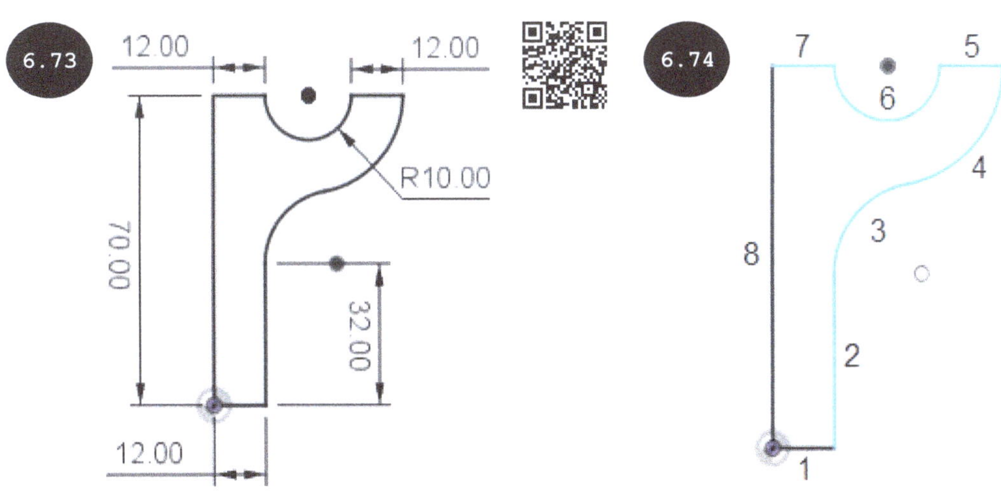

4. Click on the **Extrude** tool in the **SOLID** tab of the **Toolbar**, see Figure 6.75 or press the **E** key. The **EXTRUDE** dialog box appears and the closed sketch profile gets automatically selected in the graphics area, see Figure 6.76. If the profile does not get selected automatically, then you need to select it by clicking the left mouse button.

5. Change the orientation of the model to isometric by clicking on the **Home** icon of ViewCube, if the orientation is not changed by default.

6. Enter **60** in the **Distance** field of the **EXTRUDE** dialog box. The preview of the extrude feature appears in the graphics area, see Figure 6.77.

7. Invoke the **Direction** drop-down list in the **EXTRUDE** dialog box and then select the **Symmetric** option to extrude the sketch symmetrically on both sides of the sketching plane, see Figure 6.78. The preview of the extrude feature gets modified such that the 60 mm extrusion distance is added on both sides of the sketching plane. This is because the **Half Length** button is activated in the dialog box, by default.

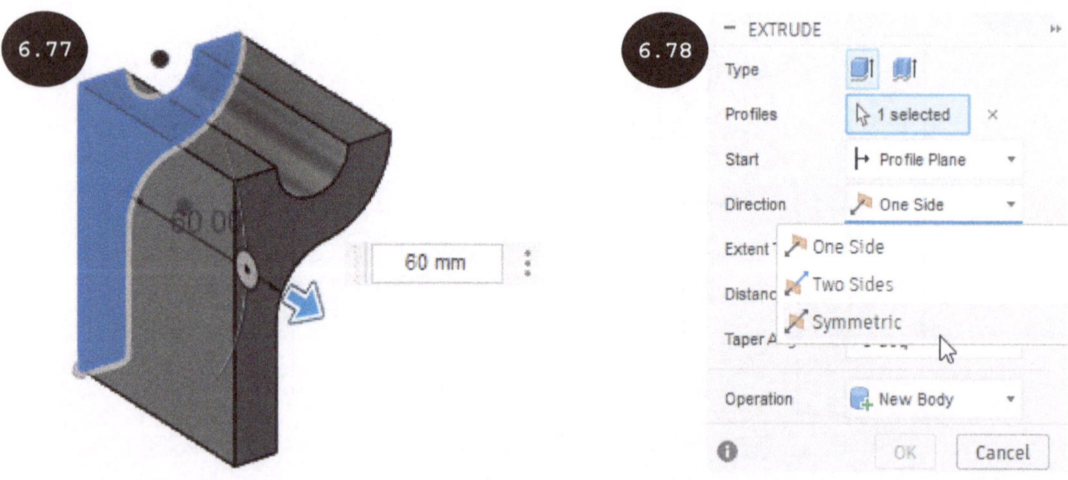

8. Click on the **Whole Length** button in the **Measurement** area of the **EXTRUDE** dialog box. The preview of the extrude feature gets modified such that the 30 mm extrusion distance is added on each side of the sketching plane and the total length of the feature is maintained at 60 mm.

9. Click on the **OK** button in the dialog box. The base feature is created, see Figure 6.79.

6.79

Section 4: Creating the Second Feature

To create the second feature of the model, you first need to create a construction plane at an offset distance of 10 mm from the right planar face of the base feature.

1. Click on the **Offset Plane** tool in the **SOLID** tab of the **Toolbar**, see Figure 6.80. The **CONSTRUCTION GEOMETRY** dialog box appears in the graphics area. Alternatively, invoke the **CONSTRUCT** drop-down menu in the **SOLID** tab of the **Toolbar** and then click on the **Offset Plane** tool.

6.80

2. Select the right planar face of the base feature, see Figure 6.81. The preview of an offset construction plane appears in the graphics area.

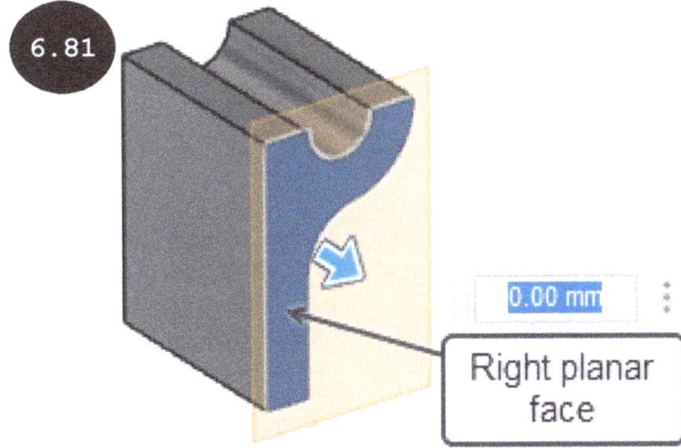

6.81

3. Enter **-10** in the **Distance** field of the dialog box. A preview of the construction plane appears at an offset distance of 10 mm from the right plane face, see Figure 6.82. Note that the negative distance value is used for reversing or flipping the direction of the plane.

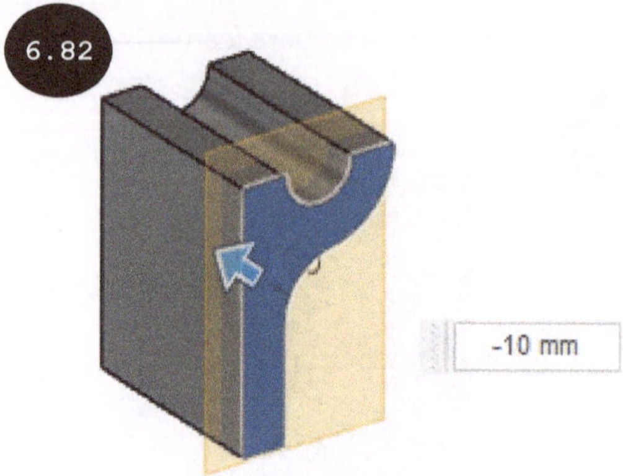

4. Click on the **OK** button in the dialog box. The offset construction plane is created.

   After creating the construction plane, you need to create the second feature of the model.

5. Click on the **Create Sketch** tool in the **Toolbar** and then select the newly created construction plane as the sketching plane. The construction plane becomes the sketching plane and is oriented normal to the viewing direction.

6. Create the sketch of the second feature and then apply the required constraints and dimensions, see Figure 6.83.

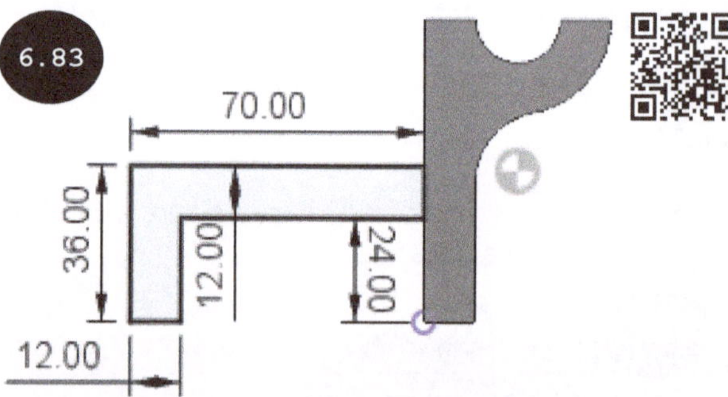

7. Click on the **SOLID** tab in the **Toolbar** to display the solid modeling tools.

8. Press the **E** key to activate the **Extrude** tool. The **EXTRUDE** dialog box appears and the closed sketch profile gets automatically selected in the graphics area, see Figure 6.84. Note that if the profile does not get selected automatically, then you need to select it by clicking the left mouse button.

9. Change the orientation of the model to isometric by clicking on the **Home** icon of ViewCube, if not changed by default.

10. Enter **-50** in the **Distance** field of the **EXTRUDE** dialog box. The preview of the extrude feature appears in the graphics area, see Figure 6.85.

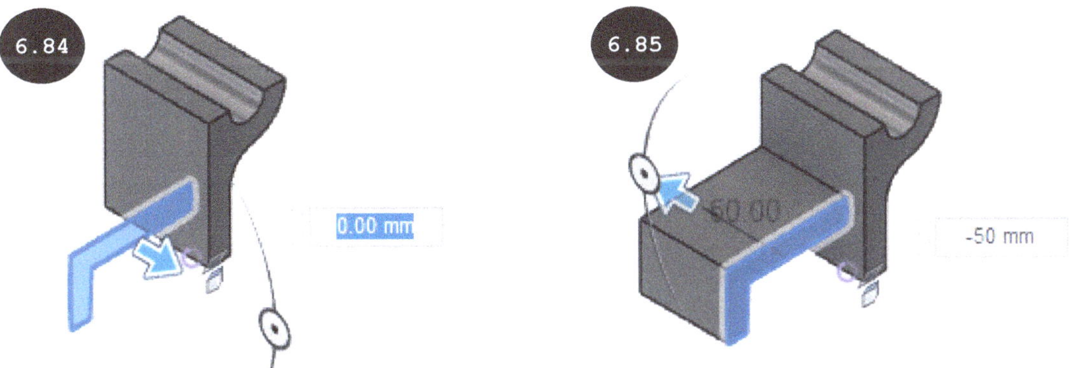

11. Ensure that the **Join** option is selected in the **Operation** drop-down list of the dialog box to join the feature with the base feature of the model. In doing so, both features will act as a single body.

12. Click on the **OK** button in the dialog box. The extrude feature is created, see Figure 6.86.

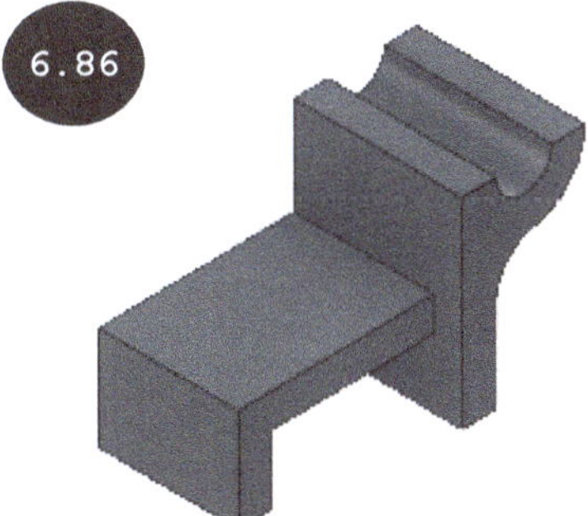

Section 5: Creating the Third Feature

To create the third feature of the model, you need to create a construction plane in the middle of the second feature.

1. Invoke the **CONSTRUCT** drop-down menu in the **SOLID** tab of the **Toolbar** and then click on the **Midplane** tool, see Figure 6.87. The **CONSTRUCTION GEOMETRY** dialog box appears, see Figure 6.88.

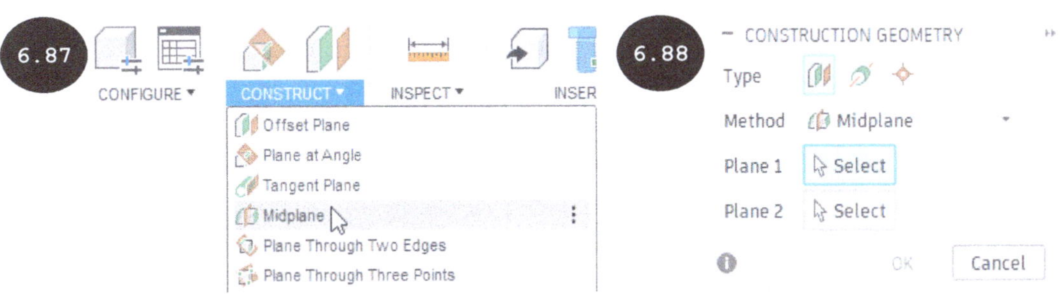

2. Select the right planar face of the second feature as the first face to create the mid-plane, see Figure 6.89.

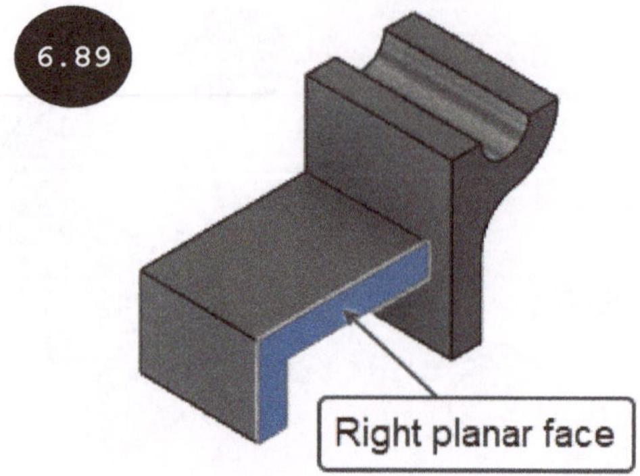

3. Rotate the model such that the left planar face of the second feature can be viewed in the graphics area, see Figure 6.90. To rotate the model, drag the cursor after pressing the SHIFT key and the middle mouse button.

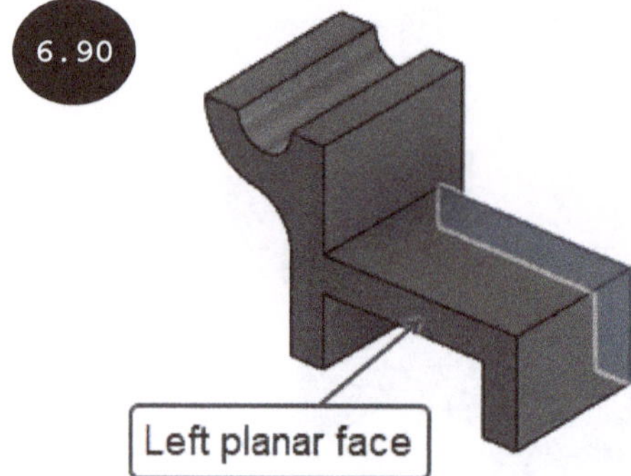

4. Select the left planar face of the second feature as the second face to create the mid-plane. The preview of the construction plane in the middle of the two selected faces appears in the graphics area, see Figure 6.91.

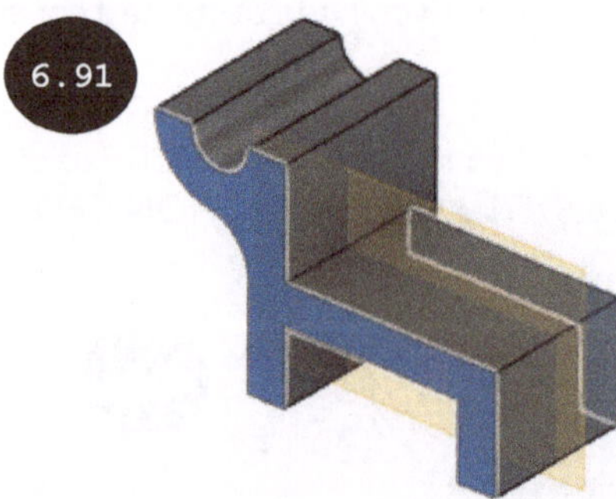

5. Change the orientation of the model to isometric by clicking on the **Home** icon of ViewCube.

6. Click on the **OK** button in the dialog box. The construction plane in the middle of the two selected faces has been created.

   After creating the construction plane, you can create the third feature of the model.

Note: The third feature of the model is a rib feature and can be easily created using the **Rib** tool. You will learn about the **Rib** tool in later chapters. In this tutorial, you will create this feature using the **Extrude** tool.

7. Click on the **Create Sketch** tool in the **Toolbar** and then select the newly created construction plane as the sketching plane. The construction plane becomes the sketching plane and is oriented normal to the viewing direction.

8. Create the closed sketch of the third feature (three-line entities), see Figure 6.92. The entities of the sketch shown in Figure 6.92 have been created by taking the reference of the vertices of the existing features of the model.

9. Press the **E** key to activate the **Extrude** tool. The **EXTRUDE** dialog box appears and the closed sketch profile gets automatically selected in the graphics area, see Figure 6.93. Note that if the profile does not get selected automatically, then you need to select it by clicking the left mouse button.

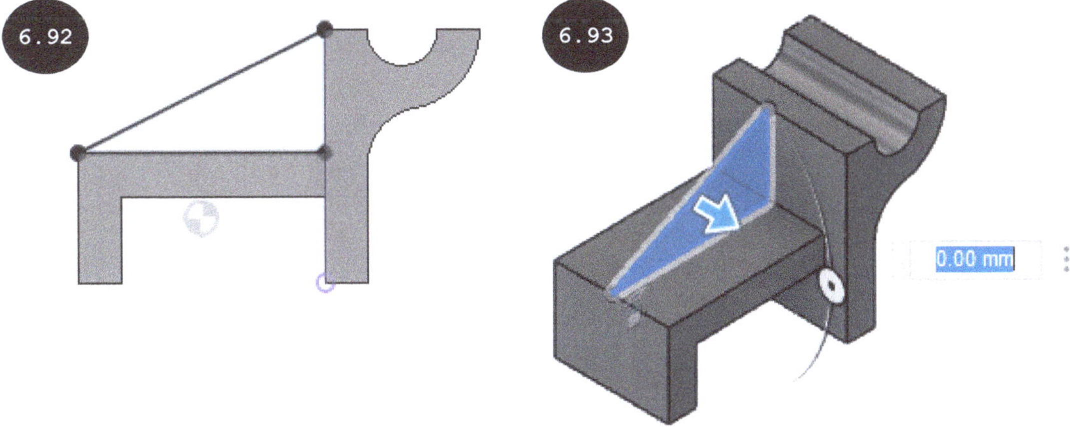

10. Change the orientation of the model to isometric by clicking on the **Home** icon of ViewCube, if not changed automatically.

11. Enter **4** in the **Distance** field of the **EXTRUDE** dialog box. The preview of the extrude feature appears in the graphics area.

12. Select the **Symmetric** option in the **Direction** drop-down list of the **EXTRUDE** dialog box. The preview of the extrude feature gets modified such that the 4 mm extrusion distance is added on both sides of the sketching plane and the total length of the feature becomes 8 mm. This is because the **Half Length** button is activated in the dialog box, by default.

13. Ensure that the **Join** option is selected in the **Operation** drop-down list of the dialog box to join the feature with the existing features of the model.

14. Click on the **OK** button in the dialog box. The extrude feature is created, see Figure 6.94.

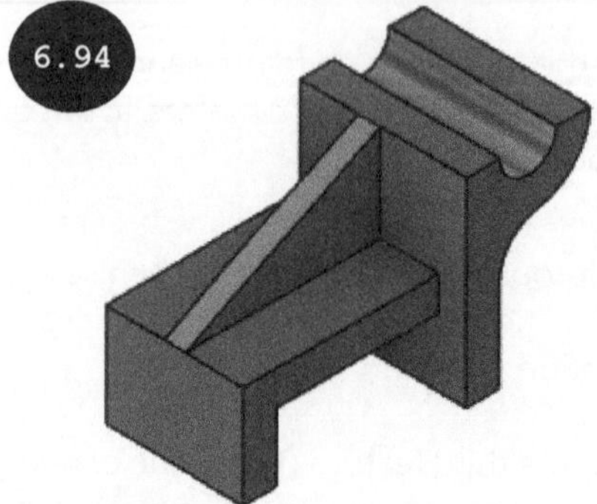

Section 6: Saving the Sketch

1. Click on the **Save** tool in the **Application Bar**. The **Save** dialog box appears.

2. Enter **Tutorial 2** in the **Name** field of the dialog box.

3. Ensure that the location ***Autodesk Fusion 360 > Chapter 06 > Tutorial*** is specified in the **Location** field of the dialog box to save the file of this tutorial. To specify the location, you need to expand the **Save** dialog box by clicking on the down arrow next to the **Location** field of the dialog box.

4. Click on the **Save** button in the dialog box. The model is saved with the name Tutorial 2 in the specified location (***Autodesk Fusion 360 > Chapter 06 > Tutorial***).

Hands-on Test Drive 1

Create the model shown in Figure 6.95. All dimensions are in mm.

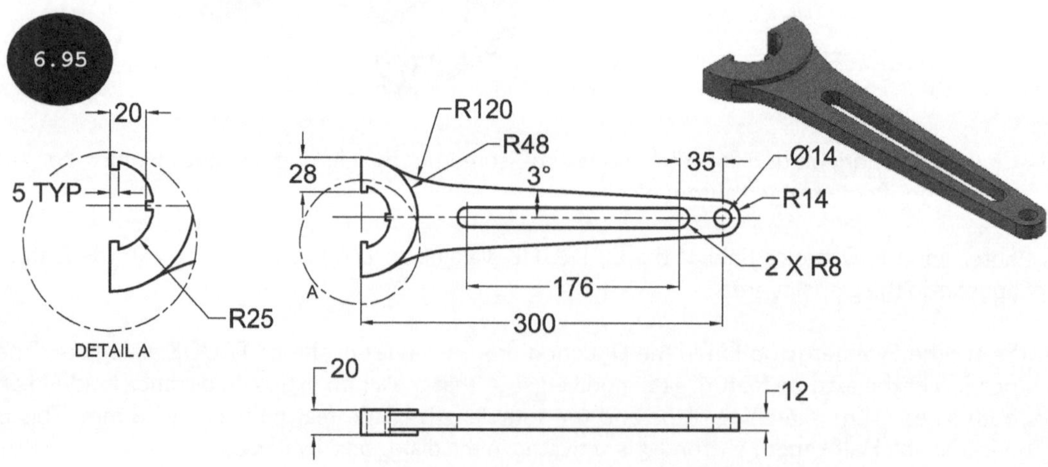

Hands-on Test Drive 2

Create the model shown in Figure 6.96. All dimensions are in mm.

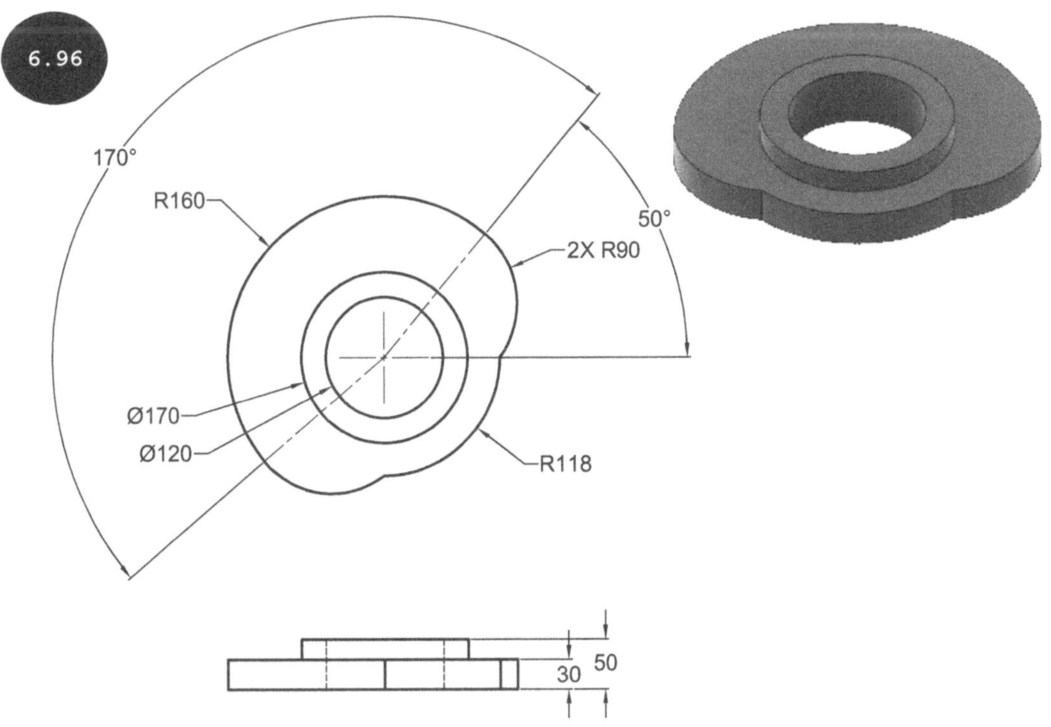

Hands-on Test Drive 3

Create the model shown in Figure 6.97. All dimensions are in mm.

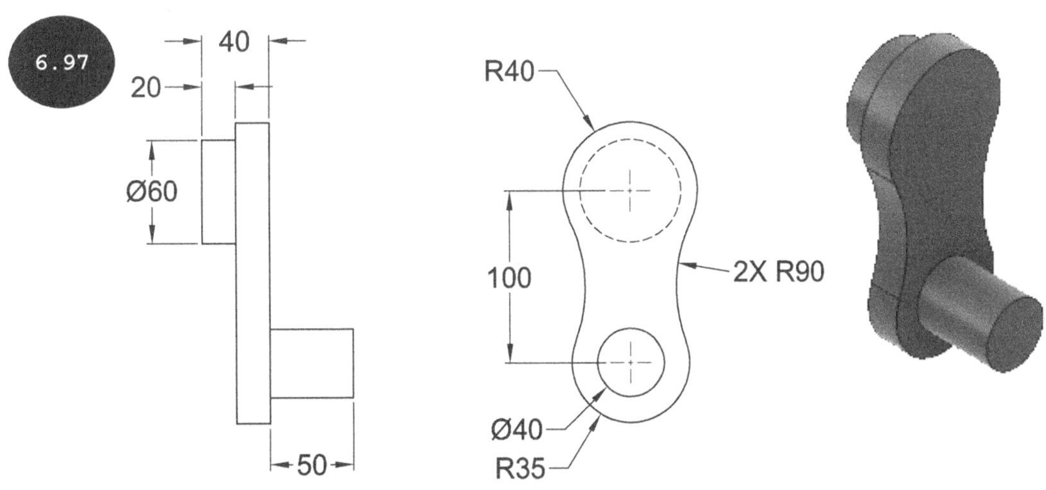

Summary

In this chapter, you learned that the three default planes: Front, Top, and Right may not be sufficient for creating all the features of a complex real-world model. To enhance your modeling capabilities, you explored how to create additional reference planes. You also discovered methods for creating construction axes and construction points, which are essential tools for building more complex and precise models.

Questions

Complete and verify the following sentences:

- You can create a construction plane at an offset distance using the _________ tool.
- You can create a construction plane at an angle using the _________ tool.
- You can create a construction plane in the middle of two faces/planes using the _________ tool.
- The _________ tool is used for creating a construction axis passing through a cylinder, cone, or torus.
- The _________ tool is used for creating a construction axis passing through two planes or planar faces.
- The _________ tool is used for creating a construction point at a vertex.
- The _________ tool is used for creating a construction point at the center of a circle, a sphere, or a torus.
- You can reverse the direction of an offset construction plane by entering a negative offset distance value. (True/False)
- You cannot select a planar face of existing features as the sketching plane for creating a feature. (True/False)

7

Advanced Modeling - I

In this chapter, the following topics will be discussed:

- Exploring Advanced Extrude Options
- Exploring Advanced Revolve Options
- Working with a Sketch having Multiple Profiles
- Projecting Edges onto a Sketching Plane
- Creating 3D Curves
- Editing a Feature and its Sketch
- Editing the Sketching Plane of a Sketch
- Applying Physical Material Properties
- Customizing Material Properties
- Calculating Mass Properties
- Measuring the Distance between Objects

In previous chapters, you learned how to create features using the **Extrude** and **Revolve** tools. In this chapter, you will explore the advanced options of these tools, including the ability to remove material from the model. Additionally, you will learn how to measure the distance between entities, apply material properties, and calculate the mass properties of a model, among other essential techniques.

Exploring Advanced Extrude Options

In earlier chapters, you learned that when you extrude a sketch using the **Extrude** tool, the EXTRUDE dialog box appears, see Figure 7.1. Some options within this dialog box have been previously covered while creating the base feature of a model. The remaining options are discussed next.

Start drop-down List

The options in the **Start** drop-down list of the dialog box allow you to define the start condition for the extrusion, see Figure 7.2. The **Profile Plane** and **Offset** options are covered earlier in the context of creating base features, while the **Object** option is discussed next.

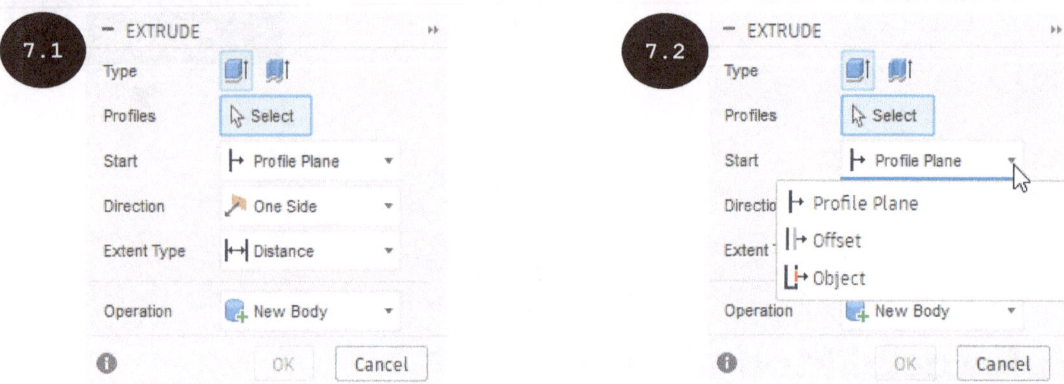

Object

The **Object** option in the **Start** drop-down list allows you to select a face, plane, or vertex to define the starting position for the extrusion. After selecting this option, you can choose a face, plane, or vertex to set as the start condition for the extrusion. Figure 7.3 shows a sketch profile to be extruded and a face to be selected as the start condition of extrusion. Figure 7.4 shows the preview of the resultant extruded feature after selecting the face as the start condition.

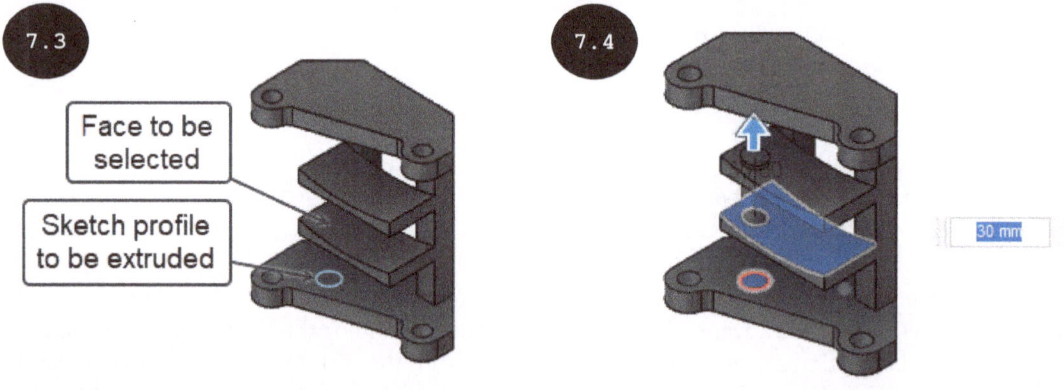

Note: By default, 0 (zero) value is entered in the **Offset** field of the dialog box. As a result, the extrusion starts exactly from the object selected (face, plane, or vertex). You can enter the required offset value in this field.

Extent Type drop-down list

The **Extent Type** drop-down list is used to define the end condition or termination method for the extrusion, see Figure 7.5. The **Distance** option in this drop-down has already been covered in the context of creating base features, while the remaining options are discussed next.

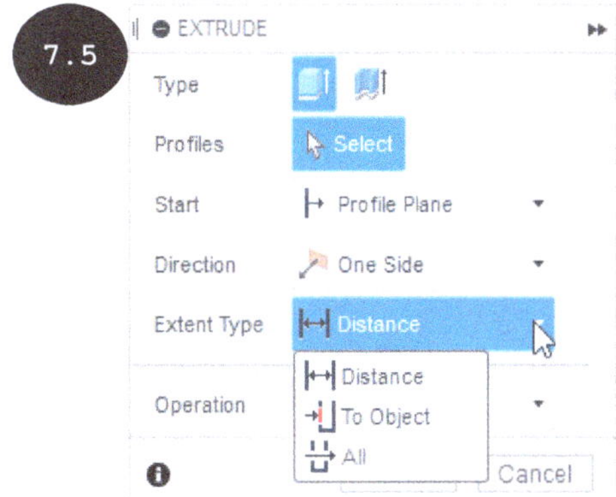

To Object

The **To Object** option is used to define the end condition or termination of the extrusion by selecting a face, a plane, a vertex, or a body. Figure 7.6 shows a sketch profile to be extruded and a face to be selected as the end condition/termination of extrusion. Figure 7.7 shows the preview of the resultant extruded feature after selecting the face as the end condition.

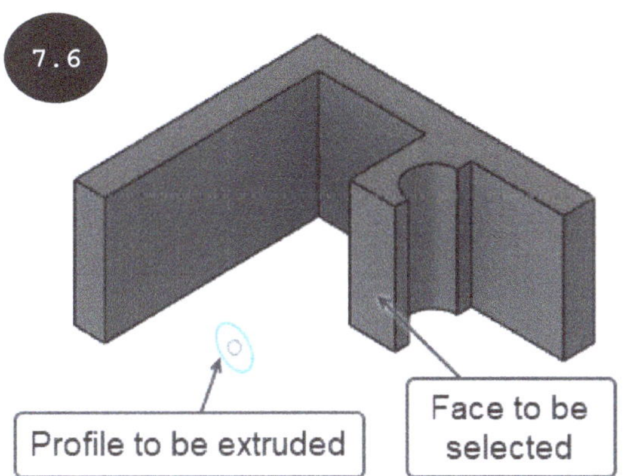

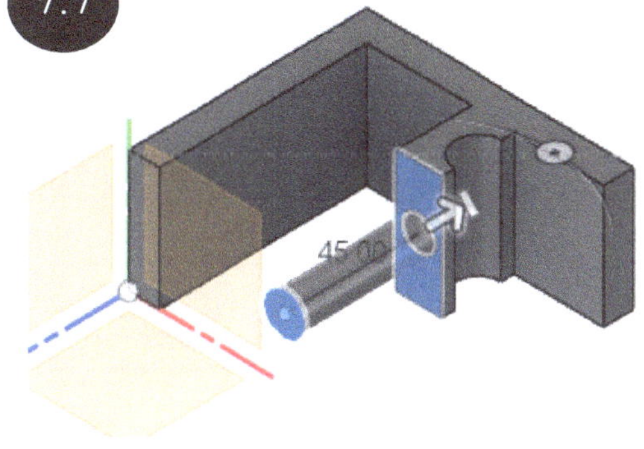

When you select a face as the end condition, the **To Selected Face** and **To Adjacent Faces** buttons appear in the dialog box, see Figure 7.8. By default, the **To Selected Face** button is activated. As a result, even if the profile to be extruded does not completely project onto the selected face, the extrusion terminates on the selected face of the model, see Figure 7.9.

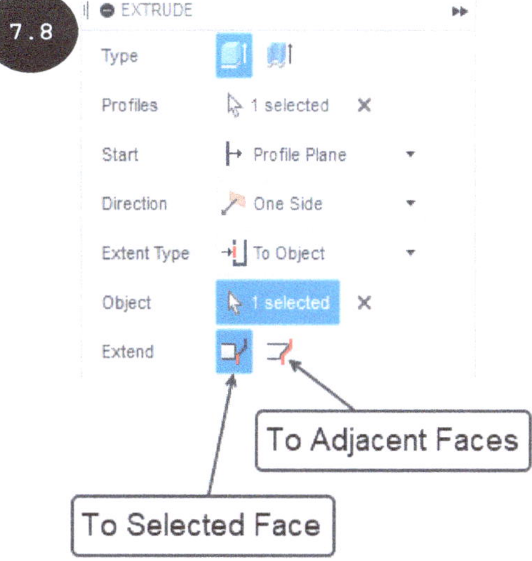

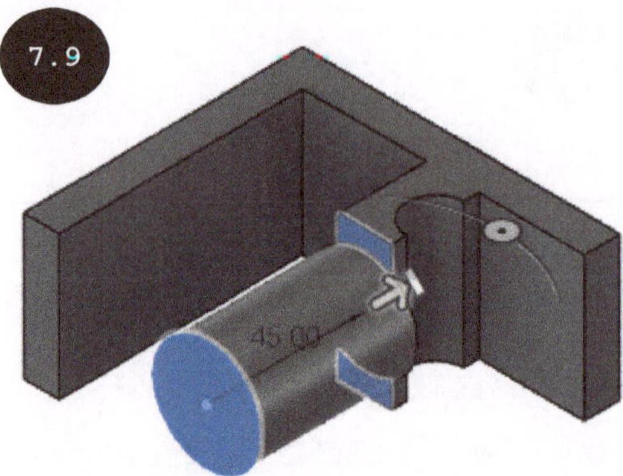

If the profile to be extruded does not fully project onto the chosen face, the extrusion extends over adjacent faces and terminates at the next intersecting face where it is completely projected, see Figures 7.10 and 7.11. Note that the existing material of the model is not overridden by the material of the newly created feature, see Figure 7.12.

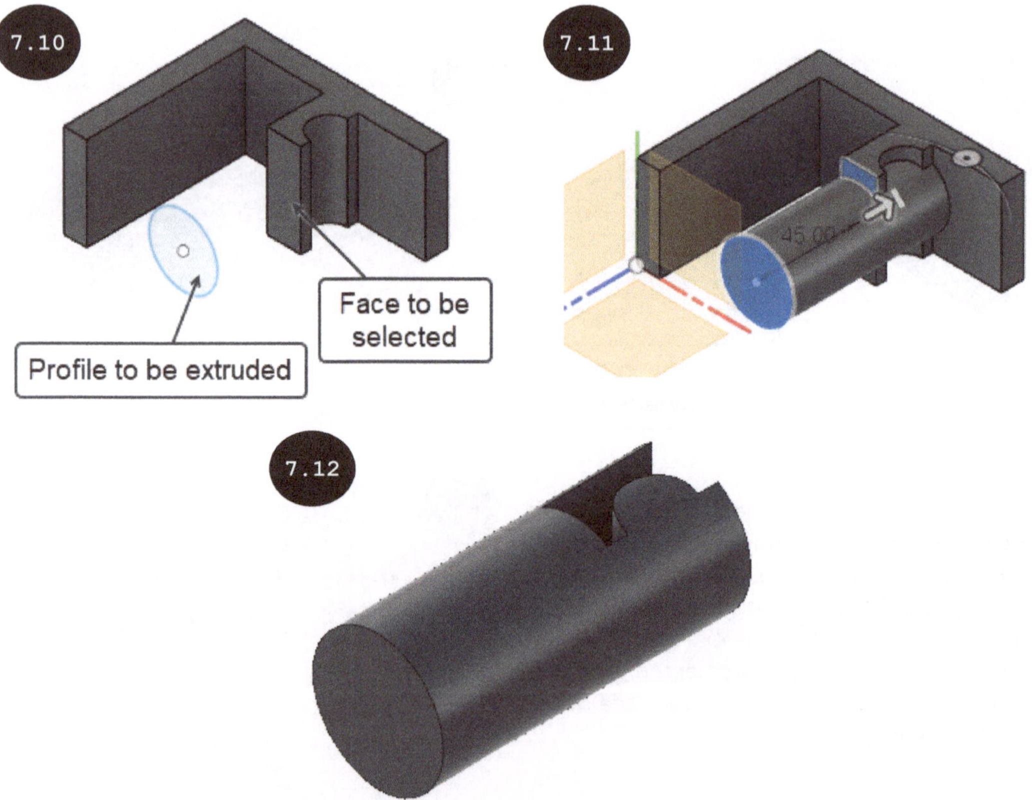

All

The **All** option of the **Extent Type** drop-down list is used to define the extrusion to pass through all faces of the model. You can also reverse the direction of extrusion from one side of the sketching plane to the other side by clicking on the **Flip** button in the dialog box. The **Flip** button becomes available in the dialog box as soon as you select the **All** option.

Operation drop-down list

The **Operation** drop-down list is used to define the type of operation for creating the extrude feature, see Figure 7.13. The options in the drop-down list are discussed next.

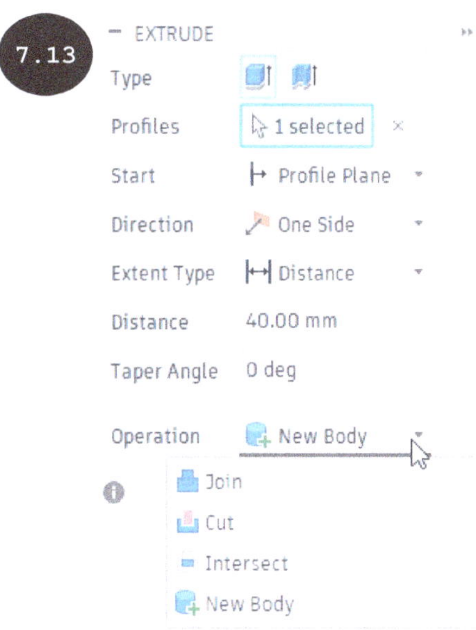

Join

The **Join** option of the **Operation** drop-down list is used to extrude the profile by adding the material as well as merging or joining the feature with the existing features of the model. The feature created by using this option merges with the existing features and together acts as a single body.

Cut

The **Cut** option of the **Operation** drop-down list is used to extrude the profile by removing material from the model. Figure 7.14 shows a sketch profile, which is created on the top planar face of the model and Figure 7.15 shows the resultant extrude cut feature.

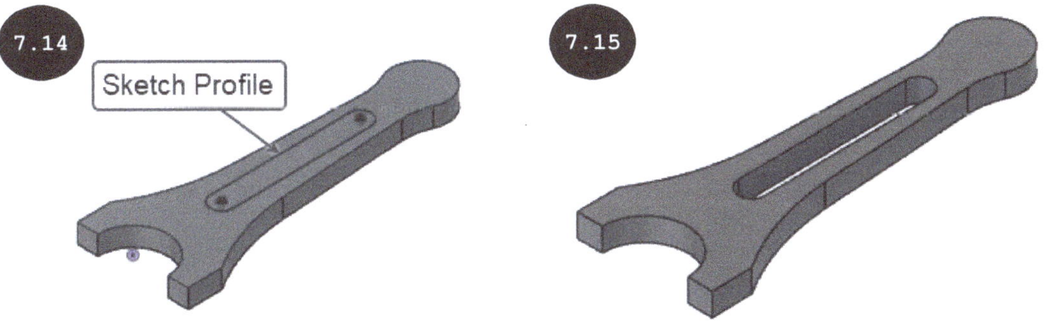

Intersect

The **Intersect** option in the **Operation** drop-down list is used to create a feature that retains only the intersecting material between the existing feature and the newly one. Figure 7.16 shows a sketch profile, which is created on the top planar face of the model and Figure 7.17 shows the resultant intersect feature.

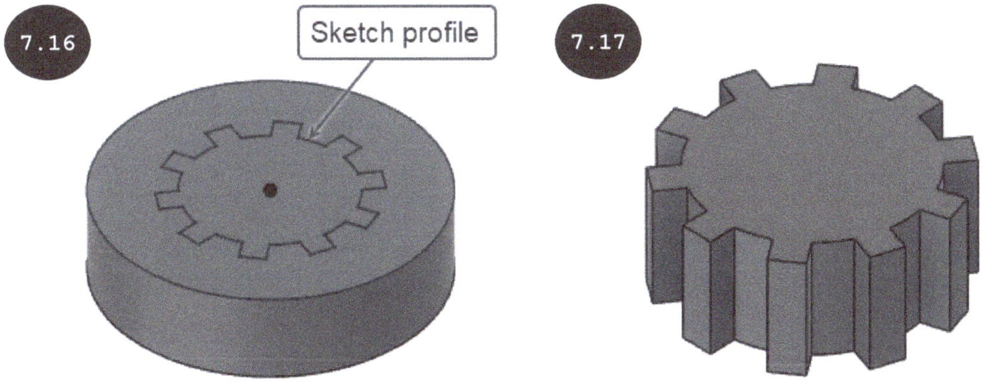

New Body

On selecting the **New Body** option, the feature being created does not merge with the existing features of the model and a separate body will be created. If you are creating a base feature of a model then this option is selected, by default.

After specifying all the required parameters in the **EXTRUDE** dialog box, click on the **OK** button. The extrude feature is created.

Exploring Advanced Revolve Options

In earlier chapters, you learned that when you revolve a sketch using the Revolve tool, the REVOLVE dialog box appears in the graphics area, see Figure 7.18. Some of the options in the REVOLVE dialog box were discussed earlier while creating the base revolve feature of a model.

The options such as Join, Cut, and Intersect in the Operation drop-down list of the REVOLVE dialog box are the same as those discussed earlier in this chapter, with the only difference being that these options are used to create a revolve feature.

Most of the options in the Extent Type drop-down list of the REVOLVE dialog box have also been discussed earlier, except the To Object option, which is used to terminate the revolve feature at a selected face or plane.

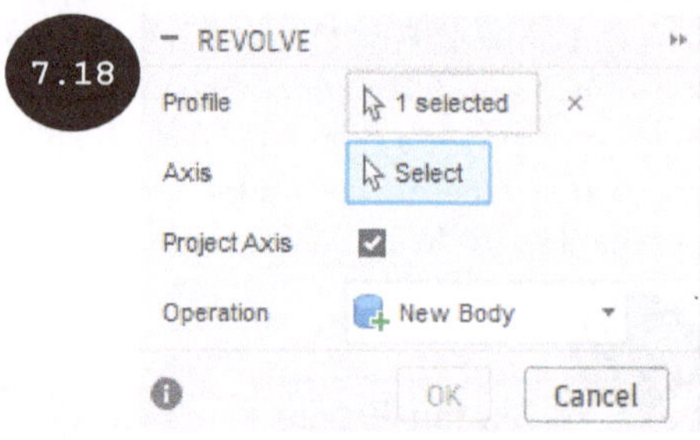

Note that the Extent Type drop-down list becomes available in the REVOLVE dialog box only after selecting an axis of revolution.

Working with a Sketch having Multiple Profiles

In Autodesk Fusion, you can create multiple features from a single sketch containing several closed profiles. Figure 7.19 shows a sketch with multiple closed profiles, while Figure 7.20 displays the resulting multi-feature model created from this sketch. The method for creating features by extruding closed profiles of a sketch is discussed below:

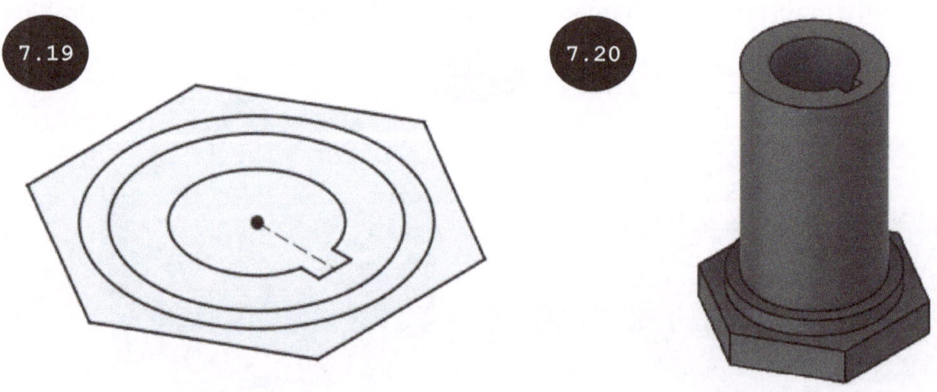

1. Create a sketch that has multiple profiles by using the sketching tools, see Figure 7.21.
2. Click on the **SOLID** tab in the **Toolbar** to display the solid modeling tools.
3. Click on the **EXTRUDE** tool in the **CREATE** panel of the **SOLID** tab or press the **E** key. The **EXTRUDE** dialog box appears.
4. Change the orientation of the sketch to isometric by clicking on the Home icon of ViewCube.
5. Move the cursor over a closed profile of the sketch to be selected and then click when it gets highlighted in the graphics area, see Figure 7.22.

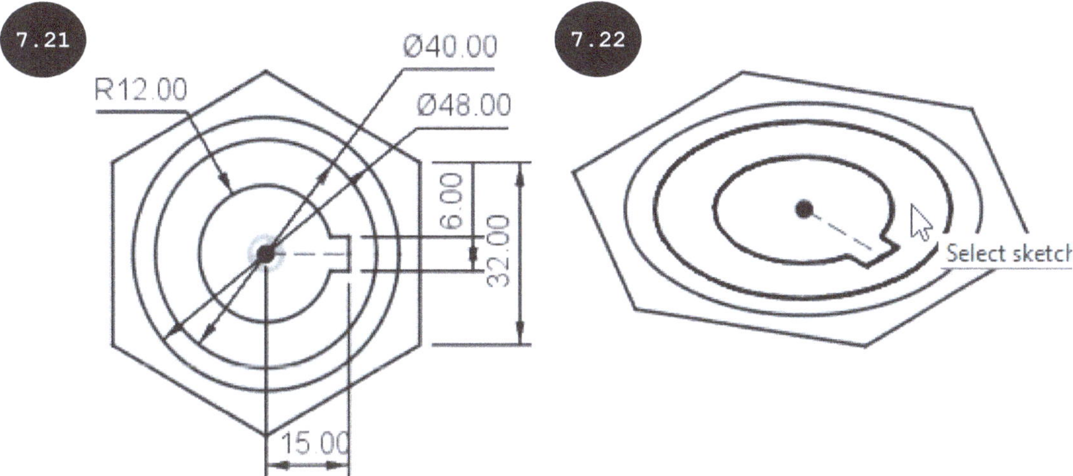

6. Specify the parameters for creating the feature in the dialog box.
7. Click on **OK** in the dialog box. The feature is created, see Figure 7.23. Also, its name is added to the **Timeline**, see Figure 7.24. Note that the sketch disappears from the graphics area. This is because the sketch is consumed by the feature. As a result, it no longer appears in the graphics area.

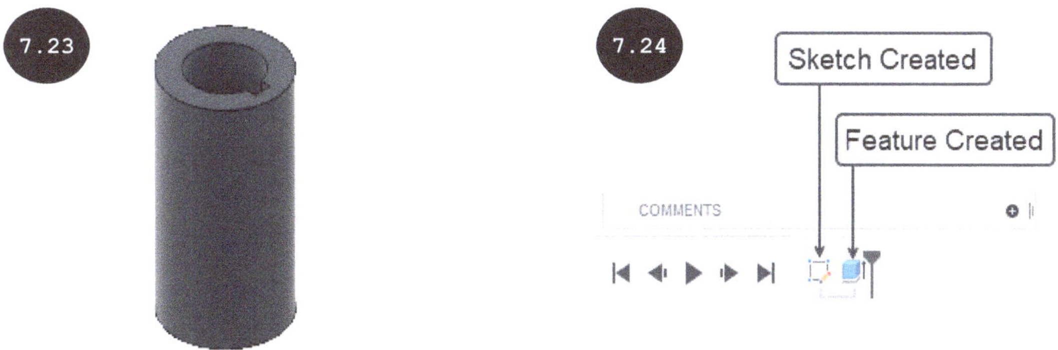

Note: The **Timeline** displays all the operations performed on a design, including sketches, features, components, and construction planes in their order of creation. However, you can change the order of the operations by dragging them in the **Timeline**.

8. In the **BROWSER**, expand the **Sketches** node by clicking on the arrow in front of it, see Figure 7.25. A list of all the sketches created in the currently active design file appears.

9. Click on the **Show** icon available in front of the sketch to turn on its visibility in the graphics area, see Figure 7.25.

10. Invoke the **Extrude** tool and then select a closed profile of the sketch, see Figure 7.26.

11. Specify the parameters for creating the feature in the dialog box and then click on the **OK** button in the dialog box. The extrude feature is created, see Figure 7.27.

12. Similarly, you can create the remaining features by using the closed profiles of a sketch, see Figure 7.28.

Projecting Edges onto a Sketching Plane

In Autodesk Fusion, while sketching, you can project edges of existing features as sketch entities onto the active sketching plane using the **Project** tool. Figure 7.29 shows a model in which the edges of the existing features have been projected as sketch entities on the active sketching plane.

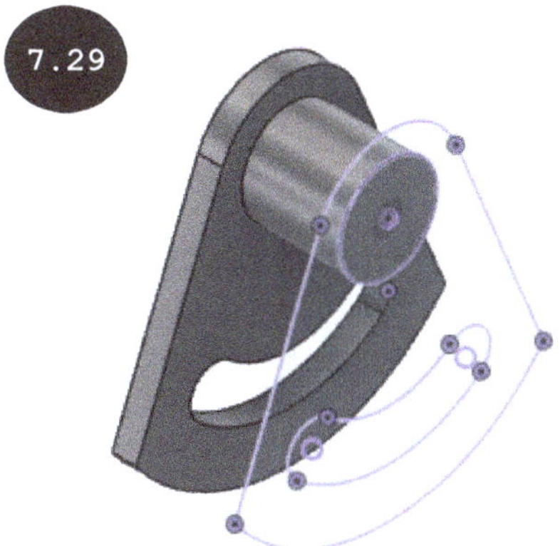

To project the edges of the existing features onto the currently active sketching plane, invoke the **CREATE** drop-down menu in the **SKETCH** contextual tab of the **Toolbar** and then click on **Project / Include > Project**, see Figure 7.30. Alternatively, press the P key. The **PROJECT** dialog box appears, see Figure 7.31. The options are discussed next.

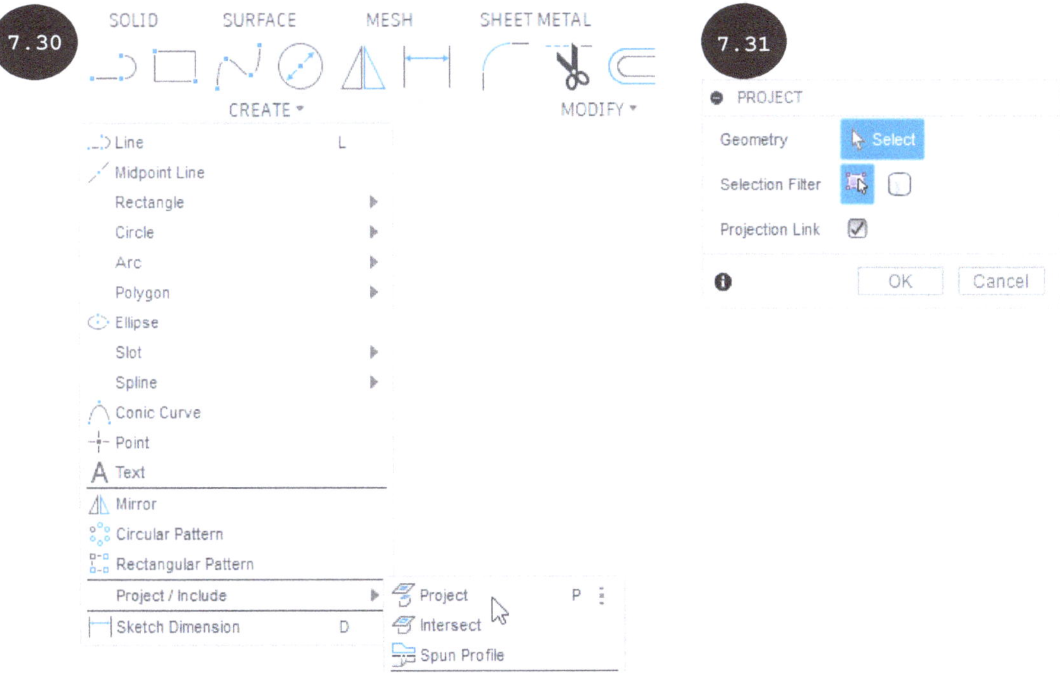

Geometry
By default, the **Geometry** selection option is activated in the dialog box. As a result, you can select edges, faces, sketch entities, and bodies as the geometries to be projected onto the currently active sketching plane.

Note that on selecting a face, all its edges get projected onto the sketching plane. You can filter the selection of geometries by using the buttons in the **Selection Filter** area of the dialog box, which is discussed next.

Selection Filter
By default, the **Specified entities** button is activated in the **Selection Filter** area of the dialog box. As a result, you can select edges, faces, and sketch entities of the model. To select bodies, you need to activate the **Bodies** button in this area of the dialog box.

Projection Link
On selecting the **Projection Link** check box, the projected sketch gets linked to its parent entity. As a result, if any change is made in the parent entity, the same change reflects on the projected entity, automatically. Note that the projected sketch cannot be modified individually if it is linked to its parent entity.

After selecting the required geometries to be projected, click on the **OK** button in the dialog box. The edges of the selected geometries are projected onto the active sketching plane as sketch entities. You can use these projected sketch entities for creating features.

Tip: If the **Auto project edges on reference** check box is selected in the **Preferences** dialog box, the edges of an existing planar face automatically project onto the sketching plane when you create a sketch on that face. To select this check box, invoke the **Preferences** dialog box and then click on the **Design** option under the **General** section in the left panel of the dialog box. Next, select the **Auto project edges on reference** check box in the right panel of the dialog box and click on the **Apply** button.

Creating 3D Curves
In Autodesk Fusion, you can create different types of curves, which are mainly used as a path, guide rail, and so on for creating features like sweep and loft. The methods for creating different types of curves are discussed next.

Creating a Projected Curve
In Autodesk Fusion, you can create a projected curve by projecting a sketch onto an existing face of a model using the **Project To Surface** tool, see Figure 7.32. You can select planar faces or curved faces to project sketch entities. The method for creating a projected curve is discussed below:

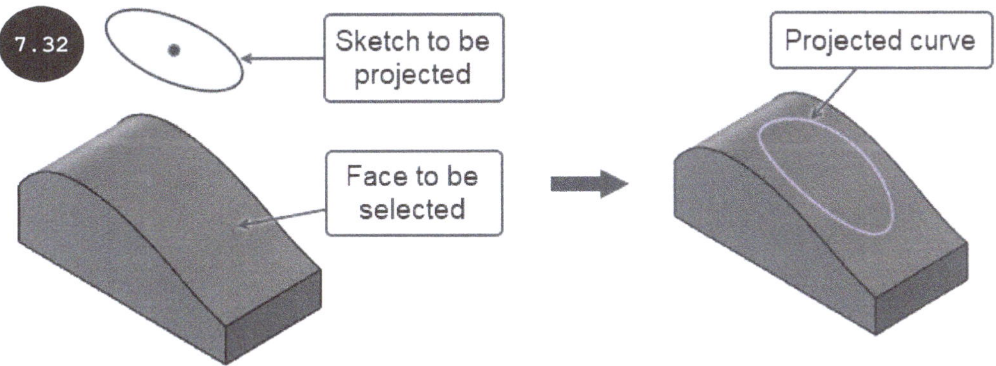

1. Invoke the Sketching environment by selecting a plane or a planar face as the sketching plane. The **SKETCH** contextual tab appears in the **Toolbar**.

2. Invoke the **CREATE** drop-down menu in the **SKETCH** contextual tab and then click on **Project / Include > Project To Surface**. The **PROJECT TO SURFACE** dialog box appears in the graphics area, see Figure 7.33.

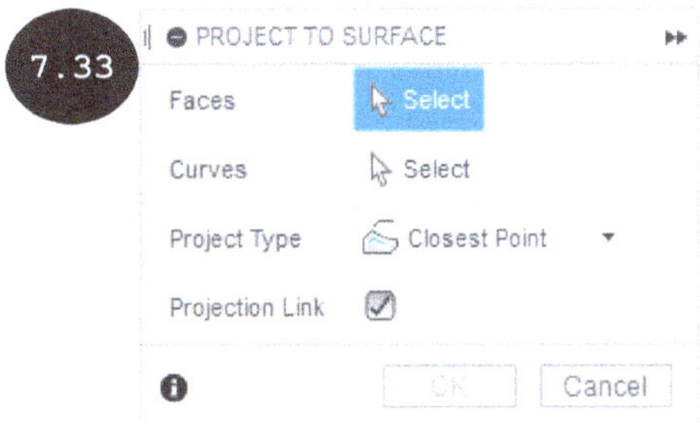

3. Change the orientation of the drawing view to isometric by clicking on the **Home** icon of ViewCube.

   By default, the **Faces** selection option is selected in the dialog box. As a result, you can select one or more faces (planar or curved) to project the sketch entities.

4. Select one or more faces of the model in the graphics area, refer to Figure 7.34.

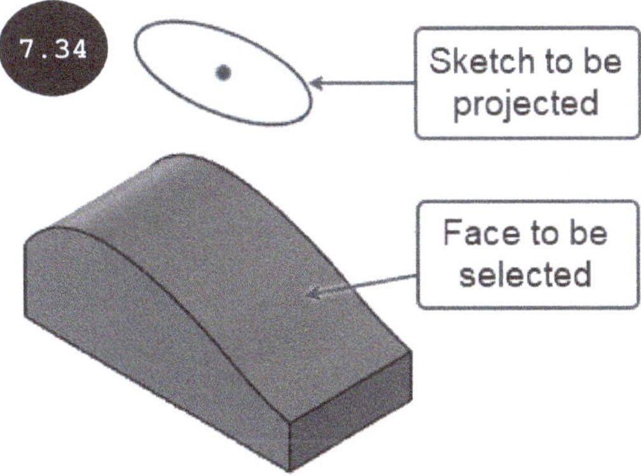

5. Click on the **Curves** selection option in the dialog box and then select the sketch entities to be projected, refer to Figure 7.34. The preview of the projected curve appears in the graphics area with the default option selected in the **Project Type** drop-down list, see Figures 7.35 and 7.36. Note that the curves to be selected should not be a part of the current sketch.

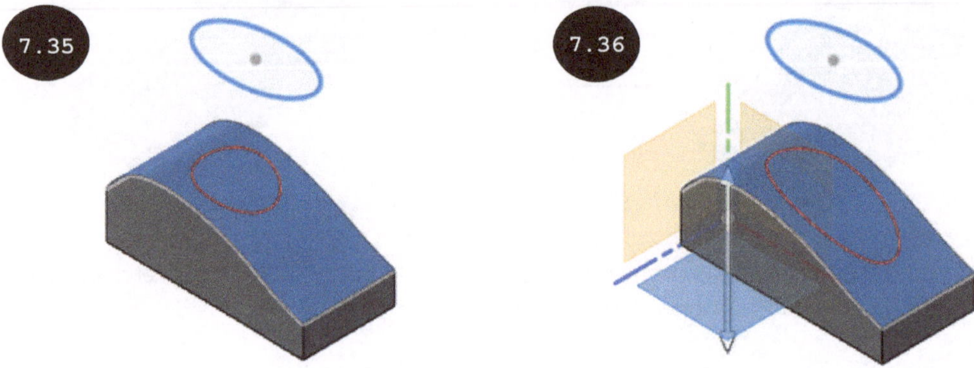

The **Closest Point** option of the **Project Type** drop-down list is used for projecting the sketch entities to the closest point on the selected face along the face vector, see Figure 7.35. On selecting the **Along Vector** option in the **Project Type** drop-down list, the **Project Direction** selection option appears in the dialog box, which is used for selecting a vector along which you want to project the entities on the selected face, see Figure 7.36. In this figure, the Top plane is selected as the vector direction.

6. Select the required option in the **Project Type** drop-down list of the dialog box. Note that, if you select the **Along Vector** option in the **Project Type** drop-down list then you also need to define the project direction by selecting a face, a plane, or an edge.

7. Select the **Projection Link** check box in the dialog box to link the projected curve with the parent sketch.

8. Click on the **OK** button in the dialog box. The projected curve is created on the selected face of the projection, see Figure 7.37.

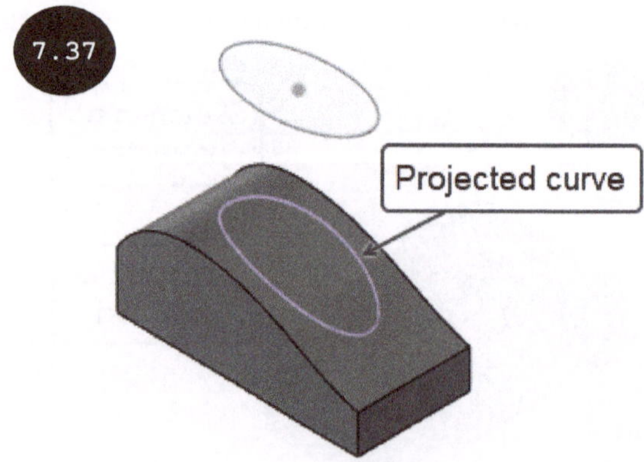

Creating an Intersection Curve

In Autodesk Fusion, you can create a 3D curve by intersecting two geometries using the **Intersection Curve** tool, see Figure 7.38. In this figure, the resultant 3D curve is created by intersecting two 2D curves (splines), each curve lying on two different planes. You can also create a 3D curve by intersecting a 2D curve with a face. The method for creating an intersection curve is discussed below:

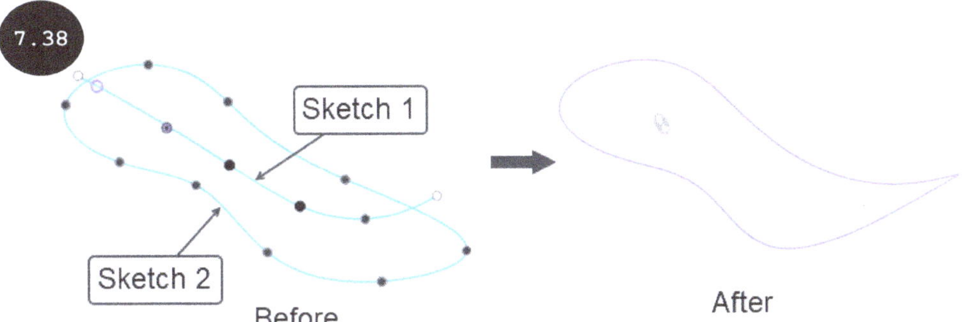

1. Invoke the Sketching environment by selecting a plane or a planar face as the sketching plane. The **SKETCH** contextual tab appears in the **Toolbar**.

2. Invoke the **CREATE** drop-down menu in the **SKETCH** contextual tab of the **Toolbar** and then click on **Project / Include > Intersection Curve**. The **INTERSECTION CURVE** dialog box appears in the graphics area, see Figure 7.39. Next, change the orientation of the drawing view to isometric by clicking on the **Home** icon of ViewCube.

   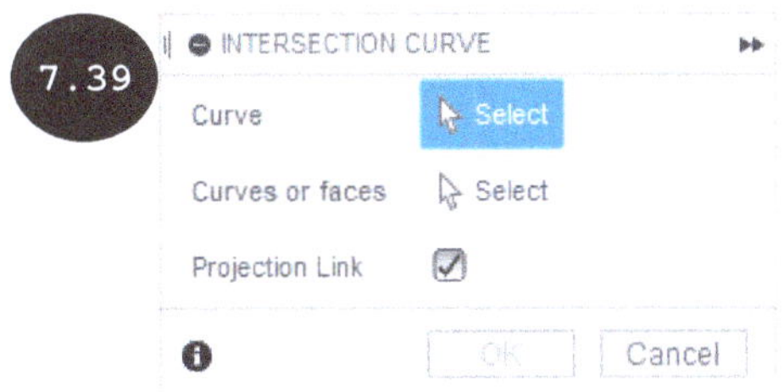

   By default, the **Curve** selection option is selected in the dialog box. As a result, you can select a 2D curve or a sketch entity to be projected on the other 2D curve or a face.

3. Select a curve/sketch entity in the drawing area. The curve is selected and the **Curves or faces** selection option is automatically activated in the dialog box.

4. Select another curve or a face in the drawing area. The preview of the intersection curve appears. Note that the curves to be selected should not be a part of the current sketch.

5. Ensure that the **Projection Link** check box is selected in the dialog box to link the projected curve with the parent sketch.

6. Click on the **OK** button in the dialog box. The intersection curve is created by intersecting the first selected curve with the second selected curve or the face.

Creating a Curve by Projecting Intersecting Geometries

You can also create a curve by projecting the geometries of the existing objects that intersect with the currently active sketching plane using the **Intersect** tool, see Figure 7.40. The method for creating a curve by projecting the geometries of the objects that intersect with the sketching plane is discussed below:

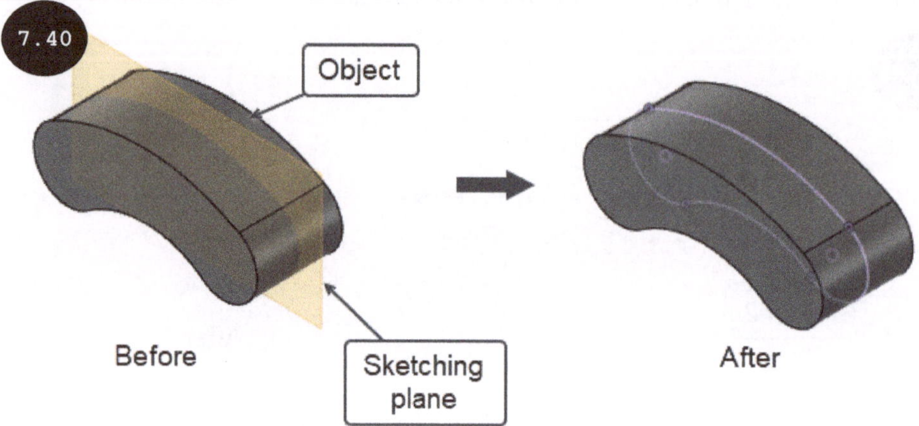

1. Invoke the Sketching environment by selecting a plane or a planar face as the sketching plane. The **SKETCH** contextual tab appears in the **Toolbar**.

2. Invoke the **CREATE** drop-down menu in the **SKETCH** contextual tab and then click on **Project / Include > Intersect**. The **INTERSECT** dialog box appears, see Figure 7.41. Change the orientation of the drawing view to isometric.

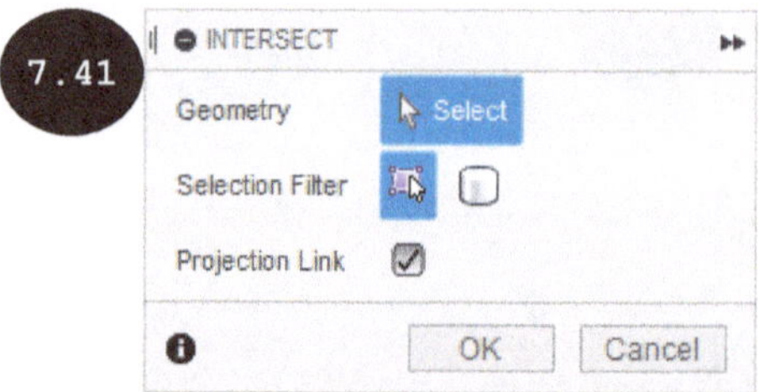

By default, the **Geometry** selection option and the **Specified entities** button are activated in the dialog box, see Figure 7.41. As a result, you can select edges and faces as the objects to be projected onto the active sketching plane. To select bodies, you need to activate the **Bodies** button in the **Selection Filter** area of the dialog box.

3. Ensure that the required button is activated in the **Selection Filter** area of the dialog box.

4. Select the objects (faces and edges) or bodies in the graphics area. The preview of the curve appears in the drawing area.

5. Ensure that the **Projection Link** check box is selected in the dialog box to link the projected curve with the parent sketch.

6. Click on the **OK** button. The curve is created by projecting the geometries of the selected objects/bodies that intersect with the sketching plane.

Editing a Feature and its Sketch

Autodesk Fusion allows you to edit features of a model at any point of design as per the design change or revision by using the **Timeline**. As discussed earlier, the **Timeline** displays a list of all features and sketches including construction geometries created for a model, see Figure 7.42. The method for editing a feature and a sketch is discussed below:

7.42

1. Right-click on the feature to be edited in the **Timeline**. A shortcut menu appears, see Figure 7.43.

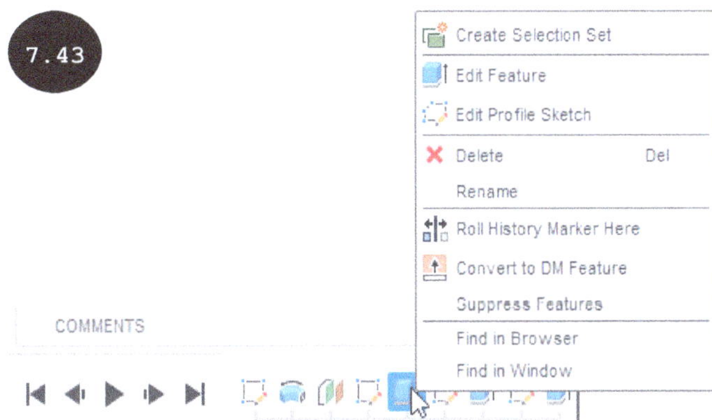

7.43

2. Click on the **Edit Feature** tool in the shortcut menu to edit the feature parameters. The respective dialog box of the feature selected appears in the graphics area.

   Note that to edit the sketch of a feature, you need to click on the **Edit Profile Sketch** tool in the shortcut menu that appears. On doing so, the sketch of the selected feature becomes active, and you can edit or modify it by using the sketching tools.

3. Change the parameters of the features as per your requirement by entering new values in the dialog box.

4. After editing the feature parameters, click on the **OK** button in the dialog box.

   Note that in case of editing the sketch of the feature, you need to click on the **FINISH SKETCH** tool in the **SKETCH** contextual tab of the **Toolbar** to finish the editing operation.

Tip: In Autodesk Fusion, you can also edit an individual sketch. To do this, right-click on the sketch to be edited in the **Timeline** and then click on the **Edit Sketch** tool in the shortcut menu that appears.

Editing the Sketching Plane of a Sketch

You can also edit or redefine the sketching plane of a sketch. To do this, right-click on the sketch whose sketching plane is to be redefined. A shortcut menu appears, see Figure 7.44. In this menu, click on the **Redefine Sketch Plane** tool. The **REDEFINE SKETCH PLANE** dialog box appears, see Figure 7.45.

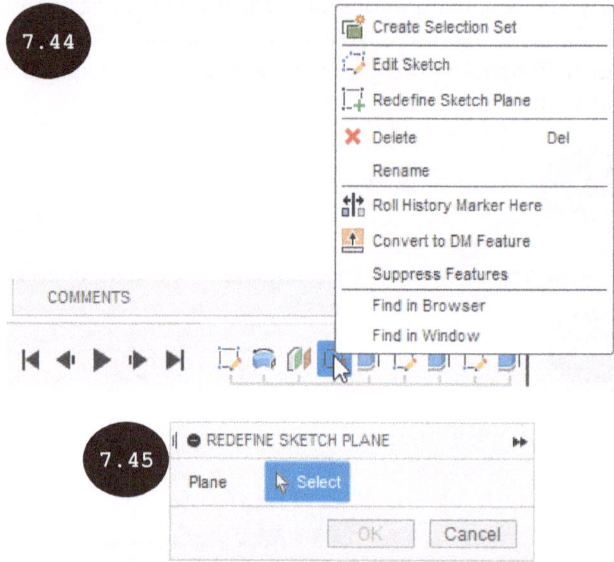

Select a new plane or a planar face as the new sketching plane of the sketch in the graphics area and then click on the **OK** button in the dialog box. The sketching plane of the sketch is redefined or changed to the newly selected plane or planar face. Also, the orientation of the sketch as well as its associated feature changes in the graphics area.

Applying Physical Material Properties

In Autodesk Fusion, you can apply physical material properties such as density, elastic modulus, and tensile strength to a model. Assigning material properties to a model is important to calculate its mass properties as well as to perform static and dynamic analysis.

By default, when you create a design/model in Autodesk Fusion, the Steel material properties are assigned. You can change the default material properties of the model by applying new material. You can do so by using the **Fusion Material Library** which contains almost all standard materials. You can also customize the material properties of applied standard material. The method for applying a standard material is discussed below:

1. Invoke the **MODIFY** drop-down menu in the **SOLID** tab of the **Toolbar**, see Figure 7.46 and then click on the **Physical Material** tool. The **PHYSICAL MATERIAL** dialog box appears, see Figure 7.47.

7.46

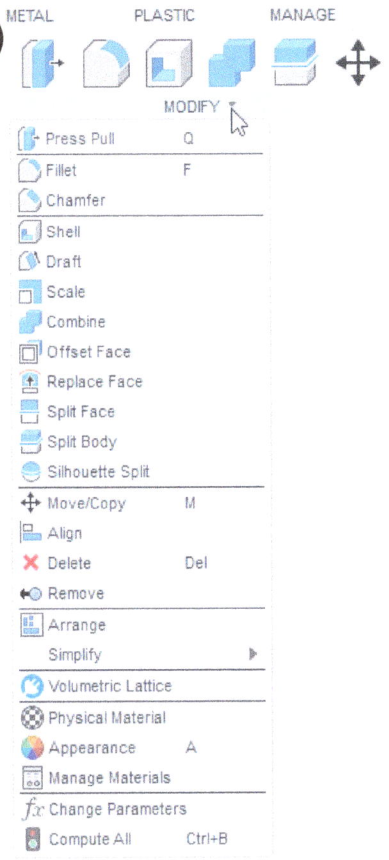

METAL
PLASTIC
MANAGE
MODIFY
Press Pull Q
Fillet F
Chamfer
Shell
Draft
Scale
Combine
Offset Face
Replace Face
Split Face
Split Body
Silhouette Split
Move/Copy M
Align
Delete Del
Remove
Arrange
Simplify
Volumetric Lattice
Physical Material
Appearance A
Manage Materials
Change Parameters
Compute All Ctrl+B

7.47

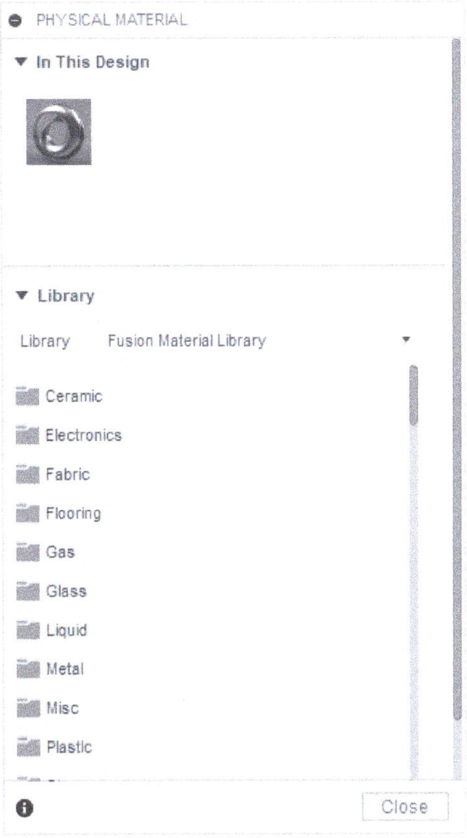

PHYSICAL MATERIAL
In This Design
Library
Library
Fusion Material Library
Ceramic
Electronics
Fabric
Flooring
Gas
Glass
Liquid
Metal
Misc
Plastic
Close

Alternatively, to invoke the **PHYSICAL MATERIAL** dialog box, select the body in the **Bodies** node of the **BROWSER** and right-click in the graphics area. A shortcut menu appears. Next, click on the **Physical Material** option in the shortcut menu. You can also right-click on the *name of the design file* in the **BROWSER** and then click on the **Physical Material** tool in the shortcut menu that appears.

By default, Steel material is added in the **In This Design** rollout of the dialog box, see Figure 7.48. As a result, Steel material is applied to the currently active design file.

7.48

PHYSICAL MATERIAL
In This Design
Steel
Steel material
Library
Library
Fusion Material Library

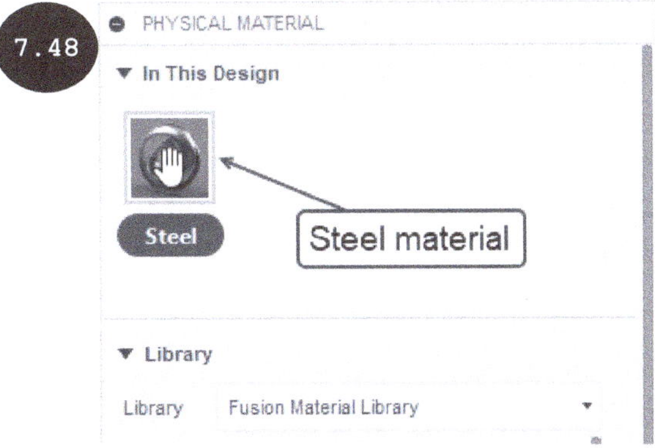

2. Ensure that **Fusion Material Library** is selected in the **Library** drop-down list of the dialog box. The different material categories such as Ceramic, Glass, Metal, Plastic, and Wood available in the material library appear in the dialog box.

3. Expand the required material category such as **Metal** or **Plastic** by clicking on its name in the dialog box. The materials available in the expanded material category appear, see Figure 7.49. This figure shows the expanded Metal category.

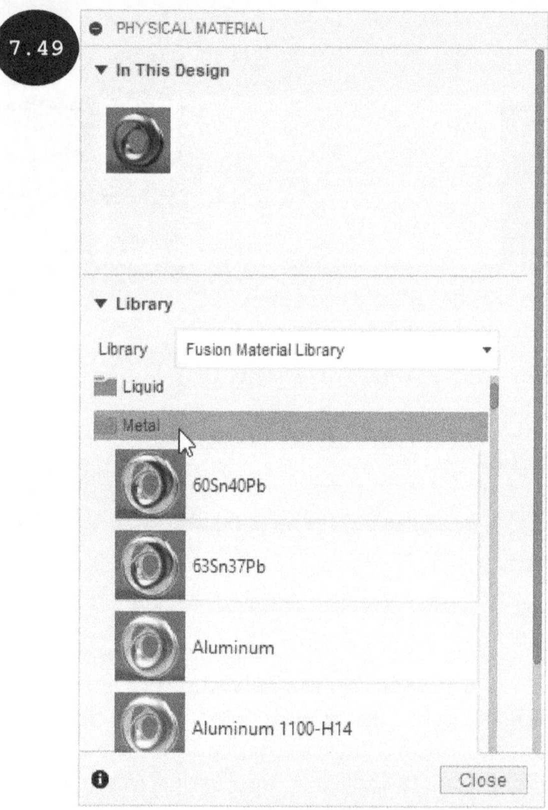

4. Drag and drop the required material from the expanded material category of the dialog box over a component or a body in the graphics area by pressing and holding the left mouse button. Material properties of the selected material are applied to the component/body. Also, a thumbnail of the applied material is added in the **In This Design** rollout of the dialog box.

5. After applying the required material, click on the **Close** button in the **PHYSICAL MATERIAL** dialog box.

Customizing Material Properties

In Autodesk Fusion, after applying the material, you can customize its material properties such as density, and elastic modulus, as required.

1. Invoke the **PHYSICAL MATERIAL** dialog box and then apply a material to the component/body, as discussed earlier.

2. Right-click on the thumbnail of the applied material in the **In This Design** rollout of the dialog box, see Figure 7.50. A shortcut menu appears.

3. Click on the **Edit** option in the shortcut menu. The respective material window appears, see Figure 7.51.

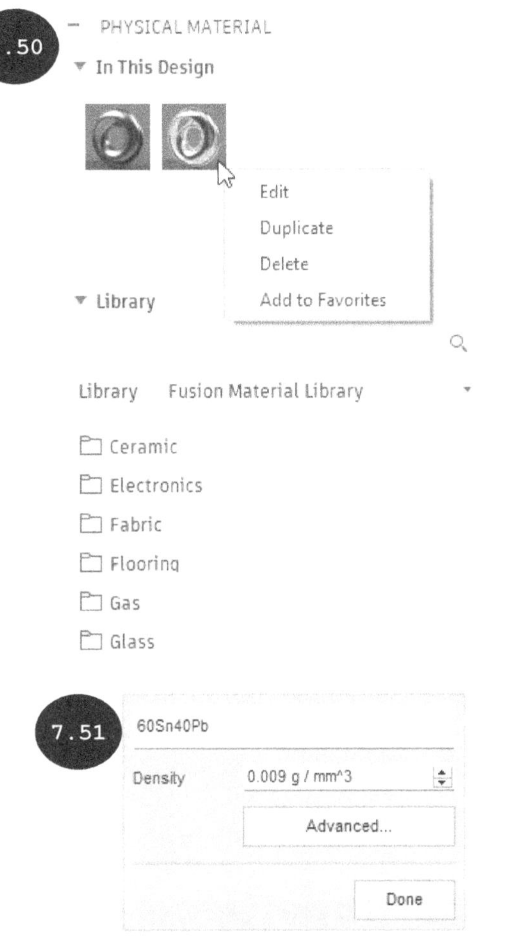

4. Click on the **Advanced** button in the material window. The **Material Editor** dialog box appears, see Figure 7.52.

   The **Material Editor** dialog box has three tabs: **Identity**, **Appearance**, and **Physical** at the top. The **Identity** tab of the dialog box displays information about the selected material. The **Appearance** tab displays options related to the appearance of the selected material. The **Physical** tab of the dialog box displays options related to the physical material properties of the material, see Figure 7.52.

5. Click on the **Physical** tab in the dialog box. The default physical material properties of the selected material appear in the dialog box, see Figure 7.52. Note that the physical properties of a material are categorized into three main sections: **Basic Thermal**, **Mechanical**, and **Strength**.

7.52

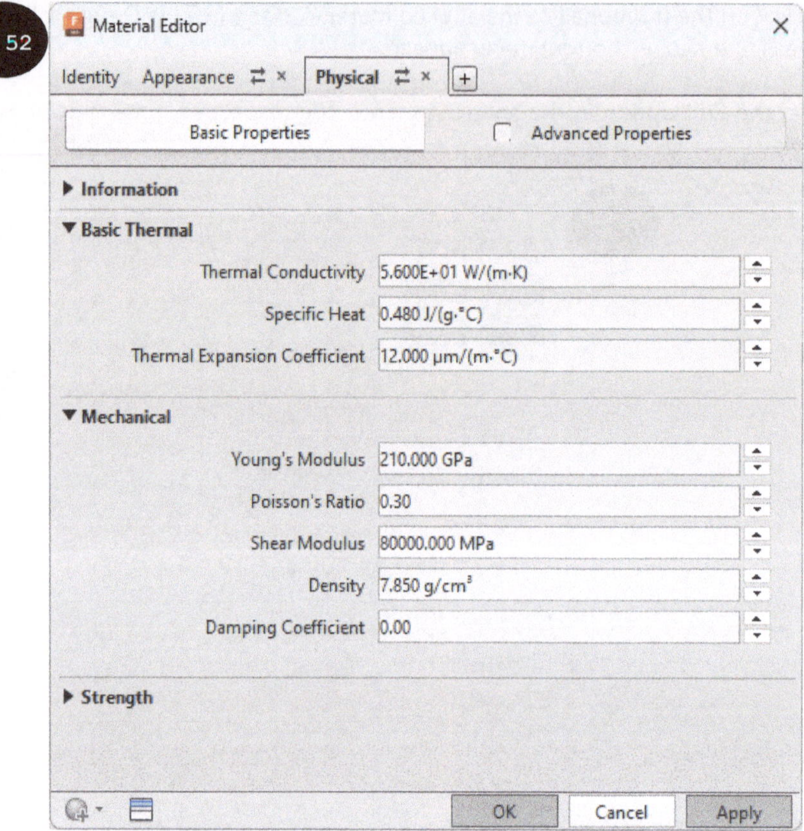

6. Edit the default physical properties of the selected material by entering new properties in the respective fields of the dialog box.

7. Click on the **Apply** button and then the **OK** button in the dialog box. The modified properties of the material are applied.

Calculating Mass Properties

After assigning the required material properties to a model, you can calculate its mass properties such as mass and volume.

To calculate the mass properties of a model, right-click on the *name of the design file* in the **BROWSER** and then click on the **Properties** tool in the shortcut menu that appears, see Figure 7.53. The **PROPERTIES** dialog box appears in the graphics area and displays the properties of the model including area, mass, volume, bounding box dimensions, center of mass, moment of inertia at center of mass, and moment of inertia at origin, see Figure 7.54. You can also copy the results to the clipboard and paste them into the required file by using the **Copy Properties to Clipboard** button of the **PROPERTIES** dialog box.

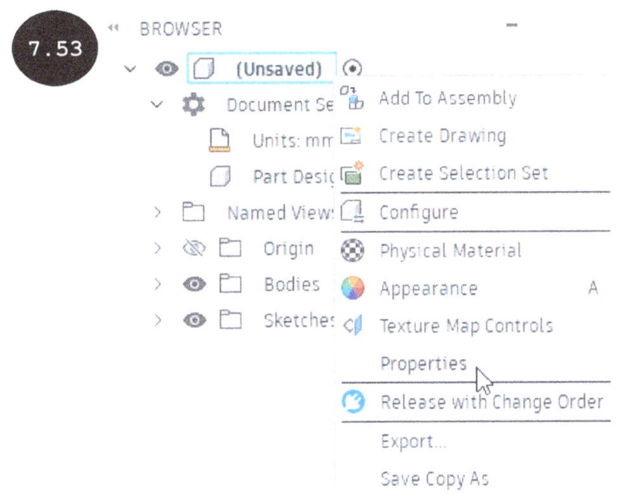
7.53
BROWSER
(Unsaved)
Document Se
Units: mm
Part Desig
Named Views
Origin
Bodies
Sketches
Add To Assembly
Create Drawing
Create Selection Set
Configure
Physical Material
Appearance
A
Texture Map Controls
Properties
Release with Change Order
Export...
Save Copy As

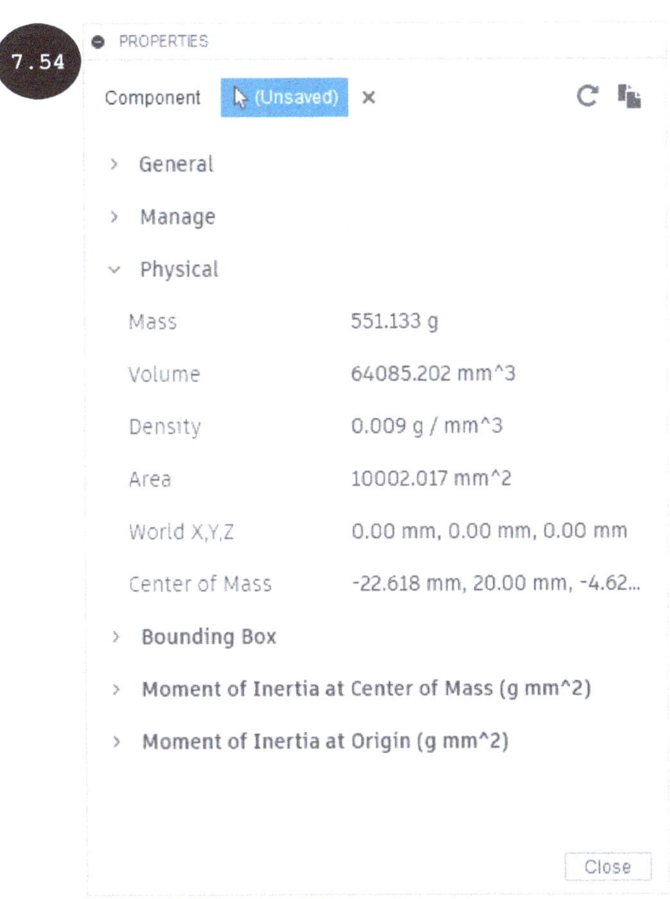
7.54
PROPERTIES
Component
(Unsaved)
General
Manage
Physical
Mass
551.133 g
Volume
64085.202 mm^3
Density
0.009 g / mm^3
Area
10002.017 mm^2
World X,Y,Z
0.00 mm, 0.00 mm, 0.00 mm
Center of Mass
-22.618 mm, 20.00 mm, -4.62...
Bounding Box
Moment of Inertia at Center of Mass (g mm^2)
Moment of Inertia at Origin (g mm^2)
Close

Note: If you invoke the **PROPERTIES** dialog box by right-clicking on the *name of the design file*, as discussed above, then the mass properties of the complete design appear. This means that, if the currently active design file has multiple components or bodies, then the **PROPERTIES** dialog box displays the overall properties of the design by combining the properties of all the components and bodies available in the active design file.

To display the properties of the individual components or bodies, right-click on the Body or Component in the **BROWSER** and then click on the **Properties** tool in the shortcut menu that appears. Note that all the bodies of a design file are listed under the **Bodies** node of the **BROWSER**.

Measuring the Distance between Objects

In Autodesk Fusion, you can measure the distance, angle, area, arc radius, and so on of one or more selected objects by using the **Measure** tool. To do this, invoke the **INSPECT** drop-down menu in the **SOLID** tab in the **Toolbar** and then click on the **Measure** tool, see Figure 7.55. Alternatively, you can press the I key. The **MEASURE** dialog box appears, see Figure 7.56. The options of the **MEASURE** dialog box are discussed next.

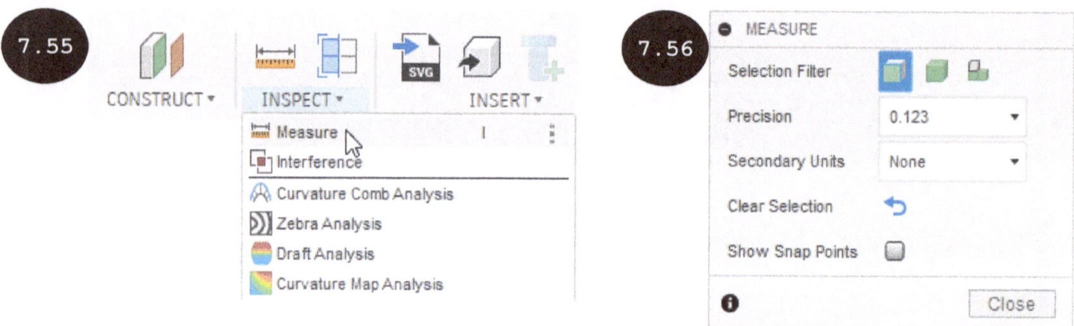

Selection Filter

By default, the **Select Face/Edge/Vertex** button is activated in the **Selection Filter** area of the dialog box. As a result, you can select a face, an edge, or a vertex of a model as the object for displaying its measurement values. You can also select multiple objects (faces, edges, or vertices) for measuring the distance between them. The **Select Body** button allows you to select one or more bodies and the **Select Component** button allows you to select one or more components to measure the distance values.

Precision

The **Precision** drop-down list in the dialog box is used for setting the precision (number of digits after the decimal point) in the measurement results.

Secondary Units

The **Secondary Units** drop-down list is used for specifying a secondary unit of measurement.

Clear Selection

The **Clear Selection** button is used for resetting or clearing the current selection set.

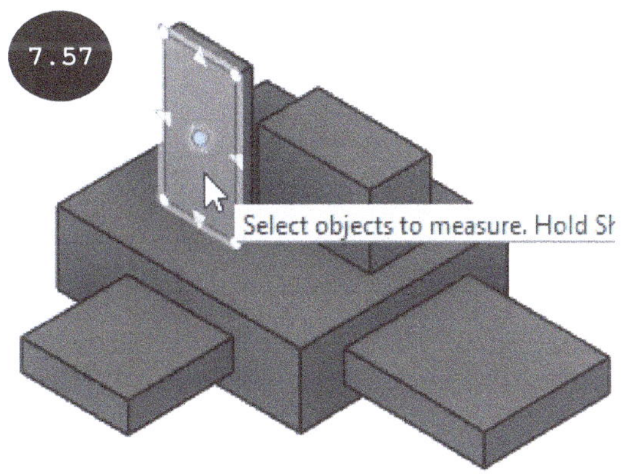

Show Snap Points

On selecting the **Show Snap Points** check box, when you hover the cursor over an object (face, edge, or vertex), the snap points of the object appear, see Figure 7.57. You can also select a snap point to display its information in the **MEASURE** dialog box. Note that this check box is available only when the **Select Face/Edge/Vertex** button is activated in the **Selection Filter** area of the dialog box.

After selecting the required selection filter and precision in the dialog box, select the object (face/edge/vertex, body, or component) in the graphics area. The respective results of the selected object appear in the **Selection 1** rollout of the dialog box, see Figure 7.58. This figure shows the measurement results of a cylindrical face.

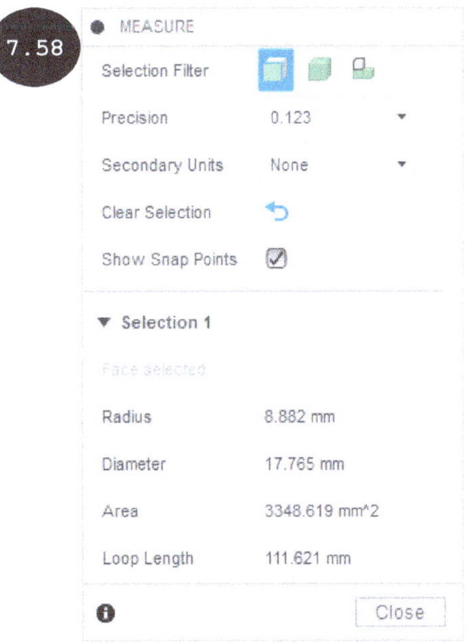

If you select two objects in the graphics area, then distance values between the selected objects appear in the **Results** rollout of the dialog box as well as in the graphics area, see Figure 7.59. Also, the measurement values of the individual objects appear in the **Selection 1** and **Selection 2** rollouts of the dialog box.

7.59

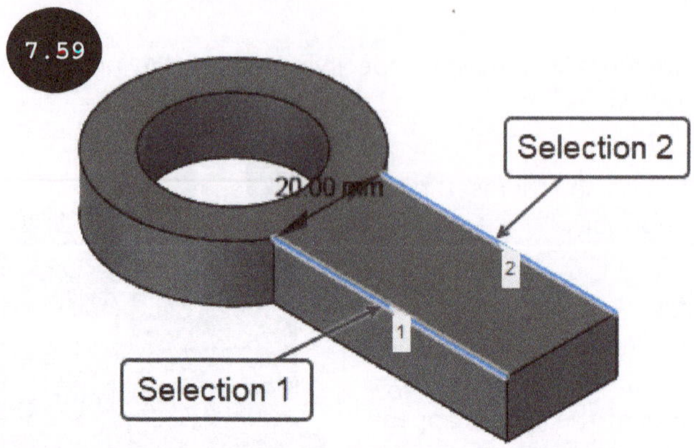

Tutorial 1

Create a model, as shown in Figure 7.60. You need to create the model by creating all its features one by one. After creating the model, assign the Stainless Steel AISI 310 material and calculate its mass properties. All dimensions are in mm.

7.60

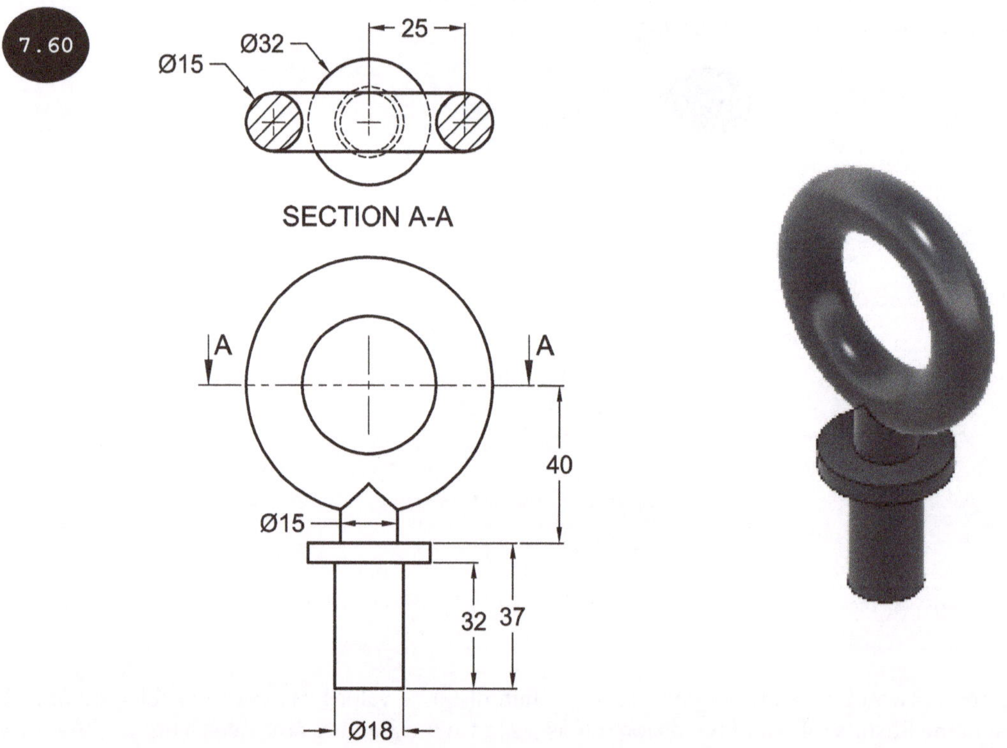

Section 1: Starting a New Part Design File

1. Click **File** > **New** in the **Application Bar** (see Figure 7.61) to display the **What do you want to design?** dialog box, see Figure 7.62.

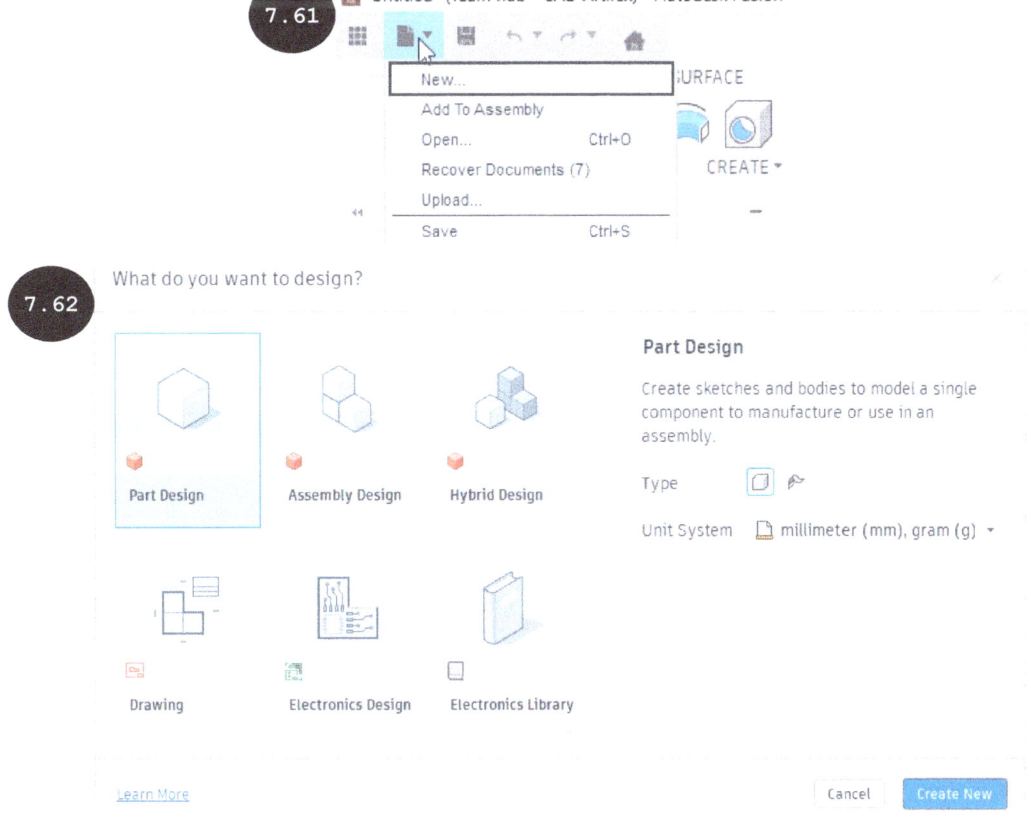

Note: If you are starting a new Autodesk Fusion session, the Part Design file opens automatically because it is set as the default design type. In this case, ensure that the **millimeter (mm), gram (g)** unit system is set for the opened Part Design file.

2. In the **What do you want to design?** dialog box, select the **Part Design** button and choose the **millimeter (mm), gram (g)** unit system from the **Unit System** drop-down list.

3. After specifying the required options, click the **Create New** button. A new Part Design file is created with the default name.

Section 2: Organizing the Data Panel

1. Invoke the **Data Panel** and then ensure that the '**Autodesk Fusion 360**' project is created in the **Data Panel**.

2. Double-click on the **Autodesk Fusion 360** project in the **Data Panel** and then create the "Chapter 07" folder by using the **New Folder** tool of the **Data Panel**.

3. Double-click on the **Chapter 07** folder in the **Data Panel** and then create the "**Tutorial**" sub-folder. Next, close the **Data Panel**.

Section 3: Creating the Base/First Feature - Revolve Feature

1. Click on the **Create Sketch** tool in the **Toolbar** and then select the Top plane as the sketching plane for creating the sketch of the base feature.

2. Create the sketch of the base feature, see Figure 7.63. Note that the base feature of the model is a revolve feature. As a result, a linear diameter dimension is applied to the sketch.

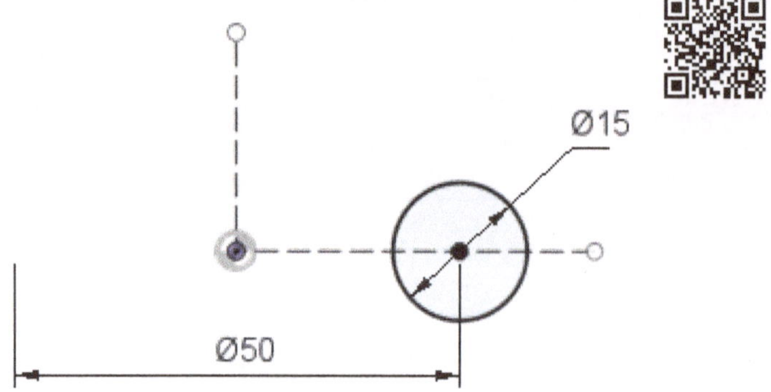

3. Click on the **SOLID** tab in the **Toolbar** to display the solid modeling tools.

4. Click on the **Revolve** tool in the **CREATE** panel of the **SOLID** tab, see Figure 7.64. The **REVOLVE** dialog box appears, see Figure 7.65. Also, the closed profile of the sketch gets selected automatically and you are prompted to select an axis of revolution.

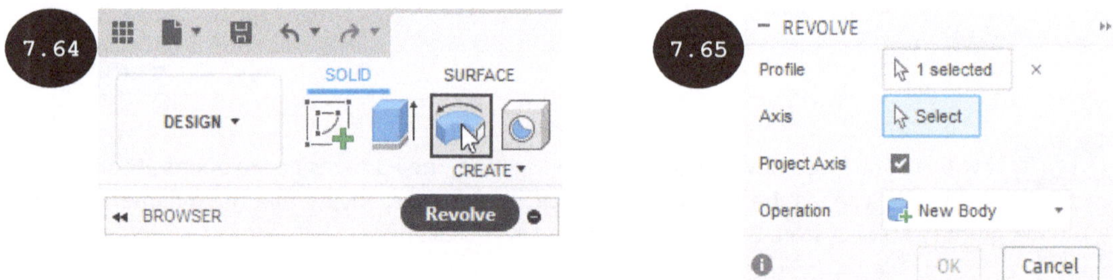

Note: In Autodesk Fusion, if a single valid profile is available in the graphics area, then it gets selected automatically on invoking the **EXTRUDE** or **REVOLVE** tool.

5. Change the orientation of the drawing view to isometric if not changed by default.

6. Select the vertical construction line of the sketch as the axis of revolution, see Figure 7.66. A preview of the revolve feature appears in the graphics area, see Figure 7.67. Also, additional options for creating a revolve feature appear in the **REVOLVE** dialog box.

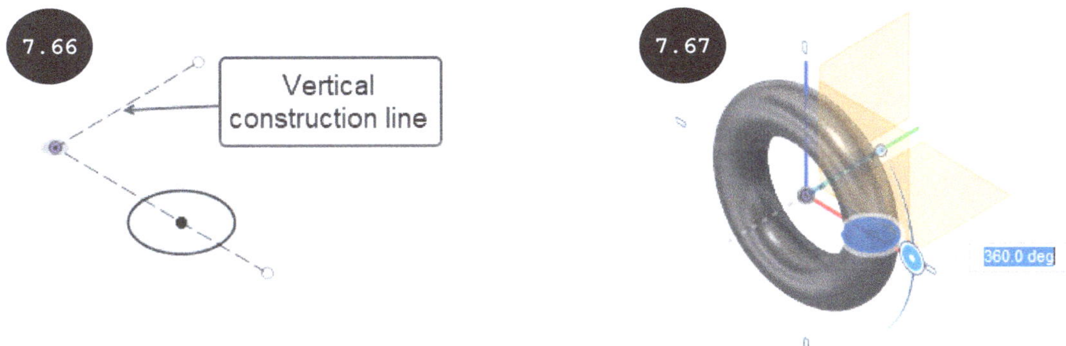

7. Ensure that the **Partial** option is selected in the **Extent Type** drop-down list and the angle of revolution is specified as 360 degrees in the **Angle** field of the dialog box. Alternatively, you can also select the **Full** option in the **Extent Type** drop-down list of the dialog box to revolve the sketch 360 degrees around the axis of revolution.

8. Click on the **OK** button in the dialog box. The revolve feature is created, see Figure 7.68.

Section 4: Creating the Second Feature - Extrude Feature

To create the second feature of the model, you first need to create a construction plane at an offset distance of 40 mm from the Top plane.

1. Invoke the **CONSTRUCT** drop-down menu in the **SOLID** tab of the **Toolbar** and then click on the **Offset Plane** tool, see Figure 7.69. The **CONSTRUCTION GEOMETRY** dialog box appears in the graphics area.

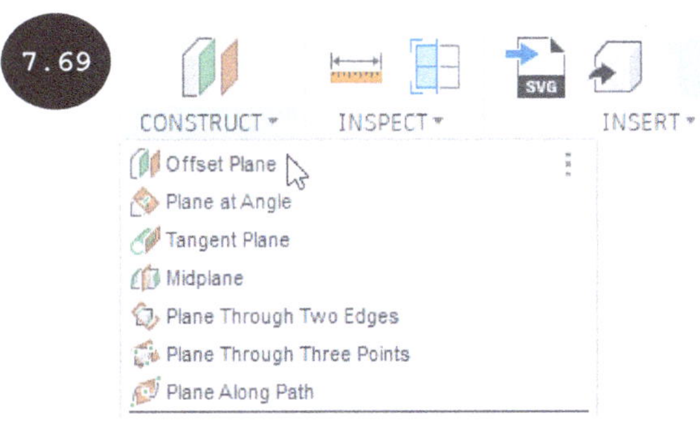

2. Click on the Top plane as a reference plane, see Figure 7.70. The Top plane gets selected, and the **Distance** field appears in the dialog box as well as in the graphics area.

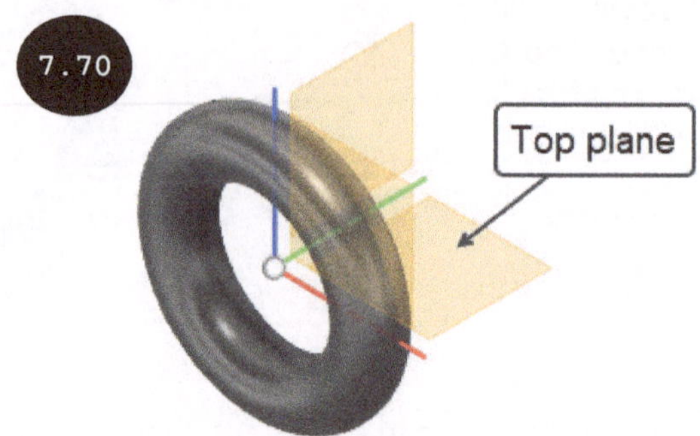

3. Enter **-40** in the **Distance** field as the offset distance for the construction plane. The preview of the plane appears downward at an offset distance of 40 mm from the Top plane, see Figure 7.71.

4. Click on the **OK** button in the dialog box. The offset construction plane is created, see Figure 7.72.

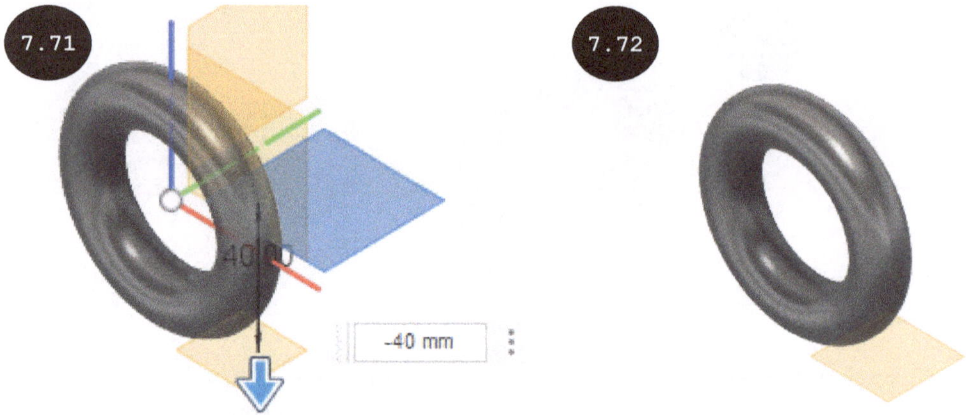

Now, you need to create the second feature of the model by selecting the newly created plane as the sketching plane.

5. Click on the **Create Sketch** tool in the **Toolbar** and then select the newly created construction plane as the sketching plane.

6. Create the sketch of the second feature (a circle of diameter 15 mm), see Figure 7.73.

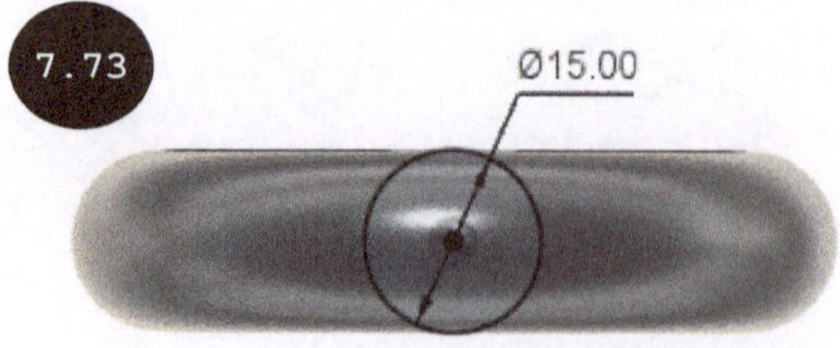

7. Click on the **SOLID** tab in the **Toolbar** to display the solid modeling tools.

8. Click on the **Extrude** tool in the **CREATE** panel of the **SOLID** tab or press the **E** key. The **EXTRUDE** dialog box appears and the closed sketch profile gets selected automatically, see Figure 7.74. Note that if the profile does not get selected automatically, then you need to select it by clicking the left mouse button.

9. Change the orientation of the model to isometric, if not changed automatically.

10. Select the **To Object** option in the **Extent Type** drop-down list of the dialog box, see Figure 7.75.

11. Select the base feature of the model as the object to terminate the extrusion. The preview of the extrude feature appears in the graphics area such that it gets terminated at its intersection with the base feature, see Figure 7.76. Also, two **Extend** areas appear in the dialog box, see Figure 7.77.

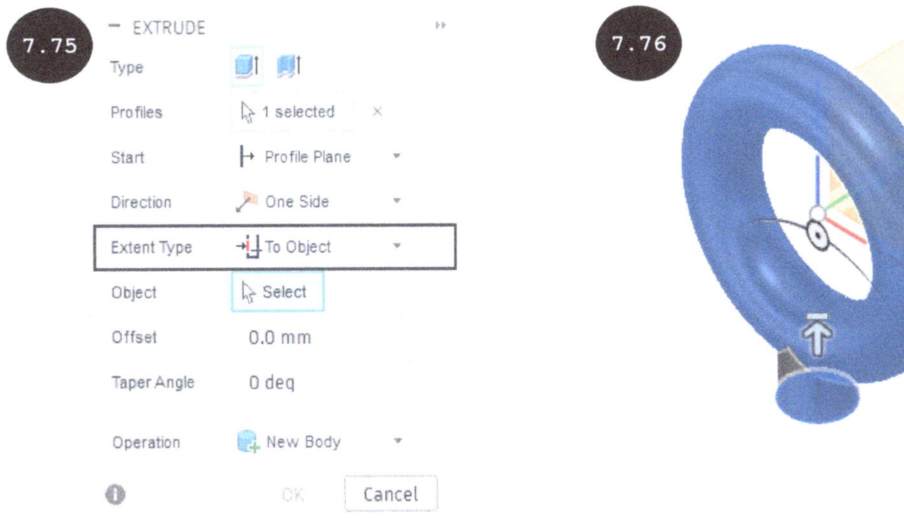

12. Ensure that the **To Object** button is activated in the first **Extend** area of the **EXTRUDE** dialog box, see Figure 7.77.

13. Ensure that the **Join** option is selected in the **Operation** drop-down list of the dialog box to merge the feature with the existing feature of the model.

14. Click on the **OK** button in the dialog box. The extrude feature is created, see Figure 7.78.

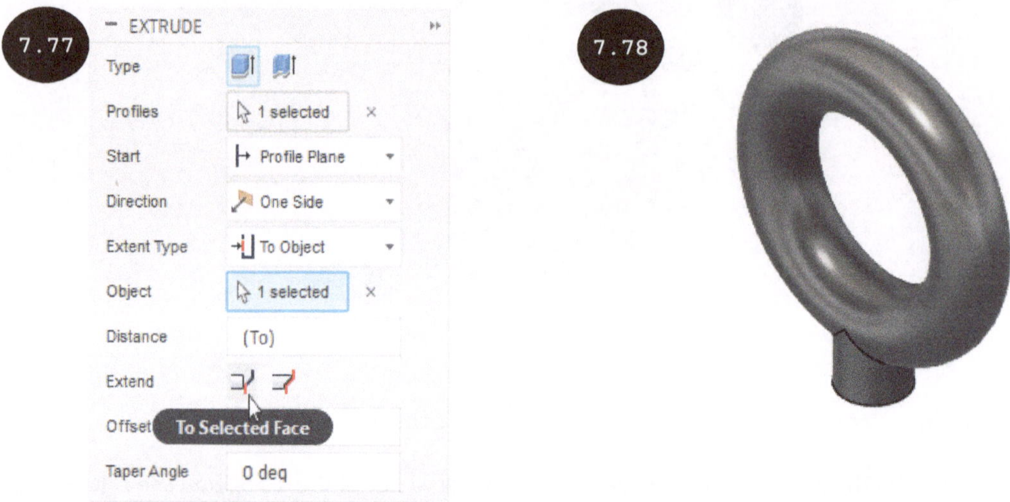

Section 5: Creating the Third Feature - Extrude Feature

1. Rotate the model such that the bottom planar face of the second feature can be viewed, see Figure 7.79.

2. Click on the **Create Sketch** tool in the **Toolbar** and then select the bottom planar face of the second feature as the sketching plane.

3. Create the sketch of the third feature (a circle of diameter 32 mm), see Figure 7.80.

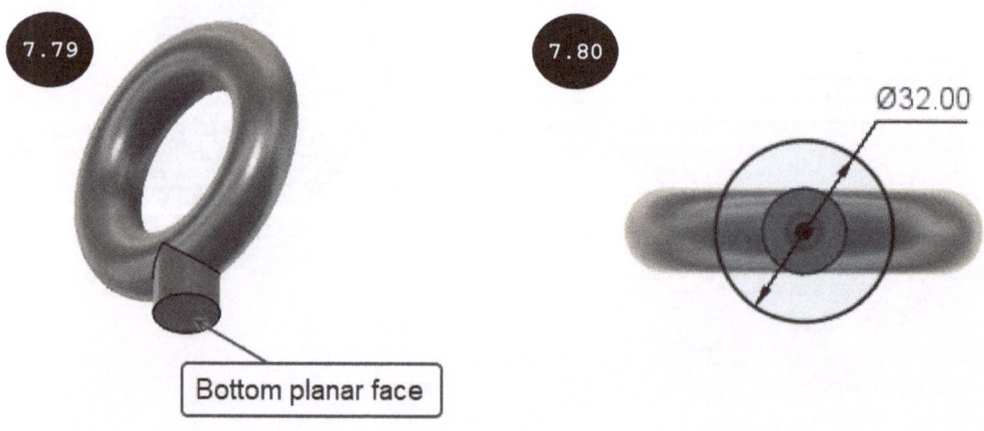

4. Click on the **SOLID** tab in the **Toolbar** to display the solid modeling tools.

5. Click on the **Extrude** tool in the **CREATE** panel of the **SOLID** tab or press the **E** key. The **EXTRUDE** dialog box appears.

6. Select the closed profiles (two profiles) created by the sketch of the third feature, see Figure 7.81.

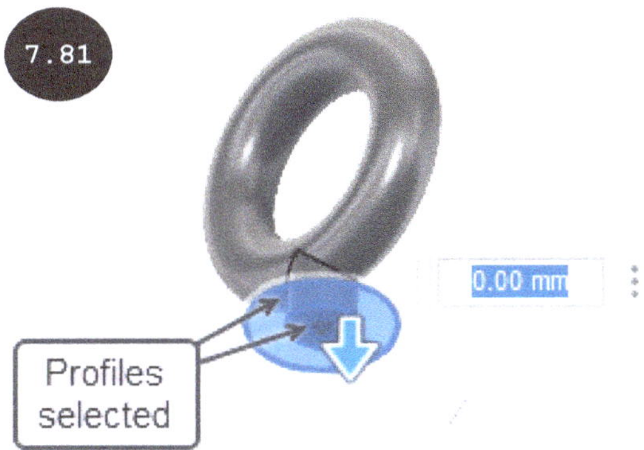

7. Change the orientation of the model to isometric and then enter **5** in the **Distance** field of the dialog box. The preview of the extrude feature appears in the graphics area, see Figure 7.82. Ensure that the direction of the extrusion is downward. You can reverse the direction of extrusion by entering a negative distance value.

8. Ensure that the **Join** option is selected in the **Operation** drop-down list of the dialog box to merge the feature with the existing features of the model.

9. Click on the **OK** button in the dialog box. The extrude feature is created, see Figure 7.83.

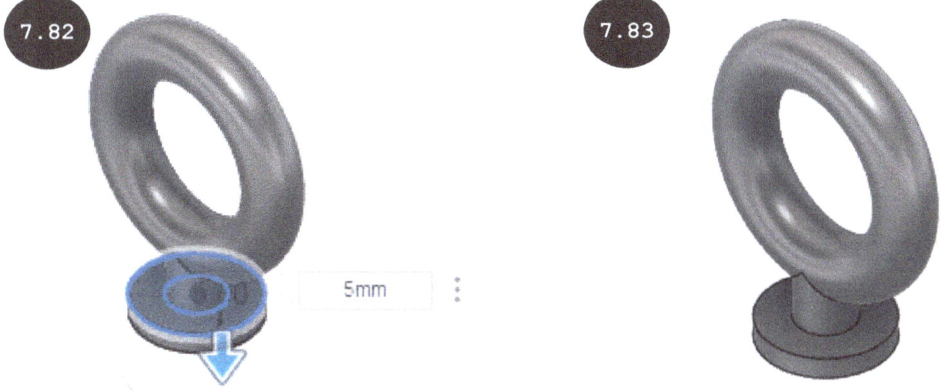

Section 6: Creating the Fourth Feature - Extrude Feature

1. Rotate the model such that the bottom planar face of the third feature can be viewed. Next, click on the **Create Sketch** tool in the **Toolbar** and then select the bottom planar face of the third feature as the sketching plane.

2. Create the sketch of the fourth feature (a circle of diameter 18 mm), see Figure 7.84.

3. Click on the **SOLID** tab in the **Toolbar** and then click on the **Extrude** tool or press the **E** key. The **EXTRUDE** dialog box appears.

4. Select the closed profile of the sketch, see Figure 7.85.

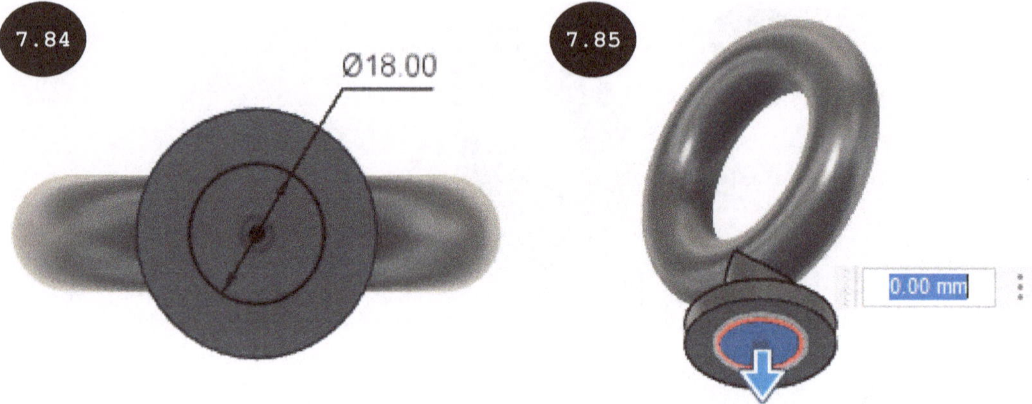

7.84 7.85

5. Change the orientation of the model to isometric and then enter **32** in the **Distance** field of the dialog box. The preview of the extrude feature appears in the graphics area. Ensure that the direction of the extrusion is downward.

6. Ensure that the **Join** option is selected in the **Operation** drop-down list of the dialog box to merge the feature with the existing features of the model.

7. Click on the **OK** button in the dialog box. The extrude feature is created, see Figure 7.86.

7.86

Section 7: Assigning the Material

As mentioned in the tutorial description, you need to apply the Stainless Steel AISI 310 material to the model.

1. Select the model in the **BROWSER** and right-click to display a shortcut menu, see Figure 7.87. Next, click on the **Physical Material** tool. The **PHYSICAL MATERIAL** dialog box appears.

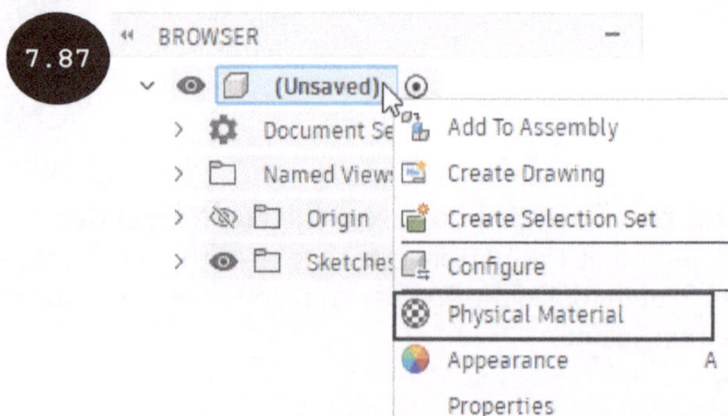

7.87

2. Ensure that the **Fusion Material Library** is selected in the **Library** drop-down list of the dialog box, see Figure 7.88.

3. Click on the **Metal** material category in the dialog box. The **Metal** material category gets expanded and all the materials available in this category appear.

4. Scroll down through the list of available materials in the Metal material category and then pause the cursor over the **Stainless Steel AISI 310** material, see Figure 7.88.

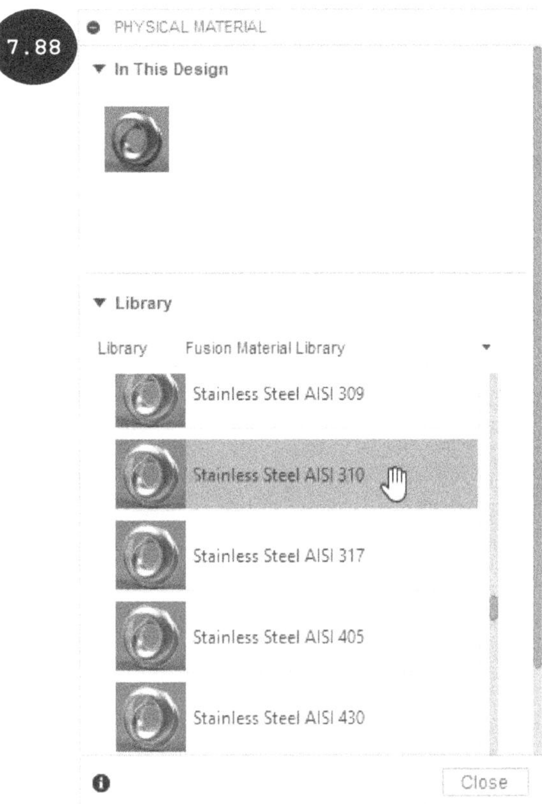

5. Drag and drop the **Stainless Steel AISI 310** material over the model in the graphics area by pressing and holding the left mouse button. The Stainless Steel AISI 310 material is applied to the model. Also, the thumbnail of the applied material is listed in the **In This Design** rollout of the dialog box. Next, close the dialog box by clicking on the **Close** button.

Section 8: Calculating Mass Properties

Now, you need to review the mass properties of the model.

1. Right-click on the *name of the design file* in the **BROWSER** and then click on the **Properties** tool in the shortcut menu that appears, see Figure 7.89. The **PROPERTIES** dialog box appears in the graphics area, which displays the properties of the model including area, mass, volume, bounding box dimensions, center of mass, moment of inertia at center of mass, and moment of inertia at origin, see Figure 7.90.

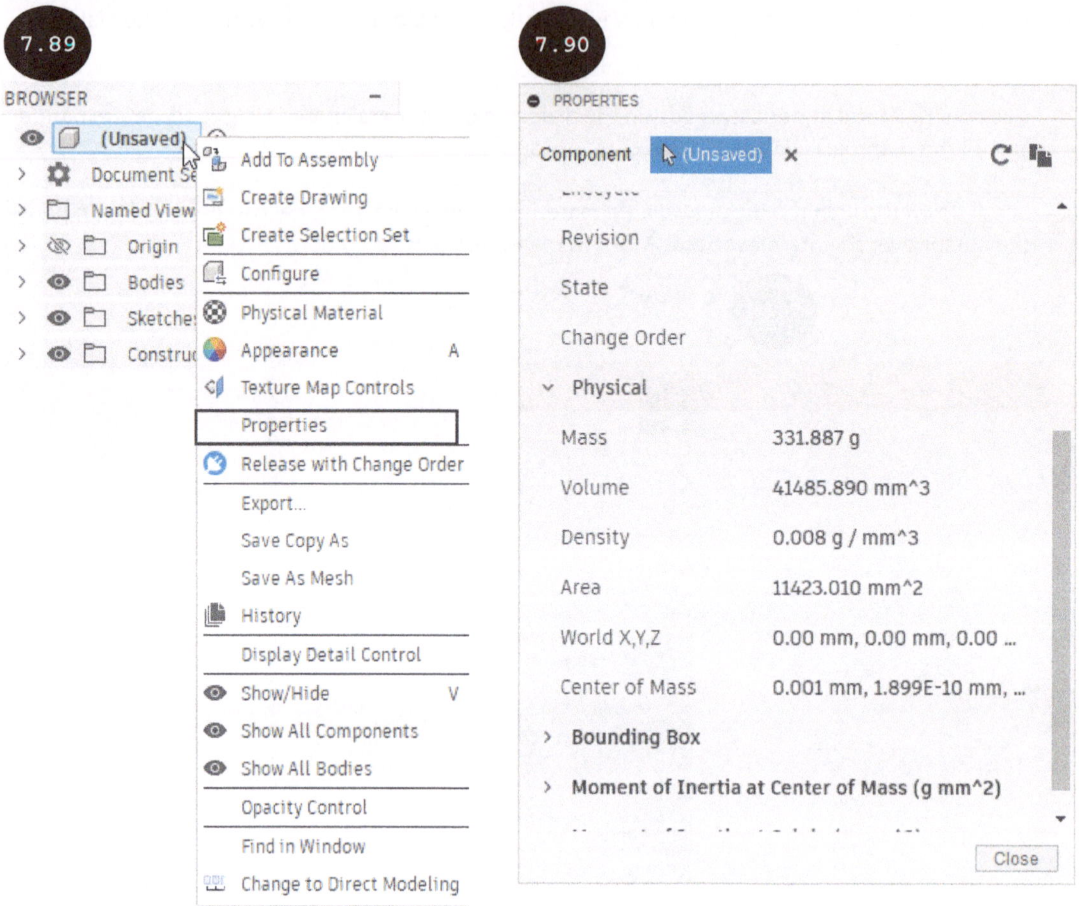

2. After reviewing the mass properties, exit the **PROPERTIES** dialog box.

Section 9: Saving the Model

1. Click on the **Save** tool in the **Application Bar**. The **Save** dialog box appears.

2. Enter **Tutorial 01** in the **Name** field of the dialog box.

3. Ensure that the location *Autodesk Fusion 360 > Chapter 07 > Tutorial* is specified in the **Location** field of the dialog box to save the file of this tutorial. To specify the location, you need to expand the **Save** dialog box by clicking on the down arrow next to the **Location** field of the dialog box.

4. Click on the **Save** button in the dialog box. The model is saved with the name Tutorial 01 in the specified location (*Autodesk Fusion 360 > Chapter 07 > Tutorial 01*).

Tutorial 2

Create a model, as shown in Figure 7.91. After creating the model, assign the Alloy Steel material and calculate the mass properties of the model. All dimensions are in mm.

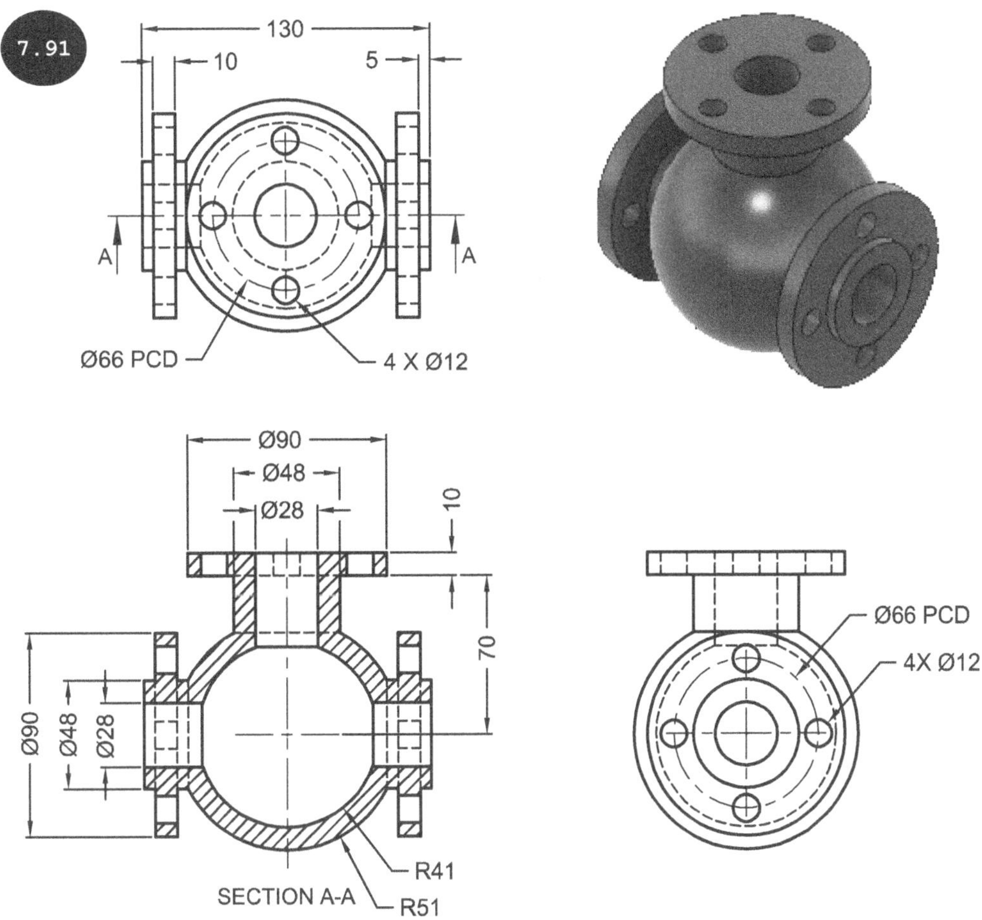

Section 1: Creating the Base/First Feature - Revolve Feature

1. Open a Part Design file with the **millimeter (mm), gram (g)** unit system.

   Now, you can create the base feature of the model.

2. Click on the **Create Sketch** tool in the **Toolbar** and then select the Front plane as the sketching plane for creating the sketch of the base feature.

3. Create the sketch of the base feature, see Figure 7.92.

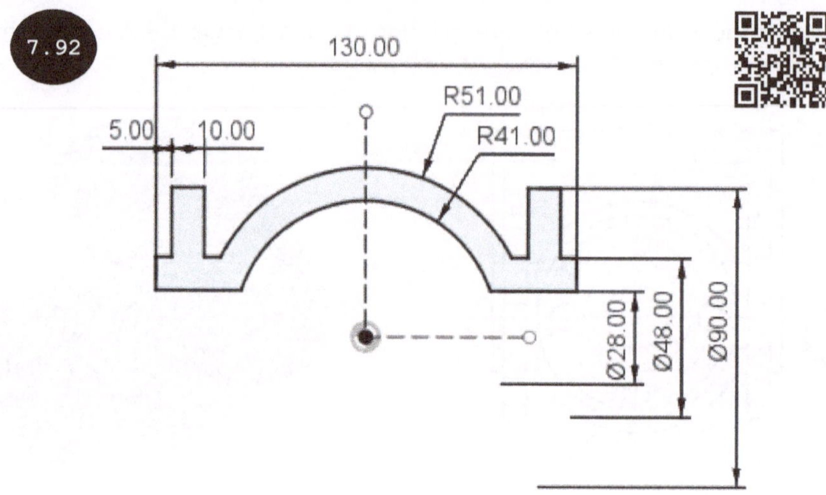

Tip: The sketch of the revolve feature shown in Figure 7.92 is symmetric about the vertical construction line. Therefore, you need to apply symmetric constraints to the sketch entities relative to the vertical construction line. Additionally, apply equal constraints between entities of equal length and collinear constraints to aligned entities in the sketch. Alternatively, you can create the line entities on one side of the vertical construction line and mirror them to create the entities on the opposite side.

4. Click on the **SOLID** tab in the **Toolbar** to display the solid modeling tools.

5. Click on the **Revolve** tool in the **CREATE** panel of the **SOLID** tab, see Figure 7.93. The **REVOLVE** dialog box appears, see Figure 7.94. Also, the closed profile of the sketch gets selected automatically and you are prompted to select an axis of revolution.

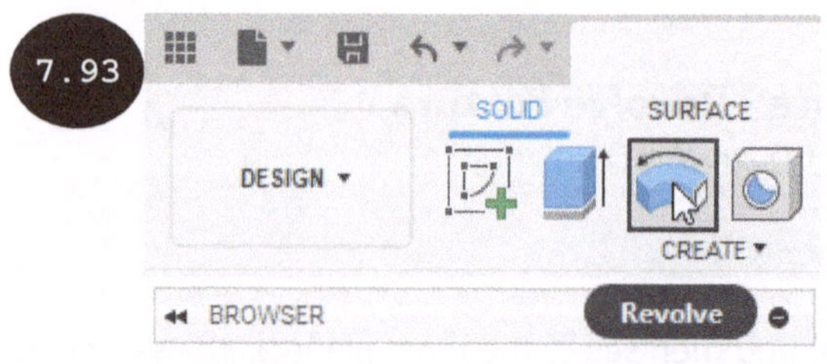

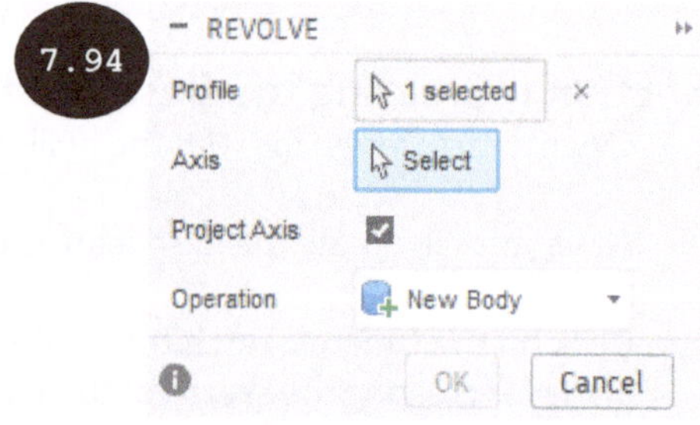

Note: In Autodesk Fusion, if a single valid profile is available in the graphics area, then it gets selected automatically on invoking the **EXTRUDE** or **REVOLVE** tool.

6. Change the orientation of the view to isometric, see Figure 7.95, if not changed by default.

7. Select the horizontal construction line of the sketch as the axis of revolution, see Figure 7.95. A preview of the revolved feature appears in the graphics area, see Figure 7.96.

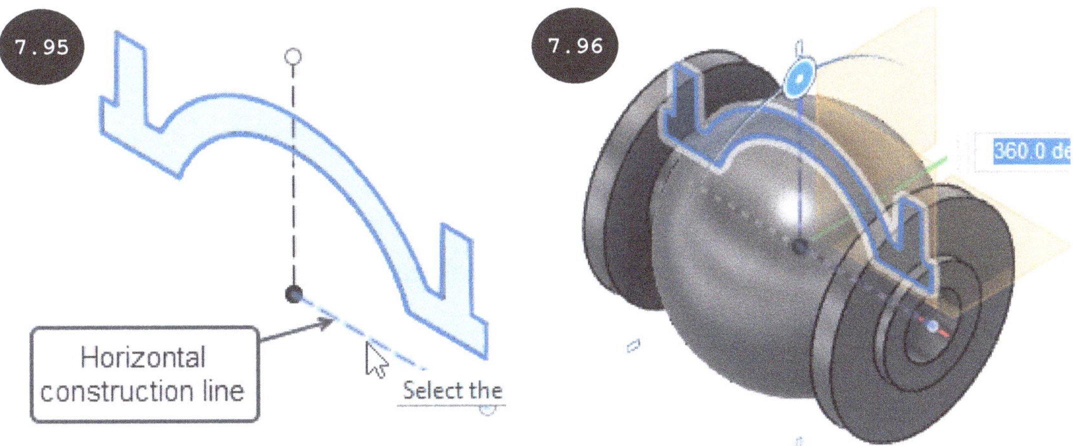

8. Ensure that the **Partial** option is selected in the **Extent Type** drop-down list and the angle of revolution is specified as 360 degrees in the **Angle** field of the dialog box. You can also select the **Full** option in the **Extent Type** drop-down list of the dialog box to revolve the sketch 360 degrees around the axis of revolution.

9. Click on the **OK** button in the dialog box. The base revolve feature is created, see Figure 7.97.

Section 2: Creating the Second Feature - Extrude Feature

To create the second feature of the model, you first need to create a construction plane at an offset distance of 70 mm from the Top plane.

1. Click on the **Offset Plane** tool in the **CONSTRUCT** panel of the **SOLID** tab, see Figure 7.98. The **CONSTRUCTION GEOMETRY** dialog box appears in the graphics area.

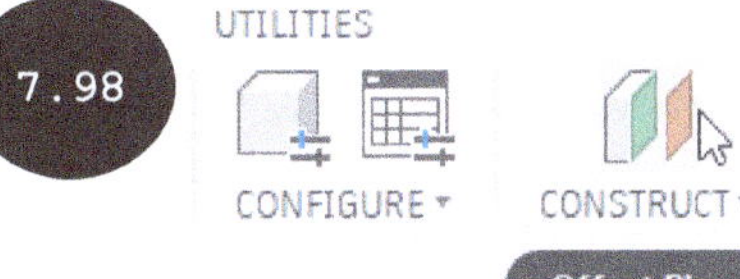

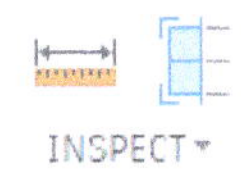

2. Click on the Top plane as a reference plane, see Figure 7.99. The Top plane gets selected, and the **Distance** field appears in the dialog box as well as in the graphics area.

3. Enter **70** in the **Distance** field. The preview of the plane appears at an offset distance of 70 mm from the Top plane in the upward direction, see Figure 7.100.

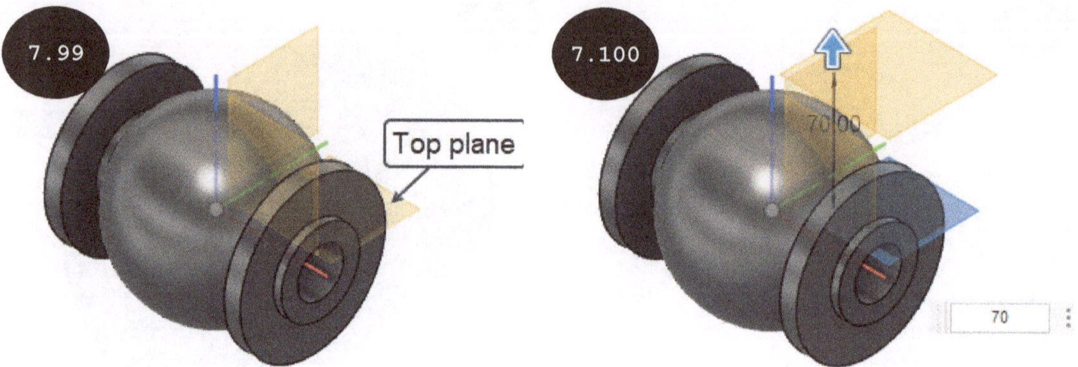

4. Click on the **OK** button in the dialog box. The offset plane is created, see Figure 7.101. Note that you can change the size of the plane by dragging its corners in the graphics area.

   Now, you need to create the second feature of the model by selecting the newly created plane as the sketching plane.

5. Click on the **Create Sketch** tool in the **Toolbar** and then select the newly created construction plane as the sketching plane.

6. Create the sketch of the second feature (a circle of diameter 48 mm), see Figure 7.102.

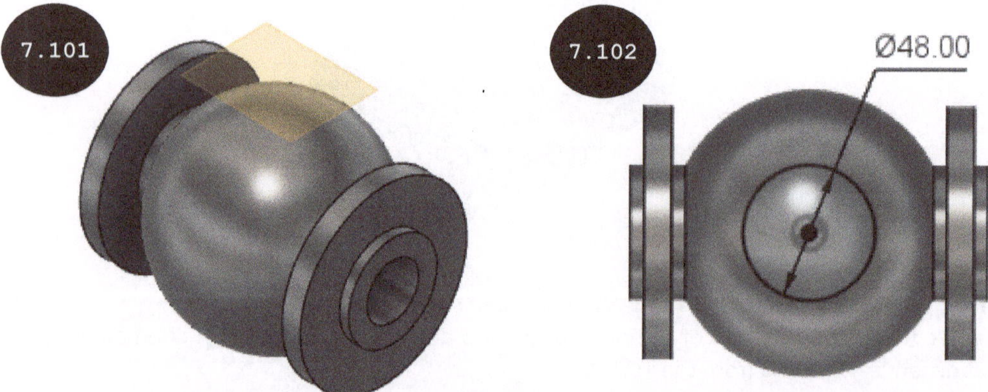

7. Click on the **SOLID** tab in the **Toolbar** to display the solid modeling tools.

8. Click on the **Extrude** tool in the **CREATE** panel of the **SOLID** tab or press the **E** key. The **EXTRUDE** dialog box appears with the closed sketch profile selected automatically. Note that if the profile does not get selected automatically, then you need to select it by clicking the left mouse button.

9. Change the orientation of the model to isometric, if not changed automatically.

10. Select the **To Object** option in the **Extent Type** drop-down list of the dialog box.

11. Select the base feature of the model as the object to terminate the extrusion. The preview of the extrude feature appears in the graphics area such that it gets terminated at its intersection with the base feature, see Figure 7.103. Also, two **Extend** areas appear in the dialog box, see Figure 7.104.

12. Ensure that the **To Body** button is activated in the first **Extend** area of the **EXTRUDE** dialog box to terminate the extrusion of the feature at its nearest intersection.

13. Ensure that the **Join** option is selected in the **Operation** drop-down list of the dialog box to merge the feature with the existing feature of the model.

14. Click on the **OK** button in the dialog box. The extrude feature is created, see Figure 7.105.

Section 3: Creating the Third Feature - Extrude Feature

1. Click on the **Create Sketch** tool in the **Toolbar** and then select the top planar face of the second feature as the sketching plane.

2. Create the sketch of the third feature (a circle of diameter 90 mm), see Figure 7.106.

3. Click on the **SOLID** tab in the **Toolbar** to display the solid modeling tools.

4. Click on the **Extrude** tool in the **CREATE** panel of the **SOLID** tab or press the **E** key. The **EXTRUDE** dialog box appears.

5. Select the closed profiles (two profiles) created by the sketch of the third feature, see Figure 7.107.

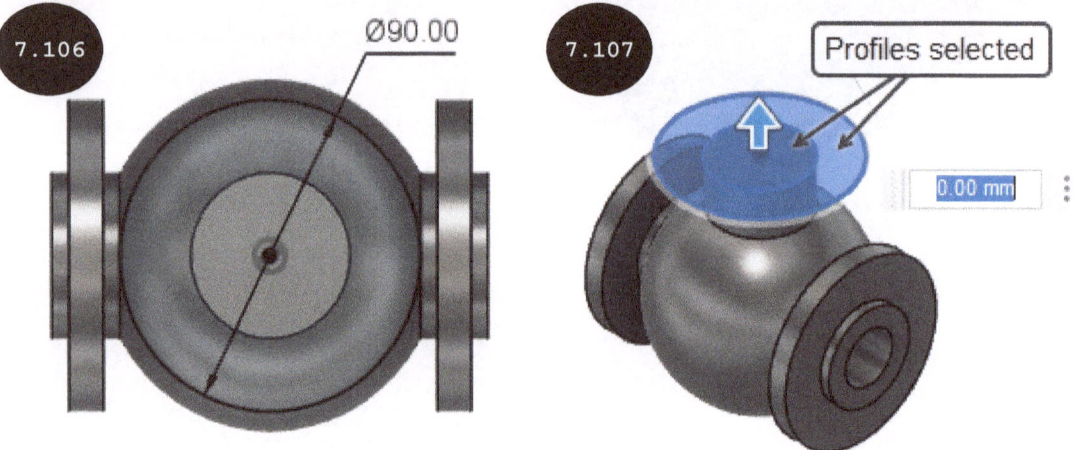

6. Enter **10** in the **Distance** field of the dialog box. The preview of the extrude feature appears in the graphics area, see Figure 7.108. Make sure that the direction of the extrusion is upward. You can reverse the direction of extrusion by entering a negative distance value.

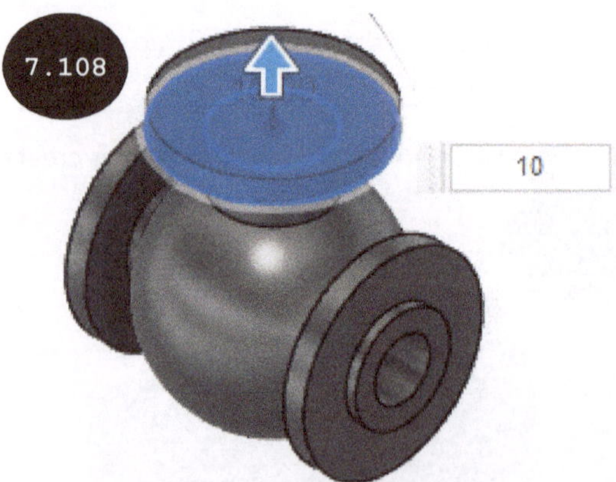

7. Ensure that the **Join** option is selected in the **Operation** drop-down list of the dialog box to merge the feature with the existing features of the model.

8. Click on the **OK** button in the dialog box. The extrude feature is created, see Figure 7.109.

Section 4: Creating the Fourth Feature - Extrude Cut Feature

1. Click on the **Create Sketch** tool in the **Toolbar** and then select the top planar face of the third feature as the sketching plane.

2. Create the sketch of the fourth feature (a circle of diameter 28 mm), see Figure 7.110.

3. Click on the **SOLID** tab in the **Toolbar** to display the solid modeling tools.

4. Click on the **Extrude** tool in the **CREATE** panel of the **SOLID** tab or press the **E** key. The **EXTRUDE** dialog box appears.

5. Select the closed profile of the sketch, see Figure 7.111.

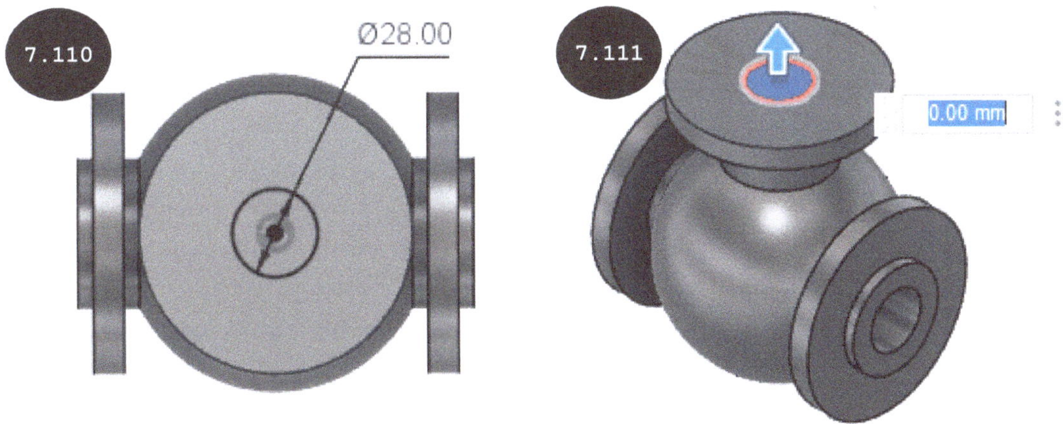

6. Select the **To Object** option in the **Extent Type** drop-down list of the dialog box.

7. Rotate the model such that the inner circular face of the base revolve feature can be viewed, see Figure 7.112.

8. Click on the inner circular face of the base feature as the face to terminate the creation of the extrude cut feature, see Figure 7.112. The preview of the extrude cut feature appears in the graphics area such that it gets terminated at its nearest intersection with the inner circular face, see Figure 7.113.

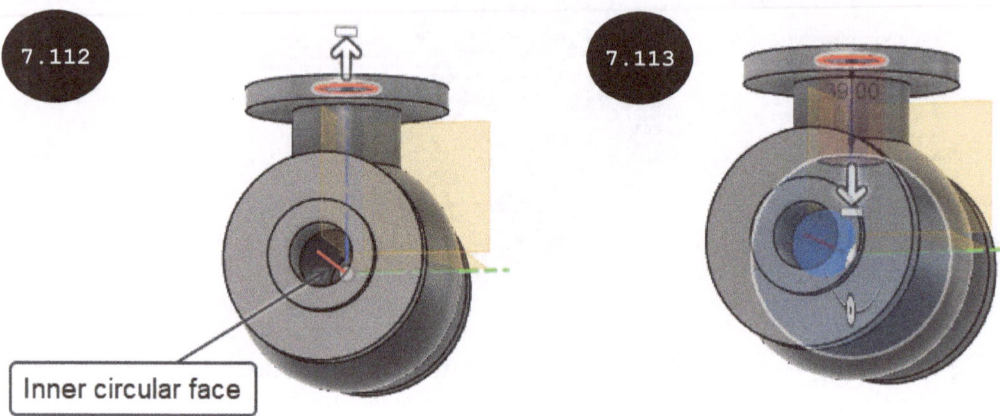

9. Ensure that the **To Body** button is activated in the first **Extend** area of the **EXTRUDE** dialog box to terminate the extrusion of the feature at its nearest intersection.

10. Ensure that the **Cut** option is selected in the **Operation** drop-down list of the dialog box to create the cut feature by removing the material.

11. Click on the **OK** button in the dialog box. The extrude cut feature is created, see Figure 7.114.

Section 5: Creating the Fifth Feature - Extrude Cut Feature

1. Click on the **Create Sketch** tool in the **Toolbar** and then select the right planar face of the model as the sketching plane, see Figure 7.115.

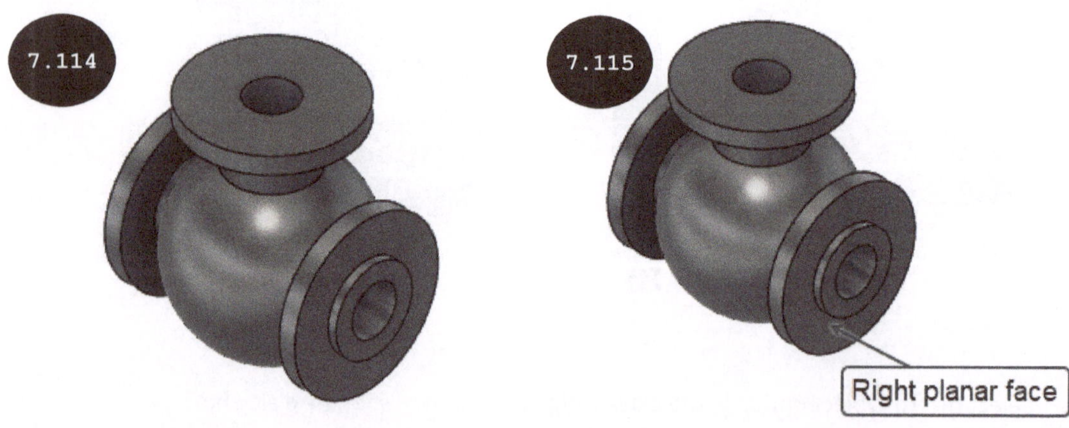

2. Create a circle of diameter 12 mm and apply the required dimensions, see Figure 7.116. Note that you need to apply a vertical constraint between the origin and the center point of the circle to make it fully defined.

3. Invoke the **Circular Pattern** tool in the **CREATE** drop-down menu of the **SKETCH** contextual tab and then create a circular pattern of the circle for creating the remaining circles of the sketch (total 4 circles), see Figure 7.117. Ensure that the center point of the circular pattern is at the origin. Next, exit the tool.

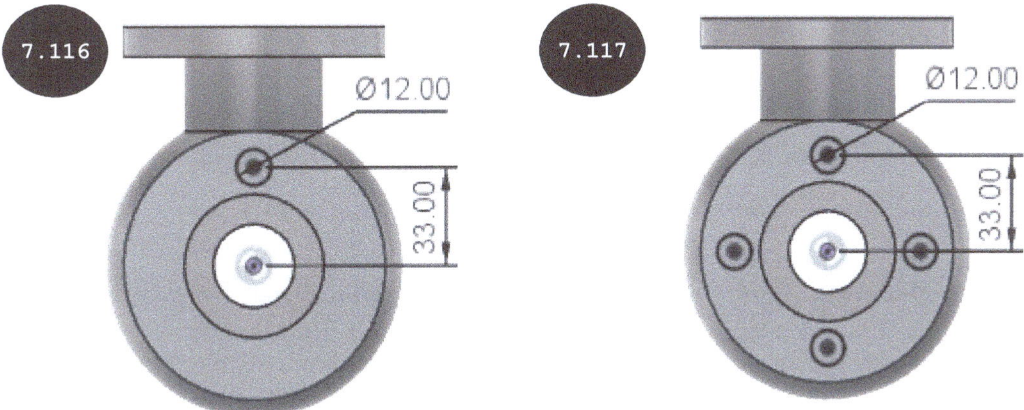

4. Click on the **SOLID** tab in the **Toolbar** to display the solid modeling tools.

5. Click on the **Extrude** tool in the **CREATE** panel of the **SOLID** tab or press the **E** key. The **EXTRUDE** dialog box appears.

6. Select the closed profiles of all the circles of the sketch one by one.

7. Ensure that the **Distance** option is selected in the **Extent Type** drop-down list of the dialog box.

8. Enter **-10** in the **Distance** field of the dialog box. A preview of the feature appears in the graphics area, see Figure 7.118.

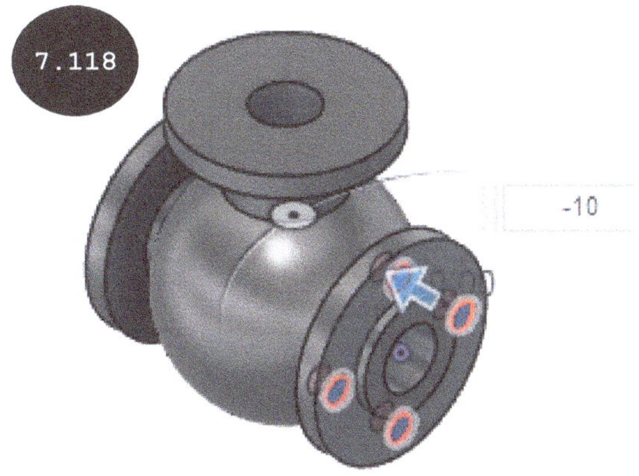

9. Ensure that the **Cut** option is selected in the **Operation** drop-down list of the dialog box to create the cut feature by removing the material.

10. Click on the **OK** button in the dialog box. The extrude cut feature is created, see Figure 7.119.

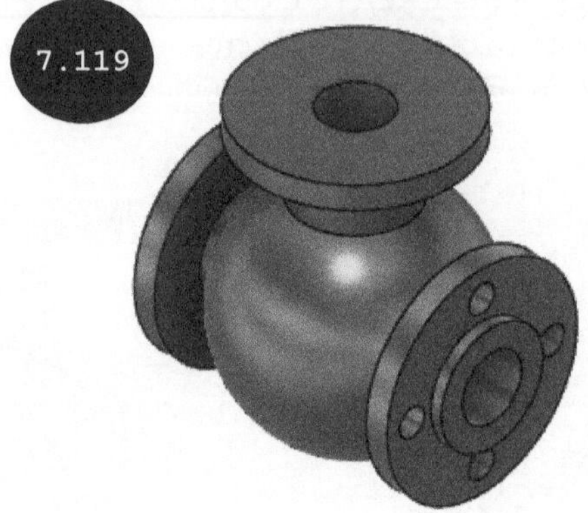

Section 6: Creating the Sixth Feature - Extrude Cut Feature

1. Similar to creating the extrude cut feature on the right planar face of the model, create the extrude cut feature on the left planar face of the model, see Figure 7.120. You can also mirror the extrude cut feature by selecting the Right plane as the mirroring plane to create the extrude cut feature on the left planar face. You will learn about mirroring features in later chapters.

Section 7: Creating the Seventh Feature - Extrude Cut Feature

1. Similar to creating the extrude cut feature on the right and left planar faces of the model, create the extrude cut feature on the top planar face of the model, see Figure 7.121.

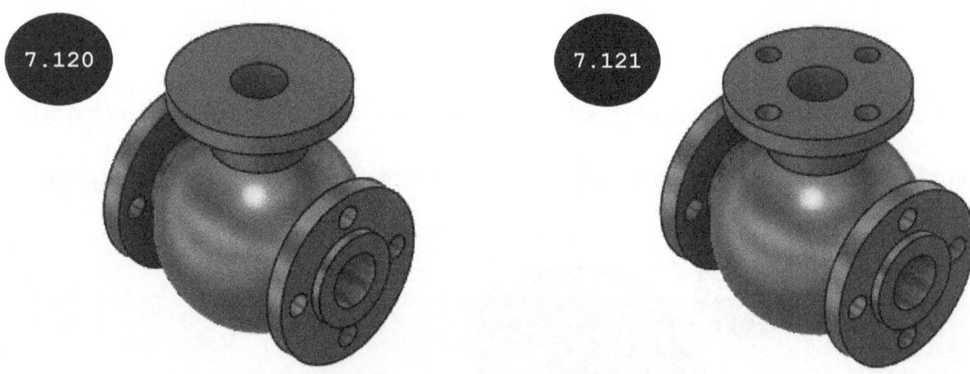

Section 8: Assigning the Material

1. Right-click on the *name of the design file* in the **BROWSER** and then click on the **Physical Material** tool in the shortcut menu that appears. The **PHYSICAL MATERIAL** dialog box appears.

2. Ensure that the **Fusion Material Library** is selected in the **Library** drop-down list of the dialog box.

3. Click on the **Metal** material category in the dialog box. The **Metal** material category gets expanded and all the materials available in this category appear.

4. Scroll down to the list of available materials in the Metal material category and then pause the cursor over the **Steel, Alloy** material, see Figure 7.122.

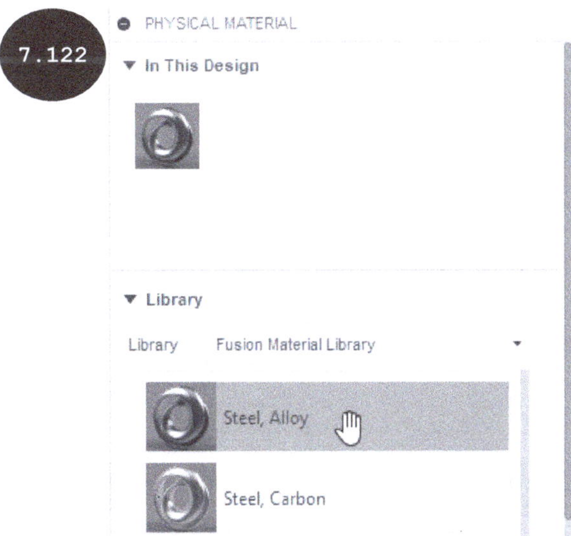

5. Drag and drop the **Steel, Alloy** material over the model in the graphics area by pressing and holding the left mouse button. The material is applied to the model. Next, close the dialog box.

Section 9: Calculating Mass Properties

Now, you need to review the mass properties of the model.

1. Right-click on the *name of the design file* in the **BROWSER** and then click on the **Properties** tool in the shortcut menu that appears, see Figure 7.123. The **PROPERTIES** dialog box appears in the graphics area, which displays the properties of the model including area, mass, volume, bounding box dimensions, center of mass, moment of inertia at center of mass, and moment of inertia at origin, see Figure 7.124.

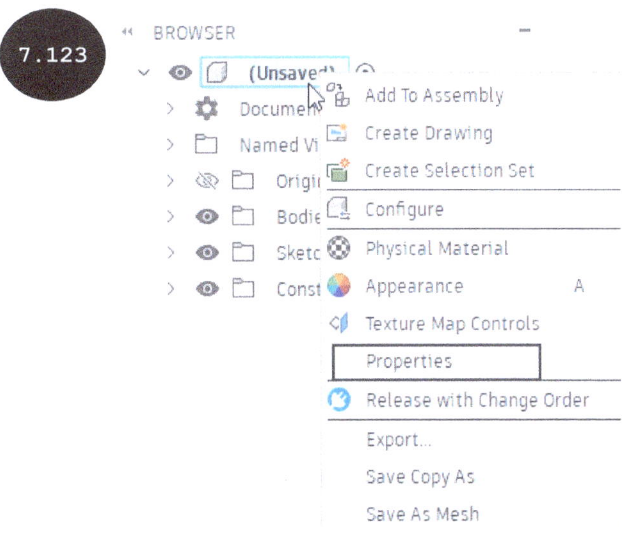

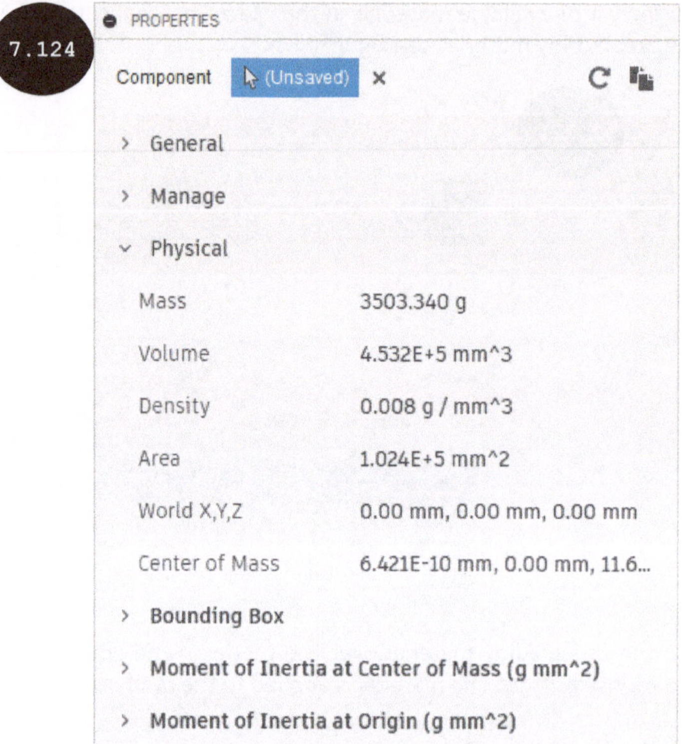

7.124

2. After reviewing the mass properties, exit the **PROPERTIES** dialog box.

Section 10: Saving the Model

1. Click on the **Save** tool in the **Application Bar**. The **Save** dialog box appears.

2. Enter **Tutorial 02** in the **Name** field of the dialog box.

3. Ensure the location ***Autodesk Fusion 360 > Chapter 07 > Tutorial*** is specified in the **Location** field of the dialog box to save the file of this tutorial. To specify the location, you need to expand the **Save** dialog box by clicking on the down arrow next to the **Location** field of the dialog box. Note that you need to create these folders in the **Data Panel**, if not created earlier.

4. Click on the **Save** button in the dialog box. The model is saved with the name Tutorial 02 in the specified location (***Autodesk Fusion 360 > Chapter 07 > Tutorial 02***).

Hands-on Test Drive 1

Create a model, as shown in Figure 7.125. After creating the model, apply the Cast Steel material to the model and calculate its mass properties. All dimensions are in mm.

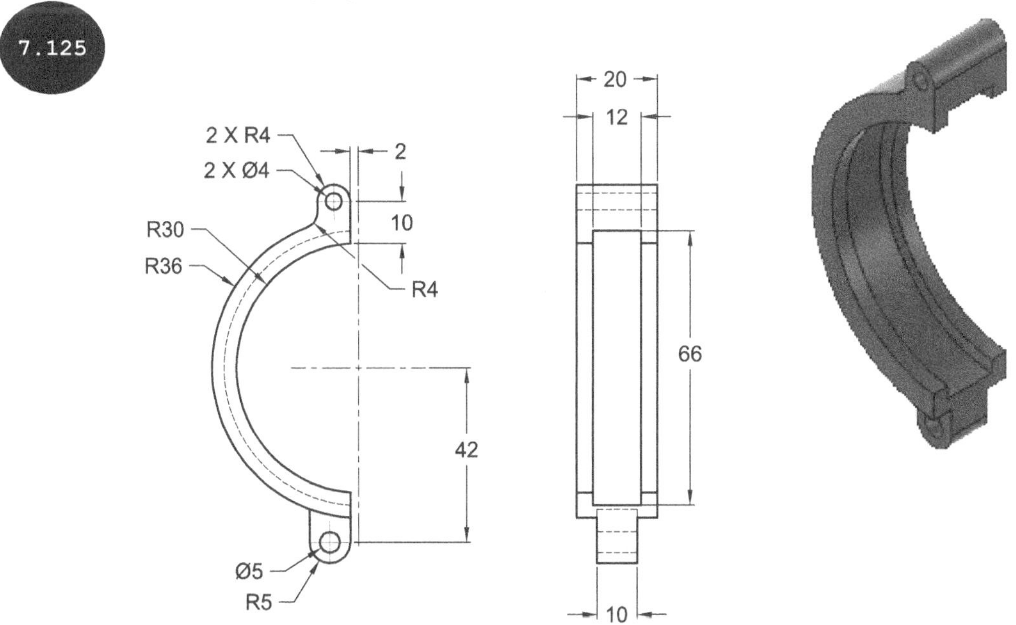

Hands-on Test Drive 2

Create a model, as shown in Figure 7.126. After creating the model, apply the Alloy Steel material to the model and calculate its mass properties. All dimensions are in mm.

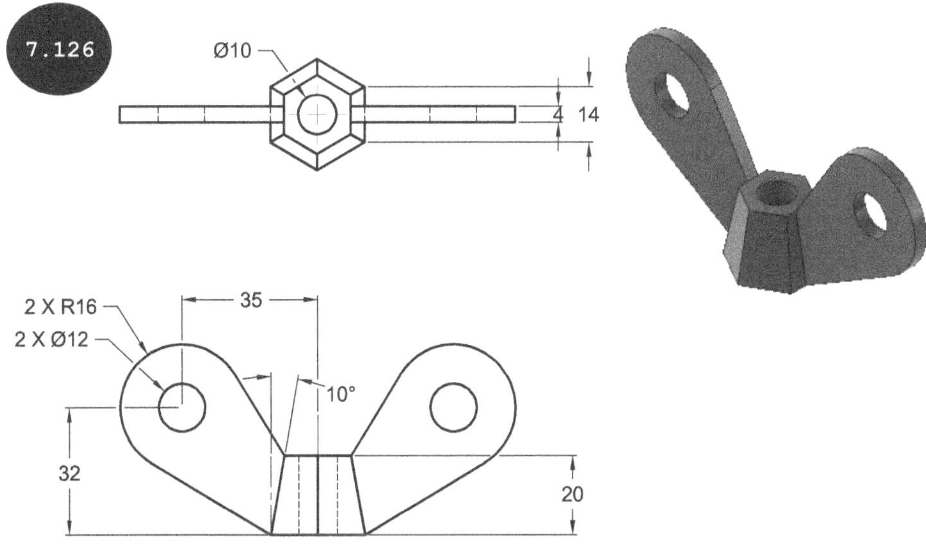

Summary

In this chapter, you explored advanced options for creating extrude and revolve features. You learned how to create cut features and retain only the intersecting material between features. The chapter also covered creating a new body or component using the **Extrude** and **Revolve** tools, as well as working with sketches that contain multiple profiles and projecting edges of existing features onto the active sketching plane. Additionally, you learned to edit existing features, sketches, and sketching planes, as well as create 3D curves using the **Project to Surface**, **Intersection Curve**, and **Intersect** tools. Finally, you learned how to assign material properties, calculate mass properties, and measure distances between objects.

Questions

Complete and verify the following sentences:

- The options in the _________ drop-down list of the **EXTRUDE** dialog box are used for defining the start condition of extrusion.
- The _________ option of the **Start** drop-down list in the **EXTRUDE** dialog box is used for selecting a face, a plane, or a vertex as the start condition of extrusion.
- The _________ option of the **Extent Type** drop-down list in the **EXTRUDE** dialog box is used for defining the termination of the extrusion by selecting a face, a plane, a vertex, or a body.
- The _________ option of the **Operation** drop-down list is used for extruding the profile by removing material from the model.
- The _________ option of the **Operation** drop-down list is used for extruding the profile by adding material and merging a feature with the existing features of the model.
- You can project the edges of the existing features onto the currently active sketching plane by using the _________ tool.
- In Autodesk Fusion, you can apply physical material properties such as density, elastic modulus, and tensile strength to a model by using the _________ tool.
- You can create a revolve cut feature by revolving a sketch around a centerline or an axis by using the **Revolve** tool. (True/False)
- You can edit individual features and their sketches as per your requirements. (True/False)
- In Autodesk Fusion, you can customize the material properties of a model. (True/False)

8

Advanced Modeling - II

In this chapter, the following topics will be discussed:

- Creating a Sweep Feature
- Creating a Loft feature
- Creating Rib Features
- Creating Web Features
- Creating Emboss Features
- Creating Holes
- Creating a Thread
- Creating an Automated Modeling
- Creating a Rectangular Box
- Creating a Cylinder
- Creating a Sphere
- Creating a Torus
- Creating a Helical and a Spiral Coil
- Creating a Pipe
- Creating 3D Sketches

In previous chapters, you learned about the primary modeling tools for creating 3D parametric models and the basic workflow, starting with the base feature and then adding the remaining features of a model step by step. In this chapter, you will explore advanced tools such as **Sweep**, **Loft**, **Rib**, **Web**, **Emboss**, **Hole**, and **Thread**. Additionally, you will dive into modifying tools like **Fillet**, **Chamfer**, **Shell**, **Draft**, **Scale**, and more, expanding your ability to create and refine complex models.

Creating a Sweep Feature

A sweep feature is created by adding or removing material as a profile is swept along a path. Figure 8.1 illustrates a profile and a path, as well as the resulting sweep feature formed by sweeping the profile along the path. In this example, the sweep feature is created by adding material.

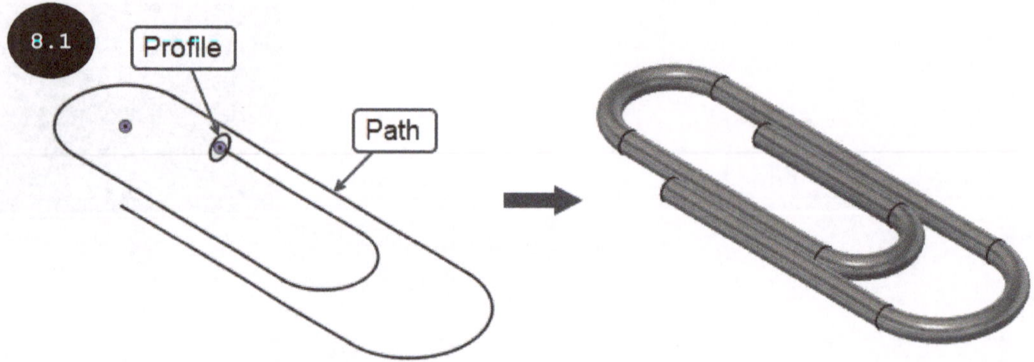

It is evident from the above figures that to create a sweep feature, you first need to create a profile and a path where the profile follows the path and creates a sweep feature. To create a profile, you need to identify the cross-section of the feature to be created. To create a path, you need to identify a route followed by the profile for creating the feature. In Autodesk Fusion, you can create a sweep feature by using the **Sweep** tool available in the **CREATE** drop-down menu of the **SOLID** tab in the **Toolbar**. Note that for creating a sweep feature, you need to ensure the following:

1. The profile must be a closed sketch. You can also select a face of a model as the profile.
2. The path can be an open or closed sketch, which is made up of a set of end-to-end connected sketched entities, a curve, or a set of model edges.
3. The starting point of the path must intersect with the plane of the profile for better results.
4. The profile, the path, and the resultant sweep feature must not be self-intersected.

After creating the path and the profile as individual sketches, invoke the **CREATE** drop-down menu in the **SOLID** tab of the **Toolbar** and then click on the **Sweep** tool, see Figure 8.2. The **SWEEP** dialog box appears, see Figure 8.3. The options in the dialog box are discussed next.

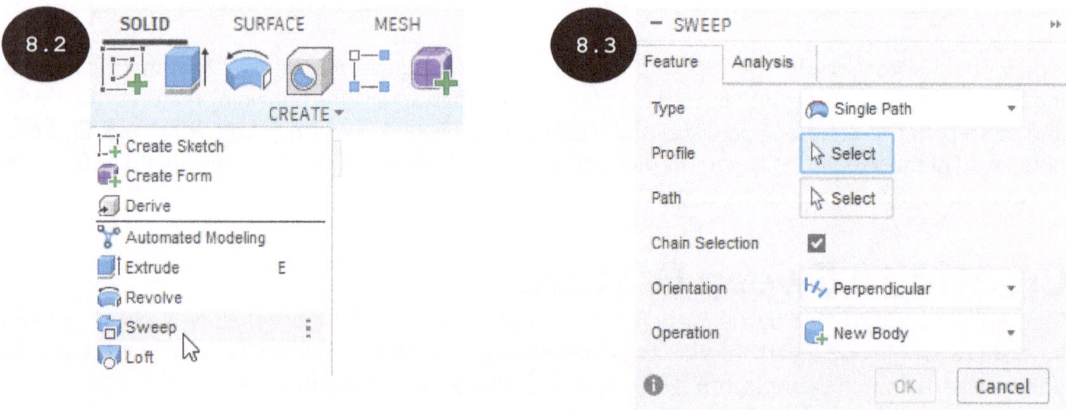

Type

The **Type** drop-down list of the **SWEEP** dialog box is used for selecting the type of sweep feature to be created. By default, the **Single Path** option is selected in this drop-down list. As a result, you can create a sweep feature by sweeping the profile along the path, see Figure 8.4.

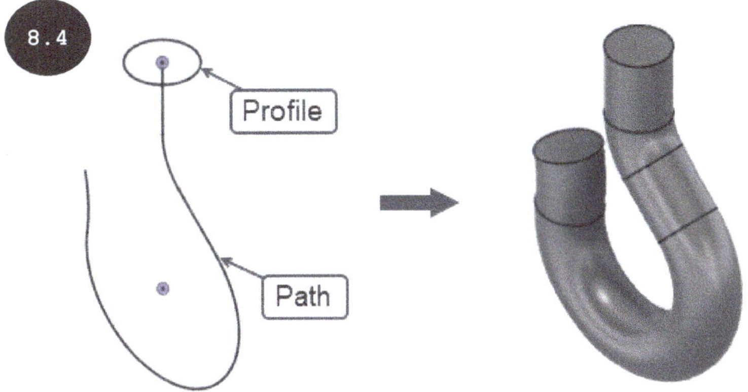

The **Path + Guide Rail** option is used for creating a sweep feature by sweeping the profile along the path, while the scale and orientation of the feature are controlled by a guide rail, see Figure 8.5.

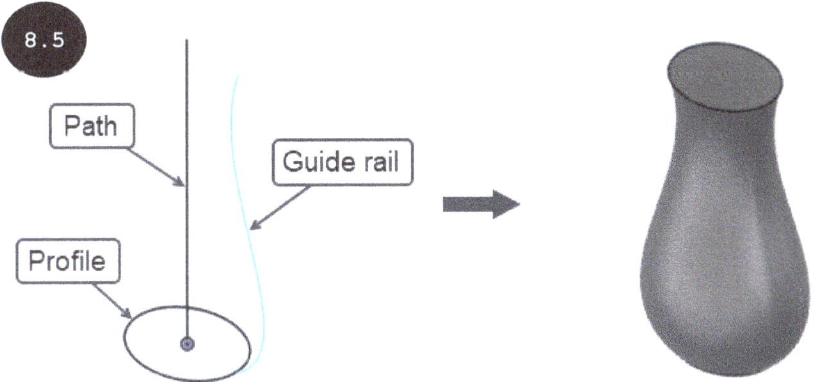

The **Path + Guide Surface** option is used for creating a sweep feature by sweeping the profile along the path and the orientation is guided by a guide surface, see Figure 8.6.

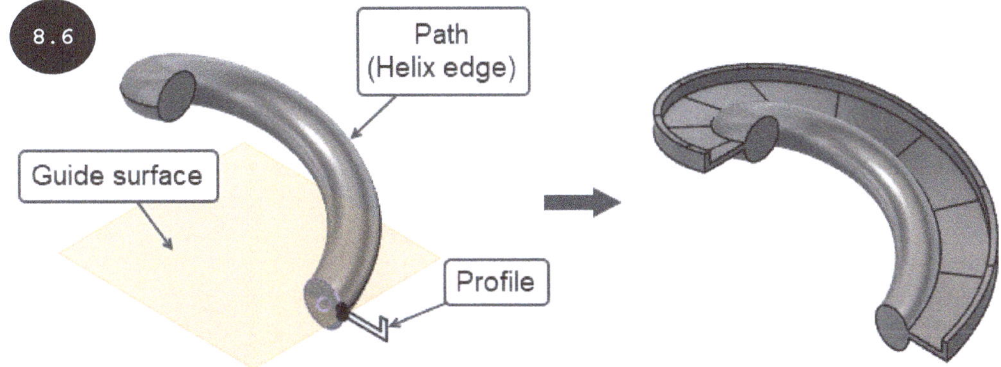

The **Solid Sweep** option is used for creating a sweep feature by sweeping a solid body along a specified path, see Figure 8.7.

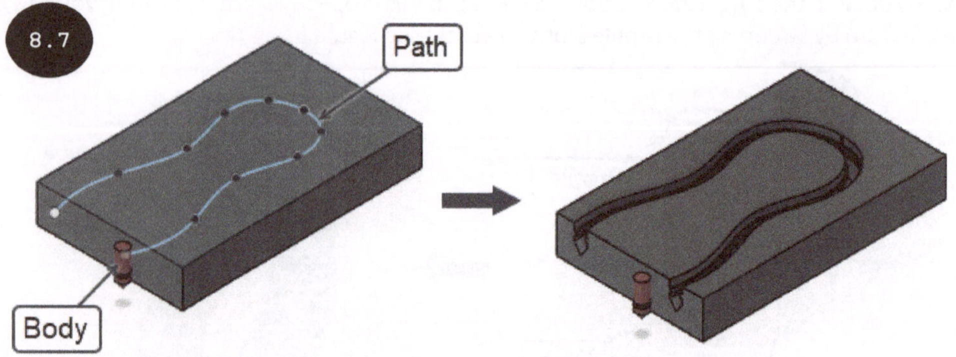

The methods for creating different types of sweep features are discussed next.

Creating a Sweep Feature with Single Path

1. Invoke the **CREATE** drop-down menu in the **SOLID** tab of the **Toolbar** and then click on the **Sweep** tool. The **SWEEP** dialog box appears, see Figure 8.8.

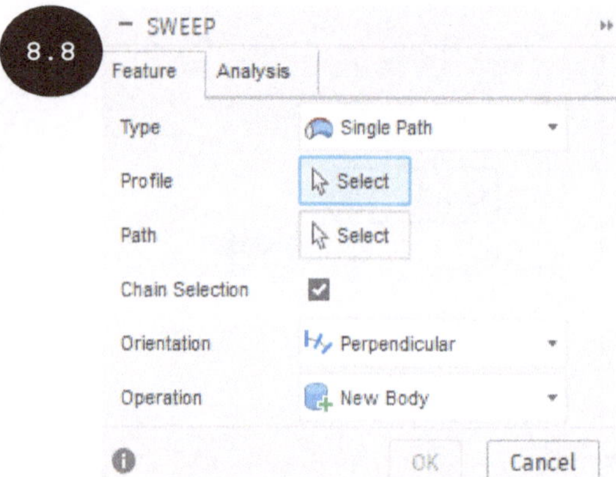

2. Ensure that the **Single Path** option is selected in the **Type** drop-down list of the dialog box.

   Profile: By default, the **Profile** selection option is activated in the dialog box. As a result, you can select the profile of a closed sketch or a face in the graphics area.

3. Select a closed profile of the sweep feature in the graphics area, see Figure 8.9.

   Chain Selection: By default, the **Chain Selection** check box is selected in the dialog box. As a result, on selecting an entity of the path created by multiple segments (entities), all the contiguous entities (closed or open loop) of the selected entity get selected, automatically.

4. Ensure that the **Chain Selection** check box is selected in the dialog box.

Path: The **Path** selection option is used for selecting a path. You can select end-to-end connected closed or opened sketch entities, edges, or a curve. Note that the starting point of the path must intersect with the plane of the profile for better results.

5. Click on the **Path** selection option in the dialog box and then select a path in the graphics area, see Figure 8.9. A preview of the sweep feature appears in the graphics area, see Figure 8.10.

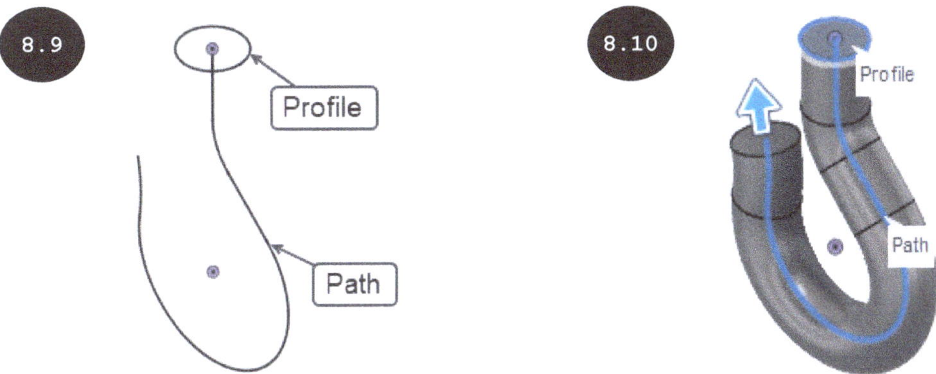

Distance: By default, the value **1** is entered in the **Distance** field of the dialog box. As a result, the profile sweeps along the total length of the path. You can specify the termination of the sweep feature by entering the required percentage value (greater than 0 and less than 1) in the **Distance** field. The percentage value is calculated in terms of the total length of the selected path. For example, the percentage value 1, sweeps the profile along the total length of the path, see Figure 8.11 and the percentage value 0.5, sweeps the profile along the half length of the path, see Figure 8.12 You can also drag the arrow that appears in the preview of the feature to define the value dynamically.

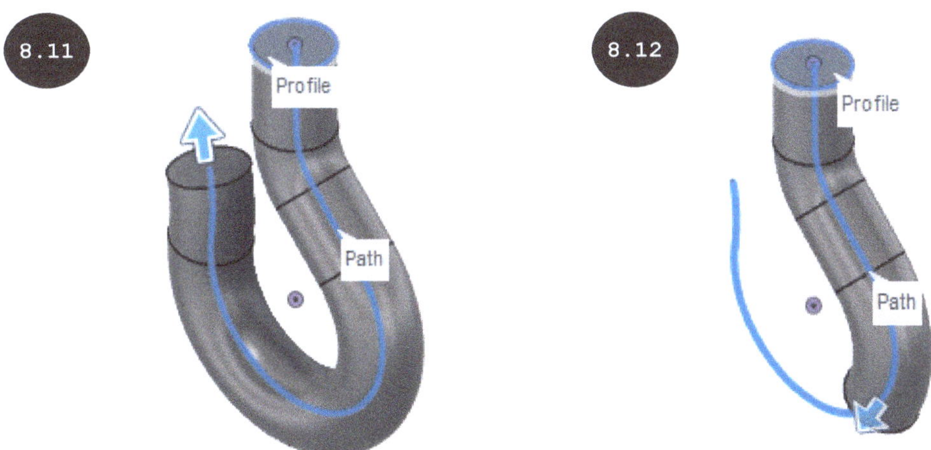

6. Enter the required percentage value in the **Distance** field of the dialog box. To sweep the profile along the total length of the path, ensure that the value **1** is entered in the **Distance** field.

Taper Angle: By default, the taper angle is specified as 0 degrees in the **Taper Angle** field of the dialog box. As a result, the resultant sweep feature is created without any tapering. You can enter the required taper angle value in this field. Figure 8.13 shows the preview of the sweep feature having a taper angle set to **-2.5** degrees. To reverse the taper direction from the outward to the inward side of the profile or vice-versa, you need to enter a negative taper angle value. Note that the **Taper Angle** field is available in the dialog box when the **Perpendicular** option is selected in the **Orientation** drop-down list of the dialog box. You will learn about the options of the **Orientation** drop-down list later in this chapter.

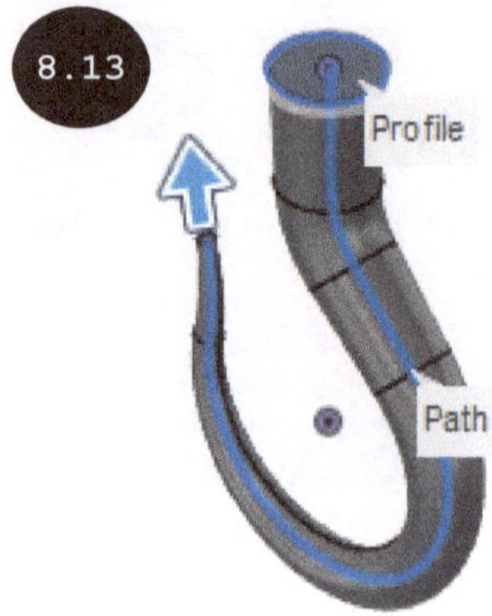

7. Enter the required taper angle value in the **Taper Angle** field. To create a sweep feature without any tapering, ensure that 0 degrees is entered in this field.

Twist Angle: By default, 0 degrees is entered in the **Twist Angle** field of the dialog box. As a result, the resultant sweep feature does not have any twisting. You can enter the required twist angle in this field to twist the profile along the path. Figure 8.14 shows the preview of a sweep feature with 0 degrees twist angle and Figure 8.15 shows the preview of the sweep feature with 90 degrees twist angle. Note that the **Twist Angle** field is available in the dialog box when the **Perpendicular** option is selected in the **Orientation** drop-down list of the dialog box.

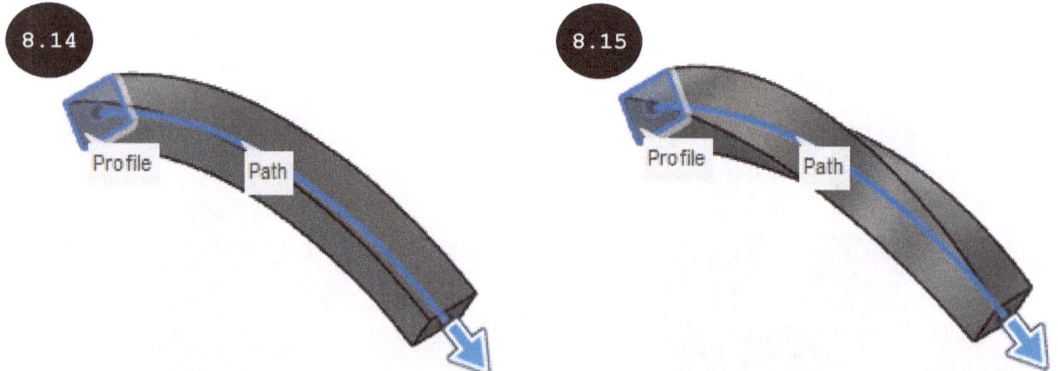

8. Enter the required twist angle in the **Twist Angle** field of the dialog box. If you do not want to create any twisting in the resultant sweep feature, then ensure that 0 degrees is entered in this field.

Orientation: By default, the **Perpendicular** option is selected in the **Orientation** drop-down list of the dialog box. As a result, the resultant sweep feature is created by keeping the profile of the feature perpendicular to the path, see Figure 8.16. On selecting the **Parallel** option in this drop-down list, the resultant sweep feature is created by keeping the profile of the sweep feature parallel to the sketching plane of the profile, see Figure 8.17

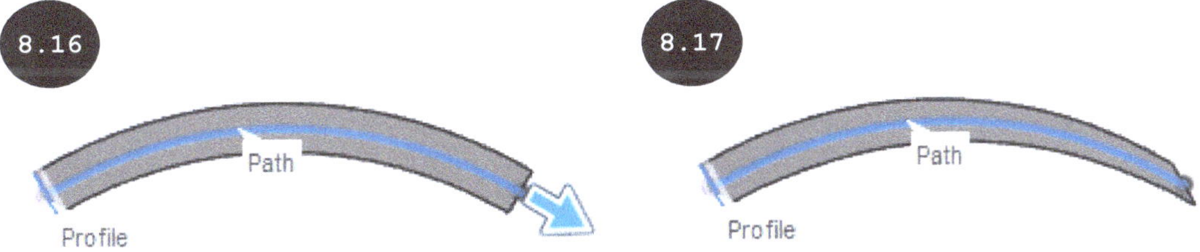

9. Select the required option (**Perpendicular** or **Parallel**) in the **Orientation** drop-down list of the dialog box.

 Operation: The options in the **Operation** drop-down list of the dialog box are the same as discussed earlier.

10. Select the required option in the **Operation** drop-down list of the dialog box.

 Analysis: The options in the **Analysis** tab of the dialog box are used for analyzing the quality of surface curvature in the preview of the sweep feature. By default, the **None** button is activated in the **Analysis Type** area of this tab. As a result, no analysis is shown in the preview of the sweep feature. On activating the **Zebra** button in the **Analysis Type** area, the curvature is shown using alternating black and white zebra stripes for analyzing the quality of the surface curvature, see Figure 8.18. On activating the **Curvature Map** button, the high and low surface curvature is shown using a color gradient, see Figure 8.19. On activating the **Isocurve** button, the surface curvature is shown using curvature combs, see Figure 8.20.

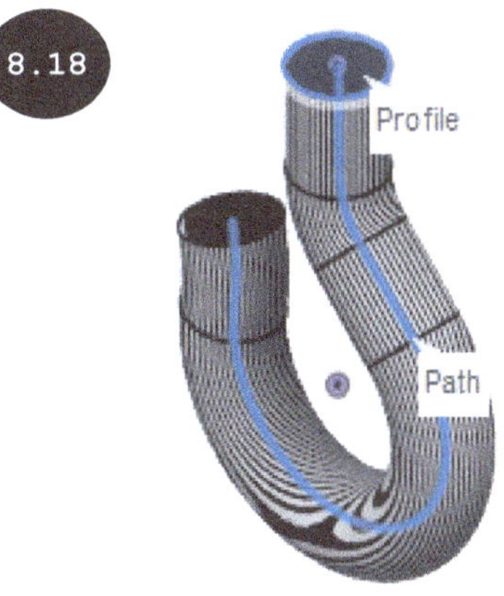

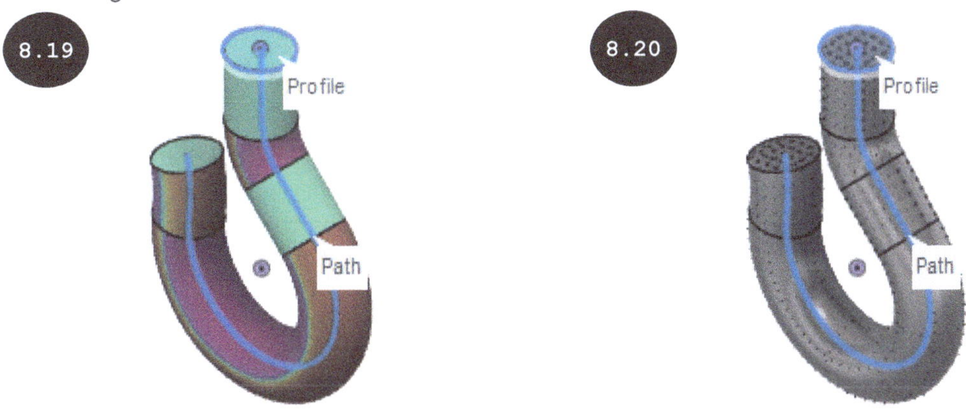

11. Click on the **Analysis** tab in the dialog box and then activate the required button (**Zebra**, **Curvature Map**, or **Isocurve**) for analyzing the surface curvature in the preview of the sweep feature, if needed.

12. Click on the **OK** button in the dialog box. The sweep feature is created by sweeping the profile along the path.

Creating a Sweep Feature with Path and Guide Rail

1. Invoke the **CREATE** drop-down menu in the **SOLID** tab of the **Toolbar** and then click on the **Sweep** tool. The **SWEEP** dialog box appears.

2. Select the **Path + Guide Rail** option in the **Type** drop-down list of the dialog box, see Figure 8.21. The options for creating a sweep feature by using the path and guide rail appear in the dialog box.

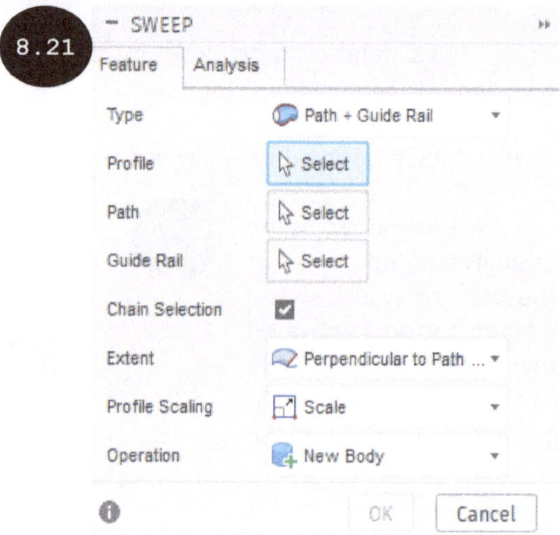

Note: Some of the options that appear in the dialog box after selecting the **Path + Guide Rail** option are the same as discussed earlier.

3. Select a closed profile of the sweep feature in the graphics area, see Figure 8.22.

4. Click on the **Path** selection option in the dialog box and then select the path of the sweep feature, see Figure 8.22.

   Guide Rail: The **Guide Rail** selection option is used for selecting a guide rail for controlling the scale and orientation of the sweep feature. Note that the starting point of the guide rail must intersect with the plane of the profile for better results.

5. Click on the **Guide Rail** selection option in the dialog box and then select the guide rail of the sweep feature, see Figure 8.22. A preview of the sweep feature appears, see Figure 8.23.

Extent: By default, the **Perpendicular to Path** option is selected in the **Extent** drop-down list in the dialog box. So, the resultant sweep feature is created by keeping the profile of the feature perpendicular to the path, see Figure 8.24. On selecting the **Full Extents** option in this drop-down list, the profile of the resultant sweep feature does not maintain a perpendicular relation to the path and extends throughout the length of the path or the guide rail, see Figure 8.25.

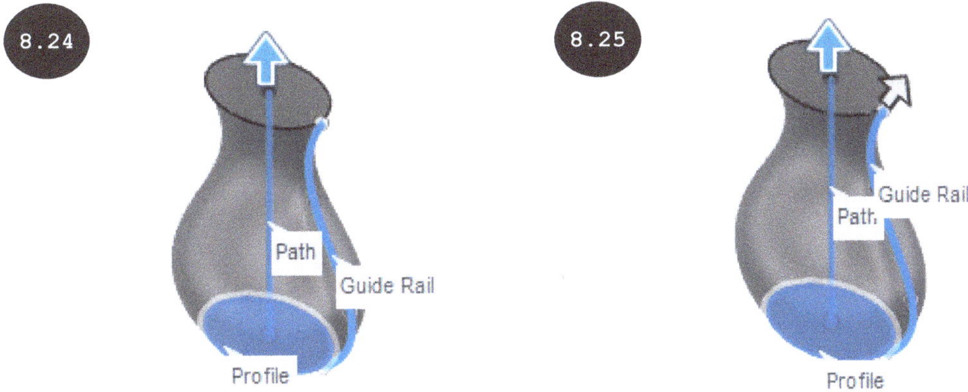

6. Select the required option in the **Extent** drop-down list of the dialog box.

   Distance: The **Distance** field is available in the dialog box when the **Perpendicular to Path** option is selected in the **Extent** drop-down list. In this field, you can specify the termination of the sweep feature by entering the required percentage value (greater than 0 and less than 1), as discussed earlier. You can also drag the arrow that appears in the preview of the feature to define the percentage value dynamically.

   Path Distance and Guide Rail Distance: The **Path Distance** and **Guide Rail Distance** fields become available in the dialog box when the **Full Extents** option is selected in the **Extent** drop-down list of the dialog box. These fields are used for specifying the termination of the sweep feature by entering the required percentage value in terms of the path length and guide rail length.

7. Specify the required percentage value to define the termination of the sweep feature in the respective field(s) of the dialog box or accept the default values.

Profile Scaling: The options in the **Profile Scaling** drop-down list control the scale and orientation of the sweep feature based on the guide rail selected. The **Scale** option creates a sweep feature by scaling the profile (section) of the feature in both the X and Y directions of the guide rail, see Figure 8.26. The **Stretch** option creates a sweep feature by scaling or stretching the profile (section) of the feature in the X direction of the guide rail only, see Figure 8.27. The **None** option creates a sweep feature by not scaling the profile (section) of the feature based on the guide rail and maintaining the same sections throughout the path, see Figure 8.28.

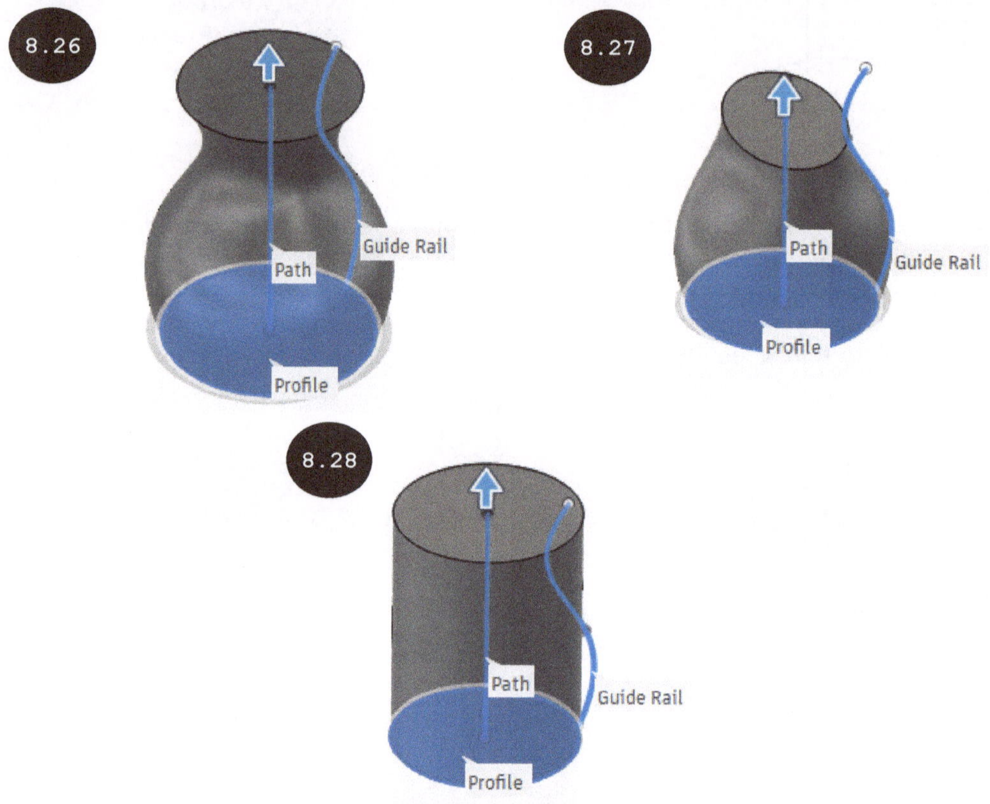

8. Select the required option in the **Profile Scaling** drop-down list of the dialog box.

9. Select the required option in the **Operation** drop-down list of the dialog box and then click on the **OK** button in the dialog box. The sweep feature is created by sweeping the profile along the path. Also, the scale and orientation of the feature are controlled by the guide rail.

Creating a Sweep Feature with Path and Guide Surface

1. Invoke the **CREATE** drop-down menu in the **SOLID** tab of the **Toolbar** and then click on the **Sweep** tool. The **SWEEP** dialog box appears.

2. Select the **Path + Guide Surface** option in the **Type** drop-down list of the dialog box, see Figure 8.29. The options for creating a sweep feature using the path and guide surface appear in the dialog box.

Note that most of the options that appear in the dialog box after selecting the **Path + Guide Surface** option are the same as discussed earlier.

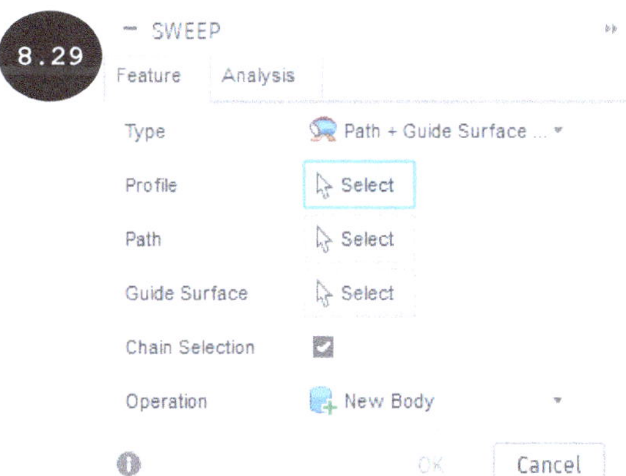

3. Select a closed profile of the sweep feature in the graphics area, see Figure 8.30.

4. Click on the **Path** selection option in the dialog box and then select the path of the sweep feature, see Figure 8.30.

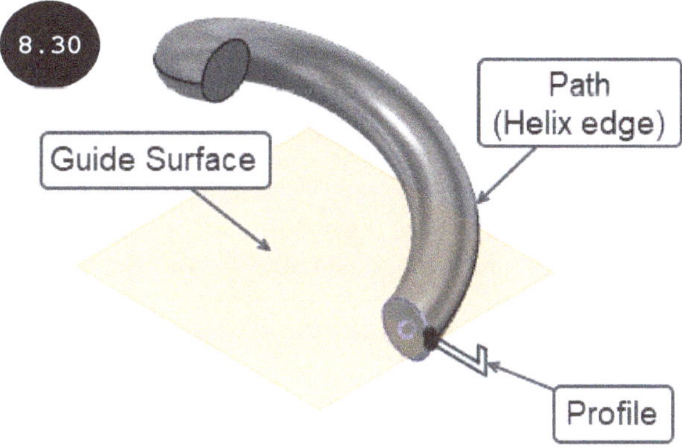

Note: In Figure 8.30, a helical edge of a coil feature is selected as the path for creating the sweep feature. You will learn about creating coil features in chapter 8.

Guide Surface: The **Guide Surface** selection option is used to select a guide surface (a face or a plane) for guiding the orientation of the profile while sweeping along the path.

5. Click on the **Guide Surface** selection option in the dialog box and then select a face or a plane as the guide surface, refer to Figure 8.30. A preview of the sweep feature appears in the graphics area such that its orientation is guided by the guide surface selected, see Figure 8.31.

You can notice the difference between the preview of the sweep feature shown in Figure 8.31 and Figure 8.32. Figure 8.31 shows the preview of a sweep feature created by selecting the profile, path, and guide surface, whereas Figure 8.32 shows the preview of the sweep feature created by selecting the profile and path using only the **Single Path** option of the **Type** drop-down list.

6. Enter the required percentage value in the **Distance** field of the dialog box, as discussed earlier.

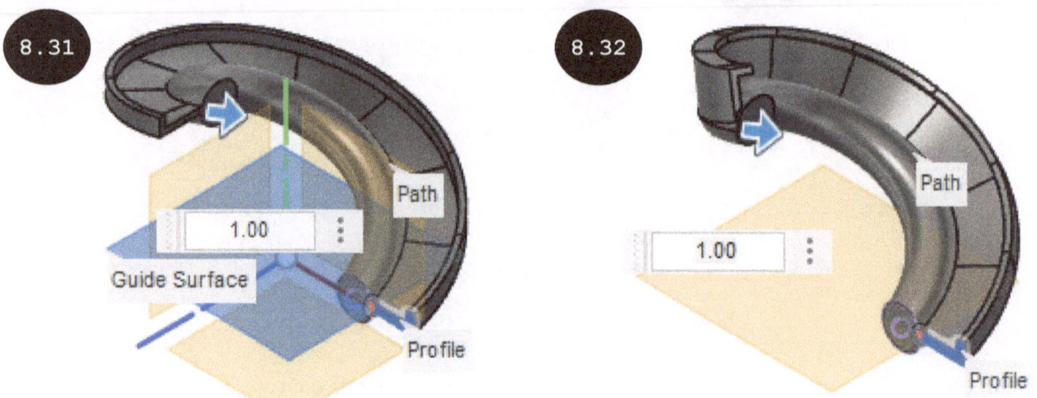

7. Select the required option in the **Operation** drop-down list of the dialog box and then click on the **OK** button in the dialog box. The sweep feature is created by sweeping the profile along the path and the orientation of the profile is maintained by the guide surface selected.

Creating a Sweep Feature with Solid Sweep

1. Invoke the **CREATE** drop-down menu in the **SOLID** tab of the **Toolbar** and then click on the **Sweep** tool. The **SWEEP** dialog box appears.

2. Select the **Solid Sweep** option in the **Type** drop-down list of the dialog box, see Figure 8.33. The options for creating a sweep feature using a solid body appear in the dialog box.

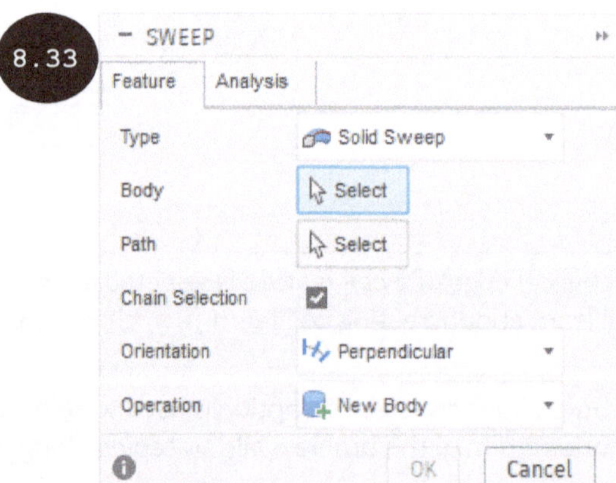

3. Select a solid body as a tool (profile) that follows the path to create the sweep feature, see Figure 8.34.

Tip: In Autodesk Fusion, while creating a feature, you can select the **New Body** option in the **Operation** drop-down list of the respective dialog box to create a new body.

4. After selecting a solid body, click to activate the **Path selection** option in the dialog box and select the path for the sweep feature, see Figure 8.34. A preview of the sweep feature appears, showing the selected solid body following the path, see Figure 8.34. The remaining options in the dialog box are same as those discussed earlier.

5. Select the required option in the **Operation** drop-down list of the dialog box, then click **OK**. The sweep feature is created by sweeping the body along the path, see Figure 8.34. In this figure, a sweep cut feature is created by selecting the **Cut** option in the **Operation** drop-down list.

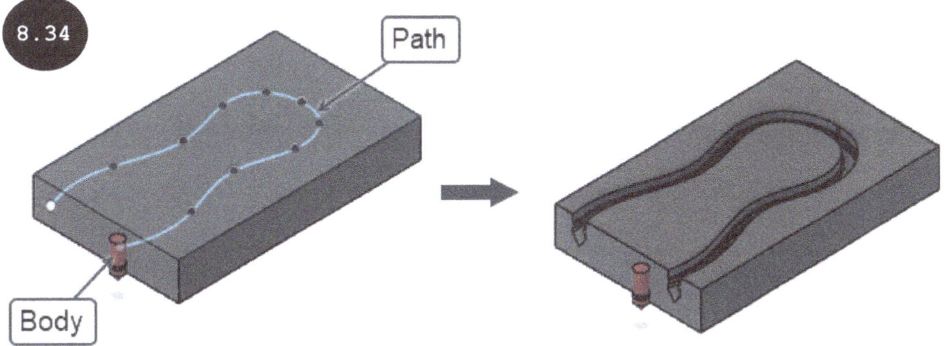

Creating a Loft feature

A loft feature is created by lofting two or more profiles (sections) such that the cross-sectional shape of the loft feature transits from one profile to another. Figure 8.35 shows two dissimilar profiles (sections) created on different planes having an offset distance between each other. Figure 8.36 shows the resultant loft feature.

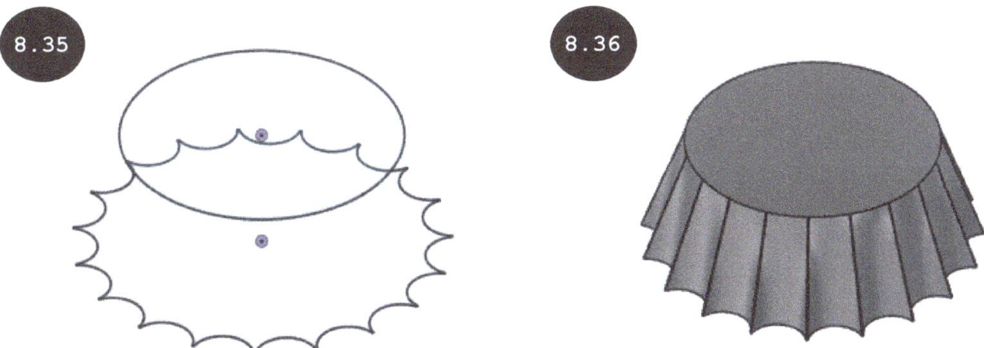

It is evident from the above figures that to create a loft feature, you first need to create all the sections that define its shape. In Autodesk Fusion, you can create a loft feature by using the **Loft** tool of the **CREATE** drop-down menu in the **SOLID** tab of the **Toolbar**. Note that for creating a loft feature, you need to ensure the following:

1. Two or more profiles (similar or dissimilar) must be available in the graphics area before invoking the **Loft** tool.

2. Profiles must be closed. You can select closed profiles of sketches and faces.

3. All profiles must be created as different sketches.

4. The profiles and the resultant lofted feature must not be self-intersected.

In Autodesk Fusion, you can create three types of loft features: with profiles, with profiles and a guide rail, and with profiles and a centerline. The methods for creating each type of loft feature are discussed next.

Creating a Loft Feature with Profiles

To create a loft feature with profiles, invoke the **CREATE** drop-down menu in the **SOLID** tab and then click on the **Loft** tool, see Figure 8.37. The **LOFT** dialog box appears, see Figure 8.38. The options of this dialog box are discussed next.

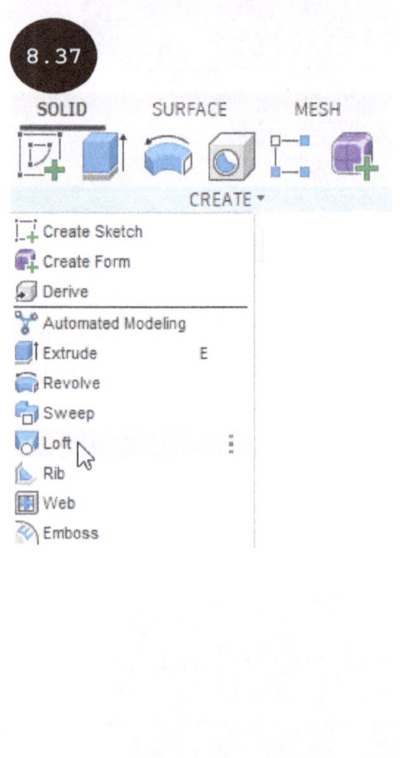

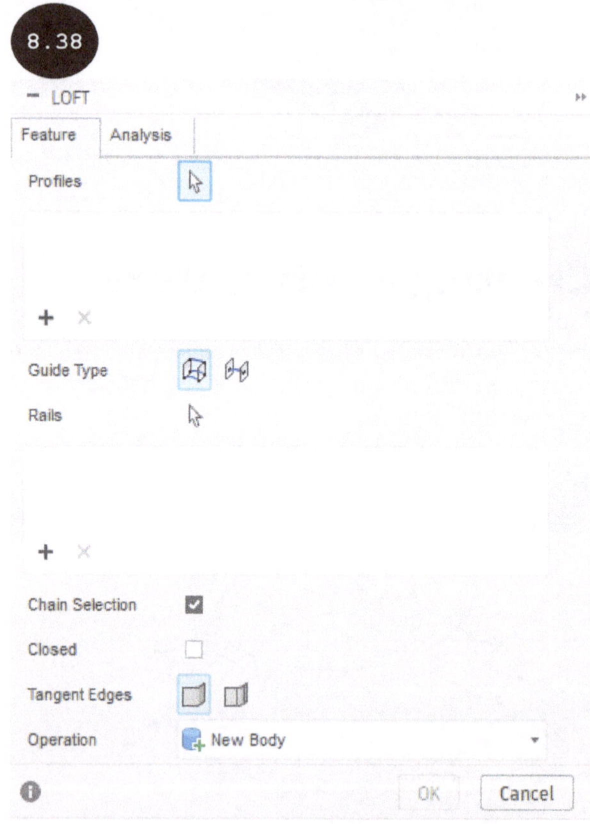

Profiles

By default, the **Profiles** selection option is activated in the dialog box. As a result, you can select closed profiles of the loft feature. You can select two or more similar or dissimilar closed profiles to create a loft feature. After selecting the profiles, a preview of the loft feature appears in the graphics area with connector points, which connect the profiles, see Figure 8.39. Also, the names of the selected profiles appear in the **Profiles** area of the dialog box in the order they are selected, see Figure 8.40.

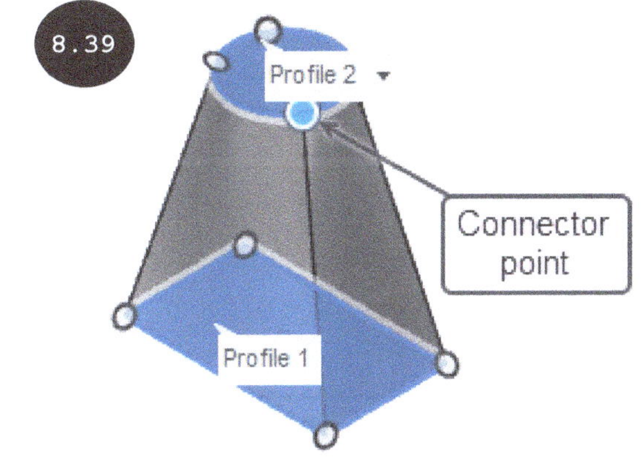

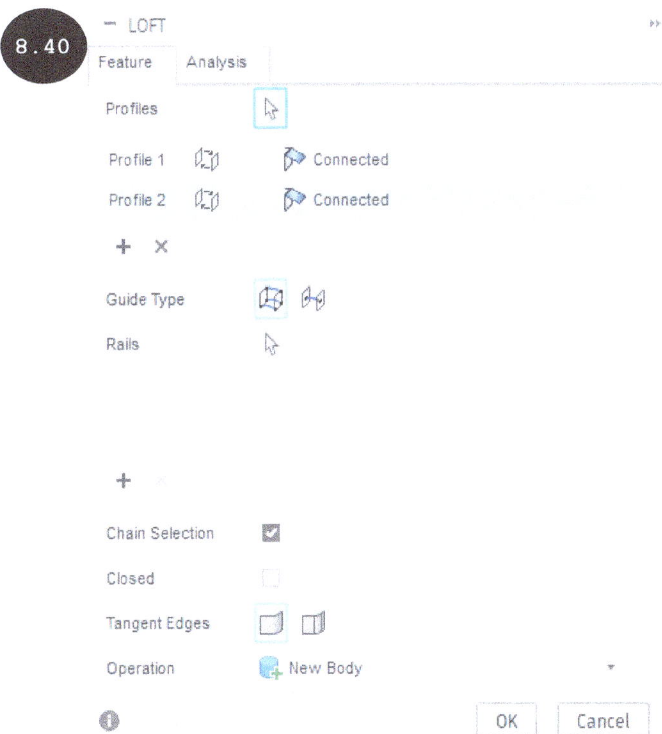

Note: You can drag the connector points that appear in the preview of a loft feature to create the twist in the feature.

The **Profiles** area of the **LOFT** dialog box is divided into three columns: **Profiles**, **Reorder,** and **End Condition**, see Figure 8.41.

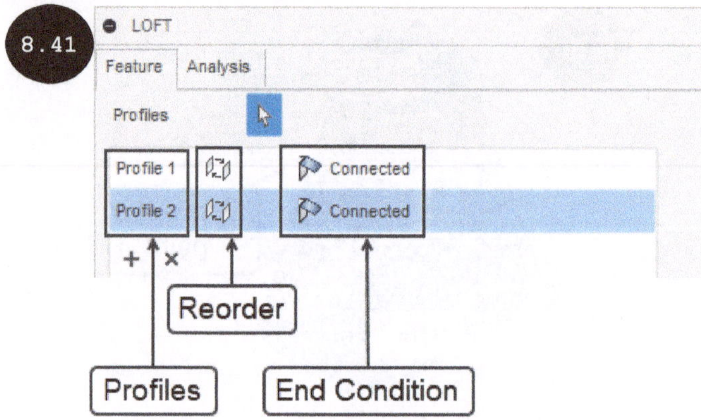

Profiles

The **Profiles** column displays the list of profiles in the order of their selection.

Reorder

To change the order of a profile, click on the **Reorder** column corresponding to the profile to be reordered. A drop-down list appears, see Figure 8.42. In this drop-down list, click on the required profile order (Profile 1, Profile 2, ... Profile n). The order of the selected profile gets changed as per the selected order in the drop-down list.

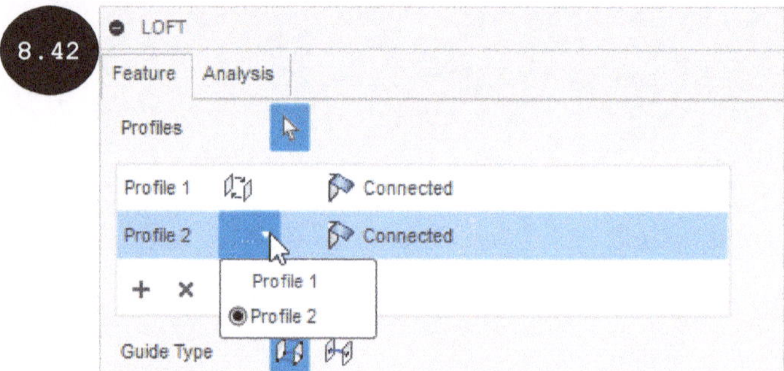

End Condition

In Autodesk Fusion, you can define the end condition for a profile to control its transition from one profile to another. To do this, click on the **End Condition** column corresponding to the profile whose end condition is to be defined. A drop-down list appears with different options to define the end condition of the selected profile, see Figure 8.43. Note that the availability of options in this drop-down list depends upon the type of geometry selected as the profile. Some of the options are discussed next.

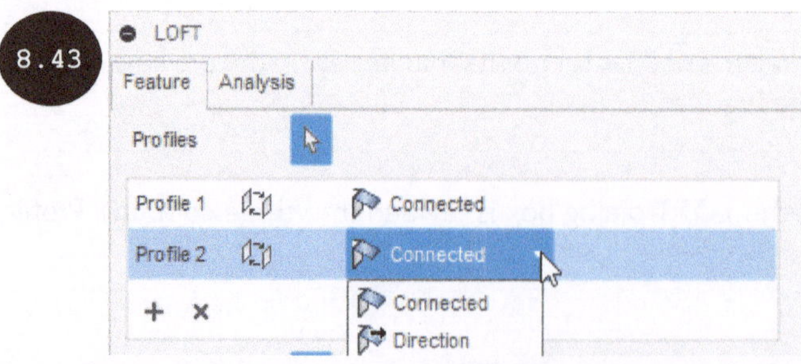

Connected: The **Connected** option is used for maintaining a straight transition between the profiles of the loft feature, see Figure 8.44.

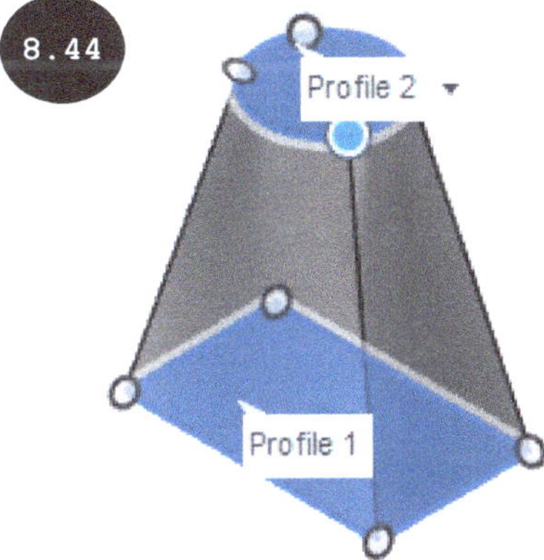

Direction: The **Direction** option is used for defining the start angle of the transition from the selected profile and its degree of influence along the loft path.

On selecting this option, the **Takeoff Weight** and **Takeoff Angle** fields appear at the bottom of the **LOFT** dialog box. The **Takeoff Weight** field is used for defining the degree of influence the start angle transition has along the loft path. The **Takeoff Angle** field is used for defining the start angle of transition, see Figures 8.45 and 8.46. In these figures, the **Direction** end condition is defined for **Profile 1** with a takeoff weight value of 1 and takeoff angle value of 0 degrees and 20 degrees, respectively. Note that the **Direction** end condition is available when the profile is a 2D sketch.

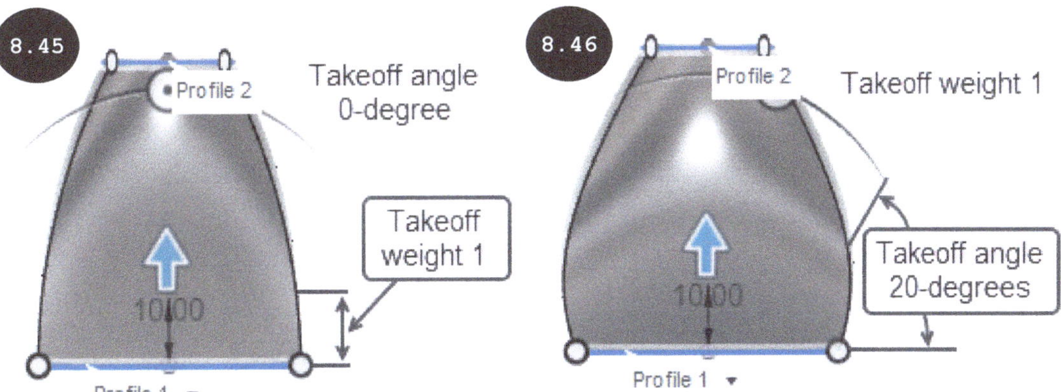

Tangent (G1): The **Tangent (G1)** option is used for defining the G1 tangency condition for the loft profile, see Figure 8.47. Note that this option is available in the drop-down list when the selected loft profile is a face of the model.

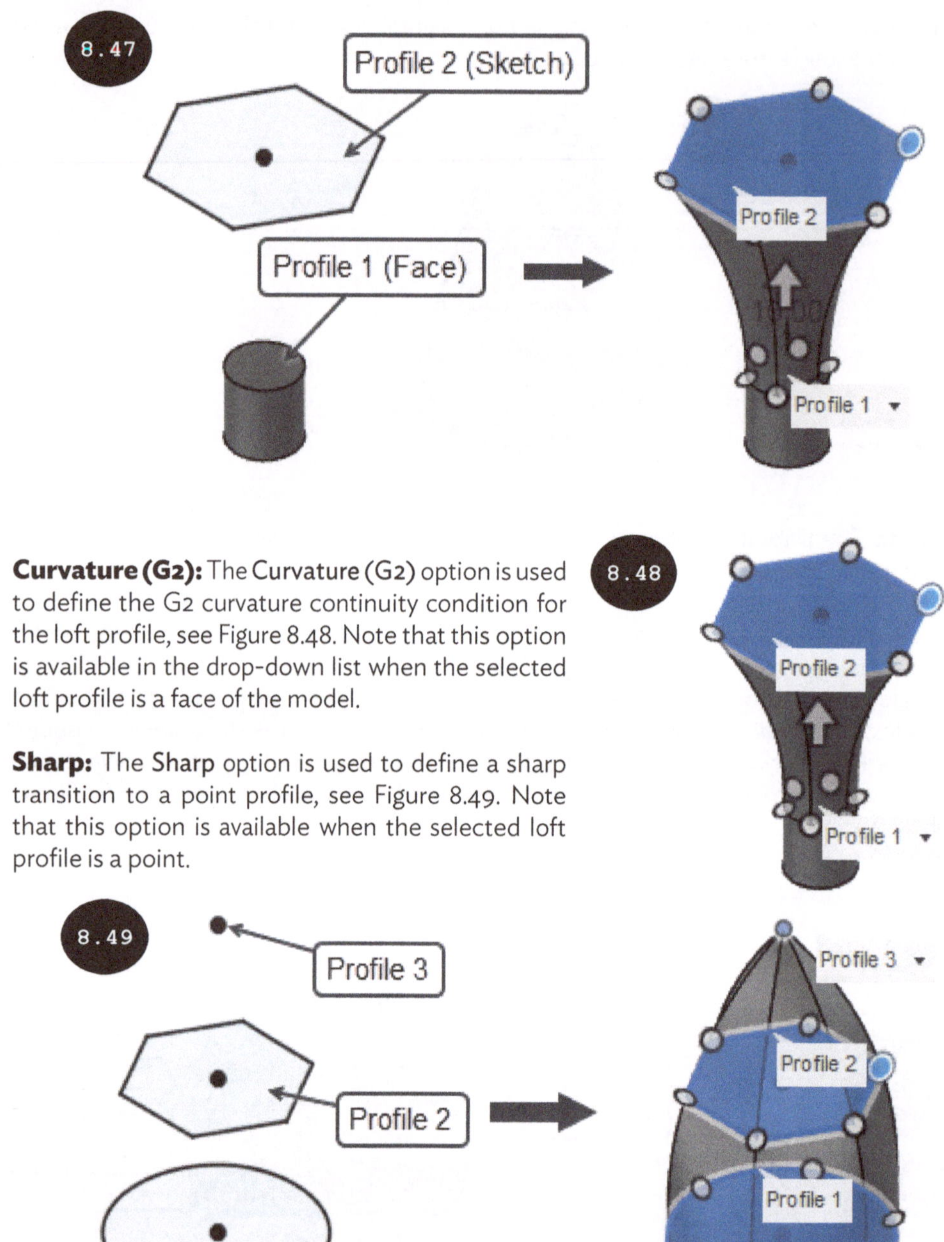

Curvature (G2): The **Curvature (G2)** option is used to define the G2 curvature continuity condition for the loft profile, see Figure 8.48. Note that this option is available in the drop-down list when the selected loft profile is a face of the model.

Sharp: The **Sharp** option is used to define a sharp transition to a point profile, see Figure 8.49. Note that this option is available when the selected loft profile is a point.

Point Tangent: The **Point Tangent** option is used to define the tangency at a point and creates a dome shape transition, see Figure 8.50. This option is available when the selected loft profile is a point. Note that on selecting the **Point Tangent** option, the **Tangency Weight** field appears at the bottom of the dialog box. In this field, you can define the tangency transition influence at the point, see Figures 8.50 and 8.51. In Figure 8.50, the value 1 is defined in the **Tangency Weight** field, whereas, in Figure 8.51, the value 4 is defined in the **Tangency Weight** field of the dialog box.

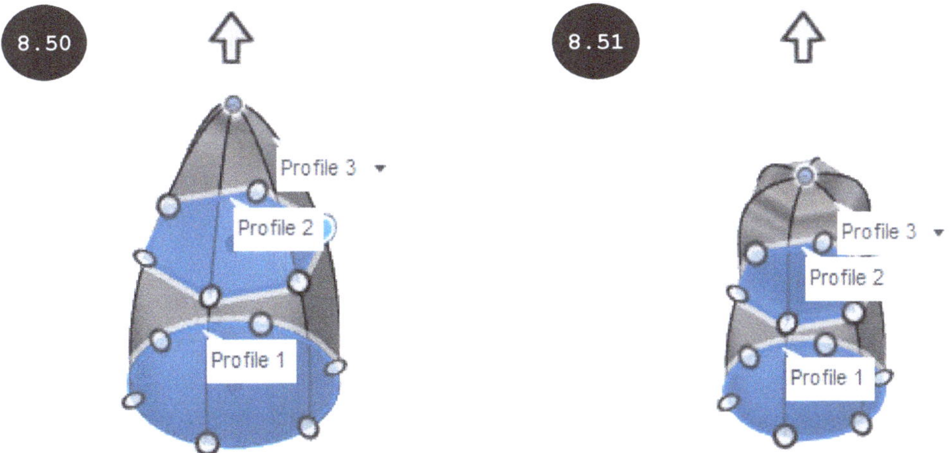

Closed

The **Closed** check box is used to create a loft feature where the start and end profiles connect, forming a closed loft feature, see Figures 8.52 and 8.53. Figure 8.52 shows the preview of an open loft feature when the **Closed** check box is cleared, and Figure 8.53 shows the preview of the loft feature when the **Closed** check box is selected in the dialog box.

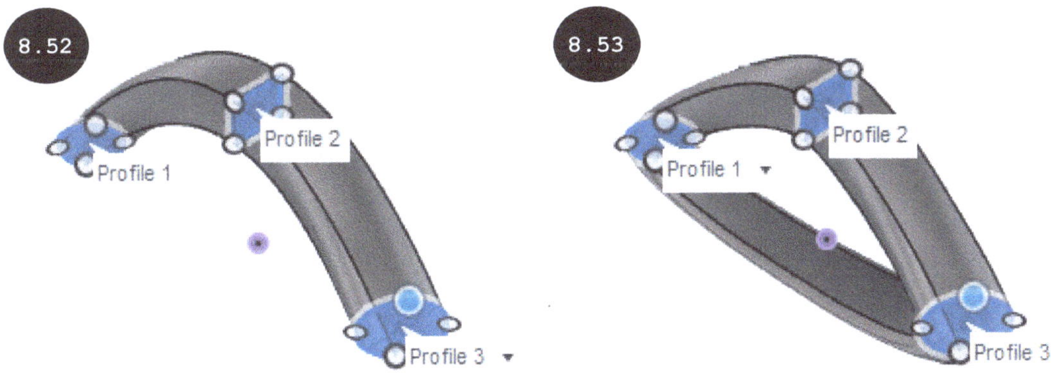

Note: To create a closed loft feature, minimum three sections are required. Also, the total angle between the start and end sections should be more than 120 degrees.

Tangent Edges

On activating the **Merge** button in the **Tangent Edges** area of the dialog box, the tangent edges of the resultant loft feature get merged, see Figure 8.54. On activating the **Keep** button, the tangent edges of the resultant loft feature remain unmerged, see Figure 8.55.

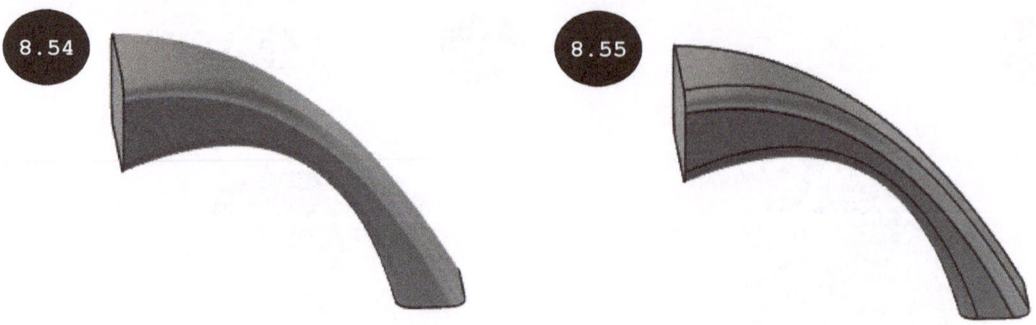

Operation
The options in the **Operation** drop-down list of the dialog box are used to define the type of operation to be performed and are the same as discussed earlier.

Analysis
The options in the **Analysis** tab of the dialog box are used to analyze the quality of surface curvature in the preview of the loft feature and are the same as discussed earlier.

After selecting the profiles for creating a loft feature and the required option in the **Operation** drop-down list, click on the **OK** button in the dialog box. The loft feature is created.

Creating a Loft Feature with Profiles and Guide Rails
In Autodesk Fusion, you can also create a loft feature using profiles and guide rails. Guide rails help control the cross-sectional shape of the loft feature, see Figure 8.56. In this figure, two profiles and one guide rail are selected, guiding the cross-sectional shape of the loft feature. You can select multiple guide rails to control the shape of the loft feature. Note that the guide rails must intersect with the profiles of the loft feature. To create a loft feature with profiles and guide rails, follow the steps given below:

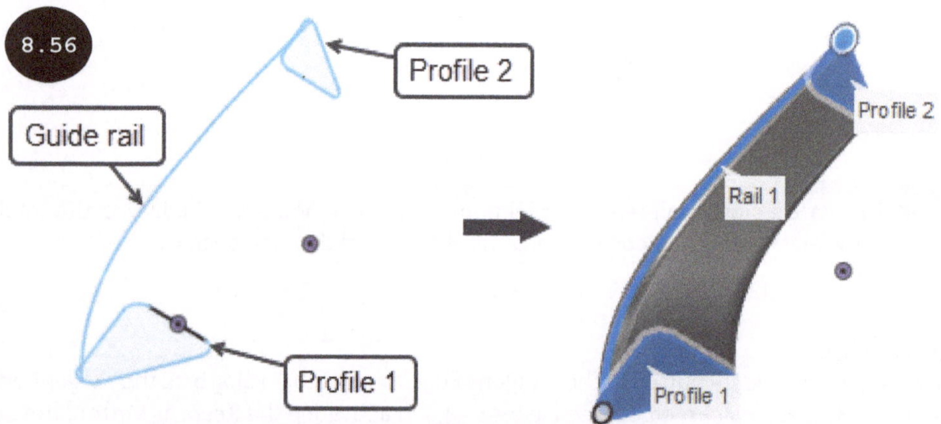

1. Invoke the **CREATE** drop-down menu in the **SOLID** tab and then click on the **Loft** tool, see Figure 8.57. The **LOFT** dialog box appears, see Figure 8.58.

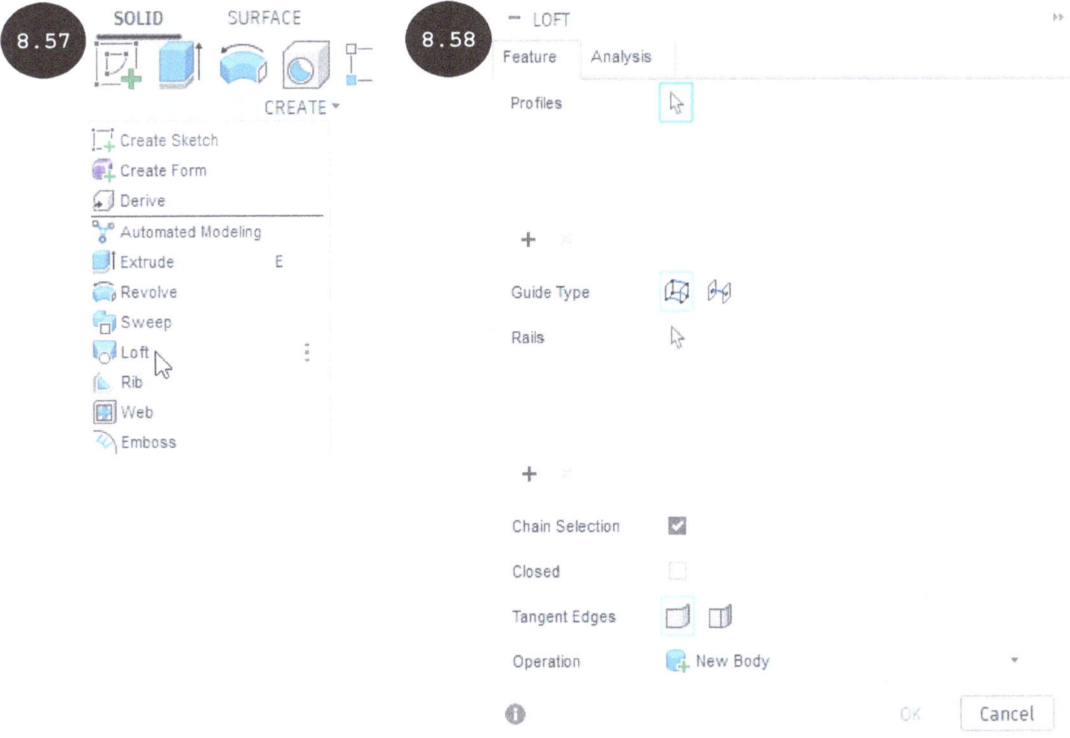

2. Select the profiles of the loft feature in the graphics area one by one, as discussed earlier. The preview of the loft feature appears, see Figure 8.59. In this figure, two closed profiles are selected. You can select multiple similar or dissimilar closed profiles for creating a loft feature. After selecting the profiles, you can also define their end conditions, as discussed earlier.

3. Ensure that the **Rails** button is activated in the **Guide Type** area of the dialog box, see Figure 8.60.

4. Click on the **Rails Selection** arrow to select the guide rails in the graphics area, see Figure 8.60.

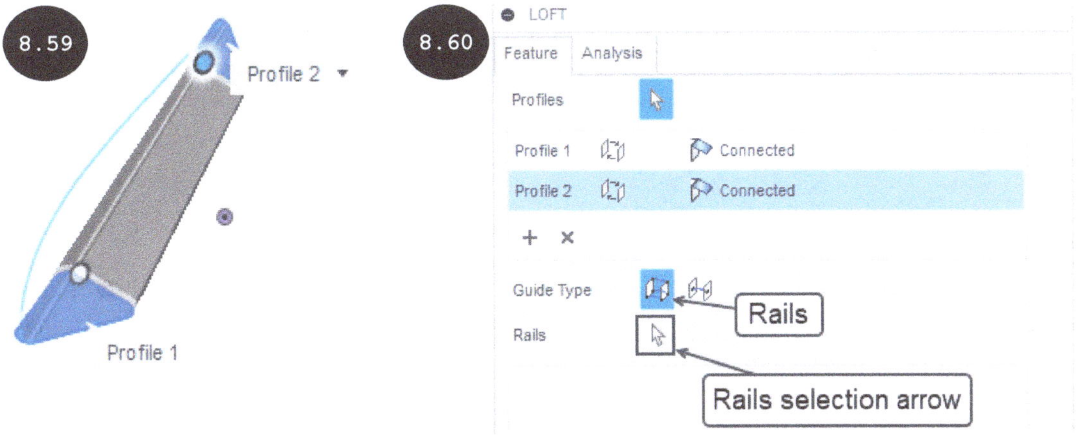

Now, you can select the guide rails to guide the cross-sectional shape of the loft feature.

5. Select the guide rails in the graphics area one by one. The preview of the loft feature is modified such that the cross-sectional shape of the feature is guided by the selected guide rails, see Figure 8.61. In this figure, one guide rail is selected. Ensure that the guide rails intersect each profile of the loft feature.

6. Select the required option in the **Operation** drop-down list and then click on the **OK** button. The loft feature is created, see Figure 8.62. To create a loft feature by removing material from the model, you need to select the **Cut** option in the **Operation** drop-down list.

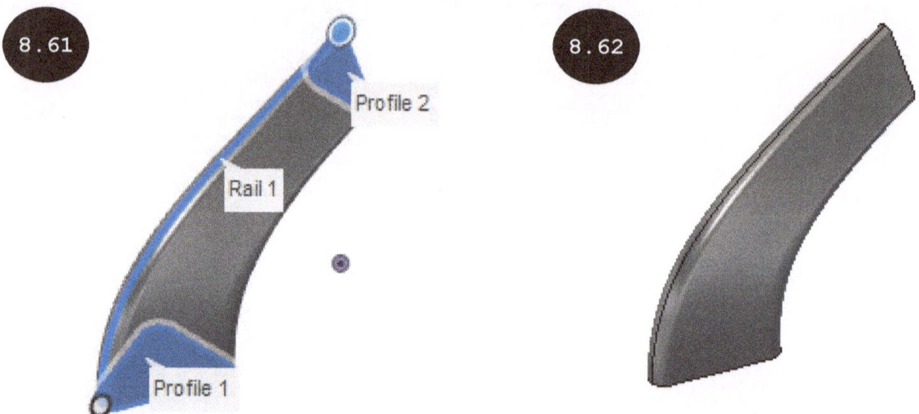

Creating a Loft Feature with Profiles and Centerline

In Autodesk Fusion, you can also create a loft feature with profiles and a centerline. A centerline is used to maintain a neutral axis for the loft feature and ensures a consistent transition between the profiles, see Figure 8.63. Note that you can select only one centerline to create a loft feature. To create a loft feature with profiles and a centerline, follow the steps given below:

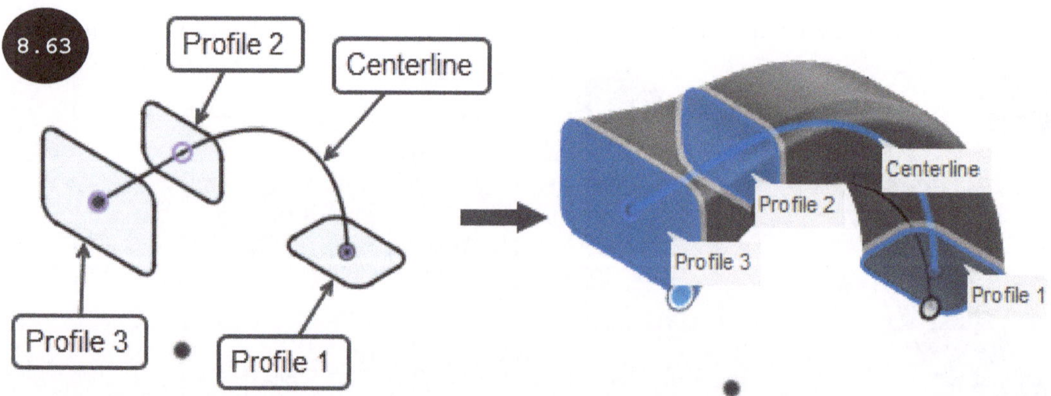

1. Invoke the **CREATE** drop-down menu in the **SOLID** tab and then click on the **Loft** tool. The **LOFT** dialog box appears.

2. Select the profiles of the loft feature in the graphics area one by one, see Figure 8.64. In this figure, both profiles are created on the same plane. As a result, a warning message appears which informs you about the failure of operation stating that closed profiles cannot be coplanar.

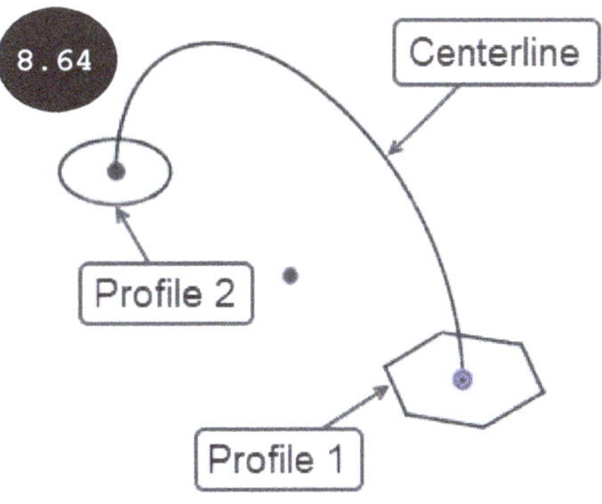

3. Click on the **Centerline** button in the **Guide Type** area of the dialog box, see Figure 8.65. The **Centerline Selection** arrow appears in the dialog box and is activated, by default.

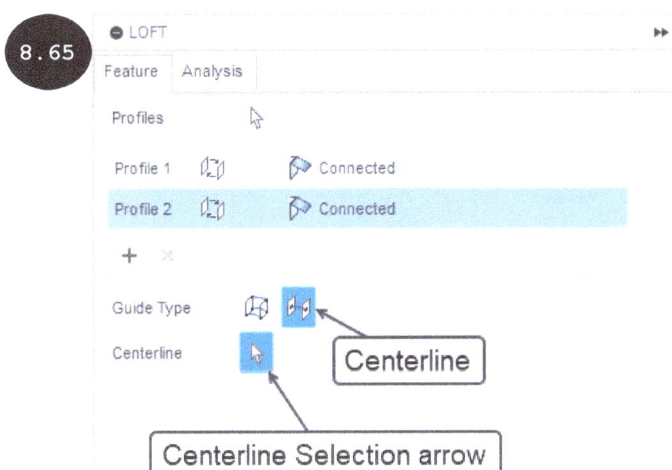

Now, you can select a centerline for creating the loft feature.

4. Select a centerline in the graphics area, refer to Figure 8.64. Ensure that the centerline intersects with the plane of all the profiles. A preview of the loft feature appears in the graphics area, see Figure 8.66.

5. Select the required option in the **Operation** drop-down list of the dialog box and then click on the **OK** button. The loft feature is created, see Figure 8.67. To create a loft feature by removing material from the model, you need to select the **Cut** option in the **Operation** drop-down list of the dialog box.

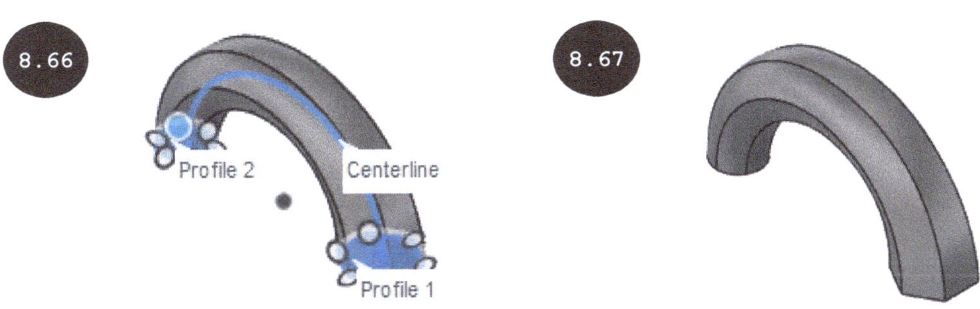

Tip: You can select a closed or open centerline to create the loft feature. On selecting a closed centerline, see Figure 8.68, you can create a closed loft feature. To do this, select the **Closed** check box in the **LOFT** dialog box. Figure 8.69 shows the preview of the closed loft feature.

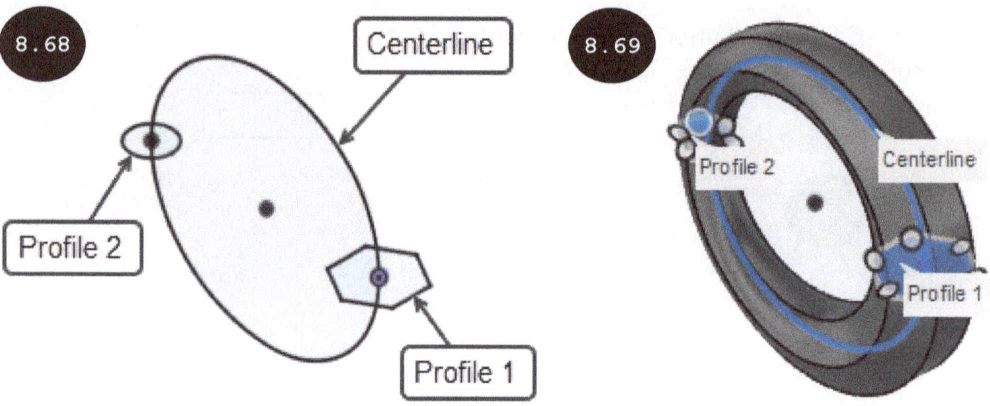

Creating Rib Features

Rib features act as supporting features and are generally used to increase the strength of a model. You can create a rib feature from a single line sketch or a curve by adding thickness in a specified direction. Figure 8.70 shows a model with a single-line sketch and the resultant rib feature created.

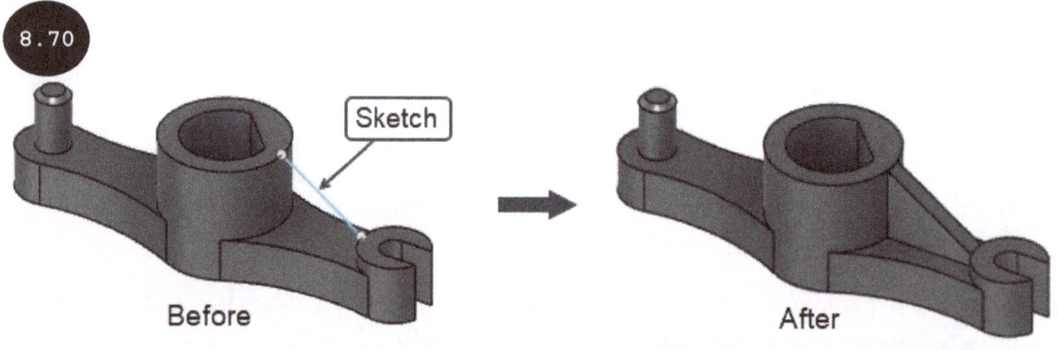

To create a rib feature, create a single-line sketch on a plane that intersects with the model, see Figure 8.71. Note that the projection of both ends of the sketch should lie on the geometry of the model. After creating a sketch of the rib feature, invoke the **CREATE** drop-down menu in the **SOLID** tab and then click on the **Rib** tool, see Figure 8.72. The **RIB** dialog box appears, see Figure 8.73. The options in the dialog box are discussed next.

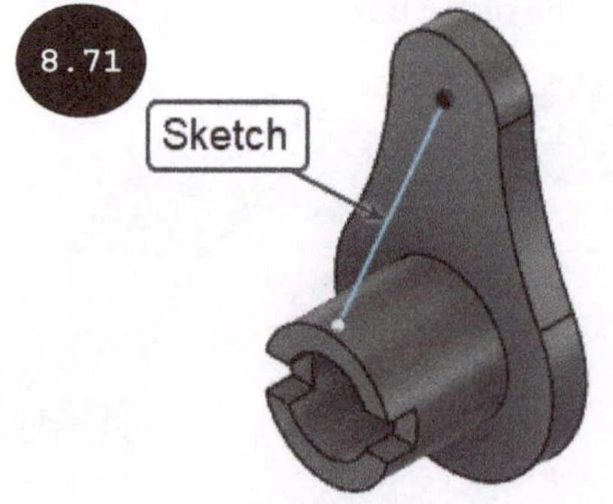

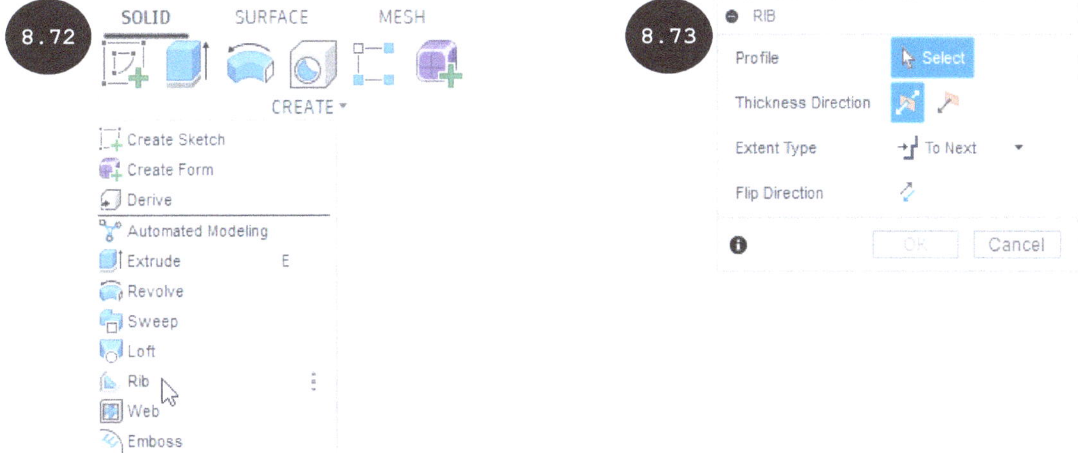

Profile

The **Profile** selection option is activated in the dialog box, by default. As a result, you can select a single line sketch or a curve to create the rib feature. Note that the projection of both ends of the sketch selected should lie on the geometry of the model. After selecting the sketch, an arrow appears in the graphics area, see Figure 8.74. Also, the **Thickness** field appears in the dialog box as well as in the graphics area.

Thickness

The **Thickness** field is used to specify the thickness of the rib feature. You can also drag the arrow that appears in the graphics area to dynamically adjust the thickness of the rib feature. As soon as you specify the thickness, the preview of the rib feature appears in the graphics area, see Figure 8.75.

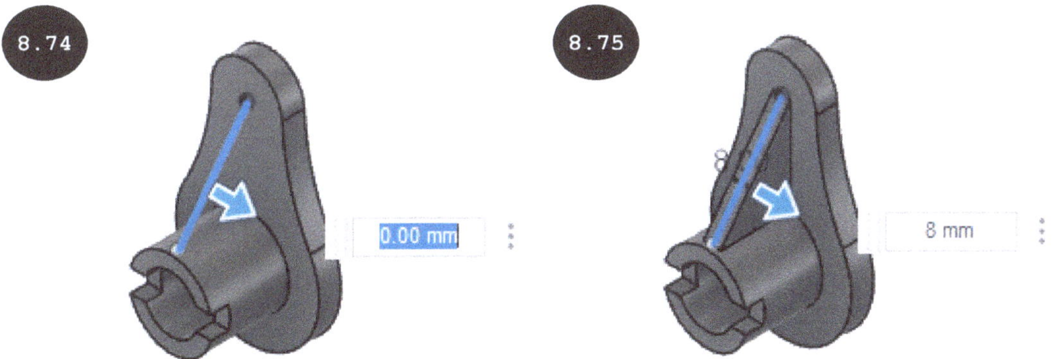

Thickness Direction

The options in the **Thickness Direction** area are used to specify the direction of thickness of the rib feature. By default, the **Symmetric** button is selected in this area. As a result, the thickness is added symmetrically on both sides of the rib sketch. On selecting the **One Side** button, you can specify the thickness on either side of the rib sketch. To reverse the direction of thickness from one side of the sketch to the other side, you need to enter a negative thickness value in the **Thickness** field of the dialog box.

Extent Type

The options in the **Extent Type** drop-down list are used to define the termination or end condition of the rib feature. By default, the **To Next** option is selected in this drop-down list. As a result, the rib feature is terminated at its next intersection, see Figure 8.76. On selecting the **Distance** option in this drop-down list, the **Depth** field appears in the dialog box. In this field, you can specify the depth value to terminate the rib feature by adding material planar to the rib sketch, see Figure 8.77. To flip the direction of termination of the rib feature, click on the **Flip Direction** button in the dialog box.

After specifying all the required parameters for creating the rib feature, click on the **OK** button in the dialog box. The rib feature is created.

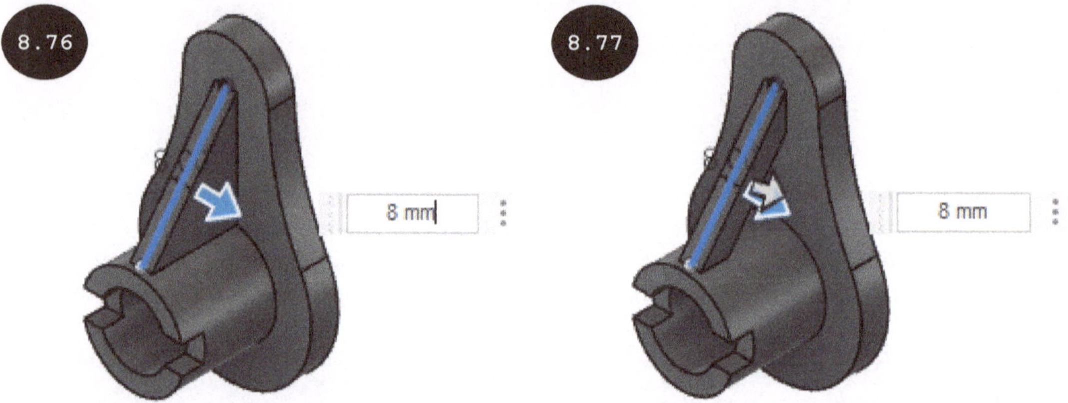

Creating Web Features

Web features are the same as the rib features with the added advantage that they can be created with multiple curves, see Figure 8.78.

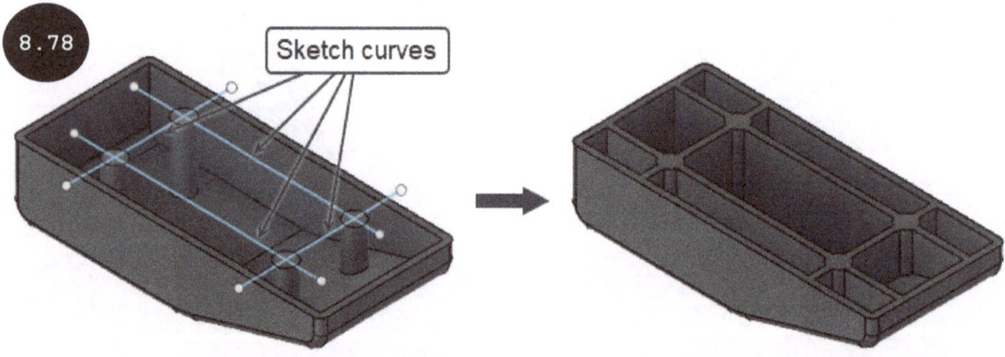

To create a web feature, invoke the **CREATE** drop-down menu in the **SOLID** tab and then click on the **Web** tool, see Figure 8.79. The **WEB** dialog box appears, see Figure 8.80.

The options in the **WEB** dialog box are discussed next.

Profile

The **Profile** selection option is activated in the dialog box, by default. As a result, you can select a sketch loop/entity to create the web feature. You can select multiple sketch loops/entities to create the web feature by clicking the left mouse button. On selecting a sketch entity, an arrow appears in the graphics area, see Figure 8.81. Also, the **Thickness** field appears in the dialog box as well as in the graphics area.

Note: If the value specified in the **Thickness** field is other than 0 (zero), then you need to press the CTRL key to select the multiple sketch curves.

Thickness

The **Thickness** field is used to specify the thickness of the web feature. You can also drag the arrow that appears in the graphics area to dynamically adjust the thickness of the web feature. As soon as you specify the thickness, the preview of the web feature appears normal to the sketching plane in the graphics area, see Figure 8.82.

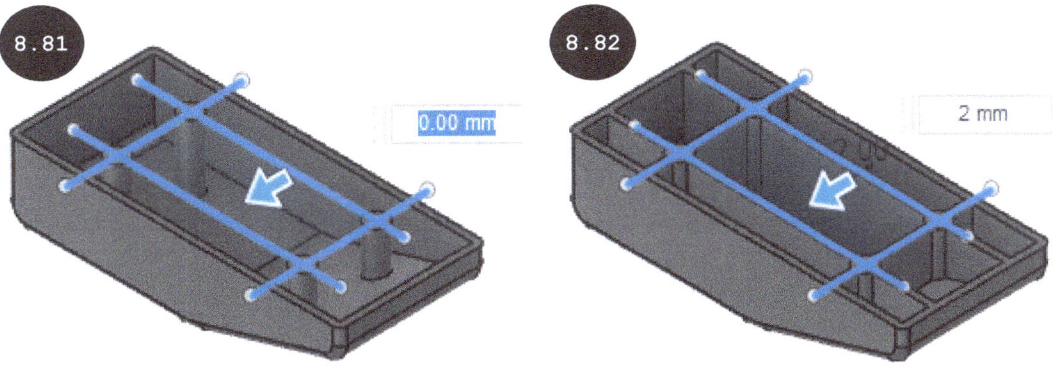

Thickness Direction and Extent Type

The options in the **Thickness Direction** area and **Extent Type** drop-down list of the dialog box are the same as those discussed earlier while creating a rib feature.

Flip Direction

The **Flip Direction** button is used to flip the direction of the material to either side of the sketching plane.

Extend Curves

By default, the **Extend Curves** check box is selected in the dialog box. As a result, the web feature is created by extending the curves up to the next intersection with the model, refer to Figure 8.80. If this check box is cleared, then the web feature is created such that the sketch curves do not extend up to the next intersection, see Figure 8.83.

After specifying all the required parameters for creating the web feature, click on the **OK** button in the dialog box. The web feature is created, see Figure 8.84. In this figure, the web feature is created by selecting the **Extend Curves** check box in the **WEB** dialog box.

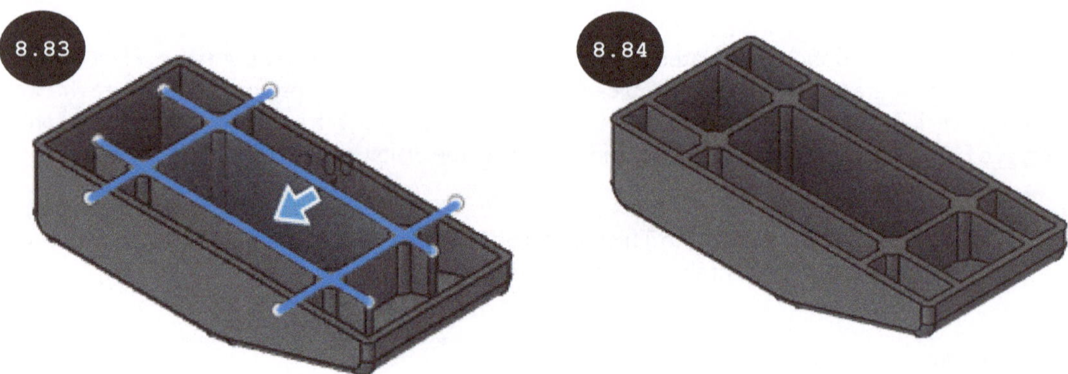

Creating Emboss Features

An emboss feature is created by wrapping a 2D sketch or text around the face of a solid body by adding or removing material. Figure 8.85 shows an emboss feature created by adding material and Figure 8.86 shows an emboss feature created by removing material.

To create an emboss feature, create a 2D sketch that is to be embossed. Next, invoke the **CREATE** drop-down menu in the **SOLID** tab and then click on the **Emboss** tool, see Figure 8.87. The **EMBOSS** dialog box appears, see Figure 8.88. The options in the dialog box are discussed next.

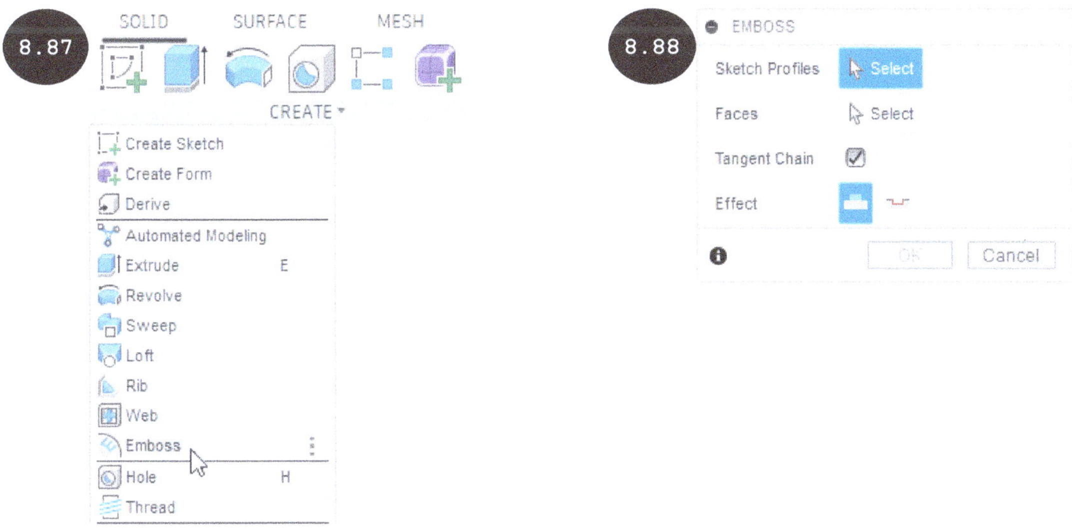

Sketch Profiles

The **Sketch Profiles** selection option is activated in the dialog box, by default. As a result, you can select a 2D sketch profile to be embossed for creating the emboss feature, see Figure 8.89.

Faces

The **Faces** selection option is used to select the faces on which the sketch is to be embossed. To do this, click on the **Faces** selection option to activate it and then select one or more faces of a model, see Figure 8.89. After selecting the sketch profiles and the faces, a preview of an emboss feature appears in the graphics area, along with arrows and a manipulator handle, see Figure 8.90. Also, additional options for defining the depth and alignment of the emboss feature appear in the dialog box, see Figure 8.91.

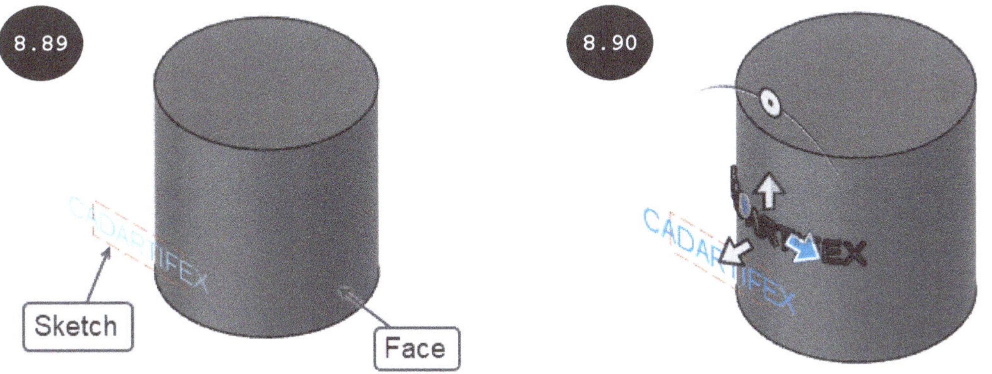

Tangent Chain

By default, the **Tangent Chain** check box is selected in the dialog box. As a result, the faces that are tangentially connected to the selected face(s) also get selected, automatically.

Depth

The **Depth** field of the dialog box is used for specifying the depth of the emboss or deboss feature. An emboss feature is created by adding material to a specified depth, whereas a deboss feature is created by removing material from the model. You can enter a negative value in this field to switch between an emboss and a deboss feature. You can also drag the arrows in the graphics area to specify the depth of the emboss or deboss feature, dynamically.

Effect

The options in the **Effect** area are used for defining the type of feature to be created, see Figure 8.92. The **Emboss** button is used for creating an emboss feature by adding material to the specified depth. The **Deboss** button is used for creating a deboss feature by removing material to the specified depth.

8.91

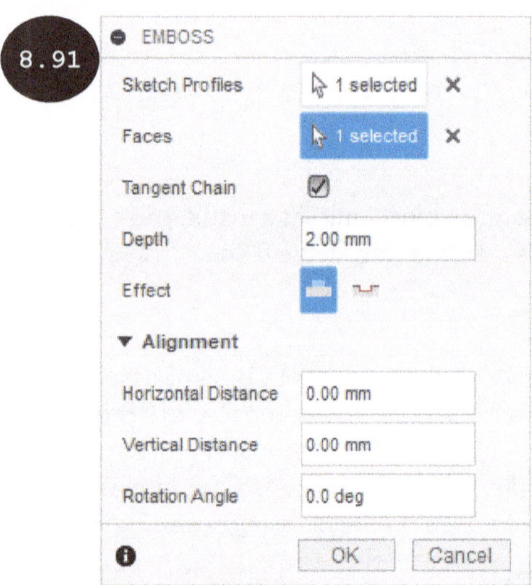

8.92

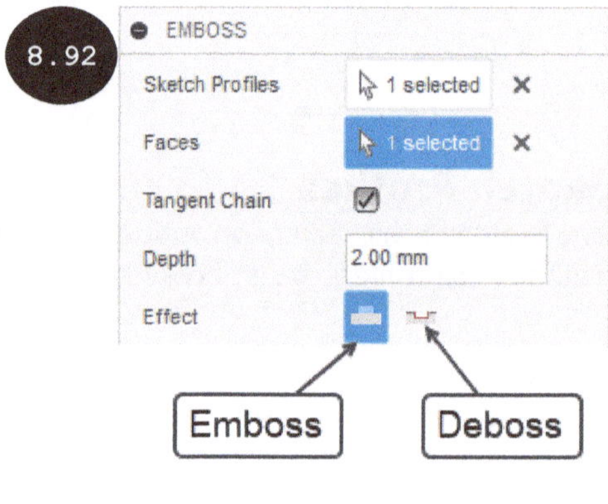

Alignment

The options in the **Alignment** rollout of the dialog box are used to define the alignment of the emboss/deboss feature in the graphics area. You can define the horizontal and vertical distance and rotation angle of the emboss/deboss feature in the respective fields of the **Alignment** rollout of the dialog box. You can also use the arrows and the manipulator handle in the graphics area to dynamically define the alignment of the feature.

After specifying all the required parameters for creating the emboss feature, click on the **OK** button in the dialog box. The emboss feature is created.

Creating Holes

In Autodesk Fusion, you can create Simple, Counterbore, and Countersink hole types by using the **Hole** tool, see Figures 8.93 through 8.95.

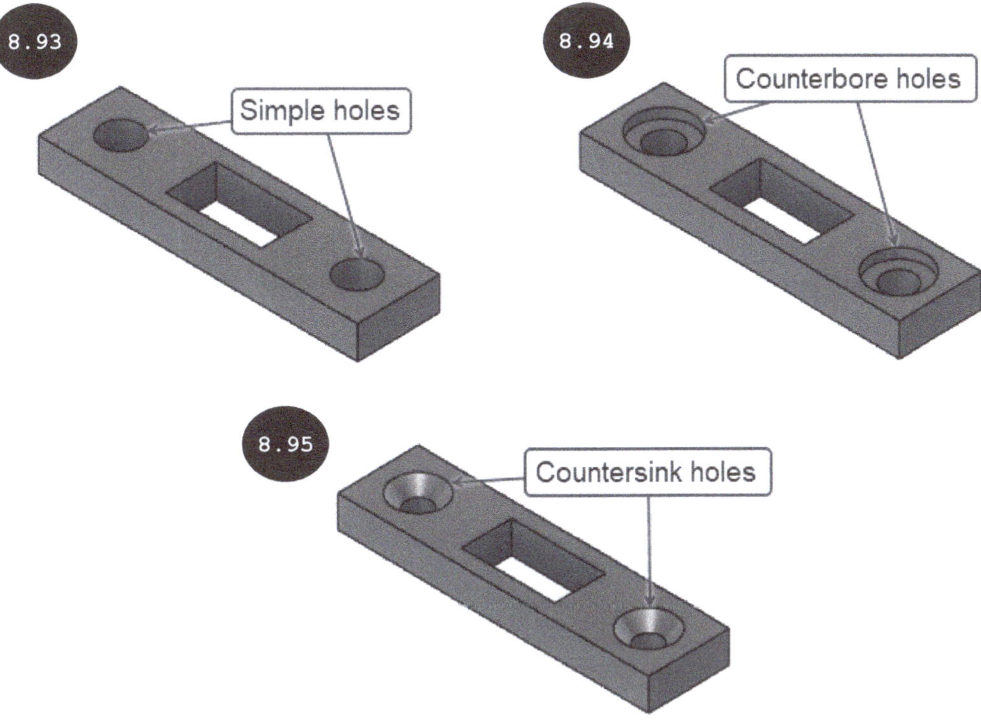

To create holes, click on the **Hole** tool in the **CREATE** panel of the **SOLID** tab, see Figure 8.96. The **HOLE** dialog box appears, see Figure 8.97. Alternatively, press the **H** key or right-click in the graphics area and then click on the **Hole** tool in the Marking Menu that appears to invoke the **HOLE** dialog box. The options in the dialog box are discussed next.

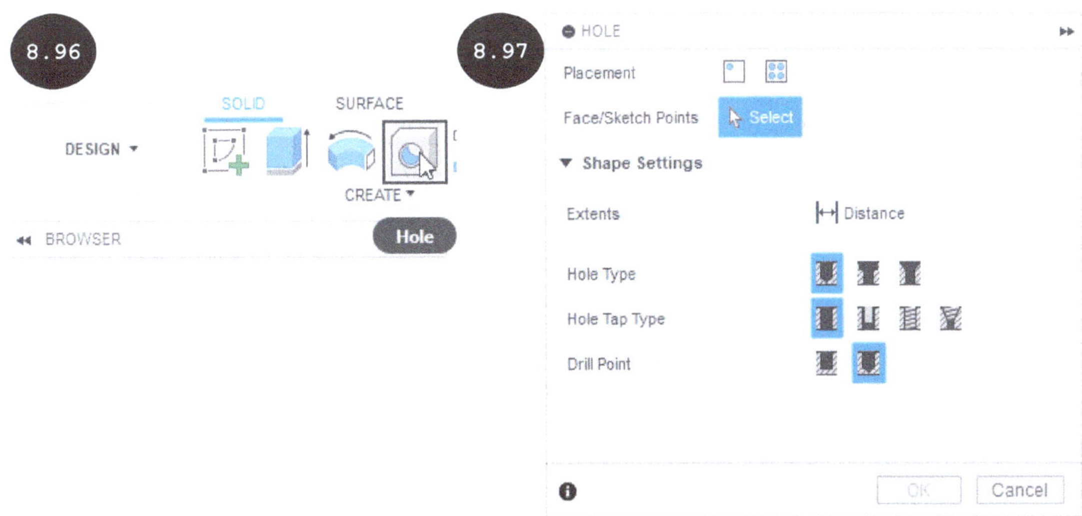

Placement

The **Placement** area of the dialog box has two buttons: **At Point (Single Hole)** and **From Sketch (Multiple Holes)**. The **At Point (Single Hole)** button is used for creating a single hole on the existing face of the model, whereas the **From Sketch (Multiple Holes)** button is used for creating multiple holes by using the sketch points of a sketch. In the latter case, the holes are created by propagating to each sketch point of the sketch. The different methods for creating holes are discussed next.

Creating a Single Hole on a Face

1. Invoke the **HOLE** dialog box and then click on the **At Point (Single Hole)** button in the **Placement** area of the dialog box to create a single hole on an existing face of the model.

   Face: The **Face** selection option is activated in the dialog box, by default. As a result, you can select a face or a plane as the placement plane for creating the hole.

2. Move the cursor over a face or a plane in the graphics area. The face gets highlighted, and its snap points appear, see Figure 8.98.

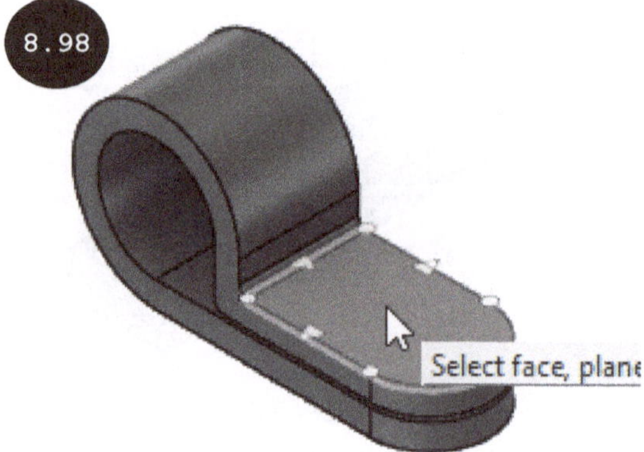

3. Click on a snap point or the face to define the placement of the hole. A preview of the hole appears in the graphics area with default parameters, see Figure 8.99. Also, additional options to create the hole appear in the dialog box, see Figure 8.100. Note that the availability of options in the dialog box depends on the type of hole selected in the **Hole Type** area of the dialog box.

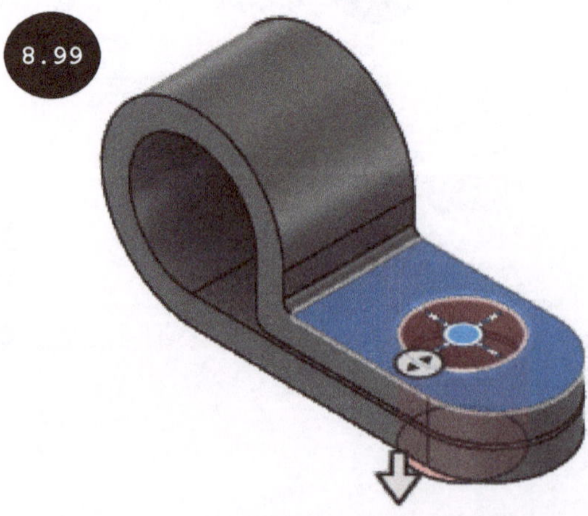

8.100

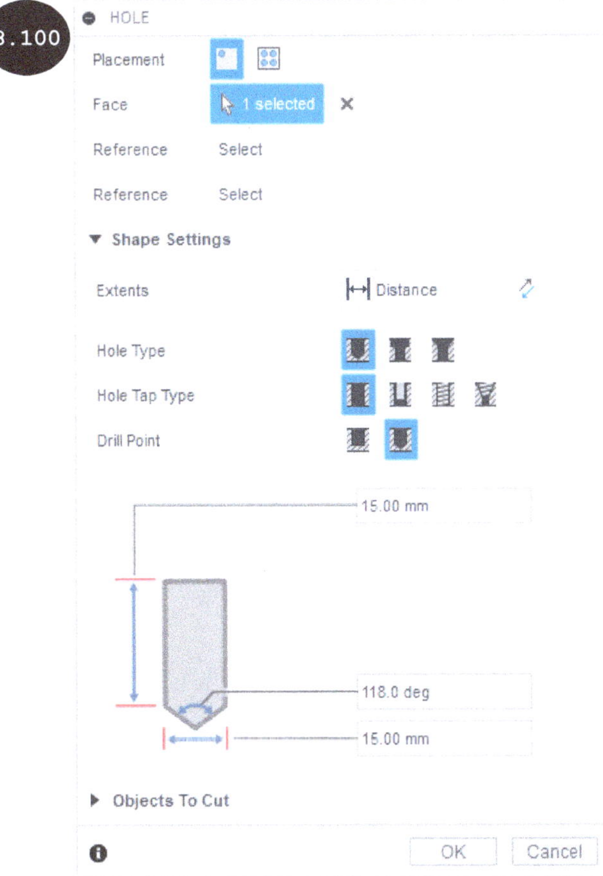

After defining the placement face, you need to define its position on the selected face.

Reference: The **Reference** selection options allow you to select edges to position the hole.

4. Move the cursor over a linear edge of the model. The distance between the edge and the center point of the hole appears, see Figure 8.101.

8.101

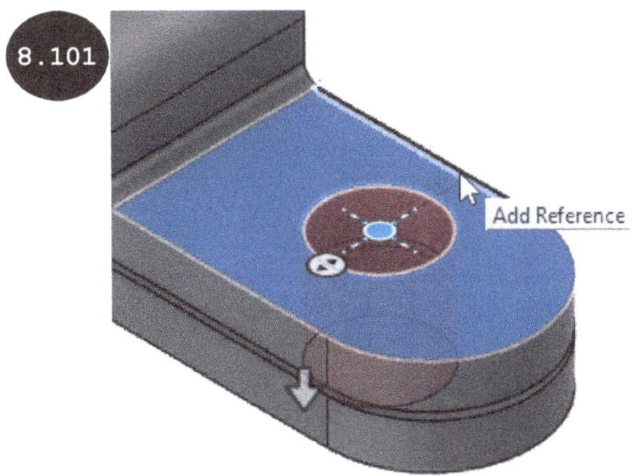

5. Click to select the edge. The **Distance** field appears in the dialog box as well as in the graphics area. Enter the required distance value in this field. Similarly, select another edge to position the second direction of the hole. Note that on selecting a circular edge, the center points of the selected circular edge and the hole become concentric with each other, see Figure 8.102.

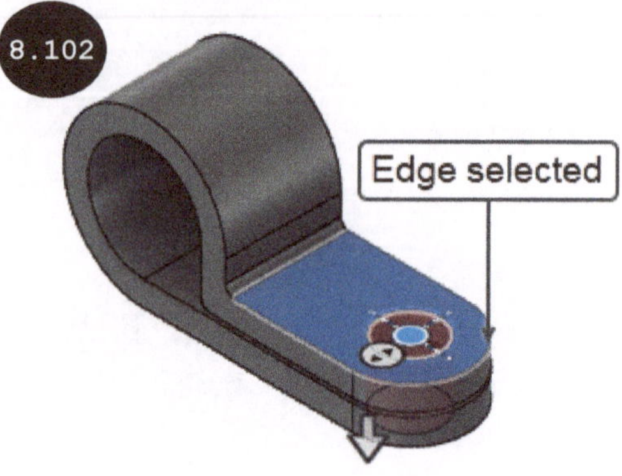

Note: You can also define the position of the hole by dragging its center point to the required location on the selected placement face.

After defining the placement face and the position of the hole, you need to select the type of hole to be created.

Hole Type: The **Hole Type** area of the dialog box is used to select the type of hole (Simple, Counterbore, or Countersink) to be created.

6. Select the **Simple**, **Counterbore**, or **Countersink** button in the **Hole Type** area of the dialog box.

Hole Tap Type: The **Hole Tap Type** area of the dialog box is used to select the hole tap type (Simple, Clearance, Tapped, or Taper Tapped) to be created.

7. Select the **Simple**, **Clearance**, **Tapped**, or **Taper Tapped** button in the **Hole Tap Type** area of the dialog box.

8. Select the **Flat** or **Angle** button in the **Drill Point** area to create the hole with either a flat end or an angled end, respectively.

Thread Offset: The **Thread Offset** area is used to specify whether to create a full-length thread or a custom-length thread in the hole by selecting the **Full** or **Offset** buttons, respectively. Note that this area is available in the dialog box only when the **Tapped** button is selected in the **Hole Tap Type** area of the dialog box.

9. Select the **Full** or **Offset** button in the **Thread Offset** area while creating the tapped hole.

10. Specify the required parameters for creating the hole in the respective fields, refer to Figures 8.103 through 8.105. Note that the availability of fields in the dialog box depends on the buttons selected in the **Hole Type**, **Hole Tap Type**, **Drill Point**, and **Thread Offset** areas of the dialog box.

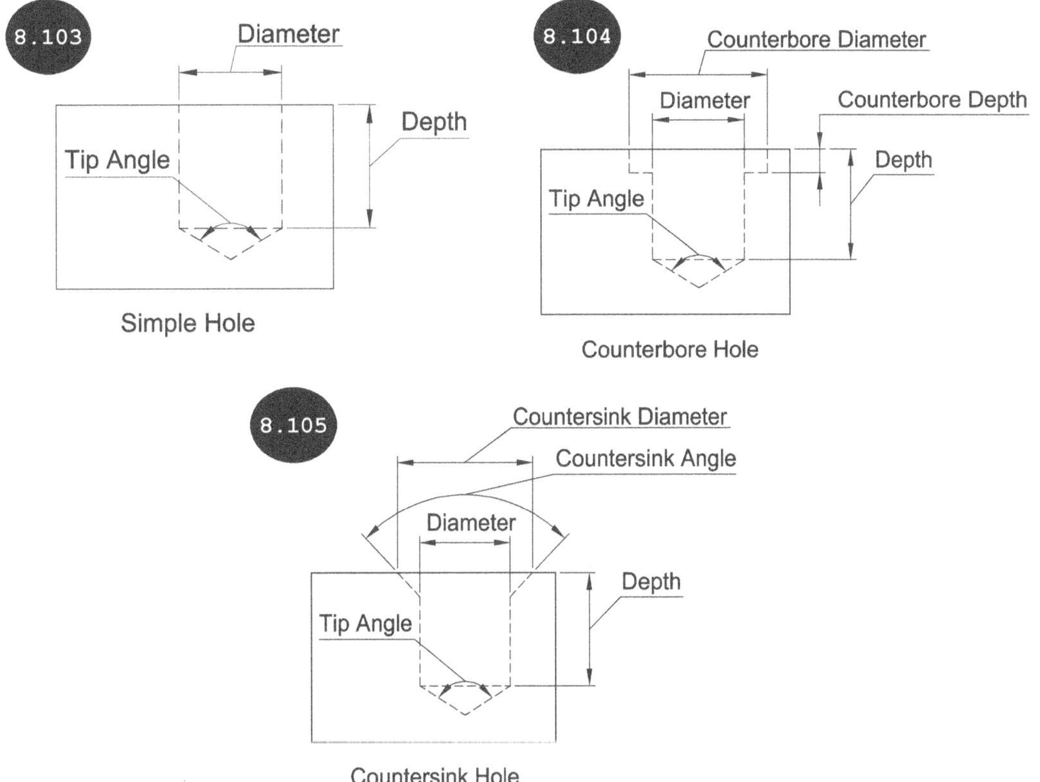

11. Specify the required options in the **Standard, Fastener Type, Size, Thread Type, Class, Direction,** and **Fit** drop-down lists of the dialog box for creating the tapped hole. Note that these drop-down lists appear only when the **Clearance, Tapped**, or **Taper Tapped** button is activated in the **Hole Tap Type** area of the dialog box.

12. Select the required option in the **Extents** drop-down list of the dialog box and define the end condition of the hole. The options in this drop-down list are the same as discussed earlier.

Tip: You can flip the direction of the hole creation to the other side of the selected face by using the **Flip Direction** button of the dialog box.

13. Click on the **OK** button. The hole is created as per specified parameters, see Figure 8.106. In this figure, the counterbore hole is created on the top planar face of the model.

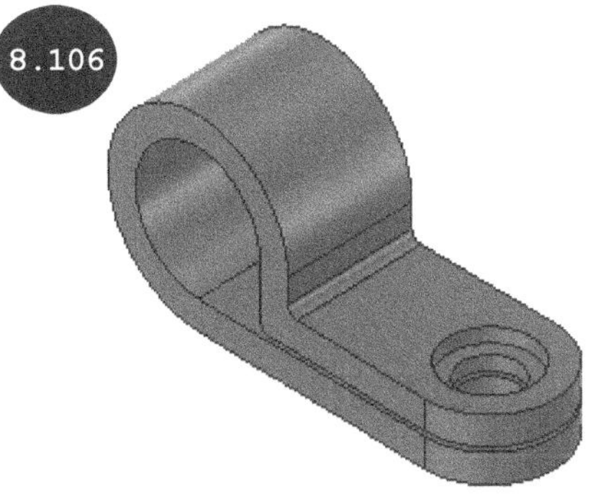

Creating Multiple Holes on Points

In Autodesk Fusion, you can also create multiple holes by selecting the sketch points or vertices.

1. Invoke the **HOLE** dialog box and then click on the **From Sketch (Multiple Holes)** button in the **Placement** area to create multiple holes by using the sketch points.

Note: The options that appear after activating the **From Sketch (Multiple Holes)** button in the dialog box are same, as discussed earlier, with the only additional advantage that you can select multiple sketch points or vertices of the model to create holes.

2. Select the sketch points or the vertices of the model one by one in the graphics area. Note that as you select the points, the preview of the holes appears with default parameters such that the center points of the holes coincide with the sketch points selected, see Figure 8.107.

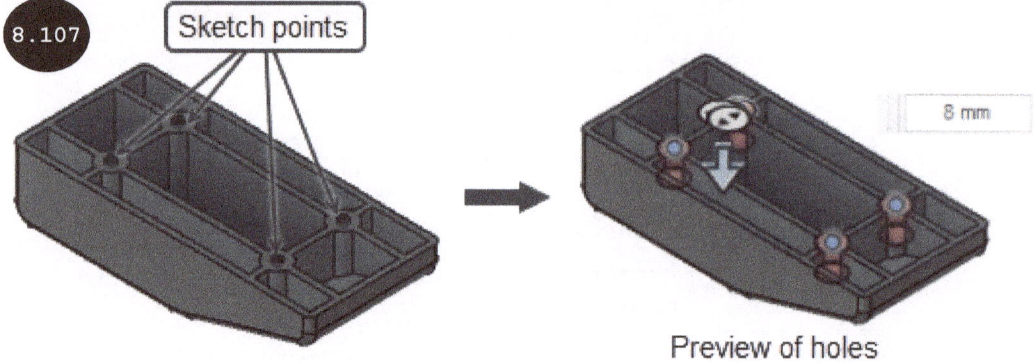

3. Select the type of hole (Simple, Counterbore, or Countersink) to be created in the **Hole Type** area of the dialog box.

4. Specify the required parameters for creating the hole in the respective fields of the dialog box, as discussed earlier.

5. Select the required option in the **Extents** drop-down list and define the end condition of the hole. The options in this drop-down list are the same as discussed earlier.

6. Click on the **OK** button. The holes are created on the points selected, see Figure 8.108. In this figure, simple holes are created by selecting the four sketch points.

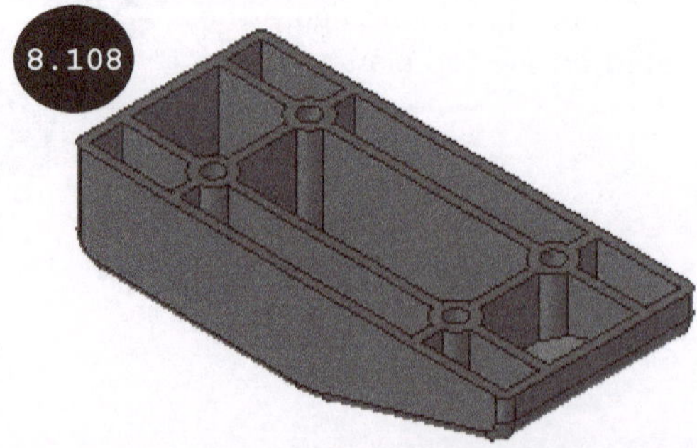

Creating a Thread

You can create internal or external threads on the cylindrical faces of the model, see Figure 8.109. In Autodesk Fusion, the threads can be cosmetic threads or modeled threads. A cosmetic thread is not a real thread and is created by applying an appearance of the thread on the selected face, whereas the modeled thread is the real thread and is created by removing material from the selected face of the model. The method for creating threads is discussed below:

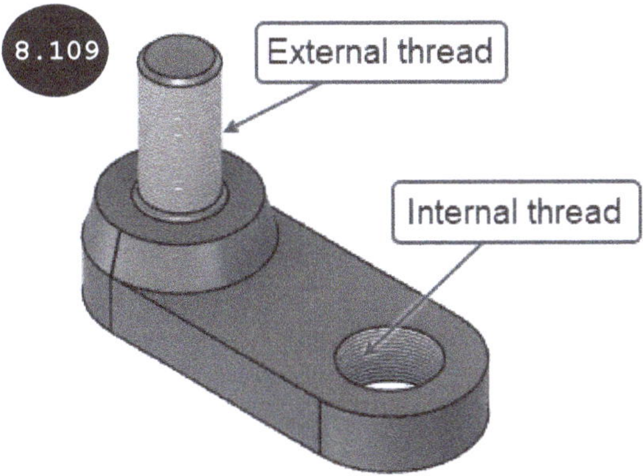

Tip: It is recommended to add cosmetic threads to holes, fasteners, or cylindrical features of a model, as it helps in reducing the complexity of the model and improves the overall performance of the system.

1. Invoke the **CREATE** drop-down menu in the **SOLID** tab of the **Toolbar** and then click on the **Thread** tool, see Figure 8.110. The **THREAD** dialog box appears, see Figure 8.111.

Faces: The **Faces** selection option is activated in the dialog box, by default. As a result, you can select cylindrical faces to create threads. You can select external or internal cylindrical faces to create external or internal threads, respectively.

2. Select a cylindrical face (internal or external) of the model. The preview of the thread with default specifications appears, see Figure 8.112. In this figure, the external cylindrical face is selected to create the thread.

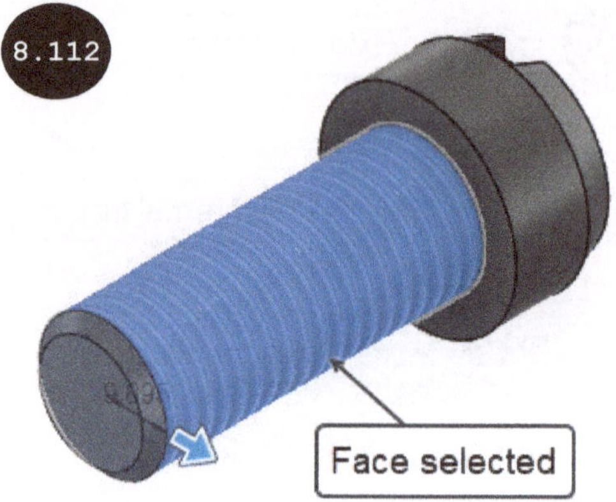

Note: You can also select multiple cylindrical faces to create threads by pressing the CTRL key.

Full Length: By default, the **Full Length** check box is selected in the dialog box. So, the resultant thread is created on the entire length of the selected face. When this check box is cleared, the **Offset** and **Length** fields appear in the dialog box. The **Offset** field is used for creating the thread at an offset distance from the starting point of the selected face, see Figure 8.113. The **Length** field is used for specifying the length of the thread, see Figure 8.113. You can also drag the arrows that appear in the preview of the thread to adjust the offset distance and length of the thread dynamically.

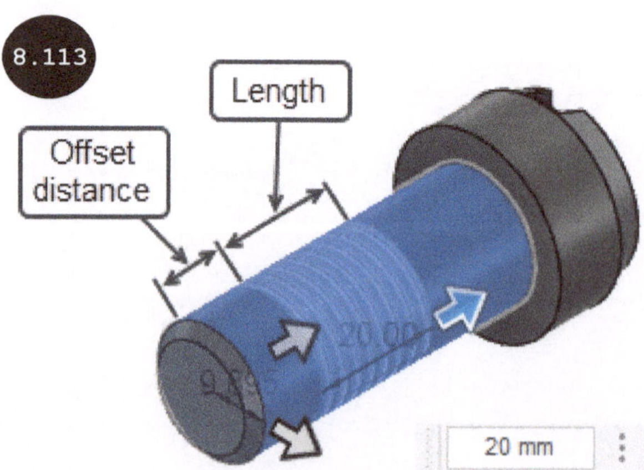

3. Select or clear the **Full Length** check box to specify a thread of full length or user-defined length, respectively.

   Modeled: By default, the **Modeled** check box is cleared in the dialog box. So, the resultant thread is created as a cosmetic thread. To create a modeled thread by cutting the actual thread on the selected face, select the **Modeled** check box in the dialog box, see Figure 8.114. This figure shows the preview of the modeled thread on an external cylindrical face.

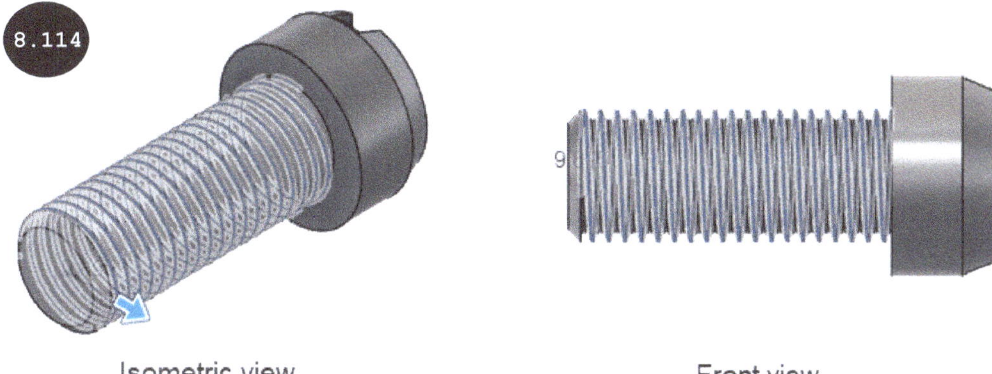

Isometric view　　　　Front view

4. Select or clear the **Modeled** check box in the dialog box for creating the modeled thread or cosmetic thread, respectively.

5. Select the required thread type in the **Thread Type** drop-down list of the dialog box.

6. Select the size of the thread to be created in the **Size** drop-down list of the dialog box. By default, the size of the thread is defined based on the diameter of the cylindrical face selected.

7. Select the pitch or designation of the thread in the **Designation** drop-down list of the dialog box. The availability of options in this drop-down list depends on the size and type of thread selected.

8. Select the thread class in the **Class** drop-down list of the dialog box. The availability of options in this drop-down list depends on the thread type selected.

9. Select the direction of the thread (right-hand thread or left-hand thread) in the **Direction** drop-down list of the dialog box.

   Remember Size: The **Remember Size** check box is used to save the specified thread settings as the default settings for the next time you invoke the **THREAD** dialog box.

10. Click on the **OK** button in the dialog box. The thread with desired specifications is created, see Figures 8.115 and 8.116. In Figure 8.115, the modeled thread is created on the external cylindrical face of the model, whereas in Figure 8.116, the modeled thread is created on the internal cylindrical face of the model.

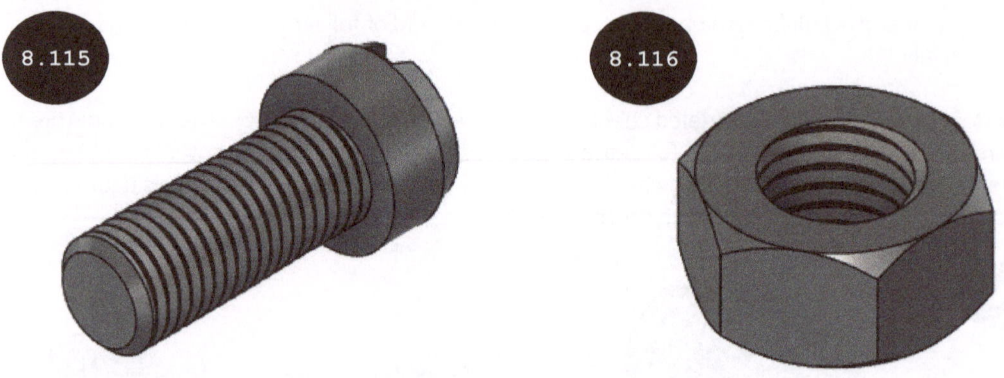

Creating an Automated Modeling

In Autodesk Fusion, automated modeling enables you to generate multiple optimized 3D design alternatives that automatically connect different geometries with just a few clicks. This approach allows designers to explore several design possibilities and select the option that best meets functional, aesthetic, or manufacturing requirements.

Automated modeling is particularly useful when exploring multiple shape variations between profiles or bodies, optimizing designs for weight, strength, or performance, and reducing repetitive manual modeling tasks. The method for creating automated design alternatives between geometries is discussed below:

1. Invoke the **CREATE** drop-down menu in the **SOLID** tab and click the **Automated Modeling** tool, see Figure 8.117. The **AUTOMATED MODELING** dialog box appears, see Figure 8.118. By default, the **Faces to Connect** selection option is activated.

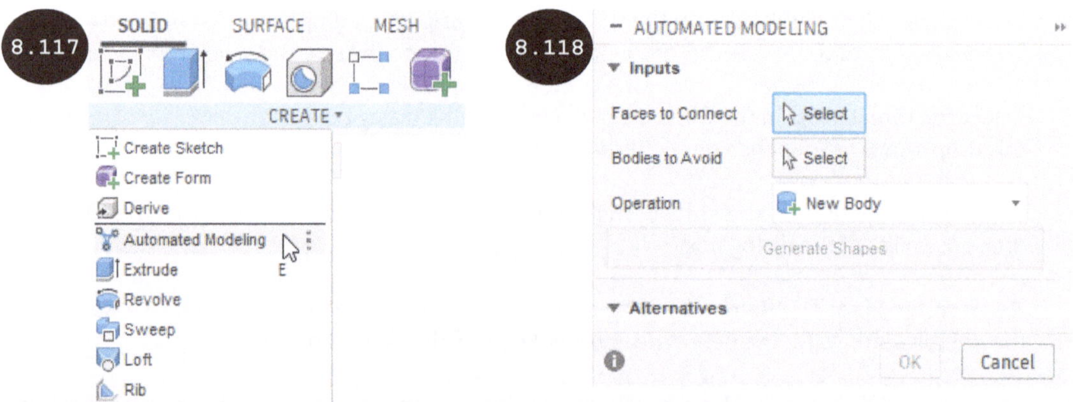

2. Select two or more faces in the graphics area between which the design alternatives are to be generated, see Figure 8.119. In this figure, four faces from two different bodies are selected.

   After selecting the faces to be connected, you can also specify bodies that should be excluded from the automated design, if required.

3. Click the **Bodies to Avoid** selection option in the **Inputs** rollout of the dialog box, and then select one or more bodies to be avoided while generating the design alternatives, if required, see Figure 8.119. In this figure, the middle body is selected as the body to be avoided during design generation.

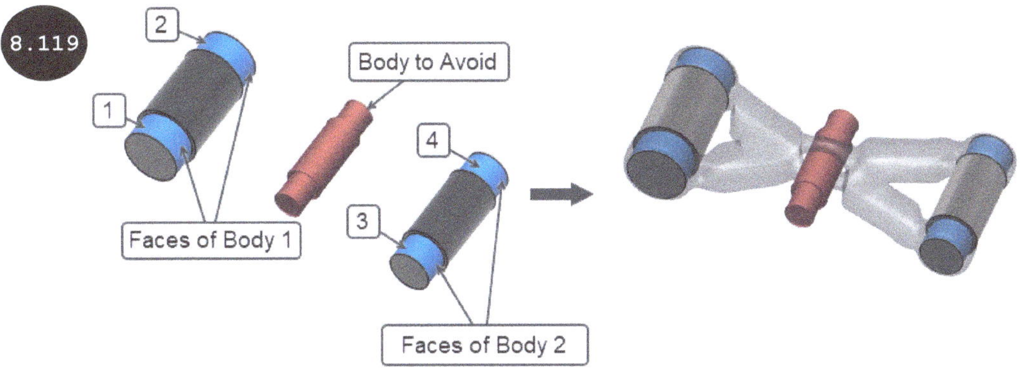

Now, you can specify the operation type for the resulting design.

4. Select the **New Body** option in the **Operation** drop-down list to create the final design as a new body within the currently active component.

5. After specifying the required inputs, click on the **Generate Shapes** button in the dialog box. Fusion begins generating multiple design alternatives based on the specified inputs.

6. Once all the design alternatives are generated, review them and select the one that best meets your design requirements. You can also increase or decrease the volume of the design using the **Volume** slider, see Figure 8.120.

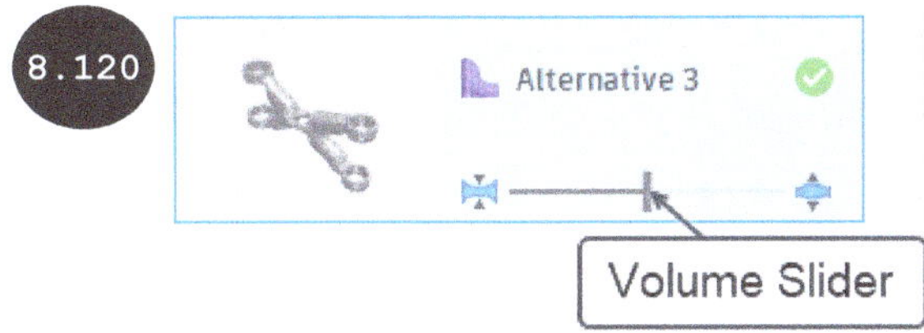

7. Click **OK** to confirm the creation of the selected design alternative in the graphics area.

Creating a Rectangular Box

In Autodesk Fusion, you can create a rectangular box using the **Box** tool. The method for creating a rectangular box is discussed below:

1. Invoke the **CREATE** drop-down menu in the **SOLID** tab of the **Toolbar** and then click on the **Box** tool, see Figure 8.121. The three default planes appear in the graphics area.

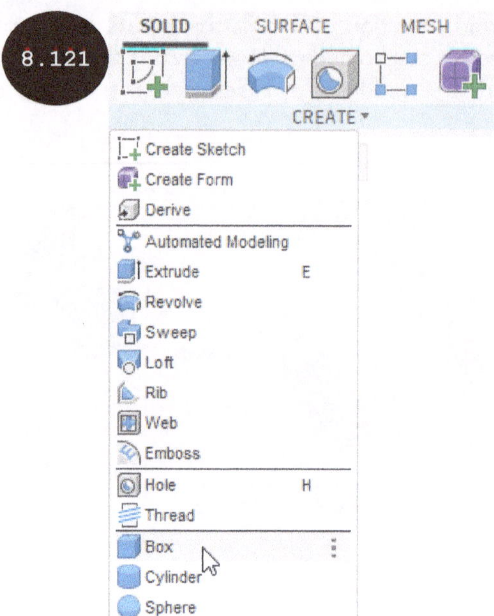

2. Select a plane or a planar face as the sketching plane to create a sketch of the rectangular box. The **2-Point Rectangle** tool gets activated automatically and you are prompted to specify two diagonally opposite corners of the rectangle.

3. Create a rectangle by specifying its two diagonally opposite corners. A preview of the rectangular box appears in the graphics area with default parameters, see Figure 8.122. Also, the **BOX** dialog box appears, see Figure 8.123.

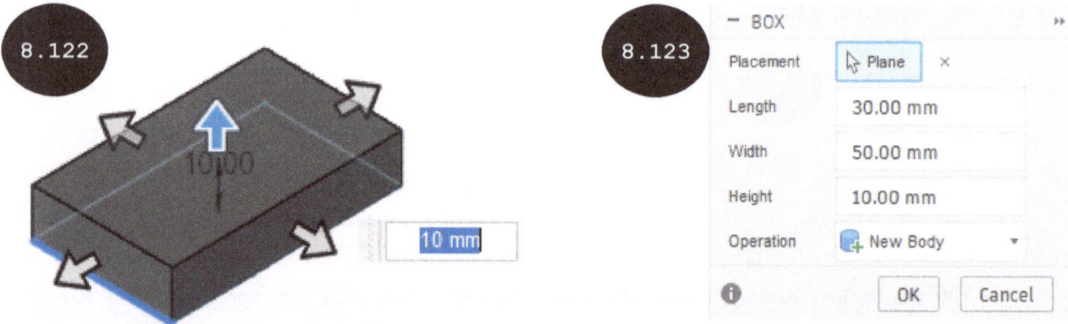

4. Specify the length, width, and height of the box in the respective fields of the dialog box. Alternatively, drag the arrows that appear in the preview of the rectangular box to set the length, width, and height of the box dynamically in the graphics area.

5. Select the required option in the **Operation** drop-down list of the dialog box. The options in this drop-down list are the same as discussed earlier.

6. Click on the **OK** button in the dialog box. The rectangular box with specified parameters is created in the graphics area.

Creating a Cylinder

You can create a cylinder using the **Cylinder** tool. The method for creating a cylinder is discussed below:

1. Invoke the **CREATE** drop-down menu in the **SOLID** tab of the **Toolbar** and then click on the **Cylinder** tool. The three default planes appear in the graphics area.

2. Select a plane or a planar face as the sketching plane to create a sketch of the cylinder. The **Center Diameter Circle** tool gets activated automatically and you are prompted to specify the center point of the circle.

3. Click to specify the center point of the circle and then the diameter. A preview of the cylinder appears in the graphics area with default parameters, see Figure 8.124. Also, the **CYLINDER** dialog box appears, see Figure 8.125.

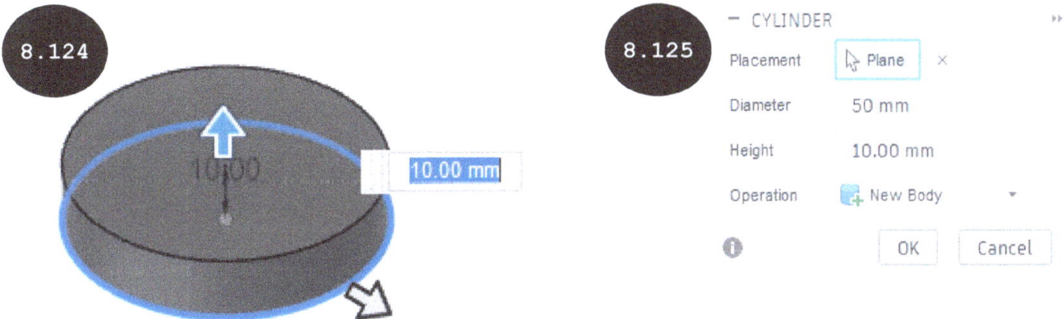

4. Specify the diameter and the height of the cylinder in the respective fields of the dialog box. Alternatively, drag the arrows that appear in the preview of the cylinder to set the diameter and height of the cylinder, dynamically in the graphics area.

5. Select the required option in the **Operation** drop-down list of the dialog box.

6. Click on the **OK** button in the dialog box. The cylinder with specified parameters is created in the graphics area.

Creating a Sphere

You can create a sphere using the **Sphere** tool. The method for creating a sphere is discussed below:

1. Invoke the **CREATE** drop-down menu in the **SOLID** tab of the **Toolbar** and then click on the **Sphere** tool.

2. Select a plane or a planar face as the sketching plane to specify the center point of the sphere. The **Point** tool gets activated automatically and you are prompted to specify the center point of the sphere.

3. Click to specify the center point of the sphere. The preview of the sphere appears in the graphics area with a default diameter, see Figure 8.126. Also, the **SPHERE** dialog box appears, see Figure 8.127.

4. Specify the diameter of the sphere in the **Diameter** field of the dialog box. Alternatively, drag the arrow that appears in the preview of the sphere to set the diameter, dynamically.

5. Select the required option in the **Operation** drop-down list of the dialog box.

6. Click on the **OK** button in the dialog box. The sphere with the specified diameter is created.

Creating a Torus

You can create a torus using the **Torus** tool. The method for creating a torus is discussed below:

1. Invoke the **CREATE** drop-down menu in the **SOLID** tab of the **Toolbar** and then click on the **Torus** tool.

2. Select a plane or a planar face as the sketching plane to create the sketch of the torus. The **Center Diameter Circle** tool gets activated automatically and you are prompted to specify the center point of the circle.

3. Click to specify the center point of the circle and then the diameter. The preview of the torus appears in the graphics area with default parameters, see Figure 8.128. Also, the **TORUS** dialog box appears, see Figure 8.129. Note that the circle defines the axis of revolution of the torus.

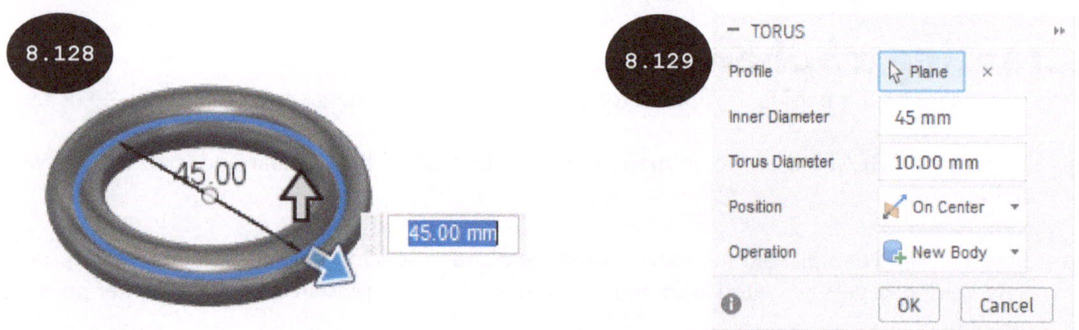

4. Specify the inner diameter of the torus in the **Inner Diameter** field of the dialog box. By default, the inner diameter defines the axis of revolution of the torus. You can also drag the arrow that appears along the axis of revolution of the torus to set its inner diameter, dynamically.

5. Specify the torus diameter in the **Torus Diameter** field. Note that the torus diameter measures the cross-sectional diameter of the torus. You can also drag the arrow that appears in the preview of the torus to dynamically set the torus diameter in the graphics area.

6. Select the required option in the **Position** drop-down list of the dialog box to define the position of the torus concerning the specified inner diameter in the **Inner Diameter** field. By default, the **On Center** option is selected. So, the resultant torus is created by positioning the center of the torus section on the specified inner diameter. On selecting the **Inside** option, the resultant torus is created by positioning the torus inside the specified inner diameter. On selecting the **Outside** option, the resultant torus is created by positioning the torus outside the specified inner diameter.

7. Select the required option in the **Operation** drop-down list of the dialog box and then click on the **OK** button. The torus with specified parameters is created.

Creating a Helical and a Spiral Coil

In Autodesk Fusion, you can create a helical and spiral coil using the **Coil** tool.

1. Invoke the **CREATE** drop-down menu in the **SOLID** tab and then click on the **Coil** tool.

2. Select a plane or a planar face as the sketching plane. The **Center Diameter Circle** tool gets activated automatically and you are prompted to specify the center point of the circle.

3. Click to specify the center point of the circle and then the diameter. The preview of a helical coil appears, see Figure 8.130. Also, the **COIL** dialog box appears, see Figure 8.131.

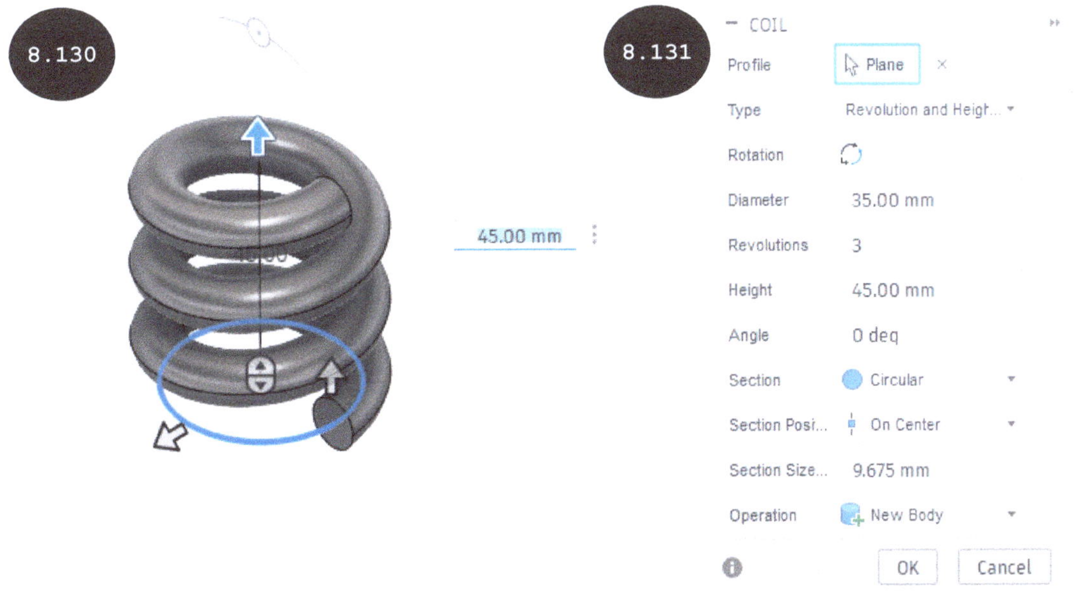

Type: The **Type** drop-down list is used to define the type of coil (helical or spiral) to be created and the method to be adopted for creating the coil, see Figure 8.132. The options are discussed next.

The **Revolution and Height** option is used to create a helical coil by defining its number of revolutions and total height. On selecting this option, the options for creating a helical coil by defining its revolutions and height are enabled in the dialog box.

The **Revolution and Pitch** option is used to create a helical coil by defining its number of revolutions and pitch.

The **Height and Pitch** option is used to create a helical coil by defining its total height and pitch.

The **Spiral** option is used to create a spiral coil by defining its pitch and number of revolutions. Figure 8.133 shows the preview of a spiral coil.

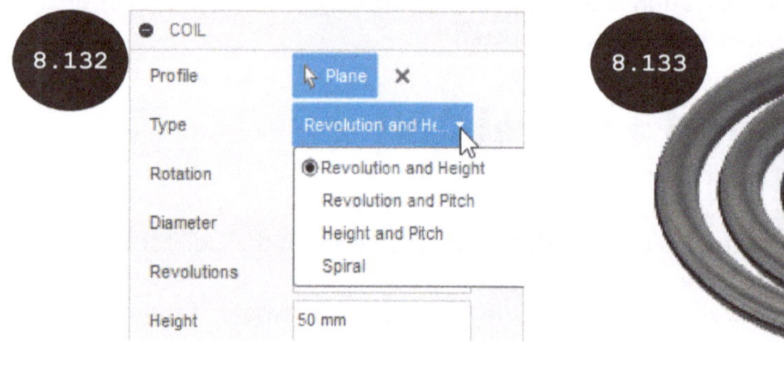

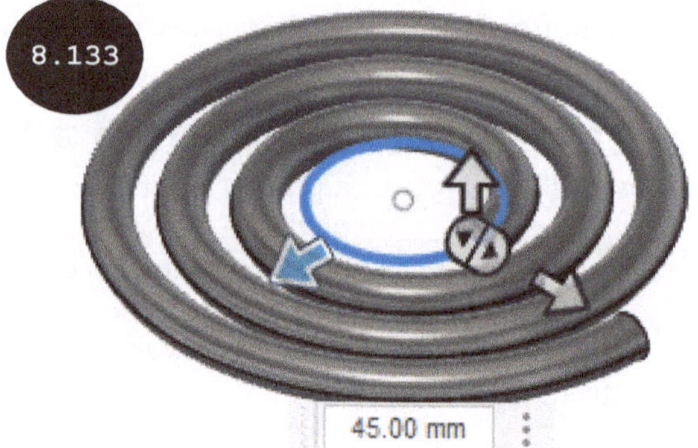

4. Select the required option (**Revolution and Height**, **Revolution and Pitch**, or **Height and Pitch**), as the method to be adopted for creating the helical coil, in the **Type** drop-down list. Note that to create a spiral coil, you need to select the **Spiral** option in the **Type** drop-down list.

5. Specify the start diameter of the coil in the **Diameter** field of the dialog box. By default, the start diameter of the coil is defined by the circle drawn.

6. Specify the parameters such as revolutions and pitch in the respective fields of the dialog box to create the coil. Note that the availability of options in the dialog box depends on the option selected in the **Type** drop-down list of the dialog box. You can also drag the arrows that appear in the preview of the coil to dynamically adjust the parameters in the graphics area.

Note: You can also create a tapered helical coil by specifying the taper angle in the **Angle** field of the **COIL** dialog box, see Figure 8.134. To reverse the direction, you need to enter a negative angle value in the field.

Section: The **Section** drop-down list is used to specify the cross-sectional shape of the coil. You can create a coil with a circular, square, external triangular, or internal triangular shape by selecting the respective option in this drop-down list, see Figures 8.135 through 8.138.

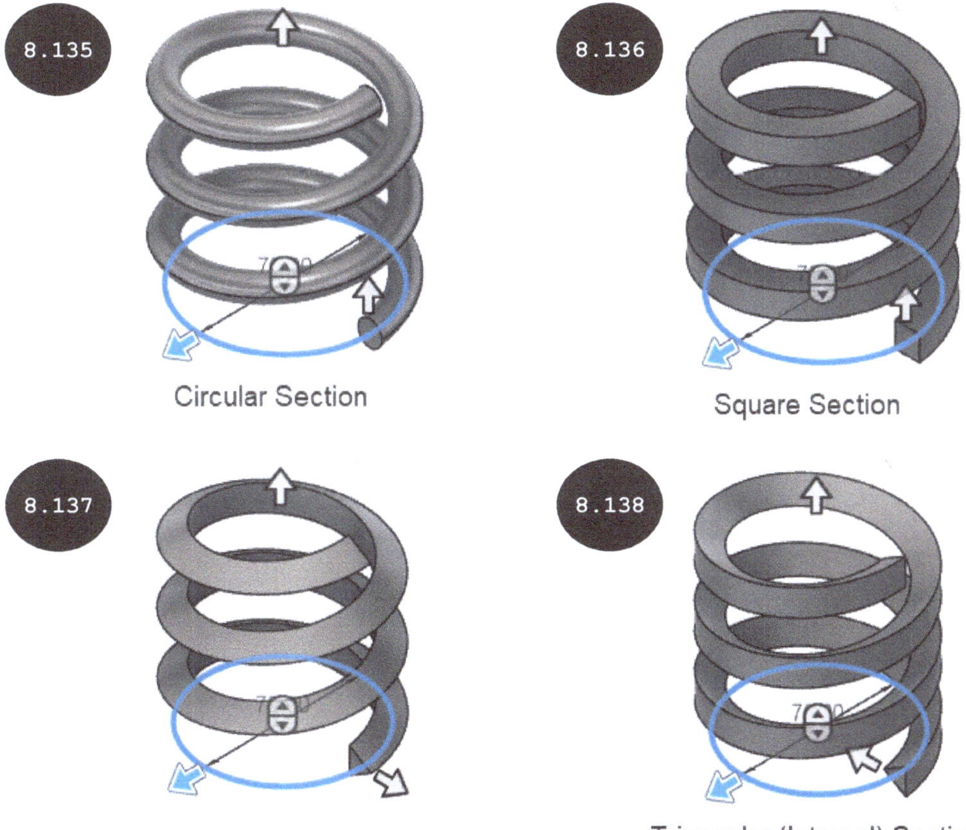

Circular Section

Square Section

Triangular (External) Section

Triangular (Internal) Section

7. Select the required option in the **Section** drop-down list to define the cross-sectional shape of the coil, refer to Figures 8.135 through 8.138.

Section Position: The **Section Position** drop-down list is used to define the position of a cross-section of the coil. By default, the **On Center** option is selected. So, the resultant coil is created by positioning the center of the coil section on the start diameter of the coil specified in the **Diameter** field. On selecting the **Inside** option, the resultant coil is created by positioning the coil section inside the specified start diameter. On selecting the **Outside** option, the resultant coil is created by positioning the coil section outside the start diameter.

8. Select the required option in the **Section Position** drop-down list of the dialog box to define the position of the coil concerning the start diameter specified in the **Diameter** field.

Section Size: The **Section Size** field is used to specify the size of the coil section.

9. Specify the size of the coil section in the **Section Size** field of the dialog box. Note that the size of the coil depends on the type of section selected in the **Section** drop-down list.

10. To reverse the direction of rotation of the coil, click on the **Rotation** button in the dialog box.

11. Select the required option in the **Operation** drop-down list of the dialog box and then click on the **OK** button. The coil with specified parameters is created. Figure 8.139 shows a helical coil having a circular section and Figure 8.140 shows a spiral coil having a circular section.

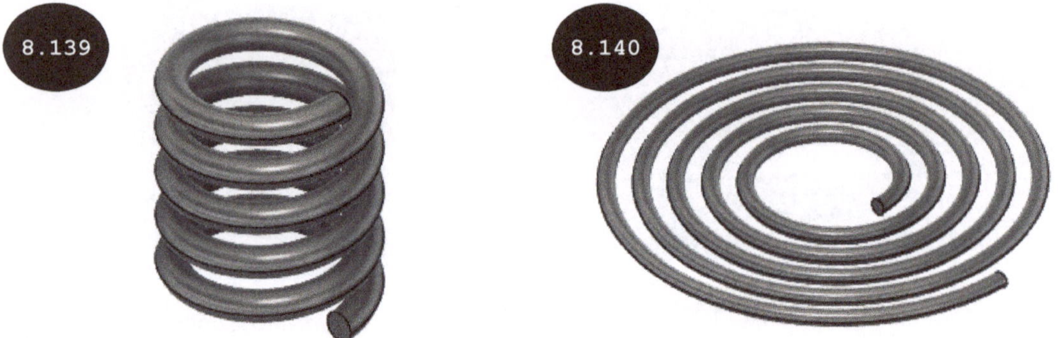

Creating a Pipe

In Autodesk Fusion, you can create a solid or hollow pipe using the **Pipe** tool. To create a pipe, you need to select an open or a closed sketch, or a curve as the path of the pipe, see Figure 8.141. You can also select an edge or a set of model edges as the path of the pipe. Note that in Figure 8.141, a 3D sketch is selected as the path. You will learn about creating 3D sketches later in this chapter.

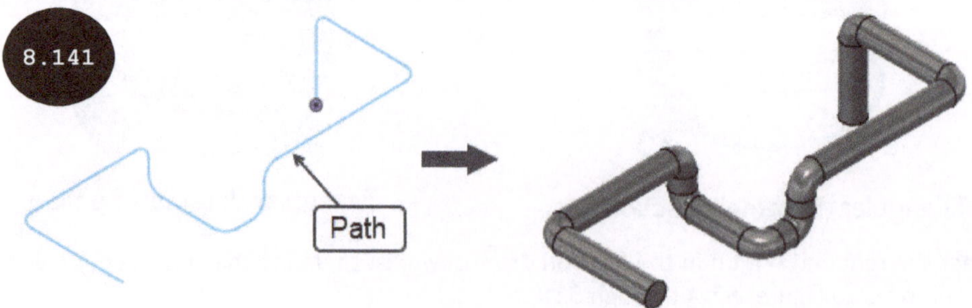

1. Create an open or closed sketch or a curve as the path by using the sketching tools.

2. Invoke the **CREATE** drop-down menu in the **SOLID** tab and then click on the **Pipe** tool, see Figure 8.142. The **PIPE** dialog box appears, see Figure 8.143.

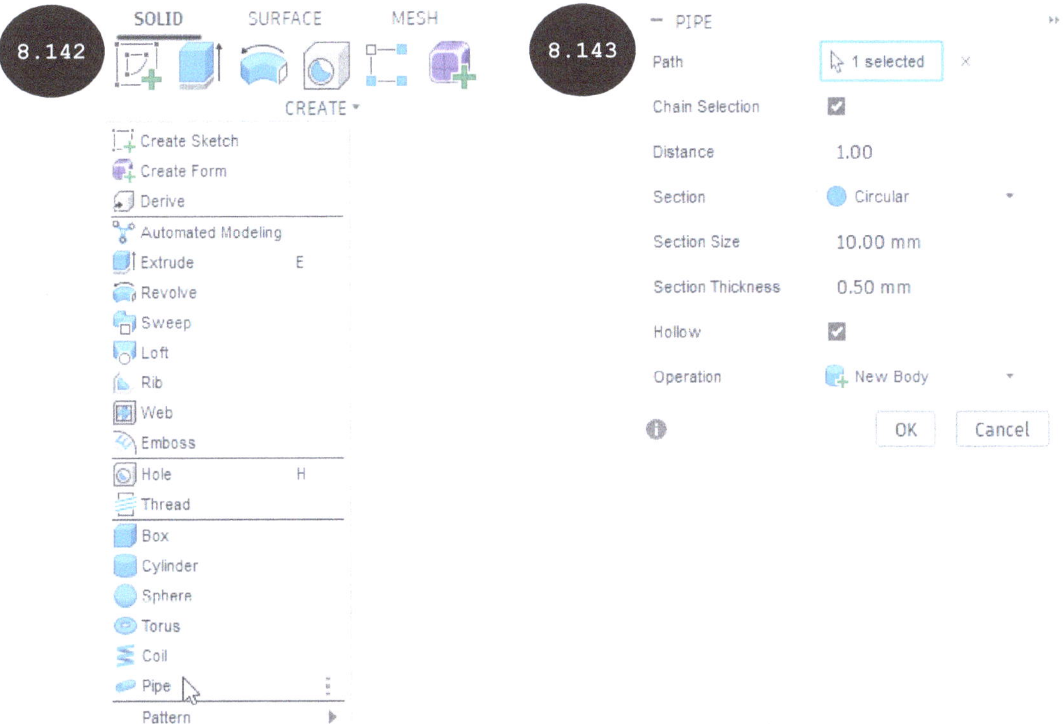

Path: By default, the **Path** selection option is activated in the dialog box. So, you can select an open or closed sketch, or a curve as the path. You can also select an edge or a set of model edges as the path. Note that the **Chain Selection** check box is selected. As a result, all its contiguous entities get selected automatically.

3. Select the path of the pipe in the graphics area, see Figure 8.144. The preview of the pipe with default parameters appears in the graphics area such that the section of the pipe follows the path selected, see Figure 8.145.

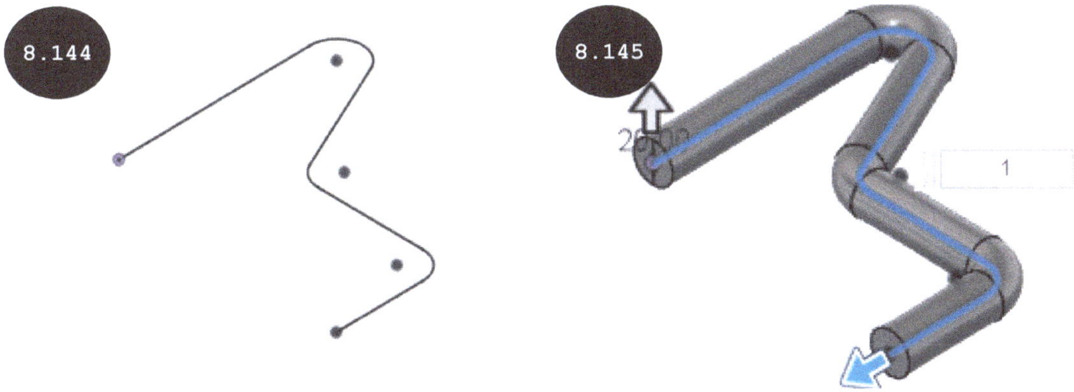

Distance: By default, the value 1 is entered in the **Distance** field of the dialog box. So, a full-length pipe is created along the path. You can specify the length of the pipe in terms of the percentage of the selected path.

4. Enter the required percentage value in the **Distance** field of the dialog box. To create a pipe of full length along the selected path, ensure that the value 1 is entered in the **Distance** field.

5. Select the required section for the pipe in the **Section** drop-down list of the dialog box. You can create a pipe with a circular section, square section, or triangular section.

6. Specify the size of the pipe section in the **Section Size** field of the dialog box.

7. Ensure that the **Hollow** check box is cleared in the dialog box for creating a solid pipe. To create a hollow pipe, you need to select the **Hollow** check box and then specify the thickness of the hollow pipe in the **Section Thickness** field that appears in the dialog box.

8. Select the required option in the **Operation** drop-down list of the dialog box and then click on the **OK** button. The pipe is created. Figure 8.146 shows a hollow pipe of a circular section and Figure 8.147 shows a solid pipe of a square section.

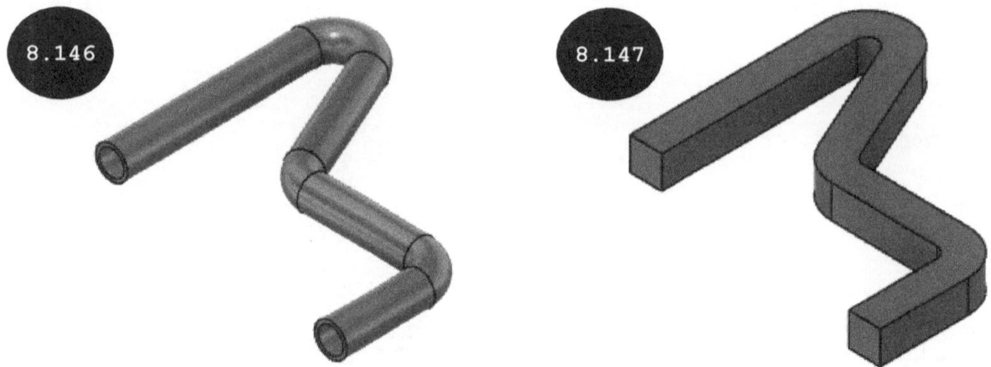

Creating 3D Sketches

In Autodesk Fusion, you can create 3D sketches using sketching tools such as **Line** and **Spline**. 3D sketches are used as a 3D path and a guide rail for creating features like sweep, loft, and pipe. The method for creating a 3D sketch by using the **Line** tool is discussed below:

1. Click on the **Create Sketch** tool in the **Toolbar**, see Figure 8.148. The three default planes appear in the graphics area.

2. Select a plane or a planar face as the sketching plane to create the sketch. The selected plane becomes the sketching plane. Also, the **SKETCH** contextual tab and the **SKETCH PALETTE** dialog box appear.

3. Select the **3D Sketch** check box in the **SKETCH PALETTE** dialog box for creating a 3D sketch, see Figure 8.149.

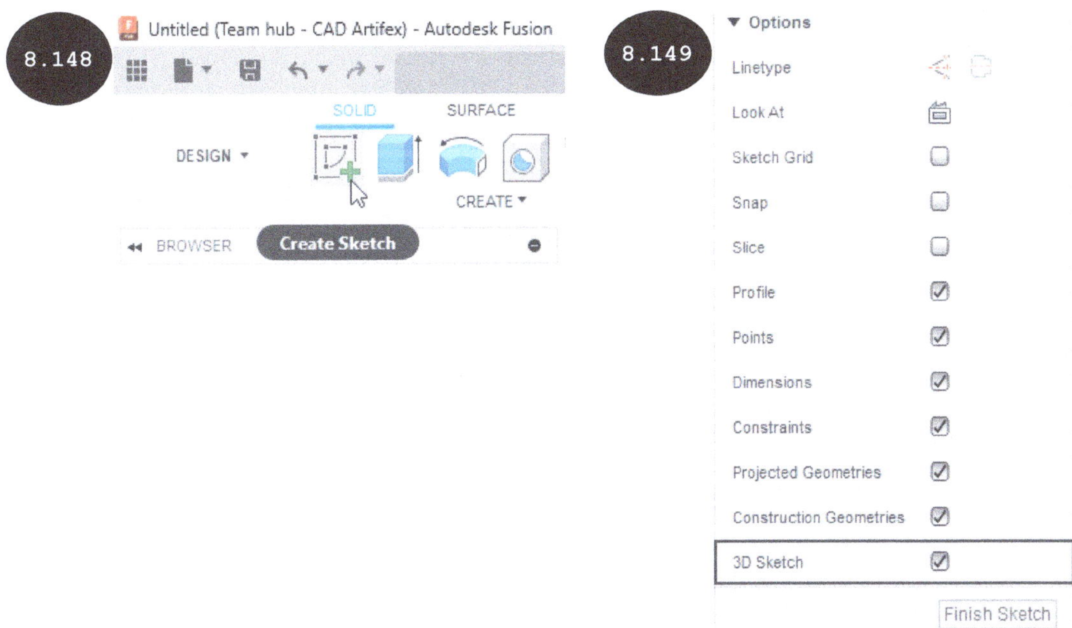

Note: If the **3D Sketch** check box is cleared in the **SKETCH PALETTE** dialog box, you can create a 2D sketch in the Sketching environment, whereas if this check box is selected, you can create a 3D sketch by using the sketching tools such as **Line** and **Spline**.

4. Change the orientation of the sketch to isometric by clicking on the **Home** icon of ViewCube.

5. Click on the **Line** tool in the **CREATE** panel of the **SKETCH** contextual tab to create a 3D sketch by using the **Line** tool. The **3D Sketch Manipulator** appears at the origin (0,0) in the graphics area, see Figure 8.150.

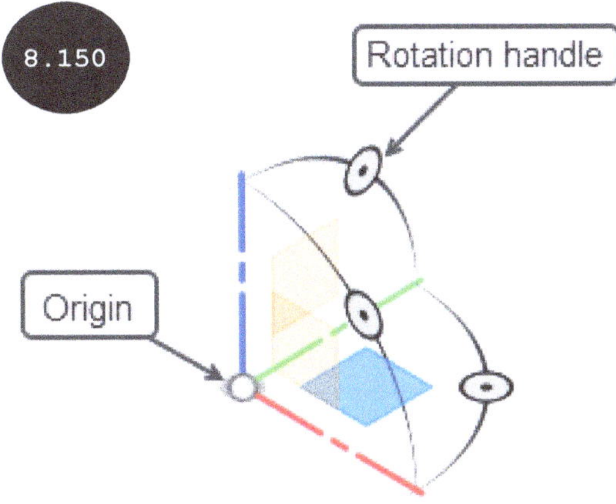

6. Click on the required plane in the **3D Sketch Manipulator** as the current sketching plane, see Figure 8.151.

Note: You can switch from one sketching plane to another for creating a 3D sketch by clicking on the required plane (XY, YZ, or XZ) in the **3D Sketch Manipulator**. You can also drag a Rotation handle of the **3D Sketch Manipulator** for rotating it about its origin, see Figure 8.152.

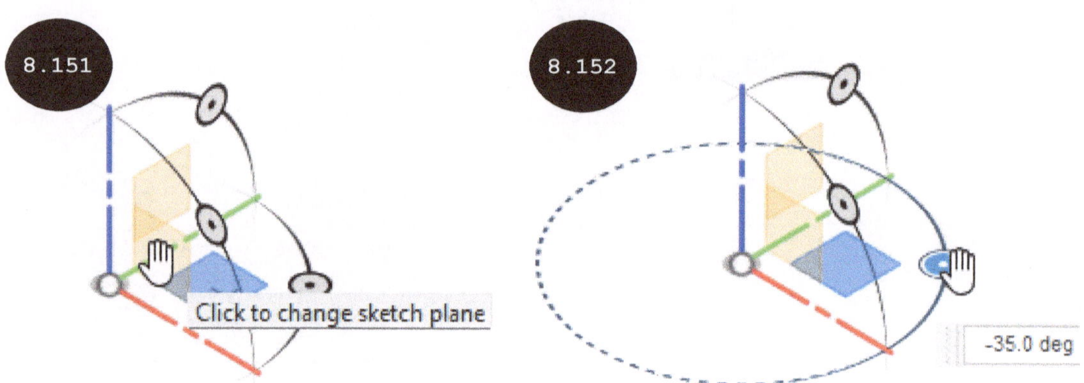

7. Click to specify the start point of the line on the active sketching plane, refer to Figure 8.153. In this figure, the start point is defined at the origin. Note that in this figure, the **Front** plane is the active plane.

8. Move the cursor to a distance from the start point. A rubber band line appears whose one end is fixed at the specified start point and the other end is attached to the cursor, see Figure 8.153.

Tip: If you move the cursor along an axis of the **3D Sketch Manipulator**, an extension line appears along it, see Figure 8.153. This extension line helps in specifying a point along the axis.

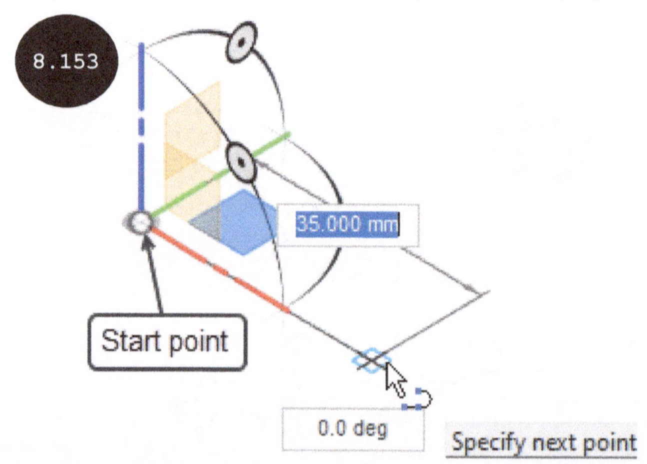

Note: You can switch to another sketching plane even after specifying the start point of the line by clicking on the required plane in the **3D Sketch Manipulator**.

9. Move the cursor to the required location in the drawing area and then click to specify the endpoint of the first line. You can also specify the length and angle of the line in the dimension boxes that appear in the graphics area. A line between the specified points gets created and the origin of the **3D Sketch Manipulator** gets shifted to the last specified point in the graphics area, see Figure 8.154. Also, a rubber band line appears attached to the cursor and you are prompted to specify the endpoint of another line.

10. Click on the required plane in the **3D Sketch Manipulator** as the sketching plane, if required.

11. Move the cursor to the required location on the active sketching plane and then click to specify the endpoint of the next line, see Figure 8.154. The line is created, and the origin of the **3D Sketch Manipulator** gets shifted to the last specified point in the graphics area.

12. Similarly, you can create the remaining lines of the 3D sketch in different planes, see Figure 8.154.

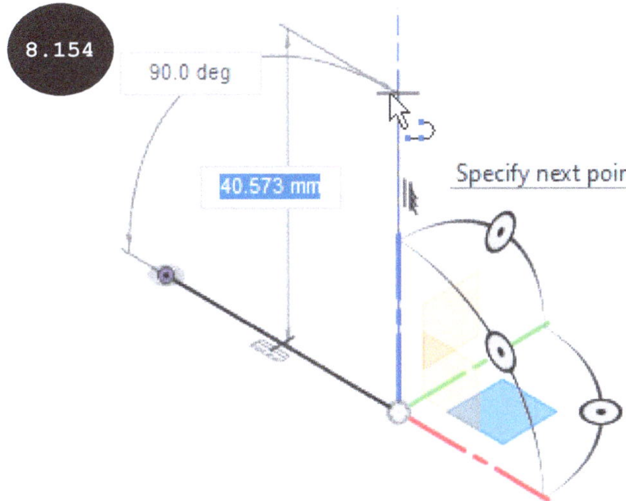

Note: You can also create fillets in the 3D sketch to remove its sharp corners by using the **Fillet** tool. Also, the method for applying dimensions to a 3D sketch is same as that for applying dimensions to a 2D sketch by using the **Sketch Dimension** tool.

13. After creating all sketch entities of the 3D sketch, press the ESC key to exit the **Line** tool. Next, click on the **FINISH SKETCH** tool in the **SKETCH** contextual tab of the **Toolbar** to exit the Sketching environment. Figure 8.155 shows a 3D sketch and Figure 8.156 shows a pipe feature created by using the **Pipe** tool.

Note: You can create 3D sketches in a similar manner by using the **Fit Point Spline** and **Control Point Spline** tools. Also, the methods for creating other sketch entities such as rectangle, arc, circle, point, and polygon are same as discussed earlier while creating 2D sketches.

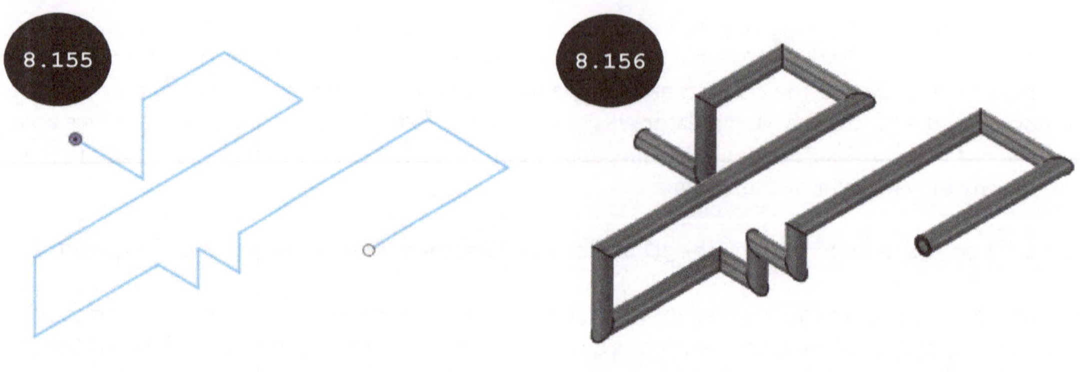

Tutorial 1

Create a model, as shown in Figure 8.157. The different views and dimensions are given in the same figure. All dimensions are in mm.

8.157

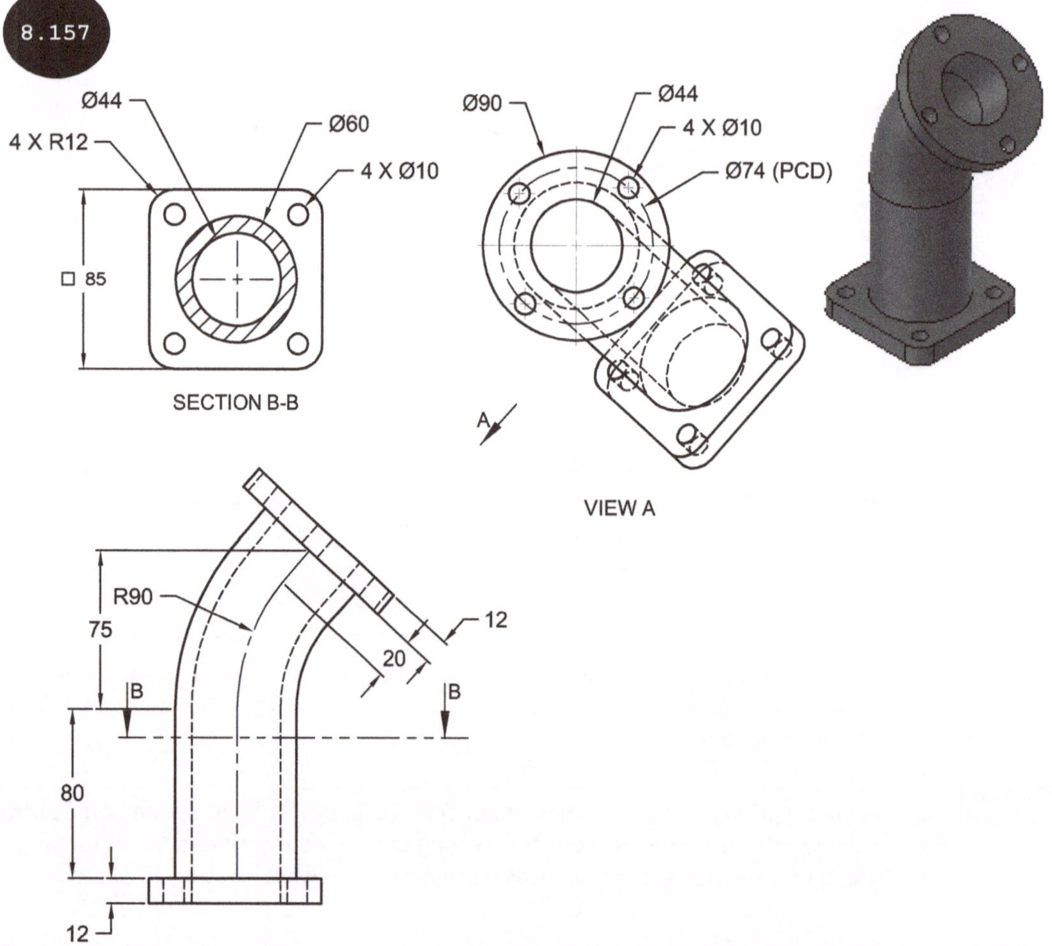

Section 1: Starting a New Part Design File

1. Click **File** > **New** in the **Application Bar** (see Figure 8.158) to display the **What do you want to design?** dialog box, see Figure 8.159.

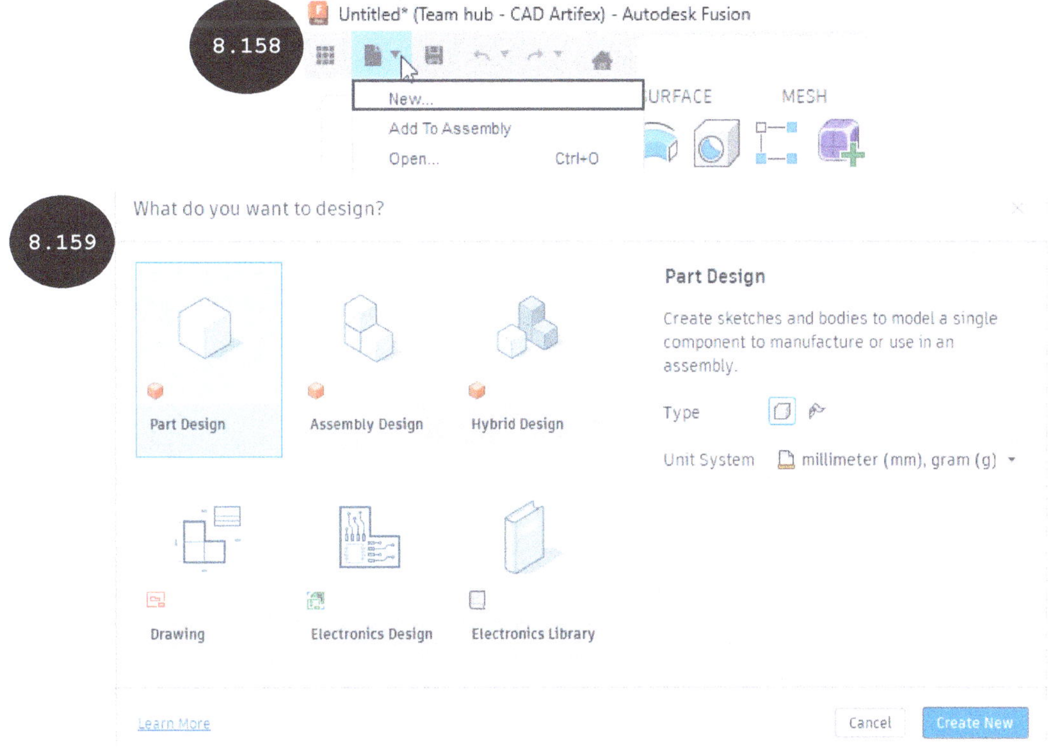

Note: If you are starting a new Autodesk Fusion session, the Part Design file opens automatically because it is set as the default design type. In this case, ensure that the **millimeter (mm), gram (g)** unit system is set for the opened Part Design file.

2. In the **What do you want to design?** dialog box, select the **Part Design** button. Also, select the **millimeter (mm), gram (g)** unit system from the **Unit System** drop-down list.

3. After specifying the required options, click the **Create New** button. A new Part Design file is created with the default name.

Section 2: Organizing the Data Panel

1. Invoke the **Data Panel** and then ensure that the '**Autodesk Fusion 360**' project is created in the **Data Panel**.

2. Double-click on the **Autodesk Fusion 360** project in the **Data Panel** and then create the "**Chapter 08**" folder by using the **New Folder** tool of the **Data Panel**.

3. Double-click on the **Chapter 08** folder and then create the "**Tutorial**" sub-folder. Next, close the **Data Panel**.

Section 3: Creating the Base Feature - Sweep Feature

1. Click on the **Create Sketch** tool in the **Toolbar** and select the Front plane as the sketching plane.

2. Create the path of the sweep feature and apply dimensions, see Figure 8.160.

3. Click on the **FINISH SKETCH** tool in the **SKETCH** contextual tab to finish the creation of the sketch.

   After creating the path, you need to create the profile of the sweep feature.

4. Click on the **Create Sketch** tool in the **Toolbar** and then select the Top plane as the sketching plane to create the profile.

5. Create the profile (two circles) of the sweep feature, see Figure 8.161.

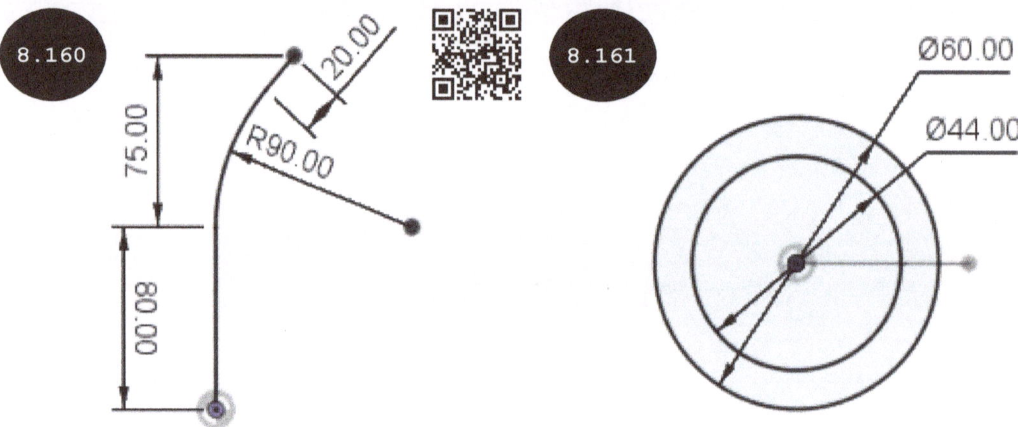

After creating the path and profile, you can create the sweep feature.

6. Click on the **SOLID** tab in the **Toolbar** to display the solid modeling tools.

7. Invoke the **CREATE** drop-down menu in the **SOLID** tab and then click on the **Sweep** tool, see Figure 8.162. The **SWEEP** dialog box appears, see Figure 8.163.

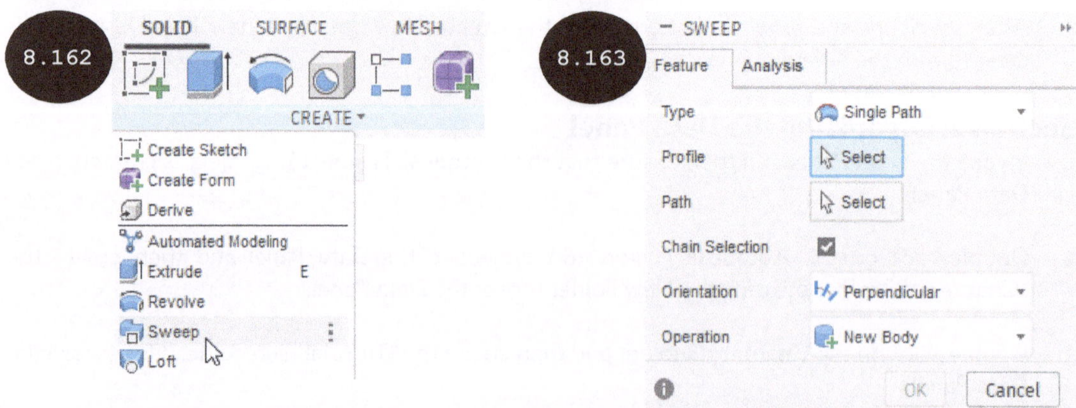

8. Ensure that the **Single Path** option is selected in the **Type** drop-down list of the **Feature** tab. Next, change the orientation of the sketch to isometric.

9. Select the profile of the sweep feature in the graphics area, see Figure 8.164.

10. Click on the **Path** selection option in the **SWEEP** dialog box and then select the path of the sweep feature, see Figure 8.164. A preview of the sweep feature appears in the graphics area, see Figure 8.165. Ensure that the **Chain Selection** check box is selected in the dialog box.

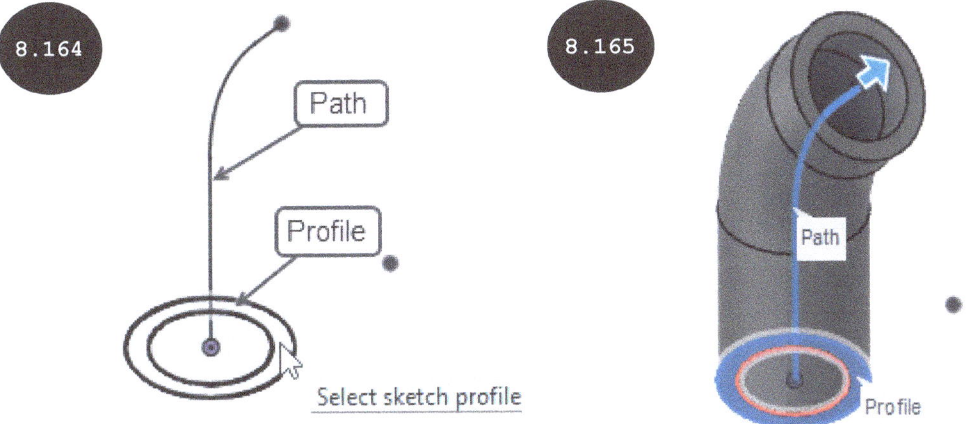

11. Ensure that the distance value **1** is specified in the **Distance** field to sweep the profile along the total length of the path.

12. Ensure that taper angle and twist angle values are specified as 0 degrees in the respective fields.

13. Ensure that the **Perpendicular** option is selected in the **Orientation** drop-down list.

14. Ensure that the **New Body** option is selected in the **Operation** drop-down list of the dialog box and then click on the **OK** button. The sweep feature is created, see Figure 8.166.

Section 4: Creating the Second Feature - Extrude Feature

1. Rotate the model such that the bottom face of the base feature can be viewed, see Figure 8.167.
2. Click on the **Create Sketch** tool in the **Toolbar** and then click on the bottom face of the base feature (sweep) as the sketching plane.
3. Create the sketch of the second feature, see Figure 8.168.

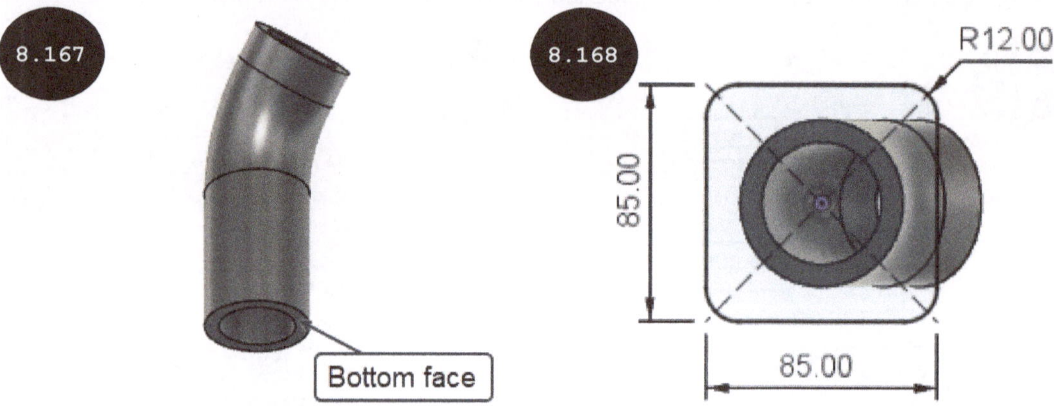

4. Press the **E** key. The **EXTRUDE** dialog box appears. Alternatively, click on the **Extrude** tool in the **CREATE** panel of the **SOLID** tab.
5. Select the closed profiles (two profiles) for creating the extrude feature, see Figure 8.169.
6. Ensure that the **Distance** option is selected in the **Extent Type** drop-down list.
7. Enter **12** in the **Distance** field. Next,
8. Ensure that the **Join** option is selected in the **Operation** drop-down list.
9. Click on the **OK** button in the dialog box. The extrude feature is created, see Figure 8.170. Change the view of the model to isometric.

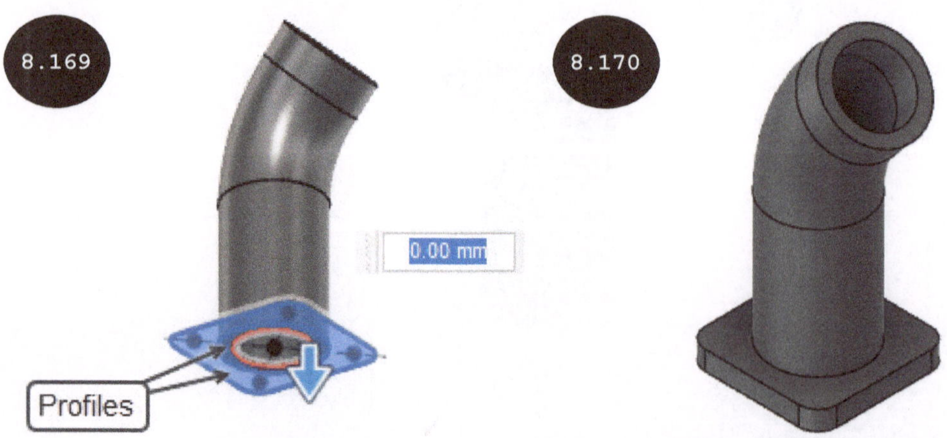

Section 5: Creating the Third Feature - Extrude Cut Feature

1. Click on the **Create Sketch** tool in the **Toolbar** and then select the top planar face of the second feature as the sketching plane, see Figure 8.171.

2. Create the sketch (four circles of diameter 10 mm) of the third feature, see Figure 8.172.

Tip: The sketch of the third feature shown in Figure 8.172 has four circles of the same diameter. Therefore, an equal constraint is applied among all circles. Also, a concentric constraint is applied between the center point of circles and the respective semi-circular edge of the second feature. You can also create one circle and then pattern it circularly to create the remaining circles.

3. Click on the **SOLID** tab in the **Toolbar** to display the solid modeling tools.

4. Click on the **Extrude** tool in the **CREATE** panel of the **SOLID** tab or press the **E** key. The **EXTRUDE** dialog box appears. Next, change the orientation of the model to isometric.

5. Select closed profiles of all four circles of the sketch one by one in the graphics area.

6. Select the **All** option in the **Extent Type** drop-down list of the dialog box.

7. Click on the **Flip** button in the dialog box to flip the direction of extrusion downwards.

8. Ensure that the **Cut** option is selected in the **Operation** drop-down list of the dialog box to create the extrude feature by removing material.

9. Click on the **OK** button in the dialog box. The extrude feature is created by removing material from the model, see Figure 8.173.

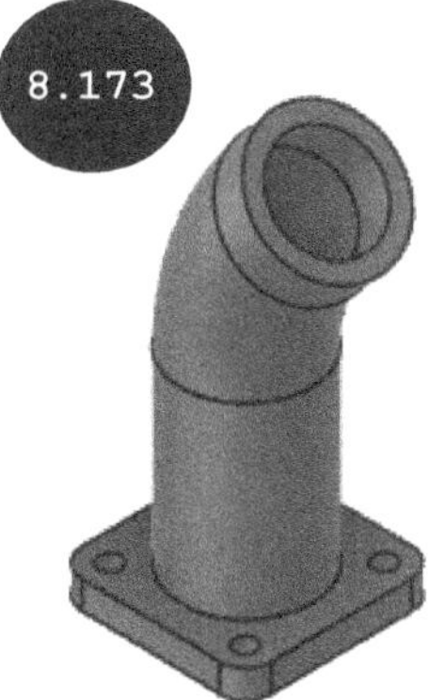

Section 6: Creating the Fourth Feature - Extrude Feature

1. Click on the **Create Sketch** tool in the **Toolbar** and then select the top planar face of the sweep feature (first feature) as the sketching plane, see Figure 8.174.

2. Create the sketch (a circle of diameter 90 mm) of the fourth feature, see Figure 8.175.

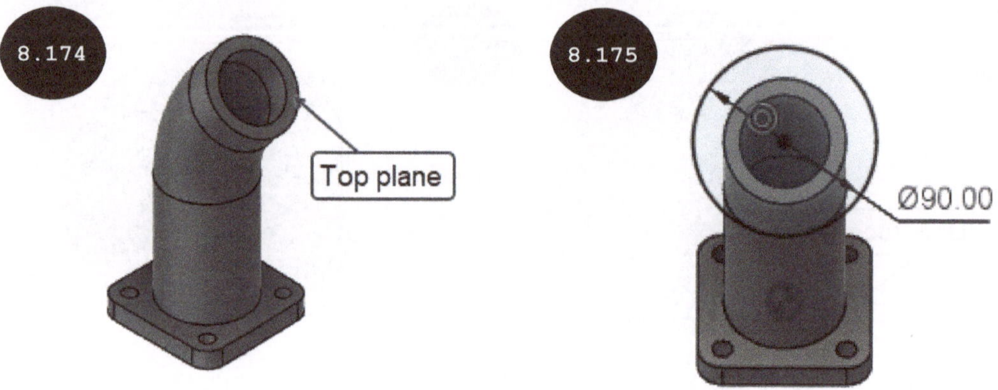

3. Click on the **SOLID** tab in the **Toolbar** to display the solid modeling tools.

4. Click on the **Extrude** tool in the **CREATE** panel of the **SOLID** tab or press the **E** key. The **EXTRUDE** dialog box appears. Next, change the orientation of the model to isometric.

5. Select the closed profiles (two profiles) for creating the extrude feature, see Figure 8.176.

6. Ensure that the **Distance** option is selected in the **Extent Type** drop-down list.

7. Enter **12** in the **Distance** field.

8. Ensure that the **Join** option is selected in the **Operation** drop-down list.

9. Click on the **OK** button in the dialog box. The extrude feature is created, see Figure 8.177.

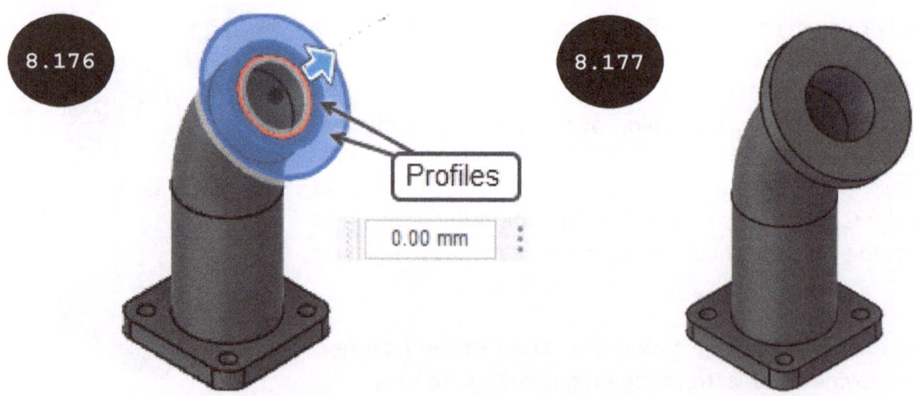

Section 7: Creating the Fifth Feature - Extrude Cut Feature

1. Click on the **Create Sketch** tool in the **Toolbar** and then select the top planar face of the fourth feature as the sketching plane.

2. Create a circle of diameter 10 mm, see Figure 8.178. Next, create the remaining circles of the same diameter by using the **Circular Pattern** tool, see Figure 8.179. Note that the center point of the circular edge of the fourth feature is defined as the center point of the circular pattern.

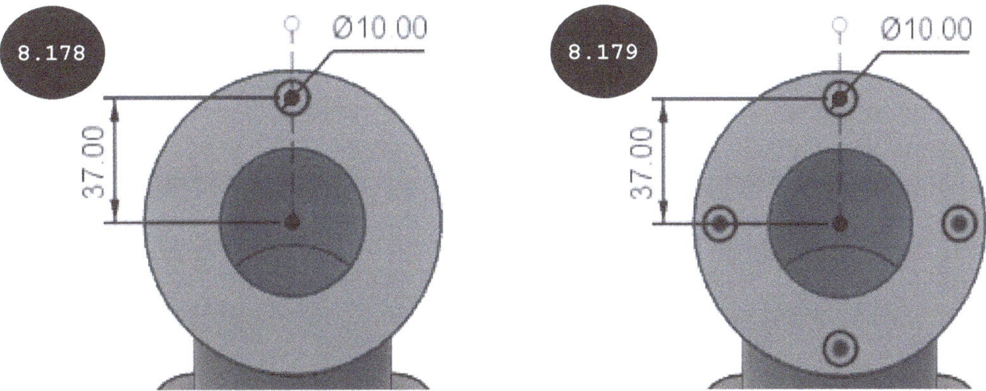

Tip: In Figure 8.179, the center point of the circle has coincident relation with the vertical construction line. Also, the start point of the vertical construction line is coincident with the center point of the circular edge of the fourth feature.

3. Click on the **SOLID** tab in the **Toolbar** to display the solid modeling tools.

4. Click on the **Extrude** tool in the **CREATE** panel of the **SOLID** tab or press the **E** key. The **EXTRUDE** dialog box appears. Next, change the orientation of the model to isometric.

5. Select closed profiles of all four circles of the sketch, one by one in the graphics area.

6. Select the **To Object** option in the **Extent Type** drop-down list of the dialog box.

7. Rotate the model such that the back face of the fourth feature can be viewed, see Figure 8.180, and then select it as the face to terminate the extruded feature.

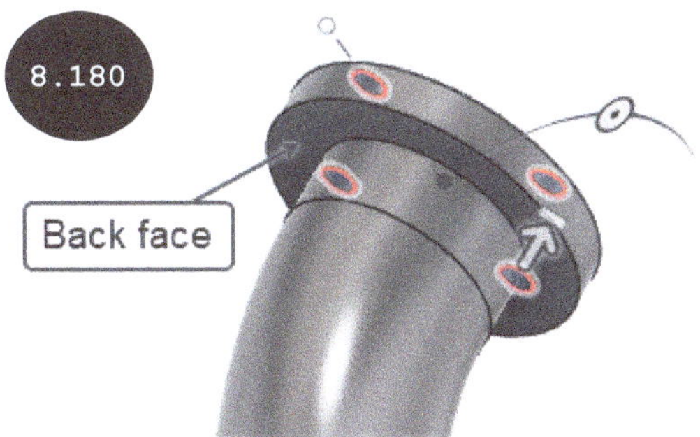

8. Ensure that the **Cut** option is selected in the **Operation** drop-down list to create the extrude feature by removing the material.

9. Click on the **OK** button in the dialog box. The extrude feature is created by removing material from the model, see Figure 8.181. Change the orientation of the model to isometric.

Section 8: Saving the Model

1. Click on the **Save** tool in the **Application Bar**. The **Save** dialog box appears.

2. Enter **Tutorial 01** in the **Name** field of the dialog box.

3. Ensure that the location ***Autodesk Fusion 360 > Chapter 08 > Tutorial 01*** is specified in the **Location** field of the dialog box to save a file of this tutorial. To specify the location, you need to expand the **Save** dialog box by clicking on the down arrow next to the **Location** field of the dialog box.

4. Click on the **Save** button in the dialog box. The model is saved with the name Tutorial 01 in the specified location (***Autodesk Fusion 360 > Chapter 08 > Tutorial 01***).

Tutorial 2

Create a model, as shown in Figure 8.182. The different views and dimensions are given in the same figure. All dimensions are in mm.

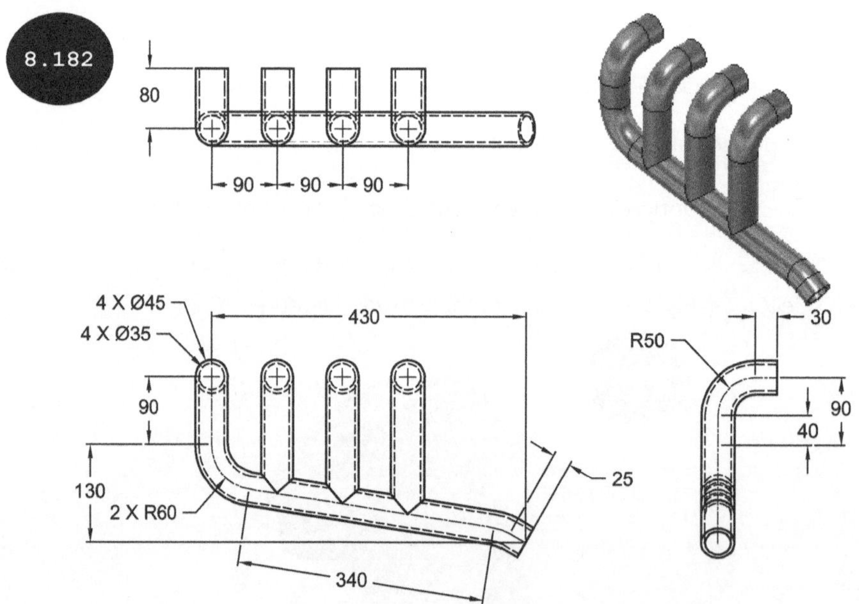

Section 1: Starting a New Part Design File

1. Click **File > New** in the **Application Bar** (see Figure 8.183) to display the **What do you want to design?** dialog box, see Figure 8.184.

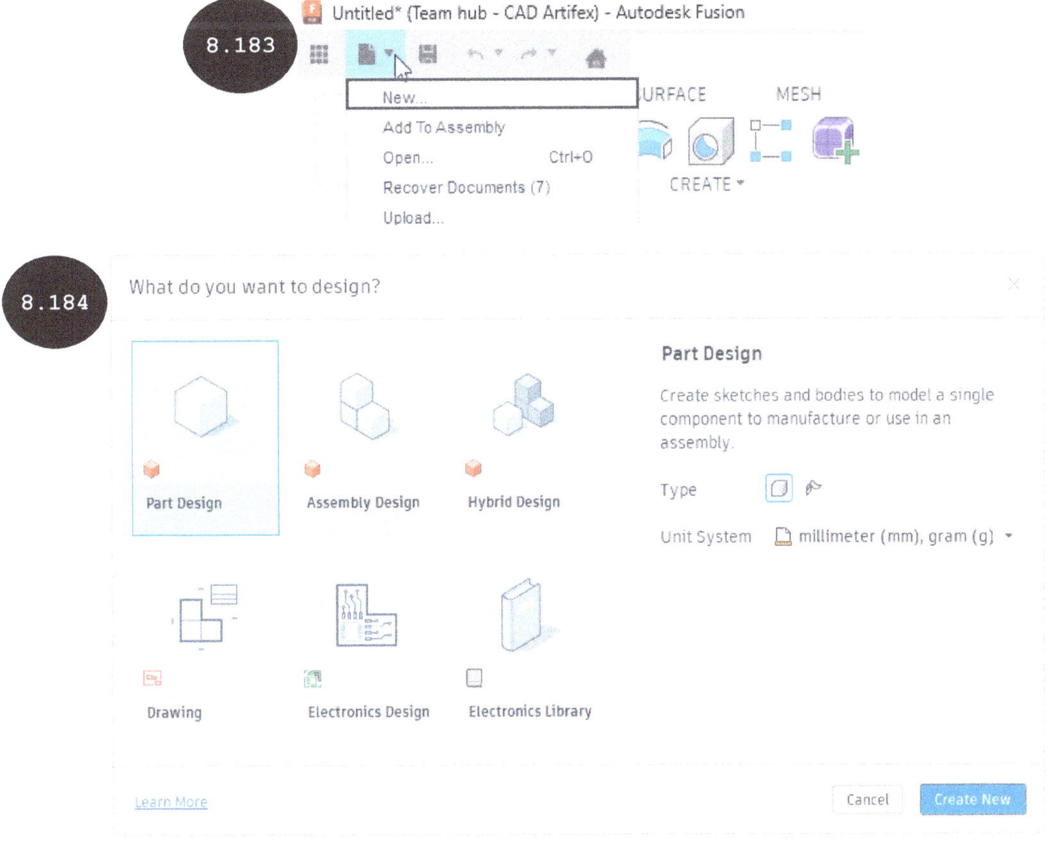

Note: If you are starting a new Autodesk Fusion session, the Part Design file opens automatically because it is set as the default design type. In this case, ensure that the **millimeter (mm), gram (g)** unit system is set for the opened Part Design file.

2. In the **What do you want to design?** dialog box, select the **Part Design** button. Also, select the **millimeter (mm), gram (g)** unit system from the **Unit System** drop-down list.

3. After specifying the required options, click the **Create New** button. A new Part Design file is created with the default name "**Untitled**".

Section 2: Creating the Base Feature - Pipe Feature

Now, you can start creating the base/first feature of the model.

1. Click on the **Create Sketch** tool in the **Toolbar** and then select the Right plane as the sketching plane.

2. Create the path of the pipe, see Figure 8.185.

3. Click on the **SOLID** tab in the **Toolbar** to display the solid modeling tools.

4. Invoke the **CREATE** drop-down menu in the **SOLID** tab and then click on the **Pipe** tool. The **PIPE** dialog box appears. Ensure that the **Chain Selection** check box is selected in the dialog box.
5. Select the path of the pipe in the graphics area. The preview of the pipe appears with default parameters, see Figure 8.186.

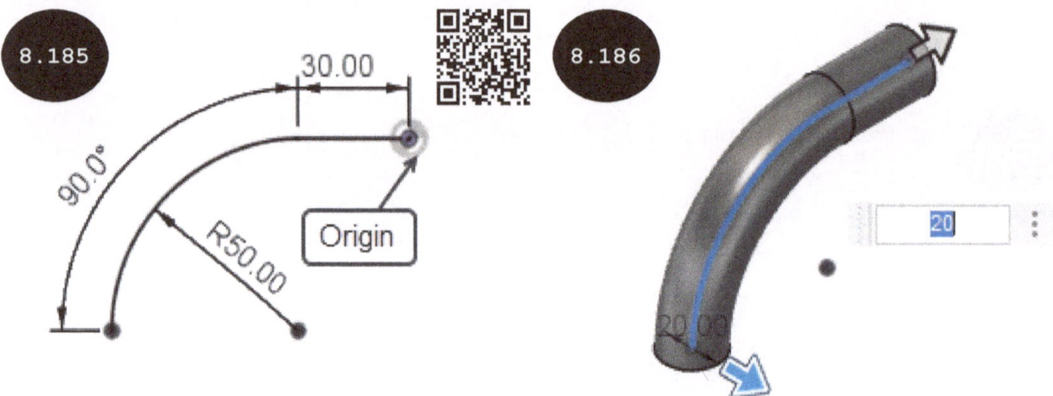

6. Ensure that the distance value **1** is specified in the **Distance** field of the dialog box to create a full-length pipe along the selected path.

7. Ensure that the **Circular** option is selected in the **Section** drop-down list of the dialog box to create a pipe of circular section.

8. Enter **45** in the **Section Size** field of the dialog box as the diameter of the circular section of the pipe.

9. Select the **Hollow** check box to create a hollow pipe. The **Section Thickness** field appears in the dialog box.

10. Enter **5** in the **Section Thickness** field as the thickness of the pipe.

11. Ensure that the **New Body** option is selected in the **Operation** drop-down list of the dialog box and then click on the **OK** button. The hollow pipe is created, see Figure 8.187.

Section 3: Creating the Second Feature - Pipe Feature

To create the second feature of the model, you first need to create a construction plane at an offset distance of 80 mm from the Front plane.

1. Click on the **Offset Plane** tool in the **CONSTRUCT** panel of the **SOLID** tab. The **CONSTRUCTION GEOMETRY** dialog box appears.

2. Click on the Front plane as a reference plane, see Figure 8.188. The Front plane gets selected, and the **Distance** field appears in the dialog box as well as in the graphics area.

3. Enter **-80** in the **Distance** field of the dialog box. The preview of the construction plane appears at an offset distance of 80 mm from the Front plane, see Figure 8.189. Ensure that the direction of the construction plane is the same as shown in Figure 8.189. To reverse the direction of the plane, you need to enter a positive offset distance value.

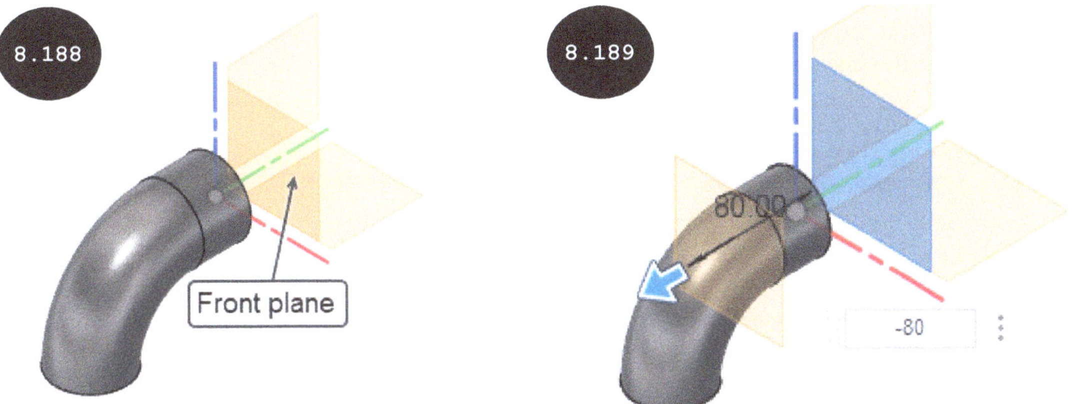

4. Click on the **OK** button in the dialog box. A construction plane at an offset distance of 80 mm from the Front plane is created.

   Now, you can create the path of the second feature (pipe) at the newly created construction plane.

5. Click on the **Create Sketch** tool in the **Toolbar** and then select the newly created construction plane as the sketching plane.

6. Create the path of the second feature (pipe), see Figure 8.190. Note that in this figure, an equal relation has been applied between both the arcs of the sketch having the same radius of 60 mm.

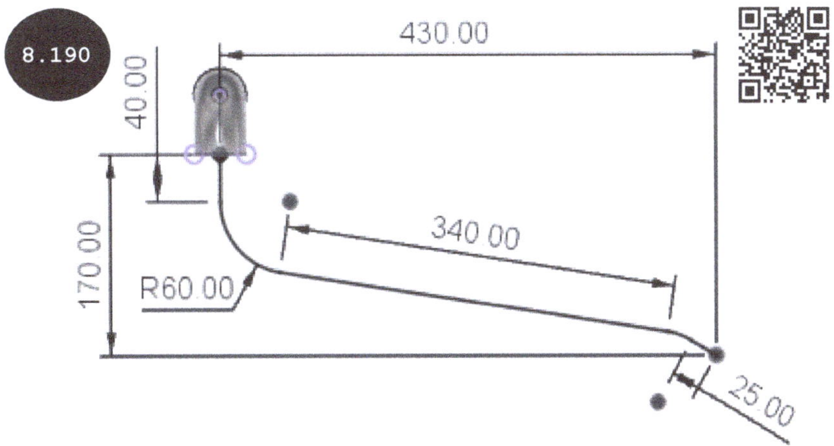

7. Invoke the **CREATE** drop-down menu in the **SOLID** tab and then click on the **Pipe** tool. The **PIPE** dialog box appears. Next, change the orientation of the model to isometric.

8. Ensure that the **Chain Selection** check box is selected in the dialog box.

9. Select the path of the pipe in the graphics area. The preview of the pipe appears with default parameters.

10. Ensure that distance **1** is specified in the **Distance** field of the dialog box to create a full-length pipe along the selected path.

11. Ensure that the **Circular** option is selected in the **Section** drop-down list of the dialog box to create a pipe of a circular section.

12. Enter **45** in the **Section Size** field of the dialog box as the diameter of the circular section of the pipe.

13. Select the **Hollow** check box in the dialog box to create a hollow pipe. The **Section Thickness** field appears in the dialog box.

14. Enter **5** in the **Section Thickness** field as the thickness of the pipe.

15. Ensure that the **Join** option is selected in the **Operation** drop-down list of the dialog box and then click on the **OK** button. The hollow pipe is created, see Figure 8.191.

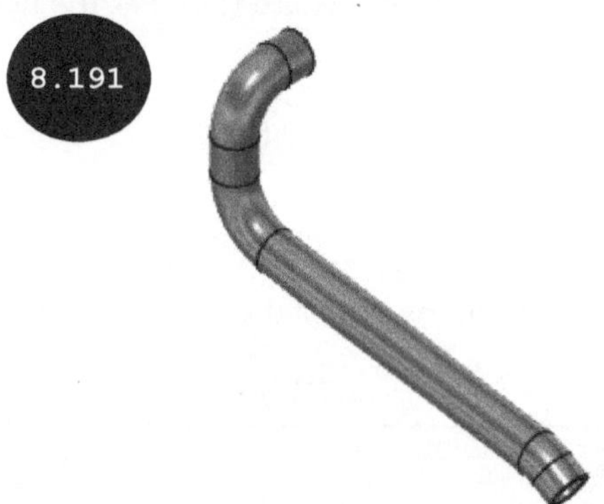

Section 4: Creating the Third Feature - Extrude Feature

To create the third feature of the model, you first need to create a construction plane at an offset distance of 50 mm from the Top plane.

1. Click on the **Offset Plane** tool in the **CONSTRUCT** panel of the **SOLID** tab. The **CONSTRUCTION GEOMETRY** dialog box appears.

2. Click on the Top plane as a reference plane. The Top plane gets selected, and the **Distance** field appears in the dialog box as well as in the graphics area.

3. Enter **-50** in the **Distance** field of the dialog box. A preview of the construction plane appears downward, at an offset distance of 50 mm from the Top plane, see Figure 8.192. Ensure that the direction of the construction plane is downward.

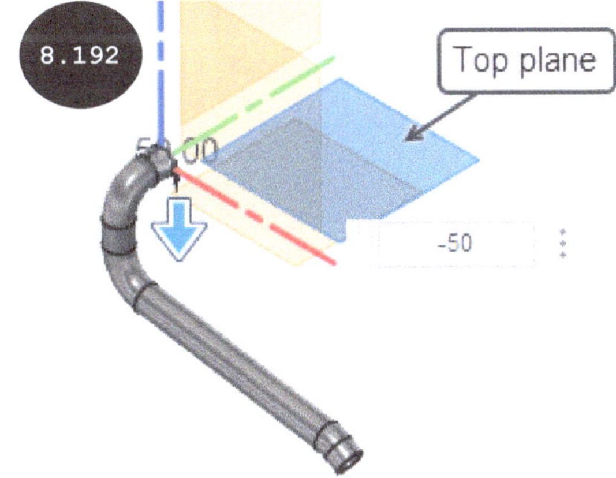

4. Click on the **OK** button in the dialog box. The construction reference plane is created.

   Now, you can create a sketch of the third feature (extrude).

5. Click on the **Create Sketch** tool in the **Toolbar** and then select the newly created construction plane as the sketching plane.

6. Create a sketch of the third feature (three circles of the same diameter), see Figure 8.193.

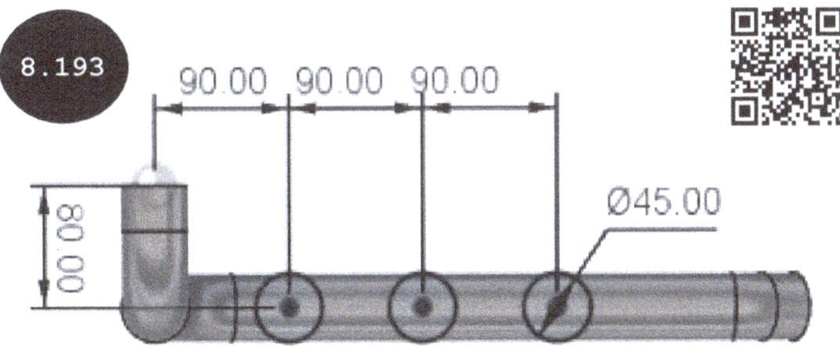

7. Click on the **SOLID** tab in the **Toolbar** to display the solid modeling tools.

8. Click on the **Extrude** tool in the **CREATE** panel of the **SOLID** tab or press the **E** key. The **EXTRUDE** dialog box appears. Next, change the orientation of the model to isometric.

9. Select closed profiles of all three circles of the sketch one by one in the graphics area.

10. Select the **To Object** option in the **Extent Type** drop-down list of the dialog box.

11. Select the outer face of the inclined pipe to terminate the extrude feature, see Figure 8.194. A preview of the extrude feature appears, see Figure 8.195.

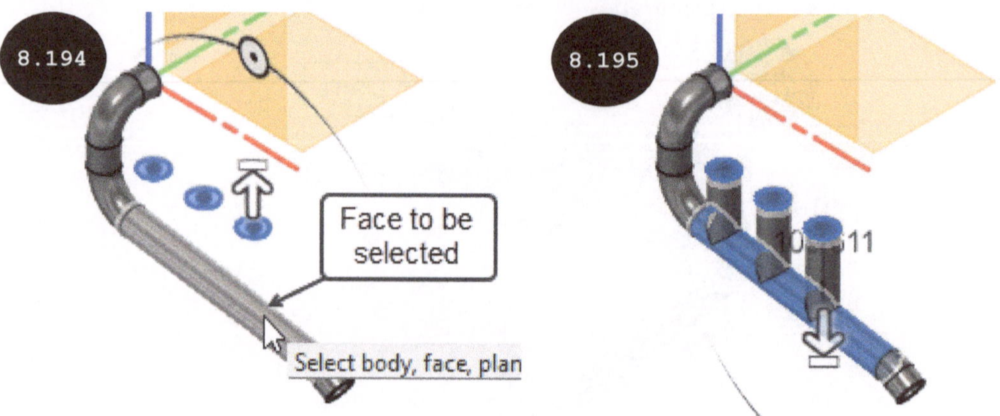

12. Ensure that the **To Body** button is activated in the first **Extend** area of the dialog box.

13. Ensure that the **Join** option is selected in the **Operation** drop-down list of the dialog box and then click on the **OK** button. The extrude feature is created.

Section 5: Creating the Fourth Feature - Extrude Cut Feature

1. Click on the **Create Sketch** tool in the **Toolbar** and then select the top planar face of the third feature as the sketching plane, see Figure 8.196.

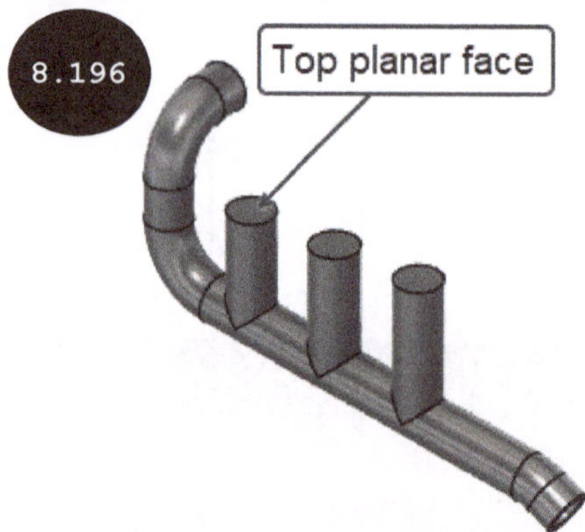

2. Create a sketch of the fourth feature (three circles of the same diameter 35 mm), see Figure 8.197.

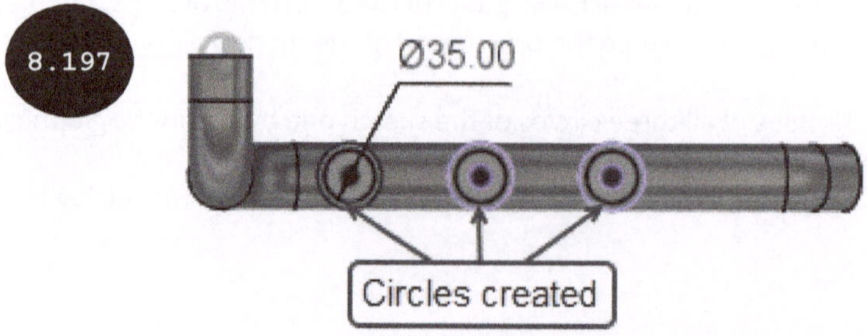

Tip: The sketch of the fourth feature shown in Figure 8.197 has three circles, which are concentric to the circular edges of the third feature (extrude). Also, an equal constraint has been applied between all the circles.

3. Click on the **SOLID** tab in the **Toolbar** to display the solid modeling tools.

4. Click on the **Extrude** tool in the **CREATE** panel of the **SOLID** tab or press the **E** key. The **EXTRUDE** dialog box appears. Next, change the orientation of the model to isometric.

5. Select closed profiles of all three circles of the sketch one by one in the graphics area.

6. Select the **To Object** option in the **Extent Type** drop-down list of the dialog box.

7. Rotate the model such that the inner circular face of the model can be viewed and then select it as the object to terminate the feature, see Figure 8.198. Next, change the orientation of the model to isometric. Also, a preview of the cut feature appears in the graphics area, see Figure 8.199.

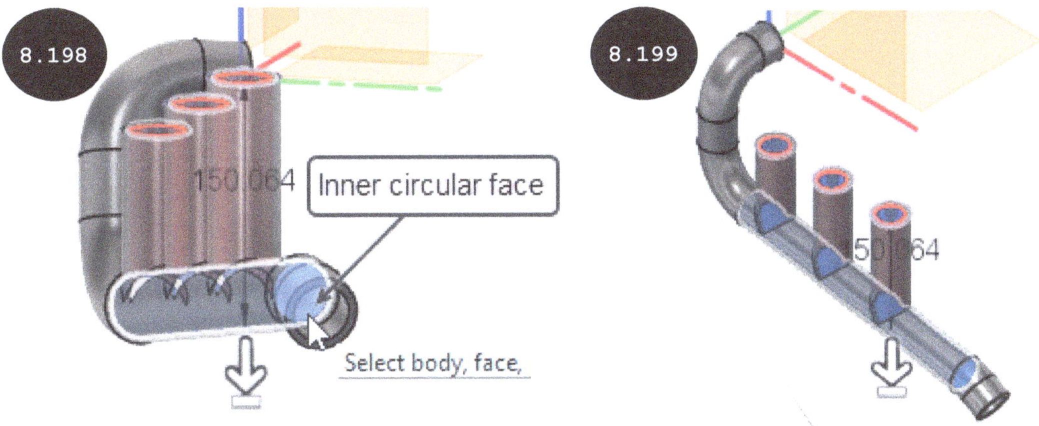

8. Ensure that the **To Body** button is activated in the first **Extend** area of the dialog box.

9. Ensure that the **Cut** option is selected in the **Operation** drop-down list of the dialog box and then click on the **OK** button. The extrude cut feature is created, see Figure 8.200.

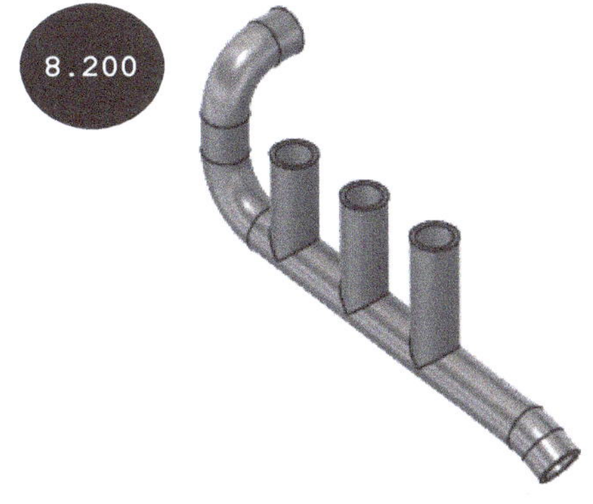

Section 6: Creating the Fifth Feature - Sweep Feature

Now, you need to create a sweep feature by selecting the sketch of the first feature as its path.

1. Expand the **Sketches** node in the **BROWSER** and then click on the **Show** icon in front of **Sketch1**, see Figure 8.201. The sketch of the first feature (pipe) is displayed in the graphics area.

2. Invoke the **CREATE** drop-down menu in the **SOLID** tab and then click on the **Sweep** tool, see Figure 8.202. The **SWEEP** dialog box appears.

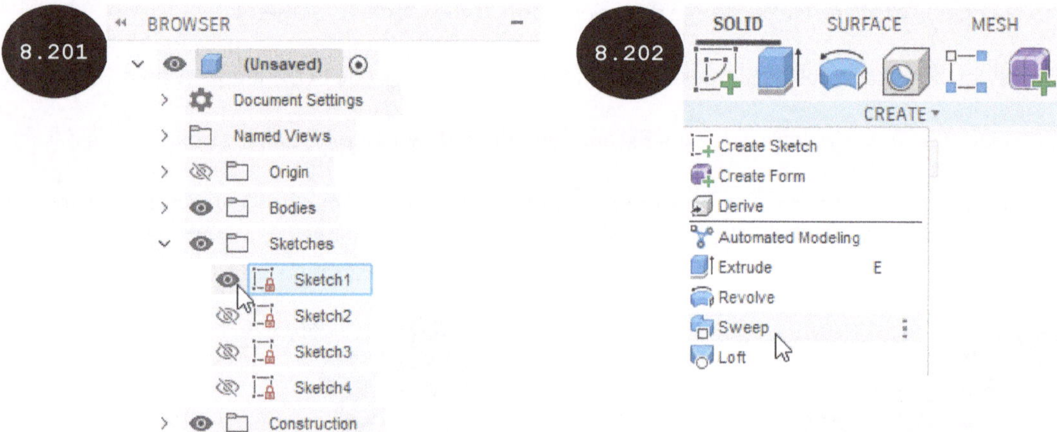

3. Ensure that the **Single Path** option is selected in the **Type** drop-down list of the dialog box.

4. Select the top planar faces (three faces) of the third feature as the profile of the sweep feature, see Figure 8.203.

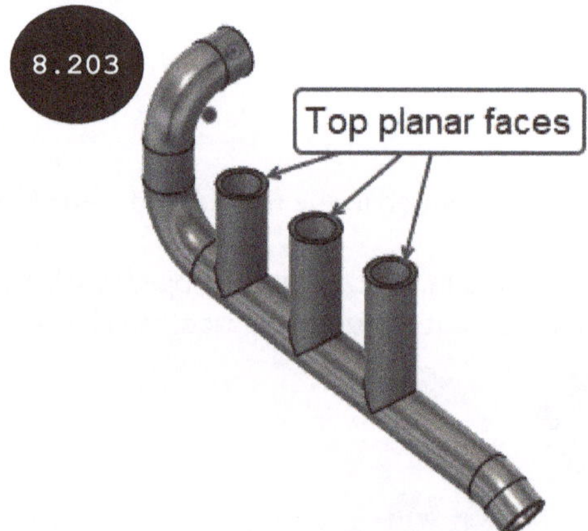

5. Click on the **Path** selection option in the dialog box and then ensure that the **Chain Selection** check box is selected.

6. Select the sketch of the first feature (pipe) as the path of the sweep feature. A preview of the sweep feature appears, see Figure 8.204.

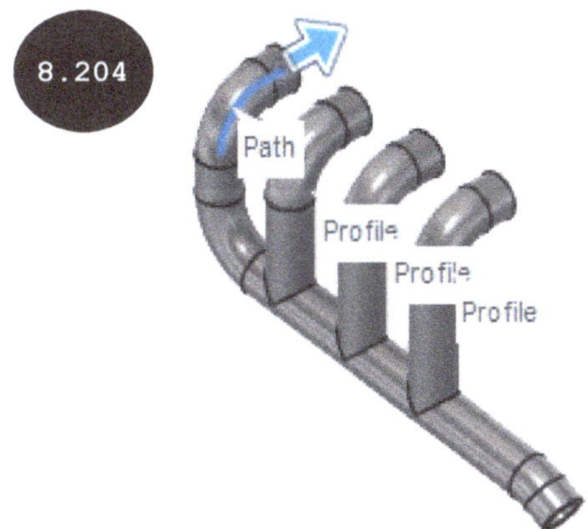

7. Ensure that the value **1** is entered in the **Distance** field of the dialog box to sweep the profile along the full length of the selected path.

8. Ensure that the **Perpendicular** option is selected in the **Orientation** drop-down list.

9. Ensure that the **Join** option is selected in the **Operation** drop-down list of the dialog box and then click on the **OK** button. The sweep feature is created, see Figure 8.205. Hide the sketch of the first feature.

Section 7: Saving the Model

1. Click on the **Save** tool in the **Application Bar**. The **Save** dialog box appears.

2. Enter **Tutorial 02** in the **Name** field of the dialog box.

3. Ensure that the location *Autodesk Fusion 360 > Chapter 08 > Tutorial* 02 is specified in the **Location** field of the dialog box to save a file of this tutorial. To specify the location, you need to expand the **Save** dialog box by clicking on the down arrow next to the **Location** field of the dialog box. Note that you need to create these folders in the **Data Panel**, if not created earlier.

4. Click on the **Save** button in the dialog box. The model is saved with the name Tutorial 02 in the specified location (*Autodesk Fusion 360 > Chapter 08 > Tutorial 02*).

Tutorial 3

Create a model, as shown in Figure 8.206. All dimensions are in mm.

8.206

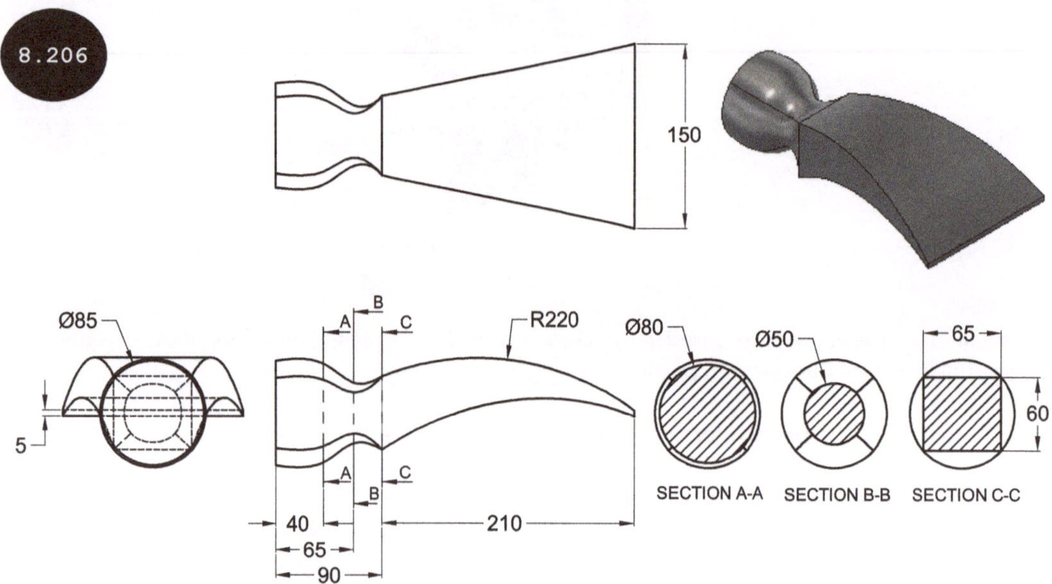

Section 1: Starting a New Part Design File

1. Click **File** > **New** in the **Application Bar** (see Figure 8.207) to display the **What do you want to design?** dialog box, see Figure 8.208.

8.207

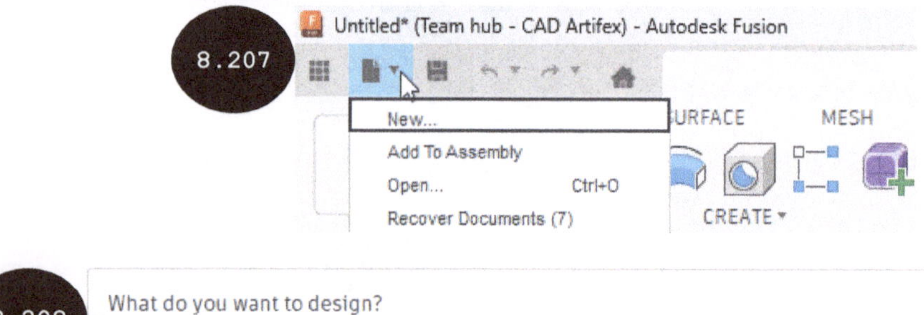

8.208

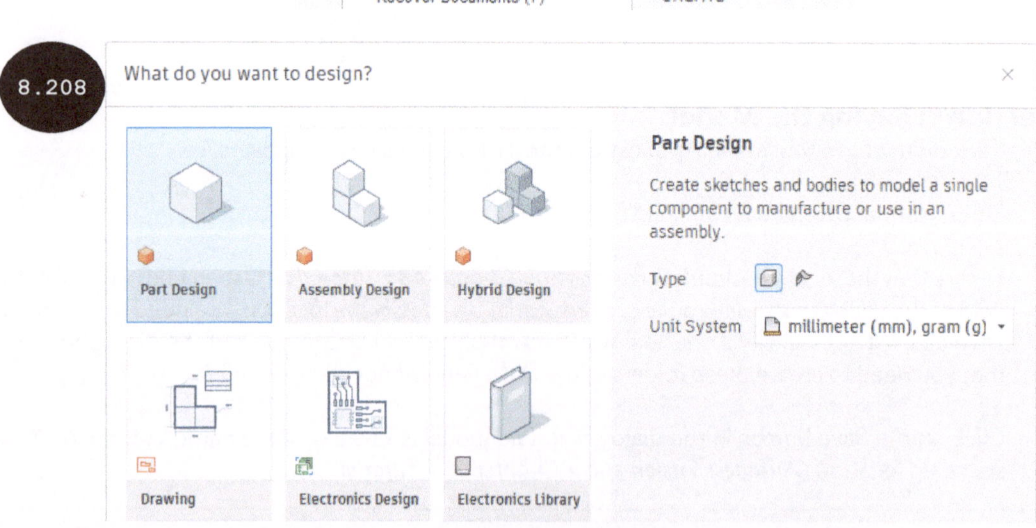

Note: If you are starting a new Autodesk Fusion session, the Part Design file opens automatically because it is set as the default design type. In this case, ensure that the **millimeter (mm), gram (g)** unit system is set for the opened Part Design file.

2. In the **What do you want to design?** dialog box, select the **Part Design** button. Also, select the **millimeter (mm), gram (g)** unit system from the **Unit System** drop-down list.

3. After specifying the required options, click the **Create New** button. A new Part Design file is created with the default name.

Section 2: Creating the Base Feature - Loft Feature

To create the base feature (loft feature) of the model, first, you need to create all its sections (profiles) on different construction planes.

1. Click on the **Create Sketch** tool in the **Toolbar** and then select the Right plane as the sketching plane.

2. Create the first section (profile) of the loft feature, which is a circle of diameter 85 mm, see Figure 8.209. Next, click on the **FINISH SKETCH** tool in the **SKETCH** contextual tab and then change the orientation of the sketch to isometric.

   After creating the first section (profile) of the loft feature, you need to create the second section at an offset distance of 40 mm from the Right plane.

3. Create a construction plane at an offset distance of 40 mm from the Right plane by using the **Offset Plane** tool of the **CONSTRUCT** panel in the **SOLID** tab, see Figure 8.210.

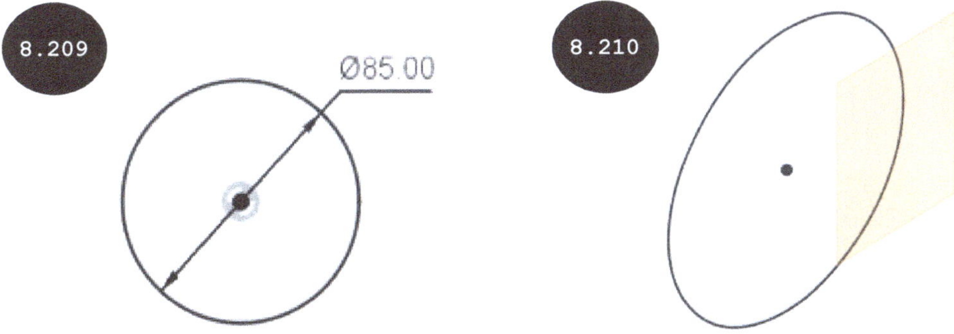

4. Click on the **Create Sketch** tool in the **Toolbar** and then select the newly created construction plane as the sketching plane.

5. Create the second section (a circle of diameter 80 mm) of the loft feature, see Figure 8.211. Next, click on the **FINISH SKETCH** tool in the **SKETCH** contextual tab and then change the orientation of the sketch to isometric.

After creating the second section (profile) of the loft feature, you need to create the third section of the feature at an offset distance of 65 mm from the Right plane.

6. Create a construction plane at an offset distance of 65 mm from the Right plane by using the **Offset Plane** tool, see Figure 8.212.

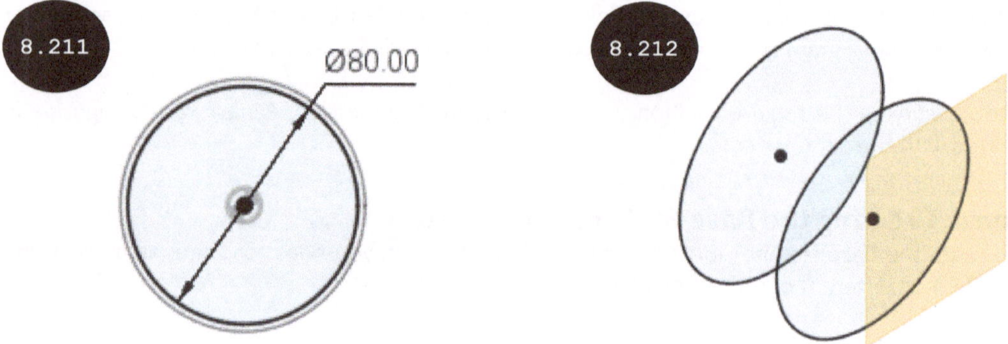

7. Click on the **Create Sketch** tool in the **Toolbar** and then select the newly created construction plane as the sketching plane.

8. Create the third section (a circle of diameter 50 mm) of the loft feature, see Figure 8.213. Next, click on the **FINISH SKETCH** tool in the **SKETCH** contextual tab and then change the orientation of the sketch to isometric.

   After creating the third section (profile) of the loft feature, you need to create the fourth section at an offset distance of 90 mm from the Right plane.

9. Create a construction plane at an offset distance of 90 mm from the Right plane by using the **Offset Plane** tool, see Figure 8.214.

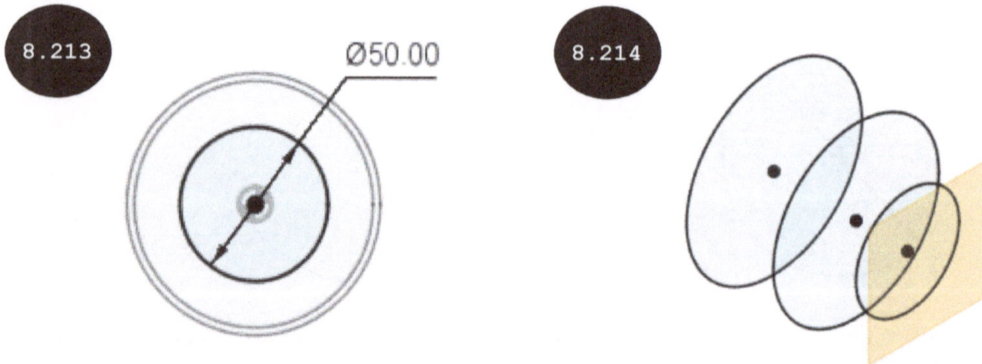

10. Click on the **Create Sketch** tool in the **Toolbar** and then select the newly created construction plane as the sketching plane.

11. Create the fourth section (rectangle of 65 X 60) of the loft feature, see Figure 8.215. Next, click on the **FINISH SKETCH** tool in the **SKETCH** contextual tab and then change the orientation of the sketch to isometric, see Figure 8.216.

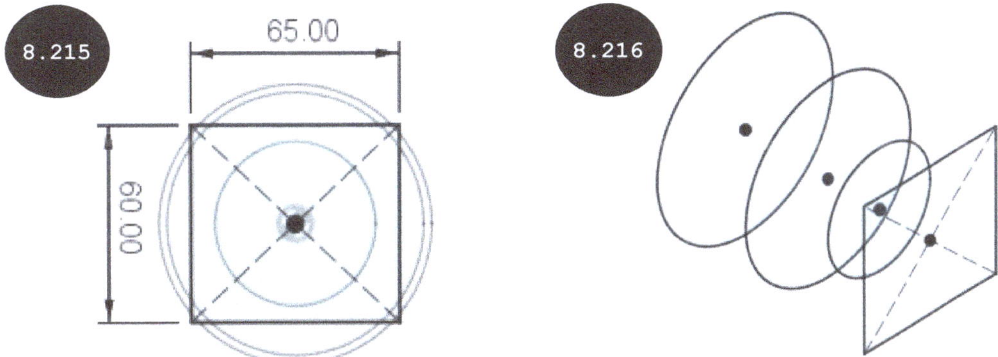

After creating all the sections of the loft feature, you can create the loft feature.

12. Click on the **SOLID** tab in the **Toolbar** to display the solid modeling tools.

13. Invoke the **CREATE** drop-down menu in the **SOLID** tab and then click on the **Loft** tool, see Figure 8.217. The **LOFT** dialog box appears.

14. Select all the sections (profiles) of the loft feature in the graphics area one by one. A preview of the loft feature appears in the graphics area, see Figure 8.218.

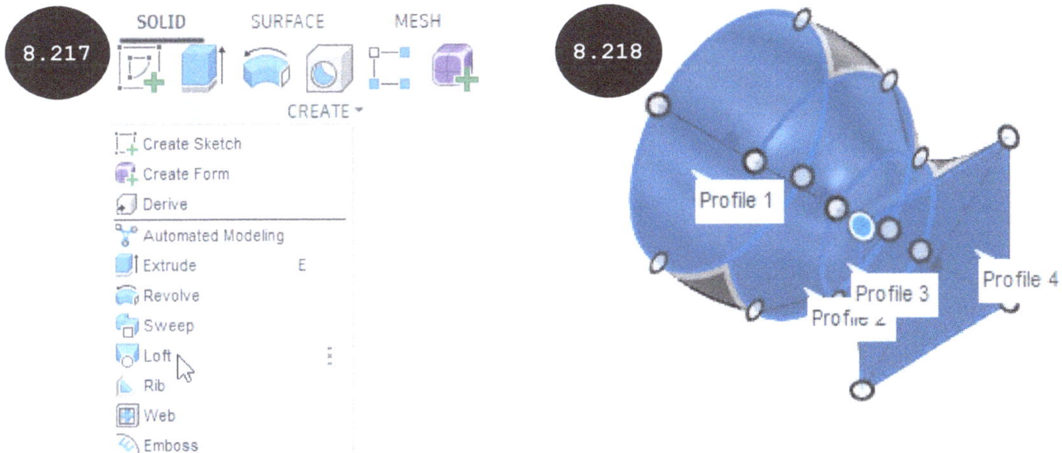

15. Click on the **OK** button in the dialog box. The loft feature is created, see Figure 8.219.

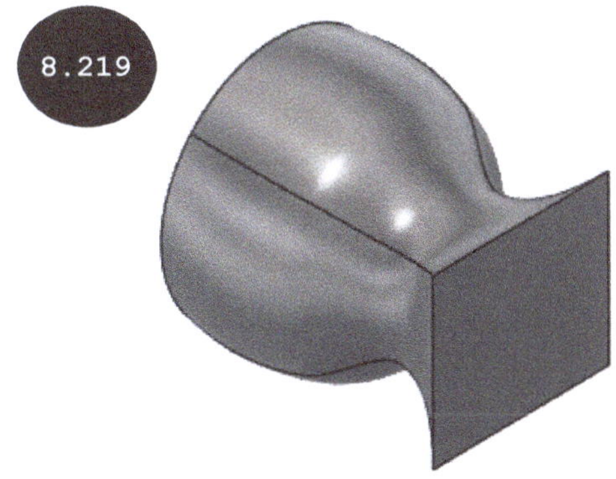

Section 3: Creating the Second Feature - Loft Feature

Now, you need to create the second feature of the model, which is also a loft feature.

1. Create a construction plane at an offset distance of 210 mm from the right planar face of the base feature by using the **Offset Plane** tool, see Figure 8.220.

2. Click on the **Create Sketch** tool in the **Toolbar** and then select the newly created construction plane as the sketching plane.

3. Create a section (rectangle of 150 X 5) of the loft feature, see Figure 8.221. Next, click on the **FINISH SKETCH** tool in the **SKETCH** contextual tab and then change the orientation of the sketch to isometric.

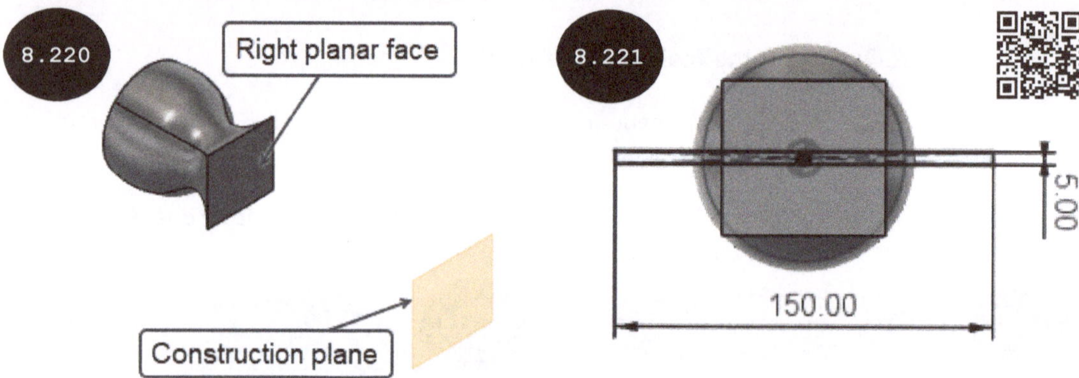

Now, you need to create a guide rail for creating the loft feature on the Front plane.

4. Click on the **Create Sketch** tool in the **Toolbar** and then select the Front plane as the sketching plane.

5. Create the guide rail (an arc of radius 220 mm), see Figure 8.222. Next, click on the **FINISH SKETCH** tool in the **SKETCH** contextual tab. Change the orientation of the sketch to isometric.

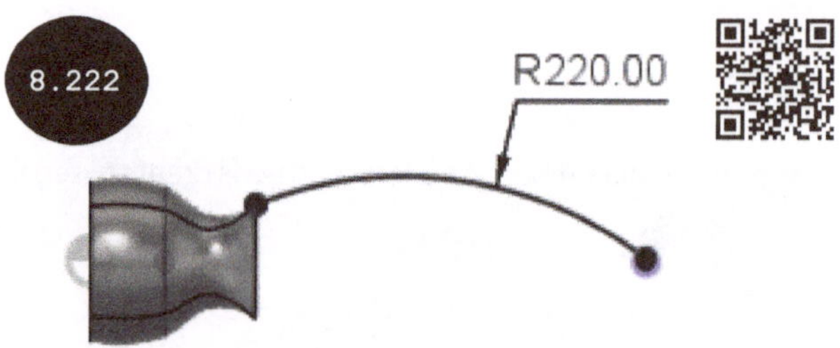

Note: The endpoints of the guide rail (arc) shown in Figure 8.222 have coincident constraint with the top entity of the rectangular section of the loft feature and the top edge of the right planar face of the base feature, respectively.

Now, you need to create the lofted feature.

6. Click on the **SOLID** tab in the **Toolbar** to display the solid modeling tools.

7. Invoke the **CREATE** drop-down menu in the **SOLID** tab and then click on the **Loft** tool. The **LOFT** dialog box appears.

8. Select the right planar face of the base feature as the first section of the loft feature and then select a rectangular section (rectangle of 150 X 5) as the second section of the loft feature. A preview of the loft feature appears in the graphics area, see Figure 8.223.

9. Ensure that the **Rails** button is activated in the **Guide Type** area of the dialog box, see Figure 8.224.

10. Click on the **Rails Selection** arrow in the dialog box to select the guide rails in the graphics area, see Figure 8.224.

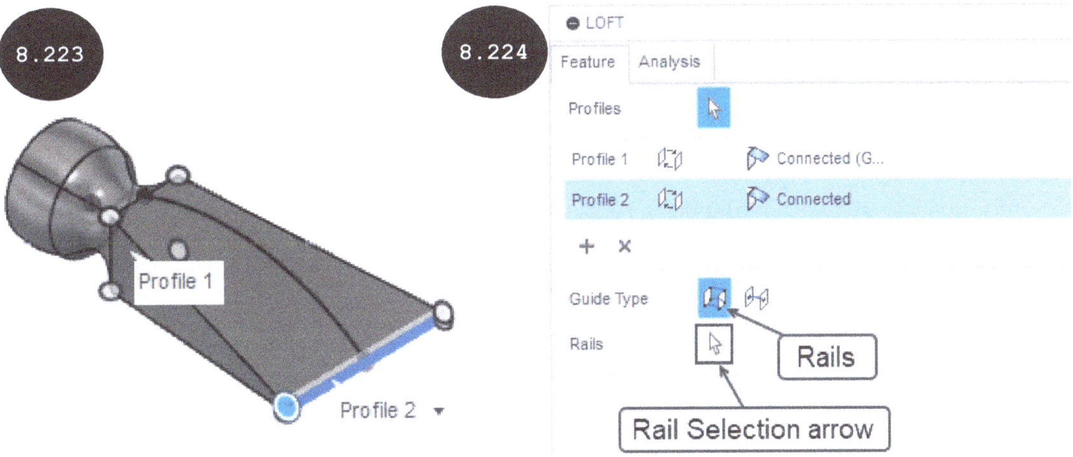

Now, you can select the guide rail to guide the cross-sectional shape of the loft feature.

11. Select the arc of radius 220 mm as the guide rail. A preview of the loft feature appears, see Figure 8.225.

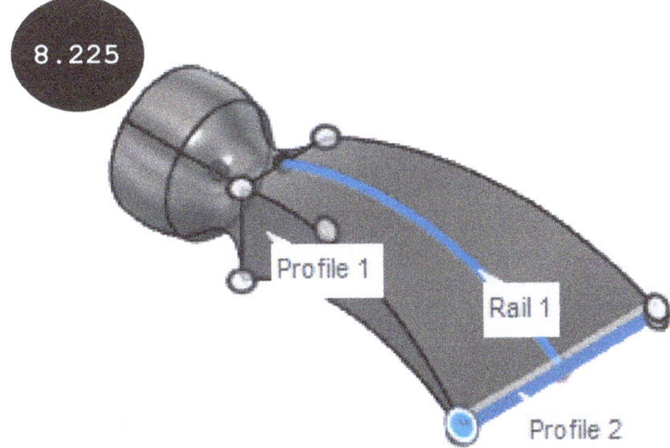

12. Ensure that the **Join** option is selected in the **Operation** drop-down list of the dialog box and then click on the **OK** button. The loft feature is created, see Figure 8.226.

8.226

Section 4: Saving the Model

1. Click on the **Save** tool in the **Application Bar**. The **Save** dialog box appears. Next, enter **Tutorial 03** in the **Name** field of the dialog box.

2. Ensure that the location ***Autodesk Fusion 360 > Chapter 08 > Tutorial 03*** is specified in the **Location** field of the dialog box to save a file of this tutorial. Note that you need to create these folders in the **Data Panel**, if not created earlier.

3. Click on the **Save** button in the dialog box. The model is saved with the name Tutorial 03 in the specified location (***Autodesk Fusion 360 > Chapter 08 > Tutorial 03***).

Tutorial 4

Create a model, as shown in Figure 8.227. All dimensions are in mm.

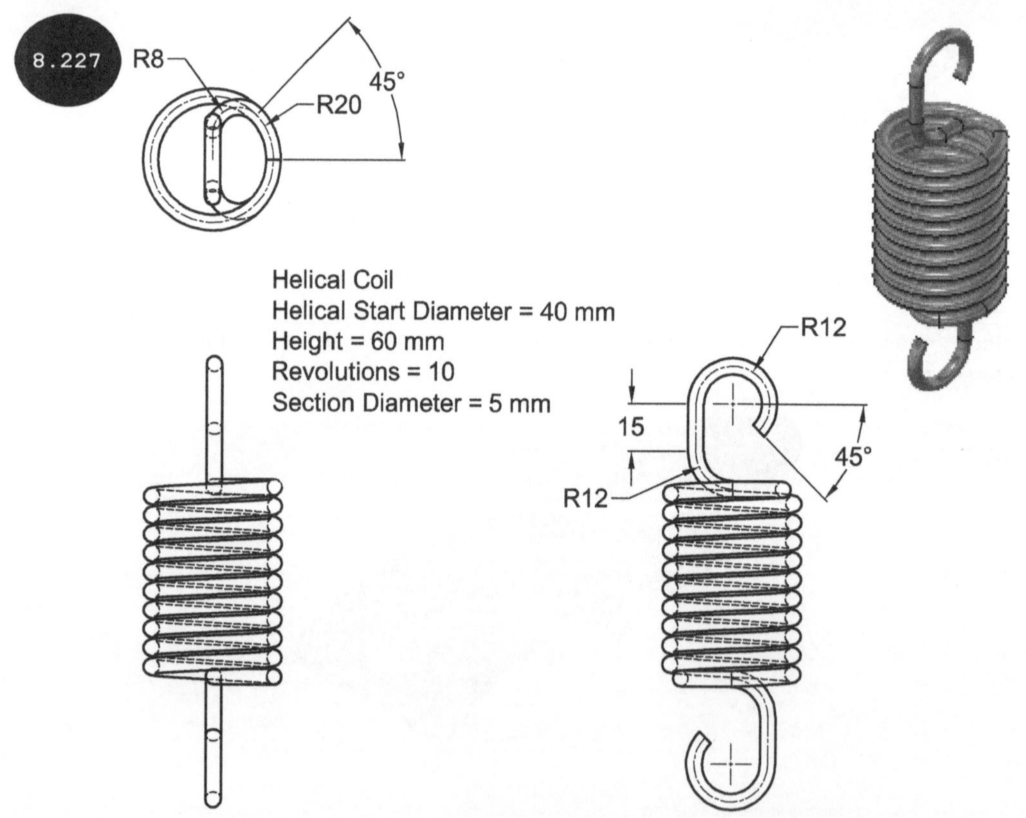

8.227

Section 1: Starting a New Part Design File

1. Click **File** > **New** in the **Application Bar** (see Figure 8.228) to display the **What do you want to design?** dialog box.

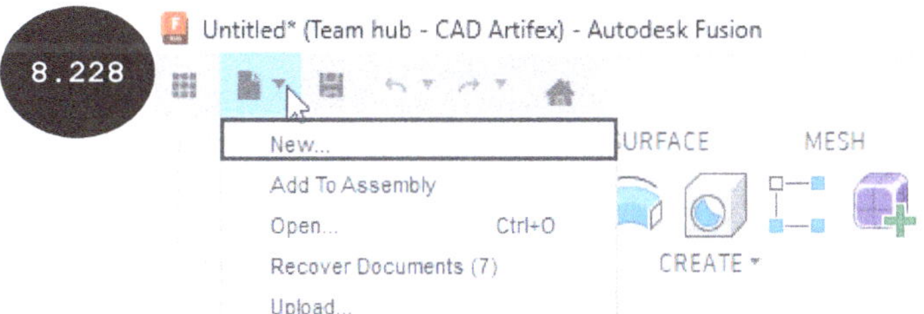

2. In the **What do you want to design?** dialog box, select the **Part Design** button. Also, select the **millimeter (mm), gram (g)** unit system from the **Unit System** drop-down list.

3. After specifying the required options, click the **Create New** button. A new Part Design file is created with the default name.

Note: If you are starting a new Autodesk Fusion session, the Part Design file opens automatically, as it is set as the default design type. In this case, ensure that the **millimeter (mm), gram (g)** unit system is set for the opened Part Design file.

Section 2: Creating the Base Feature - Helical Coil

1. Invoke the **CREATE** drop-down menu in the **SOLID** tab and then click on the **Coil** tool. You are prompted to select a sketching plane.

2. Select the Top plane as the sketching plane. The **Center Diameter Circle** tool gets activated automatically, and you are prompted to specify the center point of the circle.

3. Create a circle of diameter 40 mm by specifying its center point at the origin. A preview of the helical coil with default specifications appears, see Figure 8.229. Also, the **COIL** dialog box appears.

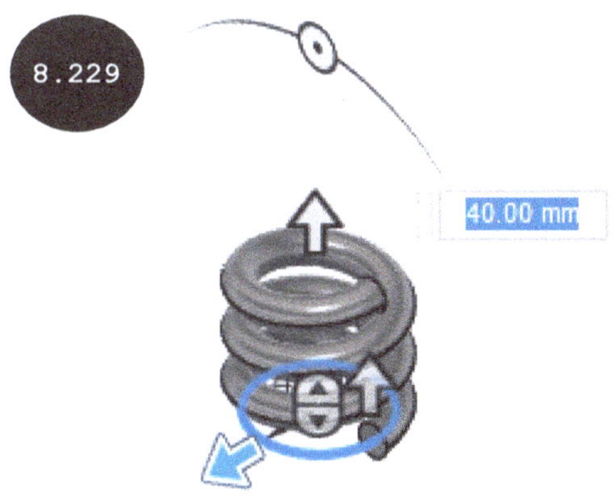

4. Ensure that the **Revolution and Height** option is selected in the **Type** drop-down list of the **COIL** dialog box, see Figure 8.230.

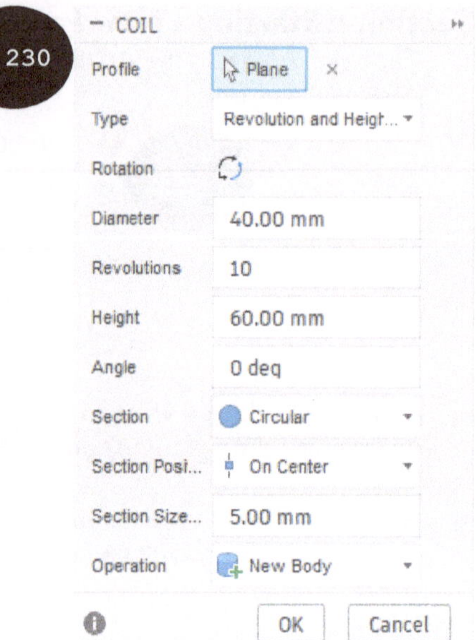

8.230

5. Enter **10** in the **Revolutions** field of the dialog box as the number of revolutions of the coil, see Figure 8.230.

6. Enter **60** in the **Height** field of the dialog box as the total height of the coil, see Figure 8.230.

7. Ensure that 0 degrees is specified in the **Angle** field.

8. Ensure that the **Circular** option is selected in the **Section** field for creating a coil of circular section.

9. Ensure that the **On Center** option is selected in the **Section Position** field, see Figure 8.230.

10. Enter **5** in the **Section Size** field of the dialog box as the size of the coil section.

11. Ensure that the **New Body** option is selected in the **Operation** drop-down list of the dialog box.

12. Click on the **OK** button in the dialog box. A helical coil of required specifications is created, see Figure 8.231.

Section 3: Creating the Second Feature - Sweep Feature

To create the path of the sweep feature, you need to create a construction plane at an offset distance of 60 mm from the Top plane.

1. Create a construction plane at an offset distance of 60 mm from the Top plane by using the **Offset Plane** tool, see Figure 8.232.

8.231

8.232

After creating the construction plane, you can create the path of the sweep feature.

2. Click on the **Create Sketch** tool in **Toolbar** and then select the newly created construction plane as the sketching plane.

3. Create a sketch of the path by using the sketching tools, see Figure 8.233.

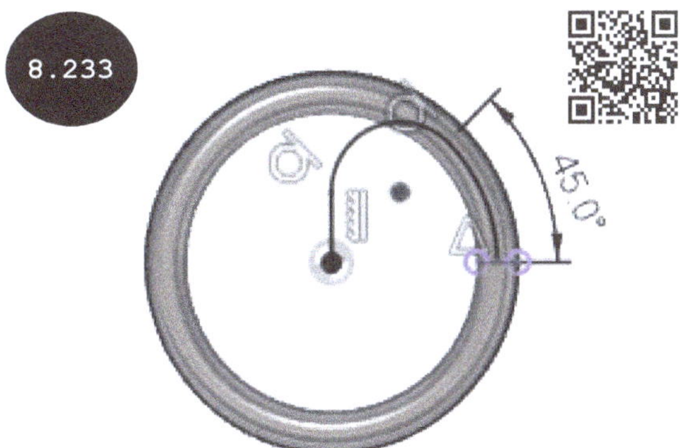

4. Click on the **SOLID** tab in the **Toolbar** to display the solid modeling tools.

5. Invoke the **CREATE** drop-down menu in the **SOLID** tab and then click on the **Sweep** tool. The **SWEEP** dialog box appears. Next, change the orientation of the model to isometric.

6. Ensure that the **Single Path** option is selected in the **Type** drop-down list of the dialog box.

7. Rotate the model and then select the end face of the coil as the profile of the sweep feature, see Figure 8.234.

8. Click on the **Path** selection option in the dialog box and then select the path of the sweep feature, see Figure 8.234. A preview of the sweep feature appears in the graphics area.

9. Ensure that the **Perpendicular** option is selected in the **Orientation** drop-down list of the dialog box.

10. Ensure that the **Join** option is selected in the **Operation** drop-down list of the dialog box.

11. Click on the **OK** button in the dialog box. The sweep feature is created, see Figure 8.235. Change the orientation of the model to isometric.

Section 4: Creating the Third Feature - Sweep Feature

1. Click on the **Create Sketch** tool in the **Toolbar** and then select the Right plane (YZ) as the sketching plane to create the path of the sweep feature.

2. Create the path of the sweep feature by using the sketching tools, see Figure 8.236.

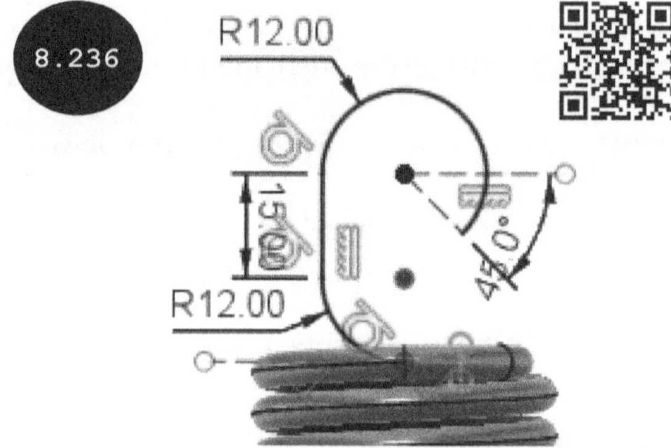

3. Click on the **SOLID** tab in the **Toolbar** to display the solid modeling tools.

4. Invoke the **CREATE** drop-down menu in the **SOLID** tab and then click on the **Sweep** tool. The **SWEEP** dialog box appears. Next, change the orientation of the model to isometric.

5. Ensure that the **Single Path** option is selected in the **Type** drop-down list of the dialog box.

6. Rotate the model and then select the end face of the previously created sweep feature as the profile, see Figure 8.237.

7. Click on the **Path** selection option in the dialog box and then select the path of the sweep feature, see Figure 8.237. A preview of the sweep feature appears in the graphics area.

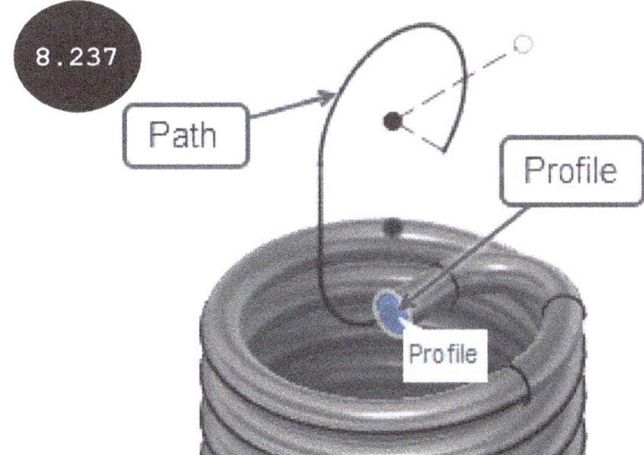

8. Ensure that the **Perpendicular** option is selected in the **Orientation** drop-down list and the **Join** option is selected in the **Operation** drop-down list of the dialog box.

9. Click on the **OK** button in the dialog box. The sweep feature is created, see Figure 8.238. Change the orientation of the model to isometric.

Section 5: Creating the Fourth Feature - Sweep Feature

1. Click on the **Create Sketch** tool in the **Toolbar** and then select the Top plane as the sketching plane.

2. Create the path of the sweep feature by using the sketching tools, see Figure 8.239.

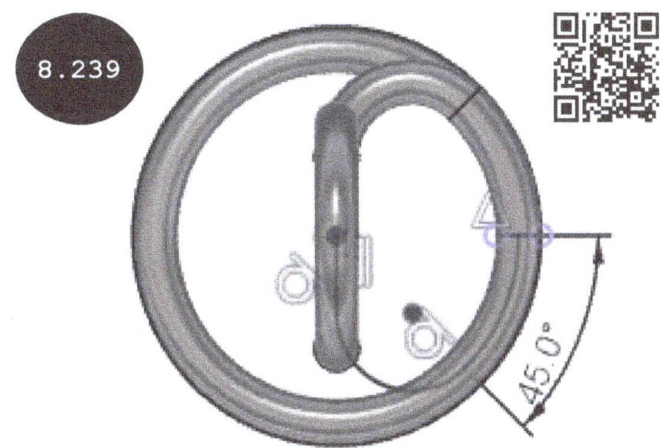

3. Click on the **SOLID** tab in the **Toolbar** to display the solid modeling tools.

4. Invoke the **CREATE** drop-down menu in the **SOLID** tab and then click on the **Sweep** tool. The **SWEEP** dialog box appears. Next, change the orientation of the model to isometric.

5. Ensure that the **Single Path** option is selected in the **Type** drop-down list of the dialog box.

6. Select the start face of the coil as the profile of the sweep feature, see Figure 8.240

7. Click on the **Path** selection option in the dialog box and then select the path of the sweep feature, see Figure 8.240. A preview of the sweep feature appears in the graphics area.

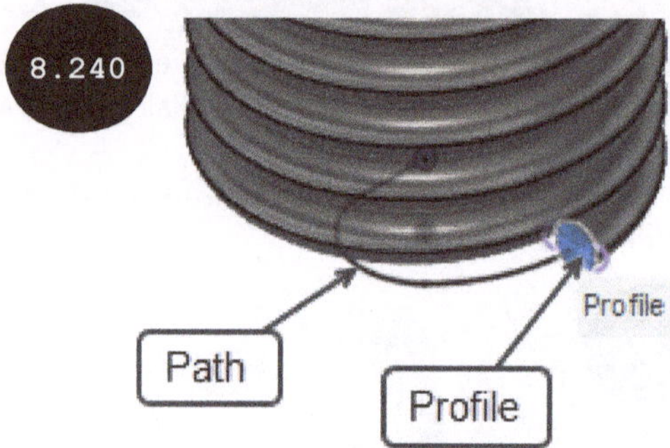

8. Ensure that the **Perpendicular** option is selected in the **Orientation** drop-down list of the dialog box.

9. Ensure that the **Join** option is selected in the **Operation** drop-down list of the dialog box.

10. Click on the **OK** button in the dialog box. The sweep feature is created, see Figure 8.241.

Section 6: Creating the Fifth Feature - Sweep Feature

1. Click on the **Create Sketch** tool in the **Toolbar** and then select the Right plane (YZ) as the sketching plane to create the path of the sweep feature.

2. Create the path of the sweep feature by using the sketching tools, see Figure 8.242.

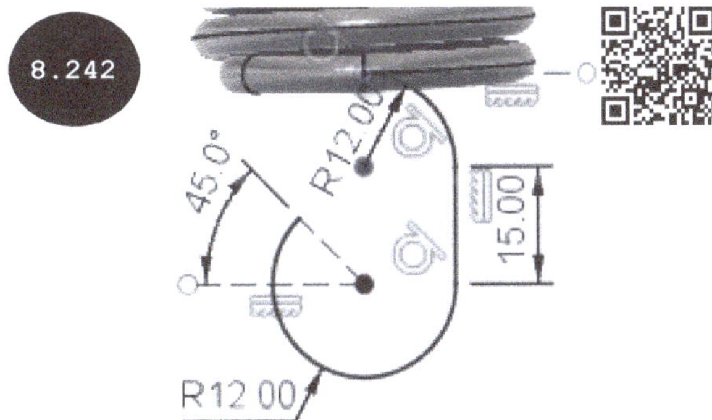

3. Click on the **SOLID** tab in the **Toolbar** to display the solid modeling tools.

4. Invoke the **CREATE** drop-down menu in the **SOLID** tab and then click on the **Sweep** tool. The **SWEEP** dialog box appears. Next, change the orientation of the model to isometric.

5. Ensure that the **Single Path** option is selected in the **Type** drop-down list of the dialog box.

6. Rotate the model and then select the end face of the previously created sweep feature as the profile, see Figure 8.243.

7. Click on the **Path** selection option in the dialog box and then select the path of the sweep feature, see Figure 8.243. A preview of the sweep feature appears in the graphics area.

8. Ensure that the **Perpendicular** option is selected in the **Orientation** drop-down list and the **Join** option is selected in the **Operation** drop-down list of the dialog box.

9. Click on the **OK** button in the dialog box. The sweep feature is created, see Figure 8.244. Change the orientation of the model to isometric.

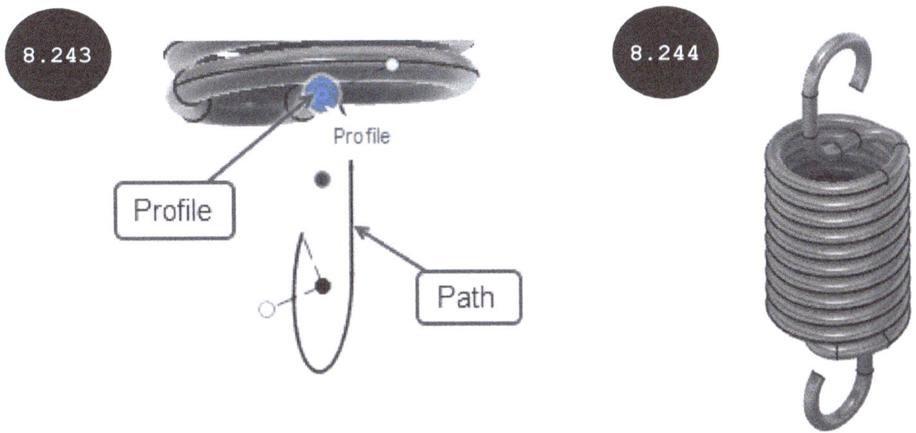

Section 7: Saving the Model

1. Click on the **Save** tool in the **Application Bar**. The **Save** dialog box appears.

2. Enter **Tutorial 04** in the **Name** field of the dialog box.

3. Ensure that the location ***Autodesk Fusion 360 > Chapter 08 > Tutorial 04*** is specified in the **Location** field of the dialog box to save a file of this tutorial. Note that you need to create these folders in the **Data Panel**, if not created earlier.

4. Click on the **Save** button in the dialog box. The model is saved with the name Tutorial 04 in the specified location (***Autodesk Fusion 360 > Chapter 08 > Tutorial 04***).

Hands-on Test Drive 1

Create a model, as shown in Figure 8.245. After creating the model, apply the Alloy Steel material and then calculate its mass properties. All dimensions are in mm.

8.245

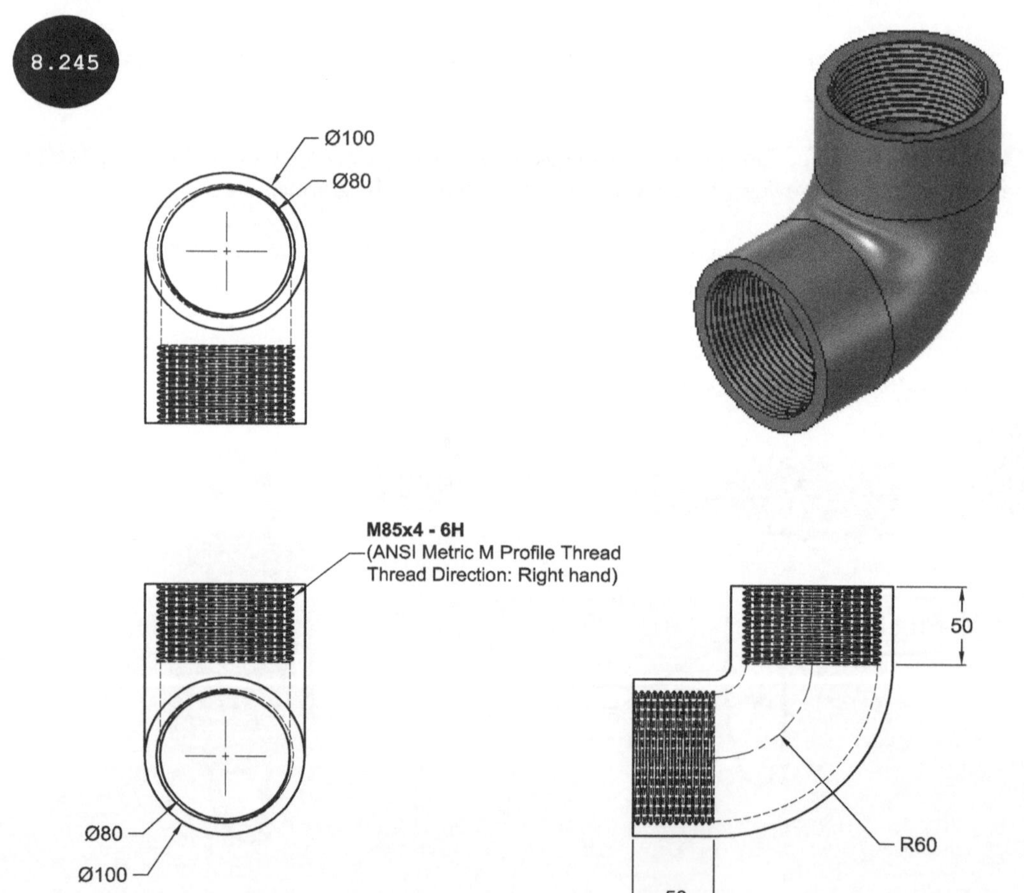

Hands-on Test Drive 2

Create a model, as shown in Figure 8.246, and then apply the Alloy Steel material. Also, calculate the mass properties of the model. All dimensions are in mm.

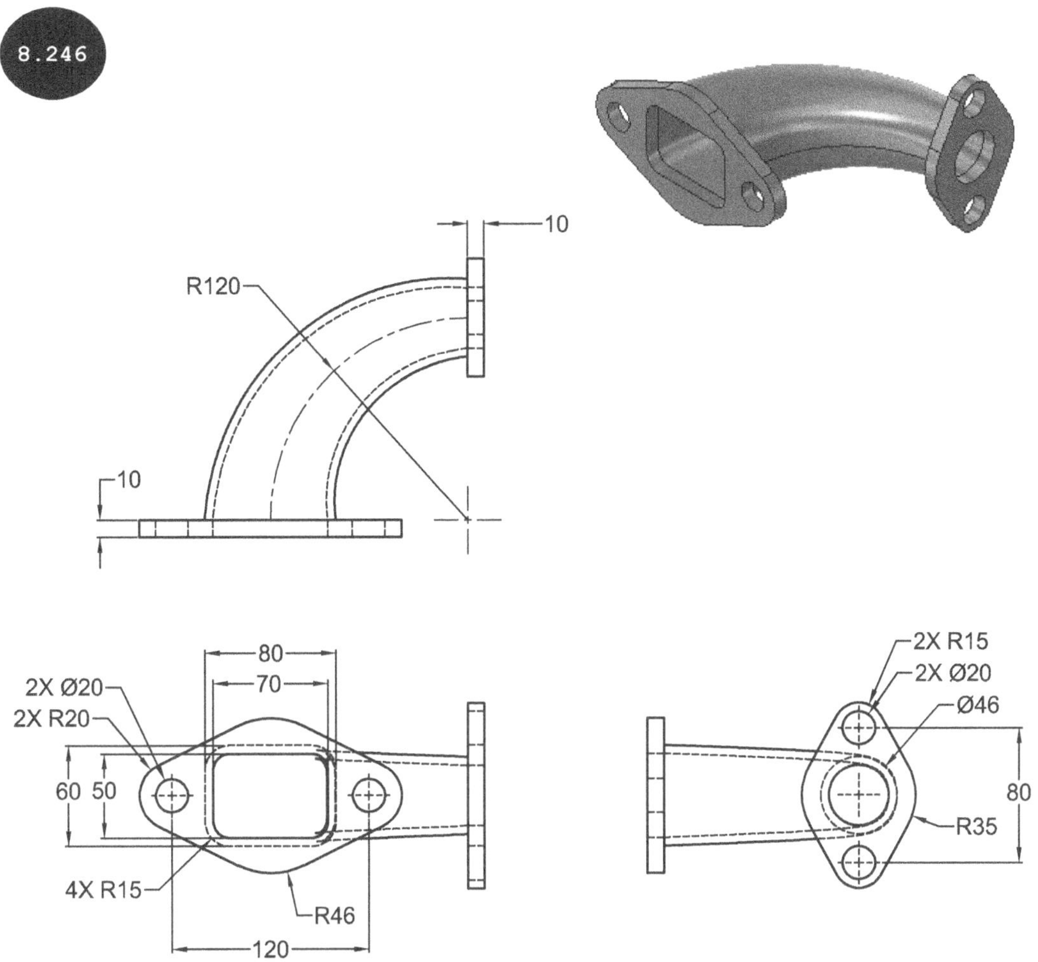

Summary

In this chapter, you explored various advanced design tools and techniques. You learned how to create sweep and loft features, which allow you to form complex shapes, along with the practical uses of rib, web, and emboss features. The chapter also covered how to create essential primitive shapes such as rectangular boxes, cylinders, spheres, and torus, as well as more specialized features like helical and spiral coils, pipes, and 3D sketches.

Additionally, you gained insight into creating cosmetic and modeled threads using the **Thread** tool and designing holes such as simple, counterbore, and countersink types using the **Hole** tool. Each of these tools enhances your ability to construct detailed and precise designs, forming the foundation for more complex modeling projects.

Questions

Complete and verify the following sentences:

- The _________ tool is used for creating a sweep feature.
- The _________ option of the **Type** drop-down list in the **SWEEP** dialog box is used for creating a sweep feature by using the profiles and a guide rail.
- The _________ field of the **SWEEP** dialog box is used for specifying the twist angle value for twisting the profile along the path.
- On selecting the _________ option, the resultant sweep feature is created by keeping the section/profile of the feature perpendicular to the path.
- You can create two types of threads: _________ and _________.
- The **Hole** tool is used for creating _________, _________, and _________ holes.
- The _________ button of the **HOLE** dialog box is used for creating multiple holes by using the sketch points.
- On selecting the _________ option, you can create a helical coil by defining its pitch and number of revolutions.
- The _________ tool is used for creating a solid or hollow pipe.
- The _________ option of the **COIL** dialog box is used for creating a spiral coil by defining its pitch and number of revolutions.
- In Autodesk Fusion, you cannot create tapered helical coils. (True/False)
- The profiles/sections of a loft feature must be closed. (True/False)
- You can drag the connector points that appear in the preview of a loft feature to create a twist in the feature. (True/False)
- You can create 3D sketches by selecting the **3D Sketch** check box in the **SKETCH PALETTE** dialog box. (True/False)

9

Patterning and Mirroring

In this chapter, the following topics will be discussed:

- Creating a Rectangular Pattern
- Creating a Circular Pattern
- Creating a Pattern along a Path
- Mirroring Features/Faces/Bodies/Components

Patterning and mirroring are powerful tools that significantly enhance design efficiency by reducing repetitive tasks and saving valuable time. For instance, if a plate requires 1000 identical holes, instead of modeling each one individually, you can simply create a single hole and then use the patterning tool to replicate the others. Likewise, if your design is symmetrical, you only need to model one side and mirror it to generate the other half.

In Autodesk Fusion, you can create rectangular, circular, and path patterns of faces, bodies, features, and components. The various types of patterns are discussed next.

Creating a Rectangular Pattern

You can create a rectangular pattern by creating multiple instances of faces, bodies, features, or components in one or two linear directions using the **Rectangular Pattern** tool, refer to Figures 9.1 through 9.3.

Figure 9.1 shows the feature to be patterned and the two linear directions: Direction 1 and Direction 2. Figure 9.2 displays the resulting pattern when the feature is patterned along Direction 1, while Figure 9.3 shows the pattern when the feature is patterned along both Direction 1 and Direction 2.

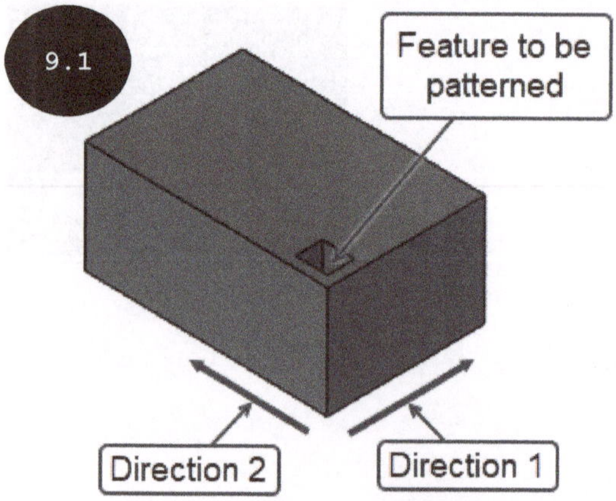

9.1

Feature to be patterned

Direction 2

Direction 1

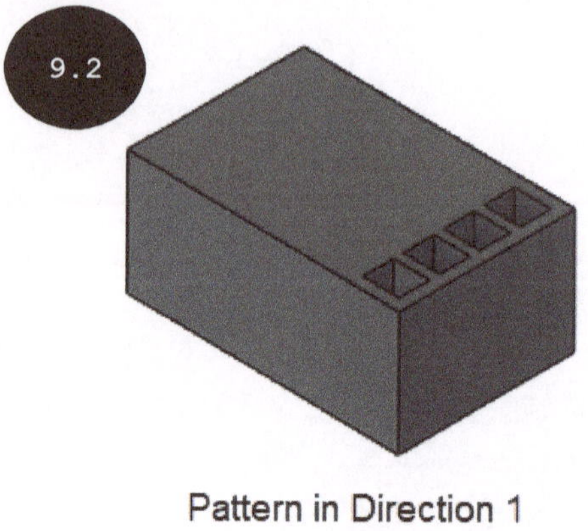

9.2

Pattern in Direction 1

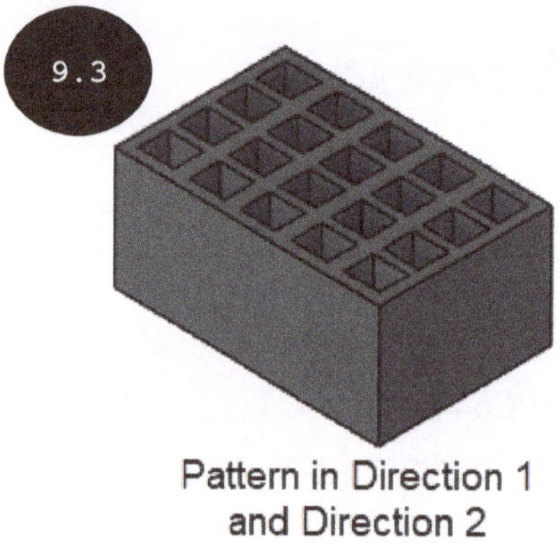

9.3

Pattern in Direction 1 and Direction 2

To create a rectangular pattern, click on the **Rectangular Pattern** tool in the **CREATE** panel of the **SOLID** tab, see Figure 9.4. The **RECTANGULAR PATTERN** dialog box appears, see Figure 9.5. Alternatively, invoke the **CREATE** drop-down menu in the **SOLID** tab and then click on **Pattern > Rectangular Pattern**. The options in this dialog box are discussed next.

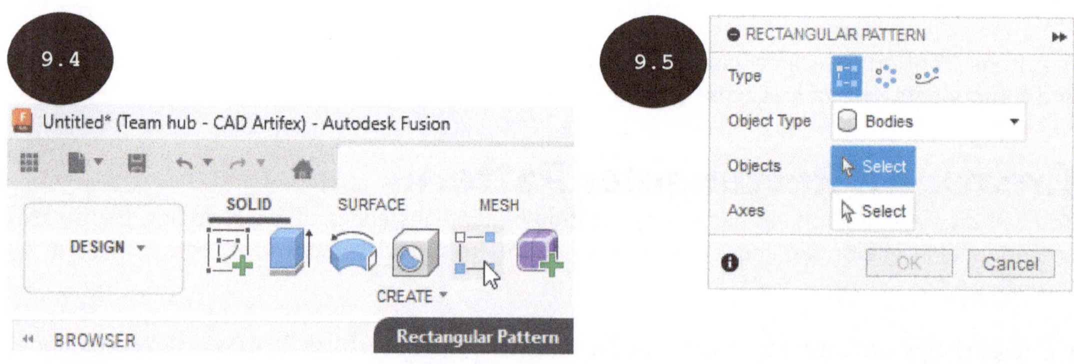

Type

The **Type** area of the **RECTANGULAR PATTERN** dialog box displays all the pattern tools (**Rectangular Pattern, Circular Pattern,** and **Pattern On Path**). You can switch between the pattern tools by activating the respective tool in this **Type** area of the dialog box if needed.

Object Type

The **Object Type** drop-down list in the dialog box is to select the type of entities to be patterned, including faces, features, bodies, or components. By selecting the **Faces** option, you can select specific faces that define the geometry of the model for patterning. Selecting the **Bodies** option enables you to choose entire bodies to pattern. If you select the **Features** option, you can pattern specific features, while choosing the **Components** option allows you to pattern components within your design.

Objects

The **Objects** selection option allows you to select objects (faces, bodies, features, or components) to be patterned. Note that the type of object selection depends upon the option selected in the **Object** Type drop-down list.

Axes

The **Axes** selection option is used to specify the first and second linear pattern directions for creating the pattern. You can select a linear edge, a linear sketch entity, or an axis as the first and second pattern directions. Note that on selecting the first pattern direction, the second pattern direction is defined perpendicular to the first selected direction, automatically. After choosing the pattern directions, the arrows appear in the graphics area pointing toward the pattern directions, see Figure 9.6.

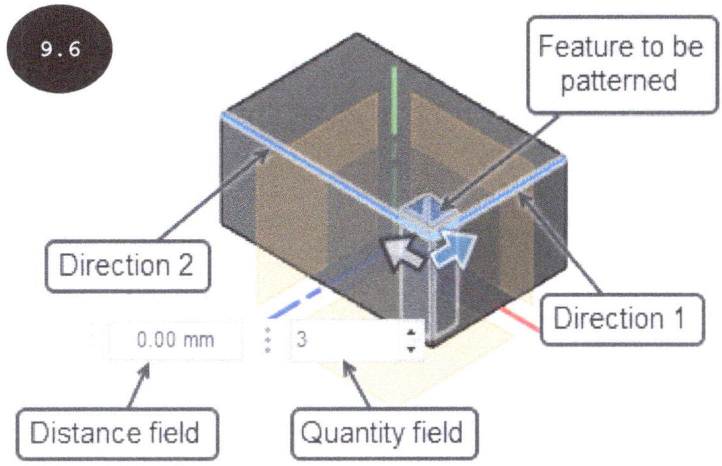

Distribution

The **Distribution** drop-down list is used to specify the type of distance measurement between the pattern instances. By default, the **Extent** option is selected in this drop-down list. As a result, the distance value specified in the **Distance** field of the dialog box is used as the spacing between the first and last pattern instances (total pattern distance). For example, if the pattern distance along a pattern direction is specified as 100 mm, then all the pattern instances will adjust within the specified pattern distance with equal spacing among all the instances.

On selecting the **Spacing** option in the **Distribution** drop-down list, the distance value specified in the **Distance** field is used as the spacing between two consecutive pattern instances.

Quantity

The **Quantity** fields in the **Axis 1** and **Axis 2** rollouts of the **RECTANGULAR PATTERN** dialog box are used to specify the number of pattern instances to be created in Direction 1 and Direction 2, respectively, see Figures 9.7 and 9.8. Figure 9.7 shows the dialog box with **Axis 1** and **Axis 2** rollouts. Figure 9.8 shows the preview of a rectangular pattern with 4 instances in Direction 1 and 5 instances in Direction 2. You can also drag the spinner arrows that appear near the source object in the preview of the pattern to increase or decrease the number of pattern instances. You can also specify the number of pattern instances to be created in the **Quantity** field that appears in the graphics area, refer to Figure 9.6.

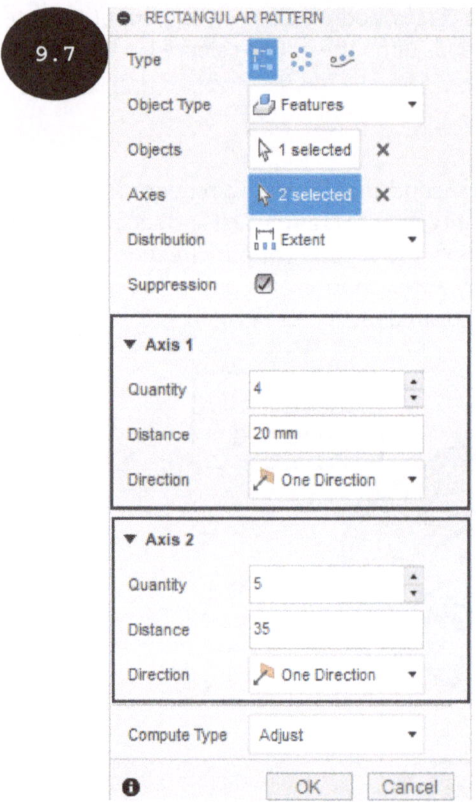

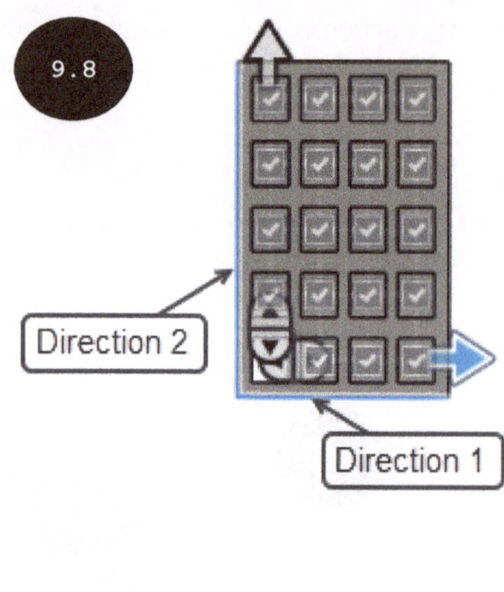

Note: The number of pattern instances specified in the **Quantity** field includes the parent or original instance. For example, if you specify **4** in the **Quantity** field, a total of 4 pattern instances will be created in the respective pattern direction, counting the original instance as one of them.

Distance

The **Distance** fields in the **Axis 1** and **Axis 2** rollouts of the dialog box are used to specify the spacing between pattern instances in Direction 1 and Direction 2, respectively. You can also drag the arrows that appear in the preview of the pattern to increase or decrease the spacing between the pattern instances. Alternatively, specify the spacing in the **Distance** field that appears in the graphics area. Also, to reverse the pattern direction, you can enter a negative distance value in the **Distance** field. Note that the distance value specified in the **Distance** field depends upon the option selected in the **Distribution** drop-down list of the dialog box.

Direction

The **Direction** drop-down lists in the **Axis 1** and **Axis 2** rollouts of the dialog box are used for defining pattern direction on one side or symmetric about the parent object(s) by selecting the **One Direction** or **Symmetric** option, respectively, see Figures 9.9 and 9.10. Figure 9.9 shows the preview of a rectangular pattern when the **One Direction** option is selected for Direction 1 and Direction 2. Figure 9.10 shows the preview of a rectangular pattern when the **Symmetric** option is selected for Direction 1.

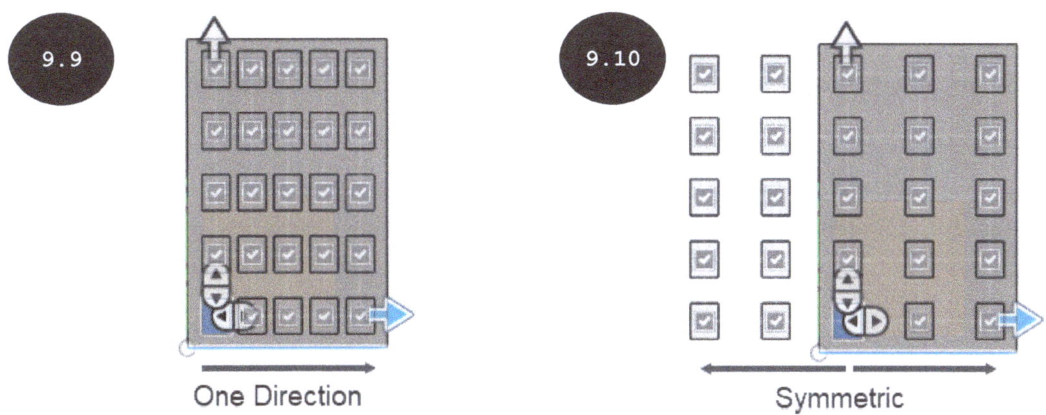

Suppression

When the **Suppression** check box is selected in the **RECTANGULAR PATTERN** dialog box, a check box appears at the center of each pattern instance in the graphics area. You can clear the check boxes of the pattern instances that you want to skip or remove from the resultant pattern. You can do so by clicking the left mouse button on the instance to be removed from the pattern. To recall or include the skipped instances of the pattern, select the check boxes that appear in the preview of the pattern.

Compute Type

The options in the **Compute Type** drop-down list of the dialog box are used to define the computational method for creating the pattern. Note that the **Compute Type** drop-down list is available when the **Features** option is selected in the **Object Type** drop-down list. The options in the **Compute Type** drop-down list are discussed next.

Optimized

The **Optimized** option is used for creating a pattern with a large number of pattern instances by optimizing the process of creating the pattern. It is the fastest way of doing so.

Identical

The **Identical** option is used for creating a pattern such that the pattern instances do not maintain the same geometrical relations as that of the parent feature. For example, Figure 9.11 shows the front view of a model, in which a cut feature is created by defining the end condition as 4 mm offset from the bottom face of the model. Figure 9.12 shows the resultant pattern of the cut feature created by selecting the **Identical** option in the **Compute Type** drop-down list.

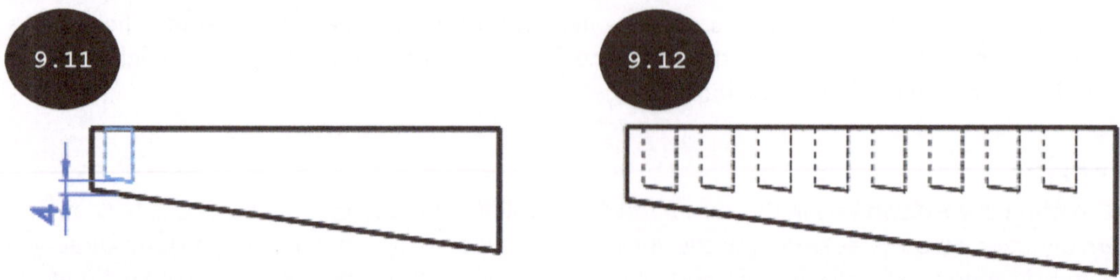

Adjust

The **Adjust** option is used for creating a pattern such that all the pattern instances maintain the same geometrical relations as that of the parent feature, see Figure 9.13. In this figure, the pattern instances maintain the geometrical relation of the parent feature, which is 4 mm offset from the bottom face of the model.

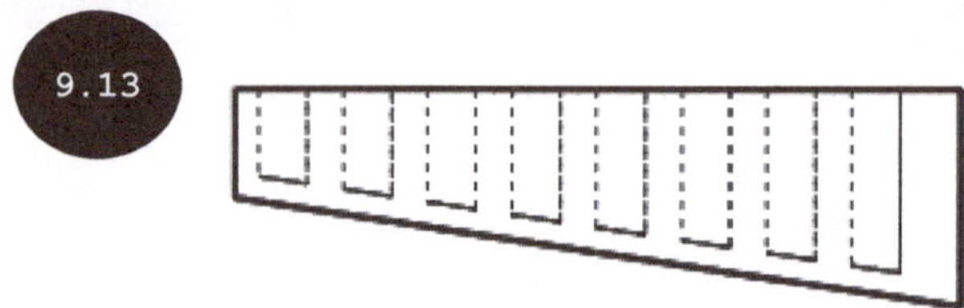

After defining parameters in the **RECTANGULAR PATTERN** dialog box, click on the **OK** button. The rectangular pattern is created, see Figure 9.14.

Creating a Circular Pattern

You can create a circular pattern by creating multiple instances of faces, bodies, features, or components, circularly around an axis using the **Circular Pattern** tool, see Figure 9.15.

9.15

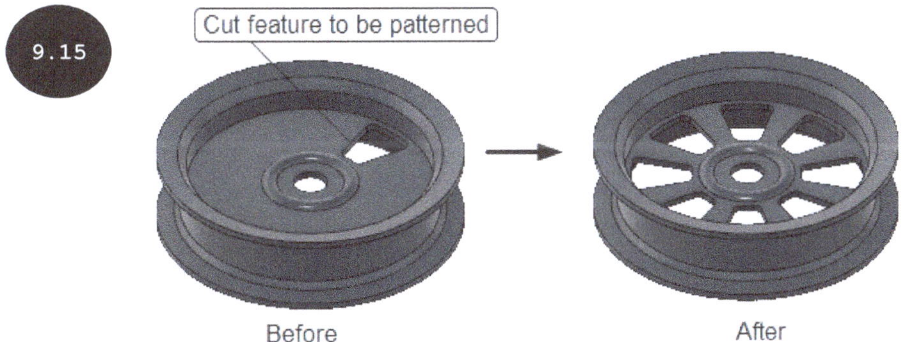

To create a circular pattern, invoke the **CREATE** drop-down menu in the **SOLID** tab and then click on **Pattern > Circular Pattern**, see Figure 9.16. The **CIRCULAR PATTERN** dialog box appears with the **Circular Pattern** tool activated in its **Type** area, by default, see Figure 9.17. The options in this dialog box are discussed next.

9.16

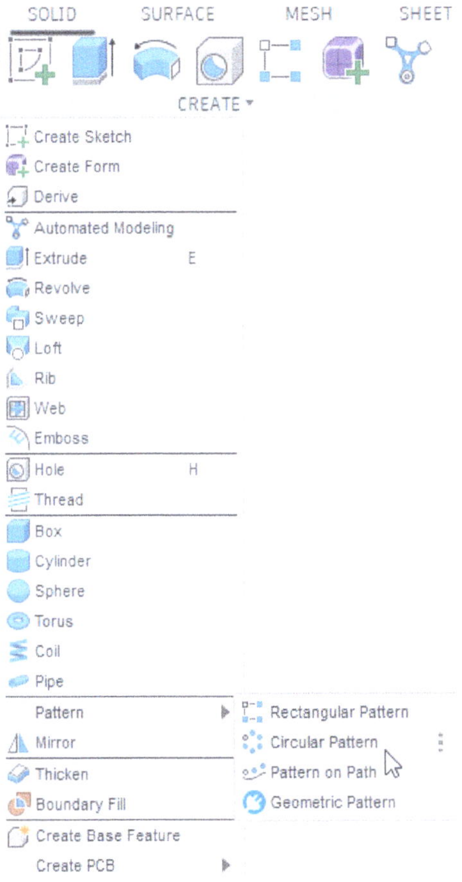

9.17

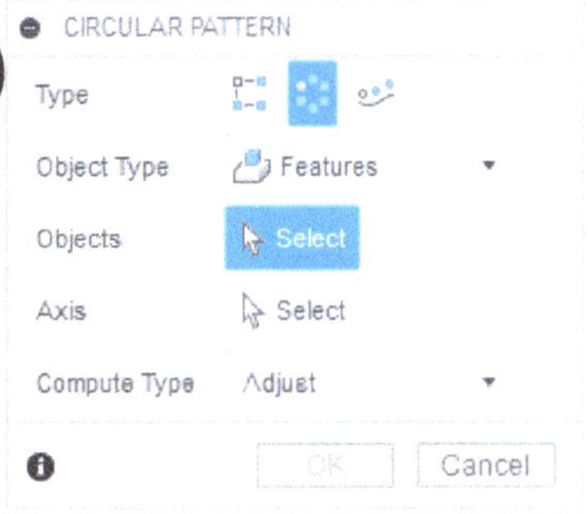

Type

The **Type** area of the **CIRCULAR PATTERN** dialog box displays all the pattern tools. You can switch between the pattern tools by activating the respective tool in this area if needed.

Object Type

The options in the **Object Type** drop-down list are used to select faces, features, bodies, or components to be patterned. On selecting the **Faces** option, you can select the faces to be patterned in the graphics area, which defines the geometry of a model. Similarly, on selecting the **Bodies** option, you can select entire bodies to be patterned. On selecting the **Features** option, you can select features to be patterned. Lastly, on selecting the **Components** option, you can select the components to be patterned.

Objects

The **Objects** selection option allows you to select objects (faces, bodies, features, or components) to be patterned. Note that the type of object selection depends upon the option selected in the **Object Type** drop-down list.

Axis

The **Axis** selection option is used to select axis around which you want to create a circular pattern. To do this, click on the **Axis** selection option in the dialog box and then select an axis, a circular face, a circular edge, or a linear sketch as the pattern axis. Note that on selecting a circular face or a circular edge as the pattern axis, the respective center axis is automatically determined and is used as the axis of the circular pattern.

Distribution

By default, the **Full** option is selected in the **Distribution** drop-down list. As a result, the circular pattern created is such that it covers 360 degrees in the pattern and the number of pattern instances specified in the **Quantity** field of the dialog box are adjusted within the total 360 degrees, equally. On selecting the **Partial** option in the **Distribution** drop-down list, the **Angle** field appears in the dialog box. In this field, you can specify the total angle value of the pattern, as required. You can also drag the arrow that appears near the last pattern instance to increase or decrease the total angle value. Note that the pattern instances are adjusted within the specified total angle value, automatically.

On selecting the **Symmetric** option in the **Distribution** drop-down list, you can create a circular pattern symmetric about the parent object selected.

Quantity

The **Quantity** field is used to specify the number of pattern instances to be created. You can also drag the spinner arrows that appear in the preview of the pattern to increase or decrease the number of pattern instances.

Note: The **Quantity** field specifies the total number of pattern instances, including the parent or original instance. For instance, if you enter **4** in the **Quantity** field, it will result in the creation of 4 pattern instances in the specified direction, with the parent instance counted as one of them.

Suppression

On selecting the **Suppression** check box, a check box appears at the center of each pattern instance in the graphics area, see Figure 9.18. You can clear the check boxes of the pattern instances that you want to skip or remove from the resultant pattern. To recall or include the skipped instances of the pattern, select the check boxes that appear in the preview of the pattern.

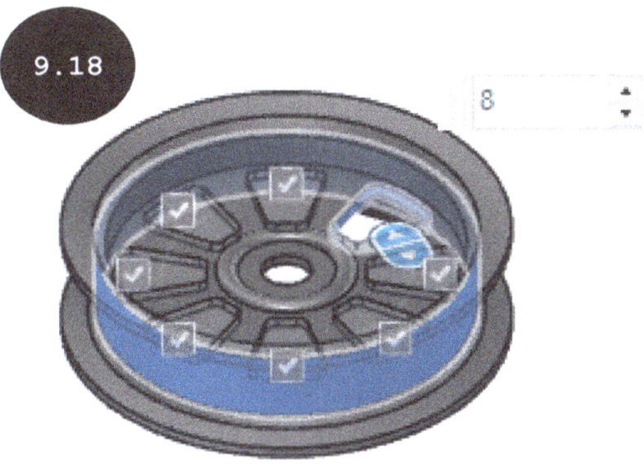

9.18

Compute Type

The options in the **Compute Type** drop-down list are used to define the computational method for creating a pattern and are the same as discussed earlier.

After defining parameters for patterning the selected objects in the **CIRCULAR PATTERN** dialog box, click on the **OK** button. The circular pattern is created, see Figure 9.19.

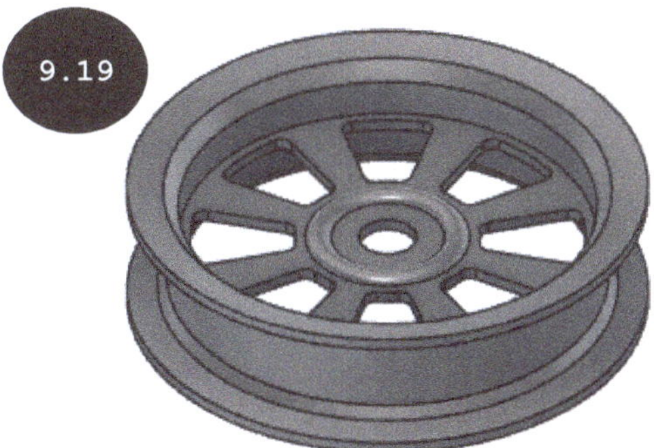

9.19

Creating a Pattern along a Path

You can create a pattern by creating multiple instances of faces, bodies, features, or components along a specified path by using the **Pattern on Path** tool, see Figure 9.20. You can select sketch curves or edges as the path to drive the pattern instances along the selected path.

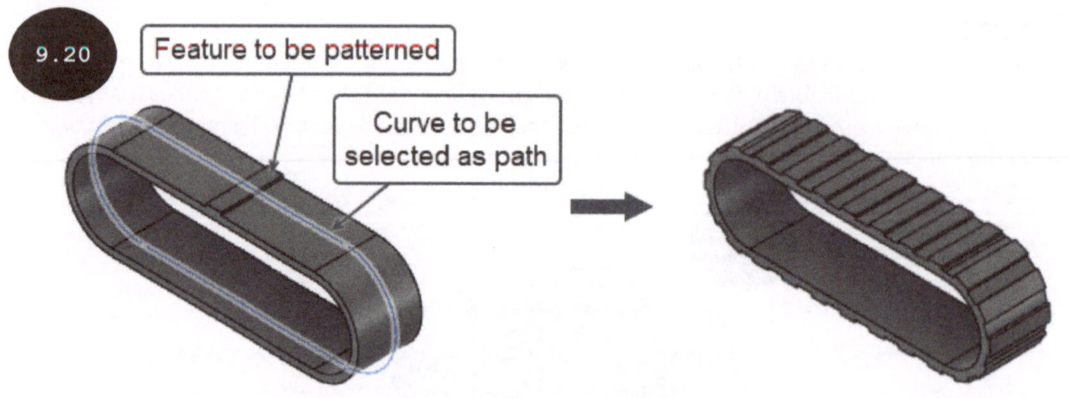

To create a pattern along a path, invoke the **CREATE** drop-down menu in the **SOLID** tab and then click on **Pattern > Pattern on Path**. The **PATTERN ON PATH** dialog box appears with the **Pattern on Path** tool activated in its **Type** area, see Figure 9.21. The options in this dialog box are discussed next.

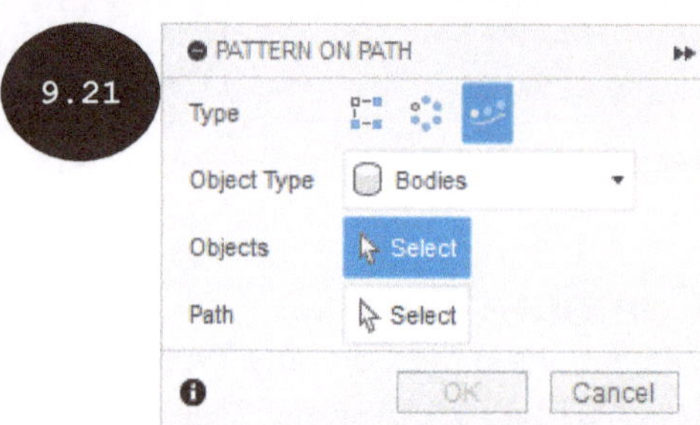

Object Type

The **Object Type** drop-down list of the dialog box is used to select faces, features, bodies, or components to be patterned.

Objects

The **Objects** selection option allows you to select objects to be patterned, see Figure 9.22. Note that the type of object selection depends upon the option selected in the **Object Type** drop-down list of the dialog box. You can select faces, features, bodies, or components in the graphics area.

Path

The **Path** selection option is used to select a curve or an edge as the path to drive the pattern instances. To do this, click on the **Path** selection option and then select the path in the graphics area, see Figure 9.22. Note that on selecting an edge or a curve, all its contiguous edges/curves are selected automatically.

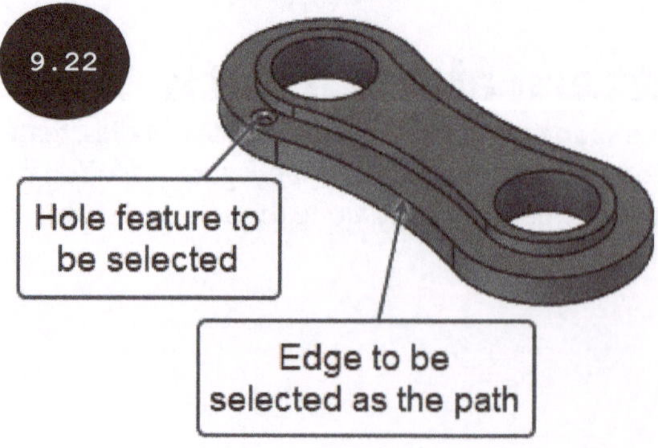

Distribution

The **Distribution** drop-down list is used to specify the type of distance measurement between the pattern instances. By default, the **Extent** option is selected in this drop-down list. As a result, the distance value specified in the **Distance** field of the dialog box is used as the spacing between the first and last pattern instances (total pattern distance). For example, if the pattern distance is specified as 100 mm, then all the pattern instances will adjust within the specified pattern distance with equal spacing between all the instances.

On selecting the **Spacing** option in the **Distribution** drop-down list, the distance value specified in the **Distance** field is used as the spacing between two consecutive pattern instances.

Distance

The **Distance** field of the dialog box is used to specify the spacing between pattern instances along the selected path. You can also drag the arrows that appear in the preview of the pattern to increase or decrease the spacing between the pattern instances. Note that the distance value specified in this field depends upon the option selected in the **Distribution** drop-down list of the dialog box.

Quantity

The **Quantity** field of the dialog box is used for specifying the number of pattern instances to be created along the path selected. You can also drag the spinner arrows that appear in the preview of the pattern to increase or decrease the number of pattern instances.

Start Point

The **Start Point** field in the dialog box defines the starting point for the pattern calculation. By default, this field is set to a value of **0** (zero), which means the pattern begins at the parent object selected for patterning. The value specified in this field is expressed as a percentage (ranging from 0 to 1) of the total length of the selected path. For example, on entering 0.5 in the **Start Point** field, the pattern starts from the middle of the path selected.

Direction

The options in the **Direction** drop-down lists are used to define pattern direction on one side or symmetric about the parent object(s) selected, as discussed earlier.

Orientation

The **Identical** option of the **Orientation** drop-down list is used to maintain the orientation of the pattern instances the same as the parent object selected, see Figure 9.23.

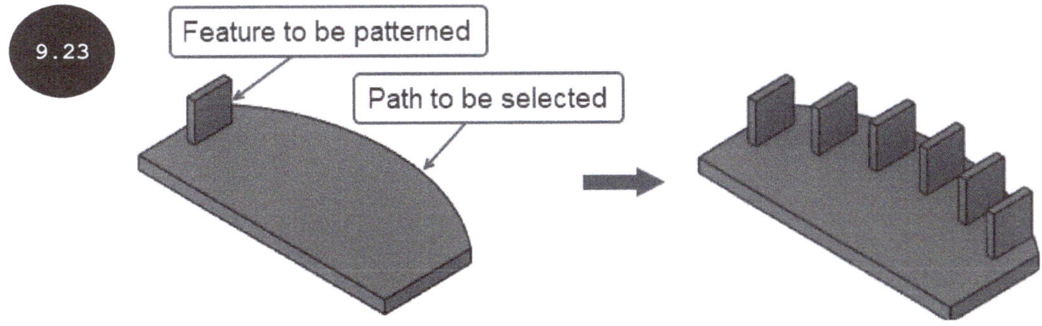

The **Path Direction** option is used to maintain the orientation of the pattern instances relative to the path selected, see Figure 9.24.

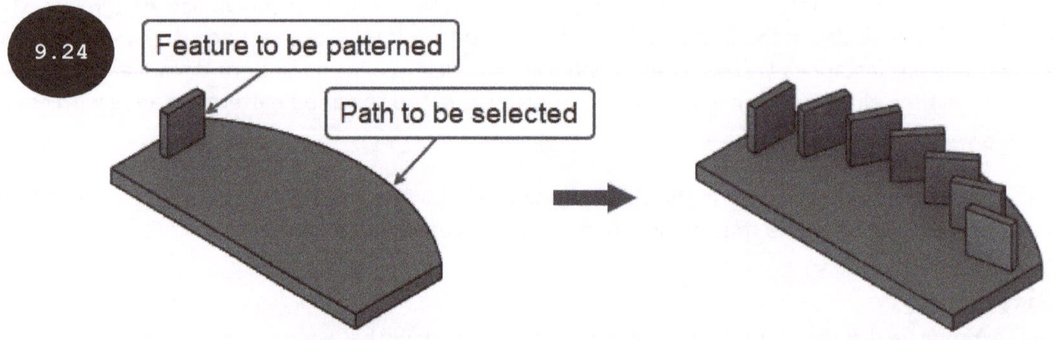

Suppression

On selecting the **Suppression** check box in the dialog box, a check box appears at the center of each pattern instance in the graphics area, see Figure 9.25. You can clear the check boxes of the pattern instances that you want to skip or remove from the resultant pattern. To recall or include the skipped instances of the pattern, select the check boxes that appear in the preview of the pattern.

Compute Type

The options in the **Compute Type** drop-down list are used to define the computational method for creating the pattern and are the same as discussed earlier.

After defining the parameters for patterning the selected object, click on the **OK** button. The pattern instances are created along the selected path, see Figure 9.26. The pattern shown in this figure is created by selecting the **Path Direction** option in the **Orientation** drop-down list of the dialog box.

Mirroring Features/Faces/Bodies/Components

You can mirror features, faces, bodies, or components about a selected mirroring plane by using the **Mirror** tool. Figure 9.27 shows features to be mirrored, mirroring plane, and the resultant mirrored feature created.

9.27

Features to be mirrored
Mirroring plane
Before
After

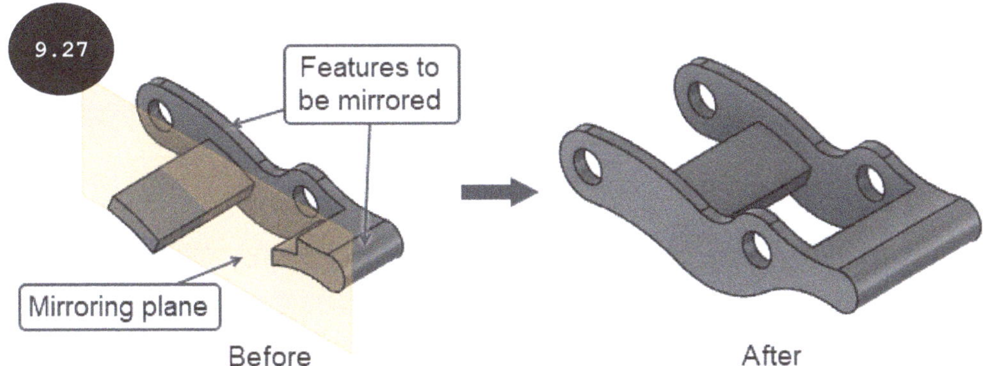

To mirror features, faces, bodies, or components, invoke the **CREATE** drop-down menu in the **SOLID** tab and then click on the **Mirror** tool, see Figure 9.28. The **MIRROR** dialog box appears, see Figure 9.29. The options in this dialog box are discussed next.

9.28

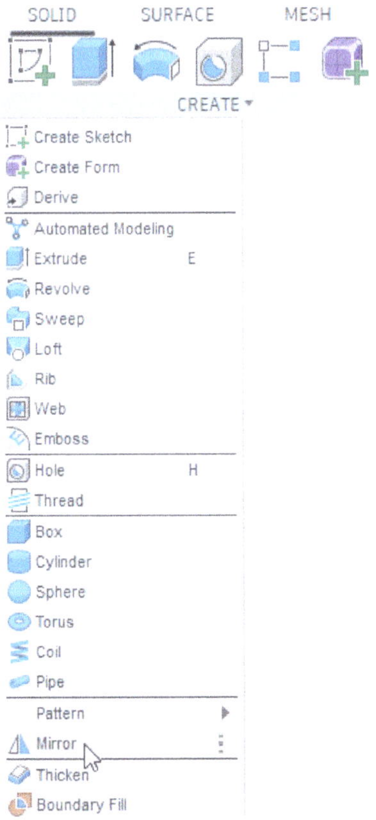

SOLID
SURFACE
MESH
CREATE
Create Sketch
Create Form
Derive
Automated Modeling
Extrude E
Revolve
Sweep
Loft
Rib
Web
Emboss
Hole H
Thread
Box
Cylinder
Sphere
Torus
Coil
Pipe
Pattern
Mirror
Thicken
Boundary Fill

9.29

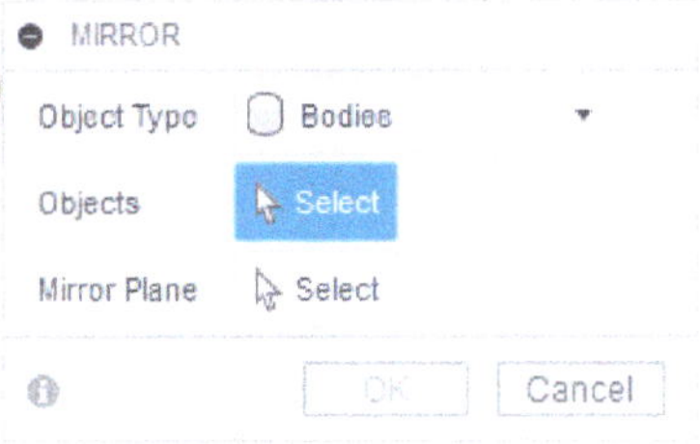

MIRROR
Object Type
Bodies
Objects
Select
Mirror Plane
Select
OK
Cancel

Object Type

The options of the **Object Type** drop-down list allow you to select faces, features, bodies, or components to be mirrored. Select the required option in this drop-down list.

Objects

The **Objects** selection option allows you to select objects to be mirrored about a mirroring plane, see Figure 9.30. Note that the type of object selection depends upon the option selected in the **Object Type** drop-down list of the dialog box.

Mirror Plane

The **Mirror Plane** selection option is used to select a mirroring plane. You can select a plane or a planar face as the mirroring plane. To do this, click on the **Mirror Plane** selection option in the dialog box and then select a mirroring plane in the graphics area, see Figure 9.30. After selecting the objects to be mirrored and a mirroring plane, the preview of the mirror feature appears in the graphics area, see Figure 9.31. In this figure, three features are selected as the objects to be mirrored.

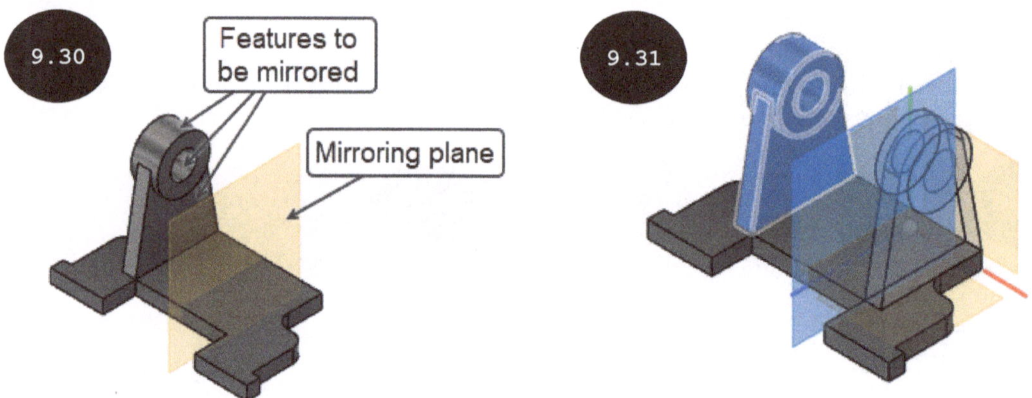

Compute Type

The options in the **Compute Type** drop-down list of the dialog box are used to define the computational method for mirroring the selected objects. Note that the **Compute Type** drop-down list is available in the dialog box when the **Features** option is selected in the **Type** drop-down list of the dialog box. The options in this drop-down list are discussed next.

Optimized

The **Optimized** option is used to optimize the process of mirroring the selected objects. It is the fastest computational method for mirroring objects.

Identical

The **Identical** option is used to mirror objects such that the resultant mirrored feature does not maintain the same geometrical relations as that of the parent object. For example, Figure 9.32 shows the front view of a model, in which the cut feature is created by defining the end condition as 4 mm offset from the bottom face of the model. Figure 9.33 shows the resultant mirrored feature created by selecting the **Identical** option in the **Compute Type** drop-down list of the dialog box.

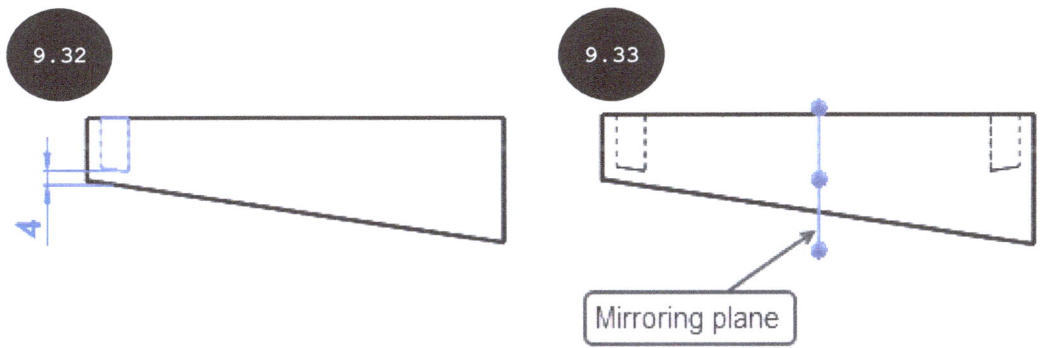

Adjust

The **Adjust** option is used to mirror objects such that the resultant mirrored feature maintains the same geometrical relations as that of the parent feature, see Figure 9.34. In this figure, the mirrored feature maintains the geometrical relation of the parent feature, which is 4 mm offset from the bottom face of the model.

After selecting the required option, click on the **OK** button in the dialog box. The selected objects get mirrored about the mirroring plane and the mirror feature is created, see Figure 9.35.

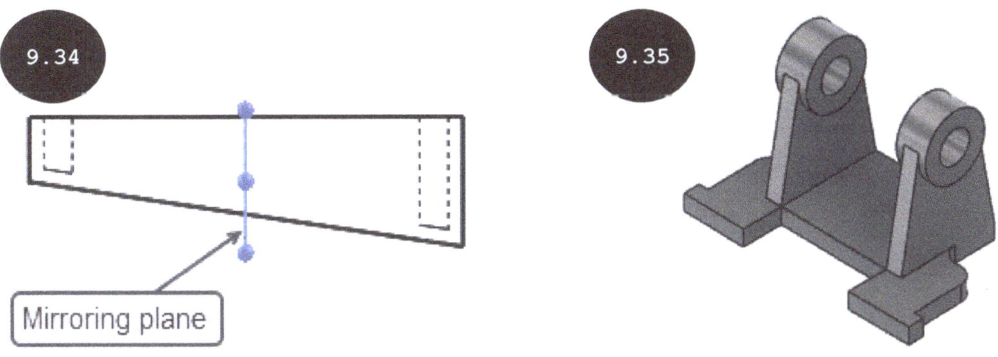

Note: When you mirror a body using the **Mirror** tool, the **Operation** drop-down list appears in the **MIRROR** dialog box. In this drop-down list, you can select the type of operation for creating the mirrored body. On selecting the **Join** option, the mirrored body gets joined or merged with the parent body and together acts as a single body in the graphics area. On selecting the **New Body** option, the mirrored body gets created as a new body in the graphics area.

Tutorial 1

Create a model, as shown in Figure 9.36. All dimensions are in mm.

9.36

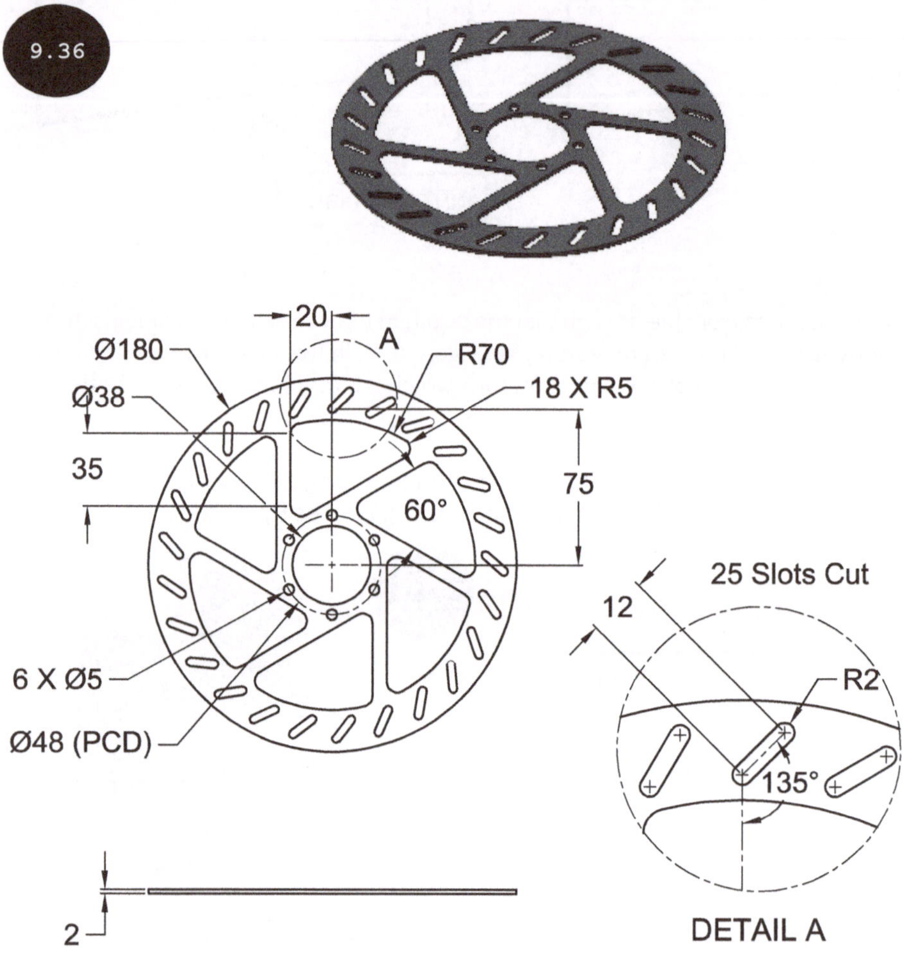

Ø180
Ø38
35
20
A
R70
18 X R5
75
60°
6 X Ø5
Ø48 (PCD)
2
12
25 Slots Cut
R2
135°
DETAIL A

Section 1: Starting a New Part Design File

1. Click **File** > **New** in the **Application Bar** (see Figure 9.37) to display the **What do you want to design?** dialog box, see Figure 9.38.

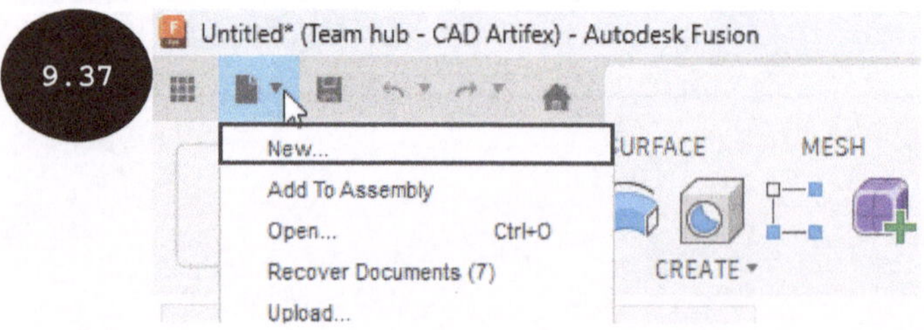

9.37

9.38

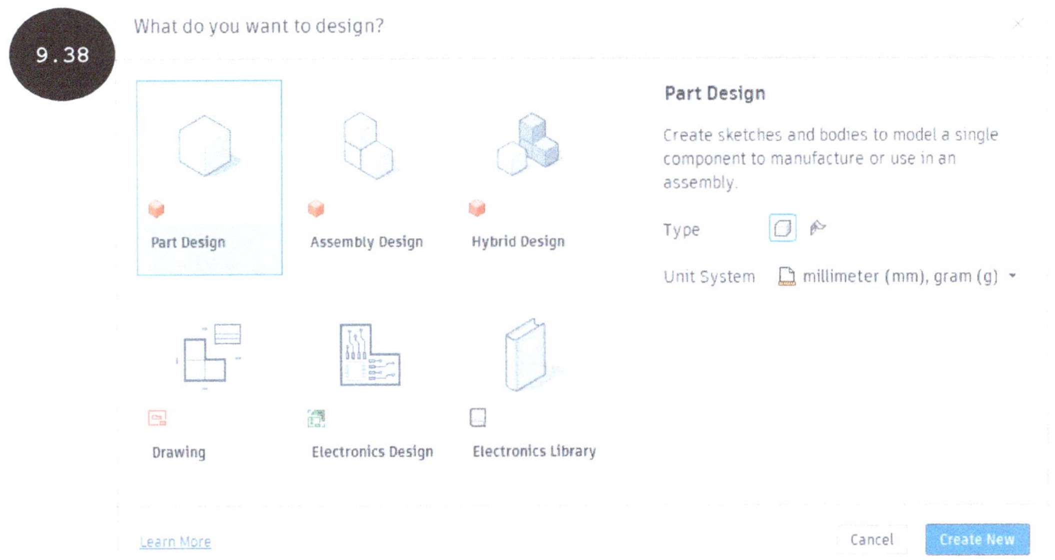

2. In this dialog box, select the **Part Design** button. Also, select the **millimeter (mm), gram (g)** unit system from the **Unit System** drop-down list.

3. After specifying the required options, click the **Create New** button. A new Part Design file is created with the default name.

Section 2: Organizing the Data Panel

1. Invoke the **Data Panel** and then ensure that the '**Autodesk Fusion 360**' project is created.

2. Double-click on the **Autodesk Fusion 360** project in the **Data Panel** and create the "**Chapter 09**" folder by using the **New Folder** tool of the **Data Panel**.

3. Double-click on the **Chapter 09** folder and then create the "**Tutorial**" sub-folder. Next, close the **Data Panel**.

Section 3: Creating the Base Feature - Extrude Feature

1. Click on the **Create Sketch** tool in the **Toolbar** and then select the Top plane as the sketching plane.

2. Create the sketch of the base feature of the model, see Figure 9.39.

3. Click on the **SOLID** tab in the **Toolbar** to display the solid modeling tools.

4. Click on the **Extrude** tool in the **CREATE** panel of the **SOLID** tab or press the **E** key. The **EXTRUDE** dialog box appears.

9.39

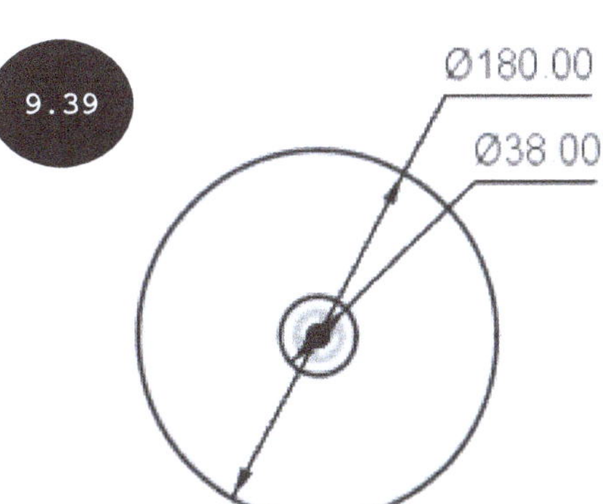

5. Change the orientation of the sketch to isometric, if not changed by default.

6. Select the outer closed profile of the sketch, see Figure 9.40.

7. Ensure that the **One Side** option is selected in the **Direction** drop-down list.

8. Ensure that the **Distance** option is selected in the **Extent Type** drop-down list.

9. Enter **2** in the **Distance** field of the dialog box. The preview of the extrude feature appears.

10. Ensure that the **New Body** option is selected in the **Operation** drop-down list.

11. Click on the **OK** button in the dialog box. The extrude feature is created, see Figure 9.41.

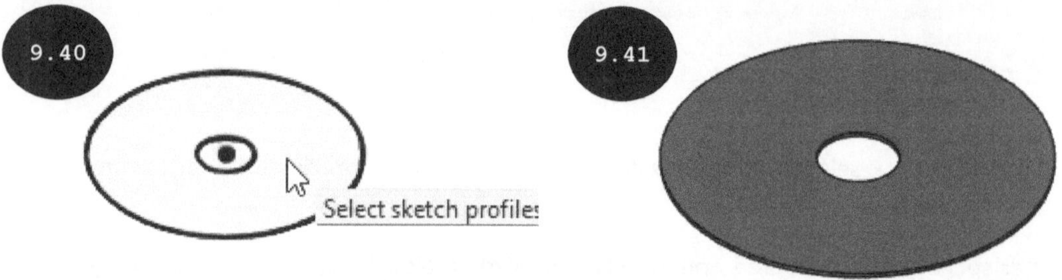

Section 4: Creating the Second Feature - Extrude Cut Feature

1. Click on the **Create Sketch** tool in the **Toolbar** and then select the top planar face of the base feature as the sketching plane.

2. Create the sketch of the second feature, see Figure 9.42.

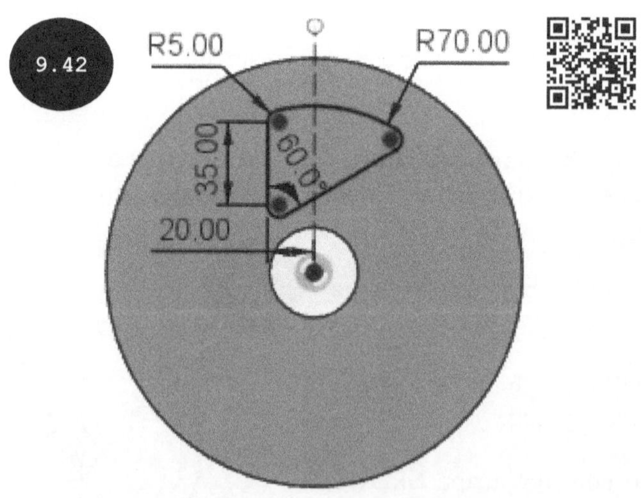

3. Click on the **SOLID** tab in the **Toolbar** to display the solid modeling tools.

4. Click on the **Extrude** tool in the **CREATE** panel of the **SOLID** tab or press the **E** key. The **EXTRUDE** dialog box appears. Next, change the orientation of the sketch to isometric, if not changed by default.

5. Select the closed profile of the sketch, see Figure 9.43.

6. Select the **All** option in the **Extent Type** drop-down list of the dialog box.

7. Click on the **Flip** button in the dialog box to flip the direction of extrusion downwards.

8. Ensure that the **Cut** option is selected in the **Operation** drop-down list to create the extrude feature by removing material.

9. Click on the **OK** button. The extrude cut feature is created, see Figure 9.44.

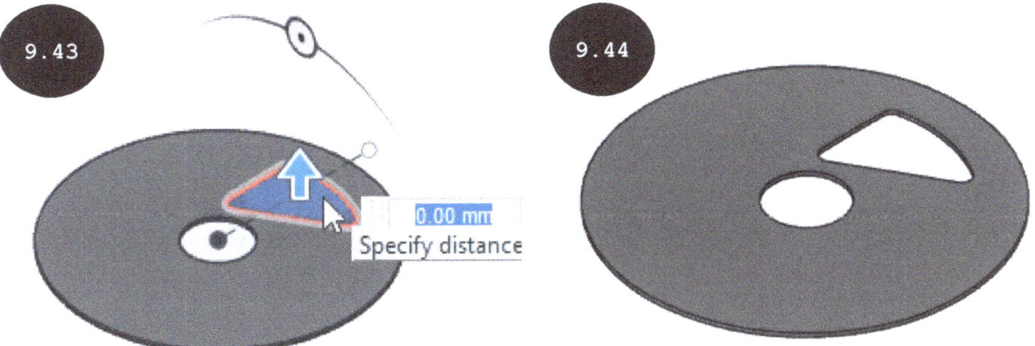

Section 5: Creating the Third Feature - Circular Pattern

1. Invoke the **CREATE** drop-down menu in the **SOLID** tab and then click on **Pattern > Circular Pattern**. The **CIRCULAR PATTERN** dialog box appears, see Figure 9.45.

2. Select the **Features** option in the **Object Type** drop-down list of the dialog box to select the cut feature as the object to be patterned.

3. Click on the **Extrude2** (previously created extrude cut feature) in the **Timeline** as the feature to be patterned, see Figure 9.46.

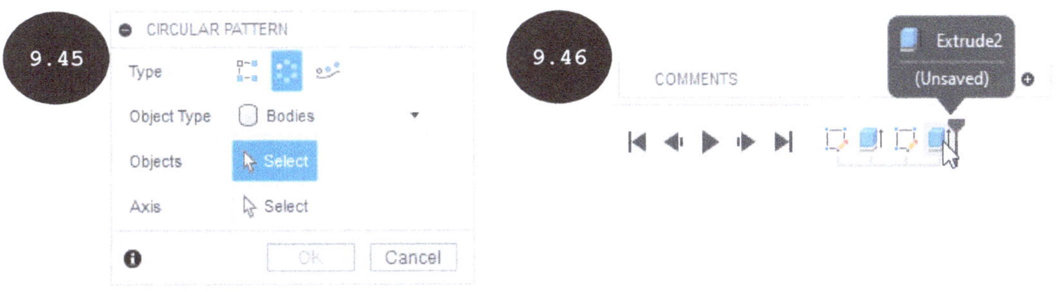

4. Click on the **Axis** selection option in the dialog box and then select the outer circular edge of the base feature to define the pattern axis, see Figure 9.47. A preview of the circular pattern appears with default parameters.

5. Ensure that the **Full** option is selected in the **Distribution** drop-down list of the dialog box.

6. Enter **6** in the **Quantity** field of the dialog box.

7. Click on the **OK** button in the dialog box. The circular pattern is created, see Figure 9.48.

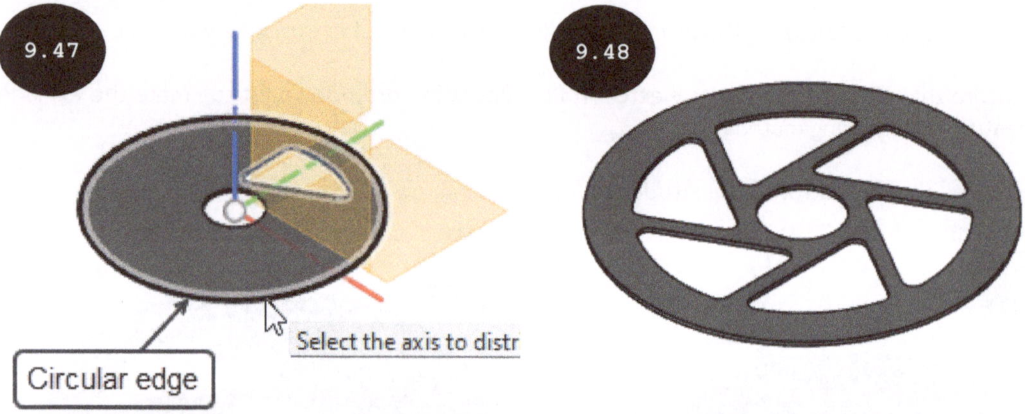

Section 6: Creating the Fourth Feature - Extrude Cut Feature

1. Click on the **Create Sketch** tool in the **Toolbar** and then select the top planar face of the base feature as the sketching plane.

2. Create a sketch of the fourth feature of the model, see Figure 9.49.

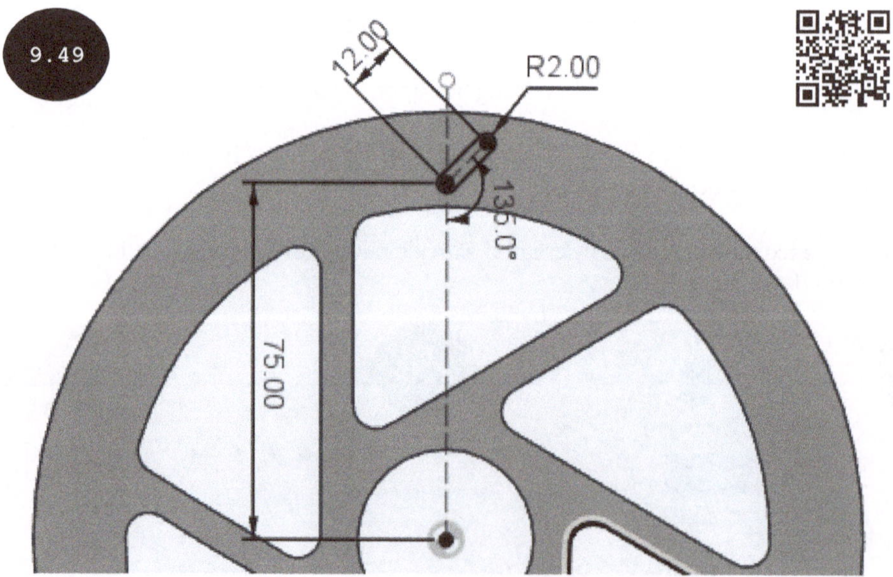

3. Click on the **SOLID** tab in the **Toolbar** to display the solid modeling tools.

4. Click on the **Extrude** tool in the **CREATE** panel of the **SOLID** tab or press the **E** key. The **EXTRUDE** dialog box appears. Next, change the orientation of the sketch to isometric, if not changed by default.

5. Select the closed profile of the sketch, see Figure 9.50.

6. Select the **All** option in the **Extent Type** drop-down list of the dialog box.

7. Click on the **Flip** button in the dialog box to flip the direction of extrusion downwards.

8. Ensure that the **Cut** option is selected in the **Operation** drop-down list of the dialog box to create the extrude feature by removing material.

9. Click on the **OK** button in the dialog box. The extrude cut feature is created, see Figure 9.51.

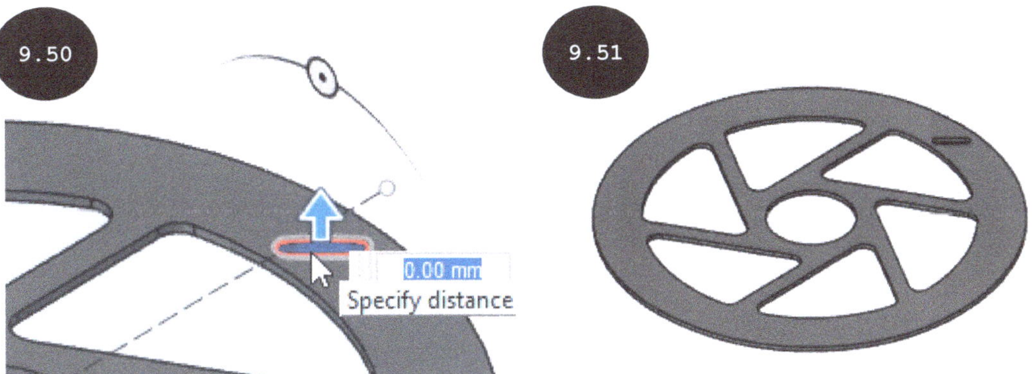

Section 7: Creating the Fifth Feature - Circular Pattern

1. Invoke the **CREATE** drop-down menu in the **SOLID** tab and then click on **Pattern > Circular Pattern**. The **CIRCULAR PATTERN** dialog box appears.

2. Select the **Features** option in the **Object Type** drop-down list of the dialog box.

3. Click on the **Extrude3** (previously created extrude cut feature) in the **Timeline** as the feature to be patterned, see Figure 9.52.

4. Click on the **Axis** selection option in the dialog box and then select the outer circular edge of the base feature to define the pattern axis, see Figure 9.53. A preview of the circular pattern appears with default parameters.

5. Ensure that the **Full** option is selected in the **Distribution** drop-down list.

6. Enter **25** in the **Quantity** field of the dialog box.

7. Click on the **OK** button. The circular pattern is created, see Figure 9.54.

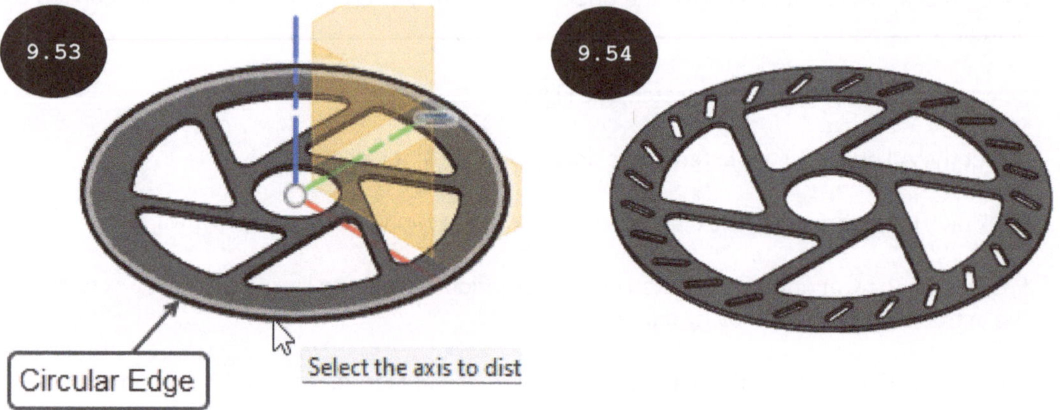

Section 8: Creating the Sixth Feature - Extrude Cut Feature

1. Click on the **Create Sketch** tool in the **Toolbar** and then select the top planar face of the base feature as the sketching plane.

2. Create a sketch of the sixth feature (circle of diameter 5 mm), see Figure 9.55.

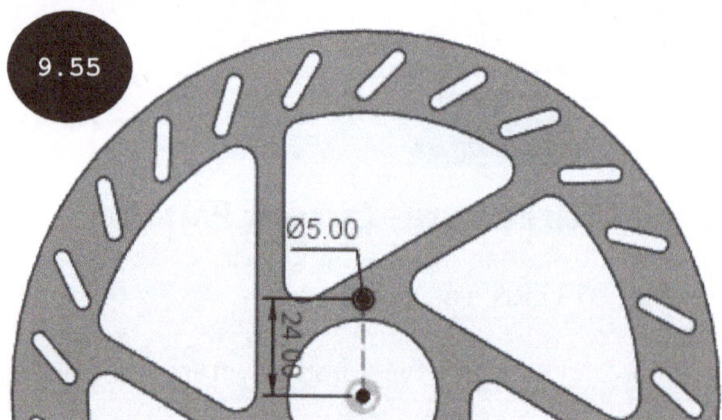

3. Click on the **SOLID** tab in the **Toolbar** to display the solid modeling tools.

4. Click on the **Extrude** tool in the **CREATE** panel of the **SOLID** tab or press the **E** key. The **EXTRUDE** dialog box appears. Next, change the orientation of the sketch to isometric, if not changed by default.

5. Select the closed profile of the previously created sketch (circle of diameter 5 mm).

6. Select the **All** option in the **Extent Type** drop-down list of the dialog box.

7. Click on the **Flip** button in the dialog box to flip the direction of extrusion downward.

8. Ensure that the **Cut** option is selected in the **Operation** drop-down list of the dialog box to create the extrude feature by removing material.

9. Click on the **OK** button in the dialog box. The extrude cut feature is created, see Figure 9.56.

Section 9: Creating the Seventh Feature - Circular Pattern

1. Invoke the **CREATE** drop-down menu in the **SOLID** tab and then click on **Pattern > Circular Pattern**. The **CIRCULAR PATTERN** dialog box appears.

2. Select the **Faces** option in the **Object Type** drop-down list of the dialog box.

3. Select the inner circular face of the previously created cut feature as the object to be patterned in the graphics area, see Figure 9.57.

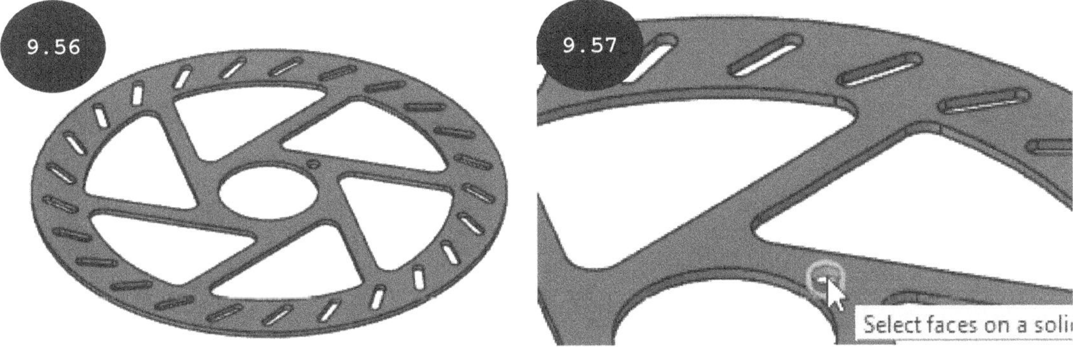

4. Click on the **Axis** selection option in the dialog box and then select the outer circular edge of the base feature to define the pattern axis. The preview of the circular pattern appears with default parameters.

5. Ensure that the **Full** option is selected in the **Distribution** drop-down list of the dialog box.

6. Enter **6** in the **Quantity** field and then click on the **OK** button. The circular pattern is created, see Figure 9.58.

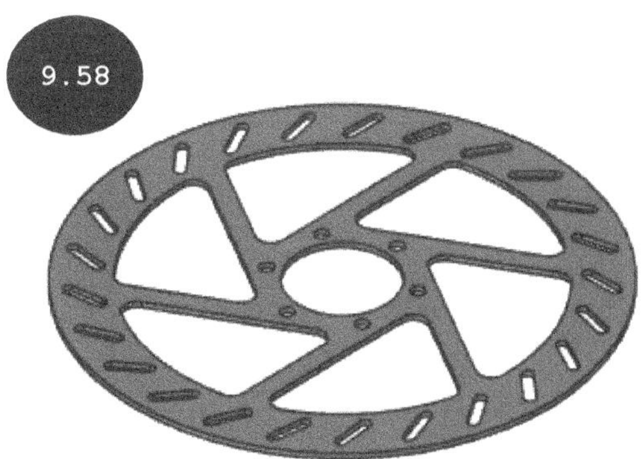

Section 10: Saving the Model

1. Click on the **Save** tool in the **Application Bar**. The **Save** dialog box appears. Next, enter **Tutorial 1** in the **Name** field of the dialog box.

2. Ensure that the location ***Autodesk Fusion 360 > Chapter 09 > Tutorial*** is specified in the **Location** field of the dialog box to save the file of this tutorial. To specify the location, you need to expand the **Save** dialog box by clicking on the down arrow next to the **Location** field of the dialog box.

3. Click on the **Save** button in the dialog box. The model is saved with the name Tutorial 1 in the specified location (***Autodesk Fusion 360 > Chapter 09 > Tutorial***).

Tutorial 2

Create a model, as shown in Figure 9.59. The different views and dimensions are given in the same figure. All dimensions are in mm.

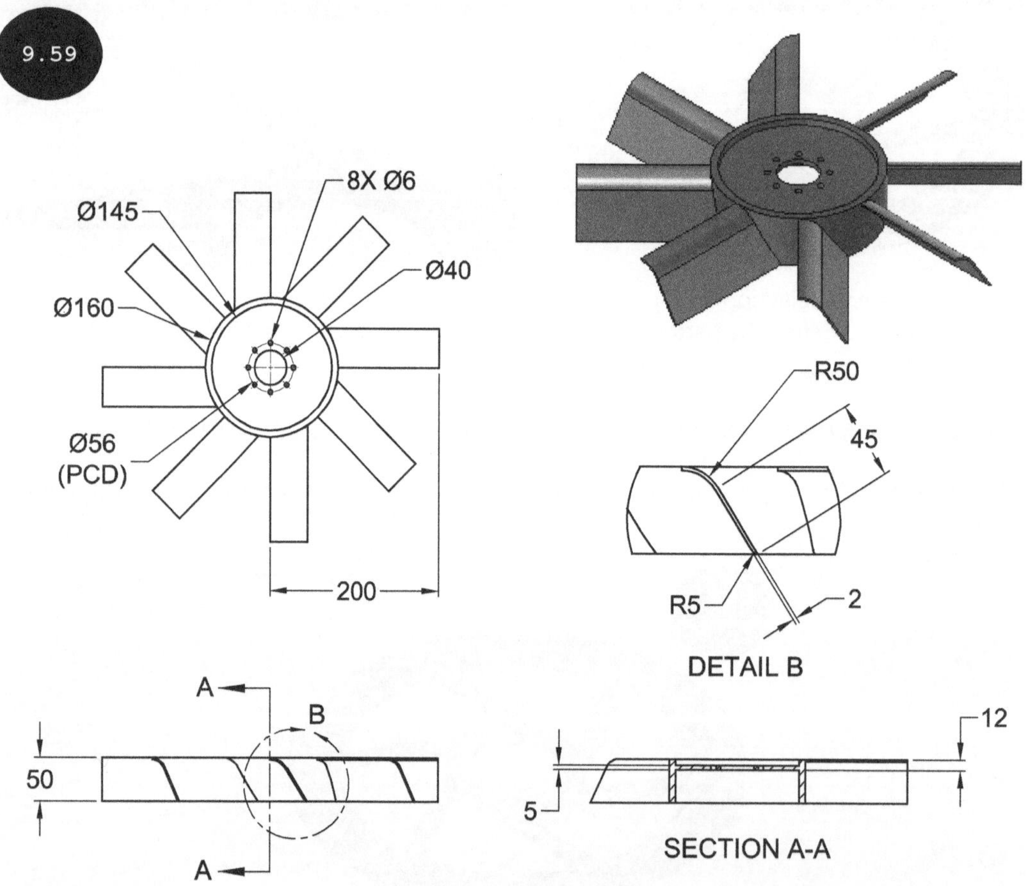

Section 1: Starting a New Part Design File

1. Click **File** > **New** in the **Application Bar** (see Figure 9.60) to display the **What do you want to design?** dialog box, see Figure 9.61.

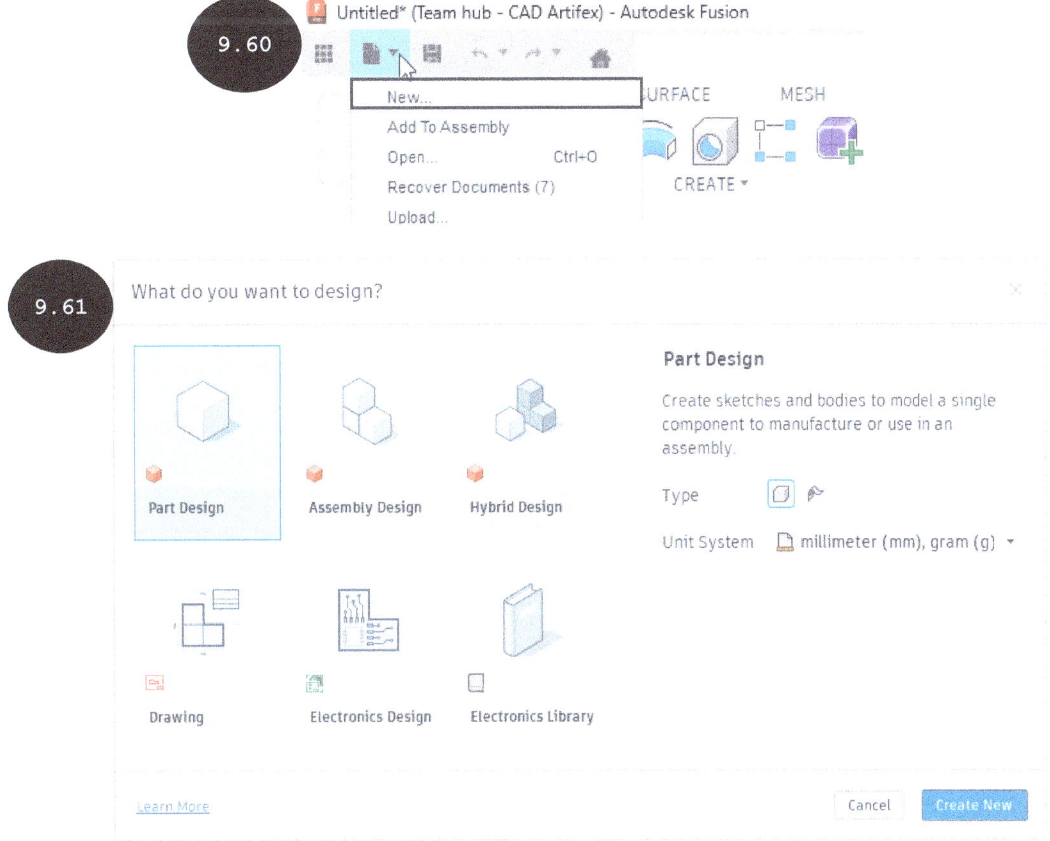

2. In this dialog box, select the **Part Design** button. Also, select the **millimeter (mm), gram (g)** unit system from the **Unit System** drop-down list.

3. After specifying the required options, click the **Create New** button. A new Part Design file is created with the default name "**Untitled**".

Section 2: Creating the Base Feature - Extrude Feature

1. Click on the **Create Sketch** tool in the **Toolbar** and then select the Top plane as the sketching plane.

2. Create the sketch of the base feature of the model, see Figure 9.62.

3. Click on the **SOLID** tab in the **Toolbar** to display the solid modeling tools.

4. Click on the **Extrude** tool in the **CREATE** panel of the **SOLID** tab or press the **E** key. The **EXTRUDE** dialog box appears. Next, change the orientation of the sketch to isometric, if not changed by default.

5. Select the outer closed profile of the sketch, see Figure 9.63.

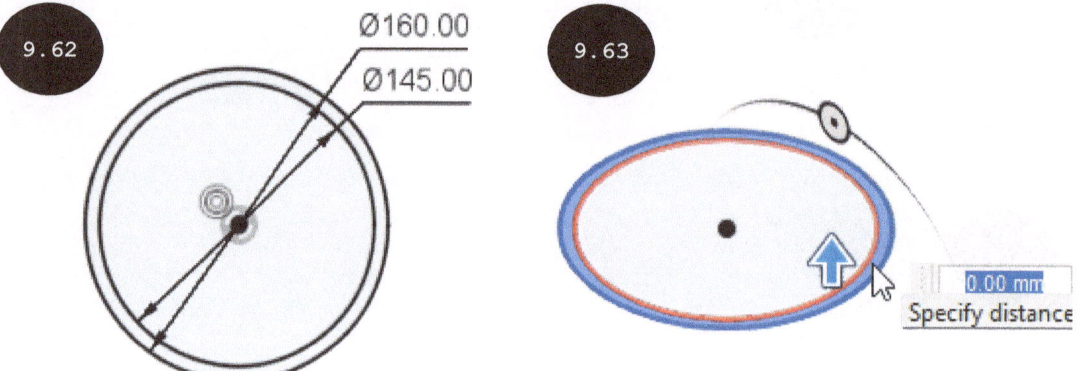

6. Select the **Symmetric** option in the **Direction** drop-down list of the dialog box.

7. Click on the **Whole Length** button in the **Measurement** area of the dialog box.

8. Enter **50** in the **Distance** field of the dialog box. A preview of the extrude feature appears, see Figure 9.64.

9. Ensure that the **New Body** option is selected in the **Operation** drop-down list.

10. Click on the **OK** button in the dialog box. The extrude feature is created, see Figure 9.65.

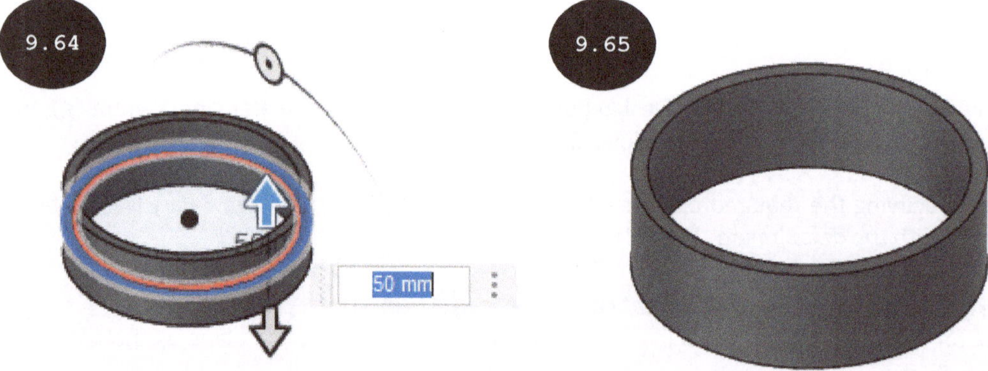

Section 3: Creating the Second Feature - Extrude Feature

1. Click on the **Create Sketch** tool in the **Toolbar** and then select the top planar face of the base feature as the sketching plane.

2. Create a circle of diameter 40 mm as the sketch of the second feature, see Figure 9.66.

3. Click on the **SOLID** tab in the **Toolbar** to display the solid modeling tools.

4. Click on the **Extrude** tool in the **CREATE** panel of the **SOLID** tab or press the **E** key. The **EXTRUDE** dialog box appears. Next, change the orientation of the sketch to isometric, if not changed by default.

5. Select the closed profile created between the circle and the inner circular edge of the base feature, see Figure 9.67.

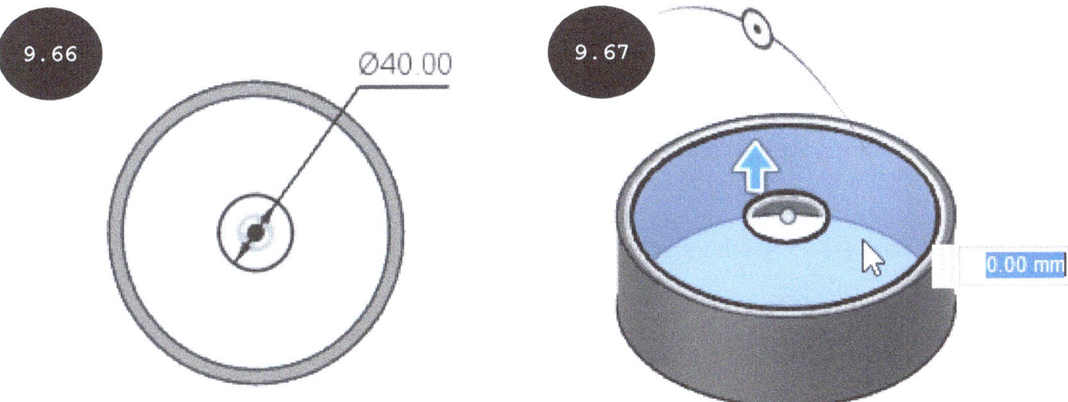

6. Select the **Offset** option in the **Start** drop-down list of the dialog box to define the start condition of extrusion.

7. Enter **-12** in the **Offset** field of the dialog box to start the extrusion at an offset distance of 12 mm downward from the sketching plane.

8. Enter **5** in the **Distance** field of the dialog box. A preview of the extrude feature appears, see Figure 9.68. Ensure that the direction of the extrusion is upward.

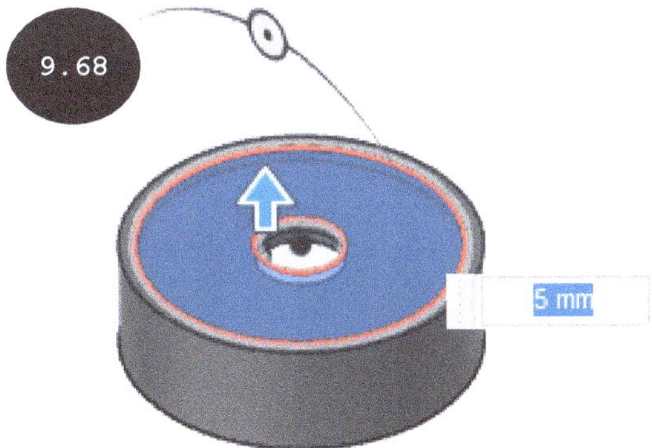

9. Ensure that the **Join** option is selected in the **Operation** drop-down list of the dialog box.

10. Click on the **OK** button in the dialog box. The extruded feature is created, see Figure 9.69.

Section 4: Creating the Third Feature - Extrude Cut Feature

1. Click on the **Create Sketch** tool in the **Toolbar** and then select the top planar face of the second feature (previously created extrude feature) as the sketching plane.

2. Create a circle of diameter 6 mm as the sketch of the third feature, see Figure 9.70.

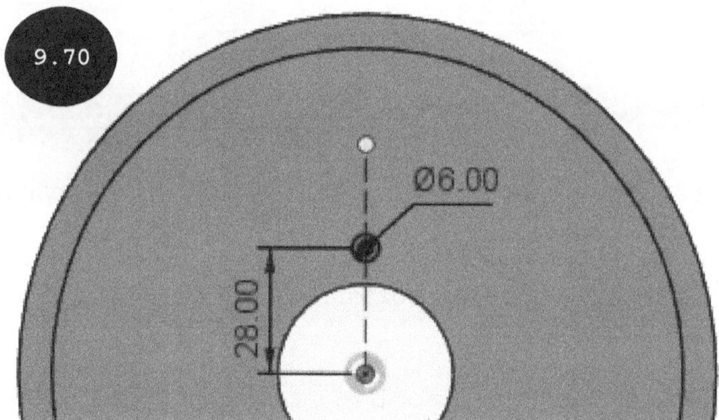

3. Click on the **SOLID** tab in the **Toolbar** and then click on the **Extrude** tool or press the **E** key. The **EXTRUDE** dialog box appears. Next, change the orientation of the sketch to isometric.

4. Select the closed profile of the previously created circle of diameter 6 mm.

5. Select **All** in the **Extent Type** drop-down list.

6. Click on the **Flip** button in the dialog box to flip the direction of extrusion downward.

7. Ensure that the **Cut** option is selected in the **Operation** drop-down list of the dialog box to create the extrude feature by removing material.

8. Click on the **OK** button in the dialog box. The extrude cut feature is created, see Figure 9.71.

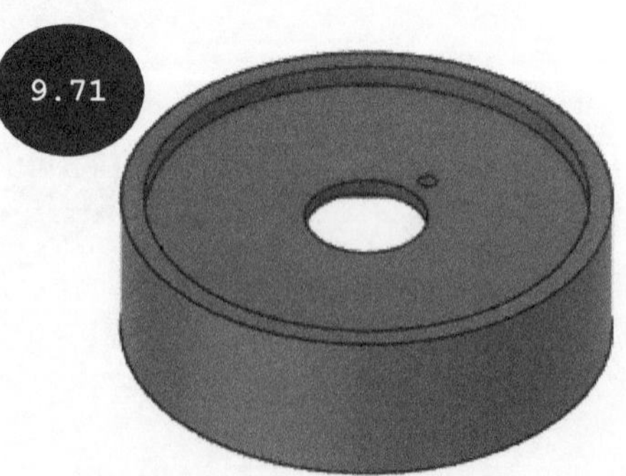

Section 5: Creating the Fourth Feature - Circular Pattern

1. Invoke the **CREATE** drop-down menu in the **SOLID** tab and then click on **Pattern** > **Circular Pattern**. The **CIRCULAR PATTERN** dialog box appears.

2. Ensure that the **Faces** option is selected in the **Object Type** drop-down list.

3. Select the inner circular face of the previously created cut feature as the object to be patterned in the graphics area, see Figure 9.72.

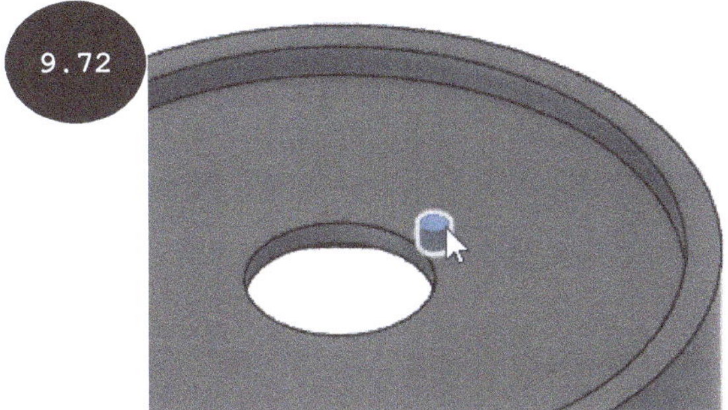

4. Click on the **Axis** selection option in the dialog box and then select the outer circular face of the base feature to define the pattern axis, see Figure 9.73. A preview of the circular pattern appears with default parameters.

5. Ensure that the **Full** option is selected in the **Distribution** drop-down list of the dialog box.

6. Enter **8** in the **Quantity** field of the dialog box as the number of pattern instances to be created.

7. Click on the **OK** button in the dialog box. The circular pattern is created, see Figure 9.74.

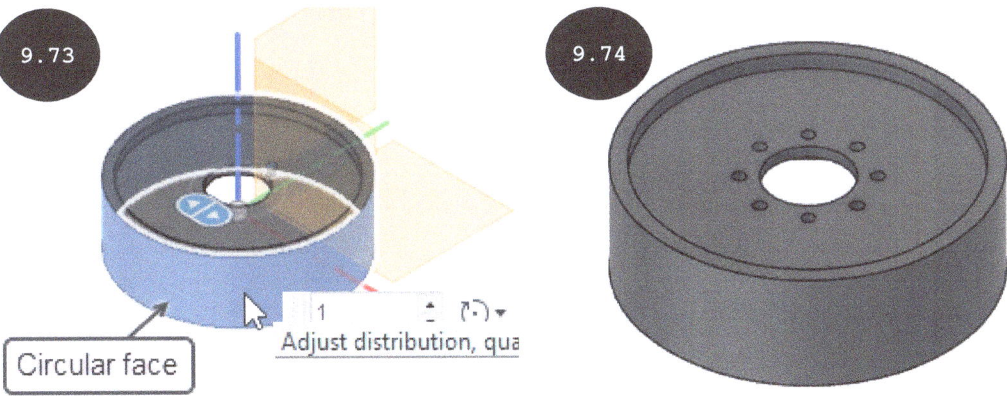

Section 6: Creating the Fifth Feature - Extrude Feature

The fifth feature of the model is an extrude feature and its sketch is to be created on a construction plane, which is at an offset distance of 200 mm from the Right plane.

1. Create a construction plane at an offset distance of 200 mm from the Right plane (YZ plane) by using the **Offset Plane** tool, see Figure 9.75.

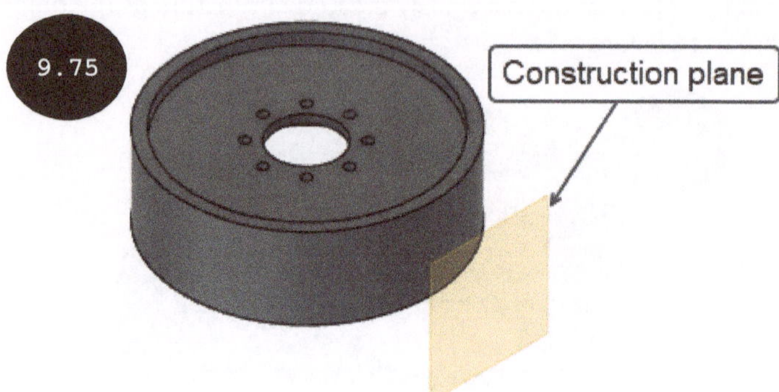

2. After creating the construction plane, click on the **Create Sketch** tool in the **Toolbar** and then select the newly created construction plane as the sketching plane.

3. Create the sketch of the extrude feature, see Figure 9.76.

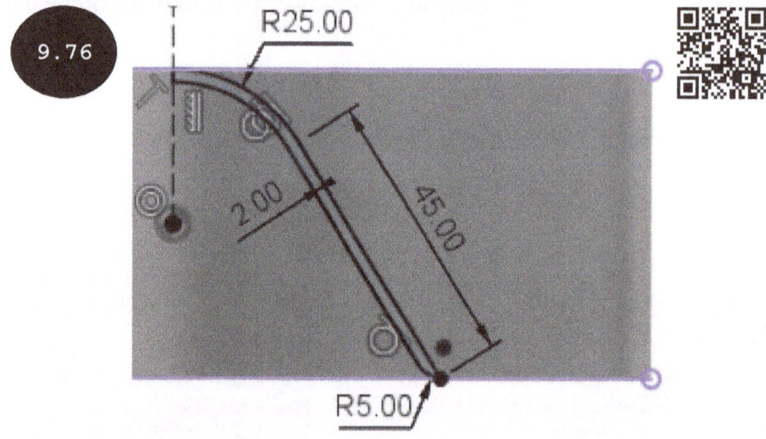

Note: In Figure 9.76, tangent constraints are applied between the connecting arcs and lines of the sketch. Also, the center point of the arc having a radius of 25 mm is coincident with the origin.

4. Click on the **SOLID** tab in the **Toolbar** to display the solid modeling tools.

5. Click on the **Extrude** tool in the **CREATE** panel of the **SOLID** tab or press E. The **EXTRUDE** dialog box appears. Next, change the orientation of the sketch to isometric, if not changed by default.

6. Select the sketch profile in the graphics area, see Figure 9.77.

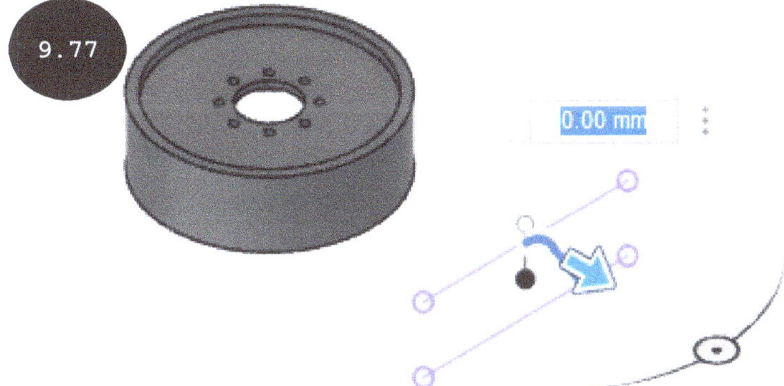

7. Select the **To Object** option in the **Extent Type** drop-down list of the dialog box.

8. Select the outer circular face of the base feature as the object to terminate the extrude feature. A preview of the extrude feature appears, see Figure 9.78.

9. Ensure that the **To Body** button is activated in the first **Extend** area of the dialog box.

10. Ensure that the **Join** option is selected in the **Operation** drop-down list of the dialog box.

11. Click on the **OK** button in the dialog box. The extrude feature is created, see Figure 9.79.

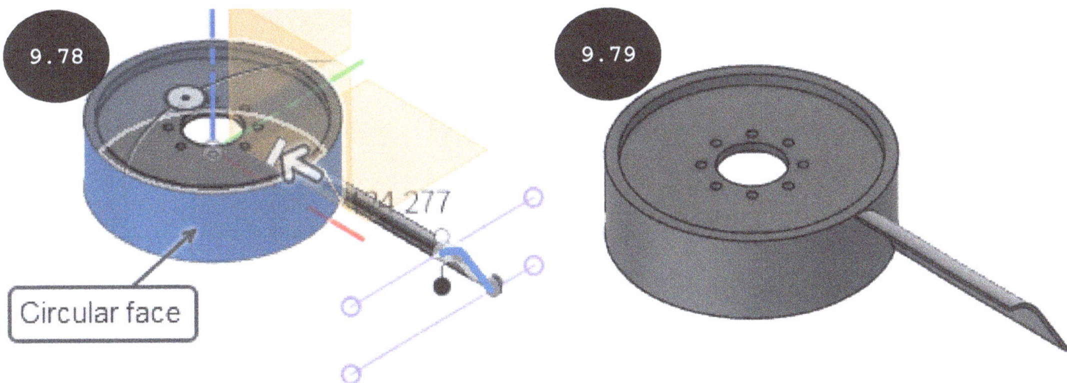

Section 7: Creating the Sixth Feature - Circular Pattern

1. Invoke the **CREATE** drop-down menu in the **SOLID** tab and then click on **Pattern** > **Circular Pattern**. The **CIRCULAR PATTERN** dialog box appears.

2. Select the **Features** option in the **Object Type** drop-down list of the dialog box and then select the previously created extrude feature in the graphics area as the feature to be patterned. Note that you can select the feature to be patterned in the graphics area or in the **Timeline**.

3. Click on the **Axis** selection option in the dialog box and then select the outer circular face of the base feature to define the pattern axis. A preview of the circular pattern appears.

4. Ensure that the **Full** option is selected in the **Distribution** drop-down list.

5. Enter **8** in the **Quantity** field of the dialog box.

6. Click on the **OK** button. The circular pattern is created, see Figure 9.80.

9.80

Section 8: Saving the Model

1. Click on the **Save** tool in the **Application Bar**. The **Save** dialog box appears.

2. Enter **Tutorial 2** in the **Name** field of the dialog box. Ensure that the location ***Autodesk Fusion 360 > Chapter 09 > Tutorial*** is specified in the **Location** field to save the file of this tutorial.

3. Click on the **Save** button in the dialog box. The model is saved with the name Tutorial 2 in the specified location (***Autodesk Fusion 360 > Chapter 09 > Tutorial***).

Hands-on Test Drive 1

Create a model, as shown in Figure 9.81. All dimensions are in mm.

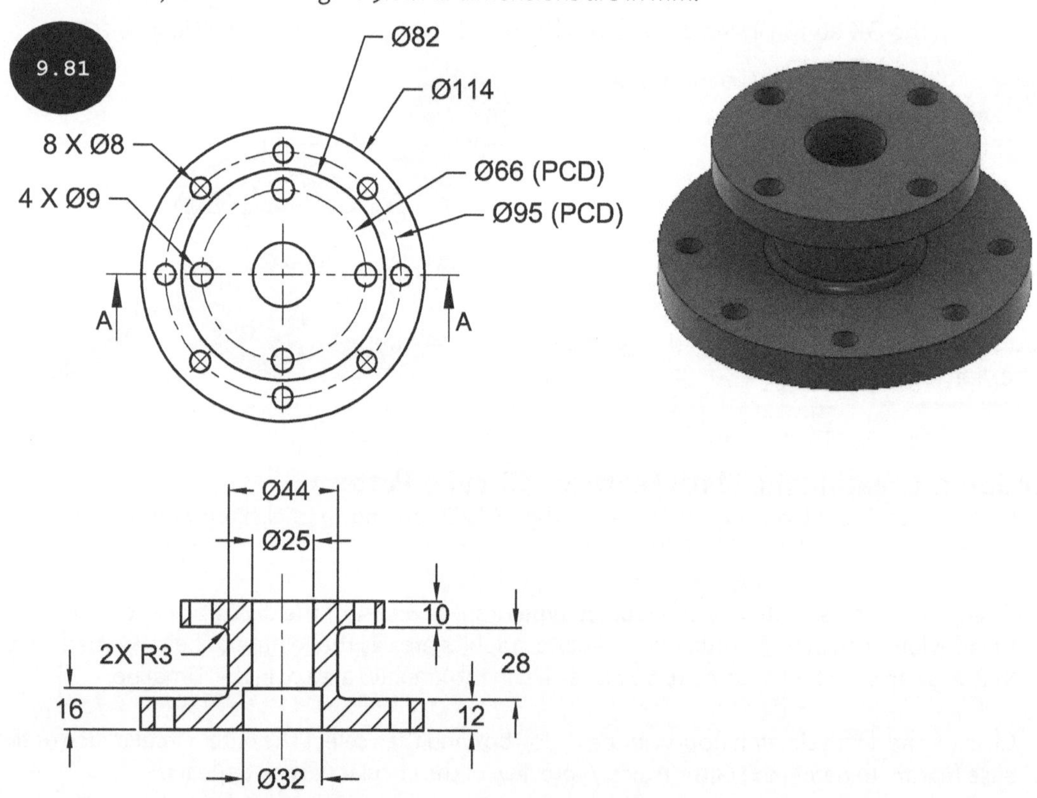

Hands-on Test Drive 2

Create a model, as shown in Figure 9.82. All dimensions are in mm.

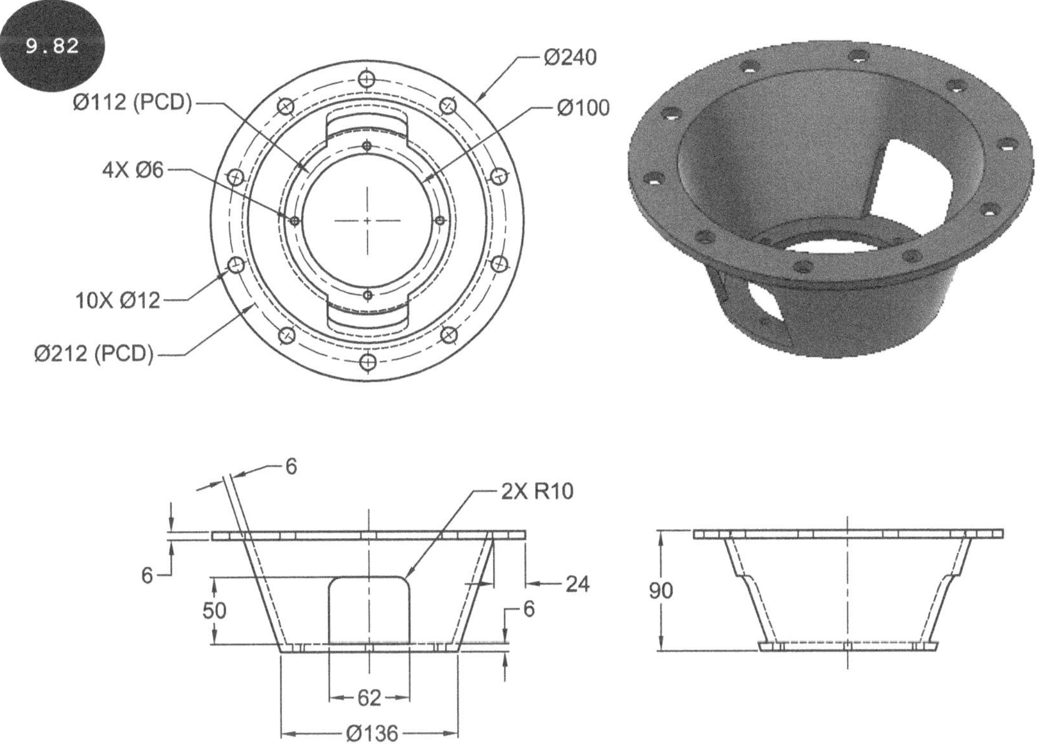

Hands-on Test Drive 3

Create a model, as shown in Figure 9.83. All dimensions are in mm.

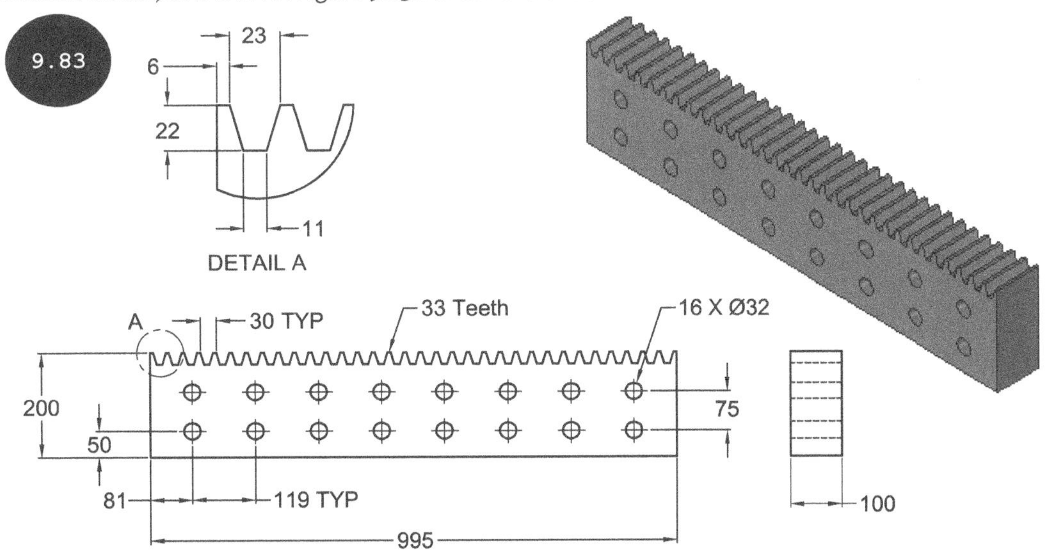

Summary

In this chapter, you explored various patterning and mirroring tools. You learned how to create different types of patterns, including rectangular patterns, circular patterns, and patterns along a path. Additionally, you gained the skills to mirror features, faces, bodies, or components about a mirroring plane. By mastering these tools, you are now better equipped to enhance your design capabilities.

Questions

Complete and verify the following sentences:

- The _________ tool is used for creating multiple instances of features, faces, bodies, or components in one to two linear directions.
- The _________ tool is used for creating multiple instances of features, faces, bodies, or components in a circular manner around an axis.
- The _________ check box in the **RECTANGULAR PATTERN** dialog box is used for displaying a check box at the center of each pattern instance in the graphics area to skip the instances.
- The _________ option is used for creating a pattern such that all the pattern instances maintain the same geometrical relations as that of the parent/source feature.
- You can create a pattern by creating multiple instances of faces, bodies, features, or components along a path by using the _________ tool.
- The _________ option is used for maintaining the orientation/position of the pattern instances relative to the path selected.
- The _________ tool is used for mirroring faces, bodies, features, or components about a mirroring plane.
- You can select features to be patterned from the _________.
- The number of pattern instances specified in the **Quantity** field is counted along with the parent/original instance. (True/False)
- In Autodesk Fusion, you cannot recall or include the skipped instances of the pattern. (True/False)

10

Editing and Modifying 3D Models

In this chapter, the following topics will be discussed:

- Working with the Press Pull Tool
- Creating Fillets
- Creating Chamfers
- Creating Shell Features
- Adding Drafts
- Scaling Objects
- Combining Solid Bodies
- Offsetting Faces of a Model
- Splitting Faces of a Model
- Splitting Bodies

In this chapter, you will learn about various methods for editing and modifying a solid model using tools such as **Press Pull**, **Shell**, **Draft**, **Scale**, **Combine**, and **Split Faces**. You will also explore how to create constant and variable radius fillets to smooth sharp edges with the Fillet tool, including how to specify chord length and rules for fillet creation. Additionally, the chapter discusses several methods for applying chamfers to the edges of a model using the **Chamfer** tool.

Working with the Press Pull Tool

The **Press Pull** tool is a useful tool for quickly and dynamically modifying a solid model. Using the **Press Pull** tool, you can offset a face, fillet an edge, or extrude a sketch profile directly in the graphics area. To do this, click on the **Press Pull** tool in the **MODIFY** panel of the **SOLID** tab, see Figure 10.1. The **PRESS PULL** dialog box appears, see Figure 10.2. Alternatively, press the **Q** key or right-click in the graphics area and click on the **Press Pull** tool in the Marking Menu that appears to invoke the **Press Pull** tool.

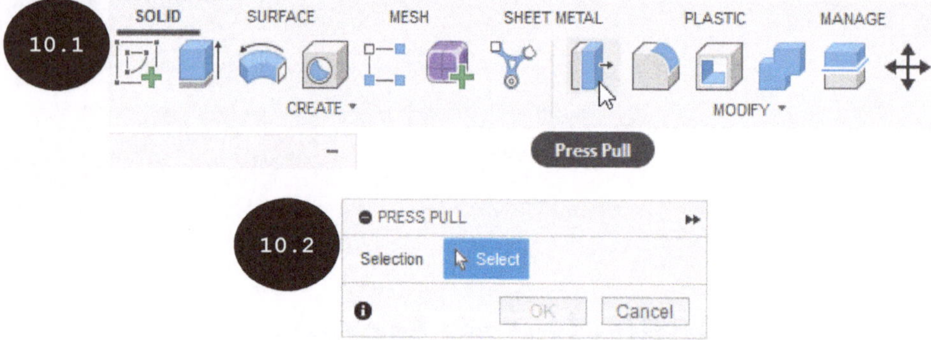

After invoking the **PRESS PULL** dialog box, you can select the geometry of the model to be modified. You can select a face or an edge of the model as the geometry to be modified. Note that the editing operation depends on the type of geometry selected. For example, on selecting a face of a model, the **OFFSET FACE** dialog box appears, which allows you to offset the selected face of the model at an offset distance, see Figure 10.3. However, on selecting an edge of a model, the **FILLET** dialog box appears, which allows you to create a constant or variable radius fillet on the selected edge of the model, see Figure 10.4. The various editing operations that can be performed by using the **Press Pull** tool are discussed next.

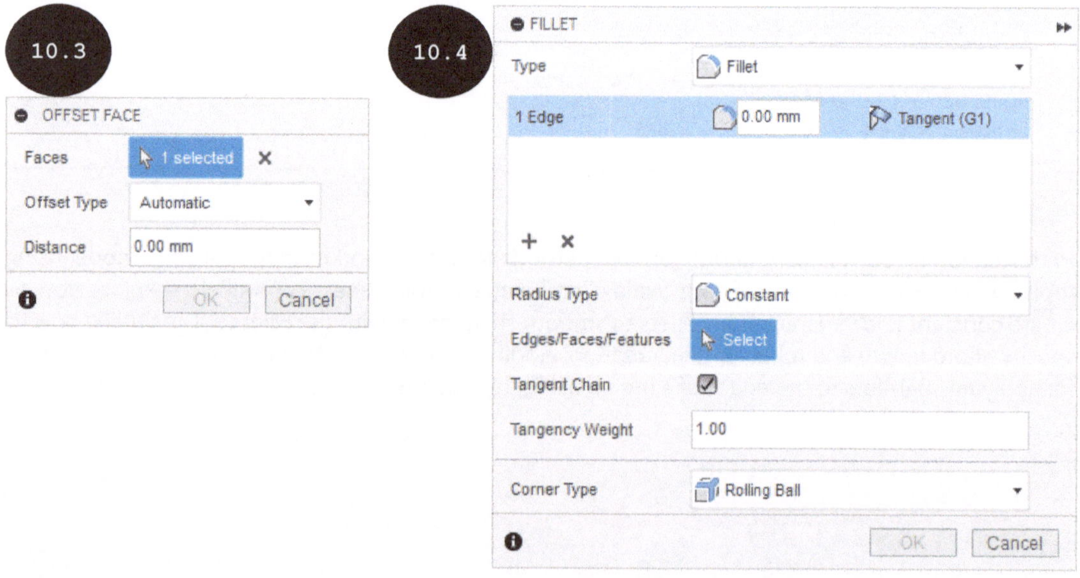

Offsetting a Face by Using the Press Pull Tool

1. Invoke the **PRESS PULL** dialog box, see Figure 10.5. You are prompted to select a geometry to be modified.

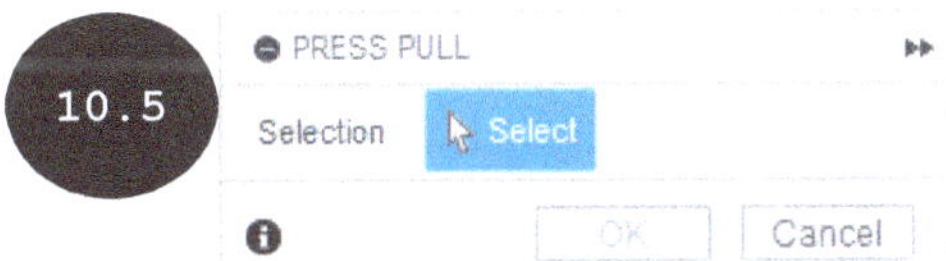

2. Select a face of the model to be modified. The **OFFSET FACE** dialog box appears, refer to Figure 10.3. Also, the selected face gets highlighted, and an arrow appears in the graphics area, see Figure 10.6.

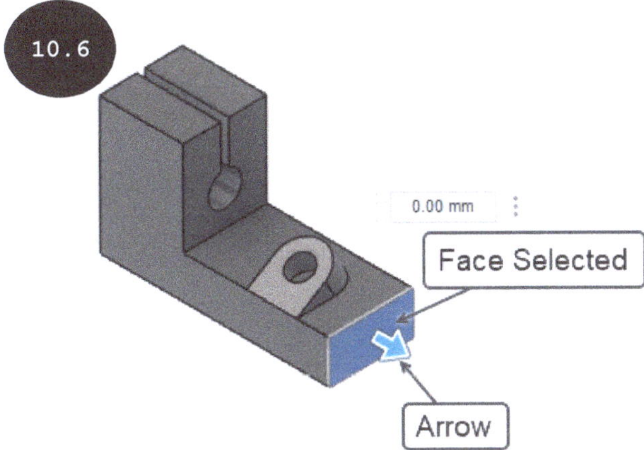

3. Drag the arrow that appears in the graphics area by pressing and holding the left mouse button to offset the selected face, dynamically in the graphics area, see Figure 10.7. Alternatively, enter the offset distance in the **Distance** field of the **OFFSET FACE** dialog box. You can also enter an offset distance in the **Distance** box that appears in the graphics area. To reverse the offset direction, you need to drag the arrow to the other side of the selected face or enter a negative offset distance value in the **Distance** field.

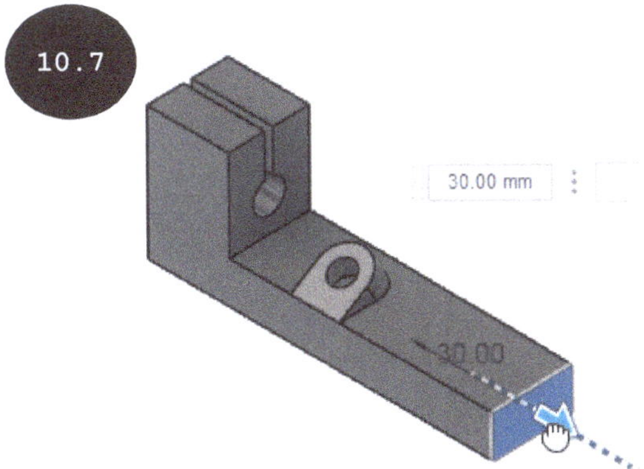

4. After offsetting a face at an offset distance, click on the **OK** button in the dialog box.

Note: The options in the **Offset Type** drop-down list of the dialog box are used for defining the method for offsetting the selected face. The **Modify Existing Feature** option is used for modifying the existing features of a model by offsetting the selected face. The **New Offset** option is used for offsetting a face starting from zero and creates a new offset feature in the **Timeline**. The **Automatic** option uses the best option (**Modify Existing Feature** or **New Offset**) to offset the selected face.

Filleting an Edge by Using the Press Pull Tool

1. Click on the **Press Pull** tool in the **MODIFY** panel of the **SOLID** tab or press the Q key. The **PRESS PULL** dialog box appears and you are prompted to select a geometry to be modified.

2. Select an edge of the model to be modified. The **FILLET** dialog box appears, see Figure 10.8. Also, the selected edge gets highlighted, and an arrow appears in the graphics area, see Figure 10.9.

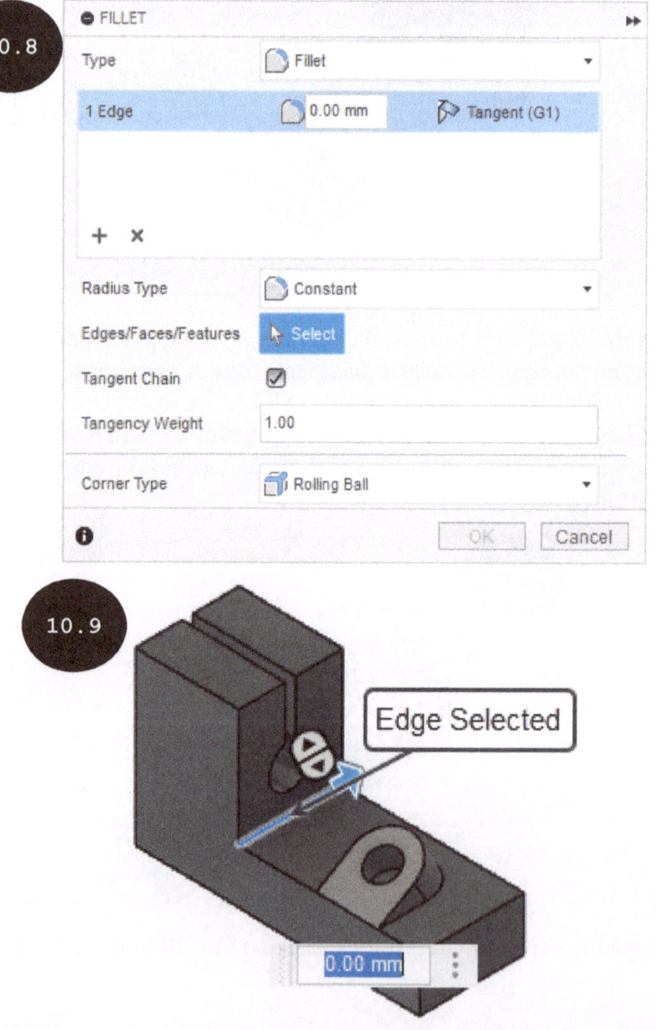

3. Drag the arrow that appears in the graphics area by pressing and holding the left mouse button to create a fillet on the selected edge, dynamically, see Figure 10.10. Alternatively, enter the fillet radius in the **Radius** field of the **FILLET** dialog box. You can also enter the fillet radius in the **Radius** box that appears in the graphics area.

Note: The type of fillet to be created on the selected edge depends on the option selected in the **Radius Type** drop-down list of the **FILLET** dialog box. By default, the **Constant** option is selected. As a result, the constant radius fillet is created on the selected edge. On selecting the **Variable** option, you can create a fillet of variable radius by entering different radius values for both ends of the selected edge in the **Radius** fields respectively, or by dragging the arrows that appear on both ends of the selected edge. On selecting the **Chord Length** option, you can create a constant radius fillet by specifying the chord length of the fillet. You will learn more about the options available in the **FILLET** dialog box later in this chapter.

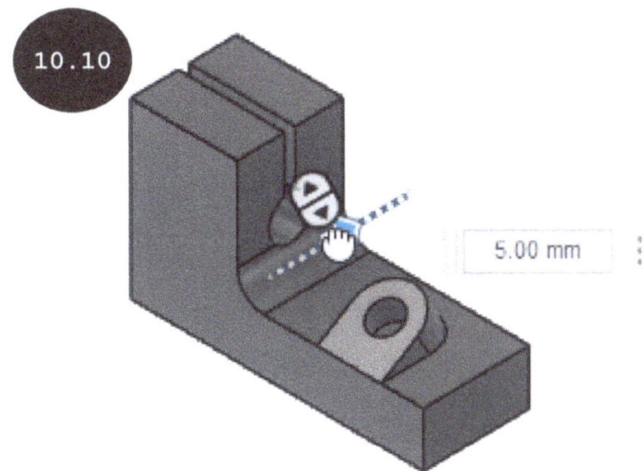

4. After creating a fillet on the selected edge, click on the **OK** button in the dialog box.

Extruding a Sketch Profile by Using the Press Pull Tool

In addition to offsetting a face and creating a fillet on an edge, you can also extrude a sketch profile using the **Press Pull** tool. The method to extrude a sketch profile is discussed below:

1. Click on the **Press Pull** tool in the **MODIFY** panel of the **SOLID** tab or press the Q key. The **PRESS PULL** dialog box appears and you are prompted to select a geometry to be modified.

2. Select a sketch profile in the graphics area to be extruded, see Figure 10.11. The **EXTRUDE** dialog box appears, see Figure 10.12. Also, the selected sketch profile gets highlighted, and an arrow, as well as a manipulator handle, appears in the graphics area, see Figure 10.13.

10.11

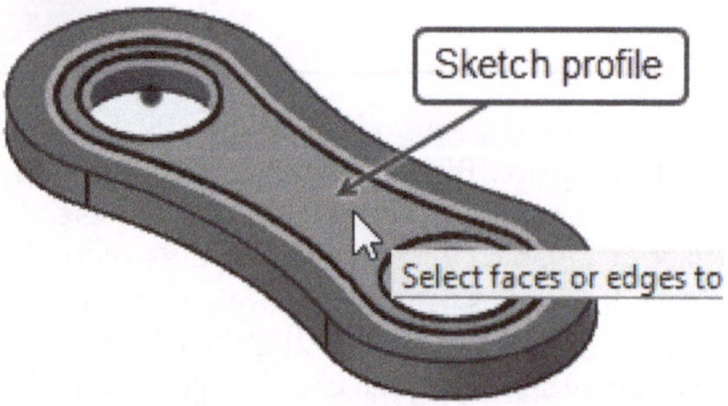

Sketch profile

Select faces or edges to

10.12

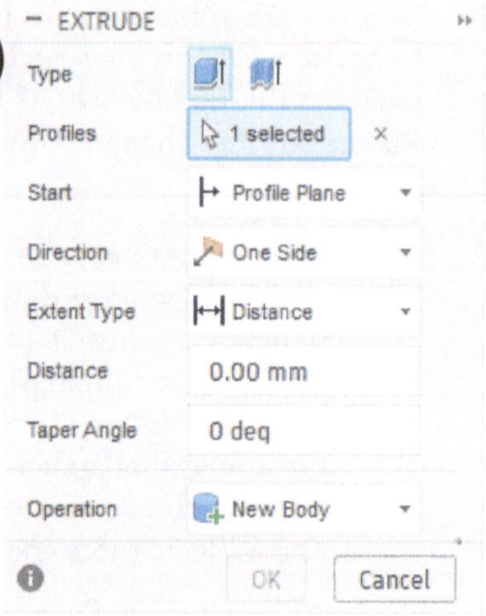

EXTRUDE

Type

Profiles: 1 selected

Start: Profile Plane

Direction: One Side

Extent Type: Distance

Distance: 0.00 mm

Taper Angle: 0 deg

Operation: New Body

OK Cancel

10.13

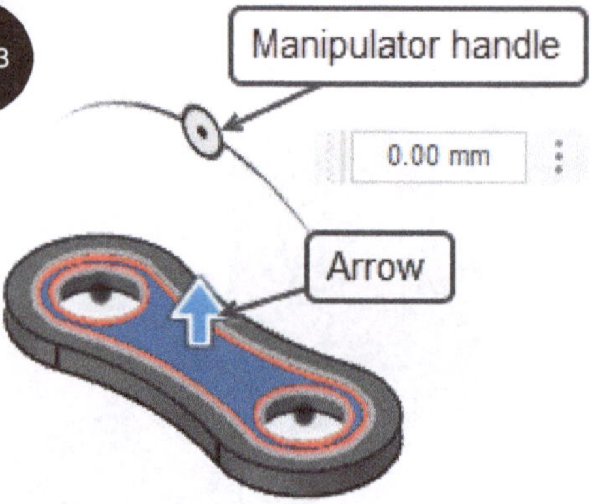

Manipulator handle

0.00 mm

Arrow

3. Drag the arrow that appears in the graphics area by pressing and holding the left mouse button to dynamically extrude the sketch profile, see Figure 10.14. Alternatively, enter the extrusion distance in the **Distance** field of the dialog box. You can also add tapering to the extrude feature by dragging the manipulator handle or entering the taper angle in the **Taper Angle** field of the dialog box. The options in the dialog box have been discussed earlier.

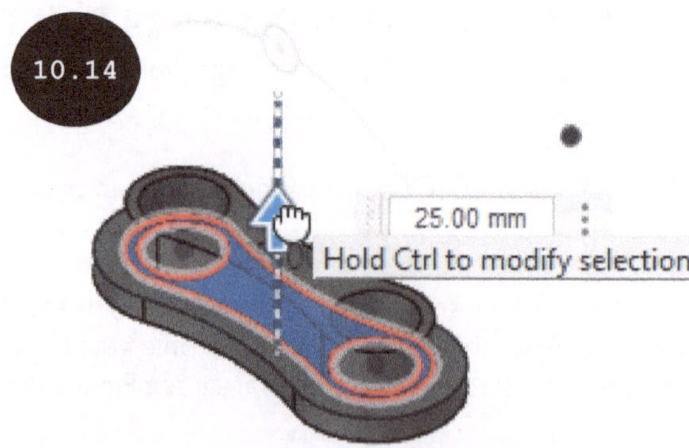

4. Select the required option in the **Operation** drop-down list of the dialog box and then click on the **OK** button. The extrude feature is created.

Creating Fillets

A fillet is a curved face of a constant or variable radius and is used for removing sharp edges of a model that may cause injury while handling the model. Figure 10.15 shows a model before and after applying a constant radius fillet.

In Autodesk Fusion, you can create a fillet of constant radius, variable radius, or by specifying the chord length using the **Fillet** tool. Additionally, you can also create rule fillets and full-round fillets by using the **Fillet** tool. The methods for creating different types of fillets are discussed next.

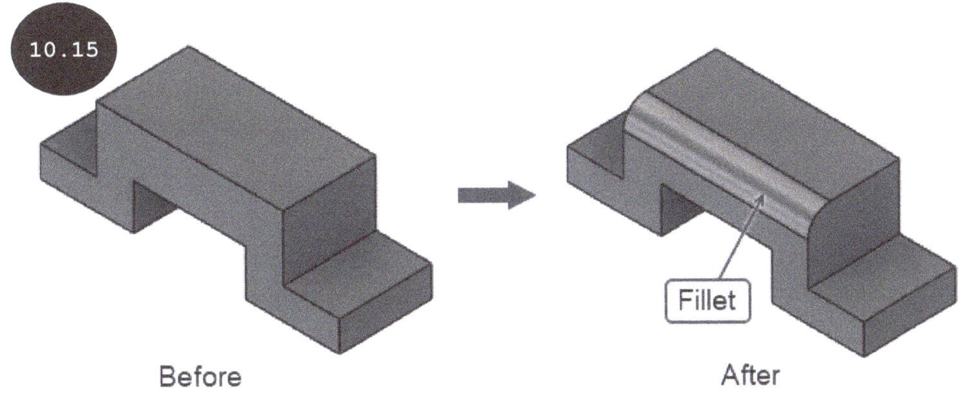

Creating a Constant Radius Fillet

1. Click on the **Fillet** tool in the **MODIFY** panel of the **SOLID** tab, see Figure 10.16. The **FILLET** dialog box appears, see Figure 10.17. Alternatively, press the F key to invoke the **FILLET** dialog box.

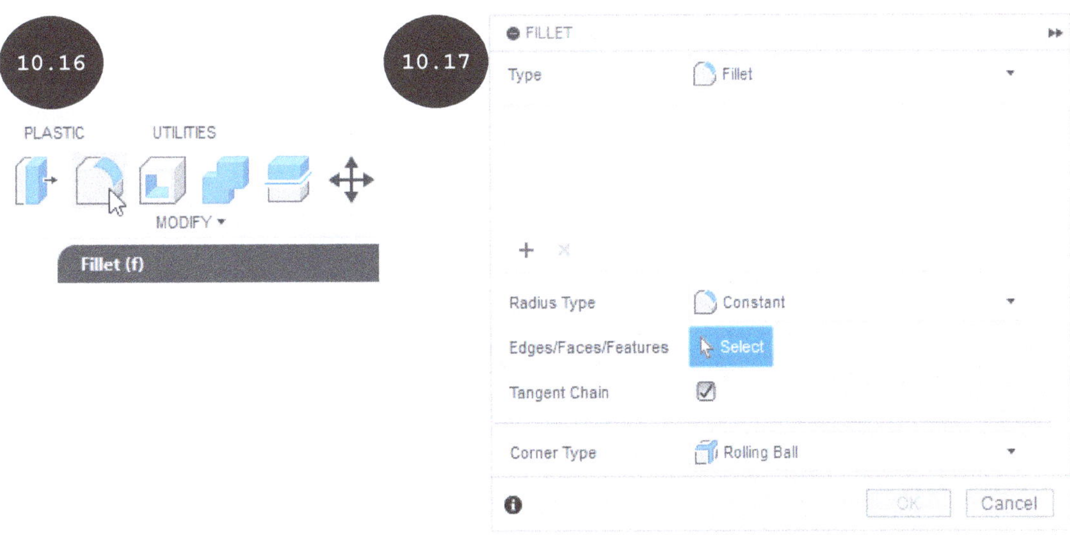

Type: By default, the **Fillet** option is selected in the **Type** drop-down list of the dialog box, see Figure 10.17. As a result, you can create a fillet of constant radius, variable radius, or by specifying chord length. The **Rule Fillet** option of the **Type** drop-down list is used for creating rule fillets. The **Full Round Fillet** option is used for creating full-round fillets. You will learn about creating a rule fillet and a full-round fillet later in this chapter.

2. Ensure the **Fillet** option is selected in the **Type** drop-down list of the dialog box.

Radius Type: By selecting the required option (**Constant**, **Variable**, or **Chord Length**) in the **Radius Type** drop-down list, you can create constant radius fillets, variable radius fillets, or chord length fillets, respectively. You will learn about creating a variable radius fillet and chord length fillet later in this chapter.

3. Select the **Constant** option in the **Radius Type** drop-down list of the dialog box to create a constant radius fillet.

Edges/Faces/Features: By default, the **Edges/Faces/Features** selection option is activated in the dialog box. As a result, you can select edges, faces, or features of the model for creating the fillets. You can select edges or faces in the graphics area, whereas the features can be selected in the **Timeline**.

Tangent Chain: The **Tangent Chain** check box is selected in the dialog box, by default. As a result, on selecting an edge, all the edges that are tangent to the selected edge, get selected automatically. Figure 10.18 shows an edge to be selected for applying the fillet. Figures 10.19 and 10.20 show the preview of the resultant fillet when the **Tangent Chain** check box is selected and cleared, respectively.

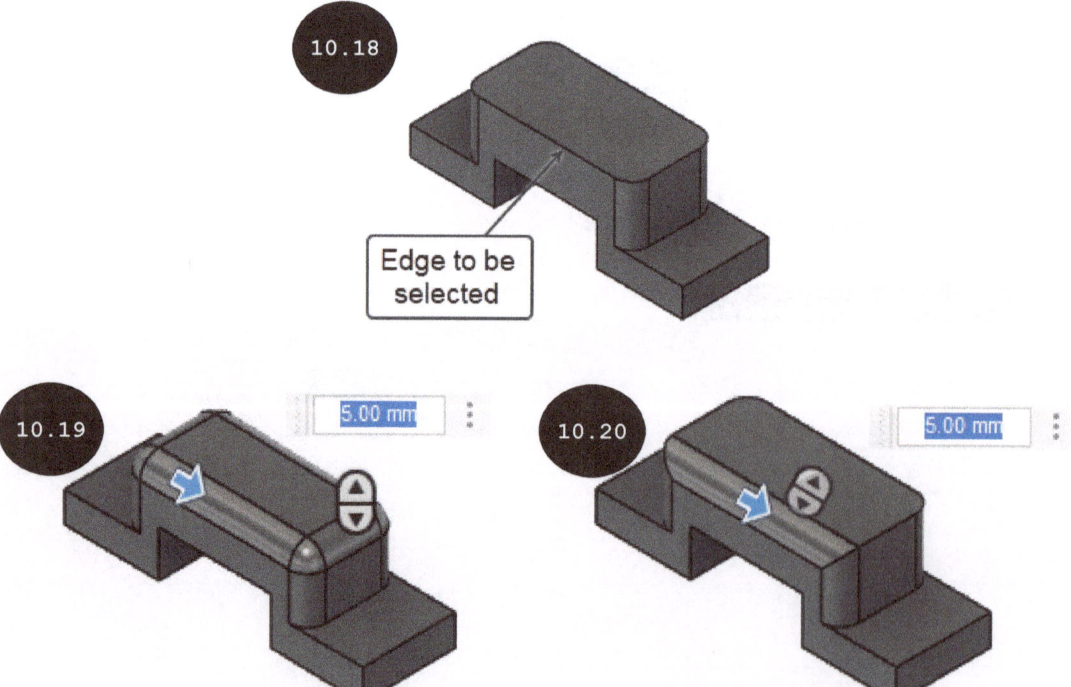

4. Ensure that the **Tangent Chain** check box is selected in the dialog box to include tangentially connected edges or faces. To create fillets on individual edges or faces, clear the **Tangent Chain** check box.

5. Select an edge, a face, or a feature of the model to create the fillet. After selecting an edge, a face, or a feature, the **FILLET** dialog box gets modified with additional options, see Figure 10.21. Also, an arrow and a spinner arrow appear on the selected entity in the graphics area, see Figure 10.22.

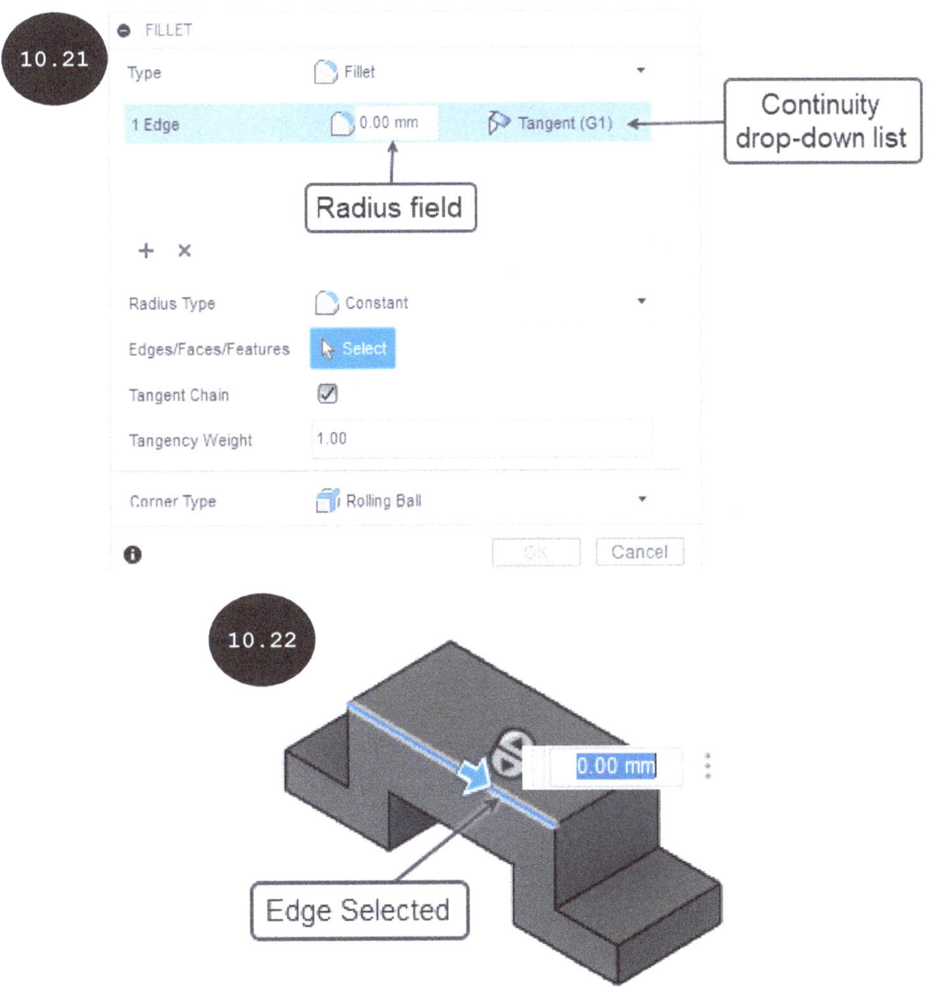

Tip: If a radius value other than 0 (zero) is specified in the **Radius** field, then you need to press the CTRL key to select multiple edges or faces to be filleted.

Radius: The **Radius** field of the dialog box is used to specify the radius value of the fillet, refer to Figure 10.21.

Continuity: The options in the **Continuity** drop-down list are used to reply the type of continuity: G1 tangent continuity or G2 curvature continuity to the fillet, respectively.

6. Select the required option: **Tangent (G1)** or **Curvature (G2)** as the type of continuity to be applied to the fillet in the **Continuity** drop-down list, see Figure 10.23.

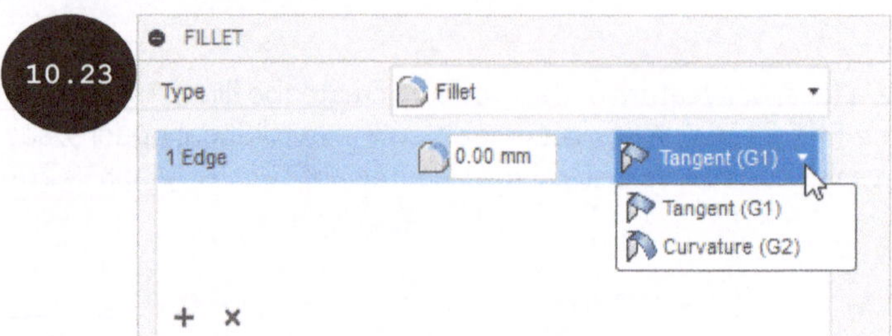

7. Enter the radius value in the **Radius** field of the dialog box or drag the arrow that appears in the graphics area to define the radius value of the fillet dynamically. The preview of a constant radius fillet appears, see Figure 10.24.

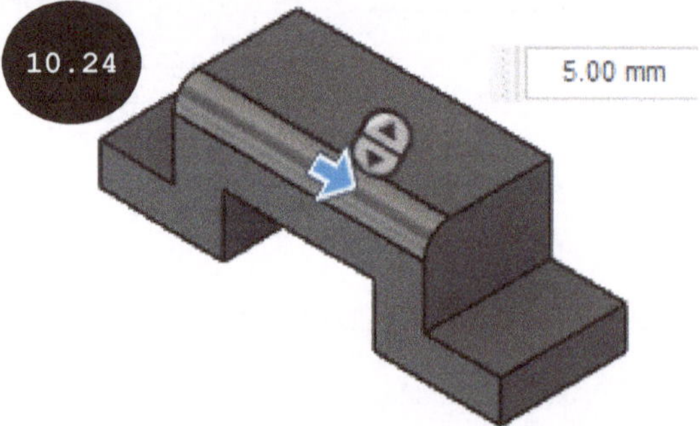

Tangency Weight: The **Tangency Weight** field in the dialog box is used to specify a tangency weight value of the fillet to alter its tangency curvature, as required. You can also dynamically change the tangency weight value of the fillet by dragging the spinner arrows that appear in the graphics area.

Corner Type: By default, the **Rolling Ball** option is selected in the **Corner Type** drop-down list of the dialog box. As a result, the rolling ball corner is created at the vertex where three or more edges intersect each other, see Figure 10.25. The **Setback** option of the **Corner Type** drop-down list of the dialog box is used for creating a setback fillet at the corner where three or more edges intersect each other, see Figure 10.26. A setback fillet corner has a smooth transition from the fillet edges to the common intersecting vertex.

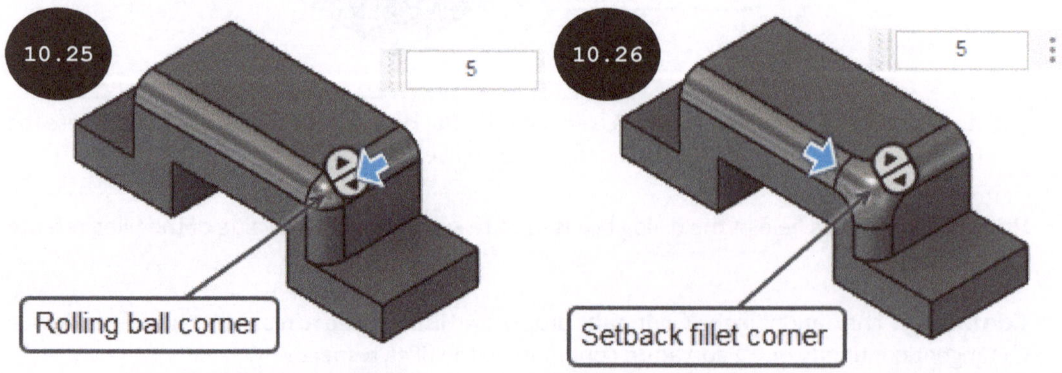

8. Select the required option in the **Corner Type** area of the dialog box.

9. Click on the **OK** button in the dialog box. The constant radius fillet is created.

Creating a Variable Radius Fillet

In Autodesk Fusion, you can also create a variable radius fillet on an edge of the model using the **Fillet** tool, see Figure 10.27. The method for creating a variable radius fillet is discussed below:

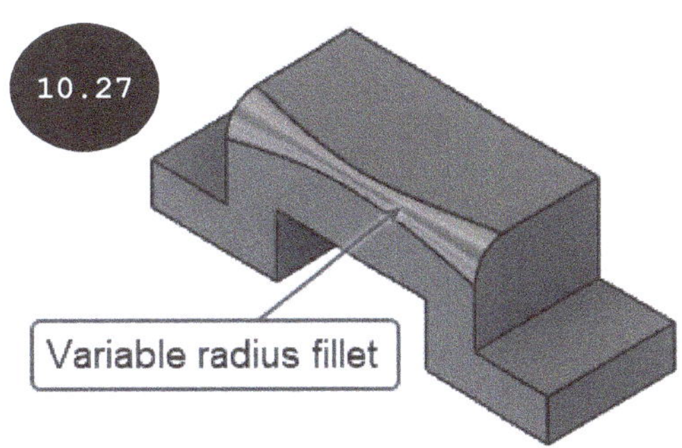

1. Click on the **Fillet** tool in the **MODIFY** panel of the **SOLID** tab or press the F key. The **FILLET** dialog box appears. Most of the options in the **FILLET** dialog box were discussed earlier.

2. Select an edge of the model to create the fillet.

3. Select the **Variable** option in the **Radius Type** drop-down list of the dialog box for creating the variable radius fillet. The **FILLET** dialog box gets modified, and the **Radius Points** area appears in the dialog box with the **Start Radius** and **End Radius** fields, see Figure 10.28. Also, an arrow appears on each end of the selected edge, see Figure 10.29.

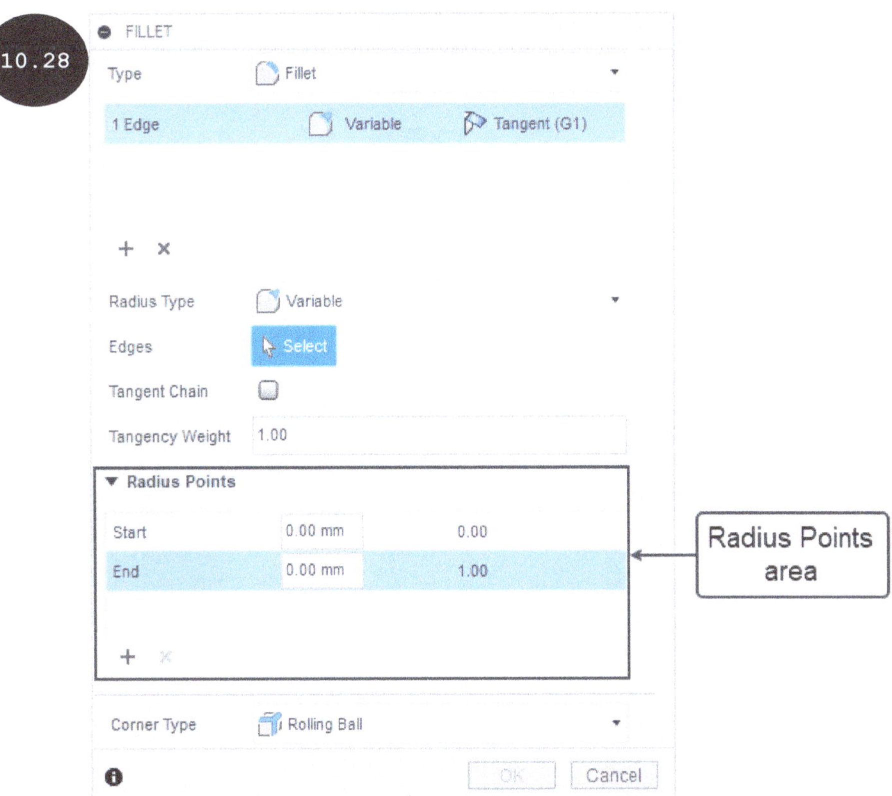

4. Specify different fillet radii on both ends of the selected edge by entering different radius values in the **Start Radius** and **End Radius** fields of the **Radius Points** area in the dialog box, see Figure 10.30. Alternatively, drag the arrows that appear in the graphics area to set different radii on both ends of the selected edge, dynamically.

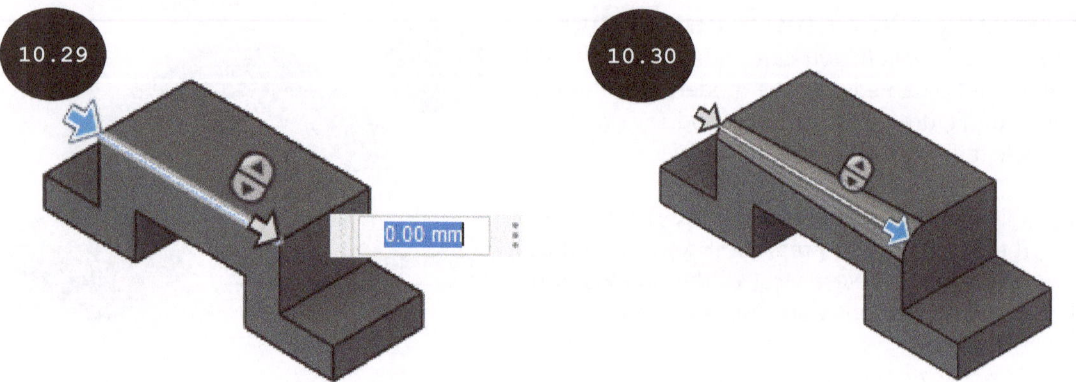

In addition to defining variable radii on both ends of the selected edge, you can add multiple control points on the edge and specify a different fillet radius for each control point.

5. To add a control point on the selected edge for specifying a different radius value, move the cursor over the selected edge. A dot appears, see Figure 10.31. Next, click the left mouse button. A new control point gets added and an arrow appears at the specified location on the edge, see Figure 10.31. Also, the respective **Radius** and **Position** fields get added in the **Radius Points** area of the dialog box and also appear in the graphics area, see Figure 10.32.

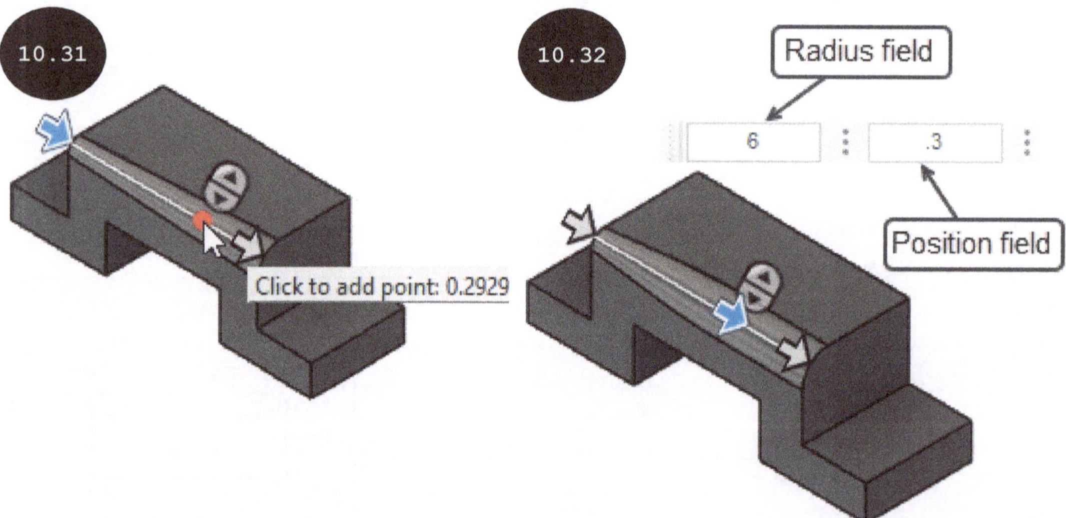

6. Specify a different radius value for the newly added control point in the respective **Radius** field or drag the arrow that appears in the graphics area, see Figure 10.33. You can also specify the position of the control point on the selected edge by entering a percentage value (0 to 1) in the **Position** field that appears in the graphics area. Note that the percentage value is calculated in terms of the total length of the selected edge.

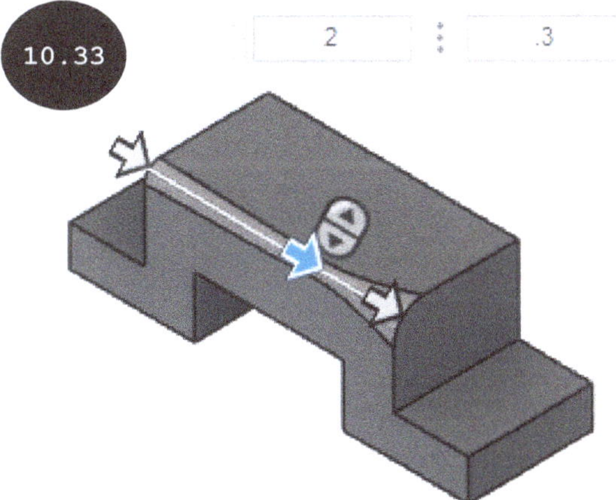

7. You can similarly add multiple control points by clicking the left mouse button on the selected edge and defining a different radius value for each control point.

   You can also delete a control point by using the **Remove selected point** button of the dialog box, which is discussed below:

   Remove selected point: The **Remove selected point** button of the dialog box is used to delete a control point added on a selected edge.

8. To delete an already added control point on the selected edge, select the control point to be deleted by clicking on its name listed in the **Radius Points** area of the dialog box or by clicking on the arrow that appears on the edge in the graphics area. Next, click on the **Remove selected point** button in the dialog box, see Figure 10.34. The selected control point gets deleted. Note that this button is enabled only when a control point is selected.

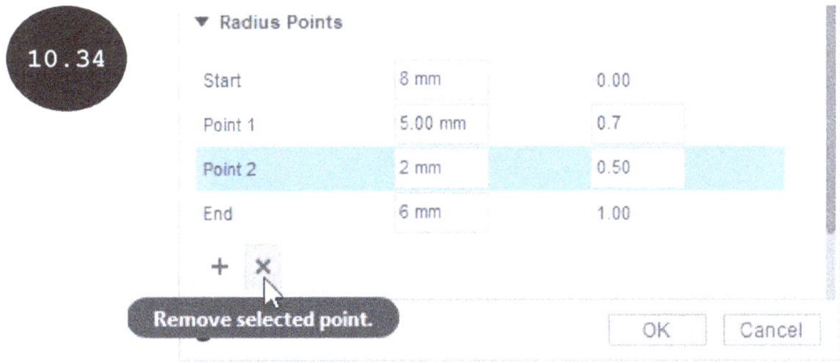

The remaining options of the **FILLET** dialog box are discussed earlier.

9. After specifying the required parameters for creating the variable radius fillet, click on the **OK** button in the dialog box. The variable radius fillet is created on the selected edge of the model.

Creating a Fillet by Specifying the Chord Length

In addition to creating a constant radius fillet by specifying its radius value, you can also create a fillet by specifying its chord length, see Figure 10.35.

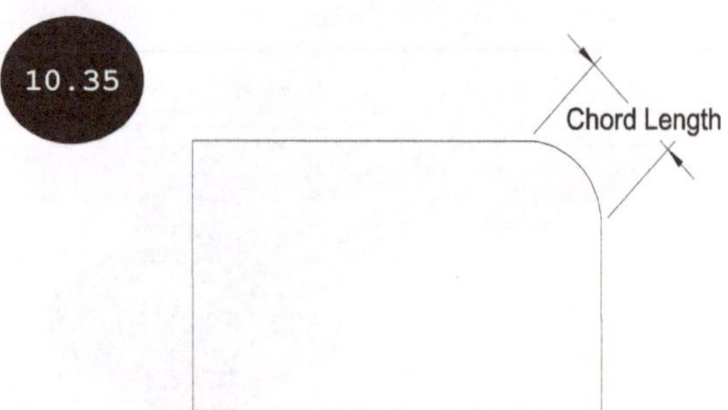

1. Click on the **Fillet** tool in the **MODIFY** panel of the **SOLID** tab or press the **F** key. The **FILLET** dialog box appears.

2. Select edges, faces, or features of the model to create the fillet. You can select edges or faces in the graphics area, whereas the features can be selected in the **Timeline**.

3. Select the **Chord Length** option in the **Radius Type** drop-down list of the dialog box, see Figure 10.36. An arrow and a spinner arrow appear on the selected edge, see Figure 10.37.

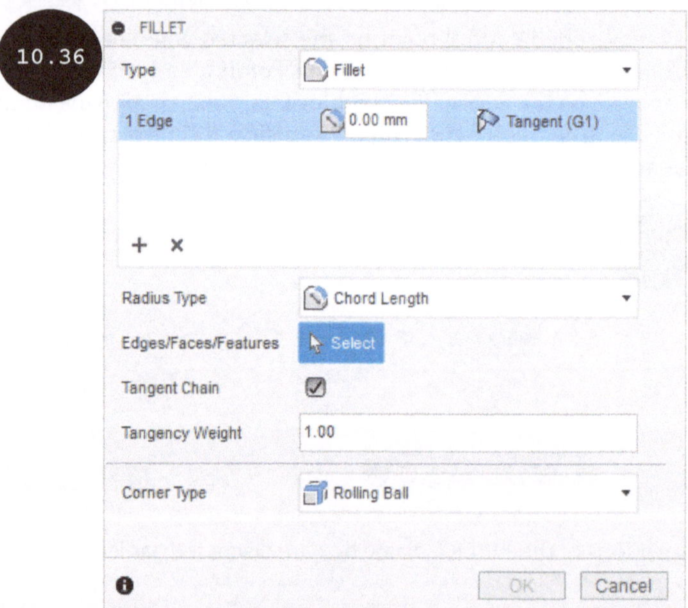

4. Drag the arrow that appears in the graphics area to define the chord length of the fillet, dynamically. The preview of the fillet appears, see Figure 10.38. You can also enter the chord length in the **Chord Length** field of the dialog box.

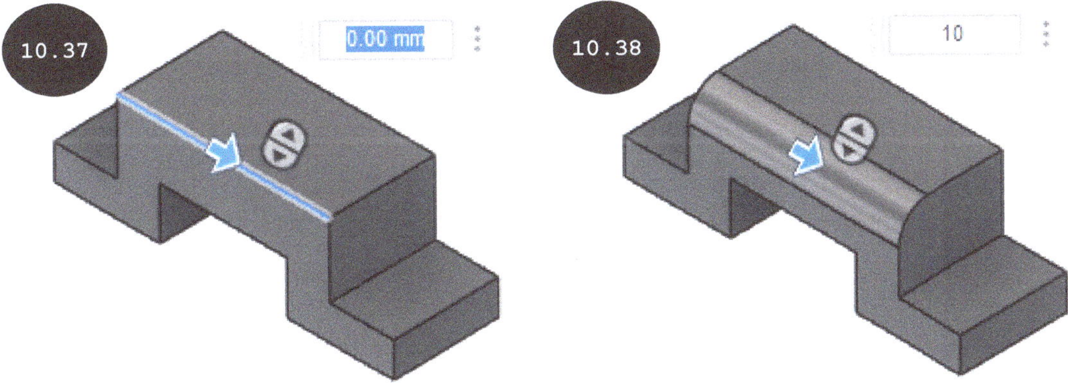

The remaining options of the **FILLET** dialog box are discussed earlier.

5. After specifying the required parameters for creating the fillet, click on the **OK** button in the dialog box. The fillet with a specified chord length is created on the selected edge of the model.

Creating Rule Fillets

Rule fillets are the same as constant radius fillets with the only difference being that in rule fillets, the edges for creating fillets are determined by specifying rules. To do this, you need to select faces and features. In Autodesk Fusion, you can create rule fillets by using the **Fillet** tool. The method for creating rule fillets is discussed below:

1. Click on the **Fillet** tool in the **MODIFY** panel of the **SOLID** tab. The **FILLET** dialog box appears. Alternatively, press the F key to invoke the **FILLET** dialog box.

2. Select the **Rule Fillet** option in the **Type** drop-down list of the dialog box, see Figure 10.39.

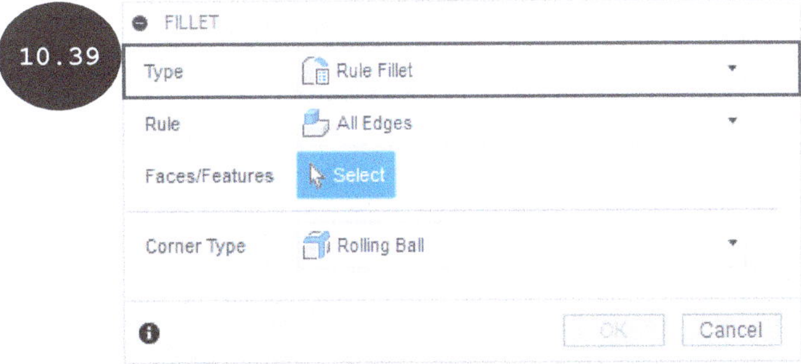

Faces/Features: The **Faces/Features** selection option is used to select faces or features to define a rule for determining the edges to create fillets. Note that you can select the faces of the model in the graphics area, whereas the features can be selected in the **Timeline**.

3. Select faces or features as the input to specify the rule, see Figure 10.40. In this figure, a face is selected as the input to define the rule. You can select single or multiple faces or features.

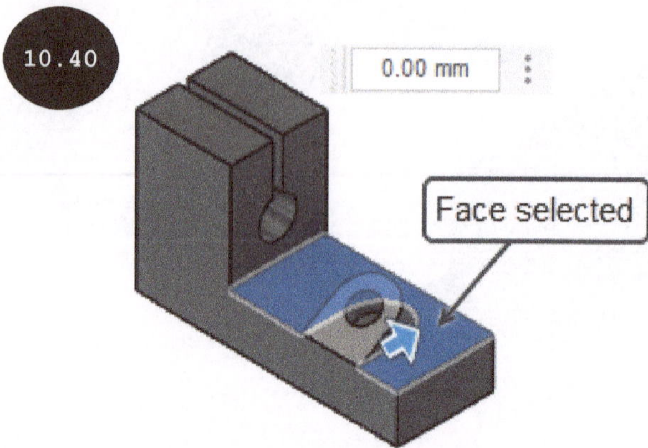

4. Enter a radius value in the **Radius** field of the dialog box or drag the arrow that appears in the graphics area. The preview of the fillets appears on the edges which are determined by the default rules specified in the **Rule** drop-down list of the dialog box. The options in the **Rule** drop-down list are discussed below:

   Rule: By default, the **All Edges** option is selected in the **Rule** drop-down list of the dialog box. As a result, the fillets are created on all the edges of the face selected, see Figure 10.41. On selecting the **Between Faces/Features** option in this drop-down list, the **Faces/Features 1** and **Faces/Features 2** selection options appear in the dialog box. By using these selection options, you can select two sets of faces/features to determine the edges between them to create fillets, see Figure 10.42. In this figure, a face is selected as set 1 and a feature is selected as set 2. As a result, the fillets are only created at the intersections of the face and the feature selected. Note that you can select the faces of the model in the graphics area, whereas the features can be selected in the **Timeline**.

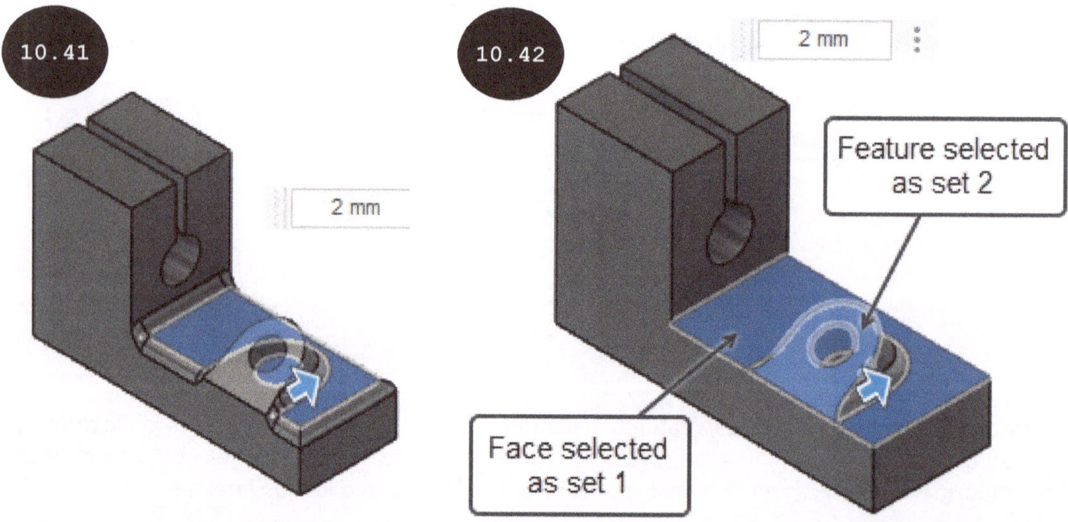

5. Select the required option (**All Edges** or **Between Faces/Features**) in the **Rule** drop-down list of the dialog box to determine the edges to be filleted. Note that on selecting the **Between Faces/Features** option, you need to select two sets of faces/features to determine the edges for creating fillets.

Topology: By default, the **Rounds and Fillets** option is selected in the **Topology** drop-down list of the dialog box. As a result, all fillets and rounds are created on the determined edges, see Figure 10.43.

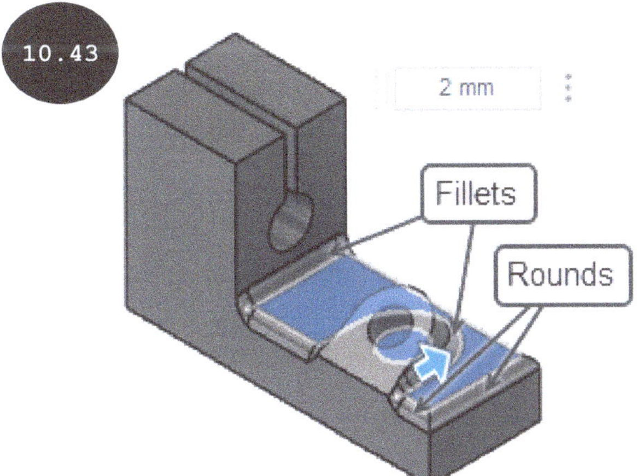

On selecting the **Fillets Only** option in the **Topology** drop-down list, only fillets are created on the respective edges, see Figure 10.44. On selecting the **Rounds Only** option, only rounds are created on the respective edges, see Figure 10.45.

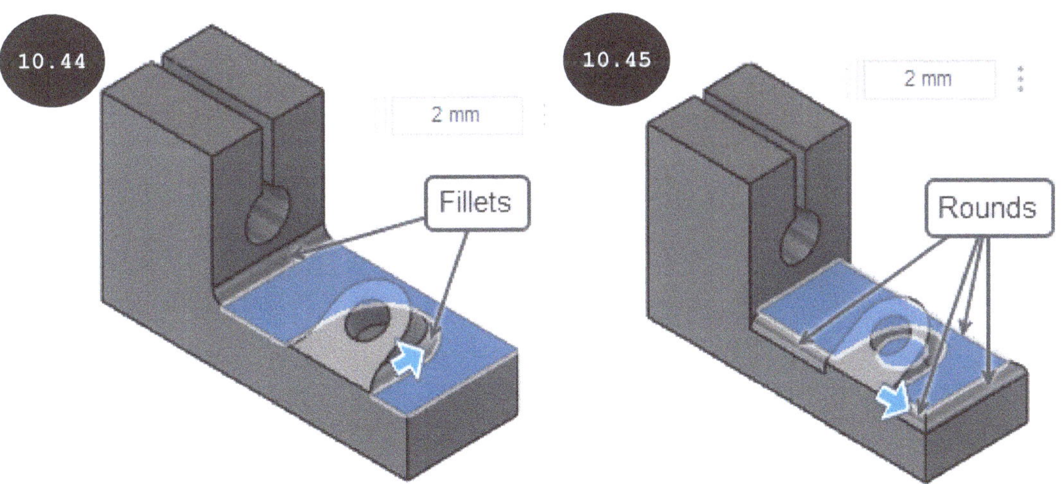

6. Select the required option (**Rounds and Fillets**, **Fillets Only**, or **Rounds Only**) in the **Topology** drop-down list of the dialog box to define the type of fillets (fillets or rounds) to be created on the determined edges of the selected faces/features.

   The remaining options of the **FILLET** dialog box are discussed earlier.

7. After defining the required input and options, click on the **OK** button. The fillets are created.

Creating Full Round Fillets

A full round fillet is created tangent to three adjacent faces of a model. In Autodesk Fusion, you can create full round fillets by using the **Fillet** tool. The method for creating a full round fillet is discussed below:

1. Click on the **Fillet** tool in the **MODIFY** panel of the **SOLID** tab. The **FILLET** dialog box appears. Alternatively, press the F key to invoke the **FILLET** dialog box.

2. Select the **Full Round Fillet** option in the **Type** drop-down list of the dialog box, see Figure 10.46.

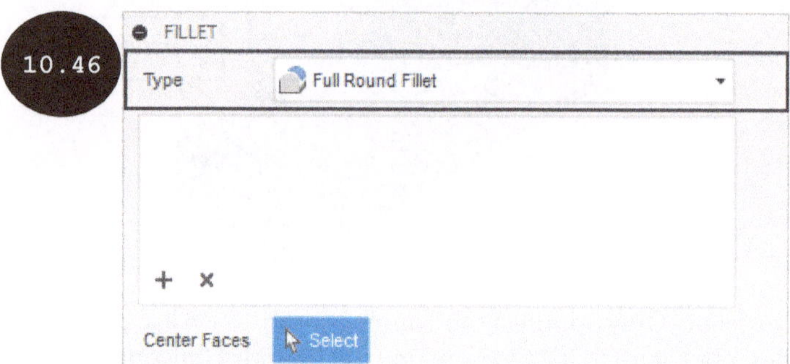

Center Faces: The **Center Faces** selection option is used to select the central face of a full round fillet, see Figure 10.47.

3. Select a face as the center face for a full round fillet, see Figure 10.47. Both the adjacent faces of the center face get selected automatically and the preview of a full round fillet appears, see Figure 10.47. You can select multiple center faces for creating multiple full round fillets by pressing the CTRL key, or by clicking the **Add selection set** button + in the dialog box.

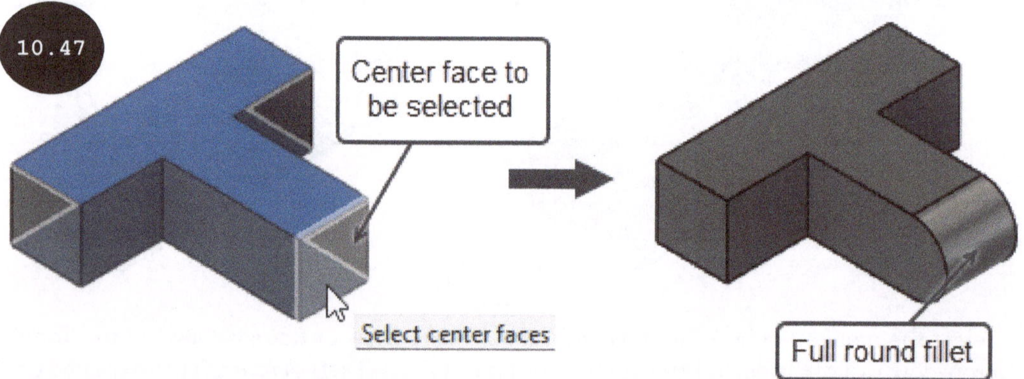

Side 1 and **Side 2:** The **Side 1** and **Side 2** selection sets are used to select the faces adjacent to the center face of the full round fillet. These selection sets appear after selecting a center face for creating a full round fillet.

Note: On selecting a center face, if the preview of a full round fillet does not appear automatically, then you need to select both its adjacent side faces manually by activating the **Side 1** and **Side 2** selection sets, respectively.

4. Click on the **OK** button. A full round fillet is created.

Creating Chamfers

A chamfer is a bevel face that is non-perpendicular to its adjacent faces, see Figure 10.48. You can create different types of chamfers: Equal Distance, Two Distances, and Distance and Angle chamfers by using the **Chamfer** tool.

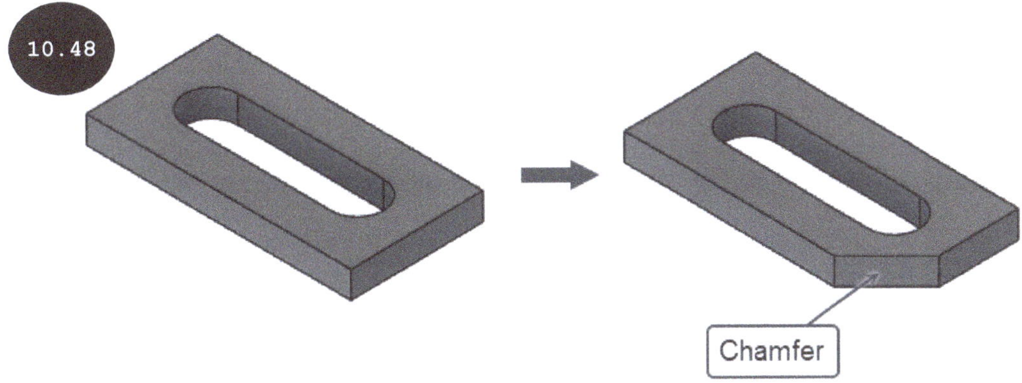

To create a chamfer, invoke the **MODIFY** drop-down menu in the **SOLID** tab and then click on the **Chamfer** tool, see Figure 10.49. The **CHAMFER** dialog box appears, see Figure 10.50. The options in this dialog box are discussed next.

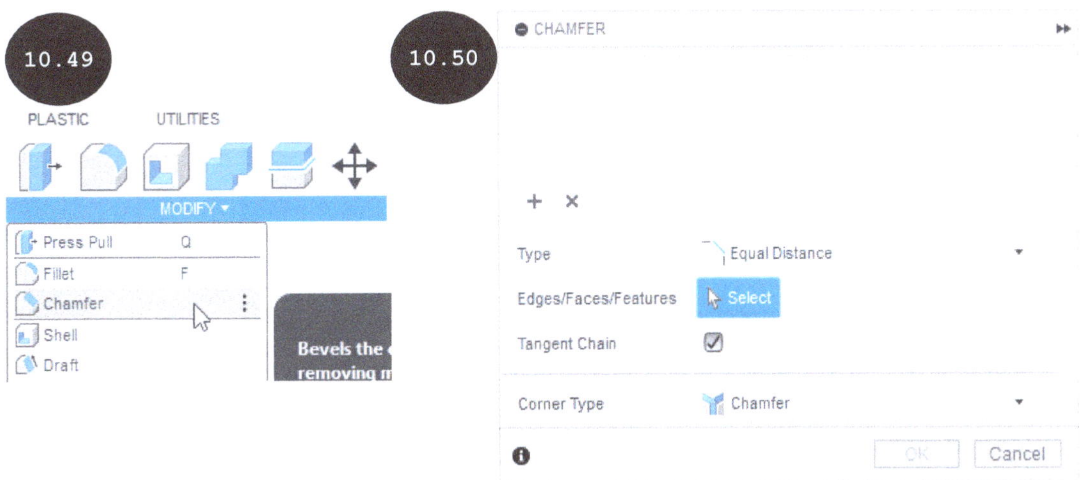

Edges/Faces/Features

By default, the **Edges/Faces/Features** selection option is activated in the dialog box. As a result, you can select one or more edges, faces, and features to create chamfers. Note that you can select the edges and faces of the model in the graphics area, whereas the features can be selected in the **Timeline**.

Tangent Chain

By default, the **Tangent Chain** check box is selected in the dialog box. As a result, on selecting an edge or a face, all the edges or faces that are tangent to the selected edge or face get selected, automatically. Figure 10.51 shows an edge to be selected for applying the chamfer. Figures 10.52 and 10.53 show the preview of the resultant chamfer when the **Tangent Chain** check box is selected and cleared, respectively.

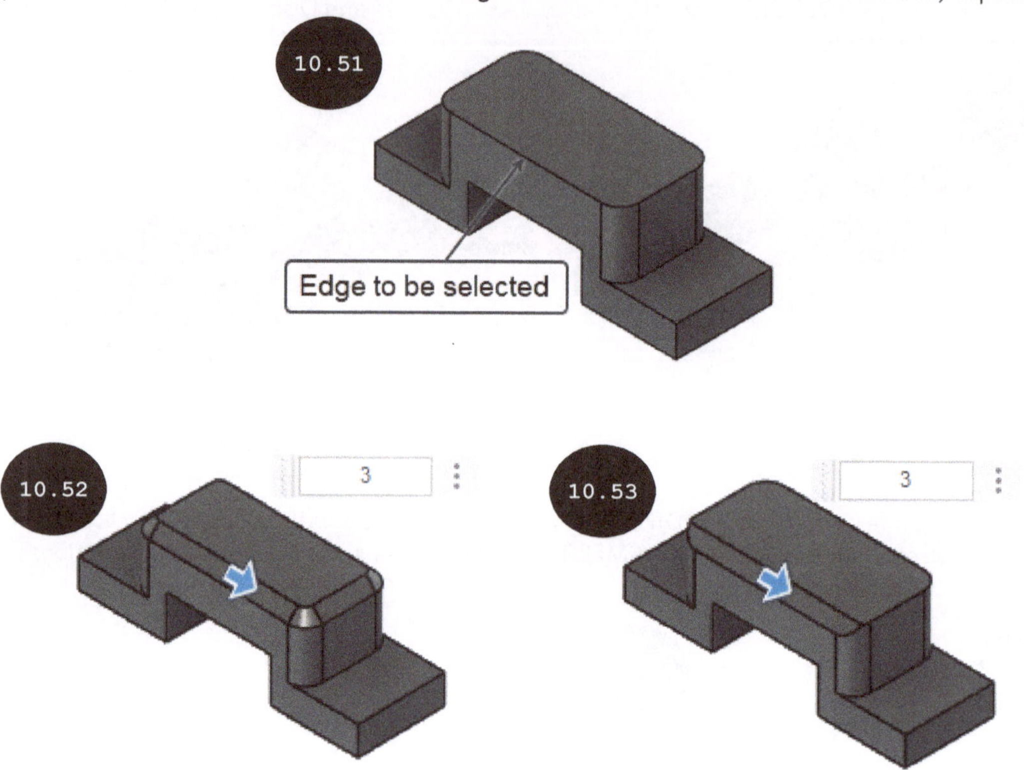

Type

The **Type** drop-down list of the dialog box is used to select the type of chamfer to be created on the selected edges and faces. The options in this drop-down list are discussed next.

Equal Distance

The **Equal Distance** option of the **Type** drop-down list is used to create a chamfer with equal/symmetric distance on both sides of the chamfer edge. By default, the **Equal Distance** option is selected in the **Type** drop-down list. As a result, on selecting an edge, face, or feature, the **Distance** field appears in the dialog box, see Figure 10.54. Also, an arrow appears in the graphics area, see Figure 10.55. Enter the distance value in the **Distance** field or drag the arrow that appears in the graphics area to specify the chamfer distance value. The preview of the chamfer appears such that the distance value specified in the **Distance** field is added equally/symmetrically on both sides of the selected edge or face, see Figure 10.56.

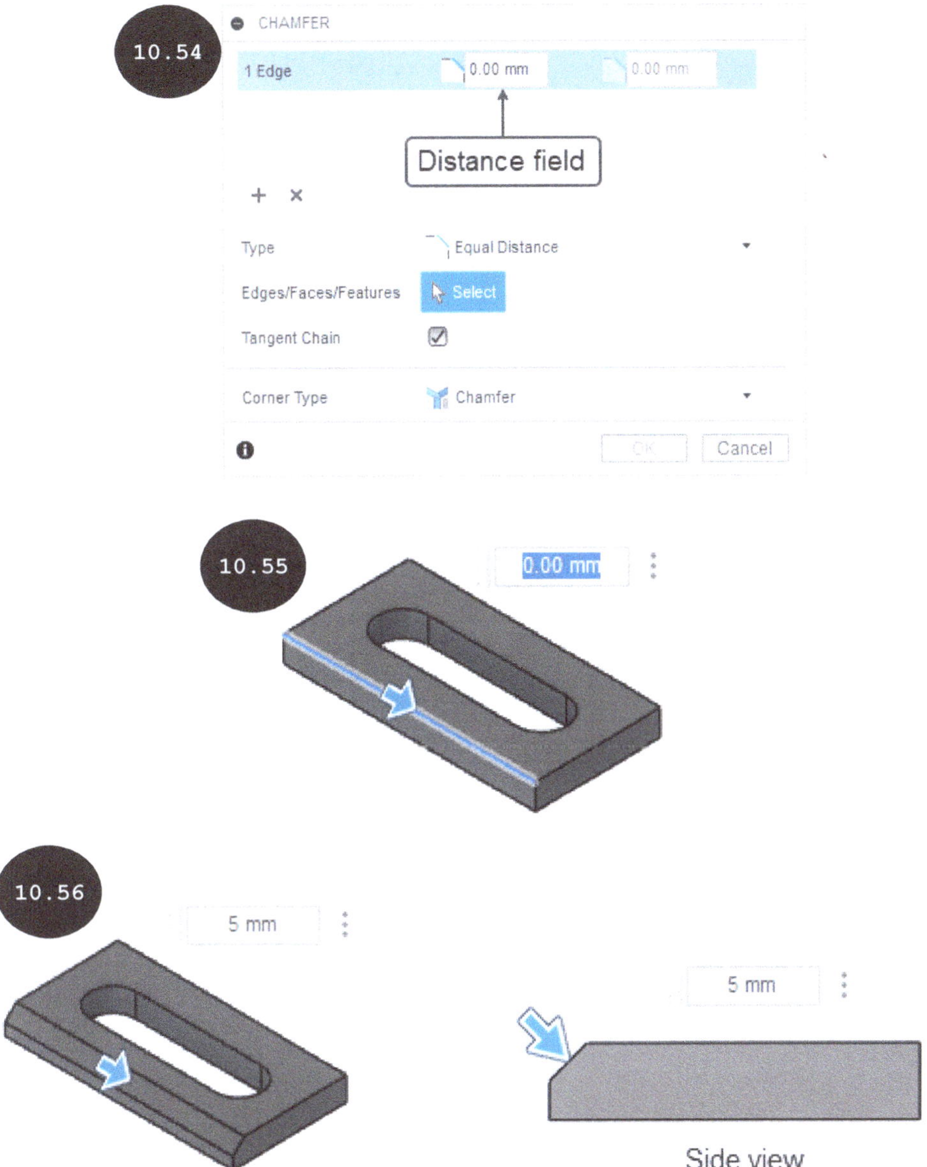

Two Distance

The **Two Distance** option of the **Type** drop-down list is used to create a chamfer with different distance values on both sides of the chamfer edge. On selecting this option, two **Distance** fields appear in the dialog box, see Figure 10.57. Also, two arrows appear in the graphics area on the edge or face selected to create the chamfer, see Figure 10.58. In these **Distance** fields, specify different distance values for both sides of the selected edge or face. On doing so, the preview of the chamfer appears with specified distance values on both sides of the edge or face selected, see Figure 10.59. You can also drag the arrows that appear in the graphics area to specify different distance values on both sides of the edge or face selected.

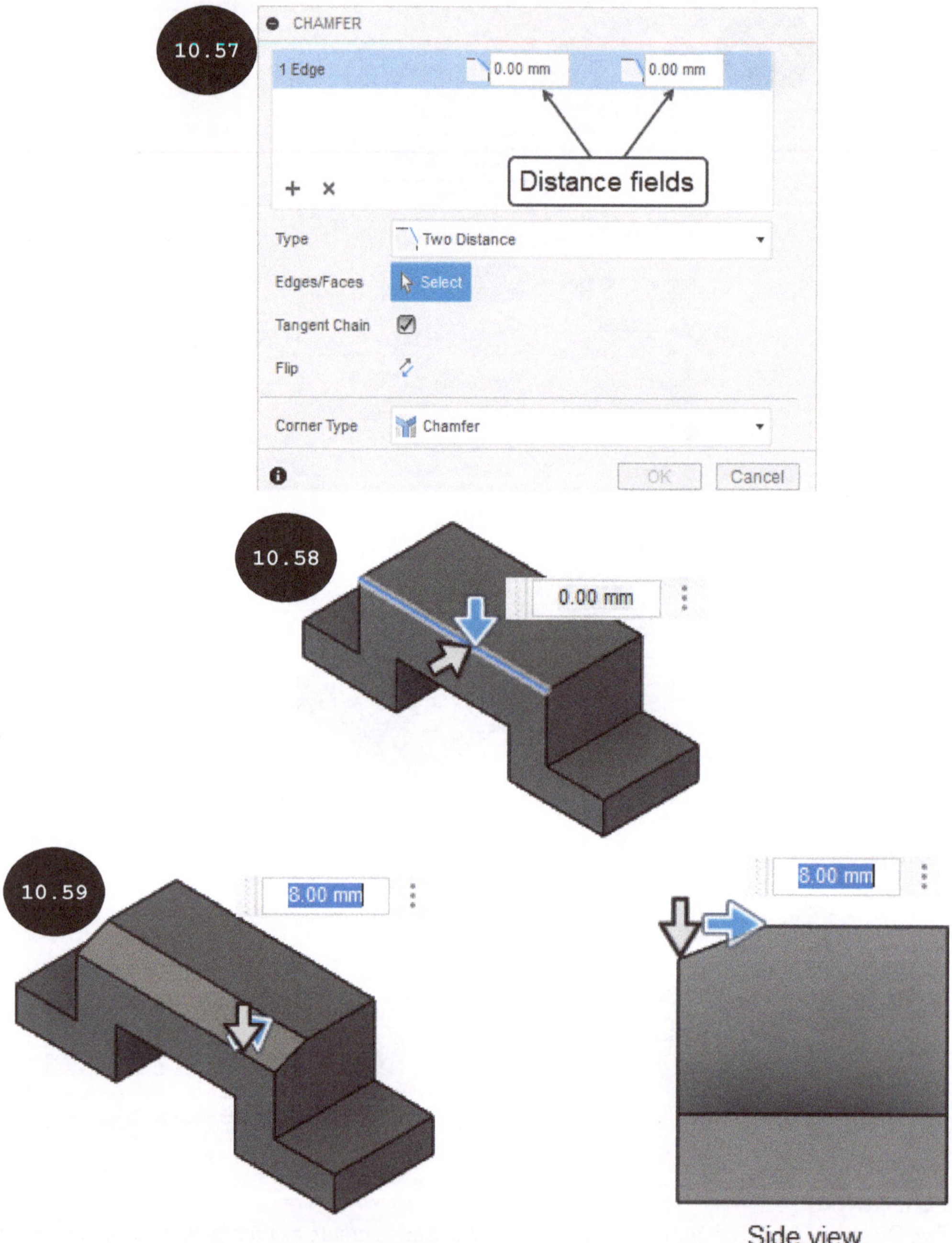

Distance and Angle

The **Distance and Angle** option of the **Type** drop-down list is used to create a chamfer by specifying its distance and angle values. On selecting this option, the **Distance** and **Angle** fields appear in the dialog box, see Figure 10.60. Also, an arrow and a manipulator handle appear in the graphics area on the edge or face selected, see Figure 10.61. Enter the required distance and angle values of the chamfer in the **Distance** and **Angle** fields of the dialog box, respectively. On doing so, the preview of the chamfer appears on the selected edge or face with specified distance and angle values, see Figure 10.62. You can also drag the arrow and the manipulator handle that appear in the graphics area to specify the distance and angle values of the chamfer. Note that in the preview of the chamfer, an arrow appears pointing toward the direction of the distance value measured.

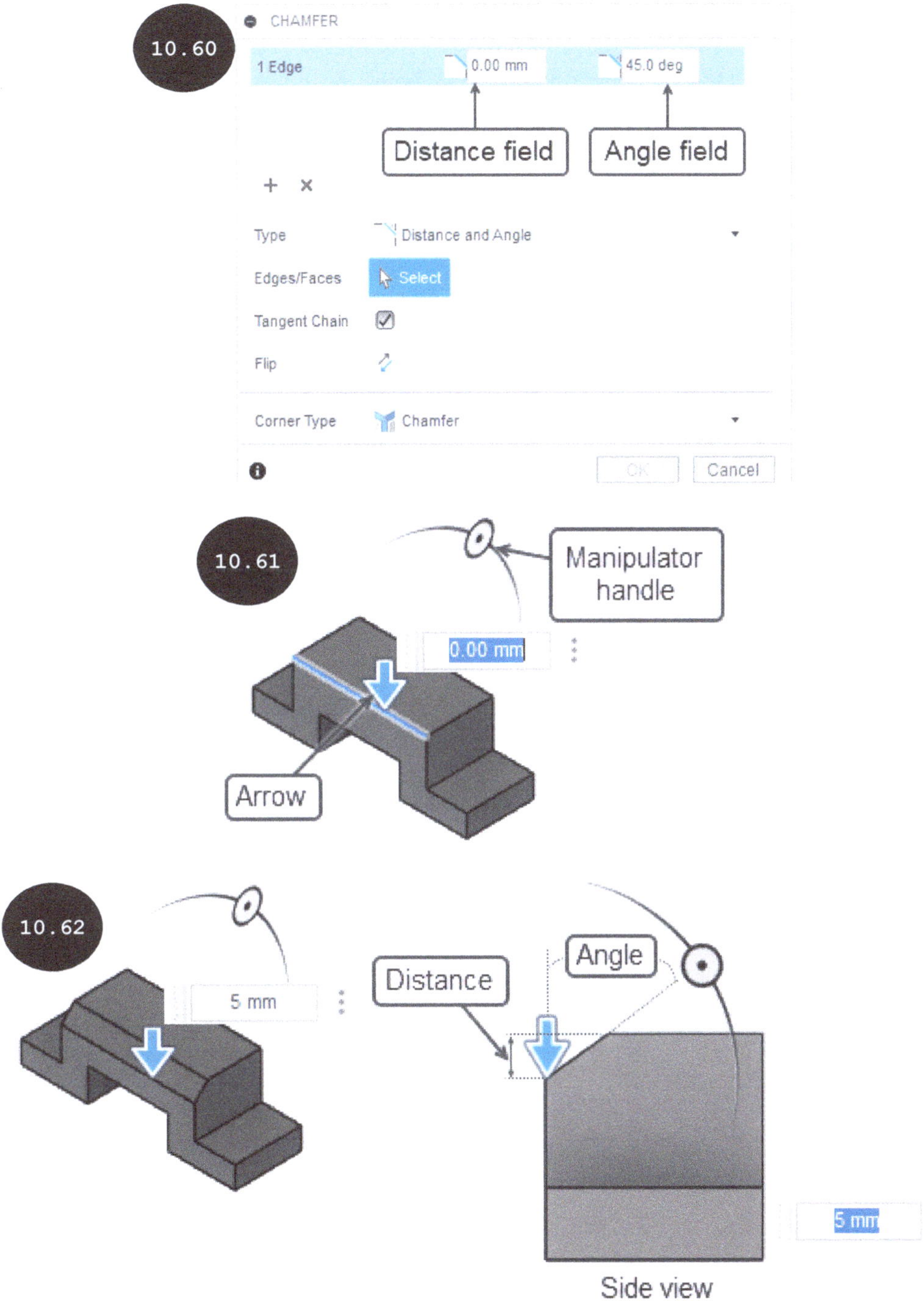

Flip

The **Flip** button is used for reversing or flipping the orientation of the chamfer to the other side of the selected edge. Note that this button is available when the **Two Distance** or **Distance and Angle** option is selected in the **Type** drop-down list of the **CHAMFER** dialog box.

Corner Type

The options (**Chamfer**, **Miter**, or **Blend**) in the **Corner Type** drop-down list of the dialog box are used for defining a type of corner to be created at the intersection of three chamfered edges of the model, see Figure 10.63.

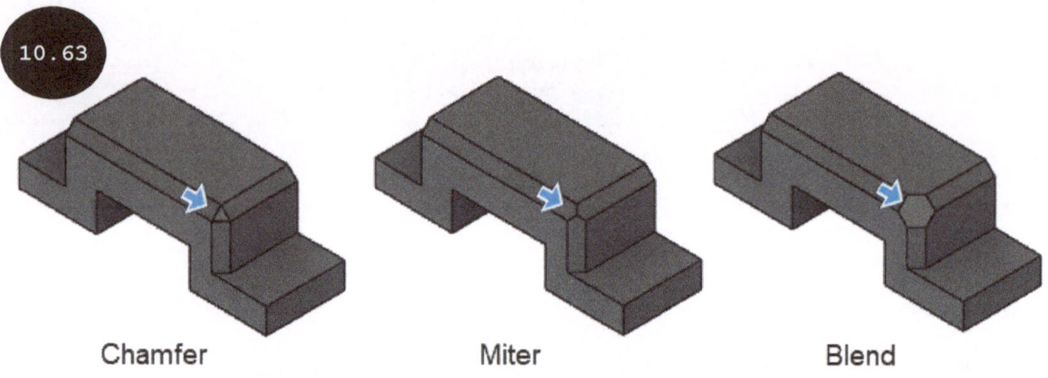

After selecting the required chamfer type and specifying the parameters, click on the **OK** button in the dialog box. The chamfer is created on the selected edge.

Creating Shell Features

A shell feature is a thin-walled feature created by hollowing out a model from the inside or by removing specific faces, see Figures 10.64 and 10.65.

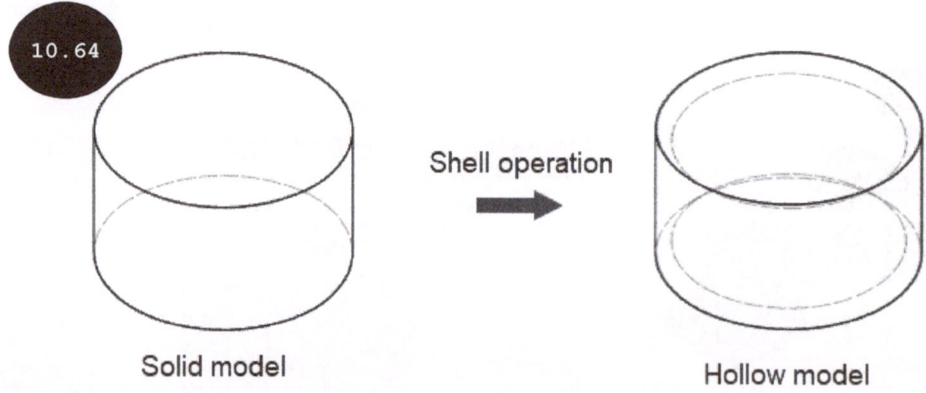

Note: In Figure 10.64, the visual style of the model has been changed to "wireframe with hidden edges" visual style so that the hidden edges of the hollow model can be visualized.

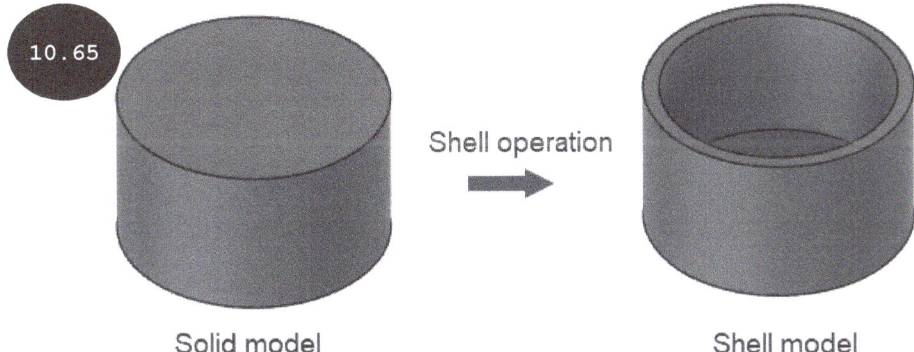

To create a shell feature, click on the **Shell** tool in the **MODIFY** panel of the **SOLID** tab, see Figure 10.66. The **SHELL** dialog box appears, see Figure 10.67. The options in this dialog box are discussed next.

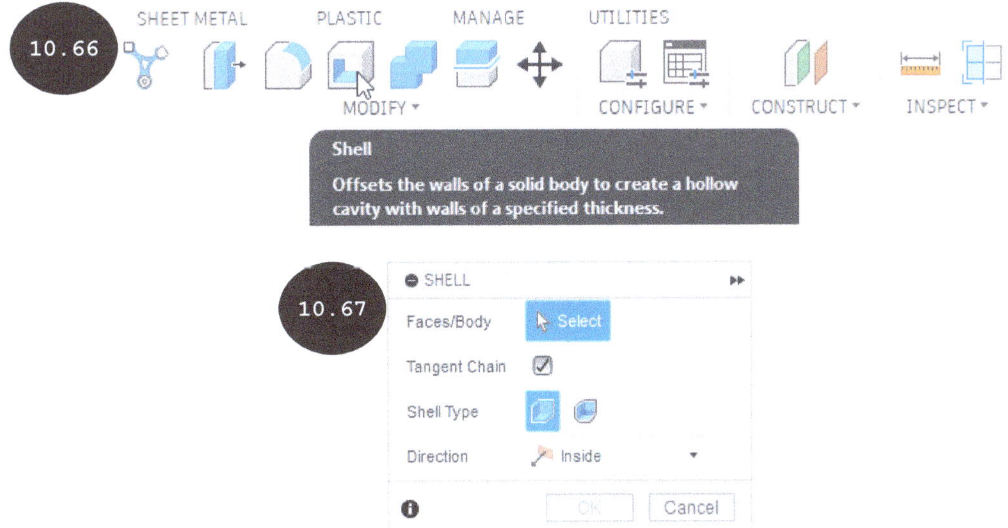

Faces/Body

By default, the **Faces/Body** selection option is activated in the dialog box. As a result, you can select faces or a body to create a shell feature of specified wall thickness. You can specify the wall thickness in the **Inside Thickness/Outside Thickness** field of the dialog box. Note that on selecting a body, the closed hollow shell model of specified wall thickness is created, refer to Figure 10.64. You can select a body in the graphics area or the **Bodies** node of the **BROWSER**. To select a body in the graphics area, move the cursor over an edge of the model and then click the left mouse button when the entire model gets highlighted.

If you select one or more faces, a shell feature with the specified wall thickness will be created, resulting in the removal of the selected face(s) from the model, see Figure 10.68.

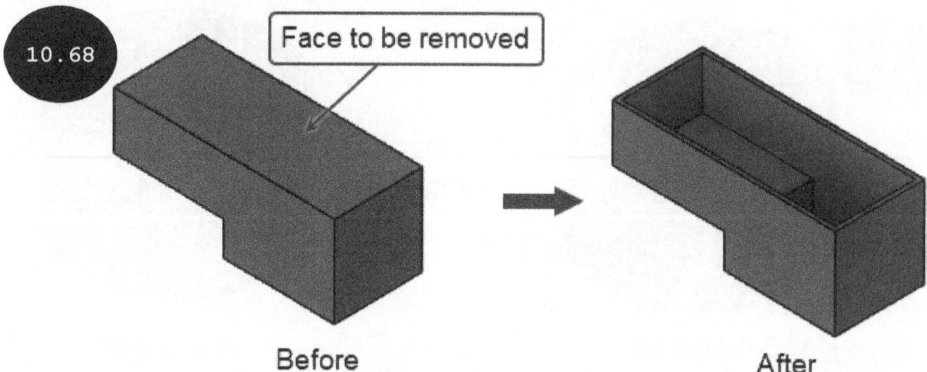

Tangent Chain

By default, the **Tangent Chain** check box is selected in the dialog box. As a result, on selecting a face to be removed, all the faces that are tangentially connected to the selected face of the model get selected, automatically.

Shell Type

By default, the **Sharp Shell** button is activated in the **Shell Type** area of the dialog box, creating a shell feature with sharp offset corners, see Figure 10.69. An offset corner refers to an internal corner formed at the intersection of the offset faces of the shell feature. If you select the **Rounded Shell** button, the shell feature will instead be created with rounded offset corners, see Figure 10.70.

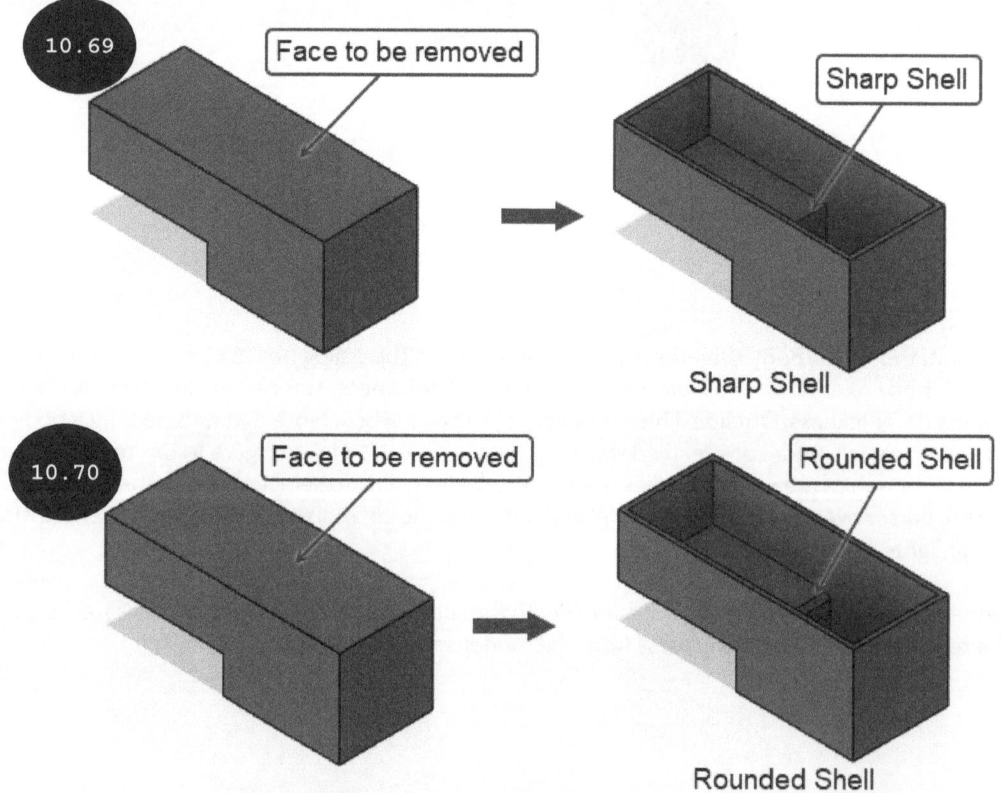

Inside Thickness/Outside Thickness

The **Inside Thickness** field in the dialog box is used to specify the wall thickness value of the shell feature that will be added inward to the model. It is important to note that this field is available only when the **Inside** or **Both** option is selected in the **Direction** drop-down list of the dialog box.

The **Outside Thickness** field in the dialog box is used to specify the wall thickness value of the shell feature that will be added outward to the model. This field is available only when the **Outside** or **Both** option is selected in the **Direction** drop-down list of the dialog box.

Direction

The **Direction** drop-down list is used for specifying whether the thickness is to be added inside, outside, or on both sides of the model by selecting the respective option.

After specifying the required parameters to create the shell feature, click on the **OK** button. The shell feature with a specified wall thickness is created.

Adding Drafts

Adding drafts is a process of tapering the faces of a model so that the model can easily get separated from its cast during its manufacturing. In Autodesk Fusion, you can taper the faces of the model by using the **Draft** tool. To do this, invoke the **MODIFY** drop-down menu in the **SOLID** tab and then click on the **Draft** tool, see Figure 10.71. The **DRAFT** dialog box appears, see Figure 10.72. In this dialog box, you can create two types of drafts: Fixed plane and Parting line. The fixed plane draft is created by selecting a plane or a planar face as a fixed plane to draft from and the faces to apply the draft, whereas the Parting line draft is created by selecting a plane, a face, an edge, or a sketch curve as a parting line to apply the draft around it. The methods for creating both these types of drafts are discussed next.

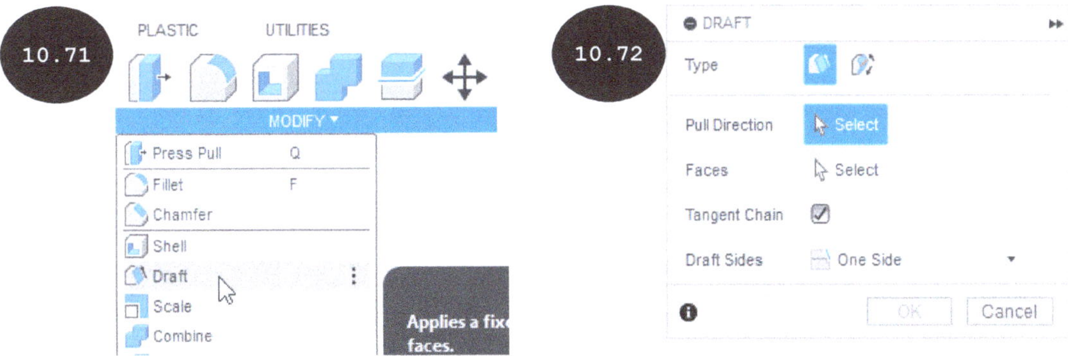

Creating the Fixed Plane Draft

1. Invoke the **DRAFT** dialog box and then ensure that the **Fixed Plane** button is activated in the **Type** area of the dialog box, refer to Figure 10.72.

   Pull Direction: By default, the **Pull Direction** selection option is activated in the dialog box. As a result, you can select a plane or a planar face as a fixed or neutral plane to define the pulling direction for adding drafts.

2. Select a plane or a planar face as a neutral plane to define the pulling direction for adding the draft, refer to Figure 10.73. In this figure, the top planar face of the model is selected as the neutral plane. Note that on selecting the neutral plane, an arrow appears on the selected face pointing toward the pulling direction. Also, the **Faces** selection option gets activated in the dialog box.

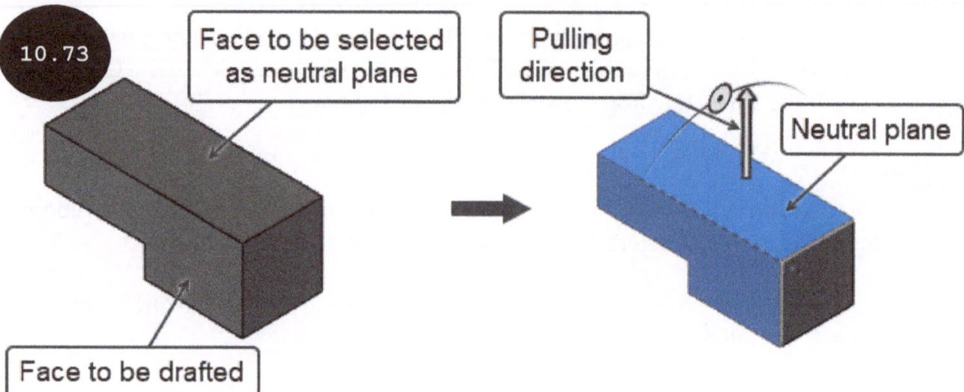

Faces: The **Faces** selection option is used for selecting faces of the model to be tapered/drafted.

3. Select one or more faces of the model to be drafted, refer to Figure 10.73. In this figure, the front planar face of the model is selected as a face to be drafted.

Tangent Chain: By default, the **Tangent Chain** check box is selected. As a result, faces that are tangentially connected to the selected face(s) also get selected.

Flip Pull Direction: The **Flip Pull Direction** button is used for flipping the pulling direction from upward to downward or vice-versa.

Note: On flipping the pulling direction, the direction of draft gets changed from outward to inward or vice-versa.

4. Click on the **Flip Pull Direction** button to flip the direction of the pull, if necessary.

Angle: The **Angle** field is used to specify draft angle to taper the selected face or faces. Note that the draft angle for the selected faces is calculated concerning the neutral plane selected. To flip the direction of the draft, you can enter a negative angle value in this field. You can also drag the manipulator handle that appears in the graphics area to specify the draft angle, dynamically.

5. Specify the draft angle in the **Angle** field of the dialog box. Alternatively, drag the manipulator handle that appears in the graphics area to specify the draft angle in the graphics area, dynamically.

Draft Sides: By default, the **One Side** option is selected in the **Draft Sides** drop-down list of the dialog box. As a result, you can specify a single draft angle in the **Angle** field of the dialog box. On selecting the **Two Side** option, the **Angle 1** and **Angle 2** fields appear in the dialog box, which allows you to specify two draft angles, above and below the neutral plane, respectively. On selecting the **Symmetric** option, the draft angle specified in the **Angle** field gets applied symmetrically above and below the neutral plane selected. Note that this drop-down list is available when a fixed plane or a fixed parting line is selected as the parting tool. You will learn about creating a draft by selecting a fixed parting line later in this chapter.

6. Specify the draft side by selecting the required option (**One Side**, **Two Side**, or **Symmetric**) in the **Draft Sides** drop-down list of the dialog box, as discussed above.

7. After specifying the required parameters, click on the **OK** button in the dialog box. A draft is created on the selected faces of the model.

Creating the Parting Line Draft

1. Invoke the **DRAFT** dialog box and then click on the **Parting Line** button in the **Type** area of the dialog box for creating a draft around the parting line, see Figure 10.74.

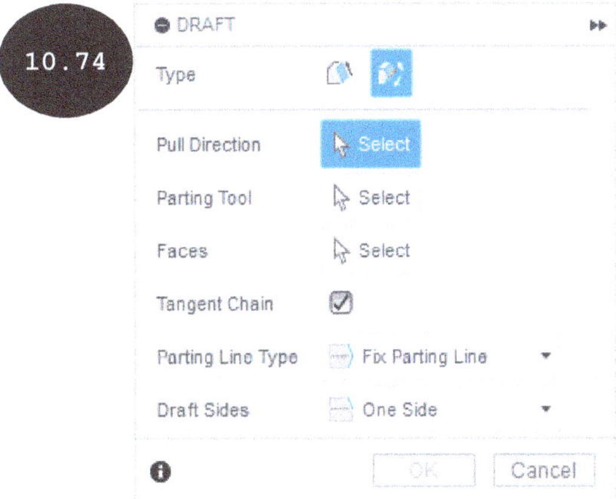

2. Select a plane or a planar face to define the pulling direction for adding a draft. An arrow appears on the selected face, pointing toward the pulling direction in the graphics area, see Figure 10.75. Also, the **Parting Tool** selection option gets activated in the dialog box.

   Parting Tool: The **Parting Tool** selection option is used to select a plane, a face, an edge, or a sketch curve on the solid body as a parting tool, see Figure 10.75.

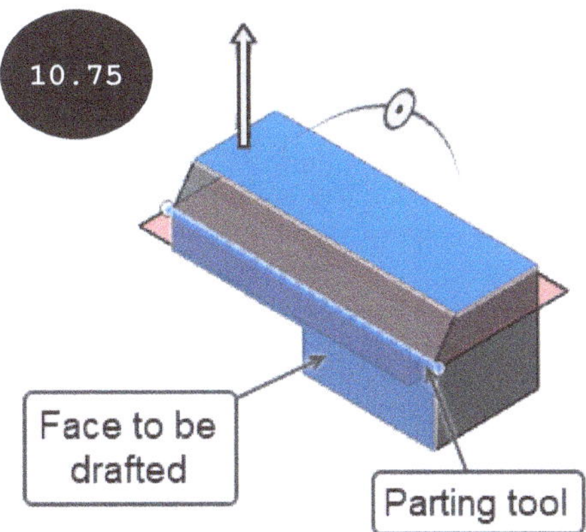

3. Select a plane, a face, an edge, or a sketch curve as the parting tool, refer to Figure 10.75. In this figure, a plane is selected as the parting line for creating the draft around it.

4. After selecting a parting line, click to activate the **Faces** selection option in the dialog box and then select one or more faces of the model for adding a draft.

5. Click on the **Flip Pull Direction** button to flip the direction of the pull, if necessary.

6. Specify the draft angle in the **Angle** field of the dialog box for adding draft on the selected faces of the model around the parting line. You can also drag the manipulator handle to specify the draft angle.

   Parting Line Type: By default, the **Fix Parting Line** option is selected in the **Parting Line Type** drop-down list of the dialog box. As a result, the position of the parting line gets fixed in place, as specified for applying the draft. On selecting the **Move Parting Line** option, the parting line position gets moved or changed for applying the draft.

7. Select the required option (**Fix Parting Line** or **Move Parting Line**) in the **Parting Line Type** drop-down list for creating the draft, as required.

8. Specify the draft side for applying the draft to one side, both sides or symmetrically around the parting line by selecting the required option in the **Draft Sides** drop-down list of the dialog box.

9. After specifying the required parameters, click on the **OK** button in the dialog box. A fixed parting line draft gets created.

Note: On selecting the **Move Parting Line** option in the **Parting Line Type** drop-down list, the **Direction** drop-down list and the **Fixed Edges** selection option appear in the dialog box. The options in the **Direction** drop-down list are used for maintaining the draft angle above, below, or on both sides of the parting line, respectively. The **Fixed Edges** selection option is used for selecting one or more edges of a model to remain fixed while the parting line gets moved to prevent deformation in the draft. Note that if the draft angle is set to a value other than 0 degree, then you need to press the CTRL key for selecting the fixed edges of the model.

Scaling Objects

In Autodesk Fusion, you can increase or decrease the scale of components, bodies, or sketch entities by using the **Scale** tool. The method for scaling an object (component, body, or sketch entity) is discussed below:

1. Invoke the **MODIFY** drop-down menu in the **SOLID** tab and then click on the **Scale** tool, see Figure 10.76. The **SCALE** dialog box appears, see Figure 10.77.

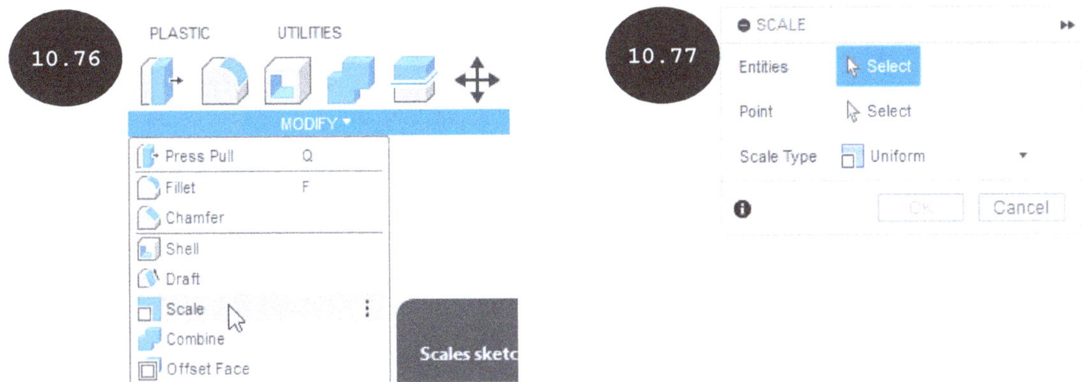

Entities: By default, the **Entities** selection option is activated in the dialog box. As a result, you can select components, bodies, or sketch entities as the objects to be scaled.

2. Select components, bodies, or sketch entities as the objects to be scaled in the graphics area.

Point: The **Point** selection option is used to specify a base point or center point for scaling the selected objects. Note that on selecting a body or a component to be scaled, a point on the selected object gets automatically selected as the base point. To specify a base point, as required, click on the **Point** selection option, and then click on the point to be selected as the base point for scaling the selected object.

3. Click on the **Point** selection option in the dialog box and then select a point in the graphics area as the base point, see Figure 10.78.

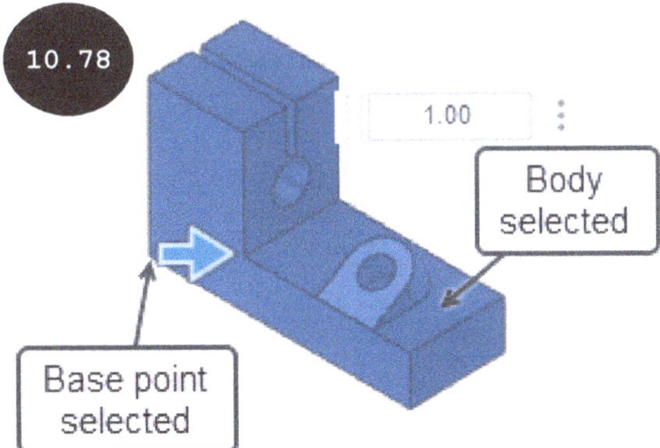

Scale Type: The **Scale Type** drop-down list of the dialog box is used to specify whether to scale the selected objects uniformly or non-uniformly about the base point. By default, the **Uniform** option is selected in this drop-down list. As a result, the selected objects get scaled uniformly in all directions about the base point as per the scale factor specified in the **Scale Factor** field of the dialog box. On selecting the **Non Uniform** option, you can specify different scale factors to scale the selected objects in the X, Y, and Z directions.

4. Select the required option (**Uniform** or **Non Uniform**) in the **Scale Type** drop-down list of the dialog box.

5. Enter the scale factor value in the **Scale Factor** field of the dialog box to scale the selected objects. You can also drag the arrow that appears in the graphics area to specify the scale factor, dynamically. Note that if the **Non Uniform** option is selected in the **Scale Type** drop-down list, then you can specify different scale factors in the **X Scale**, **Y Scale**, and **Z Scale** fields of the dialog box to scale the selected objects, non-uniformly in the X, Y, and Z directions.

6. Click on the **OK** button in the dialog box. The selected objects are scaled as per the specified scale factor.

Combining Solid Bodies

In Autodesk Fusion, you can combine solid bodies by performing boolean operations such as join, cut, or intersect between bodies by using the **Combine** tool. The method for combining solid bodies is discussed below:

1. Click on the **Combine** tool in the **MODIFY** panel of the **SOLID** tab, see Figure 10.79. The **COMBINE** dialog box appears, see Figure 10.80.

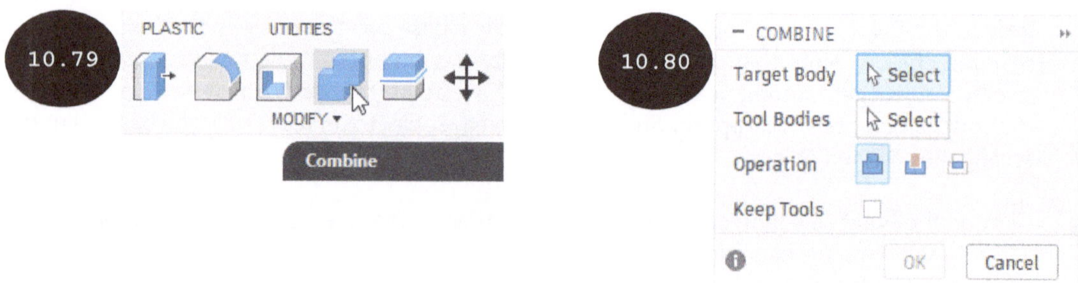

Target Body: The **Target Body** selection option is used to select a body or a component as the target body which undergoes the boolean operation.

2. Select a body or a component in the graphics area as the target body, see Figure 10.81. After selecting a target body, the **Tool Bodies** selection option gets activated in the dialog box.

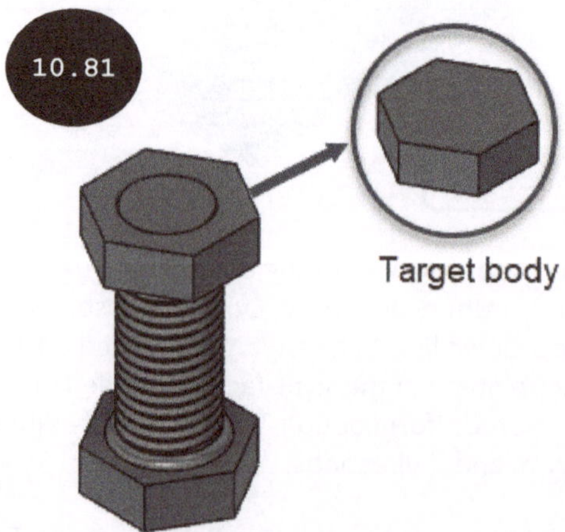

Tool Bodies: The **Tool Bodies** selection option is used to select one or more bodies as the tool bodies to guide the boolean operation to be performed on the target body selected.

3. Select one or more bodies as the tool bodies in the graphics area, see Figure 10.82. The preview of the boolean operation appears as per the default boolean operation selected in the **Operation** area of the dialog box, refer to Figure 10.83. This figure shows the preview of the boolean operation when the **Cut** button is activated in the **Operation** area of the dialog box.

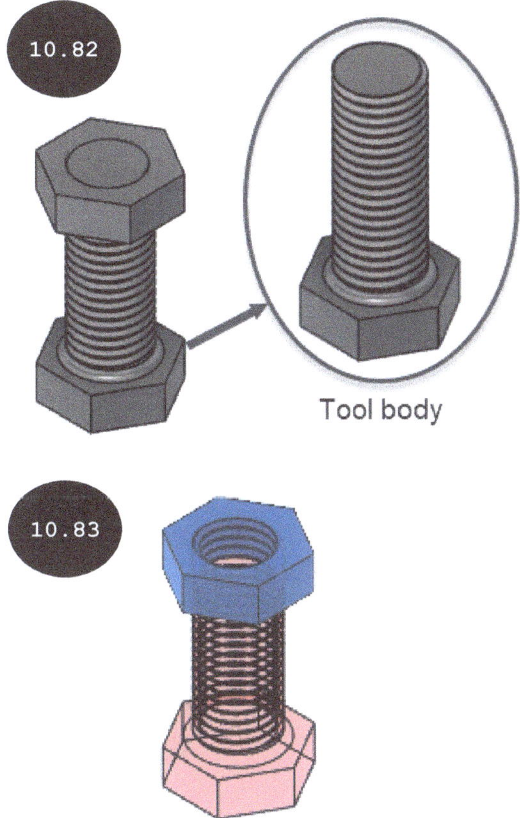

Operation: The options in the **Operation** area of the dialog box are used to select a boolean operation to be performed on the selected target body. On selecting the **Cut** button, the material gets removed from the target body. On selecting the **Join** button, the target body and the tool body get joined to each other and act as a single body. On selecting the **Intersect** button, the intersecting/common material between the target body and the tool body gets retained.

4. Select the required boolean operation in the **Operation** area of the dialog box.

Keep Tools: The **Keep Tools** check box is used to retain the tool body in the design after performing the boolean operation on the target body.

5. Select the **Keep Tools** check box in the dialog box to keep the tool body after performing the boolean operation on the target body, see Figure 10.84. To remove the tool body from the design,

clear this check box, see Figure 10.85. In Figure 10.85, the tool body is removed after performing the boolean operation on the target body as the **Keep Tools** check box is cleared.

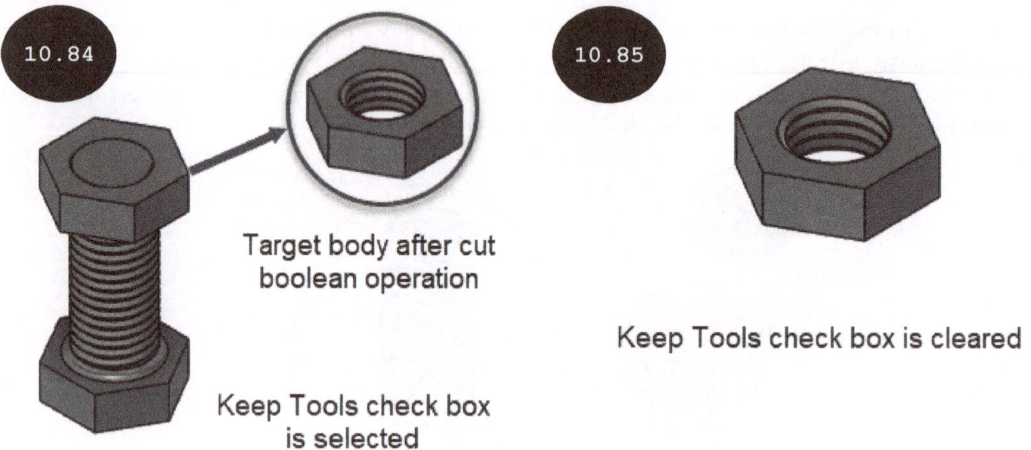

6. Click on the **OK** button in the dialog box. The selected solid bodies are combined by performing the selected boolean operation.

Offsetting Faces of a Model

In Autodesk Fusion, you can offset the selected face of a model at an offset distance using the **Offset Face** tool. The method for offsetting the faces of a model is discussed below:

1. Invoke the **MODIFY** drop-down menu in the **SOLID** tab and then click on the **Offset Face** tool, see Figure 10.86. The **OFFSET FACE** dialog box appears, see Figure 10.87.

Faces: By default, the **Faces** selection option is activated in the dialog box. As a result, you can select one or more faces to be offset.

2. Select one or more faces of the model to offset. The selected face gets highlighted, and an arrow appears in the graphics area, see Figure 10.88.

3. Drag the arrow that appears in the graphics area by pressing and holding the left mouse button to offset the selected face dynamically in the graphics area, see Figure 10.89. Alternatively, enter the offset distance in the **Distance** field of the **OFFSET FACE** dialog box. You can also enter an offset distance in the **Distance** field that appears in the graphics area. To reverse the offset direction, you need to drag the arrow to the other side of the selected face or enter a negative offset distance value in the **Distance** field.

4. After offsetting a face at an offset distance, click on the **OK** button in the dialog box.

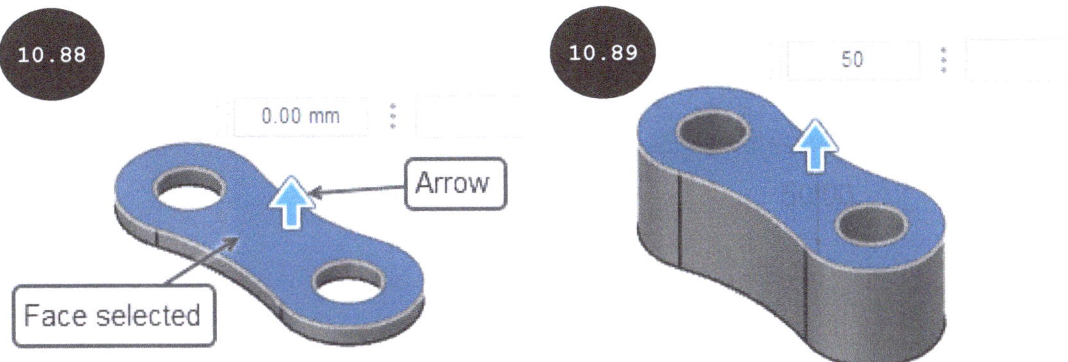

Splitting Faces of a Model

In Autodesk Fusion, you can split the faces of a model by selecting a splitting tool and manipulating each split face independently, see Figure 10.90. You can select a sketch, a plane, an edge, or a face as the splitting tool. In Figure 10.90, an open sketch is selected as the splitting tool and a draft is added to the top portion of the face after splitting it. You can split faces using the **Split Face** tool. The method for splitting faces is discussed next.

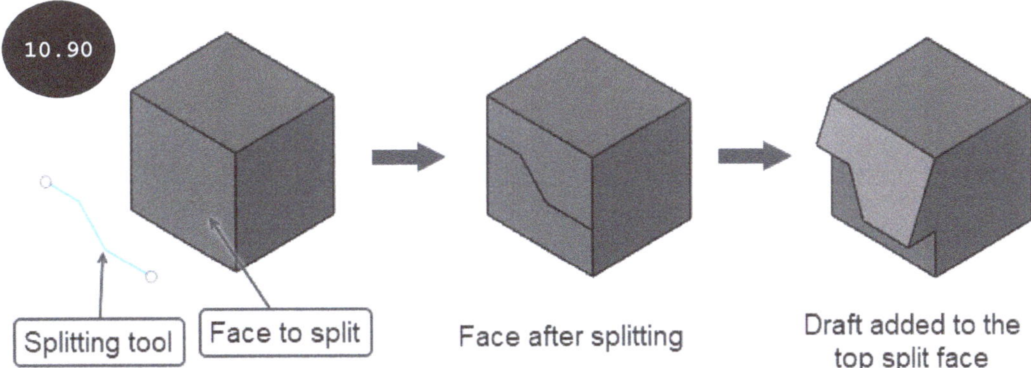

1. Invoke the **MODIFY** drop-down menu in the **SOLID** tab and then click on the **Split Face** tool, see Figure 10.91. The **SPLIT FACE** dialog box appears, see Figure 10.92.

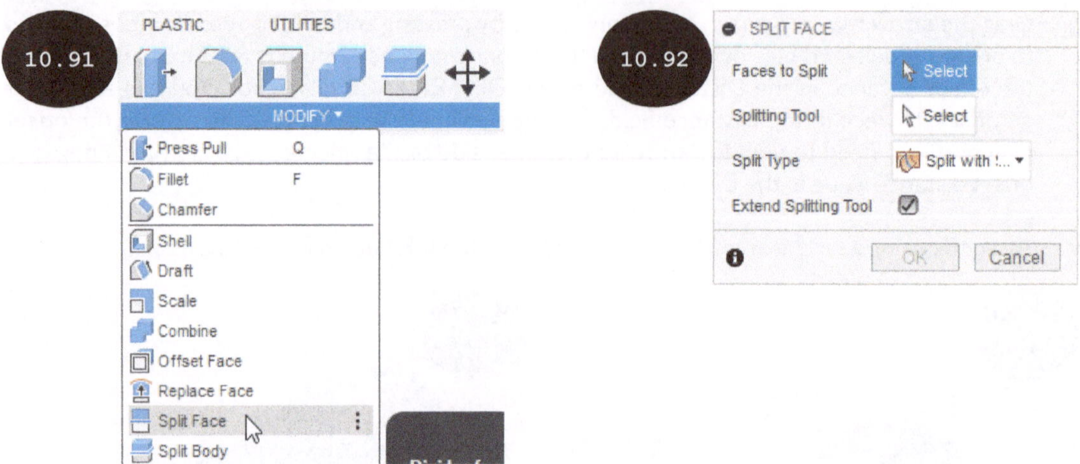

Faces to Split: By default, the **Faces to Split** selection option is activated in the dialog box. As a result, you can select one or more faces of the model to split.

2. Select one or more faces of the model to be split by clicking the left mouse button.

   Splitting Tool: The **Splitting Tool** selection option is used for selecting a splitting tool to split the selected face or faces of the model. You can select a face/surface, a plane, a sketch, or an edge as the splitting tool, see Figures 10.93 through 10.95. In Figure 10.93, a sketch is selected as the splitting tool. In Figure 10.94, a plane is selected as the splitting tool. In Figure 10.95, a surface is selected as the splitting tool.

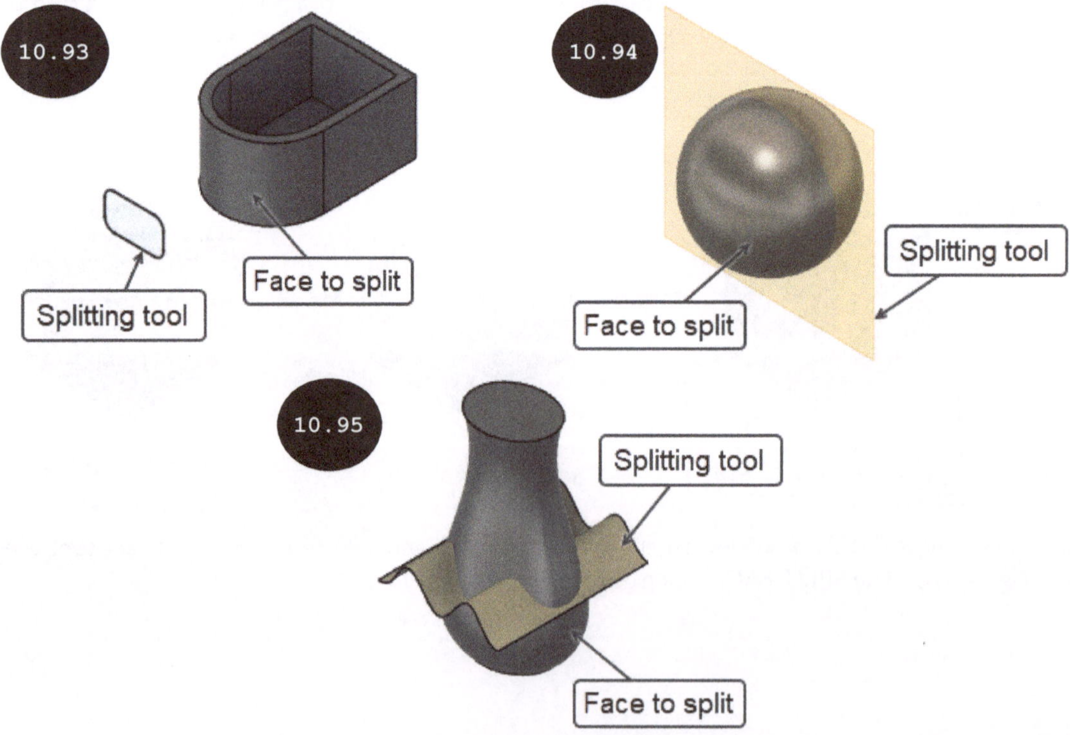

Note: In Autodesk Fusion, you can create surfaces or a surface model by using the tools in the **SURFACE** tab of the **DESIGN** workspace. Tools such as **Extrude** and **Revolve** in the **SURFACE** tab are same as discussed in the **SOLID** tab with the only difference that surface tools are used for creating surface models having zero thickness. To learn creating surface and T-Spline models, refer to "**Autodesk Fusion 360 Surface Design and Sculpting with T-Spline Surfaces (8th Edition)**" textbook by CADArtifex.

3. Click on the **Splitting Tool** selection option in the dialog box and then select a split tool in the graphics area, refer to Figures 10.96 through 10.98.

   Split Type: The **Split with Surface** option in the **Split Type** drop-down list of the dialog box is used for splitting the selected face by projecting the splitting tool on it. On selecting the **Along Vector** option, the **Project Direction** selection option appears in the dialog box, which is used for defining the direction of the projection to project the splitting tool on the selected face/faces. You can select an edge, face, plane, or axis to define the direction of the projection. On selecting the **Closest Point** option, the projection direction is defined as the closest distance between the splitting tool and the faces selected to split. Note that this drop-down list is not available on selecting a plane as the splitting tool.

4. Select the required option in the **Split Type** drop-down list of the dialog box.

   Extend Splitting Tool: The **Extend Splitting Tool** check box is used for extending the splitting tool so that it can completely intersect the faces selected to be split.

5. Select the **Extend Splitting Tool** check box in the dialog box, if needed.

6. Click on the **OK** button in the dialog box. The selected face/faces get split, see Figures 10.96 through 10.98.

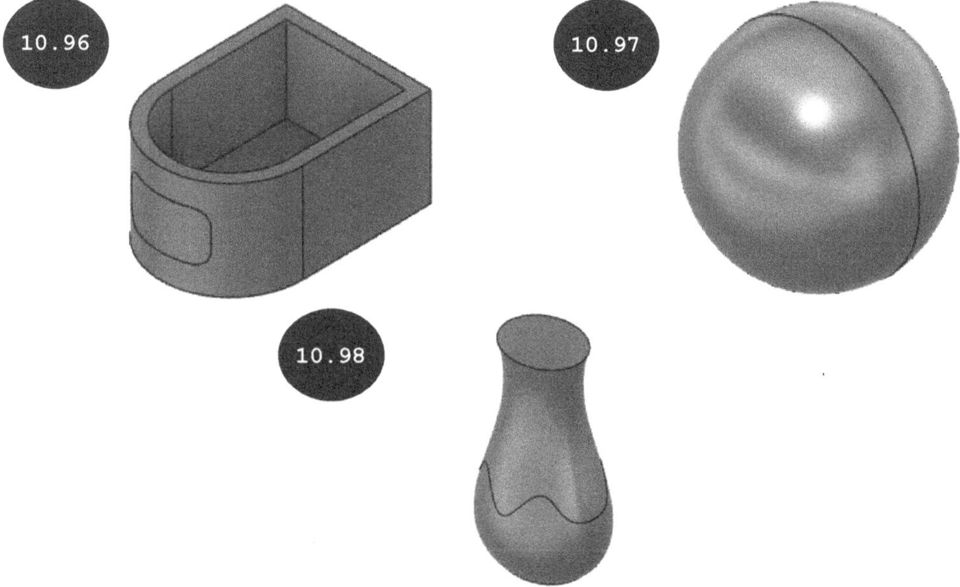

Note: In Figure 10.98, the visibility of splitting tool (surface) has been turned off after splitting the face.

Splitting Bodies

In Autodesk Fusion, you can split a body into multiple bodies by using the **Split Body** tool. The method for splitting one or more bodies is discussed below:

1. Click on the **Split Body** tool in the **MODIFY** panel of the **SOLID** tab. The **SPLIT BODY** dialog box appears, see Figure 10.99.

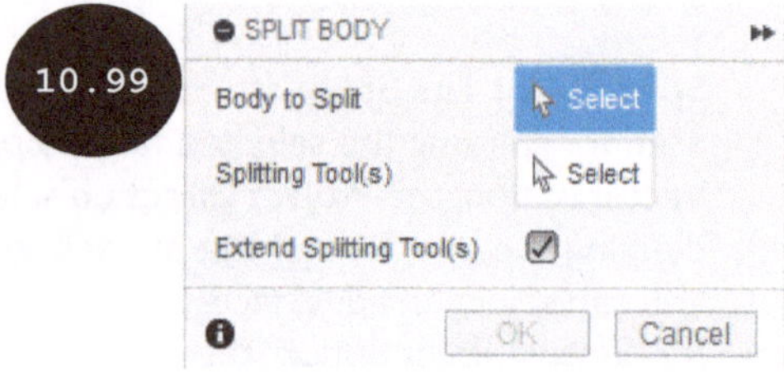

   Body to Split: By default, the **Body to Split** selection option is activated in the dialog box. As a result, you can select a body to be split into multiple bodies. You can select a single body or multiple bodies to be split.

2. Select one or more bodies to be split in the graphics area, see Figure 10.100.

   Splitting Tool(s): The **Splitting Tool(s)** selection option is used to select one or more splitting tools to split the selected body/bodies. You can select a surface, a plane, or a sketch as the splitting tool.

3. Click on the **Splitting Tool(s)** selection option in the dialog box and then select a splitting tool, see Figure 10.100. In this figure, a sketch is shown as the splitting tool. The preview appears in the graphics area by projecting the splitting tool on the body selected to split, see Figure 10.101.

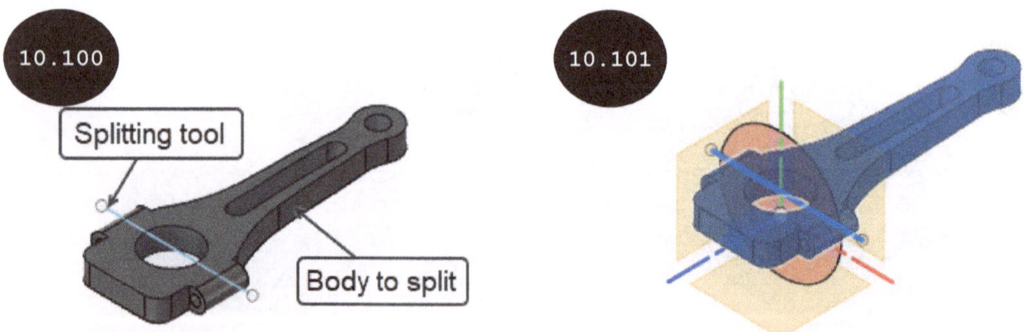

   Extend Splitting Tool(s): The **Extend Splitting Tool(s)** check box is used to extend the selected splitting tools so that they can completely intersect the selected body/bodies to split. In Figure 10.99, the **Extend Splitting Tool(s)** check box is selected.

4. Select the **Extend Splitting Tool(s)** check box in the dialog box, if needed.

5. Click on the **OK** button in the dialog box. The selected body is split into two bodies (see Figure 10.102) which are added as separate bodies in the **Bodies** node of the **BROWSER**, see Figure 10.103.

Tutorial 1

Create a model, as shown in Figure 10.104. All dimensions are in mm.

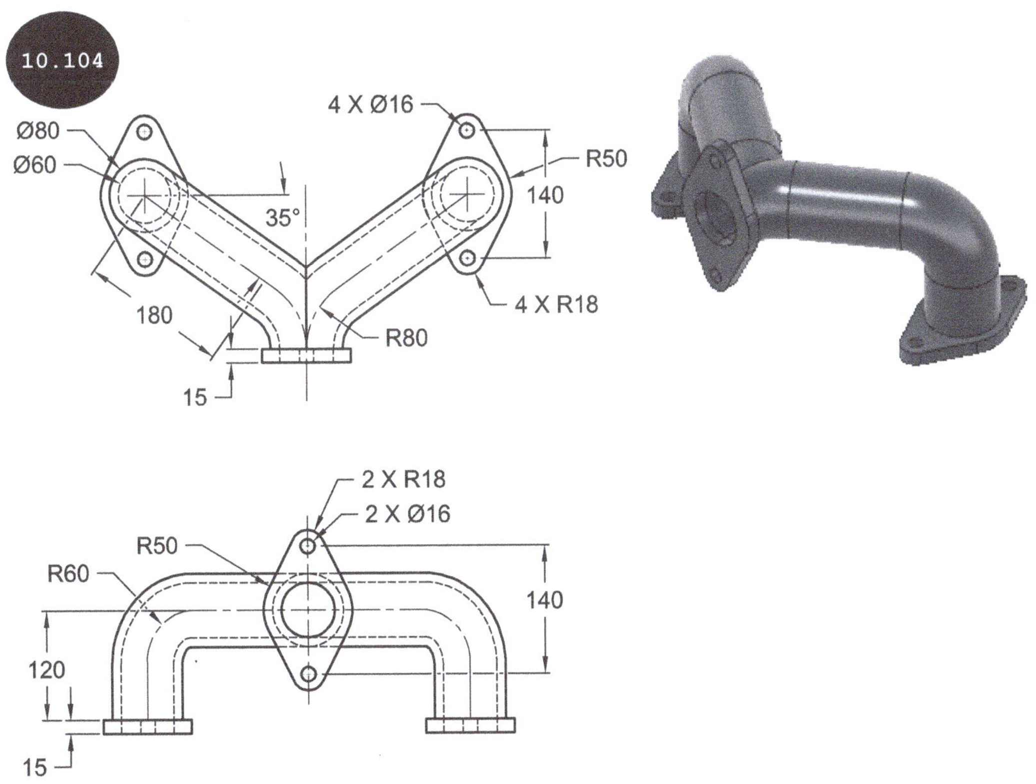

Section 1: Starting a New Part Design File

1. Click **File** > **New** in the **Application Bar** (see Figure 10.105) to display the **What do you want to design?** dialog box, see Figure 10.106.

10.105

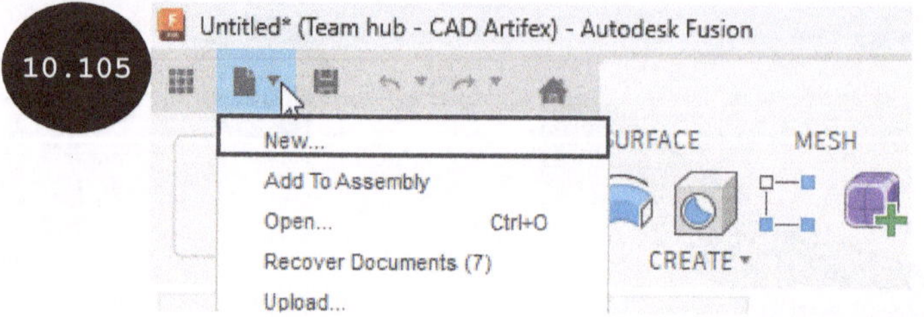

2. In this dialog box, choose the **Part Design** button and then select the **millimeter (mm), gram (g)** unit system from the **Unit System** drop-down list.

10.106

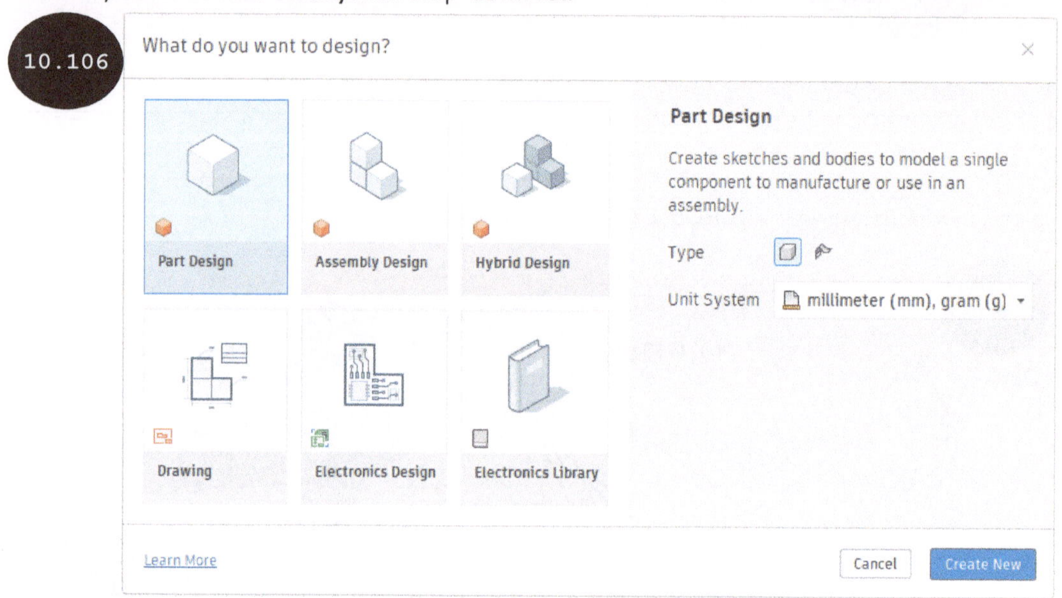

3. After specifying the required options, click the **Create New** button. A new Part Design file is created with the default name "**Untitled**".

Section 2: Creating the 3D Path - Sweep Feature

The base feature of the model is a sweep feature. To create this sweep feature, you need to first create a 3D sketch that serves as the path for the sweep.

1. Click on the **Create Sketch** tool in the **Toolbar** and then click on the Top plane as the sketching plane. The Sketching environment gets invoked.

2. Change the orientation to isometric by clicking on the **Home** icon of ViewCube.

3. Select the **3D Sketch** check box in the **SKETCH PALETTE** dialog box for creating a 3D sketch.

Tip: If the **3D Sketch** check box is selected in the **SKETCH PALETTE** dialog box, you can create a 3D sketch by using the sketching tools such as **Line** and **Spline**, whereas if this check box is cleared, you can create a 2D sketch in the Sketching environment.

4. Click on the **Line** tool in the **CREATE** panel of the **SKETCH** contextual tab or press the **L** key. The **Line** tool gets activated and the **3D Sketch Manipulator** appears at the origin (0,0) in the graphics area, see Figure 10.107. Also, the Top plane of the **3D Sketch Manipulator** is selected as the sketching plane, by default.

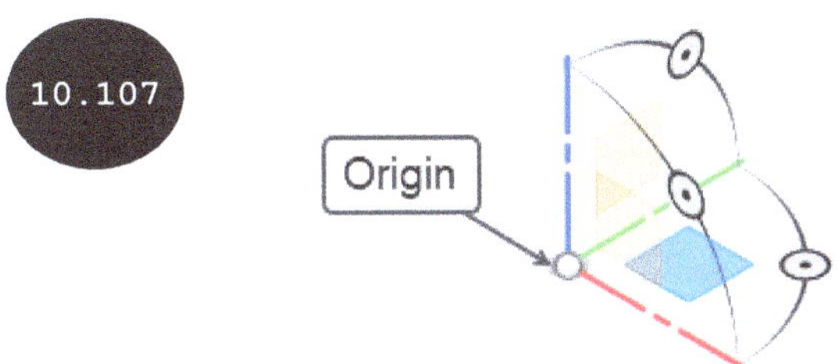

Note: You can switch from one sketching plane to another for creating a 3D sketch by clicking on the required plane (XY, YZ, or XZ) in the **3D Sketch Manipulator**.

5. Move the cursor toward the origin (0,0) and then click to specify the start point of the line when the cursor snaps to the origin.

6. Move the cursor vertically upward along an axis of the **3D Sketch Manipulator** to a distance. An extension line appears along the axis.

7. Enter **120** in the dimension box as the length of the line to be created, see Figure 10.108. The length of the line gets locked to 120 mm.

8. Click the left mouse button along the extension line that appears. A vertical line of length 120 mm gets created, see Figure 10.109. Also, the origin of the **3D Sketch Manipulator** gets shifted to the last specified point in the graphics area and a rubber band line appears attached to the cursor, see Figure 10.108.

9. Ensure that the Top plane is selected in the **3D Sketch Manipulator** as the sketching plane.

10. Move the cursor at an angle to the X-axis in the graphics area, see Figure 10.109. Next, enter **180** as the length of the line in the dimension box that appears in the graphics area, see Figure 10.109. The length of the line gets locked on the current sketching plane.

11. After specifying the length of the line, press the TAB key to switch to the next dimension box in the graphics area and then enter **35** as the angle of the line in the dimension box. The length and angle of the line get locked, see Figure 10.109.

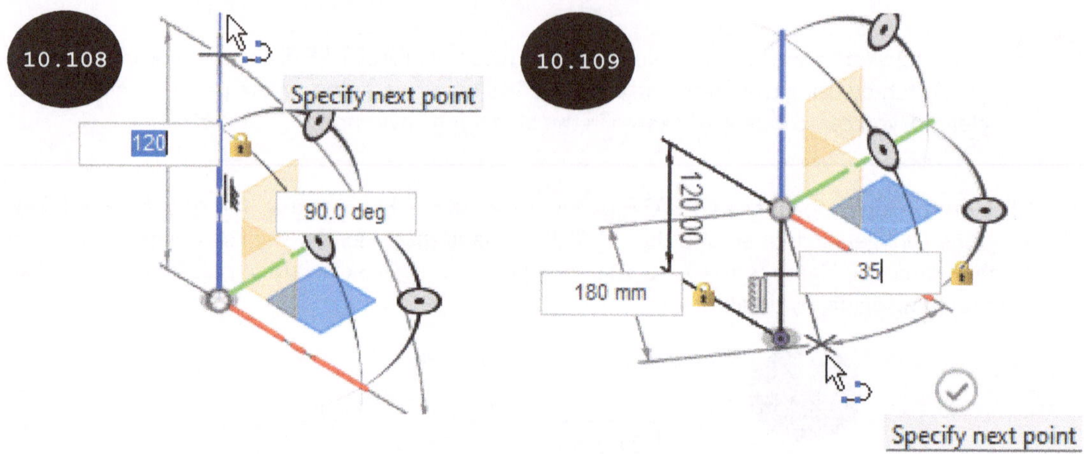

12. Click to specify the endpoint of the line. A second line of length 180 mm and angle 35 degrees from the X-axis is created. Also, the origin of the **3D Sketch Manipulator** gets shifted to the last specified point and a rubber band line appears attached to the cursor, see Figure 10.110.

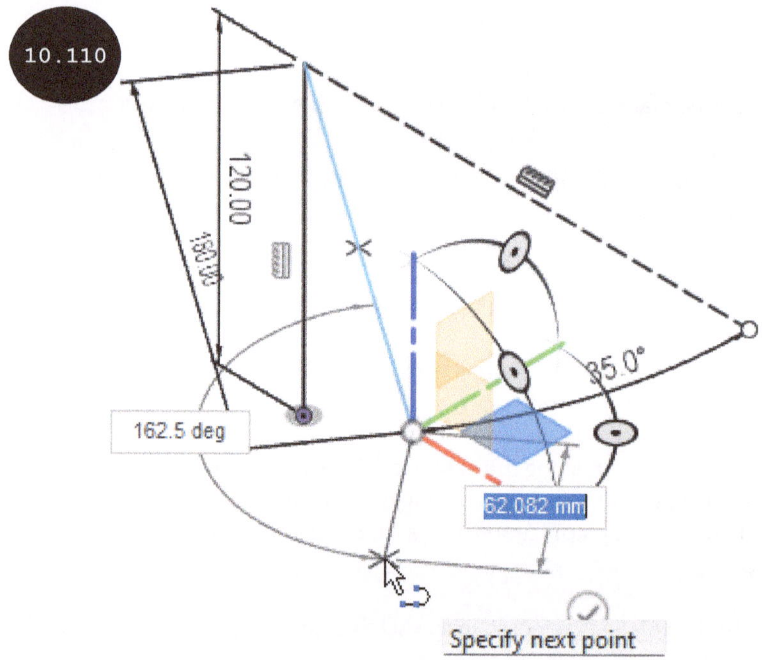

13. Press the ESC key to exit the **Line** tool.

    Now, you need to create a tangent arc.

14. Invoke the **CREATE** drop-down menu and then click on **Arc** > **Tangent Arc**, see Figure 10.111. The **Tangent Arc** tool gets activated and you are prompted to specify the start point.

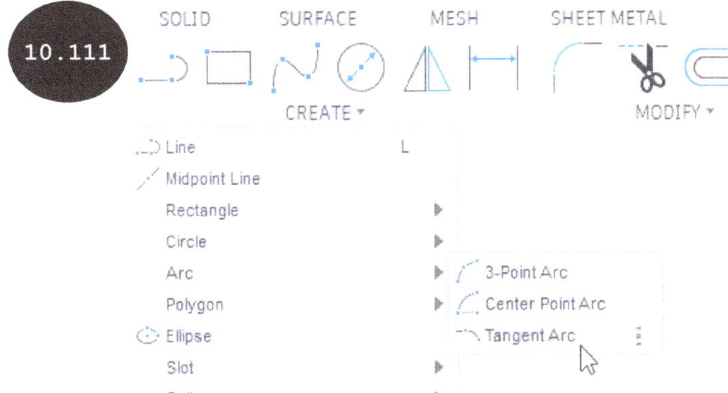

15. Click to specify the start point of the tangent arc at the endpoint of the previously created line, see Figure 10.112. The **3D Sketch Manipulator** appears at the specified start point.

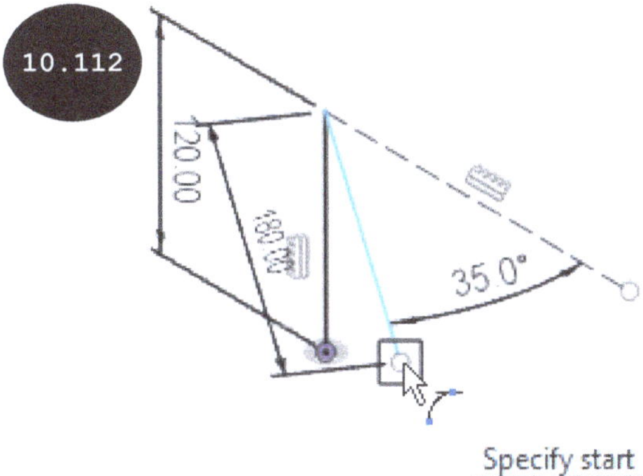

16. Ensure that the Top plane is selected in the **3D Sketch Manipulator** as the sketching plane.

17. Move the cursor to a distance. A preview of an arc tangent to the line appears.

18. Enter **80** as the radius of the tangent arc in the dimension box that appears, (see Figure 10.113) and then click anywhere in the graphics area to specify the endpoint of the arc. A tangent arc is created, see Figure 10.114. Next, press the ESC key to exit the **Tangent Arc** tool.

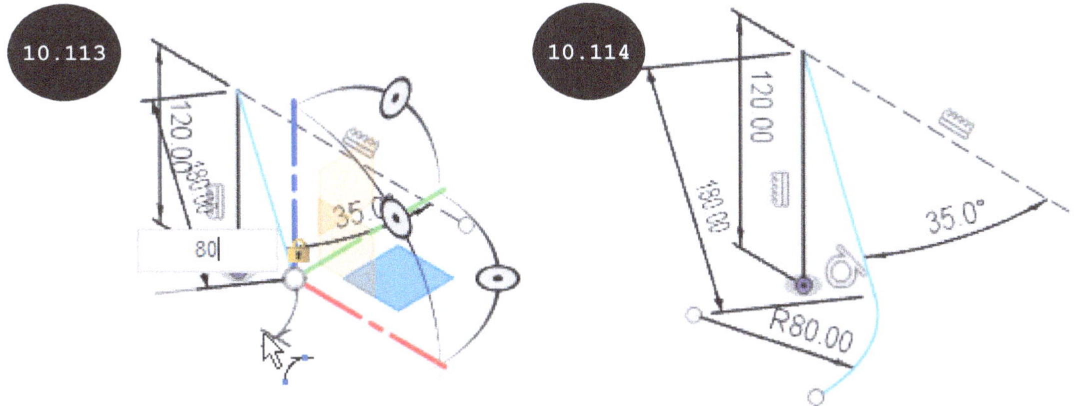

Now, you need to apply a horizontal constraint between the center point and the endpoint of the tangent arc.

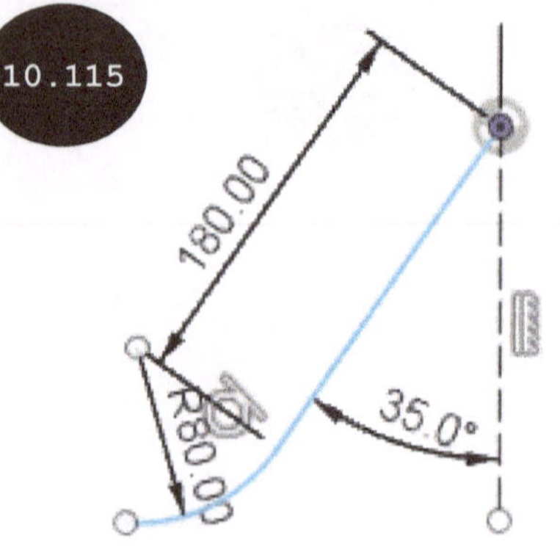

19. Change the current orientation of the sketch to the top view by clicking on the TOP face of ViewCube, see Figure 10.115.

    Now, you can apply constraints to the entities.

20. Click on the **Horizontal/Vertical** tool in the **CONSTRAINTS** panel of the **SKETCH** contextual tab, see Figure 10.116.

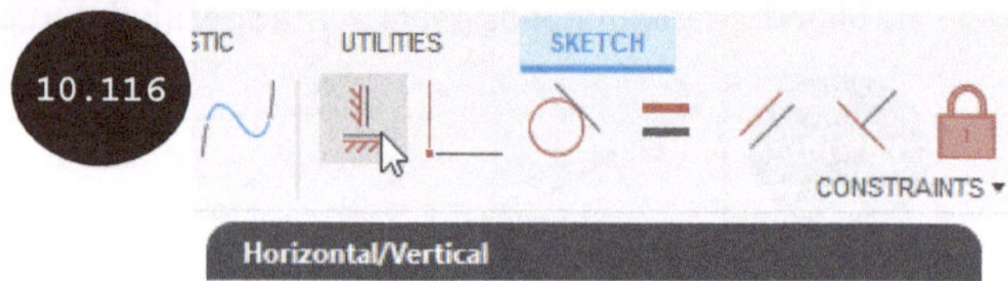

21. Click on the center point of the tangent arc and then its endpoint, see Figure 10.117. The center point and the endpoint of the tangent arc become aligned with each other. Change the orientation to isometric.

    Now, you need to add the fillet at the corner of the sketch.

22. Click on the **Fillet** tool in the **MODIFY** panel in the **SKETCH** contextual tab.

23. Click on the vertical line of the sketch as the first entity and then click on the inclined line of length 180 mm as the second entity to create the fillet. The preview of the fillet appears at the vertex of the selected entities, see Figure 10.118.

24. Enter **60** as the radius of the fillet in the **Fillet radius** field that appears, see Figure 10.118.

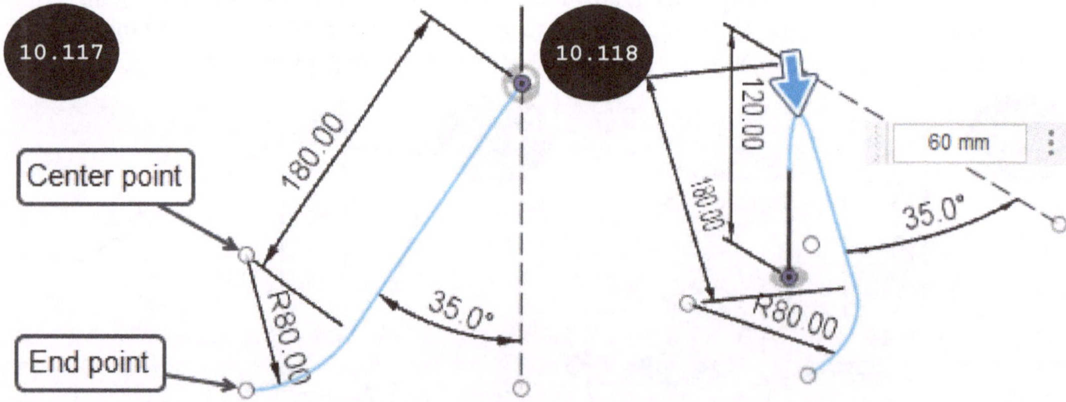

25. Press ENTER to create the fillet and exit the **Fillet** tool.

26. Apply the perpendicular constraint between vertical and horizontal line entities, see Figure 10.119.

27. If needed, apply the horizontal constraint between the endpoint of the sketch (arc entity) and the construction line to make the sketch fully defined, see Figure 10.120.

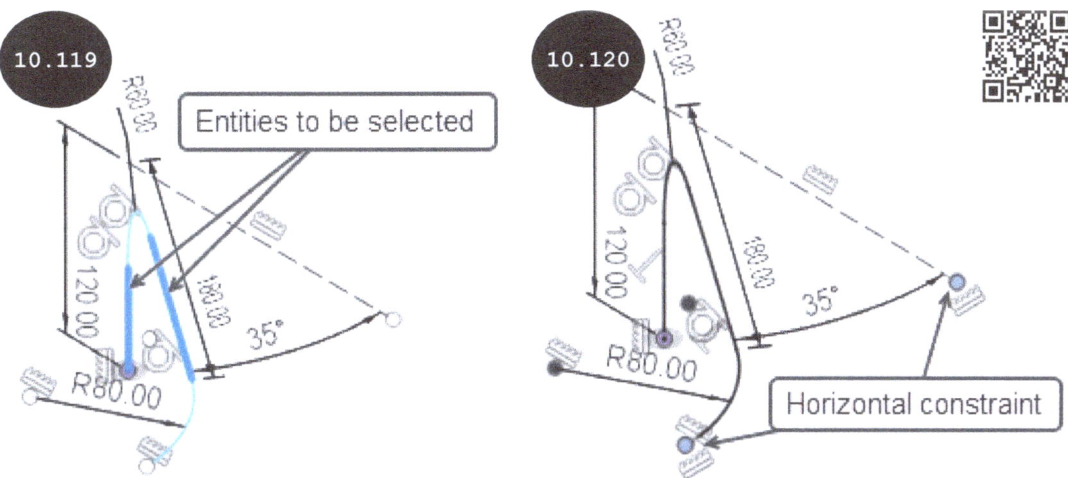

28. Click on the **FINISH SKETCH** tool in the **SKETCH** contextual tab to finish the creation of the sketch. The 3D sketch is drawn, see Figure 10.121.

Section 3: Creating the Profile - Sweep Feature

After creating the path of the sweep feature, you need to create the profile.

1. Click on the **Create Sketch** tool in the **Toolbar** and then select the Top plane as the sketching plane. The Sketching environment gets invoked and the **SKETCH PALETTE** dialog box appears.

2. Ensure that the **3D Sketch** check box is cleared in the **SKETCH PALETTE** dialog box for creating a 2D sketch.

3. Click on the **Look At** tool in the **SKETCH PALETTE** dialog box to orient the current sketching plane normal to the viewing direction.

4. Create a circle of diameter 80 mm as the profile of the sweep feature, see Figure 10.122. Note that the center point of the circle is at the origin.

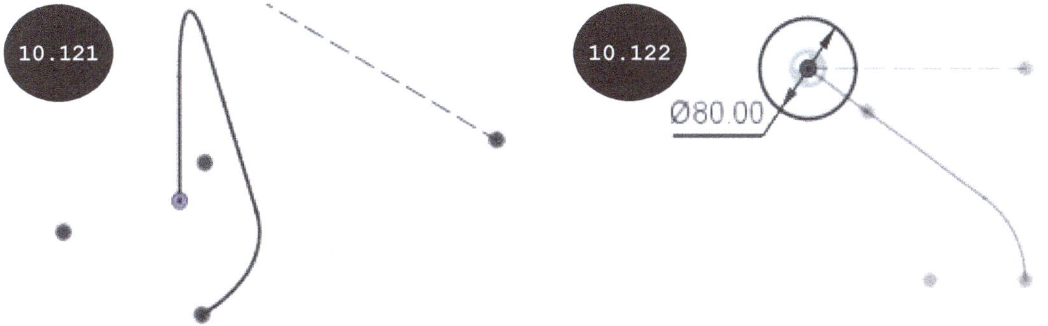

5. Click on the **FINISH SKETCH** tool in the **SKETCH** contextual tab and then change the orientation of the sketch to isometric.

Section 4: Creating the Base Feature - Sweep Feature

After creating the path and profile of the sweep feature, you can create the sweep feature.

1. Click on the **SOLID** tab in the **Toolbar** to display the solid modeling tools.

2. Invoke the **CREATE** drop-down menu in the **SOLID** tab and then click on the **Sweep** tool. The **SWEEP** dialog box appears.

3. Ensure that the **Single Path** option is selected in the **Type** drop-down list of the dialog box.

4. Select the profile of the sweep feature in the graphics area, see Figure 10.123.

5. Ensure that the **Chain Selection** check box is selected in the dialog box.

6. Click on the **Path** selection option and select the path of the sweep feature in the graphics area. The preview of the sweep feature appears, see Figure 10.123.

7. Ensure that the **Perpendicular** option is selected in the **Orientation** drop-down list.

8. Ensure that the **New Body** option is selected in the **Operation** drop-down list of the dialog box.

9. Click on the **OK** button in the dialog box. The sweep feature is created, see Figure 10.124.

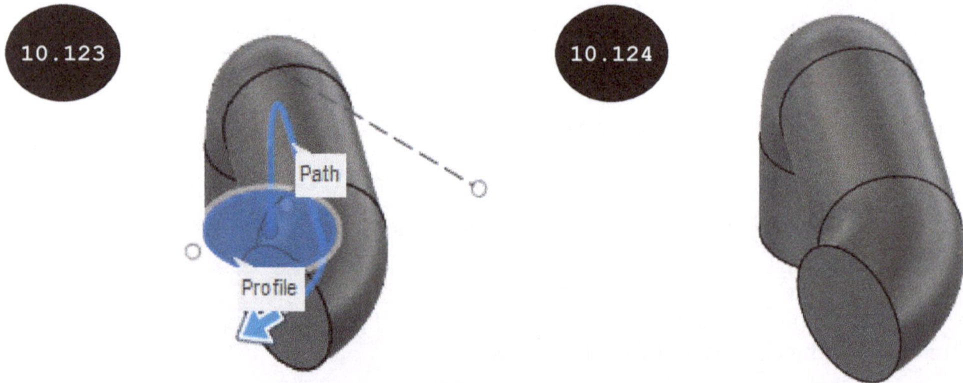

Section 5: Creating the Second Feature - Mirror Feature

The second feature of the model can be created by mirroring the first feature about a construction plane, which passes through the center of the end circular face of the first feature and is parallel to the Right plane. To create this construction plane, you need to first create a construction point at the center of the end circular face of the first feature.

1. Invoke the **CONSTRUCT** drop-down menu in the **SOLID** tab and then click on the **Point at Center of Circle/Sphere/Torus** tool. The **CONSTRUCTION GEOMETRY** dialog box appears in the graphics area.

2. Select the circular edge of the sweep feature, see Figure 10.125. The construction point at the center of the selected circular edge is created, see Figure 10.126.

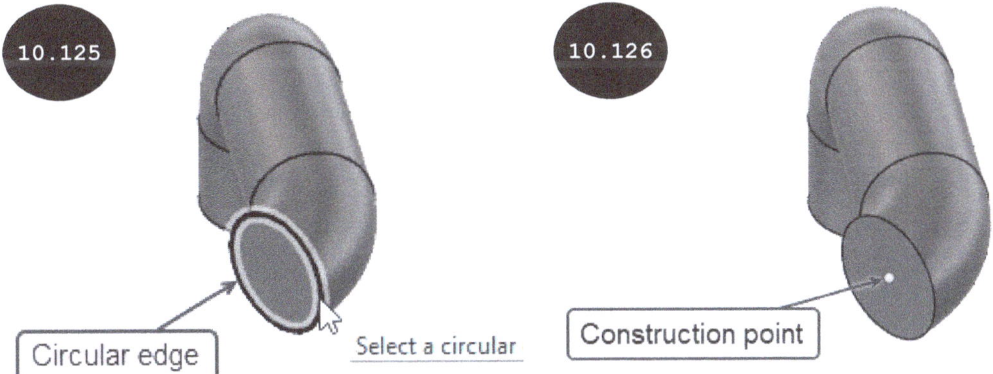

3. Click on the **OK** button in the dialog box.

   After creating the construction point, you can create the construction plane passing through it and parallel to the Right plane.

4. Click on the **Offset Plane** tool in the **CONSTRUCT** panel in the **SOLID** tab. The **CONSTRUCTION GEOMETRY** dialog box appears.

5. Expand the **Origin** node in the **BROWSER**, click on the **YZ** plane (Right plane) as the reference plane, and then click on the construction point created at the center of the circular face of the sweep feature. The preview of the construction plane passing through the construction point and parallel to the Right plane appears in the graphics area, see Figure 10.127.

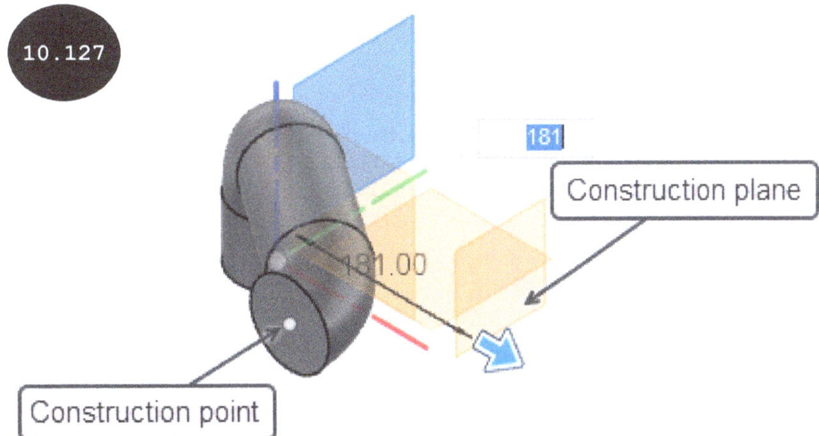

6. Click on the **OK** button in the dialog box. The construction plane is created.

   After creating the construction plane, you need to mirror the first feature (sweep).

7. Invoke the **CREATE** drop-down menu in the **SOLID** tab and then click on the **Mirror** tool. The **MIRROR** dialog box appears in the graphics area.

8. Select the **Features** option in the **Object Type** drop-down list of the dialog box.

9. Click on the **Sweep1** feature in the **Timeline** as the feature to be mirrored, see Figure 10.128.

10. Click on the **Mirror Plane** selection option in the dialog box and then select the newly created construction plane as the mirroring plane in the graphics area. The preview of the mirror feature appears, see Figure 10.129.

11. Click on the **OK** button in the **MIRROR** dialog box. The mirror feature is created, see Figure 10.130.

12. Hide the construction geometries by clicking on the **Show/Hide** icon in front of the **Construction** node in the **BROWSER**. In Figure 10.130, the construction geometries are hidden.

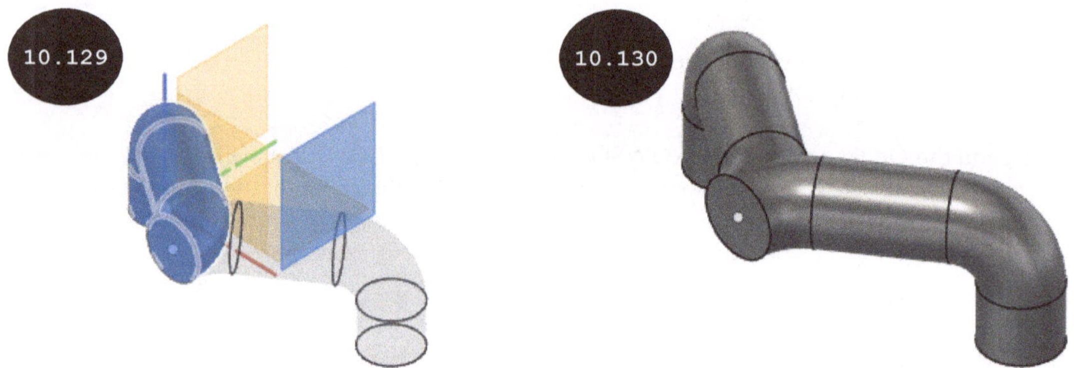

Section 6: Creating the Third Feature - Combine Feature

Notice that the newly created mirror feature is created as a new body. As a result, in the **Bodies** node of the **BROWSER**, two separate bodies (**Body1** and **Body2**) are listed. You need to merge these bodies to make a single body.

1. Click on the **Combine** tool in the **MODIFY** panel in the **SOLID** tab. The **COMBINE** dialog box appears, see Figure 10.131.

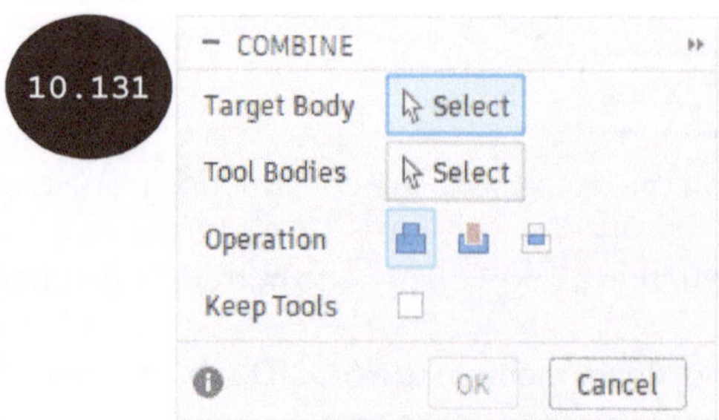

2. Select the base sweep feature as the target body and the mirror feature as the tool body in the graphics area one by one.

3. Ensure that the **Join** button is selected in the **Operation** area of the dialog box as the boolean operation to be performed on the selected bodies.

4. Ensure that the **New Component** and **Keep Tools** check boxes are cleared in the dialog box.

5. Click on the **OK** button in the dialog box. Both the selected bodies get merged and form a single body.

Section 7: Creating the Fourth Feature - Shell Feature

1. Click on the **Shell** tool in the **MODIFY** panel in the **SOLID** tab, see Figure 10.132. The **SHELL** dialog box appears, see Figure 10.133.

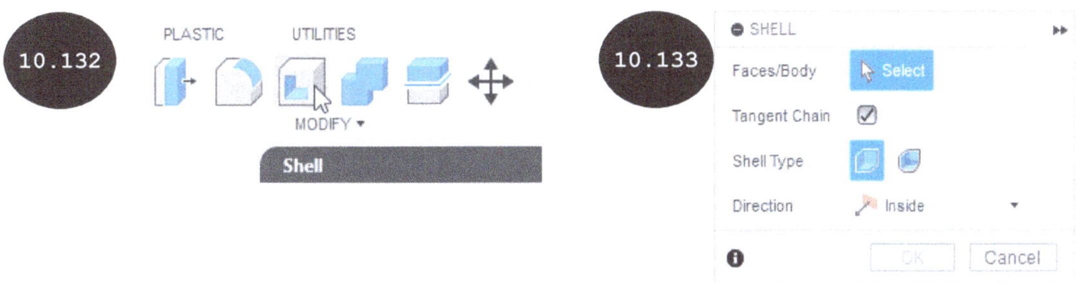

2. Click on the three circular end faces of the model as the faces to be removed, see Figure 10.134.

3. Ensure that the **Inside** option is selected in the **Direction** drop-down list of the dialog box to add thickness inside the model.

4. Enter **10** in the **Inside Thickness** field of the dialog box.

5. Click on the **OK** button in the dialog box. The shell feature of specified thickness is created by removing the selected faces of the model, see Figure 10.135.

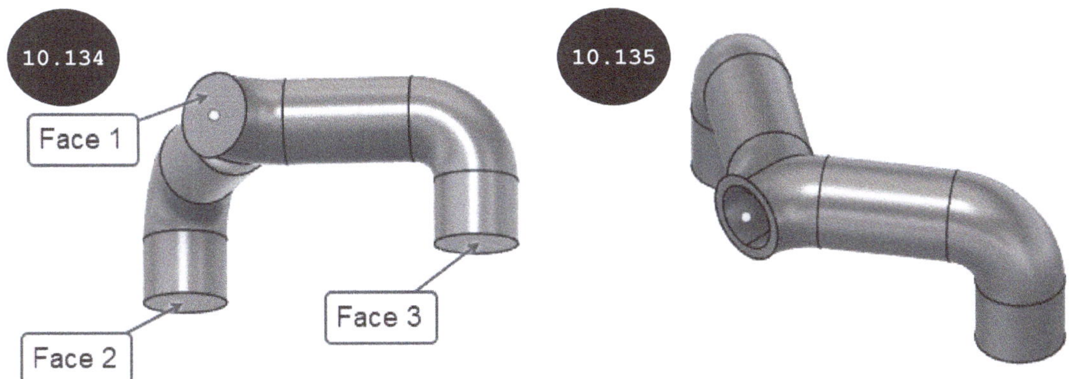

Section 8: Creating the Fifth Feature - Extrude Feature

1. Click on the **Create Sketch** tool in the **Toolbar** and select the Top plane as the sketching plane.

2. Create the sketch of the fifth feature (extrude feature), see Figure 10.136.

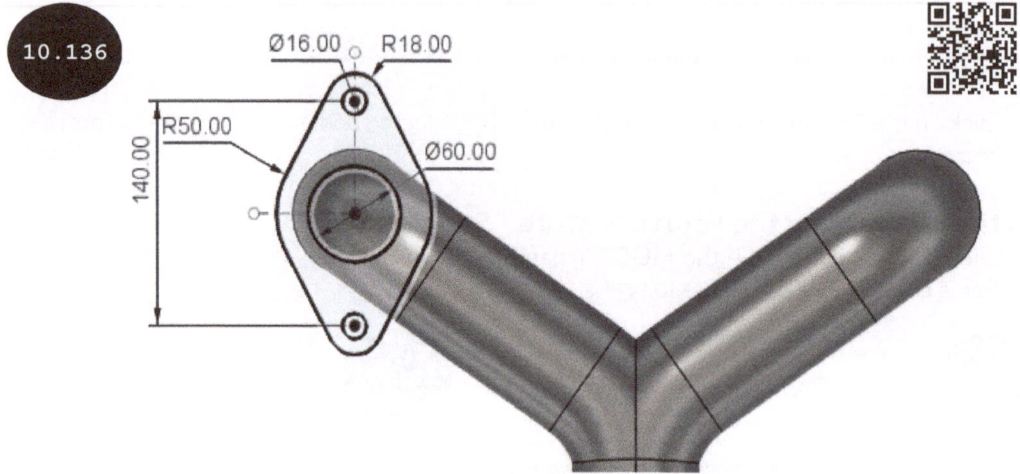

Note: The sketch of the fifth feature shown in Figure 10.136 has been fully defined by applying the required dimensions and constraints. You need to apply tangent constraints between each set of connected line and arc entities of the sketch. You also need to apply the symmetric relation between the center points of the upper and lower arcs of the sketch to the horizontal construction line. Besides, you need to apply equal relation between the upper and lower arcs of the sketch.

3. Click on the **SOLID** tab in the **Toolbar** to display the solid modeling tools.

4. Click on the **Extrude** tool in the **CREATE** panel in the **SOLID** tab or press the E key. The **EXTRUDE** dialog box appears in the graphics area. Next, change the orientation of the model to isometric.

5. Select the closed profile of the sketch in the graphics area, see Figure 10.137.

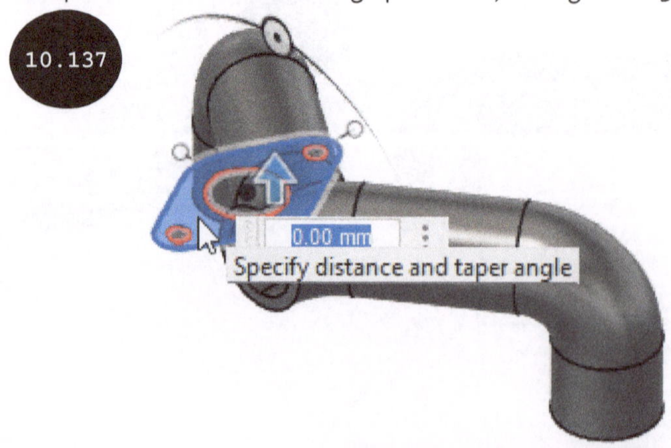

6. Ensure that the **One Side** option is selected in the **Direction** drop-down list of the dialog box.

7. Ensure that the **Distance** option is selected in the **Extent Type** drop-down list of the dialog box.

8. Enter **-15** in the **Distance** field of the dialog box as the extrusion distance. Note that the negative value is used for reversing the direction of extrusion to the downward direction, see Figure 10.138.

9. Ensure that the **Join** option is selected in the **Operation** drop-down list of the dialog box.

10. Click on the **OK** button in the dialog box. The extrude feature is created, see Figure 10.139.

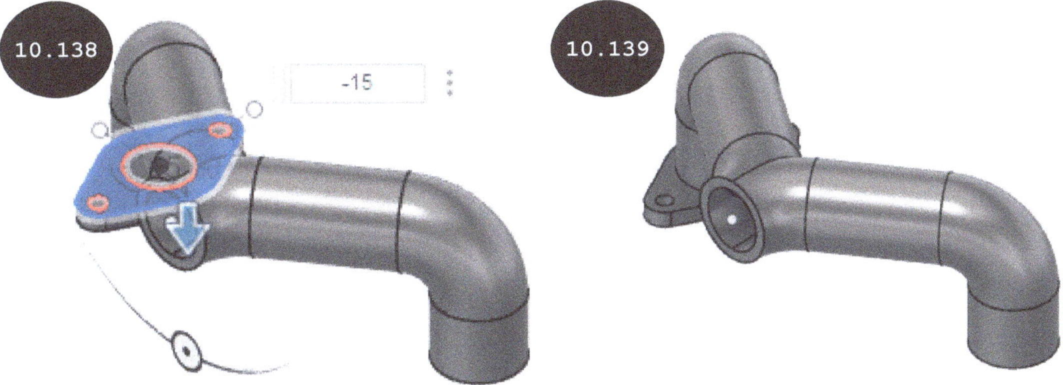

Section 9: Creating the Sixth Feature - Mirror Feature

1. Invoke the CREATE drop-down menu in the SOLID tab and then click on the **Mirror** tool. The MIRROR dialog box appears in the graphics area.

2. Select the **Features** option in the **Type** drop-down list of the dialog box.

3. Click on the previously created extrude feature (**Extrude1**) in the **Timeline** as the feature to be mirrored, see Figure 10.140.

4. Click on the **Mirror Plane** selection option in the dialog box and then select the construction plane (**Plane1**) in the expanded **Construction** node of the **BROWSER**, see Figure 10.141.

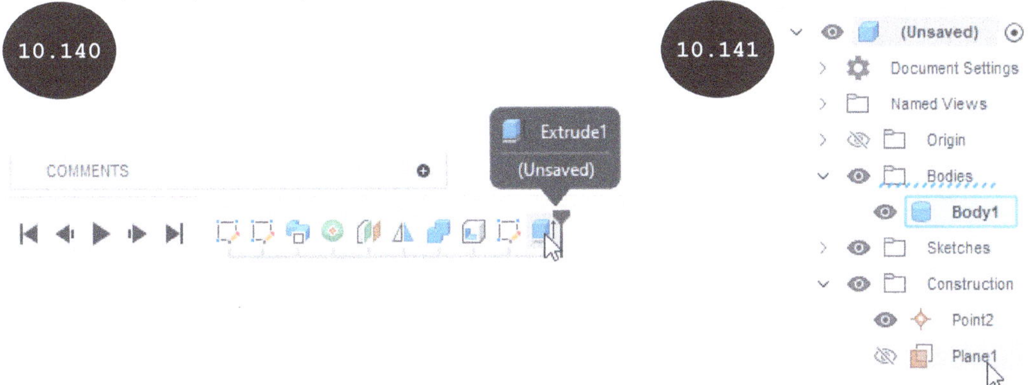

5. Ensure that the **Adjust** option is selected in the **Compute Type** drop-down list of the dialog box.

6. Click on the **OK** button in the dialog box. The mirror feature is created, see Figure 10.142.

Section 10: Creating the Seventh Feature - Extrude Feature

1. Click on the **Create Sketch** tool in the **Toolbar** and then select the front planar face of the model as the sketching plane, see Figure 10.143.

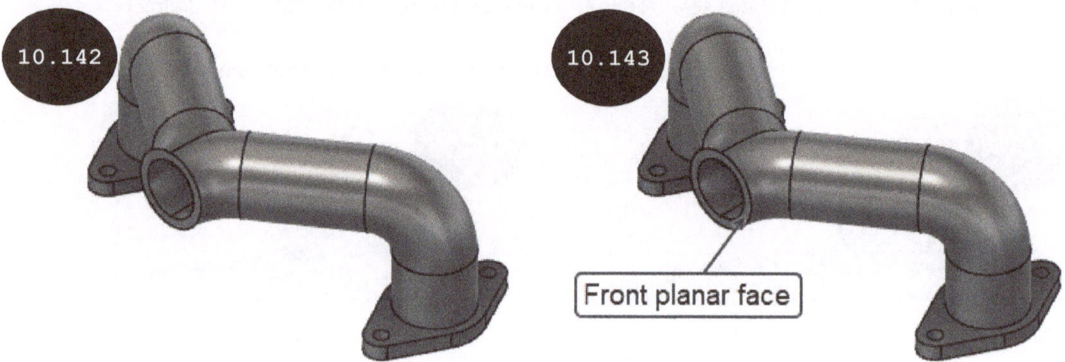

2. Create the sketch of the seventh feature (extrude feature), see Figure 10.144.

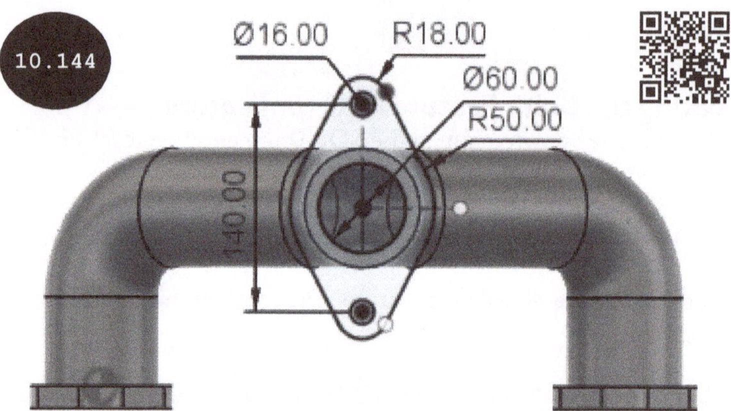

3. Click on the **SOLID** tab in the **Toolbar** and then click on the **Extrude** tool or press the **E** key. The **EXTRUDE** dialog box appears. Next, change the orientation of the model to isometric.

4. Select the two closed profiles of the sketch in the graphics area, see Figure 10.145.

5. Ensure that the **One Side** option is selected in the **Direction** drop-down list of the dialog box.

6. Ensure that the **Distance** option is selected in the **Extent Type** drop-down list of the dialog box.

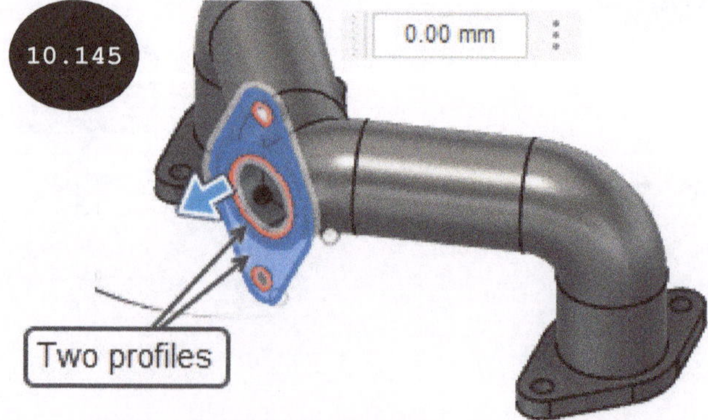

7. Enter **15** in the **Distance** field of the dialog box as the extrusion distance. The preview of the extrude feature appears, see Figure 10.146.

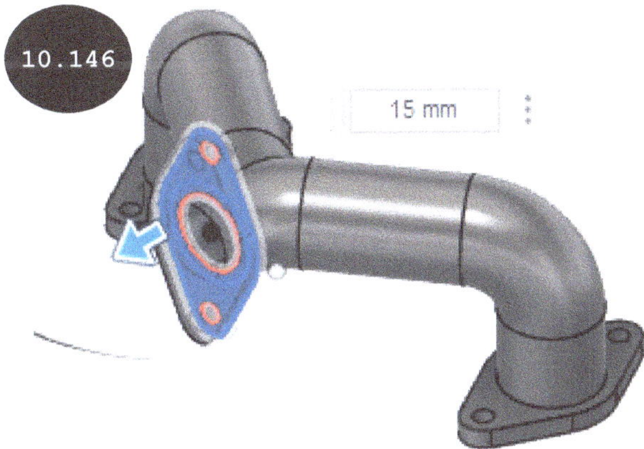

8. Ensure that the **Join** option is selected in the **Operation** drop-down list of the dialog box.

9. Click on the **OK** button in the dialog box. The extrude feature is created, see Figure 10.147.

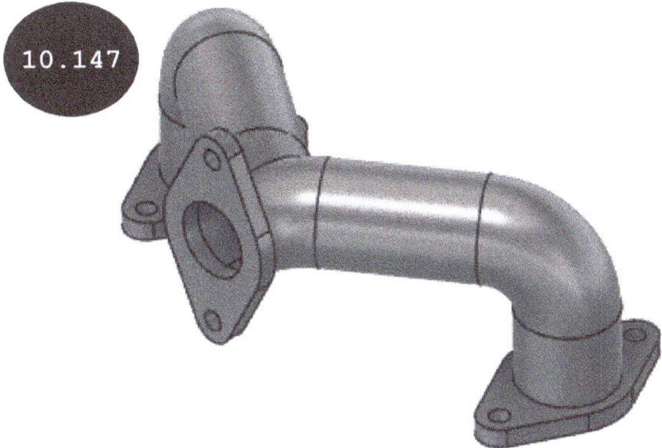

Section 11: Saving the Model

1. Click on the **Save** tool in the **Application Bar**. The **Save** dialog box appears.

2. Enter **Tutorial 1** in the **Name** field of the dialog box.

3. Ensure that the location ***Autodesk Fusion 360 > Chapter 10 > Tutorial 1*** is specified in the **Location** field of the dialog box to save the file of this tutorial. Note that you need to create these folders in the **Data Panel**, if not created earlier.

4. Click on the **Save** button in the dialog box. The model is saved with the name Tutorial 1 in the specified location (***Autodesk Fusion 360 > Chapter 10 > Tutorial 1***).

Tutorial 2

Create a model, as shown in Figure 10.148. All dimensions are in mm.

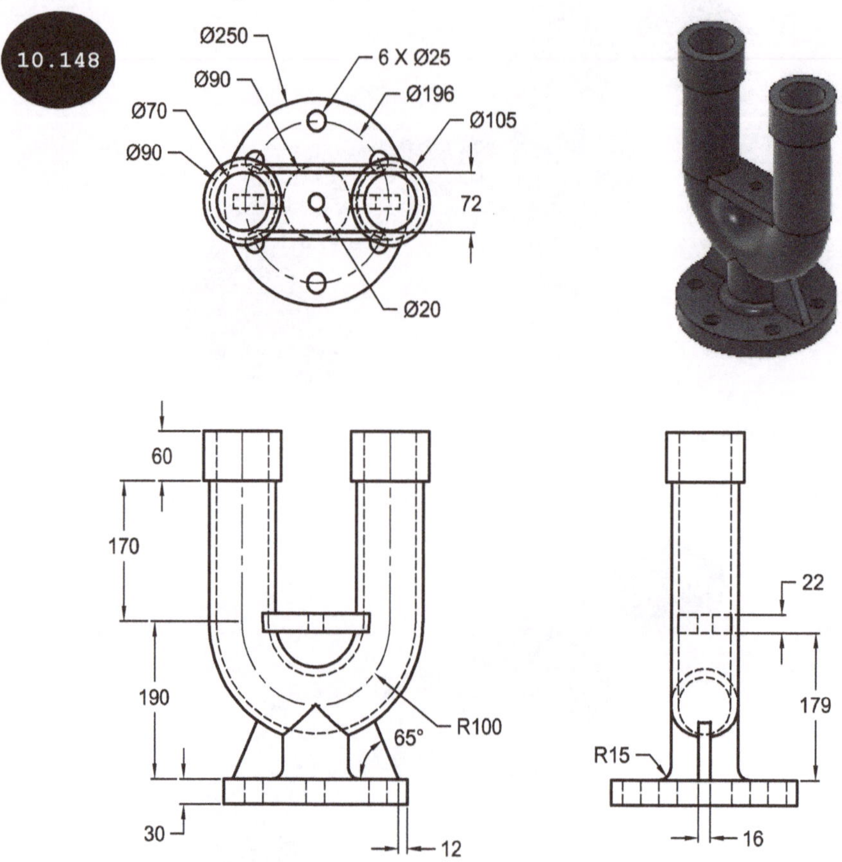

Section 1: Starting a New Design File

1. Click **File** > **New** in the **Application Bar** (see Figure 10.149) to display the **What do you want to design?** dialog box.

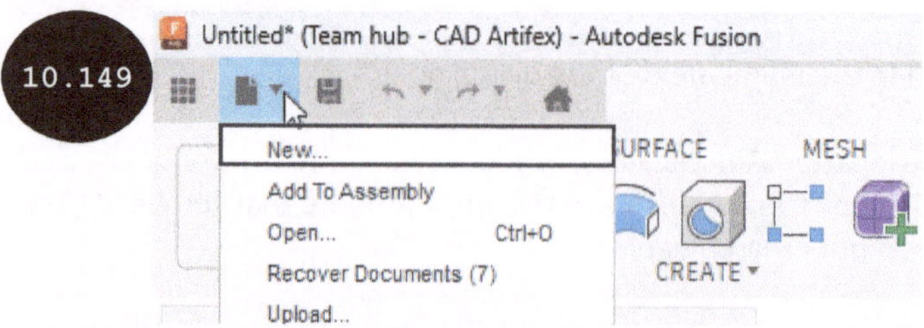

2. In the **What do you want to design?** dialog box, choose the **Part Design** button and then select the **millimeter (mm), gram (g)** unit system from the **Unit System** drop-down list.

3. After specifying the required options, click the **Create New** button. A new Part Design file is created with the default name.

Section 2: Creating the Base Feature - Pipe Feature

The base feature of the model is a pipe feature. To create a pipe feature, you need to first create its path.

1. Click on the **Create Sketch** tool in the **Toolbar** and then select the Front plane as the sketching plane.

2. Create the path of the pipe feature, see Figure 10.150.

Note: In Figure 10.150, the center point of the arc has coincident constraint with the origin. Also, the connecting line and arc entities of the sketch have tangent constraints with each other. In addition, an equal constraint has been applied between the vertical lines of the sketch.

After creating the path, you need to create the pipe feature.

3. Click on the **SOLID** tab in the **Toolbar** to display the solid modeling tools.

4. Invoke the **CREATE** drop-down menu in the **SOLID** tab and then click on the **Pipe** tool. The **PIPE** dialog box appears in the graphics area. Change the orientation of the sketch to isometric.

5. Ensure that the **Chain Selection** check box is selected in the dialog box.

6. Select the path of the pipe feature in the graphics area. The preview of the pipe feature appears with default parameters, see Figure 10.151.

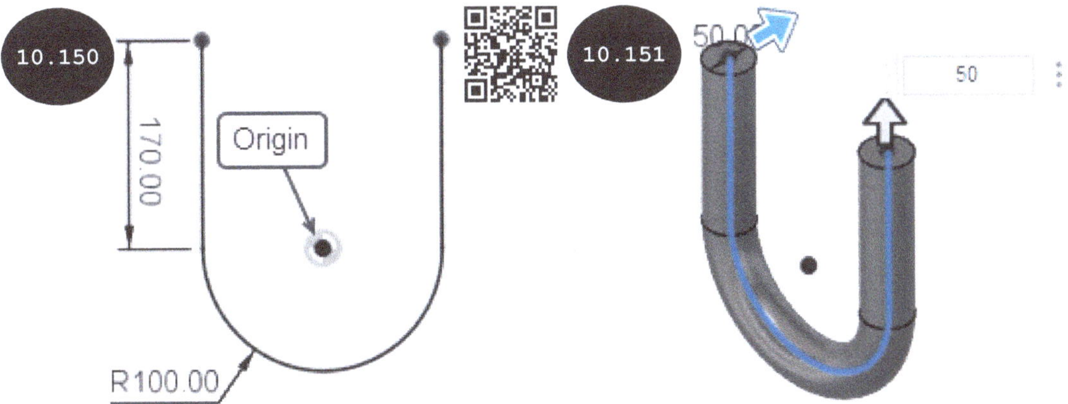

7. Ensure that the distance value **1** is specified in the **Distance** field of the dialog box.

8. Ensure that the **Circular** option is selected in the **Section** drop-down list of the dialog box as the section of the pipe feature.

9. Enter **90** in the **Section Size** drop-down list of the dialog box.

10. Select the **Hollow** check box in the dialog box to create a hollow pipe. The **Section Thickness** field appears in the dialog box.

11. Enter **10** in the **Section Thickness** field of the dialog box as the thickness of the pipe feature.

12. Ensure that the **New Body** option is selected in the **Operation** drop-down list of the dialog box.

13. Click on the **OK** button in the dialog box. The pipe feature is created, see Figure 10.152.

Section 3: Creating the Second Feature - Extrude Feature

1. Click on the **Create Sketch** tool in the **Toolbar** and then select the top planar face of the base feature (pipe) as the sketching plane, see Figure 10.153.

2. Create a circle of diameter 105 mm as the sketch of the second feature, see Figure 10.154.

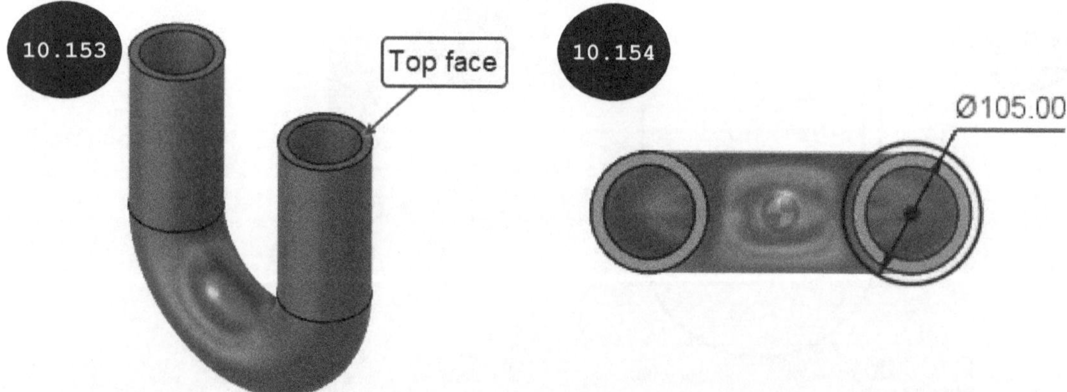

3. Click on the **SOLID** tab in the **Toolbar** to display the solid modeling tools.

4. Click on the **Extrude** tool in the **CREATE** panel of the **SOLID** tab or press the **E** key. The **EXTRUDE** dialog box appears in the graphics area. Next, change the orientation of the model to isometric.

5. Select the two closed profiles of the sketch in the graphics area, see Figure 10.155.

6. Ensure that the **One Side** option is selected in the **Direction** drop-down list of the dialog box.

7. Ensure that the **Distance** option is selected in the **Extent Type** drop-down list of the dialog box.

8. Enter **60** in the **Distance** field of the dialog box as the extrusion distance. The preview of the extrude feature appears, see Figure 10.156.

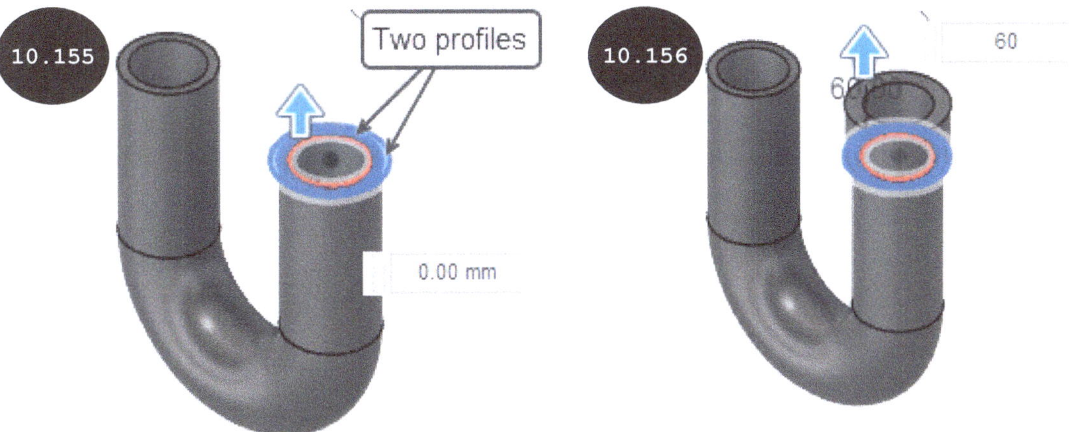

9. Ensure that the **Join** option is selected in the **Operation** drop-down list of the dialog box.

10. Click on the **OK** button in the dialog box. The extrude feature is created, see Figure 10.157.

Section 4: Creating the Third Feature - Mirror Feature

1. Invoke the **CREATE** drop-down menu in the **SOLID** tab and then click on the **Mirror** tool. The **MIRROR** dialog box appears in the graphics area.

2. Select the **Features** option in the **Pattern Type** drop-down list of the dialog box.

3. Select the previously created extrude feature (**Extrude1**) in the **Timeline** or the graphics area as the feature to be mirrored.

4. Click on the **Mirror Plane** selection option in the dialog box and then select the Right plane (YZ plane) as the mirroring plane in the graphics area. The preview of the mirror feature appears, see Figure 10.158.

5. Ensure that the **Adjust** option is selected in the **Compute Type** drop-down list of the dialog box.

6. Click on the **OK** button in the dialog box. The mirror feature is created, see Figure 10.159.

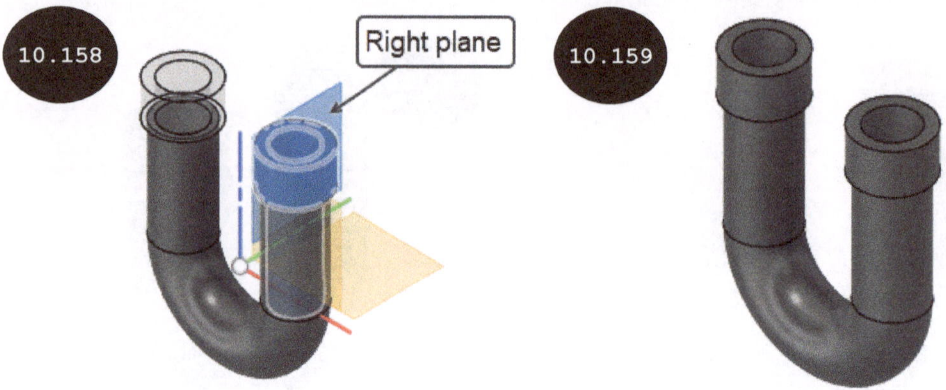

Section 5: Creating the Fourth Feature - Extrude Feature

To create the sketch of the fourth feature (extrude), you need to create a construction plane at an offset distance from the Top plane.

1. Click on the **Offset Plane** tool in the **CONSTRUCT** panel. The **CONSTRUCTION GEOMETRY** dialog box appears.

2. Click on the Top plane as the reference plane. The Top plane gets selected, and the **Distance** field appears in the dialog box as well as in the graphics area.

3. Enter **-190** in the **Distance** field of the dialog box to create a construction plane at an offset distance of 190 mm, downward.

4. Click on the **OK** button in the dialog box. The construction plane is created, see Figure 10.160.

5. Click on the **Create Sketch** tool in the **Toolbar** and then select the newly created construction plane as the sketching plane.

6. Create a circle of diameter 90 mm as the sketch of the fourth feature, see Figure 10.161. Note that the center point of the circle is at the origin.

7. Click on the **SOLID** tab in the **Toolbar** to display the solid modeling tools.

8. Click on the **Extrude** tool in the **CREATE** panel of the **SOLID** tab or press the **E** key. The **EXTRUDE** dialog box appears in the graphics area and the closed profile of the sketch gets selected, automatically, see Figure 10.162. Note that if the profile does not get selected automatically, then you need to select it by clicking the left mouse button.

9. Change the orientation of the model to isometric, if not changed automatically.

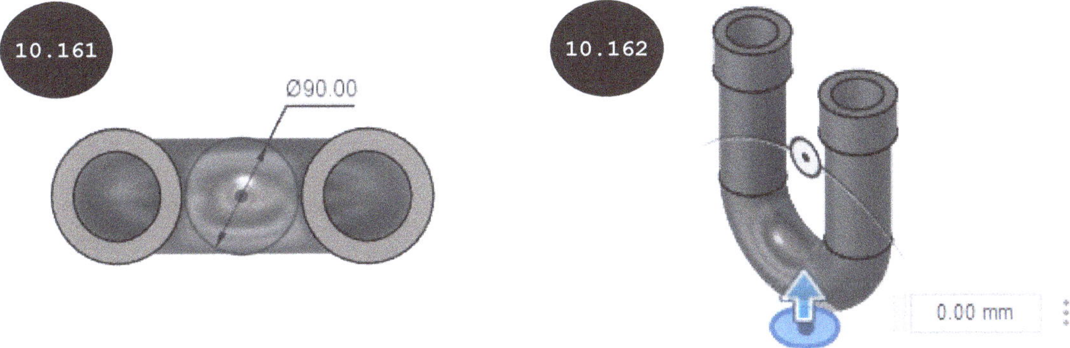

10. Ensure that the **One Side** option is selected in the **Direction** drop-down list of the dialog box.

11. Select the **To Object** option in the **Extent Type** drop-down list of the dialog box.

12. Select the outer circular face of the model as the face to terminate the extrusion, see Figure 10.163. The preview of the extrude feature appears in the graphics area, see Figure 10.164.

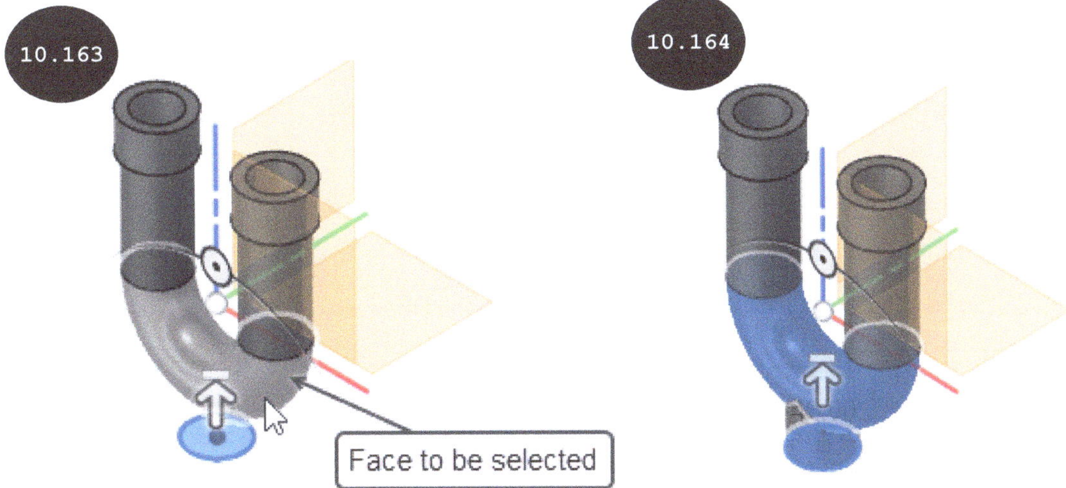

13. Ensure that the **To Body** button is activated in the first **Extend** area of the dialog box.

14. Ensure that the **Join** option is selected in the **Operation** drop-down list of the dialog box.

15. Click on the **OK** button in the dialog box. The extrude feature is created, see Figure 10.165.

Section 6: Creating the Fifth Feature - Extrude Feature

1. Click on the **Create Sketch** tool in the **Toolbar**. You are prompted to select a plane or a planar face as the sketching plane.

2. Expand the **Construction** node in the **BROWSER** and then click on **Plane1** (construction plane) as the sketching plane. Alternatively, you can select the bottom planar face of the previously created extrude feature as the sketching plane.

3. Create a circle of diameter 250 mm as the sketch of the fifth feature, see Figure 10.166.

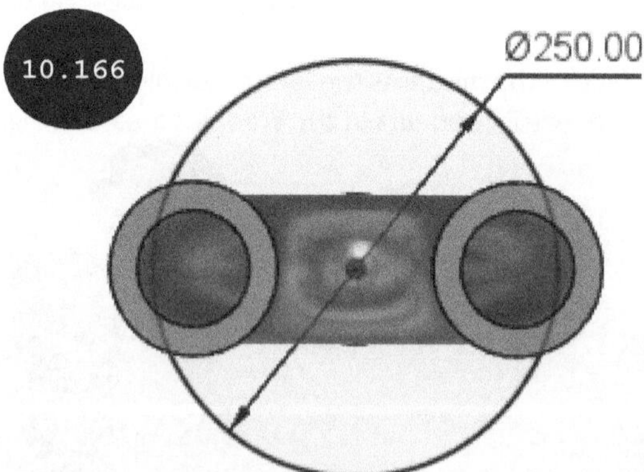

4. Click on the **SOLID** tab in the **Toolbar** to display the solid modeling tools.

5. Click on the **Extrude** tool in the **CREATE** panel of the **SOLID** tab or press the **E** key to invoke the **EXTRUDE** dialog box. The **EXTRUDE** dialog box appears in the graphics area and the closed profile of the sketch gets selected, automatically. Note that if the profile does not get selected automatically, then you need to select it by clicking the left mouse button.

6. Change the orientation of the model to isometric, if not changed automatically.

7. Ensure that the **One Side** option is selected in the **Direction** drop-down list and the **Distance** option is selected in the **Extent Type** drop-down list of the dialog box.

8. Enter **-30** in the **Distance** field of the dialog box. The preview of the extrude feature appears, see Figure 10.167.

9. Ensure that the **Join** option is selected in the **Operation** drop-down list of the dialog box.

10. Click on the **OK** button in the dialog box. The extrude feature is created, see Figure 10.168.

Section 7: Creating the Sixth Feature - Extrude Cut Feature

1. Click on the **Create Sketch** tool in the **Toolbar** and then select the top planar face of the previously created extrude feature as the sketching plane, see Figure 10.169.

2. Create a circle of diameter 25 mm as the sketch of the sixth feature, see Figure 10.170.

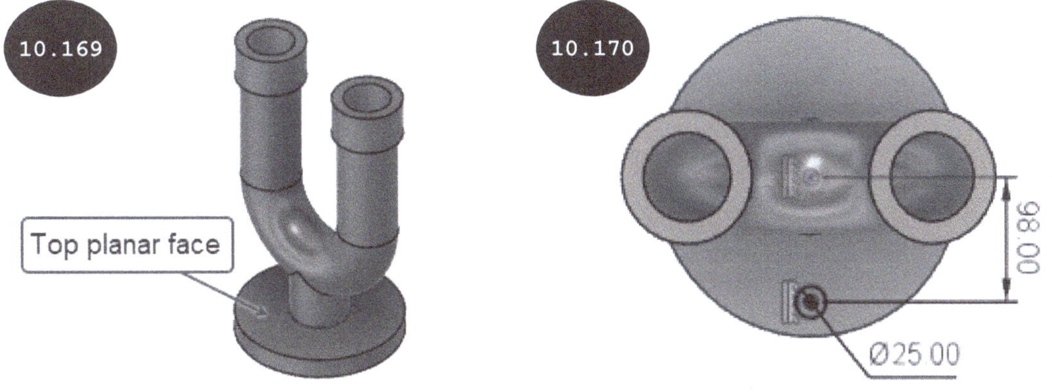

Note: In Figure 10.170, a vertical constraint has been applied between the center point of the circle and the origin to make the sketch fully defined.

3. Click on the **SOLID** tab in the **Toolbar** to display the solid modeling tools.

4. Click on the **Extrude** tool in the **CREATE** panel of the **SOLID** tab or press the **E** key to invoke the **EXTRUDE** dialog box. Next, change the orientation of the model to isometric.

5. Select the closed profile of the sketch in the graphics area.

6. Select the **All** option in the **Extent Type** drop-down list of the dialog box.

7. Click on the **Flip** button in the dialog box to flip the direction of extrusion downward.

8. Ensure that the **Cut** option is selected in the **Operation** drop-down list of the dialog box to create the feature by removing the material.

9. Click on the **OK** button in the dialog box. The extrude cut feature is created, see Figure 10.171.

10.171

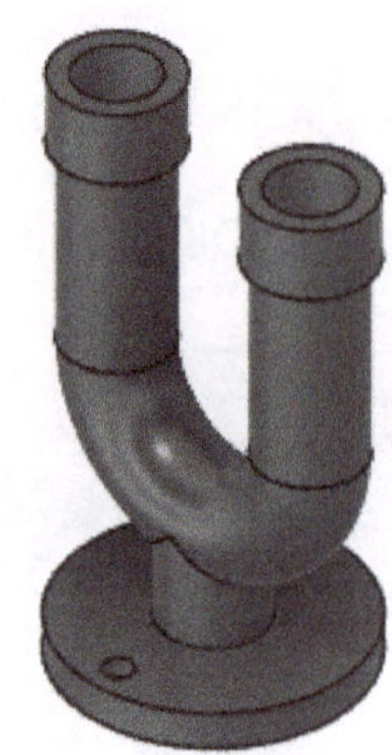

Section 8: Creating the Seventh Feature - Circular Pattern

1. Invoke the **CREATE** drop-down menu in the **SOLID** tab and then click on **Pattern** > **Circular Pattern**. The **CIRCULAR PATTERN** dialog box appears in the graphics area.

2. Select the **Faces** option in the **Object Type** drop-down list of the dialog box.

3. Select the inner circular face of the previously created extrude cut feature to be patterned, see Figure 10.172.

4. Click on the **Axis** selection option in the dialog box and then select the axis of revolution, see Figure 10.172. A preview of the circular pattern appears.

10.172

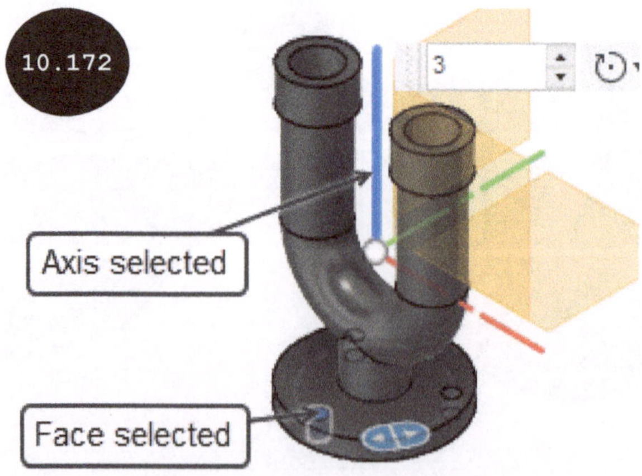

5. Ensure that the **Full** option is selected in the **Distribution** drop-down list of the dialog box.

6. Enter **6** in the **Quantity** field of the dialog box as the number of pattern instances to be created.

7. Click on the **OK** button in the dialog box. The circular pattern is created, see Figure 10.173.

Section 9: Creating the Eighth Feature - Fillet

1. Click on the **Fillet** tool in the **MODIFY** panel of the **SOLID** tab. The **FILLET** dialog box appears. Alternatively, press the **F** key to invoke the **FILLET** dialog box.

2. Click on the circular edge of the model to apply the fillet, see Figure 10.174.

3. Ensure that the **Constant** option is selected in the **Radius Type** drop-down list of the dialog box.

4. Enter **15** as the radius of the fillet in the **Radius** field of the dialog box.

5. Click on the **OK** button in the dialog box. A fillet with a radius of 15 mm is created, see Figure 10.175.

Section 10: Creating the Ninth Feature - Rib Feature

1. Click on the **Create Sketch** tool in the **Toolbar** and then select the Front plane as the sketching plane.

2. Create an inclined line as the sketch of the rib feature, see Figure 10.176. In this figure, the inclined line is created by taking reference of a projected line which is created by using the **Project** tool.

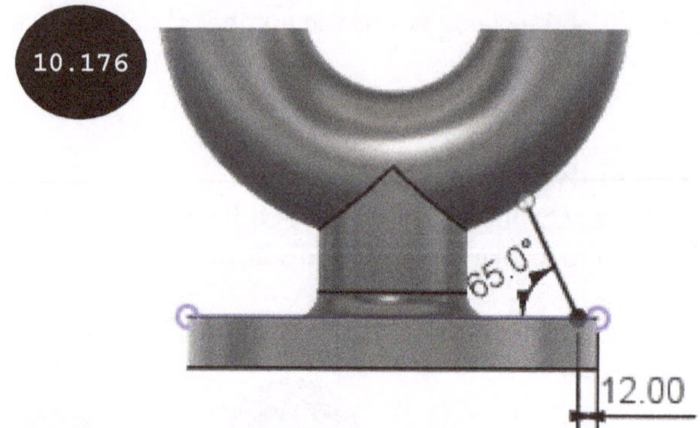

3. Click on the **SOLID** tab in the **Toolbar** to display the solid modeling tools.

4. Invoke the **CREATE** drop-down menu in the **SOLID** tab and then click on the **Rib** tool. The **RIB** dialog box appears. Next, change the orientation of the model to isometric.

5. Select the inclined line as the curve to create the rib feature.

6. Ensure that the **Symmetric** option is selected in the **Thickness Direction** drop-down list of the dialog box.

7. Ensure that the **To Next** option is selected in the **Extent Type** drop-down list of the dialog box.

8. Enter **16** in the **Thickness** field of the dialog box as the thickness of the rib feature. A preview of the rib feature appears in the graphics area.

9. Click on the **Flip Direction** button to change the direction of the rib feature to inward, if required.

10. Click on the **OK** button in the dialog box. The rib feature is created, see Figure 10.177.

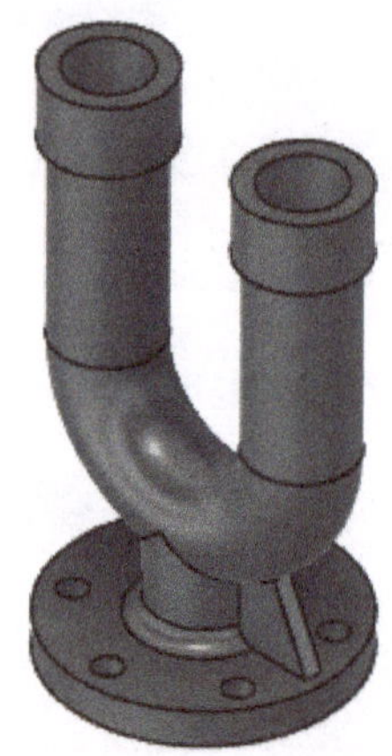

Section 11: Creating the Tenth Feature - Mirror Feature

1. Invoke the **CREATE** drop-down menu in the **SOLID** tab and then click on the **Mirror** tool. The **MIRROR** dialog box appears in the graphics area.

2. Select the **Features** option in the **Object Type** drop-down list of the dialog box.

3. Click on the previously created rib feature as the feature to be mirrored.

4. Click on the **Mirror Plane** selection option in the dialog box and then select the Right plane (YZ plane) as the mirroring plane. A preview of the mirror feature appears.

5. Ensure that the **Adjust** option is selected in the **Compute Type** drop-down list of the dialog box.

6. Click on the **OK** button in the dialog box. The mirror feature is created, see Figure 10.178.

Section 12: Creating the Eleventh Feature - Extruded Feature

1. Click on the **Create Sketch** tool in the **Toolbar** and then select the Right plane (YZ plane) as the sketching plane.

2. Select the **Slice** check box in the **SKETCH PALETTE** dialog box to cut the object by using the sketching plane of the sketch so that the sketching plane appears in the front to create the sketch of the feature.

3. Create a rectangle as the sketch of the eleventh feature, see Figure 10.179. Note that the center of the rectangle is at the origin.

4. Clear the **Slice** check box in the **SKETCH PALETTE** dialog box after creating the sketch.

10.179

72.00

22.00

5. Click on the **SOLID** tab in the **Toolbar** to display the solid modeling tools.

6. Click on the **Extrude** tool in the **CREATE** panel of the **SOLID** tab or press the **E** key. The **EXTRUDE** dialog box appears and the closed profile of the sketch gets selected, automatically. Note that if the profile does not get selected automatically, then you need to select it by clicking the left mouse button.

7. Change the orientation of the model to isometric, if not changed automatically.

8. Select the **Two Sides** option in the **Direction** drop-down list of the dialog box. The **Side 1** and **Side 2** rollouts appear in the dialog box.

9. Select the **To Object** option in the **Extent Type** drop-down list of the **Side 1** rollout in the dialog box.

10. Select the circular face of the model as the face to terminate side 1 of the extrude feature, see Figure 10.180.

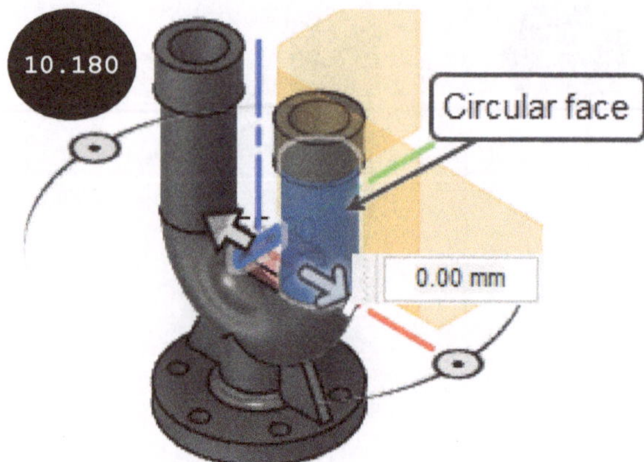

11. Ensure that the **To Body** option is selected in the first **Extend** area of the **Side 1** rollout.

12. Select the **To Object** option in the **Extent Type** drop-down list of the **Side 2** rollout in the dialog box.

13. Select the circular face of the other side of the model to terminate side 2 of the extrude feature, see Figure 10.181.

14. Ensure that the **To Body** option is selected in the first **Extend** area of the **Side 2** rollout.

15. Ensure that the **Join** option is selected in the **Operation** drop-down list of the dialog box.

16. Click on the **OK** button in the dialog box. The extrude feature is created, see Figure 10.182.

Section 13: Creating the Twelfth Feature - Extrude Cut Feature

1. Click on the **Create Sketch** tool in the **Toolbar** and then select the top planar face of the previously created extrude feature as the sketching plane.

2. Create a circle of diameter 20 mm, whose center point is at the origin, see Figure 10.183.

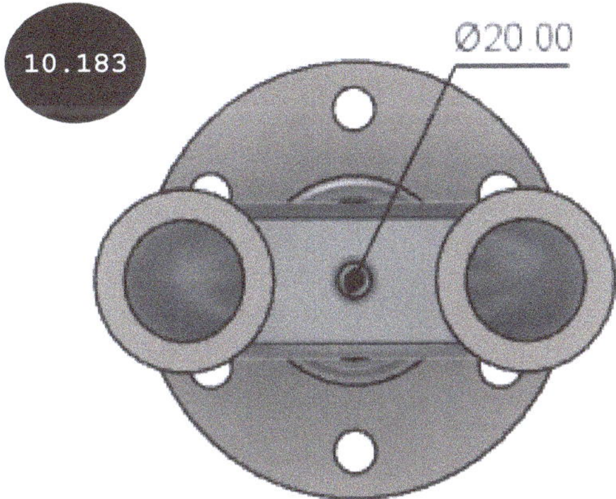

3. Click on the **SOLID** tab in the **Toolbar** to display the solid modeling tools.

4. Click on the **Extrude** tool in the **CREATE** panel of the **SOLID** tab or press the **E** key to invoke the **EXTRUDE** dialog box. Next, change the orientation of the model to isometric.

5. Select the closed profile of the sketch in the graphics area.

6. Select the **To Object** option in the **Extent Type** drop-down list of the dialog box.

7. Rotate the model and then select the bottom planar face of the previously created extrude feature as the face to terminate the extrusion, see Figure 10.184.

8. Ensure that the **Cut** option is selected in the **Operation** drop-down list of the dialog box.

9. Click on the **OK** button in the dialog box. The extrude cut feature is created, see Figure 10.185. Change the orientation of the model to isometric.

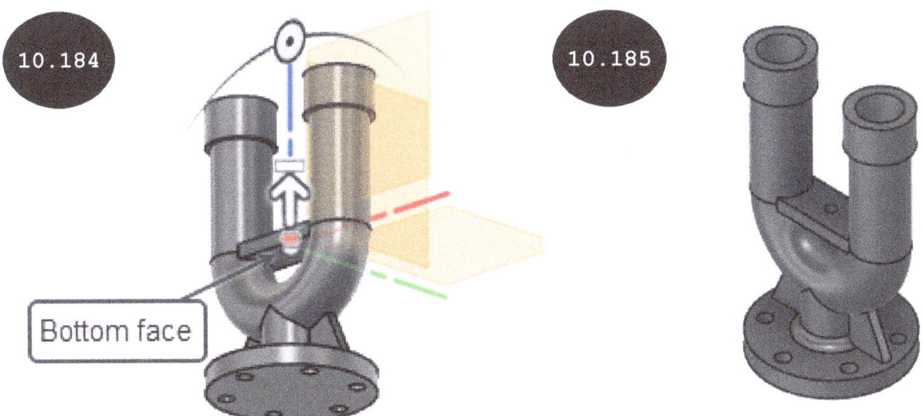

Section 14: Saving the Model

1. Click on the **Save** tool in the **Application Bar**. The **Save** dialog box appears.
2. Enter **Tutorial 2** in the **Name** field of the dialog box.
3. Ensure that the location ***Autodesk Fusion 360 > Chapter 10 > Tutorial*** is specified in the **Location** field of the dialog box to save the file of this tutorial. Note that you need to create these folders in the **Data Panel**, if not created earlier.
4. Click on the **Save** button in the dialog box. The model is saved with the name Tutorial 2 in the specified location (***Autodesk Fusion 360 > Chapter 10 > Tutorial***).

Hands-on Test Drive 1

Create a model, as shown in Figure 10.186. All dimensions are in mm.

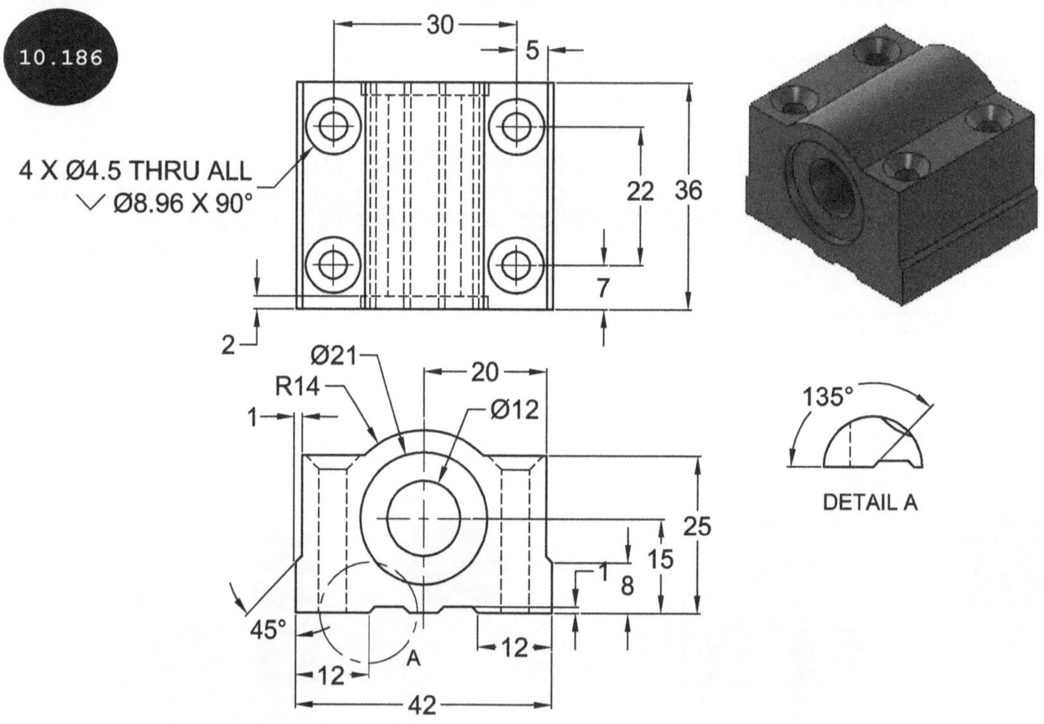

Hands-on Test Drive 2

Create a model, as shown in Figure 10.187. All dimensions are in mm.

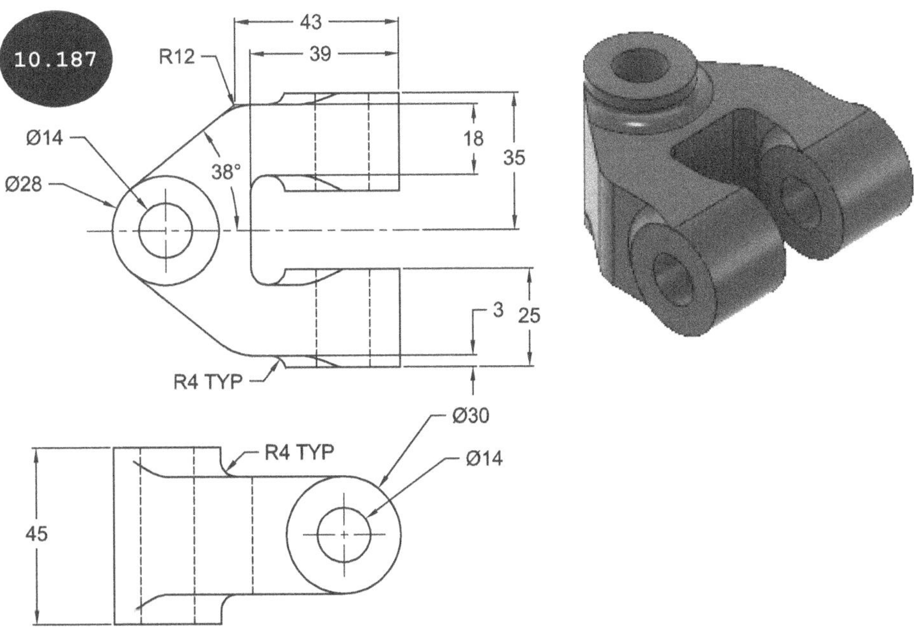

Summary

In this chapter, you learned how to modify or edit a 3D solid model using the Press Pull tool. You explored methods for creating constant and variable radius fillets to eliminate sharp edges, as well as techniques for specifying chord length, rule fillets, and full round fillets. The chapter also covered various methods for creating chamfers. Additionally, you discovered how to create shell features, add drafts, scale objects, combine solid bodies, offset faces, and split faces or bodies. This comprehensive overview equips you with the necessary skills to enhance your modeling capabilities.

Questions

Complete and verify the following sentences:

- Using the **Fillet** tool, you can create _________, _________, _________, _________, and _________ fillets.

- The _________ tool is used for offsetting a face of a model, filleting an edge of a model, and extruding a sketch profile, dynamically in the graphics area.

- The **Chamfer** tool is used for creating _________, _________, and _________ chamfers.

- The _________ tool is used for creating a thin-walled feature by making a model hollow from the inside or removing the faces of the model.
- In Autodesk Fusion, you can taper the faces of a model by using the _________ tool.
- You can increase or decrease the scale of components, bodies, or sketch entities by using the _________ tool.
- The **Combine** tool is used for combining solid bodies by performing _________ , _________ , or _________ boolean operations.
- The _________ tool is used for splitting faces of a model for manipulating each split face, independently.

11

Working with Assemblies - I

In this chapter, the following topics will be discussed:

- Understanding Different Assembly Approaches
- Getting Started with Bottom-up Assembly
- Inserting Components in a Design File
- Fixing/Grounding the First Component
- Working with Degrees of Freedom
- Applying Joints
- Defining the Position of the Joint Origin
- Editing Joints
- Defining Joint Limits
- Animating a Joint
- Animating the Model
- Locking/Unlocking the Motion of a Joint
- Driving a Joint
- Defining Relative Motion between Two Joints
- Applying Constraints
- Grouping Components Together
- Enabling Contact Sets between Components
- Capturing the Position of Components

In earlier chapters, you learned both basic and advanced techniques for creating real-world mechanical components. In this chapter, you will explore various techniques for creating mechanical assemblies. An assembly consists of two or more components connected using specific joints or constraints. Figure 11.1 illustrates an example of an assembly in which multiple components are connected by applying the appropriate joints/constraints.

Understanding Different Assembly Approaches

In Autodesk Fusion, you can create an assembly using two primary approaches: the Bottom-up Assembly Approach and the Top-down Assembly Approach. You can also combine these approaches to create an assembly. Both approaches are discussed next.

Bottom-up Assembly Approach

The **Bottom-up Assembly** Approach is the most commonly used method for assembling components. In this approach, all the components of an assembly are created individually as separate design files and saved in a common location. Later, these components are inserted one by one into an Assembly Design file, where they are assembled by applying the necessary joints and constraints.

Tip: Autodesk Fusion has bidirectional association capabilities, meaning that any changes or modifications made to a component are automatically reflected in the assembly, as well as in any associated drawings and other workspaces. These updates occur automatically when the respective files are updated, ensuring consistency across the design.

Top-down Assembly Approach

In the **Top-down Assembly Approach**, all the components of an assembly are created within a single Assembly Design file. This approach is useful for concept-based designs, where new components are created by referencing existing components in the assembly. You will learn more about creating assemblies using the Top-down approach in the next chapter. In this chapter, the focus will be on creating assemblies using the **Bottom-up Assembly** Approach.

Getting Started with Bottom-up Assembly

After creating all the components of an assembly as separate design files and saving them in a common location, you need to insert them one by one into an Assembly Design file to assemble them by applying the appropriate joints and constraints.

To do this, invoke the **What do you want to design?** dialog box by clicking on **File > New** in the **Application Bar**. Then, click on the **Assembly Design** button in the dialog box, see Figure 11.2. Next, specify the desired unit system, such as **millimeter (mm), gram (g); centimeter (cm), gram (g);** or **meter (m), kilogram (kg)**, from the **Unit System** drop-down list in the dialog box.

11.2

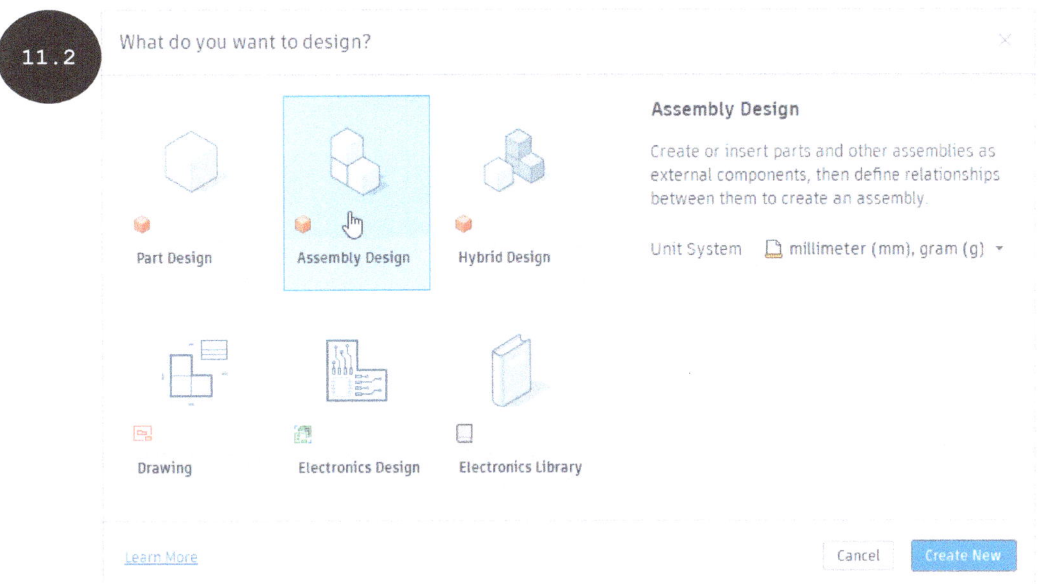

After specifying the required options, click on the **Create New** button. A new Assembly Design file is opened with the default name in a separate tab, and the **BROWSER** appears on the left side of the graphics area, see Figure 11.3.

11.3

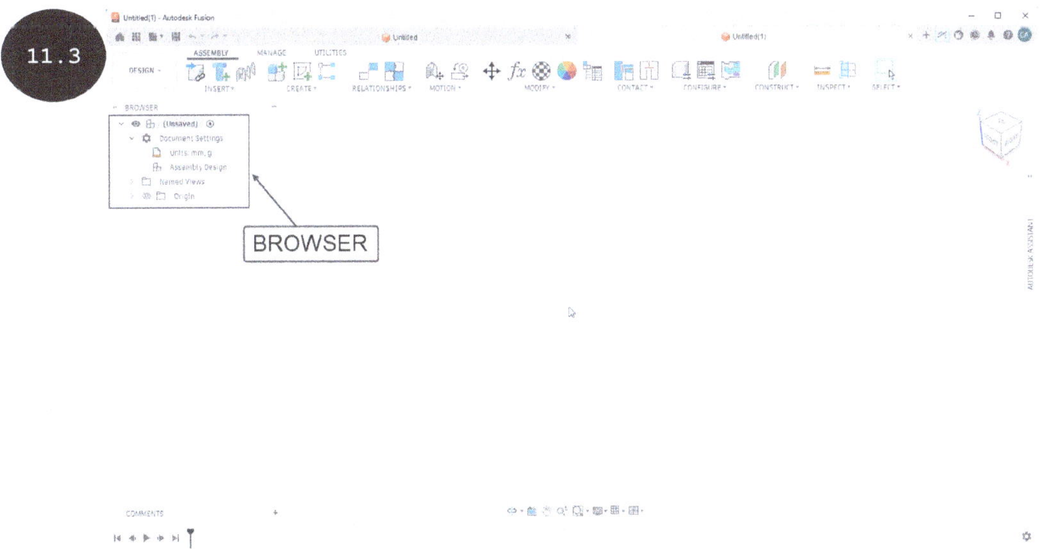

Note that in the **BROWSER**, the **Assembly Design** option appears under the **Document Settings** node, indicating that the current file is an Assembly Design file.

However, if required, you can easily convert an Assembly Design file to a Part Design or Hybrid Design file, and vice versa. To do this, move the cursor over the **Assembly Design** option under the **Document Settings** node. Then, click the **Convert Design Type** icon that appears, see Figure 12.4. The **CONVERT UNTITLED** dialog box appears, see Figure 12.5.

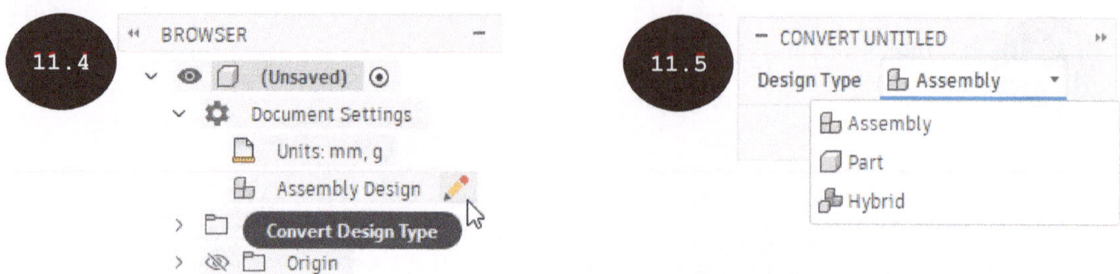

In the **CONVERT UNTITLED** dialog box, select the desired design type and click the **Convert** button. The current file is then converted to the selected design type. Similarly, you can convert Part Design and Hybrid Design files into an Assembly Design or vice versa.

Inserting Components in an Assembly Design File

The method for inserting the components of an assembly into an Assembly Design file is discussed below:

1. In the Assembly Design file, open the **Data Panel** by clicking on the **Show Data Panel** tool in the **Application Bar**, see Figure 11.6.

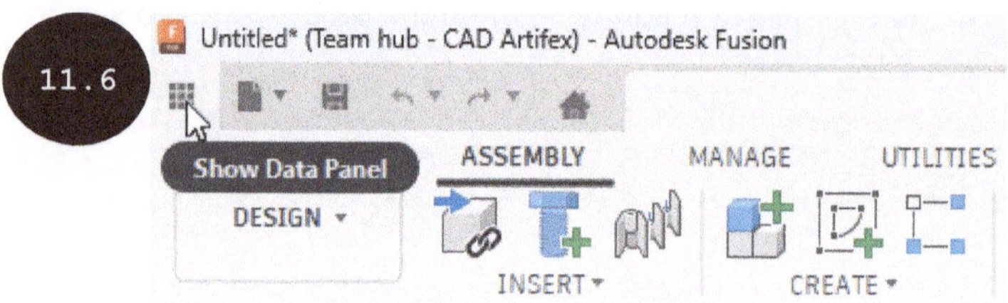

2. In the **Data Panel**, browse to the location where all the components of the assembly are saved.

3. Right-click on the name of the component to be inserted into the active design file. A shortcut menu appears, see Figure 11.7.

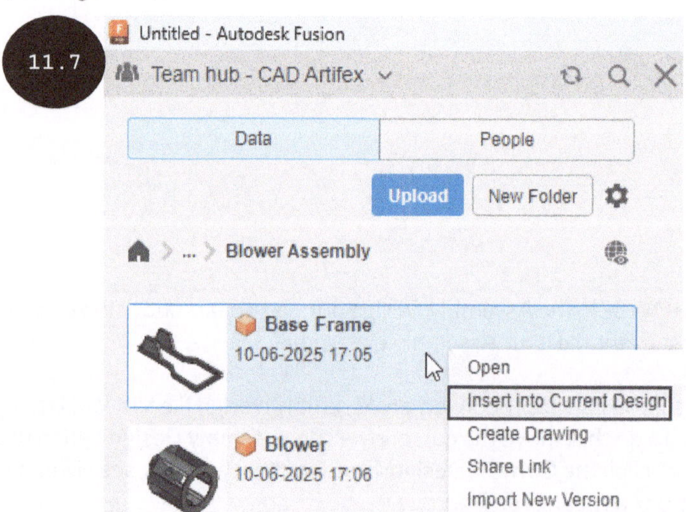

4. Select the **Insert into Current Design** option in the shortcut menu. The selected component gets inserted into the currently active file along with the display of the translational and manipulator handles, see Figure 11.8. Also, the **INITIAL POSITION** dialog box appears automatically.

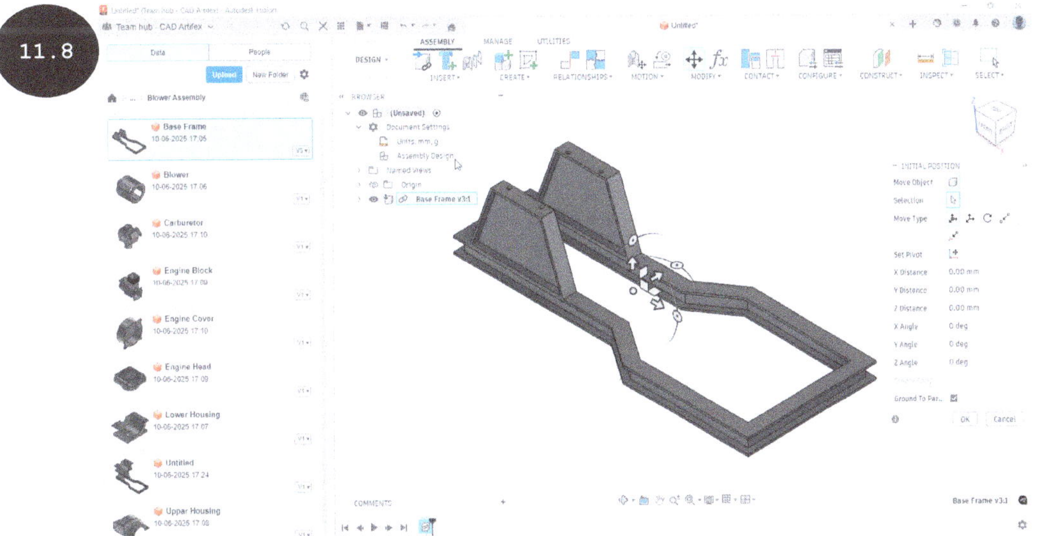

5. If needed, drag the translational and manipulator handles that appears to define the position and orientation of the inserted component in the design file as needed. By default, the component is placed at the origin of the active design file.

6. Ensure that the **Ground to Parent** check box is selected in the **INITIAL POSITION** dialog box to fix or ground the first component. A fixed or grounded component does not allow any translational or rotational movement. In Autodesk Fusion, this check box is selected by default when inserting the first component into the design file.

7. After defining the position of the component in the graphics area, click on the **OK** button in the **INITIAL POSITION** dialog box. The component is placed at the specified position in the design file and becomes a fixed component, by default. Note that the inserted component appears in the **BROWSER** with an anchor symbol and a link icon, see Figure 11.9.

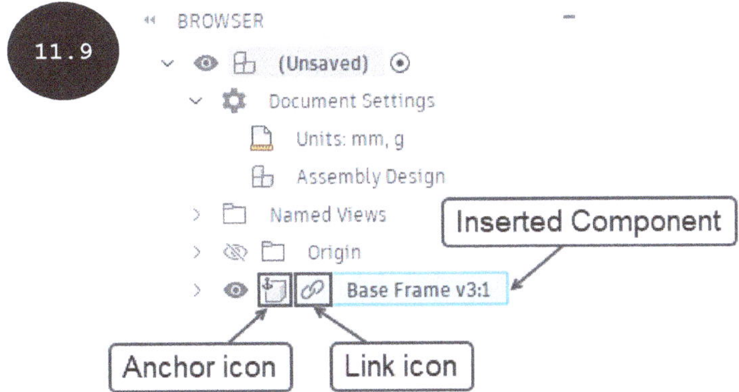

The anchor symbol indicates that the component is grounded (fixed) and all its degrees of freedom are fixed. The link icon indicates that the component has been inserted as an externally referenced file within the assembly.

Tip: You can also insert a component in the active design file by dragging and dropping it from the **Data Panel** to the design file.

Note: In Autodesk Fusion, you can change a grounded (fixed) component to an ungrounded component, where all degrees of freedom are free, or vice versa, at any time during design. To do this, right-click on the name of the component in the **BROWSER**, then select the **Unground From Parent** or **Ground From Parent** option from the shortcut menu that appears. Note that the available option depends on the current state of the component.

After inserting the first component, you can insert the second component of the assembly.

8. Invoke the **Data Panel** by clicking on the **Show Data Panel** tool in the **Application Bar**, see Figure 11.10.

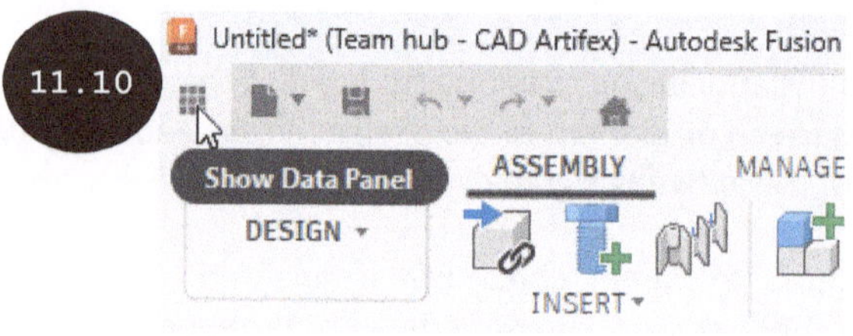

9. Right-click on the component to be inserted into the design file and then select the **Insert into Current Design** option in the shortcut menu that appears, see Figure 11.11. The selected component gets inserted into the design file along with the display of the translational and manipulator handles, see Figure 11.12. Also, the **INITIAL POSITION** dialog box appears automatically.

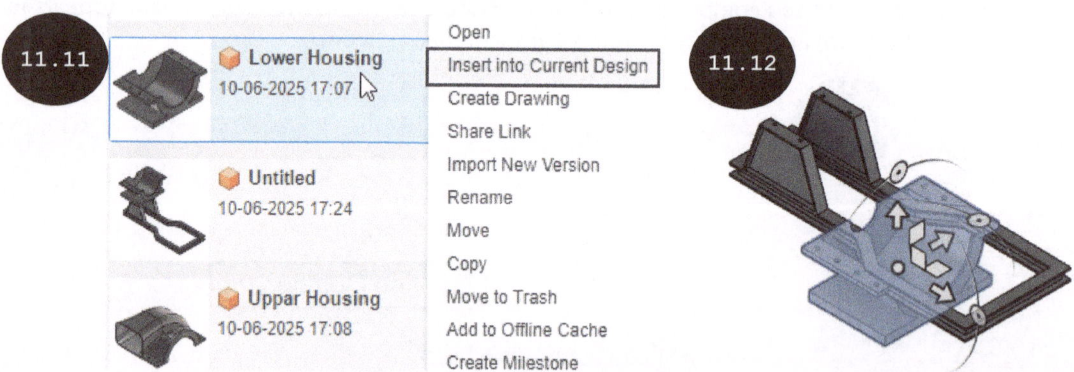

10. Define the position of the component in the graphics area by dragging the translational and manipulator handles such that it does not intersect the existing component of the assembly.

11. After positioning the component, click the **OK** button in the **INITIAL POSITION** dialog box. The component is placed at the specified position in the design file.

Note: In Autodesk Fusion, every component of an assembly has its own independent origin, bodies, sketches, and construction geometries. When you expand the node of a component in the **BROWSER**, the **Origin, Bodies, Sketches, construction** and **Assembly Context** sub-nodes containing the respective geometries of the component appear, see Figure 11.13.

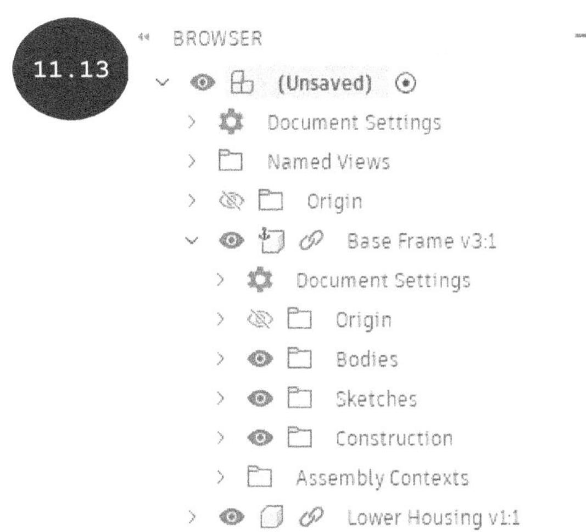

By default, the second component you insert into the design file is ungrounded, with all degrees of freedom free, allowing it to move or rotate in any direction within the graphics area. Therefore, it is recommended to assemble it with the first component by applying the necessary joints or constraints before inserting the third or any subsequent components of the assembly. Joints and constraints define the relationship between components in the assembly. However, before learning to apply joints and constraints between assembly components, it's important to understand degrees of freedom, which is discussed next.

Working with Degrees of Freedom

An ungrounded component within the design file has six degrees of freedom: three translational (along the X, Y, and Z axes) and three rotational (around the X, Y, and Z axes).

As discussed earlier, the first component inserted in the design file is fixed, or grounded, by default, which restricts all translational and rotational movement. However, the second and subsequent components are ungrounded and free to move in all directions, so they must be assembled by applying appropriate joints. Joints restrict specific degrees of freedom and define the relationships between components in an assembly. For instance, if a shaft in an assembly is meant to rotate about its axis, a joint would be applied to allow this rotational degree of freedom while constraining others.

Note: To check the degrees of freedom of a component, you can move or rotate the component along or about its free degrees of freedom by using the **Move/Copy** tool. You can also move a component along its free degrees of freedom by dragging it in the graphics area.

Applying Joints

In Autodesk Fusion, you can apply various types of joints such as rigid, revolute, slider, cylindrical, pin-slot, ball, and planar to define relationships between components in an assembly using the **Joint** and **As-Built Joint** tools. In the next chapter, you will learn about applying joints with the **As-Built Joint** tool. This chapter focuses on applying joints using the **Joint** tool.

To apply a joint between assembly components using the **Joint** tool, invoke the **RELATIONSHIPS** drop-down menu in the **ASSEMBLY** tab of the **Toolbar** and then click on the **Joint** tool, see Figure 11.14. The **JOINT** dialog box appears, see Figure 12.15. Alternatively, you can simply press the J key to open the **JOINT** dialog box.

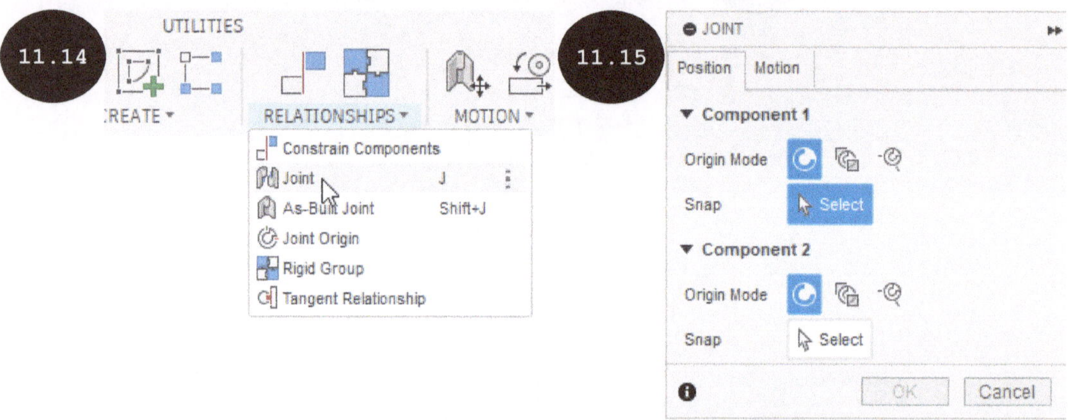

The **JOINT** dialog box has two tabs: **Position** and **Motion**. The options in the **Position** tab define the components to join and their alignment, while the options in the **Motion** tab define the type of joint to be applied between the components. The methods for applying various types of joints are discussed next.

Applying a Rigid Joint

The rigid joint is used to lock or fix two components together by removing all degrees of freedom, preventing any relative motion between them, see Figure 11.16. This joint is primarily applied between components that are welded or bolted together, where no motion is allowed between them. The method for applying a rigid joint is discussed below:

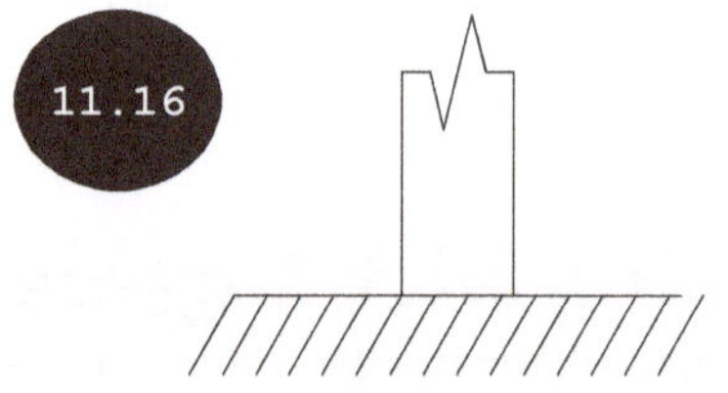

Rigid Joint
(No translational or rotational movements)

1. Invoke the **RELATIONSHIPS** drop-down menu in the **ASSEMBLY** tab and click on the **Joint** tool (refer to Figure 11.14) or press the J key. The **JOINT** dialog box appears.

   Now, you need to define the joint origin on the two components to apply a joint.

   Component 1: The options available in the **Component 1** rollout of the **Position** tab are used to define the position of the joint origin on the first component (movable component). By default, the **Simple** button is selected in the **Origin Mode** area of the **Component 1** rollout. This option allows you to define the joint origin directly by selecting a snap point on a face, edge, or vertex of the first component.

Note: The **Between Two Faces** and **Two Edge Intersection** options of this area will be discussed in detail later in this chapter. In this session, the joint origin is defined using only the **Simple** option.

2. Ensure that the **Simple** button is selected in the **Origin Mode** area of the **Component 1** rollout for defining the position of the joint origin on a face, an edge, or a point of the first component.

3. After selecting the **Simple** button in the **Origin Mode** area of the **Component 1** rollout, move the cursor over a face, edge, or vertex of the first component (the moveable component). The face, edge, or vertex gets highlighted, and its snap points appear, see Figure 11.17. Additionally, the joint origin appears attached to the cursor tip (also shown in Figure 11.17). In this figure, the cursor is moved over the face of a component.

11.17

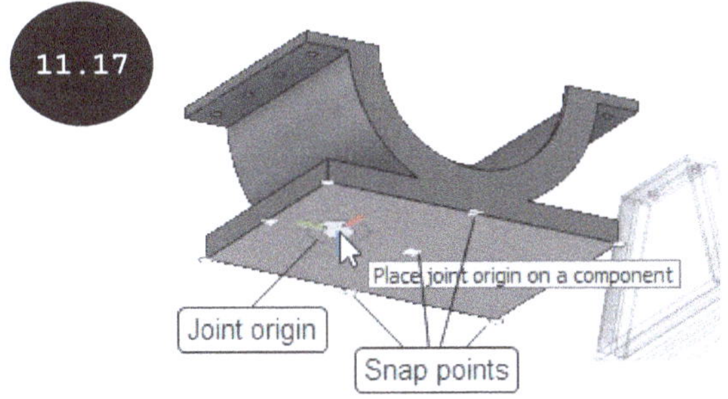

Tip: A triangular snap point indicates a midpoint, a circular snap point indicates a corner, and a square snap point indicates a center.

Now, you need to define the position of the joint origin on the highlighted face, edge, or vertex of the first component.

4. Specify the position of the joint origin on the required snap point available on the highlighted face, edge, or vertex of the first component by clicking the left mouse button. As soon as you define the position of the joint origin on the first component, the **Snap** selection option in the **Component 2** rollout gets activated, and you are prompted to define the joint origin on the second component. Additionally, the first component becomes transparent in the graphics area, and the joint origin symbol appears at the specified position, see Figure 11.18.

11.18

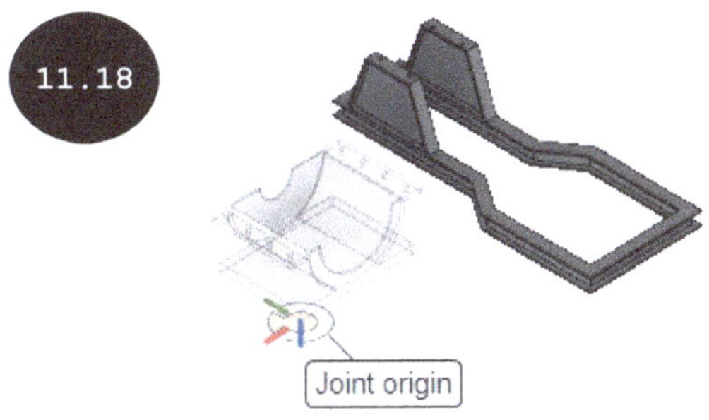

Component 2: The options available in the **Component 2** rollout of the **Position** tab are the same as those in the **Component 1** rollout. However, the options in the **Component 2** rollout are used to define the position of the joint origin on the second component. These options will be discussed in detail later in this chapter.

5. Ensure that the **Simple** button is selected in the **Origin Mode** area of the **Component 2** rollout to define the position of the joint origin on a face, edge, or point of the second component.

6. Move the cursor over a face, edge, or vertex of the second component. The snap points appear (see Figure 11.19), and the joint origin is attached to the cursor tip.

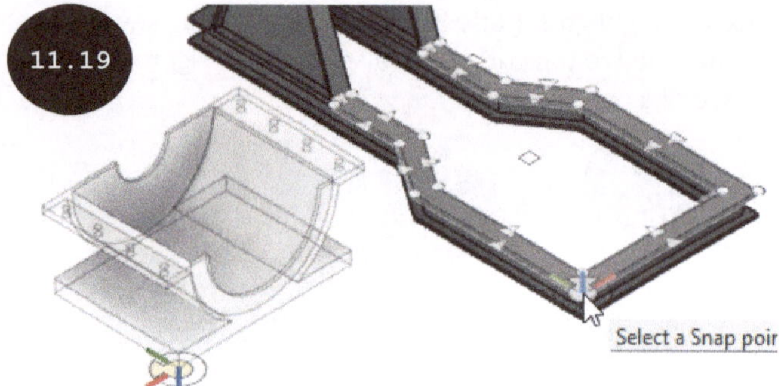

7. Specify the position of the joint origin on the required snap point available on the face, edge, or vertex of the second component by clicking the left mouse button. The first component moves toward the second component, and the joint origins of both components coincide with each other in the graphics area, see Figure 11.20.

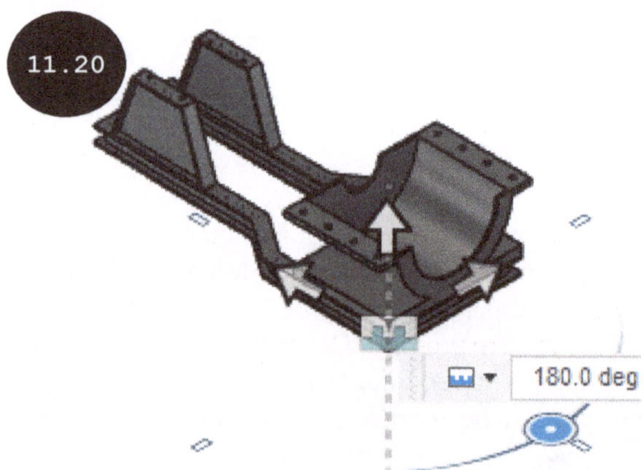

Note: Sometimes, when you move the cursor toward a snap point on the highlighted face or edge to define the joint origin, the snap points of another nearby face or edge on the component may become highlighted instead.

To avoid this, you can lock the intended face or edge before selecting its snap point. When the snap points of the required face or edge appear, press and hold the CTRL key, and then click the desired snap point using the left mouse button. After selecting the snap point, release the CTRL key.

Alignment: The options available in the **Alignment** rollout of the **Position** tab allow you to define the alignment between the components. By default, the **Offset X**, **Offset Y**, and **Offset Z** fields are set to **0**, which causes the joint origins of both components to coincide.

You can enter specific values in these offset fields to adjust the relative position of the components as required. Additionally, you can specify a value in the **Angle** field to define the orientation of the first component relative to the second.

Note that the **Alignment** rollout appears in the **Position** tab only after defining the joint origins on two components in the assembly. To reverse the alignment, use the **Flip** button, refer to Figures 11.21 and 11.22.

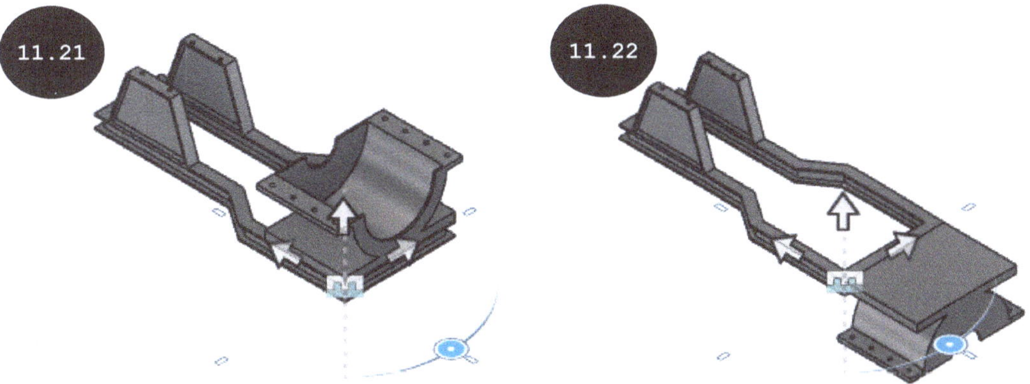

8. Specify the alignment between the components by using the **Alignment** rollout in the **Position** tab of the dialog box, if needed.

   After defining the joint origins on the two components using the options in the **Position** tab, you must specify the type of joint to be applied between them using the options available in the **Motion** tab.

9. Click on the **Motion** tab in the dialog box, see Figure 11.23.

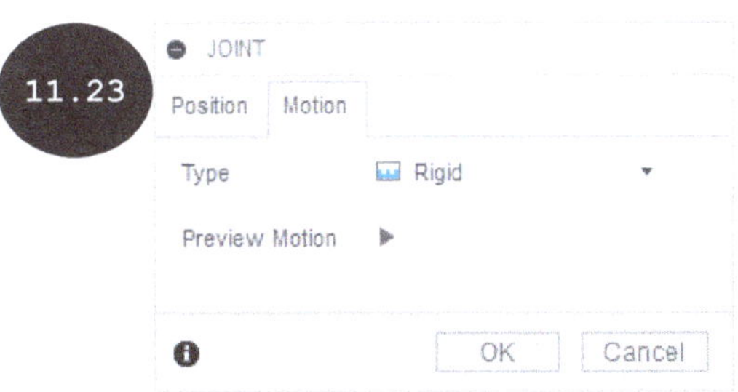

   Type: The options available in the **Type** drop-down list of the **Motion** tab are used to define the type of joint or motion to be applied between the selected components. You can specify Rigid, Revolute, Slider, Cylindrical, Pin-Slot, Planar, or Ball motion by selecting the appropriate option from this drop-down list. In this session, only the **Rigid** motion is discussed. The remaining joint types are covered individually in subsequent sessions.

10. Select the **Rigid** option in the **Type** drop-down list of the **Motion** tab of the dialog box to apply a rigid connection between the components, refer to Figure 11.23.

Preview Motion: The **Play** button in the **Preview Motion** area of the **Motion** tab is used to animate the allowable motion between the components after applying the joint. It helps to identify the free degrees of freedom of the components based on the joint applied.

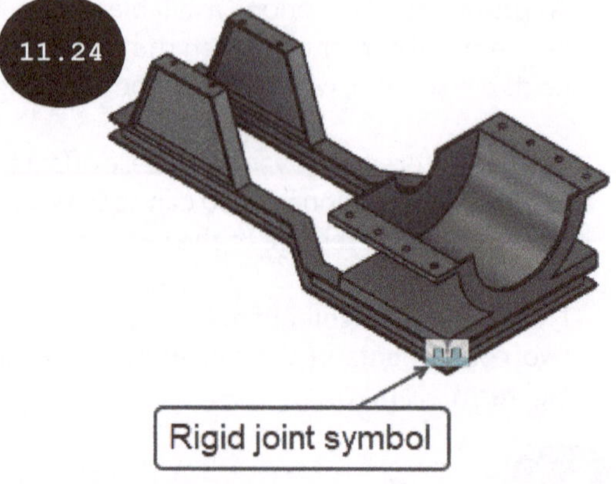

11. Click on the **OK** button in the dialog box. The rigid joint is applied between the components such that all degrees of freedom of the components are removed and the components are locked together, see Figure 11.24. Also, a symbol of a rigid joint appears in the graphics area.

Note: By default, the visibility of applied joints is turned on, causing the symbols of all applied joints to appear in the graphics area. To toggle the visibility of applied joints, invoke the **Display Settings** flyout in the **Display Settings**, see Figure 11.25. Then, move the cursor over the **Object Visibility** option in the flyout. A cascading menu appears, see Figure 11.26. In this menu, select or clear the **Joints** check box to turn the visibility of joints on or off in the graphics area.

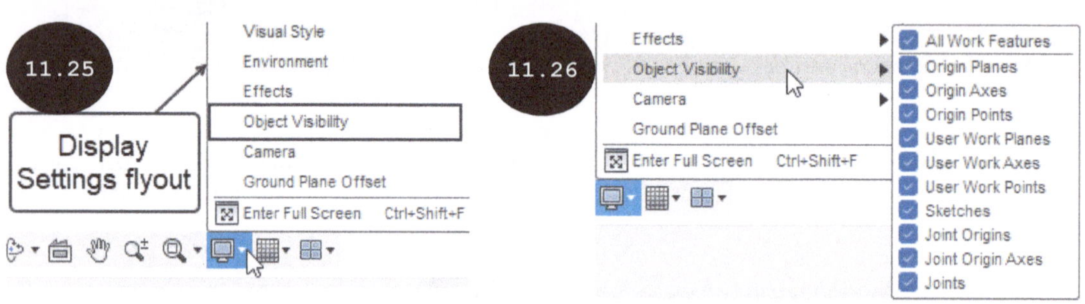

You can similarly apply other joints, such as revolute, slider, cylindrical, pin-slot, planar, and ball joints, which are discussed next.

Applying a Slider Joint

The slider joint allows a component to move or slide along a single axis by restricting all other degrees of freedom, see Figure 11.27. This joint allows only one translational degree of freedom, making it ideal for linear sliding motions. The method for applying a slider joint is discussed below:

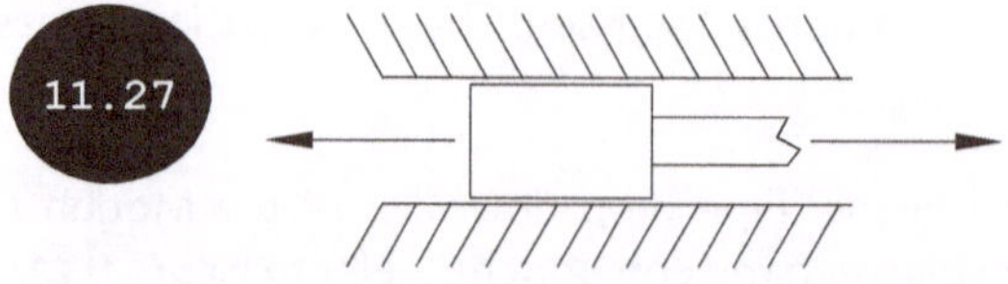

Slider Joint
(Moves freely along a single axis)

1. Press the J key or invoke the **RELATIONSHIPS** drop-down menu and click on the **Joint** tool. The **JOINT** dialog box appears, and the **Simple** button is activated in the **Origin Mode** area of the **Component 1** rollout.

2. Move the cursor over a face or an edge of the first component (moveable component). The face or edge gets highlighted, and its snap points appear, see Figure 11.28.

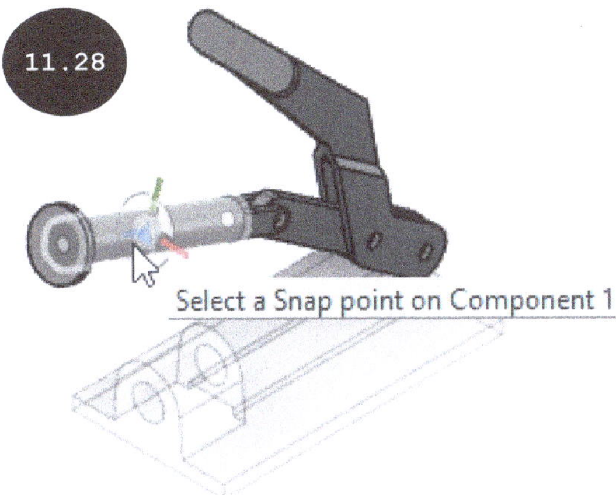

3. Click on a snap point to define the position of the joint origin on the first component. You can also lock a face or an edge to select its snap point easily by pressing the **CTRL** key. The joint origin is defined at the specified snap point and the component becomes transparent.

   Now, you need to define the joint origin on the second component.

Note: The **Simple** button is activated in the **Origin Mode** area of the **Component 2** rollout, by default. As a result, you can define the position of the joint origin on a face, an edge, or a point of a component. You can also select the **Between Two Faces** or **Two Edge Intersection** button for defining the position of the joint origin, as required. Both these options are discussed later in this chapter.

4. Move the cursor over a face, an edge, or a vertex of the second component. The snap points appear, see Figure 11.29. In this figure, the cursor is moved over a circular edge. As a result, only one snap point appears at the center of the circular edge and the joint origin is snapped to it, by default.

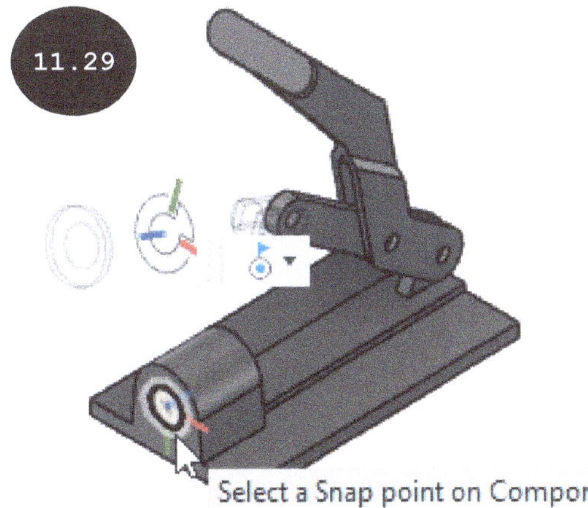

5. Click on the snap point to define the position of the joint origin on the second component. The joint origins of both components

coincide with each other in the graphics area, see Figure 11.30. Also, a preview of the motion between the components appears as an animation in the graphics area as per the default selected joint type in the **Type** drop-down list of the dialog box.

Now, you need to define the type of joint to be applied between the selected components.

11.30

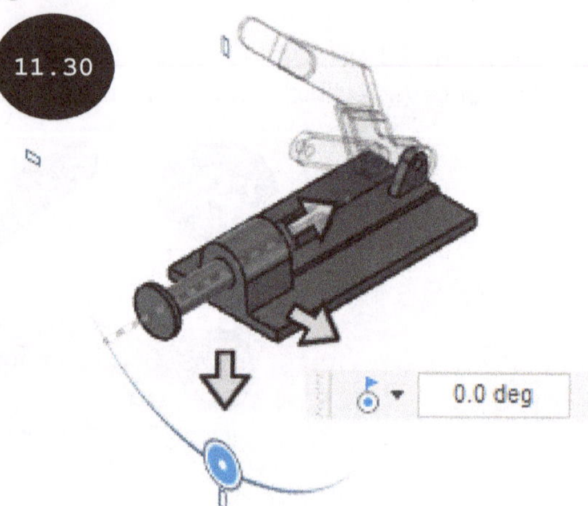

6. Click on the **Motion** tab in the dialog box and then select the **Slider** option in the **Type** drop-down list of the dialog box to slide the moveable component along an axis.

7. Select the required option in the **Slide** drop-down list in the **Motion** tab for defining the translational movement of the component.

Note: You can define the translational movement of the component along the X, Y, or Z axis by selecting the corresponding option from the **Slide** drop-down list.

Alternatively, you can define a custom axis other than the standard X, Y, or Z axes by selecting the **Custom** option in the **Slide** drop-down list. After selecting **Custom**, choose an edge or a face to define the axis along which the component will translate. If you select an edge, the component will slide along that edge. If you select a face, an axis normal (perpendicular) to the selected face is automatically defined for the translational movement.

Now, you can define minimum and maximum limits for the joint, if needed.

Joint Motion Limits: The options in the **Joint Motion Limits** rollout are used to define the minimum and maximum limits for the selected joint. The options are discussed next.

Minimum and Maximum: The **Minimum** and **Maximum** fields in the **Joint Motion Limits** rollout of the **Motion** tab are used to define the minimum and maximum motion limits for the selected joint to control the movement of the component along or about its free degrees of freedom. By default, the component is free to rotate or translate without any limitation about its free degrees of freedom, since minimum and maximum limits not defined in the respective fields, refer to Figure 11.31.

11.31

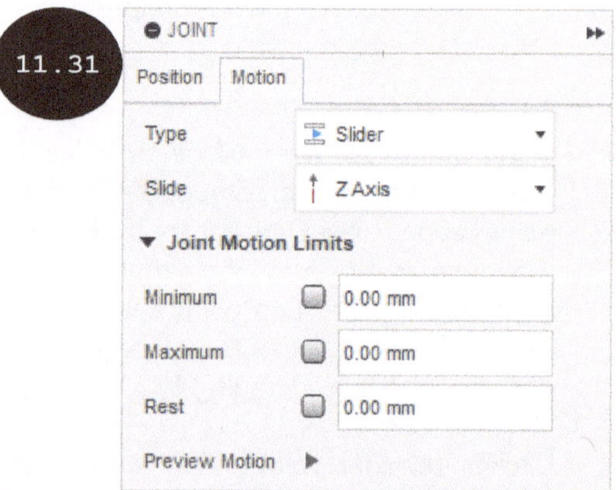

To define the minimum and maximum limits for a joint, select the **Minimum** and **Maximum** check boxes in the **Joint Motion Limits** rollout of **Motion** tab. The respective edit fields get enabled. After selecting the **Minimum** and **Maximum** check boxes, you can specify the minimum and maximum limits for the motion of the selected joint type in the respective fields, see Figures 11.32 and 11.33. Note that the limits are measured between the locations of the joint origins defined on the components.

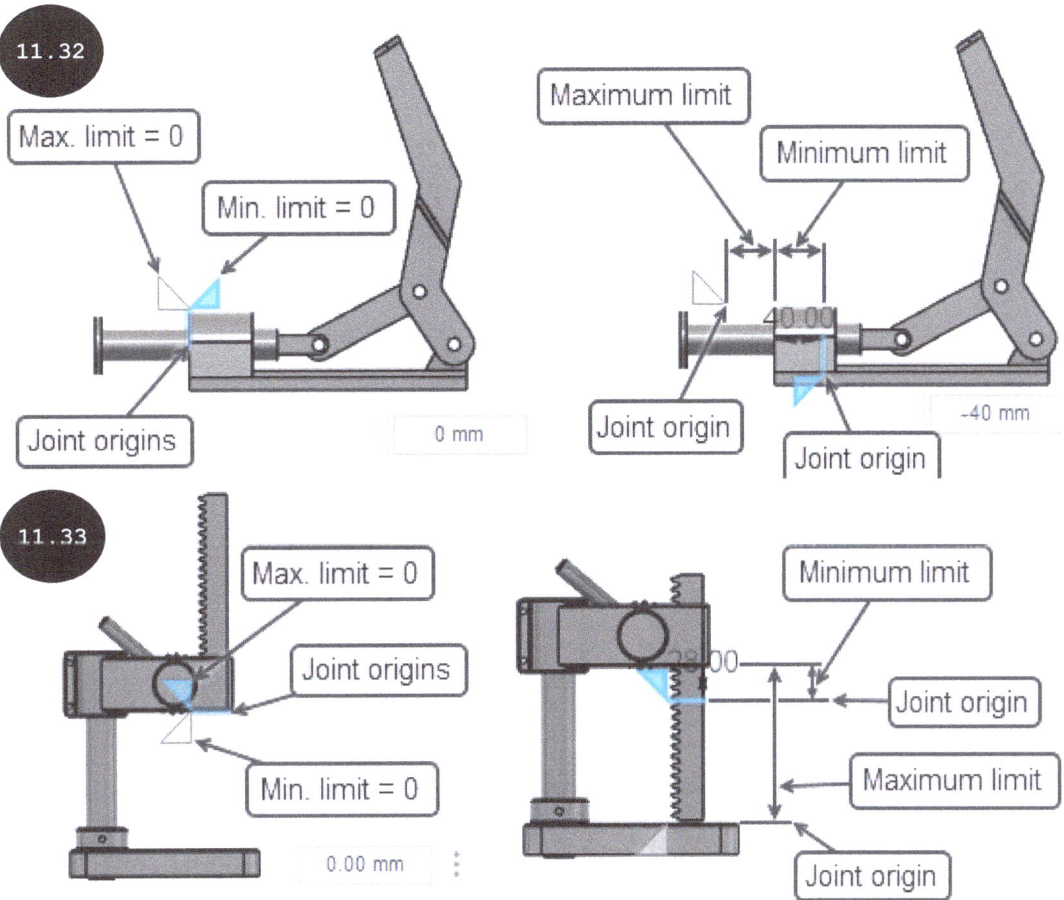

Rest: The **Rest** check box in the **Joint Motion Limits** rollout is used for defining the rest position of the component. The rest position of the component is the position where the component will come to rest after the motion. On selecting the **Rest** check box, the respective edit field gets enabled in its front in the dialog box. In this field, you can specify the rest position of the component. You can define the rest position of the component anywhere between the minimum and maximum limits defined.

Preview Limits: The **Preview Limits** button ▶ in the **Joint Motion Limits** rollout is used for animating the movement of the component between the specified minimum and maximum limits of the joint, see Figures 11.34 and 11.35.

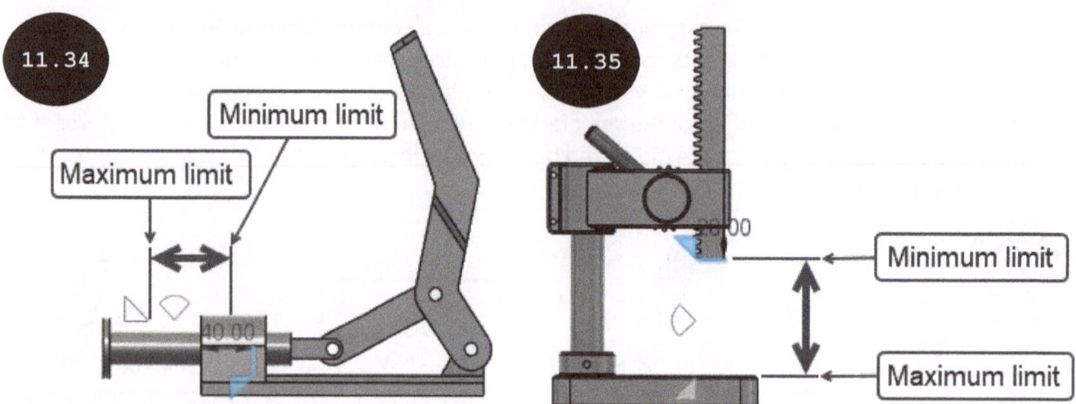

8. Define the minimum and maximum motion limits for the selected joint by selecting the respective check boxes in the **Joint Motion Limits** rollout of the **Motion** tab as discussed above, if needed.

9. Click on the **OK** button in the dialog box. The slider joint is applied between the components such that all degrees of freedom of the components are removed except a single translational degree of freedom and the component can slide along the specified axis, within the defined minimum and maximum limits, see Figures 11.34 and 11.35.

Tip: To review the movement of a component after applying a joint, select the component and then drag it along or about its free degree of freedom.

Applying a Revolute Joint

The revolute joint allows a component to rotate about an axis by removing all degrees of freedom except one rotational degree of freedom, see Figure 11.36. This joint type is used for rotating the component around an axis which is defined by the joint origins of the components. The method for applying a revolute joint is discussed below:

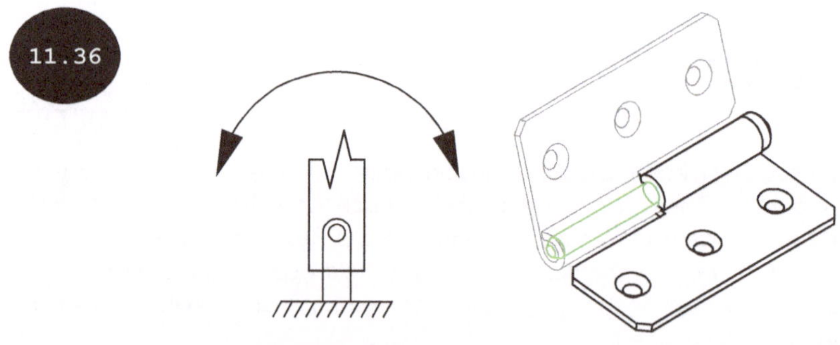

Revolute Joint
(No translational movement, only one rotational movement is allowed)

1. Press the J key or invoke the **RELATIONSHIPS** drop-down menu and click on the **Joint** tool. The **JOINT** dialog box appears.

2. Ensure that the **Simple** button is activated in the **Origin Mode** area of the **Component 1** rollout to define the position of the joint origin on a face, an edge, or a point of a component.

Note: To define the joint origin on a plane located at the center between two selected faces, or at the intersection of two selected edges of a component, select the **Between Two Faces** or **Two Edge Intersection** button in the **Origin Mode** area of the **Component 1** rollout. These options are discussed in detail later in this chapter.

3. Move the cursor over a face or an edge of the first component (moveable component). The face/edge gets highlighted, and the snap points appear, see Figure 11.37. In this figure, the cursor has been moved on a circular edge of the component. As a result, only one snap point appears at the center of the edge and the joint origin is snapped to it, by default.

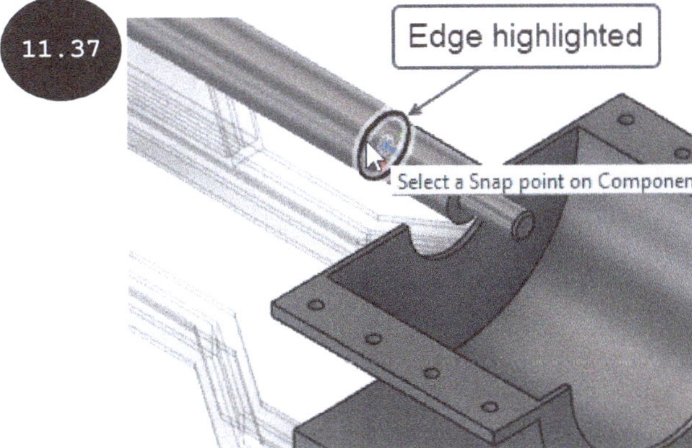

4. Click on the snap point to define the position of the joint origin on the first component. Note that to lock a face or an edge to select its snap point easily, you need to press the CTRL key. The joint origin is defined, and the component becomes transparent.

   Now, you need to define the joint origin on the second component.

5. Move the cursor over a face or an edge of the second component. The face or edge gets highlighted, and its snap points appear, see Figure 11.38. In this figure, the cursor has been moved on a circular edge of the component. As a result, only one snap point appears at the center of the edge and the joint origin is snapped to it, by default.

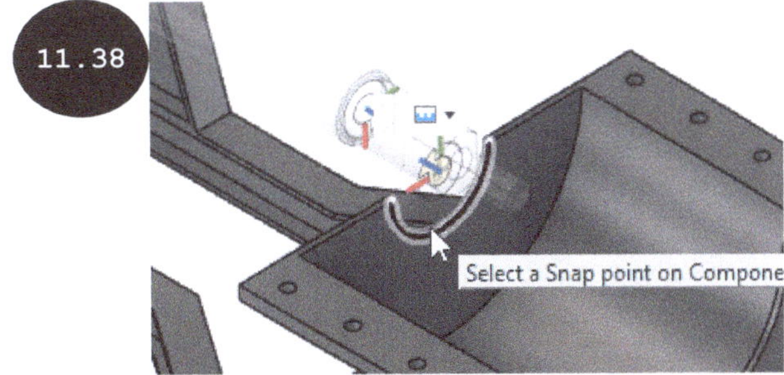

6. Click on the snap point to define the position of the joint origin on the second component. The first component moves toward the second component and the joint origins of both components

coincide with each other in the graphics area, see Figure 11.39. Also, a preview of the motion between the components begins to animate in the graphics area as per the default selected joint type in the **Motion** tab of the dialog box.

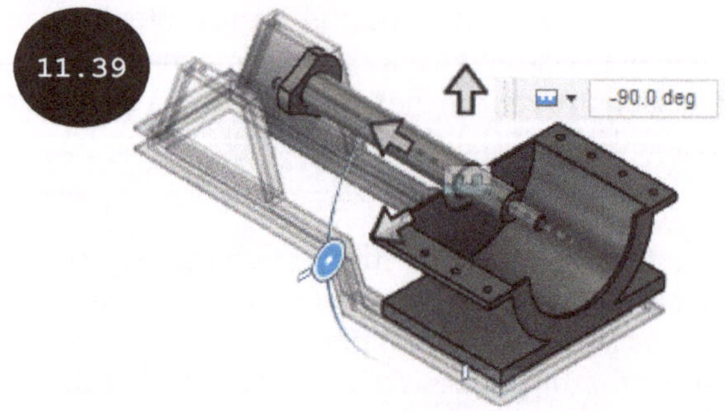

Note: You can lock a face or an edge of the component to easily select its snap point by pressing and holding the CTRL key.

7. Specify the alignment between the components by using the **Alignment** rollout in the **Position** tab of the dialog box, if needed.

Now, you need to define the type of joint to be applied.

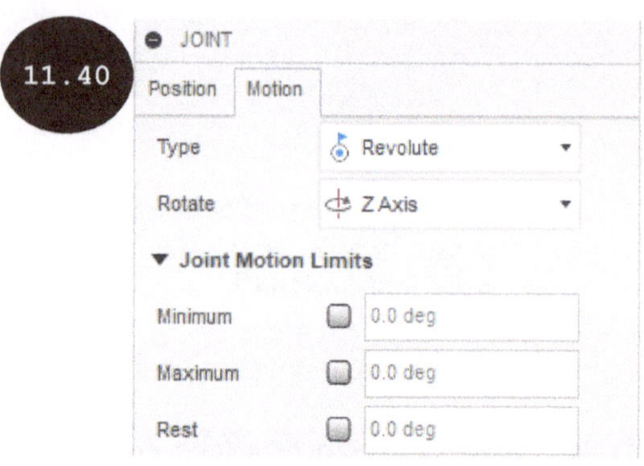

8. Click on the **Motion** tab in the dialog box to select a type of joint to be applied between the selected components, see Figure 11.40.

9. Select the **Revolute** option in the **Type** drop-down list of the **Motion** tab for applying the revolute joint.

10. Define the required axis of rotation for the component by selecting the required option in the **Rotate** drop-down list of the **Motion** tab.

Note: You can define the rotational movement of the component about the X, Y, or Z axis by selecting the corresponding option from the **Rotate** drop-down list.

Alternatively, you can specify a custom axis other than the standard X, Y, and Z axes by selecting the **Custom** option from the **Rotate** drop-down list. After selecting **Custom**, choose an edge or a face to define the axis about which the component will rotate. If you select an edge, the component rotates about that edge. If you select a face, an axis normal (perpendicular) to the selected face is automatically defined for the rotational movement.

11. Define the minimum and maximum limits for the rotational degree of freedom of the component by selecting the respective check boxes in the **Joint Motion Limits** rollout of the **Motion** tab as

discussed earlier, if needed. You can also define the rest position of the component by selecting the **Rest** check box.

Note: By default, the component can rotate or translate freely without any restriction on its degrees of freedom, because no minimum or maximum values are defined in the respective fields of the **Joint Motion Limits** rollout. If needed, you can define limits, as discussed earlier.

12. Click the **OK** button in the dialog box. The Revolute joint is applied between the components such that all degrees of freedom are restricted except the rotational degree of freedom. As a result, the component can rotate about the specified axis.

    You can verify the motion of the component after applying the joint by dragging it along or about its available degree of freedom.

Applying a Cylindrical Joint

The cylindrical joint allows a component to both translate and rotate along the same axis by restricting all other degrees of freedom, as shown in Figure 11.41. This joint is typically used to create a screw mechanism, where the component can move linearly and rotate along a common axis. The method for applying a cylindrical joint is discussed below:

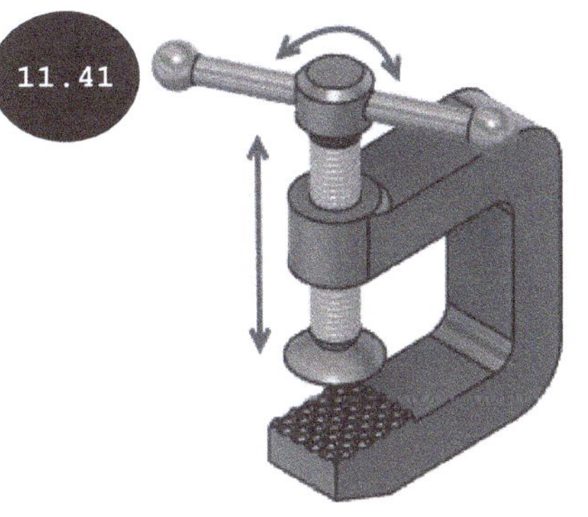

1. Press the J key. The **JOINT** dialog box appears, and the **Simple** button  is activated in the **Origin Mode** area of the **Component 1** rollout.

2. Move the cursor over a face or an edge of the first component (moveable component). The face or edge gets highlighted, and its snap points appear, see Figure 11.42.

3. Click on the snap point to define the position of the joint origin on the first component. The joint origin is defined at the specified snap point and the component becomes transparent.

   Now, you need to define the joint origin on the second component.

4. Move the cursor over a face, an edge, or a vertex of the second component. The snap points appear, see Figure 11.43.

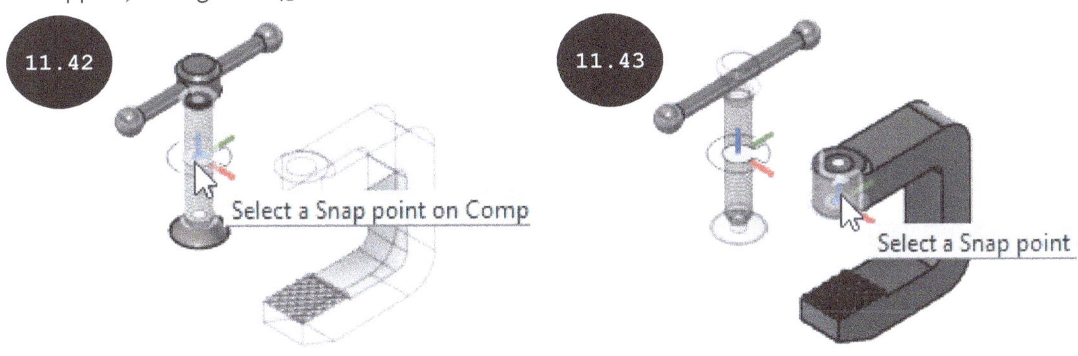

5. Click the left mouse button when the joint origin snaps to the required snap point for defining its position on the second component. The first component moves toward the second component and the joint origins of both components coincide in the graphics area, see Figure 11.44.

   Now, you need to define the type of joint to be applied between the selected components.

6. Click on the **Motion** tab and select the **Cylindrical** option in the **Type** drop-down list to allow the component to rotate as well as translate along the same axis, see Figure 11.45.

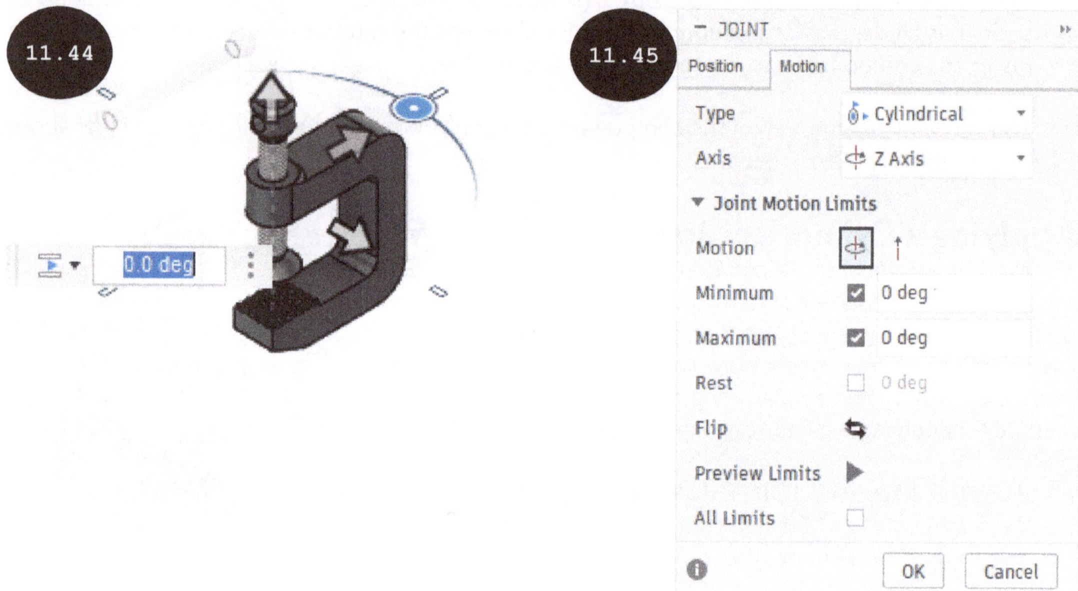

7. Select the required axis to define the rotation and translation of the component in the **Axis** drop-down list in the **Motion** tab of the dialog box.

   Joint Motion Limits: After selecting the **Cylindrical** joint type, you can define the minimum and maximum limits for both the rotational and translational free degrees of freedom of the component by using the options available in the **Joint Motion Limits** rollout of the dialog box.

   To specify the minimum and maximum limits for the rotational motion of the cylindrical joint, first ensure that the **Rotate** button is activated in the **Motion** area of the **Joint Motion Limits** rollout (refer to Figure 11.45). Next, select the **Minimum** and **Maximum** check boxes, and then enter the required rotational limit values in the respective fields that become available in the rollout.

   You can also define a rest position for the rotational motion by selecting the **Rest** check box and specifying the desired value.

8. After defining the minimum and maximum limits for the rotational and translational free degrees of freedom of the component, if required, using the options in the **Joint Motion Limits** rollout as discussed above, you can preview both motions simultaneously. To do this, select the **All Limits** check box and then click the **Preview Motion** button.

9. Click on the **OK** button in the dialog box. The cylindrical joint is applied between the components such that the component can rotate as well as translate along the specified axis, see Figure 11.46.

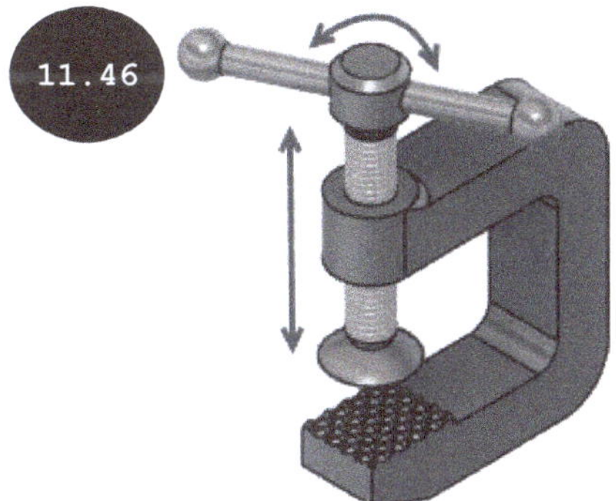

Applying a Pin-slot Joint

The pin-slot joint allows a component to translate along one axis and rotate around a different axis by limiting all degrees of freedom except for a single translational and a single rotational motion, as shown in Figure 11.47. This joint is typically used to create a pin-slot mechanism, where the pin can move along the length of the slot and rotate around its axis. The method for applying a pin-slot joint is discussed below:

1. Press the J key or invoke the **RELATIONSHIPS** drop-down menu and click on the **Joint** tool. The **JOINT** dialog box appears, and the **Simple** button is activated in the **Origin Mode** area of the **Component 1** rollout.

2. Move the cursor over a face or an edge of the first component (moveable component) and then specify the location of the joint origin on the required snap point, see Figure 11.48.

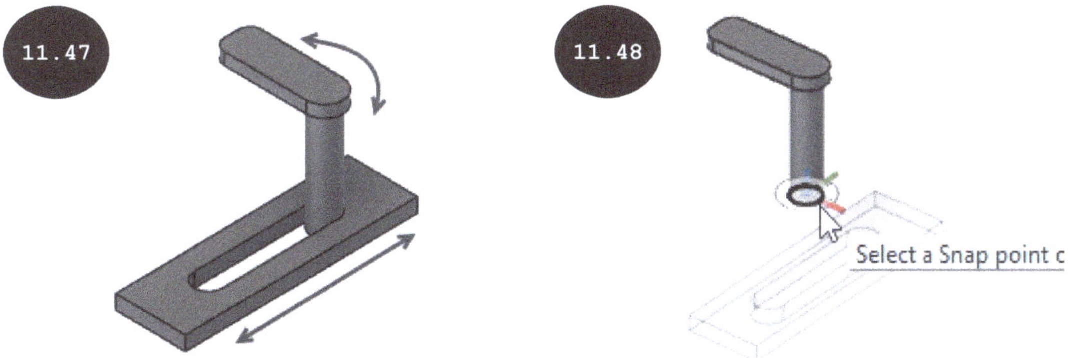

3. Move the cursor over a face or an edge of the second component and then specify the location of the joint origin on the required snap point, see Figure 11.49. The joint origins of both components coincide with each other in the graphics area, see Figure 11.50.

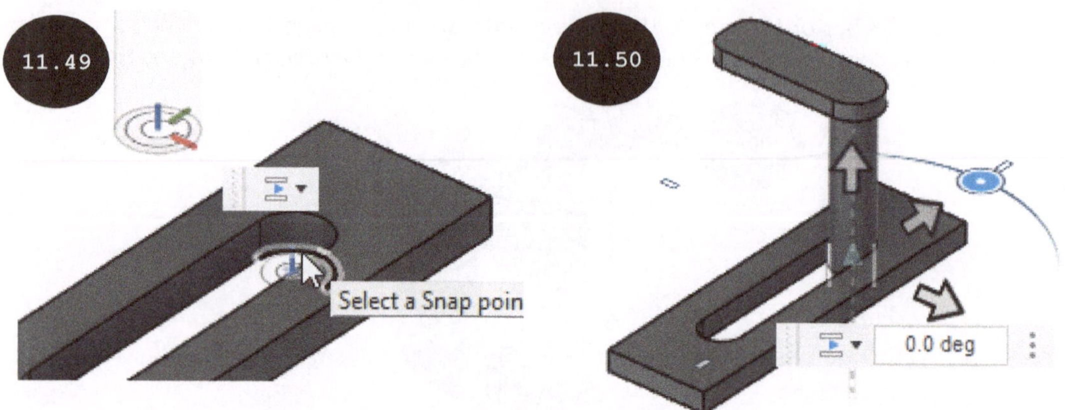

Now, you need to define the type of joint to be applied between the selected components.

4. Click on the **Motion** tab and select the **Pin-slot** option in the **Type** drop-down list to allow the component to rotate about an axis and translate along a different axis, see Figure 11.51.

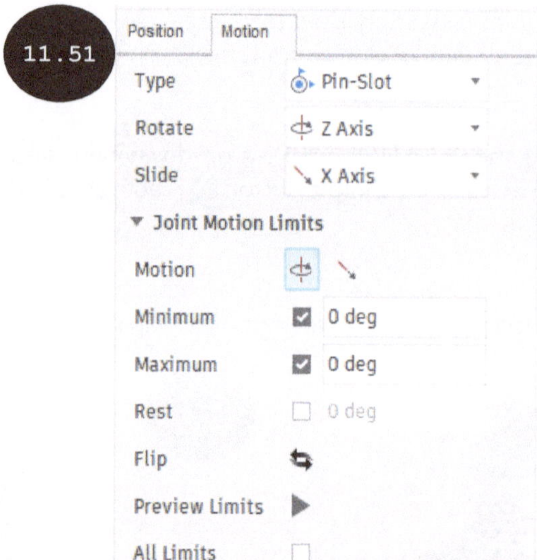

5. Select the required axis of rotation in the **Rotate** drop-down list of the **Motion** tab.

6. Select the required direction of translation in the **Slide** drop-down list of the **Motion** tab.

Note: You can also define a custom axis for the rotation or translation direction of the component by using the **Custom** option. To do this, select the **Custom** option in the **Rotate** or **Slide** drop-down list and then select an edge or a face to define the custom axis for the rotation or translation direction of the component, respectively.

7. If required, define the minimum and maximum limits for the rotational and translational free degrees of freedom of the component by activating the respective **Rotate** and **Slide** buttons in

the **Motion** area of the **Joint Motion Limits** rollout. The available options are the same as those discussed earlier.

After defining the limits, you can preview both motions simultaneously by selecting the **All Limits** check box and clicking the **Preview Motion** button.

8. Click on the **OK** button in the dialog box. The pin-slot joint is applied between the components such that the components can rotate and translate along different axes, see Figure 11.52.

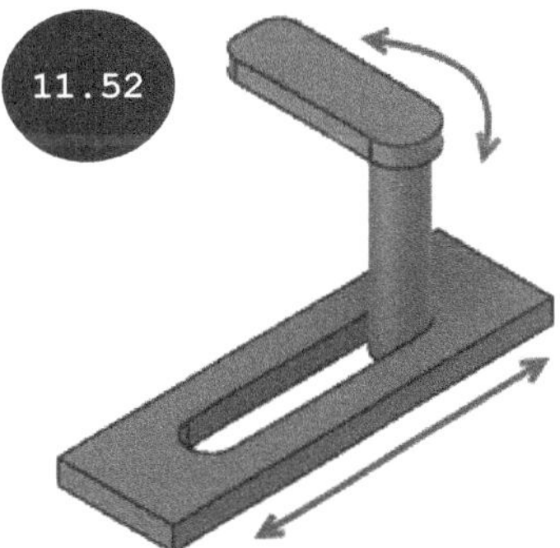

Applying a Planar Joint

The planar joint allows a component to translate along two axes and rotate about a single axis, see Figure 11.53. This joint restricts the component's movement in the direction normal to a planar face of another component while allowing motion within the plane of that face. The component can also rotate around an axis normal to the planar face. For instance, an object can slide on the surface of a tabletop and also rotate around an axis perpendicular to the tabletop. The method for applying a planar joint is discussed below:

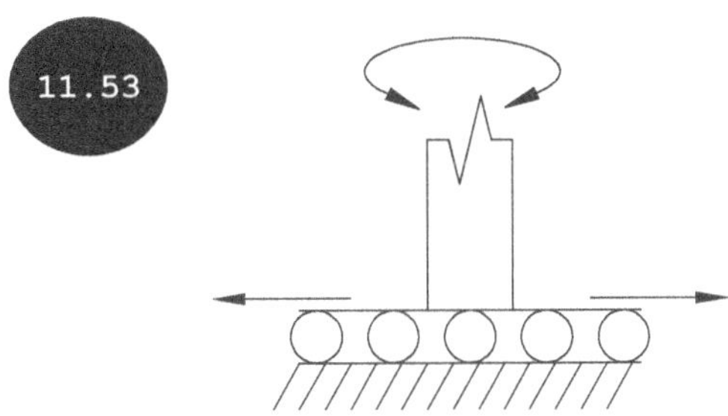

Planar Joint
(Moves freely within the plane of face with no movement in the direction normal to the planar face. Also, allows a rotational movement about an axis)

1. Invoke the **JOINT** dialog box and then move the cursor over a face or an edge of the first component (moveable component) and then specify the location of the joint origin on a required snap point, see Figure 11.54. Note that you can lock a face or an edge to select its snap point easily by pressing the CTRL key.

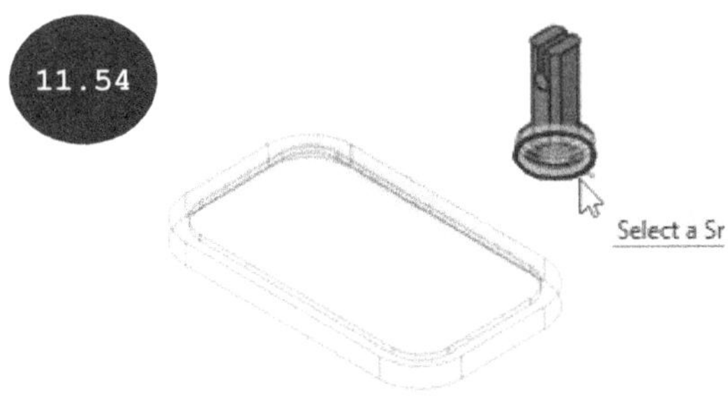

2. Move the cursor over a face or an edge of the second component and then specify the location of the joint origin on a required snap point, see Figure 11.55. The joint origins of both components coincide with each other in the graphics area, see Figure 11.56.

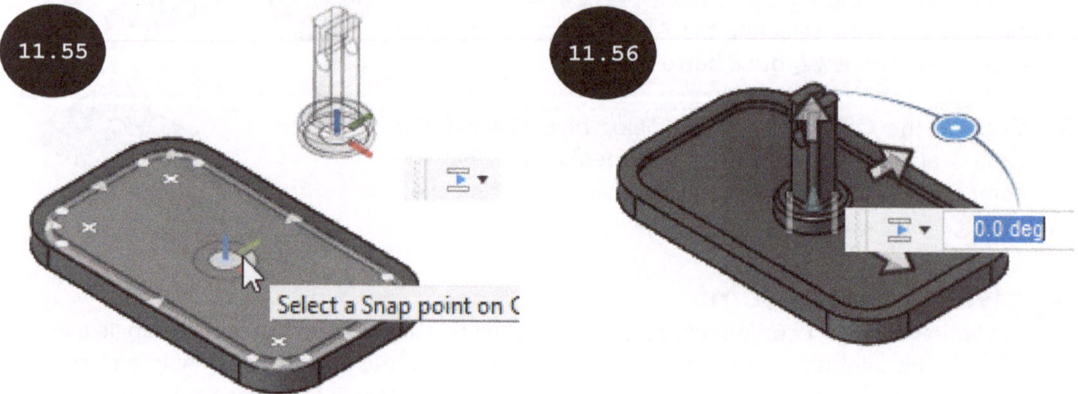

Now, you need to define the type of joint to be applied between the selected components.

3. Click on the **Motion** tab and select the **Planar** option in the **Type** drop-down list to allow the component to translate along two axes as well as rotate about a single axis, see Figure 11.57.

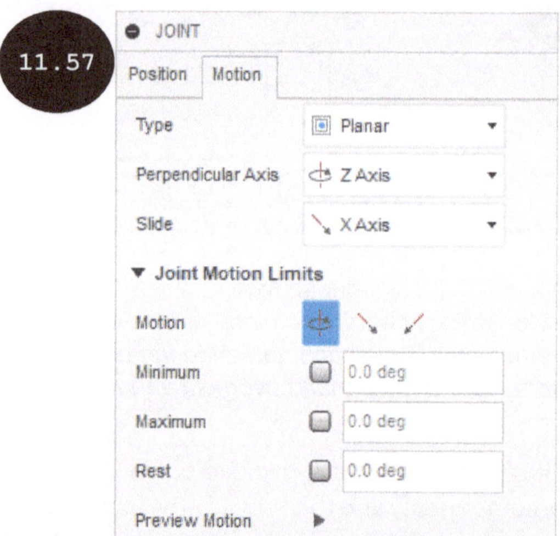

4. Select the required axis to define the rotation of the component in the **Perpendicular Axis** drop-down list of the **Motion** tab.

5. Select the required axis in the **Slide** drop-down list to define the two translational movements of the component within the plane of the face. By default, it is defined based on the option selected in the **Perpendicular Axis** drop-down list of the dialog box.

6. If required, define the minimum and maximum limits for the one rotational and two translational free degrees of freedom of the component by activating the respective **Rotate**, **Slide 1**, and **Slide 2** buttons in the **Motion** area of the **Joint Motion Limits** rollout.

After defining the limits, you can preview all the motions simultaneously by selecting the **All Limits** check box and clicking the **Preview Motion** button.

7. Click on the OK button in the dialog box. The planar joint is applied between the components such that the component can translate along two axes (plane of the face) as well as rotate about the specified axis, see Figure 11.58.

11.58

Applying a Ball Joint

The ball joint allows a component to rotate around all three rotational axes, see Figure 11.59. This joint restricts all translational degrees of freedom, meaning the component cannot move linearly in any direction. Instead, it can freely rotate around the three axes with respect to a fixed point known as the joint origin. The method for applying a ball joint is discussed below:

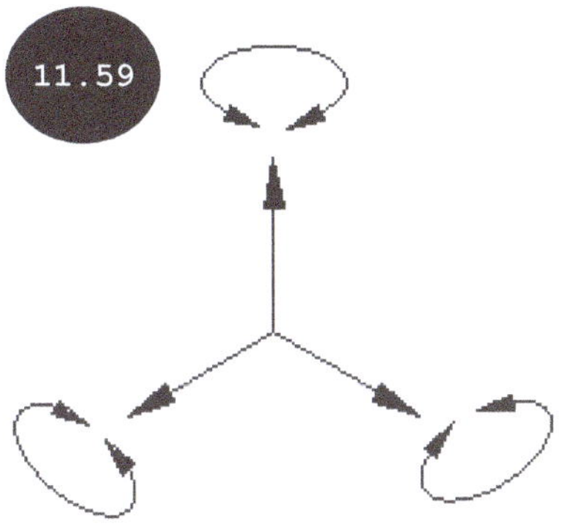

11.59

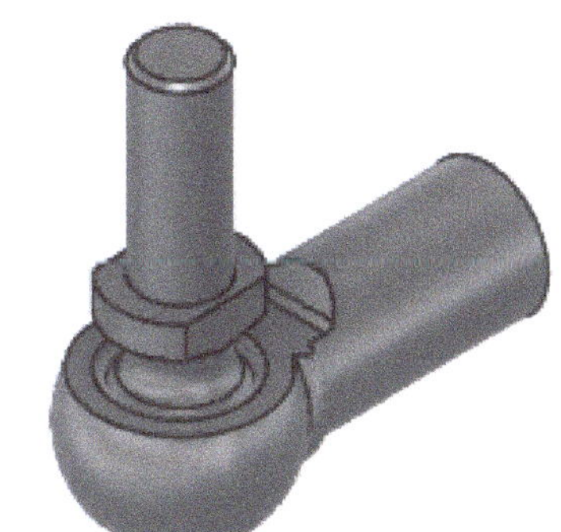

1. Invoke the JOINT dialog box. The options in this dialog box were discussed earlier.

2. Move the cursor over the spherical face of the first component (moveable component) and then click to specify the location of the joint origin at its center snap point, see Figure 11.60.

   Now, you need to define the joint origin of the second component.

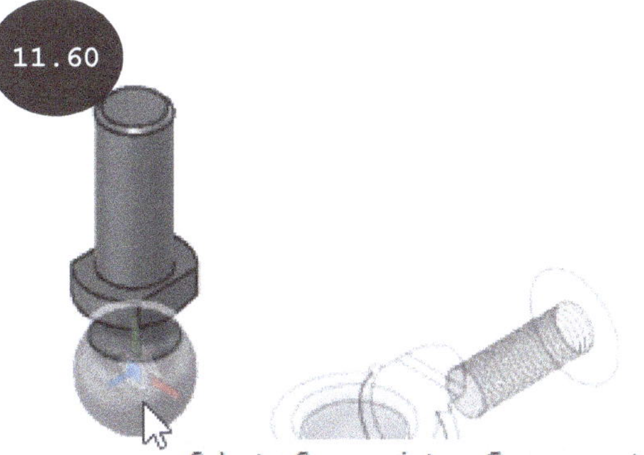

11.60

3. Move the cursor over the spherical face of the second component and then click to specify the location of the joint origin at its center snap point that appears, see Figure 11.61. The joint origins of both components coincide with each other in the graphics area, see Figure 11.62.

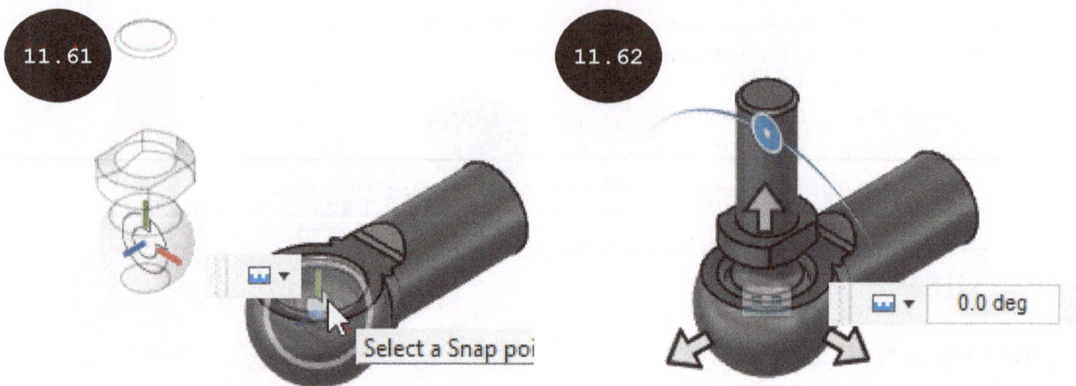

Now, you need to define the type of joint to be applied between the selected components.

4. Click on the **Motion** tab and select the **Ball** option in the **Type** drop-down list to allow the component to rotate about three axes, see Figure 11.63.

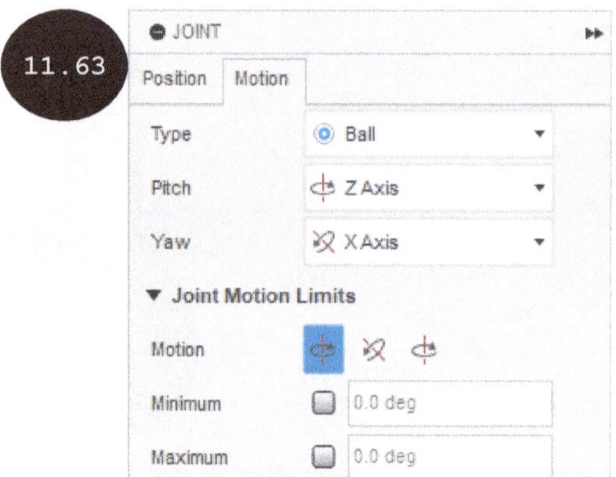

5. Select the axis as the lateral axis of the component in the **Pitch** drop-down list of the **Motion** tab.

6. Select the axis as the longitudinal/perpendicular axis of the component in the **Yaw** drop-down list of the **Motion** tab.

7. Define the minimum and maximum limits for the three rotational degrees of freedom of the component by activating the respective buttons (**Pitch** , **Yaw** , and **Roll**) in the **Motion** area of the **Joint Motion Limits** rollout, if needed. The options are the same as discussed earlier.

8. Click on the **OK** button in the dialog box. The ball joint is applied between the components such that the component can rotate about three axes and all its translational movements are restricted.

Defining the Position of the Joint Origin

As discussed earlier, to apply a joint, you must define the position of the joint origin on two different components. In Autodesk Fusion, the joint origin position can be defined using three options: **Simple**, **Between Two Faces**, and **Two Edge Intersection**. These options are available in the **JOINT** dialog box that appears when applying a joint using the **Joint** tool, see Figure 12.64. The options are discussed next.

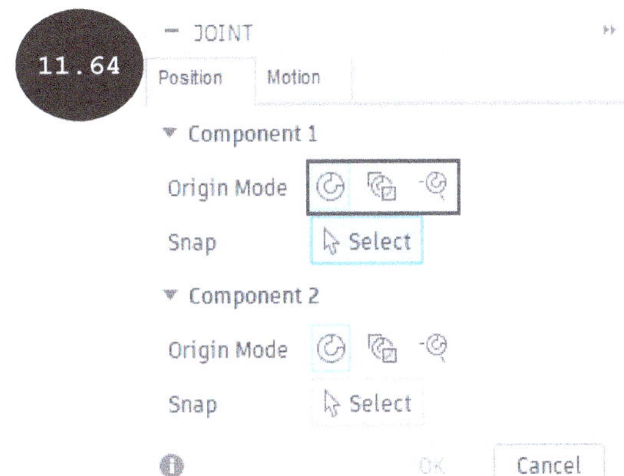

Simple

By default, the **Simple** button is activated. This option allows you to define the joint origin directly by selecting a snap point on a face, edge, or vertex of the component, as discussed earlier.

Between Two Faces

The **Between Two Faces** button is used to define the joint origin on a plane located midway between two selected faces of a component.

To define the joint origin on the component using this option, activate the **Between Two Faces** button in the **Origin Mode** area of the **Component 1** rollout. This enables the **Plane 1** and **Plane 2** selection options, see Figure 11.65. By default, the **Plane 1** option is active, allowing you to select the first face of the component, see Figure 11.66.

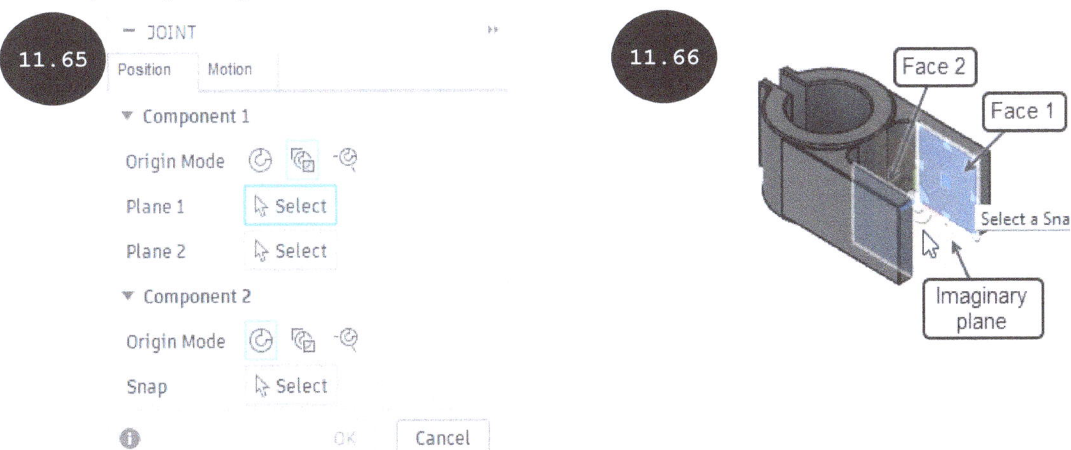

After selecting the first face, the **Plane 2** option automatically becomes active, enabling you to select the second face, refer to Figure 11.66. Once both faces are selected, the **Snap** selection option becomes available in the **Component 1** rollout.

Next, move the cursor over a geometry element (face, edge, or point) of the component. The selected geometry is highlighted, and its snap points appear. Move the cursor over the desired snap point of the highlighted geometry. The joint origin corresponding to that snap point is projected onto an imaginary plane displayed midway between the two selected faces, as illustrated in Figure 11.66.

Finally, click the desired snap point. The joint origin position is defined by projecting the selected snap point onto the imaginary mid-plane located between the two selected faces.

Similarly, you can define the joint origin on the second component by activating the **Between Two Faces** button in the **Component 2** rollout.

Two Edge Intersection

The **Two Edge Intersection** button is used to define the joint origin at the intersection of two edges of a component.

To define the joint origin on the first component using this option, click the **Two Edge Intersection** button in the **Origin Mode** area of the **Component 1** rollout. The **Edge 1** and **Edge 2** selection options become available, see Figure 11.67. By default, the **Edge 1** option is active, allowing you to select the first edge of the component, see Figure 11.68.

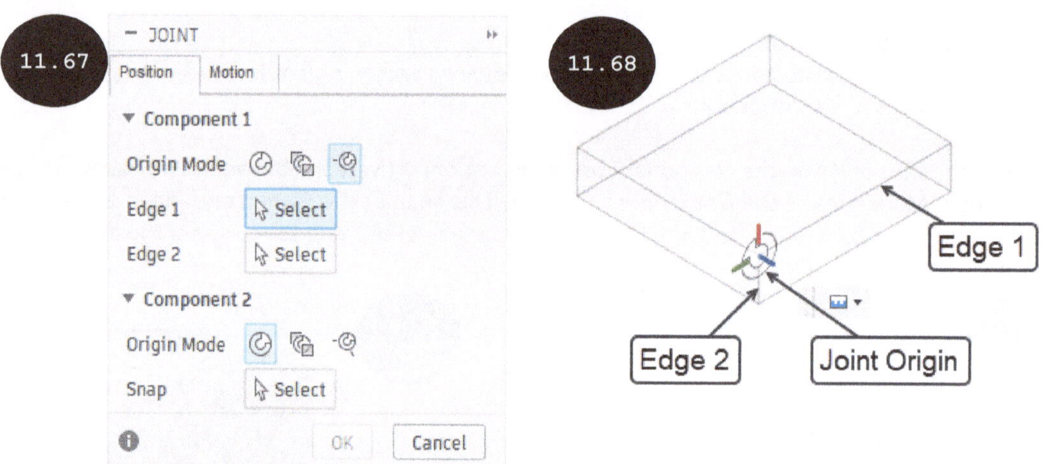

After selecting the first edge, the **Edge 2** option automatically becomes active. Select the second edge of the component, refer to Figure 11.68. The joint origin is then defined at the intersection of the two selected edges.

Note: Once the joint origin is defined on a component, the component becomes transparent in the graphics area. This helps you clearly visualize the defined joint origin and makes it easier to define the joint origin on the other component, refer to Figure 11.68

Similarly, you can define the joint origin on the second component by activating the **Two Edge Intersection** button in the **Component 2** rollout.

Editing Joints

In Autodesk Fusion, you can edit joints that have already been applied between components in an assembly. To edit an existing joint, expand the **Joints** node in the **BROWSER**, see Figure 11.69.

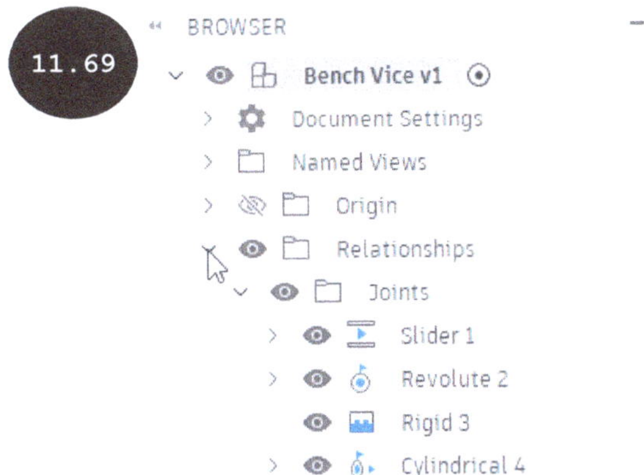

The **Joints** node displays a list of all joints applied between the components in the assembly. Expand this node in the **BROWSER**, and then right-click the joint you want to edit. A shortcut menu appears (see Figure 11.70), and the selected joint is highlighted in the graphics area. Next, click the **Edit Joint** option in the shortcut menu. The **EDIT JOINT** dialog box appears, see Figure 11.71.

Alternatively, you can right click the joint in the **Timeline** and select the **Edit Joint** option from the shortcut menu to open the **EDIT JOINT** dialog box.

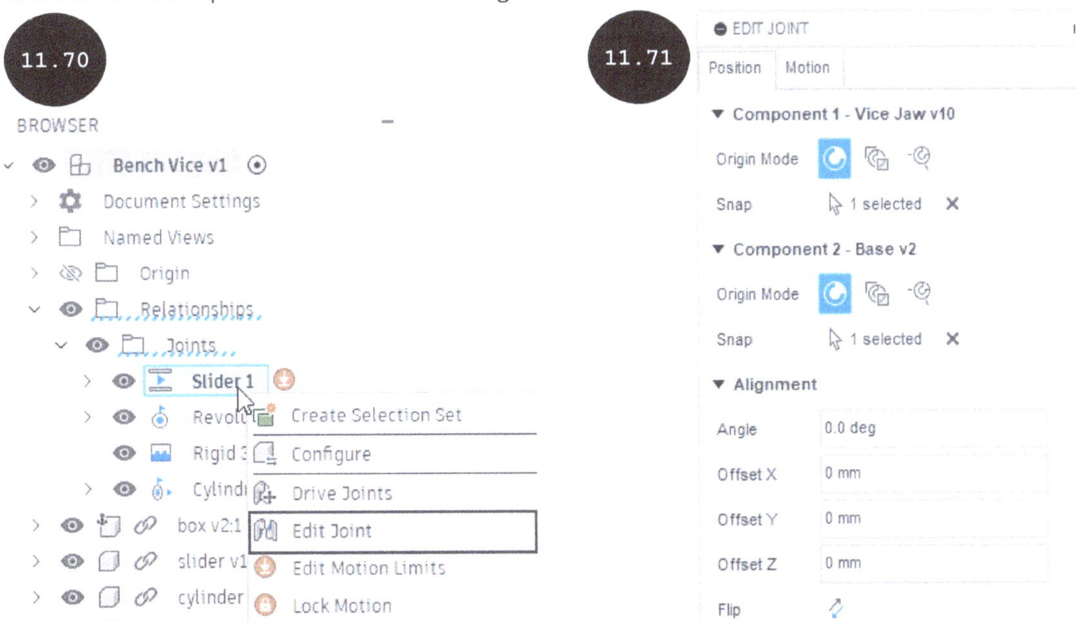

By using the options of the **EDIT JOINT** dialog box, you can define new positions for the joint origins of the components, change the type of joint, edit alignment, and so on. Once the editing has been done, click on the **OK** button in the dialog box to accept the changes and exit the **EDIT JOINT** dialog box.

Editing Joint Limits

In Autodesk Fusion, you can edit the minimum and maximum limits of an existing joint of an assembly. To edit the limits of an already applied joint, expand the **Joints** node in the **BROWSER**, refer to Figure 11.72.

11.72

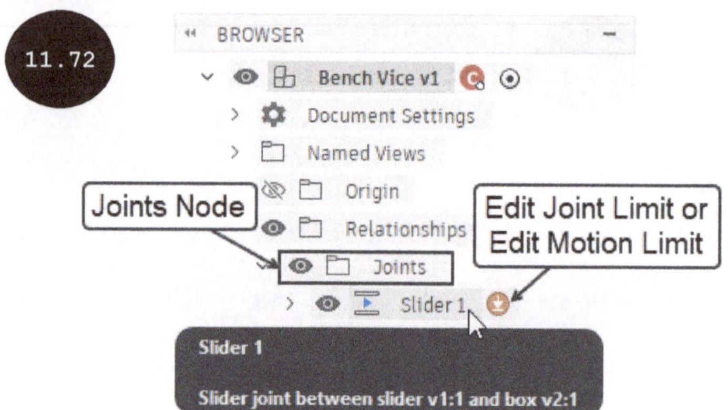

In the expanded **Joints** node, move the cursor over the joint to edit its limits. The **Edit Motion Limits** icon appears next to the name of the joint, refer to Figure 11.72. Next, click on this **Edit Motion Limits** icon. The **EDIT MOTION LIMITS** dialog box appears, see Figure 11.73. Alternatively, right-click on the joint in the expanded **Joints** node of the **BROWSER** or the **Timeline** and then click on the **Edit Motion Limits** option in the shortcut menu that appears to invoke the **EDIT MOTION LIMITS** dialog box. The options in this dialog box are used for editing or defining the minimum and maximum limits of the selected joint. The options are the same as discussed earlier.

11.73

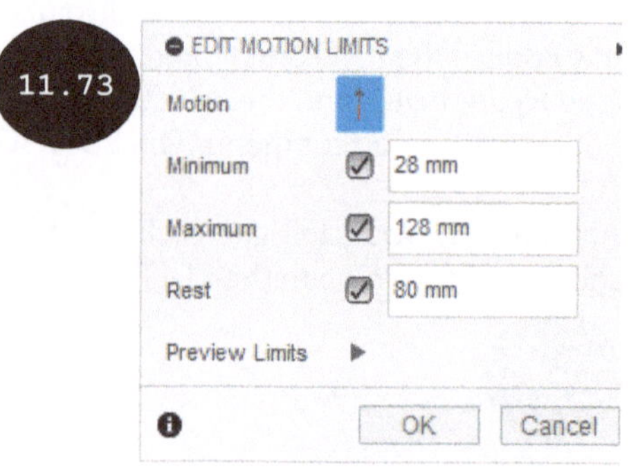

Tip: The **Motion** area in the **EDIT MOTION LIMITS** dialog box displays the types of available motions for the selected joint. For instance, a slider joint has only one translational motion. As a result, only the **Slide** button is available in the **Motion** area for defining the limits for the slider joint. However, the cylindrical joint has two motions: rotational and translational. As a result, the **Rotate** and **Slide** buttons are available in the **Motion** area for the cylindrical joint and you can define the limits for both the available motions by selecting them in this area.

After editing or defining the minimum and maximum limits for the motion of the joint in the dialog box, click on the **OK** button. The limits get modified as defined and the component can move within the specified limits.

Animating a Joint

In Autodesk Fusion, after applying a joint, you can animate it to review its motion. To do this, expand the **Joints** node in the **BROWSER** and then right-click on the joint whose motion is to be animated. A shortcut menu appears, see Figure 11.74. In this shortcut menu, click on the **Animate Joint** option. The motion of the selected joint starts animating in the graphics area. To stop/end the animation, press the ESC key.

11.74

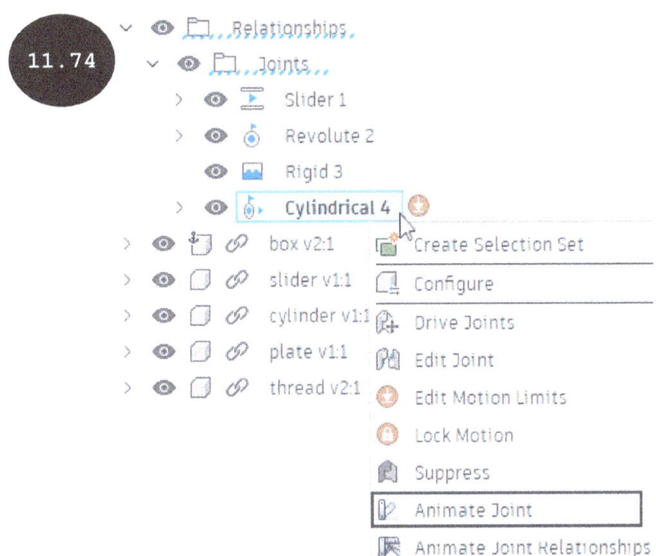

Animating the Model

11.75

In Autodesk Fusion, in addition to animating a joint, you can animate the model/assembly to review its working conditions and the behavior of its components concerning each other. To do this, right-click on the joint in the expanded **Joints** node of the **BROWSER** and then click on the **Animate Joint Relationships** option in the shortcut menu that appears. The model starts animating in the graphics area based on the joints applied. For example, in Figure 11.75, on animating the revolute joint of the crank shaft, the crank shaft starts rotating about its axis, and simultaneously the piston starts sliding up and down, which is connected to the crank shaft through the connecting rod. Note that to animate an assembly in the same way as its real-world working conditions, you need to apply proper joints between its components.

Locking/Unlocking the Motion of a Joint

In Autodesk Fusion, you can temporarily lock the motion of a joint. To do this, right-click on the joint to be locked in the expanded **Joints** node of the **BROWSER** or in the **Timeline** and then click on the **Lock Motion** option in the shortcut menu that appears, see Figure 11.76. The motion of the selected joint gets locked temporarily in its current position.

To unlock the motion of a locked joint, right-click on the joint and then click on the **Unlock Motion** option in the shortcut menu that appears. Alternatively, click on the **Revert Position** tool in the contextual **POSITION** panel that appears at the end of the **Toolbar**, see Figure 11.77.

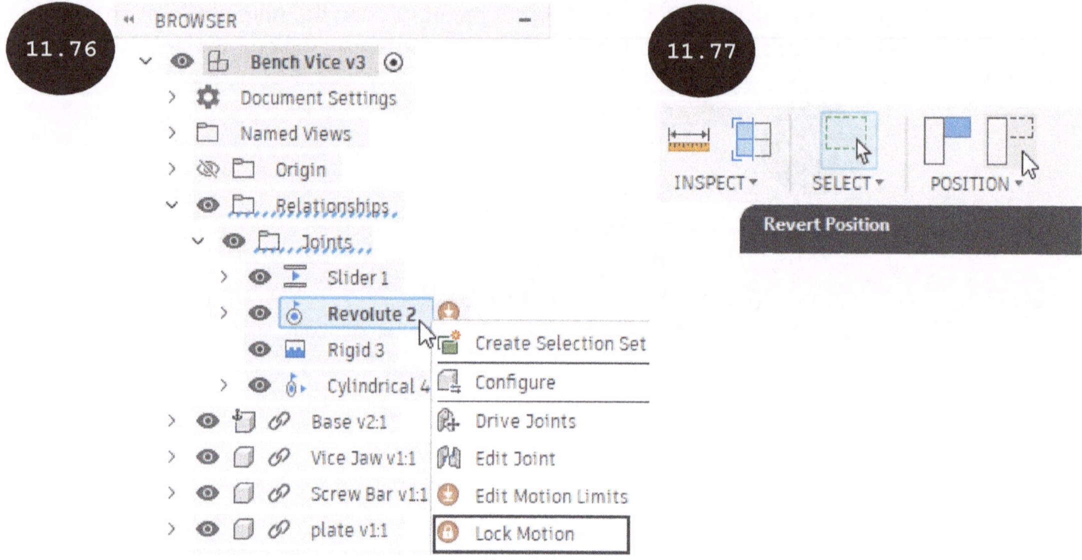

Driving a Joint

In Autodesk Fusion, you can drive a joint within its free degrees of freedom to define a new position of the component using the **Drive Joints** tool. To do this, invoke the **MOTION** drop-down menu in the **ASSEMBLY** tab and then click on the **Drive Joints** tool, see Figure 11.78. The **DRIVE JOINTS** dialog box appears, see Figure 11.79.

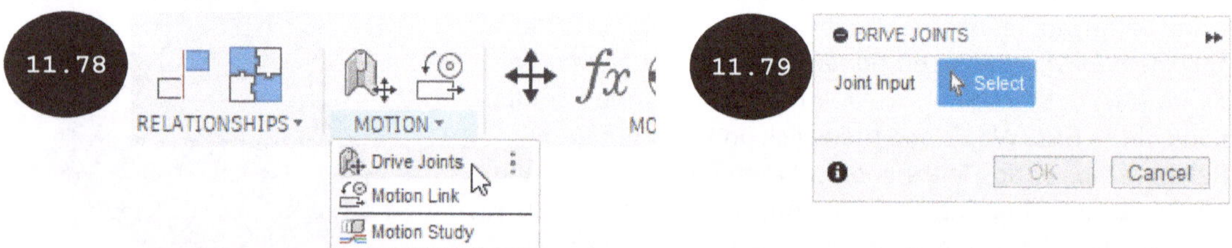

After invoking the **DRIVE JOINT** dialog box, select the joint to be driven within its available degrees of freedom from the expanded **Joints** node in the **BROWSER** or from the **Timeline**. The **Distance** and/or **Rotation** fields appear in the dialog box, refer to Figure 11.80.

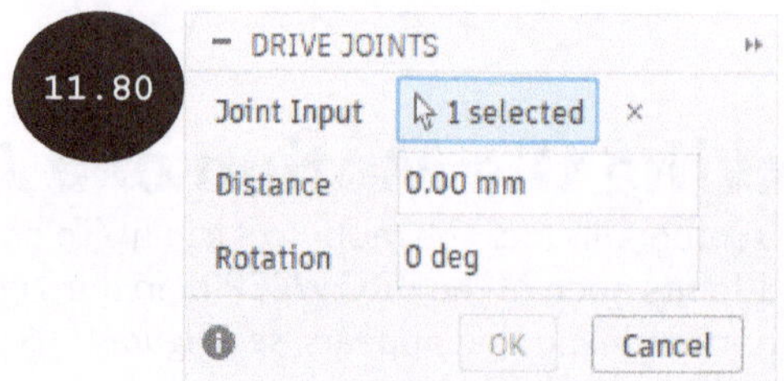

Note that the fields displayed in the dialog box depend on the type of joint selected. For example, when a Cylindrical joint is selected, both the **Distance** and **Rotation** fields appear, allowing you to drive the translational as well as rotational motion of the joint. In contrast, when a Slider joint is selected, only the **Distance** field appears, as it supports only translational motion.

Enter the required values in the available fields to drive the selected joint and define the new position of the corresponding component in the graphics area. Alternatively, you can drag the arrows displayed in the graphics area to drive the joint interactively. After driving the joint, click the **OK** button in the dialog box to confirm the changes. You can also reposition a component directly by dragging it along its available degrees of freedom in the graphics area.

Defining Relative Motion between Two Joints

In Autodesk Fusion, you can also define relative motion between two joints by using the **Motion Link** tool. For example, you can define the relative motion between the slider and revolute joints such that the linear motion of one component translates to the rotational motion of another component and vice-versa, see Figure 11.81.

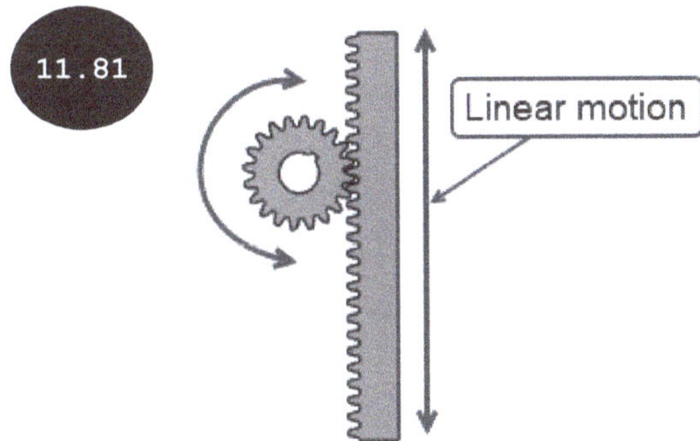

To define the relative motion between two joints, invoke the **MOTION** drop-down menu in the **ASSEMBLY** tab and then click on the **Motion Link** tool, see Figure 11.82. The **MOTION LINK** dialog box appears, see Figure 11.83.

Once the **MOTION LINK** dialog box is invoked, select two joints in the **Joints** node of the **BROWSER** or in the **Timeline**, one by one. The dialog box gets modified with additional options, which are used for controlling the relative motion between the selected joints. Note that the availability of options in the dialog box depends upon the type of joints selected, see Figure 11.84.

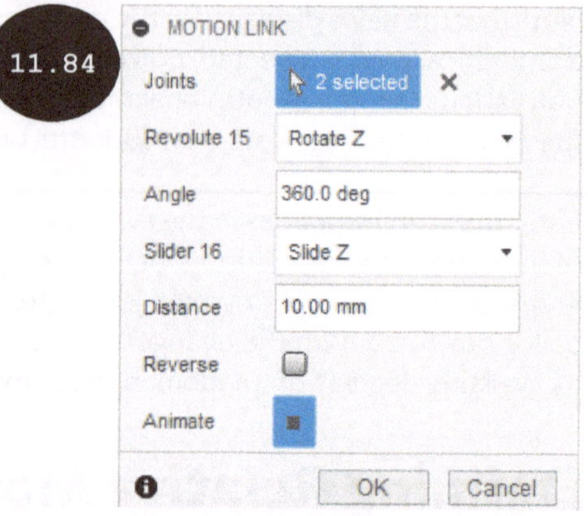

In Figure 11.84, the slider and revolute joints are selected. As a result, you can specify the distance traveled by one component concerning the angle of revolution of the other component in the **Distance** and **Angle** fields of the dialog box, respectively.

Note that the relative motion between the joints animates in the graphics area as per the values specified in the respective fields of the dialog box. You can also reverse the direction of motion by selecting the **Reverse** check box in the dialog box. You can play or stop the animation by using the **Play/Stop** button in the **Animate** area of the dialog box, respectively. After defining the relative motion between the selected joints, click on the **OK** button in the dialog box. The relative motion between the selected joints is defined and you can review it by dragging the respective components in the graphics area.

Applying Constraints

In addition to applying joints, you can also apply different types of constraints such as Align, Angle, Center, and Tangent to assemble components. Constraints are used to position components in an assembly by restricting or reducing their degrees of freedom. This is the traditional method of assembling components.

To apply a constraint between components, click the **Constrain Components** tool in the **RELATIONSHIPS** panel of the **Assembly** tab (refer to Figure 11.85) or press the C key. The **CONSTRAIN COMPONENTS** dialog box appears, see Figure 11.86. By default, the **Align** button is activated in the **Type** area of the dialog box. You can select the required constraint type to apply between the components from this area. The methods for applying different types of constraints are discussed next.

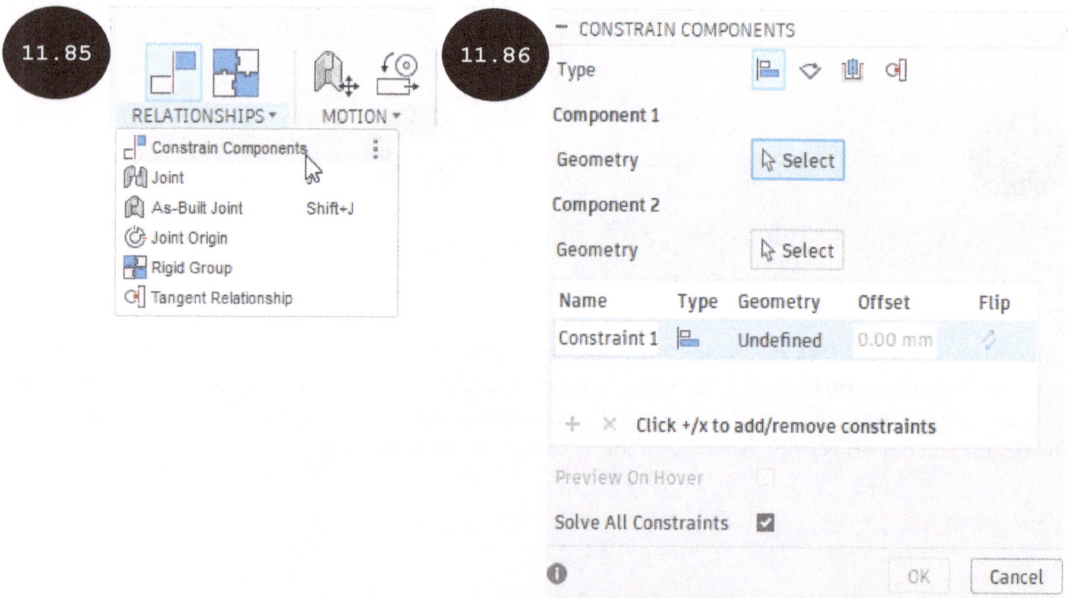

Applying an Align Constraint

The Align constraint is used to make the selected geometries of two different components aligned with each other, see Figure 11.87. You can select face (planar or cylindrical), edges, or axes of two different components as the reference geometries for applying the Align constraint.

Note that on selecting planar faces, both the selected geometries becomes coincident whereas on selecting the cylindrical faces, they becomes concentric, see Figures 11.87 and 11.88. In Figure 11.87, the the Align constraint is applied between two planar faces. In Figure 11.88, the Align constraint is applied between two cylindrical faces. The method for applying an Align constraint is discussed below:

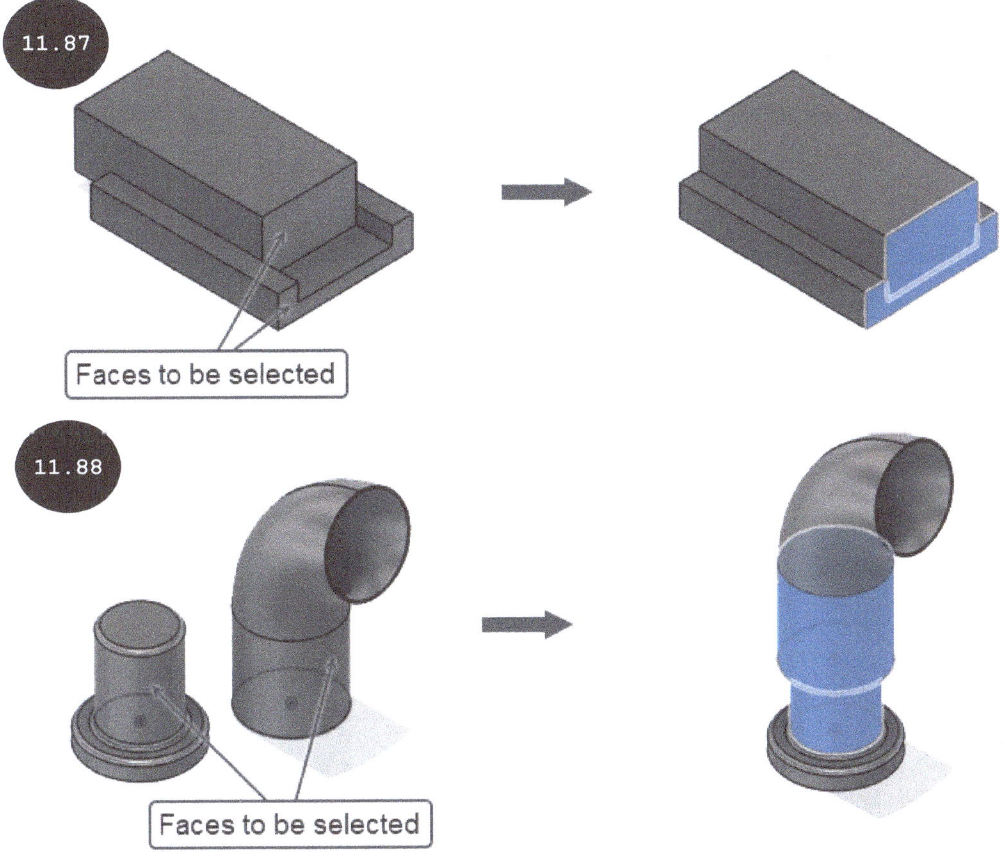

1. After invoking the **CONSTRAIN COMPONENTS** dialog box, ensure that the **Align** button is activated in the **Type** area. By default, the **Geometry** selection option for **Component 1** is active in the dialog box. As a result, you are prompted to select a geometry (face, edge, or vertex) of the first component.

2. Select the required face (planar or cylindrical), edge, or vertex as the geometry of the first component in the graphics area, see Figure 11.89. The selected component becomes transparent and the **Geometry** selection option of **Component 2** is activated automatically in the dialog box.

3. Select the required face, edge, or vertex of the second component, see Figure 11.89. The Align constraint is applied such that both the selected faces of the components become coincident.

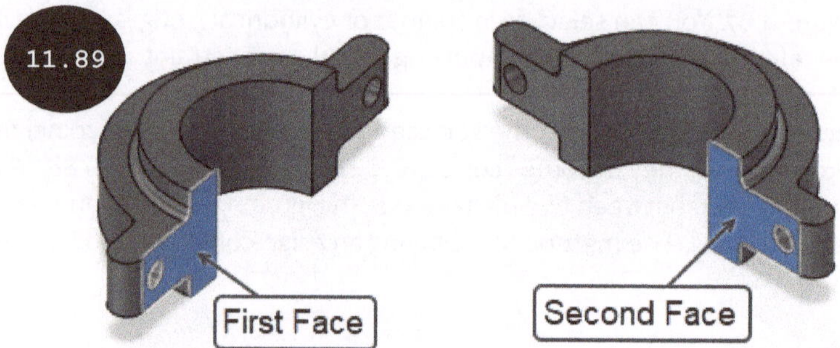

4. The Component 1 will automatically move and get attached to the selected face/edge of the Component 2, see Figure 11.90. Give the required offset value in the **Offset Distance** field, if needed.

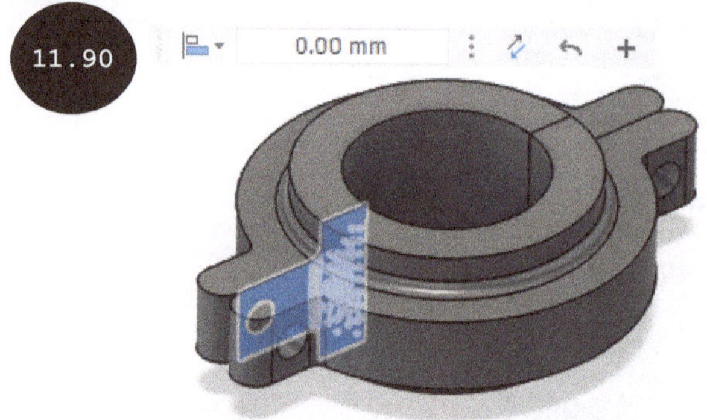

Note: When you select planar faces, the Align constraint is applied such that both faces become coincident. However, when you select two cylindrical faces, the selected faces become concentric.

5. If needed, you can reverse the alignment between the components by clicking on the **Flip** button in the dialog box.

Offset: By default, the offset value in the **Offset** column of the applied Align constraint is set to 0. As a result, the selected geometries of the two components become perfectly coincident. If required, you can enter a specific offset value to define the desired distance between the selected geometries of the components.

Add Constraint +: The **Add Constraint** button + is used to apply additional constraints between the geometries of two components in a similar manner. When you click this button +, a new constraint entry with a default name is added to the dialog box, allowing you to define another constraint between the selected geometries of the components.

Delete Constraint ×: The **Delete Constraint** button × is used to remove the selected constraint from the assembly.

6. After applying the aligned constraint between the components, click on the **OK** button.

Applying an Angle Constraint

The Angle constraint is used for restricting geometries of two different components at a specified angular distance. You can select two planar faces or linear edges of two different components as geometries for applying the angle constraint, see Figure 11.91. The method for applying an Angle constraint is discussed below:

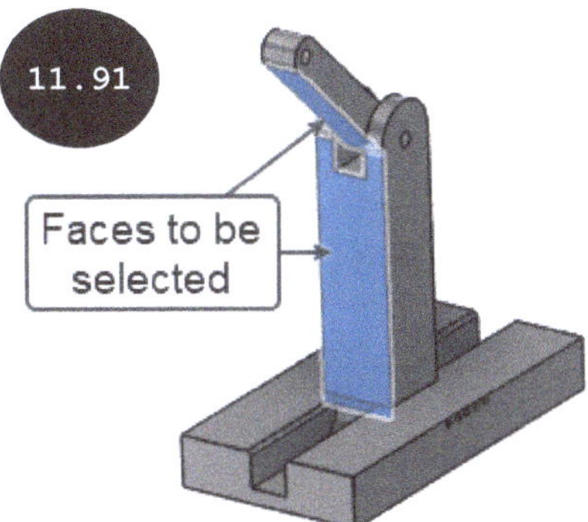

1. Invoke the **CONSTRAIN COMPONENTS** dialog box by clicking on the **Constrain Components** tool in the **RELATIONSHIPS** panel (see Figure 11.92) or pressing the **C** key.

2. Activate the **Angle** button in the **Type** area of the dialog box to apply an Angle constraint between the components. By default, the **Geometry** selection option for **Component 1** is active in the dialog box, allowing you to select a geometry (face, edge, or vertex) of the first component.

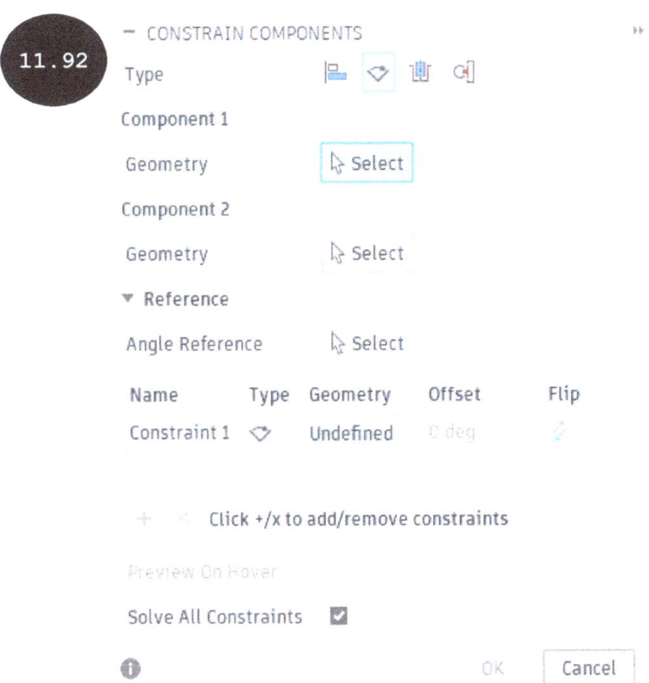

3. Select the required face or edge of the first component in the graphics area, see Figure 11.93. The selected component becomes transparent, and the **Geometry** selection option for **Component 2** is activated automatically in the dialog box.

   Now, you can select a geometry of the second component.

4. Select the required face or edge of the second component, see Figure 11.93. The Angle constraint is applied between the components with default angle value. Also, the **Angle Reference** selection option gets enabled.

11.93

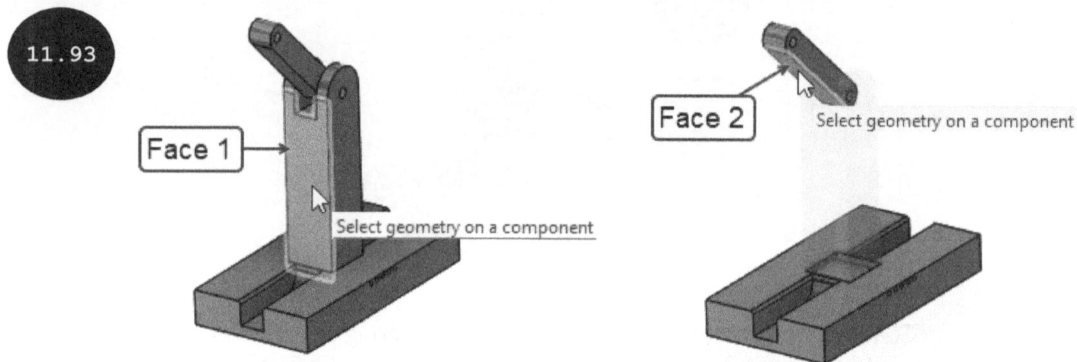

   Now, you need to define a reference geometry to control the angle between the geometries of the components.

5. Select an edge or face of a component as the reference geometry to define the angle between the selected geometries of the components.

   Now, you can define the angle value.

6. Enter the required angle value in the **Offset Angle** field of the dialog box.

7. If needed, reverse the angle between the components by clicking the **Flip** button in the dialog box.

8. After setting the desired angle, click the **OK** button. The Angle constraint with the defined angle value is applied.

Applying a Center Constraint

The Center constraint is used to position one or two planar faces of first component centrally between two parallel planar faces of second component (or vice versa), see Figures 11.94 and 11.95. This constraint ensures equal spacing on both sides and is commonly used to achieve symmetric placement in an assembly.

11.94

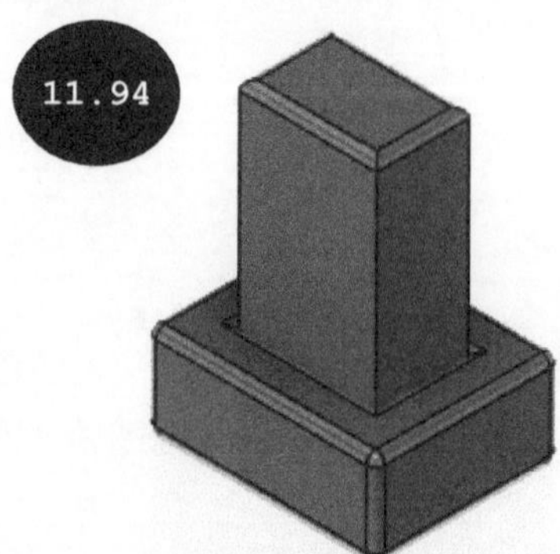

To apply this constraint, you must select two pairs of planar faces: the first pair is referred to as Component 1, while the second pair is referred to as Component 2.

In Figure 11.95, two planar faces are selected for Component 1, and two parallel planar faces are selected for Component 2. The figure also shows the resultant model after applying the Center constraint, where the first component is positioned exactly midway between the selected faces of the second component. The method of applying Center constraint is discussed below:

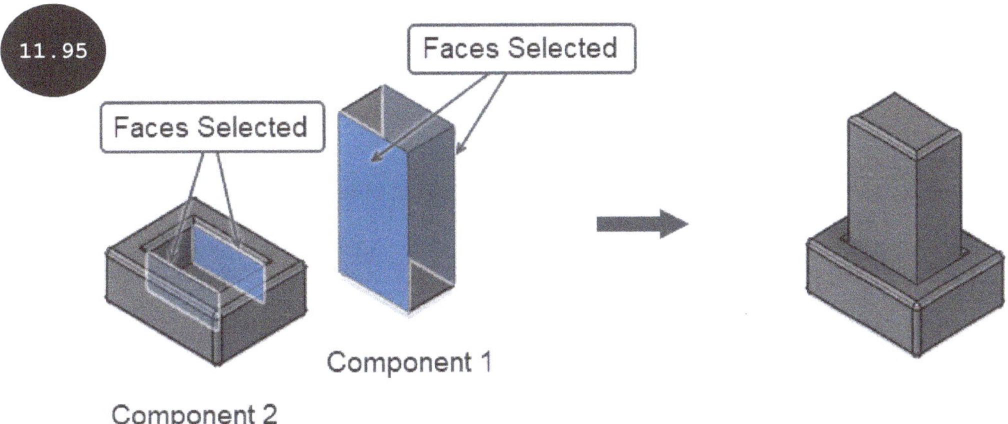

1. Invoke the **CONSTRAIN COMPONENTS** dialog box by clicking on the **Constrain Components** tool in the **RELATIONSHIPS** panel (see Figure 11.96) or by pressing the **C** key.

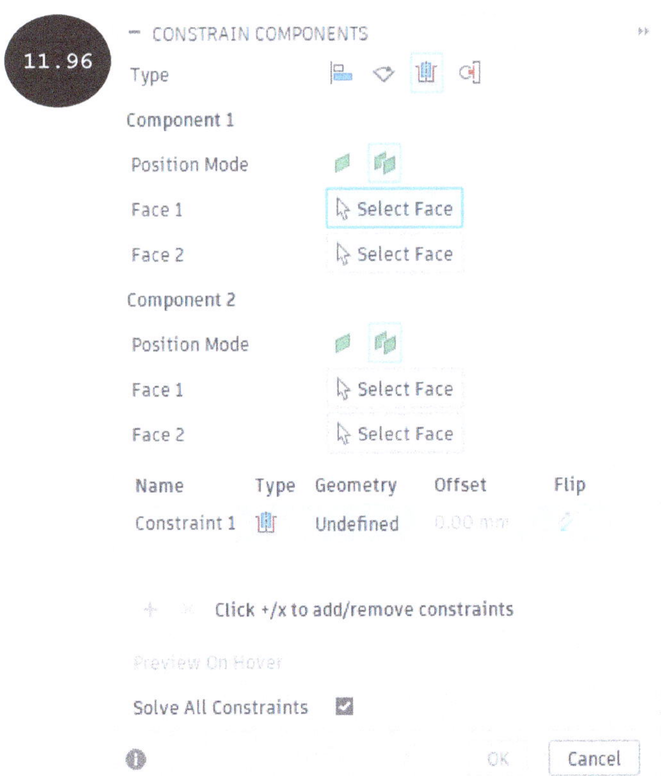

2. Activate the **Center** button in the **Type** area of the dialog box to apply a Center constraint between the components, refer to Figure 11.96.

   By default, the **Between Two Faces** button is activated in the **Position Mode** area of **Component 1**. As a result, you can select two planar faces for Component 1. To select only one planar face for Component 1, activate the **Simple** button in the **Position Mode** area.

3. Activate the required button (**Between Two Faces** or **Simple**) in the **Position Mode** area of **Component 1**.

4. Select one or two planar faces of the first component in the graphics area, depending upon the option selected in the **Position Mode** area, see Figure 11.97 (a). In this figure, two planar faces of the first component are selected.

11.97

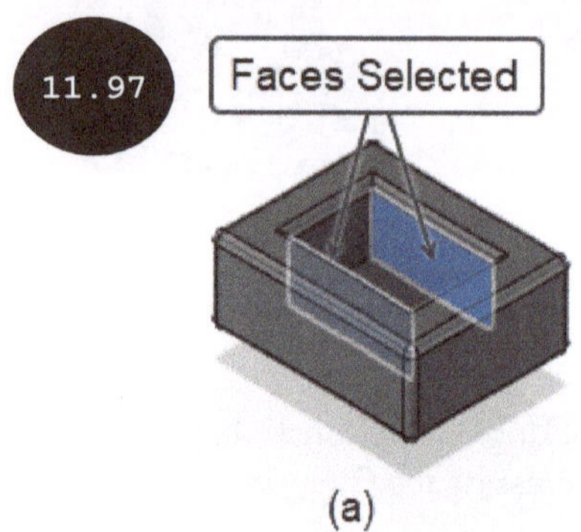

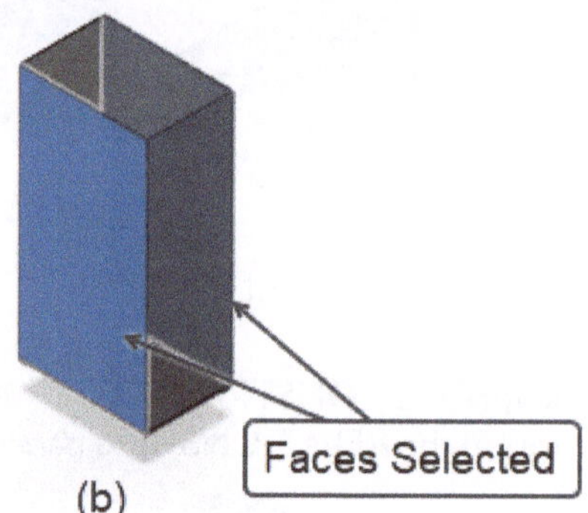

   Now, define the planar face(s) for the second component.

5. Ensure that the required button (**Between Two Faces** or **Simple**) is activated in the **Position Mode** area of **Component 2** to select two or only one planar face, respectively

Note: You must select two planar faces either for Component 1 or for Component 2. If you activate the **Simple** button in the **Position Mode** area of **Component 1** (to select only one face), the **Simple** button will not be available for **Component 2**.

6. Select the required planar face(s) of the second component in the graphics area according to the selected **Position Mode** option, refer to Figure 11.97 (b). After completing the selections, the planar face(s) of the first component become centrally aligned between the planar faces of the second component, see Figure 11.98.

11.98

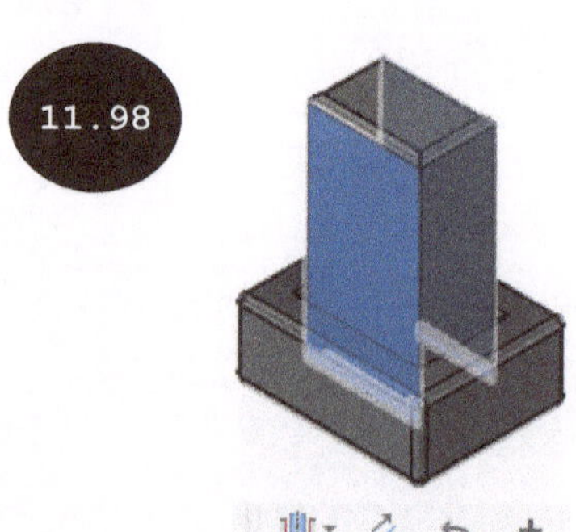

7. If needed, you can reverse the orientation of the selected geometry by clicking the **Flip** button in the dialog box.

8. Click **OK** to confirm the application of the constraint.

Applying a Tangent Constraint

The Tangent constraint is used for making the selected geometries of two different components tangent to each other, see Figure 11.99. You can select a planar face, a curved face, an edge, or a plane as the first geometry and a cylindrical, conical, or spherical face as the second geometry for applying the Tangent constraint. The method for applying a Tangent constraint is discussed below:

1. Press the **C** key to invoke the **CONSTRAIN COMPONENTS** dialog box.

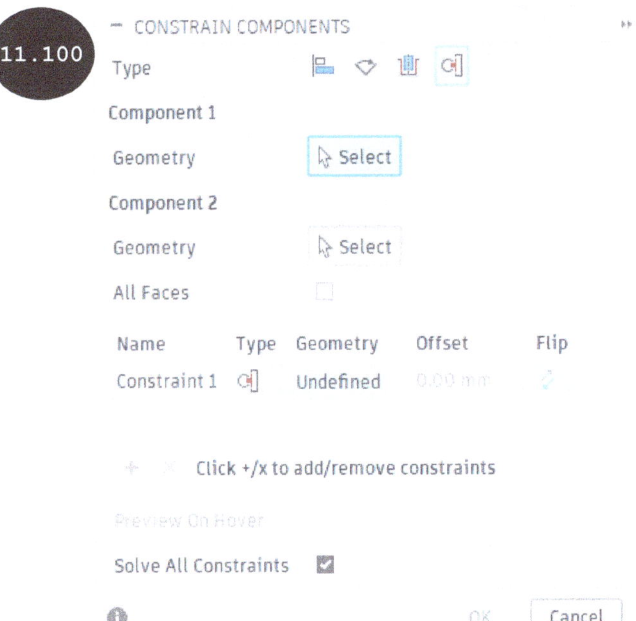

2. Activate the **Tangent** button in the **Type** area of the dialog box to apply a Tangent constraint between the geometries of two different components, see Figure 11.100. The **Geometry** selection option of **Component 1** becomes activated and you are prompted to select a geometry of the first component.

3. Select a planar face, a curved face, an edge, or a plane of a component as the first geometry for applying the Tangent constraint, see Figure 11.101 (a). The geometry gets selected, and the component becomes transparent. Also, the **Geometry** selection option for **Component 2** becomes activated automatically.

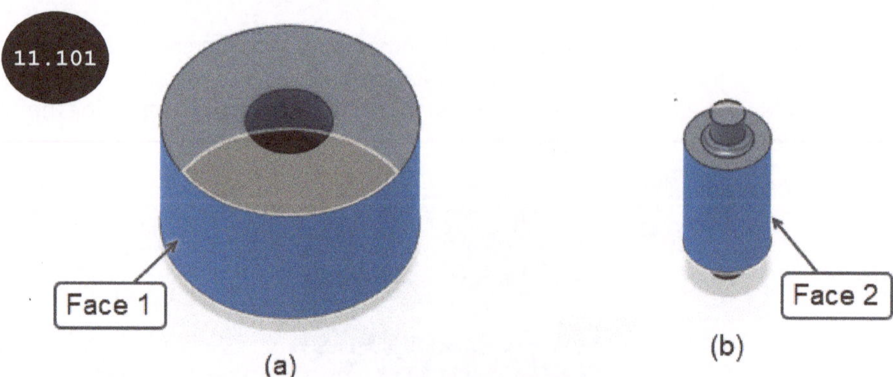

4. Select a cylindrical, conical, or spherical face of another component as the second geometry, refer to Figure 11.101 (b). The Tangent constraint gets applied such that the selected geometries become tangent to each other in the graphics area, see Figure 11.102.

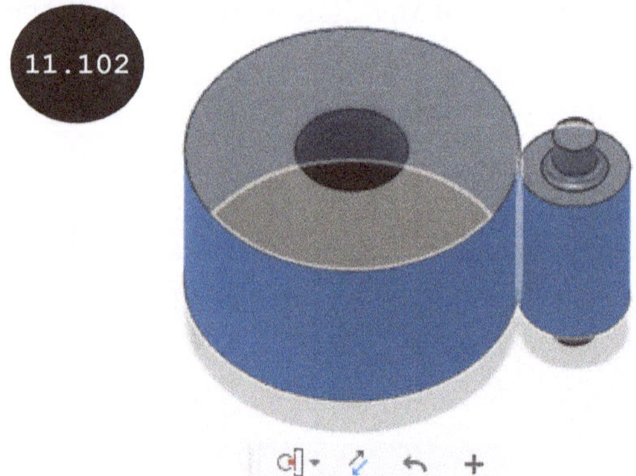

5. If needed, you can reverse the orientation of the selected geometry by clicking on the **Flip** button.

6. Click on the **OK** button to confirm the application of the constraint.

Grouping Components Together

In Autodesk Fusion, you can group components such that the relative position of the components gets locked and acts as a single object. To do this, invoke the **RELATIONSHIPS** drop-down menu in the **ASSEMBLY** tab and then click on the **Rigid Group** tool, see Figure 11.103. The **RIGID GROUP** dialog box appears, see Figure 11.104. Next, select the components to be grouped in the graphics area.

Note that the **Include Child Components** check box is selected in the dialog box, by default. As a result, the child components of the selected components get included in the selection set. After selecting the components to be grouped, click on the **OK** button. The selected components get grouped such that the relative position of the components gets locked, and they act as a single object.

Enabling Contact Sets between Components

By default, the movement of a component along its free degrees of freedom is not restricted by interference or collisions with other components in the assembly. This means the component can move freely, even if it comes into contact with another component, see Figure 11.105. This occurs because contact sets are not established between components, by default.

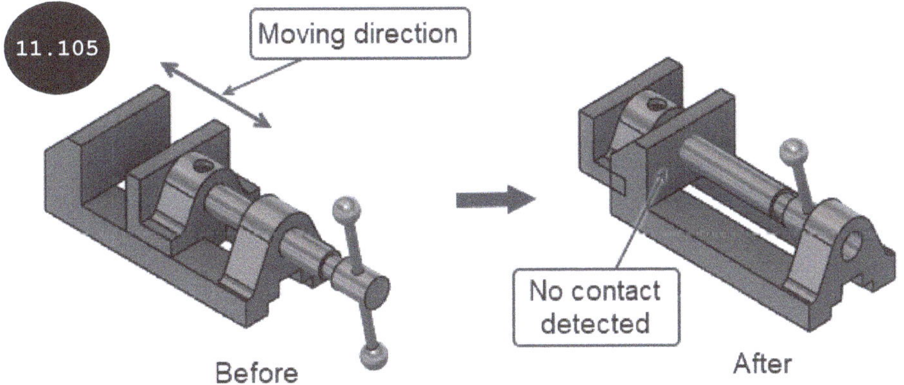

To establish contact sets between components, invoke the **CONTACT** drop-down menu in the **ASSEMBLY** tab and then click on the **Enable Contact Sets** tool, see Figure 11.106. The **Contact: sets** option is added in the **BROWSER**, which is used for managing contact sets, see Figure 11.107. Next, right-click on the **Contact: sets** option in the **BROWSER** and then click on the **New Contact Set** option in the shortcut menu that appears, see Figure 11.108. The **NEW CONTACT SET** dialog box appears, see Figure 11.109.

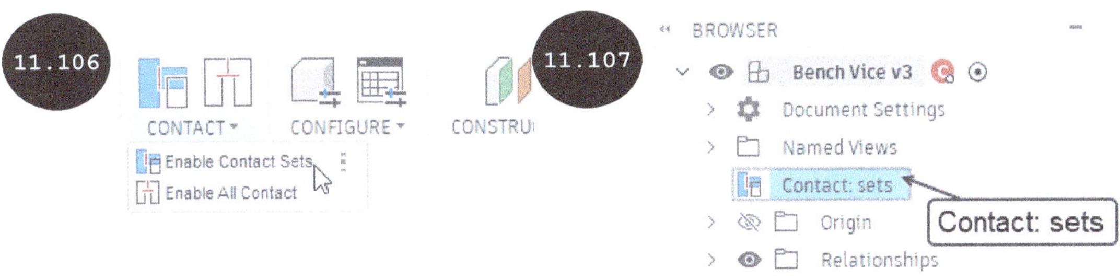

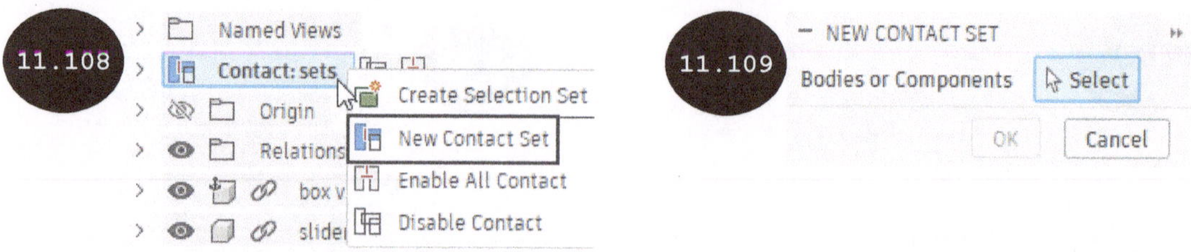

Once the **NEW CONTACT SET** dialog box is invoked, select components in the graphics area to establish the contact sets between them. Next, click on the **OK** button in the dialog box. The contact set is defined between the selected components. Now, when the moveable component touches the other component, the collision gets detected and the component cannot move further or forces the other component to move, see Figure 11.110.

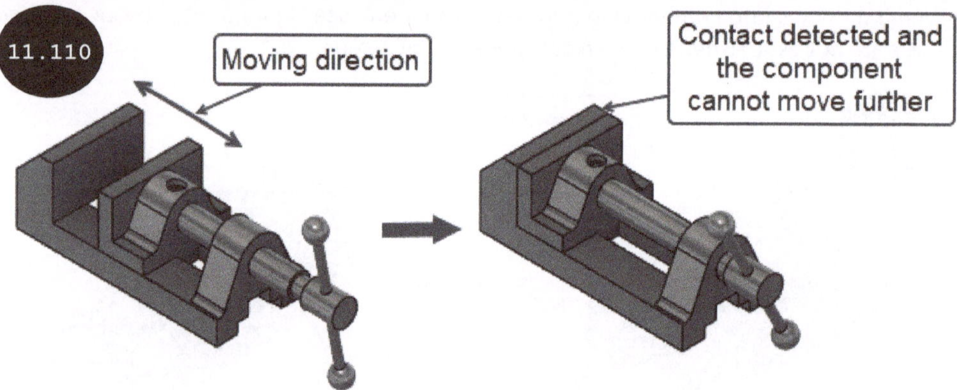

In addition to defining the contact sets between components, you can enable all contacts of the assembly. To do this, right-click on the **Contact: sets** option in the **BROWSER** and then click on the **Enable All Contact** tool in the shortcut menu that appears. Alternatively, invoke the **CONTACT** drop-down menu in the **ASSEMBLY** tab and then click on the **Enable All Contact** option to enable all contacts of the assembly in the contact sets. You can also move the cursor over the **Contact: sets** option in the **BROWSER** and then click on the **All bodies contact** button that appears, see Figure 11.111.

To disable the contact sets, right-click on the **Contact: sets** option in the **BROWSER** and then click on the **Disable Contact** option in the shortcut menu that appears. You can also move the cursor over the **Contact: sets** option in the **BROWSER** and then click on the **No contact** button that appears, see Figure 11.111.

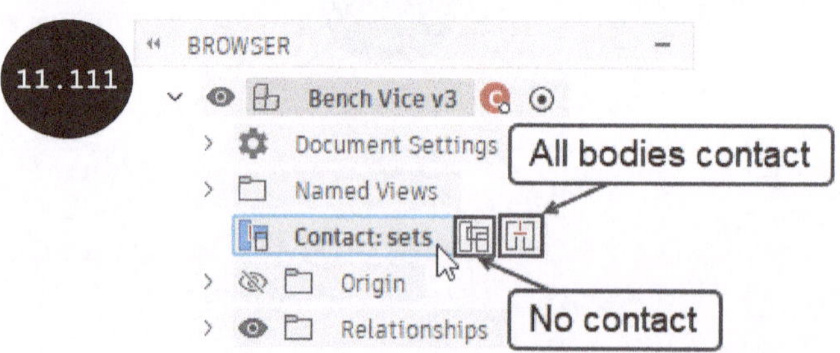

Capturing the Position of Components

When you move a component of an assembly to a new position in the graphics area, the contextual **POSITION** panel appears at the end of the **Toolbar** with two tools: **Capture Position** and **Revert Position**, see Figure 11.112.

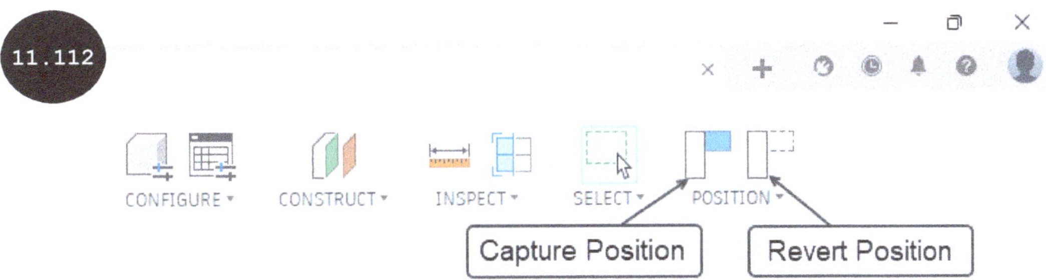

On clicking the **Capture Position** tool in the contextual **POSITION** panel, the new position of the components gets captured and added to the **Timeline**, see Figure 11.113. You can also delete or suppress the capture position of the components. To do this, right-click on the capture position to be deleted/suppressed in the **Timeline** and then click on the **Delete/Suppress Features** option in the shortcut menu that appears, respectively.

The **Revert** tool of the contextual **POSITION** panel is used for reverting the position of the components to the previous position.

Note: If you did not capture the new position of a moved component, then the **Capture or revert component positions** message window may appear on invoking a tool, see Figure 11.114. This message window informs that some component positions have changed from their previous positions. In this window, click on the **Capture Position** button to capture the new position of the components or click on the **Revert Position** button to revert to the previous position of the components.

Tutorial 1

Create an assembly, as shown in Figure 11.115 by applying the joints and then animate it. The exploded view of the assembly is also shown in Figure 11.115 for your reference. Different views and dimensions of individual components of the assembly are shown in Figures 11.116 through 11.120. All dimensions are in mm.

11.115

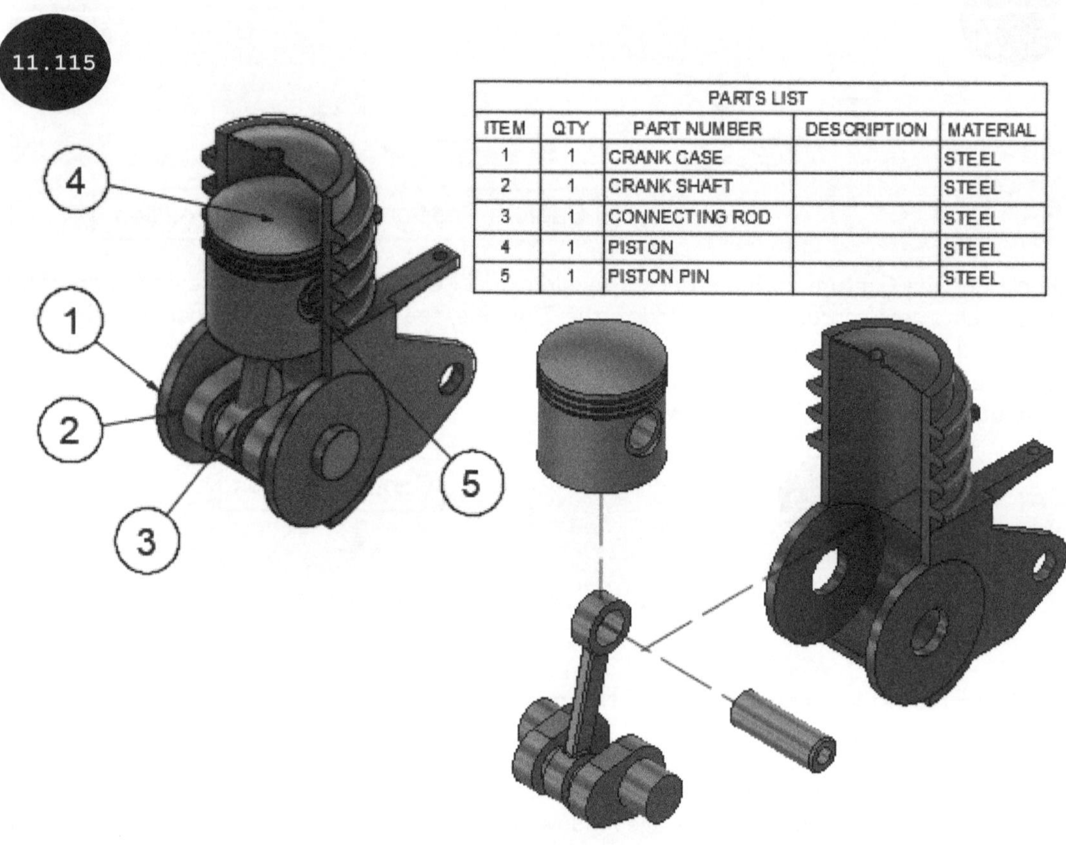

PARTS LIST				
ITEM	QTY	PART NUMBER	DESCRIPTION	MATERIAL
1	1	CRANK CASE		STEEL
2	1	CRANK SHAFT		STEEL
3	1	CONNECTING ROD		STEEL
4	1	PISTON		STEEL
5	1	PISTON PIN		STEEL

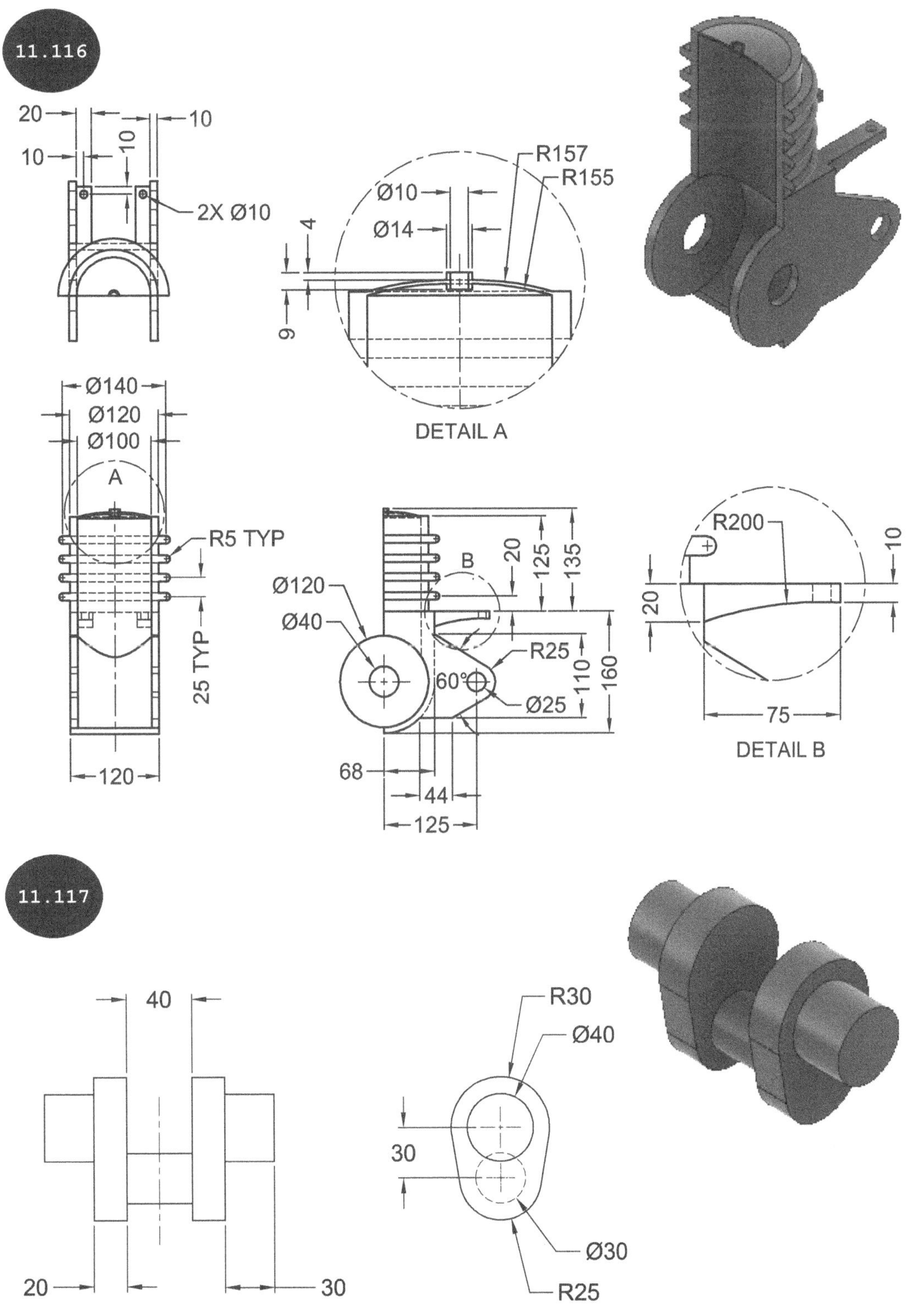
11.116
20
10
10
10
2X Ø10
Ø10
Ø14
R157
R155
4
9
DETAIL A
Ø140
Ø120
Ø100
A
R5 TYP
25 TYP
120
Ø120
Ø40
B
20
125
135
R25
60°
Ø25
110
160
68
44
125
R200
10
20
75
DETAIL B
11.117
40
20
30
R30
Ø40
30
Ø30
R25

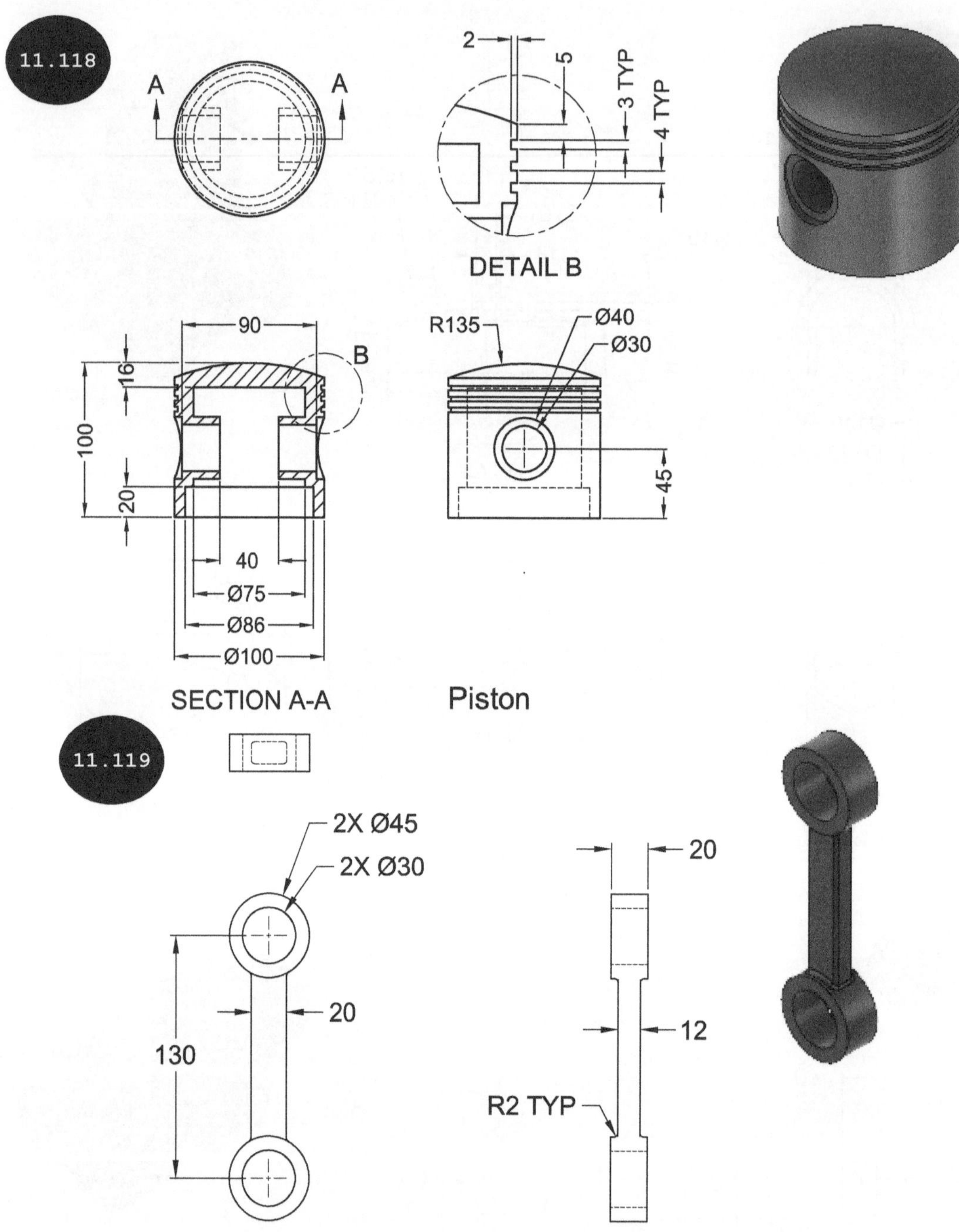

11.118
A
A
2
5
3 TYP
4 TYP
DETAIL B
90
16
B
100
20
40
Ø75
Ø86
Ø100
SECTION A-A
R135
Ø40
Ø30
45
Piston
11.119
2X Ø45
2X Ø30
20
130
20
12
R2 TYP

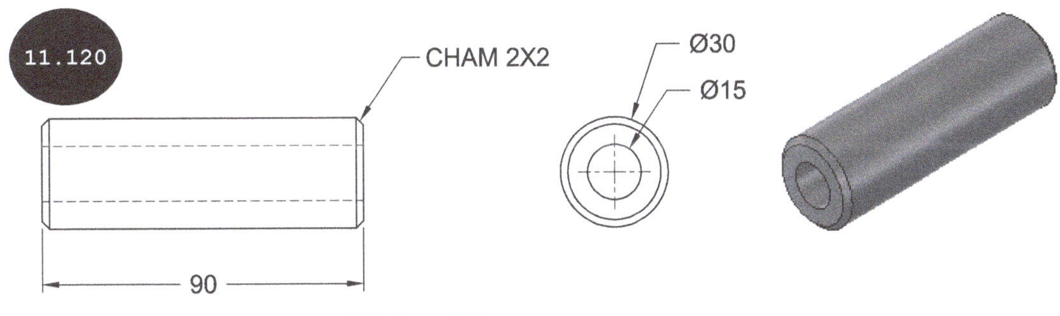

Section 1: Starting Autodesk Fusion and Creating All Components

In this section, you will create all components of the assembly.

1. Launch Autodesk Fusion and create all the components of the assembly one by one as a separate Part Design file. Refer to Figures 11.116 through 11.120 for the dimensions of each component. After creating all the components, save them at a common location *Autodesk Fusion 360 > Chapter 11 > Tutorial > Tutorial 1* in the **Data Panel**. You need to create these folders in the **Data Panel**.

Note: You can also download all the components of the assembly by logging into your account on the CADArtifex website (*cadartifex.com/login*). If you are a new user, you need to first register yourself on the CADArtifex website (*cadartifex.com/register*) to access the online resources. After downloading, you need to upload the components of this assembly to the "*Autodesk Fusion 360 > Chapter 11 > Tutorial > Tutorial 1*" location in the **Data Panel**.

Section 2: Creating the Assembly - Single Cylinder Engine

Now, you can create the assembly (**Single Cylinder Engine**).

1. Start Autodesk Fusion, if it is not already running and invoke the **What do you want to design?** dialog box, see Figure 11.121.

Note: You can invoke the **What do you want to design?** dialog box by clicking on **File > New** in the **Application Bar**, see Figure 11.122. Alternatively, you can click on the + icon next to the name of the active design tab.

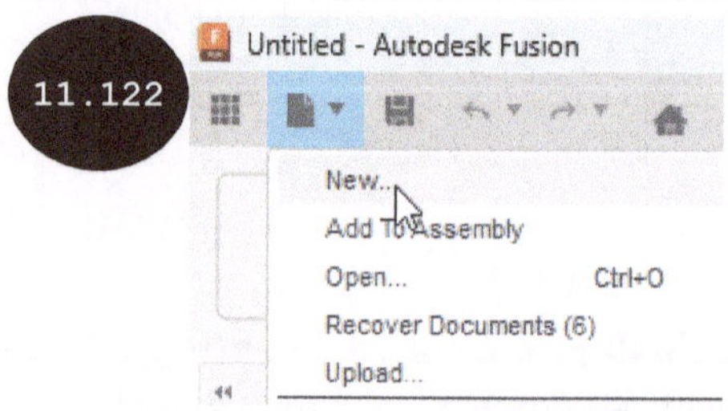

2. In the **What do you want to design?** dialog box, choose the **Assembly Design** button. Next, select the **millimeter (mm), gram (g)** unit system from the **Unit System** drop-down list.

3. After specifying the required options, click the **Create New** button. A new Assembly Design file is opened with the default name in a separate tab.

4. Invoke the **Data Panel** and then browse to the location where all the components of the assembly have been saved (***Autodesk Fusion 360 > Chapter 11 > Tutorial > Tutorial 1***), see Figure 11.123. The preview of all the components of the assembly appears in the **Data Panel**.

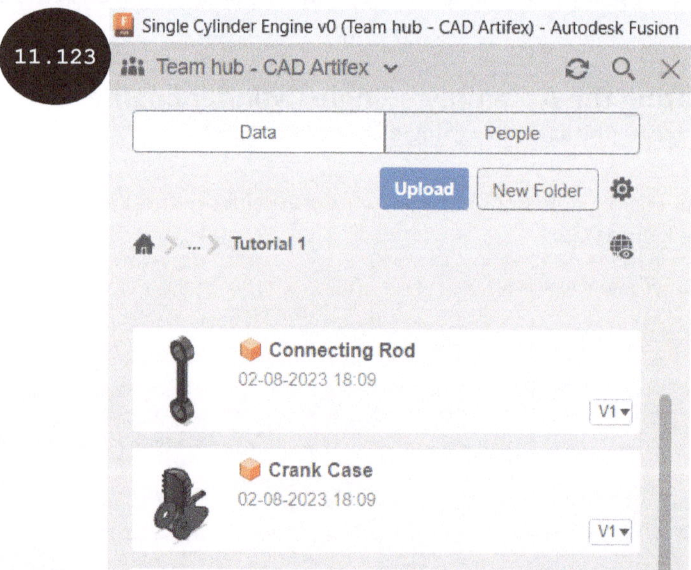

5. Right-click on the **Crank Case** component in the **Data Panel** and then click on the **Insert into Current Design** option in the shortcut menu that appears, see Figure 11.124. The **Crank Case** component gets inserted into the design file with the display of translational and manipulator handles, see Figure 11.125. Also, the **INITIAL POSITION** dialog box appears in the graphics area.

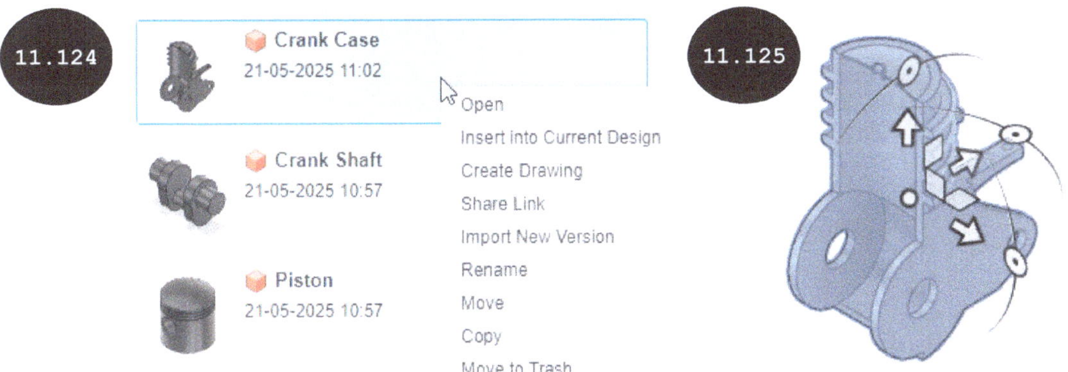

6. Ensure that the orientation of the component appears similar to the one shown in Figure 11.125 in the graphics area. If needed, you can change the orientation of the component by using the translational and manipulator handles that appear in the graphics area.

7. Click on the **OK** button in the **INITIAL POSITION** dialog box. The **Crank Case** component is inserted into the design file and becomes the fixed component by default. Next, close the **Data Panel** by clicking on the cross mark at its top right corner.

Section 3: Inserting the Second Component

Now, you need to insert the second component (**Crank Shaft**) of the assembly.

1. Invoke the **Data Panel** and then right-click on the **Crank Shaft** component. A shortcut menu appears, see Figure 11.126. In this shortcut menu, click on the **Insert into Current Design** option. The **Crank Shaft** component gets inserted into the design file with the display of translational and manipulator handles.

Now, you need to position the second component (**Crank Shaft**).

2. Change the position of the second component (**Crank Shaft**) in the graphics area such that it does not intersect with the first component, see Figure 11.127. You can change the position of the component by dragging its translational and manipulator handles that appear in the graphics area.

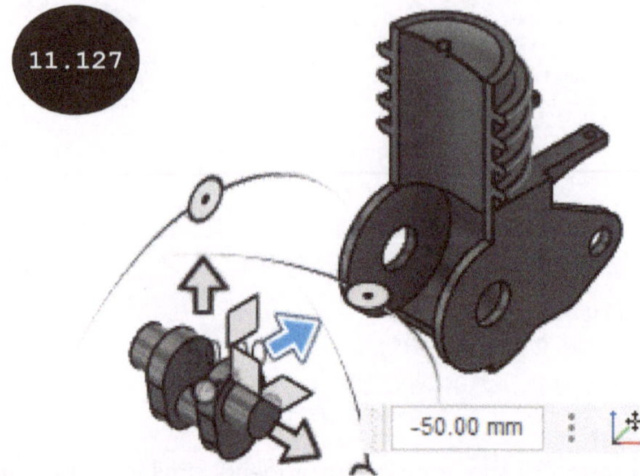

3. Click on the **OK** button in the **INITIAL POSITION** dialog box. The **Crank Shaft** component is inserted and placed at the specified position in the design file. Next, close the **Data Panel** by clicking on the cross mark at its top right corner.

Section 4: Applying the Revolute Joint

Now, you need to apply the revolute joint between the second (**Crank Shaft**) and the first (**Crank Case**) components of the assembly, so that the **Crank Shaft** component can rotate about an axis.

1. Click on the **Joint** tool in the **RELATIONSHIPS** drop-down menu in the **ASSEMBLY** tab, see Figure 11.128 or press the J key. The **JOINT** dialog box appears, see Figure 11.129 and you are prompted to define the position of the joint origin on the second component (moveable component).

2. Ensure that the **Simple** button is selected in the **Origin Mode** area of the **Component 1** rollout in the dialog box for defining the joint origin on a face, an edge, or a point of the component.

3. Move the cursor over the right circular edge of the **Crank Shaft** component, see Figure 11.130. The edge gets highlighted, and the joint origin snaps to the snap point that appears at the center of the edge.

4. Click the left mouse button when the joint origin snaps to the center of the circular edge, see Figure 11.130. The position of the joint origin is defined at the center of the circular edge. Also,

the **Crank Shaft** component becomes transparent in the graphics area, and you are prompted to define the position of the joint origin on the other component (**Crank Case**).

5. Move the cursor over the right inner circular edge of the second component (**Crank Case**), see Figure 11.131. The edge gets highlighted and the joint origin snaps to the center of the edge.

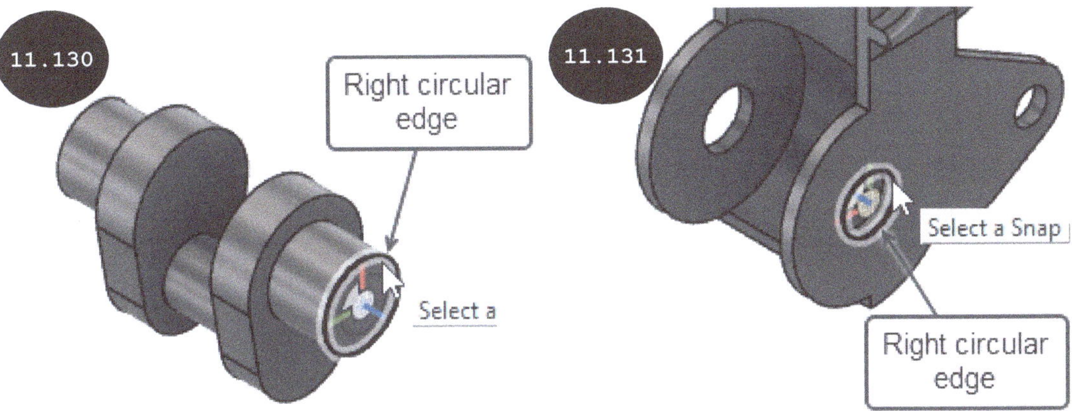

6. Click the left mouse button when the joint origin snaps to the center of the edge, see Figure 11.131. The position of the joint origin is defined, and the second component moves toward the first component such that the defined joint origins of both components coincide with each other in the graphics area, see Figure 11.132.

7. Enter **-10** in the **Offset Z** field of the **Alignment** rollout as the offset distance between the joint origins of both components, see Figures 11.133 and 11.134. Figure 11.133 highlights the **Offset Z** field in the dialog box and Figure 11.134 shows the preview of the offset distance applied between the joints.

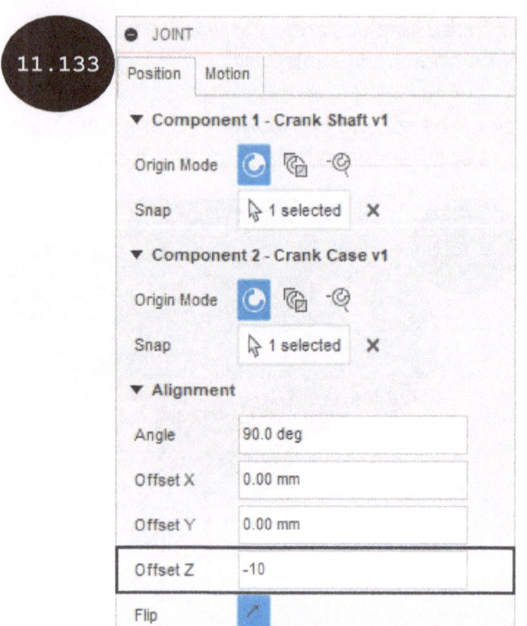

11.133

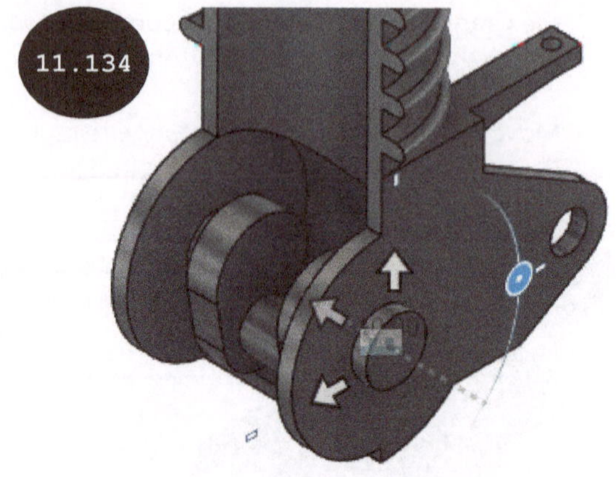
11.134

Now, you need to define the joint to be applied between the components.

8. Click on the **Motion** tab in the dialog box and then select the **Revolute** option in the **Type** drop-down list of the dialog box as the joint to be applied between the components.

9. Click on the **OK** button in the dialog box. The revolute joint is applied such that all degrees of freedom of the **Crank Shaft** component become fixed except one rotational degree of freedom. As a result, the component can rotate about its axis.

Section 5: Inserting and Assembling the Third Component

Now, you need to insert and assemble the **Connecting Rod** component of the assembly.

1. Insert the third component (**Connecting Rod**) in the design file by using the **Data Panel**. Note that you need to define its position and orientation in the graphics area similar to the one shown in Figure 11.135 by using the translational and manipulator handles that appear.

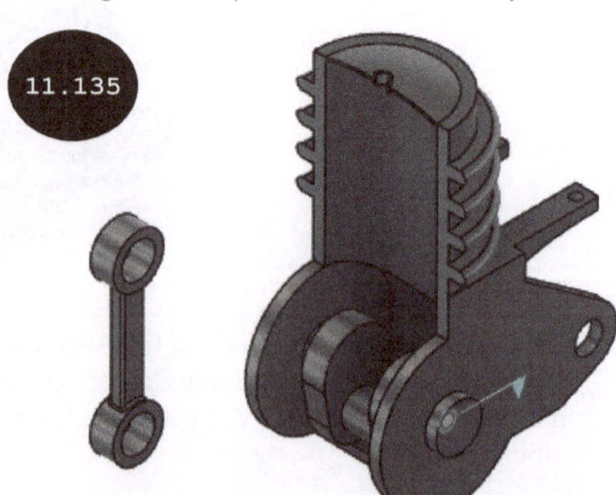
11.135

Now, you need to assemble the third component (**Connecting Rod**) by applying the rotational joint.

2. Click on the **Joint** tool in the **RELATIONSHIPS** drop-down menu of the **ASSEMBLY** tab, see Figure 11.136 or press the **J** key. The **JOINT** dialog box appears in the graphics area.

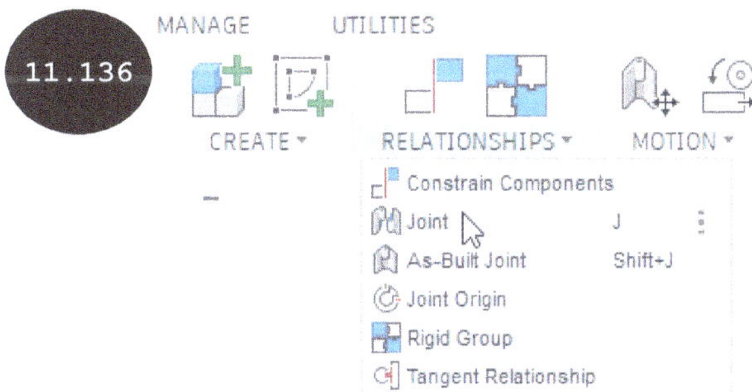

3. Ensure that the **Simple** button is selected in the **Origin Mode** area of the **Component 1** rollout for defining the joint origin on a face, an edge, or a point.

4. Move the cursor over the inner circular face of the third component (**Connecting Rod**), see Figure 11.137. The face gets highlighted and its three snap points (front, middle, and back) appear.

5. Press and hold the CTRL key to lock the highlighted face so that you can easily select the required (middle) snap point of the face to define the position of the joint origin

6. Move the cursor over the middle snap point of the face and then click the left mouse button when the joint origin snaps to it, see Figure 11.137. The position of the joint origin on the **Connecting Rod** component is defined and you are prompted to define the position of the joint origin on the other component. Release the CTRL key.

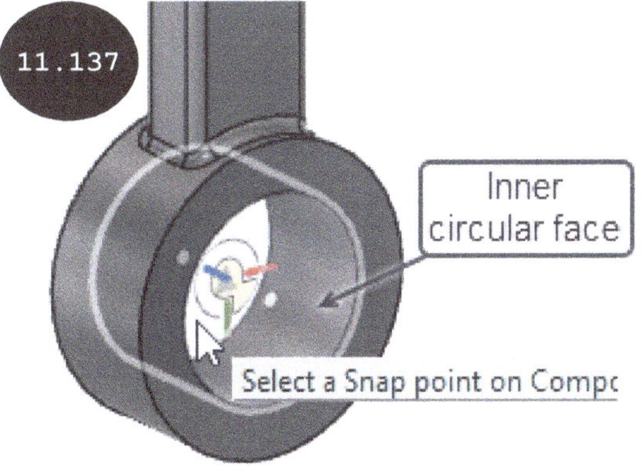

7. Move the cursor over the circular face of the second component (**Crank Shaft**), see Figure 11.138. The face gets highlighted, and its snap points appear.

8. Press the CTRL key and then click the left mouse button when the joint origin snaps to the middle snap point of the highlighted face of the second component (**Crank Shaft**), see Figure 11.138. The position of the joint origin is defined, and the **Connecting Rod** component moves toward the

Crank Shaft component such that the defined joint origins of both components coincide with each other in the graphics area, see Figure 11.139. Also, the component begins to animate in the graphics area based on the default joint type selected in the **Type** drop-down list of the dialog box.

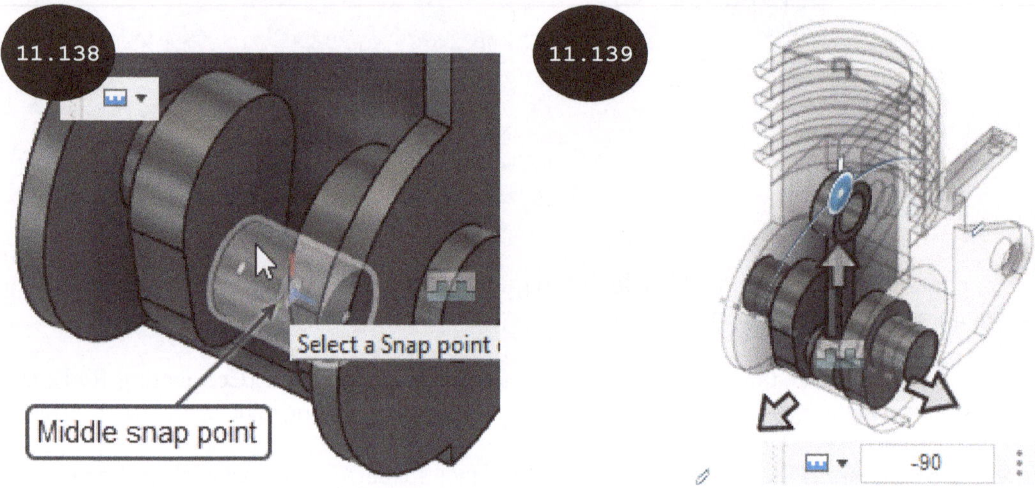

Now, you need to define the joint to be applied between the components.

9. Click on the **Motion** tab in the dialog box and then select the **Revolute** option in the **Type** drop-down list of the dialog box as the joint to be applied between the components.

10. Click on the **OK** button in the dialog box. The revolute joint is applied such that all degrees of freedom of the **Crank Shaft** component become fixed except one rotational degree of freedom. As a result, the component can rotate about its axis, see Figure 11.140.

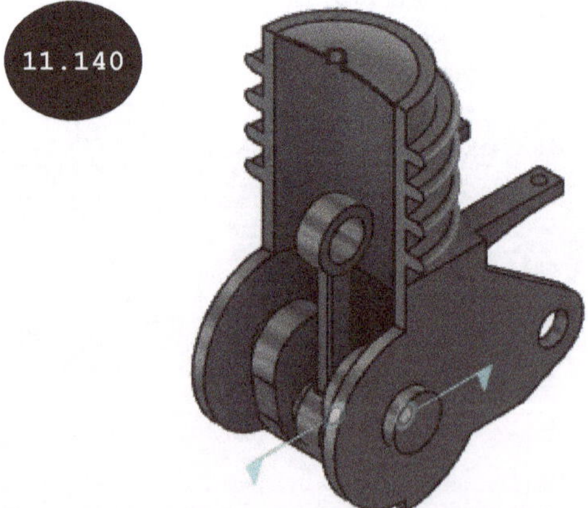

Section 6: Inserting and Assembling the Fourth Component

Now, you need to insert and assemble the **Piston Pin** of the assembly.

1. Insert the fourth component (**Piston Pin**) in the design file by using the **Data Panel**, see Figure 11.141. Note that you need to define the position of the **Piston Pin** component in the graphics area by

using the translational and manipulator handles such that it does not intersect with existing components of the assembly.

Now, you need to assemble the fourth component (**Piston Pin**) by applying the rotational joint.

2. Invoke the **Joint** dialog box by clicking on the **Joint** tool in the **RELATIONSHIPS** drop-down menu of **ASSEMBLY** tab. You are prompted to specify the position of the joint origin.

3. Move the cursor over the outer circular face of the fourth component (**Piston Pin**), see Figure 11.142. The face gets highlighted, and its three snap points appear.

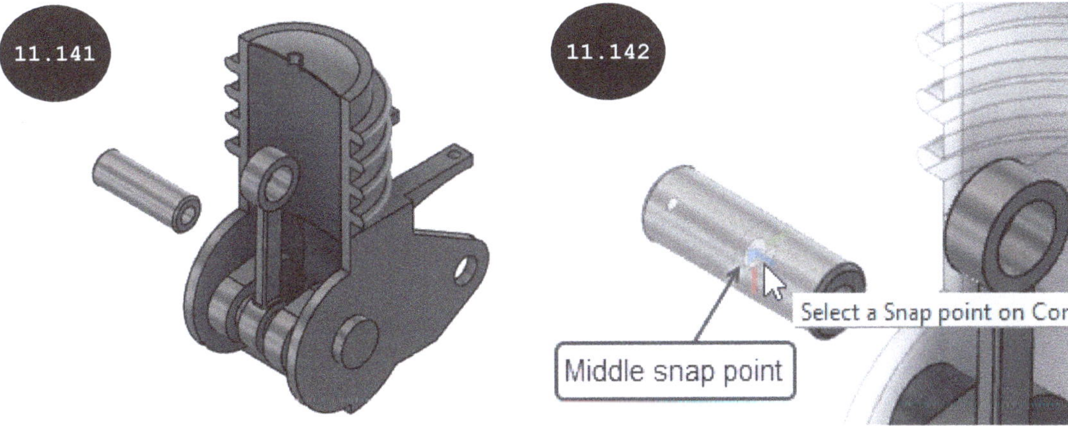

4. Press the CTRL key and then click the left mouse button when the joint origin snaps to the middle snap point of the highlighted face, see Figure 11.142. Next, release the CTRL key. The position of the joint origin is defined on the **Piston Pin**, and you are prompted to define the position of the joint origin on the other component.

5. Move the cursor over the inner circular face of the third component (**Connecting Rod**), see Figure 11.143. The face gets highlighted, and its three snap points appear.

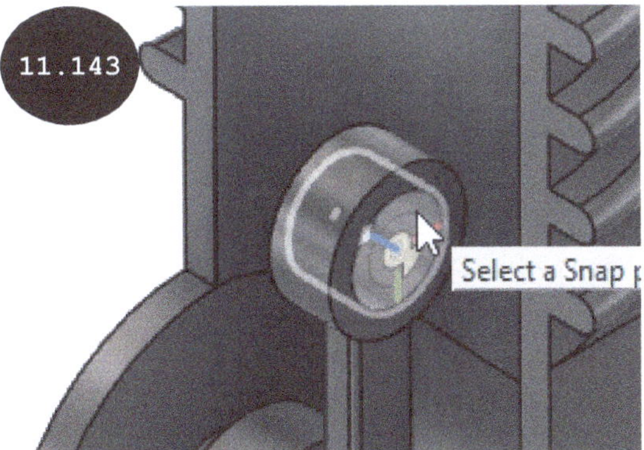

6. Move the cursor over the middle snap point of the face and then click the left mouse button when the joint origin snaps to it, see Figure 11.144. The position of the joint origin is defined, and the **Piston Pin** component moves toward the **Connecting Rod** component such that the defined joint

origins of both components coincide, see Figure 11.145. Also, the component begins to animate based on the default joint type selected.

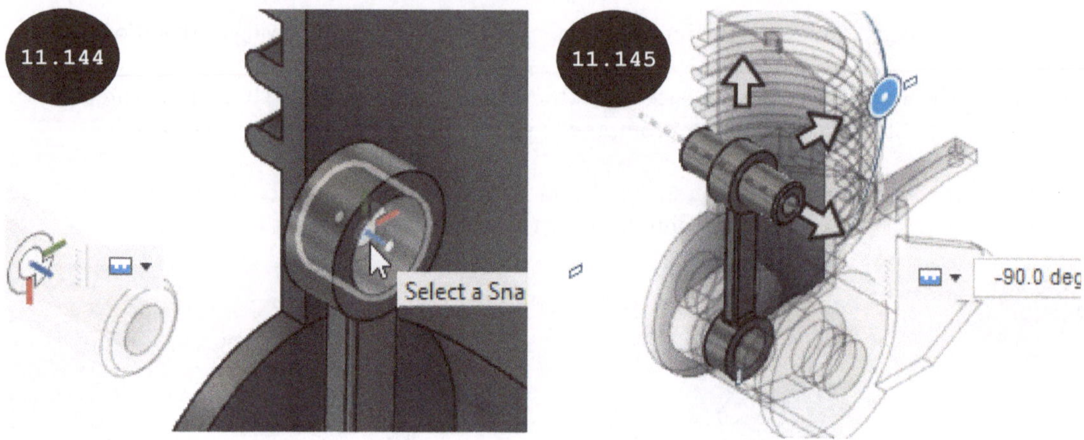

11.144

11.145

Now, you need to define the joint to be applied between the components.

7. Click on the **Motion** tab and select the **Revolute** option in the **Type** drop-down list of the dialog box, see Figure 11.146.

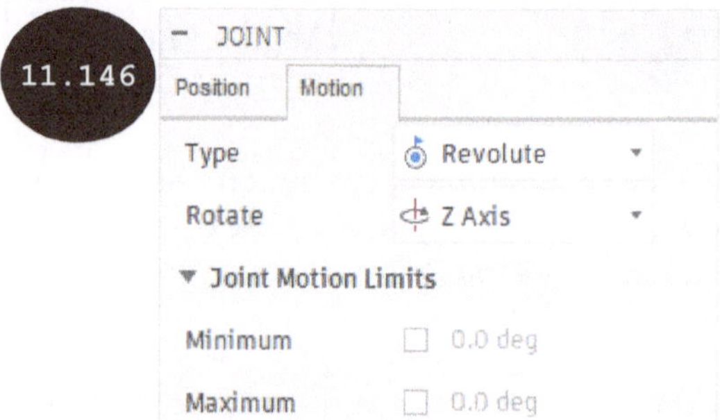

11.146

8. Click on the **OK** button in the dialog box. The revolute joint is applied such that all degrees of freedom of the **Piston Pin** component become fixed except one rotational degree of freedom. As a result, the component can rotate about its axis, refer to Figure 11.147.

11.147

Section 7: Inserting and Assembling the Fifth Component

Now, you need to insert and assemble the **Piston** of the assembly.

1. Insert the fifth component (**Piston**) in the design file by using the **Data Panel**, see Figure 11.148. Note that you need to define the position of the **Piston** component in the graphics area by using its translational and manipulator handles such that it does not intersect with existing components of the assembly.

   Now, you need to assemble the fifth component (**Piston**).

2. Invoke the **Joint** dialog box by clicking on the **Joint** tool in the **RELATIONSHIPS** drop-down menu of **ASSEMBLY** tab. You are prompted to specify the position of the joint origin.

3. Move the cursor over the inner circular edge of the **Piston** component, see Figure 11.149. The edge gets highlighted and the joint origin snaps to the center of the edge.

4. Click the left mouse button when the joint origin snaps to the center of the circular edge, see Figure 11.149. The position of the joint origin is defined on the **Piston** component, and you are prompted to define the position of the joint origin on the other component.

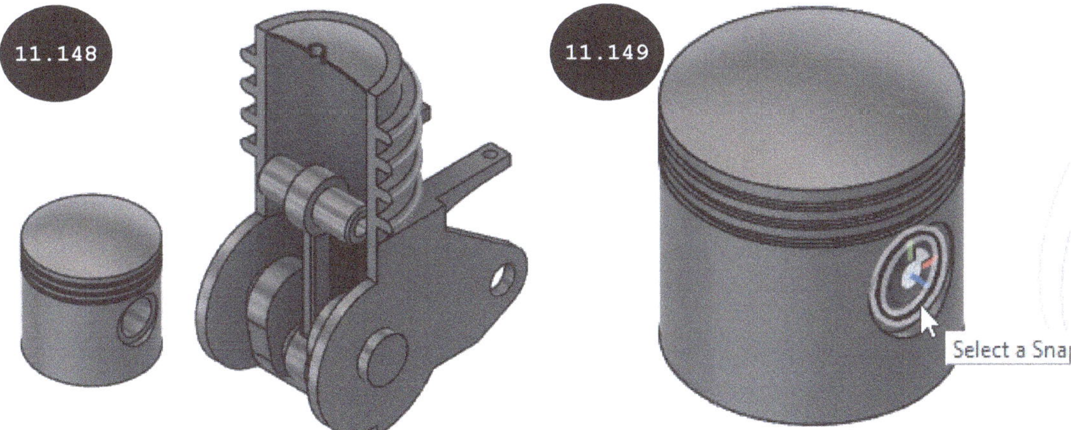

5. Move the cursor over the outermost circular edge of the **Piston Pin** component, see Figure 11.150. The edge gets highlighted and the joint origin snaps to the center of the edge.

6. Click the left mouse button when the joint origin snaps to the center of the circular edge, see Figure 11.150. The defined joint origins of both components coincide with each other in the graphics area, see Figure 11.151. Also, the component begins to animate in the graphics area based on the default joint type selected in the **Type** drop-down list of the **Motion** tab in the dialog box.

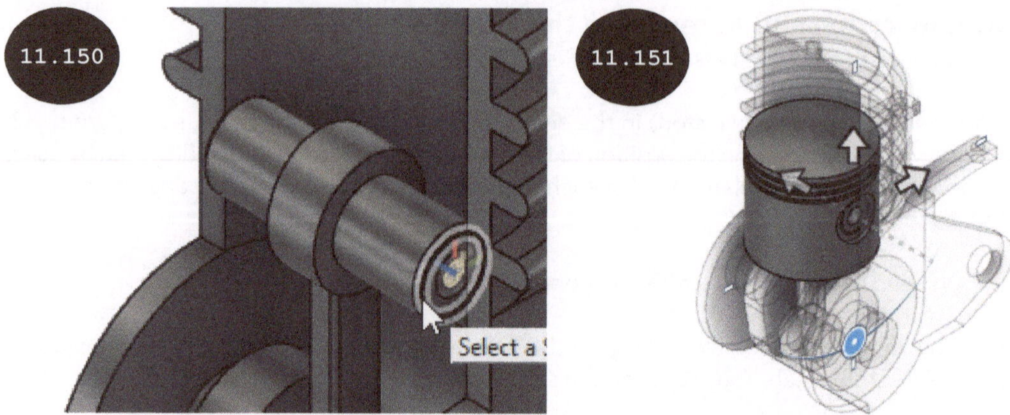

Now, you need to define the joint to be applied between the components.

7. Click on the **Motion** tab in the dialog box and then select the **Revolute** option in the **Type** drop-down list of the dialog box as the joint to be applied between the components.

8. Click on the **OK** button in the dialog box. The revolute joint is applied such that all degrees of freedom of the **Piston** component become fixed except one rotational degree of freedom. As a result, the component can rotate about its axis, see Figure 11.152

Section 8: Applying Slider Joints

Now, you need to apply the slider joint between the **Piston** and the **Crank Case** components so that the **Piston** can slide along the axis of the **Crank Case** component.

1. Invoke the **JOINT** dialog box by pressing the J key.

2. Move the cursor over the outer circular face of the **Piston** component, see Figure 11.153. The circular face gets highlighted and its three snap points (bottom, middle, and top) appear.

3. Press the CTRL key and then click the left mouse button when the cursor snaps to the middle snap point, see Figure 11.154. The joint origin is defined on the **Piston** component, and you are prompted to define the joint origin on the other component. Next, release the CTRL key.

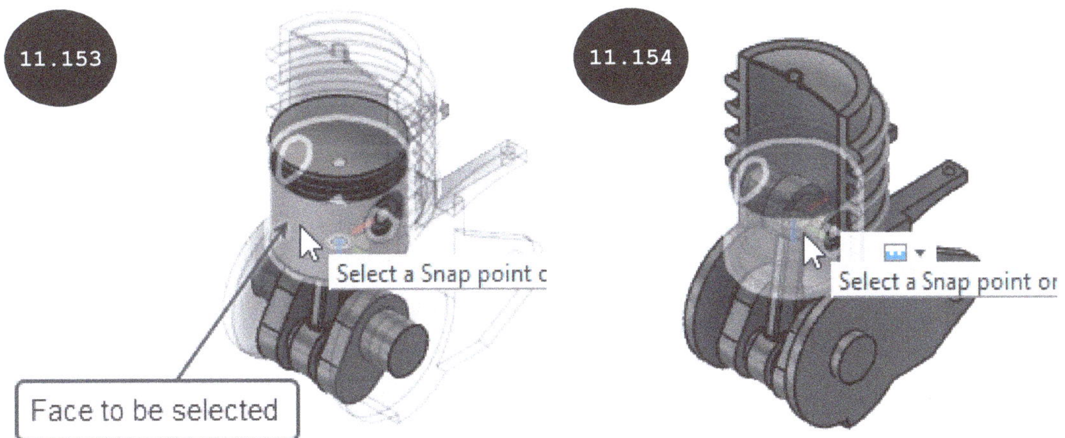

4. Move the cursor over the inner circular face of the **Crank Case** component and then click the left mouse button when the cursor snaps to its middle snap point, see Figure 11.155. Both the defined joint origins coincide with each other, see Figure 11.156.

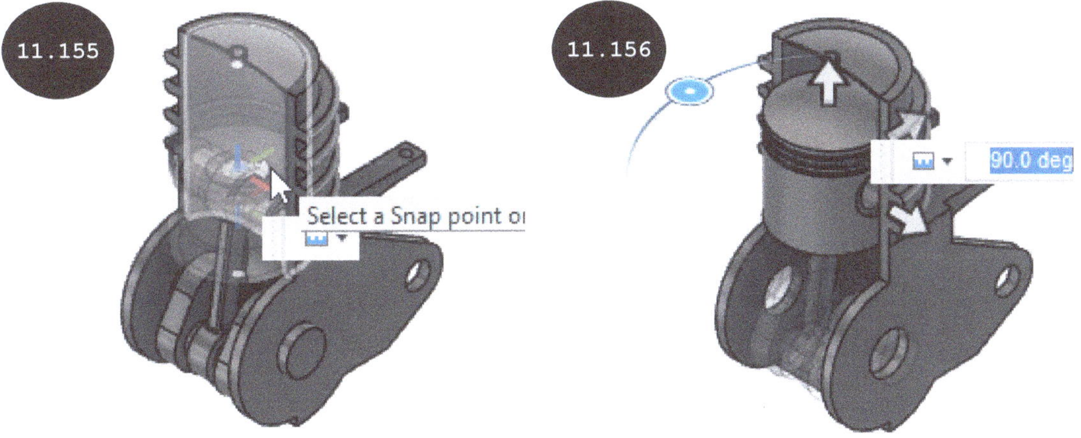

Tip: Ignore the warning message that may appear at the lower right corner of the screen informing that the selected joint type will result in conflict.

5. Click on the **Motion** tab and select the **Slider** option in the **Type** drop-down list of the dialog box. Next, click on the **OK** button in the dialog box. The slider joint is applied such that the **Piston** component can slide along the axis of the respective face of the **Crank Case** component, see Figure 11.157.

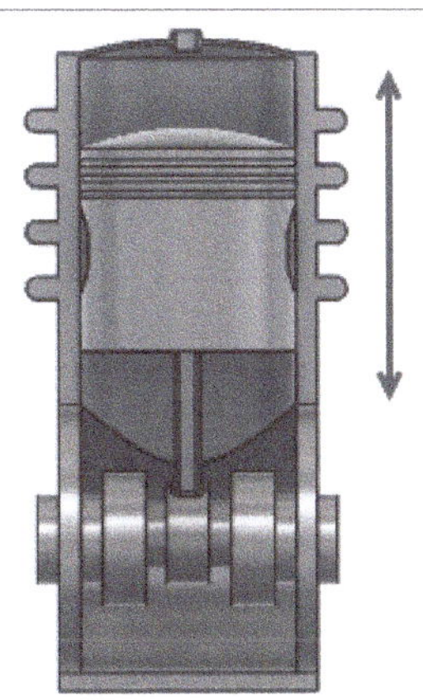

Section 9: Animating Assembly

Now, you can animate the entire assembly to review the behavior (motion) of all its components concerning each other.

1. Expand the **Joints** node in the **BROWSER**. A list of all the applied joints appears, see Figure 11.158.

2. Right-click on the first revolute joint (**Revolute 1**) in the expanded **Joints** node. A shortcut menu appears, see Figure 11.158.

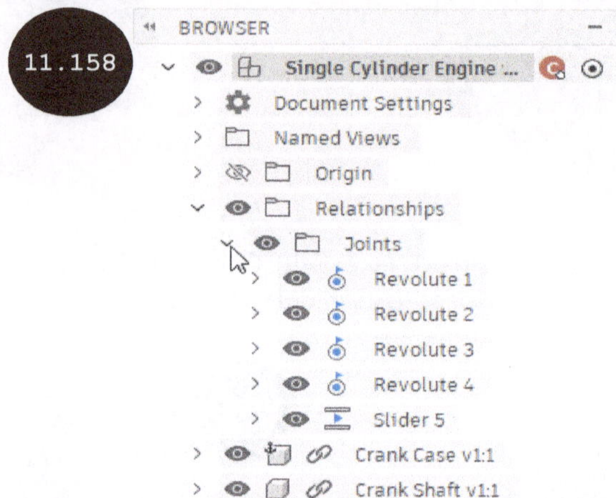

3. Click on the **Animate Joint Relationships** option in the shortcut menu, refer to Figure 11.159. The components of the assembly begin to animate concerning each other in the graphics area based on the joints applied.

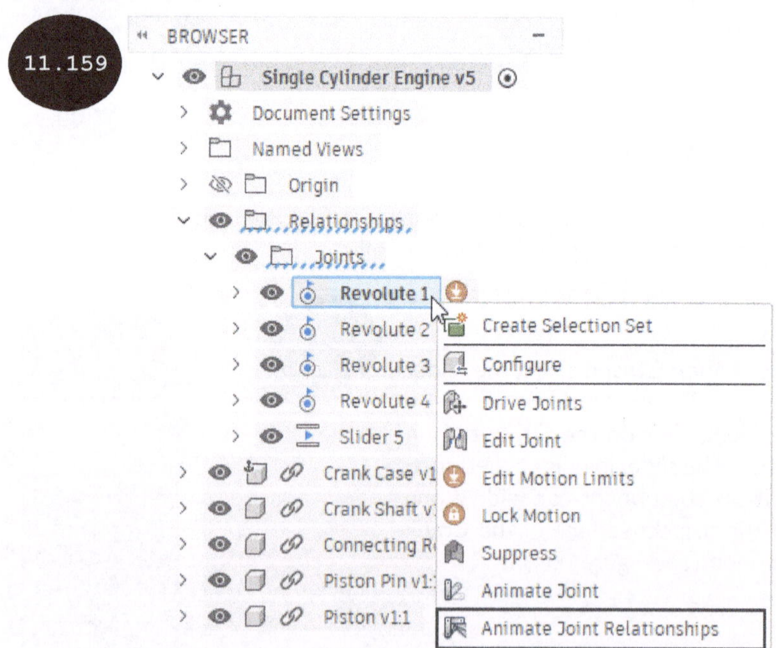

4. Press the ESC key to stop the animation.

Section 10: Saving the Model

1. Click on the **Save** tool in the **Application Bar**, see Figure 11.160. The **Save** dialog box appears.

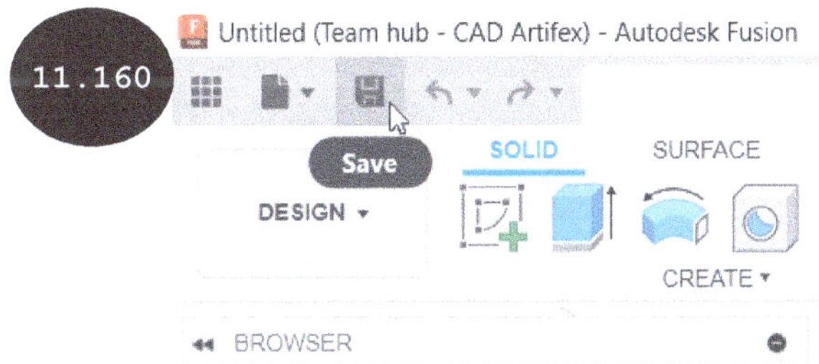

2. Enter **Single Cylinder Engine** in the **Name** field of the dialog box as the name of the assembly.

3. Ensure that the location ***Autodesk Fusion 360 > Chapter 11 > Tutorial > Tutorial 1*** is specified in the **Location** field of the dialog box to save the file.

4. Click on the **Save** button in the dialog box. The design file is saved with the name **Single Cylinder Engine** in the specified location (***Autodesk Fusion 360 > Chapter 11 > Tutorial > Tutorial 1***).

Note: In Autodesk Fusion, every time you save a design file, a new version of the file gets saved without overriding its existing versions.

5. Click on the **OK** button in the window. The new or updated version of the assembly file is saved at the specified location (***Autodesk Fusion 360 > Chapter 11 > Tutorial > Tutorial 1***).

Tutorial 2

Create an assembly, as shown in Figure 11.161 by applying all the required joints and then animate it. Different views and dimensions of individual components of the assembly are shown in Figures 11.162 through 11.165. You can also download all components of the assembly by logging on to the CADArtifex website (www.cadartifex.com). All dimensions are in mm.

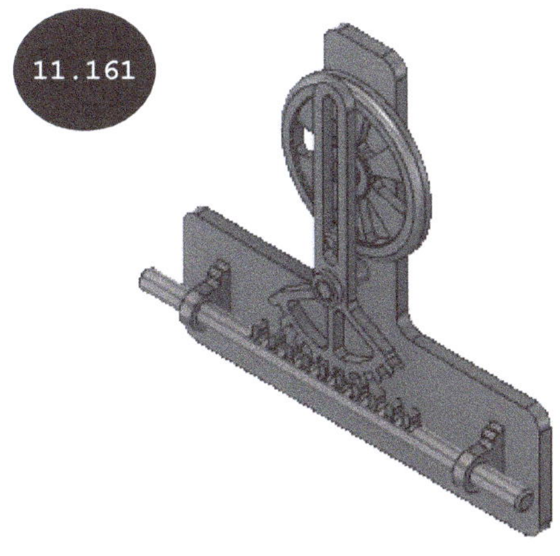

11.162

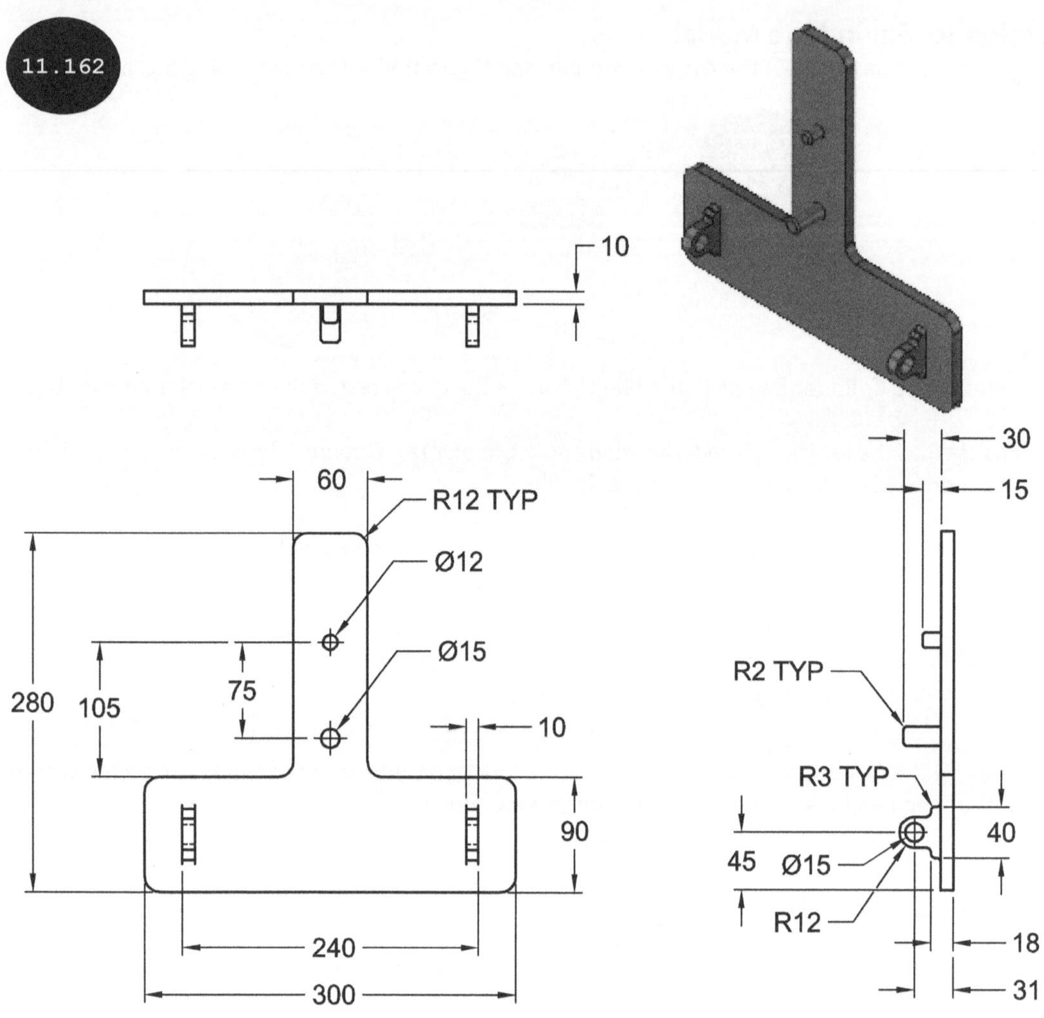

Mounting Board

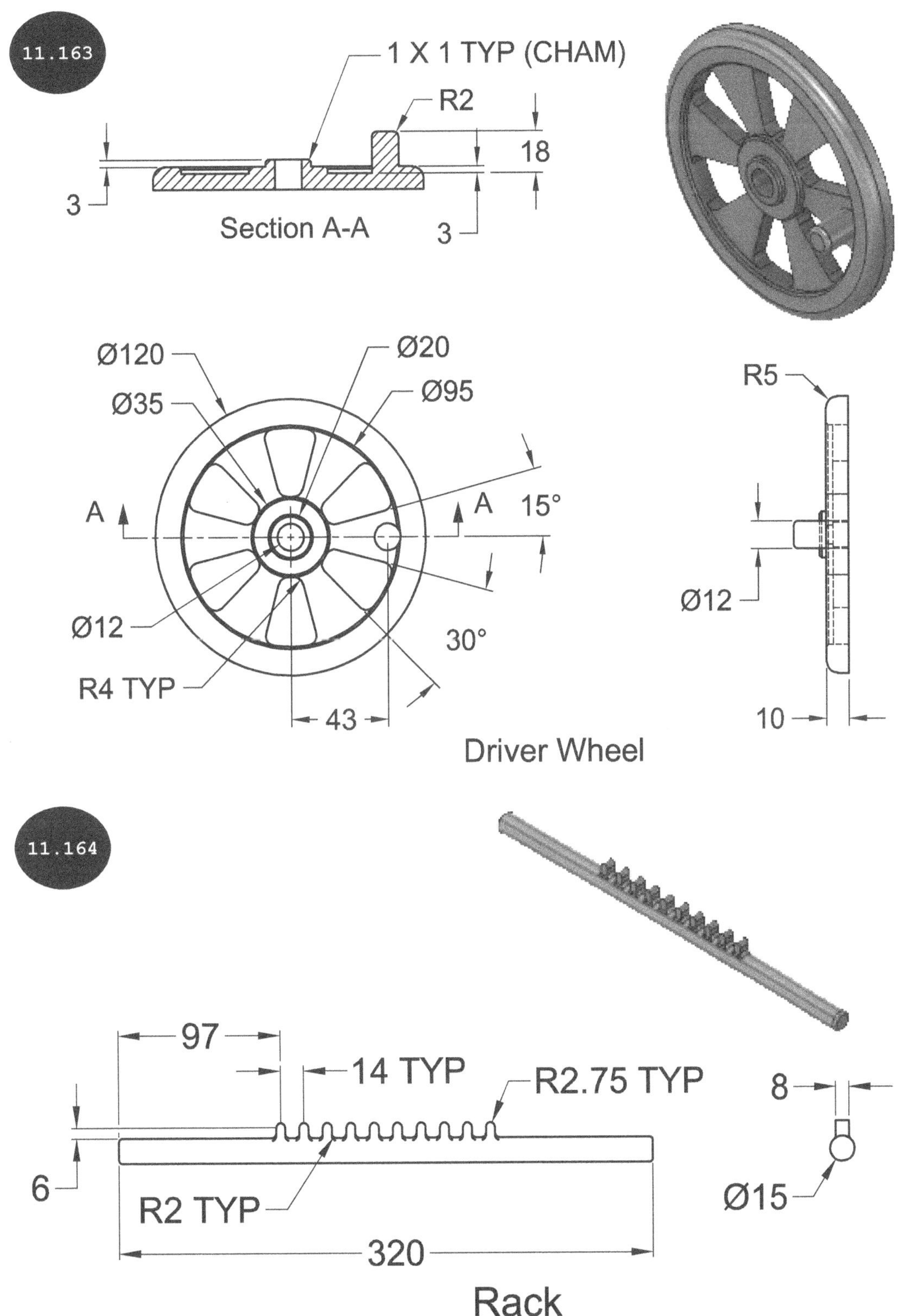
11.163
1 X 1 TYP (CHAM)
R2
18
3
Section A-A
3
Ø120
Ø20
Ø35
Ø95
A
A
15°
Ø12
30°
R4 TYP
43
R5
Ø12
10
Driver Wheel
11.164
97
14 TYP
R2.75 TYP
8
6
R2 TYP
Ø15
320
Rack

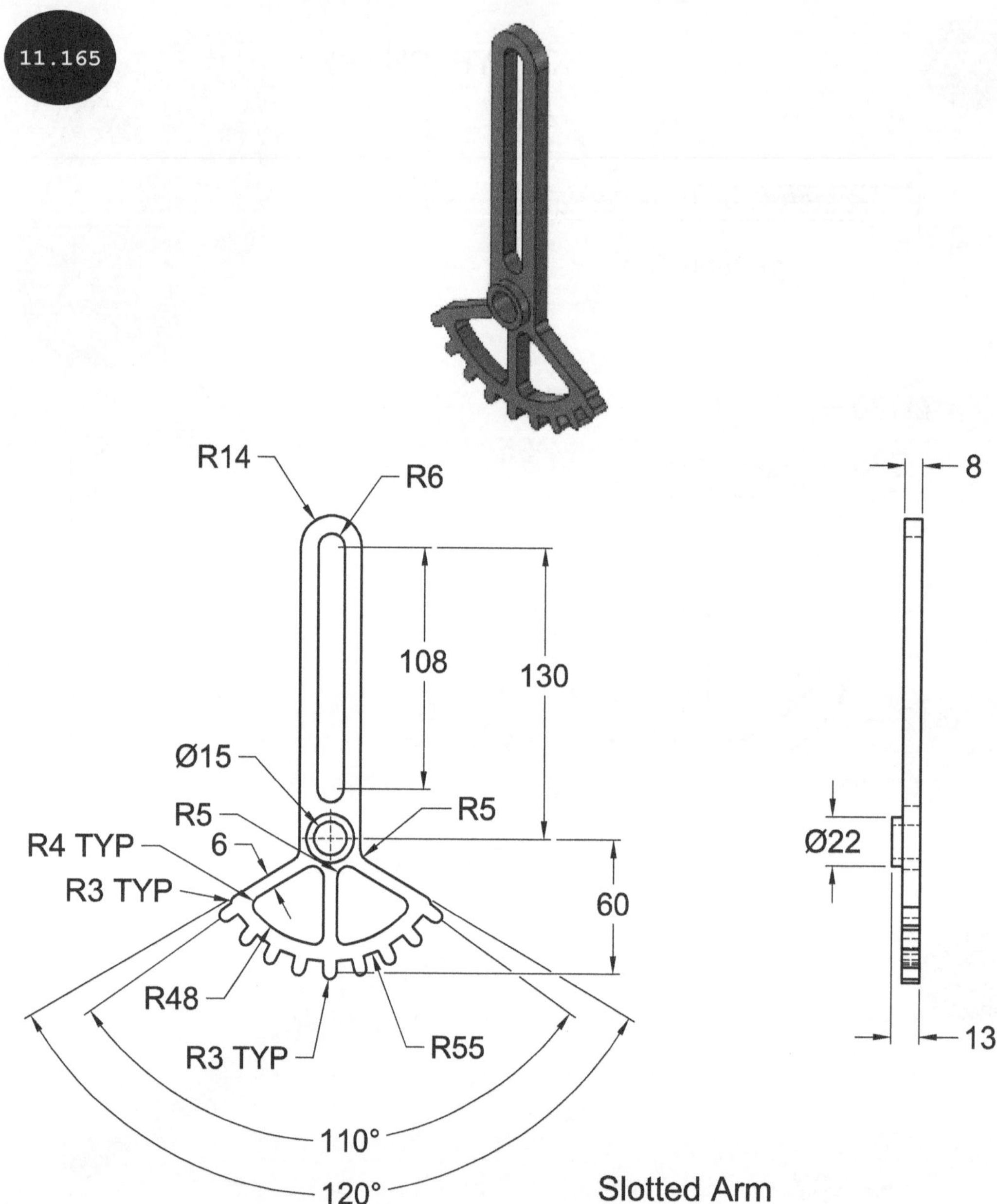

Slotted Arm

Section 1: Starting Autodesk Fusion and Creating All Components

In this section, you will create all components of the assembly.

1. Launch Autodesk Fusion and create all the components of the assembly one by one as a separate Part Design file. Refer to Figures 11.162 through 11.165 for the dimensions of each component. After creating all the components, save them at a common location *Autodesk Fusion 360 > Chapter 11 > Tutorial > Tutorial 2* in the **Data Panel**. You need to create these folders in the **Data Panel**.

Note: You can also download all the components of the assembly by logging in to your account on CADArtifex website (*cadartifex.com/login*). If you are a new user, you need to first register yourself on the CADArtifex website (*cadartifex.com/register*) to access the online resources.

Section 2: Creating the Assembly - Quick Return Mechanism

In this section, you need to create the assembly (*Quick Return Mechanism*).

1. Click **File > New** in the **Application Bar** (see Figure 11.166) to display the **What do you want to design?** dialog box, see Figure 11.167.

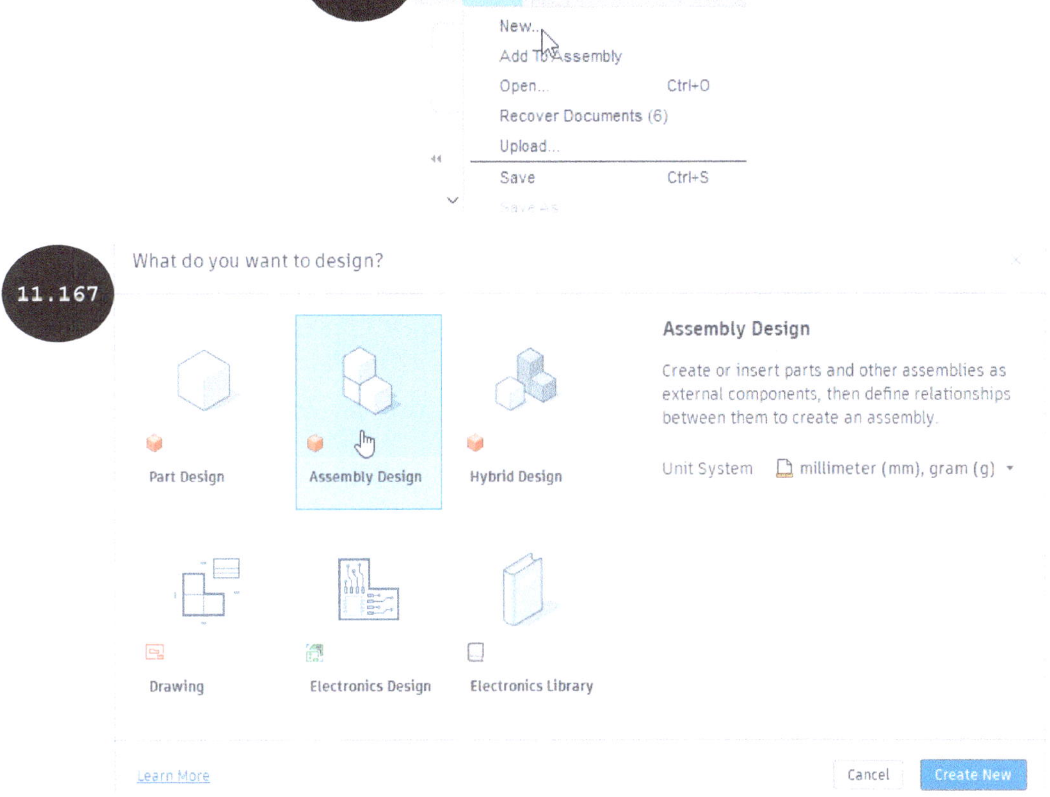

2. In this dialog box, select the **Assembly Design** button. Next, select the **millimeter (mm), gram (g)** unit system from the **Unit System** drop-down list.

3. After specifying the required options, click the **Create New** button. A new Assembly Design file is opened with the default name in a separate tab.

4. Invoke the **Data Panel** and then browse to the location where all the components of the assembly have been saved (***Autodesk Fusion 360** > **Chapter 11** > **Tutorial** > **Tutorial 2***). A preview of all the components of the assembly appears in the **Data Panel**.

5. Right-click on the **Mounting Board** component in the **Data Panel** and then click on the **Insert into Current Design** option in the shortcut menu that appears, see Figure 11.168. The **Mounting Board** component gets inserted into the design file with the display of translational and manipulator handles. Also, the **INITIAL POSITION** dialog box appears in the graphics area.

6. Accept the default position of the component in the graphics area and then click on the **OK** button in the **INITIAL POSITION** dialog box. The **Mounting Board** component is inserted into the Assembly design file and becomes the fixed component, by default. Next, close the **Data Panel** by clicking on the cross mark at its top right corner.

Section 3: Inserting the Second Component

Now, you need to insert the second component of the assembly into the design file.

1. Invoke the **Data Panel** and then right-click on the **Driver Wheel** component. A shortcut menu appears, see Figure 11.169. In this shortcut menu, click on the **Insert into Current Design** option. The **Driver Wheel** component gets inserted into the design file with the display of translational and manipulator handles attached to it.

2. Change the position of the second component (**Driver Wheel**) in the graphics area such that it does not intersect with the first component, see Figure 11.170. You can change the position of the component by dragging its translational handles that appear in the graphics area.

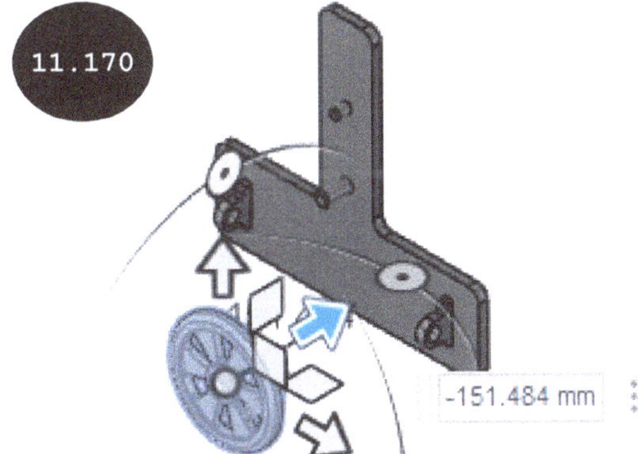

3. Click on the **OK** button in the INITIAL POSITION dialog box. The **Driver Wheel** component is inserted and placed in the specified position in the design file. Next, close the **Data Panel**.

Section 4: Applying the Revolute Joint

1. Press the **J** key or click on the **Joint** tool in the **RELATIONSHIPS** drop-down menu of the **ASSEMBLY** tab, see Figure 11.171. The **JOINT** dialog box appears, and the **Simple** button is activated in the **Origin Mode** area of its **Component 1** rollout, see Figure 11.172 and you are prompted to define the position of the joint origin on the second component (moveable component).

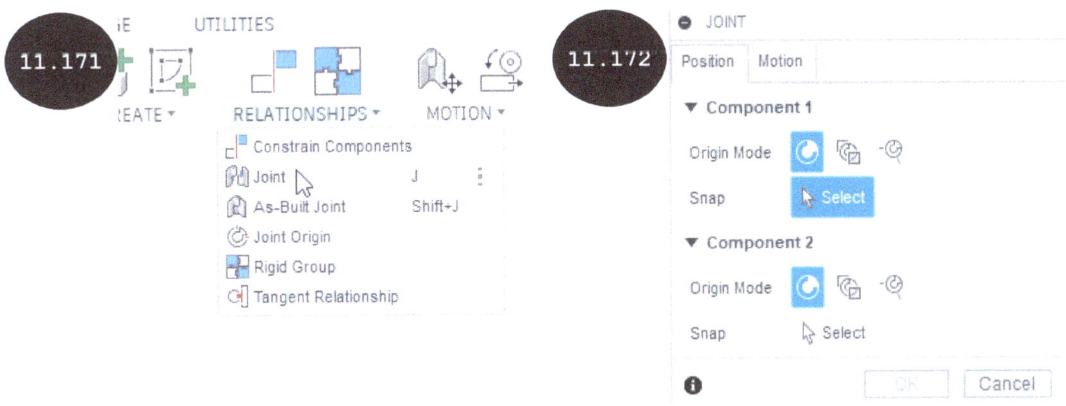

2. Rotate the assembly such that the back planar face of the second component (**Driver Wheel**) can be viewed, see Figure 11.173.

3. Move the cursor over the inner circular edge of the second component (**Driver Wheel**), see Figure 11.173. The edge gets highlighted and the joint origin snaps to its center.

4. Click the left mouse button when the joint origin snaps to the center of the inner circular edge, see Figure 11.173. The position of the joint origin is defined, and the **Driver Wheel** component becomes transparent in the graphics area. Also, you are prompted to define the position of the joint origin on another component (**Mounting Board**). Next, change the orientation of the assembly back to isometric.

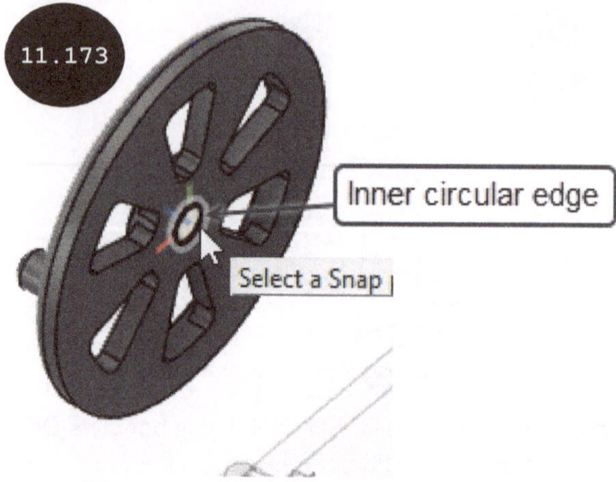

Note: The **Simple** button is activated in the **Origin Mode** area of the **Component 2** rollout, by default. As a result, you can define the position of the joint origin on a face, an edge, or a point of a component.

5. Move the cursor over the circular face of the top cylindrical feature of the **Mounting Board** component, see Figure 11.174. The circular face gets highlighted and its snap points (front, middle, and back) appear in the graphics area.

6. Press the CTRL key to lock the highlighted face and then move the cursor over its back snap point, see Figure 11.174. Next, click the left mouse button when the joint origin snaps to it. The position of the joint origin is defined, and the **Driver Wheel** component moves toward the **Mounting Board** component such that the defined joint origins of both components coincide with each other, see Figure 11.175. Also, the component animates in the graphics area based on the default joint type selected in the **Motion** tab of the dialog box.

   Now, you need to define the joint to be applied between the components.

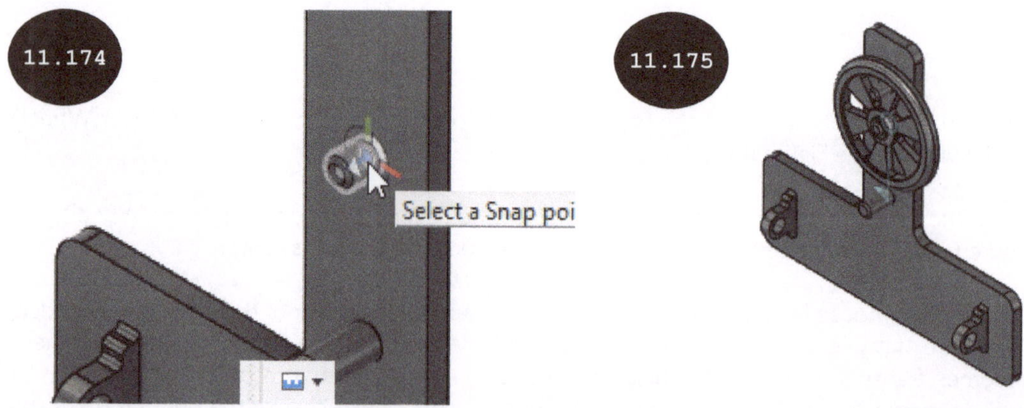

7. Click on the **Motion** tab in the dialog box and then select the **Revolute** option in the **Type** drop-down list of the dialog box as the joint to be applied between the components. The **Driver Wheel** component starts rotating for a while about an axis which is selected in the **Rotate** drop-down list of the dialog box.

8. Ensure that the **Z Axis** option is selected in the **Rotate** drop-down list of the dialog box.

9. Click on the **OK** button in the dialog box. The revolute joint is applied such that all degrees of freedom of the second component become fixed except one rotational degree of freedom.

Section 5: Inserting the Third Component

1. Invoke the **Data Panel** and then insert the **Slotted Arm** component into the design file such that it does not intersect with the existing components of the assembly, see Figure 11.176.

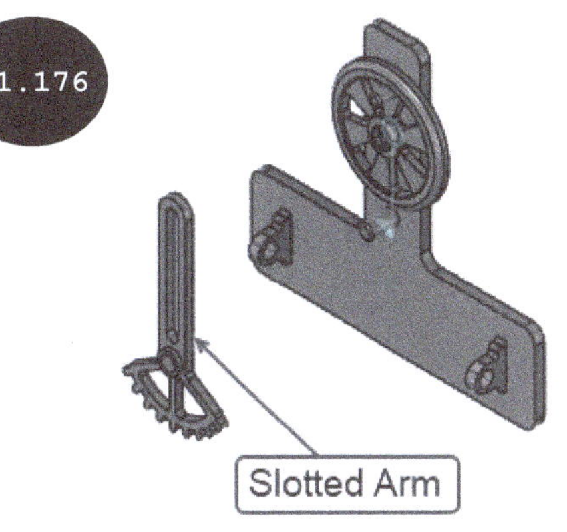

Section 6: Applying the Revolute Joint

You need to assemble the **Slotted Arm** component by applying the revolute and pin-slot joints.

1. Press the J key or click on the **Joint** tool in the **RELATIONSHIPS** drop-down menu of the **ASSEMBLY** tab. The **JOINT** dialog box appears, and the **Simple** button is activated in the **Origin Mode** area of the **Component 1** rollout.

2. Move the cursor over the inner circular edge of the **Slotted Arm** component and then click the left mouse button when the joint origin snaps to its center, see Figure 11.177. The position of the joint origin is defined on the **Slotted Arm** component. Also, you are prompted to define the position of the joint origin on another component.

3. Move the cursor over the top circular edge of the bottom cylindrical feature of the **Mounting Board** component and then click the left mouse button when the joint origin snaps to its center, see Figure 11.178. The **Slotted Arm** component moves toward the **Mounting Board** component such that the defined joint origins of both components coincide with each other in the graphics area,

see Figure 11.179. Also, the component animates in the graphics area based on the default joint type selected in the **Motion** tab of the dialog box.

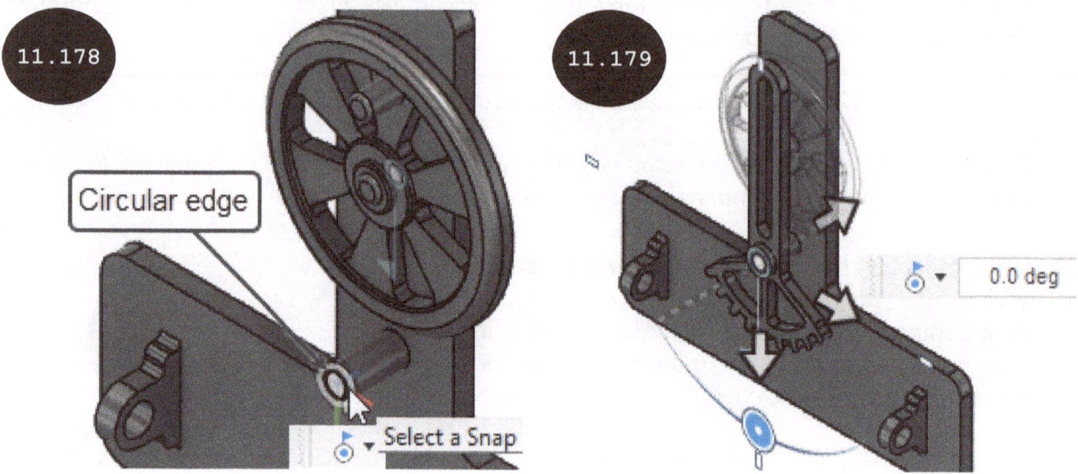

Now, you need to define the joint to be applied between the components.

4. Click on the **Motion** tab and then select the **Revolute** option in the **Type** drop-down list of the dialog box as the joint to be applied between the components.

5. Click on the **OK** button in the dialog box. The revolute joint is applied such that all degrees of freedom of the second component become fixed except one rotational degree of freedom.

Section 7: Applying the Pin-Slot Joint

1. Press the J key. The **JOINT** dialog box appears, and the **Simple** button is activated in the **Origin Mode** area of the **Component 1** rollout.

2. Move the cursor over the top circular edge of the pin (cylindrical feature) in the **Driver Wheel** component and then click the left mouse button when the joint origin snaps to its center, see Figure 11.180. The position of the joint origin is defined on the **Driver Wheel** component, and you are prompted to define the joint origin on another component.

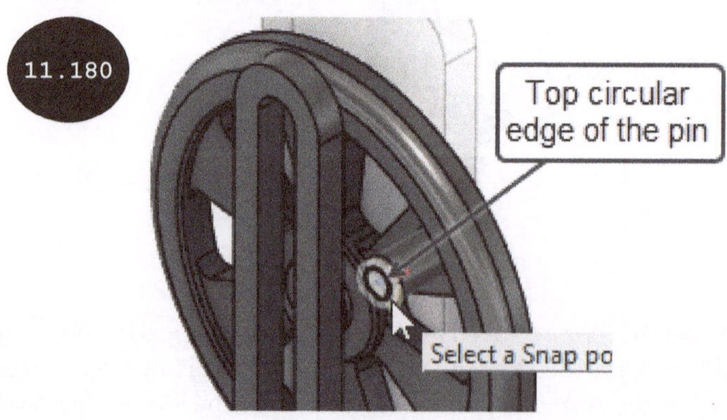

3. Move the cursor over the top slot arc of the **Slotted Arm** component and then click the left mouse button when the joint origin snaps to its center, see Figure 11.181. The defined joint origins of both components coincide with each other. Also, a warning message appears at the lower right corner of the screen informing that the selected joint type will result in conflict.

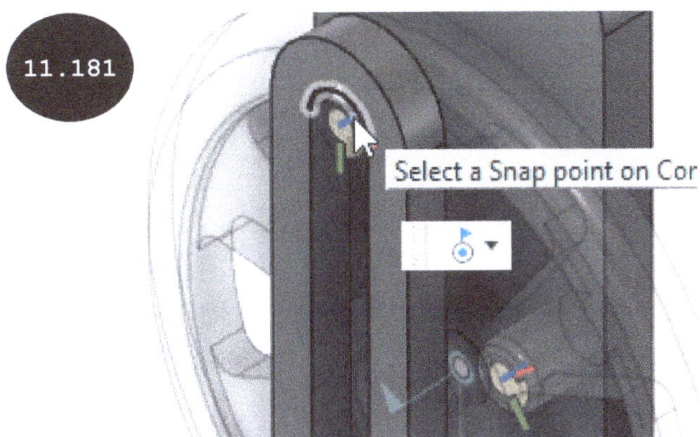

4. Click on the **Motion** tab in the dialog box and then select the **Pin-Slot** option in the **Type** drop-down list of the dialog box as the joint to be applied between the components, see Figure 11.182.

5. Ensure that the **Z Axis** option is selected in the **Rotate** drop-down list of the dialog box as the axis of revolution, see Figure 11.182.

   Now, you need to define the sliding direction for the pin-slot joint.

6. Select the **Y Axis** option in the **Slide** drop-down list of the **Motion** tab as the sliding direction, see Figure 11.182.

7. Click on the **OK** button in the dialog box. The pin-slot joint is applied between the components, see Figure 11.183.

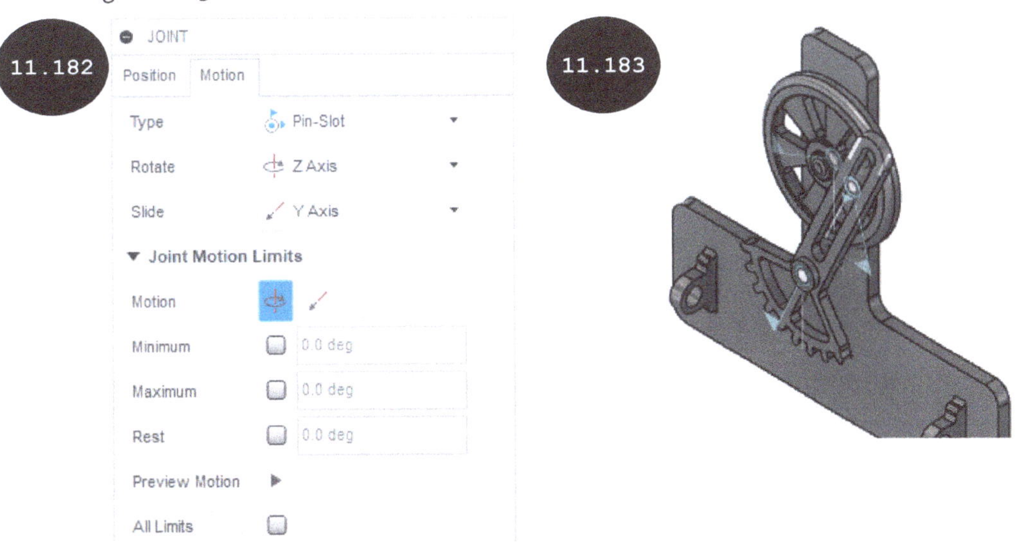

Section 8: Inserting and Assembling the Fourth Component

Now, you need to insert and assemble the fourth component of the assembly.

1. Invoke the **Data Panel** and then insert the **Rack** component into the Assembly design file such that it does not intersect with the existing components of the assembly, see Figure 11.184.

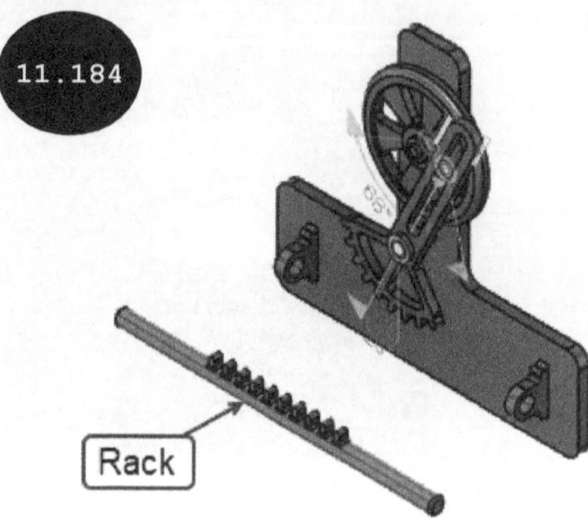

Now, you need to assemble the **Rack** component by applying the slider joint.

2. Press the J key or click on the **Joint** tool in the **RELATIONSHIPS** drop-down menu of the **ASSEMBLY** tab. The **JOINT** dialog box appears.

3. Move the cursor over the right circular edge of the **Rack** component and then click the left mouse button when the joint origin snaps to its center, see Figure 11.185. The position of the joint origin is defined on the **Rack** component, and you are prompted to define the joint origin on another component.

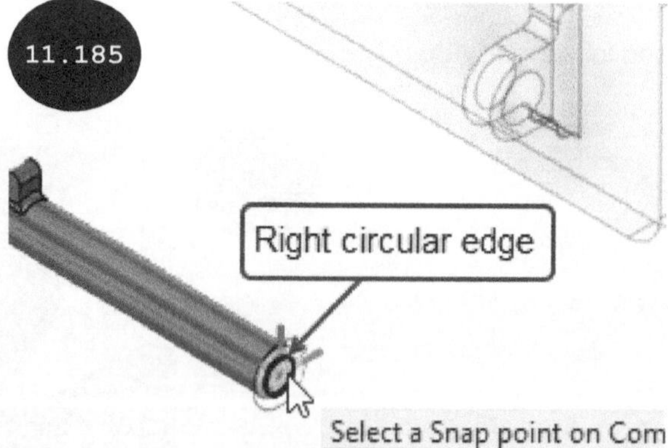

4. Move the cursor over the circular edge of the right bracket of the **Mounting Board** component and then click the left mouse button when the joint origin snaps to its center, see Figure 11.186. The defined joint origins of both components coincide with each other in the graphics area.

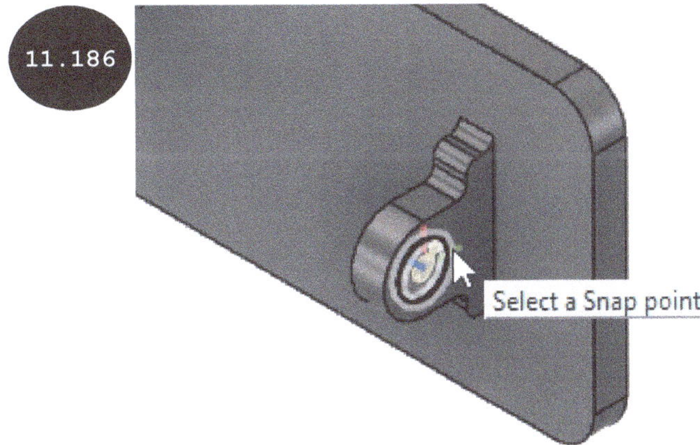

5. Enter **-40** in the **Offset Z** field of the **Alignment** rollout of the dialog box as the offset distance between the defined joint origins of the components.

6. Click on the **Motion** tab in the dialog box and then select the **Slider** option in the **Type** drop-down list of the dialog box as the joint to be applied between the components.

   Now, you need to define the maximum and minimum joint limits for the slider joint.

Tip: By default, when you apply a joint, the component is free to rotate or translate, without any limitation along its free degrees of freedom. Consider the case of the slider joint, where the component can translate freely, without any limitation along its sliding direction. You can avoid this by defining the maximum and minimum limits for the joint to control its free movement.

7. Select the **Minimum** check box in the **Joint Motion Limits** rollout of the **JOINT** dialog box. Next, enter **-40** mm in the field that appears in front of the **Minimum** check box in the dialog box as the minimum limit for the slider joint, see Figure 11.187.

8. Select the **Maximum** check box in the dialog box. Next, enter **40** mm in the field that appears in front of the **Maximum** check box as the maximum limit for the slider joint.

Note: The minimum and maximum limits are measured between the locations of the joint origins defined on the components.

9. Select the **Rest** check box in the dialog box and then enter **0** mm in the field that appears in front of this check box as the rest position for the slider joint, see Figure 11.187.

10. Click on the **OK** button in the **JOINT** dialog box. The minimum and maximum joint limits for the slider joint are defined. Now, the **Rack** component can slide within the specified minimum and maximum joint limits, see Figure 11.188.

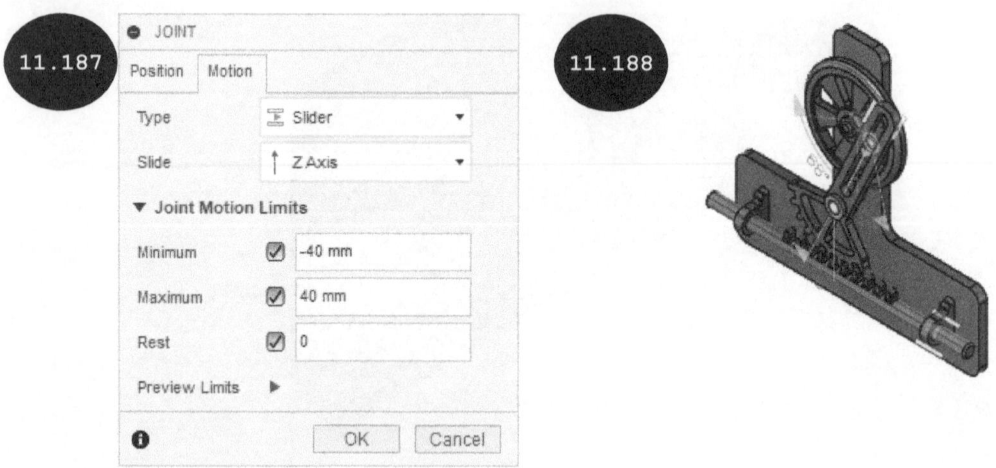

Section 9: Defining Relative Motion between Two Joints

Now, you need to define the relative motion between the revolute joint of the **Slotted Arm** component and the slider joint of the **Rack** component such that the rotational motion of the **Slotted Arm** translates to the translational motion of the **Rack** and vice-versa.

1. Change the orientation of the assembly to Front view, see Figure 11.189. Next, define the position of the **Slotted Arm** component to the middle (vertically aligned) by dragging it, similar to the one shown in Figure 11.189. Keeping the **Slotted Arm** position in the middle helps it swing symmetrically to both its sides like a pendulum swing while the **Driver Wheel** component rotates 360 degrees. Now, you can define the relative motion between the components.

2. Invoke the **MOTION** drop-down menu in the **Toolbar** and then click on the **Motion Link** tool, see Figure 11.190. The **Capture or revert component positions** message window appears informing that some components have been moved.

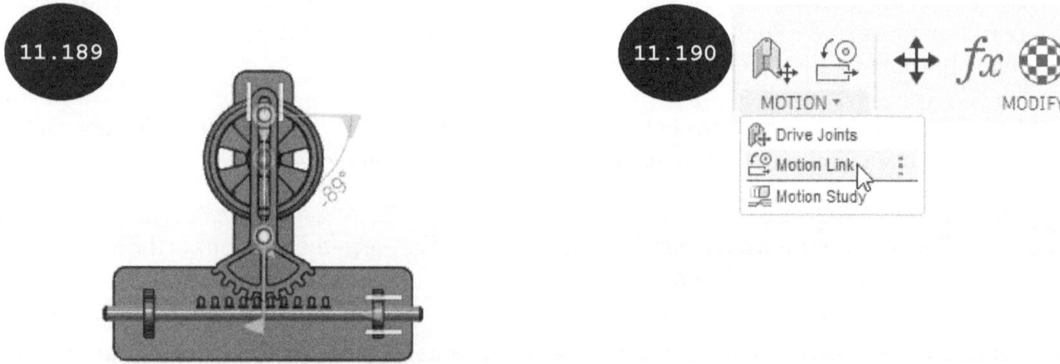

3. Click on the **Capture Position** button in the **Capture or revert component positions** message window. The **MOTION LINK** dialog box appears.

4. Expand the **Joints** node in the **BROWSER** and then select the revolute joint (**Revolute 2**) applied to the **Slotted Arm** and the slider joint (**Slider 4**) applied to the **Rack** component of the assembly

one by one, refer to Figure 11.191. On selecting the joints, the **MOTION LINK** dialog box gets modified with additional options, which are used for controlling the relative motion between the selected joints, see Figure 11.192.

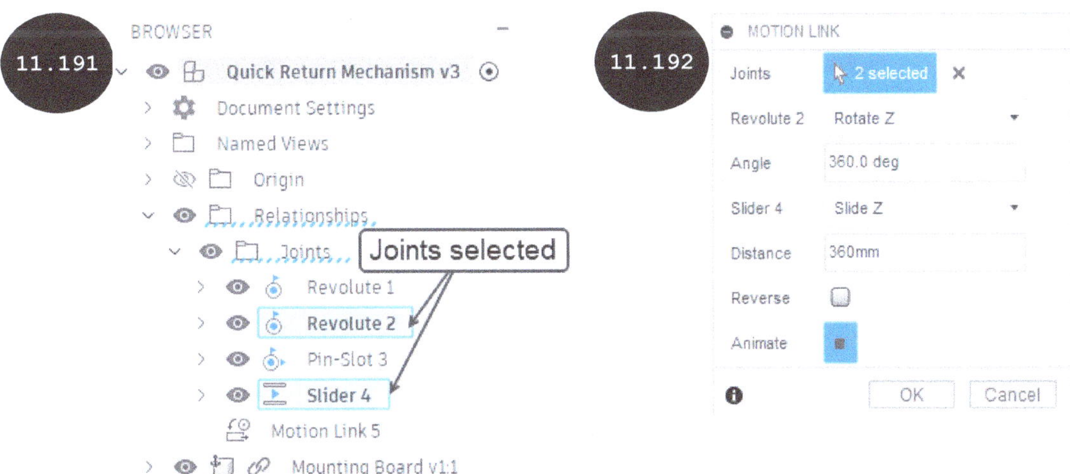

5. Ensure that **360** degrees is specified in the **Angle** field of the dialog box as the angle of revolution of the **Slotted Arm** component.

6. Enter **360** mm in the **Distance** field of the dialog box as the distance traveled by the **Rack** component per 360 degrees of revolution of the **Slotted Arm** component.

7. Click on the **OK** button in the dialog box. The relative motion between the selected joints is defined. Change the orientation of the assembly to isometric. Figure 11.193 shows the final assembly.

Section 10: Animating Assembly

Now, you can animate the entire assembly to review the behavior (motion) of all its components.

1. Expand the **Joints** node in the **BROWSER**. A list of all the applied joints appears.

2. Right-click on the first revolute joint (**Revolute 1**) in the expanded **Joints** node and then click on the **Animate Joint Relationships** option in the shortcut menu that appears, see Figure 11.194. The

components of the assembly start animating concerning each other in the graphics area based on the joints applied.

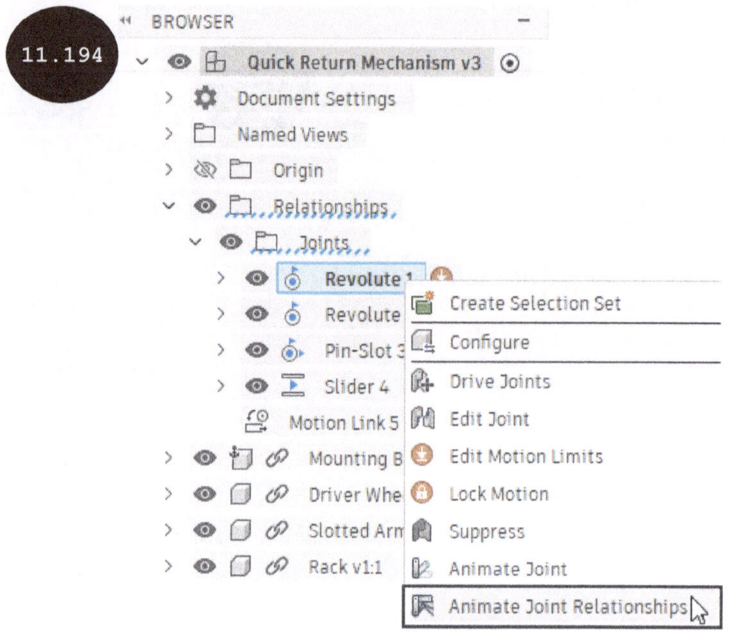

3. After reviewing the behavior (motion) of all assembly components, press the ESC key to stop the animation.

Section 11: Saving the Model

1. Click on the **Save** tool in the **Application Bar**. The **Save** window appears.

2. Enter **Quick Return Mechanism** in the **Name** field of the dialog box as the name of the assembly.

3. Ensure that the location ***Autodesk Fusion 360 > Chapter 11 > Tutorial > Tutorial 2*** is specified in the **Location** field of the dialog box to save the file.

4. Click on the **OK** button in the window. The new version of the assembly file is saved at the specified location (***Autodesk Fusion 360 > Chapter 11 > Tutorial > Tutorial 2***).

Hands-on Test Drive 1

Create an assembly, as shown in Figure 11.195 by applying the required joints. The exploded view of the assembly is shown in Figure 11.196 for your reference only. Different views and dimensions of individual components of the assembly are shown in Figures 11.197 through 11.204. You can also download all components of the assembly by logging on to the CADArtifex website (www.cadartifex.com). All dimensions are in mm.

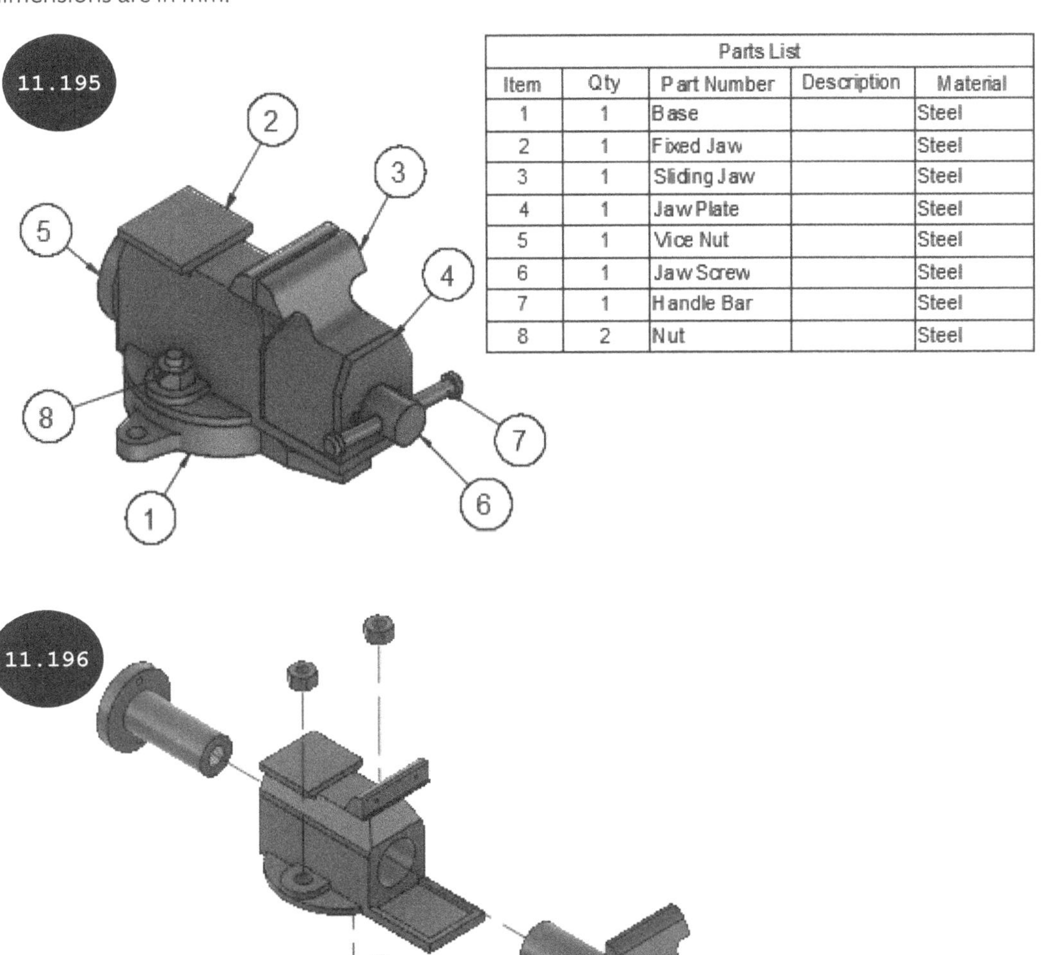

Parts List				
Item	Qty	Part Number	Description	Material
1	1	Base		Steel
2	1	Fixed Jaw		Steel
3	1	Sliding Jaw		Steel
4	1	Jaw Plate		Steel
5	1	Vice Nut		Steel
6	1	Jaw Screw		Steel
7	1	Handle Bar		Steel
8	2	Nut		Steel

11.197

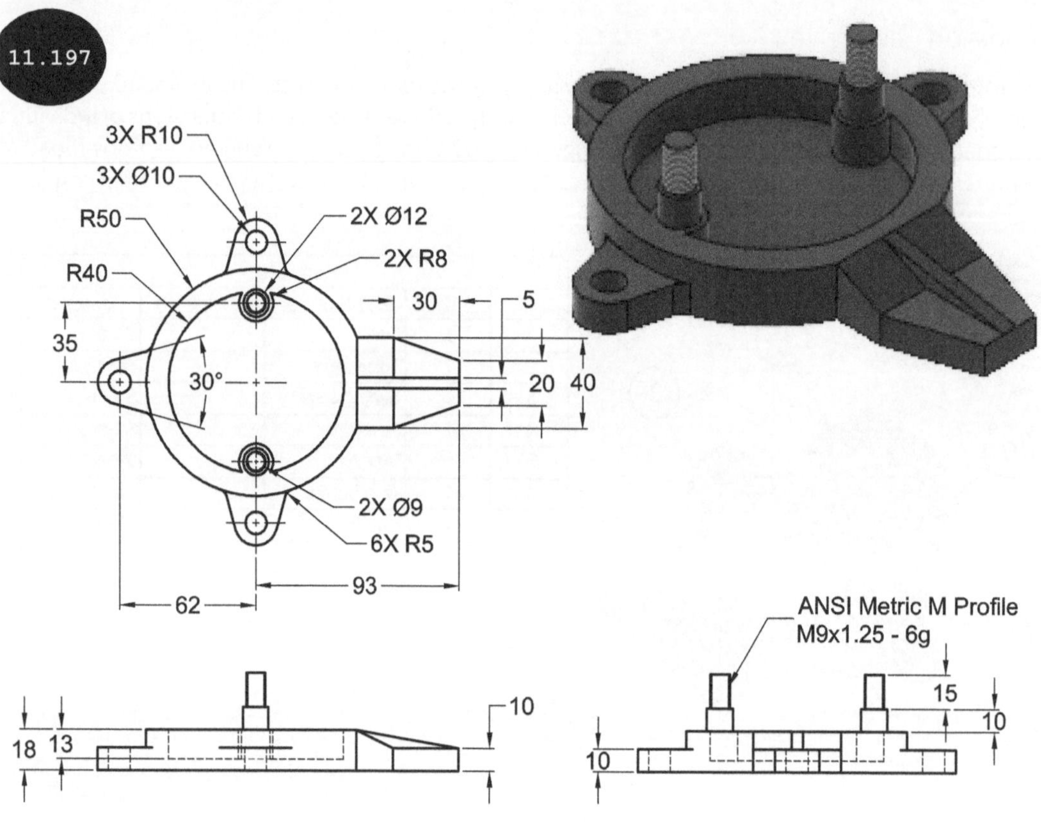
3X R10
3X Ø10
R50
R40
2X Ø12
2X R8
30
5
35
30°
20
40
2X Ø9
6X R5
62
93
ANSI Metric M Profile
M9x1.25 - 6g
15
10
18
13
10
10

11.198

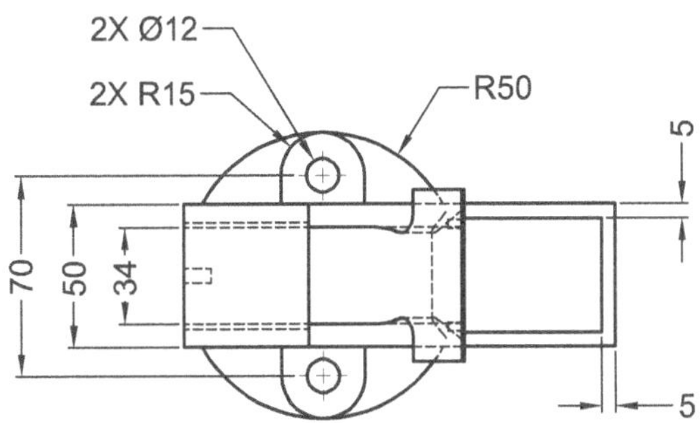
2X Ø12
2X R15
R50
5
70
50
34
5

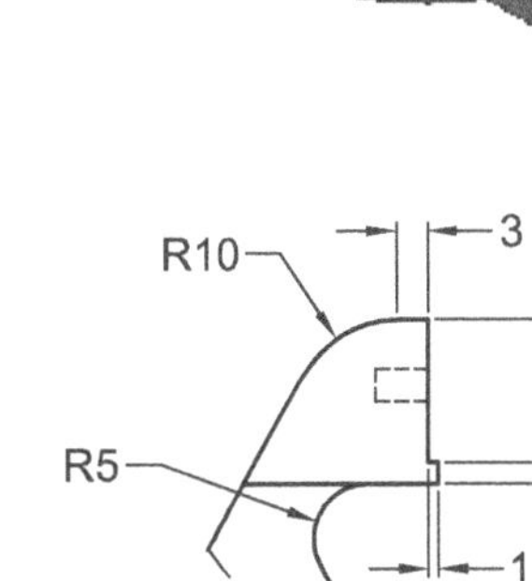
R10
3
2
15
R5
1
Detail A

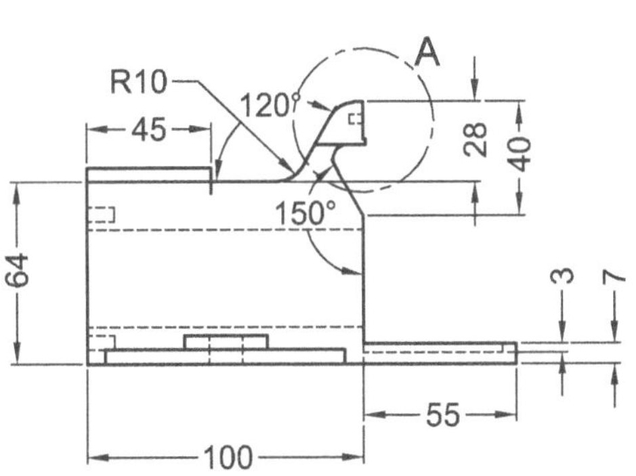
A
R10
120°
45
28
40
150°
64
3
7
55
100

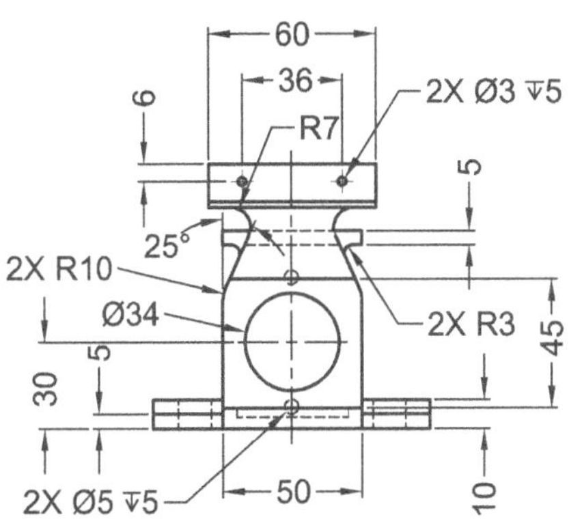
60
36
6
2X Ø3 ↧5
R7
5
25°
2X R10
Ø34
2X R3
45
5
30
2X Ø5 ↧5
50
10

11.199

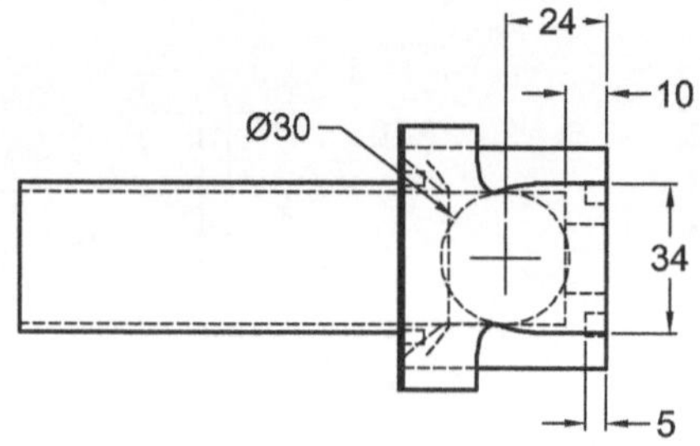
24
10
Ø30
34
5

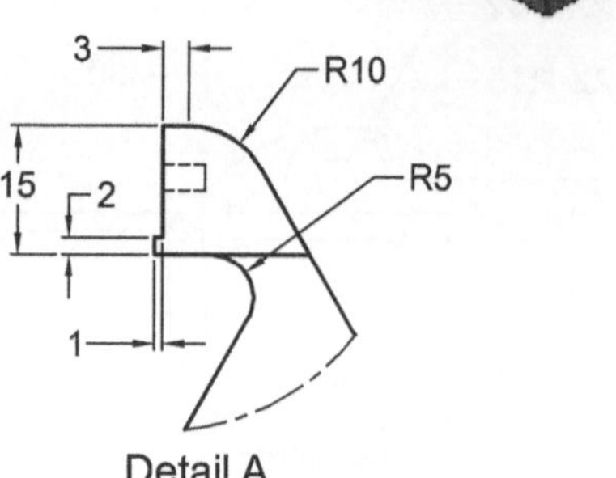
3
R10
15
2
R5
1
Detail A

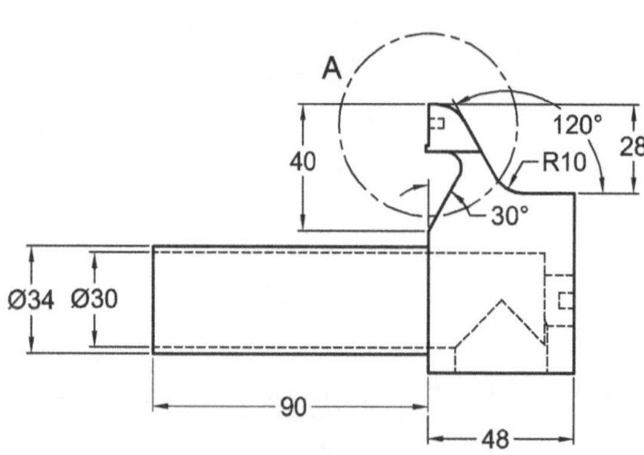
A
120°
40
28
R10
30°
Ø34 Ø30
90
48

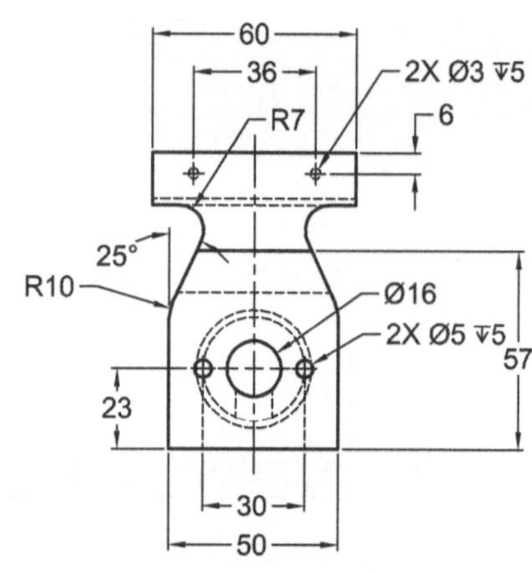
60
36
2X Ø3 ↧5
R7
6
25°
R10
Ø16
2X Ø5 ↧5
57
23
30
50

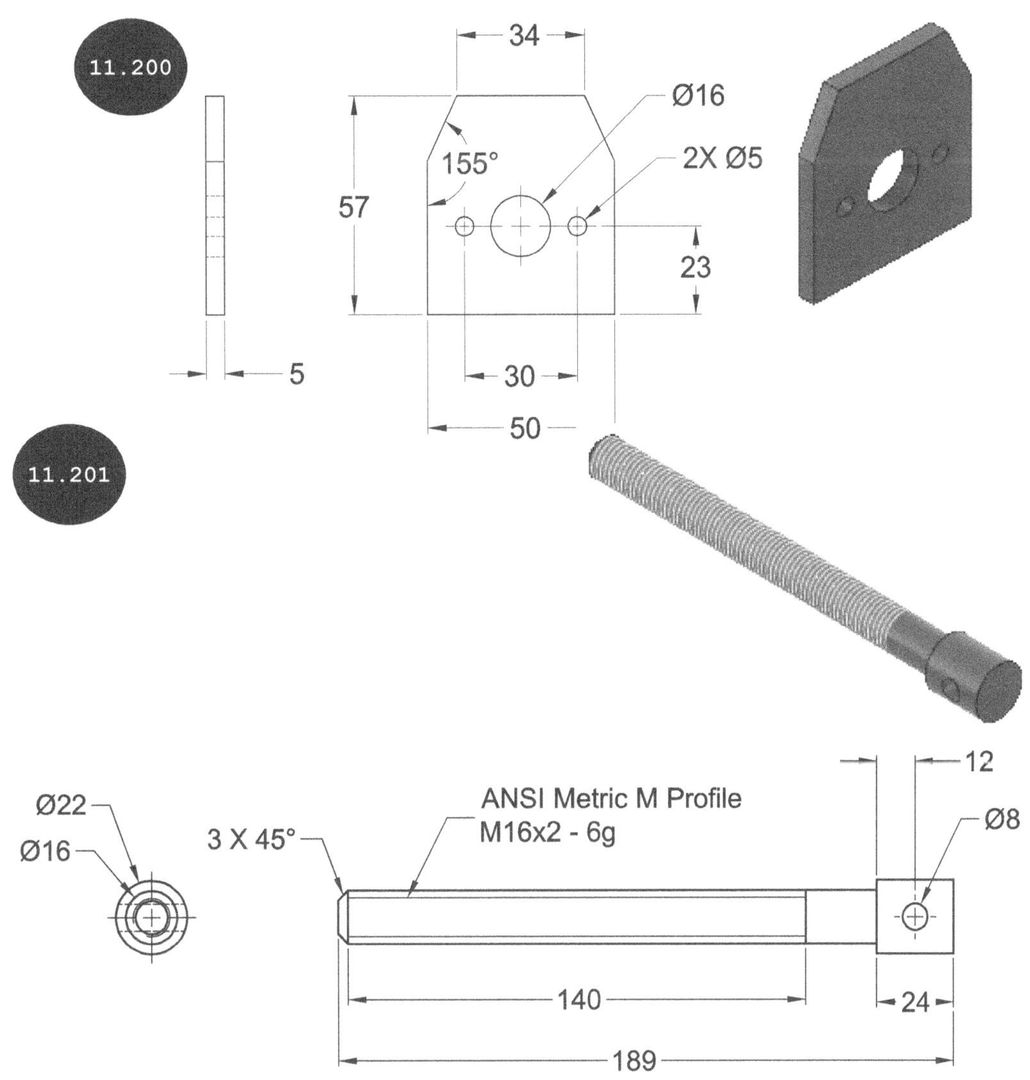
11.200
34
Ø16
2X Ø5
155°
57
23
5
30
50
11.201
12
Ø22
ANSI Metric M Profile
M16x2 - 6g
Ø8
3 X 45°
Ø16
140
24
189

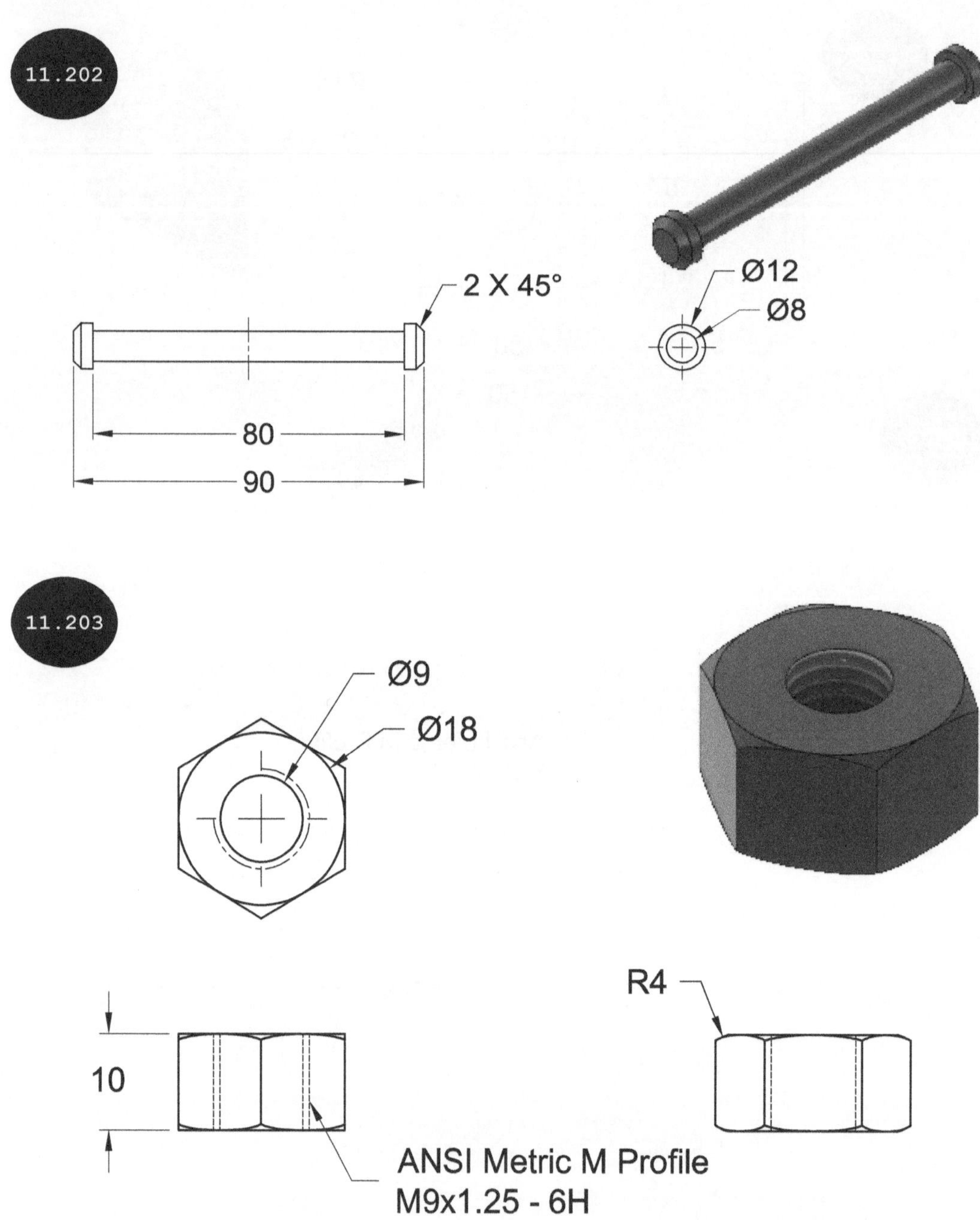
11.202
2 X 45°
Ø12
Ø8
80
90
11.203
Ø9
Ø18
R4
10
ANSI Metric M Profile
M9x1.25 - 6H

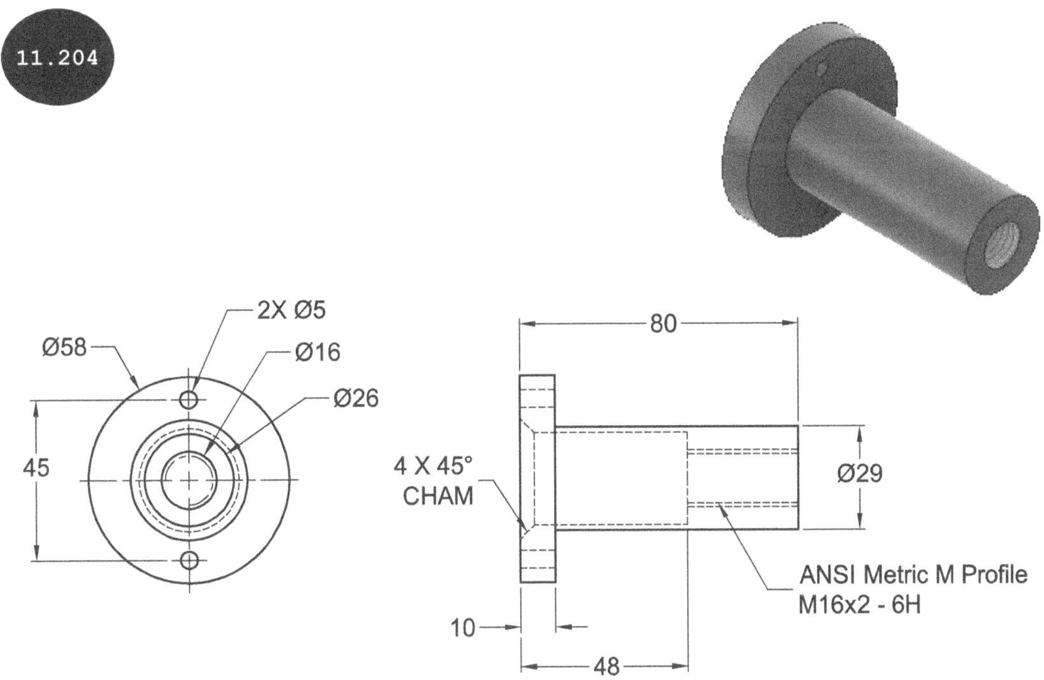

Summary

In this chapter, you learned how to create assemblies using the bottom-up assembly approach. You explored how to apply various joint types such as rigid, revolute, slider, cylindrical, pin-slot, planar, and ball joints to assemble components and define their relative motion. You also learned how to insert components into a design file, apply and edit joints, set joint limits, animate joints as well as the entire assembly, and lock or unlock movement between joints. Additionally, this chapter covered how to group components, enable contact sets, and capture component positions, equipping you with essential tools for managing assemblies effectively.

Questions

Complete and verify the following sentences:

- In Autodesk Fusion, you can create assemblies by using the ________ and ________ approaches.
- Autodesk Fusion has ________ capabilities. As a result, if you make any change in a component, the same change reflects in the component used in the assembly as well as in the drawing and other respective workspaces of Autodesk Fusion, automatically updating the respective file.
- The ________ dialog box appears every time on inserting a component in a design file and allows you to define the position and orientation of the component in the design file.

- A free/unground component of an assembly has _________ degrees of freedom.
- The _________ joint allows the component to rotate about an axis by removing all degrees of freedom except one rotational degree of freedom.
- The _________ joint allows the component to translate along a single axis by removing all degrees of freedom except one translational degree of freedom.
- The _________ joint allows the component to translate along an axis as well as rotate about a different axis.
- The _________ tool is used for animating the model or assembly to review its working conditions and the behavior of its components concerning each other.
- You can move the individual components of an assembly along its degrees of freedom. (True/False)
- You can define minimum and maximum limits for a joint. (True/False)
- In Autodesk Fusion, you cannot define relative motion between two joints. (True/False)

12

Working with Assemblies - II

In this chapter, the following topics will be discussed:

- Creating an Assembly by Using Top-down Approach
- Creating Components within an Assembly File
- Creating Feature of an Empty Component
- Applying As-Built Joints
- Defining a Joint Origin on a Component
- Editing Assembly Components

In the previous chapter, you explored the Bottom-up Assembly Approach to creating assemblies. You also gained an understanding of the different types of joints and how to apply them to assemble components relative to one another. Additionally, you learned how to edit joints, set joint limits, animate joints, and animate models.

In this chapter, you'll dive into the Top-down Assembly Approach, where you'll learn to build assemblies by creating components directly within the assembly. You'll also discover how to apply As-built Joints between components to establish their correct relationships.

Creating an Assembly Using Top-down Approach

In the Top-down Assembly approach, all the components of an assembly are created within a single Assembly Design file. It helps in taking references from the existing components of the assembly. By using this approach, you can create a concept-based design, where new components of an assembly can be created by taking reference from the existing components.

Creating Components within an Assembly File

In Autodesk Fusion, you can create components of an assembly within a single Assembly Design file by using one of the following methods:

Creating a New Empty Component

The method for creating a new empty component within an Assembly Design file is discussed below:

1. Start Autodesk Fusion, if it is not already running, and open a new Assembly Design file.

2. In the Assembly Design file, invoke the **CREATE** drop-down menu and then click on the **New Component** tool, see Figure 12.1. The **NEW COMPONENT** dialog box appears, see Figure 12.2.

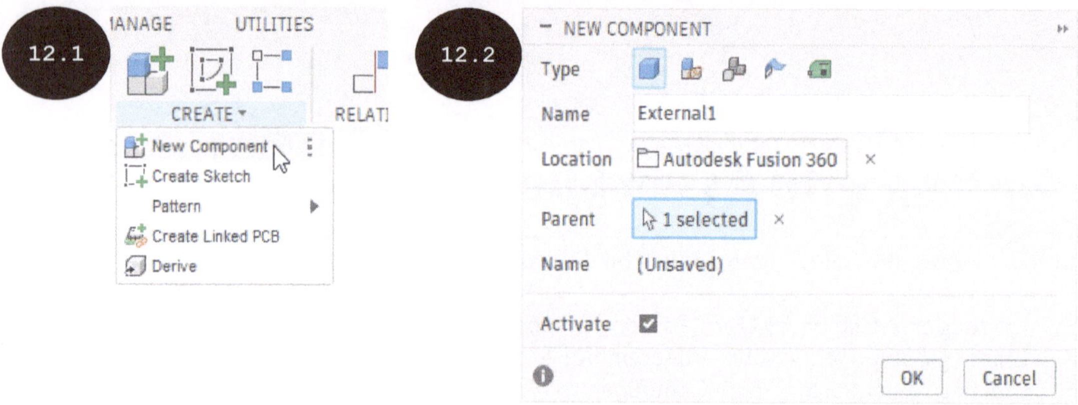

Tip: You can also invoke the **NEW COMPONENT** dialog box by right-clicking on the name of the assembly file (top browser node) in the **BROWSER** and then clicking on the **New Component** tool in the shortcut menu that appears, see Figure 12.3.

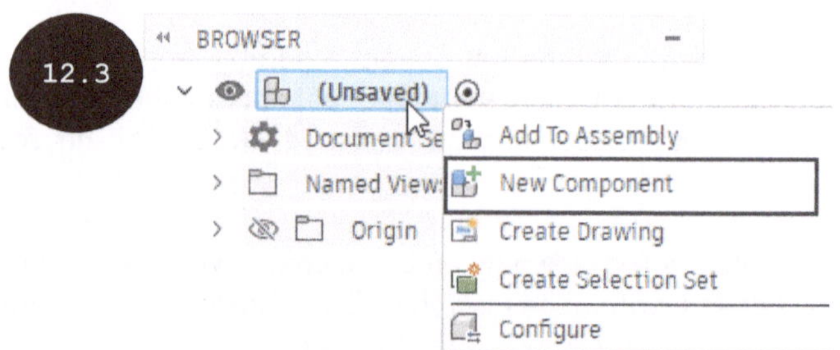

Type: By default, the **Part** button is activated in the **Type** area, refer to Figure 12.2. It is used to create an empty Part Design file for modeling a part as an external file within the assembly.

The **Assembly** button is used to create an empty Assembly Design file, allowing you to create a sub-assembly within the main assembly file. The **Hybrid** button is used to create an empty Hybrid Design file, enabling you to work in a hybrid design environment with access to both part and assembly design tools. The **Sheet Metal** button is used to create an empty Part Design file for modeling a sheet metal component within the assembly file. The **Linked PCB** button is used to create an empty Electronics Design file for designing a PCB within the assembly file.

Name: The **Name** field allows you to enter a name for the new design file.

Location: The **Location** area allows you to select a location (project folder) in the **Data Panel** to save the design file as an external file.

Parent: In the **Parent** selection field, the active design file in the **BROWSER** is selected by default as the parent for the new design file being created. To change the parent, click the cross mark × next to the **Parent** field in the dialog box to clear the default selection. Then, select the desired design file in the **BROWSER** to set it as the new parent.

Activate: By default, the **Activate** check box is selected in the dialog box. This makes the new design file the active design file in the assembly, allowing you to create the component within it.

3. Ensure that the **Part** button is activated to create an empty Part Design file for modeling a solid component within the assembly file.

4. Enter a name for the new design file in the **Name** field of the dialog box.

5. Ensure that the required location to save the design file is specified in the **Location** field. To define a new location, click the currently selected folder in this field or click the cross mark next to it to open the **Select Folder** dialog box. Next, choose the required project folder and click the **Select** button. It is recommended to save all files related to an assembly within a single project folder.

6. Accept the default parent selection for the new design file in the **Parent** field of the dialog box. If required, you can specify a different parent file, as discussed earlier.

7. Ensure that the **Activate** check box is selected to make it the active file in the assembly.

8. After defining all the required options, click the **OK** button. A new empty design file is created as a child of the selected parent file in the **BROWSER** with its specified name, see Figure 12.4. The file also becomes the active design file for creating the component.

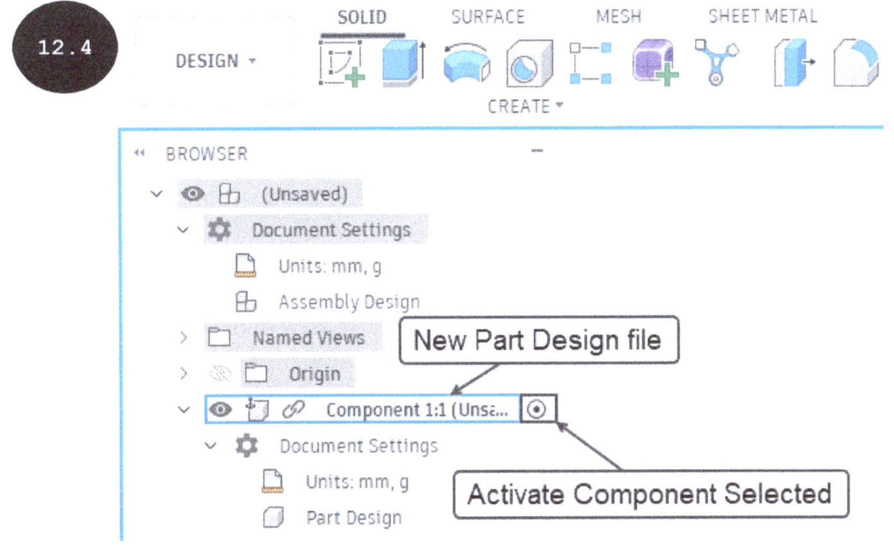

Note: By default, the first design file created within an assembly file is fixed (grounded). This means that all its degrees of freedom are constrained, preventing it from moving. It therefore acts as a reference component for assembling other components around it.

Now, you can create the component in the active design file by building its features one by one using the feature modeling tools available in the **SOLID** tab of the **Toolbar**.

Creating Features of an Empty Component

1. Click on the **Create Sketch** tool in the **Toolbar** and then select a plane as the sketching plane to create the sketch of the first feature of the active component. The sketching plane becomes normal to the viewing direction and the **SKETCH** contextual tab appears in the **Toolbar**. Also, the **SKETCH PALETTE** dialog box appears.

2. Ensure that the **3D Sketch** check box is cleared in the **SKETCH PALETTE** dialog box for creating a 2D sketch.

3. Draw the sketch of the base/first feature using the sketching tools, see Figure 12.5. In this figure, the sketch is created on the Top plane. All dimensions are in mm.

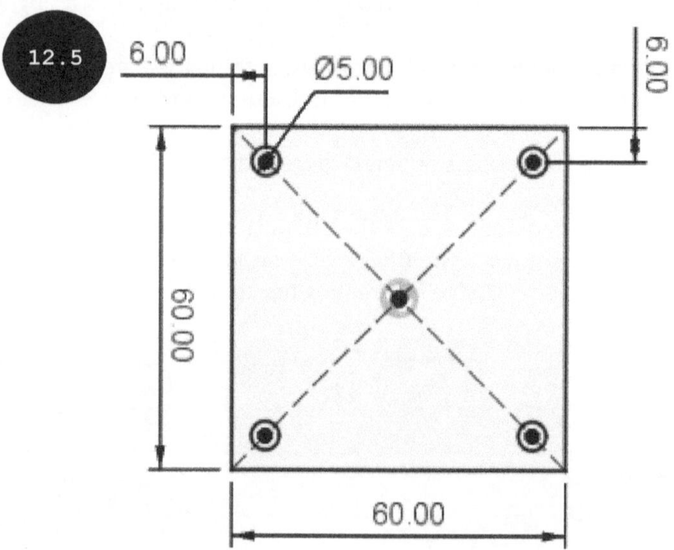

After creating the sketch, you need to convert it into a solid feature.

4. Convert the sketch into a solid feature by using solid modeling tools such as **Extrude**, **Revolve**, or **Sweep**, see Figure 12.6. In this figure, the sketch profile is extruded to a distance of 15 mm by using the **Extrude** tool.

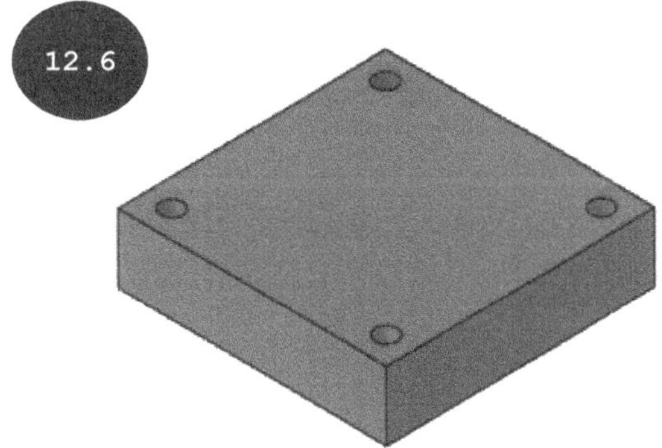
12.6

Now, you need to create the second feature of the first component.

5. Click on the **Create Sketch** tool in the **Toolbar** and then select a plane or a planar face as the sketching plane to create a sketch of the second feature.

6. Create the sketch of the second feature, see Figure 12.7. In this figure, the sketch is created on the top planar face of the first feature.

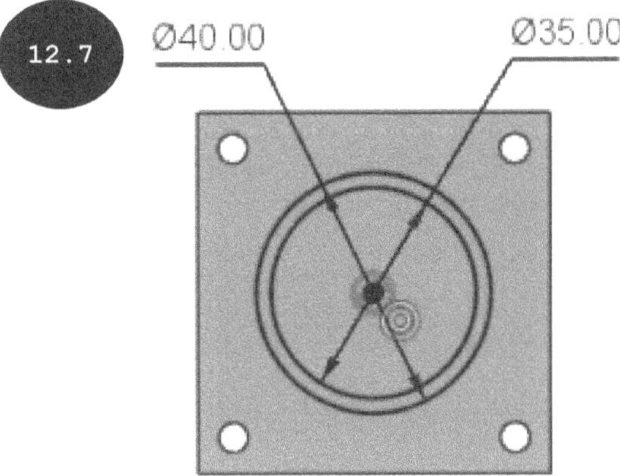

12.7

7. Convert the sketch into a feature by using the solid modeling tool, see Figure 12.8. In this figure, the sketch profile is extruded to a distance of 75 mm by using the **Extrude** tool.

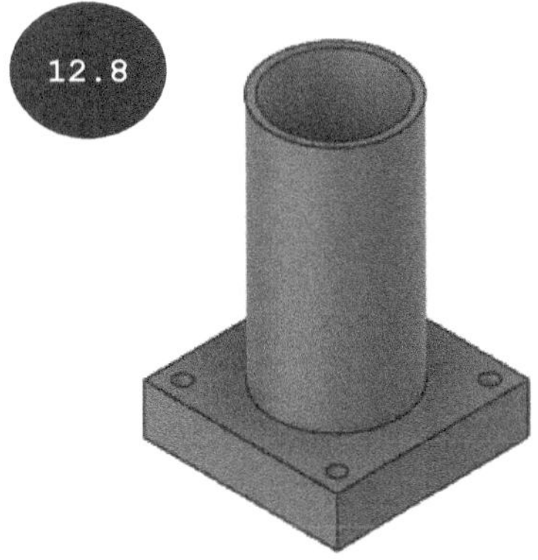
12.8

8. You can similarly create the remaining features of the first component one after the other.

   After creating the first component, you can create the second component of the assembly.

9. After creating all the required features, click the **Finish Edit In Place** button located at the top center of the graphics area to confirm the creation of the component, see Figure 12.9. The first component is created and the main assembly becomes activated automatically.

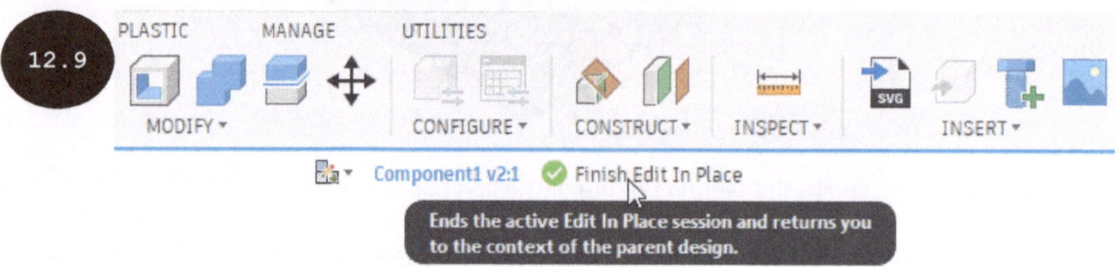

   Now, you can proceed to create a new design file to model the second component of the assembly.

10. Invoke the **CREATE** drop-down menu in the **ASSEMBLY** tab and select the **New Component** tool, see Figure 12.10. The **NEW COMPONENT** dialog box appears, see Figure 12.11.

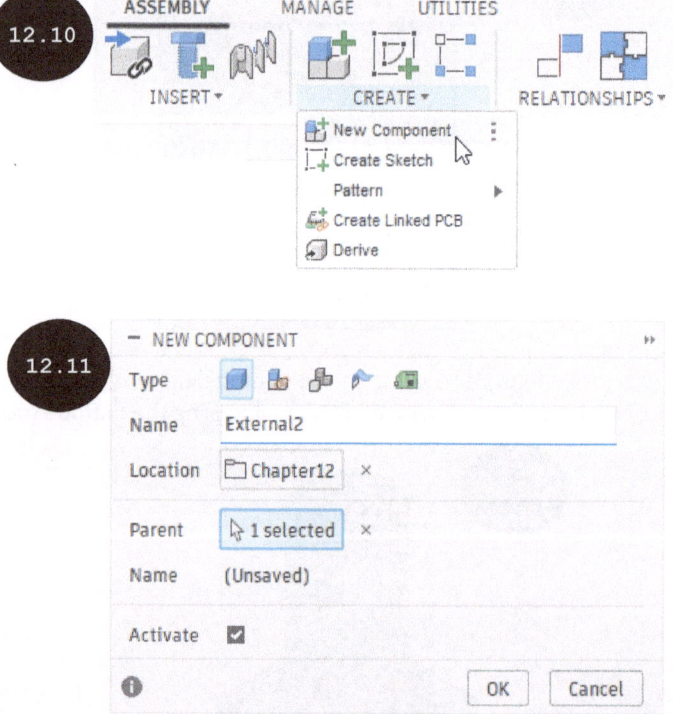

Tip: You can also invoke the **NEW COMPONENT** dialog box by right-clicking on the name of the assembly file (top browser node) in the **BROWSER** and then clicking on the **New Component** tool in the shortcut menu that appears, see Figure 12.12.

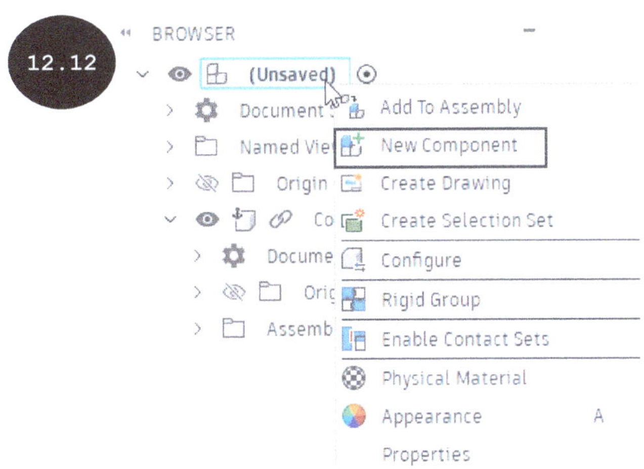

11. Ensure that the **Part** button is activated to create an empty Part Design file for modeling a solid component within the assembly file.

12. Enter a name for the component in the **Name** field of the dialog box.

13. Accept the default parent selection for the new design file in the **Parent** field of the dialog box. By default, it is set to the currently active file in the **BROWSER**, which is the main assembly (top browser node), see Figure 12.13.

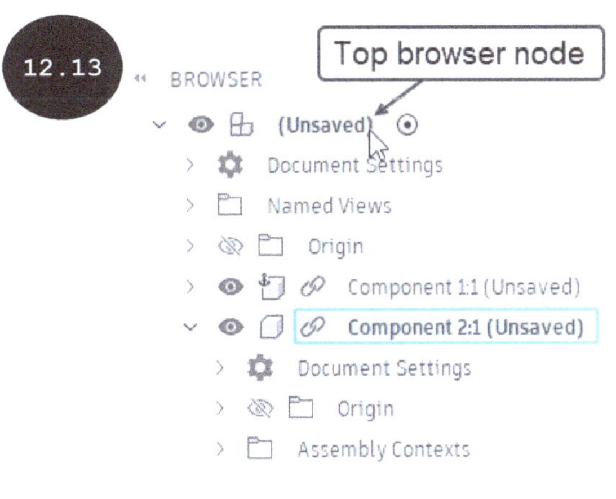

Tip: The **Activate Component** radio button displayed next to the design file name in the **BROWSER** is selected, indicating that it is the currently active design file.

14. Ensure that the **Activate** check box is selected to make the new design file the active file in the assembly.

15. After defining all the required options, click the **OK** button. A new empty design file (second component) is created as a child of the selected parent assembly file in the **BROWSER**, see Figure 12.14. It also becomes the active design file for creating the component. Additionally, the first component becomes transparent in the graphics area, allowing you to easily create the second component by taking reference from the first one during modeling, see Figure 12.15.

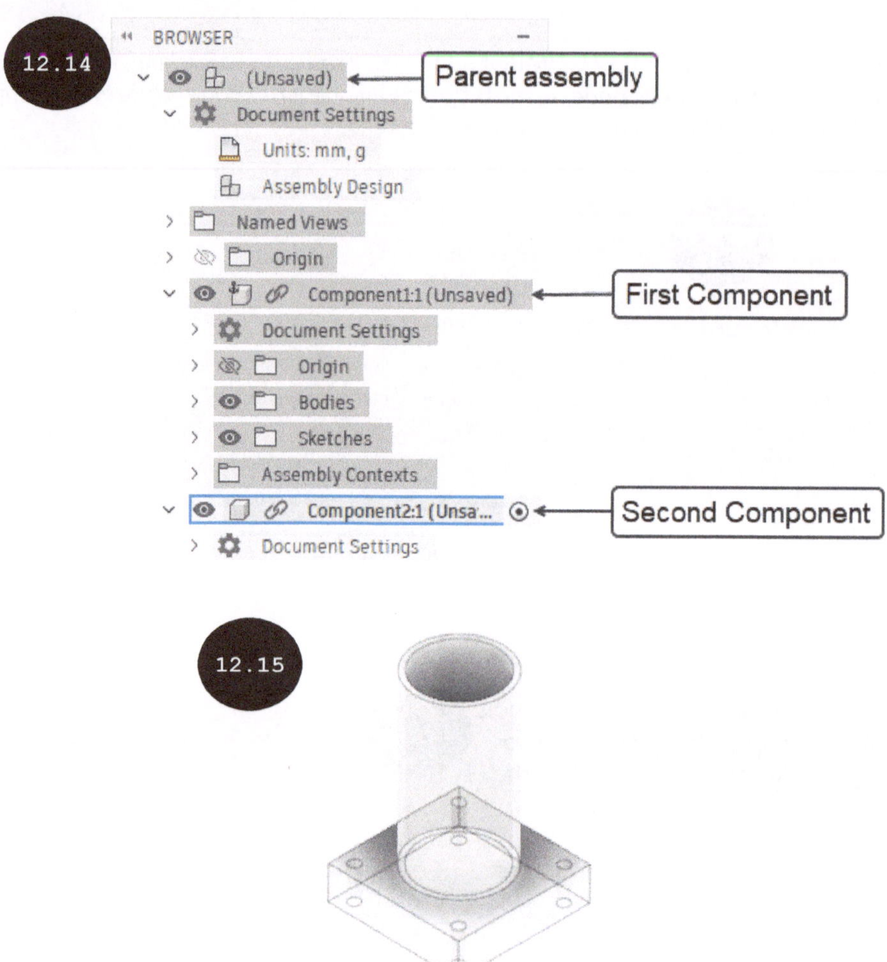

Now, you can add features to the newly added empty design file (second component).

16. Click on the **Create Sketch** tool in the **Toolbar** and then select a plane or a planar face of the existing component as the sketching plane for creating the sketch of the first feature of the active component (second component). The sketching plane becomes normal to the viewing direction and the **SKETCH** contextual tab appears in the **Toolbar**.

17. Draw the sketch of the first feature of the second component using the sketching tools, see Figure 12.16. In this figure, a rectangle and four circles have been created by projecting the edges of the first component onto the sketching plane. Also, the orientation has been changed to isometric to better understand the sketch.

18. Convert the sketch into a solid feature by using a solid modeling tool, see Figure 12.17. In this figure, the sketch is extruded to a distance of 15 mm by using the **Extrude** tool. Note that the second component is still activated, and you can create its remaining features one by one.

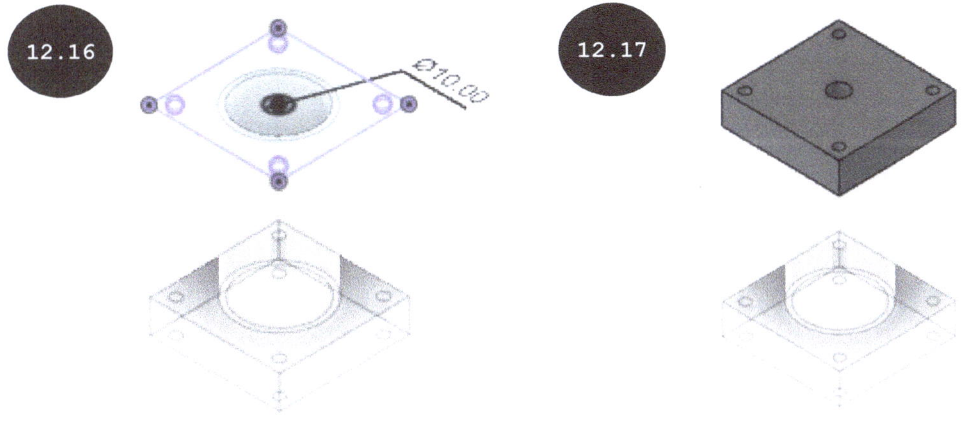

19. Click the **Finish Edit In Place** button located at the top center of the graphics area to confirm the creation of the second component, see Figure 12.18. The second component is created and the main assembly becomes activated again.

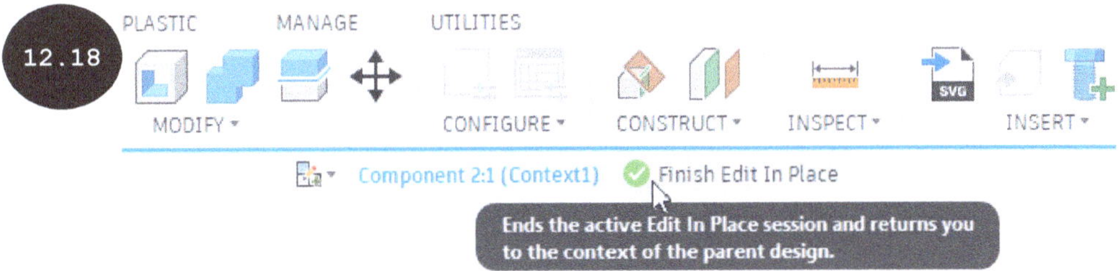

After creating the second component, you can create the third component of the assembly.

20. Ensure that the **Part** button is activated in the dialog box.

21. Enter a name for the component in the **Name** field of the dialog box.

22. Accept the default parent selection for the new design file in the **Parent** field of the dialog box. By default, it is set to the currently active file in the **BROWSER**, which is the main assembly (top browser node).

23. Ensure that the **Activate** check box is selected to make the new design file the active file in the assembly.

24. Click the **OK** button. A new empty design file (third component) is created as a child of the parent assembly file with its specified name, see Figure 12.19. It also becomes the active design file for creating the component. Additionally, the existing components become transparent in the graphics area, allowing you to easily create the third component by taking reference from them during modeling, see Figure 12.20.

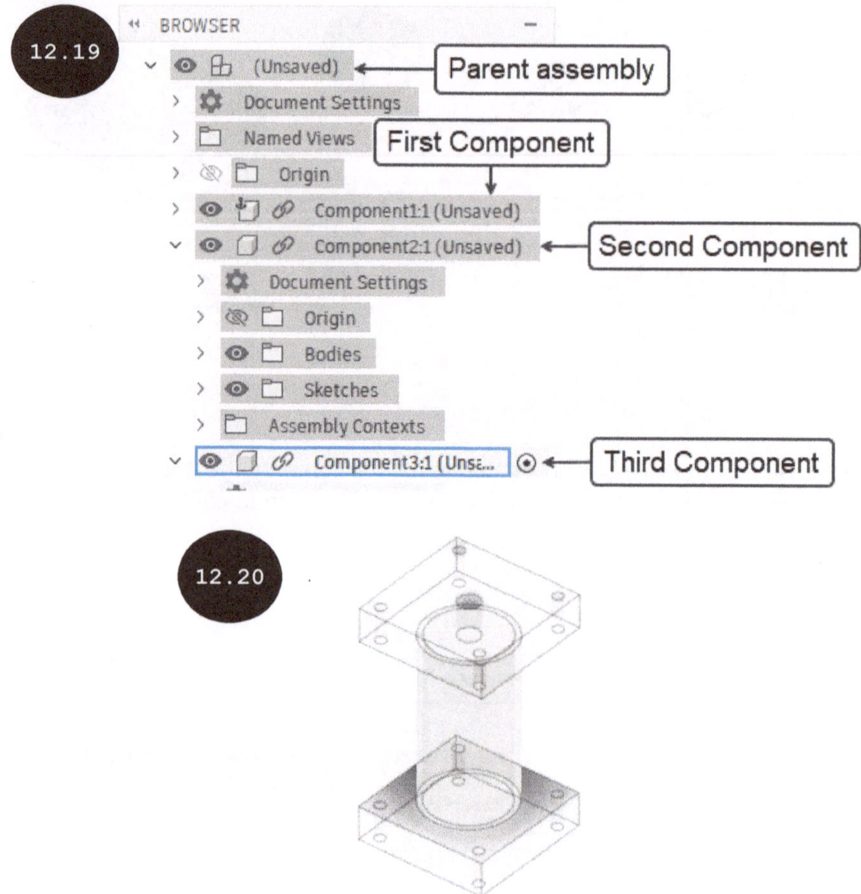

Now, you can add features to the newly added empty component (third component).

25. Click on the **Create Sketch** tool in the **Toolbar** and then select a plane or a planar face of the existing component as the sketching plane for creating the sketch of the first feature of the active component (third component). The sketching plane becomes normal to the viewing direction and the **SKETCH** contextual tab appears in the **Toolbar**.

26. Draw a sketch of the first feature of the third component by using the sketching tools, see Figure 12.21. In this figure, a circle has been created by projecting the circular edge of the second component onto the sketching plane.

27. Convert the sketch into a solid feature by using a solid modeling tool, see Figure 12.22. In this figure, the circle is extruded to a distance of 120 mm (whole length), symmetrically on both sides of the sketching plane by using the **Extrude** tool. Note that the third component is still activated, and you can create its remaining features.

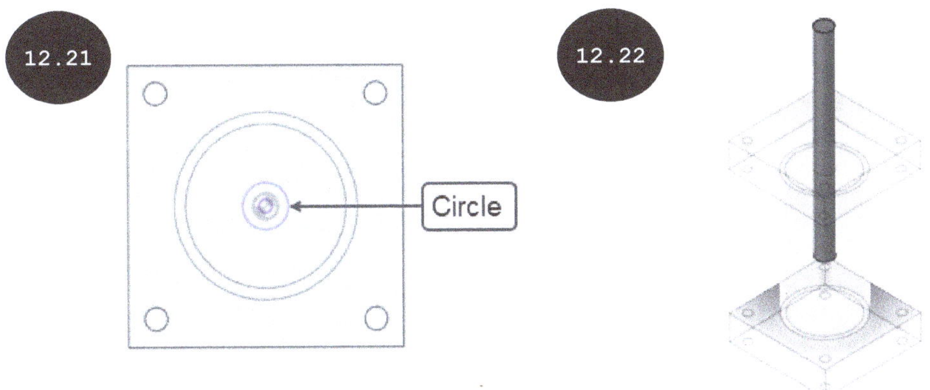

28. Create the second feature of the third component, see Figure 12.23. In this figure, the sketch (circle) of the second feature is created on the bottom planar face of the first component and extruded to a distance of 6 mm.

29. Similarly, create the remaining features of the third component one by one, see Figure 12.24.

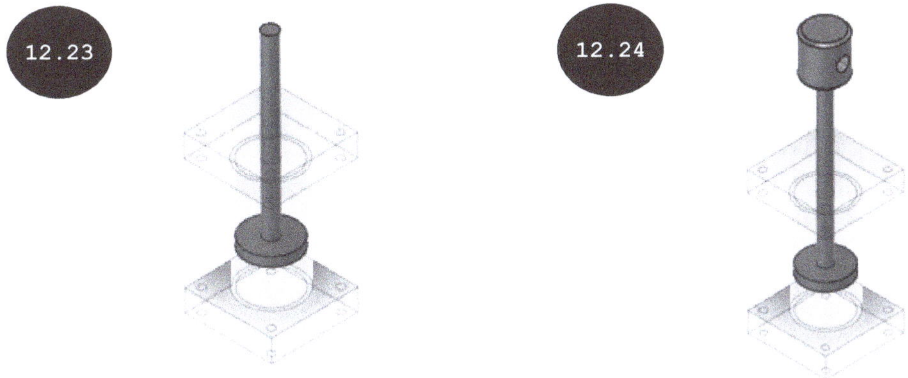

30. Click the **Finish Edit In Place** button located at the top center of the graphics area to confirm the creation of the third component, see Figure 12.25. The third component is created and the main assembly becomes activated again.

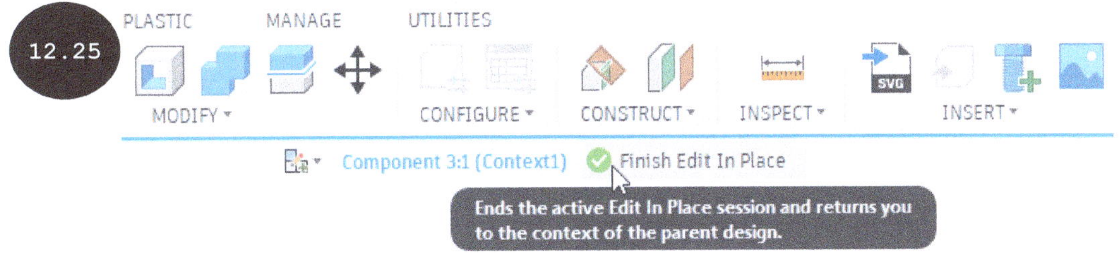

After creating the third component, you can create the fourth and subsequent components of the assembly one by one, see Figure 12.26.

12.26

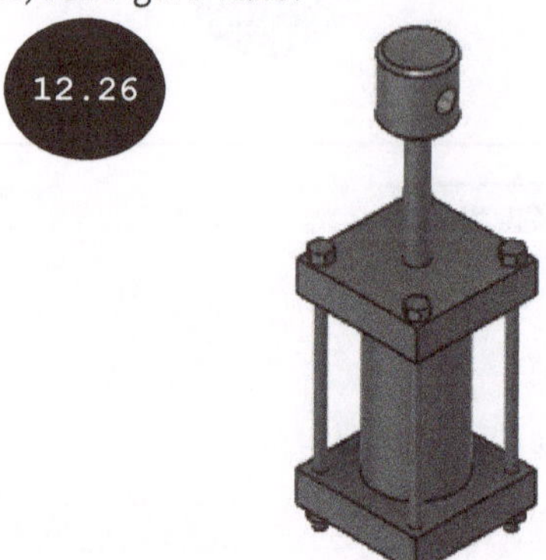

Tip: You can pattern a component for creating its multiple instances. The method for patterning a component is same as patterning a feature of a component.

Note: After creating all the components of the assembly, ensure that the main assembly (top browser node) is activated in the **BROWSER** so that all its components appear in the default visible style (Shaded with Visible Edges Only), refer to Figure 12.26.

To do so, move the cursor over the main assembly (top browser node) in the **BROWSER**. The **Activate Component** radio button appears, see Figure 12.27. Click this radio button to activate the main assembly, if it is not already activated by default.

12.27

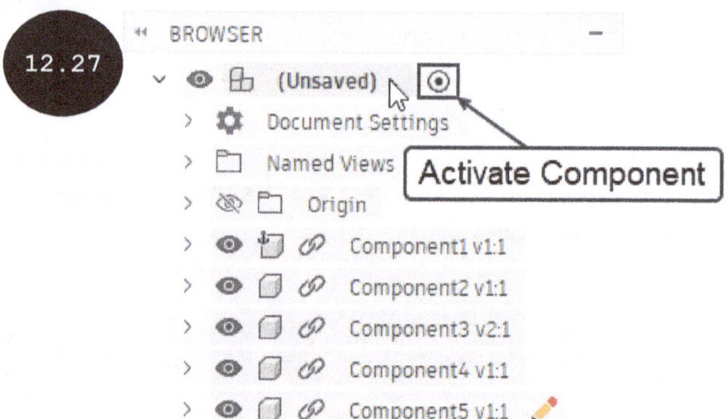

After creating all the components of an assembly within a single design file using the Top-down Assembly approach, the next step is to define relationships between the components by applying joints.

In Autodesk Fusion, you can apply joints such as rigid, revolute, slider, cylindrical, pin-slot, ball, and planar using the Joint tool and the As-Built Joint tool. While the previous chapter covered how to apply various types of joints using the Joint tool, this chapter will focus on guiding you through the process of applying joints using the As-Built Joint tool, which is discussed next.

Applying As-Built Joints

The **As-Built Joint** tool is used for applying joints to define the relative motion between the components in their current position as they are built. It is mainly used when the components of an assembly are created in context to each other by using the Top-down assembly approach and are already positioned properly concerning each other. The method for applying a joint by using the **As-Built Joint** tool is discussed below:

1. Invoke the **RELATIONSHIPS** drop-down menu in the **ASSEMBLY** tab and then click on the **As-Built Joint** tool, see Figure 12.28. The **AS-BUILT JOINT** dialog box appears, see Figure 12.29. Alternatively, press the SHIFT + J key to invoke the **AS-BUILT JOINT** dialog box.

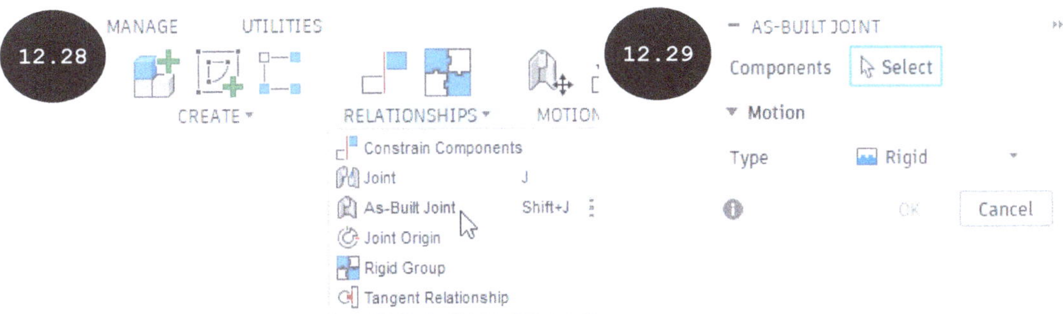

2. Select two components in the graphics area one by one to apply a joint by maintaining their current position, see Figure 12.30.

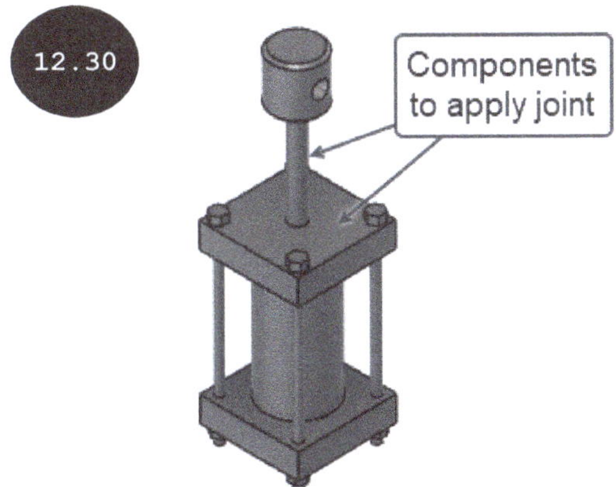

3. Select the joint type in the **Type** drop-down list of the dialog box.

Note: If you select a joint other than the **Rigid** joint in the **Type** drop-down list, then the **Origin Mode** area and **Snap** selection option appear in the dialog box, which are used for defining the position of the joint origin. The joint origin is used for defining the location where two components have relative motion with respect to each other.

4. Ensure that the **Simple** button is selected in the **Origin Mode** area of the dialog box for defining the joint origin on a face, an edge, or a point of the component.

5. Specify the position of the joint origin where the components have relative motion concerning one another. To do this, move the cursor over a face or an edge of the component (movable component). The face or edge gets highlighted, and its snap points appear in the graphics area. Next, click on the required snap point of the highlighted face or edge to define the position of the joint origin.

6. Select the required option in the respective drop-down list or lists that appear below the **Type** drop-down list in the dialog box. Note that the drop-down lists that appear below the **Type** drop-down list depend upon the joint type selected and are the same as discussed earlier.

7. Click on the **OK** button in the dialog box. The joint is applied between the components.

8. You can similarly apply joints between the other set of components to define relative motion between them.

Note: The methods for defining joint limits, driving a joint, animating a joint or a model, editing a joint, and so on are same as discussed in the previous chapter.

Defining a Joint Origin on a Component

In Autodesk Fusion, you can also define a joint origin anywhere on a component by using the **Joint Origin** tool. To do this, invoke the **RELATIONSHIPS** drop-down menu in the ASSEMBLY tab and then click on the **Joint Origin** tool, see Figure 12.31. The **JOINT ORIGIN** dialog box appears, see Figure 12.32. The options in this dialog box are discussed next.

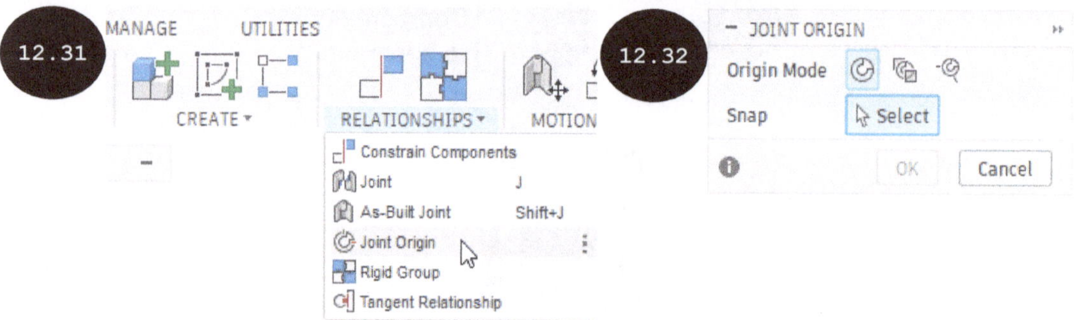

Simple

The **Simple** button in the **Origin Mode** area of the dialog box is used for placing the joint origin on a face, an edge, or a point of the component and then manipulating its location, as required.

To do this, ensure that the **Simple** button is selected in the **Origin Mode** area of the dialog box and then move the cursor over a face of a component. The face gets highlighted, and its snap points appear, see Figure 12.33. Click on a snap point to define the initial position of the joint origin. The translational and manipulator handles appear in the graphics area, see Figure 12.34. Also, the **JOINT ORIGIN** dialog box gets modified with additional options to manipulate the position of the joint origin, see Figure 12.35.

12.33

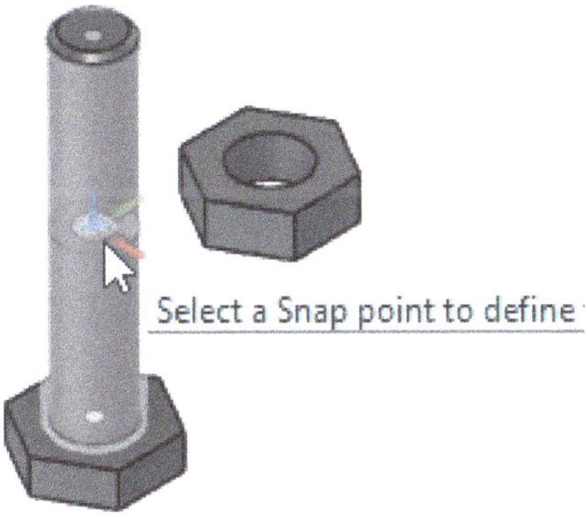

Select a Snap point to define

12.34

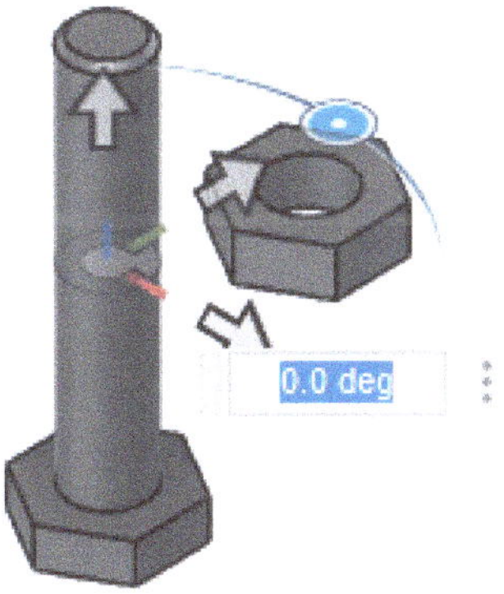

0.0 deg

12.35

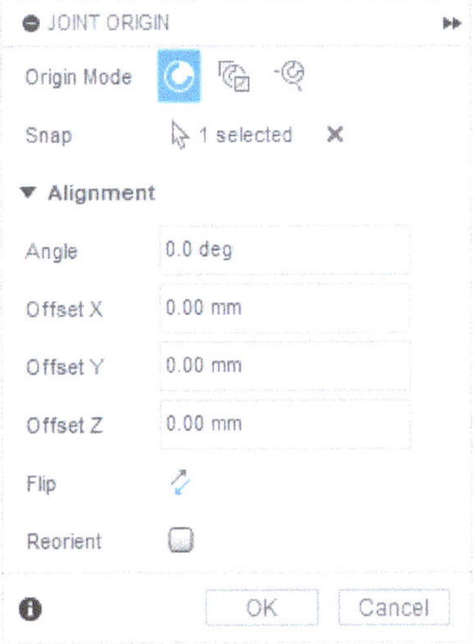

JOINT ORIGIN
Origin Mode
Snap
1 selected
Alignment
Angle
0.0 deg
Offset X
0.00 mm
Offset Y
0.00 mm
Offset Z
0.00 mm
Flip
Reorient
OK
Cancel

Now, you can define the position of the joint origin, as required, by dragging the translational and manipulator handles that appear in the graphics area. You can also specify the angle and offset values in the dialog box to define the position of the joint origin, as required. After defining the position of the joint origin, click on the **OK** button in the dialog box. The position of the joint origin is defined, see Figure 12.36.

After defining the joint origin on a component, you can select it for applying a joint by using the **Joint** tool, see Figure 12.37.

12.36

Joint origin defined

12.37

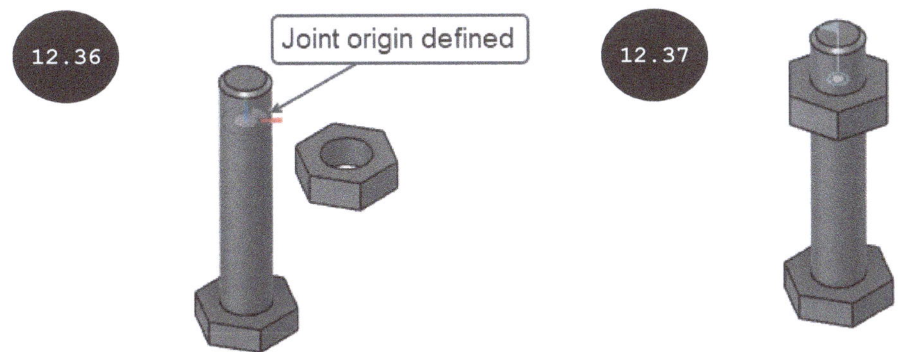

Between Two Faces

The **Between Two Faces** button of the **Origin Mode** area is used for placing the joint origin on a plane in the middle of two selected faces of a component. To do this, select the **Between Two Faces** button. The **Plane 1** and **Plane 2** selection options appear in the dialog box. By default, the **Plane 1** selection option is activated. As a result, you can select the first face of a component.

After selecting the first face of a component, the **Plane 2** selection option gets activated. Next, select the second face of the component. The **Snap** selection option appears in the dialog box. Next, move the cursor over a face, an edge, or a point in between the selected faces of the component. The snap points appear, and an imaginary plane is displayed in the middle of the faces selected, see Figure 12.38. Next, click on a snap point. The joint origin is placed in the middle of the faces selected such that the selected snap point gets projected onto the imaginary plane that appears in the middle of the faces, see Figure 12.39. Also, the translational and manipulator handles appear in the graphics area and the **JOINT ORIGIN** dialog box gets modified with additional options for manipulating the position of the joint origin.

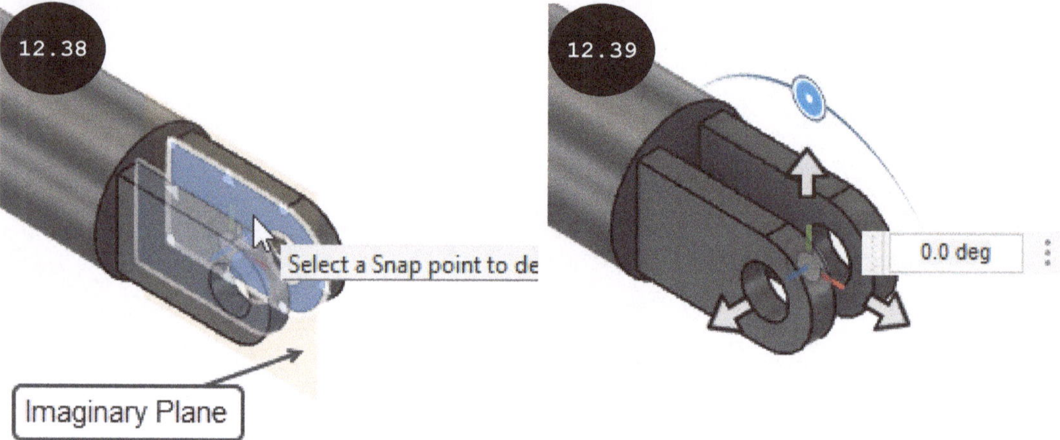

Define the position of the joint origin as required, by dragging the translational and manipulator handles that appear in the graphics area or by specifying the angle and offset values in the dialog box. After defining the position of the joint origin, click on the **OK** button in the dialog box. The position of the joint origin is defined in the middle of the faces selected. Now, you can apply a joint by using the **Joint** tool and selecting it to define the position of the joint origin, see Figure 12.40.

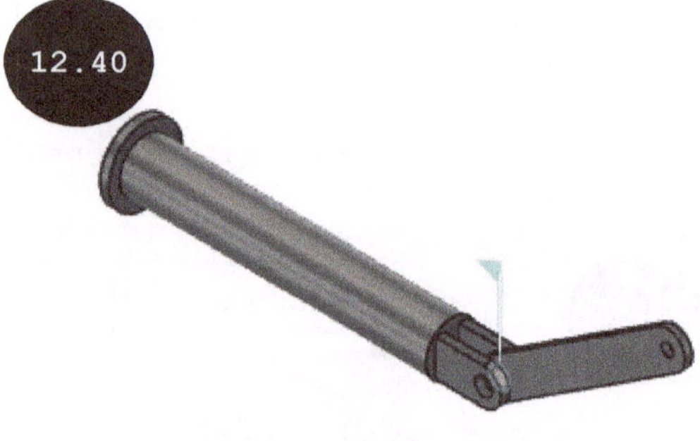

Two Edge Intersection

The **Two Edge Intersection** button of the **Origin Mode** area is used for placing the joint origin at the intersection of two selected edges of a component. To do this, select the **Two Edge Intersection** button of the **Origin Mode** area. The **Edge 1** and **Edge 2** selection options appear in the dialog box. By default, the **Edge 1** selection option is activated. As a result, you can select the first edge of a component.

After selecting the first edge of a component, the **Edge 2** selection option gets activated. Next, select the second edge of the component. After selecting the edges, a joint origin gets defined at the intersection of the selected edges, see Figure 12.41. Also, the translational and manipulator handles appear in the graphics area and the **JOINT ORIGIN** dialog box gets modified with additional options for manipulating the position of the joint origin.

Define the position of the joint origin as required, by dragging the translational and manipulator handles that appear in the graphics area or by specifying the angle and offset values in the dialog box. After defining the position of the joint origin, click on the **OK** button in the dialog box. The position of the joint origin is defined at the intersection of the edges selected. After defining the joint origin on a component, you can select it for applying a joint by using the **Joint** tool, see Figure 12.42.

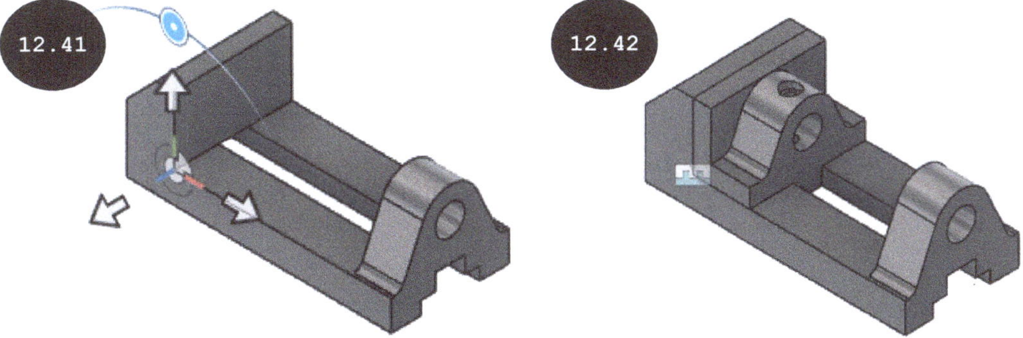

Editing Assembly Components

In the process of creating an assembly, you may need to edit its components depending on the changes in the design, revisions, or so on. Autodesk Fusion allows you to edit components of an assembly at any stage of the design process. The methods for editing components are discussed below.

To edit a component of an assembly that is created within a single file by using the Top-down Assembly approach, you need to first activate the component to be edited, as discussed earlier. Once the component gets activated, you can edit its features and sketches. To edit a feature or a sketch, right-click on the feature or sketch to be edited in the **Timeline** and then click on the **Edit Feature** tool or **Edit Sketch** tool in the shortcut menu that appears, respectively, see Figures 12.43 and 12.44. Next, make the necessary modifications to the feature parameters or the sketch selected. You can also create new features in the component by using solid modeling tools.

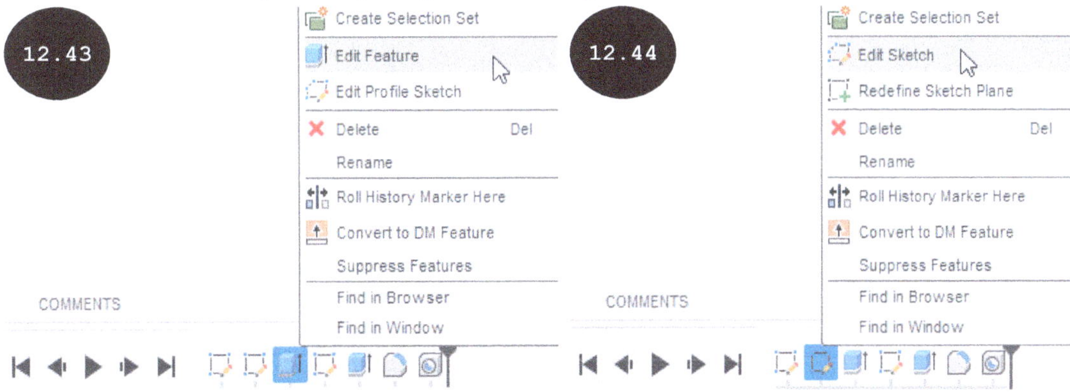

Note: If the assembly is created by inserting the components as external references, then you can open the component to be edited on a separate file for editing its features and sketches. To do this, right-click on the component to be edited in the **BROWSER** and then click on the **Open** tool in the shortcut menu that appears. The selected component gets opened on a separate design file. Now, you can edit its features and sketches, as discussed earlier. After editing the component, save it by using the **Save** tool. Next, switch to the assembly file. In the assembly file, you will notice the Update icon on the name of the edited component in the **BROWSER** as well as in the **Application Bar**, see Figure 12.45. Click on the **Update** icon in the **Application Bar** to update all the components of the assembly.

You can also update an external component in the same position as that in the assembly. To do this, move the cursor over the name of the component in the **BROWSER** and click on the **Edit in Place** tool that appears besides the name of the component, see Figure 12.46. An edit window appears, and you can edit the component as required by taking reference from other components of the assembly, which become transparent in the graphics area. After making the required changes, click on the **Finish Edit in Place** tool that appears at the top center of the edit window, see Figure 12.47. The component gets updated.

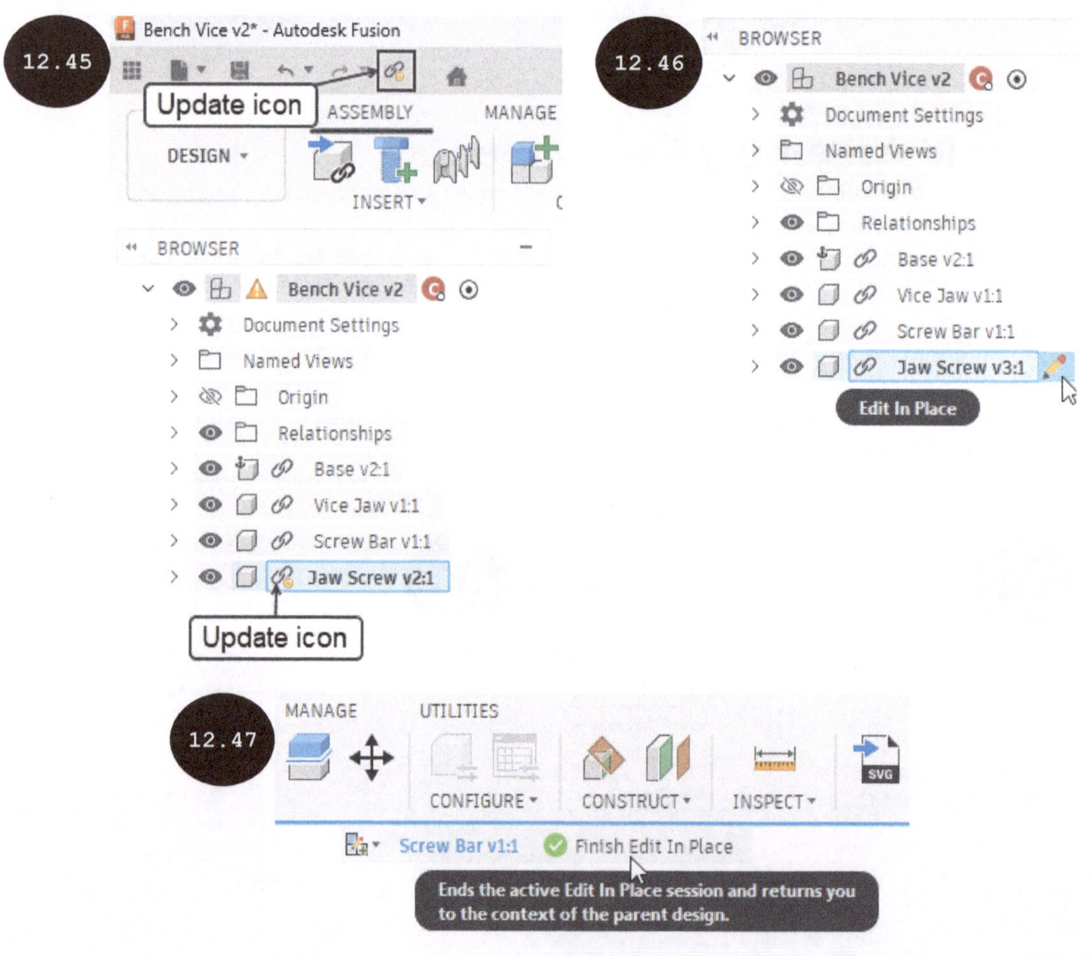

Tutorial 1

Create an assembly, as shown in Figure 12.48 by using the Top-down Assembly approach. Different views and dimensions of each component are shown in Figures 12.49 through 12.52. After creating the assembly, you must apply joints using the **As-Built Joint** tool. All dimensions are in mm.

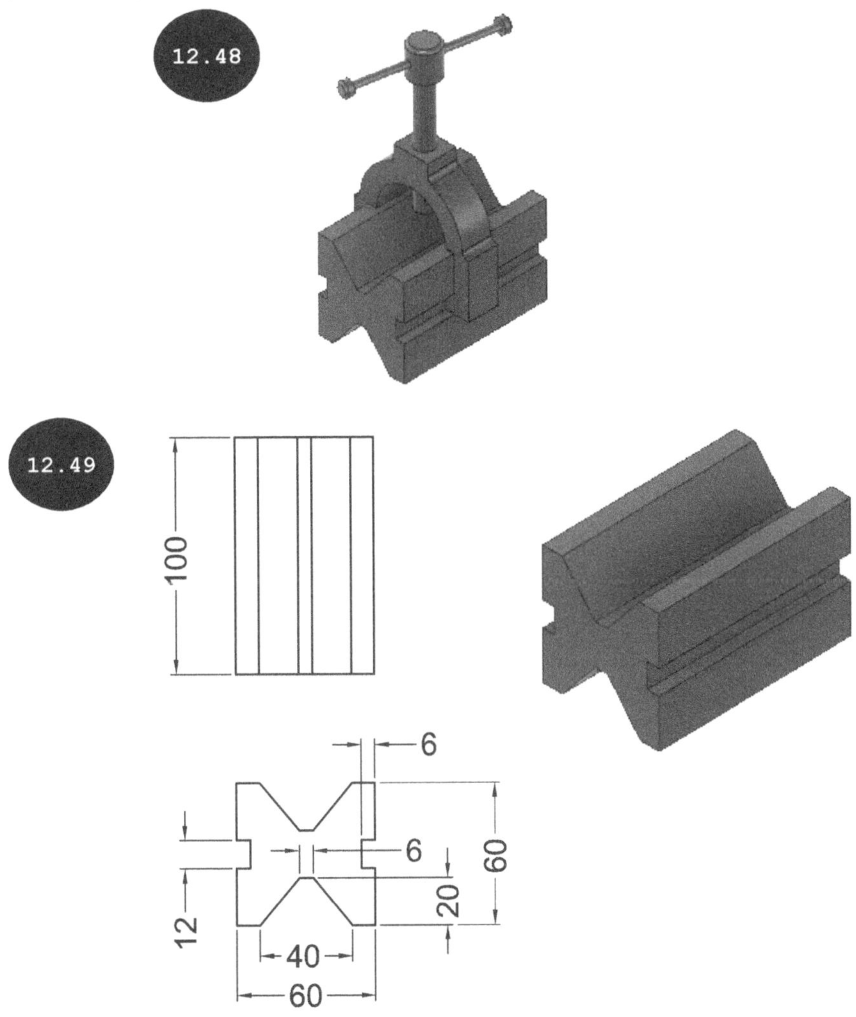

First Component

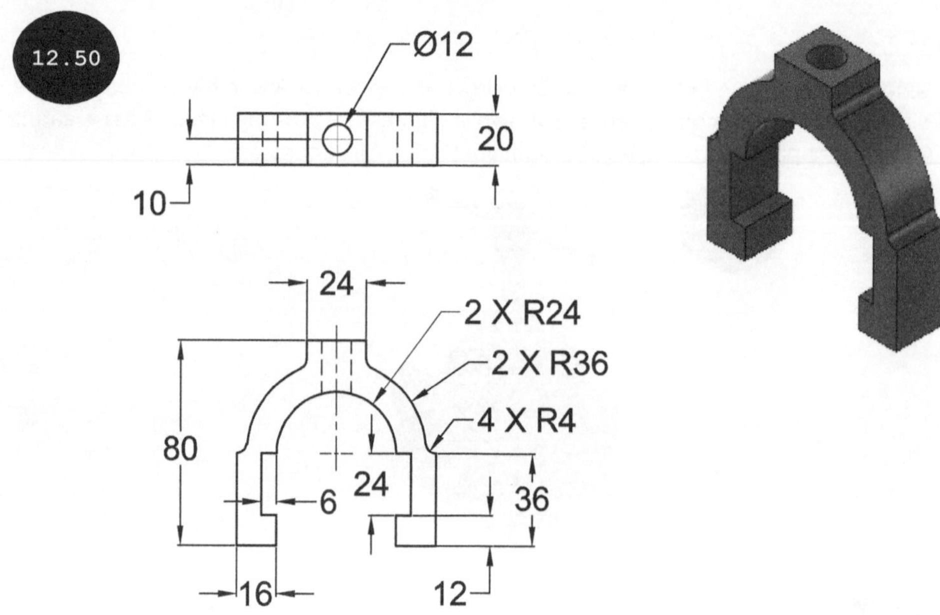

Second Component

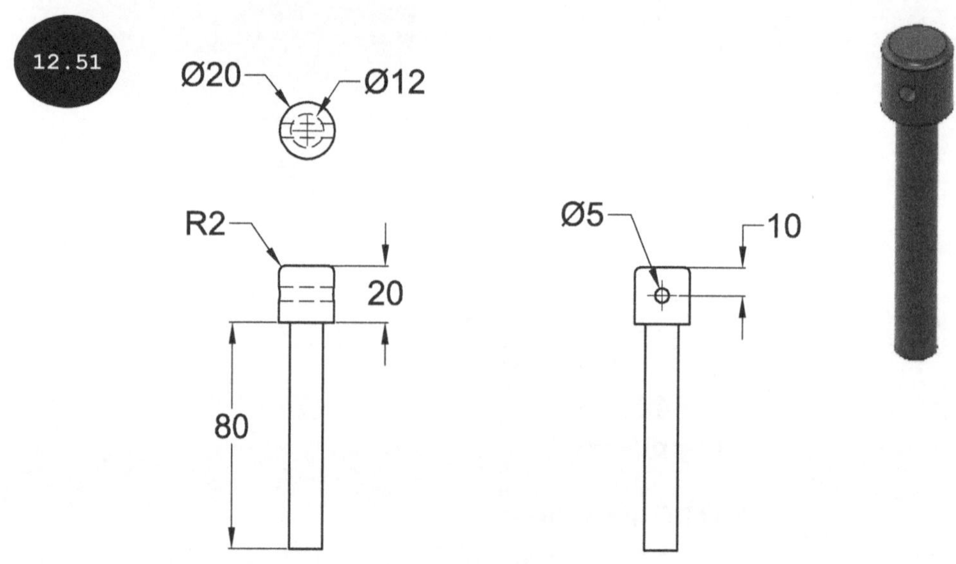

Third Component

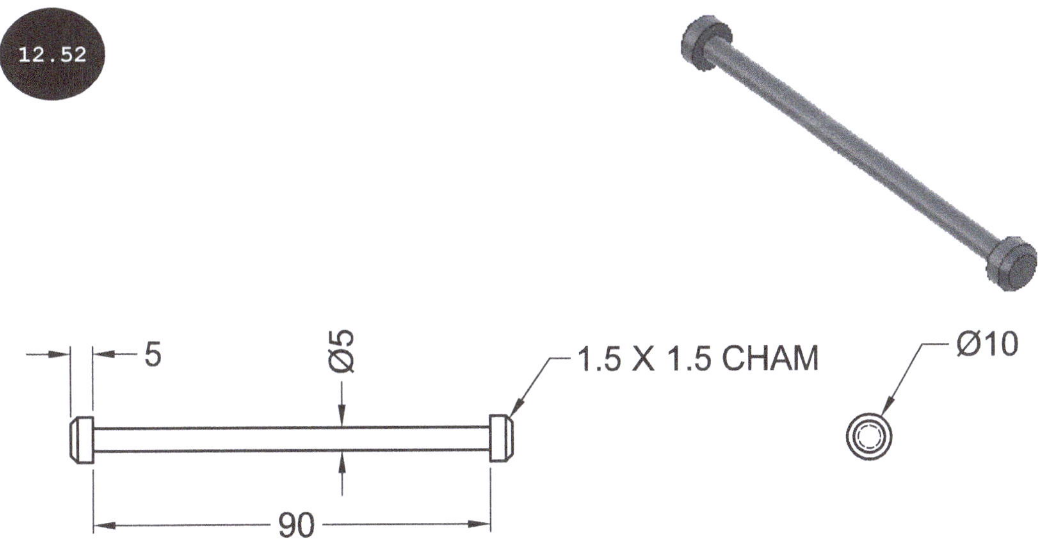

Section 1: Starting Autodesk Fusion and a New Design File

1. Start Fusion by double-clicking on the Autodesk Fusion icon on your desktop, if not started already. Next, invoke the **What do you want to design?** dialog box, see Figure 12.53.

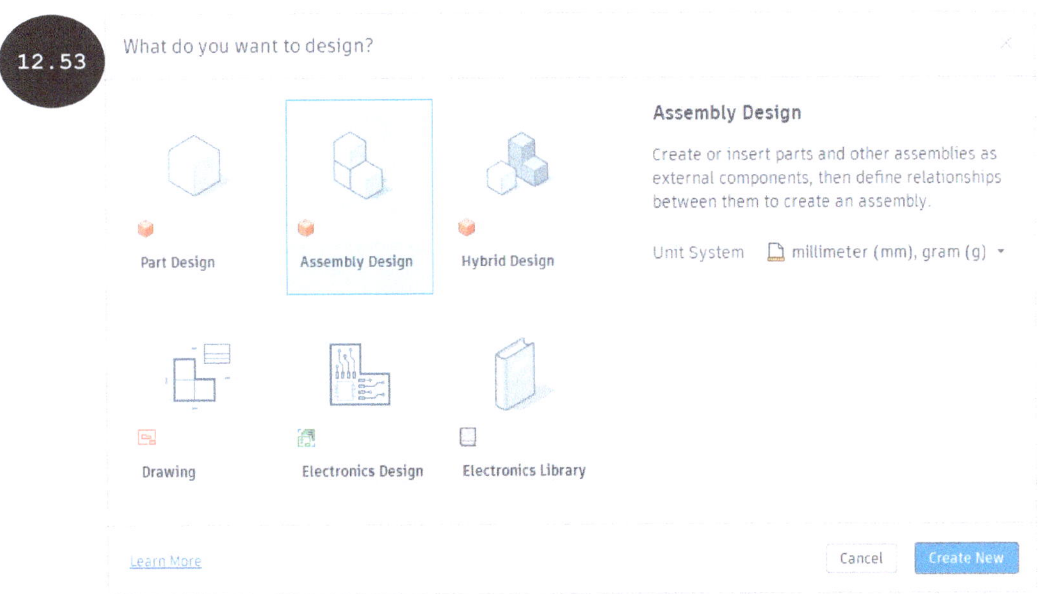

Note: You can invoke the **What do you want to design?** dialog box by clicking on **File > New** in the **Application Bar**, see Figure 12.54. This dialog box allows you to select the desired design file type and the required unit system.

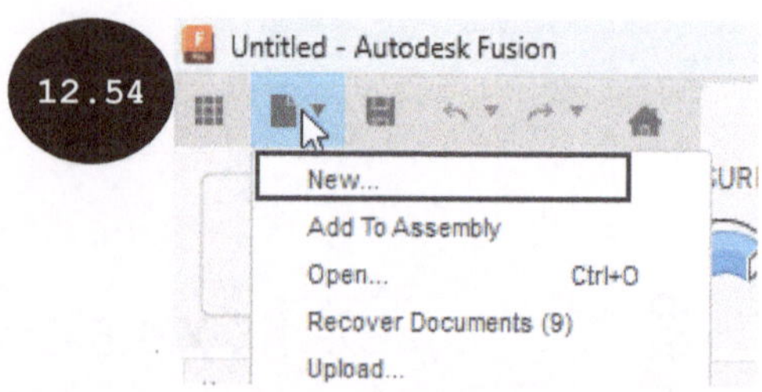

2. In the **What do you want to design?** dialog box, select the **Assembly Design** button and choose the **millimeter (mm), gram (g)** unit system from the **Unit System** drop-down list.

3. After specifying the required options, click the **Create New** button. A new Assembly Design file is opened with the default name.

Section 2: Creating the First Component

1. Invoke the **CREATE** drop-down menu in the **ASSEMBLY** tab and then click on the **New Component** tool, see Figure 12.55. The **NEW COMPONENT** dialog box appears, see Figure 12.56.

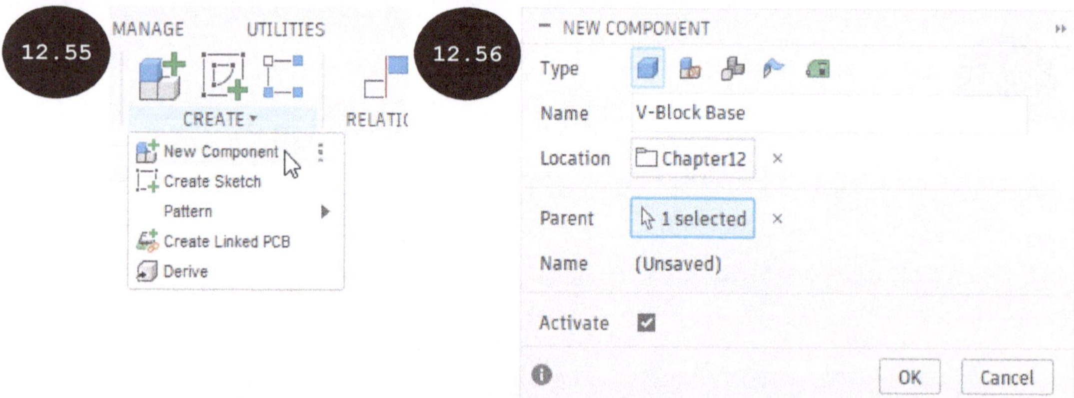

2. Ensure that the **Part** button is activated to create an empty Part Design file for modeling a solid part within the assembly file.

3. Enter **V-Block Base** as the name for the new design file in the **Name** field of the dialog box.

4. Click the currently selected folder in the **Location** field, and then browse to **Autodesk Fusion 360 > Chapter 12 > Tutorial** to save the file. You need to create the **Chapter 12** and **Tutorial 1** folders inside the **Autodesk Fusion 360** project folder to store all the files related to this assembly.

5. Accept the default parent selection for the design file in the **Parent** field of the dialog box.

6. Ensure that the **Activate** check box is selected to make it the active file in the assembly.

7. Click the **OK** button. A new empty design file is created as a child of the parent assembly file in the **BROWSER** with its specified name, see Figure 12.57. The file also becomes the active design file for creating the component.

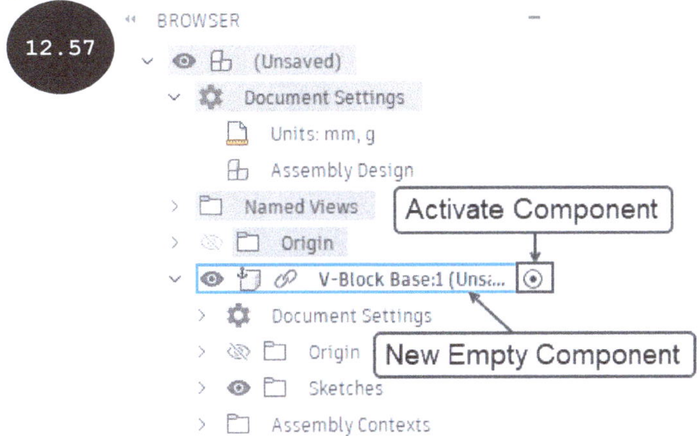

Note: By default, the first design file created within an assembly file is fixed (grounded). This means that all its degrees of freedom are constrained, preventing it from moving. It therefore acts as a reference component for assembling other components around it.

You can now begin creating the features of the component.

8. Click on the **Create Sketch** tool in the **Toolbar** and then select the Front plane as the sketching plane to create the sketch of the first feature. The sketching plane becomes normal to the viewing direction and the **SKETCH** contextual tab appears in the **Toolbar**. Also, the **SKETCH PALETTE** dialog box appears.

9. Ensure that the **3D Sketch** check box is cleared in the **SKETCH PALETTE** dialog box for creating a 2D sketch.

10. Draw the sketch of the first feature, see Figure 12.58.

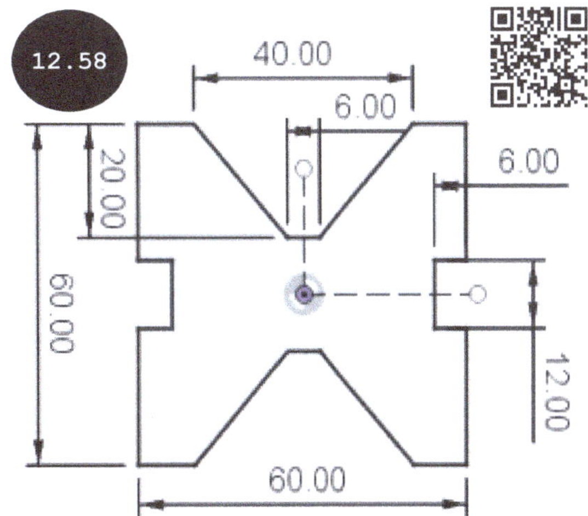

11. Click on the **SOLID** tab in the **Toolbar** and then click on the **Extrude** tool in the **CREATE** panel. Alternatively, press the **E** key. The **EXTRUDE** dialog box appears in the graphics area.

12. Select the sketch profile in the graphics area, if not selected automatically.

13. Select the **Symmetric** option in the **Direction**

drop-down list of the dialog box and then enter **50 mm** in the **Distance** field of the dialog box. Ensure that the **Half Length** button is activated in the **Measurement** area of the dialog box.

14. Ensure that the **New Body** option is selected in the **Operation** drop-down list of the dialog box.

15. Click on the **OK** button in the dialog box. The extrude feature of the first component is created, see Figure 12.59.

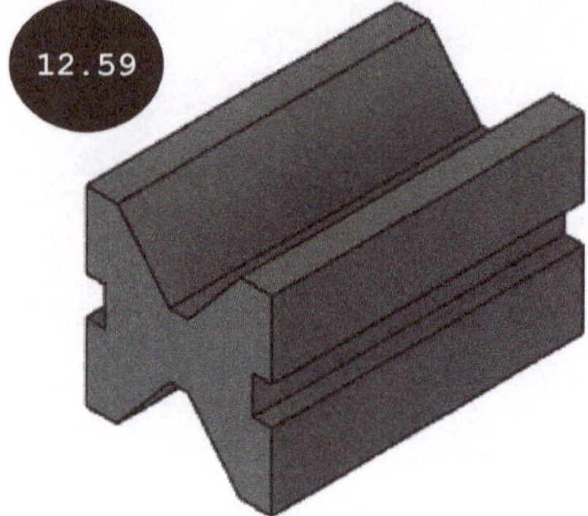

16. Click the **Finish Edit In Place** button located at the top center of the graphics area to confirm the creation of the first component, see Figure 12.60. The first component is created and the main assembly becomes activated again.

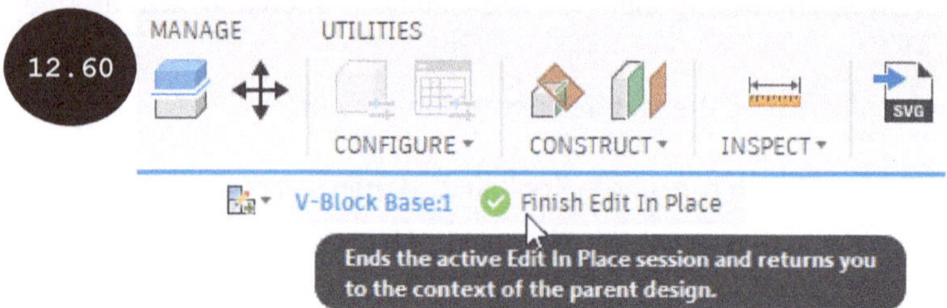

Section 3: Creating the Second Component

Now, you need to create the second component.

1. Right-click on the top browser node and then click on the **New Component** tool in the shortcut menu that appears, see Figure 12.61. The **NEW COMPONENT** dialog box appears.

2. Ensure that the **Part** button is activated in the dialog box.

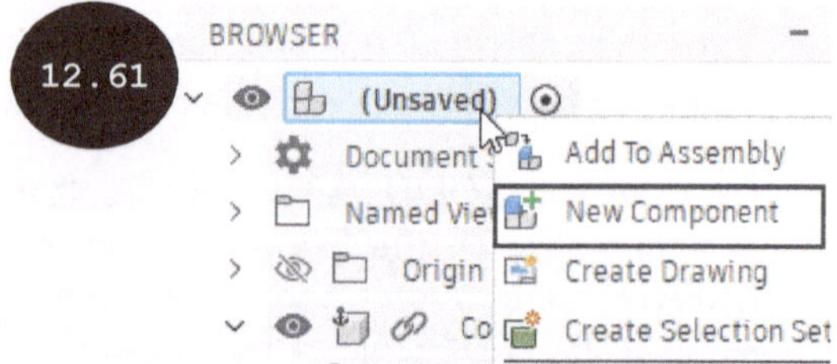

3. Enter **Clamp Bracket** as the name for the design file (second component) in the **Name** field of the dialog box.

4. Accept the remaining default options, and click the **OK** button in the dialog box. A new empty design file is created as a child of the parent assembly file in the **BROWSER** with its specified

name, see Figure 12.62. The file also becomes the active design file for creating the features of the second component. Notice that the first component becomes transparent in the graphics area.

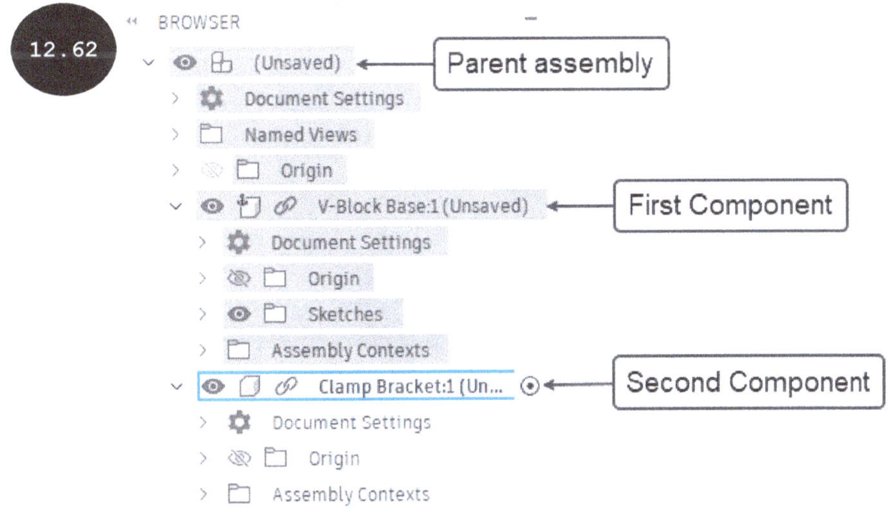

Now, you can add features to the newly created empty component (second component).

5. Click on the **Create Sketch** tool in the **Toolbar** and then select the Front plane as the sketching plane to create the sketch of the first feature of the second component. The sketching plane becomes normal to the viewing direction and the **SKETCH** contextual tab appears in the **Toolbar**.

6. Draw a sketch of the first feature of the second component, see Figure 12.63.

Note: To create the sketch of the first feature of the second component as shown in Figure 12.61, you need to project the edges of the first component onto the sketching plane by using the **Project** tool.

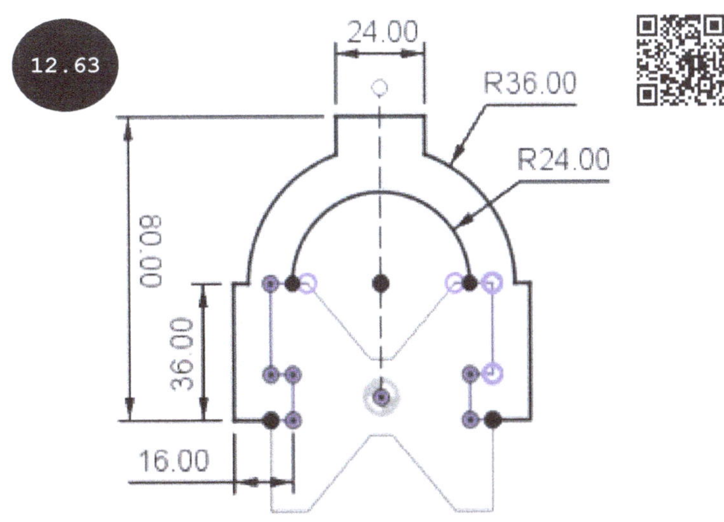

7. Extrude the sketch profile to a distance of 10 mm symmetrically, on both sides of the sketching plane by using the **Extrude** tool, see Figure 12.64. Note that the total extrusion distance is 20 mm, and you need to select the **New Body** option in the **Operation** drop-down list of the **EXTRUDE** dialog box. The first feature is created, and the second component is still activated.

12.64

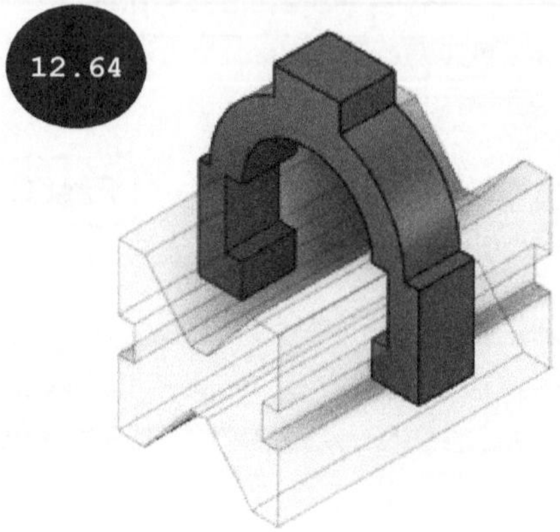

Now, you need to create the second feature of the component. The second feature of the component is a cut feature.

8. Click on the **Create Sketch** tool in the **Toolbar** and then select the top planar face of the first feature of the second component as the sketching plane.

9. Create a circle of diameter 12 mm as the sketch of the second feature, see Figure 12.65.

12.65

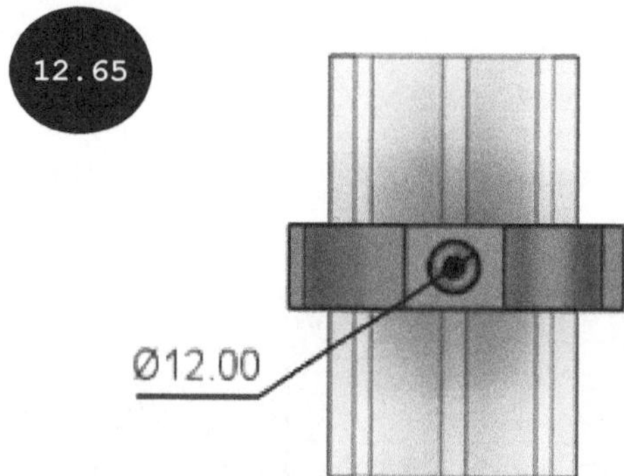

10. Invoke the **EXTRUDE** dialog box and then select the sketch profile in the graphics area.

11. Select the **To Object** option in the **Extent Type** drop-down list of the dialog box and then select the bottom semi-circular face of the first feature as the object to terminate the extrude feature, see Figure 12.66.

12. Ensure that the **Cut** option is selected in the **Operation** drop-down list of the dialog box.

13. Click on the **OK** button in the **EXTRUDE** dialog box. The second feature (cut feature) of the second component is created, see Figure 12.67. Also, the second component is still activated.

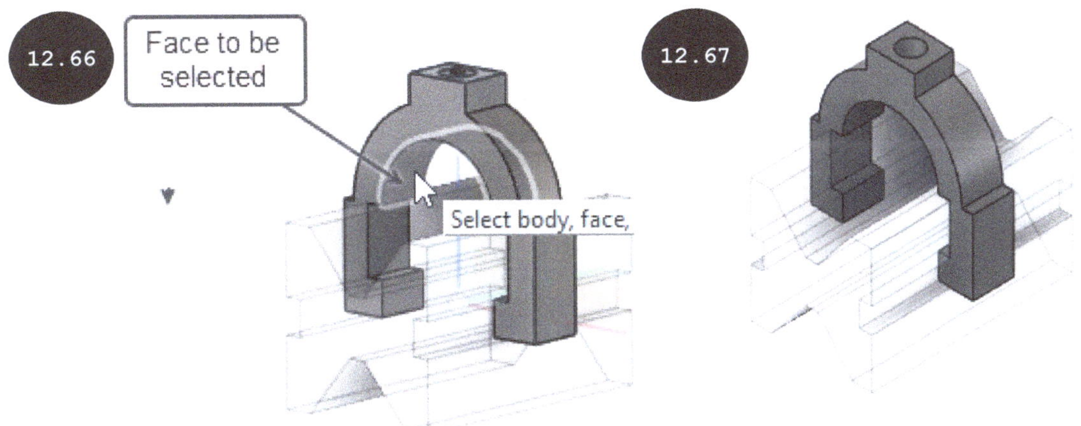

Now, you need to create the third feature of the second component. The third feature of the component is a fillet feature.

14. Click on **MODIFY** > **Fillet** in the **SOLID** tab or press the **F** key. The **FILLET** dialog box appears.

15. Select the edges (4 edges) of the second component to be filleted, see Figure 12.68.

16. Enter 4 in the **Radius** field of the dialog box and then click on the **OK** button. The third feature (fillet) of the second component is created, see Figure 12.69.

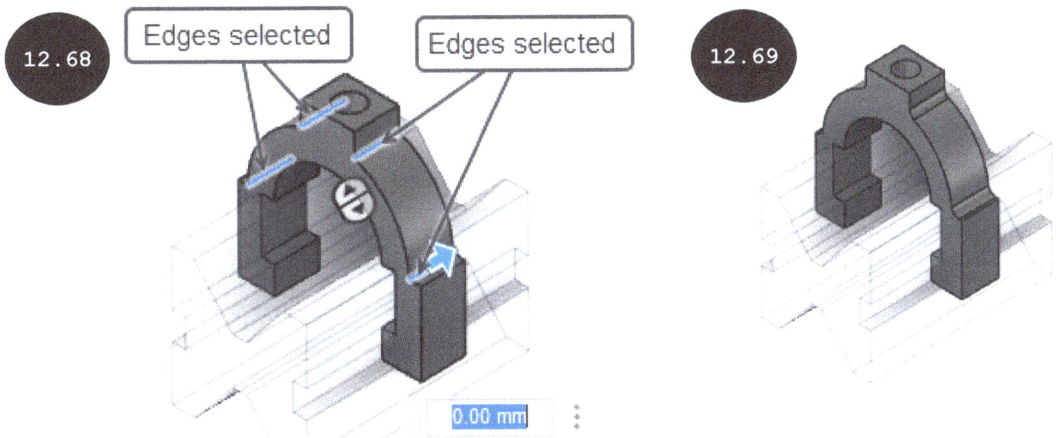

17. Click the **Finish Edit In Place** button located at the top center of the graphics area to confirm the creation of the second component, see Figure 12.70. The second component is created and the main assembly becomes activated again.

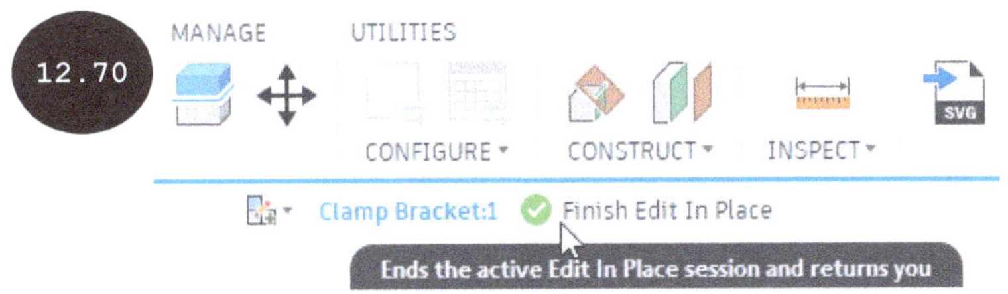

Section 4: Creating the Third Component

Now, you need to create the third component.

1. Right-click on the top browser node as the parent component and then click on the **New Component** tool in the shortcut menu that appears, see Figure 12.71. The **NEW COMPONENT** dialog box appears.

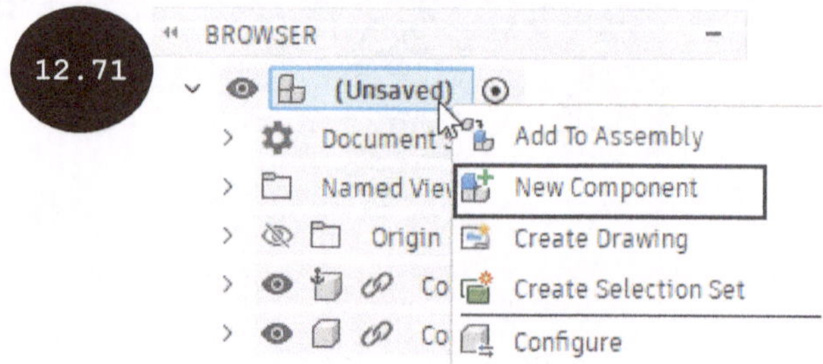

2. Ensure that the **Part** button is activated in the dialog box.

3. Enter **Clamping Screw** as the name for the design file (third component) in the **Name** field of the dialog box.

4. Accept the remaining default options, and click the **OK** button in the dialog box. A new empty design file is created as a child of the parent assembly file in the **BROWSER** with its specified name, see Figure 12.72. The file also becomes the active design file for creating its features. Notice that the existing components of the assembly becomes transparent in the graphics area.

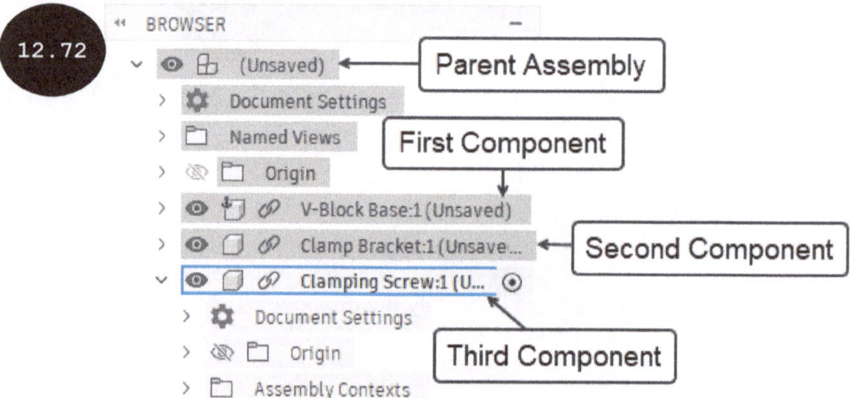

Now, you can add features to the newly created empty component (third component).

5. Click on the **Create Sketch** tool in the **Toolbar** and then select the top planar face of the second component as the sketching plane.

6. Project the circular edge of the second component by using the **Project** tool, see Figure 12.73.

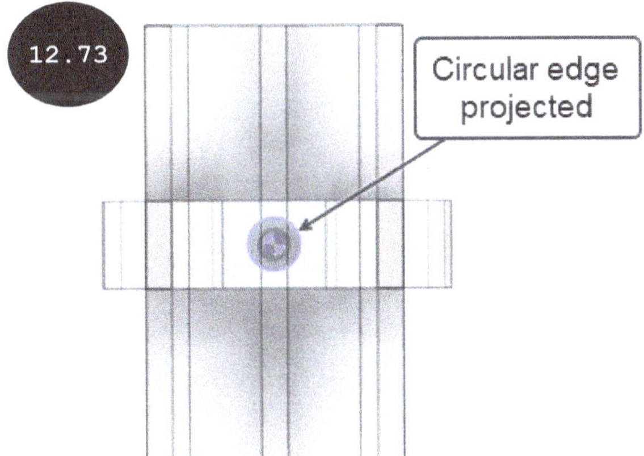

7. Invoke the **EXTRUDE** dialog box and then extrude the projected profile to a distance of 80 mm symmetrically on both sides of the sketching plane by selecting the **Whole Length** button in the **Measurement** area of the dialog box, see Figure 12.74. Note that you need to select the **New Body** option in the **Operation** drop-down list of the **EXTRUDE** dialog box. The first feature is created, and the third component is still activated.

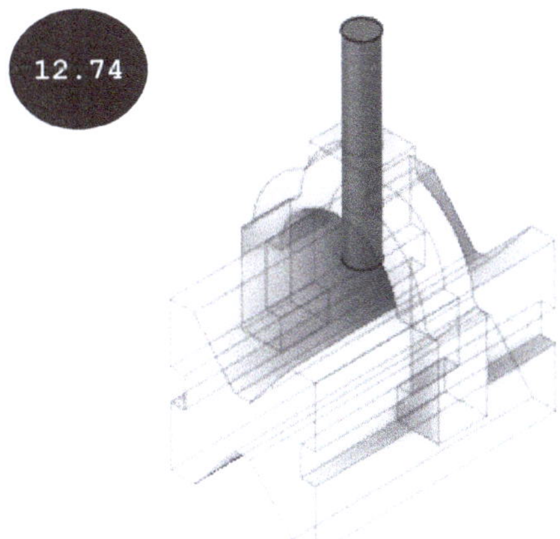

Now, you need to create the second feature of the third component.

8. Click on the **Create Sketch** tool in the **Toolbar** and then select the top planar face of the first feature of the third component as the sketching plane.

9. Create a circle of diameter 20 mm as the sketch of the second feature, see Figure 12.75.

10. Extrude the sketch profile to a distance of 20 mm in the upward direction by using the **Extrude** tool, see Figure 12.76. Ensure that the **Join** option is selected in the **Operation** drop-down list of the **EXTRUDE** dialog box.

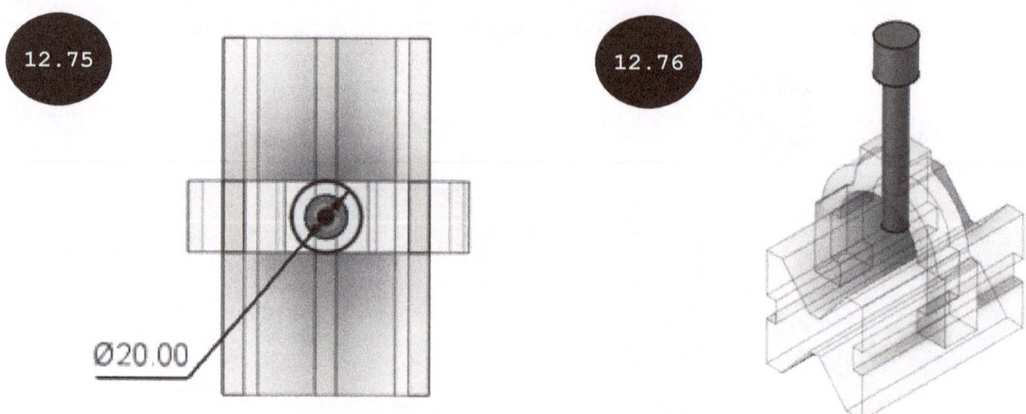

Now, you need to create the third feature of the component.

11. Click on the **Create Sketch** tool in the **Toolbar** and then select the Right plane as the sketching plane.

12. Create a circle of diameter 5 mm as the sketch of the third feature, see Figure 12.77.

13. Create a cut feature by extruding the sketch through all, on both sides of the sketching plane, see Figure 12.78.

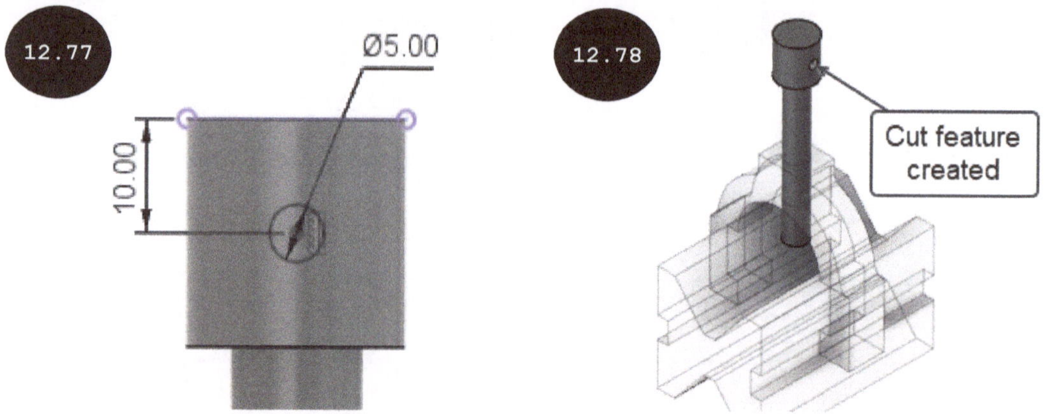

Now, you need to create the fourth feature of the third component. The fourth feature is a fillet feature.

14. Create a fillet of radius 2 mm on the top circular edge of the third component by using the **Fillet** tool, see Figure 12.79.

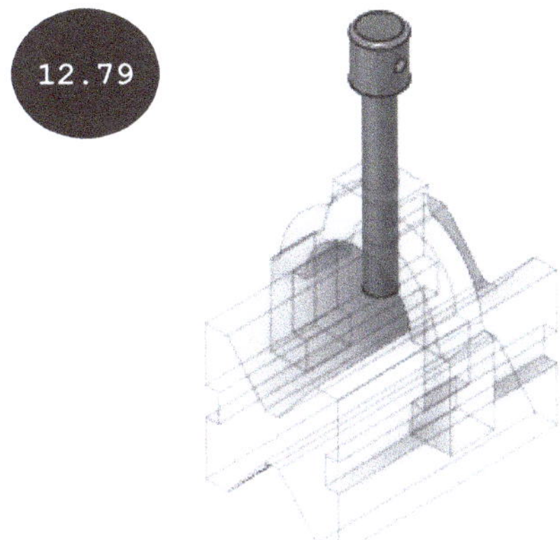

15. Click the **Finish Edit In Place** button located at the top center of the graphics area to confirm the creation of the third component, see Figure 12.80. The third component is created and the main assembly becomes activated again.

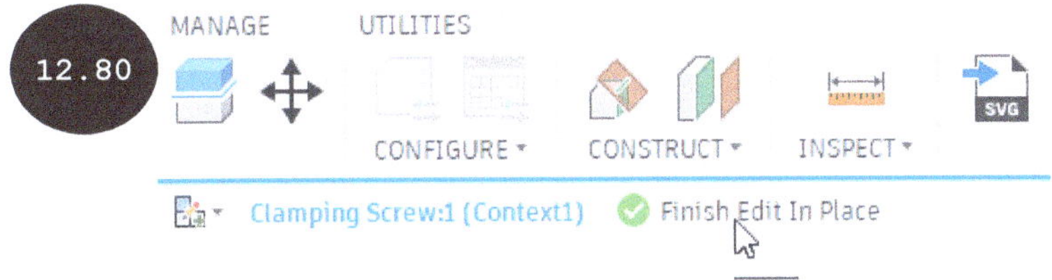

Section 5: Creating the Fourth Component

Now, you need to create the fourth component.

1. Right-click on the top browser node as the parent component and then click on the **New Component** tool in the shortcut menu that appears. The **NEW COMPONENT** dialog box appears.

2. Ensure that the **Part** button is activated in the dialog box.

3. Enter **Handle Rod** as the name for the design file (fourth component) in the **Name** field of the dialog box.

4. Accept the remaining default options, and click the **OK** button in the dialog box. A new empty design file is created as a child of the parent assembly file in the **BROWSER** with its specified name, see Figure 12.81. The file also becomes the active design file for creating its features. The existing components of the assembly becomes transparent in the graphics area.

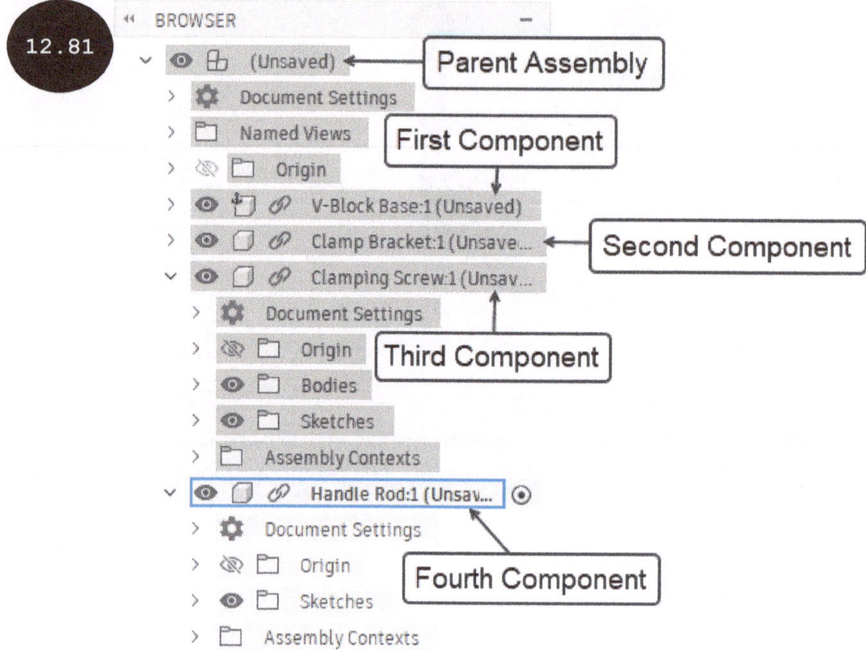

Now, you can add features to the newly created empty component (fourth component).

5. Click on the **Create Sketch** tool in the **Toolbar** and then select the Right plane as the sketching plane.

6. Create a circle of diameter 5 mm as the sketch of the first feature, see Figure 12.82.

7. Extrude the sketch profile to a distance of 45 mm, symmetrically on both sides of the sketching plane by using the **Extrude** tool, see Figure 12.83. Note that the total extrusion distance is 90 mm, and you need to select the **New Body** option in the **Operation** drop-down list of the **EXTRUDE** dialog box. The first feature is created, and the fourth component is still activated.

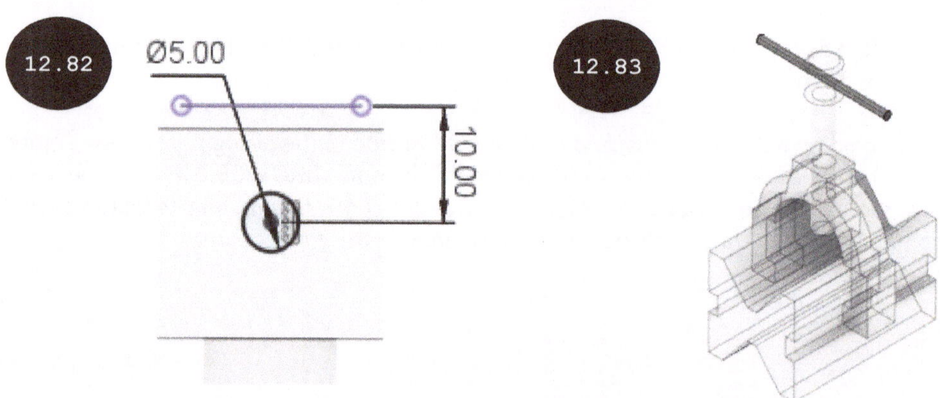

Now, you need to create the second feature of the fourth component.

8. Click on the **Create Sketch** tool in the **Toolbar** and then select the right planar face of the first feature of the fourth component as the sketching plane.

9. Create a circle of diameter 10 mm as the sketch of the second feature, see Figure 12.84.

10. Extrude the sketch profile to a distance of 5 mm by using the **Extrude** tool, see Figure 12.85. The second feature of the fourth component is created.

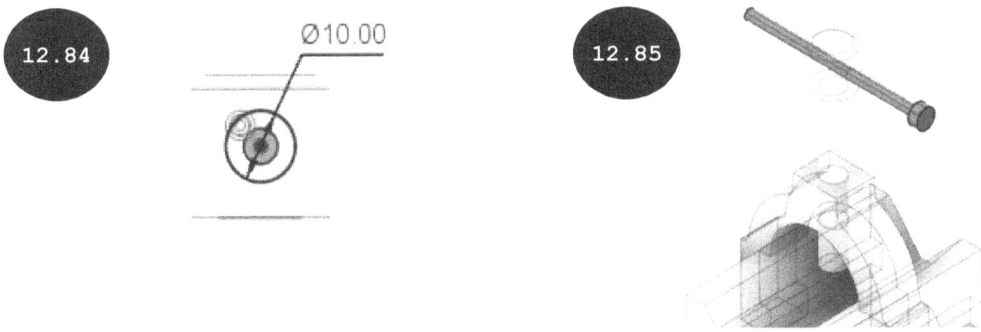

Now, you need to create the third feature of the fourth component. The third feature of the component is a chamfer.

11. Create an equidistant chamfer of 1.5 mm on the right circular edge of the second feature of the fourth component, see Figure 12.86.

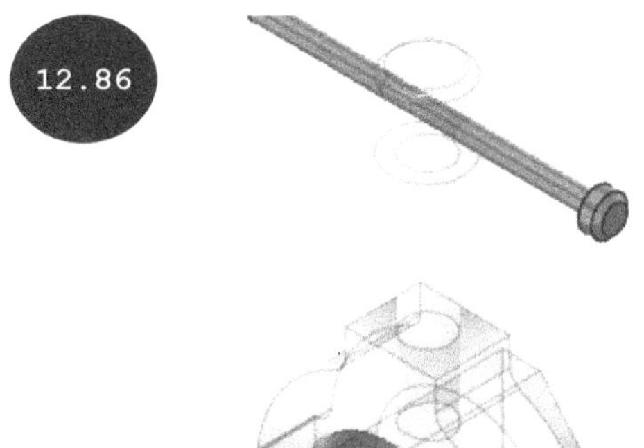

Now, you need to create the fourth feature of the component. The fourth feature of the component is a mirror feature.

12. Invoke the **MIRROR** dialog box and then select the **Features** option in the **Object Type** drop-down list of the dialog box.

13. Click on the previously created two features (**Extrude2** and **Chamfer1**) in the **Timeline** or the graphics area as the features to be mirrored.

14. Click on the **Mirror Plane** selection option in the **MIRROR** dialog box and then select the Right plane as the mirroring plane in the graphics area.

15. Click on the **OK** button in the **MIRROR** dialog box. The selected features get mirrored about the mirroring plane, see Figure 12.87. The fourth component is created.

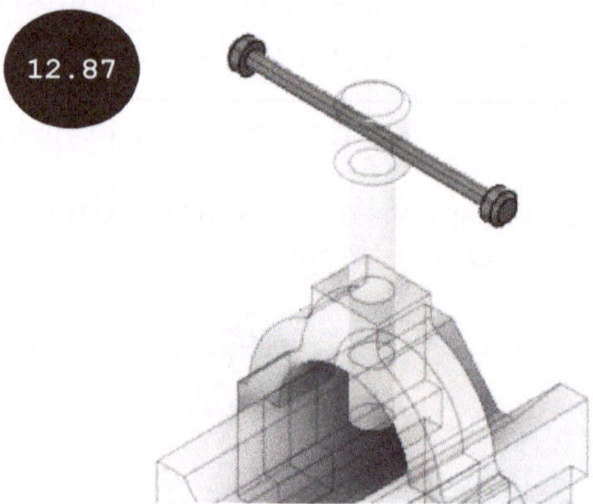

16. Click the **Finish Edit In Place** button located at the top center of the graphics area to confirm the creation of the fourth component, see Figure 12.88. The fourth component is created and the main assembly becomes activated again. All the child components of the assembly appear in the default visual style, see Figure 12.89. This figure shows the assembly after creating its components.

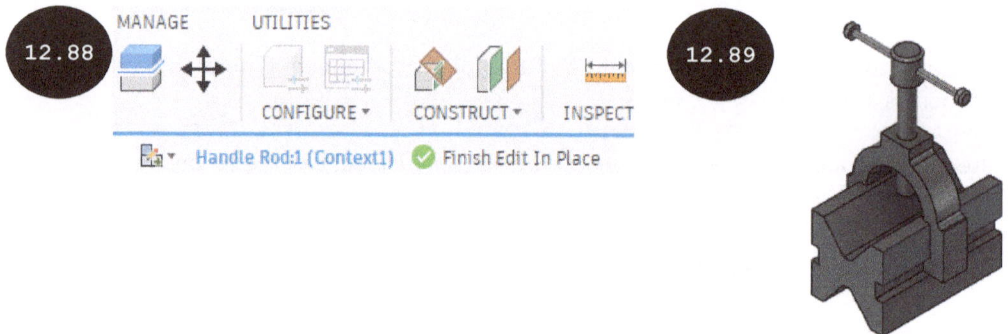

Section 6: Applying Joints

After creating all the components of the assembly, you need to apply joints to define the relative motion between them. As all the assembly components are in the correct position, you can apply joints using the **As-Built Joint** tool.

1. Invoke the **RELATIONSHIPS** drop-down menu in the **ASSEMBLY** tab and then click on the **As-Built Joint** tool, see Figure 12.90. The **AS-BUILT JOINT** dialog box appears, see Figure 12.91. Alternatively, press the SHIFT + J keys to invoke the **AS-BUILT JOINT** dialog box.

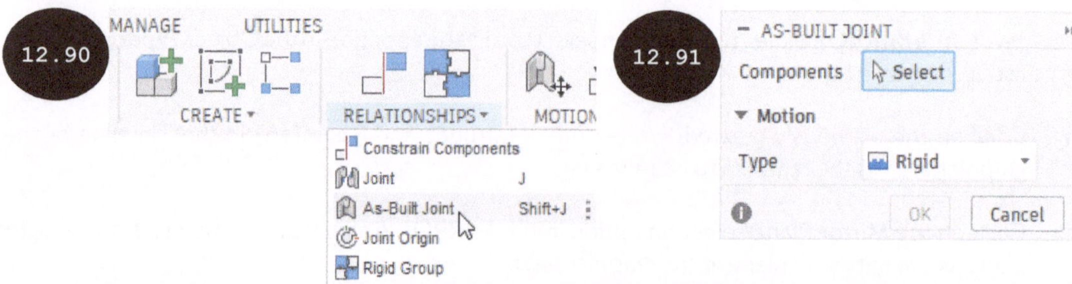

2. Select the second component (moveable component) and then the first component (fixed component) in the graphics area one by one to apply the joint.

3. Select the **Slider** option in the **Type** drop-down list of the dialog box as the joint to be applied between the selected components. The **Origin Mode** area and **Snap** selection option appear in the dialog box, and you are prompted to specify the position of the joint origin.

4. Ensure that the **Simple** button is selected in the **Origin Mode** area of the dialog box for defining the joint origin on a face, an edge, or a point of the component, see Figure 12.92.

5. Move the cursor over a linear edge of the first component to define the position of the joint origin and the direction of translation, see Figure 12.93. The edge gets highlighted, and its snap points appear.

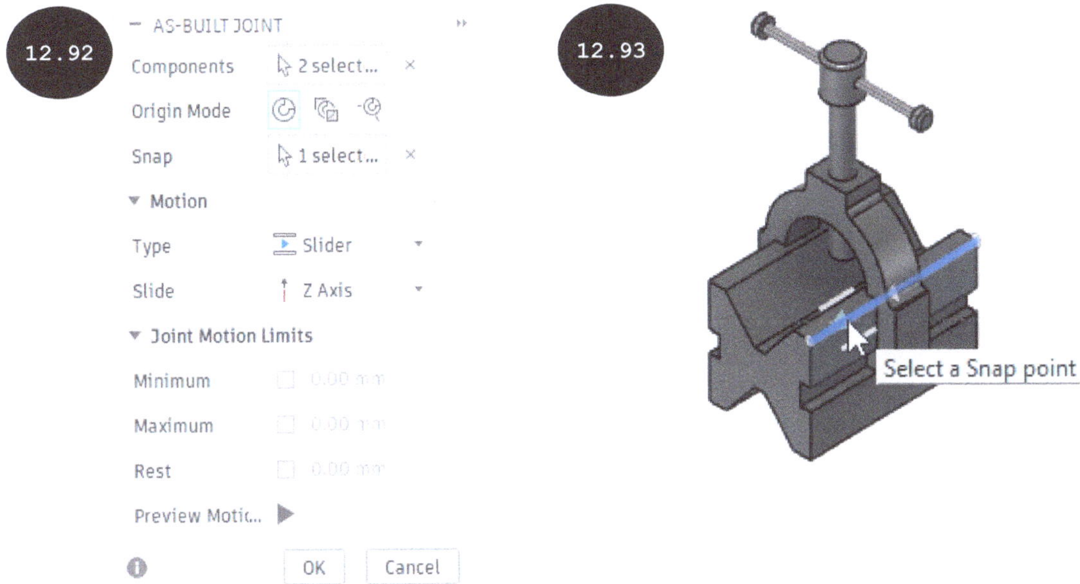

6. Press the CTRL key to lock the highlighted edge and then click to specify the position of the joint origin when the cursor snaps to the middle snap point of the highlighted edge. The second component starts sliding along the joint origin defined.

7. Click on the **OK** button in the dialog box. The slider joint is applied between the selected components.

   Now, you need to apply a cylindrical joint between the third and second components of the assembly.

8. Invoke the **AS-BUILT JOINT** dialog box and then select the third and second components to apply the cylindrical joint between them.

9. Select the **Cylindrical** option in the **Type** drop-down list of the dialog box. The **Origin Mode** area and **Snap** selection option appear in the dialog box, and you are prompted to specify the position of the joint origin.

10. Ensure that the **Simple** option is selected in the **Origin Mode** area of the dialog box.
11. Move the cursor over the cylindrical face of the third component, see Figure 12.94. The face gets highlighted, and its snap points appear.

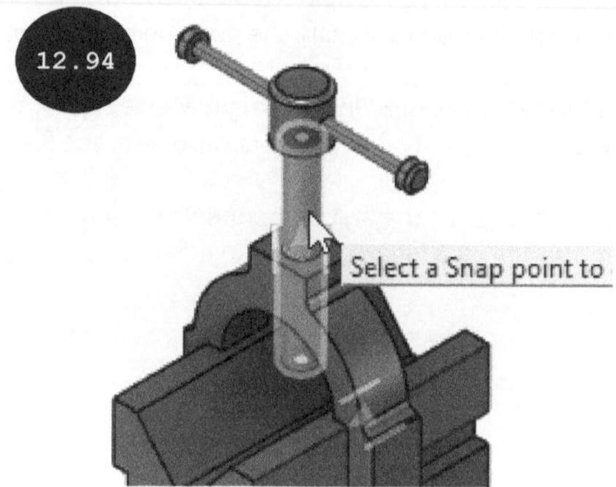

12. Press the CTRL key to lock the highlighted face and then click to specify the position of the joint origin when the cursor snaps to its middle snap point. The third component starts sliding as well as rotating about the joint origin defined.
13. Click on the **OK** button in the dialog box. The cylindrical joint is applied between the selected components.

    Now, you need to apply a rigid joint between the fourth and third components.

14. Invoke the **AS-BUILT JOINT** dialog box and then select the fourth and third components in the graphics area.
15. Select the **Rigid** option in the **Type** drop-down list of the dialog box and then click on the **OK** button. The rigid joint is applied between the selected components. Figure 12.95 shows the final assembly after applying the joints.

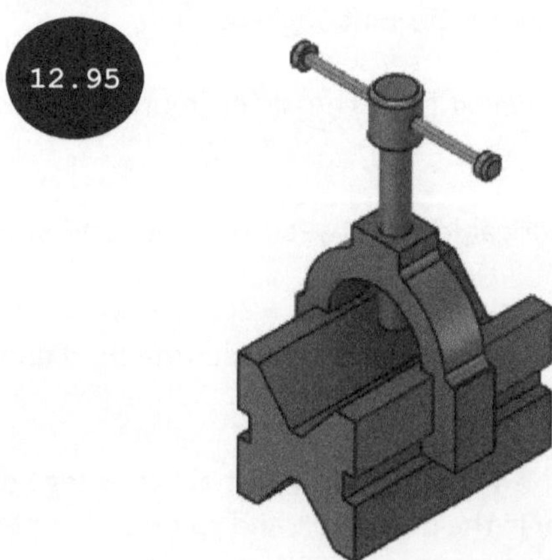

Note: In Figure 12.95, the visibility of the applied joints symbols is turned off. To toggle the visibility of the applied joints, click on the **Display Settings > Object Visibility > Joints** in the **Navigation Bar**, see Figure 12.96.

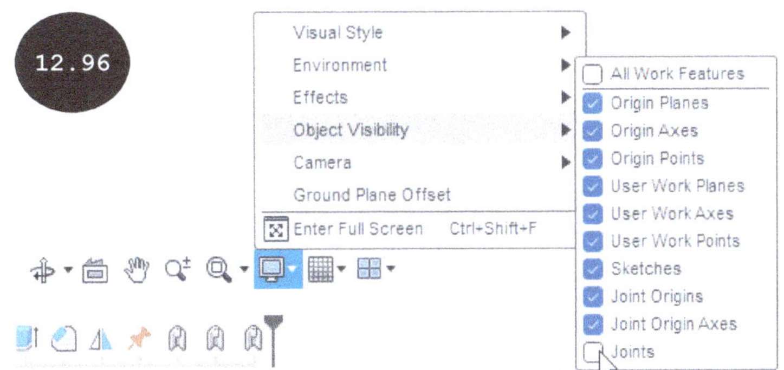

Section 7: Saving the Assembly File

1. Click on the **Save** tool in the **Application Bar**. The **Save** dialog box appears.

2. Enter **Tutorial 1** in the **Name** field of the dialog box.

3. Ensure that the location ***Autodesk Fusion 360 > Chapter 12 > Tutorial*** is specified in the **Location** field of the dialog box to save the file of this tutorial. Note that you need to create these folders in the **Data Panel**, if not created earlier.

4. Click on the **Save** button in the dialog box. The model is saved with the name Tutorial 1 in the specified location (***Autodesk Fusion 360 > Chapter 12 > Tutorial > Tutorial 1***).

Hands-on Test Drive 1

Create an assembly, as shown in Figure 12.97 by using the Top-down approach. Different views and dimensions of the individual components of the assembly are shown in Figures 12.98 through 12.103. After creating the assembly, you need to apply the joints by using the **As-Built Joint** tool. All dimensions are in mm.

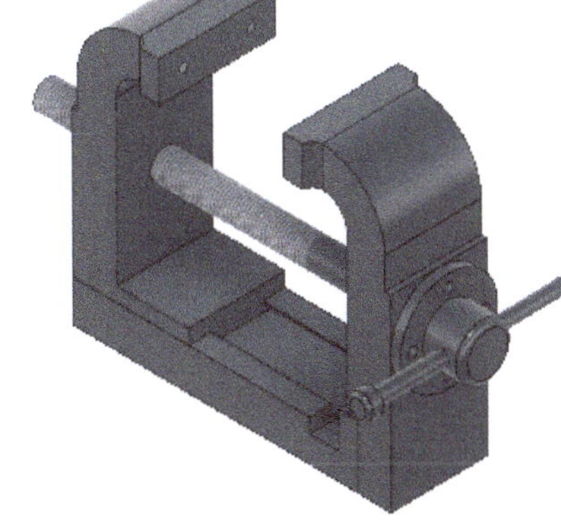

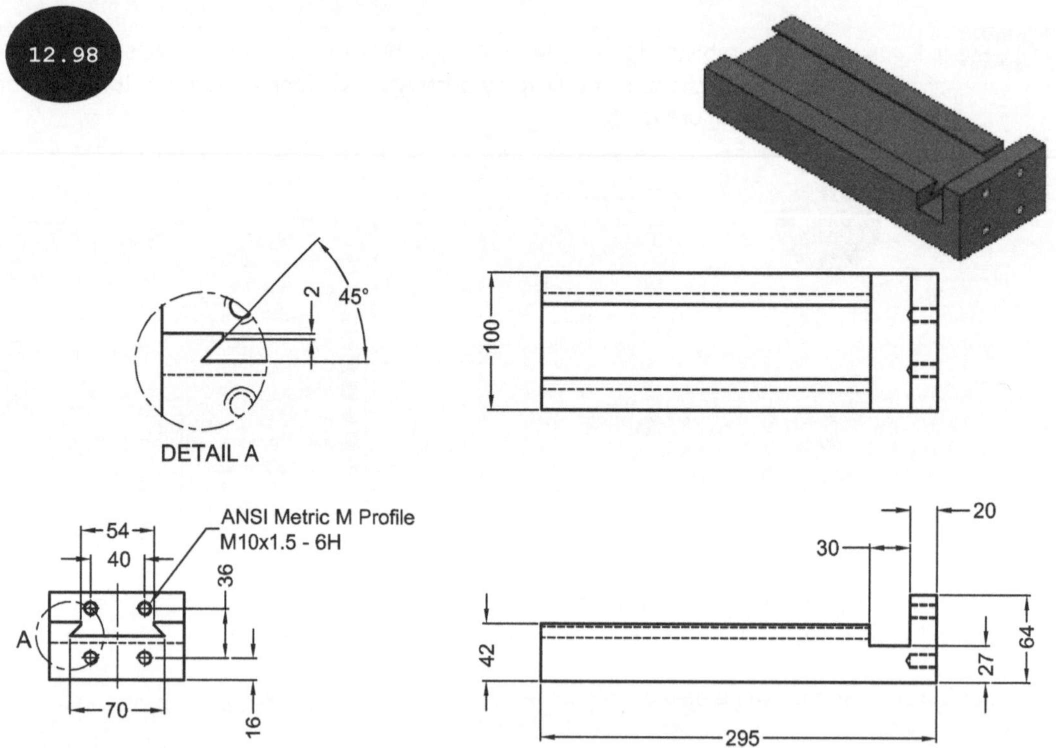
12.98
2
45°
100
DETAIL A
54
40
ANSI Metric M Profile
M10x1.5 - 6H
36
A
70
16
30
20
42
64
27
295

Base

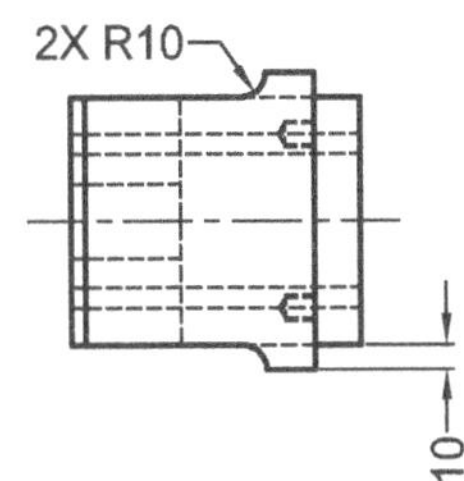

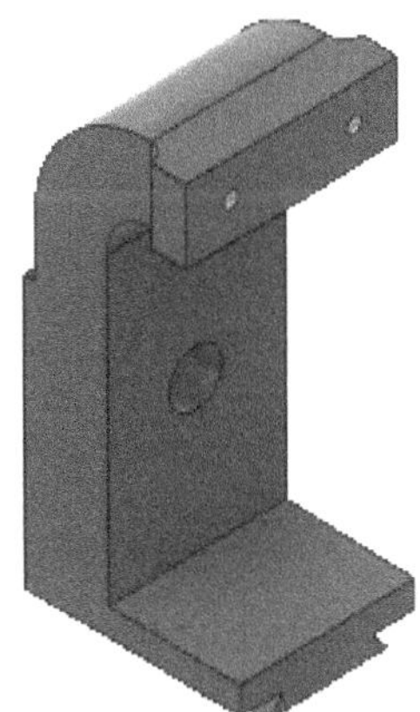

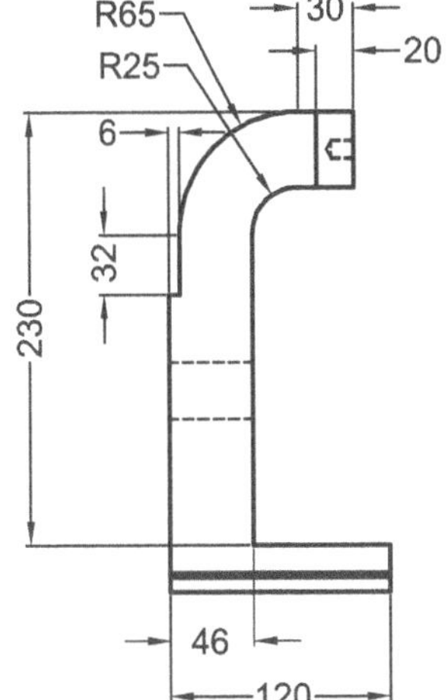

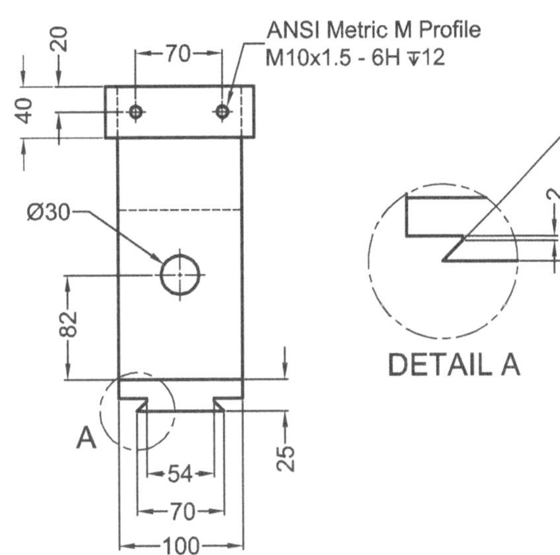

Moveable Jaw

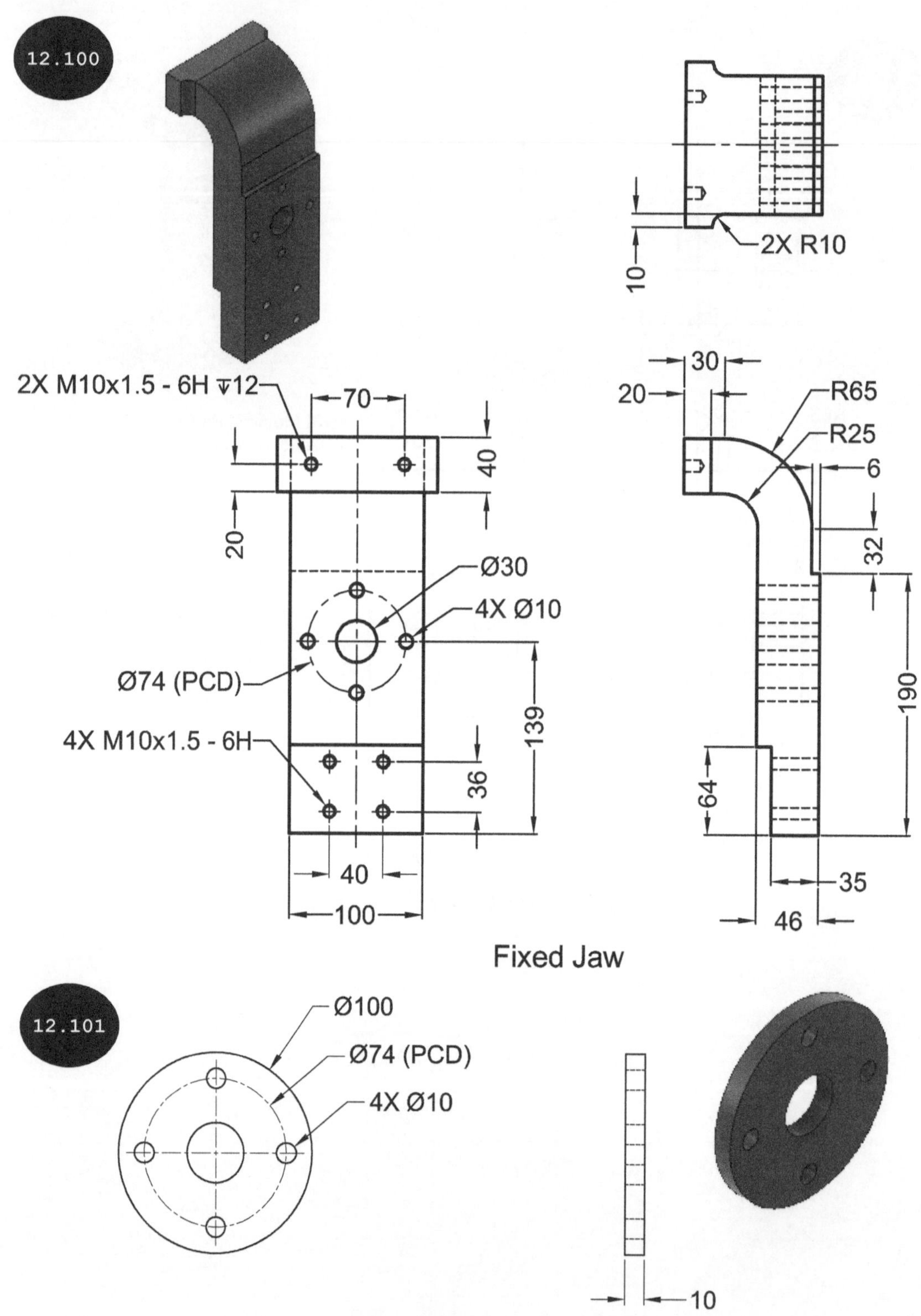

Fixed Jaw

Washer

12.102

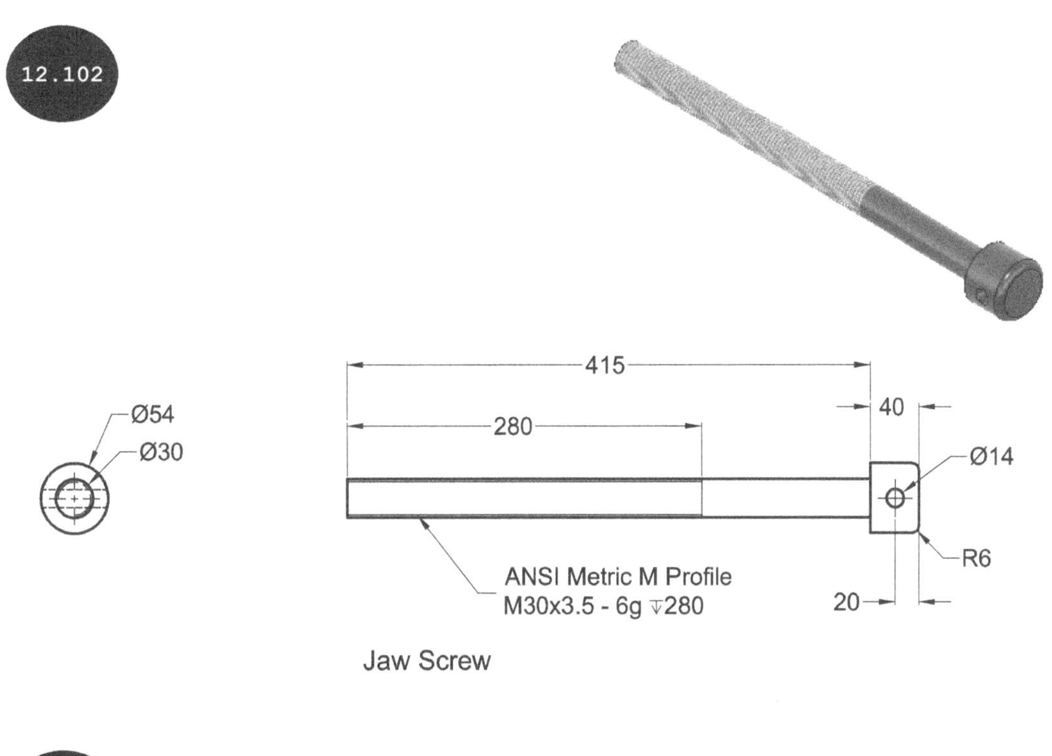

Jaw Screw

12.103

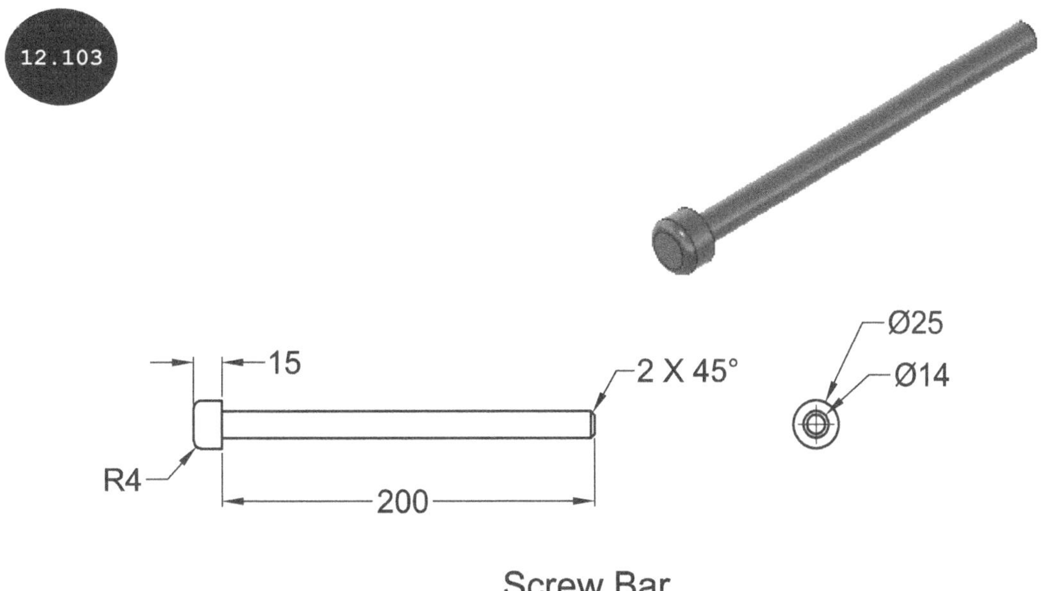

Screw Bar

Summary

In this chapter, you learned how to create assemblies using the Top-down assembly approach. You explored the process of applying As-Built joints between components using the **As-Built Joint** tool. Additionally, you gained an understanding of how to define a joint origin for components and edit components within an assembly to ensure proper alignment and functionality. This knowledge will help you efficiently manage assemblies and their relationships as you continue your design process.

Questions

Complete and verify the following sentences:

- In the _________ approach, all components of an assembly are created within a single design file.
- The _________ dialog box is used for creating an empty component or converting the existing bodies into a component.
- The _________ selection option of the **NEW COMPONENT** dialog box is used for selecting the parent for the component being created.
- The _________ tool is used for applying joints between the components in their current position as they are built.
- The _________ tool is used for creating a joint origin anywhere on a component.
- The _________ button of the **JOINT ORIGIN** dialog box is used for placing the joint origin on a face of the component and then manipulating its location, as required.
- The _________ button of the **JOINT ORIGIN** dialog box is used for placing the joint origin in the middle of two selected faces of a component.
- In Autodesk Fusion, to add features to a component, you need to ensure that the component is active. (True/False)
- In Autodesk Fusion, you cannot edit components of the assembly created by using the Top-down assembly approach. (True/False)

CHAPTER

13

Creating Animation of a Design

In this chapter, the following topics will be discussed:

- Invoking the ANIMATION Workspace
- Capturing Views on the Timeline
- Capturing Actions on the Timeline
- Customizing Views and Actions on the Timeline
- Deleting Views and Actions of a Storyboard
- Creating a New Storyboard
- Toggling On or Off Capturing Views
- Playing and Publishing Animation

In Autodesk Fusion, you can animate a design to demonstrate how the components of an assembly are assembled, operated, or repaired. Animations also serve as an excellent marketing tool, allowing you to showcase your product or explain its functionality effectively.

To create an animation, you can use the ANIMATION workspace in Autodesk Fusion. The process for accessing this workspace and creating an animation is explained in the following sections.

Invoking the ANIMATION Workspace

After creating an assembly in the DESIGN workspace, you need to switch to the ANIMATION workspace to create its animation. To do this, open the **Workspace** drop-down menu in the design file (see Figure 13.1) and select ANIMATION. The user interface of the ANIMATION workspace appears, see Figure 13.2.

13.1

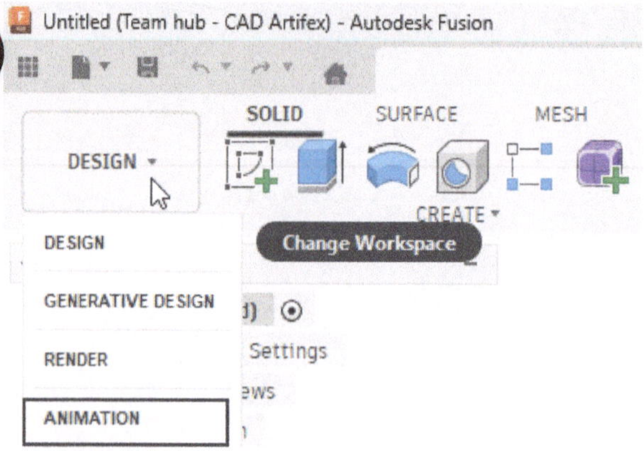

Untitled (Team hub - CAD Artifex) - Autodesk Fusion

DESIGN

SOLID SURFACE MESH

CREATE

Change Workspace

DESIGN

GENERATIVE DESIGN

RENDER

ANIMATION

13.2

Toolbar

ANIMATION TIMELINE

Time 0

Actions

Playhead

Storyboard

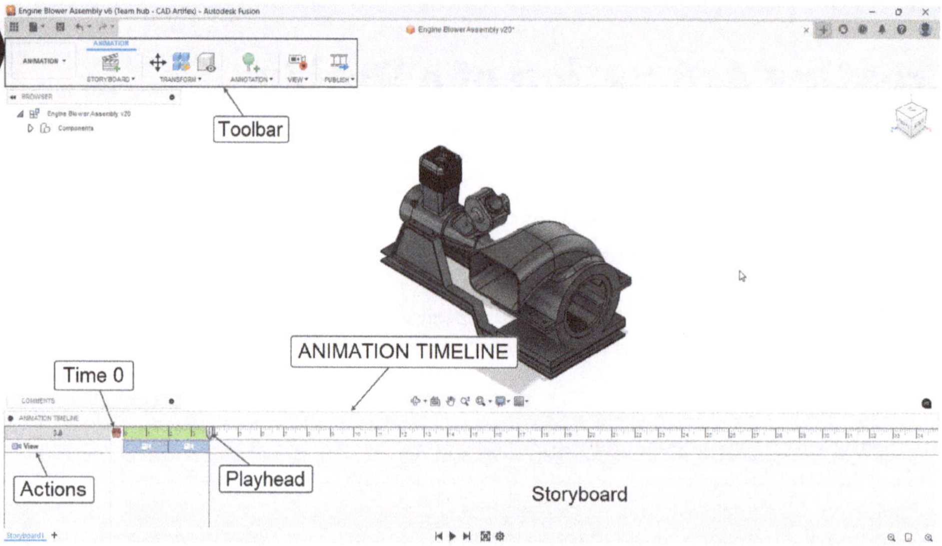

In Autodesk Fusion, to create an animation of a design, you need to capture views and actions along the **Timeline** in a storyboard, see Figure 13.3. Note that all navigating operations such as zoom in, zoom out, and orbit, performed at a given point in time on the design or assembly are captured on the **Timeline** as views. On the other hand, all transforming operations such as move and rotate, performed at a given point in time on individual components of an assembly are captured on the **Timeline** as actions. The methods for capturing views and actions on the **Timeline** of a storyboard are discussed next.

13.3

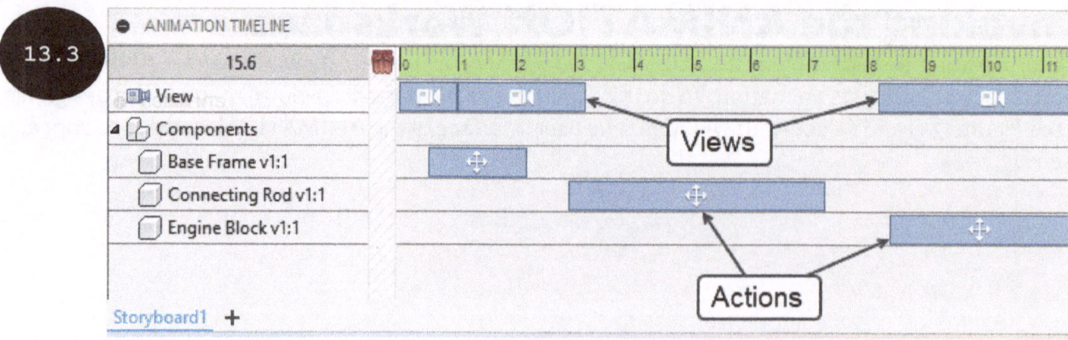

Capturing Views on the Timeline

To capture a view such as a zoom or an orbit, you need to first, define the position of the **Playhead** on the **Timeline** at a positive point in time, see Figure 13.4. In this figure, the **Playhead** is placed on the **Timeline** at time 2 seconds. Note that, if the position of the **Playhead** is defined on the **Timeline** at **Time 0** (red mark), then the view will not be captured on performing any navigating operation on the design or assembly, see Figure 13.5. You can also turn on or off the recording or capturing of views by clicking on the **View** tool in the **Toolbar**.

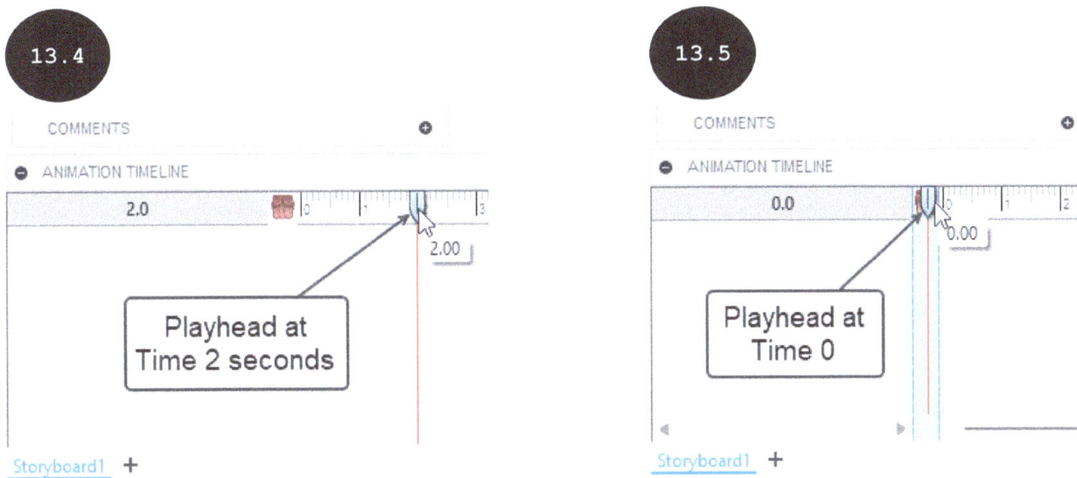

After defining the **Playhead** position at a positive point in time, perform a navigating operation on the design or assembly by using the mouse buttons or the navigating tools. The navigating operation performed is captured as a view on the **Timeline** at a defined point in time, see Figure 13.6. Now, you can play the animation to review the captured view by clicking on the **Play** button in the lower middle part of the storyboard, see Figure 13.6. You can similarly capture multiple views on the **Timeline** at different points in time.

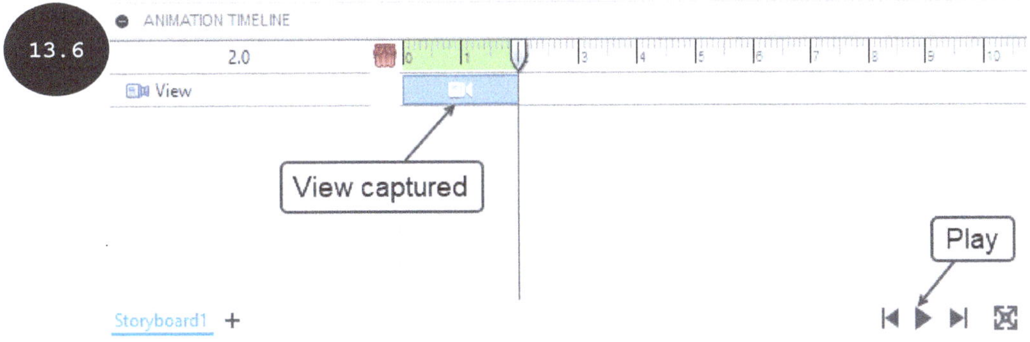

Note: After capturing a view, if you further perform any navigating operation without changing the **Playhead** position on the **Timeline**, then the existing view gets overridden by the newly performed navigating operation.

Capturing Actions on the Timeline

In Autodesk Fusion, you can capture actions at a given point in time on the **Timeline** by performing operations such as moving and rotating on individual components of an assembly. You can also capture actions by creating exploded views of an assembly, turning on or off the visibility of the components, and creating callouts with annotations. The methods for capturing actions are discussed next.

Transforming Components (Move or Rotate)

In Autodesk Fusion, any transforming operation such as move or rotate performed at a given point in time on a component of an assembly is captured as an action. You can perform a transforming operation by using the **Transform Components** tool. To do this, first, define the position of the **Playhead** on the **Timeline** at a positive point in time, see Figure 13.7. In this figure, the **Playhead** is positioned on the **Timeline** at a time of 4 seconds. Note that if the position of the **Playhead** is defined on the **Timeline** at **Time 0** (red mark), then the action will not be captured.

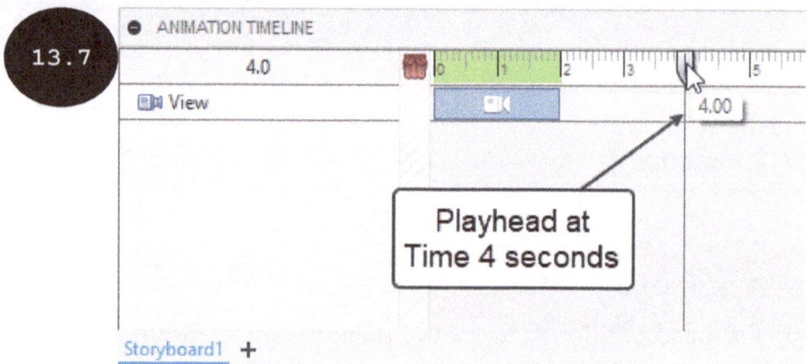

After defining the **Playhead** position at a positive point in time, click on the **Transform Components** tool in the **Toolbar**, see Figure 13.8 or press the M key. The **TRANSFORM COMPONENTS** dialog box appears, see Figure 13.9. Next, select a component to be transformed in the graphics area. You can also select multiple components by pressing the CTRL key. The **TRANSFORM COMPONENTS** dialog box gets modified, see Figure 13.10. Also, the translational and manipulator handles appear on the selected component in the graphics area, see Figure 13.11. Now, you can transform (move and rotate) the selected component by dragging the translational and manipulator handles or by entering the distance and angle values in the respective fields of the dialog box.

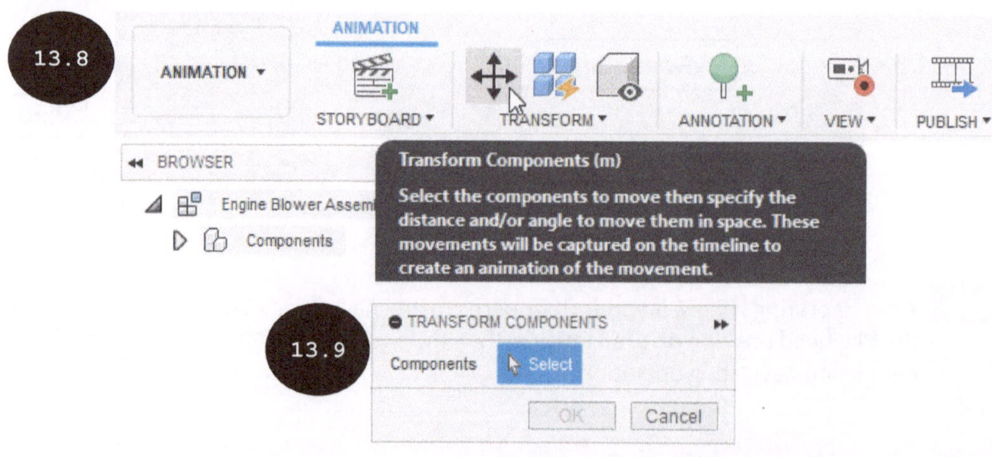

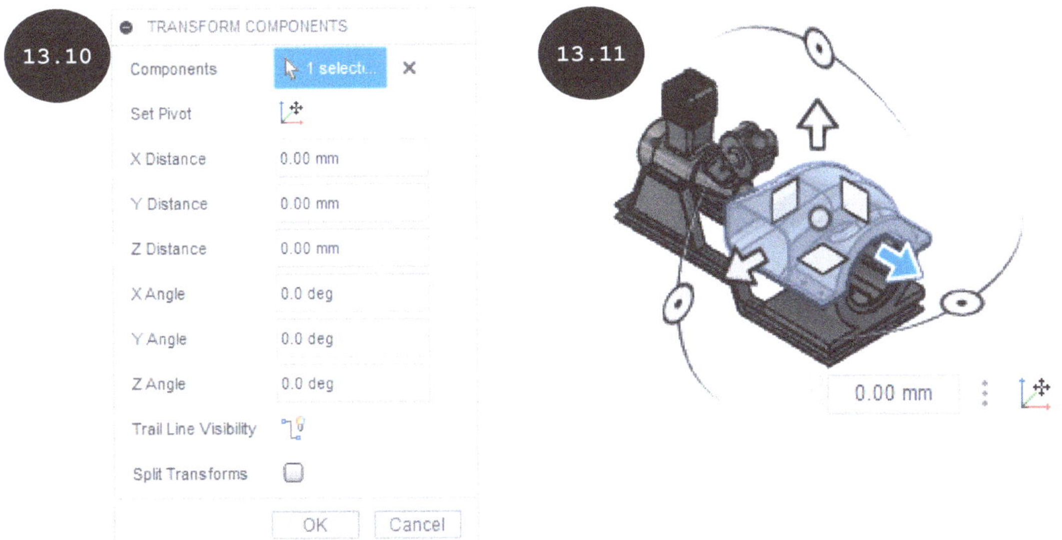

The **Trail Line Visibility** button of the **TRANSFORM COMPONENTS** dialog box is used for toggling the visibility of the trail line in the graphics area. The trail line defines the path and the direction in which the component is assembled, see Figure 13.12. By default, the **Split Transforms** check box is cleared in the dialog box. As a result, a straight trail line appears in the graphics area, see Figure 13.12. On selecting the **Split Transforms** check box, the trail line gets split into horizontal and vertical lines in the graphics area depending upon the transforming operation performed, see Figure 13.13.

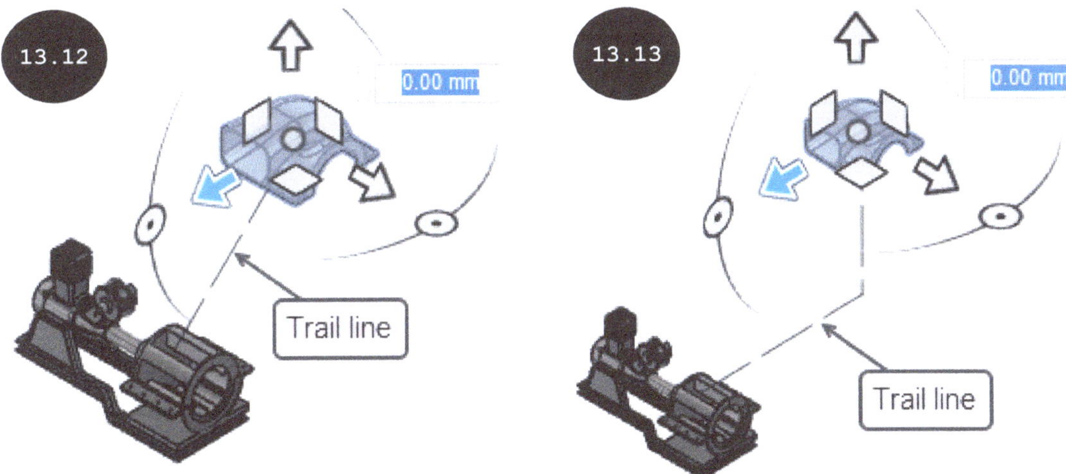

After transforming a component, click on the **OK** button in the **TRANSFORM COMPONENTS** dialog box. The transforming operation performed on the component is captured as an action on the **Timeline** at the defined point in time, see Figure 13.14. In Autodesk Fusion, after creating an action, you can customize it by editing its start and end times. You will learn about customizing an action later in this chapter.

13.14

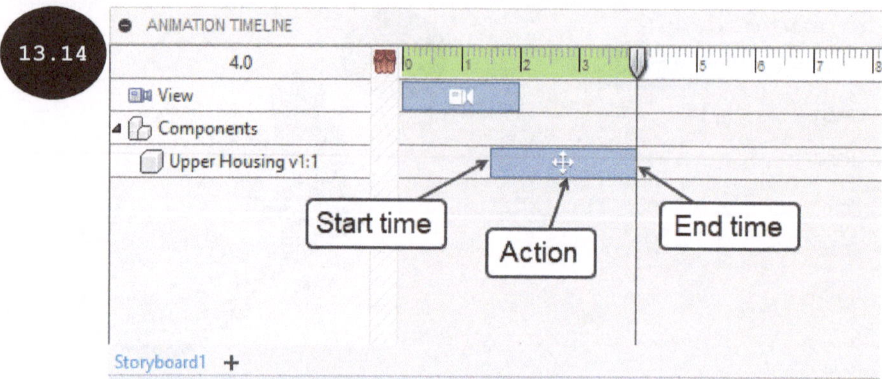

Note: If you move as well as rotate the component by dragging the translational and manipulator handles or by entering the distance and angle values in the respective fields of the **TRANSFORM COMPONENTS** dialog box, then both the move and rotate actions will be captured separately on the **Timeline**, see Figure 13.15.

13.15

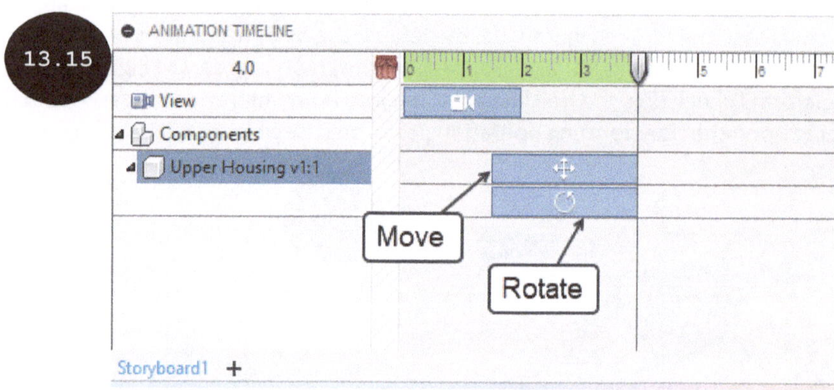

You can similarly capture multiple actions on the **Timeline** at different points in time by performing transforming operations on other components of the assembly one by one. After capturing the actions on the **Timeline** of a storyboard, you can play the animation by clicking on the **Play** button in the lower middle part of the storyboard.

Tip: You can also invoke the **Transform Components** tool by using the Marking Menu. To do this, right-click on the component to be transformed in the graphics area. The Marking Menu appears, see Figure 13.16. In this Marking Menu, click on the **Transform Components** tool.

Creating an Exploded View of an Assembly

In Autodesk Fusion, you can also capture actions on the **Timeline** by creating an exploded view of an assembly. An exploded view of an assembly helps in easily identifying the position of each component in the assembly. In Autodesk Fusion, you can create exploded views by using the **Auto Explode: One Level**, **Auto Explode: All Levels**, or **Manual Explode** tools, see Figure 13.17. The different tools used for exploding an assembly are discussed next.

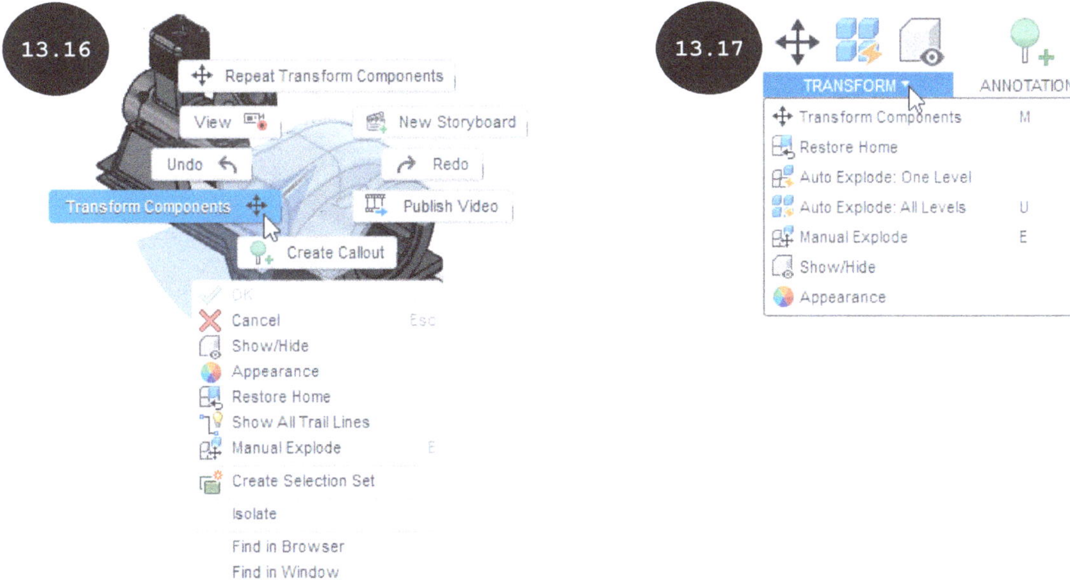

Auto Explode: One Level Tool

The **Auto Explode: One Level** tool is used for exploding only the first-level children's components of the assembly, automatically. This means that, if the assembly consists of sub-assemblies, then the components of sub-assemblies will not explode. To do this, expand the **Components** node in the **BROWSER** and then click on the assembly node to select it, see Figure 13.18. All the components of the assembly get selected and highlighted in the graphics area.

Next, invoke the **TRANSFORM** drop-down menu in the **Toolbar** (refer to Figure 13.17) and click on the **Auto Explode: One Level** tool. The process of exploding the first level children's components of the selected assembly gets started and once it is completed, the preview of the exploded view of the assembly and the **Auto Explode** toolbar appear in the graphics area, see Figure 13.19. Also, the actions of the exploded view of individual components of the assembly are captured on the **Timeline**, and the Green and Red sliders appear, see Figure 13.20.

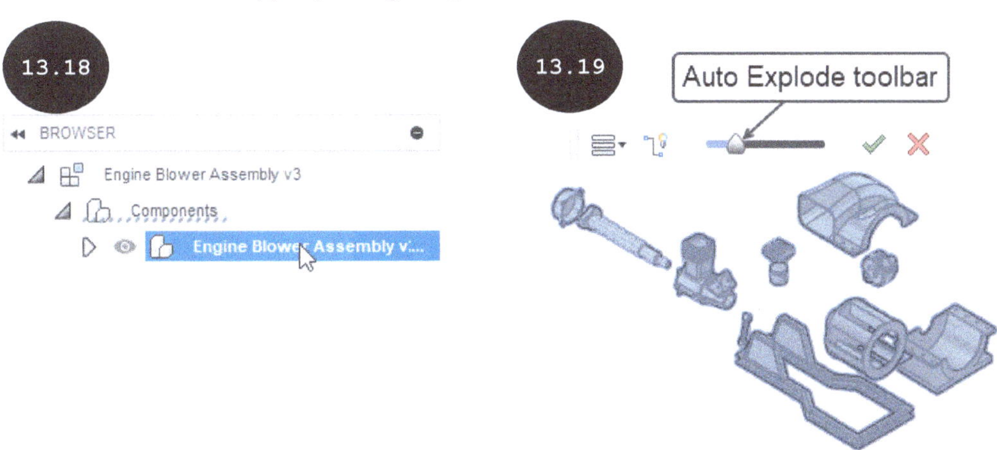

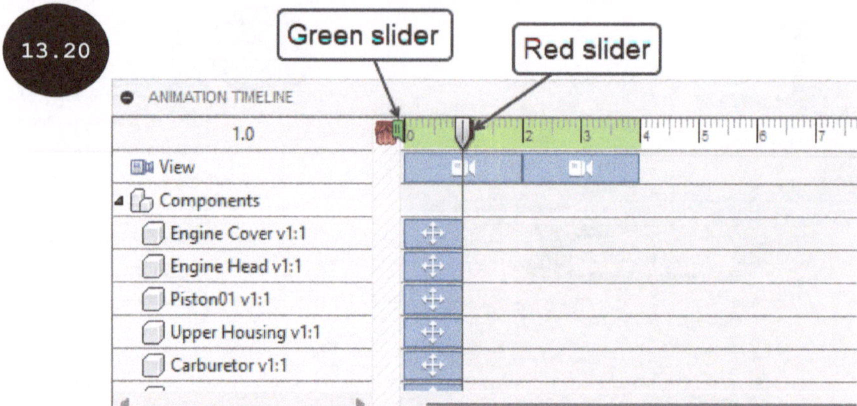

The Green slider defines the start time and the Red slider (appearing in the background of the Playhead) defines the end time of the exploded view on the **Timeline**. You can change the start and end times of the exploded view by dragging them along the **Timeline**, as required.

The **Auto Explode** toolbar that appears in the graphics area is used for controlling the type, trail line visibility, and explosion scale of the exploded view, see Figure 13.21. By default, the **One-Step Explosion** option is selected as the type of explosion in the **Type** drop-down list, see Figure 13.22. As a result, all components of the assembly are exploded at the same time. To explode each component of the assembly in sequential order, select the **Sequential Explosion** option in the **Type** drop-down list of the **Auto Explode** toolbar. Note that, depending upon the option selected in the **Type** drop-down list, the actions of the exploded view are captured accordingly on the **Timeline**. Figure 13.23 shows the actions captured on the **Timeline** when the **One-Step Explosion** option is selected, and Figure 13.24 shows the actions captured on the **Timeline** when the **Sequential Explosion** option is selected.

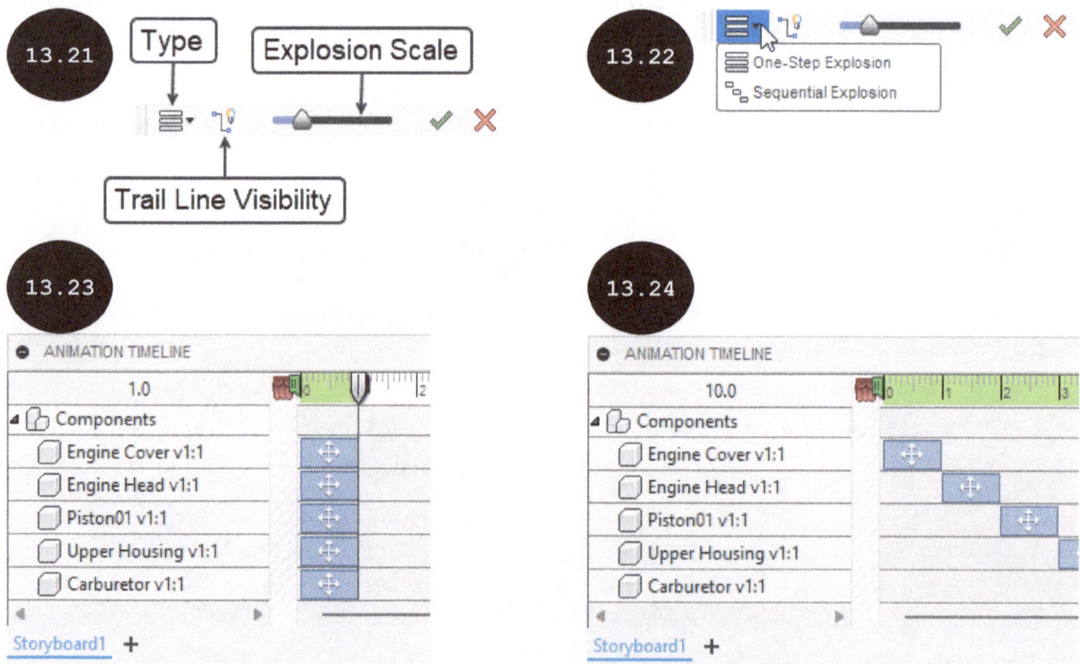

After defining the required options for the exploded view, click on the **OK** button (green tick-mark) in the **Auto Explode** toolbar. The exploded view is created and the actions of each exploded component of the assembly are captured on the **Timeline**. Now, you can animate the exploded view by clicking on the **Play** button of the Storyboard.

Auto Explode: All Levels Tool

The **Auto Explode: All Levels** tool is used for exploding all levels of the assembly, automatically. This means that, if the assembly consists of sub-assemblies, then the components of sub-assemblies will also explode. The method for exploding all levels of the assembly by using the **Auto Explode: All Levels** tool is the same as discussed earlier.

Manual Explode Tool

The **Manual Explode** tool is used to explode the components of the assembly, manually. To do this, invoke the **TRANSFORM** drop-down menu in the **Toolbar** and then click on the **Manual Explode** tool, see Figure 13.25. The **Auto Explode** toolbar appears in the graphics area. Also, the Green and Red sliders appear on the **Timeline**, see Figure 13.26. Next, select a component to be exploded manually, in the graphics area. A Triad with different axes appears along with the selected component in the graphics area, see Figure 13.27.

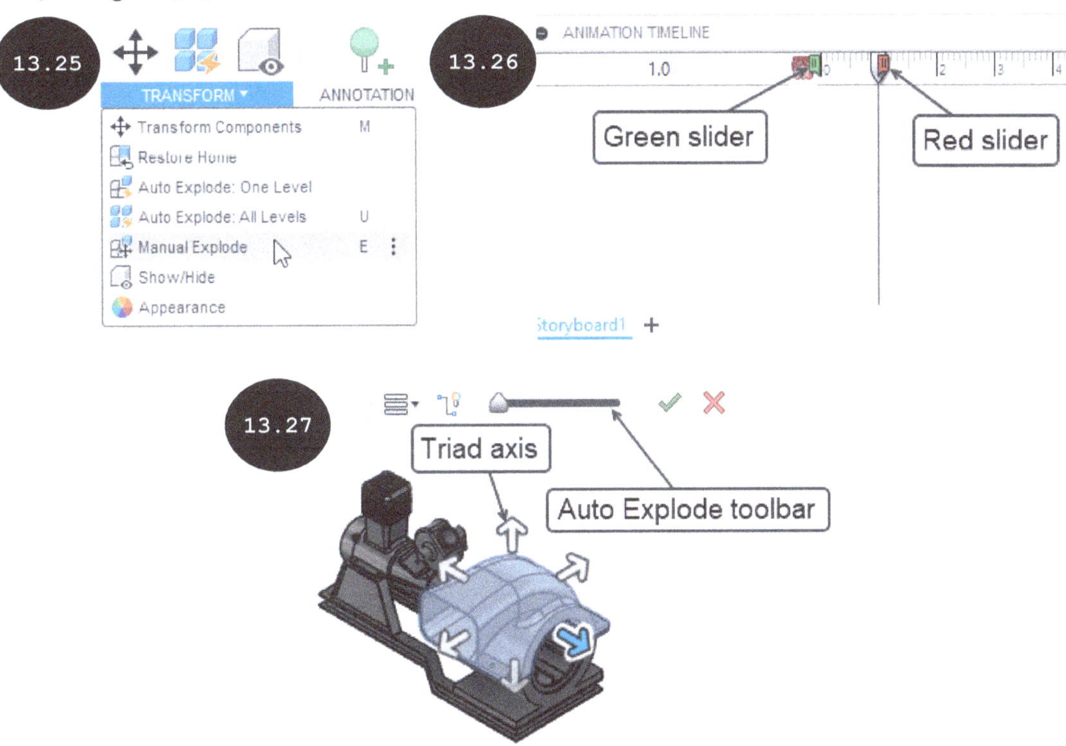

Select an axis of the Triad as the direction of explosion for the selected component in the graphics area. You can similarly select other components to be exploded and define the direction of the explosion, one by one in the graphics area. You can also select a set of components by pressing the CTRL key. After selecting the components and defining the direction of the explosion, specify the type of explosion (**One-Step Explosion** or **Sequential Explosion**), trail lines visibility, and explosion scale in the **Auto Explode** toolbar, as discussed earlier. A preview of the exploded view of the selected components appears in the graphics area, see Figure 13.28. Also, the exploded actions are captured on the **Timeline**. Now, specify the start and end times for the exploded actions by dragging the Red and Green sliders that appear in the **Timeline**. Next, click on the **OK** button (green tick-mark) in the **Auto Explode** toolbar. The exploded view is created, and the exploded actions are captured on the **Timeline**. You can similarly explode other components of the assembly, manually. After creating the exploded view, you can animate it by clicking on the **Play** button on the storyboard.

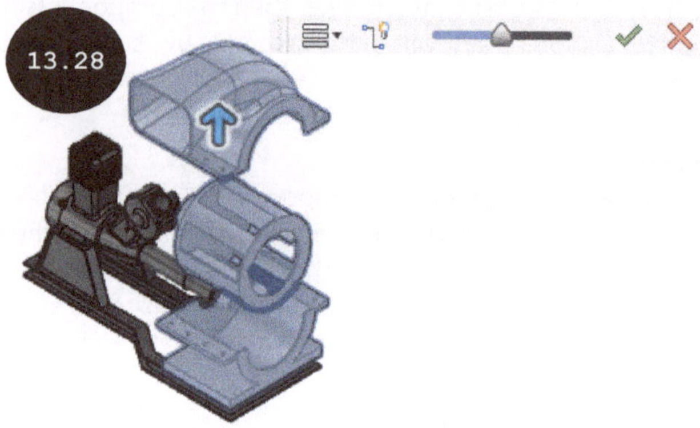

Toggling on or off the Visibility of Components

In Autodesk Fusion, you can capture actions on the **Timeline** by turning on or off the visibility of components at a given point in time on the **Timeline**. To do this, first define the position of the **Playhead** on the **Timeline** at a positive point in time, where the visibility of the component is to be turned off. Next, select the component in the graphics area. After selecting the component, click on the **Show/Hide** tool in the **TRANSFORM** panel of the **Toolbar**, see Figure 13.29. The visibility of the selected component gets turned off in the graphics area. Also, a visibility action is captured and added below the name of the selected component on the **Timeline**, see Figure 13.30.

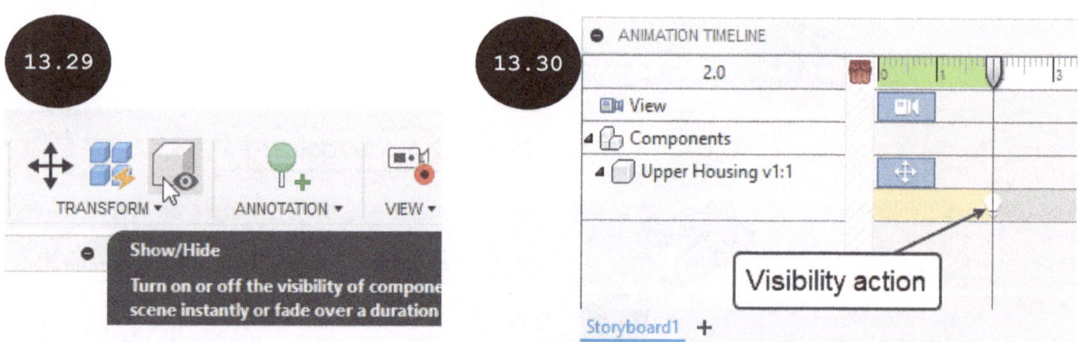

Now, when you play the animation, you will notice that the visibility of the selected component gets turned off instantly at the specified point in time. This is because, the **Instant** option is defined for the visibility action, by default. You can define the start and end times for the visibility action so that the component fades slowly. To do this, right-click on the light bulb icon of the visibility action in the **Timeline** and then click on the **Edit Start/End** option in the shortcut menu that appears, see Figure 13.31. The **Start/End** toolbar appears with the **Start** field only, see Figure 13.32. Click on the arrow next to the

Instant option in the **Toolbar** and then select the **Duration** option, see Figure 13.32. Both **Start** and **End** fields appear in the **Toolbar**, see Figure 13.33. Now, you can specify the start and end times of the action in the respective fields of the **Toolbar** and then click on the **OK** button. Now, when you play the animation, you will notice that the component starts fading from its start time and gets hidden at its end time on the **Timeline**. You will learn more about editing actions later in this chapter.

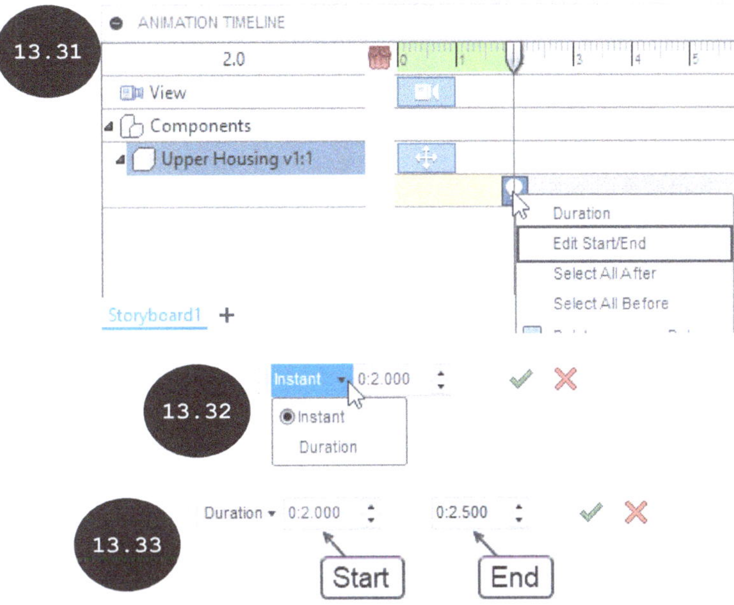

Creating a Callout with Annotation

In Autodesk Fusion, you can also capture the action on the **Timeline** by tagging a callout with text or annotation on a component. To do this, first, define the position of the **Playhead** on the **Timeline** and then click on the **Create Callout** tool in the **ANNOTATION** panel of the **Toolbar**. A callout gets attached to the cursor. Next, click on the component to tag the callout. A Text window appears, see Figure 13.34. Enter the information to be tagged with the selected component in the Text window and then click on the green tick-mark that appears above it. The callout is tagged to the selected component. Also, the callout action is captured at the specified point in time on the **Timeline**. Now, when you hover the cursor over the callout, the text appears in the graphics area.

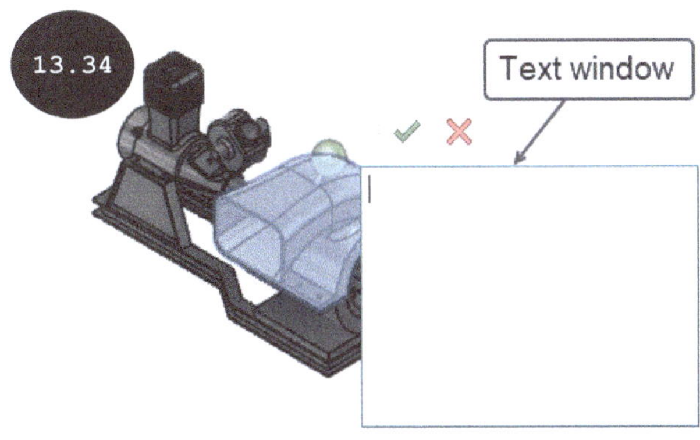

Customizing Views and Actions on the Timeline

In Autodesk Fusion, after capturing views and actions on the **Timeline**, you can customize them by editing their start and end times. To edit the start time of an action, move the cursor over its start time (left end) on the **Timeline** until the cursor changes to a double arrow, see Figure 13.35. Next, drag the cursor to set the new start time for the action on the **Timeline**, see Figure 13.36. You can similarly edit the end time of the action, as required. On editing the start and end times of an action, you can control the total duration of the action on the **Timeline**. You can also edit the duration of an action as discussed earlier.

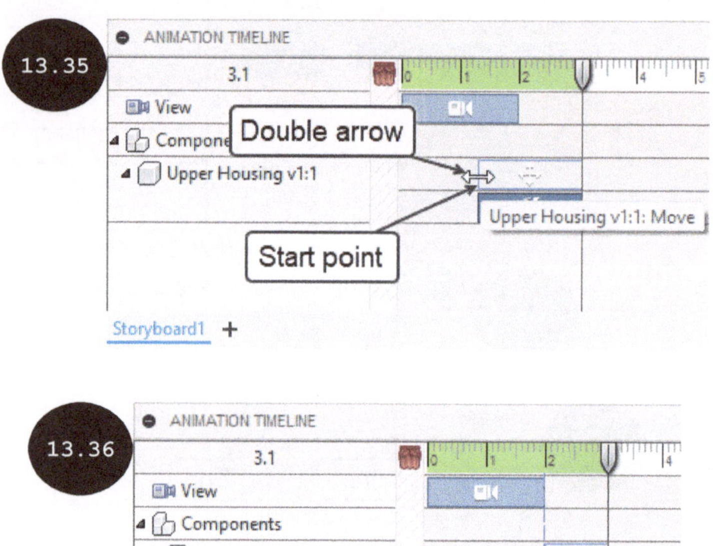

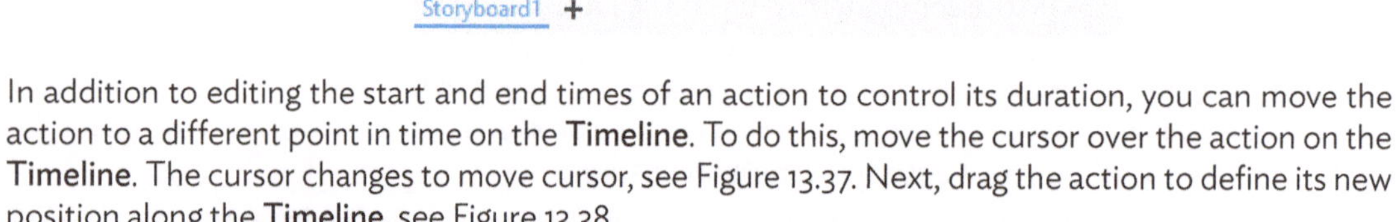

In addition to editing the start and end times of an action to control its duration, you can move the action to a different point in time on the **Timeline**. To do this, move the cursor over the action on the **Timeline**. The cursor changes to move cursor, see Figure 13.37. Next, drag the action to define its new position along the **Timeline**, see Figure 13.38.

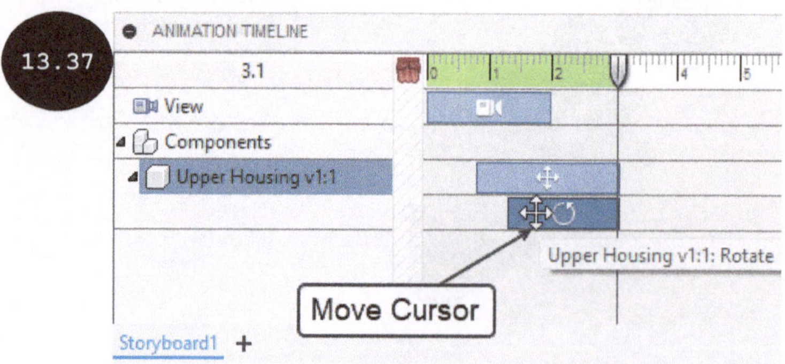

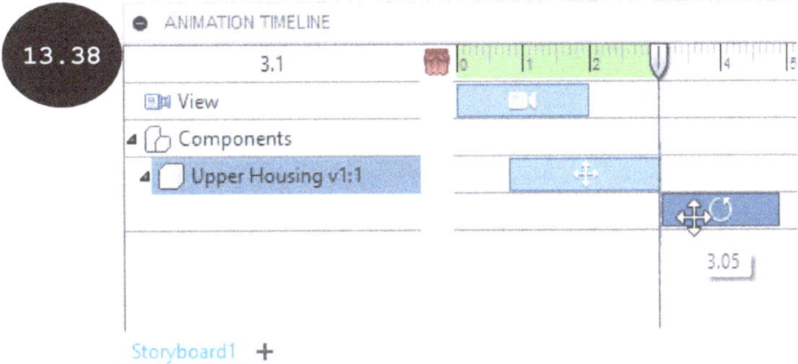

After creating the required actions and views for a storyboard, you can play the animation by clicking on the **Play** button available at the lower middle part of the storyboard, see Figure 13.39.

Deleting Views and Actions of a Storyboard

In Autodesk Fusion, you can also delete views and actions of a storyboard. To do this, right-click on a view or an action to be deleted on the **Timeline** of a storyboard. A shortcut menu appears, see Figure 13.40. In this shortcut menu, click on the **Delete** option. The selected view or action gets deleted from the **Timeline** of the storyboard.

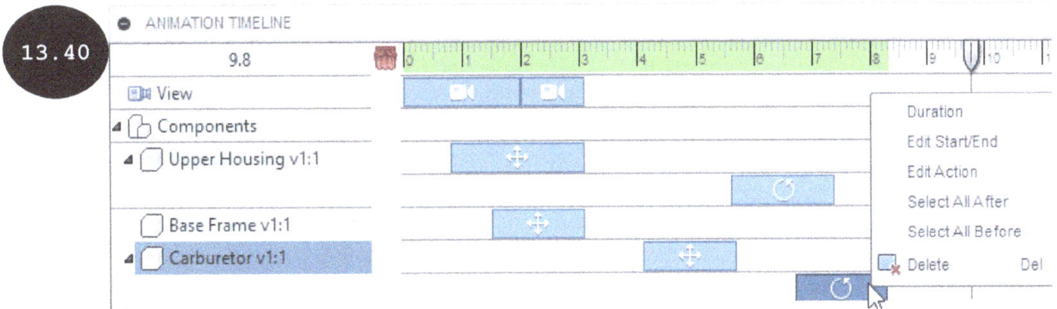

Creating a New Storyboard

In Autodesk Fusion, on invoking the **ANIMATION** workspace, an empty storyboard is created with a default name (**Storyboard1**) automatically, at the bottom of the screen. In addition to the default storyboard created, you can create a new storyboard and add the required views and actions. To do this, click on the **New Storyboard** tool in the **STORYBOARD** panel of the **Toolbar**, see Figure 13.41. The **NEW STORYBOARD** dialog box appears, see Figure 13.42. On selecting the **Clean** option in the **Storyboard Type** drop-down list of the dialog box, a new empty storyboard is created with no action and the transformation of the components is the same as they are brought from the **DESIGN** workspace. On selecting the **Start from end of previous** option, a new empty storyboard is created with no action and the transformation of the components is the same as they are at the end of the previous storyboard.

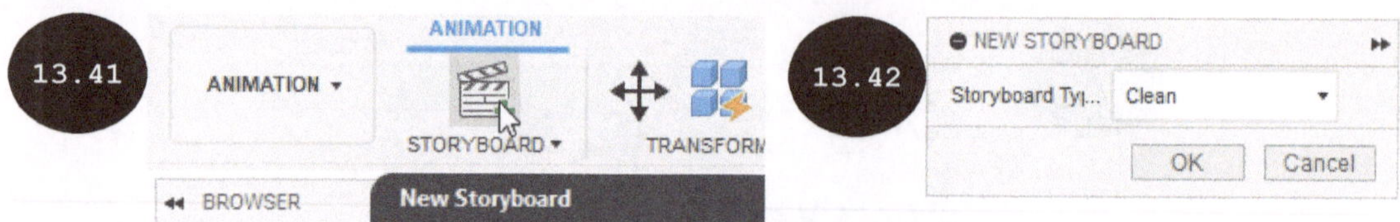

Select the required option in the **Storyboard Type** drop-down list of the dialog box and then click on the **OK** button. A new empty storyboard is created with a default name and becomes the active storyboard, see Figure 13.43. Now, you can add different views and actions for the newly created storyboard, as discussed earlier. Alternatively, you can create a new storyboard by clicking on the **Plus** sign next to the existing storyboard tab, see Figure 13.43.

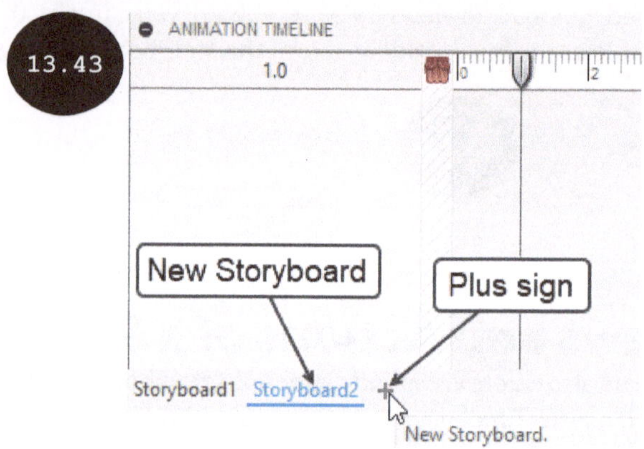

Note: When you publish the animation of a storyboard, the name of the storyboard appears on the web as its title. As a result, it is recommended to rename the storyboard accordingly. To do this, right-click on the storyboard tab at the lower left corner of the screen and then click on the **Rename** option in the shortcut menu that appears, see Figure 13.44. Now, you can enter a new name for the storyboard. You will learn about publishing the animation of a storyboard later in this chapter.

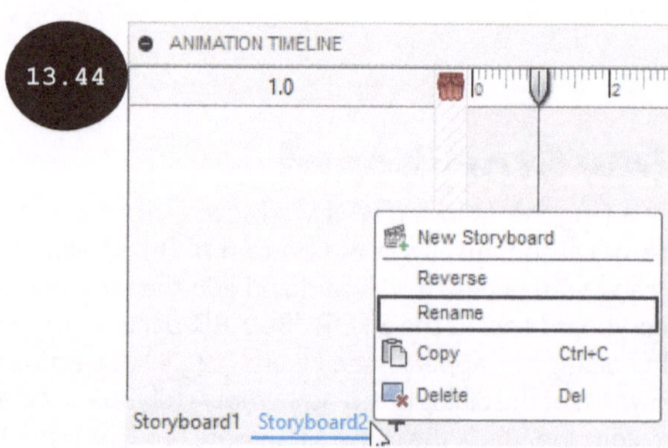

Toggling On or Off Capturing Views

In Autodesk Fusion, when the **Playhead** is positioned at a positive point in time on the **Timeline**, the views get captured or recorded automatically on performing the navigating operations. However, to set up a scene in preparation for animation, you may need to turn off the capturing of views. To turn on or off the capturing of views, click on the **View** tool in the **Toolbar** (see Figure 13.45), or press **CTRL + R**. The automatic capturing of navigation operations as views can be turned on or off, respectively. Note that it is a toggle button.

13.45

ANNOTATION
VIEW
PUBLISH
View (Ctrl+R)

Note: In Autodesk Fusion, you can capture the actions, even if the recording/capturing of views are turned off by using the **View** tool of the **Toolbar**.

Playing and Publishing Animation

After capturing all views and actions on the **Timeline** of a storyboard, you can play the animation as well as publish it to a video file format. To play the animation, click on the **Play** button at the lower middle part of the storyboard, see Figure 13.46.

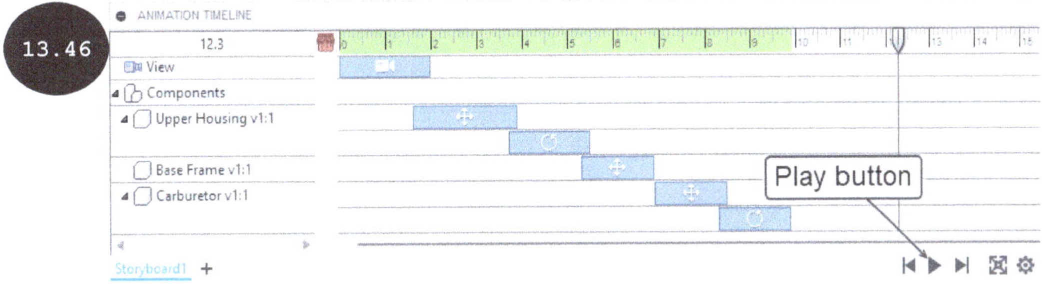

To publish the animation as a video file format, click on the **Publish Video** tool in the **PUBLISH** panel of the **Toolbar**, (see Figure 13.47) or press the **P** key. The **Video Options** dialog box appears, see Figure 13.48. In the **Storyboard** drop-down list of the dialog box, specify whether to publish the animation of all storyboards or only the currently active storyboard by selecting the **All Storyboards** or the **Current Storyboard** option, respectively.

In the **Video Resolution** area of the dialog box, specify the resolution/size of the video file to be published. The **Current Document Window Size** option in this area is used for publishing the video using the pixel size and resolution of the current environment. Next, click on the **OK** button in the dialog box. The **Save As** dialog box appears. In this dialog box, enter the name of the video file and specify the location to save the video in a local drive of your computer or a project in the Autodesk cloud. Next, click on the **Save** button. The video file (*.avi*) is saved in the specified location.

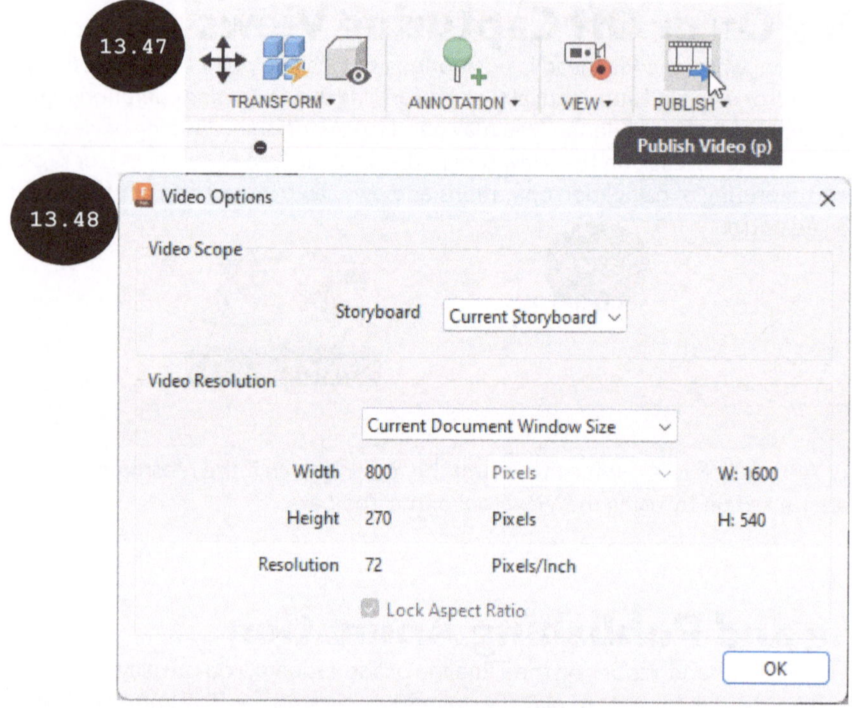

Tutorial 1

Open the assembly created in Tutorial 1 of Chapter 11 (see Figure 13.49) and then create the animation by exploding its components sequentially one after the other in the **ANIMATION** workspace.

Section 1: Opening Tutorial 1 of Chapter 11

1. Launch Autodesk Fusion, if it is not already running.

2. Open the assembly created in Tutorial 1 of Chapter 11, see Figure 13.49.

Section 2: Invoking the ANIMATION Workspace

1. Invoke the **Workspace** drop-down menu, see (Figure 13.50) and then click on ANIMATION. The startup user interface of the ANIMATION workspace appears, see Figure 13.51.

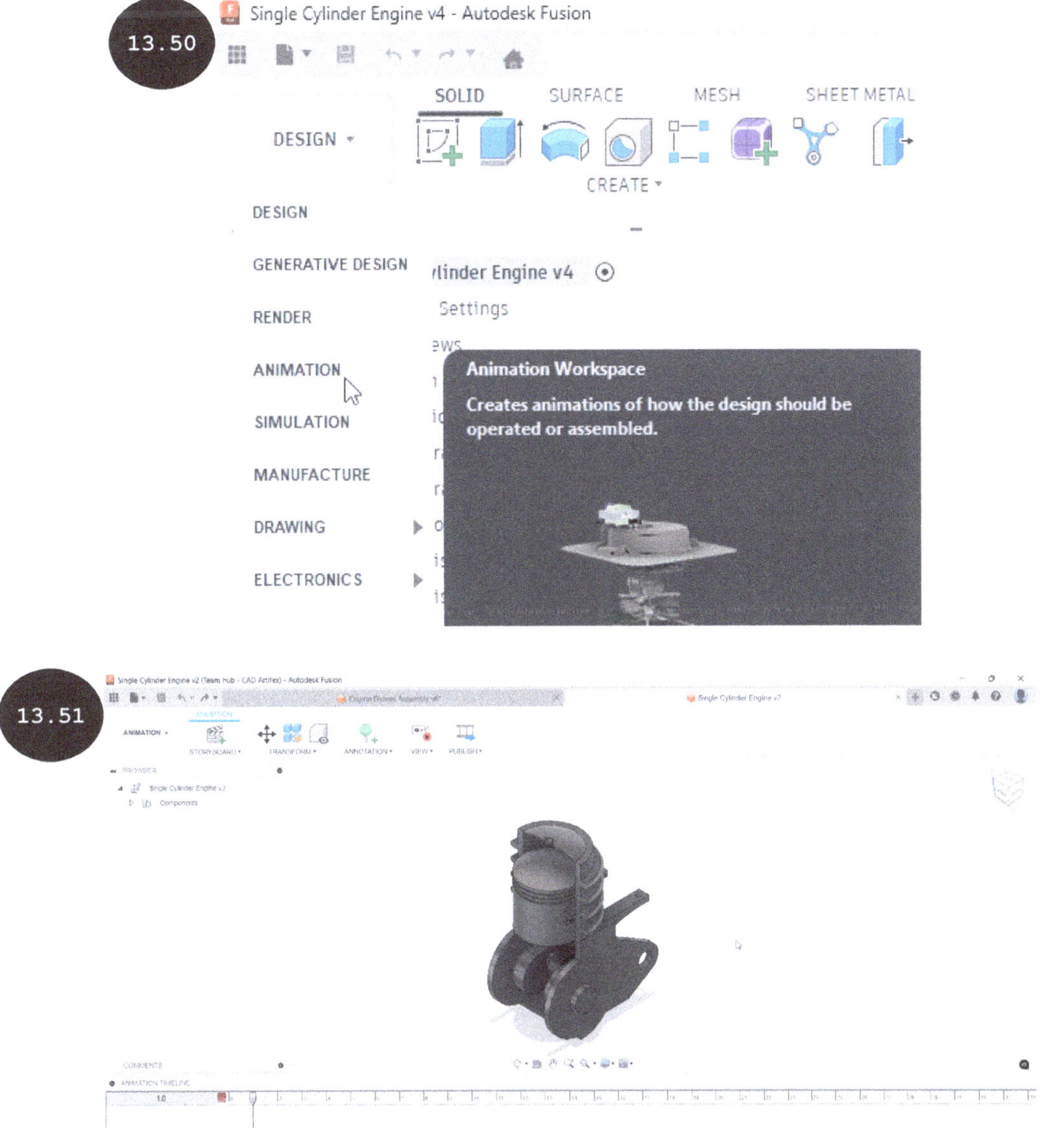

Section 3: Creating Exploded View

1. Define the **Playhead** position to time 2 seconds on the **Timeline** to capture the view, see Figure 13.52.

2. Navigate the assembly such that it fits within the screen. The view is captured at time 2 seconds on the **Timeline**, see Figure 13.53.

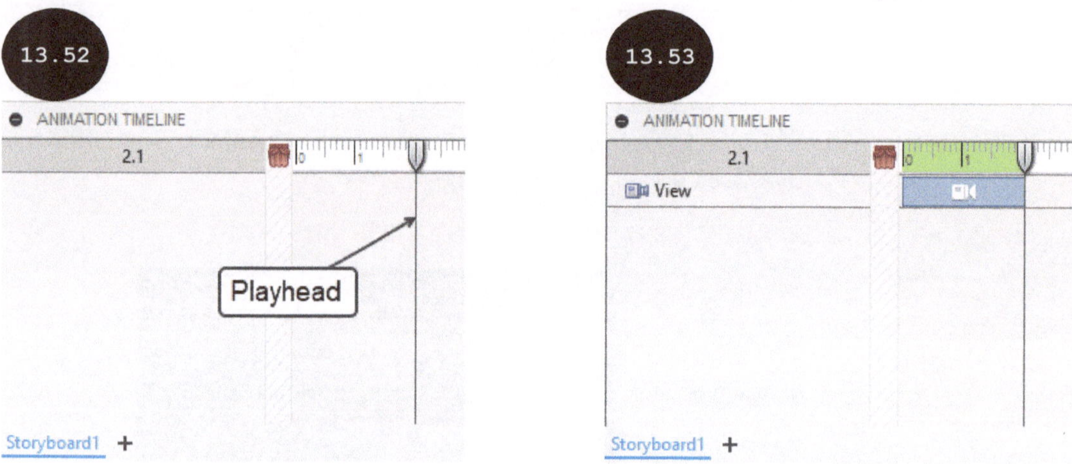

3. Expand the **Components** node in the **BROWSER** and then click on the **Single Cylinder Engine** (*name of the assembly*), see Figure 13.54. All components of the assembly get selected and highlighted in the graphics area.

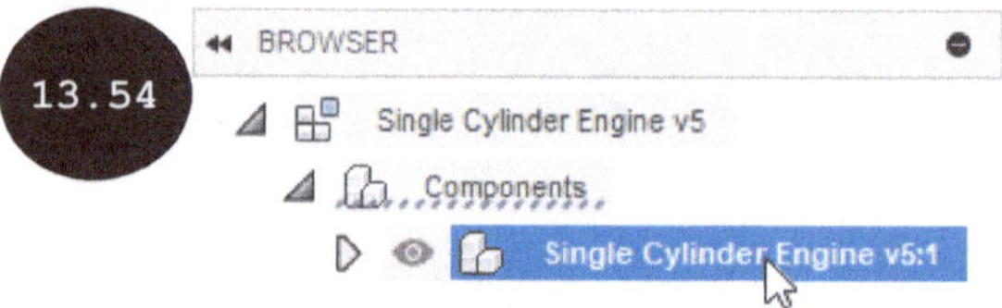

4. Click on the **Auto Explode: All Levels** tool in the **TRANSFORM** panel in the **Toolbar** (see Figure 13.55) to explode all components of the assembly including sub-assemblies, if any. The process of exploding all components of the assembly gets started and once it is completed, the preview of the exploded view of the assembly and the **Auto Explode** toolbar appears in the graphics area, see Figure 13.56. Also, the Green and Red sliders appear on the **Timeline** representing the start and end times of the explosion. By default, the **One-Step Explosion** option is selected in the **Auto Explode** toolbar. As a result, all components of the assembly are exploded at the same time and the exploded actions are captured, accordingly on the **Timeline**, see Figure 13.56.

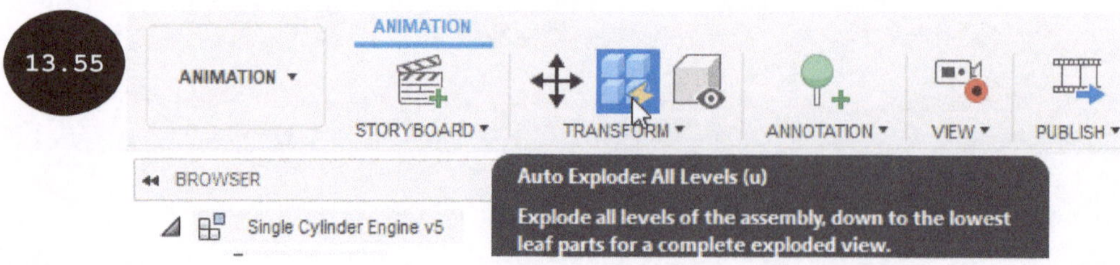

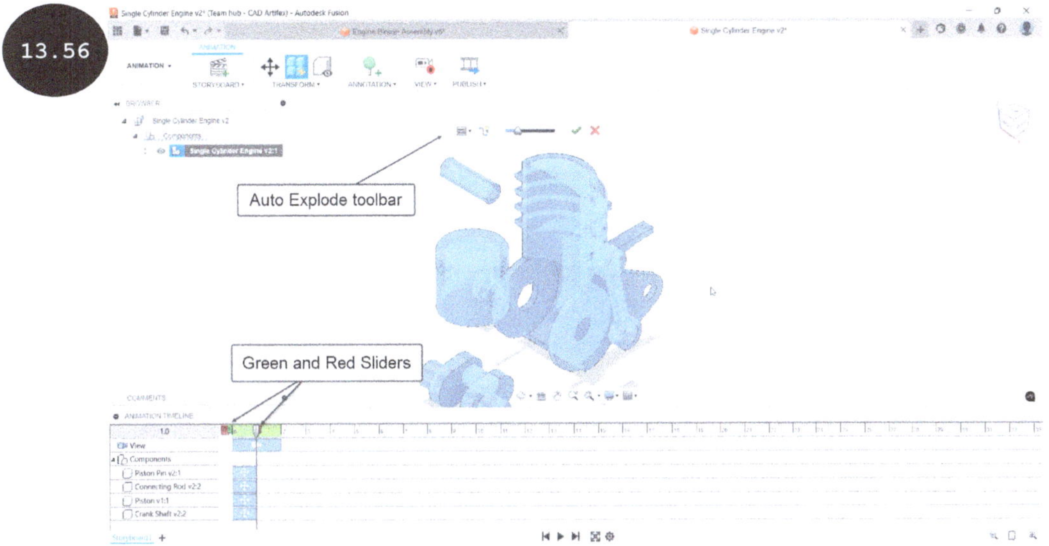

5. In the **Auto Explode** toolbar, invoke the **Type** drop-down list, (see Figure 13.57) and then click on the **Sequential Explosion** tool. Each component of the assembly gets exploded sequentially and the actions are captured accordingly on the **Timeline**, see Figure 13.58.

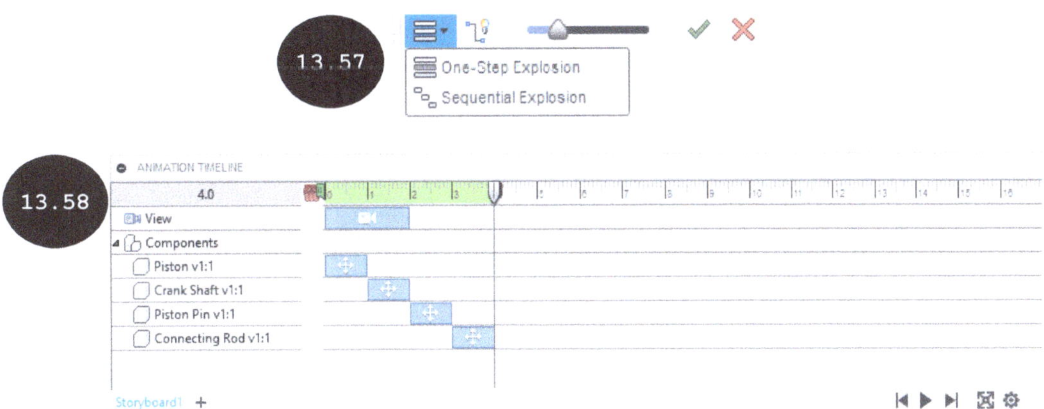

6. Adjust the expansion scale by dragging the **Explosion Scale** slider of the **Auto Explode** toolbar, as required.

7. Drag the Green slider to time 2.15 seconds on the **Timeline** as the start time of the explosion, see Figure 13.59.

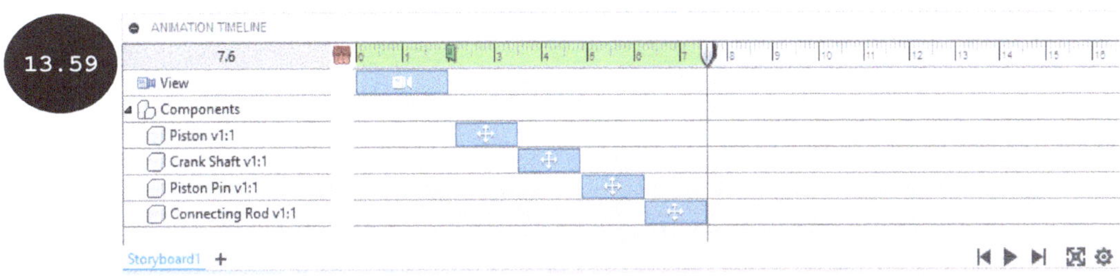

8. Drag the Red slider to time **10** seconds on the **Timeline** as the end time of the explosion. Note that if the slider does not snap to time **10** seconds, you can specify any time close to **10** seconds and then edit it manually.

9. Click on the **OK** button (green tick-mark) in the **Auto Explode** toolbar. The exploded view is created, and the explosion actions are captured on the **Timeline**. Next, click anywhere in the graphics area to exit the selection set.

10. Navigate the assembly such that the exploded view fits within the screen. A view is captured on Timeline.

Section 4: Editing Actions

1. Move the cursor over the left end of the first action captured on the **Timeline**. The cursor changes to a double arrow, see Figure 13.60. Next, drag the cursor to time 2 seconds on the **Timeline** as the start time of the first action, see Figure 13.60.

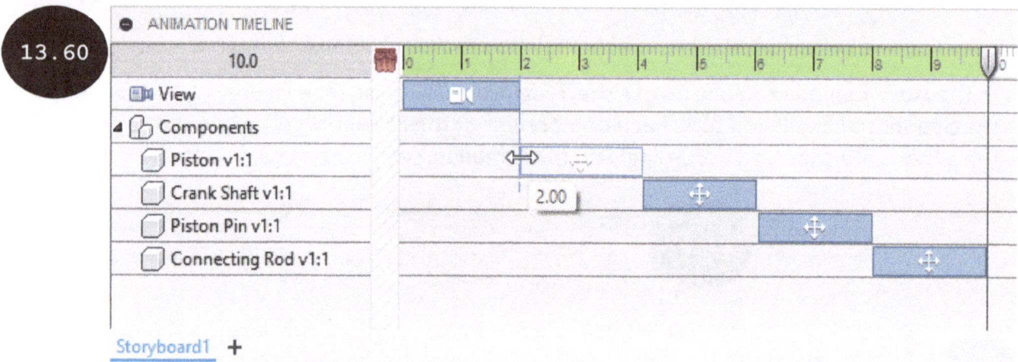

2. Similarly, scroll down the **Timeline** and then edit the end time of the last action to time 10 seconds.

Section 5: Renaming the Storyboard

1. Right-click on the Storyboard tab at the lower left corner of the screen. The shortcut menu appears, see Figure 13.61.

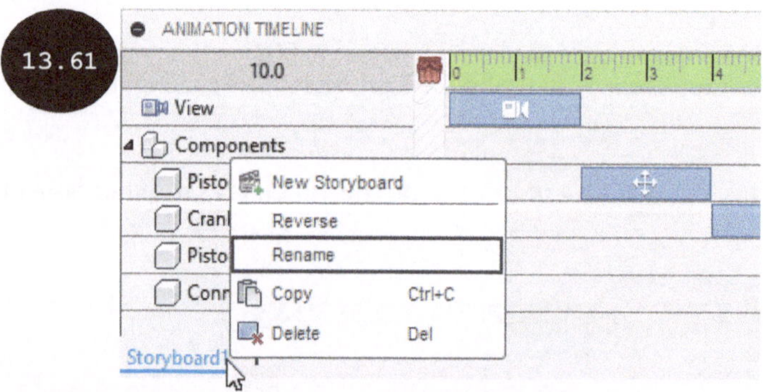

2. Click on the **Rename** option in the shortcut menu. An edit field appears.

3. Enter **Exploded View Animation** in the edit field as the name of the storyboard.

Section 6: Playing Animation

1. Click on the **Play** button at the lower middle part of the storyboard. The animation of the exploded view starts in the graphics area.

Section 7: Publishing and Saving the Animation

1. Click on the **Publish Video** tool in the **PUBLISH** panel of the **Toolbar**. The **Video Options** dialog box appears, see Figure 13.62.

2. Ensure that the **Current Storyboard** option is selected in the **Storyboard** drop-down list of the **Video Options** dialog box.

3. Accept the remaining options of the dialog box and then click on the **OK** button. The **Save As** dialog box appears.

4. Enter **Single Cylinder Engine Exploded View** in the **Name** field of the dialog box as the name of the video file.

5. Ensure that the **Save to a project in the cloud** check box is cleared in the dialog box.

6. Select the **Save to my computer** check box in the dialog box and then click on the **Browse** button available to the right of the **Location** field of the dialog box. The **Save to my computer** dialog box appears.

7. Browse to the location where you want to save the video file in the local drive of your computer.

8. Click on the **Save** button in the dialog box. The **Publish Video** window appears, which displays the process of publishing the video, and once the process is completed, the video file is saved with the specified name in the *.avi* file format.

Hands-on Test Drive 1

Open the assembly created in Hands-on Test Drive 2 of Chapter 11 (see Figure 13.63) and then create the exploded view of the assembly manually, by exploding its components one by one in the **ANIMATION** workspace, see Figure 13.64. After creating the exploded view, save the animated video in the *.avi* file format on a local drive of your computer.

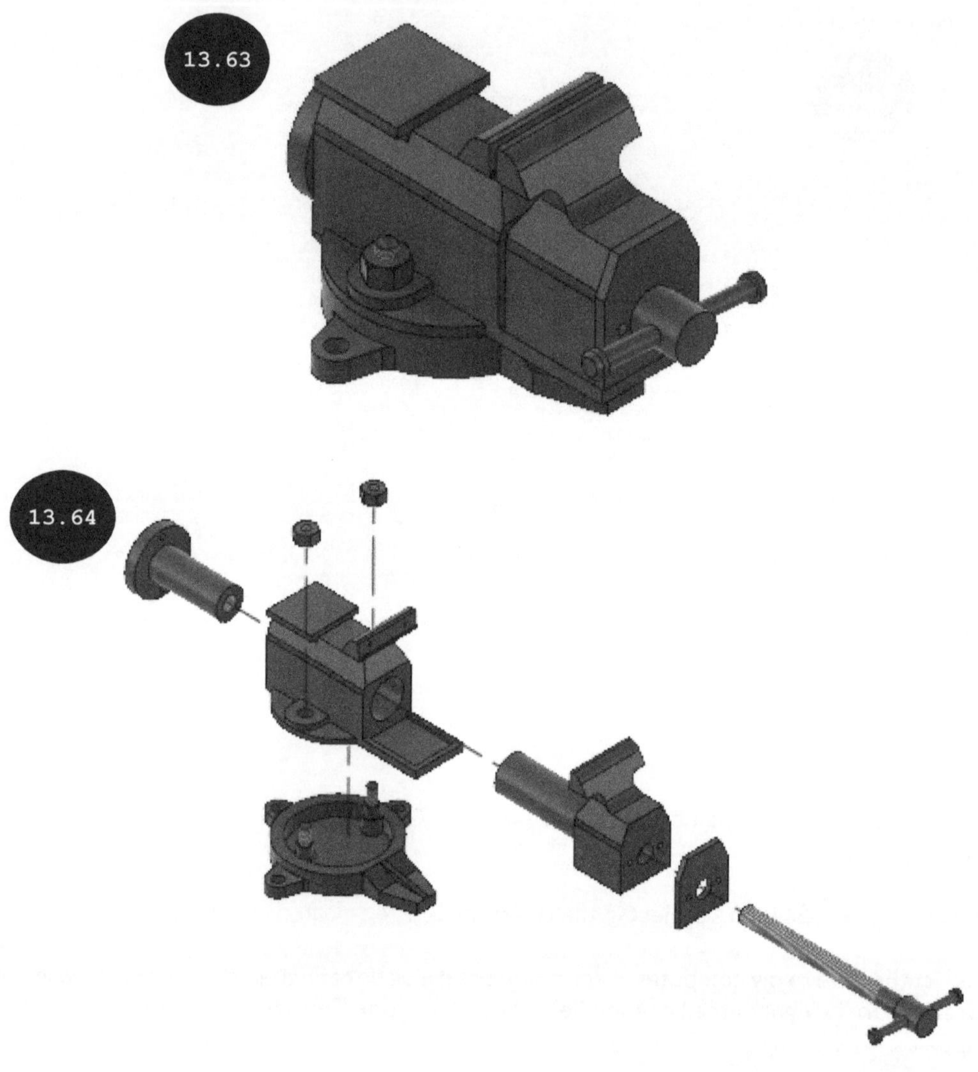

Summary

In this chapter, you learned how to create animations for designs or assemblies in the ANIMATION Workspace of Autodesk Fusion. You explored capturing views and actions on the Timeline, where navigation operations like zooming or orbiting are recorded as views, and transformations such as moving or rotating components are recorded as actions. The chapter also covered creating exploded views (manually or automatically), toggling component visibility, adding callouts, and customizing or deleting Timeline elements. Finally, you learned how to create new storyboards, manage recording options, and publish animations in .avi format, enabling you to effectively animate and present your designs.

Questions

Complete and verify the following sentences:

- In Autodesk Fusion, you can create the animation of a design in the _________ workspace.
- If the position of the _________ is defined on the **Timeline** at **Time 0** (red mark), then the views and actions will not be captured.
- In Autodesk Fusion, any transforming operation such as move or rotate performed at a point in time on a component of an assembly is captured as an _________.
- The _________ button of the **TRANSFORM COMPONENTS** dialog box is used for toggling the visibility of the trail line on or off in the graphics area.
- In Autodesk Fusion, you can create an exploded view of an assembly by using the _________, _________, and _________ tools.
- The _________ tool is used to explode the first-level children's components of the assembly, automatically.
- The _________ tool is used for exploding all levels of the assembly including the sub-assemblies of the components, automatically.
- The _________ option is used for exploding all the components at the same time.
- The _________ option is used for exploding each component of the assembly in sequential order, one after the other.
- The _________ tool is used for turning on or off the visibility of components at a point in time on the **Timeline**.
- The _________ tool is used for adding a callout with text or annotation on a component.
- The _________ tool is used for creating a new empty storyboard.
- The _________ tool is used for publishing the animation as a video file format.

- In Autodesk Fusion, after capturing views and actions on the **Timeline**, you can customize them by editing their start and end times. (True/False)
- In Autodesk Fusion, you cannot delete views and actions of a storyboard. (True/False)
- When you publish the animation of a storyboard, the name of the storyboard appears on the web as its title. (True/False)

14

Working with Drawings

In this chapter, the following topics will be discussed:

- Invoking the DRAWING Workspace
- Creating the Base View of a Design
- Creating Projected Views
- Working with the Angle of Projection
- Defining the Angle of Projection
- Defining Drawing Preferences
- Editing Document and Sheet Settings
- Editing and Inserting a New Title Block
- Creating Section Views
- Creating Detail Views
- Creating Break Views
- Creating an Exploded Drawing View
- Invoking DRAWING Workspace From Animation
- Editing Properties of a Drawing View
- Editing Hatch Properties of a Section View
- Creating a Sketch
- Moving a Drawing View
- Rotating a Drawing View
- Deleting a Drawing View
- Adding Geometries in Drawing Views
- Applying Dimensions
- Editing a Dimension
- Arranging Dimensions
- Breaking Dimension Lines
- Adding Text/Note
- Adding Text/Note With Leader
- Adding the Surface Texture Symbol
- Creating the Bill of Material (BOM)/Part List
- Adding Balloons Manually
- Renumbering Balloons
- Adding Drawing Sheets
- Creating a New Drawing Template
- Exporting a Drawing

After creating parts and assemblies, the next step is to generate 2D drawings. These technical drawings serve as the primary means of communication, conveying detailed information about the end product to be manufactured. 2D drawings are not just visual representations; they act as a language used by engineers to express ideas and provide crucial details about engineered products. Through these drawings, a designer can effectively communicate the specifications of components to the engineers on the shop floor.

The accuracy of these drawings is critical; any errors or missing information can result in faulty production. Therefore, the role of the designer in producing precise and error-free drawings is crucial. To support this, Autodesk Fusion offers a dedicated workspace known as **DRAWING**, designed to facilitate the generation of reliable, error-free 2D drawings for production.

The **DRAWING** workspace in Autodesk Fusion enables you to create precise 2D drawings of individual components or assemblies created in the **DESIGN** workspace. It also allows you to generate 2D drawings of exploded assembly views created in the **ANIMATION** workspace.

Invoking the DRAWING Workspace

Once you have created a design (part or assembly) in the **DESIGN** workspace, you can switch to the **DRAWING** workspace to generate its drawings. To do this, invoke the **Workspace** drop-down menu in the design file and click on **DRAWING > From Design**, see Figure 14.1. The **CREATE DRAWING** dialog box appears, see Figure 14.2.

Tip: If the design file has not been saved, the **Save** dialog box appears first, prompting you to save the design before creating its drawing.

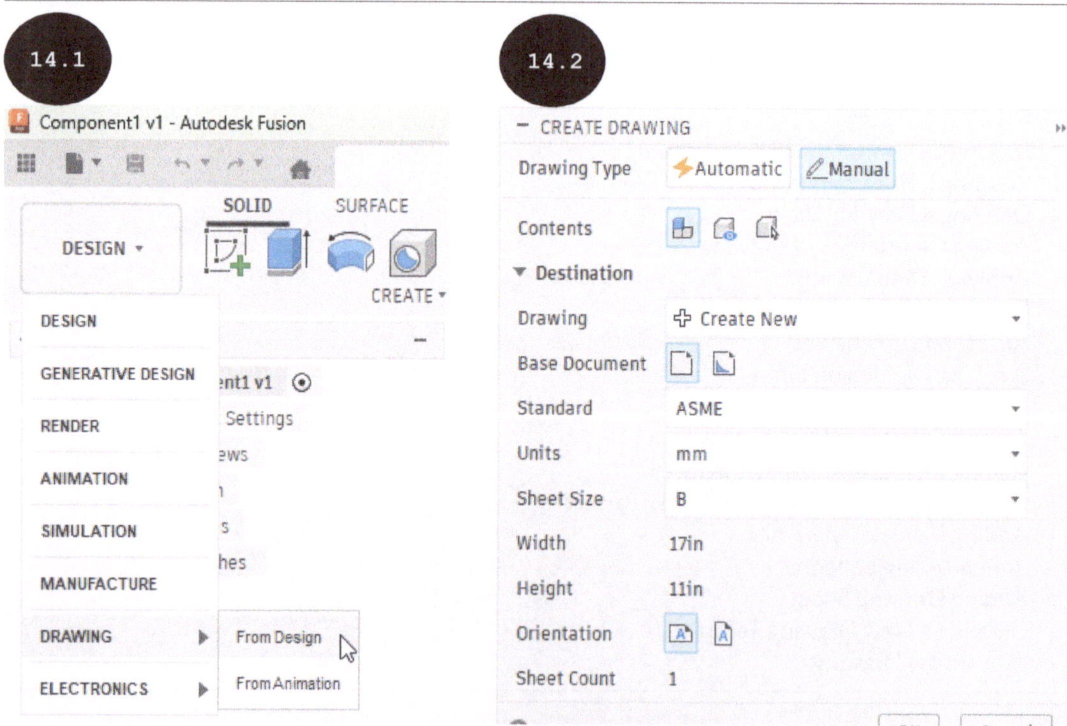

The options in the **CREATE DRAWING** dialog box allow you to define the drawing type (Automatic or Manual), drawing contents, drafting standard, units, sheet size, sheet orientation, and other related settings before creating the drawing, refer to Figure 14.2.

Note: Autodesk Fusion allows you to invoke the **DRAWING** workspace from either a design file or an animation file by selecting the respective option: **From Design** or **From Animation**, refer to Figure 14.2.

The **From Design** option is used to create drawing views from a design file (part or assembly), whereas the **From Animation** option is used to create drawing views from the exploded views of an assembly created in the **ANIMATION** workspace. You will learn how to invoke the **DRAWING** workspace from an animation file later in this chapter.

Alternatively, right-click the design name (top browser node) in the **BROWSER** and select the **Create Drawing** option from the shortcut menu, see Figure 14.3. The **CREATE DRAWING** dialog box appears, where you can define the drawing settings.

You can also invoke the **CREATE DRAWING** dialog box by clicking on the **Drawing** button in the **What do you want to design?** dialog box, which appears each time you start a new design file in Autodesk Fusion, see Figure 14.4. You can also choose **Design** or **Animation** from the **From** drop-down list in this dialog box.

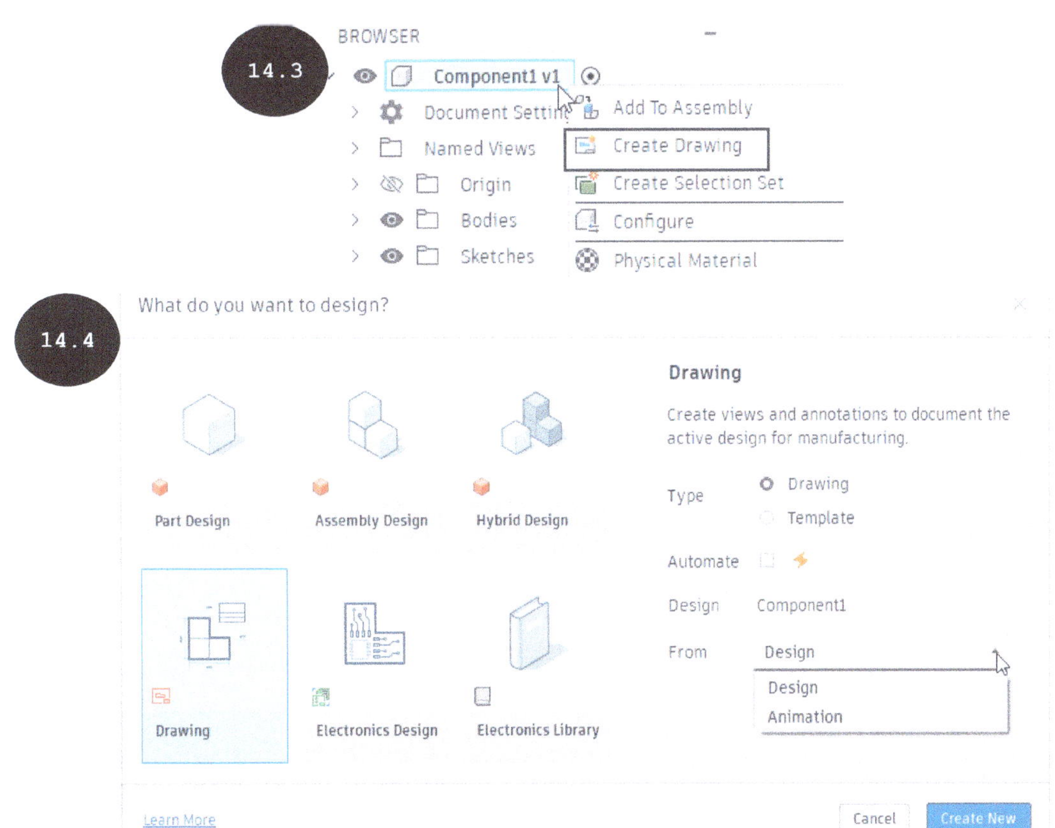

The options in the **CREATE DRAWING** dialog box are discussed next.

Drawing Type

The **Drawing Type** area of the dialog box provides two options: **Automatic** and **Manual**. The **Automatic** option generates multiple drawing view layouts of the design, along with dimensions, based on the defined automation preferences such as base document, drafting standard, units, sheet size, and sheet orientation in the **Automation** rollout of the dialog box. After the layouts are generated, you can select the most suitable arrangement.

The **Manual** option allows you to create the drawing views of the design manually as required.

Contents

The **Contents** area of the dialog box has three buttons: **Full Assembly**, **Visible Only**, and **Select**, see Figure 14.5. On selecting the **Full Assembly** option, all the components of the assembly get selected automatically for creating the drawing. Even if the visibility of some of the components of the assembly is turned off or hidden in the graphics area, they will still be included in the selection set for creating the drawing. On selecting the **Visible Only** option, only the visible components of the assembly get selected for creating the drawing. On selecting the **Select** option, the **Components** selection option appears in the dialog box, which is used for selecting components of the assembly for creating the drawing.

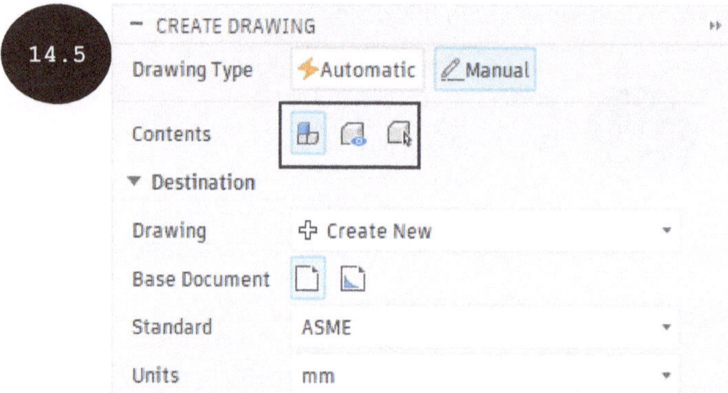

Destination

The options in the **Destination** rollout of the dialog box are used to specify the drawing destination (either create a new drawing or add to an existing drawing), select the base document (from scratch or from a template), and define other related settings. The options are discussed next.

Note: The **Destination** rollout is not enabled when creating a drawing using the **Automatic** option, and some of its settings are instead available in the **Automation** rollout.

Drawing

By default, the **Create New** option is selected in the **Drawing** drop-down list of the dialog box. As a result, you can create a new drawing from scratch. The **Drawing** drop-down list also displays a list of existing drawings created for the design. You can select an existing drawing created for the design in this drop-down list. On doing so, you can add a new sheet of drawing or create drawing views in a sheet of the existing drawing.

Base Document

The **Base Document** area provides two buttons: **From Scratch** and **Template**. These allow you to choose whether to create a drawing from scratch or by using an existing drawing template, respectively.

When you select the **From Scratch** button, you can manually define the required drawing settings such as units, drafting standard, sheet size, orientation, and other document properties using the respective options available in the dialog box, see Figure 14.6.

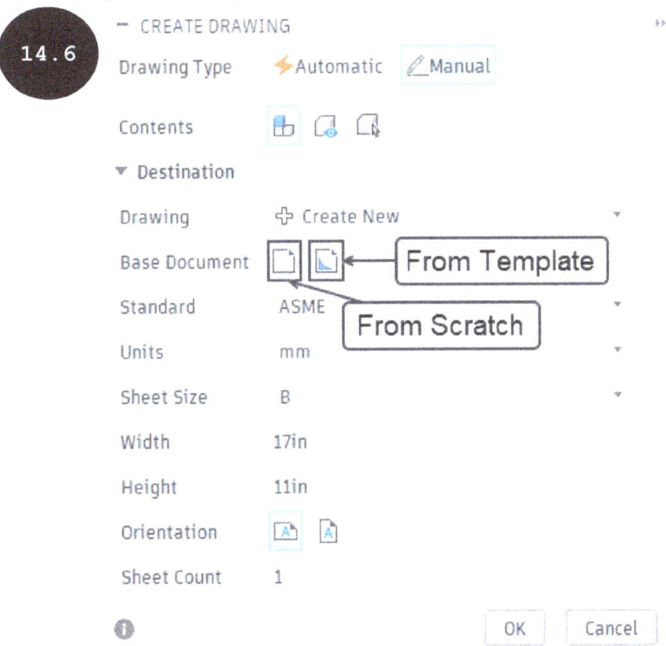

When you select the **Template** button, you can choose the required template from the **Drawing Template** drop-down list. The selected template defines drawing settings such as units, standards, and formats. To select an existing drawing template, choose the **Browse** option from the **Template** drop-down list, see Figure 14.7. The **Select Template** dialog box appears, allowing you to choose the required drawing template for creating the drawing. After selecting the required drawing template, click on the **Select** button in the dialog box. You will learn about creating drawing templates later in this chapter.

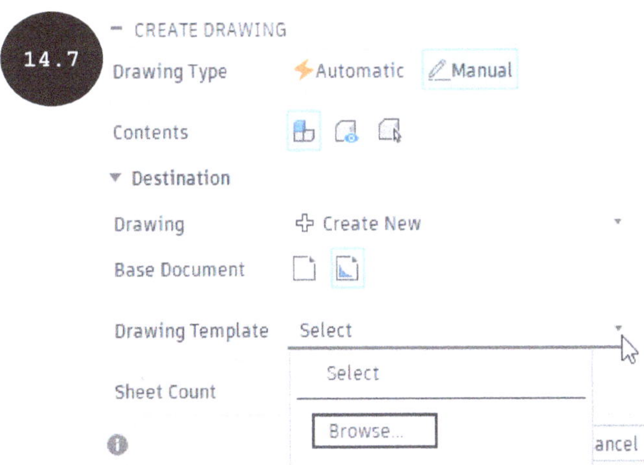

Standard

The **Standard** drop-down list is used to select the drawing standard, such as **ASME** or **ISO**, for creating the drawing. Note that this drop-down list is enabled only when creating a drawing from scratch by activating the **From Scratch** button in the **Base Document** area.

Units

The **Units** drop-down list is used to select the unit of measurement for the drawing. Note that this drop-down list is enabled in the dialog box only when creating a drawing from scratch.

Sheet Size

The **Sheet Size** drop-down list is used for selecting a sheet size for creating the drawing. Note that this drop-down list is enabled when creating a drawing from scratch.

Orientation

The **Orientation** area of the dialog box allows you to define the drawing orientation by selecting either the **Landscape** or **Portrait** button, as required.

Automation

The **Automation** rollout appears only when the **Automatic** button is activated in the **Drawing Type** area to define the automation preferences for creating the drawing automatically, see Figure 14.8.

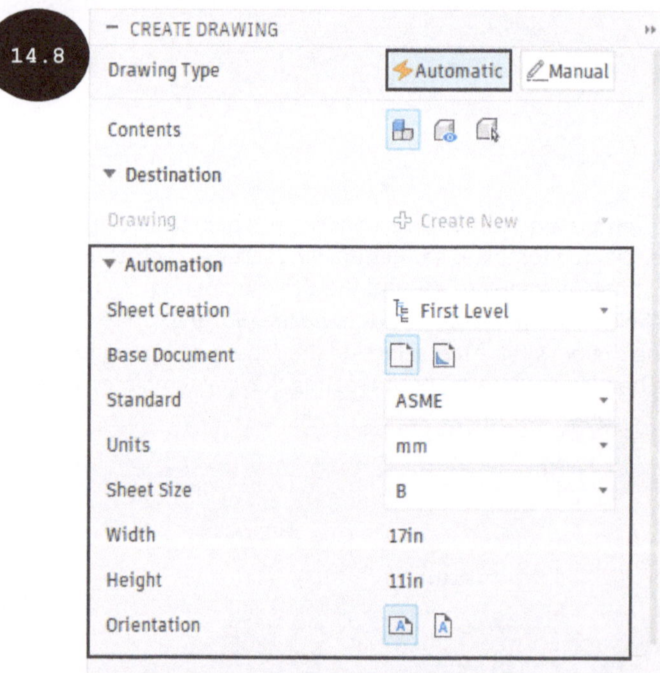

Most of the options available in this rollout are similar to those discussed earlier, except for the options provided in the **Sheet Creation** drop-down list. By default, the **First Level** option is selected in this drop-down list. This option creates drawing sheets only for the first-level components of the assembly. In contrast, the **All Levels** option creates drawing sheets for components across all levels of the assembly hierarchy.

After selecting the required options in the **CREATE DRAWING** dialog box, click the **OK** button.

If you are creating a drawing manually by activating the **Manual** button in the **Drawing Type** area of the dialog box, the **DRAWING** workspace is invoked with a drawing sheet of the specified size, see Figure 14.9. Also, the **DRAWING VIEW** dialog box is displayed, and the base view of the selected design (component or assembly) is attached to the cursor. You are prompted to specify the placement location for the base view. Click to define the placement point, and then specify the required options such as orientation, style, and scale in the dialog box. The options available in this dialog box are discussed later in this chapter. Next, click **OK**. A base view with the specified settings is created on the drawing sheet.

14.9

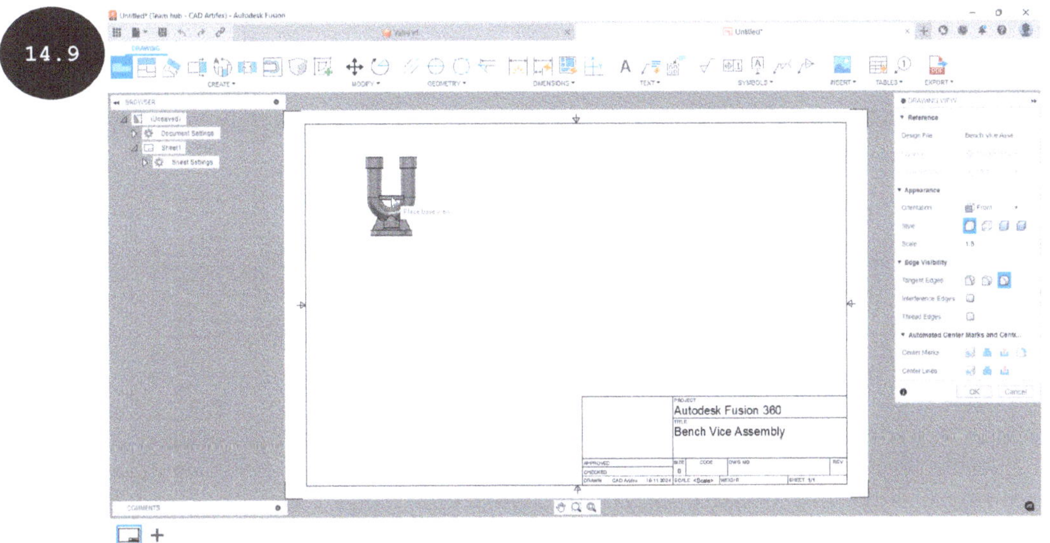

However, if you are creating a drawing automatically by activating the **Automatic** button in the **Drawing Type** area, the system begins generating various drawing layouts in the background after you click the **OK** button. Once the process is complete, the **DRAWING** workspace is invoked, and the **EDIT AUTO DIMENSIONS** dialog box appears displaying multiple alternative drawing view layouts, see Figure 14.10. Select the layout that best meets your requirements, and then click **OK**. The drawing views are generated based on the selected option.

14.10

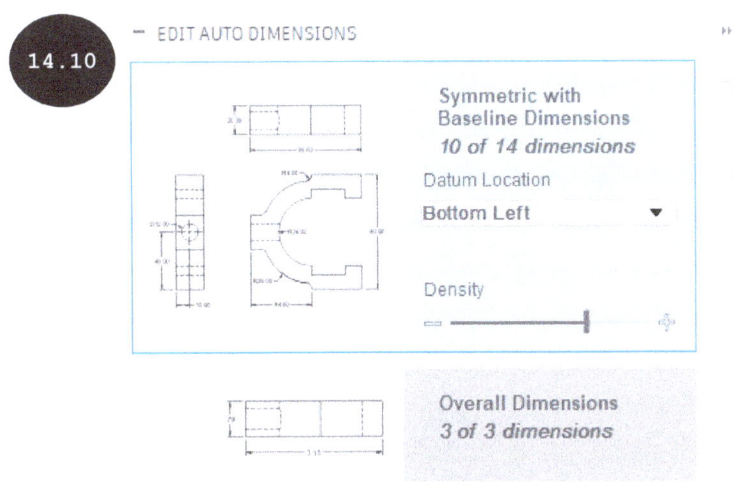

Note: In Autodesk Fusion, each time you invoke the **DRAWING** workspace using the manual method, the **DRAWING VIEW** dialog box appears automatically because the **Base View** tool in the **Toolbar** is activated by default when the **DRAWING** workspace is opened. The options available in the **DRAWING VIEW** dialog box are discussed next.

Creating the Base View of a Design

The base view is an independent view of a design. It is also known as the first or the parent view for generating the orthogonal and isometric projected views of the design. You can create a base view using the **DRAWING VIEW** dialog box, which appears automatically when the **DRAWING** workspace is invoked while creating a drawing manually. You can also invoke the **DRAWING VIEW** dialog box using the **Base View** tool in the **CREATE** panel of the **Toolbar**, see Figure 14.11. The options in the **DRAWING VIEW** dialog box are discussed next.

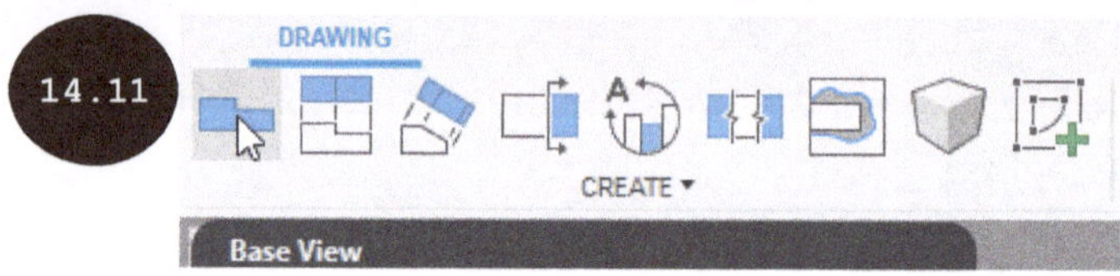

Instance

By default, the **Create New** option is selected in the **Instance** drop-down list of the dialog box. As a result, a new base view instance is added in the **BROWSER** after creating the base view, see Figure 14.12. The **Instance** drop-down list also displays a list of existing base view instances created in the current drawing sheet, see Figure 14.13. You can select any of the existing base view instances in this drop-down list as a reference for the base view to be created. Note that the **Instance** drop-down list is not enabled when the **DRAWING VIEW** dialog box is invoked automatically on invoking the **DRAWING** workspace.

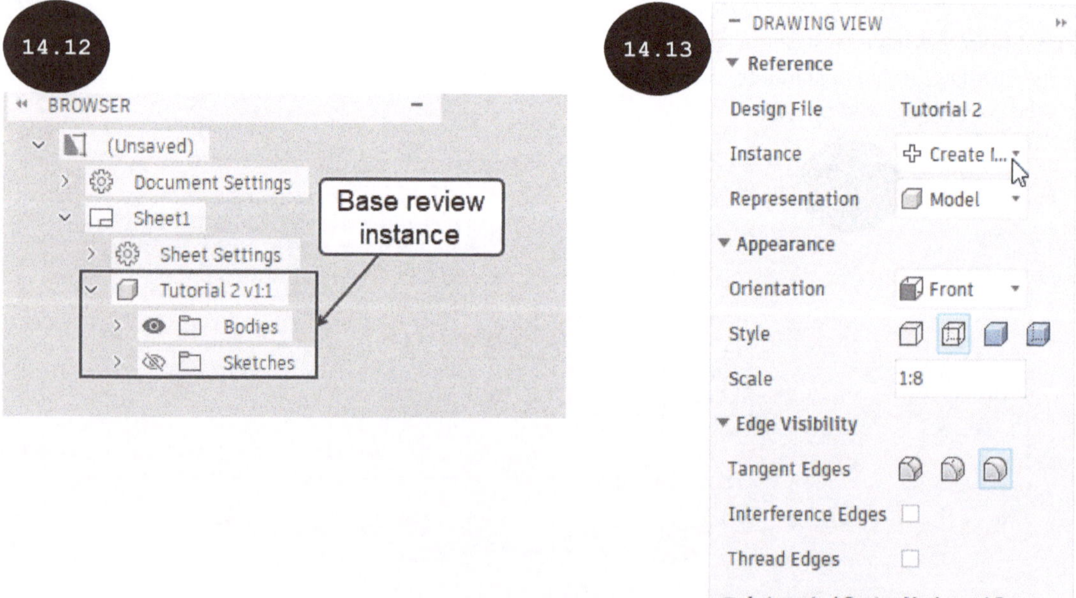

Representation

The **Representation** drop-down list allows you to specify the representation of the base view either as a model or as an exploded view from a storyboard. This drop-down list displays a list of storyboards created for the current design in the **ANIMATION** workspace. By default, the **Model** option is selected in this drop-down list when the **DRAWING** workspace is invoked from a design. So, the base view is represented as a model. You can select a storyboard in this drop-down list to create an exploded view of the design as the base view. Note that the **Representation** drop-down list is not enabled when the **DRAWING VIEW** dialog box is opened automatically on invoking the **DRAWING** workspace from a design.

Appearance

The options in the **Appearance** rollout of the dialog box are used for defining the orientation, visual style, and scale for the base view of the model. The options are discussed next.

Orientation

The **Orientation** drop-down list is used for selecting the orientation such as Front, Top, or Right for the base view of the design to be created.

Style

The **Style** area is used for specifying a visual style for the base view to be created, see Figure 14.14. You can select the **Visible Edges**, **Visible and Hidden Edges**, **Shaded**, or **Shaded with Hidden Edges** button in this area to define the visual style of the model.

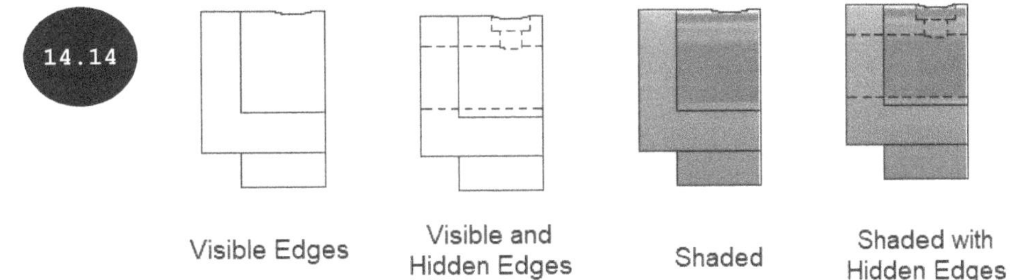

Scale

The **Scale** field is used for specifying a scale for the base view. By default, Autodesk Fusion calculates the most appropriate scale for the base view depending on the sheet size and the volume of the model.

Tangent Edges

The **Tangent Edges** area is used for controlling the display of the tangent edges of the model in the base view. Tangent edges are a smooth transition (tangent continuity) between the faces and the rounded edges (filleted edges). The **Full Length** button of the **Tangent Edges** area is used for displaying the full-length tangent edges of the model in the base view, see Figure 14.15. The **Shortened** button is used for displaying shortened tangent edges in the base view, see Figure 14.15. The **Off** button is used for turning off the display of tangent edges in the base view, see Figure 14.15.

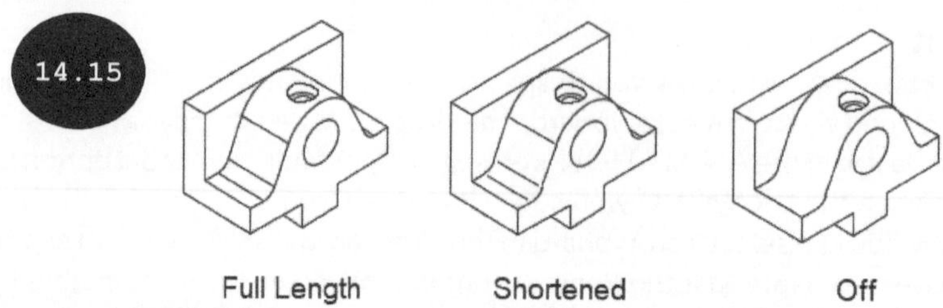

Interference Edges

The **Interference Edges** check box is used for turning on or off the display of interference edges of the model in the base view. Interference edges are edges that occur when the faces of two components intersect each other. By default, the **Interference Edges** check box is cleared in the dialog box. As a result, the display of interference edges is turned off in the base view, see Figure 14.16. On selecting this check box, the display of interference edges is turned on in the base view, see Figure 14.16.

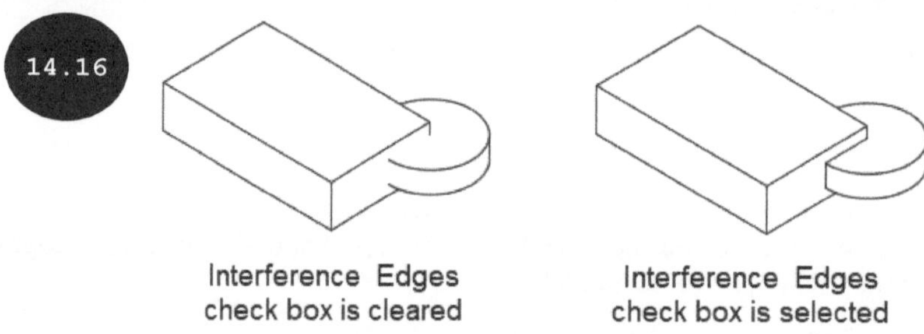

Thread Edges

On selecting the **Thread Edges** check box in the dialog box, the thread edges are represented as dash lines in the drawing views, see Figure 14.17. On clearing this check box, the thread edges representation gets turned off in the drawing views, see Figure 14.18.

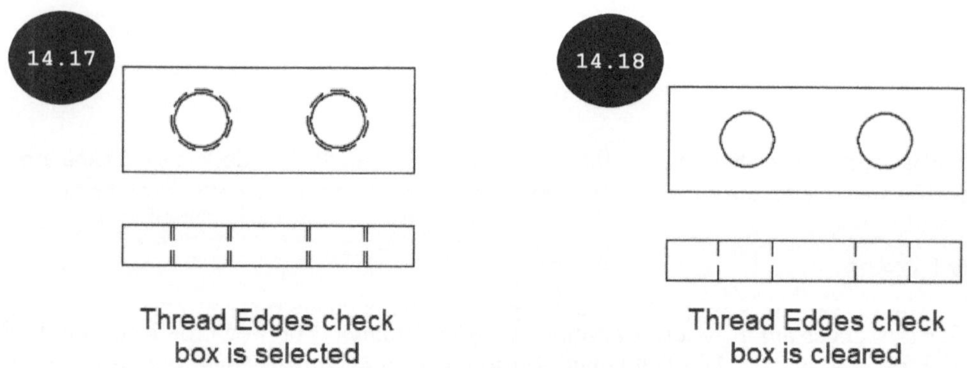

Automated Center Marks and Centerlines

The options in the **Automated Center Marks and Centerlines** rollout are discussed next.

Center Marks

The **Center Marks** area is used for adding center marks to holes, round extrudes, round cuts, patterns, and fillets of the model in the base view by activating the respective buttons. Note that on activating the **Fillet** button for adding center marks to fillets, the **Minimum fillet radius** and **Maximum fillet radius** fields appear in the **Automated Center Marks and Centerlines** rollout. In these fields, you can specify a minimum and a maximum fillet radius between which the center marks are to be added in the base view.

Centerlines

The **Centerlines** area is used for adding centerlines to holes, round extrudes, and round cuts of the model in the base view by activating the respective buttons.After specifying the required settings for creating the base view such as orientation, visual style, and scale factor, click on the drawing sheet to position the base view. The **OK** button of the **DRAWING VIEW** dialog box is enabled. Click on the **OK** button in the dialog box. A base with the specified settings is created in the drawing sheet. After creating the base view of the model, you can generate the orthogonal and isometric projected views from it. The method for generating the projected views is discussed next.

Creating Projected Views

Projected views are orthogonal and isometric views of an object, which are created by viewing the object from different projection sides such as top, front, side, and at a 45 degrees angle. Figure 14.19 and Figure 14.20 show different projected views of an object.

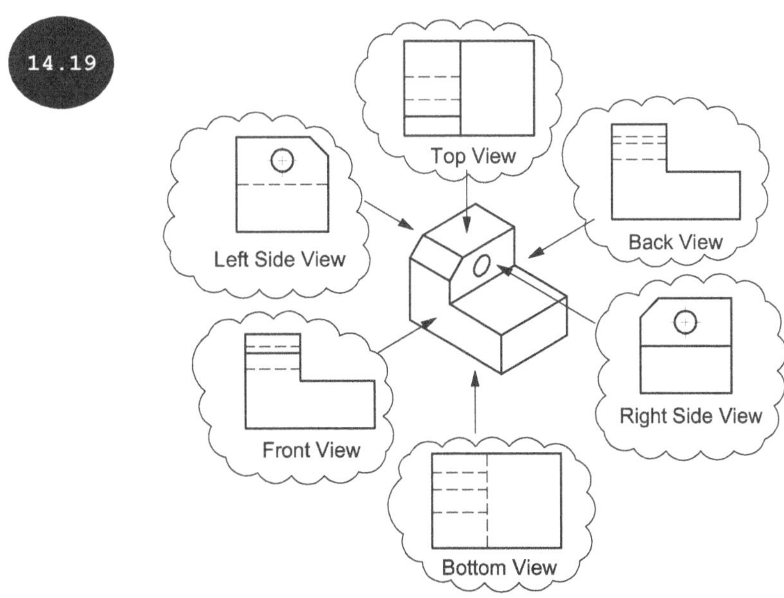

Projected Views

14.20

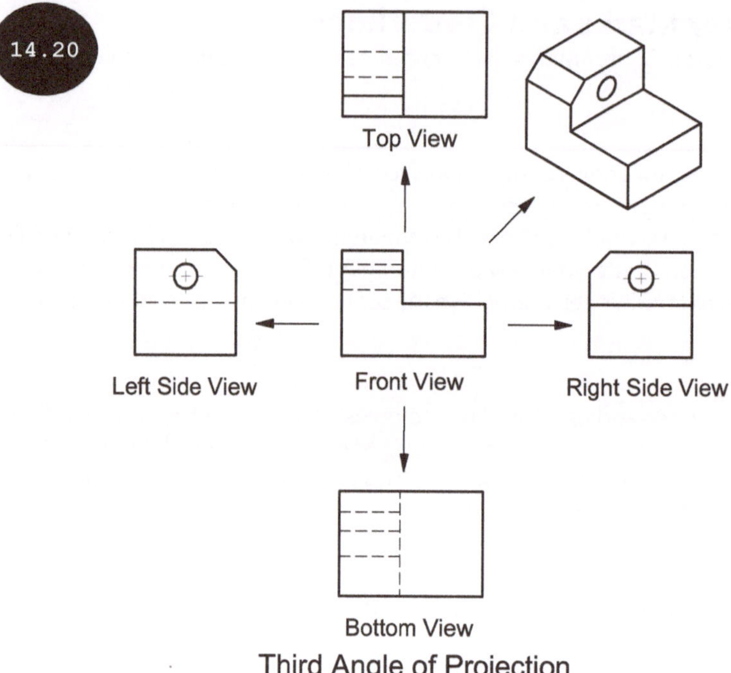

Third Angle of Projection

In Autodesk Fusion, you can create different projected views from a base view using the **Projected View** tool. The method for creating projected views is discussed below:

1. Click on the **Projected View** tool in the **CREATE** panel of the **Toolbar**, see Figure 14.21 or press the P key. The **Projected View** tool gets activated and you are prompted to select a drawing view as the base or parent view for creating its projected views.

14.21

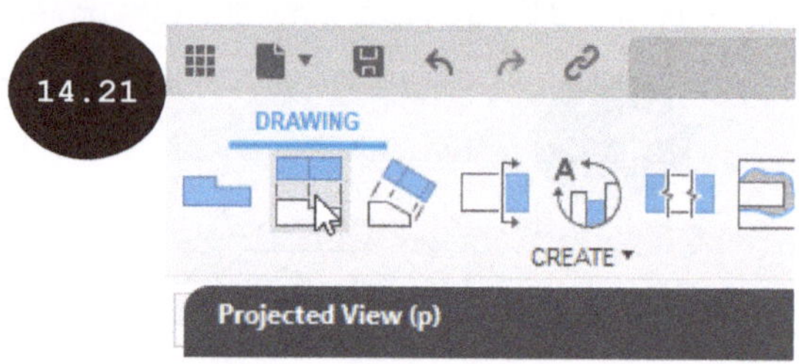

2. Select a drawing view as the base view whose projected views are to be created.

3. Move the cursor to the required location in the drawing sheet. The preview of the projected view appears attached to the cursor depending upon the direction of movement.

Note: The creation of projected views; orthogonal or isometric; depends upon the movement of the cursor. When the cursor is moved at a right angle (horizontally or vertically) to the base view, an orthogonal view gets created, whereas when it is moved at a 45 degrees angle to the base view, an isometric view gets created.

4. Click to specify the placement point for the projected view in the drawing sheet. The projected view is created. Also, a preview of the other projected view appears attached to the cursor.

Note: On creating a projected view, the **Rollback placement and continue** button as well as the **Create and continue** button appear near the projected view. The **Rollback placement and continue** button is used for undoing the creation of the last created projected view and continuing with the creation of projected views. The **Create and continue** button is used for accepting the creation of projected views and exiting the tool.

5. You can continue creating other projected views one after the other by specifying the placement points in the drawing area.

6. After creating all the projected views, press the ENTER key or click on the **Create and continue** button that appears near the last created projected view. The projected views are created. Note that the properties of the base view are propagated to the projected views.

In Autodesk Fusion, the creation of orthogonal projected views depends upon the angle of projection defined for the drawing sheet. You can define the first angle of projection or the third angle of projection for creating the projected views. The concept of the angle of projection and the procedure for defining the angle of projection for a drawing sheet are discussed next.

Working with the Angle of Projection

Engineering drawings follow two types of angles of projection: the first angle of projection and the third angle of projection. In the first angle of projection, the object is assumed to be kept in the first quadrant and the viewer views the object from the direction as shown in Figure 14.22. As the object has been kept in the first quadrant, its projections of views are on the respective planes as shown in Figure 14.22.

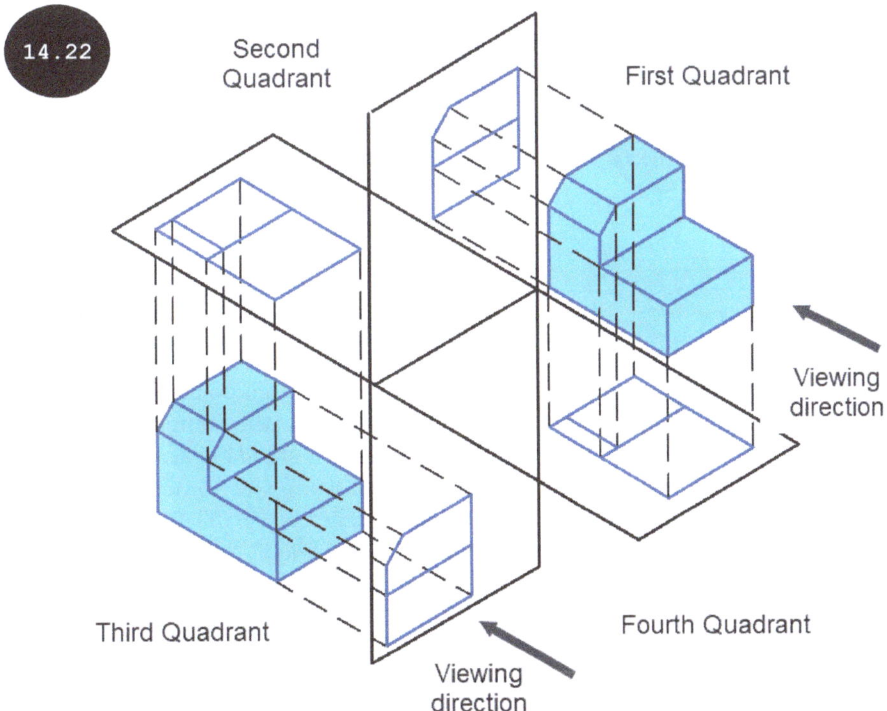

Now on unfolding the planes of projections, the front view appears on the upper side and the top view appears on the bottom side. Also, the right-side view appears on the left and the left-side view appears on the right of the front view, see Figure 14.23. Similarly, in the third angle of projection, the object is assumed to be kept in the third quadrant, refer to Figure 14.22. In this case, the projection of the front view appears on the bottom and the projection of the top view appears on the top side of the drawing. Also, the right-side view appears on the right and the left-side view appears on the left of the front view, see Figure 14.24.

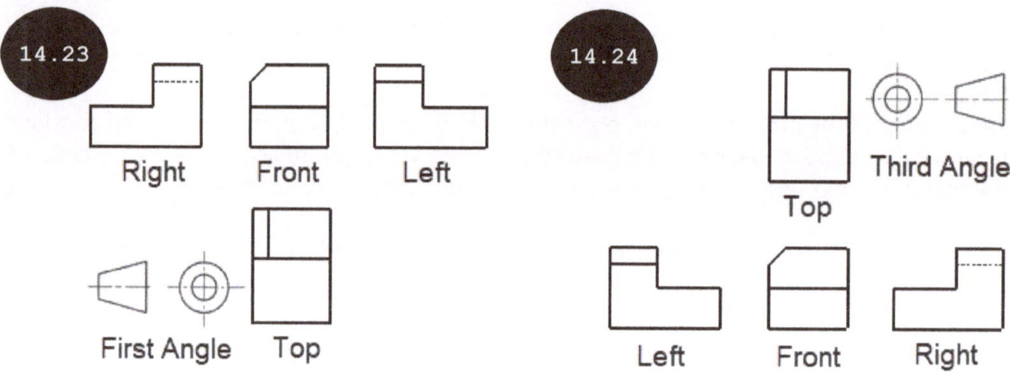

Defining the Angle of Projection

By default, when you create a drawing as per the ISO standard, the first angle of projection is used for generating the projected views, whereas when creating a drawing as per the ASME standard, the third angle of projection is used. However, you can customize the default projection angle, as required. To do this, click on your profile in the upper right corner of Autodesk Fusion. The **User Account** drop-down menu appears, see Figure 14.25. In this drop-down menu, click on the **Preferences** tool. The **Preferences** dialog box appears.

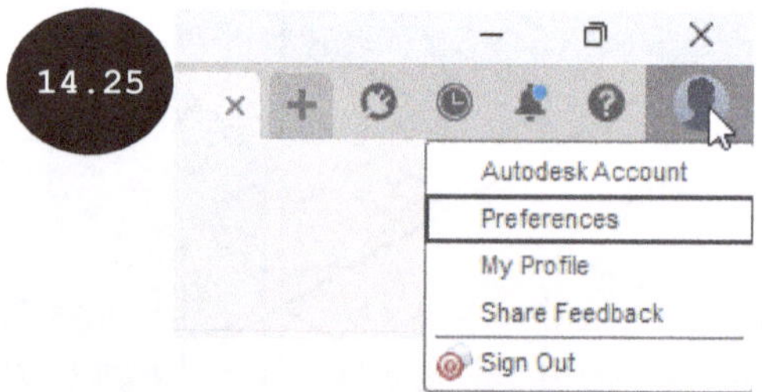

In the left panel of the **Preferences** dialog box, click on the **Drawing** option under the **General** node, see Figure 14.26. Next, select the drawing standard (**ASME** or **ISO**) in the **Standard** drop-down list to customize its default projection angle. After selecting the drawing standard, all its default properties or preferences appear in the dialog box, see Figure 14.26. In this figure, the **ASME** standard is selected. Next, select the **Override or Restore Format Defaults Below** check box in the dialog box to customize the default properties of the selected drawing standard. All the default properties become editable. Now, you can select the projection angle, as required in the **Projection Angle** drop-down list of the dialog box. Next, click on the **Apply** button in the dialog box to accept the change and then click on the **OK** button to exit the dialog box. Note that the changes made in the projection angle for a standard will be applied only to new drawings and will not reflect on the current drawing or any of the existing drawings.

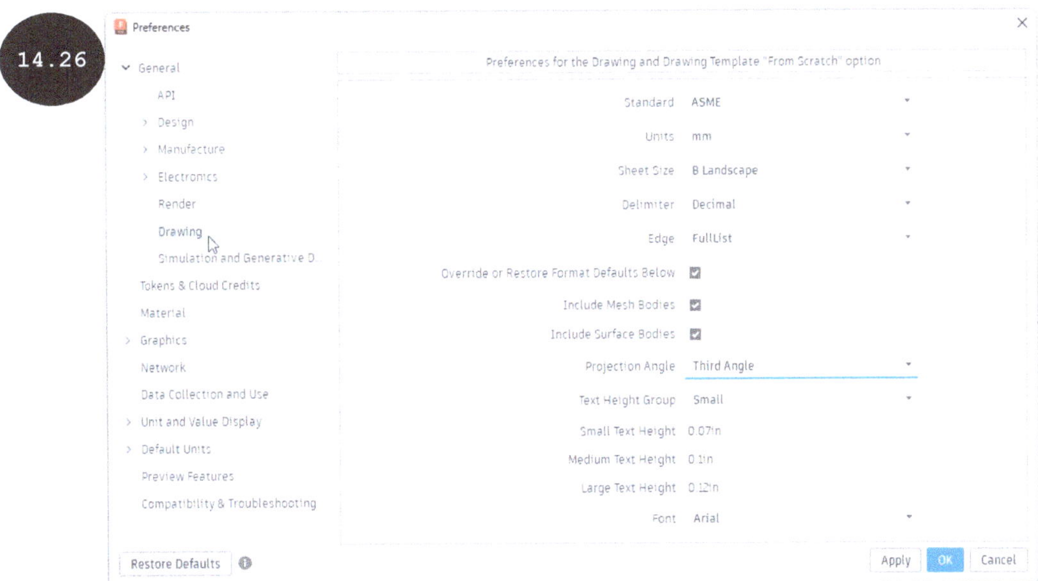

Defining Drawing Preferences

In Autodesk Fusion, you can define default preferences for creating drawings, including drawing annotation format, annotation units, drawing sheet size, annotation style, annotation font, and dimension precision. To do this, invoke the **Preferences** dialog box, as discussed earlier, see Figure 14.27. Next, click the **Drawing** option under the **General** node in the left panel of the dialog box. The options for specifying the default drawing preferences appear in the right panel.

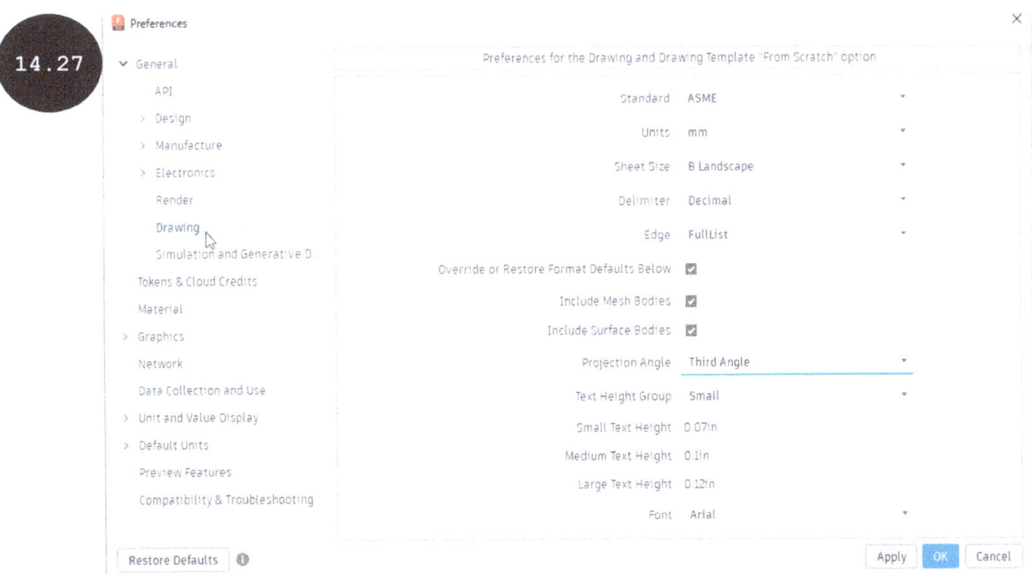

In the **Standard** drop-down list on the right panel, select the required drafting standard (**ASME** or **ISO**) for the drawing. If you select the **Inherit From Design** option in the **Standard** drop-down list, each new drawing will use the same standard specified for the design. Similarly, you can define the required unit preferences for the drawing using the **Units** drop-down list.

By selecting the **Override or Restore Format Defaults Below** check box, the options for customizing default preferences such as text height, font, dimension precision, and related settings for the selected standard are enabled in the dialog box for modification.

After customizing the default preferences for a standard, click the **Apply** button to accept the changes, and then click the **OK** button to close the dialog box. Note that the changes made to the default preferences apply only to new drawings and do not affect the current drawing or any existing drawings.

Editing Document and Sheet Settings

In Autodesk Fusion, after creating a new drawing, you can modify its document settings and sheet size. To modify the document settings, expand the **Document Settings** node in the **BROWSER** by clicking on the arrow in front of it, see Figure 14.28.

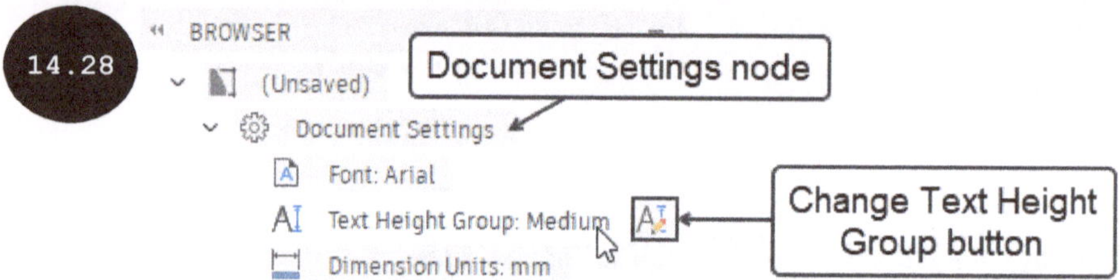

In the expanded **Document Settings** node, you can change the font, text height, dimension units, and line width by using the respective options. For example, to edit the text height, move the cursor over the **Text Height Group** option in the expanded **Document Settings** node and then click on the **Change Text Height Group** button that appears beside this option, refer to Figure 14.28. The **DOCUMENT SETTINGS** dialog box appears, see Figure 14.29.

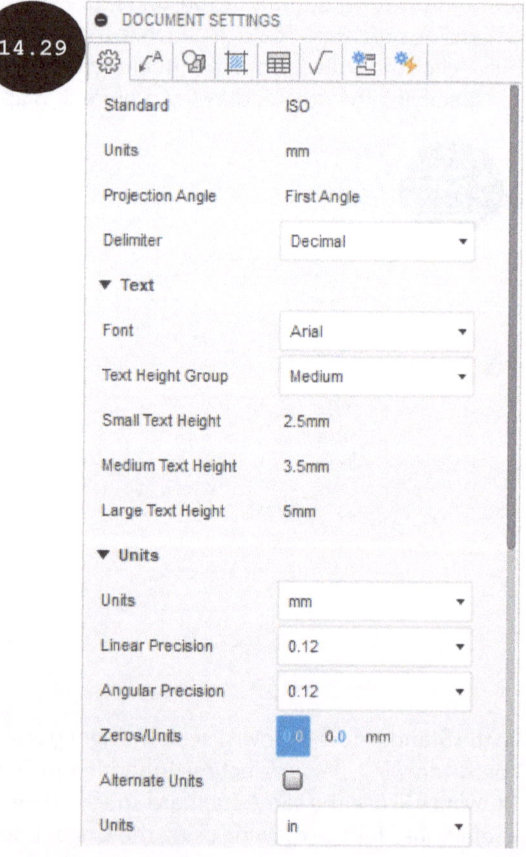

In this dialog box, you can make the necessary changes. You can also turn on or off the display of trailing and leading zeros in the decimal dimensions of the drawing by using the **Leading Zeros** and **Trailing Zeros** buttons in the **Zeros/Units** area of the **DOCUMENT SETTINGS** dialog box, respectively. On deactivating the **Trailing Zeros** button, the display of the trailing zeros in all decimal dimensions gets turned off. For example, if the dimension is 15.500 units, then by deactivating this button it becomes 15.5, and 15.000 units becomes 15. Similarly, on deactivating the **Leading Zeros** button, the display of leading zeros in the decimal dimensions gets turned off. For example, if the dimension is 0.800 units, then by deactivating this button it becomes .800.

To modify the sheet settings such as sheet size and title block for the current drawing, expand the **Sheet Settings** node in the **BROWSER** by clicking on the arrow in front of it, see Figure 14.30.

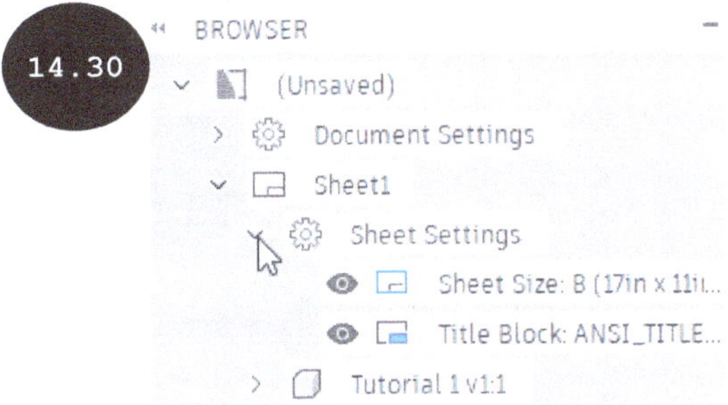

In the expanded **Sheet Settings** node, to modify the sheet size, move the cursor over the **Sheet Size** option and click the **Change Sheet Size** button that appears, see Figure 14.31. The **SHEET SIZE** dialog box is displayed. In this dialog box, select the required sheet size (see Figure 14.32), and then click the **OK** button.

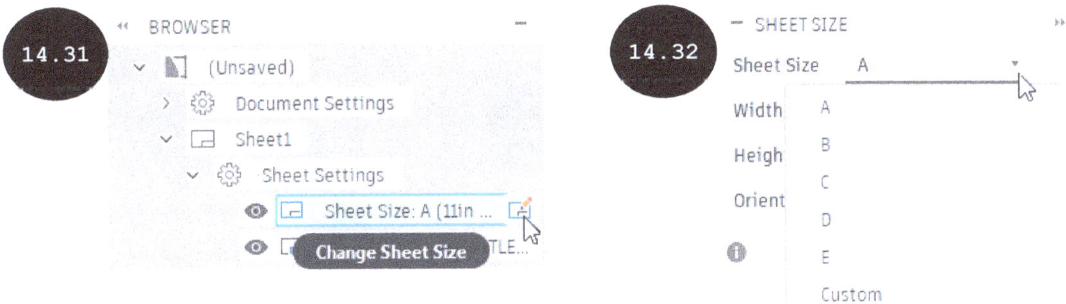

Similarly, you can change or rename a title block using the **Title Block** option under the expanded **Sheet Settings** node. However, the default title block cannot be renamed. The procedure for creating a new title block is discussed later in this chapter. You can also turn the display of the title block on or off by clicking the **Show/Hide** button available next to its name in the **BROWSER**.

Editing and Inserting a New Title Block

In Autodesk Fusion, when you create a new drawing, the default title block appears automatically at the bottom of the drawing sheet, depending upon the drawing standard (ASME or ISO) selected for creating the drawing, see Figure 14.33. The title block contains drawing attributes such as project name, drawn by, checked by, approved by, date, sheet size, drawing number, revision, and so on. You can edit the title block attributes or insert a new custom title block such that it matches the standard format of your company.

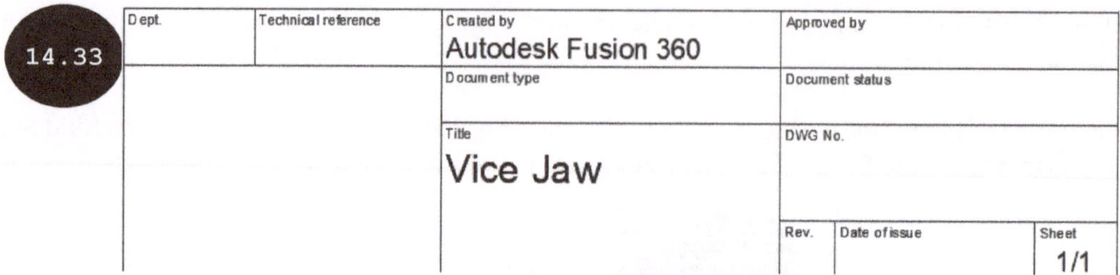

To edit the title block attributes, double-click the title block. The **PROPERTIES** dialog box appears, see Figure 14.34. Also, the title block gets zoomed in on the screen and you are prompted to select attributes to be edited or you can press ENTER to exit. Click on the required attribute of the title block to be edited. The selected attribute appears in edit mode. Now, you can edit the selected attribute or enter a new attribute, as required. Next, press ENTER to exit the edit mode. You can similarly edit the other attributes of the title block, as required. After editing the attributes of the title block, press the ENTER key or click on the **Finish Properties** button in the **PROPERTIES** dialog box.

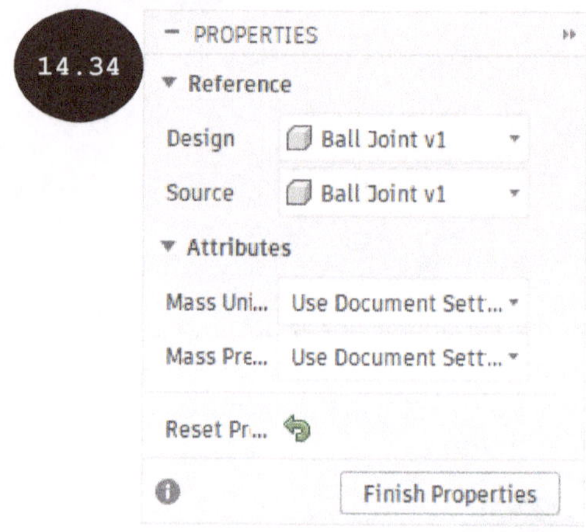

You can also insert your company logo in the title block. To do this, click on the **INSERT> Insert Image** in the **Toolbar**, see Figure 14.35. The **Insert** dialog box appears. Next, browse to the required location in a project folder of the **Insert** dialog box, where the image file to be inserted is saved, or click on the **Insert from my computer** button to insert an image from a local drive of your system. On clicking the **Insert from my computer** button, the **Open** dialog box appears. In this dialog box, browse to the location where the image (logo) to be inserted is saved and then select it. Next, click on the **Open** button. The selected image gets attached to the cursor. Also, the **INSERT IMAGE** dialog box appears. Next, place the image in the title block, see Figure 14.36. After inserting the image, you can control its scale, X and Y distance values, and angle of rotation by using the fields that appear in the **INSERT IMAGE** dialog box, see Figure 14.37. Next, click **OK** to exit the dialog box.

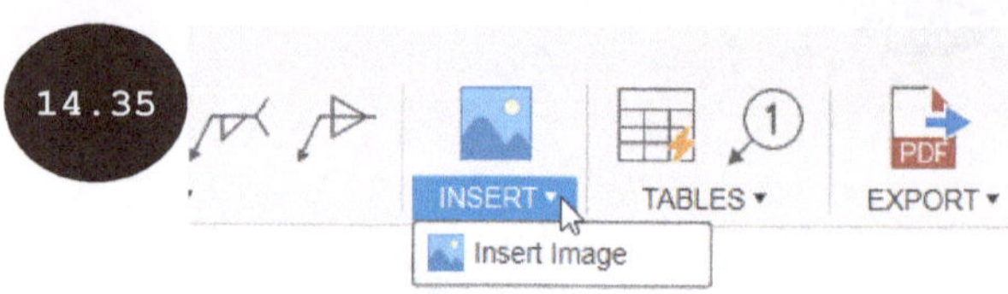

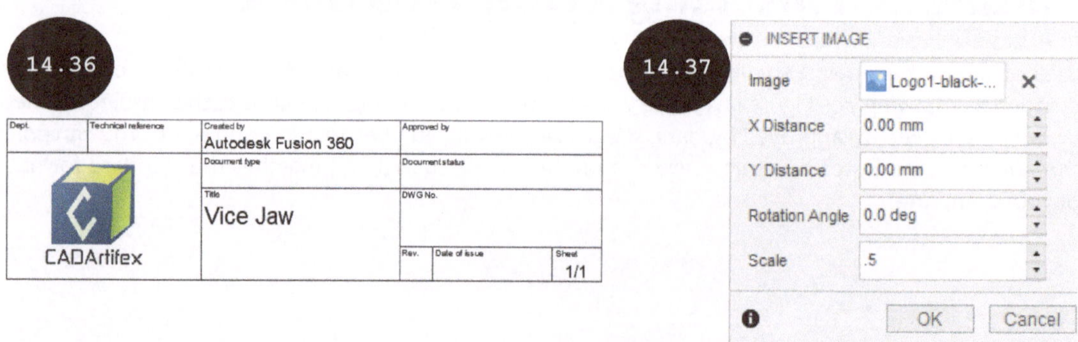

In Autodesk Fusion, you can also create a new custom title block as per your company standard. To do this, expand the **Sheet Settings** node in the **BROWSER** and then right-click on the **Title Block** option in it, see Figure 14.38. Next, select the **New Title Block** tool in the shortcut menu that appears. The **NEW TITLE BLOCK** dialog box appears, see Figure 14.39. Alternatively, select the title block in the drawing area and then right-click to display the Marking Menu, see Figure 14.40. Next, select the **New Title Block** tool in the Marking Menu to invoke the **NEW TITLE BLOCK** dialog box. By using this dialog box, you can create a new title block using an existing title block as a reference, from scratch, or import an existing title block that is saved in .DWG file format by activating the respective button in the **Source** area of the dialog box. The options are discussed next.

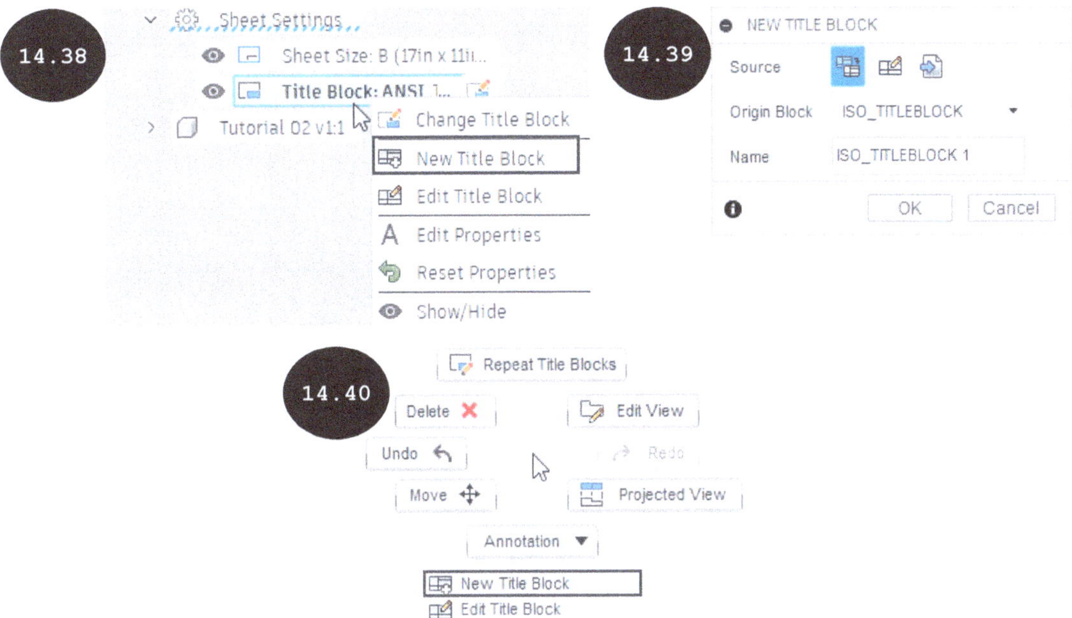

From Existing

To create a new title block using an existing title block as a reference, ensure that the **From Existing** button is activated in the **Source** area of the dialog box. Next, select an existing title block in the **Origin Block** drop-down list of the dialog box and then enter a name for the new title block to be created in the **Name** field of the dialog box. Next, click on the **OK** button. The selected title block appears in an edit mode with the display of the **TITLE BLOCK** dialog box, see Figure 14.41. Now, make the necessary changes in the title block as required, by using the sketch tools of the **Toolbar.** You can also delete the existing lines of the title block and create new lines. After making the necessary changes in the title block, click on the **Finish Title Block** button in the **TITLE BLOCK** dialog box. The new title block is created and appears in the drawing sheet.

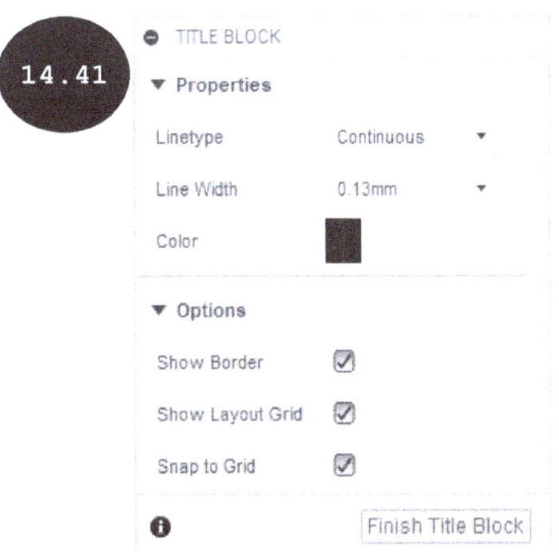

From Scratch

To create a new title block from scratch, invoke the **NEW TITLE BLOCK** dialog box and then activate the **From Scratch** button in the **Source** area of the dialog box, see Figure 14.42. Next, enter the name of the title block in the **Name** field and then click on the **OK** button. The edit mode appears with the display of the **TITLE BLOCK** dialog box. Now, you can create a new title block by using the tools available in the **Toolbar**. After creating the title block, click on the **Finish Title Block** button in the **TITLE BLOCK** dialog box. The new title block is created and appears in the drawing sheet.

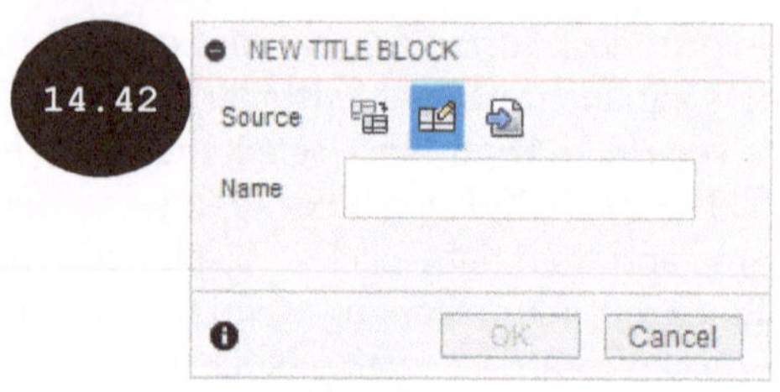

From DWG File

You can also import an existing title block that is saved in .DWG file format. To do this, invoke the **NEW TITLE BLOCK** dialog box and then activate the **From DWG File** button. Next, click on the **DWG File** button in the dialog box. The **Open** dialog box appears. In this dialog box, browse to the location where the .DWG file to be imported is saved and then select it. Next, click on the **Open** button in the dialog box. The name of the selected. DWG file appears in the **Name** field of the **NEW TITLE BLOCK** dialog box. Next, click on the **OK** button. The selected .DWG file is imported as the title block in the drawing.

Note that you can change the position of the title block in the sheet by dragging it or by using the **Move** tool of the **Toolbar** if needed. You will learn more about the **Move** tool later in this chapter.

Creating Auxiliary Views

An auxiliary view is created by projecting the edges of the model normal to a specified edge or line of an existing view, see Figure 14.43. You can create an auxiliary view by using the **Auxiliary View** tool. The method for creating an auxiliary view is discussed below:

1. Click on the **Auxiliary View** tool in the **CREATE** panel of the **Toolbar**, see Figure 14.44. You are prompted to select a parent view.

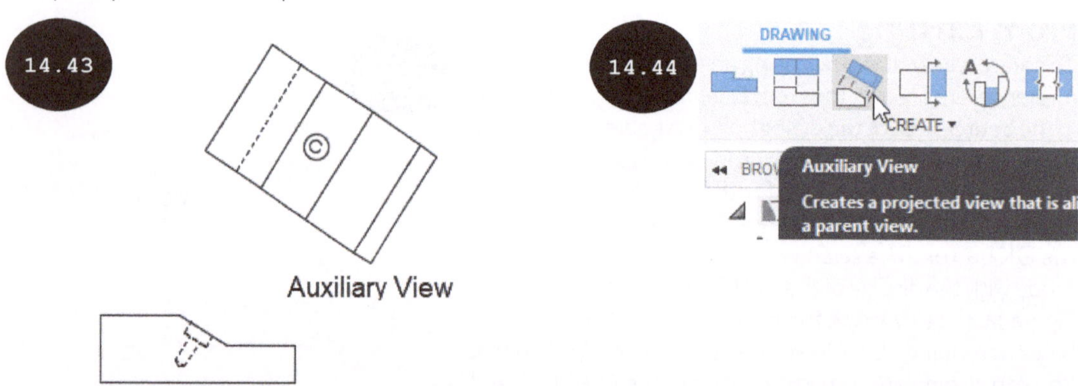

2. Select an edge of an existing drawing view for creating an auxiliary view. The preview of an auxiliary view normal to the selected edge appears attached to the cursor, see Figure 14.45. Also, the **AUXILIARY VIEW** dialog box appears (see Figure 14.46), and you are prompted to specify a placement point for the auxiliary view on the sheet.

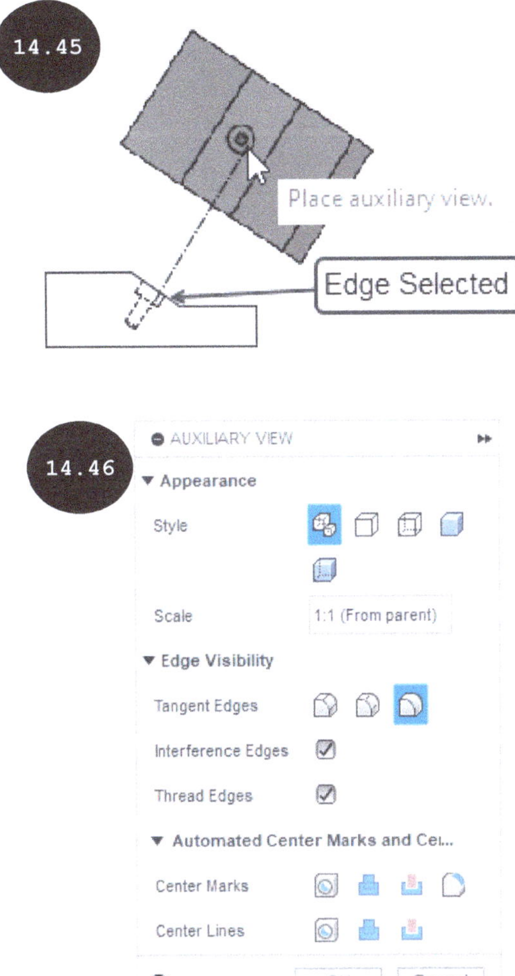

3. Click to specify the placement point for the auxiliary view in the drawing sheet.

   Now, you need to define the required settings by using the **AUXILIARY VIEW** dialog box.

4. Define the settings such as appearance, scale, and visibility of tangent edges in the auxiliary view by using the **AUXILIARY VIEW** dialog box. Note that the **From Parent** button is activated in the **Style** area of the dialog box, by default. As a result, the properties of the parent view get propagated to the auxiliary view. The remaining options in the **AUXILIARY VIEW** dialog box are the same as discussed earlier.

5. After specifying the required settings such as orientation, visual style, and scale factor for creating the auxiliary view, click on the **OK** button in the dialog box. An auxiliary view of specified settings gets created, see Figure 14.47.

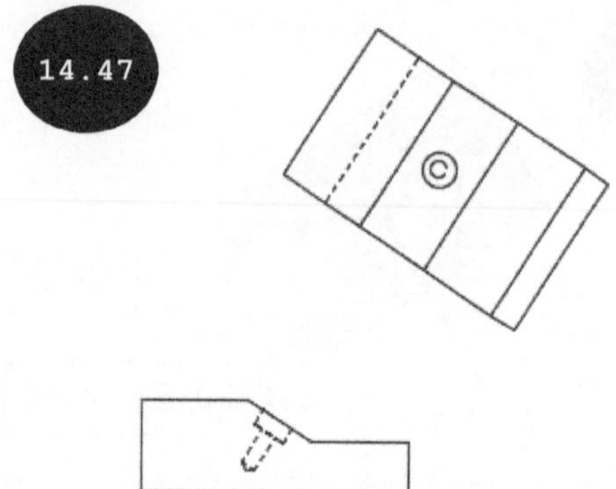

Creating Section Views

In Autodesk Fusion, in addition to creating orthogonal and isometric projected views, you can create section views. A section view is created by cutting an object by using an imaginary cutting plane or a section line and then viewing the object from a direction normal to the section line. Figure 14.48 shows a section view created by cutting an object using a section line. A section view is used to illustrate the internal features of an object clearly. It also reduces the number of hidden-detail lines, facilitates the dimensioning of internal features, shows cross-sections, and so on. In Autodesk Fusion, you can create the following types of section views by using the **Section View** tool.

- Full Section View
- Half Section View
- Offset Section View
- Aligned Section View

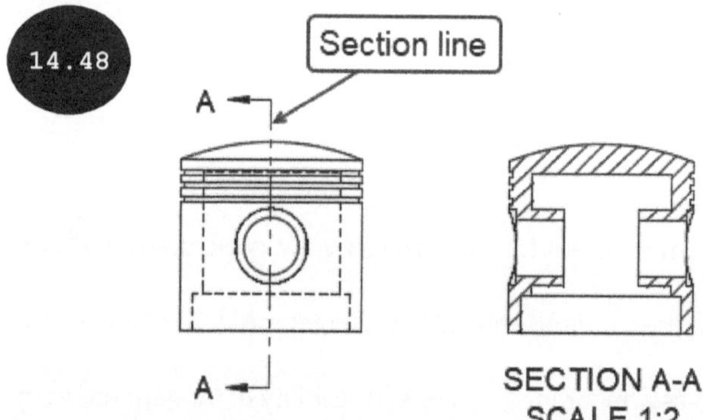

Creating Full Section Views

Full section views are the most widely used section views in engineering drawings. In a full section view, an object is assumed to be cut through its entire length by an imaginary cutting plane or a section line, see Figure 14.49. In Autodesk Fusion, you can create a full section view by using the **Section View** tool. The method for creating a full section view is discussed next.

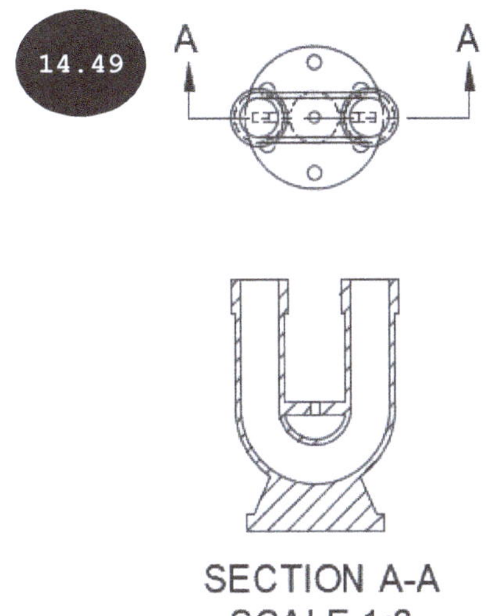

1. Click on the **Section View** tool in the CREATE panel of the **Toolbar**, see Figure 14.50. You are prompted to select a parent view.

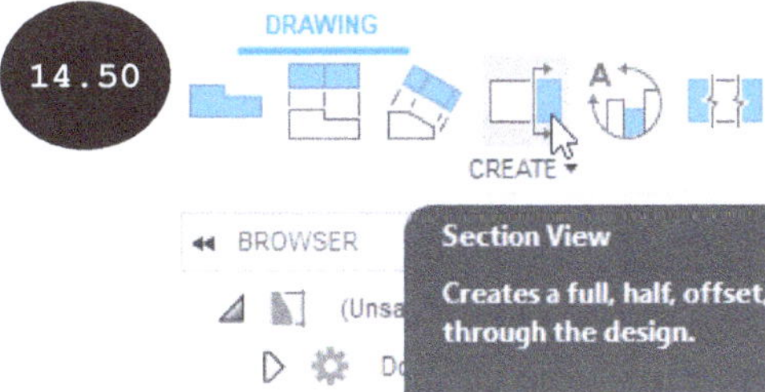

2. Select an existing drawing view as the parent for creating the section view. An arrow appears attached to the cursor and you are prompted to specify the start point of the section line. Also, the DRAWING VIEW dialog box appears.

3. Click to specify the start point of the section line, see Figure 14.51. Note that to specify the start point, you can use the object snap tracking line, which appears when you move the cursor away from an object snap point of the parent view, see Figure 14.51. After specifying the start point, the section line appears such that its end arrow is attached to the cursor, see Figure 14.52. Also, you are prompted to specify the endpoint of the section line.

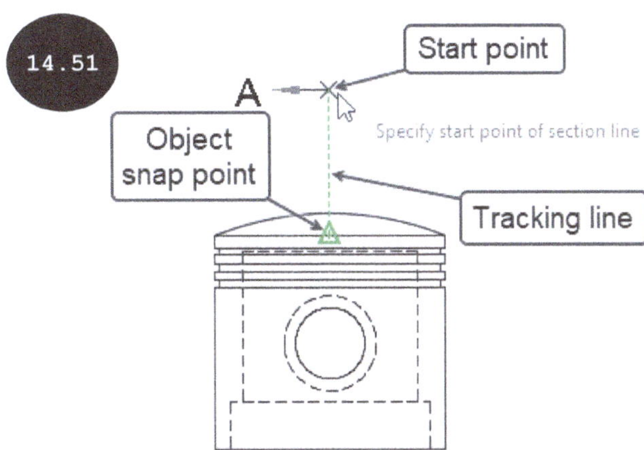

4. Click to specify the endpoint of the section line, see Figure 14.52. Another segment of the section line appears attached to the cursor and you are prompted to either specify the next point of the section line or press ENTER to end the creation of the section line, see Figure 14.53. In Autodesk Fusion, you can create a section line by specifying multiple points one after the other.

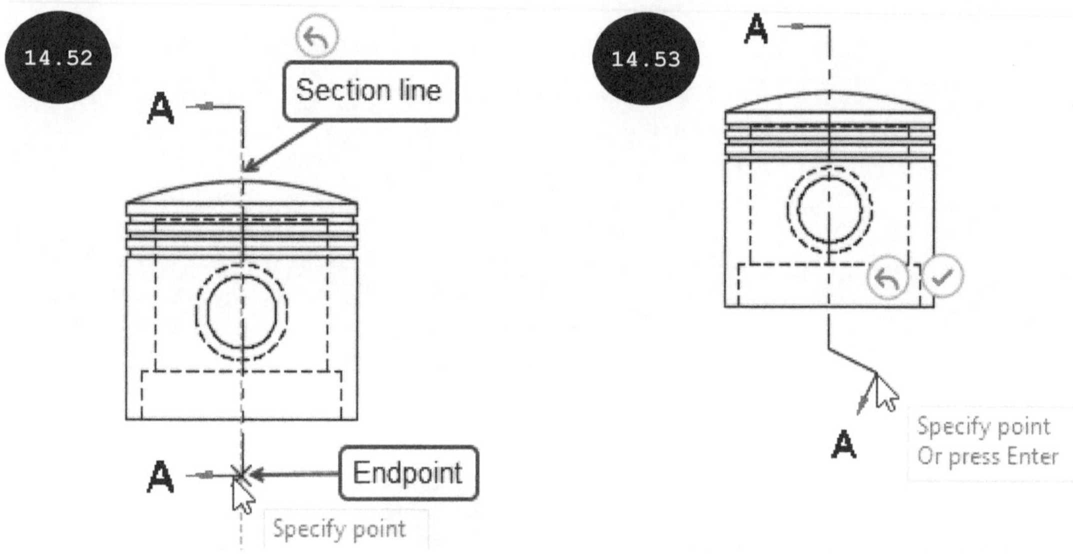

Note: On specifying the endpoint of a section line, the **Rollback placement and continue** button as well as the **Create and continue** button appear near it in the drawing sheet. The **Rollback placement and continue** button is used for undoing the creation of the last specified endpoint of the section line and continuing with specifying other endpoints. The **Create and continue** button is used for accepting the creation of section line.

5. Press the ENTER key or click on the **Create and continue** button that appears near the line to end the creation of the section line. The preview of the section view appears attached to the cursor and you are prompted to specify its placement in the drawing sheet, see Figure 14.54.

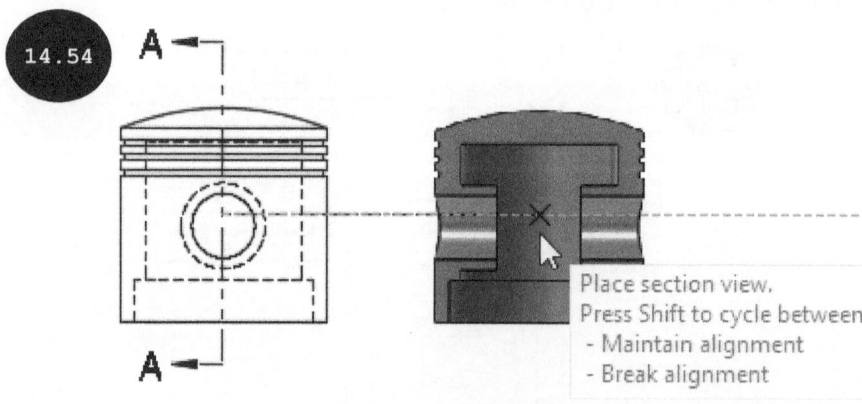

Tip: To create a full section view, you need to define the start and end points of the section line such that its passes through the entire length of the object.

Note: By default, the section view maintains a horizontal or vertical alignment to the section line, see Figure 14.54. To break the alignment of the section view, press the SHIFT key. You can again press the SHIFT key to restore the horizontal or vertical alignment of the section view.

6. Click to define the placement point for the section view in the drawing sheet. After defining the placement for the section view, you can define the appearance, scale, and visibility of tangent edges in the section view by using the **DRAWING VIEW** dialog box. The options in this dialog box are the same as discussed earlier, except for the **Section Depth** and **Objects To Cut** rollouts, which are discussed next.

   Section Depth: By default, the **Full** option is selected in the **Depth** drop-down list of the **Section Depth** rollout. As a result, the section view is created such that all geometries of the object beyond the section line are visible in the resultant section view. On selecting the **Slice** option, the sliced section view is created such that only the geometries that cut through the section line are visible. On selecting the **Distance** option, the **Distance** field gets enabled below the drop-down list. In this field, you can specify a distance of viewing in the object beyond the section line.

   Objects To Cut: The **Objects To Cut** rollout of the **DRAWING VIEW** dialog box displays a list of bodies included in the section cut. If you are creating the section view of a component, then it displays only one body, see Figure 14.55. On the other hand, if you are creating the section view of an assembly, then it displays a list of all bodies included in the section cut, see Figure 14.56. In this rollout, you can clear the check boxes that appear in front of the bodies like fasteners, to exclude them from the section cut.

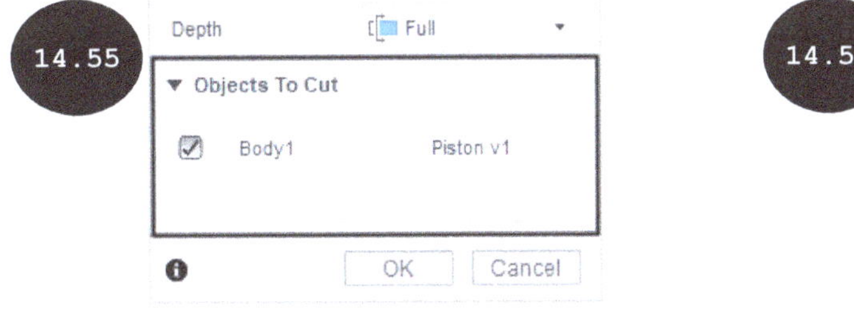

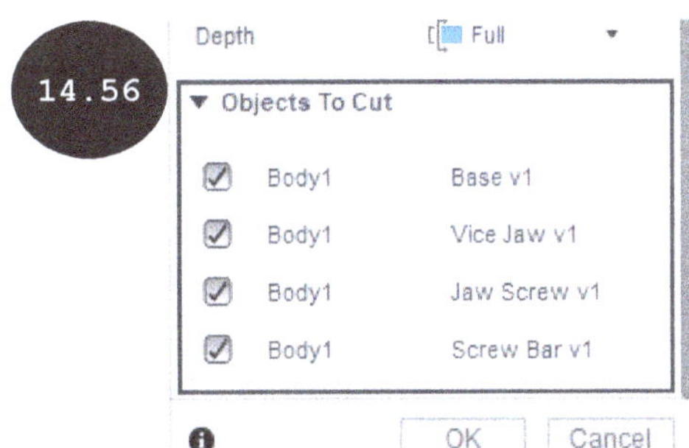

7. Accept the default option in the **DRAWING VIEW** dialog box and then click on the **OK** button. The section view is created, see Figures 14.57 and 14.58. Figure 14.57 shows the section view of a component, whereas Figure 14.58 shows the section view of an assembly in which the **Jaw Screw** component has been excluded from the section cut.

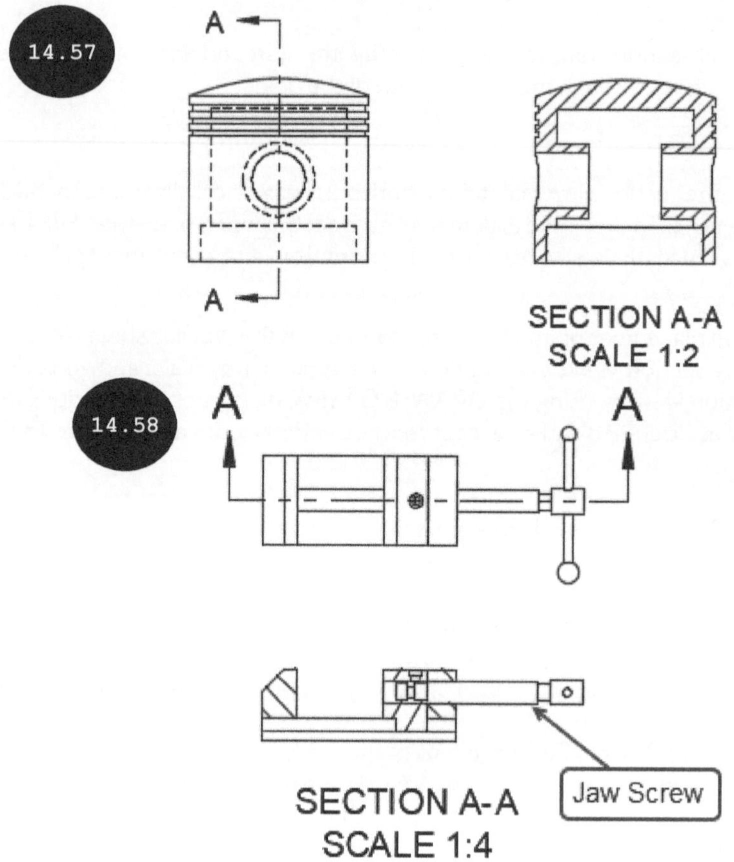

Note: The direction of the arrows of the section line represents the viewing direction.

Creating Half Section Views

A half section view is created by cutting an object using an imaginary cutting plane or section line that passes halfway or through a portion of a drawing view, see Figure 14.59. In Autodesk Fusion, you can create a half section view by using the **Section View** tool. The method for creating a half section view is discussed below:

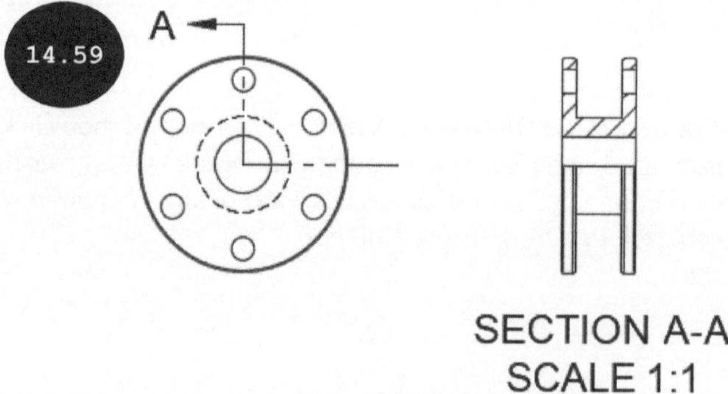

1. Click on the **Section View** tool in the **CREATE** panel in the **Toolbar**, see Figure 14.60. You are prompted to select a parent view.

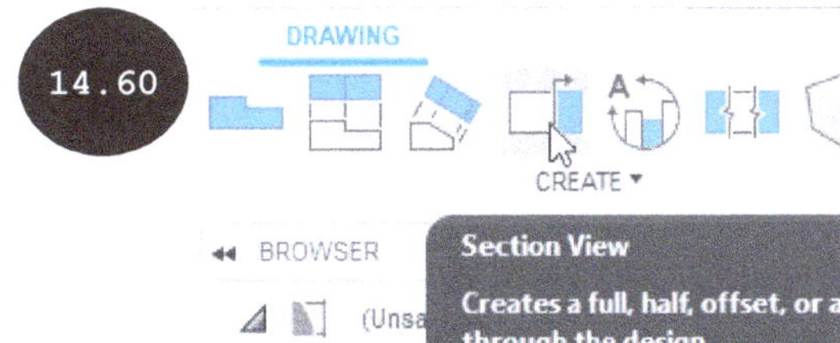

2. Select an existing drawing view as the parent view for creating the section view. An arrow appears attached to the cursor and you are prompted to specify the start point of the section line. Also, the **DRAWING VIEW** dialog box appears.

3. Click to specify the start point of the section line, see Figure 14.61. Note that, to specify the start point, you can use the object snap tracking line, which appears when you move the cursor away from an object snap point of the parent view, see Figure 14.61. After specifying the start point, the section line appears such that its end arrow is attached to the cursor.

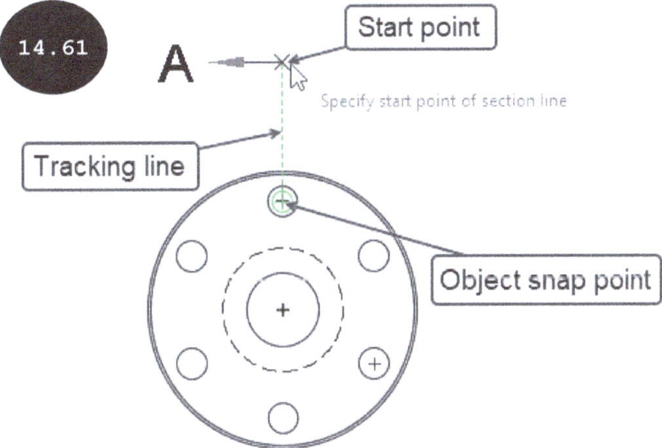

4. Click in the drawing view to specify the endpoint of the first segment of the section line, see Figure 14.62. The second segment of the section line appears attached to the cursor and you are prompted to either specify the next point of the section line or press ENTER to end the creation of the section line.

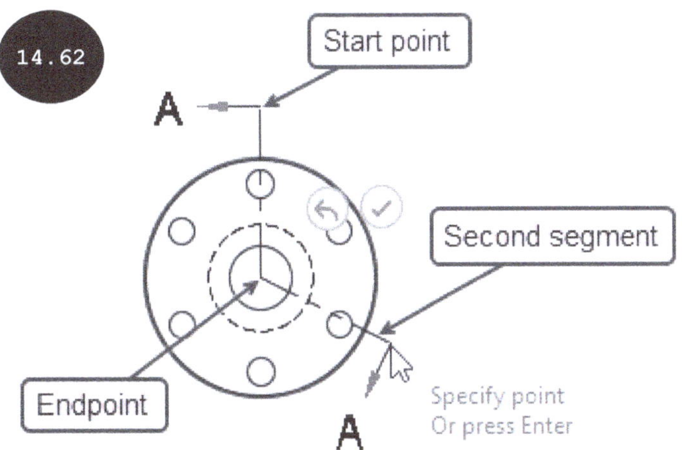

5. Click to specify the endpoint of the section line outside the drawing view, see Figure 14.63. The third segment of the section line appears attached to the cursor.

6. Press the ENTER key or click on the **Create and continue** button that appears near the line to end the creation of the section line. The preview of the half section view appears attached to the cursor and you are prompted to specify its placement in the drawing sheet, see Figure 14.64.

Note: By default, the section view maintains a horizontal or vertical alignment to the section line, see Figure 14.64. To break the alignment of the section view, press the SHIFT key. You can again press the SHIFT key to restore the horizontal or vertical alignment of the section view.

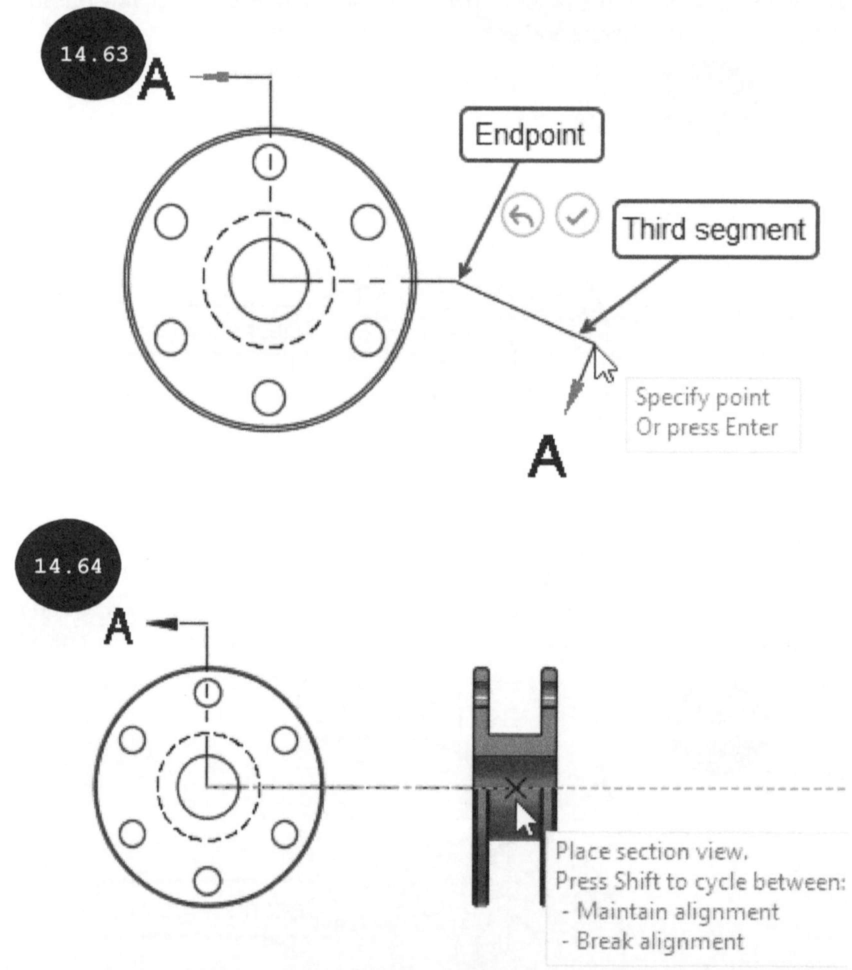

7. Click to define the placement point for the section view in the drawing sheet. After defining the placement for the section view, you can define the appearance, scale, and visibility of tangent edges in the section view by using the **DRAWING VIEW** dialog box.

Note: If you are creating the section view of an assembly, you can also define the bodies to be included or excluded from the section cut by using the **Objects To Cut** rollout of the **DRAWING VIEW** dialog box, as discussed earlier.

8. Accept the default option in the **DRAWING VIEW** dialog box and then click on the **OK** button. The half section view is created, see Figure 14.65.

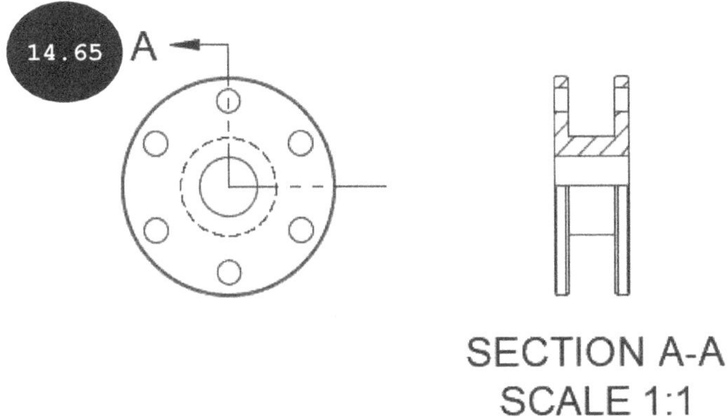

Creating Offset Section Views

An offset section view is created by jogging or bending the imaginary cutting plane or section line such that it cuts the portion of the object that cannot be sectioned through a straight line, see Figure 14.66. In Autodesk Fusion, you can create an offset section view by using the **Section View** tool. The method for creating an offset section view is discussed below:

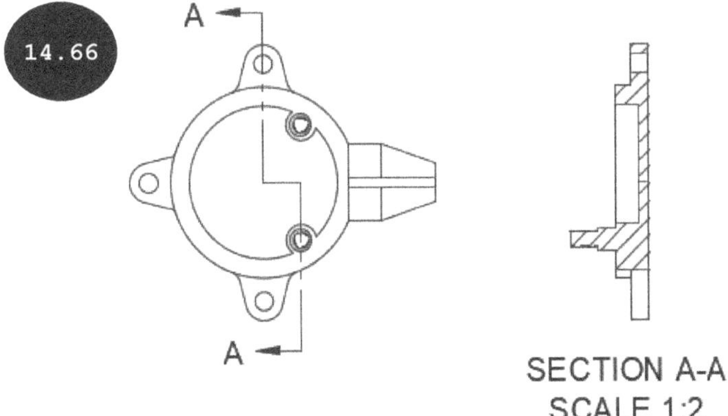

1. Click on the **Section View** tool in the **CREATE** panel of the **Toolbar**. You are prompted to select a parent view.

2. Select an existing drawing view as the parent for creating the section view. An arrow appears attached to the cursor and you are prompted to specify the start point of the section line. Also, the **DRAWING VIEW** dialog box appears.

3. Click to specify the start point of the section line, see Figure 14.67. You are prompted to specify the endpoint of the section line.

4. Click on the drawing view to specify the second point of the section line, see Figure 14.67.

5. Click on the drawing view to specify the third point of the section line, see Figure 14.67.

6. Click to specify the fourth point of the section line outside the drawing view, see Figure 14.67.

7. Press the ENTER key or click on the **Create and continue** button that appears near the line to end the creation of section lines. The jogged section line is created, and a preview of the offset section view appears attached to the cursor.

8. Click to define the placement point for the section view in the drawing sheet. Note that, you can switch between maintaining or breaking the horizontal or vertical alignment of the section view by pressing the SHIFT key.

9. Accept the default options in the **DRAWING VIEW** dialog box and then click on the **OK** button. The offset section view is created, see Figure 14.67.

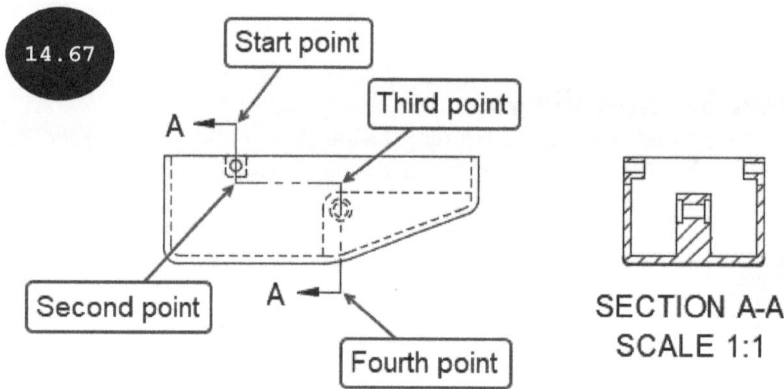

Creating Aligned Section Views

An aligned section view is created by cutting an object using the section line, which comprises two non-parallel lines, and then straightening the cross-section by revolving it around the center point of the section line, see Figure 14.68.

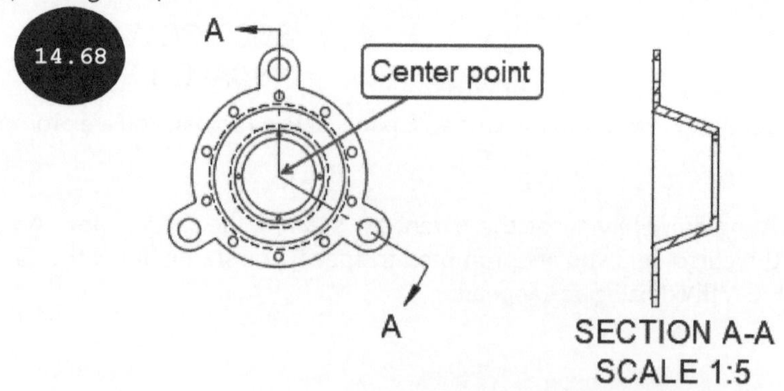

You can create an aligned section view by using the **Section View** tool. The method for creating an aligned section view is the same as discussed earlier with the only difference being that to create the aligned section view, you need to create a section line having two non-parallel line segments.

Creating Detail Views

A detail view is used for showing a portion of an existing drawing view in an enlarged scale, see Figure 14.69. You can define the portion of an existing drawing view to be enlarged by drawing a boundary using the **Detail View** tool. The method for creating a detailed view is discussed below:

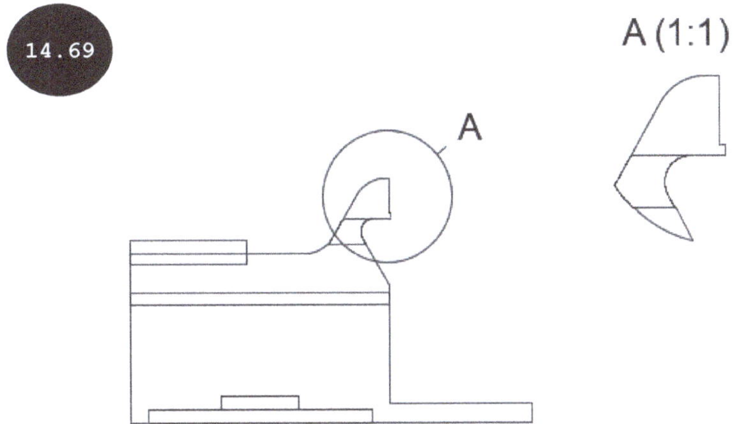

1. Click on the **Detail View** tool in the **CREATE** panel in the **Toolbar**, see Figure 14.70. You are prompted to select a parent view.

2. Select an existing drawing view as the parent for creating the detail view. You are prompted to specify the center point of the detail boundary. Also, the **DRAWING VIEW** dialog box appears. Note that the detail boundary defines the portion of the drawing view to be enlarged.

3. Click to specify the center point of the detail boundary, see Figure 14.71. You are prompted to define the size of the detail boundary by clicking the left mouse button.

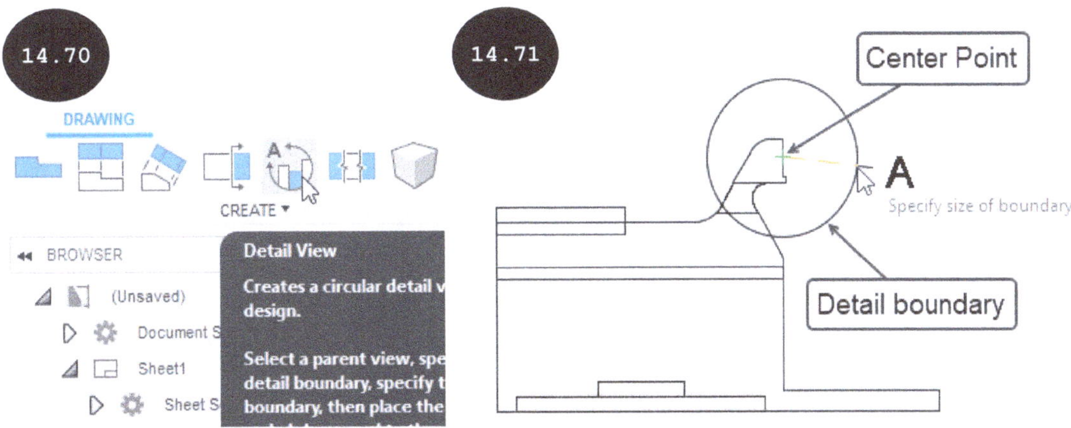

4. Click to define the size of the boundary. A preview of the enlarged view of the portion enclosed within the boundary gets attached to the cursor.

5. Click to define the placement point for the detail view in the drawing sheet.

6. Specify the enlarged scale of the detail view in the **Scale** field of the dialog box. You can also specify other properties of the detail view in the dialog box, as discussed earlier.

7. Click on the **OK** button in the dialog box. The detail view is created.

Note: On editing the boundary of a detail view, the detail view gets updated, dynamically. To do this, click on the boundary, the grips appear, see Figure 14.72. You can edit the boundary by using these grips. For example, to change the location of the boundary, click on its center grip and then specify its new position on the drawing view by clicking the left mouse button. Similarly, to increase or decrease the size of the boundary, click on a grip appearing along the boundary and then click to specify its new position.

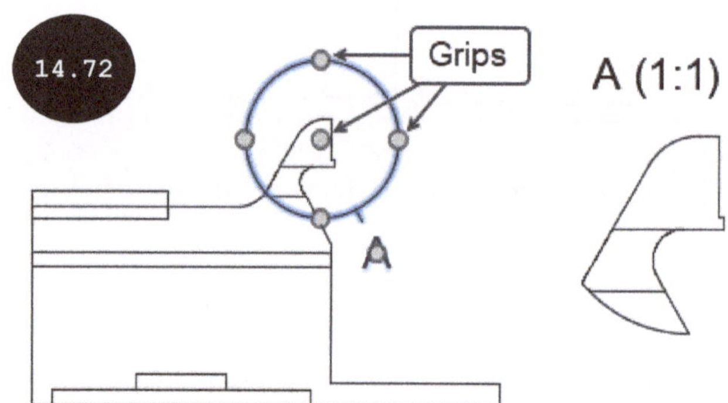

Creating Break Views

A break view is used for displaying a large scaled view on a small scale sheet by removing a portion of the view that has the same cross-section. A break view is created by breaking an existing base, projection, or section view using a pair of horizontal or vertical lines such that the portion existing between the break lines is removed from the view, see Figure 14.73. The method for creating a break view is discussed below:

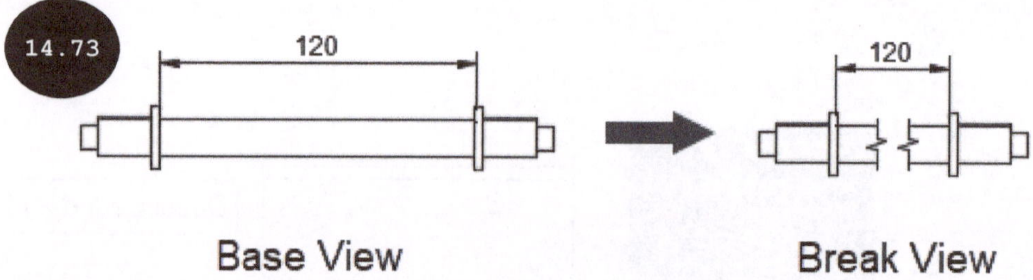

1. Click on the **Break View** tool in the **CREATE** panel in the **Toolbar**, see Figure 14.74. The **BREAK VIEW** dialog box appears, see Figure 14.75, and you are prompted to select a parent view.

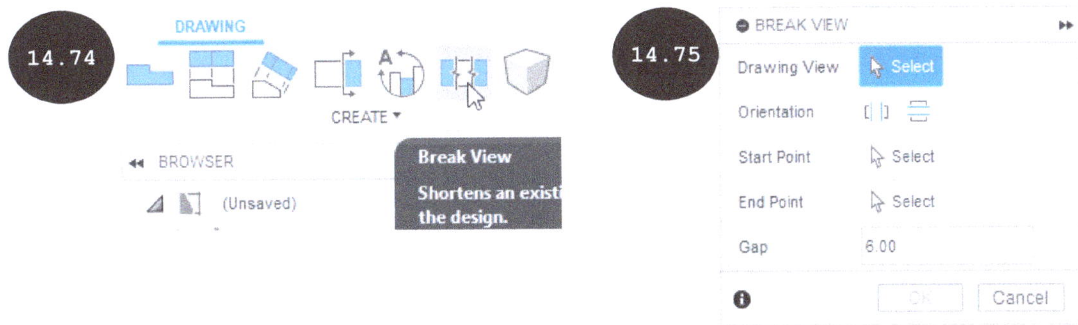

2. Select an existing drawing view as the parent view for creating the break view. You are prompted to specify the start point for the break line. Note that the orientation of the break lines is defined automatically based on the parent view selected. You can change the orientation of the break lines by selecting the required option (**Horizontal** or **Vertical**) in the **Orientation** area of the dialog box.

3. Click to specify the start point of the break line, see Figure 14.76. You are prompted to specify the endpoint of the break line.

4. Click to specify the endpoint of the break line, see Figure 14.76.

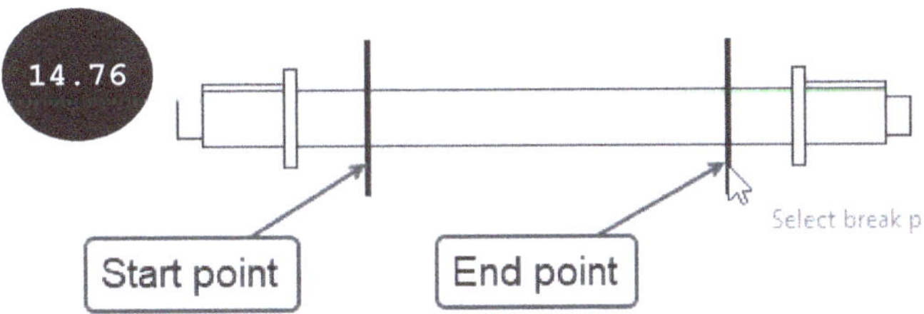

5. Specify the gap between the break lines in the **Gap** field of the dialog box and then click on the **OK** button in the dialog box. The break view is created.

Creating an Exploded Drawing View

In Autodesk Fusion, you can also create an exploded drawing view of an assembly as the base view by using the **Base View** tool, see Figure 14.77. The method for creating an exploded view is discussed below:

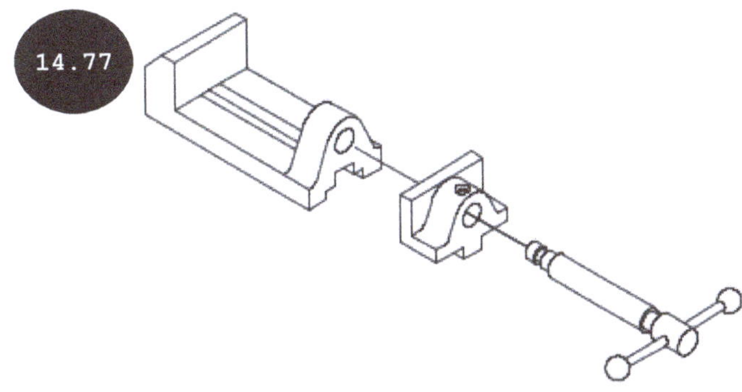

1. Click on the **Base View** tool in the **CREATE** panel of the **Toolbar**. The **DRAWING VIEW** dialog box appears. The options in this dialog box are the same as discussed earlier.

2. Invoke the **Representation** drop-down list in the dialog box, see Figure 14.78. A list of all the storyboards created in the **ANIMATION** workspace appears.

14.78

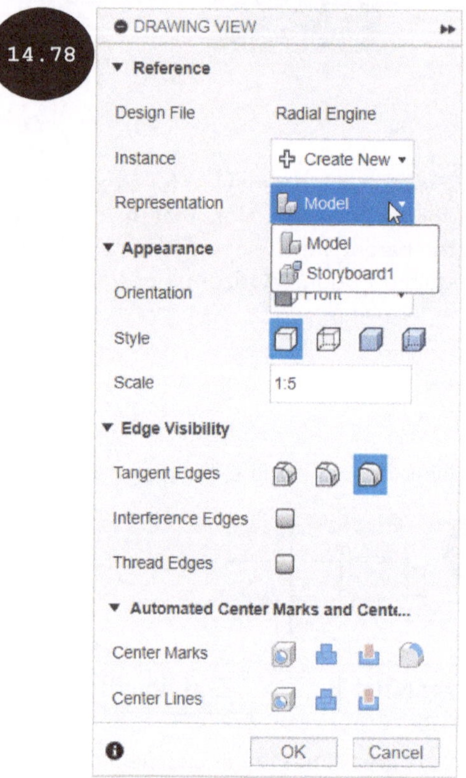

Note: If the animation storyboards are not created for the assembly in the **ANIMATION** workspace, then only the **Model** option appears in this drop-down list.

3. Select a storyboard that represents an exploded view of the assembly in the **Representation** drop-down list in the dialog box. A preview of the exploded view created in the **ANIMATION** workspace for the selected storyboard appears attached to the cursor.

4. Click to define the placement point for the exploded view in the drawing sheet. Next, specify the properties for the exploded view such as orientation, style, and scale in the **DRAWING VIEW** dialog box.

5. Click on the **OK** button. The exploded drawing view of the assembly is created as a base view in the drawing sheet, see Figure 14.79.

14.79

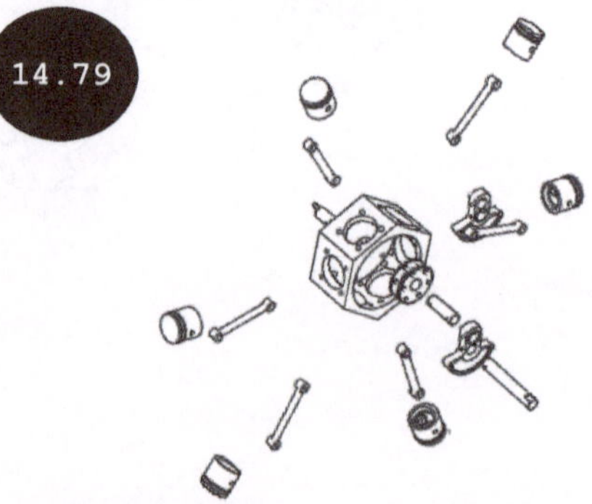

Invoking DRAWING Workspace From Animation

In Autodesk Fusion, you can create an exploded view of an assembly by invoking the DRAWING workspace using the **From Animation** option, see Figures 14.80. On selecting the **From Animation** option, the ANIMATION Workspace is invoked with the display of the CREATE DRAWING dialog box. The options in this dialog box are the same as discussed earlier. Select the required storyboard in the **Storyboard** drop-down list of the dialog box and then specify other settings such as drawing template, standard, units, and sheet size. Next, click on the OK button. The DRAWING environment is invoked, and the exploded view of the assembly appears attached to the cursor. Also, the DRAWING VIEW dialog box appears. The options in this dialog box are the same as discussed earlier. Next, click to specify the position of the exploded view in the drawing sheet and then click on the OK button in the dialog box. The exploded view is created.

Editing Properties of a Drawing View

In Autodesk Fusion, after creating a drawing view, you can edit its properties such as orientation, style, scale, and visibility of tangent edges. To do this, double-click on a drawing view. The DRAWING VIEW dialog box appears. By using this dialog box, you can edit the properties of the selected drawing view. The options in this dialog box are the same as discussed earlier.

Note: On editing the properties of the parent view, the properties of the projected views also change, accordingly. However, if you edit the properties of a projected view, the parent view remains the same and no change is reflected in its properties.

Editing Hatch Properties of a Section View

In Autodesk Fusion, after creating a section view, you can edit its default hatching properties such as hatch pattern, scale factor, and hatch angle. To do this, double-click on the hatch pattern of a section view to be edited. The HATCH dialog box appears, see Figure 14.81.

14.81

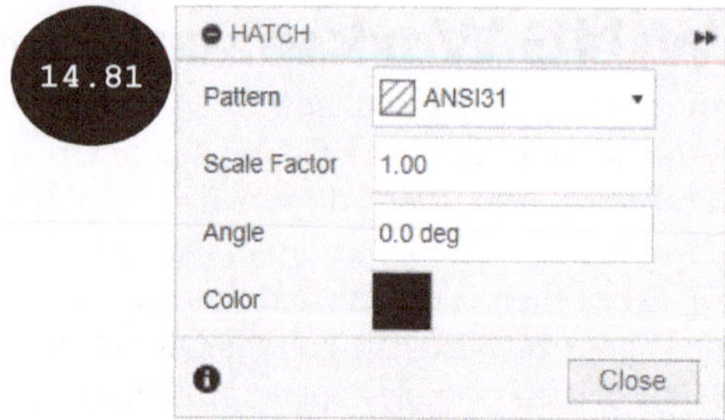

The **Pattern** drop-down list of the dialog box is used for selecting the required hatch pattern. The **Scale Factor** field is used for specifying the required scale factor and the **Angle** field is used for specifying the angle of the hatch pattern. After editing the properties of the selected hatch, click on the **Close** button to exit the dialog box. Similarly, you can edit or modify the properties of each hatch.

Creating a Sketch

In Autodesk Fusion, you can create a sketch on the current drawing sheet in the same way as creating a sketch in the **DESIGN** workspace. You can create a sketch on the drawing sheet to represent a supplementary geometry or custom symbol such as weld and surface symbols. To do this, click on the **Create Sketch** tool in the **CREATE** panel in the **Toolbar**, see Figure 14.82. The **SKETCH** contextual tab appears with various sketching tools, see Figure 14.83. Also, the **SKETCH** dialog box is displayed, see Figure 14.84.

14.82

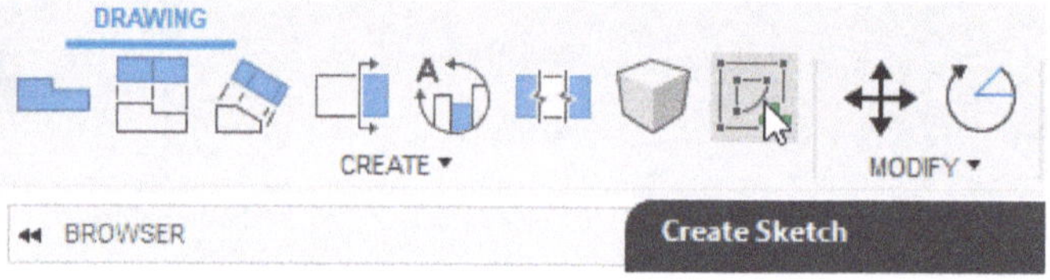

14.83

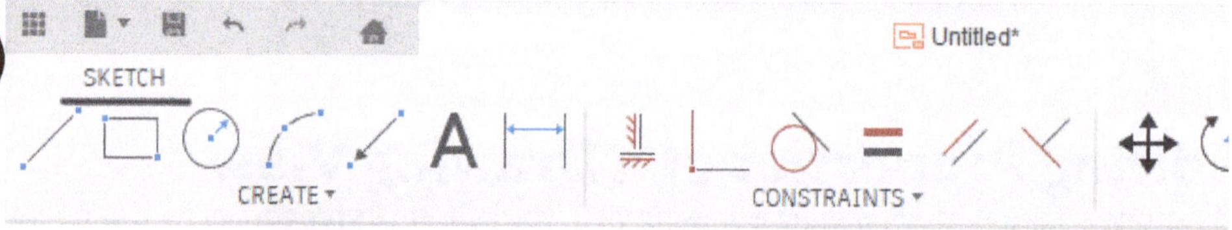

14.84

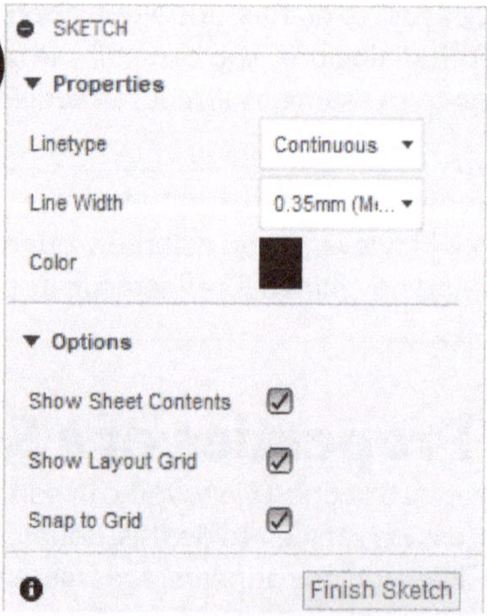

You can draw sketch entities using the sketch tools such as **Line**, **2-Point Rectangle**, **Center Radius Circle**, and **3-Point Arc** the same way as discussed earlier. If needed, you can also apply the required constraints such as horizontal, vertical, and tangent to the sketch entities using the respective constraint tools available in the **CONSTRAINTS** panel. Additionally, you can perform modifying operations such as moving, rotating, copying, trimming, extending, offsetting, and deleting sketch entities using the respective tools in the **MODIFY** panel in the **SKETCH** contextual tab. You can also add text using the **Text** tool of the **SKETCH** contextual tab. After creating the sketch, click on the **FINISH SKETCH** tool in the **SKETCH** contextual tab to exit the **SKETCH** contextual environment.

Note: The sketches drawn on a drawing sheet appear under its **Sheet** node, inside the **Sketches** sub-node of the **BROWSER**.

Moving a Drawing View

In Autodesk Fusion, after placing a drawing view in the drawing sheet, you can move it to define its new position in the drawing sheet by using the **Move** tool or by simply dragging it. The method for moving a drawing view is discussed below:

1. Click on the **Move** tool in the **MODIFY** panel of the **Toolbar** see Figure 14.85 or press the **M** key. The **MOVE** dialog box appears, see Figure 14.86. Also, you are prompted to select drawing views to be moved.

2. Select a drawing view to be moved. The **Transform** area appears in the dialog box with the **Point to Point** tool, see Figure 14.87. You can select single or multiple drawing views to be moved.

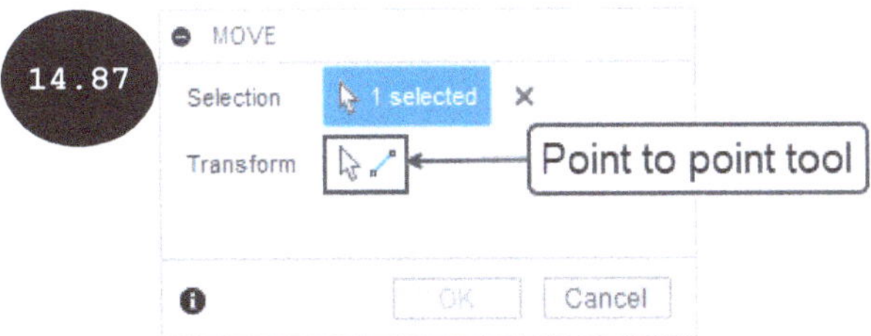

3. After selecting one or more drawing views, click on the **Point to Point** tool in the **Transform** area of the dialog box. You are prompted to specify a base point. Note that the base point acts as a reference point for moving the selected drawing view(s).

4. Click to specify a base point. You are prompted to specify a placement point for the selected drawing view or views. Also, the preview of the selected view(s) is attached to the cursor.

5. Click to specify the second point in the drawing area as the placement point. The selected drawing view(s) are moved to the specified location in the drawing sheet.

Note: On moving a drawing view, the geometries associated with it such as dimensions, centerlines, or section lines will also move along with the drawing view.

To move a drawing view by dragging, move the cursor over the view to be moved and then drag it to the new location on the drawing sheet by pressing and holding the left mouse button on the boundary of the view that appears.

Rotating a Drawing View

In Autodesk Fusion, you can also rotate a drawing view at an angle in two dimensional space by using the **Rotate** tool. The method for rotating a drawing view is discussed below:

1. Click on the **Rotate** tool in the **MODIFY** panel in the **Toolbar**, see Figure 14.88. The **ROTATE** dialog box appears see Figure 14.89 and you are prompted to select drawing views to be rotated. Alternatively, invoke the **MODIFY** drop-down menu in the **Toolbar** and then click on the **Rotate** tool to invoke the **ROTATE** dialog box.

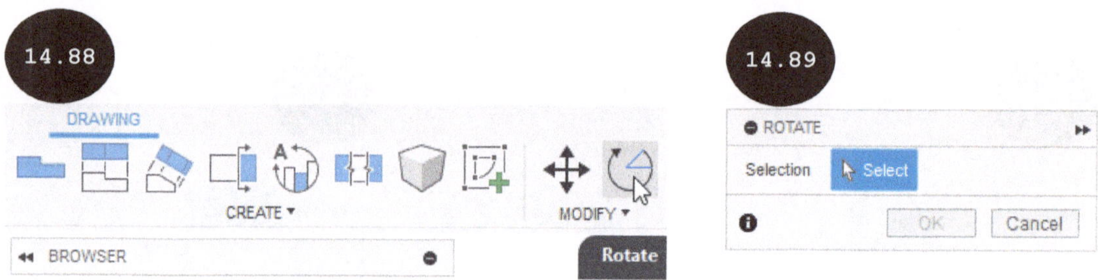

2. Select a drawing view to be rotated. The **Transform** area appears in the dialog box with the **Rotate** tool, see Figure 14.90. You can select single or multiple drawing views to be rotated.

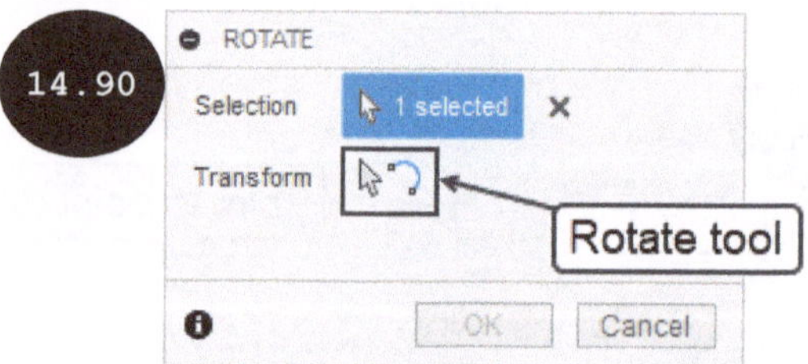

3. After selecting a drawing view(s), click on the **Rotate** tool in the **Transform** area of the dialog box. You are prompted to specify a base point. Note that the base point acts as a reference or center point for rotating the selected drawing view(s).

4. Click to specify the base point. The **Angle** field appears in the dialog box, and you are prompted to specify the rotational angle. Also, a preview of the selected drawing view(s) is attached to the cursor.

5. Enter a rotational angle value in the **Angle** field of the dialog box and then click on the **OK** button. Alternatively, you can also click in the drawing area to define the rotational angle. The selected drawing view(s) is rotated in the drawing sheet at the specified rotational angle.

Deleting a Drawing View

To delete an existing drawing view, invoke the **MODIFY** drop-down menu in the **Toolbar**, see Figure 14.91 and then click on the **Delete** tool. The **DELETE** dialog box appears. Next, select the drawing view to be deleted. You can select single or multiple drawing views. After selecting the drawing view, click on the **OK** button. The selected drawing view is deleted from the drawing sheet and is no longer a part of the drawing. Note that you can select drawing views to be deleted before or after invoking the **Delete** tool. Alternatively, select the drawing views to be deleted and then press the DELETE key to delete the selected views.

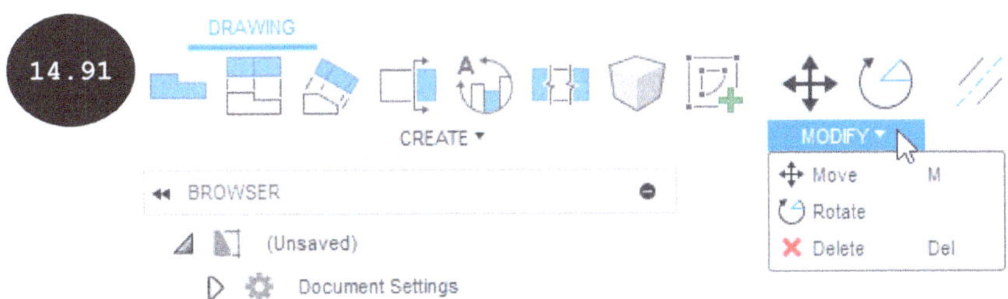

Note: On deleting a drawing view, the geometries associated with it such as dimensions, centerlines, or section lines will also be deleted.

Also, if you delete a parent view, the dependent views such as detail views and section views will also be deleted. However, the projected views remain available in the drawing sheet even on deleting the parent view.

Adding Geometries in Drawing Views

After creating the drawing views of an object, you need to add geometries such as centerlines, center marks, and center mark patterns to identify geometric relationships. For example, the center marks in the drawing views are used for identifying the center of the rounded or circular edges, and the centerlines are used for identifying the center between two lines or edges representing hole features in the drawing views. The different types of geometries are discussed next.

Adding Centerlines

Centerlines are used as references for identifying the center of circular cut features in drawing views, see Figure 14.92. In Autodesk Fusion, you can add a centerline between two linear edges that represent a circular cut or hole feature in a drawing view by using the **Centerline** tool. The method for adding centerlines is discussed below:

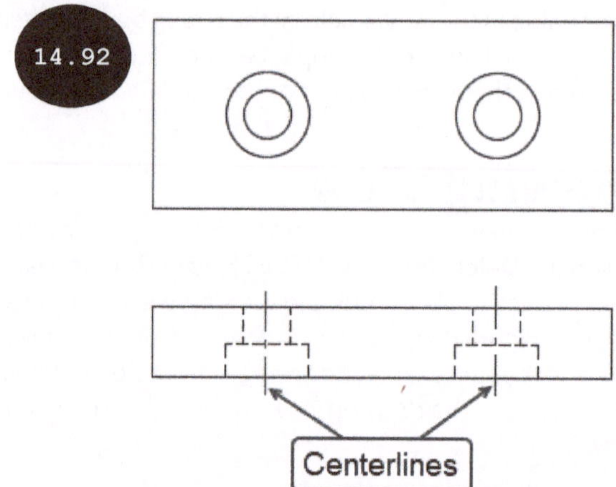

1. Click on the **Centerline** tool in the **GEOMETRY** panel of the **Toolbar**, see Figure 14.93. You are prompted to select the first linear edge.

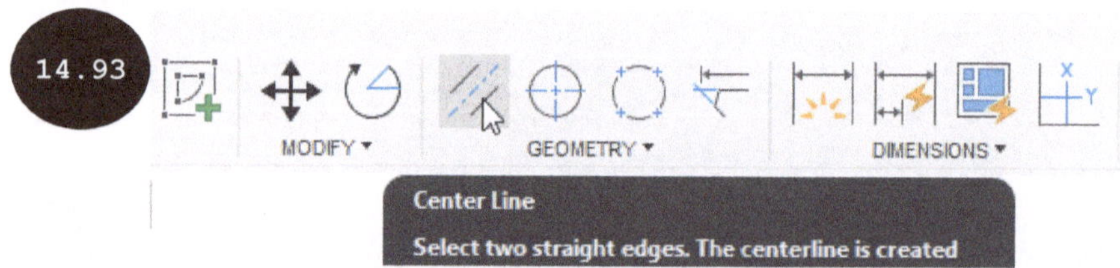

2. Click to select the first linear edge in the drawing view. You are prompted to select the second linear edge.

3. Click to select the second linear edge in the drawing view. The centerline is added at the center of the two selected linear edges in the drawing view.

4. Similarly, you can add centerlines between the other set of linear edges.

Note: After adding a centerline, you can edit its length. To do this, select the centerline to be edited. Arrows appear on both sides of the selected centerline, see Figure 14.94. Now, you can drag these arrows to increase or decrease its length.

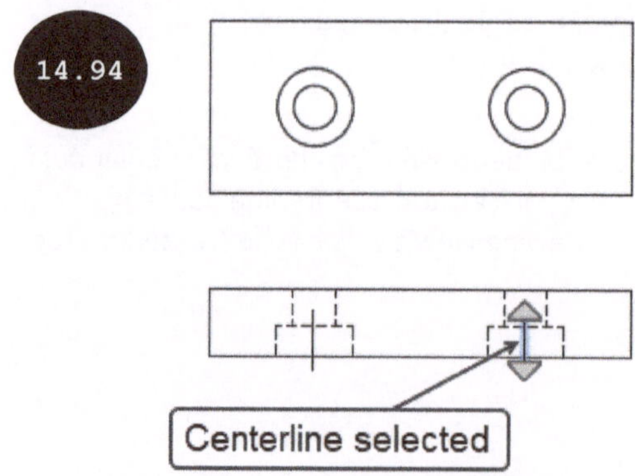

Adding Center Marks

Center marks are used as references for identifying the center of the rounded or circular edges in drawing views, see Figure 14.95. You can add center marks on rounded or circular edges by using the **Center Mark** tool. The method for adding center marks is discussed below:

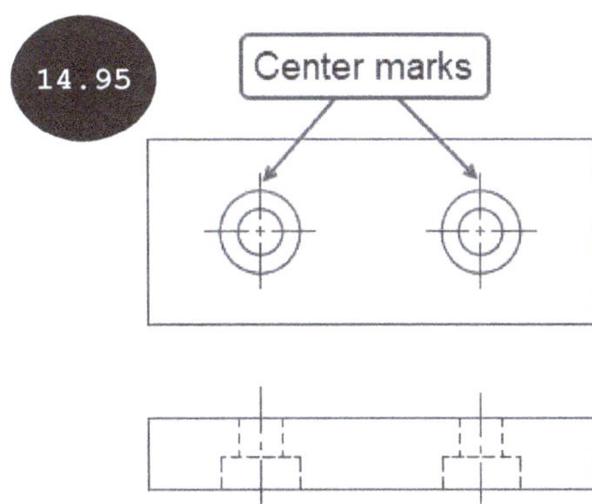

1. Click on the **Center Mark** tool in the **GEOMETRY** panel of the **Toolbar**, see Figure 14.96 or press the **C** key. You are prompted to select a hole or rounded edge in the drawing view.

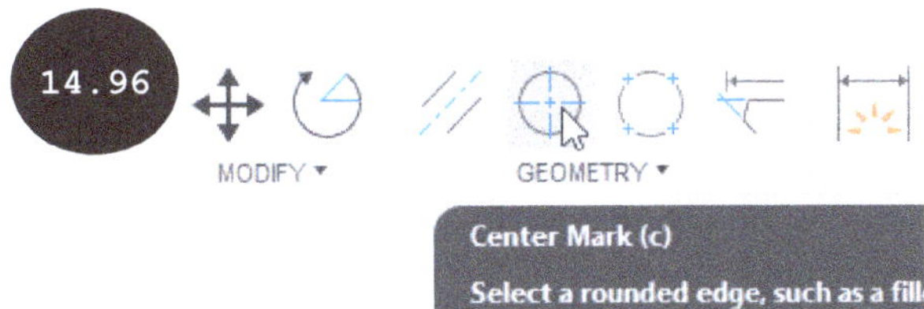

2. Click to select a circular or rounded edge of the drawing view. The center mark is created at the center of the selected circular edge. Also, the **Center Mark** tool is still activated, and you are prompted to select a hole or rounded edge in the drawing view.

3. You can select multiple circular or rounded edges one after the other to create the center marks.

4. After adding all center marks in the drawing views, right-click on the drawing sheet and then click on the **OK** tool in the Marking Menu that appears to exit the **Center Mark** tool.

Note: After adding a center mark, you can edit the length of each of its line entity. To do this, select the center mark to be edited. The arrows appear on both sides of each line entity of the center mark, see Figure 14.97. Now, you can drag these arrows to increase or decrease the length of the line entities.

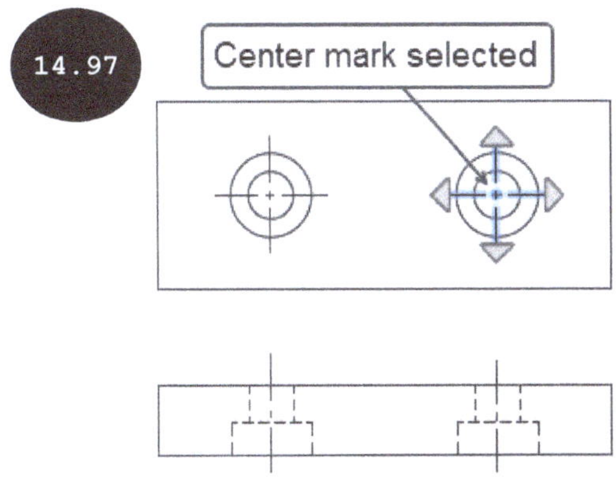

Adding Center Mark Pattern

Center mark pattern geometry is used as a reference for identifying the center and PCD (Pitch Circle Diameter) of the pattern feature in a drawing view, see Figure 14.98. The method for adding center mark pattern geometry is discussed below:

1. Click on the **Center Mark Pattern** tool in the **GEOMETRY** panel in the **Toolbar**, see Figure 14.99. The **CENTER MARK PATTERN** dialog box appears, and you are prompted to select a hole or rounded edge of a pattern instance in the drawing view.

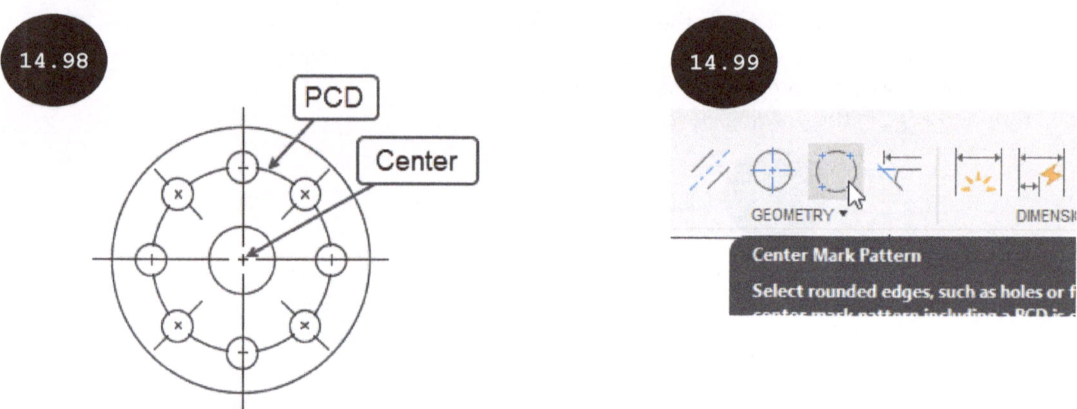

2. Click to select a circular or rounded edge of a pattern instance. Center marks are created on all the pattern instances along with the addition of the PCD, since the **Auto-complete** check box is selected in the dialog box, by default. If you clear this check box, then a center mark is created at the center of the selected circular edge only. Also, you are prompted to select a hole or rounded edge of another pattern instance.

3. Click to select the circular or rounded edge of the second pattern instance. The center mark is created. Also, you are prompted to select a hole or rounded edge of another pattern instance.

4. Similarly, select the circular edges of the remaining pattern instances one after the other. The center marks are created at the center of each selected circular edge. Also, the PCD is added.

5. Select the **Full PCD** check box in the **CENTER MARK PATTERN** dialog box to create a full representation of the PCD. Note that this check box appears on selecting a minimum of three circular edges.

6. Select the **Center Mark** check box in the dialog box for adding the center mark to represent the center of the PCD. Note that this check box appears on selecting a minimum of three circular edges.

7. Click on the **OK** button in the dialog box. The center mark pattern is created.

Note: After adding a center mark pattern, you can edit the length of its line entities, as discussed earlier.

Adding Edge Extension between Two Intersecting Edges

In Autodesk Fusion, you can add edge extension between two intersecting, non-parallel edges by using the **Edge Extension** tool, see Figure 14.100. This tool is used for representing the extension and intersection of two non-parallel edges. It also acts as a reference for applying dimensions. The method for adding edge extension is discussed below:

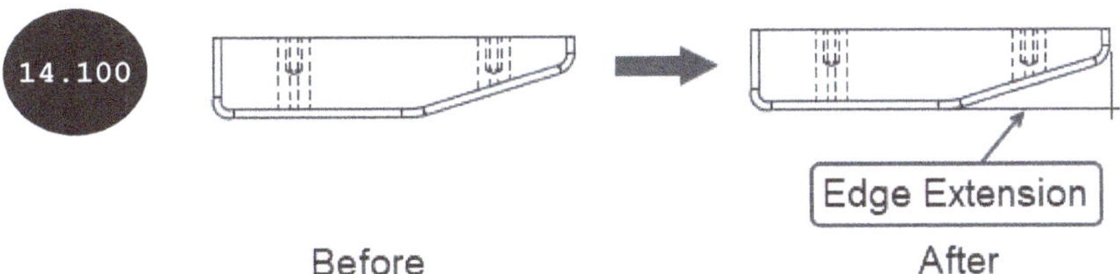

1. Click on the **Edge Extension** tool in the **GEOMETRY** panel of the **Toolbar**, see Figure 14.101. You are prompted to select the first edge.

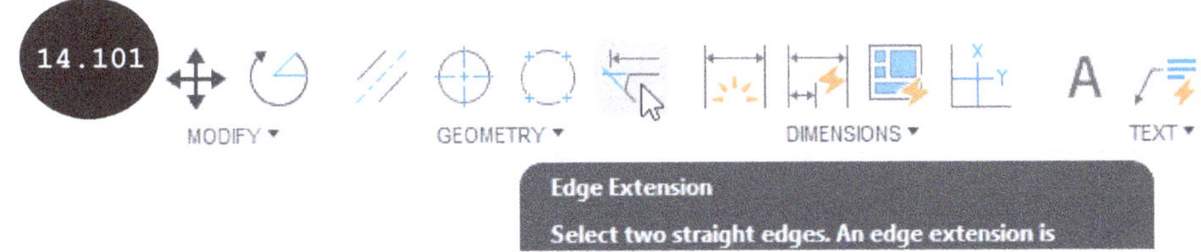

2. Click to select the first edge of the drawing view. You are prompted to select the second edge.

3. Click to select the second non-parallel edge of the drawing view. The edge extension is added between the selected edges. Next, press the ESC key to exit the **Edge Extension** tool.

Applying Dimensions

After creating various drawing views of a component or an assembly, you need to apply dimensions to them. In Autodesk Fusion, you can apply various types of dimensions by using the tools available in the **DIMENSIONS** drop-down menu of the **Toolbar**, see Figure 14.102. The methods for applying various types of dimensions are discussed next.

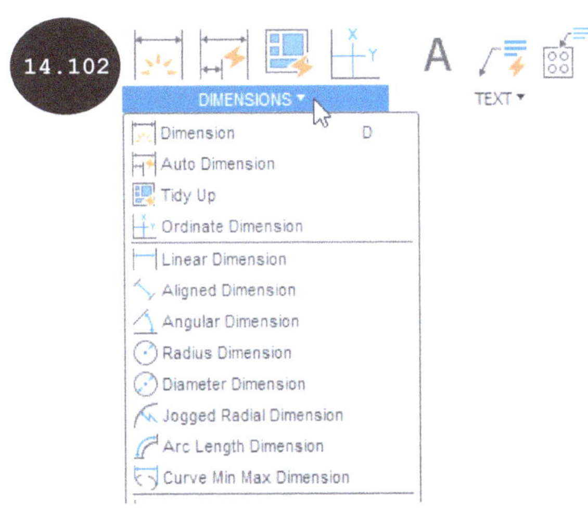

Applying Linear, Aligned, Angular, Radius, and Diameter Dimensions

In Autodesk Fusion, you can apply various types of dimensions such as linear, aligned, angular, and radius using the **Dimension** tool. This tool is used for applying dimension, depending upon the type of entity selected. For example, if you select a circular edge, the diameter dimension is applied, and if you select a linear edge, the linear dimension is applied. Also, if you select two edges or points/vertices, the dimension between the selected edges/points is applied. You can select an edge, two edges, or two vertices to apply a dimension using the **Dimension** tool. The methods for applying various types of dimensions using this tool are the same as discussed earlier while applying dimensions to sketch entities.

Note that, you can invoke this tool by clicking on the **Dimension** tool in the **DIMENSIONS** panel in the **Toolbar**, see Figure 14.102 or by pressing the **D** key. Alternatively, you can right-click in the drawing area and then select **Dimensions > Dimension** in the Marking Menu that appears.

Once the **Dimension** tool is activated, select an edge, two edges, or two vertices to apply dimension. The dimension gets attached to the cursor depending upon the entity or entities selected. Next, click to define the placement point for the dimension in the drawing sheet. Note that after applying a dimension, the **Dimension** tool is still activated and you can apply the remaining dimensions one by one in the drawing views, see Figure 14.104.

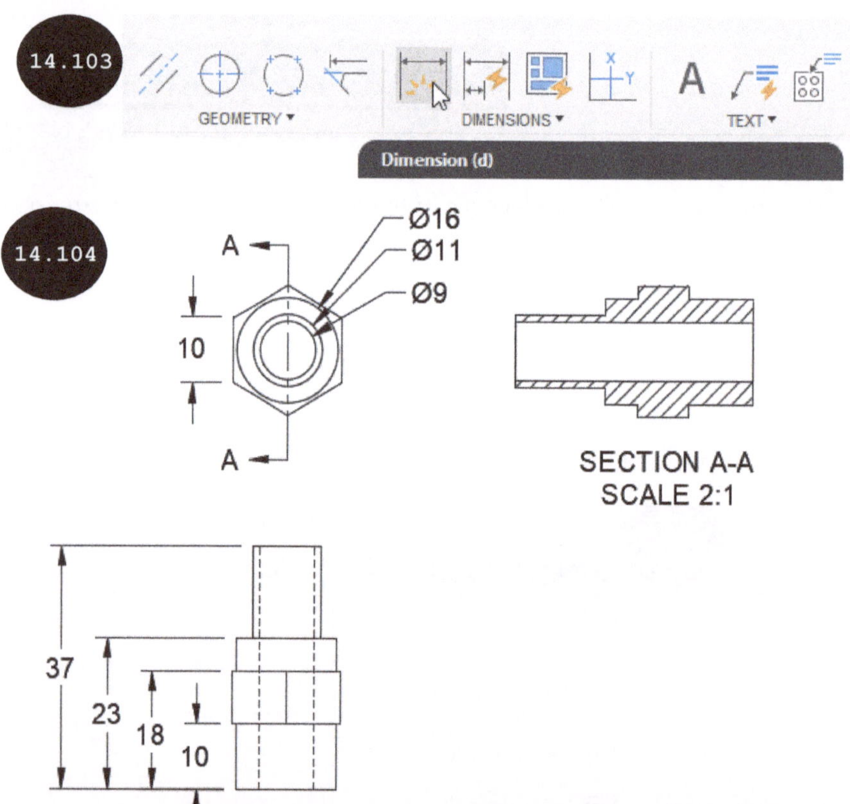

In addition to applying various types of dimensions by using the **Dimension** tool, you can also apply individual dimensions by using the respective dimension tool available in the **DIMENSION** drop-down menu of the **Toolbar**. For example, to apply linear dimensions, you can activate the **Linear Dimension** tool and to apply radius dimensions, you can activate the **Radius Dimension** tool.

Applying Ordinate Dimensions

The **Ordinate Dimension** tool is used for applying ordinate dimensions in drawing views. Ordinate dimensions are used for dimensioning machine parts for maintaining accuracy and measuring distance in the X and Y directions from a specified base point, see Figure 14.105. The method for applying ordinate dimensions is discussed below:

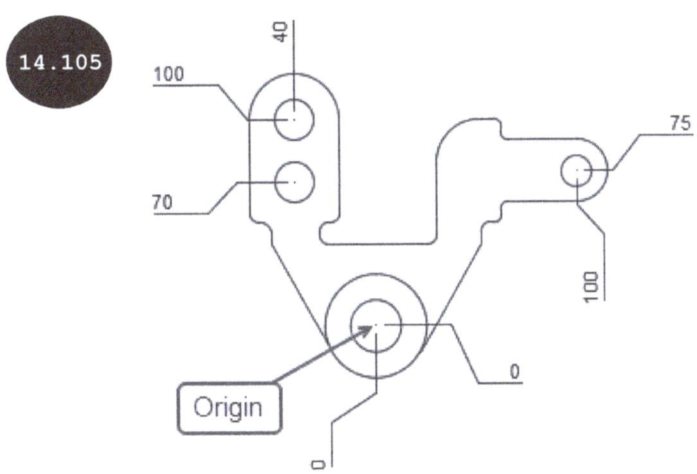

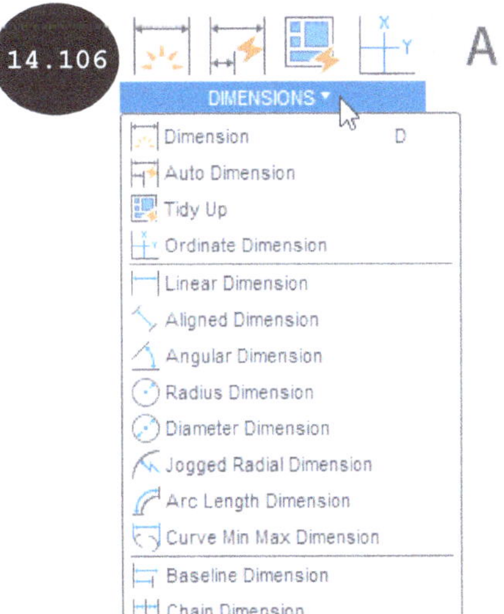

1. Invoke the **DIMENSION** drop-down menu of the **Toolbar** and then click on the **Ordinate Dimension** tool, see Figure 14.106. The 0 dimension leader appears attached to the cursor and you are prompted to define a base point to measure all dimensions.

2. Click on an entity of the drawing view to define it as the origin. The origin is defined, and you are prompted to specify the placement point for the 0 dimension.

3. Click on the drawing sheet to define the placement of the 0 dimension. The 0 dimension is applied, and a dimension leader appears attached to the cursor. Also, you are prompted to select the reference entity to be measured from the origin (0 dimension).

4. Click on an entity of the drawing view to be dimensioned from the origin. The ordinate dimension appears attached to the selected entity and you are prompted to define its placement point.

5. Click to define the placement for the ordinate dimension. You are prompted to select another reference entity to be measured from the origin (0 dimension).

6. You can similarly select reference entities to be measured from the origin one by one and apply ordinate dimensions.

Applying Baseline Dimensions

Baseline dimensions are a series of parallel linear dimensions that share the same base point, see Figure 14.107. The baseline dimensions are used for eliminating cumulative errors that can occur due to the rounded dimension values between consecutive adjacent dimensions or due to the upper and lower dimension limits. In Autodesk Fusion, you can apply baseline dimensions by using the **Baseline Dimension** tool. The method for applying baseline dimensions is discussed below:

1. Apply a linear dimension in a drawing view as the base dimension by using the **Dimension** tool, see Figure 14.108.

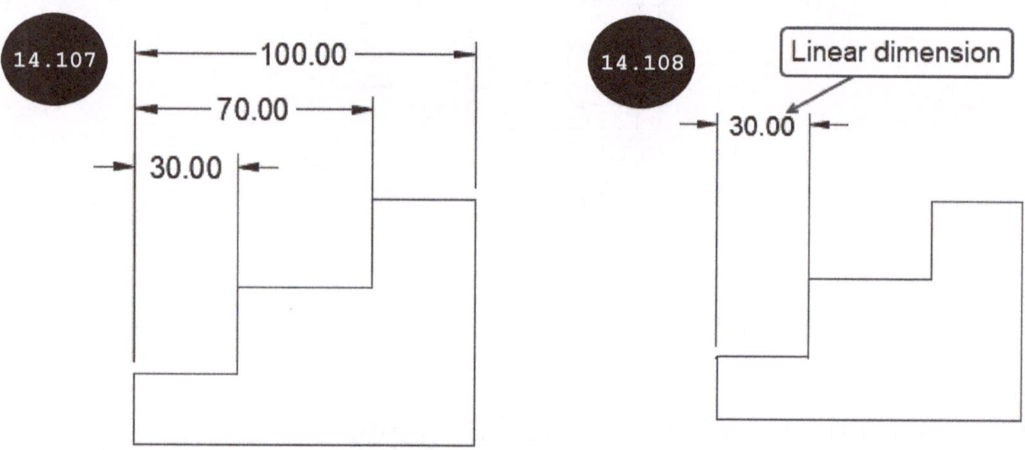

Note: In Autodesk Fusion, before you start applying the baseline dimensions, you need to apply a linear dimension which will be used as the base dimension.

2. Invoke the **DIMENSION** drop-down menu of the **Toolbar** and then click on the **Baseline Dimension** tool, see Figure 14.109. You are prompted to select a base dimension.

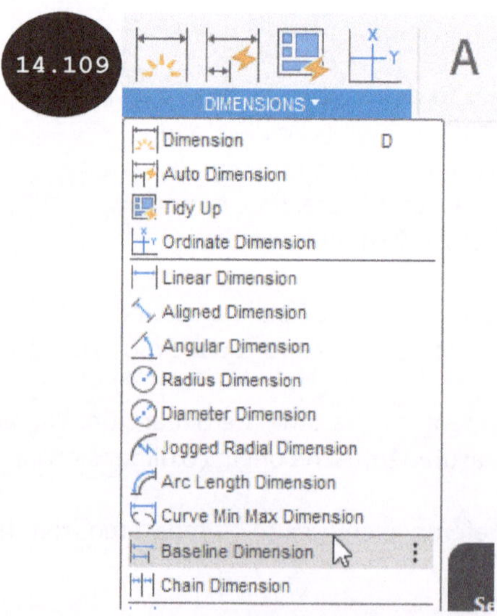

3. Select a linear dimension as the base dimension by clicking the left mouse button, closer to its first extension line. The baseline dimension appears attached to the cursor such that its first extension line is fixed, and you are prompted to specify the origin of its second extension line.

4. Click to specify the origin of the second extension line of the baseline dimension. The first baseline dimension is applied. A preview of the second baseline dimension appears and you are prompted to specify the origin of its second extension line.

5. Click to specify the origin of the second baseline dimension. The second baseline dimension is applied. A preview of the third baseline dimension appears and you are prompted to specify the origin of its second extension line.

Note: In Autodesk Fusion, the first extension line of the base dimension is used as the first extension line of all the baseline dimensions, see Figure 14.110.

6. You can similarly apply multiple baseline dimensions one after the other by specifying the origin of the second extension lines, see Figure 14.110. Next, press the ENTER key to exit the tool.

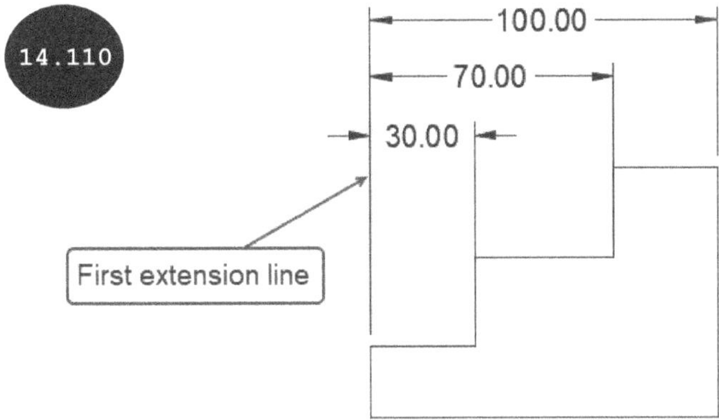

Applying Chain Dimensions

Similar to applying baseline dimensions, you can apply chain dimensions in a drawing, see Figure 14.111. Chain dimensions are a chain of linear dimensions placed end to end (the second extension line of the first linear dimension is used as the first extension line for the next linear dimension).

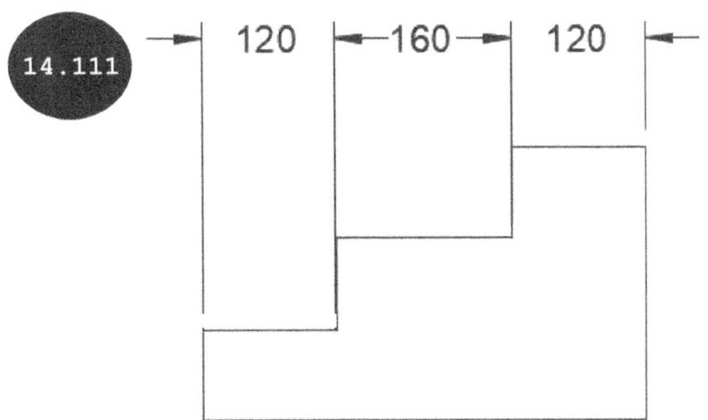

In Autodesk Fusion, you can apply chain dimensions by using the **Chain Dimension** tool. The method for applying chain dimensions is discussed below:

1. Apply a linear dimension in a drawing view as the base dimension by using the **Dimension** tool, see Figure 14.112. Note that to apply chain dimensions, you need to first create a linear dimension as the base dimension.

2. Invoke the **DIMENSION** drop-down menu of the **Toolbar** and then click on the **Chain Dimension** tool, see Figure 14.113. You are prompted to select a base dimension.

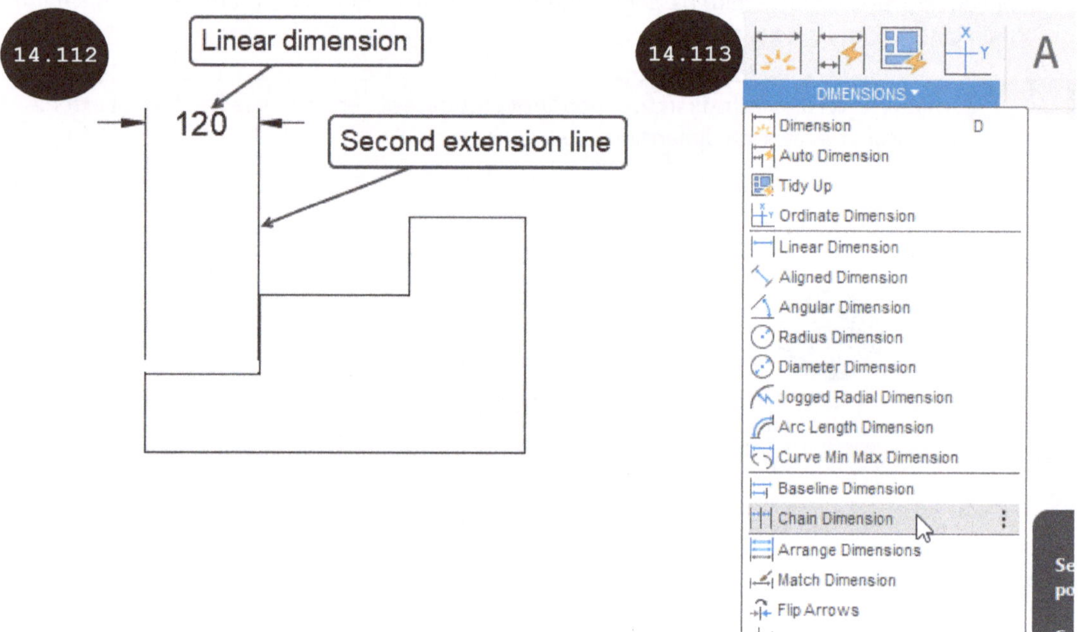

3. Select a linear dimension as the base dimension by clicking the left mouse button closer to its second extension line. A preview of the baseline dimension appears with the origin of the first extension line fixed at the second extension line of the base dimension and you are prompted to specify the origin of the second extension line of the dimension.

4. Click to specify the origin of the second extension of the dimension in the drawing view. The chain dimension is applied, a preview of the next dimension appears, and you are prompted to specify the origin of its second extension line.

5. Similarly, you can apply multiple chain dimensions one after another by specifying the origin of the second extension lines. After applying chain dimensions, press the ENTER key to exit the tool.

Applying Dimensions Automatically

In Autodesk Fusion, you can also automatically apply various types of dimensions to drawing views using the **Auto Dimension** tool. To do this, click on the **Auto Dimension** tool in the **DIMENSIONS** panel, see Figure 14.114. The **AUTO DIMENSION** dialog box appears, where you can select the required dimension types to apply to the drawing views. When you select the dimension types, a preview of the selected dimensions displays directly on the drawing views. You can also adjust settings such as the datum location and the density of the selected dimension types. After configuring the desired dimension settings, click the **OK** button to automatically apply the dimensions to the drawing views.

Editing a Dimension

In Autodesk Fusion, after applying a dimension, you can edit it to override its dimension value, insert symbols, specify tolerances, and so on. To do this, double-click on the dimension value to be edited. The **DIMENSION** dialog box appears, see Figure 14.115. Also, the dimension value appears as "<*value*>" in an edit field. Note that the availability of options in the **DIMENSION** dialog box depends upon the type of dimension selected. In Figure 14.114, the **DIMENSION** dialog box appears while editing the linear dimension by double-clicking on it.

14.115

DIMENSION
Text
Repres... XX XX XX
Insert ... Ø
Properties
Type General
Design Tutorial 1 animati...
Source Tutorial 1 animati...
Proper... Part Number
Insert Property
Primary Units
Primar... mm
Linear ... 0.12
Linear ... 0.12
Zeros/... 0.0 0.0 mm
Alternate Units
Tolerances
Inspection
Close

To override the dimension value, enter a new dimension value in the edit field that appears. In the **DIMENSION** dialog box, the **Linear Precision** or **Angular Precision** drop-down list is used for selecting the precision for the selected linear or angular dimension, respectively. The **Primary Units** drop-down list is used for selecting the unit for the selected dimension. You can choose to show the leading zeros, trailing zeros, and unit abbreviation by activating the respective button in the **Zeros/Units** area of the dialog box.

To display an alternate unit of the dimension, select the **Alternate Units** check box to activate the **Alternate Units** rollout. You can specify the unit, format, and precision for the alternate unit by using the respective options that appear on selecting the **Alternate Units** check box in the dialog box.
To insert a symbol, place the cursor on the required side of the dimension value in the edit field where you want to insert the symbol.

Next, click on the down arrow in the **Insert Symbol** area of the dialog box. The **Symbol** flyout appears, see Figure 14.116. In this flyout, select the required symbol. The selected symbol is inserted on the specified side of the dimension value in the edit field, see Figure 14.117. In this figure, the diameter symbol is inserted into the linear dimension.

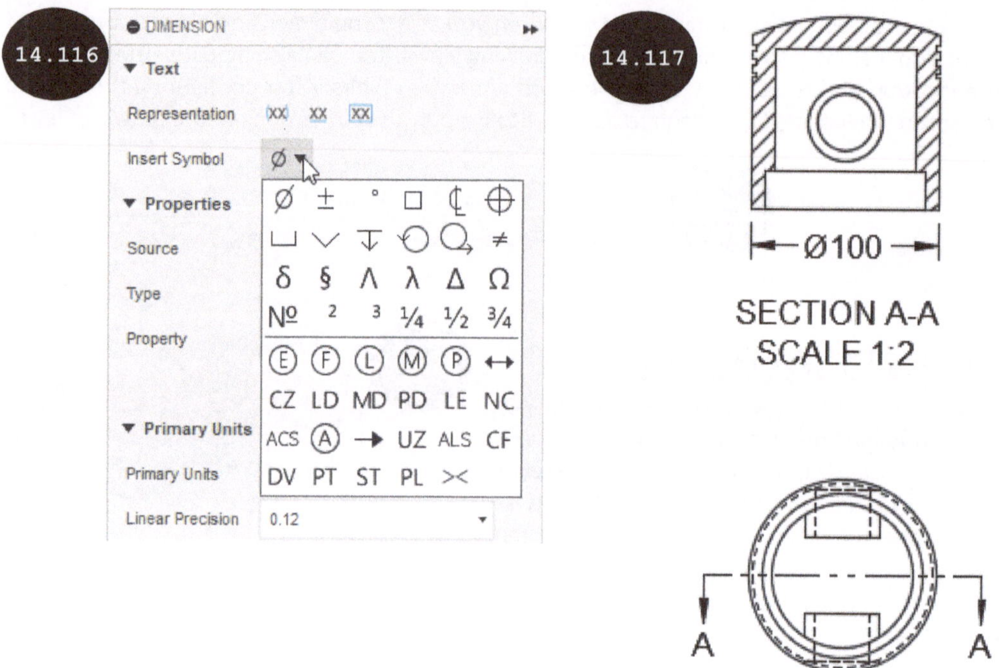

You can also specify the required type of tolerance for the selected dimension using the **Type** drop-down list in the **Tolerances** rollout of the dialog box. Besides, you can also specify inspection options for the selected dimension by using the **Inspection** rollout of the dialog box. You can specify the representation options for the selected dimension by using the options in the **Representation** area of the **Text** rollout of the dialog box. After editing the dimension, close the dialog box by clicking on the **Close** button.

Arranging Dimensions

In Autodesk Fusion, you can arrange linear and angular dimensions concerning a base dimension by using the **Arrange Dimensions** tool. The method for arranging dimensions is discussed below:

1. Invoke the **DIMENSION** drop-down menu in the **Toolbar** and then click on the **Arrange Dimensions** tool. The **ARRANGE DIMENSIONS** dialog box appears, see Figure 14.118.

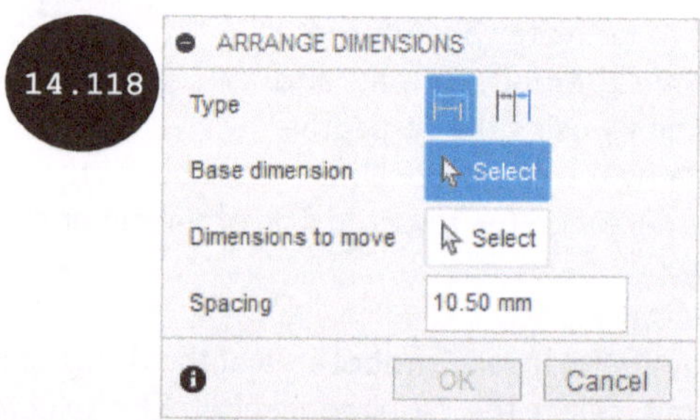

Type: By default, the **Stack** button is activated in the **Type** area of the dialog box. As a result, the selected dimensions will be stacked one over the other. On activating the **Align** button, the selected dimensions will be arranged side by side to a base dimension.

2. Select the required button (**Stack** or **Align**) in the **Type** area of the dialog box.

3. Select a dimension in the drawing area as the base dimension.

4. Select one or more dimensions to be arranged concerning the base dimension selected.

5. Specify the required spacing between the selected dimensions in the **Spacing** field.

6. Click on the **OK** button. The dimensions get arranged.

Breaking Dimension Lines

In Autodesk Fusion, you can break dimensions or leader lines that intersect with other dimensions or leader lines to avoid overlapping or confusion by using the **Dimension Break** tool, see Figures 14.119 and 14.120. Figure 14.119 shows the intersecting dimension lines and Figure 14.120 shows the dimensions after breaking a dimension line. The method for breaking dimensions or leader lines is discussed below:

1. Invoke the **DIMENSION** drop-down menu in the **Toolbar** and then click on the **Dimension Break** tool. The **DIMENSION BREAK** dialog box appears, see Figure 14.121.

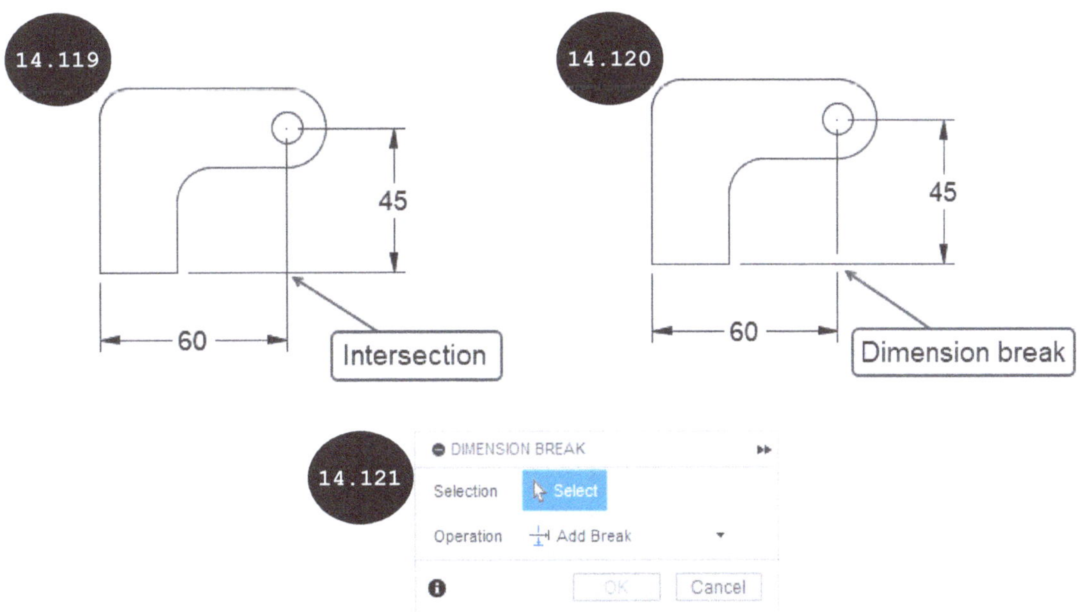

2. Select the dimensions or leader lines that are intersecting with each other one by one.

3. Ensure that the **Add Break** option is selected in the **Operation** drop-down list of the dialog box.

Note: The **Add Break** option is used for adding a break between the selected dimension or leader lines, whereas the **Remove Break** option is used for removing the existing break from the selected dimension lines.

4. Click on the **OK** button in the dialog box. The first selected dimension line gets broken to avoid overlapping.

Similar to breaking dimension or leader lines, you can remove the existing break applied between the dimension or leader lines by selecting the **Remove Break** option in the **Operation** drop-down list of the **DIMENSION BREAK** dialog box.

Adding Text/Note

In Autodesk Fusion, you can add text or notes on a drawing sheet using the **Text** tool. Generally, adding text or notes in drawings is used for conveying additional information that is not available in the drawing views. The method for adding text is discussed below:

1. Click on the **Text** tool in the **TEXT** panel of the **Toolbar** see Figure 14.122 or press the T key. You are prompted to specify the first corner of the text box.

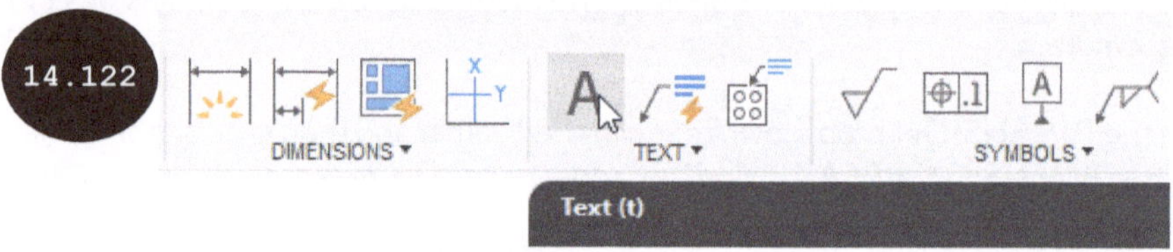

2. Click to specify the first corner of the text box in the drawing sheet, see Figure 14.123. A preview of the text box appears such that its first corner is fixed at the specified location and the diagonally opposite corner is attached to the cursor. Also, you are prompted to specify the opposite corner of the text box.

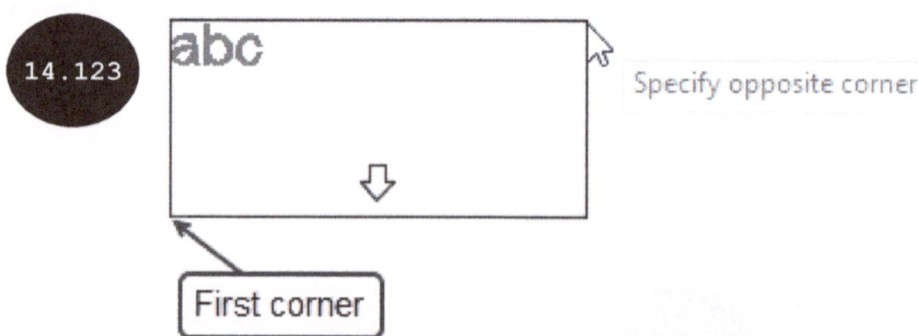

3. Click to specify the diagonally opposite corner of the text box in the drawing sheet. A text box with an indent ruler appears in the drawing area for writing the text, see Figure 14.124. Also, the **TEXT** dialog box appears, see Figure 14.125.

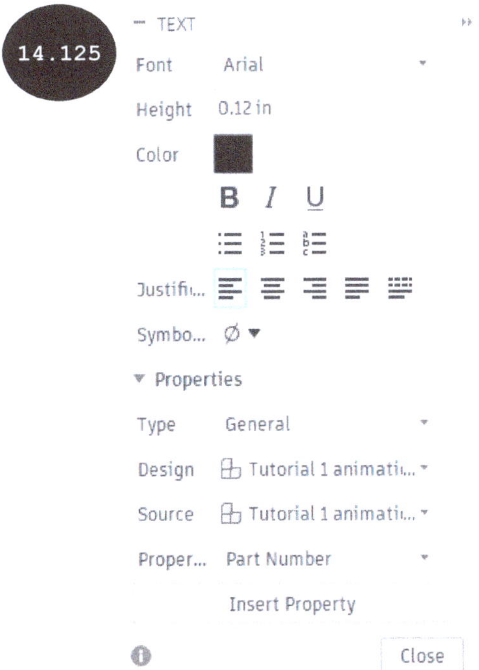

4. Write the required text in the text box. Next, specify the required text font, height, color, and justification in the **TEXT** dialog box.

5. Click anywhere outside the text box. The text is added in the specified location of the drawing sheet.

Note: You can also edit the existing text of the drawing. To do this, double-click on the text to be edited. The text box and **TEXT** dialog box appear for editing the text and its style. You can also change the width and height of the text box by dragging the ends of the text box or the ruler. After editing the text, click anywhere in the drawing area.

Adding Text/Note With Leader

You can add a custom or user-defined text or note attached to an edge of a drawing view with a leader by using the **Note** and **Leader Note** tools of the **TEXT** drop-down menu in the **Toolbar**, see Figure 14.126. Moreover, you can also add a hole, thread, or bend note on a hole, a thread, or a bend edge of a drawing view by using the **Hole and Thread Note** tool and the **Bend Note** tool, respectively. The method for adding a note or text with a leader is discussed below:

1. Invoke the **TEXT** drop-down menu in the **Toolbar**, see Figure 14.126 and then click on the required tool (**Note**, **Leader Note**, **Hole and Thread Note**, or **Bend Note**). The **NOTE** dialog box appears, see Figure 14.127. Also, you are prompted to select an edge of a drawing view.

Note: The default option selected in the **Type** drop-down list of the **NOTE** dialog box depends on the tool selected. On selecting the **Note** tool, the **Automatic** option is selected in the **Type** drop-down list by default. Similarly, on selecting the **Leader Note** or **Hole and Thread Note** tool, the respective options are selected in the **Type** drop-down list by default.

2. Click to select an edge of a drawing view. The leader arrow is attached to the selected edge, and you are prompted to specify the placement point for the text. Note that if the **Hole and Thread Note** option is selected in the **Type** drop-down list, then you can only select the edges of a hole or thread.

3. Click on the drawing sheet to define the placement of the text. An edit box and the **TEXT** dialog box appear. Note that if a hole is selected, then the details of the hole appear automatically on defining the placement of the text.

4. Write the text in the edit box, as required. Next, specify the required text font, height, and justification in the **TEXT** dialog box.

5. Click anywhere on the drawing sheet. The text or note is added, attached to the selected edge of the drawing view, with a leader, see Figure 14.128.

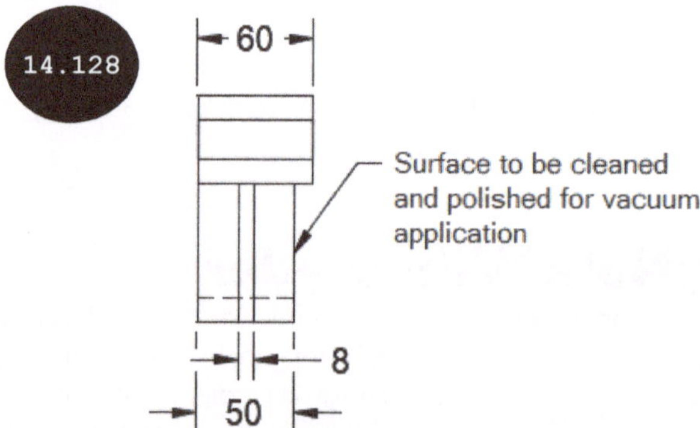

Adding the Surface Texture Symbol

In Fusion, you can add a surface texture symbol to specify the surface texture or finish for a face of a model. A surface texture symbol has three components: surface roughness, waviness, and lay, see Figure 14.129. The specifications given in a surface texture symbol are used for machining the respective surface of the object. You can add a surface texture symbol to an edge of a surface in a drawing view by using the **Surface Texture** tool. The method for adding surface texture is discussed below:

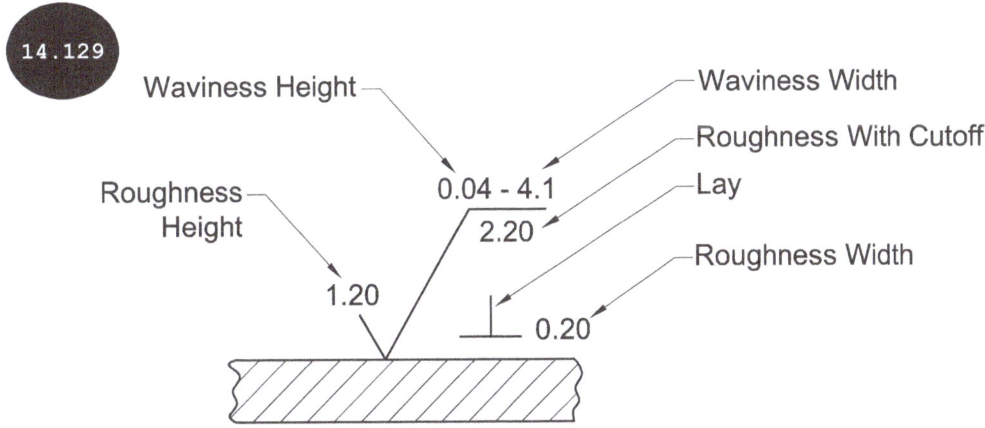

1. Click on the **Surface Texture** tool in the **SYMBOLS** panel of the **Toolbar**, see Figure 14.130. You are prompted to select an object.

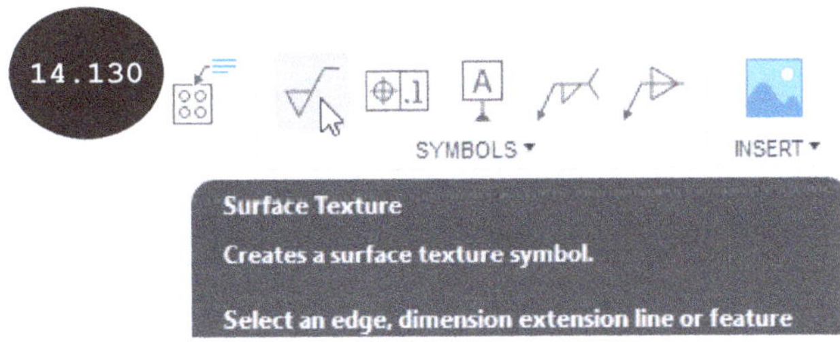

2. Select an edge of a drawing view. The surface texture symbol is attached to the selected edge, and you are prompted to define its start point on the edge selected.

3. Click to specify the start point of the surface texture symbol along the selected edge. The surface texture symbol is attached to the selected edge with a leader, and you are prompted to define its placement on the drawing sheet.

4. Click to specify the placement point and then press ENTER. The surface texture symbol is placed on the specified location and is attached to the selected edge of the drawing view with a leader. Also, the **SURFACE TEXTURE** dialog box appears, see Figure 14.131.

Note: The availability of the options in the **SURFACE TEXTURE** dialog box depends upon the type of drawing standard (ASME or ISO) and the surface symbol selected.

5. Select the required type of surface finish symbol in the **Symbol Type** area of the dialog box.

6. Specify the required specification for the surface texture such as roughness, waviness, or process, and lay in the respective fields of the dialog box. Next, click on the **OK** button. The surface texture is applied to the selected edge of the drawing view, see Figure 14.132.

14.131

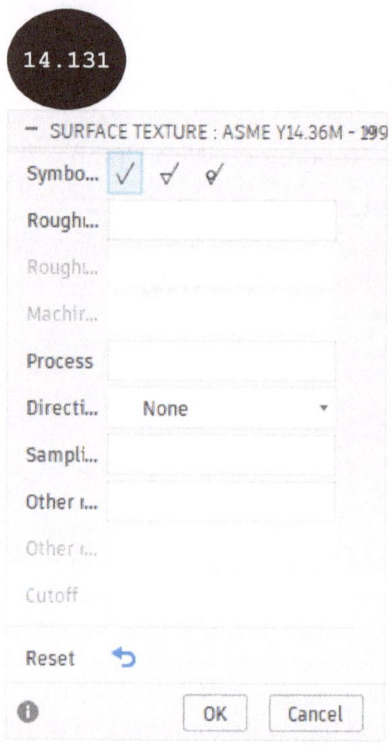

14.132

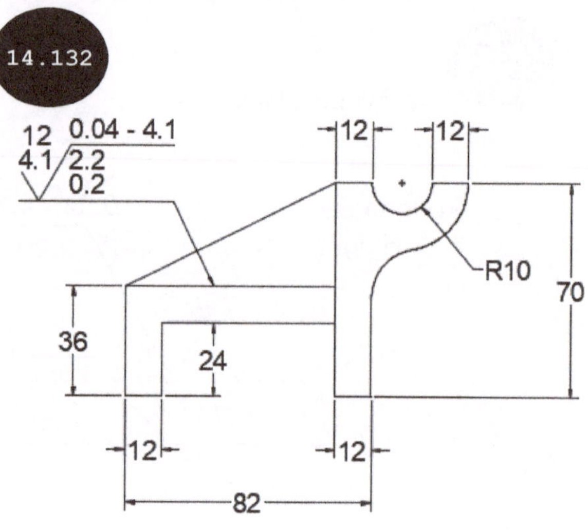

Creating the Bill of Material (BOM)/Part List

After creating all the required drawing views of an assembly, you need to create the Bill of Material/Part list. The Bill of Material (BOM)/Part list contains all the required information such as the number of parts used in an assembly, part number, quantity of each part, material, and so on. Since the Bill of Material (BOM) contains all the information, it serves as a primary source of communication between the manufacturer and the vendors as well as the suppliers. The method for creating a Bill of Material (BOM)/Part list for an assembly is discussed below:

1. Click on the **Table** tool in the **TABLES** panel of the **Toolbar**, see Figure 14.133. The preview of a table appears attached to the cursor. Also, the **TABLE** dialog box appears, see Figure 14.134.

14.133

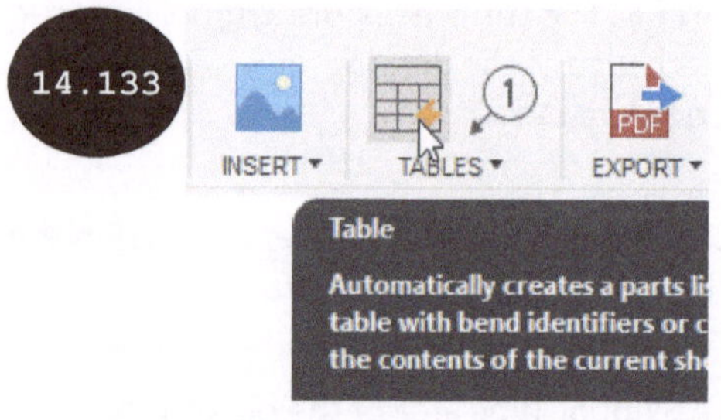

14.134

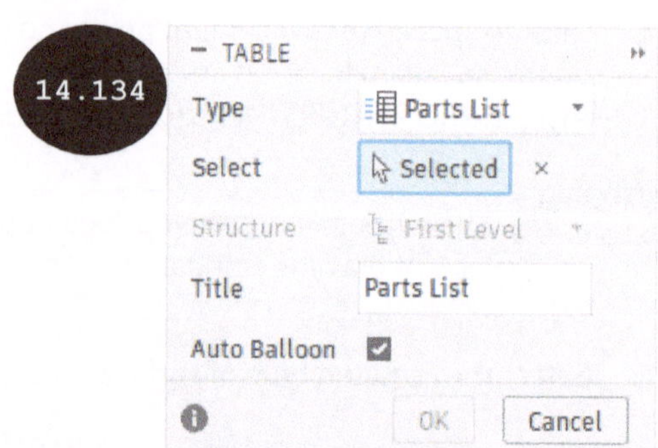

Note: If the current drawing sheet has more than one base view reference created, then on invoking the **Table** tool, you are prompted to select a drawing view for creating the part list and adding the balloons. Select the drawing view by clicking on it in the drawing sheet. You can create a custom empty table with custom number of rows and columns in the drawing sheet by selecting the **Custom Table** option in the **Type** drop-down list of the **TABLE** dialog box. On selecting the **Parts List** option, you can create a parts list in the drawing area. You can also create a bend table, hole table, and revision history by selecting the respective option in the **Type** drop-down list. By default, the **Automatic** option is selected, hence a suitable table is created automatically depending on the components present in the drawing sheet. In case of an assembly, the **Part List** option will be selected in this drop-down list, by default.

Structure: The **First Level** option of the **Structure** drop-down list is used for including only the top-level assembly components in the parts list. The **All Levels** option of the **Structure** drop-down list is used for including sub-assemblies also in the parts list.

2. Select the required option in the **Structure** drop-down list of the dialog box.

Auto Balloon: By default, the **Auto Balloon** check box is selected in the dialog box. As a result, balloons are automatically added to each component of the assembly when you specify the placement point of the Part List in the drawing area.

3. Click on the drawing sheet to specify the position of the BOM/Part list. The BOM/Part list is placed in the specified position in the drawing sheet and the balloons are added automaticaly to each component of the assembly in the selected drawing view, see Figure 14.135. Note that if the Part list is placed on the upper half of the drawing sheet, then the part numbering is from top to bottom, whereas if the part list is placed on the lower half of the sheet, then the part numbering is from bottom to top.

PARTS LIST				
ITEM	QTY	PART NUMBER	DESCRIPTION	MATERIAL
1	1	BASE		STEEL
2	1	VICE JAW		STEEL
3	1	JAW SCREW		STEEL
4	1	SCREW BAR		STEEL

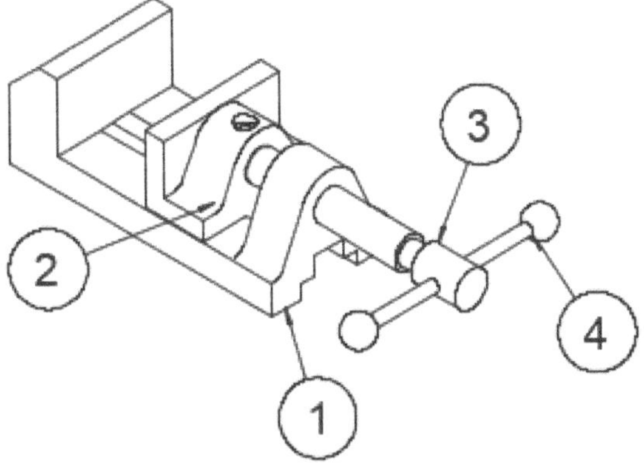

Tip: Before specifying the position of the Parts list, you can flip its position to either side of the cursor by pressing the SHIFT key.

Note: In Autodesk Fusion, you can also customize the BOM/Parts list by adding or removing item columns, as required in the BOM. To do this, double-click on the Parts list in the drawing sheet. The **PARTS LIST** dialog box appears. In this dialog box, you can select the check boxes of the columns to be added in the Parts list and clear the check boxes of the columns to be removed or not included in the Parts list. Next, close the dialog box.

Note: As discussed, the balloons are added automatically to each component of the assembly on inserting the parts list. However, you may need to edit the default balloon locations to arrange them properly on the drawing sheet. To do this, select the balloon and then move it to a new location in the drawing sheet by using its grips.

Adding Balloons Manually

A Balloon is attached to a component with a leader line and displays the respective part number assigned in the Bill of Material (BOM)/Parts list. In the drawings, balloons are generally added to the individual components of an assembly to identify them easily concerning the part number assigned in the Bill of Materials (BOM)/Parts list. In Autodesk Fusion, when you add the BOM/Parts list by using the **Table** tool, the balloons are added to each component of the assembly, automatically. Besides, you can also add balloons to the components of an assembly, manually by using the **Balloon** tool. The method for adding balloons manually is discussed below:

1. Click on the **Balloon** tool in the **TABLES** panel of the **Toolbar**, see Figure 14.136 or press the **B** key. The **BALLOON** dialog box appears, see Figure 14.137 and you are prompted to select an edge of the component in a drawing view to add a balloon.

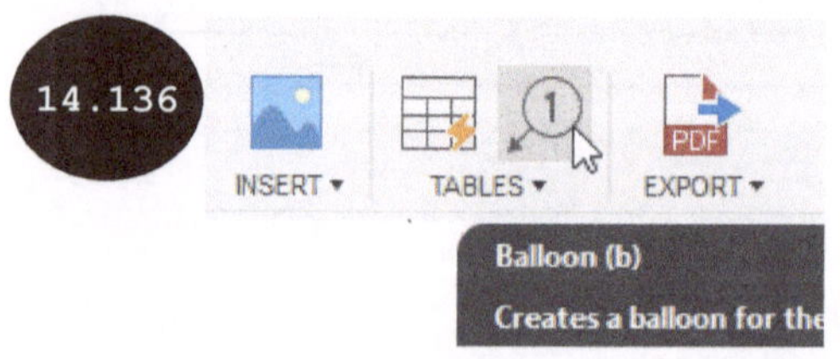

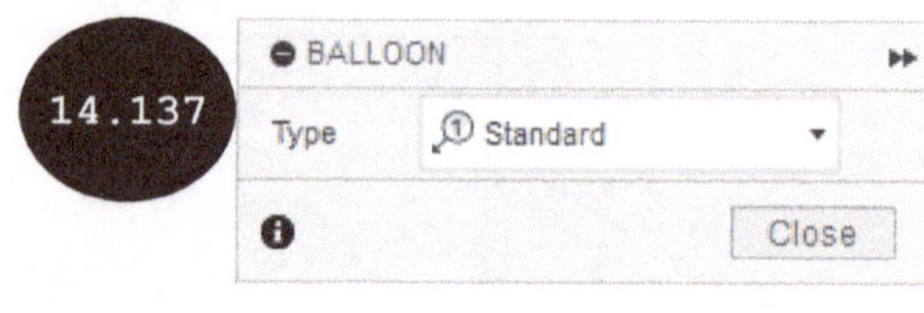

2. Ensure that the **Standard** option is selected in the **Type** drop-down list of the **BALLOON** dialog box to add a balloon with a standard leader type. You can also add a balloon with a curved leader by selecting the **Patent** option in this drop-down list.

3. Click on an edge of a component in a drawing view. The leader arrow is attached to the selected edge, and you are prompted to specify the placement of the balloon.

4. Click to specify the placement of the balloon in the drawing sheet. The balloon is added to the selected edge of the component with a display of its part number, see Figures 14.138 and 14.139. Figure 14.138 shows the standard balloon, whereas Figure 14.139 shows the patent balloon with a curved leader.

5. You can similarly add balloons to other components one after the other, manually.

Note: In Autodesk Fusion, you can suppress or unsuppress the components of an assembly in the drawing view by clearing or selecting the check boxes of the components, respectively in the **BROWSER**, see Figure 14.140. If you suppress a component of the assembly by clearing its check box in the **BROWSER**, then the component will be removed from the drawing views and the Part list will be updated, accordingly.

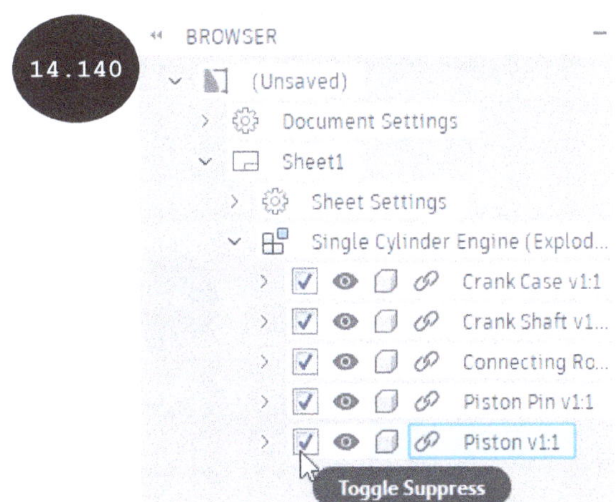

Renumbering Balloons

In Autodesk Fusion, after adding balloons to each component of the assembly in a drawing view, you can renumber them by using the **Renumber** tool. To do this, invoke the **TABLES** drop-down menu in the **Toolbar** and then click on the **Renumber** tool, see Figure 14.141. The **RENUMBER** dialog box appears, see Figure 14.142.

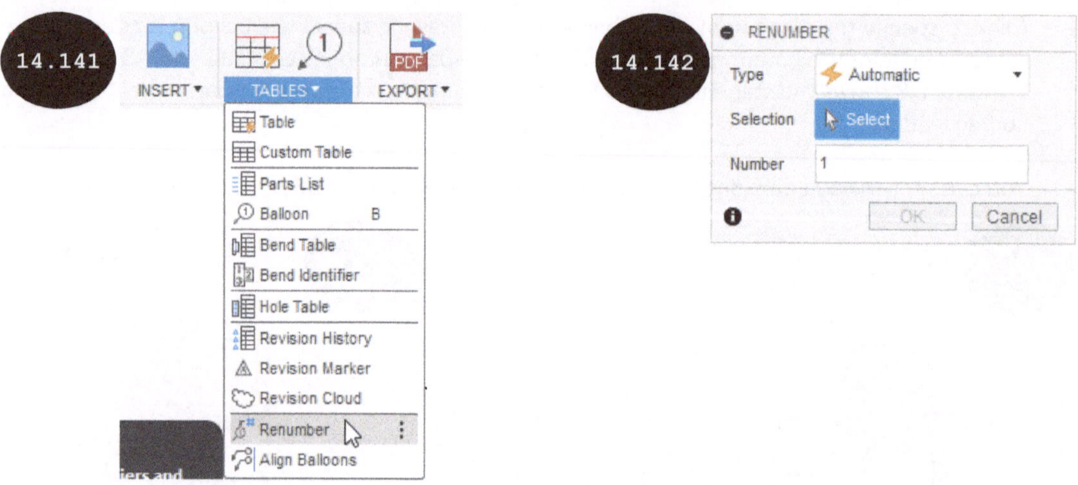

Ensure that the **Automatic** or **Balloon** option is selected in the **Type** drop-down list. Enter the starting number for a balloon in the **Number** field of the dialog box and then select a balloon in the drawing view. The numbering of the selected balloon is renumbered as specified. Also, the numbering of other balloons is renumbered, and the Part list is updated, accordingly. Click on the other balloons one by one to renumber them as per the starting number specified. Next, click on the **OK** button to exit the dialog box.

Adding Drawing Sheets

In Autodesk Fusion, you can add multiple drawing sheets for creating different drawing views of a project. For creating all drawing views of a real-world mechanical model, a single drawing sheet may not be sufficient, and you may need to add multiple drawing sheets. To add a new drawing sheet for creating different drawing views, click on the + button in the lower left corner of the screen, see Figure 14.143. A new drawing sheet is added as per the specifications of the existing drawing sheet and its tab is highlighted with a blue border at the lower left corner of the screen, see Figure 14.144. Note that the blue border around the tab of a drawing sheet indicates that it is currently activated. Similarly, you can add multiple drawing sheets, one after the other. To switch between the drawing sheets, you need to click on the respective tab of the drawing sheet in the lower left corner of the screen.

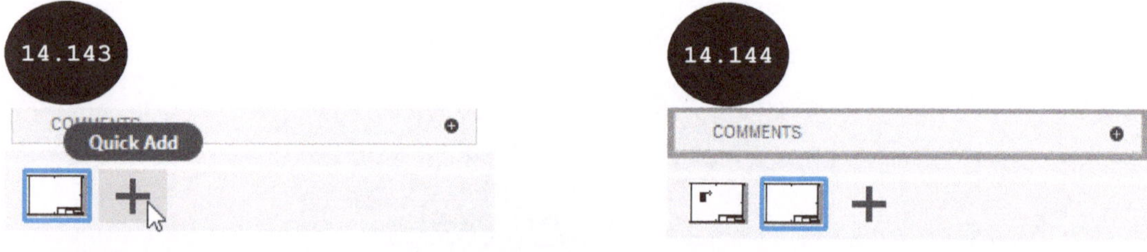

Note: In Autodesk Fusion, you can also create a duplicate copy of an existing drawing sheet. To do this, right-click on the sheet tab at the lower left corner of the screen and then click on the **Duplicate Sheet** option in the shortcut menu that appears, see Figure 14.145.

14.145

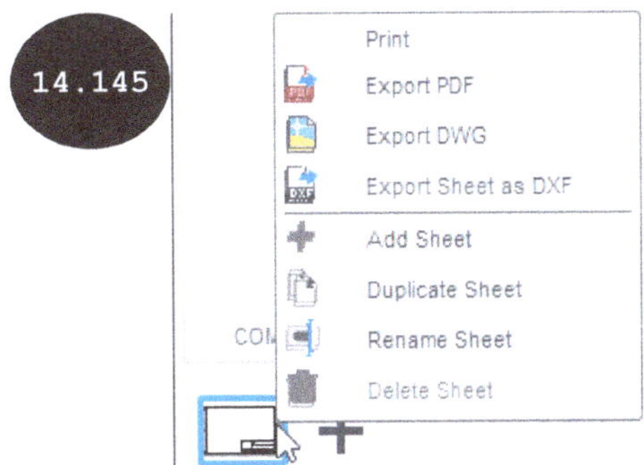

Creating a New Drawing Template

In Autodesk Fusion, you can create a new drawing template, as per your company standard or project requirement, and use it to create drawings. To create a new drawing template, invoke the **What do you want to design?** dialog box, see Figure 14.146. This dialog box appears each time you launch Autodesk Fusion or start a new design file.

14.146

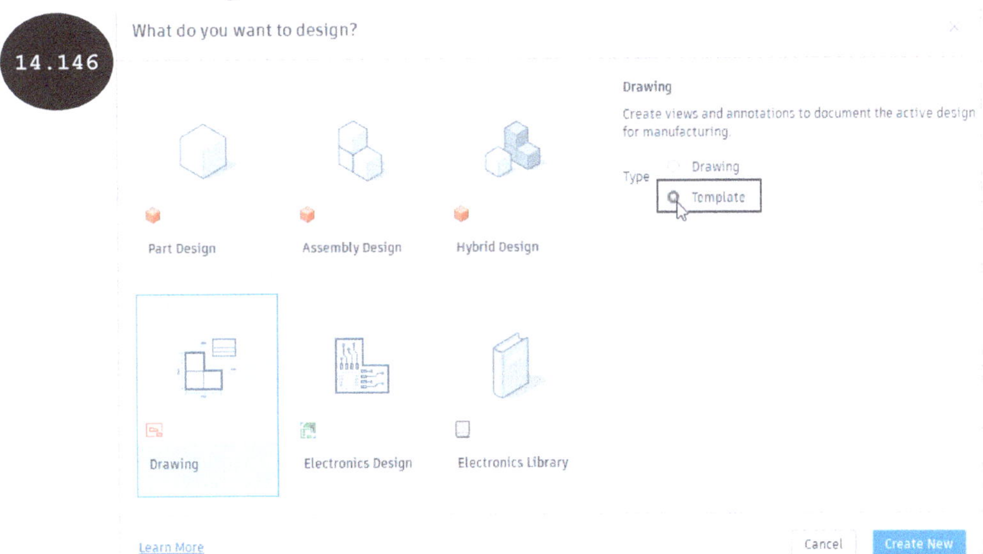

In this dialog box, click the **Drawing** button, and then select the **Template** radio button in the **Type** area on the right panel, refer to Figure 14.146. Next, click the **Create New** button. The **CREATE DRAWING TEMPLATE** dialog box appears, see Figure 14.147.

14.147

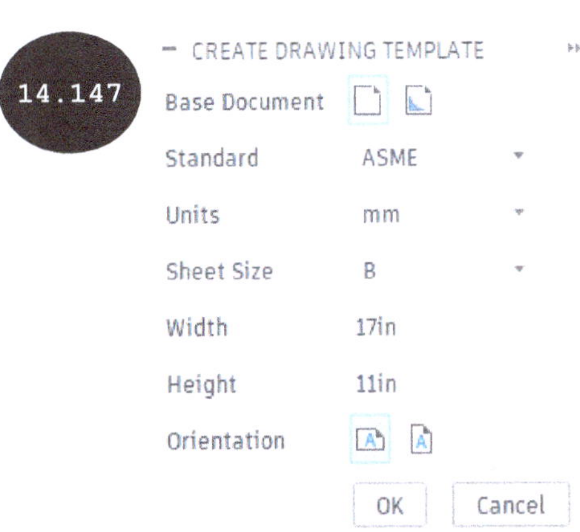

In this dialog box, specify the required options such as standard, units, and sheet size, and then click on the **OK** button. A new drawing template with specified options appears. Now, customize the drawing template by adding the required number of sheets, text, table, and so on. Also, customize the title block, as required. After customizing the drawing template, click on the **Save** tool in the **Application Bar**. The **Save** dialog box appears. In this dialog box, enter the name of the drawing template and specify the location to save it. Next, click on the **Save** button in the dialog box. The custom drawing template is saved in the specified location. Now, you can use this custom drawing template to start a new drawing file for creating drawings.

Exporting a Drawing

In Autodesk Fusion, after creating a drawing, you can export it as a PDF, DWG, DXF, or CSV file. The method for the same is discussed next.

Exporting a Drawing as a PDF File

1. Click on the **Export PDF** tool in the **Toolbar**, see Figure 14.148. The **EXPORT PDF** dialog box appears, see Figure 14.149.

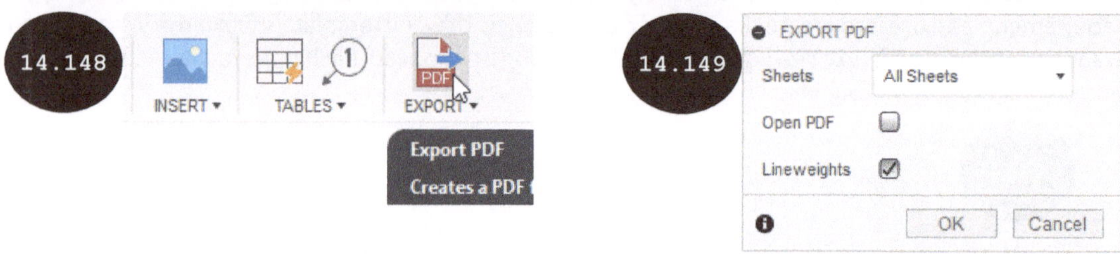

2. Select the required option in the **Sheets** drop-down list of the dialog box. Note that the options in the **Sheets** drop-down list are used for specifying the drawing sheets to be included in the exported PDF file. The **All Sheets** option is used for including all the drawing sheets in the exported PDF file. The **Current Sheet** option is used to include only the current drawing sheet in the exported PDF file. The **Range** option is used for specifying a range of sheets to be included in the PDF file. The **Selected Sheets** option is used to include only the selected drawing sheets in the PDF file. You can select multiple sheets in the bottom left corner by pressing the CTRL key.

3. Select the **Open PDF** file check box in the dialog box to automatically open the PDF file when the exported file is generated.

4. Ensure that the **Lineweights** check box is selected to generate the PDF file with thicker drawing lines, see Figure 14.150. To generate the PDF file with thinner lines (see Figure 14.151), clear this check box in the dialog box.

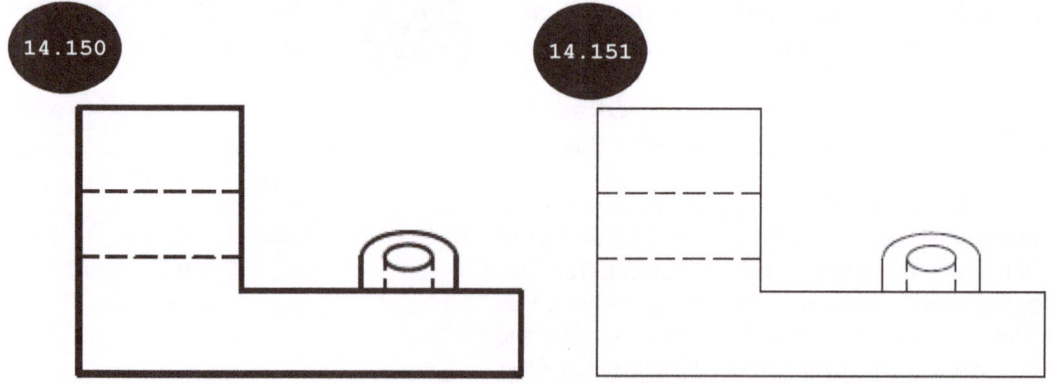

5. After selecting the required options to generate the PDF file, click on the **OK** button. The **Export PDF** dialog box appears. In this dialog box, specify the name of the PDF file in the **File name** field and then browse to the required location for saving the file.

6. Click on the **Save** button in the dialog box. The PDF file is saved in the specified location.

Exporting a Drawing as a DWG File

1. Invoke the **EXPORT** drop-down menu in the **Toolbar** and then click on the **Export DWG** tool, see Figure 14.152. The **EXPORT DWG** dialog box appears.

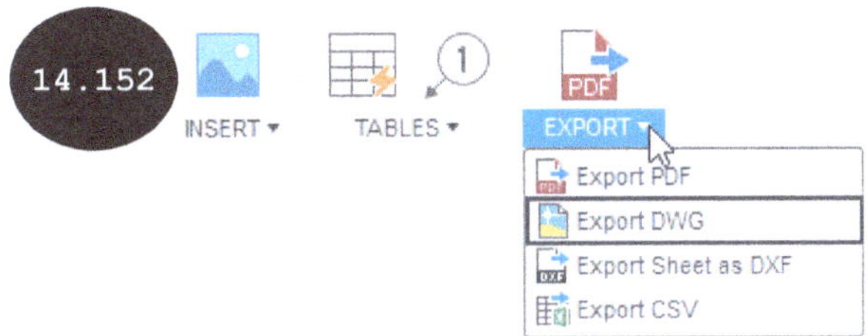

2. Select the required option in the **Format** drop-down list of the dialog box. The **AutoCAD DWG** option of this drop-down list is used for including all the drawing sheets in the exported DWG file. The **Simplified DWG** option is used to include only the current drawing sheet in the exported DWG file. After selecting the required option, click on the **OK** button in the dialog box. The **Output DWG** dialog box appears.

3. Enter the name of the DWG file in the **File name** field in the dialog box. Next, browse to the required location for saving the file.

4. Click on the **Save** button in the **Output DWG** dialog box. The DWG file is saved in the specified location.

Exporting a Drawing as a DXF File

1. Invoke the **EXPORT** drop-down menu in the **Toolbar** and then click on the **Export Sheet as DXF** tool, see Figure 14.153. The **Output Sheet as DXF** dialog box appears.

2. Enter the name of the DXF file in the **File name** field of the dialog box. Next, browse to the required location for saving the file.

3. Click on the **Save** button in the **Output Sheet as DXF** dialog box. The DXF file is saved in the specified location.

Exporting the Drawing Part List as a CSV File

1. To export the Parts list/BOQ (Bill of Quantity) of the drawing as a CSV file, invoke the **EXPORT** drop-down menu in the **Toolbar** and then click on the **Export CSV** tool. The **Output Table** dialog box appears.

2. Enter the name of the CSV file in the **File name** field in the dialog box. Next, browse to the required location for saving the file.

3. Click on the **Save** button in the **Output Table** dialog box. The CSV file of the Parts list is saved in the specified location.

Tutorial 1

Open the model created in Tutorial 2 of Chapter 7 and then create drawing views: front, top, side, isometric, section, and detail, as shown in Figure 14.154 in the B (17in x 11in) sheet size. After creating the drawing views, apply dimensions. You need to use the **ASME** drawing standard for creating this drawing.

14.154

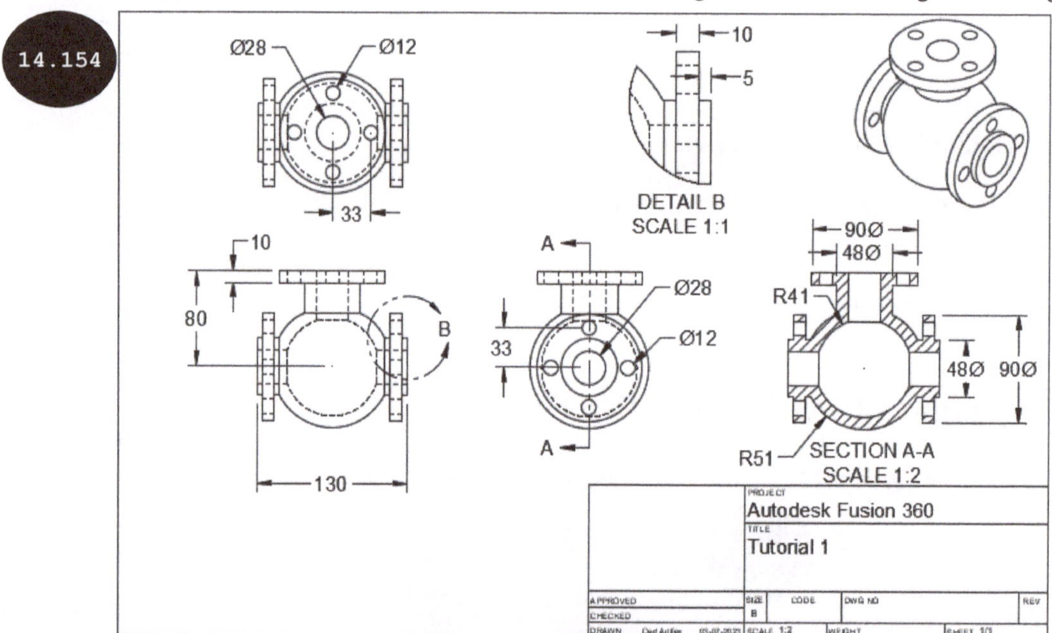

Section 1: Opening and Saving Tutorial 2 of Chapter 7

1. Launch Autodesk Fusion, if not already running.

   Now, open the model to create its drawing.

2. Click **File** > **Open** in the **Application Menu**, see Figure 14.155. The **Open** dialog box appears.

14.155

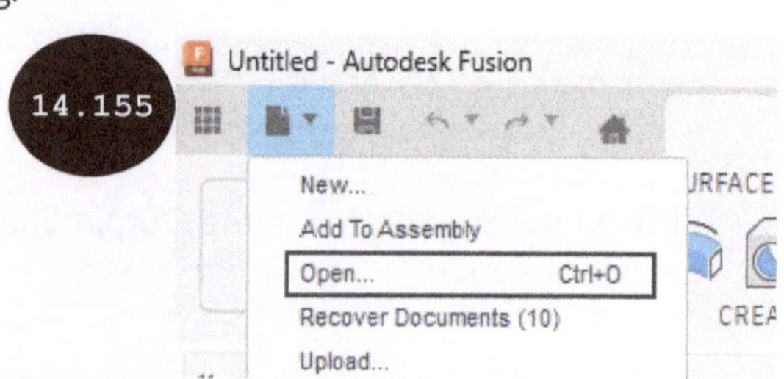

3. In the **Open** dialog box, browse to the **Chapter 7** folder and select the model named **Tutorial 2**.

4. Click the **Open** button in the dialog box. The model created as Tutorial 2 in Chapter 7 opens in Autodesk Fusion, see Figure 14.156.

Now, you need to save the model with the name "Tutorial 1" in the Chapter 14 folder of the project.

5. Click on **File > Save As** in the **Application Bar**. The **Save As** dialog box appears. Save the model with the name "Tutorial 1" in the ***Autodesk Fusion 360 > Chapter 14 > Tutorial*** location. You need to create these folders inside the "Autodesk Fusion 360" project folder in the **Data Panel**.

Section 2: Invoking the DRAWING Workspace and Creating Front View

1. Invoke the **Workspace** drop-down menu and then click on **DRAWING > From Design**, see Figure 14.157. The **CREATE DRAWING** dialog box appears, see Figure 14.158.

14.158

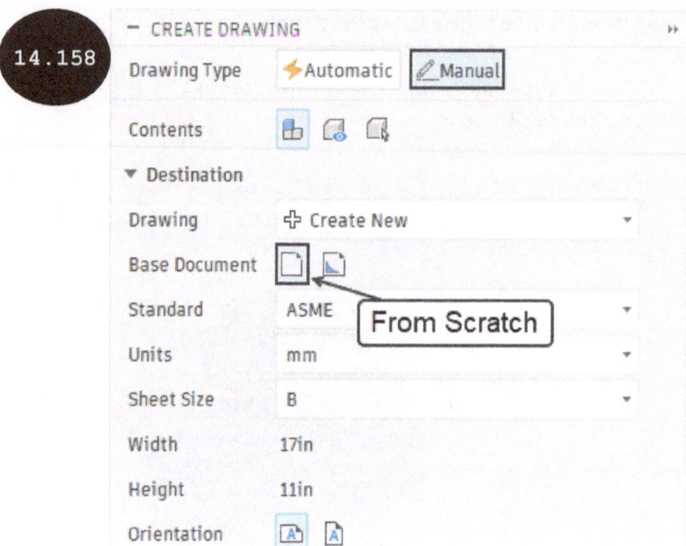

2. Activate the **Manual** button in the **Drawing Type** area of the dialog box to create drawing views manually.

3. Ensure that the **Create New** option is selected in the **Drawing** drop-down list and the **From Scratch** button is activated in the **Base Document** area of the dialog box, refer to Figure 14.158.

4. Select the **ASME** standard in the **Standard** drop-down list of the dialog box.

5. Ensure that the **mm** unit is selected in the **Units** drop-down list of the dialog box.

6. Select the **B** (17in x 11in) sheet size in the **Sheet Size** drop-down list of the dialog box.

7. Click on the **OK** button. The DRAWING workspace is invoked and a drawing sheet with the specified standard and size appears, see Figure 14.159. Also, the **DRAWING VIEW** dialog box appears on the right side of the drawing sheet and a preview of the default base view appears attached to the cursor.

14.159

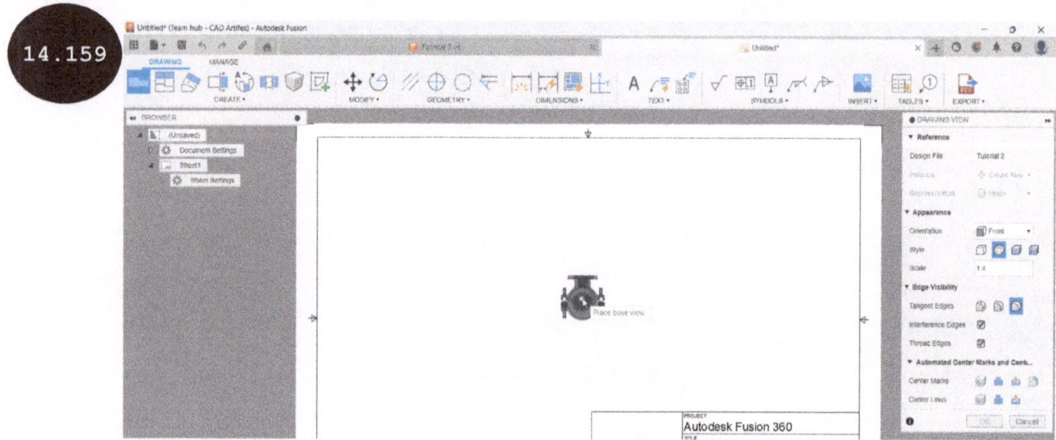

8. Click to specify the position of the base view in the lower left corner of the drawing sheet, see Figure 14.160. The Front view is placed in the specified location.

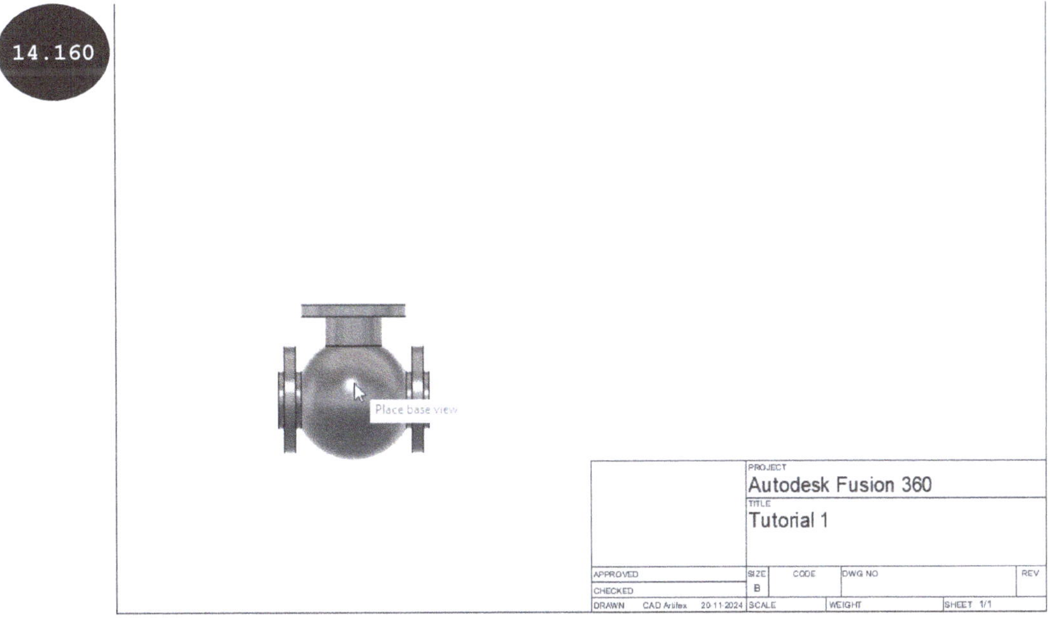

9. Ensure that the **Front** option is selected in the **Orientation** drop-down list of the **DRAWING VIEW** dialog box.

10. Ensure that the **Visible and Hidden Edges** button is activated in the **Style** area of the dialog box.

11. Enter **1:2** in the **Scale** field of the dialog box as the scale of the base view.

12. Accept the remaining options in the **DRAWING VIEW** dialog box and then click on the **OK** button. The Front view is placed in the specified location as per the parameters specified in the dialog box.

Section 3: Creating Projected Views

Now, you need to create the orthogonal and isometric projected views of the Base view.

1. Click on the **Projected View** tool in the **CREATE** panel in the **Toolbar**, (see Figure 14.161) or press the **P** key. You are prompted to select the parent view.

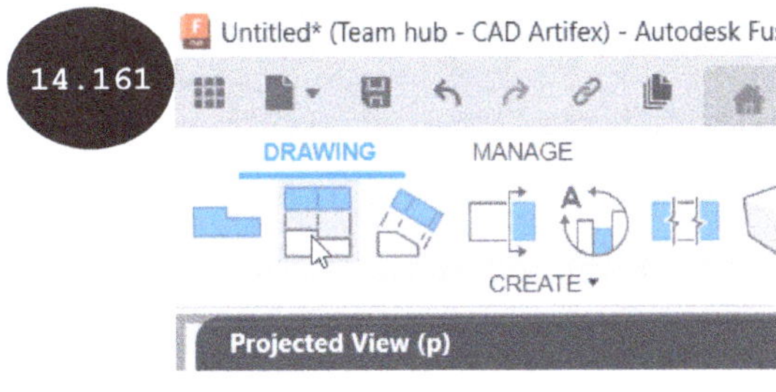

2. Select the Front view as the parent view for creating the projected views. A projected view is attached to the cursor.

3. Move the cursor vertically upward. The projected view (Top view) appears attached to the cursor, see Figure 14.162.

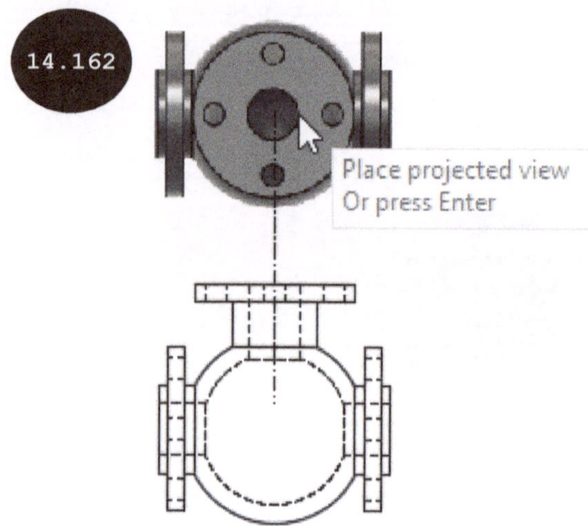

4. Click on the drawing sheet to specify the position for the Top view, see Figure 14.163.

5. Move the cursor horizontally towards the right. The projected view (Right view) of the model appears attached to the cursor.

6. Click on the drawing sheet to specify the position for the Right view, see Figure 14.163.

7. Move the cursor at an angle to the Front view (Base view). The isometric view of the model appears attached to the cursor. Next, click to specify its position on the upper right corner of the drawing sheet, see Figure 14.163.

8. After creating all the projected views, press ENTER or click on the **Create and continue** button that appears near the last created projected view to exit the tool. The projected views are created. Now, you need to change the visible style of the isometric projected view. By default, the properties of the parent view (Front view) are propagated to the projected views.

9. Double-click on the isometric projected view. The **DRAWING VIEW** dialog box appears. In this dialog box, the **From Parent** button is activated in the **Style** area, by default. As a result, properties of the parent view (Front view) are propagated to the projected view.

10. Click on the **Visible Edges** button in the dialog box to change the visible style of the isometric projected view.

11. Click on the **Close** button to exit the dialog box. Figure 14.163 shows the drawing sheet after creating all the projected views.

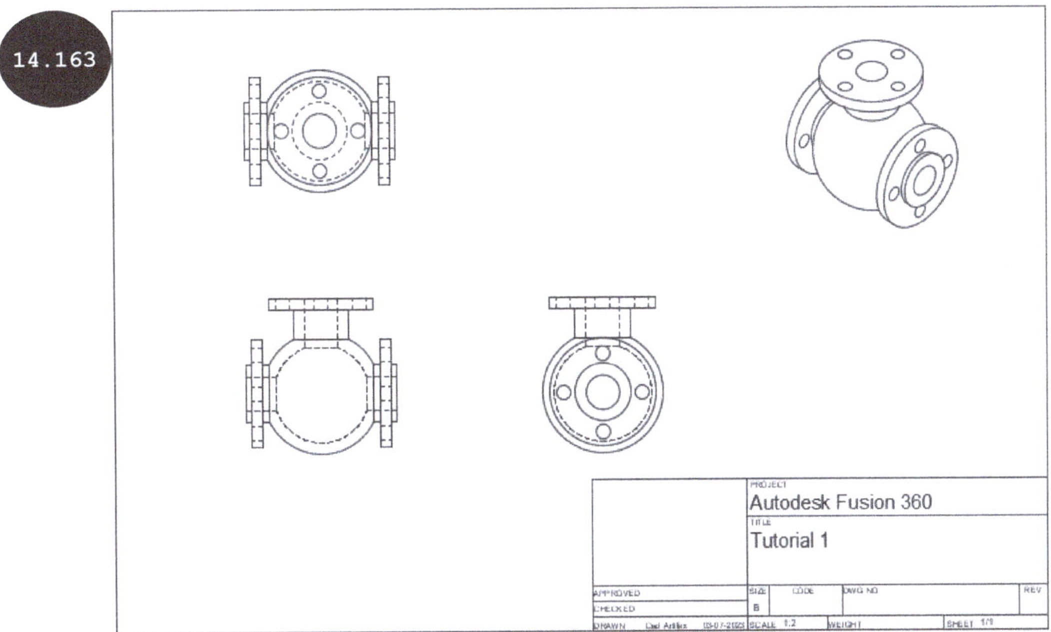

Section 4: Creating Section View

Now, you need to create the section view by selecting the Right view as the parent view.

1. Click on the **Section View** tool in the **CREATE** panel in the **Toolbar**. You are prompted to select the parent view.

2. Select the Right view as the parent view for creating the section view. The **DRAWING VIEW** dialog box appears, and you are prompted to specify the start point of the section line.

3. Move the cursor to the midpoint of the upper horizontal edge of the Right view, (see Figure 14.164) and then move the cursor vertically upward. A tracking line appears, see Figure 14.165.

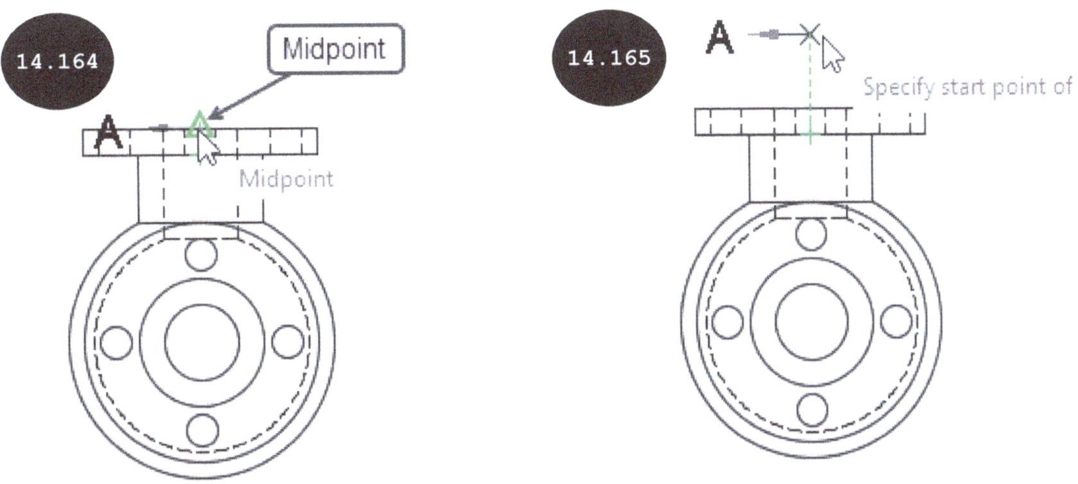

4. Follow the tracking line and then click to specify the start point of the section line. You are prompted to specify the endpoint of the section line.

5. Move the cursor vertically downward and then click to specify the endpoint of the section line anywhere outside the Right view.

6. Press ENTER or click on the **Create and continue** button that appears near the line to end the creation of the section line. A preview of the section view appears attached to the cursor.

7. Move the cursor horizontally toward the right and then click to specify the position of the section view on the drawing sheet.

8. Click on the **OK** button in the dialog box. The section view is created, see Figure 14.166. Note that if the text of the section view overrides the title block. You need to place this text below the section view such that it should not overlap with the title block. You can move the text by selecting it and then dragging its grip point.

14.166

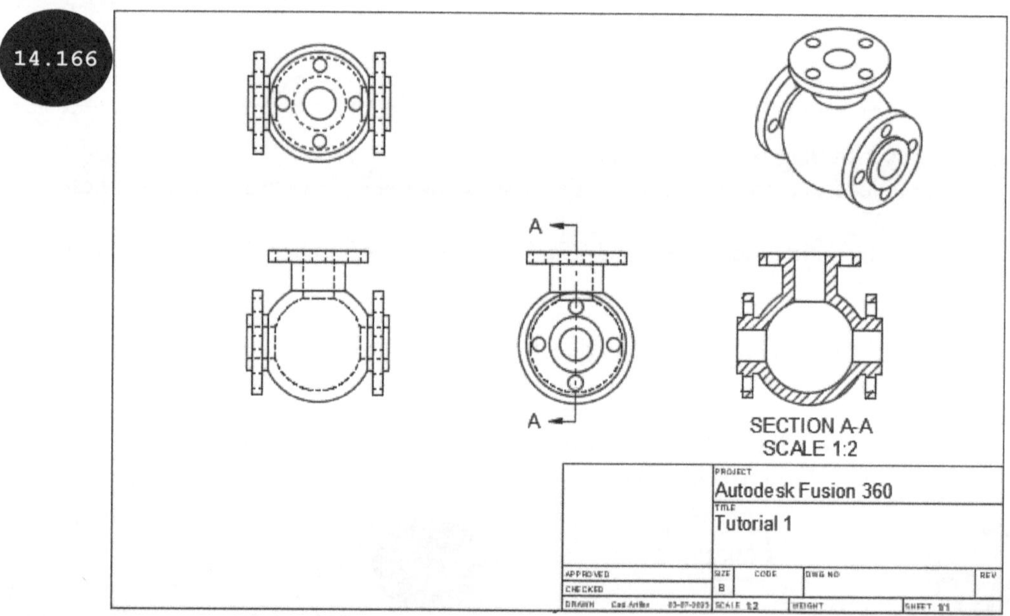

Section 5: Creating Detail View

Now, you need to create a detail view of a portion of the Front view.

1. Click on the **Detail View** tool in the **Toolbar**. You are prompted to select the parent view.

2. Select the Front view as the parent view for creating the detail view. The **DRAWING VIEW** dialog box appears, and you are prompted to specify the center point of the detail boundary.

3. Move the cursor over the upper rightmost vertex of the Front view and then click to specify the center point of the detail boundary when the cursor snaps to it, see Figure 14.167. You are prompted to specify the size of the detail boundary.

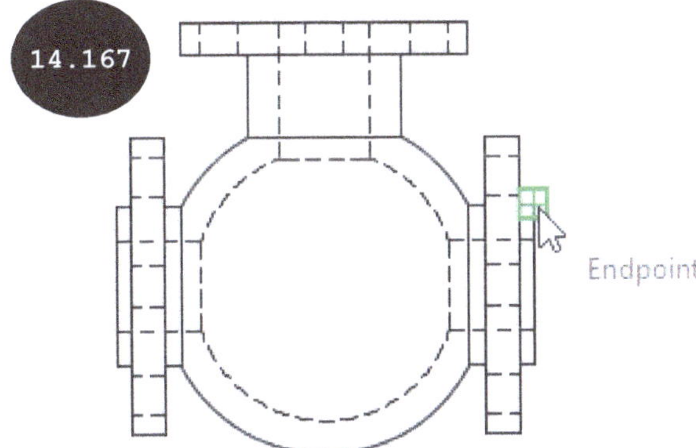

4. Move the cursor to a distance and then click to define the size of the boundary. The preview of the detail view of the portion that lies inside the boundary appears attached to the cursor.

5. Click to specify the position of the detail view on the drawing sheet, see Figure 14.168.

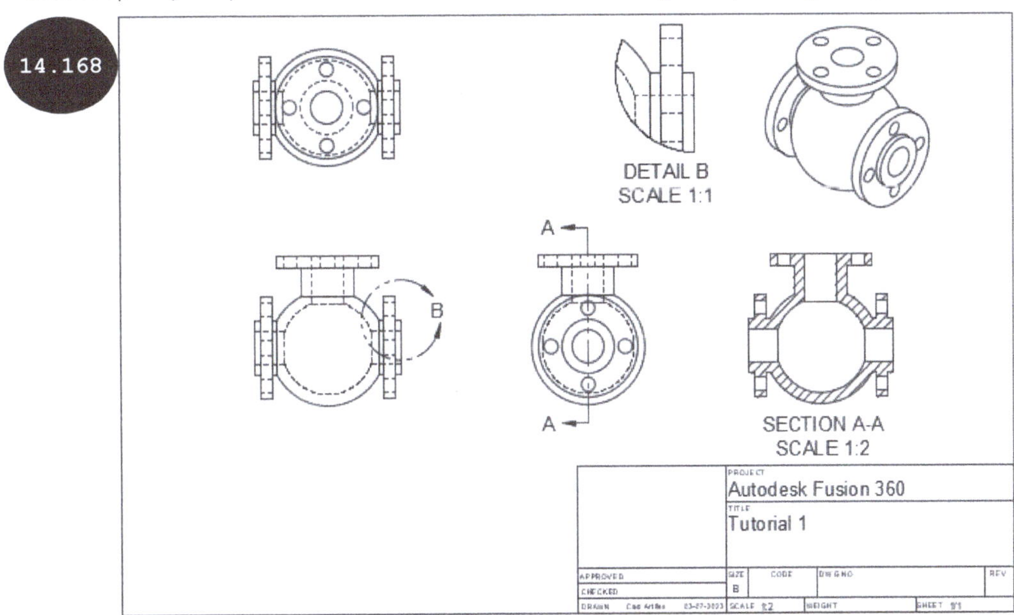

6. Ensure that **1:1** is specified as the scale factor of the detail view in the dialog box. Next, click on the **OK** button. A detail view is created in the specified position, see Figure 14.169. Note that, if the text of the detail view intersects with any existing drawing view, then you need to change its position such that it should not intersect with any drawing view.

Section 6: Applying Dimensions

1. Click on the **Dimension** tool in the **DIMENSIONS** panel in the **Toolbar** or press the D key. You are prompted to select an edge or specify points to apply dimensions.

2. Click on the upper rightmost vertex of the Section view, see Figure 14.167. You are prompted to specify the second point to apply dimension.

3. Click on the lower rightmost vertex of the Section view, see Figure 14.169. The linear dimension between the selected vertices is attached to the cursor. Next, click on the right side of the Section view to define the position of the dimension. The linear dimension is applied between the selected vertices, see Figure 14.169.

14.169

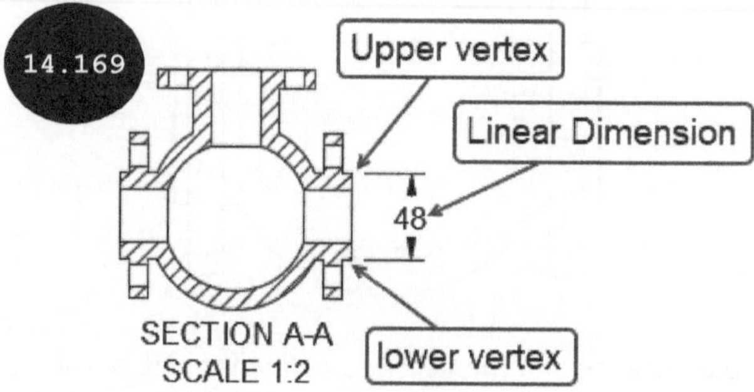

4. Similarly, apply the remaining dimensions on the drawing views, see Figure 14.170.

14.170

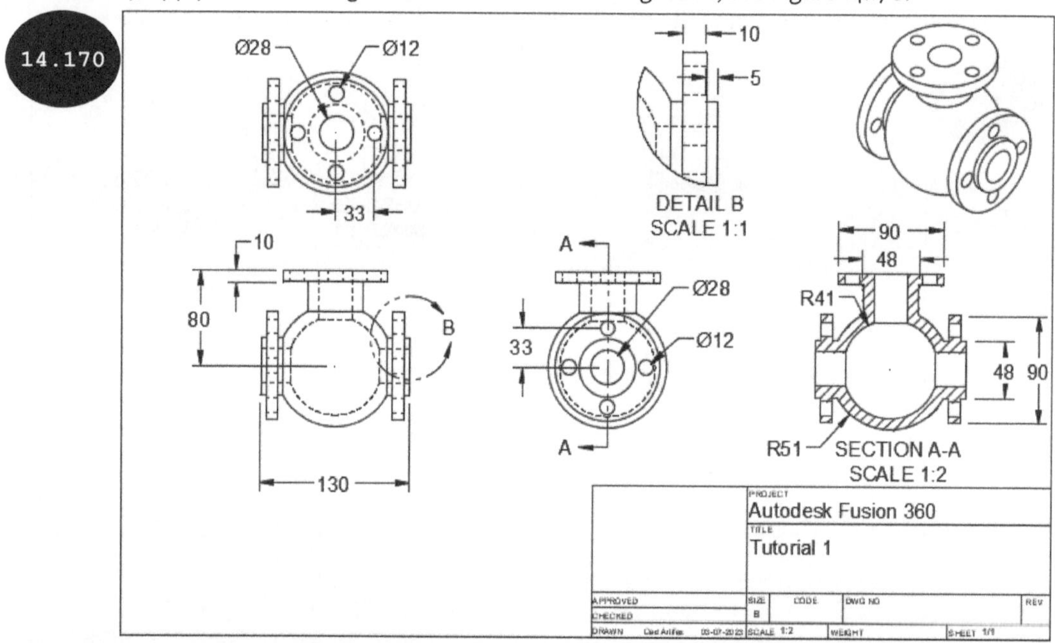

Note: After applying a dimension, you may need to change its position to avoid any intersection or overlapping with other dimensions. To do this, select a dimension and then click the grip point that appeare on the dimension text. Next, specify the new position for the dimension.

Section 7: Editing Dimensions

Now, you need to edit the linear dimensions applied on the Section view to insert the diameter symbol.

1. Double-click on the linear dimension 90 mm, applied on the right of the Section view. The **DIMENSION** dialog box appears. Also, the dimension value appears in an edit field.

2. Place the cursor in front of the dimension value in the edit field and then invoke the **Insert Symbol** flyout in the **DIMENSION** dialog box, see Figure 14.171.

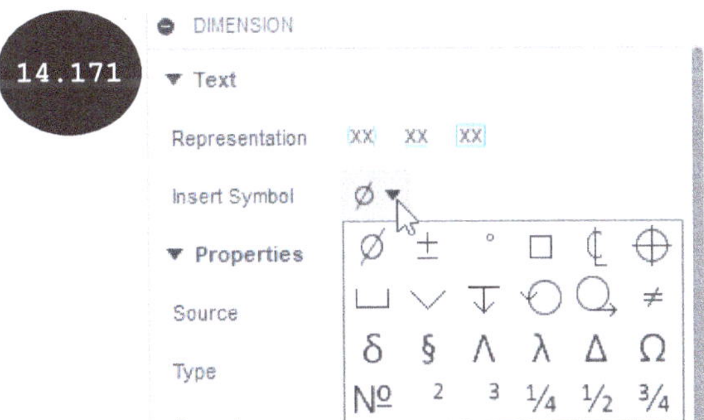

3. Select the **Diameter** symbol in the **Insert Symbol** flyout and then click on the **Close** button to exit the dialog box. The diameter symbol is inserted in front of the dimension value, see Figure 14.172.

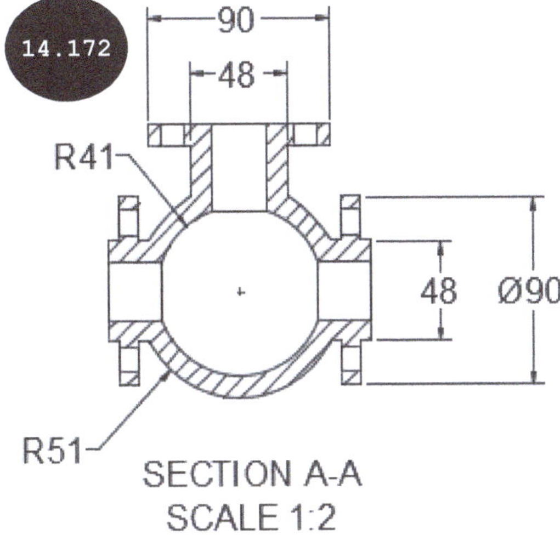

4. Similarly, insert the diameter symbol into other linear dimensions of the Section view, see Figure 14.173.

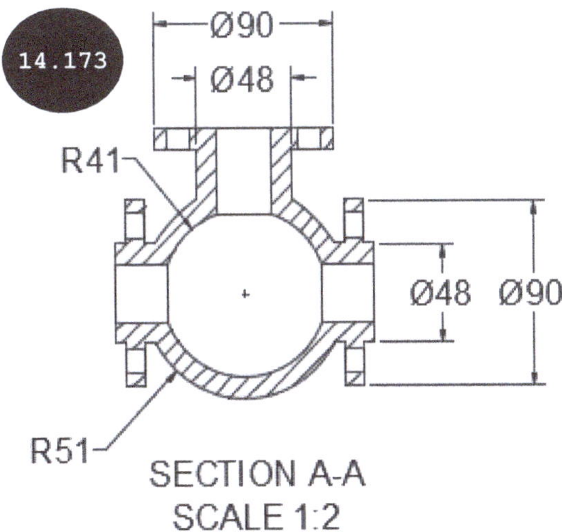

5. Arrange the position of the dimensions to maintain proper spacing between each other. Figure 14.174 shows the final drawing creating all the drawing views and applying dimensions.

14.174

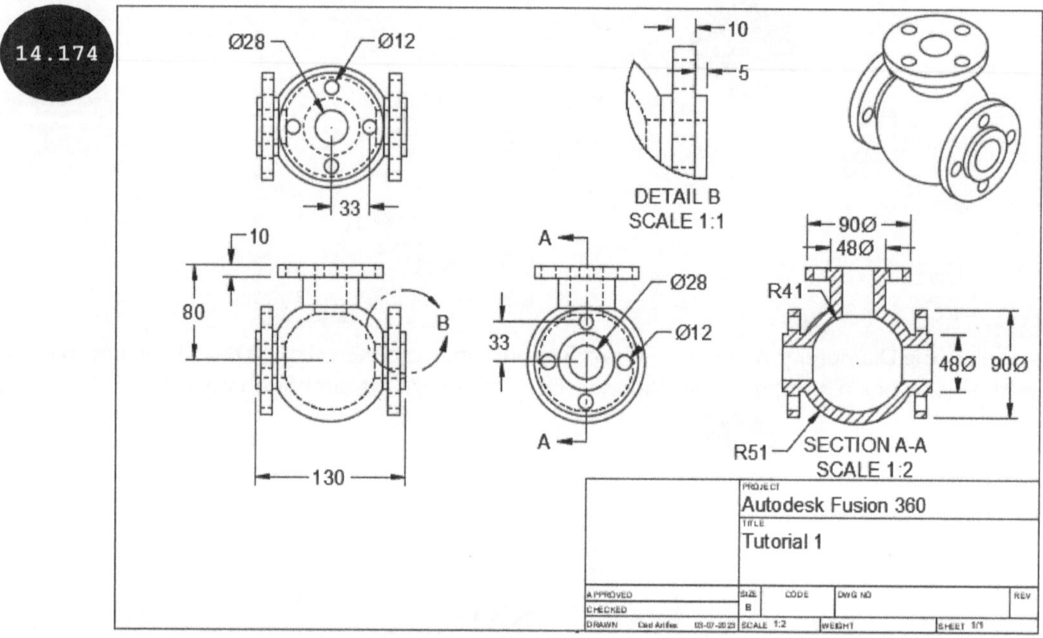

Section 8: Saving the Drawing

Now, you can save the drawing.

1. Click on the **Save** tool in the Application Bar. The **Save** dialog box appears. Next, ensure that the location to save the file is specified as ***Autodesk Fusion 360 > Chapter 14 > Tutorial*** in the **Location** field of the dialog box.

2. Click on the **Save** button in the dialog box. The drawing file is saved in the specified location with the default specified name "Tutorial 1".

Hands-on Test Drive 1

Open the assembly created in Hands-on Test Drive 1 of Chapter 13, (see Figure 14.175) and then create the different drawing views: Front, Top, and Right of the assembly in the B (17in x 11in) sheet size.

Also, create an exploded view of the assembly and add the Parts list with balloons to each component of the assembly in the exploded view.

14.175

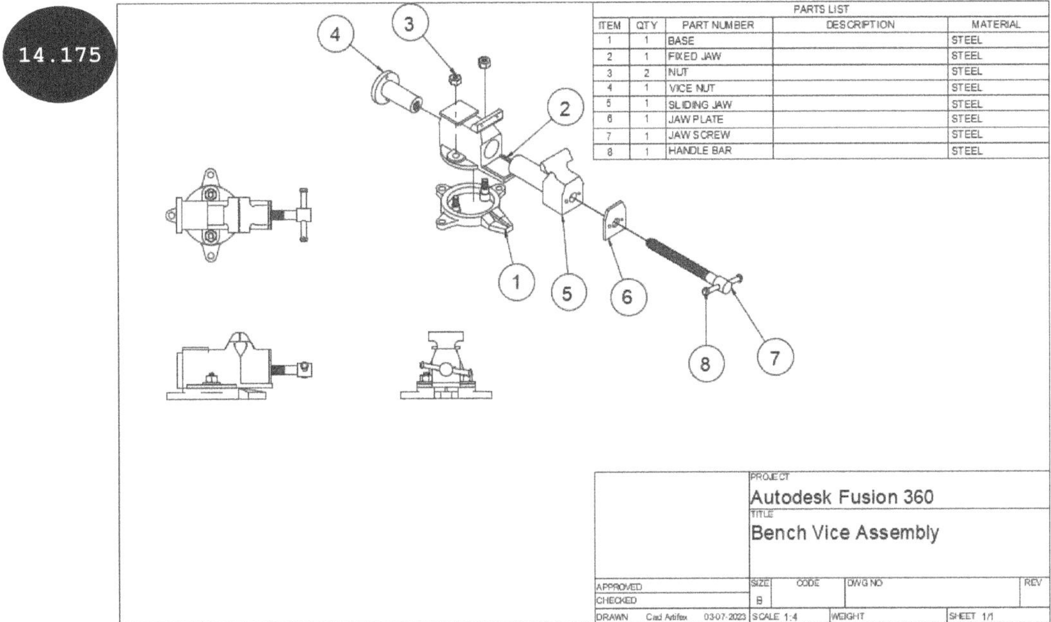

PARTS LIST				
ITEM	QTY	PART NUMBER	DESCRIPTION	MATERIAL
1	1	BASE		STEEL
2	1	FIXED JAW		STEEL
3	2	NUT		STEEL
4	1	VICE NUT		STEEL
5	1	SLIDING JAW		STEEL
6	1	JAW PLATE		STEEL
7	1	JAW SCREW		STEEL
8	1	HANDLE BAR		STEEL

Summary

In this chapter, you learned how to create 2D drawings of components and assemblies. You explored the concept of projection angles and the process of editing documents and sheet settings. The chapter also covered methods for creating sketches, exploded views of assemblies, and applying and editing dimensions. Additionally, you discovered how to manage hatch properties, add notes, and include geometries such as center marks, centerlines, and surface texture symbols in drawing views. The chapter further explained how to create the Bill of Materials (BOM)/Parts List, add and renumber balloons, insert drawing sheets, create drawing templates, and export drawings. These skills enable you to generate precise and comprehensive technical drawings, ensuring effective communication throughout the design and manufacturing processes.

Questions

Complete and verify the following sentences:

- In _________ workspace of Autodesk Fusion, you can generate 2D drawings of a component or an assembly.
- Autodesk Fusion allows you to invoke the DRAWING workspace from a design or an animation file by selecting the respective option: _________ and _________.
- On selecting the _________ check box in the **DRAWING VIEW** dialog box, the thread edges are represented as dash lines in the drawing views.

- Engineering drawings follow the _________ and the _________ angles of projections.
- Projected views are _________ and _________ views of an object, which are created by viewing the object from its different projection sides.
- A _________ view is created by cutting an object by using an imaginary cutting plane or a section line and then viewing the object from a direction normal to the section line.
- In Autodesk Fusion, you can create _________, _________, _________, and _________ section views by using the **Section View** tool.
- On creating the section view of an assembly, a list of all bodies included in the section cut appears in the _________ rollout of the **DRAWING VIEW** dialog box.
- A _________ view is used for showing a portion of an existing drawing view on an enlarged scale.
- You can add center marks on rounded/circular edges by using the _________ tool.
- The _________ contains all the required information of an assembly such as part number, quantity, material, and so on.
- A surface finish symbol has three components: _________, _________, and _________.
- In Autodesk Fusion, after creating a section view, you can edit its hatching properties such as hatch pattern, scale factor, and hatch angle. (True/False)
- In Autodesk Fusion, after creating a drawing view, you can edit its properties such as orientation, style, scale, and visibility of tangent edges. (True/False)
- In Autodesk Fusion, after applying a dimension, you can edit it to override its dimension value, insert a symbol, specify tolerances, and so on. (True/False)

INDEX

Symbols

A

B

C

R

S

T

U

V

W

Z

Other Publications by CADArtifex

Some of the other Publications by CADArtifex are given below:

AutoCAD Textbooks

AutoCAD 2026: A Power Guide for Beginners and Intermediate Users
AutoCAD 2025: A Power Guide for Beginners and Intermediate Users
AutoCAD 2024: A Power Guide for Beginners and Intermediate Users
and more

AutoCAD For Architectural Design Textbooks

AutoCAD 2023 for Architectural Design: A Power Guide for Beginners and Intermediate Users
AutoCAD 2022 for Architectural Design: A Power Guide for Beginners and Intermediate Users
and more

Autodesk Fusion 360 Textbooks

Autodesk Fusion 360: A Power Guide for Beginners and Intermediate Users (8th Edition)
Autodesk Fusion 360: A Power Guide for Beginners and Intermediate Users (7th Edition)
Autodesk Fusion 360: A Power Guide for Beginners and Intermediate Users (6th Edition)
and more

Autodesk Fusion 360 Surface and T-Spline Textbooks

Autodesk Fusion 360 Surface Design and Sculpting with T-Spline Surfaces (8th Edition)
Autodesk Fusion 360 Surface Design and Sculpting with T-Spline Surfaces (7th Edition)
and more

Autodesk Inventor Textbooks

Autodesk Inventor 2026: A Power Guide for Beginners and Intermediate Users
Autodesk Inventor 2025: A Power Guide for Beginners and Intermediate Users
Autodesk Inventor 2024: A Power Guide for Beginners and Intermediate Users
and more

FreeCAD Textbooks

FreeCAD 1.0: A Power Guide for Beginners and Intermediate Users
FreeCAD 0.21: A Power Guide for Beginners and Intermediate Users
and more

Onshape Textbooks

Onshape 2025: A Power Guide for Beginners and Intermediate Users
and more

PTC Creo Parametric Textbooks
Creo Parametric 12.0: A Power Guide for Beginners and Intermediate Users
Creo Parametric 11.0: A Power Guide for Beginners and Intermediate Users
and more

SOLIDWORKS Textbooks
SOLIDWORKS 2026: A Power Guide for Beginners and Intermediate User
SOLIDWORKS 2025: A Power Guide for Beginners and Intermediate User
SOLIDWORKS 2024: A Power Guide for Beginners and Intermediate User
and more

SOLIDWORKS Sheet Metal and Surface Design Textbooks
SOLIDWORKS Sheet Metal and Surface Design 2026 for Beginners and Intermediate Users
SOLIDWORKS Sheet Metal and Surface Design 2025 for Beginners and Intermediate Users
and more

SOLIDWORKS Simulation Textbooks
SOLIDWORKS Simulation 2026: A Power Guide for Beginners and Intermediate User
SOLIDWORKS Simulation 2025: A Power Guide for Beginners and Intermediate User
SOLIDWORKS Simulation 2024: A Power Guide for Beginners and Intermediate User
and more

Exercises Books
100 AutoCAD Exercises - Learn by Practicing (2 Edition)
Autodesk Inventor Exercises - Learn by Practicing
Autodesk Fusion 360 Exercises Learn by Practicing (2023-24)
SOLIDWORKS Exercises - Learn by Practicing (3 Edition)

Video Courses by CADArtifex
CADArtifex offers a range of video courses designed to support students, educators, and professionals in developing practical CAD skills through structured, project-based learning. Available video courses include:

- SOLIDWORKS Mastery Pack – 11 Courses in 1 | Complete Beginner to Industry Training
- Fusion 360 Mastery Pack: Design, Sculpt & Build Real Projects (6-in-1 Course Combo)
- Learn SOLIDWORKS Sheet Metal: From Concept to Creation
- Complete Fusion 360 All-in-One Course for Beginners (2025)
- Fusion 360 Surface Design & T-Spline Sculpting
- Complete FreeCAD for Beginners – No Experience Needed
- Complete Onshape for Beginners: Project-Based Approach
- Master Autodesk Inventor: From Basics to Advanced
- Mastering AutoCAD 2D & 3D for Beginners

For full course details and access, visit: ***cadartifex.com***

Printed at Repro India Ltd.